MW01097718

"**This is the unparalleled "how-to" book for investigators and fraud experts.** Diana is undoubtedly the reigning expert on online dating scams. I've personally seen the effort and diligence she put into her books, and no one else has the insider knowledge that she possesses. Working with private investigators and attorneys for over a decade has clearly developed a perseverance that's unmatched in this arena. **Diana not only captures the "how's" of the scammers' trade, she's also managed to get them to confide in her and divulge the elusive "why's". TV experts claim to know how these scams work, but Diana isn't talking theory.** This is practical (and personal) knowledge. **You will learn much from her. Stay tuned; more secrets will be revealed in her other books on online dating scams.**"

— MICHAEL J. WEST, *Criminologist and Certified Fraud Examiner, Arkansas*

"**This book will awaken every one of your emotions!** Who is the Real Man Behind the Screen is a rousing expose' of online scammers. While reading, I became enthralled in the tactics of deception, agendas, and the reach of those who will drain not only the finances of their victims but their emotions and spirits as well. I was furious that the scammers have no limit to their greed or their plots. *Who is the Real Man Behind the Screen* **will enlighten, warn, and prevent others from losing their money and the one thing you never gain back – time! It is a must-read for every person who has even thought about online dating or simply "friending" on the Internet.** D. L. Garren allowed herself to be vulnerable in order to help prevent millions from drowning in disappointment, hurt, and shame."

— YUNICE J. PATRICK, *Business Owner, Georgia*

"Diana went deep. Real deep. So deep that I was concerned for her safety and well-being. During the last few years she used her natural skills and determination to uncover the TRUTH about online dating scams. She did this to prevent the very thing that happened to her from happening to YOU. **You must read** *Who is the Real Man Behind the Screen?* The knowledge she has gained from the Private Investigation, Security and Surveillance industries from years of marketing and business development with them put her in a unique position to tackle online dating scams with all the resources of a team of professionals and the subtlety of a double agent. Unbelievable what is happening, worldwide."

— S. WALKER, *Business Owner, Atlanta, Georgia*

"**This book is a must-read for anyone who wants to avoid being a victim of online scammers and thieves.** Unfortunately we live in a world of consumer beware. I found this book very informative and very clearly written. I have fully recommended this book to family and friends as an excellent source and guide to avoid becoming a victim of foul play. CONGRATULATIONS AND BEST OF LUCK!"

— DANIEL GAGNON, *Canada*

"**If you or someone you know is currently involved in or considering online dating,** *Who is the Real Man Behind the Screen?* **is a "must read."** Having been scammed herself, Diana Garren began tracking down and identifying her online scammer. Not only did Ms. Garren track down and identify the real man behind the screen, she persuaded him to tell his story and reveal detailed information about how online dating scammers ensnare their victims. Ms. Garren went on to obtain additional information from other scammers involved in online dating. **Both men and women will benefit from reading Diana Garren's latest book, Who is the Real Man Behind the Screen?**"

— CLAUDE L. BOOKOUT, *CEO/Chief Investigator, United International Investigations, Austin, Texas*

"What makes fraud different from other crime is the response of victims. Most victims of crime immediately report the incident to the police. In online dating fraud, there is a sense of embarrassment and a reluctance to acknowledge that one has been taken. As a result, many online dating frauds are not reported, making the continuation of the scam easier and more profitable to the scammers.

Diana Garren was a victim of online dating fraud. Instead of keeping the details of how she was separated from her money, she bravely went forward gathering additional information to let others know how online dating schemes work and who is behind them. Her efforts detailed in this excellent book now empower others who find themselves in similar situations. **Readers of this book are better equipped to protect themselves with the advantage of knowing the red flags". I highly recommend this book to all of those searching for a relationship with others online, so they can protect themselves against wolves in sheep's clothing. I also recommend this book to law enforcement investigators to provide them with a deeper understanding of not just how fraud schemes are implemented but a more complete understanding of online dating fraud in general.**"

— THOMAS M. RUCKE, *Certified Fraud Investigator, Minnesota*

"Diana Garren has written an accurate and astonishing account of the world of the online scammer, those individuals who exploit and lure women into emotional relationships that can wreak havoc, not only on the hearts but the wallets of the innocent. In Who is the Real Man Behind the Screen Diana's honesty, courage and integrity shines brightly, as does the spotlight she focuses on these criminals. This book is an extensive and enlightening investigative report on a dark and despicable enterprise, most of which is cast from Nigeria.

Diana's many years of business experience in working with attorneys and professional investigators has paid off – **she knows how to build a case. Her investigation on the subject matter is forensically sound and her ability to bring the scammers into her confidence is first-rate investigative work.** Diana has learned from her mistake and she is now sharing those lessons with the rest of us. Great job, Diana."

— DON C. JOHNSON, CLI, CII, *President, Trace Investigations, Inc., Bloomington, Indiana Assistant National Director, National Association of Legal Investigators, Indiana*

"Diana is a diligent investigator (Merriam-Webster defines investigator as one who observes or studies by close examination and systematic inquiry). I, too, am an investigator, and I, too, fell for a scammer. Diana has put a lot of work into making this book informative and educational for everyone about the online dating scams. We talked about the scammers, as I confided in her about my escapade with one. She empathized with my pain and understood why I felt like I did. As we discussed the scams, I knew Diana had to write this book. I am a Certified Fraud Investigator, and I can attest that Diana has done a lot of research into the scammers. Diana has answered just about all the who's, the what's, the why's, the where's and the how's, just like a detective investigating a case. She has gone the whole course on this. She even was able to get scammers to confide in her, the whole program. Not only are women victims of these scammers, men are too. **Everyone will learn from Diana's book,** and knowing Diana, there will be more to come! Congratulations, Diana. I am proud of this accomplishment, I am proud of you for sharing your story. You will help millions of good women and men protect themselves from these scammers."

— ALICE E GOLD, *Retired detective, Certified Fraud Examiner, MAcc (Forensic), Florida*

"**Diana has done her research and produced knowledge that every woman should acquire.** I get a call at least 3 times a week at my agency from women who have sent money to these con artists. Now I will refer them to the expert!"

— GAYLE MARTIN, *Certified Investigator, Florida*

"I have been a Deputy/Detective for ten years and a Professional Private Investigator for 28 years. My specialty is organized crime and intelligence (LEIU), crime pattern analysis, sexual abuse and exploitation cases. I have my Ed.D. Doctor of Education in Human Sexuality, and it is from the perspective of my background that I want to applaud Diana Garren for the time and effort she has put into this book "Who Is the Real Man Behind the Screen." Not only has she done a thorough forensic investigation without any bias, she has also identified the human element of the romance scam as being "molestation for money" and detailed how scammers mimic the manipulation and grooming tactics used by child molesters. Both the child molester and the scammer use the grooming process of trust, isolation, manipulation and "you will do this if you love me." **I highly recommend this book to those who are or want to online date. This book will provide you the knowledge to keep you and your money safe. I also recommend this book and the awareness program to those who have already been scammed. It is only through breaking the silence that you will no longer be a victim and be able to reclaim that part of yourself and help others do the same**."

— HARVEY C. SHAPIRO, *Ed.D., California*

"Being an FBI Special Agent for 28 years and a Certified Fraud Examiner for 22 years, plus having a Bachelor's in both Business and Psychology and a Master's in Criminal Justice, I know a solid educational book when I see one. This is exactly what Who Is the Real Man Behind the Screen? is. This book was developed through personal experience, a thorough two-year investigation and inside knowledge provided by scammers themselves. Diana Garren has created an educational handbook that is filled with valuable red flags and practical knowledge that will help people protect their hearts and money, as well as an awareness campaign to break the silence and allow victims to become victorious. Understanding that all human beings are vulnerable to being scammed, **I highly recommend anyone who has been scammed through a dating site, who is currently or contemplating online dating, along with law enforcement and investigators to read this book.**

Once you start reading it is almost impossible to put down as you follow the emotions between Diana and the scammer as he weaves a web of deceit. **The reader will get so caught up in the raw emotions that they will be thankful they are reading these in the book instead of discovering the deceit for themselves in an online romance.**

Once the reader learns the techniques of the scammer, they will be able to protect themselves from a similar fate."

— BROCKMAN C. SELF, *Masters of Science in Criminal Justice and Certified Fraud Examiner, Florida*

"It is estimated that as many as 58% of women and 48% of men in the United States engage in online dating. Diana Garren's book, **Who is the Man behind the Screen** **should be mandatory reading for every single one of these dating site clients.** Not only that, but every investigator in the country who has ever dealt with one of these dating scams owes it to their clients to be familiar with the tell-tale signs that a scam is being or about to be committed.

To those who have fallen victim to such a crime in the past, you will see from this book that you are not alone. To those who may unwittingly engage with an online fraudster in the future – commit the invaluable real-life information to memory and refuse to be a victim.

Diana has herself stepped into the light in order to reveal the scammers' "tricks of the trade." While most others would rather stay silent and not let it be known that they themselves had been swindled, Diana courageously bares her soul and shares with us the way in which she was used. In much the same way as "Penn and Teller" have become infamous for revealing magicians' secrets, she takes us by the hand and navigates us through the inner working of an online scammer. She methodically penetrates well-constructed webs of deceit and strips away layer by layer of subterfuge, until the criminal is left shivering and unprotected in the cold light of day."

— JOHN SEXTON, CII, CST, *President, Council of International Investigators and Author of; "How to make a Killing as a Bodyguard". Washington, DC*

"Trusting and falling in love… online! I've heard it happens to a lucky few. I personally knew a couple who met online and who are happily married today, living their dreams of having a family and a blessed life together. We have all heard many stories like that. You do so want to be part of that lucky few… after all, you do your homework to check things out. However, unknown to us, the scammer makes sure he has backstops to cover himself, his lies, and his scams! The scammer tells you what he knows you want to hear, but he does not stop there.

"Diana has revealed her heart in telling her story in order to help others. She appears vulnerable, yet she is a strong and courageous woman. Diana tells you how she fell in love in spite of feeling some things were not quite right. The truth in her story and her research will set others free to be strong, courageous, and knowledgeable in matters of the heart and their finances when dealing with people on-line. **Diana's story is a must read for all people, young and old; those looking for a relationship, or those looking for a deal that's "too good to be true**."

— JULIE MARTIN, *Retired FBI, Austin, Texas*

"Having been a private investigator for more than thirty years, I have heard many stories from very intelligent people who have been swindled by skilled criminals. Some came to mind as I read Diana's own account of how she plunged headlong into victimhood. Knowing well her strength of character, professionalism, and inquisitive nature, I found it hard to fathom how Diana was taken. In her book she frankly explains how her emotions overrode her sensibilities, right in line with the con artist's plan as he sized up and exploited her. **I applaud her honesty in recounting her experience, her tenacity in turning the table on the scammer, and her devoted investment of time and money to create this roadmap that is certain to help others detour around the warning signs of online dating fraud**."

— J.R. SKAGGS, *Texas*

"**If you are serious about protecting yourself from scammers, Who Is the Real Man Behind the Screen is an important tool for you to add to your survival kit. Do yourself a favor and buy it.** Better still, buy the book, visit her awareness campaign and get yourself to one of Diana's workshops.

Whether you are learning from her in person or from her book, Diana's teaching style is straight-up, fact-filled, enriching, joyful and thorough. This energetic and generous author is passionate about her craft; her enthusiasm is infectious. I do not know how she does it, but her style of communication imparts confidence to the reader whether you are vulnerable or have been scammed. Better still, she tells you how to recognize potential scammers. Because she has walked the road of the scammed, her advice is based on experience, inside sources and research. She is honest, she is human and she wants you to be safe. Kudos to you, Diana! I look forward to more books from you."

— TERRY O'CONNOR, *PhD, Arkansas*

"Who is the Real Man Behind the Screen? is an authoritative commentary that exhaustively exposes the tactics used against innocent people partaking in online dating. As more of my customers turn to online dating as a means of finding companionship, I find great comfort in knowing that **Diana Garren has provided this resource, which reveals the red flags my customers should watch for.** Although I grieve that she personally had to endure such pain and deceit, I applaud her ability to use her experience for the good of others. Diana's investigative and marketing skills are masterfully played out through the pages of this book. I look forward to her next!"

— GERALD SCARBROUGH, *Owner, Computer Helper, Georgia*

"**This is a book for smart people. People who already know the dangers of online dating and would never dream of sharing personally identifying information with a stranger.** People who know what "phishing" is and who delete suspicious messages and ignore unsolicited email offers. This is a book for people who, upon making a new online connection, immediately Google search their new friend to verify their identity; people who cross-check Google, LinkedIn, Facebook, Twitter, and whitepages.com to confirm that the person they are connecting with online is really who they say they are. If you are smart enough to do all those things, this book is definitely for you!

Diana Garren is a smart woman. She did all those things. She got scammed anyway. Her book is compelling because she lays bare the harsh realities of online dating scams, the harshest of which may be that you never really know who is behind the screen. No one does. Ms. Garren's book cuts through the romantic notions and wishful thinking that can impair the strongest among us and make us easy prey.

Ms. Garren writes with honesty, compassion, and utter commitment to her mission. Hers is a rallying cry to awaken the gut instinct and native intelligence we rely on for our wellbeing and survival. This book will change you for the better."

—SALLY M. BACCHETTA, *Author of The Adoptive Parent and Freelance Writer, New York*

"**Who is the Real Man Behind the Screen is a must read for anyone looking for love with online dating services or social media groups.**

D.L. Garren shares her experience and explains in detail what to look out for so you can avoid being scammed.

I strongly recommend this book to everyone so you can learn from her experience instead of your own."

— DIANNE GREGG, C.C., *Author, The Hidden Dangers of Soy, Georgia*

"Diana has captured the essence of Internet scammers and how they infiltrate hearts to commit crimes that are virtually non-prosecutable and destroy trust and financial stability. **This is a must read book for Internet dating**."

—UNDERSHERIFF RICK STALY, *Retired Orange County Sheriff's Office, Florida*

"Diana Garren has written a heart-wrenching story of a search for happiness gone awry, placing trust above all. **This is a must-read for not only those who search for relationships on the Internet but also for investigators called up to assist.** Ms. Garren has written the definitive primer and pleads her case exceptionally well for due diligence to avoid a disastrous emotional roller coaster ride. **Read it, learn from it or weep**."

—JIM CARINO, *Retired Special Agent AFOSI & Founder & Executive Director Emeritus, Intellnet, Pennsylvania*

"Who Is the Real Man Behind the Screen? and Is It a Real Soldier Behind the Screen? are enlightenment to the old biblical saying, "Beware of false prophets. They come to you disguised as sheep, but in their hearts they are vicious wolves." Diana brilliantly combines her regrettable encounter with an unscrupulous scammer with her years of experience working with private investigators and attorneys to create scholastic exposes of online scammers' tradecraft. **She uncovers how scammers employ the internet and social media to find their targets and manipulate them to extort their money, pride and innocence, while, like false prophets, disguising their true malevolent intentions.**

I applaud this passionate author's bravery because despite great emotional and financial loss, she found the courage to write these books. **Her diligent efforts and example will not only educate and equip others with the advantage of knowing online scams red flags and scammers' trade craft, they will empower people to protect themselves from the emotional, physical and financial hardships of a online scam victims.**

These books are MUST READ books for persons engaged in online dating, everyone who has a social media account, and professional private investigators, law enforcement officials and investigative reporters entrusted to help protect innocent sufferers from online predators."

— ARNOLD RODRIGUEZ, *Retired AFOSI Special Agent & CEO of Investigative Security Consultants, LLC, Arizona*

"Congratulations on your book. Courage and determination are what it takes to write a book like this. Diana was emotionally involved and rational at the same time. Trusting our instincts always ends up being rewarding. **A MUST READ book**."

—MARIE-HÉLÈNE GAGNON, *Canada*

"A remarkable story, rich in unknown details about a vastly lucrative business. **This is the perfect book for anyone online dating who wants to know what to look for in a Scammer.** It is unbelievable how the author has channeled her hurt, pain and embarrassment into an extraordinary work and a wealth of information that will truly help those who are innocently seeking real relationships online. **Read this book and avoid a lot of heartache and trouble.**"

— E. BRYANT, *Business Owner, Georgia*

"Who is the Real Man Behind the Screen?, and Is It a Real Soldier Behind the Screen?, are two of the most riveting works I have ever read. If I did not know Diana personally, and know the passion with which she has pursued these books, I would have sworn I was reading works of fiction. There is only one way someone could write about this horrific crime with such conviction — to have been the victim of such. Diana took what could have been—for some people—a life-ending experience, and with dignity, turned her crisis into these heart-wrenching guides. **I recommend to anyone who might be even remotely contemplating online dating, read these books! Law enforcement officers, private investigators, fraud examiners — these books should be required reading!** Congratulations, Diana, on this accomplishment. I know it has ruled your life for several years. Thank you for allowing me to tiptoe briefly into the project with you. I wish you love and Godspeed."

— SHERYL M. JACKSON, *Retired Executive Director, Texas Association of Licensed Investigators, Texas*

"Online Dating Scams are a dishonest way to make money and they are conducted by deceiving people. This criminal act has been and is still very in vogue in Nigeria. It has left so many victims in a state of depression, some even to the extent of committing suicide. Can you imagine someone who claims to love you and in the end they swindle you out of millions of dollars. There is always an end to evil acts and this one (online dating scamming) is no exception. **People need to read** *Who is the Real Man Behind the Screen* **not because its just another book on the market, but because it is written with in-depth research, real life occurrences and much more, with its sole aim of eliminating the online dating scamming menace.** Above all, the author is a passionate, intelligent, dedicated woman who has deemed it fit for the public to be highly educated on the tricks these scammers use to hunt and hurt their victims."

— ADEWALE KEHINDE, *Lagos State, Nigeria*

"This book is a cautionary tale of one woman's short but intense encounter with the shadowy side of the Internet. The other day Diana Garren called me and in the course of the conversation told me she had written a couple of books. She described this first-hand account of her encounter with online dating. As I listened I recalled my own experience with the "Sweetheart Swindle" that I have encountered several times over the years. It seems that sweetheart swindle scams and Nigerian 419 scams have coalesced into the near perfect method of extracting money from the unsuspecting aided by the Internet and technology.

This book is a detailed account of Diana's first internet dating experience. **What she learned, at great expense to her heart and her pocketbook, is a worthwhile read for those thinking about entering the Internet dating scene. This book is intentionally detailed because unless you see each detail you will continue to say what most folks say: "That couldn't happen to me."** For over thirty years I have heard that phrase from victims. It did happen to them. This book explains dating scams and the warning signs to look for so you can keep your hard earned money. Diana was able to convince several of the scammers to cooperate with her, in a manner of speaking, and tell their personal stories as well as revealing exactly how these schemes work. I found it interesting to learn the hierarchy that exists in this endeavor. This not just a bunch of folks working independently; it is an organized effort to extract money, complete with scripts and an organizational chart.

Internet dating is not a bad thing but it is an area where you must exercise extreme caution and not allow your heart to lead your head. Due diligence is necessary to avoid being taken advantage of from afar."

—BURT HODGES, *Florida Licensed Investigator and Certified Fraud Examiner, Florida*

"Diana Garren's book *Who is the Man Behind the Screen* **is a must-read for every person. Even if you yourself are not attempting to meet people online, you have friends and family who are.** We have several friends who met online and are now married. Those are the success stories. Far too often the story goes like Diana's experience, where the victim has been deceived, emotionally abused, and financially defrauded. I had no idea this type of crime was so prevalent, and after reading Diana's book, I have a much better understanding about how to protect myself from any type of online crime, not just Internet dating. I have known Diana many years. I am continually impressed by her passion and willingness to be transparent to save others from this fate. **Read this book and tell your friends about it**. Thank you, Diana, for this imperative work."

— WENDY E. MURNAN, *Licensed Investigator, Complete Legal Investigations, Inc., Florida*

"**A MUST READ for anyone contemplating online dating. I would go further and add, for ANYONE who has an account on any social media platform. Eye opening and informative, this book connects the dots on how scammers find their "clients" and how they manipulate and extort while hiding behind a computer screen.** It is astonishing to learn the extremes these people go to – casting spells, using emotional guilt and loving dialogue – preying on people who want to find a loving relationship, cleaning out their bank accounts and destroying future financial security. I worked as a researcher for a Private Investigator and cases of this type were the norm; people who had lost thousands of dollars, suffered the humiliation of being duped, and dealing with broken emotions looking for restitution from a scammer thousands of miles away that would never be located or prosecuted. **This book is a definite "Bible" for all in the business of investigation of online crimes and scams so they can better understand how these scams work.** I have a few friends that have online dating accounts and I would LOVE to give them copies."

—DELIA SALAZAR, *California*

"Heart-breaking and eye-opening, this is a must-read for anyone trying out online dating. Don't be afraid of it; just **make sure to read this book first!**"

— MATTHEW TYLER, *Principal, ASI, Texas*

"Writing this book has been an emotional roller coaster for my friend Diana. I have watched her struggle to keep her sense of well-being and sanity while researching for this book. Not only was Diana herself a victim of a scam, in her diligence to write this book, she deliberately put herself in harm's way again and again in order to make sure this book was the best possible resource on the topic. Diana was dedicated and determined to write a book full of hard facts and details, so anyone who reads her book will have valuable knowledge that can prevent them from also being a victim of an online dating scam. They say "An ounce of prevention is better than a pound of cure" and that is what Diana has tried to do in writing this book: prevent others from going through the emotional and physical heartache that she went through. I liken this book to the Boy Scouts "Be Prepared" motto. **Don't just read this book once and put it down; read it again and again. Be prepared, be knowledgeable, be smart and be safe.** I am so glad to have my friend back. Her writing of this book has been a long emotional journey for us both."

— RD FOSTER, *Georgia*

WHO IS THE REAL MAN BEHIND THE SCREEN?

ONLINE DATING: HOW TO PROTECT YOUR HEART AND MONEY

DL Garren

Who Is the Real Man Behind the Screen?
Online Dating: How to Protect Your Heart and Money

Publisher:
True Perceptions, Inc.®
P.O. Box 20826, Atlanta, GA 30320
678-583-0401

Awareness Program
info@silentvictimnomore.com
www.silentvictimnomore.com

Printed in the United States of America

International Standard Book Numbers:

ISBN-10: 0-9907611-0-X
ISBN-13: 978-0-9907611-0-5 (Paperback)

First Edition

Crime Prevention/Self-help

The author can be reached at diana@dlgarren.com or via the Web at www.dlgarren.com or follow her on Twitter at twitter.com/DianaLGarren and FaceBook at www.facebook.com/authordlgarren

Edited by Sally M. Bacchetta
Content layout and format by AuthorVista LLC
Cover design, graphics, icons and awareness logo designed by Stephen R. Walker

DEDICATION

This book is dedicated to all the men and women who fell in love, had their hearts broken and money stolen by an online dating scammer, especially those who took their lives because of the cruel criminal act known as the romance scam; to those men and women who are now, or plan to, online date, with the hope that the information in this book will keep your heart and money safe; and to the government agencies, non-government organizations, corporations and individuals dedicated to educating the public on romance scams.

CONTENTS

Acknowledgements

First and foremost I thank God for this divine setup. I wasn't even looking to online date. However, the Singlesbee dating site literally popped off my computer screen when it came in my inbox, and for a divine reason I arose to the calling and instantly stopped working, put up my profile and emailed the scammer (unknown to me at the time). From this act came the experience of being scammed. Sometime later came an inner knowing that I was supposed to do research for this book and start an awareness program. This surely wasn't easy and it wasn't in my plan for my life! However, it was God's plan and I give God all the glory, honor and praise for what he has already done and what he will continue to do to take this teaching and healing around the world.

Next I want to thank my dearest friend of over twenty years and a member of our team, Terry O'Connor. Thank you for always believing in me and supporting everything I do, including this book. You are a real Godsend. I value you and our friendship, and I love you!

I want to thank my awesome team and say how grateful I am for your support and hours upon hours of work. Without you, this book would not have come to fruition. Stephen R. Walker who has been a great friend and the fabulous creative arm for True Perceptions, Inc. for 14 years designed the cover, icons and graphics for this book, our awareness program logo and website and my author website.. Sally M. Bacchetta who has been a friend for the last five years and who provides her talent to edit and write for True Perceptions. She works her magic with the written word to make us all look good. Thank you Sally for your phenomenal work with me and for drudging through all the emotions this work brought forth in your spirit.

Thank you to Patricia Wallenburg for starting the layout process, which seeing it in a formatted style pushed me to write after the long years of research.

Thank you to Eugene F. Ferraro (my wingman and shepherd) and his firm AuthorVista LLC for creating the beautiful layout that makes reading easy for our readers and making sure this book was ready for print. I know it wasn't easy to have several chapters that were actually the size of an entire book. Without you, this book would have never gone to print.

Thank you to my clients and friends Michael J. West, Thomas M. Rucke and Brockman C. Self for your expertise as I swam through the murky waters of the scamming world. Without your training and expertise I would have been stuck more than once.

Thank you to Paul Price for writing the fabulous Foreword and teaching me things I didn't know, for encouraging me, and supporting this book and the awareness program because you know that education is the key to stopping romance scams.

Thank you to everyone who took the time to read this book and write a testimonial. I know this took a lot of your precious time, and I greatly appreciate that you found this work important enough.

Thank you to Sheila Franks (God mother), my sister-in-law Bev Yalch, my brother Jonathan Garren, my niece Stephanie Garren and my incredible friends Daniel Gannon, Ruby Foster, Sheryl M. Jackson, Shelia Middleton, Ronald Waugh, Alice Gold, Yunice Patrick, Delia Vasquez Salazar, Tim Little, Shawn Anderson, Gayle Martin, Danielle Black, Julie Martin, Jeannie Finelli, Harvey Shapiro, Neema Carter, Dianne Gregg, Tyler Mabry, Christopher A, Kaiz and Elaine Bryant. You all believed in me and this book and you supported me in many ways. You were there to push me when I needed it, remind me to stay balanced, help level out my emotions when things got really heavy and dark, get me away from the keyboard to take a break and have some fun every now and then, and remind me that I need rest for my health. Without all of you, this journey would have been much harder. Thank you for staying with me through the good and the bad!

Last but not least, I want to thank my inside sources in Nigeria: Bob Jugant, Chris Terumun and Kelvin Mitchell for teaching me the inner workings of the scam world and protecting me as I continued chatting to obtain intelligence for this book. I also want to thank Bobo Ighosogie Ogbomo and N.U. for verifying information I was provided and for your many translations. Because of you the information in this book is forensically sound.

FOREWORD

Online dating has become very popular for obvious reasons. It provides an opportunity to expand your search for that "perfect someone" from the comfort and safety of your home. It's not the type of scenario where you expect to attract thieves looking to steal your money, but these predators enjoy a great deal of financial success because they know how to manipulate your heart and bank account.

I spent a good part of my law enforcement career that spanned over 20 years investigating online fraud, and it involved people from all walks of life and socioeconomic groups. The one universal truth is that *anyone can be a victim*. Predators focus their collective efforts on learning what to say and do to legitimize their online identity and gain your trust. They share their methods with other predators to ensure further success. Any amount of money they can get, from $5.00 to $100,000.00 or more, is considered a victory because their single goal is to get your money.

Who is the Real Man Behind the Screen? is an in-depth look at online dating fraud and some of the tactics predators use. The book follows the fraud from start to finish, with detailed chats, emails, websites, posted pictures, and most importantly the "red flags." Red Flags are the subtle cues that something is wrong. These red flags are something the average person may overlook, but after reading this book you will see just how important they really are to prevent yourself from being victimized.

The most dangerous attitude is, *"It will never happen to me."* Predators expend almost unlimited resources to hone their skills to separate your from your money and will continue to use the anonymity of the Internet to target their victims. It *can* happen to you, and education is the key to keeping yourself safe. Knowing what to look for and the methods used by predators will help you to identify the true intentions of the person behind the screen.

Paul Price

CEO, Beyond IT

Houston, Texas

AUTHOR'S NOTE

People understand what they feel. Please do not just *read* this book. Please put yourself in my place and *feel* this book so you do not have to experience that which I did.

You will find this book will take you on a journey of every human emotion. It will help you heal if you have been victimized and your heart has been broken. It will provide insight from real live intimate chats, emails, text, images and emotions. Red flags are provided to help prevent you from becoming a victim and one of the millions whose money has been stolen and heart played and broken.

Good luck and best wishes,

DL Garren

DISCLAIMER

The contents of this book are for educational purposes only. The author's intent is not to glorify scams or scammers but to reveal how scammers operate and the red flags that can help identify potential scams. Neither the author nor True Perceptions, Inc.® assume any liability for any results or outcomes that may result from the use, misuse or failure to use any of the information contained in this book. Neither the author nor True Perceptions, Inc. offers services to recover funds for victims of fraud.

No guarantee, implied or implicit is given or offered that following the information contained herein will keep you safe from scams or scammers, nor should this information be the basis for your action or inaction. Neither this work nor the opinions and advice contained herein should be construed as legal advice or relied upon as such. Should such advice be necessary, it is suggested that competent professional assistance be sought. Furthermore, while many of the practices, methodologies, and insights which are presented are considered sound, specific circumstances and fact patterns should drive your effort and approach. If unsure as to how to properly proceed, stop and seek the advice of a competent professional.

All of the images of individuals, other than those of herself, in this book were provided to DL Garren by scammers. No attempt to exploit these individuals or the unfortunate misuse of their images has been made or attempted by either the publisher or the author. The reader should note that most images used by scammers are stolen from third parties. The author has included them solely so that the reader will know the manner and methods of their inappropriate use. The author has tried unsuccessfully to find the individuals whose images that were misappropriated by scammers and used as examples in this book. In an attempt to protect their identity, she has blurred their faces.

CHAPTER 1

MOLESTATION FOR MONEY

I have been thinking about you for two and a half years, and I am so happy to finally be speaking directly to you, my readers; anyone who is currently or thinking about online dating, anyone who has friends and/or family who are dating online, and anyone who has been or knows someone who has been scammed via the Internet dating romance scam. For those who have committed suicide over the heartbreak and loss of money, my heart bleeds and I send sincere condolences to your family. This book is also for you. All heartache and loss is now not in vain.

Only *after* I was scammed did I learn a few red flags and the enormity of the Internet dating problem. Like all who have been scammed I learned after the fact, after my money was gone! This helped me realize we need to teach and take preventative measures. So, I continued to chat online to learn the inside details about various scams so I could educate you and other people worldwide.

All through the two and a half years I spent chatting with scammers, talking via telephone almost daily to my five inside sources in Nigeria, and logging untold number of hours researching online, you were on my mind. You strengthened me so I could stay in the trenches and learn all I could. I knew you needed the information I was mining. Thank you for always being in the forefront of my mind and giving me the strength and courage to continue! With every stroke on my keyboard, I knew thousands (if not millions) of men and women all over the world were getting their hearts broken and money stolen at that very moment, all because they were not armed with the knowledge they needed to keep their hearts and money safe.

Once I became adept at identifying scammers, I would send them an email, and of course they would take my bait, hook, line and sinker. I sometimes chatted with up to six scammers at the same time. I am a woman of truth and integrity, so all this lying and deception took a toll on me. At times I felt I was in a very dark place as a person because I was doing what the scammer does. I was lying and telling them I love them all to get something from them. The only difference was that I wanted information and they wanted money. I went to this dark place in order to help people, and scammers live in this dark place in order to hurt people. My close friends noticed a change in me during this time and they rode the emotional roller coaster with me. They watched me sink into the black hole and thankfully were still there by my side when I resurfaced to the light. I must tell you, I have never received so many flower bouquets, teddy bears, chocolates and false promises as I did during the time in which I was chatting to gather the intelligence for this book. I live in a small town so I had to tell my florist what I was doing so they didn't have the wrong perception of me. I have also never said, "I love you" without meaning it. But I sure did while chatting to obtain the information for this book. It was a wild ride, to say the least! The journey this book will take you on will touch every one of your human emotions, so buckle up!

I will show you the dangers entwined with online dating through intimate chats, emails, text, red flags, language, formats and scam stories the scammers employ. You will learn how scammers gain your trust to swindle your money; tools of the scammer trade used to fool you and the inner workings of the scamming world… revealed by scammers themselves.

In chapter two (p. 9) I will take you through my own personal journey of being scammed by a professional scammer from beginning to end. The rest of the book was all research so you have everything you need to be safe.

There are two ways to read this book. You can read every word, which will allow you to really understand and *feel* it for yourself, or you can read just the red flags that are bolded and italicized and summarized throughout each of the scam stories. The choice is yours, however you will learn much more if you read it word for word.

Many people have asked if I was writing this book to heal from my own experience, and my answer has always been, no. I had already forgiven the man who scammed me and was healed. This book has nothing to do with my healing or any revenge. My experience awakened my awareness and fueled my dedication to educate you. Through my experience I realized that Internet dating scams are a huge problem that no one is tackling head on. Most people don't seek out information about online scams until after they have been scammed, if ever. The only way to stop the romance scams forever is to build worldwide awareness and prevention. That is why I wrote this book and started the awareness campaign. Everything you are going to read is so much bigger than me. So big that it has a global reach and will help men and women heal, protect their hearts and money, and learn the online dating rules everyone needs to know *before* venturing online to find love.

I believe this book will change laws and help governments, because every dollar that is stolen through the Internet romance scam bleeds money from the country it is stolen from. I urge citizens in every country to promote this book to their community and law enforcement so they can stop the bleeding and strengthen their economies.

Estimates are that out of 54 Million single people in the U.S., 40 Million of them have tried online dating, and online dating has generated annual revenues of over $2.2 Billion dollars in the U.S. alone. comScore Research found that over 122 million people worldwide are dating online. NBC News staff writer M. Alex Johnson writes, "romance scams make up more than 10 percent of all financial losses to online fraud — and women 50 and older account for 61 percent of those losses" (Johnson, 2013). Online Dating Magazine estimates that there are approximately 2,500 online dating sites in the United States and more than 5,000 online dating sites worldwide. These numbers make online dating a goldmine for scammers.

Stopping these predators through legal means appears impossible. Educating people to identify a scammer upfront, and providing a way to break the silence concerning this *molestation for money*, may be the only way to end this evil. Most people do not talk about or report being scammed, so there are no accurate reports of the number of people who are scammed or how much money has been stolen.

"There is nothing more deceptive than an obvious fact."
— Arthur Conan Doyle

The one thing every human being wants is to love and be loved. In today's world online dating is a way to meet people, and getting into online dating is easy. What's not so easy is to know going into it that you need to beware of scammers and "here are the tools to teach you what to look for." Granted, many dating sites have this information…somewhere…buried on their website. A few are actually responsible and post warnings in several places. But for the most part, people new to online dating are unaware of the online predator called the "scammer". *Many don't even think about getting scammed because after all, when you sign up for online dating you are looking for love, not watching out for a scammer.* I hope this book, which is filled with complete scam stories from the beginning to end and with profiles, pictures, live chats, emails, text and red flags, will provide the education needed to make it impossible for the scammer to ever scam another person via the Internet romance scam.

You are at a great disadvantage when you venture into the virtual world and start online dating. Many of the safeguards and natural instincts you have built up over your lifetime are greatly diminished because you never see the person to see their eyes and read their body language. You lose the benefits of sight, smell and touch. The virtual world is very different from the world you are accustomed to. The virtual world operates more on emotion than anything else. Most people are not prepared or knowledgeable enough about what happens in the virtual world to play safely, and sooner or later they become a victim. It's not "if" you will become a victim, it's "when."

People are born with a threat detection instinct that allows us to quickly determine whether someone is friend or foe by the way they look or act. Think about a baby crying the first time she sees a relative with a beard or a toddler hiding behind his parents when a stranger approaches. These natural fight or flight responses are designed to keep you safe. When you meet someone online these natural safeguards are defeated; you feel no threat sitting safely behind a keyboard in your own home. You falsely feel in control of the situation. Trust me, the man behind the screen will take his time and put his full effort into gaining your trust before attempting the scam, and your best weapon – your natural threat detection instinct – is asleep at the wheel because you are interacting online rather than in person.

"We're all friends here" is a prelude to fraud. "I am sincere" is a prelude to lying.
— *Mason Cooley*

Those who were molested as a child are particularly susceptible to the romance scam because the scammer uses the same grooming process of gaining your trust, telling you they love you, and then using "You will do this if you love me." I don't know why, but whenever someone has been molested, predators can easily spot it and they prey upon that vulnerability.

Think you're too smart to be scammed? Let's hope so, but would it surprise you to know that even highly intelligent people — people with advanced degrees; doctors; lawyers — fall for cleverly planned and executed online scams? *It happens every day.*

If you think, *"It will never happen to me"* I'll just say, "Yeah. I thought the same thing." I have worked with fraud investigators for over a decade, and I know a lot about different types of fraud. In the end, I was wrong. I didn't know what I needed to be safe online. Confidence that gets you to relax and let your guard down can really get you in trouble online. Scammers are trained and they are slick. A scammer himself told me, "Everyone can be scammed, including me. If someone gets to that certain place in your heart or to your vulnerability, the scam will work. Everyone has a spot where they are vulnerable, even the smartest and toughest person." *Never say never!*

Because I was not educated about the romance scam, I got my heart broken and was scammed by the first man I met online. Not only was he a pro at making a woman fall in love with him, but I was the perfect target because I was naïve about online dating. I didn't even know how to chat on Yahoo! Messenger until he taught me. I did not know how dangerous online dating could be. It can be far more dangerous than most people would ever think. That's why I dedicated an entire chapter to the unknown dangers.

Being scammed and writing books about romance scams was not even on my radar screen the day I put up a profile on an online dating site. The only thing on my mind that day was the possibility of finding my "forever" love. *Please, please, please* hear me when I tell you that you too can easily be scammed if you don't know the red flags. I know private investigators, attorneys, prior law enforcement, CIA and FBI agents who have been scammed. All of these individuals are very smart people. Being scammed has nothing to do with your IQ. It comes from the lack of education *about the scam and the scammer.* This book will not only provide you with the education you need, it will allow you to feel and experience the emotional roller coaster ride a scammer will take you on.

In many ways, the victim unwittingly assists in their own deceit. Think about it. Who doesn't love the euphoria of falling in love? The excitement of meeting and connecting with someone who may be your forever love is intoxicating, whether you meet in person or online. Your imagination cascades through one possible future to another, picking up speed and intensity with every conversation. When dating online your desire for love, your attraction to a person's picture and your own imagination help the scammer do his job. So much so that you can be swept up and not even realize you are being scammed until after your money is gone. **Scammers know and play on this. It is how they make a living.** They work at making you fall in love, and they are fast, furious and hypnotic. For them it is like writing a movie and casting you as the main character.

Scammers know that the first thing they need from you is your trust. Trust is a prerequisite for you to overlook minor discrepancies and dismiss your doubts. Trust can blind you to the ragged edges and disconnected dots of a false reality. This book will steel you to hold fast to your trust and your intellect so you can pay careful attention to every detail, because the slightest inconsistency will uncover the illusion, and the truth behind the illusion will become revealed. In this book the illusions are being uncovered and the truth is being revealed.

If you get involved with a scammer, the emotional journey will create a trust issue within you and alter your life forever! Many people including myself trust others too easily. In today's world, we cannot do this. I surely do not do this anymore. That has been changed in me forever. To aid in changing this, I created a trust formula that I think we can all benefit from.

First you need to realize that trust is NOT to be given freely, it is to be EARNED!

Second, draw a horizontal line on a piece of paper. On the far left of the line write "DON'T TRUST." On the far right of the line write "TRUST." In the center write "I DON'T KNOW YOU." When you meet someone new they get placed dead center..."I DON'T KNOW YOU." This isn't harsh or unfair, it's REALITY! You DON'T know them. Then for 90 DAYS MINIMUM LISTEN to their WORDS and PAY CLOSE ATTENTION to their ACTIONS. Every time their WORDS and ACTIONS don't align move them closer to DON'T TRUST. During this time, share very little about yourself. Instead, listen closely and learn about them to discern if they have pure or impure motives. PAY ATTENTION!

People can always talk "good jive," BUT they can only keep up a facade for a short period of time. If you are not sure after 90 days, extend the time period. Here is the CRITICAL part: IF you find reasons they CANNOT be trusted, DO NOT talk yourself into thinking they are someone they are not. Believe what they are showing you instead of what they are telling you and CUT THEM OUT OF YOUR LIFE instead of starting a relationship with them. If you do this you won't be knocked down and have to pick yourself back up.

Have You Already Been Scammed?

If you have already been scammed by the romance scam, please forgive yourself. The only thing you did was trust someone who was untrustworthy and undeserving of your trust. It was blindness that put you in the path of who betrayed you. Sometimes a good heart doesn't see bad. Please know you are not stupid and you did nothing wrong. You were manipulated and too close to even see it happening until it was too late. It is human nature to not be able to see when we are emotionally or financially attached. I believe George Orwell said it best, "To see what is in front of one's nose requires a constant struggle."

When someone hurts or betrays you, please know it has NOTHING to do with you. They did it because it's WHO THEY ARE. Now your job is to say "Thank you for showing me who you are, now I can CHOOSE if I want you in my life. Then CHOOSE WISELY!

It's Time to Break the Silence

If you are still beating yourself up, feeling embarrassed and ashamed, please stop. As long as you do this, you will not heal. You will remain a victim of the scammer and he will always be able to haunt you and control your life. I want you to become victorious and take your power back. You take your power back by forgiving yourself and by talking about it and educating others. Education can break the silence of shame and embarrassment and stop others from being scammed. If you want to take your power back and join our effort to educate the world – we would love for you to share your story at www.silentvictimnomore.com.

What You Need to Know if the Scammer Reveals Himself to You

Many times a scammer will reveal himself to you to continue the scam. Nobody wants to admit they have been played and denial is a powerful thing, so many women continue their relationship with the scammer. I would think it would be the toughest relationship ever because it was founded on lies and deceit, and trust could never be formed. However, some women do this and choose to live an illusion, one that allows them to continue to be deceived by false realities. If you are going through this, please know you deserve so much better. Please watch the video found at www.youtube.com/watch?v=53A0zfaab0s

Before Dating Online

If you are going to date online, know all the red flags, keep this book close by and refer to the quick guide in the back of this book. Do your due diligence and hire a professional if need be. Remember, once a scammer infiltrates your heart, you become easy prey and he can easily obtain your money. For additional assistance in identifying who you are chatting with contact us at www.dlgarren.com. We can help you. We want you to be safe!

I always believed in the power of intention and I love adventure, but never, in my wildest dreams, did I expect this adventure. Life really is like a box of chocolates — you never know what you're going to get.

In this journey there are unexpected, bizarre twists and turns that are deeply steeped with love, disappointment, sadness, lies, heartbreak, revealed truths, repentance, shame, embarrassment, loss of money and along the way three scammers on the other side of the world that became sources...

So are you ready to take a ride and experience some of the characters I dealt with? It started with Jerry who took me in and out of love with him in just eleven days, then there was Bob, the teacher of many things, then Jeff who used a story that would rip any woman's heart out, then there was Bret, Bret taught me the real dangers of online dating and then last but not least there was Jimmy, or was he Robin?

References:

http://h-dating-online.blogspot.com/2013/02/online-dating-statistics.html

www.examiner.com/article/online-dating-and-statistics

www.onlinedatingmagazine.com/faq/howmanyonlinedatingsitesarethere.html

www.reuters.com/article/2011/12/22/us-usa-scams-romance-idUSTRE7BK12620111222

www.huffingtonpost.com/2012/02/14/online-dating-scams_n_1263837.html

Johnson, M. Alex, 2013. *Older women most likely to click with online romance scam artist.*

www.youtube.com/watch?v=53A0zfaab0s

CHAPTER 2

IN AND OUT OF LOVE IN
ELEVEN DAYS!

T his is how it all started. This is the man who scammed me. This is my personal experience. The worst thing for me is I initiated our meeting. Yep, I hit on his profile. If I had known then what I know now (and what you will know from reading this book) I would not have been scammed. I would not ever have had a conversation with him. I would have recognized the red flags in his profile. But because I didn't know the red flags, I was easy prey and I got stung. Although I did not enjoy the emotional pain, I do not regret it happened. I have always felt this is how it was supposed to be. If I wasn't scammed, I would not know how it feels, and I could not have written books and started an awareness program to educate others and elicit change.

Was I stupid? Not at all. I am a very intelligent, street smart woman. Was I desperate? No, not at all. I am a beautiful and successful woman any man would be proud to be with. Was I lonely? I would say yes, sometimes on holidays and weekends because I have no family living close to me, and I do not go out a lot. I am busy working, and besides, where does a 48 year old woman go to meet men? Most times, I didn't even see where there was time for a relationship, and I chose not to date for eight years while I built my business. This chapter of the book picks up the chapter of my life when I found myself ready to build a relationship. In January, I made the decision to date and I met this man at the end of March. I knew what I wanted in a man and knew nothing about the dangers of online dating. This man supposedly had many of the qualities I was looking for. He portrayed himself as a Christian, a man who was kind, romantic, and emotionally available. He claimed to own his own business and live in my favorite city of San Diego. He was sweet and attentive and said he had a grown son in college, which gave me hopes of having a family since I have no children. The key words here are "supposedly" and "portrayed." He honed in on my romantic nature and played this trait of mine like a fiddle. He was very good at his game, and I fell hard and fast for his sweet words. Because my heart was guiding me instead of my logic, I didn't ask enough pertinent questions about his background. When I discovered he was definitely not who he pretended to be and realized he scammed me, I actually thanked him for making me aware this happens, so I could do something to change it.

This is difficult for me to admit, but it is very important for you to understand: I knew I was mesmerized by his sweet words filled with honey and I also knew better than to send the money, but I sent it anyway. I am still shaking my head in disbelief. My head knew better, but my heart won out. He later told me, "I knew you were a smart woman, and I was surprised you sent the money". So again, I go back to believing all this was supposed to happen.

This man was a professional scammer with tools and charm, and he was damn good at what he did. He told me "The boss needs me because he has no clue how to make women fall in love with him, so my job is to make women fall in love with me so they will give me their money, and I am damn good at it!"

What I didn't know then was I was the perfect target. I fit every qualification a scammer looks for in a victim. In addition to fitting the target profile demographically, I was naïve. I am by nature too trusting, and I want to believe the best about people.

Once I realized I had been scammed, I felt stupid, embarrassed and ashamed. However, I quickly realized the only thing I did wrong was make the mistake of trusting someone untrustworthy. This is the only mistake every victim makes. If you have been a victim, please know that this is all you did wrong; you were manipulated, not stupid. This was a good lesson learned and now I pray everyone who reads my books will learn through me and spare themselves the experience of a broken heart and lost money.

As I developed the red flags in this chapter, it was definitely strange to "see" myself in a relationship in black and white print. It gave me an opportunity to examine myself from a different perspective, and I hope this speaks to you and helps you as well. If I didn't want to help people, I surely would not expose myself like this. I know that nothing will change if those of us who have been scammed stay silent. We have to break the silence to change this crime plaguing so many. I hope you learn much from the bumpy emotional ride this professional scammer will take you on in this chapter!

His profile as found on *Singlesbee*:

Profile: libertaren50

Come live in my heart rent free
50-year-old in San Diego, CA
Seeking 39 to 65-year-old women

My Headline
Come Live in my heart and pay no rent!! Live rent free

My Current Status
619 add 796 add 1879

My Basics

- Height: 5'10"
- Body type: Average
- Hair color: Black
- Ethnicity: White / Caucasian
- Looks: Very attractive
- Education: Some college
- *Occupation: Construction and installation*
- Income: $100,000
- I speak: English
- Religion: Christian - other
- *Relationship status: Widowed*
- Children: Yes, not living at home
- Wants children: Undecided
- Smoking: Never
- Drinking: Occasionally

My Type of Girl

- Looking for: Dating Only, Dating / Long-term Potential, Long-term Only
- *With: Women 39 to 65-year-old*
- Distance: Within 10000 miles of San Diego
- Height: 5'0" to 6'0"
- Body type: Any
- Hair color: Any
- Ethnicity: Doesn't Matter
- Education: Doesn't Matter
- Occupation: Any
- Income: Doesn't Matter
- Language(s): English
- Religion: Any
- Relationship status: Any
- Children: Doesn't Matter
- Wants children: Doesn't Matter
- Smoking: Doesn't Matter
- Drinking: Doesn't Matter

About Me

Thanks for taking the time to learn more about me. I feel truly blessed. I'm healthy, and have a big heart. I have had a successful career. I'm well-mannered and treat women respectfully. I believe in opening doors and pulling out chairs. I understand that you are fully capable of opening a door or pulling a chair out for yourself, but it's just a sign of respect. It's just a nonverbal way of saying that you mean something to me. I'm a pretty romantic guy. I just believe in free will and ***trust a lot too.*** I cook then starve.

That's probably my strongest traits, along with the desire to talk to my partner. If we can't talk, then what are we doing really? I 'm very affectionate with my woman and she gets my undivided attention when we are together. My woman will always feel secure, safe, and loved by me. When I say "my woman", I don't mean that in a possessive way, but rather the one I love and I 'm dedicated too. I 'm a one woman guy, and I believe I have a lot to offer the right woman. I never thought that I would resort to online dating, but I think I must give it a try.

If we found ways to make each day special, and every now and then, found a way to sneak in a real adventure too, that would be great... but all in all, it will be the sharing that makes it special. We are each far from perfect, but together... We are perfection... let's converse and see what we can offer to each other.

Who I'd Like To Meet

I'd like to share my life with someone special; someone with whom I am emotionally compatible; someone with whom I share electric interpersonal chemistry and physical attraction . . . my soul mate if you will. I appreciate a good heart, good conversation and physical activities. I am a talkative, bold, good-humored, quick-witted, and playful man. Ideally, you're a confident, sassy, graceful, natural woman with a good sense of humor. Please feel free to write me a note if you think we're a good match. Thank you for your time.

RED FLAGS

- The occupation of construction and installation. Many scammers say this is their occupation.
- He is 50 and looking for women in the age group of 39 to 65. This is the age group many scammers target.
- Relationship is "widowed." Yes, it's a red flag but many "real" people in this age group are widowed. You need to assess the profile as a whole. The odds are 99.9% that a man who claims to be widowed AND looking for women in the age group of 39 to 65 AND employed in construction and installation is a scammer. Do not even embark on any conversation with them. Stop right here!

In my profile I shared what I was looking for in a man and he used this to manipulate me. Naïvely, I disclosed this:

> I am looking for a Christian man who is genuine, honest, kind, sincere, fun, emotionally available and who wants to be in a long-term relationship. A man who loves to travel and experience new things. A sharp dressed man is a definite turn on for me...hint, hint. I love surprises and love giving surprises. I am goal-oriented and looking for a man who also has goals and a bucket list of things he wants to do. I know that all great relationships are based on friendship and open communication, so I am looking for a man who will be my friend first and who is good at communicating, willing to work through things, and go the distance. I am looking for my best friend that I can share everything with, and who will be my safe place to fall and I will be his. I am not interested in a one night stand, and no games please!

This is the correspondence I sent that started it all:

From: ladedi
To: libertaren50
Subject: Hello libertaren
Sent: 3/28/2012

Hello Libertaren!

How are you? You live in one of my favorite cities. Sweet! I am new to on line dating. I was surfing and found you. I was at first attracted to your headline – good one! Then I was attracted to the kindness in your eyes, so I started reading your profile. I am glad I did! If you wrote this yourself, you are a good writer and know how to openly communicate. I love that! Open communication is a must for me too. Without it, why bother! Opening doors and pulling out chairs. I love this too. It means a lot to me to be treated like the lady that I am and to be respected, and I must be able to respect the man I am with. For me, respect and admiration are critical in a relationship. I really do not believe love can be formed without first having respect and admiration.

I am glad to hear you are a one woman man. Nice! I am a one man woman and very selective.

My real name is Diana and my friends say "Diana is your name and blunt is your game". With me, what you see is who I am. I do not like pretense. I believe truth is the only way to go. It appears you are the same.

If you would please be so kind to check out my profile I would appreciate it. I am looking forward to hearing back from you. I would like to explore and learn more about you. Btw, I travel a lot, so jaunting from Atlanta to San Diego is no big deal!

Lady Di

For three days I patiently waited for a reply. Though I never received an email reply, he left me three messages to text him on a different part of the dating site that I didn't know about. Once I finally saw these messages on 3/30/12 I texted him. Unfortunately, I lost those texts. I didn't know at the time I would be writing a book. I remember we texted back and forth for a good hour. We talked about where we lived, our businesses, his son and what we wanted in the future. There was nothing in these texts that made me think he wasn't who he said he was. We set a time to meet on Yahoo! messenger at 7:00ET. I remember having a nice time while we texted. I was very interested in this man and wanted to see where it could go. I was a little like a fish out of water, because I hadn't dated in eight years and never did online dating. This was all new territory for me.

From: Jerry Wesley [mailto:fallinghrt22@yahoo.com]
Sent: Friday, March 30, 2012 12:46 PM
To: Diana Garren
Subject: Hi Diana. I sent you pictures

Hope you like what you saw....

From: Diana Garren
Sent: Friday, March 30, 2012 1:06 PM
To: Jerry Wesley [mailto:fallinghrt22@yahoo.com]
Subject: RE: Hi Diana. I sent you pictures

Hi Jerry,

I do like what I see! Thank you for sending. I have attached some pictures. One was taken in Benecia, CA and one in Napa, CA. Talk with you at 4:00 PST. Diana.

From: Jerry Wesley [mailto:fallinghrt22@yahoo.com]
Sent: Friday, March 30, 2012 2:09 PM
To: Diana Garren
Subject: Re: Hi Diana. I sent you pictures

thanks for the pictures...I must say you are Beautiful and *you were created in the Morning*....Nice smile.

From: Jerry Wesley [mailto:fallinghrt22@yahoo.com]
Sent: Friday, March 30, 2012 2:13 PM
To: Diana Garren
Subject: More about me!!!

Hi Diana,

Thanks for the pictures and text I must tell you that I was excited to hear from you. I am interested in getting to know you better and see where it takes us. I would use this opportunity to tell you more about me.

I am 49...My son's name is William and he is 18, he lives in the *school dormitory*. He is a very cool headed kid and puts a smile on my face. I love every good thing that life has got to offer, the outdoors, camping, gardening, swimming, hiking, skating, golfing, cooking, home chores and spending quality time with loved ones.

I am originally from Denmark and have lived in the States for 19 yrs now. My mother was originally from California.

I am into **Residential & Industrial Construction and real estate**, I have been doing this for over 15 years and I love what I do. *I travel a lot with my job*, but I really need to settle down. I miss being loved. I have been single and lonely for 5 years and don't think I want to experience loneliness any further. I think we have a few things in common and can get a good result if we take things one day at a time.

Actually, I really do not think that having all things in common is what determines compatibility but the ability of each of the mates to adapt or be flexible as to each other's wants, needs and interests. It would be great to do a live chat and get to know each other better. 4:00 pm. I will stop here for now and wait to hear more from you about yourself.

Until then I remain the same.
Jerry

From: Diana Garren
Sent: Friday, March 30, 2012 2:20 PM
To: Jerry Wesley [mailto:fallinghrt22@yahoo.com]
Subject: RE: Hi Diana. I sent you pictures

Wow...you are good! I was born at 11:35 AM! I do love to smile.

From: Diana Garren
Sent: Friday, March 30, 2012 2:53 PM
To: Jerry Wesley [mailto:fallinghrt22@yahoo.com]
Subject: RE: More about me!!!

Hi Jerry,

Thank you for telling me more about yourself and William. I do not have any kids. I will be 49 in November. Denmark. Do you miss Denmark? Do you like it here in the states? Do you like California? I am originally from Pennsylvania and have lived in Georgia for the last 15 years. I know this is not where I will live forever. I want to live by the water. I love the ocean! I love to swim, boat, drive my convertible, picnic, sample wines, dance, read, write, golf (just learning), ice skate, travel, cuddle and roast marshmallows over an open fire to name a few. There is so much that I want to try. I also like being with friends and loved ones.

Registered through: GoDaddy.com, LLC (http://www.godaddy.com)
Domain Name: BEHRKYLANCONSTRUCTIONS.COM
Created on: 19-Mar-12
Expires on: 19-Mar-13
Last Updated on: 19-Mar-12

Administrative Contact:
Hopkins, Abraham@ContractorProWebsites.com
Contractor Pro Websites

From: Diana Garren
Sent: Friday, March 30, 2012 4:25 PM
To: Jerry Wesley [mailto:fallinghrt22@yahoo.com]
Subject: Re: Hey

Hi Jerry,

You are very good looking! Is this your company? Beautiful work!

Diana

From: Jerry Wesley [mailto:fallinghrt22@yahoo.com]
Sent: Friday, March 30, 2012 4:34 PM
To: Diana Garren
Subject: Re: Hey

Awwwww sure and you are Awesome...Yes it's my company...thanks for the compliments.

From: Diana Garren
Sent: Friday, March 30, 2012 4:40 PM
To: Jerry Wesley [mailto:fallinghrt22@yahoo.com]
Subject: Re: Hey

Hi Jerry,

Seriously, you really do nice work. Do you currently rent or own? How far are you from the water?

Diana

From: Jerry Wesley [mailto:fallinghrt22@yahoo.com]
Sent: Friday, March 30, 2012 4:59 PM
To: Diana Garren
Subject: Re: Hey

I still *live on rent*. I just want to settle down and get my own house, which I don't know where yet....**I live 40 minutes from the water.**

From: Jerry Wesley [mailto:fallinghrt22@yahoo.com]
Sent: Friday, March 30, 2012 5:50 PM
To: Diana Garren
Subject: More about me!!!

Hi *Sweetness*.

thanks so much for the e-mail, I want you to know that I am interested in getting to know you much better and see where it takes us to...Yes I do miss *denmark* but love it here in the *state.* Oh You are November and I am October 5th...I have just 1 brother and he is disabled and lives in Denmark. I do take care of him financially. With the economy I still work hard because *my job is based on traveling* it pays better *lol...*I want to use this opportunity to tell you more about me.

I like literature, music, and cinema. Personality traits are calm, honest, kind, loyal, flexible, elegant, sociable, sensitive, gentle, cheerful, optimistic, romantic.

I would like to see near me a clever and reliable woman, which would require my emotional heat, capable to like and respect. I have to let you know as well, that am an honest person as *i* have said, and *i* have to be honest with that, *i* don't have any girl friend now and am not in any serious relationship. Am a great giver because I so much believe in the Multiplied returns and that's why I don't lack anything.

I would show up at your door with a small bouquet of flowers. We would go to a dimly lit restaurant and find a table in the corner where we would not be disturbed. We could then walk hand in hand through the mall enjoying each other's company. We could then rent a movie and go home (whoever is closer) and cuddle on the couch while watching the movie. We would gentle kiss periodically throughout the movie. We might even have a glass of wine. Just one glass.

I've asked God to bring someone into my life who will want me for me and be good to me and my boy because I know that there has to be someone out there for me because he never does anything without a reason even if we can't figure it out. I know the lord has someone in mind for me to share the rest of my life with because he doesn't want us to be alone or lonely. *I did take my profile off the site* for you because you seem very unique from other women and *i* thought it would be nice to see where this could possible lead us if you are willing to do the same.

I am an adventurous, risk-taker that's chosen to live an uncommon life. I love great food, wine, friends, and conversation. I believe I have another lifetime in front of me and I would like to meet someone with whom I connect emotionally and spiritually to share it with.

Someone I can get very, very close to. Someone to share a bond and trust with. Someone I can be silly with. Someone I can play with. I bring out the little girl in you and you the little boy in me. I'd love to let you know that *i* am easygoing and an optimistic man who fly's solo, *i* am content to most of what life brings and always want to explore and aspire great possibilities. You know the saying, when life gives you lemon, you should make lemonade out of it. *i* am also a pretty upbeat person and with a decent and healthy outlook of passion, humor, honesty, spirituality, sensuality, intelligence, kindhearted and *i* am also a person with a great sense of humor..

I'd love someone that is serious, confident, purposeful, persistent, smart, responsible, honest, modest, kind, flexible, elegant, sociable, communicative, sensitive, gentle, cheerful, romantic, **considered,** someone that still believes in true love, soul mates, love notes, walks, holding hands, and talking to each other. That special someone would be attractive, sexy, romantic, affectionate, caring, funny, confident, and family oriented. Accept my son because he's an important part of my life. Someone who will work at keeping the relationship alive. Want that feeling of looking forward to seeing each other after work, and when were away from each other, we can't wait to go home!

I enjoy chick flicks but I also like those movies you have to watch every little thing so you understand the plot and the ending, movies that make you think. Horror movies usually scare me, so I don't watch them often. Action movies about blowing everything up are okay, comedy movies to make you laugh until you can hardly breathe are wonderful too.

I am a Christian and do go to church to learn about the lord. I know that if the lord wasn't in my life that there are days I would just give up but because he keeps me going. Do you like sports or outdoor activities? I like going to ball games *i* like watching them on TV.

I do like to watch the skaters on TV, *i* love football. What do you like to do with that special someone when it is raining? I like snuggling on the couch or holding hands watching the rain or when it is just raining a little sitting on the porch on the swing watching and talking. We can also kiss, share jokes and tell stories.

I'd like to use this opportunity and tell you all about me and my Son. My Son is the Love of my Life...Not many kids his age have known what they wanted to do, and have actually gone for it...My son William, will be 19 on July 7th (if he lives that long!!!). he has been high-maintenance since the beginning. I struggle daily to keep things under control. I am many things, and I don't really know where to start..I guess I'm not a "typical" man. I love, love, LOVE football!!!

On Sundays, you usually can't get me out from in front of the TV, at least till the game is over!! I love the satisfaction of taking something apart when it doesn't work and being able to fix it, put it back together again, and have it work!

There's not much better than that!! I love music and movies. I love cuddling..I love kissing...I love being held when I've had a bad day, and that seems to be pretty regularly here lately. I miss having someone there when I get home to say that everything is gonna be okay..I miss just having someone to share things with. I miss conversation..I miss so many things..I dream of sharing my life with the woman who was meant to be my soul-mate.

I dream of having that special connection with someone where it doesn't matter what you say, or even if you say anything..you always understand each other and respect what the other has to say or feel..I miss laying in a woman's arms at night and knowing that she will protect me from whatever life brings at me.

I hope this is kind of what you were wanting from me. I hope I didn't bore you or scare you off. I think this could just be the start of something.

I look forward to chatting with you and to know you better. Hugs.

Jerry

At the time I wasn't looking for anything to be wrong or for this man to not be who he claimed to be. However, I was interested in him and did my due diligence. He had a business website with his name, phone number and address listed on it, and it was a California telephone number. When I looked for him online I found a listing with the same address and phone number on Switchboard, White pages and Checkmate [the images can be found on the following page].

When I looked up his website domain name, I didn't see anything funny other than that it was just launched 11 days prior. But that really didn't send any red flags because I work with businesses and they could be in business a long time before launching a website. One thing I didn't do that I should have was look to see if he was a licensed contractor in California.

I did mail him an Easter card and it didn't come back return to sender until after he got my money. Once the card came back, I called one of my client's, Mr. Thomas M. Rucke to ask about the address. Tom is the owner of Cadfael Investigative Group, was a United States Postal Inspector for 31 years and is a Certified Fraud Examiner. Tom told me there was no way possible that address could exist.

If you want to know about the validity of an address call Mr. Tom M. Rucke at 763-694-6086.

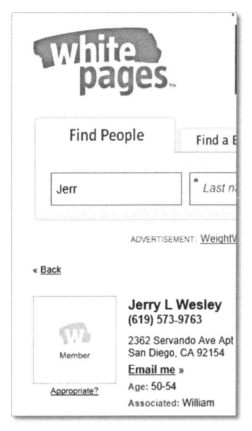

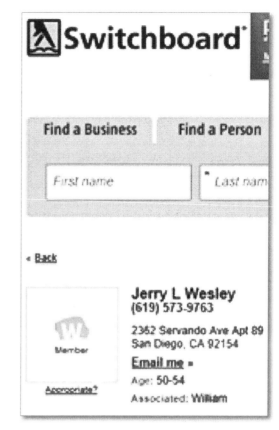

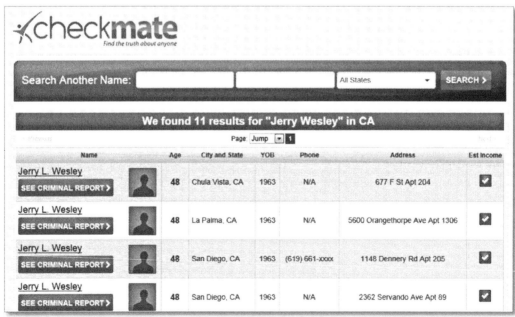

The following red flags are what I would have seen if I knew what to look for.

RED FLAGS

- The occupation of residential and industrial construction and real estate.
- He travels a lot with his job. Most scammers say they travel.
- "You were created in the Morning". I have seen this phrase used by other scammers. It's part of a format that is circulating among them.
- In his profile he says he is 50, and in the email he says he is 49. I never looked back at the profile to see if there was a discrepancy. You should always compare facts with what they have on their profile.
- He says school dormitory instead of college campus.
- He says "I am originally from Denmark and have lived in the States for 19 yrs years now. My mother was originally from California." Many scammers claim to be from another country to explain their accent when they talk to you on the phone.
- He says "still live on rent". In English we would say, "I still rent". I just thought it was because he was from Denmark so English was his second language. This is exactly what he wanted me to think so he could get away with errors in grammar and knowledge. This is another reason why scammers say they are from another country. I didn't think it strange that he rented because he said he traveled and was waiting to settle down.
- His "I's" are a mixture of capital and lower case. Most scammers do not capitalize their "I's" when they write but they are capitalized when they copy and paste, so many times you will see a mixture.
- He tells me he took his profile off the dating site in hopes that I would do the same thing. This seemed normal to me and something I appreciated. However, scammers want to get you off the dating site so no other scammers get to you.
- This man had the tools of a website and United States phone number and had his supposed name listed several places on line. These are all signs that he is a "professional" scammer.

And the chatting quickly began on *Yahoo! Messenger*:

IM Mar 30, 2012 6:58:55 PM

6:58:55 PM **ladydi2011**: Hi Jerry! I just got home.

7:00:42 PM **fallinghrt22**: Hi Diana. 😊
7:05:56 PM **fallinghrt22**: You are invisible.
7:06:08 PM **ladydi2011**: How do I become visible?

7:06:23 PM **ladydi2011**: Can you tell I am new to this? lol

7:07:36 PM **fallinghrt22**: look up to your yahoo messenger...where your ID or name is written click it you will see available.

7:08:27 PM **fallinghrt22**: I am glad to teach you

7:08:31 PM **ladydi2011**: Ok. Thank you!

7:08:32 PM **fallinghrt22**: you learn fast

7:08:43 PM **ladydi2011**: but if course...you are a good teacher

7:09:24 PM **ladydi2011**: I love the hearts!!!

7:09:33 PM **ladydi2011**: How did you do that?

7:10:22 PM **fallinghrt22**: thanks. I am glad to help always

7:10:40 PM **fallinghrt22**: the heart comes with yahoo messenger...lol

7:10:56 PM **ladydi2011**: Ahhh! Technology sure has changed many things.

7:11:41 PM **fallinghrt22**: I am glad you are here

7:11:45 PM **fallinghrt22**: so how is work?

7:12:52 PM **ladydi2011**: It was good.

7:15:56 PM **ladydi2011**: I read part of your last email

7:16:23 PM **ladydi2011**: October 5th is your birthday...

7:16:29 PM **fallinghrt22**: Yes.

7:16:35 PM **fallinghrt22**: take your time to read all..

7:16:42 PM **fallinghrt22**: I could wait forever

7:17:23 PM **ladydi2011**: Do you have a job or are you talking about your business?

7:17:43 PM **fallinghrt22**: Yes my business.

7:18:18 PM **ladydi2011**: How far do you travel?

7:19:01 PM **ladydi2011**: The fact that you like literature explains a lot about your writing...

7:19:37 PM **fallinghrt22**: I have been to New York, Sweden, Finland, **Uland**, Philippines, Russia, **German**, Switzerland, Australia, Greece, France, Portugal, Brazil, Canada, Jamaica, Italy and UK.

7:19:45 PM **fallinghrt22**: do you travel?

7:21:13 PM **ladydi2011**: I do. You have me beat! I have been to almost every state in the United States, Paris, Mexico, Africa, Caribbean and the West Indies Islands.

7:21:42 PM **ladydi2011**: How many languages do you speak?

7:21:43 PM **fallinghrt22**: *Wow...where in Africa?*

7:21:52 PM **ladydi2011**: Niger

7:22:08 PM **fallinghrt22**: *Wow what did you go there to do?*

7:22:29 PM **ladydi2011**: It was a 2 week mission trip. I brought hope to the women and let them know that God loves them and has not forgotten about them and visited the orphanage.

7:22:30 PM **fallinghrt22**: *I have been planning to go to South Africa.*

7:23:03 PM **ladydi2011**: I would love to go to South Africa. I have a friend there.

7:23:23 PM **fallinghrt22**: I see

7:23:31 PM **fallinghrt22**: we have so much in common and same dream.

7:23:40 PM **fallinghrt22**: maybe we would go together

7:23:51 PM **ladydi2011**: That would be nice.

7:24:24 PM **fallinghrt22**: cool we will work towards that.

7:24:36 PM **fallinghrt22**: *so tell me how long were you on the site?*

7:27:15 PM **ladydi2011**: 2 days.

7:28:49 PM **ladydi2011**: I am reading your email again...I love your personality traits!

7:29:36 PM **fallinghrt22**: all I got on the site want's a one night stand...which I am not there for that.

7:30:09 PM **ladydi2011**: I am clever, smart, reliable, and honest and I am sure I could handle your emotional heart

7:30:18 PM **fallinghrt22**: was on the site for 4days now

7:31:30 PM **ladydi2011**: I am glad to know you do not have a girlfriend and are not in a serious relationship. When was the last time you were out on a date?

7:31:51 PM **ladydi2011**: 4 day only. You are new to the site also.

7:32:44 PM **fallinghrt22**: I dated 2yrs ago...but it didn't work out she drinks and smokes....and she was not ready to settle down...what hurt me the most *she ran away with my best friend and with my funds...*I have not set my eyes on them...

7:32:51 PM **fallinghrt22**: I am 100% single

7:32:59 PM **ladydi2011**: I can tell you are a giver. I am a giver too. I also lack for nothing except for a special man in my life.

7:34:21 PM **fallinghrt22**: Oh you don't have to search any futher...

7:36:21 PM **ladydi2011**: This was not good! I am sure she hurt you deeply. I was married for 8 years. I got a divorce in 1998. I didn't date until the end of 1999. We were together for 4 years and his betrayal devastated me. Then I threw myself into my business and haven't dated for 8 years.

7:37:56 PM **fallinghrt22**: so you have been single for 8yrs now?

7:38:05 PM **ladydi2011**: In December I met a man and went out on a couple dates but we were not compatible.

7:38:33 PM **fallinghrt22**: I see. Could I be the one you are waiting for?

7:39:27 PM **ladydi2011**: Possibly, let's see what happens.

7:40:16 PM **fallinghrt22**: loneliness is No fun.

7:40:33 PM **fallinghrt22**: *so tell me do you live alone?*

7:40:43 PM **ladydi2011**: I must be honest, my heart is finally opened, but I am scared to get hurt again. However, if I don't put myself out there I will never have what I want, which is love...

7:42:00 PM **fallinghrt22**: You are right.

7:42:03 PM **ladydi2011**: Yes, well kind of. I have an inside kitty and 4 outside kitties. What about you?

7:42:43 PM **fallinghrt22:** I Live alone.

7:43:03 PM **ladydi2011**: No animals?

7:43:12 PM **fallinghrt22**: No.

7:43:29 PM **fallinghrt22**: I am a very busy man thou...and I want to settle down.

7:43:43 PM **fallinghrt22**: I'm sorry you don't have children.

7:43:50 PM **fallinghrt22**: hope you will Love to share

7:43:58 PM **ladydi2011**: What is your favorite food?

7:45:14 PM **ladydi2011**: I do love to share. If we get together, I would embrace having William and his future wife and children in my life.

7:45:25 PM **fallinghrt22**: I love southern "soul food" - italian - thai - chinese - turkish.. favorite fast food - pizza with fresh moz and basil drizzled with olive oil..and you

7:47:50 PM **ladydi2011**: Italian is my favorite! The pizza sounds yummy. I have never had Turkish food but would love to try it. I also like Mexican and Chinese and I love the Japanese hibachi!

7:48:06 PM **fallinghrt22**: cool.

7:48:12 PM **ladydi2011**: You really took yourself off the site?

7:48:37 PM **fallinghrt22**: Yes I want too...I don't know about you.

7:49:14 PM **ladydi2011**: Yes, I will take myself off the site.

7:50:09 PM **fallinghrt22**: Good,

7:51:26 PM **ladydi2011**: I am laughing because I am also an adventurous risk taker. I also love wine, friends and conversation. Most of all I love to cuddle and be silly and have fun.

7:51:45 PM **fallinghrt22**: Awwww thats nice.

7:52:38 PM **ladydi2011**: What do you mean when you say you fly solo?

7:53:44 PM **fallinghrt22**: Oh...I take things the way life brings them. lol

7:54:20 PM **ladydi2011**: Me too...One of my favorite sayings is "It is what it is".

7:54:33 PM **fallinghrt22**: sounds Nice.

7:54:53 PM **fallinghrt22**: *I know that God will not give you what you won't be able to carry.*

7:55:03 PM **fallinghrt22**: *What do you feel about me when you first saw my picture and read my profile?*

7:55:14 PM **ladydi2011**: You definitely know who you are and what you want in a woman.

7:55:53 PM **fallinghrt22**: Awww you are a hand writing written from heaven

7:56:43 PM **ladydi2011**: I said WOW! I have to email this man. You are very good looking. In good shape and when I read your profile I said WOW...either this man is for real or someone else wrote his profile.

7:56:59 PM **ladydi2011**: Awww. All your compliments make me blush.

7:57:07 PM **fallinghrt22**: lol...I am just me Cinderella.

7:57:31 PM **ladydi2011**: Lol...Cinderella!

8:05:23 PM **ladydi2011**: So, being from Denmark do you have an accent?

8:05:40 PM **fallinghrt22**: Yes I have an accent...you?

8:05:45 PM **ladydi2011**: I don't think you told me. How many languages do you speak?

8:06:43 PM **fallinghrt22**: I speak 3 danish spanish and english...but I can write danish better.

8:06:45 PM **fallinghrt22**: you?

8:07:03 PM **ladydi2011**: Well, I am from the North and live in the South, so the Southerner's say I have an accent. When I speak people think I am from the mid-west.

8:07:25 PM **fallinghrt22**: Oh I see

8:07:30 PM **fallinghrt22**: do you Love accent?

8:08:03 PM **ladydi2011**: I only speak English.

8:08:13 PM **ladydi2011**: Yes, I do love accents!

8:08:25 PM **fallinghrt22:** cool.

8:08:46 PM **fallinghrt22**: *What do you feel about me when you first saw my picture and read my profile?*

8:09:51 PM **ladydi2011**: This might sound crazy, but for the last couple of months I have felt in my heart that the man for me was not going to be from the states and that he would have an accent.

8:10:12 PM **ladydi2011**: That I was attracted to you and wanted to get to know you.

8:10:26 PM **fallinghrt22**: Awwwww could this be a pray answered

8:10:29 PM **ladydi2011**: I could tell by your email that you had an accent.

8:10:53 PM **ladydi2011**: It could be another desire of my heart being fulfilled

8:12:17 PM **fallinghrt22**: As I came across your profile you seem to possess some sort of magnetic charm that elicited my interest and fascination. My admiration and physical attraction drew forth my immediate response without hesitation because you appeal to my dreams, desire and taste. My sudden instinctive response was based primarily on a spontaneous mutual attraction which rendered me helpless and unable to resist communicating with you immediately..

8:13:05 PM **ladydi2011**: Jerry, I have heard many horror stories about people not being who they say on on-line dating sites. I am a little apprehensive. It has nothing to do with you. It is me being a little cautious. Trust is something that is earned. If you feel I am holding back a little it is due to this and not you.

8:13:38 PM **ladydi2011**: Wow! How do you write like this? You were persistent to get back to me.

8:14:35 PM **fallinghrt22**: Oh how do you know whats on my mind...***I am very honest and trust worthy if we can trust each other with every bit*** then I am ready...***I will never disappoint you***.

8:15:18 PM **ladydi2011**: I did feel an instant attraction to you when I saw your picture. I am lonely at times, but I am not desperate! I would not have emailed you if I wasn't attracted.

8:17:08 PM **fallinghrt22**: Awwww ***you melt me***. I am just me Diana. I am glad you feel this way..and you make me feel special.

8:18:47 PM **fallinghrt22**: I really was marveled reading your profile. The first thing that came to my mind when *i* saw your picture was. "WOW" you're drop dead GORGEOUS. I thought it will be nice to let you know that someone out here care's to know more about you, and what I care about is to be the man you've always wanted and i'm sure you and I would work things nicely being together.

8:20:11 PM **ladydi2011**: You are special!

8:20:42 PM **fallinghrt22**: You are extra special..I don't know why you are still single with the Beauty you possess.

8:21:12 PM **fallinghrt22**: I would want to ask you a question.

8:21:15 PM **ladydi2011**: I didn't spend much time on my profile. I am pretty, but I don't know about drop dead gorgeous! But thank you.

8:21:32 PM **fallinghrt22**: don't you have singles men living around you?

8:21:55 PM **ladydi2011**: Thank you for letting me know that you are interested.

8:22:29 PM **ladydi2011**: I had my heart closed for the last 8 years.

8:26:14 PM **ladydi2011**: Yes, there are single men living around me.

8:28:42 PM **fallinghrt22**: Be right back sweety

8:29:03 PM **ladydi2011**: Ok...

8:32:23 PM **ladydi2011**: R U there?

8:38:37 PM **fallinghrt22**: ***Baby I got booted***

8:39:02 PM **fallinghrt22**: are you there?

8:39:26 PM **ladydi2011**: I am here and just received a big kiss. Thank you!

8:40:08 PM **fallinghrt22**: lol.

8:40:13 PM **fallinghrt22**: you are welcome.

8:40:21 PM **fallinghrt22**: so answer my question.

8:41:27 PM **ladydi2011**: I thought I did. Please scroll up.

8:42:47 PM **fallinghrt22**: do you know why I asked that question...cause I will want to say that the men are all blind.

8:42:49 PM **fallinghrt22**: lol

8:43:04 PM **fallinghrt22**: only God creation can compare the Beauty I see in you.

8:43:30 PM **ladydi2011**: Lol! Thank you...now you are making me blush!

8:43:54 PM **ladydi2011**: A couple men have hit on me throughout the years, but I wasn't interested.

8:43:54 PM **fallinghrt22**: has anyone told you that you have a smile that only heaven can bring?

8:44:05 PM **ladydi2011**: You are turning the charm on pretty high!

8:44:17 PM **ladydi2011**: So, may I ask you a question?

8:44:36 PM **fallinghrt22**: go ahead sweetness

8:44:59 PM **ladydi2011**: When you travel, is it for an extended period of time?

8:45:47 PM **fallinghrt22**: 6 months hightest...but I have not gone that much for long now.. sometimes 3 months 2 months 1 month..it depends.

8:45:49 PM **fallinghrt22**: and you?

8:46:15 PM **ladydi2011**: I only go for a couple days to a week.

8:46:29 PM **fallinghrt22**: cool.

8:46:34 PM **ladydi2011**: So, can you have someone travel with you?

8:46:48 PM **fallinghrt22**: Yes that special someone.

8:47:12 PM **fallinghrt22**: *Are you a christian?*

8:47:26 PM **ladydi2011**: I can run my business from anywhere in the world as long as I have phone and Internet connection.

8:47:39 PM **fallinghrt22**: thats cool.

8:47:45 PM **fallinghrt22**: what do you do for work?

8:48:41 PM **ladydi2011**: Yes, I am a Christian. I accepted Christ when I was 22. I love the Lord with all my heart. I try my best to live according to His Word. However, I do fall short because I am not perfect.

8:48:53 PM **ladydi2011**: I am a business consult and transformational speaker.

8:49:08 PM **fallinghrt22**: I am christian by faith and a catholic by choice., *i*'ve been all my life..

8:49:40 PM **ladydi2011**: So, you like the Catholic religion?

8:50:26 PM **fallinghrt22**: Yes I do.

8:51:00 PM **fallinghrt22**: does that bother you? I do Love God and I try my best to live according to his word.

8:52:07 PM **ladydi2011**: I have tried many different organized religions and I have not found one that 100% fits my beliefs. I was raised Methodist. Went to a Catholic school for 3 years, tried Baptist and Charismatic churches here in the south.

8:53:06 PM **fallinghrt22**: I see.

8:53:07 PM **fallinghrt22**: Do you smoke or drink alcohol?

8:53:36 PM **ladydi2011**: I have read the Bible many times and even teach biblical principles. I believe that the Bible is truth and it is my plumline.

8:54:01 PM **fallinghrt22**: You are right I believe in the bible.

8:55:01 PM **ladydi2011**: No, I do not smoke. I drink a wine occasionally.

8:56:41 PM **fallinghrt22**: I don't smoke, I am ok with just two glass of wine with my partner having a nice and an interesting conversation.

8:56:44 PM **ladydi2011**: I think drinking and smoking are the least of what we need to pay attention to. It is the 10 commandments that we need to live by. If we live by the first one ---Love one another, than the other nine will not be an issue. What do you think?

8:58:10 PM **fallinghrt22**: Yes you are right...I Love you belief.

8:58:56 PM **ladydi2011**: I am a very simple person! If you think about it, God is very simple. He said even little children can understand his word.

8:59:34 PM **fallinghrt22**: sure you are right.

9:00:27 PM **fallinghrt22**: he created us like his own image we are just like him so we should act like him..

9:00:44 PM **ladydi2011**: I have seen many people hurt in the church and many cults overcome people due to the lack of people's own knowledge and need to be loved and accepted.

9:01:01 PM **fallinghrt22**: this is true.

9:01:29 PM **ladydi2011**: Scripture says to study to show yourself approved. Yet, most don't even read.

9:02:02 PM **ladydi2011**: How can anyone tell a counterfeit if they don't know the truth???

9:03:03 PM **fallinghrt22**: I believe you and you are very right.

9:03:10 PM **ladydi2011**: God is my Father. He is the provider of all things. I am SO blessed that I have an intimate relationship with him through his word.

9:03:12 PM **fallinghrt22**: I am better to tell the bitter truth.

9:03:22 PM **fallinghrt22**: same as me.

9:03:52 PM **ladydi2011**: Yep! My kitty is into something. BRB

9:04:08 PM **fallinghrt22**: Ok.

9:07:05 PM **fallinghrt22**: *what do you do for work?*

9:07:13 PM **ladydi2011**: She likes scratching my wood baseboards when I am not attentive to her...

9:07:27 PM **fallinghrt22**: Ahhhhh soon someone would take her place..lol

9:08:29 PM **fallinghrt22**: *what do you do for work?*

9:10:33 PM **ladydi2011**: Did you know in Matthew 23:9 it says to call no man your father upon the earth: for one is your Father, which is in heaven. When I studied this out, it is talking about in a spiritual sense.

9:11:26 PM **fallinghrt22:** You are right...you are wonderful Diana.

9:11:36 PM **fallinghrt22**: I still dont know why you are still single

9:12:40 PM **ladydi2011**: I am a business consultant / strategist. I make businesses profitable. I can work with any business. I predominantly work with private investigators, subject matter experts, data and cellular forensic experts and attorneys.

9:13:22 PM **ladydi2011**: Thank you. I guess I am still single because God is saving me for the man He made for me.

9:13:35 PM **fallinghrt22**: true.

9:14:05 PM **ladydi2011**: You are wonderful also. So, why are you still single? Aren't there single women in your circle?

9:15:09 PM **fallinghrt22**: well I think God is keeping me for the right one..CA ladies Oh nothing serious but bar and club and to hook up..even the ladies with no teeth late 60 lol.

9:18:06 PM **ladydi2011**: Many married men have approached me, especially when I travel. I say, "Yes, maybe we could hook up as long as I get to talk to your wife first and she approves." The look on their face is priceless!

9:18:31 PM **fallinghrt22**: lol Nice.

9:18:49 PM **fallinghrt22**: it is better I get married and settle down...I Love commitment

9:20:15 PM **ladydi2011**: You are rare. Many men hate commitment. I also want to be committed. I am a one man woman. Always have been!

9:21:07 PM **fallinghrt22**: thanks..I am also a one woman man.

9:22:24 PM **ladydi2011**: I like that. I do not want to be with someone I do not trust. I had a relationship like that in my early 20's and I hated it. I would rather be alone than in a mess like that.

9:22:50 PM **fallinghrt22**: same with me I want to love and trust.

9:24:57 PM **ladydi2011**: I finally finished all of your email. We like the same kind of movies. I also get scared with scary movies and prefer not to watch them.

9:25:23 PM **fallinghrt22**: I see.

9:25:32 PM **fallinghrt22**: *What do you do for fun?*

9:26:35 PM **ladydi2011**: Dance, read, watch TV, wine tasting, movies, theatre, swim, drive with the top down on my car, shop and go to nice dinners

9:27:15 PM **ladydi2011**: For the past 10 years I worked way too much and had way too little fun!

9:27:24 PM **ladydi2011**: I read in your email what you like to do for fun.

9:29:40 PM **fallinghrt22**: I play 5 musical instruments...I play the piano, guitar, violin, harmonica and saxophone. but it has been a long time since I played any

9:31:37 PM **ladydi2011**: Wow...5 musical instruments. The sax is my favorite.

9:32:27 PM **ladydi2011**: Can you still play the sax?

9:32:49 PM **fallinghrt22**: Yes I can and would Love to play for you while you dance.

9:35:45 PM **fallinghrt22**: Are you a jealous person?

9:36:20 PM **ladydi2011**: Yes, if I there is broken trust. What about you?

9:38:03 PM **ladydi2011**: I would love to dance for you while you played the sax. I want to learn how to ballroom dance, but I need a partner. Do you dance?

9:38:22 PM **fallinghrt22**: Making your partner jealous is so immature. This is someone you are supposed to be in love with, not someone you are trying to hurt. This is supposed to be for a lifetime, not just for a while or until you find something else. It is not like buying a house, this is a true soul mate, someone you would not trade for anything. Someone you would put your life on the line for. Someone that makes you feel so wonderful you DON'T ever want to live without them.

9:38:43 PM **fallinghrt22**: Yes I dance and would love to hold your hands and dance slow with you.

9:40:38 PM **ladydi2011**: Jerry, I am trying to type and am just in awe. WOW! Let's dance my dear!

9:40:59 PM **fallinghrt22**: Awwwww *you melt me*.

9:41:39 PM **ladydi2011**: Are you for real? Please tell me again why you are still single....

9:42:00 PM **fallinghrt22**: maybe I am waiting for you.

9:42:12 PM **ladydi2011**: Have you seen the movie, Shall We Dance?

9:42:30 PM **fallinghrt22**: I should be asking you if you for real because you are Beautiful and any man will want to keep you forever.

9:42:34 PM **fallinghrt22**: No I have not.

9:42:48 PM **ladydi2011**: You know I will be praying tonight asking God to reveal if you are the man He has for me, right?

9:43:12 PM **fallinghrt22**: please do..same as I will pray.

9:43:16 PM **ladydi2011**: You have to see this movie. I am sure you will love it.

9:43:22 PM **fallinghrt22**: I will.

9:43:32 PM **ladydi2011**: Do you ever travel to Georgia?

9:43:48 PM **fallinghrt22**: No but I think it is my next place to visit

9:43:50 PM **ladydi2011**: Anywhere close to Georgia?

9:44:02 PM **fallinghrt22**: No I have not... *soonest*

9:44:06 PM **ladydi2011**: LOL....Sounds like a plan to me.

9:44:51 PM **fallinghrt22**: cool.

9:47:11 PM **fallinghrt22**: You are getting closer to my heart

9:47:26 PM **ladydi2011**: Lol...can I live there rent free?

9:47:45 PM **fallinghrt22**: Wow....Yes forever as long as you want.

9:48:06 PM **ladydi2011**: I am looking for my forever

9:48:44 PM **fallinghrt22**: so tell me what exactly are you looking for in a man and what qualities do you desire?

9:49:45 PM **ladydi2011**: I already experienced one divorce and do not want to go through that again.

9:55:13 PM **ladydi2011**: First, I am looking for a man that loves the Lord and emotionally available.

9:55:24 PM **fallinghrt22**: Yes I do and I am.

9:56:21 PM **ladydi2011**: If not, there is no reason to go any further. Would you agree?

9:56:44 PM **fallinghrt22**: I agree

9:57:42 PM **ladydi2011**: Honest, kind, faithful, a one woman man, able to and wants to communicate

9:58:21 PM **fallinghrt22**:

9:58:59 PM **ladydi2011**: Willing to work through everything life has to throw at us as a couple

9:59:26 PM **ladydi2011**: Passionate...I am a very passionate woman!

9:59:52 PM **ladydi2011**: Romantic...I love romance.

10:00:01 PM **ladydi2011**: Loves to kiss...I love to kiss

10:00:06 PM **ladydi2011**: Compassionate

10:00:29 PM **ladydi2011**: Are you still there or have I scared you away?

10:01:20 PM **fallinghrt22**: I'm here listening.

10:01:30 PM **fallinghrt22**: continue please

10:01:38 PM **ladydi2011**: Sensitive and gentle

10:02:03 PM **ladydi2011**: His own man...with his own opinions

10:02:16 PM **ladydi2011**: Can we talk about this one?

10:02:31 PM **fallinghrt22**: Yes.

10:03:08 PM **ladydi2011**: So, how strong are you when it comes to what you want?

10:03:43 PM **fallinghrt22**: I am very strong..I don't give up easily.

10:03:45 PM **fallinghrt22**: and you?

10:05:19 PM **ladydi2011**: I am also very strong. I need a man who will challenge me a little.

10:05:51 PM **fallinghrt22**: Yes I know I can challenge you..I have muscles. lol

10:06:27 PM **ladydi2011**: One of my clients said I am still single because I am too strong. He is right that I am strong. But the right man will be able to handle my strength.

10:06:44 PM **ladydi2011**: I saw that you have muscles and I like them!

10:07:46 PM **fallinghrt22**: Look no further I have got what you need right here, so come share my world

10:08:33 PM **ladydi2011**: Ok...I am not looking any further.

10:09:05 PM **fallinghrt22**: I desire someone who is down to earth, simple, kind, caring, romantic, passionate, loving, goal oriented, affectionate, focused, honest, decisive, sense of humor and responsible. To add..a good cook

10:10:25 PM **ladydi2011**: I am all the above...You just might have hit the jackpot!!!

10:11:15 PM **fallinghrt22**: My dreams is finding the right woman and that will really make my dreams come true and I'll also make hers come true too, Who knows maybe its you..Well when I find her I really will love to hold hands with her walking side by side on the street and kissing each other. And also go to the beach together and watching the sunset and also looking into each others eyes and saying the sweetest thing in the world..I will love her, cherish her, adore her, respect her, care for her, treat her like an Angel and be by her side always and forever..Share my good and bad times with her..Show her how special, precious, and beautiful she is to my heart..

10:12:59 PM **ladydi2011**: You have done it again with your words...

10:13:08 PM **fallinghrt22**: when I find her and we love and care for each other so much like no couple was ever loved and adored before, I'll make her happy, put great and wonderful smiles in her heart and soul forever.

10:13:16 PM **fallinghrt22**: Awwwwww

10:13:50 PM **ladydi2011**: You have really thought this through and are good at copying and pasting...

10:14:57 PM **ladydi2011**: WOW again....Please tell me you are for real and not a player. Please do not play with my heart. It is a true and delicate heart that has lots of love to give to the right man.

10:16:21 PM **fallinghrt22**: I am a nice, intelligent, caring, fun loving, sensitive man who is looking for someone to share the rest of my life with. I know that developing a good and solid friendship is the first step finding the woman I of my dreams. So, I know that it will take time for us to get acquainted come to trust and respect each other. If you are interested in a serious relationship, one that will also take time to develop, then I may be your man!

10:16:59 PM **fallinghrt22**: Diana, I want you to know that we are not Kids...this is so important to me and I am loving getting to know you...*your heart is very safe with me*.

10:23:03 PM **ladydi2011**: Thank you Jerry. No, we are not kids. This is important to me too. I am not the normal woman. I have real values and I am who I say I am. Thank you for reassuring me and letting me know my heart is safe with you. Yours is also safe with me. Yes, it will take time to build a friendship and come to trust and respect each other. I want to take this time with you.

10:23:28 PM **fallinghrt22**: I would like someone that will love and respect me for who I am, that likes to hold my hand and surprise me with a little kiss when I least expect it, or give me a wink from across the room to let me know she's thinking about me or give me a call just to let me know she's thinking about me..Because I will be doing the same.

10:23:46 PM **ladydi2011**: *I just found the disadvantage of on-line dating. I cannot see your eyes. The eyes are the window to the soul and say many things.*

10:25:13 PM **ladydi2011:** I also love my man to be a gentleman and who opens my doors and pulls out my chair.

10:26:27 PM **ladydi2011:** I love surprising my man and I love surprises. I love to let my man know I am thinking about him and I love when he does the same. I love to walk hand in hand, side by side. I don't want him to walk in front or behind me.

10:26:40 PM **fallinghrt22**: I would love someone who is fun to be around, likes to laugh, joke around, being outdoors, going for long romantic walks, enjoys looking at the stars at night, and watching the sun set and rise over the ocean. I am looking for someone that enjoys the simple things in life, just as I do. I would like to meet someone special that I can grow old with, and that we can always look into each other's eyes and know that the love between us is just as wonderful and exciting as the day we met..

10:27:41 PM **ladydi2011**: I want the same thing. It is sad, but true that I haven't seen many couple like this. When I do, I recognize it and I want it!

10:30:30 PM **fallinghrt22**: I want to love a woman for who she is, to spoil her, and love her, and let her know just how much she means to me, by the little things I do or say to make her feel special. while at the same time she treats me in the same way with love and respect I'm really looking for Someone Honest, Caring, Romantic, Kind, Posses Great Sense of Humor, Loyal, gentle, cheerful, ***Has the fear of God in hear life***, LOVES KIDS, responsible, someone that still believes in true love, Affectionate, Passionate, Understanding, Intelligent, Respectful and Trust Worthy...

10:32:16 PM **ladydi2011**: Do you want more kids?

10:34:32 PM **fallinghrt22**: I'm searching for my life long partner to share a Great Life of Love with; romance, long slow kisses, feeling very special, intimacy, spirituality, pleasurable communication, dancing, meeting of the minds, opening a door for you, flowers, traveling and other exciting adventures, A GREAT LIFE of LOVE! I am one who strongly believes in respect and that without respect, you can't experience true love and generate a healthy relationship. I believe in a smaller "wow" when it is first a friendship and then a larger "Wow" later as it evolves into a Beautiful Loving committed relationship. I believe it's not just what you are like on the outside, but more about what you are like on the inside. I'm seeking friendship first, (no game playing please)

10:35:04 PM **fallinghrt22**: Oh do you think you can give birth to kids with your age? I am satisfied with William if you are willing to share.

10:37:02 PM **ladydi2011**: I am not playing games. I do unto others as I want done unto myself. No, I do not think I can birth kids at my age. I would love to share William with you. Speaking of William, what type of problems are you having with him?

10:37:40 PM **ladydi2011**: I asked if you wanted more kids to be sure we are on the same page with this.

10:38:27 PM **fallinghrt22**: I'm a gentle soul, quiet and certainly not what most people would assume - a social butterfly. Instead I'm the quiet watchful, listener who will provide you with a listening ear after a tough day, and not judge, or assume or tell you what to do. I love nature, and feel an especial kinship to just being near water and having water right near my home. I feel the peace of the world in the breeze across the water, the lapping of the waves on the shore, the unassuming nature of water and nature. I am one with nature, and could spend hours just sitting by the beach, river, lake, ocean and read, listen to music and feel at the end of a day that I've had an incredible day...

10:39:03 PM **fallinghrt22**: *I am not having problems with him*..we are first of friends..and he wants me to be happy again..he was the one that put me on the site we met.

10:39:52 PM **ladydi2011**: I am sure he wants you happy. Go William! Please tell him thank you.

10:41:40 PM **fallinghrt22**: I am a person who looks beyond what may be the obvious. Character is worth more than flashiness. I am a person who appreciates honesty and a great sense of humor. I love to laugh and to enjoy the simple things in life. I can appreciate a woman who sees a man as a friend and a partner..

10:41:47 PM **fallinghrt22**: sure will do.

10:41:58 PM **ladydi2011**: I also love nature, especially water. Jerry, you really should be a writer!

10:42:31 PM **fallinghrt22**: thanks..I love poetry. I think I will write.

10:46:05 PM **fallinghrt22**: I know that men and women all have an inner child within and that is why I would appreciate days filled with fun and laughter. I respect and am here to take care of business in life--family, work, community, etc. Yet, I know life involves balance. I look for the good in most situations and choose to look for the good in others. I know that life involves give and take and that what you seek--is that you must be willing to give and demonstrate yourself. I am a romantic at heart. I like to be appreciated and complimented to which I would do the same for that special someone..

10:46:10 PM **ladydi2011**: I also look for character. Looks and things will fade, but character is who someone is. Like I told you, I am a simple person. I have been told that when I walk into a room, everyone knows that I have walked in. I don't know why or what it is, or if it is even true. I love to laugh. It is the best medicine in the world. I have a clear picture of my direction in life. What about you. Other than true love, what else do you want in life? What do you see for your future? I want my man to be my best friend and partner. My safe place to fall and I want to be his safe place to fall. No secrets, just honesty and openness.

10:49:58 PM **fallinghrt22**: I like discovering new things about the person *i* meet. I am a person who looks for the possibilities versus what cannot be achieved. Life is better going through with a special one instead of just any one. I like poetry I like trying new things. I respect the direct approach--that is saying what you mean and meaning what you say. I believe in smiling--even when things are not going as perfect as you had hoped. A smile can brighten someone's day--I liken smiling--it is one of my trademarks..

10:51:34 PM **ladydi2011**: I believe the same as you that one must be and demonstrate what they seek. You cannot seek what you do not know. I feel very blessed that William sent you to the site. How else would we meet being almost 2,000 miles apart?

10:52:27 PM **fallinghrt22**: I am an honest dependable person and I want someone I can depend on to talk to me when I feel disappointed or sad..I want someone that can provide an emotional balance for me and in return I will give the same..when things happen to the one I love I take that seriously and try to focus on a solution to the problem by talking about it..give and take..I expect the same thing..I don't believe that is to much to ask for. It keeps things real and most of all it provides someone in your life you know you can count on.

10:52:51 PM **fallinghrt22**: I am glad we met this way. *I know it has destined to be so..*I just thank God.

10:53:03 PM **fallinghrt22**: thanks so much for the compliments you make me feel special.

10:55:46 PM **ladydi2011**: You are special! The more you write, the more I see who we are, what we want and what we will give are the same. I must tell you, I am a little taken back because I was not expecting to meet anyone on the site!

10:57:33 PM **ladydi2011**: You have definitely caught me by surprise. I am speechless. How often is it that we get exactly what our heart desires? It only happens when the Lords hands are on it because he knows our hearts and needs better than we do.

10:57:55 PM **fallinghrt22**: I am a true romantic and believe that there is such a thing as a soul mate, but they are not easily found..out of millions of people those 2 souls must meet by chance and circumstance. I believe that you should consider your soul mate, your best friend and be able to talk about any and everything, not feel strange if there is silence between you. I feel true love and connection doesn't require constant talking, as a glance or longing stare says everything and more than words could ever convey. I believe in holding hands, and public displays of affection, as I would want everyone to know that the person who I am with is truly special to me. I believe that being able to be your true self with someone without judgment is one of the best things in life.

10:58:51 PM **fallinghrt22**: You are right God is at work. I wasn't expecting such Beauty from the site but now that I found you I am not letting go.

10:59:12 PM **ladydi2011**: I think all I can say is ditto.

11:01:14 PM **ladydi2011**: Let's see where God is taking us. I have gone through many emotions with you today. Excitement, fear, happiness and joy! You are rocking my world my dear!

11:02:09 PM **ladydi2011**: Most of all I am in awe. It takes a lot to make Diana speechless, but you have done it by just being you!

11:02:28 PM **fallinghrt22**: Awwwww that's sweet

11:02:51 PM **fallinghrt22**: I'm so glad to meet you and would love to see where it takes us too

11:03:05 PM **fallinghrt22**: You did put a smile on my face.

11:03:13 PM **fallinghrt22**: I did enjoyed talking to you

11:03:39 PM **fallinghrt22**: *Baby* I need to fix something. Can we continue later??

11:06:15 PM **ladydi2011**: I am so glad I put a smile on your face. I did enjoy talking and look forward to talking again.

11:07:26 PM **fallinghrt22**: You will be in my thought. ***Wet kisses and hugs***

11:07:27 PM **ladydi2011**: Night! Please tell William I said hello...

11:07:29 PM **fallinghrt22**: Night *baby*

11:07:36 PM **ladydi2011**: Night!

11:07:40 PM **fallinghrt22**: Sure will do *baby*

11:07:42 PM **fallinghrt22**: Kisses

Wow. At the time, I was taken by his words. Now that I read them with knowledge of what scammers do, I am sure he took them from what a woman wrote to him. He did a lot of copying and pasting, and I didn't think much about that at the time. It seemed a reasonable way to save time. It is clear now that he was playing to what I said I wanted in my profile. His words were very effective in getting to my heart.

RED FLAGS

 🚩   When we talk about where we have traveled the only place he asks about is Africa.

- He asks how long I have been on the site. He is trying to find out if I might already have dealt with a scammer.
- Many times scammers say their prior girlfriend or wife ran off with their friend and sometimes with their money.
- He asks if I live alone, what I do for work and for fun. This is part of the question format a scammer asks so they know how to manipulate you.
- He talks about God and wants to know if I am a Christian. Scammers like using God to gain trust. They capture many Christian women this way.
- He asks what I felt about him when I first saw his picture and read his profile. Most scammers will ask this to get a feel for how likely you are to fall in love with them.
- He gets booted. Most scammers get booted a lot due to being in a third world country.
- "Soonest" is a word used in Nigeria.
- "Your heart is safe with me" is something most scammers tell you to get you to let down your defenses.
- He says "we are destined to be". Many scammers say this to get you to believe "this is it."
- On day one he calls me baby. Scammers always rush into calling you endearing names.
- When we're not having regular conversation he is copying and pasting from his format. You might not think much about that because many people will do that instead of typing it out. Scammers usually do mostly copy and paste in the first chat.
- In his email he said he was having problems with William but in his chat he said he wasn't. This is inconsistent.
- This chat was four hours long. Scammers like to spend a lot of time chatting with their victims, especially in the beginning.

From: Jerry Wesley [mailto:fallinghrt22@yahoo.com]
Sent: Saturday, March 31, 2012 6:08 AM
To: Diana Garren
Subject: Re: Hey

Hi Baby,

I am so excited to meet you that I just thought I'd write you a short note to tell you how much I enjoyed meeting you. I can't recall when I had a more pleasant time. Everything felt so natural, and you were very easy to talk to. It's hard for me to identify what it is about you that attracts me so. I suppose it might be the combination of your great sense of humor, your charming personality and your good-looks. Whatever it is, I can sense its presence. You could call it chemistry, or better yet, the possibility that we are on the same wavelength.

I felt very calm when I talked to with you yesterday. I truly want to give our friendship a chance to grow and turn into hopefully a relationship. Well, I guess I've said enough for the time being. Have a wonderful day and, hopefully, I'll hear from you. If you get a chance, write me and tell me your thoughts. You'll be in my thoughts.

Jerry

From: Diana Garren
Sent: Sunday, April 01, 2012 3:08 PM
To: Jerry Wesley [mailto:fallinghrt22@yahoo.com]
Subject: Hi

Hi!

I am so glad you called today. I enjoyed talking to you! *I got to hear your voice for a brief second. I am thinking that you are having problems with your phone*. Am I right? What about your computer? Are you also having issues with your computer? Either or both of these issues cannot be good for your business. I know I would be in a real panic without communication for my business.

Btw...I never even asked you if you are in California or some other part of the world at this time...so, I am going to ask now. Where in God's beautiful world are you at this time? There are many things about you that's drawing me to you and this is so out of character for me.

To be honest with you it is even a little scary. It makes me realize that my heart is wide open and I am allowing myself to be vulnerable. I have not done this for a very long time.

I forgot what this felt like. Hmmm, reality of these feeling just set in to tell me that I have been out of the game of dating and love for a long time! Being vulnerable like this is a risk...a risk that I am willing to take with you!

Diana

From: Jerry Wesley [mailto:fallinghrt22@yahoo.com]
Sent: Monday, April 02, 2012 12:51 PM
To: Diana Garren
Subject: Good Morning.

Good Morning *Sweetheart..*How are you doing today and how was your night? I missed you tremendously..*Baby an Electric pole fell so my light went off*...thats why we have not been able to connect. I hope all is well with you. Can we chat now? I went to sleep last night with a smile because I knew I'd be dreaming of you ..but I woke up this morning with a smile because you weren't a dream. I enjoy talking to you every day and I like the feeling that knowing I have you gives me, I never want to loose this feeling rather I want it to grow stronger by the minute. *Like the* *sunshine in the morning, may this brighten your day, and remind you that you're thought of in a very warm way.* Please take care of yourself and don't work too much today know that you are in my thoughts.

Hugs & Kisses
Jerry

When he says a pole fell and his lights went off it raises questions for me, but it didn't even enter my mind that he might be a scammer. I later learned that electricity goes out often in Nigeria. I was frustrated with how when we talk his phone cuts off and I didn't know why. I later learned from my sources that this happens when a scammer runs out of credit. At this time I am trying to learn if this man is compatible with me, not if he is a scammer.

RED FLAGS

- When he calls the connection is extremely brief. This is another red flag that it is a scammer.
- He says "light went off;" we would say our "electricity was off". This tells me he had no way to charge his phone or laptop because the power was off, as it often is in Nigeria.
- The following is copied from a love poem website www.lovingyou.com, "Like the sunshine in the morning, may this brighten your day, and remind you that you're thought of in a very warm way".

IM Apr 2, 2012 1:04:42 PM

1:04:42 PM **fallinghrt22**: Good Moning Sunshine.
1:05:09 PM **ladydi2011**: Good morning Handsome! It is afternoon here.
1:05:23 PM **fallinghrt22**: 10:05am here.
1:06:25 PM **fallinghrt22**: are you at work?
1:06:47 PM **ladydi2011**: Yes. I am.
1:07:15 PM **ladydi2011**: What about you? Are you at work?
1:07:21 PM **fallinghrt22**: I missed you tremendously.
1:07:45 PM **fallinghrt22**: No I am home I work from home.
1:08:12 PM **fallinghrt22**: But very busy week for me thou.
1:08:15 PM **ladydi2011**: A friend of mine who is a kick boxer came over last night to show me a different workout routine.
1:08:33 PM **fallinghrt22**: so tell me how are you and how was your weekend?
1:09:03 PM **ladydi2011**: It is very busy for me too. I have to pack and prepare to leave.
1:10:08 PM **fallinghrt22**: Lol...once we are together I be your friend and I will be the one showing you the workout routine.
1:10:42 PM **ladydi2011**: I am looking forward to that. How was your weekend?
1:11:58 PM **ladydi2011**: Was there a storm that knocked the pole on your house?
1:12:06 PM **fallinghrt22**: my weekend was terrific.... I went shopping and also ran errands and the most beautiful thing you were in my every thought. I have been smiling.

1:12:27 PM **fallinghrt22**: I don't know what knocked it down Baby.

1:13:05 PM **ladydi2011**: Awwwwww. You have been in mine also.

1:15:21 PM **ladydi2011**: To answer your question. I am speaking in Georgia

1:15:31 PM **fallinghrt22**: did you get my email Baby.

1:15:49 PM **ladydi2011**: The one you sent me this morning?

1:16:23 PM **fallinghrt22**: Yes.

1:17:13 PM **ladydi2011**: I will be leaving Thursday early afternoon and spending the night since I speak from 8:00-12:00.

1:17:34 PM **fallinghrt22**: Oh I see.

1:17:55 PM **fallinghrt22**: will I get the opportunity to talk to my heartbeat while you are gone?

1:20:02 PM **ladydi2011**: Of course I will make time somehow to talk to you. I can always call you while I am driving. However, it is supposed to be sunny so you know my top will be down.

1:20:28 PM **fallinghrt22**: cool.

1:20:39 PM **ladydi2011**: I can send and receive text and emails. I am accessible.

1:20:47 PM **fallinghrt22**: can't wait to spend so much time with you on the beach Baby it will be breath taken. *you melt me* in every way.

1:27:03 PM **fallinghrt22**: we can be blessed with much more if we can work together as one.

1:27:17 PM **ladydi2011**: Jerry, you scare me, but in a good way. If I wasn't a risk taker, I would be running as fast as I could...

1:28:51 PM **fallinghrt22**: why do I scare you Diana please tell me.

1:29:11 PM **ladydi2011**: Yes, we can. See, you are doing it again. I want to work as one. I want to communicate about everything and work through every obstacle that would come our way.

1:33:16 PM **fallinghrt22**: 🐶

1:39:36 PM **fallinghrt22**: I will so much appreciate it if you are mine and mine only. I always thought that dreams were just dreams, but you made them all come true and even better, you built new dreams with me! I can not thank you enough for being more than perfect because you showed me that even all the things that seem wrong are actually opportunities to work at them together and bring us closer together. No matter how far you are and no matter what you do, I always want you to know how much you mean to me, and how much I truly care for you.

1:40:16 PM **fallinghrt22**: Oh William was so happy for us..he said we are compatable

1:40:22 PM **fallinghrt22**: William is a sweet talker.

1:40:28 PM **fallinghrt22**: he is so happy for me.

1:42:03 PM **ladydi2011**: I am glad he thinks we are compatible and is happy for you. So, he takes after his dad in the sweet talking department...

1:43:07 PM **fallinghrt22**: it runs in the blood

1:44:12 PM **ladydi2011**: Lol... Please send me a picture of William.

1:44:39 PM **fallinghrt22**: Ok wait let me look. [images on next page]

IM Apr 2, 2012 1:48:05 PM Continued

1:48:05 PM **ladydi2011**: Thank you for the pictures. He is extremely good looking like his dad. I am in trouble if the two of you gang up on me to get what you want....

1:48:56 PM **fallinghrt22**: You are welcome..lol

1:49:06 PM **fallinghrt22**: you do really know how beautiful you are, don't you?

1:49:33 PM **fallinghrt22**: no one realizes their own beauty

1:52:31 PM **ladydi2011**: Thank you. I think I was beautiful on the outside when I was younger. I think at almost 50, I am holding my own. I also know on the inside I am more beautiful today than I ever was when I was young.

1:53:14 PM **ladydi2011**: How far away is William's school from you?

1:54:36 PM **fallinghrt22**: whats an Ideal relationship for you?

1:55:06 PM **ladydi2011**: So, if we like each other this much before we meet in person, what is going to happen when we meet in person?

1:55:48 PM **fallinghrt22**: William is in Sacramento....

1:56:12 PM **fallinghrt22**: I can't wait for our first meeting.

1:57:39 PM **fallinghrt22**: 7 hours from Sacramento to San Diego...

2:00:30 PM **ladydi2011**: Ok. I have also been to Sacramento several times. I have been to Napa and Monterey. I love Monterey.

2:06:46 PM **ladydi2011**: Thank you for asking. The ideal relationship for me has to be built on trust. Without trust, there is no relationship. I want a man that I respect and admire. I want to be with my best friend. I want to share everything. I want to complete him and him complete me. I want a committed relationship. I want to be his cheerleader in him achieving all his goals, and I want him to be my cheerleader. I want us to be partners in everything. I want to dance, play and build what we want together. I want everyone to know I am his and he is mine. I want true intimacy. I want to experience everything together.

2:10:26 PM **ladydi2011**: Life is short and I want to live it to its fullest with my partner. I want to travel together. It is important for me to fulfill my dreams of being an author and international speaker. I knew since I was 8 years old I was to do this. I want my man to be supportive of this. I know you want to settle down. However, I would love to travel with you when you travel. One day, I would love to live on an island. Many times, I almost moved to Aruba. I want to be by the water.

2:14:50 PM **fallinghrt22**: An ideal relationship for me would be one where be both respect and show one another that we care for each other. It would be loving and intimate. We would do things for each other because that is what we want, to please each other. It should not be stressful it should be mutual, honest, caring and loving..I like very much how you look. I will be honest, I don't ever look at the outside to learn about someone, I feel the real person is who is inside. Oh, of course there has to be some kind of physical attraction but that is not the only part of a person, I am good and kind and loving, I am always there to give help to anyone who needs it. I am always told I am too good to everyone else.

2:24:18 PM **fallinghrt22**: But that is my nature and I feel rewarded just knowing I have helped that someone no matter what it is. *Well I would let you lead me around the room, introducing me to all your friends. And then I would try to get to know them better. If we were to get parted in the room, I would very romantically look over at you through the crowd and smile at you very softly and then think to myself, you are all mine and I am so lucky to be going home with you and how passionate the love is going to be when we get home. I wouldn't hang on to you desprately because I think that makes poeple feel smothered, I would expect you to get me a drink though before leaving me alone with any of your friends. A glass of wine would be great.*

2:42:58 PM **ladydi2011**: Baby, it looks like we want the same thing. This makes my heart skip a beat! You would always feel secure. You would never have any reason not to feel secure. You would know that I was ALWAYS going home with you or to you if I was traveling alone. I am a one man woman. I always have been. I do not know what it is like to date several people at a time. I would always want you by my side. I would want you in the room to watch me on stage speaking. You would be proud because I am a very honest speaker. I am a transformational speaker. I speak truth because I know this sets people free and advances them. I would not smother you. I think it is healthy in a relationship for you to do guy things with the guys and me do girl things with the girls from time to time. I might be asking for too much but I want it ALL... I believe if you are with the right person and there is respect, love, trust and open communication you can have it all.

2:49:13 PM **ladydi2011**: R U there baby?

2:54:42 PM **fallinghrt22**: *I got booted*

2:54:48 PM **fallinghrt22**: Wow I am speechless

2:55:46 PM **fallinghrt22**: You are so sweet and have taken my breath away love.

2:56:07 PM **fallinghrt22**: I don't know what I did right to deserve you, but knowing I have you I will never let go of you.

2:57:46 PM **fallinghrt22**: Here in my heart, that´s where you will be....I promise to Cherish and adore what we have built forever.

2:59:54 PM **ladydi2011**: I love being in your heart. I keep hearing my one friend's voice telling me, "Diana, it is better to give your heart away and love than to not take the chance and never love." She is a very wise woman and I love her dearly.

3:00:41 PM **fallinghrt22**: thats so sweet and I am glad we are good match for each other.

3:00:51 PM **ladydi2011**: What do you see and want in your future? What are your dreams?

3:01:25 PM **fallinghrt22**: my dreams are with you..which I will soon take time to write you an email about my future with you.

3:02:46 PM **ladydi2011**: Ok. I look forward to this email. I know there has to be things that you want to achieve. I want to know what they are. Please.

3:05:34 PM **fallinghrt22**: Hmmmmmmmmmm Ok.

3:06:03 PM **fallinghrt22**: *what is a perfect first date for you?*

3:06:35 PM **ladydi2011**: I am so glad you asked.

3:07:17 PM **ladydi2011**: Well, with you, I think it would be different than someone I have not had the opportunity to learn so much about already.

3:10:42 PM **ladydi2011**: A perfect first date would be to go to a quiet, cozy, dimly lit restaurant. Then I would like to go dancing. Then, I would want to hear you play the saxophone.

3:11:41 PM **fallinghrt22**: The perfect first date for me would be a quiet intimate dinner somewhere romantic where we spend the evening getting to know each other by conversation that just seem to endlessly flow and before too long we realize that hours have passed yet it only seemed like minutes. We would never want the night to end. The night would possibly end with a romantic kiss and we would both go home and think of each other till we fell asleep.

3:11:50 PM **ladydi2011**: Or...If we were close to a beach, I would want to go to the beach and walk on the beach and look at the stars and I would want to kiss you. Did I ever tell you that I love to kiss?

3:12:35 PM **fallinghrt22**: Yes and I am a great Kisser.

3:14:41 PM **ladydi2011**: I somehow already knew this...I am a great kisser too! We both have similar visions of our first date. I do not want to rush anything Jerry. I want to take our time and make memories that we will continue to talk about to Williams children. Be an example to them of what true love is and how to be respectful and true.

3:15:04 PM **fallinghrt22**: You speak what I feel and to know that the intense emotions run the same through me as they do you. I can not explain what is happening between you and I, I just know that there is a reason for why we are here and if it is for each other, then I will not let go. It's amazing that you think the way that I do for I have had the most unhappy 5 years of my life and for some reason the events of today have taken me to you. If this is what love is, then may I feel it forever, for it fills me with want and desire again and for that I am truly thankful.

3:20:03 PM **ladydi2011**: I cannot imagine the pain and loneliness you have felt for the last five years. I cannot explain the intense emotions I am feeling either. All I know is that I am drawn to you like a magnet. I have butterflies in my stomach. I can't wait to meet you. I never really believed in love at first sight or falling in love on line until I met people that experienced both successfully. Maybe it will be like this for us.

3:21:47 PM **fallinghrt22**: You're everything I dreamed of. A woman after God's heart. So kind and compassionate. Beyond your rugged exterior Is a sweet and gentle spirit You walked in when others walked out. You are my peace in the midst of the storm. You are my best friend and I could not ask for more. The perfect gentle lady. You could teach others a thing or two about how to treat a guy and what the word respect means.

3:22:48 PM **fallinghrt22**: Awwwwww Diana, *I just don't know what I did right to deserve you.*

3:27:19 PM **fallinghrt22**: I've never felt so special. So much love and tenderness. I tried not to feel the way that i'm feeling right now with you for I did not know who you were but began to desire your touch, and your smile. I need you to know that you complete me baby and this stirring desire of passion and want is what love is all about. I will be here for you, waiting till the day that I will be in your arms forever. Take me as I am, as I will do the same for you. Love me for who I am and know that I am yours. And can not wait to tell you those words, to see the passion in your eyes, and the love that you will have forever.

3:28:34 PM **ladydi2011**: I do have a rugged exterior that has been placed there as a protective barrier by things that have happened to me in my life. Most people do not know who I really am. I do not allow myself to be vulnerable with many. For some reason, I have allowed this with you. I think it is because you told me I can trust you with my heart. I do love the Lord with ALL my heart. He has never left or forsaken me when others have. He has made me the woman I am today. Yes, I am kind and compassionate under the rugged shell. Somehow you were able to see through the shell and even crack it. I love that I am your peace in the midst of the storm. Yes, I could teach women how to respect themselves so they could then respect their man. So many people are hurting in our world.

3:30:52 PM **fallinghrt22**: *it is impossible to completely and effectively love someone without being* *included in that other person's history*. Our history has made us who we are. The images, scars and victories that we live with have shaped us into the people we have become. We will never know who a person is until we understand where they have been.

3:33:46 PM **fallinghrt22**: The secret of being transformed from a vulnerable victim to a victorious, loving person is found in *the ability to open your past to someone responsible enough to share your weakness and pains with. "Bear ye one another's burdens, and so fulfil the law of Christ" writes Paul in Galatians 6:2. You don't have to keep reliving it. You can release it.*

3:34:55 PM **ladydi2011**: Thank you. I do take you as you are. Thank you for taking me as I am. I am not perfect. Please know this. I also have battle wounds. I am feeling the same passion for you. Please examine and make sure that it is me you are feeling this for and that it is not just to eliminate loneliness. I already did this examination over the weekend.

3:36:52 PM **fallinghrt22**: *Give Him All Your Secrets- The enemy wanted to change your destiny through a series of events, but God will restore you to wholeness as if the events had never happened. The Triumphant person locked inside shall come forth to where he belongs. He's delivering you. He's releasing you. he's restoring you. he's building you back. He's bringing you out. he's delivering by the power of his Spirit. "...Not by might, nor by power, but by my spirit, said the Lord of Hosts'(Zechariah4:6)*

3:37:19 PM **fallinghrt22**: Awwwww Baby I want you to know that I have searched my heart....my heart calls for you and I hope you feel this way.

3:37:31 PM **ladydi2011**: You are so right about the history and from going from victim to victorious. I am victorious and so are you. I am again speechless at what you wrote. We are so much on the same page! Jerry Wesley, where did you come from?

3:38:13 PM **fallinghrt22**: maybe we are perfect match made from heaven waiting for the right time to show the world what true Love means.

3:40:01 PM **ladydi2011**: Jerry, two other men from the site have emailed me over the weekend. To be courteous, I emailed them back. Please tell me what I have to do to take my profile off the site.

3:40:49 PM **fallinghrt22**: God has already determined your need. He looked down from heaven long ago and saw your pain. He evaluated your situation and decided that you needed a good man. He knew that you would need someone to reach down and lift you up. He saw that you needed to recognize how important you are. It is impossible to know all that was in the mind of God when he looked down on broken humanity, but we can know that he looked past our broken hearts, wounded histories and saw our need.

3:41:39 PM **fallinghrt22**: Oh Baby you just made my heart to skip a beat...you mean you did this for me...the men want to bite more than they can chew. I am glad your mind tells you that you have been taken.

3:42:52 PM **fallinghrt22**: go to the site, click my account, look down you will see cancel my membership.

3:44:30 PM **ladydi2011**: *Ok. You do know that your profile is still on the site, right?*

3:44:45 PM **fallinghrt22**: *I am doing the same right now...cancel.*

3:45:01 PM **fallinghrt22**: are you doing yours.?

3:45:03 PM **ladydi2011**: *I thought you had done this the other day????*

3:45:17 PM **fallinghrt22**: *I didn't go on there...but I will do it now*.

3:45:55 PM **ladydi2011**: Hmmm, I will do mine when I get onto my main computer. I do not have it on this computer and cannot remember my password.

3:46:09 PM **fallinghrt22**: Ok.

3:46:43 PM **ladydi2011**: So, please tell me when I will have the opportunity to hear your voice?

3:47:25 PM **fallinghrt22**: tonight Baby....you are so sweet and charming.

3:47:39 PM **ladydi2011**: I look forward to your call.

3:47:51 PM **fallinghrt22**: same here.

3:47:59 PM **fallinghrt22**: I want you to know something from the bible.

3:48:21 PM **ladydi2011**: Ok. Please share...

3:51:59 PM **fallinghrt22**: *The Bible says," Love doesn't hold a grudge. Love doesn't harbor unforgiveness "(1 Corinthians 13:5) You may have people in your life who have done you great wrong, and you have right to be angry and bitter. You may feel as though your whole life has been stolen away by somebody who has mistreated you or deceived you. But if you will choose to let go of your grudge and forgive them, you can overcome that evil with good. You can get to the point where you can look at the people who have hurt you and return good for evil. If you do that, God will pour out His favor in your life in a fresh way. He will honor you; He will reward you, and He'll make those wrongs right. No matter what you've gone through, no matter who hurt you or whose fault it was, let it go. Don't hold a grudge. Don't try to pay them back. God says show mercy. Aim for kindness. You may be thinking, No, it's not fair. We have to remember that God is the One keeping the score. He is in control. And when you bless your enemies, you will never lose. God will always make it up to you...this is what I did when the woman I dated 2yrs ago hurt me. Our words are vital in bringing our dreams to pass. It's not enough to see your dreams simply by faith or in your imagination. You have to begin speaking words of faith over your life. The moment you speak something out, you give birth to it. This is a spiritual principle, and it works whether what you are saying is good or bad, positive or negative.*

4:00:35 PM **ladydi2011**: This woman hurt you dearly.

4:01:11 PM **ladydi2011**: I agree about speaking it. Remember, I am a perception management specialist.

4:01:29 PM **fallinghrt22**: yeah I Love everything about you.

4:02:59 PM **fallinghrt22**: I so enjoyed our conversation.

4:03:07 PM **fallinghrt22**: honey I need to run now....

4:03:17 PM **fallinghrt22**: when will be a chance to talk again?

4:03:44 PM **fallinghrt22**: thanks for giving me your time I appreciate.

4:03:58 PM **ladydi2011**: Baby, I read a fabulous book written by a pastor called How to Stop the Pain. One golden nugget changed my entire perception and how I live my life. It says that when someone does something to violate, hurt, disrespect or betray us that it has nothing to do with us. It is who they are, we just happened to be in the cross fire. Now, when this happens, I say, "thank you for letting me know who you are" and I chose to not have you in my life.

4:05:23 PM **fallinghrt22**: You are right Baby.

4:05:55 PM **ladydi2011**: I love everything about you too. I also enjoy our conversations. I also need to run because it is already 4:00 here. I am busy. However, you are very important to me.

4:06:30 PM **fallinghrt22**: Awwwww you are important to me too Baby.

4:06:40 PM **ladydi2011**: I also appreciate your time. Please call me tonight around 6:00 if you can.

4:06:45 PM **fallinghrt22**: take good care of yourself...Wet Kisses and Hugs.

4:06:48 PM **fallinghrt22**: I will.

4:06:56 PM **fallinghrt22**: *give me your address Baby.*

4:07:12 PM **ladydi2011**: Many kisses and (((hugs)))

4:07:58 PM **ladydi2011**: Ok. I will give it to you when you call.

4:08:12 PM **fallinghrt22**: Ok .

4:08:23 PM **fallinghrt22**: will talk to you later...Wet Kisses and Hugs sweety

4:08:30 PM **fallinghrt22**: *take good care of yourself.*

4:08:32 PM **ladydi2011**: Take care of you. Tell William I said hello.

4:08:33 PM **fallinghrt22**: Kisses to your lips Cinderella
4:09:02 PM **ladydi2011**: Wet kisses and hugs back to you my love.
4:09:27 PM **ladydi2011**: Oh, do you happen to have my glass slipper. I know that only my prince can possess this.

Other than him not taking his profile down, I still have no clue that he is a scammer. I am such a romantic at heart that I am sucked right into his sweet words and the "*fairytale*" he is painting. I am falling hook, line and sinker. I remember thinking "This is like back in the day when people who were apart wrote love letters to each other." He did take his profile down that night.

RED FLAGS

- ⚑ The part about being in a room and introducing him to all my friends would not normally put up a red flag. However, I now know that this is part of a format that many scammers use.
- ⚑ "What is a perfect first date?" seems like a logical question, but it is a question that scammers use to get to your heart.
- ⚑ He talks about past events, and this is also something scammers use trying to get you to remember bad events and them be the one to comfort you. This is part of their format.
- ⚑ He doesn't take his profile down when he tells me he will. This is a definite red flag.
- ⚑ He uses scripture again to talk about unforgivness. Looking at it now, it is almost like he is asking for forgiveness for what he is about to do. Please know that many, but not all scammers do know scripture, go to church and believe in God; I would think that those who do probably wrestle with their acts of deception and theft but then justify them.
- ⚑ He asks for my address. This is also what scammers will do unless they take the initiative to find you on line.
- ⚑ "Take good care of yourself" is something else scammers say.
- ⚑ Many scammers will say they don't know what they did to deserve you.

Jerry called me in the middle of the night to play the piano and sing me a song he wrote for me. I was blown away by this. He called me a lot in the middle of the night and I never really thought too much about it because he was supposedly in California, but the middle of the night here is morning in Nigeria.

From: Diana Garren
Sent: Tuesday, April 03, 2012 3:14 AM
To: Jerry Wesley [mailto:fallinghrt22@yahoo.com]
Subject: Thank you Baby!

Hi Baby!

Thank you SO much for taking the time to write a song for me. Nobody has ever done this for me. It was beautiful! You are truly an amazing man! I am so blessed to have you in my life. I am again in awe and smiling from ear to ear. My heart is filled with joy and I have tons of butterflies in my stomach. You take my breath away! I have always been the one to give and give and give in a relationship, but never the one to receive. Here you are giving to me. I now know what it is to receive! I SO treasure and appreciate you!

Please send me the words to the beautiful song you wrote for me. I am going to start a scrap book that tells our story. Every time I think about how I already feel about you I think of the movie "Fast and Furious" because my feelings for you have developed so fast and they are intense and real! Me putting my profile on the site was such a fluke... or was it God? I only did it because I received an email in my inbox and it jumped off the computer screen at me so I thought "Why not?" I was not expecting to meet anyone that I would be interested in. Especially not a man like you!

Several years ago I went on Match.com and emailed and talked to men who wanted nothing but one night stands. As you know, I am not interested in one night stands. I had one man tell me that online dating was the best candy store around and that he was sleeping with 10 different women in 10 different states. That did it for me. I cancelled my membership within three days.

I watched Dancing with the Stars tonight and thought about how wonderful it would be to be dancing with you. I have always wanted to learn how to ballroom dance, and I am thrilled that you will be the one to teach me and the one that I will be dancing with. Well my love, I am going to try to go back to sleep. Get a good night's sleep.

Kisses and hugs.

Diana

From: Jerry Wesley [mailto:fallinghrt22@yahoo.com]
Sent: Tuesday, April 03, 2012 3:19 AM
To: Diana Garren
Subject: Picture.

today with friends.

From: Jerry Wesley [mailto:fallinghrt22@yahoo.com]
Sent: Tuesday, April 03, 2012 3:34 AM
To: Diana Garren
Subject: Trust and Commitment!!

Hi Sweetie.

I miss you so much I just can't get you off my mind reading your note did put a smile on my face I am glad that we found each other. I most want to tell you that you are beginning to occupy every space in my heart... I just wanted to let you know that, Commitment is the greatest key to a successful relationship. If you are committed you will always find a way to work things out. Communication... talking and open honest communication about how you feel. What makes you happy and what upsets you. If you don't tell your partner then they can't do what makes you happy and vice versa. I feel that a relationship should always be based upon honesty and acceptance. When you can fully accept yourself, honesty will come naturally. This in return will leave your partner feeling comfortable with you, knowing there is nothing to hide. If two people can see each other in full view with complete acceptance, they can build a successful relationship from this I believe that the most important 'key' to a successful relationship would have to be 'trust'. I believe that with trust, love will follow. However, what I have noticed is that many people think trust, or expect that trust is to be earned by the other person when in all actuality it is something that comes from within yourself. All too many times people will say they don't trust due to past experiences. What they don't realize is that they have built up those proverbial walls to protect them from the very thing they are searching for...yes, there is a risk in trusting someone, but when you finally find that 'right' person, it makes all the past experiences and lessons learned very much worth the risk. All of life's little lessons do not have to be painful... even when they seem so at the time. You just have to chalk it up to experience and move on.

Nothing is worth closing your heart. Nothing is worth living in a world of fearing what bad 'may' come to you. Without trust, you close your heart to the happiness and joy that true love brings. It's only my experience... and it's what I believe has given me the wonderful gift of 'true' love. It's a hard thing to do, a scary thing, but very much worth it. This is not to go without saying that some people may betray your trust... that's the risk... but why allow past betrayals to prolong the pain by building a fortress around your heart that not only protects you from pain/betrayal, but also denies you the ability to experience happiness and joy Most have been hurt enough by one person, why allow them and their actions to stop us from finding what we search for? I say open your hearts to trust and bask in the beauty, happiness, and joy, of the true love that will follow.

For everyone there is a someone, you just can't find them if you hide away all your life. Not expecting your partner to think and react to things the way you do. Resolving any conflict in your relationship depends on this. It's important to respect your partner's feelings, even if they are different from your own. If you and your partner both do this you can usually resolve bad situations I think a good relationship requires being each others best friend, and trusting one another. I think each should respect the others opinion and that stupid arguments over stupid things are healthy, as long as they are not taken too far. Good communication. Never being ashamed of each other for any reason. On occasion surprising your mate with a nice romantic date or evening together and telling each other I love you. There is a lot of love and caring in the relationship.

There has to be love in order for a relationship to work. A good relationship is when your partner is more than just a partner... they should be your best friend. A good relationship is when two lovers understand each other, they're concerned for each other and they respect one another. A good relationship is one purely based on trust, if nothing else. Being able to be miles apart yet never worrying a minute about what they're doing.

Communication at all times is so important, and most importantly, respect for each other and their need for alone time as well as together time. Two people trusting each other fully, not being afraid to tell the other what one thinks, whether it be good or bad, and the other respecting their opinion. Being able to enjoy the same things with each other, enjoying each other, and being able to take their separate lives and smoothly combine their lifestyles into a couple's lifestyle a good relationship exists when either individual has the freedom to leave but neither wants to.

I honestly think that a good relationship is one where there are no secrets. You are completely open with each other. But the biggest key is that the other person knows the worst possible thing about you and they love you even more for it. On top of that you have to have faith and trust. So that when your man goes out with an old female friend you can completely trust him and know that no matter what happens, he will always come home to you. I know it may not seem like much but as long as you have that and love, you are in a wonderful relationship. :)

I define a good relationship by the way you treat each other. You could hold them and run your fingers down the side of their face. Feel comfortable you know. And you can also define it with fighting. Fighting or arguing is not my favorite thing to do with my Partner. But it needs to be done. It's not a real relationship until you do argue. I would have to say good communication! Equality, Love, not just lust, and most of all, friendship is needed. For me, a good relationship is being able to open up to each other even about the simple things in life. A relationship between two people cannot grow without trust. Loving a person is not enough, because if you've got doubts building up inside then your relationship won't work.

A good relationship is when the two of you can actually feel better about your relationship after an argument; it's when you can really respect each others differences and openly discuss feelings at all times you have good relationship where there is compromise, honesty, sensitivity, and a feel for the needs and wants of the other person and yourself When the couple listens and doesn't interrupt when they're trying to work out a fight. They care for each other deeply. They share similar interests. A good relationship is when both parties can freely express themselves with one another and to have that open connection to be able to say anything to each other. To have trust and faith in one another. Basically a honest, trusting, loving and open relationship. A good relationship is frankness and open-minded communication between friends. It is a two-way communication without dominance and/or hypocrisy in it.

A good relationship isn't necessarily flawless, because human beings aren't flawless. It's more important that you can grow with the person you love. If you can learn and grow each day with your best friend standing by you in body and in spirit-then you have a good relationship. When you can feel comfortable about everything together. Always being able to talk and joke. Taking your commitment seriously with one another and never taking each other for granted. A good relationship must be a give and take basis, in order for you to understand each other. Never fail to listen and understand the situation you're in to. Be open minded and be ready for any obstacle that will come your way. A good relationship is when both members fully trust each other and can have a blast with each other, knowing how to laugh and be there for each other. It's something divine. Where the understanding between the two partners is mutual, no talking required, but it's something you can just feel, something special. Where you can just believe in each other, really believe. How there is a difference between saying it and actually feeling it so this is my opinion towards a commitment relationship.

I'll be waiting for your response...wet kisses and hugs....

Jerry

From: Jerry Wesley [mailto:fallinghrt22@yahoo.com]
Sent: Tuesday, April 03, 2012 9:24 AM
To: Diana Garren
Subject: Re: Thank you Baby!

Hi Sweetie,

How are you doing today and how was your sleep? I just want you to know that I couldn't get you off my mind last night which I know that you have been through a lot of things in your life to make you believe that love can't be found again but I am here to show you that love is still out there and I mean real love. *Your past is your past but I am your present and I want us to build a trust-filled future together.*

All my days and all my life I have searched the world for happiness but since I met you I have been smiling and I wake up at morning with a smile on my face just knowing that you are there. Thoughts of you takes me to a place that I have never known before and all I am asking is that you give me a chance to break those walls that you have built and show you a whole new world filled with laughter and abundant love.

I know all these sounds so new to your ears but in time you will see all what I mean. My heart has been stolen by you and even if I had the antidote, I wouldn't take it. My heart is yours forever my dear. I thank God for someone like you because I can't seem to remember what I did right to deserve you, but for the fact that I have you, I want to show you so much more....I will stop here now and wait to hear from you, just know that I am thinking about you. Take care of yourself for me. Hoping to hear from you.

Hugs & Kisses
Jerry

From: Diana Garren
Sent: Tuesday, April 03, 2012 10:05 AM
To: Jerry Wesley [mailto:fallinghrt22@yahoo.com]
Subject: Re: Thank you Baby!

Good morning Baby! My sleep was good, and yours? I had this dream that you wrote me a fabulous song and then sang it to me! I am glad that I am occupying your mind and heart. You are doing the same in mine! You make me smile. I also want us to build a trust-filled fabulous future. You are very perceptive my dear. I want you to know that my heart is open. I do not think I have walls up, but I might. You know sometimes we cannot see in our self what others see. I think I was just being cautious because I have lived long enough to know people can say anything. So, I have trained myself to take my time to be able to see if their actions match their words. Actions will always tell us who someone really is.

I think what else you are seeing is that I promised myself that when I met a man I would take my time to get to really know him before I gave him my heart because I was looking for my forever. I didn't want to make a mistake...however, here you are and you have swept me off my feet. *It just all seems too good to be true.* But, it is true and now I am going with the flow of the beautiful current we are riding and I am going to take it day-by-day and savor everything!

I am letting myself freefall. So, please continue to show me your love, sweep me all the way off my feet and carry me into the sea of love. Take my heart and hand and lead the way my darling and I will follow!

Big hugs and kisses,
Diana

From: Jerry Wesley [mailto:fallinghrt22@yahoo.com]
Sent: Wednesday, April 04, 2012 2:17 PM
To: Diana Garren
Subject: Re: A song for you

My Dearest One,
I miss you so much and I can't seem to get you off my mind, I sit here and I imagine what my life has been like these few days of knowing you and knowing you are mine. I want to keep you forever and always make you happy. I enjoy being with you and I look forward to the day when we will spend every waking moment together.

You gladden my heart and I can't help but to be grateful everyday that I have found the woman who makes my heart pump more blood than usual, the woman that makes me smile even while I am asleep....

You are a dream come true for me and everyday I will cherish what we have..Hope to chat soon.

Jerry

From: Diana Garren
Sent: Wednesday, April 04, 2012 2:45 PM
To: Jerry Wesley [mailto:fallinghrt22@yahoo.com]
Subject: RE: A song for you

My love,
I cannot get you off my mind either. This is a good thing, right? We have started a new chapter in our lives. I am looking forward to the day we will meet in person! I have to run and get things done or I will never be ready to leave tomorrow...Yikes! Not feeling well has slowed me down...

Btw, what are you doing for Easter? Will William be coming home? KISSES AND (((HUGS)))

Diana

From: Jerry Wesley [mailto:fallinghrt22@yahoo.com]
Sent: Thursday, April 05, 2012 4:32 AM
To: Diana Garren
Subject: Thinking about the Future.

Good Morning Sweetie,

I want you to know that you have occupied my heart with so much thought of you. There is so much I want to tell you, a lot has been running through my head lately. I'm having trouble putting my thoughts into words so you will have to bare with me through this.

I keep thinking about the future, about life, and what I want out of it. I keep thinking about us and what this relationship means to me. I keep thinking about these things and I realize they go hand in hand. This relationship is our future together, it's what I want out of life. I want to grow old with you I want to experience this thing called Love again. I want to see you walk around our house in a big t-shirt **with your hair down** and catch me staring at how gorgeous you are. I want you to pull the covers off me at night and then I have to get even closer, if it's possible, to you to keep warm. I want to see you laugh like crazy at me when I do stupid stuff. I want to hold you when you cry and smile with you when you smile. I want to fall asleep every night with you in my arms. I want you to fall asleep on my chest listening to the beat of my heart and know it beats for you. I want you to be the first thing I see when I wake up and the last thing I see when I go to sleep. I want to see your morning hair, I think it will be so cute. I want to sit on the beach with you and watch the sun set, and I want all the people who pass us to envy the love that we obviously have for each other.

I want to see you walk down that isle and I want to take your hand for the rest of my life. I want to spend all night, and maybe the next day, making love to you with an undying passion (sorry to be so blunt), I want to sit there talking to you for hours about nothing at all but in the same time everything or maybe we won't talk at all and just grin at each other realizing how lucky we are lucky to have found each other. I want you to get mad at me for doing something stupid, and I want you to bust out laughing when you try to yell at me.

I want to lay with you in front of a fireplace and keep the heat going long after the fire goes out. I want to take trips with you to places we've never been and experience them together. I want us to go skinny-dipping in a hotel pool and get caught and streak back to our room waking everyone up because we're laughing so hard. I want us to go and pick out the hot tub we want with the biggest grins on our faces the whole time. I want our friends to come over and get totally jealous because they don't share a love like we do. I want us to run outside in the rain and act like total kids getting completely soaked, and when we come back in stripping down to nothing as we stumble into the bedroom, or the kitchen counter, or the balcony, or the dining room table, or an office desk, or the shower, which ever one we feel like at the time. I want it to take your breath away every time I say, "I love you" because you know it's coming from the heart. I want us to sit down with a box of strawberries, a bottle of chocolate syrup, and a thing of mint chocolate ice cream, well, I'll let your imagination finish that one. I want to love you and be with you for at least forever if not a little longer.

I couldn't really express in words what I'm feeling right now so I decided to share with you some of the images and thoughts that have been running through my head. I just want you to know that I had never found someone I wanted to spend the rest of my life with until I met you......will be looking forward to hear from you... and hope we get to talk later...Wet Kisses and Hugs

Yours Jerry

From: Jerry Wesley [mailto:fallinghrt22@yahoo.com]
Sent: Friday, April 06, 2012 7:23 AM
To: Diana Garren
Subject: You are special.

Hey Sweetheart,

I really miss you while I lay here waiting to talk to you, I can't help thinking about you it is like you have become a part of me. Waiting and wanting you has been the focus of my thoughts these days, knowing that one day, all that I have envisioned of us being together, will finally happen.

You give me reason to wake up in the morning and smile. Just smile for no particular reason except the fact that you are here. As days go by I feel myself growing closer and closer and my heart is suddenly coming out of its shy spot and wanting to feel what it feels like to be loved again. I don't ever want to lose this feeling. I don't ever want to lose you.

it's like a feeling I don't want to leave, you give me comfort and joy. Yet, still as I continue to lay here and think about everything you are making me feel now, I can't help but wonder, what's on your mind? How much do you feel, and how real do you think this really is?

Still, I just want you to know that wherever this road may take us, and how far it may be to finally get where we want to go, always know you are in my heart and in my heart is where you'll always be. You melt me Thank God I found you.

Thanks for being you. What I'd like to say next, I'd like to say to you personally. Until then....

Hugs & Kisses
Jerry

Jerry then called on the phone and spoke more sweet words to me and told me he was bidding on a construction job in China. I didn't think much about it because he told me all along that he travels for his business.

From: Diana Garren
Sent: Saturday, April 07, 2012 1:11 PM
To: Jerry Wesley [mailto:fallinghrt22@yahoo.com]
Subject: My innermost feelings....

Good morning my love!

I have typed and erased my first sentence of this email several times because I don't even know where to start or how to explain what I am feeling.
So I first want to tell you that I believe we have something really special between us and I want it to grow and last forever. So I am going to honestly share everything that I am feeling with you.

There is a part of me telling me that I love you and that we will have a wonderful life together. I know this is my heart speaking.

Then there is a part of me saying, "Don't be silly Diana, you have never even met this man in person so loving him is impossible" I am sure this is part of my brain trying to figure out what is going on and being its rational self. I believe this will not go away until we do meet in person. I really need to meet you in person.

Then there is another part of my brain saying, "anything is possible". I love this side of my brain and I am trying to let this guide and lead me.

Then there is a part of me that is like a school girl who is giddy and excited and who loves the feeling of being in love. I believe this is my hopes. I want this!

Then there is a part of me that is saying, "Stop. What if you allow yourself to love this man and then you never meet him or can never be with him? Your heart will be crushed and take forever to heal."

This I am sure is my skeptical mind at work once again. I continually push this away and replace it with *"Diana, it is time to go with the flow and see where this takes you."*

Then there is a part of me that is saying "Jerry is so perfect for you, things "feel" so right, something has to be wrong." I am sure this is my skeptical brain at work again. When this pops up, I say to myself, *"Diana, you deserve a man who is perfect for you and a dynamic relationship; it is time so stop questioning it." Then there is the question that keeps popping up that says "What if this man isn't being honest with you?"* I hate this question with a passion. I hate having doubt about anything you tell me. This question started appearing after several times of our phone conversations going dead and you not answering the phone when I call.

I guess all this is going on inside of me because of pure common sense and how we met is so foreign to me. What I do know is what I want. I want to meet you! If you can, please help me make sense of all these thoughts, feelings and emotions.

Please help me crush any doubts and skepticism. Take my hand and heart and lead me to still waters. Hold on to me baby and don't let me go. I am a real Cinderella who has been through more than you can imagine and been victorious over them. I am waiting for my handsome prince to bring me the glass slipper I lost so long ago. I await my forever prince. He is the one that makes my heart skip beats and stirs up all the butterflies within me. The prince that makes me feel like a little girl and a passionate woman.

The prince that loves, cares for, and protects me. The prince that makes me feel safe and loved. *Oh please tell me that this is happening in real life and doesn't just happen in fairy tales.* Oh please tell me I will meet you soon and that you ARE my prince and that we will spend FOREVER together.

Thanks for letting me share my innermost feelings with you my love. Thank you for being YOU!

Kisses and hugs
Diana

From: Jerry Wesley [mailto:fallinghrt22@yahoo.com]
Sent: Saturday, April 07, 2012 2:35 PM
To: Diana Garren
Subject: Re: My innermost feelings....

Hi Sweetie,

Wow...I had to re read your email and I was speechless of words , but all I want you to know is that I'm your present so don't judge with your past please... Diana. I met you **some weeks ago** on the Internet, and since that time, I have grown to love you so deeply. I have heard it said that online romances don't last, but I disagree. I know that what we are doing may be considered wrong by some, but I also know what I feel in my heart, and I know that it's real.

I lay awake at night, and miss you so much. I know that we can't change whatever has happen in our past, and I know that we can't predict the future, but my heart does not lie ... I am in love with you. When I look at your pictures and into your beautiful eyes, I can see how much I want you in my life.... I just want you to know that you are precious to me and ***no matter how this story turns out***, I am ready for any and everything with you and a wonderful life together. You are my Cinderella and my heart desire.

Love always
Jerry

From: Diana Garren
Sent: Saturday, April 07, 2012 2:59 PM
To: Jerry Wesley [mailto:fallinghrt22@yahoo.com]
Subject: Re: My innermost feelings....

Yes, my love. You are my present and my future. My heart knows this. I promise you that I will no longer allow my past to interfere with my heart or how I feel for you. Yes, there are many that have bad experiences from online dating and many who have met their soul mate. Like you, I know what my heart is telling me. It is the same that your heart is telling you!

Like you, I am ready for everything our life together holds.

Love,
Diana

From: Jerry Wesley [mailto:fallinghrt22@yahoo.com]
Sent: Saturday, April 07, 2012 3:04 PM
To: Diana Garren
Subject: Re: My innermost feelings....

Thanks, I feel at peace and comfortable now...you make me feel butterflies in my stomach...I can't get enough of you... I had a dream which I would love to share with you...but I'm shy.....don't know how you will feel...when I woke up I wrote it down...but I can't send it. lol

Love always
Jerry

From: Diana Garren
Sent: Saturday, April 07, 2012 3:09 PM
To: Jerry Wesley [mailto:fallinghrt22@yahoo.com]
Subject: Re: My innermost feelings....

Baby, please don't feel shy with me. We need to share everything. Please tell me.

Love,
Diana

From: Jerry Wesley [mailto:fallinghrt22@yahoo.com]
Sent: Saturday, April 07, 2012 3:13 PM
To: Diana Garren
Subject: Re: My innermost feelings....

Ok I will send it...you would really need a cold shower thou...lol

---

From: Jerry Wesley [mailto:fallinghrt22@yahoo.com]
Sent: Saturday, April 07, 2012 3:16 PM
To: Diana Garren
Subject: Dream about us!!!

It started with me sitting on the couch, talking on the phone. You walked over to me and as you stood there, I caressed your leg, running my hands up your thigh, then up under your denim shorts. My caresses instantly got your passion stirring and you leaned over to kiss me. I hung up the phone and you crawled on the couch over me, straddling me and kissing me deeper.

let me start by asking you...is sex important for you? For me it is important with the right person...so my dreams goes like this...We started to get more into it the more we kissed. My hands were roaming your body now, then caressing your neck and face as I slowly kissed you. I felt you moan softly in my mouth as you lowered yourself a little more onto me, and start to grind against me, feeling how hard and excited I was. The next thing I knew, you were tugging at my shirt, pulling it up and over my head--then you ran your hands all over my chest. My hands grabbed your hips, pulling you down against me, and then I slid them under your shirt, slowly caressing your back. You arched your back a little as my hands moved back around the front, up under your breasts.

As I caressed you, you reached down and pulled your T-shirt up and off, tossing it aside. Then you gave me a sex-filled look as you undid your bra, sliding it down and dropping it to the floor. I took my time to view your gorgeous breasts. I sat up, kind of on the edge of the seat cushion--we were still kissing, but now you were in my lap, with your legs wrapped around me and arms around my neck. I had my hands on your back, caressing your silky skin. I broke our kiss and start to kiss across your cheek, over to your ear, nibbling on it. Then, I slowly kissed down your neck. I continued down along your shoulder, then back across your throat, then back up to your other ear. Apparently you were enjoying the sensation, because I heard you softly moan as I kissed you.

I kissed back down your neck, then down the front of your chest.

You arched your back at this point, moaning a little louder, wanting more. I half stood up and then laid you down on your back on the couch. I knelt on the floor and took one of your feet in my hands, as I massaged your foot, I leaned forward to kiss your ankle. Mmmmmm... I continued to rub your leg as I slowly kissed up your calf as you lay there on the couch.

As I started to kiss and lick my way along your inner thigh...I just can't wait Wet kisses...
P.S don't see me as a bad person I have never done this before it is just a dream which I want to fulfill with you.

I love you so much Jerry

From: Diana Garren
Sent: Saturday, April 07, 2012 3:25 PM
To: Jerry Wesley [mailto:fallinghrt22@yahoo.com]
Subject: Re: Dream about us!!!

Wow...

Now I do have to take a cold shower!!!

Love you, Diana

From: Jerry Wesley [mailto:fallinghrt22@yahoo.com]
Sent: Sunday, April 08, 2012 3:32 AM
To: Diana Garren
Subject: Hey

Sweetheart,

On this beautiful day I wish to pour my heart out to you as you have already captured my heart. I never thought I could feel this way for anyone again, but today here I am thinking about spending every waking moment with you, thinking about you and having your picture in front of me so that I can see your pretty face.

You occupy my every thought and I begin to wonder where you have been all my life, I am glad that you are here though and I plan to keep you happy and fulfilled.

I hope you slept well and that you are thinking about me as I am of you....

Hope that you have a wonderful day and that all goes well with you today. Please be safe for me and I will chat with you soon.

All my love Jerry

From: Jerry Wesley [mailto:fallinghrt22@yahoo.com]
Sent: Friday, April 08, 2012 4:05 AM
To: Diana Garren
Subject: China

My Sweetheart,

I got the bid for china. This will provide enough money to give you the wedding you want and build the house of our dreams.

Love Always,

Jerry

Jerry called in the middle of the night to tell me to read my email about China. He was so excited and again his phone shut off. I now wonder if he called me in the middle of the night to wear me down so I wasn't thinking clearly when he asked for money.

From: Diana Garren
Sent: Saturday, April 08, 2012 4:47 AM
To: Jerry Wesley [mailto:fallinghrt22@yahoo.com]
Subject: China

Hi Baby!

Congratulations on winning the bid for the work in China! Please be sure to take and send lots of pictures. I must tell you that when I read your email and saw China, all I could think was "China is a lot further away from me than San Diego." For a couple minutes I found myself saying "China" several times. Now 2,000 miles away seems close...Lol!

I am sorry if I didn't make sense on the phone. I was trying to wake up. I was so bummed out when *your phone died and our communication was again cut off.* I am frustrated with our conversations being cut off in mid-stream. I am so glad you are going to fix this problem. As we both know, communication is critical in a relationship. Having my best friend be inaccessible to me is not good!!!

Ok my love, I am going back to bed. I am anxiously awaiting another call from you.

I mailed you something on Thursday. I hope it arrives before you leave for China!!!

Good night my love!
Kisses and hugs
Diana

From: Jerry Wesley [mailto:fallinghrt22@yahoo.com]
Sent: Sunday, April 08, 2012 4:57 AM
To: Diana Garren
Subject: picture.

On April 3rd I made the comment that "this all seems too good to be true. My instinct was starting to kick in and it tried to overrule my heart and my hopes.

On April 7th after he described letting my hair down, I really started questioning what I was feeling and whether or not all this could be true. I wrote all I was feeling to him. I even asked him to tell me this wasn't a "fairytale". One of my sources told me scammers create the "fairytale," but I didn't know this at the time.

My clients are private investigators, and although I hear them talk about many different types of fraud, I never heard them talk about online dating scams. When I started having questions, I should have gone to look for information about online dating scams, but I didn't. I wasn't even thinking "scammer".

I believed the research I had already done on this man was sufficient, and I allowed my heart to rule over my mind. This is exactly what happens; this is exactly how scammers get money from their victims. It is "NEVER" an issue of your intelligence; it is always an issue of your heart!

On April 8th he tells me he got the contract in China. I would surmise he now moved quickly because I started expressing doubts, and he knew I was starting to think with my head instead of my heart.

RED FLAGS

- 🚩 He uses the past and trust issues to manipulate.
- 🚩 He makes the comment "I want to see you walk around our house in a big t-shirt *with your hair down*". I have short hair. Watch for things that don't describe you.
- 🚩 Once I tell him about my fears he introduces "sex" into the picture. This is also part of the format designed to pull you in further and make you more attached and in love with the idea of him and of "you as a couple".
- 🚩 He is now traveling to a foreign country. Scammers always say they are traveling somewhere. Usually when they claim to travel, they also claim to need money and claim that you're the only person who can help them.

IM Apr 8, 2012 5:11:17 AM

5:11:17 AM **fallinghrt22**: Sweetness
5:13:06 AM **ladydi2011**: Hi Baby. I am here.
5:14:08 AM **fallinghrt22**: *you melt me* with that Kiss earlier on the phone
5:14:16 AM **fallinghrt22**: wish it was the real one Baby.
5:15:11 AM **ladydi2011**: I just received your pictures. Thank you Baby! You are SO SEXY!!!!
5:15:41 AM **fallinghrt22**: Awwwww you make me blush. I want you to know that every moment we've spent together since that first day holds a special place in my heart. I was afraid at first that if I let you in I'd regret it, but I haven't regretted a single moment.
5:15:54 AM **ladydi2011**: I also wish it were a real kiss. I cannot wait to kiss you!
5:16:11 AM **fallinghrt22**: Ditto, it *would* be breath taken Baby.
5:16:46 AM **ladydi2011**: Baby, thank you for letting me in. I promise that you will never regret it. I will always honor, cherish and respect you.

5:17:03 AM **fallinghrt22**: You just make me feel extra special; make me feel a sense of warmth inside. I want you to know that I love you for this!

5:18:11 AM **ladydi2011**: You are special. You deserve the best of everything.

5:19:31 AM **fallinghrt22**: Wow..we are great match

5:20:14 AM **ladydi2011**: I agree with what you say about communication. It doesn't always need to be words. Much will be spoken between us with just a look.

5:21:30 AM **ladydi2011**: My prayer was to be equally yoked in all areas. I believe we are equally yoked in all areas. This really excites me!!!

5:22:01 AM **fallinghrt22**: I want you to know that I want the best for you as well. I want you to succeed and I want all your dreams and fantasies to come true. I know that in me you see a man full of kindness, understanding, and compassion. A man with an open heart. A man who puts a smile on your face everyday. I will be that man who's there for you just as you're there for me, the one who encourages you through life's ups and downs. I want you to know that I sincerely appreciate you!

5:24:48 AM **ladydi2011**: Baby, the first time I ever heard the song Breathe by Faith Hill, I said, "This is what I want in a relationship".

5:26:22 AM **ladydi2011**: Please watch the video Breathe by Faith Hill.

5:28:40 AM **fallinghrt22**: watching the video..you are so romantic Baby..I have video I want you to listen to cause I Love good music.

5:29:07 AM **ladydi2011**: Yes baby. I do see this in you and love this about you. I so appreciate you!

5:29:20 AM **fallinghrt22**: click. (Video was Sara Evans- Could Not Ask for More)

5:29:29 AM **fallinghrt22**: let me know when you listen.

5:30:38 AM **ladydi2011**: I am listening.

5:30:49 AM **fallinghrt22**: sweet

5:31:08 AM **fallinghrt22**: I don't really know how I can express my feelings to you because I wasn't myself the first time I set my eyes on your pictures...

5:32:20 AM **ladydi2011**: I love this song and I agree. Every prayer has been answered and every dream has come true. I am in awe that God has brought us together and fulfilled both our heart's desires.

5:32:28 AM **ladydi2011**: We are so blessed!

5:32:41 AM **fallinghrt22**: (Video wasTim McGraw feat Faith Hill - I Need You)

5:32:44 AM **fallinghrt22**: listen.

5:33:34 AM **ladydi2011**: The first time I saw your picture I knew that I had to get to know you!

5:34:07 AM **fallinghrt22**: I have seen and met great beauties, I have also learned how I gaze at them but for once, and with you only, I lost control. I believe through this epistle you will understand me..

5:35:09 AM **fallinghrt22**: I found you and now that I have you I'm never letting you go. Babe, just confide in me your deepest feelings. Tell me your fantasies and they shall be fulfilled. I will do anything it takes to make you happy because that is the only thing that matters to me anymore.

5:37:03 AM **ladydi2011**: Thank you baby. I am sure you have seen, met and even dated beautiful women. I am glad what you see and have with me is different and special. I am glad you lost control...

5:39:10 AM **fallinghrt22**: You are perfect in my eyes, and there is absolutely nothing that I would ever change about you. I know that none is perfect, but baby, in my eyes you are. It leaves me amazed yet blessed to have found someone as special as you. Baby, this little distance between us is going to drive me crazy but it'll all work out just fine. So I will just be waiting till the day we will be together..

5:39:51 AM **ladydi2011**: Babe, please don't ever let go of me. I will never let go of you! I will always share with you my deepest feelings, needs and fantasies. I ask that you promise to do the same. I want you to always be happy and have joy in your heart. When something happens in life to make you sad, I promise I will be there to lift you. I will always be by your side. How could I not, I love you!

5:41:31 AM **fallinghrt22**: I will love you regardless what happens through the years in our relationship. I hope to grow old with you for the rest of my life, to celebrate good times with you and support each other through the bad times. Marriage is a journey that we will grow together through. We will learn things about each other every day.

5:43:11 AM **fallinghrt22**: We will not always have good times but we will always love each other and work through our problems. Marriage is forever. So I promise you forever.

5:43:49 AM **ladydi2011**: I will not do anything to hurt you.

5:46:41 AM **fallinghrt22**: I live for the day that I can sit next to you and whisper into your ear and tell you that I love you, and kiss you ever so lightly but passionately on your lips, and to look into your beautiful eyes as you take my breath away. I live for that first look into your eyes, that first passionate kiss, that first embrace and that first time that we make love together. I live to spend a lifetime with you as your Husband and to grow old with you, loving you for all times from now to eternity.

5:46:59 AM **ladydi2011**: I will love you regardless of what happens throughout the rest of our lives. We will grow old together. We will celebrate good times and support each other through bad times. Yes, marriage is a journey, one that we will travel together, and one that I am committed to. Jerry, when we say "I DO", it is forever. There is no divorce. There is no way out. I want our commitment to be that no matter what comes along we work and pray through it together. Can you commit to this with me?

5:50:07 AM **fallinghrt22**: YES I'm committed. *I PROMISE YOU i will NEVER take advantage of you it has never been in my nature* and *I could NEVER hurt anyone that way i too have a huge heart*......and have so wanted that one person to love me for me and to love me with every breath they have as that is what I will do..love them with every breath that *i* have *i* truly feel so blessed to have you in my life..You're so special and now that *i* have found you *i* dont plan on letting you go.. *I know God brought you into my life for a reason and I am so thankful..*

5:53:55 AM **ladydi2011**: I think society has made divorce so easy that many people today don't even think about marriage being a commitment.

5:54:13 AM **fallinghrt22**: Communication is one of the foundations of our relationship, so I want you to feel free to tell me anything. *i* will be your best friend, you confidant and your cheerleader *i* will not judge you *i* will only love you and *i* know that with honesty and communication as a strong foundation, and **with us Standing on the Word of God and going to the Rock for all of our blessings and guidance..**we can do anything and all things. As single people we have a purpose..but as a couple we have one purpose together that is what God has for us. Our purpose together..

5:58:01 AM **ladydi2011**: Yes, I agree. We need to pray together. Communication is one of the foundations. Thank you for being my best friend, confidant and cheerleader. I am also yours. I will not judge you. Thank you for not judging me either.

5:59:54 AM **fallinghrt22**: I wish I could see through your eyes so I would know what you like to see. I wish I knew your wishes, so I could give you everything you want. I wish I dreamed the same dreams you do, and together we could make them come true. I wish I knew what makes you happy, so I could make you the happiest person in the whole world. And lastly, I wish I were a cell in your blood, so I would be sure I was somewhere in your heart.

6:01:30 AM **ladydi2011**: Oh baby...You are definitely in my heart.

6:02:35 AM **fallinghrt22**: *Just because something good ends doesn't mean something better won't begin..Sometimes we must get hurt in order to grow, we must fail in order to know, Sometimes our vision clears only after our eyes are washed away with tears, Somebody out there has the keys* *to your heart..you just haven't found the right set yet, I can only wonder how touching you would make me feel..*

6:03:15 AM **ladydi2011**: Neither of us can read minds, so we must tell each other what we need.

6:06:23 AM **ladydi2011**: I agree with you. I also know I was not ready for you until now. God has taught, shaped and molded me over the years into the woman I am today. I was not always who I am today. I surrendered my life to Christ when I was 22 and asked him to shape me into the woman he created me to be, not the woman people said I was or the world tried to make me believe I was. It was a painful process but also beautiful.

6:07:53 AM **fallinghrt22**: I would rather risk my heart to the possibility of pain, than to never feel love again. To live without love is merely existing. There is no greater pain than that. Why keep your life on hold, when there is hope you can find that special person who will make your life complete..Throughout life you will meet one person who is unlike any other. This person is one you could forever talk to. They understand you in a way that no one else does or ever could. This person is your soul mate, your best friend. Don't ever let them go, for they are your guardian angel sent from heaven up above.

6:08:51 AM **ladydi2011**: I do not see anything being the same for us baby. There is something very different here.

6:09:31 AM **fallinghrt22**: You are so much more than you can see. You are so much more than you think you are. There are some things in life that don't go the way you want them to or the way you think they should, but you can't dwell on these because you'll miss out on other opportunities. Don't give up on something just because you don't think things will work, you won't know unless you give it a try. I'm so glad we are ready to give each other a chance and right now I know things will work out perfect for us..I will never let go of you *Diana Wesley*.

6:11:51 AM **ladydi2011**: I agree. I have told you today that I am all in with you. I am taking the risk with you. I agree that without love, we just exist.

6:12:14 AM **fallinghrt22**: from the day we met, I knew that you would hold my heart in your hands and you more than do that - you completely own me..every part of me. When I think of you, my heart is so full of love and passion for you that I can hardly contain myself!

6:13:57 AM **ladydi2011**: I feel the same. I have to tell you that waiting another month to be able to kiss your lips and be in your arms is NOT going to be easy for me..

6:15:18 AM **fallinghrt22**: I thank God everyday for letting me meet you and for you falling in love with me because I know that it would never be as perfect any other way. I love you with all that I am. Life seems to be full of trials of this type which test our inner strength, and more importantly, our devotion and love for one another. After all, it is said that "True Love" is boundless and immeasurable and overcomes all forms of adversity.

6:17:07 AM **ladydi2011**: I agree that true Love is boundless and immeasurable and does overcome all forms of adversity. I think God is going to show us in the next month just how strong our love for each other is.

6:20:16 AM **fallinghrt22**: Proverbs 18:22 says that "He who finds a wife, finds a good thing and obtains and receives favor from the Lord..my life has been a total preparation for someone like you preparation and consecration for a woman who will love me like Christ loves the church..cherish me like Christ cherishes the church..and for me to do the same in return *i* so love to be loved and *i* love to love *i* know that the person in my life will totally and fully complete me. *Diana L Wesley*.

6:24:07 AM **fallinghrt22**: *Baby my eyes are closing..I would want to go to bed* and I am so glad you did put a smile on my face and I know I will sleep like a babe with your voice still ringing in my ears and I still feel your cute smile..

6:24:42 AM **ladydi2011**: Yes, this is what Proverbs says. God has given you a heart to know and

follow his Word and He has done the same for me. As long as we stand on His Word, we cannot fail.
6:24:44 AM **fallinghrt22**: You are so sweet with words Baby *I promise you I will never fail you*..let me sleep. Wet Kisses and Hugs
6:25:12 AM **fallinghrt22**: keep on smiling because you have done same to me.

6:25:19 AM **fallinghrt22**:
6:25:32 AM **fallinghrt22**: night Baby
6:25:36 AM **ladydi2011**: Good night my love.

From: Diana Garren
Sent: Sunday, April 08, 2012 11:02 PM
To: Jerry Wesley [mailto:fallinghrt22@yahoo.com]
Subject: Miss You...You have mail

Happy Easter, Baby!

You have been in my thoughts all day today. I miss you! It is Easter, and I am wondering how your Easter has been. I have thought about what next Easter will be like. Will we be cooking Easter dinner together? Will William be with us?

Will we be at a friend's house? Will we be traveling together somewhere? Any of these would work for me as long as we were together! I tried calling you but couldn't reach you so I hope all is well.

Love,
Diana

Jerry called and we talked on the phone prior to him supposedly leaving for China. He promised to get a laptop so we could Skype.

He proclaimed his love for me and promised that he would do anything to make me happy.

From: Diana Garren
Sent: Monday, April 09, 2012 7:10 PM
To: Jerry Wesley [mailto:fallinghrt22@yahoo.com]
Subject: A love letter for you...

Hello Baby!

I hope you had a productive and stress free day. Did you get your laptop? Is everything ready for you to leave in the morning?

Thank you for the wonderful conversation this morning. As always, you made me smile. I have been thinking about our morning conversation. I so appreciate that you want to make me happy. Please know that I want to make you happy too.

Baby, I have learned that money comes and money goes, things come and things go, jobs come and jobs go. Businesses flourish and businesses fail. None of these things makes one happy. They are all false security.

Your love, honesty, faithfulness, loyalty, you holding my hand, kissing my lips, touching me, holding me, dancing with me, walking on the beach together, little surprises, doing silly and fun things together, just "being" without saying any words, your smile, giving me that special look or wink that lets me know you're mine, being my best friend, confidant, lover and safe place to fall. These are the things that will make me happy and feel secure. These are my heart's desires.

So, don't think you have to be anybody but yourself or give me anything that you don't already have to make me happy. What I need, you already possess.

I have had much and I have had little and everything in between. I was content and grateful with little or much. However, what my heart desired most was missing. This put me in the place of existing. No matter what happened in my day, at the end of the day I didn't have that special someone to share it with. I had all this love to give and nobody to give it to.

This left emptiness in me that only the man for me could fill. Not just any man, but the right man for me. I am sure you know what I am talking about.

I already know that our relationship is going to be an easy relationship. It is not one where we will have to strive and toil. We will just have to nurture it and love each other. This is how love is supposed to be.

When you are in China, please focus on your task and do not worry about me going anywhere. I will be here waiting to talk with you.

May God give you all that you need in abundance. May His angels go before you and prepare the way, and then travel with you to and from to bring you safely there and then safely home.

I love you. Kisses and big (((hugs)))

Your lady,

Diana

I am not sure if I picked up on the following statements at the time and let them slide, or if I missed them altogether. As I read this section to identify red flags, his words catch my attention, and it is almost as if he is telling me what is about to happen. *"Just because something good ends doesn't mean something better won't begin...Sometimes we must get hurt in order to grow, we must fail in order to know, Sometimes our vision clears only after our eyes are washed away with tears, Somebody out there has the keys to your heart..you just haven't found the right set yet, I can only wonder how touching you would make me feel.."*

There are only a couple of "real red flags". However, he did throw up some "relationship red flags" such as using the word *"would"* instead of *"will,"* and he didn't wish me Happy Easter, which didn't set right with me. All along I wasn't looking for red flags of a scammer, but relationship red flags.

RED FLAGS

- He uses lower case "I's."
- He once again tells me *"I promise you I will never fail you".* This is a term scammers say.
- He once again uses scripture.
- He calls me Diana Wesley. Scammers do what they can to make you feel you are already, or will soon be, their wife. They do this because they think a wife will do anything for her husband.
- I never picked up that he wanted to go to bed at 11:00 am. Many scammers work throughout the night and sleep in the day.

On April 8th Jerry sent me a Verbena plant with a teddy bear and a message that said, "Hey Sweetness Diana, I want you to know that you have captured my heart…I want you to keep it safe baby…I will always cherish and adore you…hold this teddy bear until I am able to get there to hold you. Wet kisses and hugs…Your Admirer."

IM Apr 9, 2012 9:48:50 AM

9:48:50 AM **fallinghrt22**: Good morning my heartbeat
9:49:30 AM **ladydi2011**: Good morning love
9:49:56 AM **fallinghrt22**: How are you doing and how was your night?
9:51:23 AM **ladydi2011**: I am good. I got some rest. How are you? Did you sleep well?
9:54:01 AM **fallinghrt22**: I am glad to know that you slept well..wish I was there to keep you warm.
9:54:19 AM **fallinghrt22**: I'm better now that I can talk to you
9:55:24 AM **ladydi2011**: I would love if you were here to keep me warm.
9:55:47 AM **ladydi2011**: Did you have a nice Easter?
9:56:29 AM **fallinghrt22**: busy *easter* needed to prepare but I had to make *chips and barbecue chicken*, and also clean up. wish you were here to help me out....you distract me thou
9:57:04 AM **fallinghrt22**: so tell me how was your day?
9:58:02 AM **ladydi2011**: Is distracting you a bad thing?
9:58:18 AM **fallinghrt22**: Nah, I would love it
9:58:37 AM **ladydi2011**: You distract me too...but I love it!
9:58:52 AM **fallinghrt22**: Wow,
9:59:46 AM **fallinghrt22**: I am glad I have all your time and attention. It means more to me than you can think of
10:01:20 AM **ladydi2011**: Of course you have my time and attention.

10:03:05 AM **fallinghrt22**: *You melt me.*

10:04:10 AM **fallinghrt22**: don't worry when we are together you will take as much time as you want to rest...while I cook and also do all the dishes and cleaning.

10:04:14 AM **ladydi2011**: What are your plans for next year?

10:04:55 AM **fallinghrt22**: my plans have already started...a great life of Love with you.

10:05:52 AM **ladydi2011**: Baby. That is so sweet.

10:06:01 AM **fallinghrt22**: did you get my texts, and email?

10:07:30 AM **ladydi2011**: No baby I didn't.

10:08:37 AM **fallinghrt22**: run I will run with you.

10:08:48 AM **fallinghrt22**: I reached your world. I summon you to my world.

10:09:50 AM **ladydi2011**: Oh wow, I have never been summoned before

10:10:33 AM **fallinghrt22**: *I Live to Love you Baby.*

10:10:53 AM **ladydi2011**: I love being in your world and I hope you love being in mine.

10:11:30 AM **fallinghrt22**: I know I would Love it with every breath I take.

10:11:35 AM **fallinghrt22**: be right back Baby.

Break in Time

10:11:42 AM **ladydi2011**: Awwww Baby, I love that you love me and live to do so.

10:12:18 AM **fallinghrt22**: are you at work?

10:12:54 AM **ladydi2011**: No, I took the day off.

10:13:03 AM **fallinghrt22**: good..what are you doing now?

10:13:11 AM **ladydi2011**: Lying down

10:13:12 AM **fallinghrt22**: on bed? Naked

10:13:43 AM **ladydi2011**: I need to clean the house, write a chapter or two and wash the car.

10:14:57 AM **fallinghrt22**: I should be the one to wash the car.

10:15:41 AM **fallinghrt22**: I am in my office doing paper work....and talking to my heart...will soon start my day. I am glad I am starting my day with you.

10:15:56 AM **ladydi2011**: Yes, that would be nice. It is not my favorite job. I also do not like cutting the grass.

10:16:12 AM **fallinghrt22**: I will do that for you baby.

10:16:22 AM **ladydi2011**: I am glad to start my day with you too!

10:16:45 AM **fallinghrt22**: be right back baby.

10:17:23 AM **ladydi2011**: Will you please be sure to text me when you arrive in China. I have been praying for safe travel.

10:18:58 AM **ladydi2011**: Thank you for the plant, teddy bear and wonderful message. Is the plant a verbena honey?

10:19:52 AM **fallinghrt22:** Awwwwww thats sweet, let the teddy bear keep you warm until *i* am there Baby.....Yes it's verbena

10:21:30 AM **fallinghrt22:** look your email.

10:21:30 AM **ladydi2011**: Maybe your green thumb will wear off on me...Lol

10:21:41 AM **ladydi2011**: Ok. Brb

From: Jerry Wesley [mailto:fallinghrt22@yahoo.com]
Sent: Monday, April 09, 2012 10:21 AM
To: Diana Garren
Subject: pic

Office...

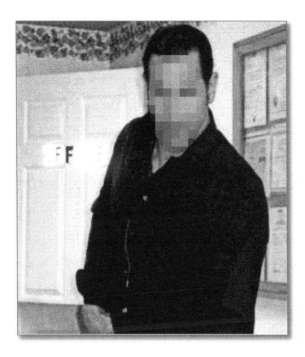

10:23:14 AM **ladydi2011**: Thank you for the picture baby! You are so handsome! Are you sure you are still single?
10:24:10 AM **fallinghrt22**: 100% single.
10:24:22 AM **fallinghrt22**: did you see a ring on my hand
10:25:02 AM **ladydi2011**: Baby, you are the complete package.
10:25:23 AM **fallinghrt22**: You make me feel special.
10:26:56 AM **ladydi2011**: No, I do not see a ring on your hand.
10:27:24 AM **fallinghrt22**: *I can't wait to kneel down with a ring asking for your hand in marriage*.
10:30:59 AM **ladydi2011**: I must keep myself busy the next month because I already know it is going to be a long month!
10:32:27 AM **fallinghrt22**: Hmmmmmm you fill me with passion for life once again..
10:33:11 AM **fallinghrt22**: *I will always be on to talk to you Baby and also prepare for our meeting..I am planning on coming to Atlanta straight from China.*
10:33:22 AM **ladydi2011**: I know you have much to do today. I would love to keep your attention on me but I do not want you stressed out. Please do call me tonight. Please do take care of yourself.
10:34:13 AM **ladydi2011**: Wait...Really! You are coming here straight from China!!!
10:35:42 AM **fallinghrt22**: Yes I will call you tonight baby once I am packed and have rested
10:36:03 AM **fallinghrt22**: Yes thats my plans. I don't know how you feel about it..
10:36:09 AM **ladydi2011**: I was so hoping that you would come straight to Atlanta.
10:36:29 AM **fallinghrt22**: Hmmmmmm were you in my thoughts to know what I was thinking
10:37:52 AM **ladydi2011**: We are in each other's thoughts baby.
10:39:08 AM **fallinghrt22**: I Love you.
10:40:03 AM **ladydi2011**: I Love You too Jerry.

10:43:28 AM **fallinghrt22**: *I wish and I wish and I wish that I can feel The warmth of your kiss, that I can touch A lock of your hair, that our bodies can meet In the same air, that time can pass quickly and the waiting be done so our lives can begin. That the longing I feel disappears with the breeze and in your arms I can know the strength of your squeeze..*

10:46:04 AM **ladydi2011**: You really need to write a book of poetry my dear.

10:47:26 AM **fallinghrt22**: lol...we can work on that together Baby.

10:48:09 AM **fallinghrt22**: you make me feel butterflies in my stomach and I love it

10:48:27 AM **ladydi2011**: Yes, we can work on this together.

10:49:22 AM **fallinghrt22**: I just want to love you like you have never felt, I am a confidant lover, just been out of practice, saving myself for someone like you..very much get pleasure out of pleasing my woman..when we meet I want to flirt with you all day by gentle touches, looking into your eyes, brushing up against you..then, when evening falls..all that flirting will make me want you even more when we lay you down

10:49:46 AM **ladydi2011**: I have butterflies too and I love it! Baby, I am never going to let you go!

10:51:57 AM **fallinghrt22**: you have a way with words that touches my heart..*I don't know what I did right to deserve you*..but knowing I have you I will never let go of you too Baby.

10:53:18 AM **ladydi2011**: Baby, I want the same thing. I love to flirt!

10:55:02 AM **fallinghrt22**: If only you could guess how I hear your voice, for you hold the key to my happiness, and it's always you my soul seeks. If only you could feel, how your very presence has the power to heal, all the wounds inside me. You've made me abandon the pain of yesterday, and you've shown me that the past can no longer stand in the way of what I hope to achieve..If only you knew..

10:56:50 AM **ladydi2011**: I am not questioning anything anymore. I will never let you fall. Your heart will never be broken. God has given you a good woman in me. We will live our life in truth, integrity and love.

11:01:43 AM **fallinghrt22**: If only you knew, how my heart overflows with love for you. If only you could see the way you fill my hopes and dreams. You're the owner of my heart, the ruler supreme. Even in the dark of night, I have only to think about you to feel your loving light and from this world I drift feeling as if I will never touch the ground again..If only you knew.

Break In Time

11:06:50 AM **fallinghrt22**: Babe, you have changed my life completely. You're the one who makes me strong. You're the one who makes me so important; you're everything to me..

11:09:55 AM **ladydi2011**: You make me want to be the best I can be. You and I have the same values, desires, dreams and hopes.

11:15:40 AM **fallinghrt22**: Every day that passes, my feelings for you grows. You are my dream come true and I can't wait to spend forever in your arms, get lost in your eyes, be warmed by your smile, melt with every kiss, and fall deeper in love when we make love.

Break In Time

11:20:56 AM **fallinghrt22**: <ding>

11:21:01 AM **fallinghrt22**: If only you could realize the way you've shown me that it's better to give than to take, and whatever I do, I do for your sake. I'm willing to give you my all and expect nothing in return. But, oh how I yearn for you... if only you knew....

Break In Time

11:23:37 AM **fallinghrt22**: <ding>

11:24:53 AM **fallinghrt22**: Baby I enjoyed talking to you..I need to get going now..thanks for talking to me..

11:24:57 AM **fallinghrt22**: I will miss you

11:25:05 AM **ladydi2011**: Honey, everything I say to you I mean. If you ask anyone, they would tell you this is very out of character for me. How I love and trust you is something I usually don't do so easily. I have let go of my protective shields and my "I will take care of me" attitude.
11:25:10 AM **fallinghrt22**: *take good care of yourself*.....Wet Kisses and Hugs
11:27:09 AM **fallinghrt22**: I promise I will do my best to make you happy
11:27:12 AM **fallinghrt22**: Love you.
11:28:47 AM **ladydi2011**: You have already made me happy. I love you. Take care of you.

The "gush" is a little too much in this last chat. I found the words he was saying to me on an e-card at www.passionup.com/fun/fun377.htm. I guess he pours it on heavy because he knows he will soon ask me for money. He ate chicken and chips for Easter. Chicken and Chips is something that is eaten on a regular basis in Nigeria, but I didn't know this at the time, I just thought it was odd and chalked it up to him being a bachelor from Denmark.

 RED FLAGS

- Many scammers send flowers, teddy bears, chocolate, jewelry and even money if they are going to ask for a large amount of money. They want to make you think that they and the relationship are real and that they have money.
- I notice a pattern with how his picture files are labeled. They have the same long sequence of numbers and then a capital A, B, C, etc. I notice a similar pattern with other scammers.
- He tells me he plans to come directly to Atlanta from China. Scammers will tell you this so you believe they are really coming to be with you.

From: Diana Garren
Sent: Tuesday, April 10, 2012 7:30 AM
To: Jerry Wesley [mailto:fallinghrt22@yahoo.com]
Subject: Good Morning!

Good morning, Sweetheart! It is 4:30 am in San Diego. If I remember correctly your flight leaves at 7:30. I would think you are on your way or already at the airport. I hope I hear from you before you board the plane. If not, I hope you have an enjoyable and safe flight. You should be in the air about 13 hours. And there is a 12 hour difference from Atlanta to China.
Continually thinking about you...I love you

Diana

From: Jerry Wesley [mailto:fallinghrt22@yahoo.com]
Sent: Tuesday, April 10, 2012 8:32 AM

To: Diana Garren
Subject: Re: A love letter for you...

Morning Love,

How are you doing and how was your night? Thanks so much for the wonderful email. I missed you so much and I want to tell you how much you mean to me, and to thank you for coming into my life. You are something I never thought could exist for me.

You are one of the best things that has happened in my life, I don't and will never regret being with you.

When I am with you, I feel alive. You bring to me a happiness that no one else ever could. You bring to me a love I have never known before. I could not imagine what my life would be like without you. You have touched my heart in ways no one could ever comprehend. I love being with you and I want to spend the rest of my life with you.

Every day I wake up thanking God for you. You have given me so much, and I don't know if I will be able to give back all that you have given me. Sometimes I feel lost and out of touch, but when you're there, I feel safe.

I could sit here and try to tell you just how I feel, but I can't find the words other than I am ecstatic we met.

I want to tell you that the love I have for you is undying and unconditional. It is a love that is strong, deep and enduring, it will stand the test of time. I truly feel blessed that you have become a part of my life, and I cannot wait for the day that we can join our lives together. I want to lay next to you at night and have you fall asleep in my arms while I watch over you like a baby.

I want to wake up to your beautiful smile. I want to share in your joys and sorrows. I want to be your everything, because you are everything to me. I promise to always love you and always hold you in my heart. I will always be here for you when you need me, and I will love you no matter what life brings us. I am so certain that you are my soul mate....Wet Kisses and Hugs

Yours,
Jerry,

Jerry called and we talked on the phone prior to him supposedly leaving for the airport. He told me that he went shopping and bought our wedding set and was going to propose to me in the airport so I needed to be sure to bring my friends to the airport to pick him up.

I asked him what size ring I wear, and he guessed it right. I was shocked that he guessed it right.

From: Diana Garren
Sent: Tuesday, April 10, 2012 10:32 AM
To: Jerry Wesley [mailto:fallinghrt22@yahoo.com]
Subject: Hit me like a brick

Baby, I promise to take care of me while you are gone. I look forward to the day when we take care of each other. Please take care of you. Honey, I must tell you that I have been very independent. "I am with you because I want to be, not because I need to be".

If I was in denial of being in love with you, the denial lifted this morning. When we once again got disconnected, my love for you hit me like a brick. I was not expecting the feelings that came over me.

Our hearts don't lie! This is the craziest and most beautiful thing. Wow...if someone would tell me that this was going to happen, I wouldn't have believed them! You, my dear, have a VERY important date in Atlanta when your work in China is done...

I love you!

Diana

From: Jerry Wesley [mailto:fallinghrt22@yahoo.com]
Sent: Tuesday, April 10, 2012 10:36 AM
To: Diana Garren
Subject: Hit me like a brick

I'm also glad to hear your voice, I feel better now...I Love you so much Baby please take good care of yourself for me until I am able to take care of you myself...

I sent you email, and thanks for the breath taken email you sent to me....you melt me and I will never let go of you...bye for now Baby...your man.

Wet Kisses and Hugs.

Love,
Jerry

From: Diana Garren
Sent: Tuesday, April 10, 2012 12:10 PM
To: Jerry Wesley [mailto:fallinghrt22@yahoo.com]
Subject: I now live in your heart rent free...

Baby,

I have only known you for *11 days*...yet I feel like I have known you for so long! Today I am living in your heart rent free. Wow...wow...wow! I thought this stuff only happened in fairy tales and to other people.

I just talked to one of my clients who knew within the first five minutes of meeting his wife that she was his wife. They married within a week and have been married for 40 years. I have been in their company many times and they are still so "in love".

It allowed me to hope that it could happen for me. What they have is what I was looking for and I believe I have found it with you. I asked him this morning how he knew, and his response was, "I can't explain it, I just knew". Yep, this is how I feel. I can't explain it. I just know!

Thinking of you and missing you baby....Your woman who lives in your heart rent free.

Diana

From: Diana Garren
Sent: Wednesday, April 11, 2012 8:52 AM
To: Jerry Wesley [mailto:fallinghrt22@yahoo.com]
Subject: Good morning!

Good morning/evening, Sweetheart,

I hope you got some rest on the flight. You should have landed or be landing soon. It is 8:50 in the evening in China. I don't know about you, but I am always hungry after a flight. I hope you have a good dinner and then rest well.

I am so proud of you for winning this bid. I wouldn't have a clue how to navigate in another country like you do. I admire you baby! I know I will always feel safe when I am with you. I am looking forward to you being by my side. Because I trust you, I will be able to rest a little and not always have to be on guard and handle everything. I have not been able to do this in a very long time. I am sure it will feel foreign to me at first but I know I will adjust quickly to letting you be my man. I am anxious to see how much more we can accomplish together than we ever did solo.

Baby, as far as your career, what do you want for the future? Please tell me more details about the job that will allow you to retire. I am anxiously awaiting your call so I know you are there safely. Knock them dead baby with your brilliance and creativity.

Please remember to take lots of pictures for me.

All my love,
Diana

Jerry called, and we talked long enough for him to say he needed to chat with me and tell me he loves me.

IM Apr 11, 2012 5:54:56 PM

5:45:56 PM **fallinghrt22:** <ding>

5:46:10 PM **ladydi2011:** Hi Baby!

5:46:53 PM **fallinghrt22:** Baby I am so exhausted... I could use a good massage from you right now

5:47:21 PM **ladydi2011:** Baby, if I was there I would give you a great massage!

5:47:55 PM **fallinghrt22:** I know you would baby

5:48:00 PM **fallinghrt22:** How is my baby doing?

5:48:25 PM **ladydi2011:** I am excellent now that I am chatting with you.

5:48:28 PM **fallinghrt22:** I really wish you were here, I need you so bad

5:48:40 PM **fallinghrt22:** Awwwwww baby, you are so sweet. *You melt me* with your sweet words

5:48:52 PM **ladydi2011:** I wish I were there too!

5:49:22 PM **ladydi2011:** I had a meeting today and everyone wanted to know why I was glowing....

5:49:24 PM **fallinghrt22:** I could use a lot of you right now

5:49:33 PM **fallinghrt22:** Oh yeah glowing

5:50:03 PM **fallinghrt22:** I know why, they should ask me

5:50:27 PM **ladydi2011:** You know why! I told them. The women are jealous and the men are sad!

5:53:47 PM **fallinghrt22:** Oh baby, I have a picture of you with me everywhere I go and I also got one in my mind's eye.

5:54:56 PM **ladydi2011:** Your picture is on my phone

5:55:41 PM **fallinghrt22:** Soon baby we will spend every waking moment together and we can do all the things that lovers do...I promise

5:56:44 PM **ladydi2011:** Is everything ok for you over there baby?

5:57:10 PM **fallinghrt22:** *I am trying not to bombard you but the only person I can reach out to is you..Baby everything is not ok right now*

5:57:55 PM **ladydi2011:** please tell me honey.

5:58:47 PM **fallinghrt22:** *Well I got here and I had issues with customs, they tagged my luggage contraband and seized it. They said I was not supposed to bring in my tools that way and I should have used a Courier service. Now they have all my tools and other things except for my carry-on*

5:59:19 PM **ladydi2011:** Oh no. Can you get them back?

5:59:48 PM **fallinghrt22:** *Yes I can get them back but they said I have broken the rules and I have to be charged to court or pay a fine for $3500*

6:00:02 PM **ladydi2011:** What????

6:00:44 PM **fallinghrt22:** *Yes and I think that paying the fine is the fastest way for me because I have a deadline on the job and the court case will take some time, it will all just be a big setback for me*

6:01:28 PM **ladydi2011:** It sounds like paying the fine is the fastest way for you baby. What the heck does charged to court mean anyway???

6:02:25 PM **fallinghrt22:** *I will be taken to court for breaking the rules of the country and I might end up in jail for a couple of weeks then be granted bail*

6:02:46 PM **ladydi2011:** Oh.....no, no, no...Pay the fine!

6:02:51 PM **fallinghrt22:** *But right now the problem is that my cashiers check is in the luggage and I can't get it. That's why I am stressed.*

6:03:41 PM **ladydi2011:** Where did you get the cashier's check from?

6:03:57 PM **fallinghrt22:** *from my bank.*

6:04:15 PM **fallinghrt22:** *I was told it wasn't safe to carry cash so I made it into cashiers check*

6:04:34 PM **ladydi2011:** Can they cancel that cashier's check and wire you money?

6:05:28 PM **fallinghrt22:** *Called my bank, it will take forever because they need to verify that I am the one making the changes..will take days.. I just don't have enough time, I need your help*

6:05:42 PM **ladydi2011:** What can I do?

6:06:15 PM **fallinghrt22:** *Can you please lend me $3500 and as soon as I get my luggage and cash the check, I will send the money back asap.*

6:06:43 PM **ladydi2011:** Of course...How do I get it to you?

6:07:16 PM **fallinghrt22:** *Hold on, I need to ask the hotel manager. I don't know anything about here*

6:07:29 PM **ladydi2011:** Ok.Baby, in the future, we are going to do research about the country in which you are traveling

6:13:39 PM **fallinghrt22:** Ok baby I am back.

6:14:05 PM **fallinghrt22:** *Ok can you do a bank transfer?*

6:14:26 PM **ladydi2011:** Bank transfer to where?

6:14:48 PM **fallinghrt22:** *To China. The hotel's bank account and I will get the money from them*

6:15:58 PM **ladydi2011:** I have to ask my bank how to do this. Please provide me what I need.

6:16:59 PM **fallinghrt22:** *I will give you the bank info baby and all you have to do is an International Wire Transfer from the bank*

6:17:59 PM **fallinghrt22:** Will email it now.

6:18:31 PM **ladydi2011:** Ok...Does it cost extra for the wire transfer?

6:18:50 PM **fallinghrt22:** *Yes about $40 - 60*

6:20:26 PM **ladydi2011:** Please give me the info I need and the hotel address and phone number.

Break In Time

6:32:17 PM **ladydi2011:** R U there baby?

6:32:30 PM **fallinghrt22:** Yes baby sending you an email

6:32:59 PM **ladydi2011:** Ok. Please breathe and know all will be ok.

6:33:49 PM **fallinghrt22:** Ok baby I just sent you the email.

He then sends me this email.

From: Jerry Wesley [mailto:fallinghrt22@yahoo.com]
Sent: Wednesday, April 11, 2012 6:34 PM
To: Diana Garren
Subject: Info for transfer

Agricultural bank of china zhejiang branch
swift code: aboccnbj110
a/c no: 19230 11404 8400 122
benef: Wihu International Limited.

Address: 369 Desheng Middle Road
+862034261324

6:44:31 PM **fallinghrt22:** *I sent the email with the information you need.*
6:44:39 PM **ladydi2011:** I got your email. I will go to my bank tomorrow.
6:45:00 PM **fallinghrt22:** *Ok baby thanks a lot*
6:45:08 PM **fallinghrt22:** *I am extremely grateful.*
6:45:11 PM **ladydi2011:** You are welcome.
6:45:55 PM **fallinghrt22:** Have you had dinner?
6:45:55 PM **ladydi2011:** I know you are baby. I will need this back if possible before the 25th of this month. Do you think this is possible?
6:46:10 PM **ladydi2011:** No, not yet. What about you honey?
6:46:25 PM **fallinghrt22:** *Of course it is possible honey, you will get it back in 2 days at most*
6:46:32 PM **fallinghrt22:** I don't know what I can eat here..
6:47:14 PM **ladydi2011:** Baby, please tell me what you need researched about China and I will do it for you while you sleep..
6:47:34 PM **fallinghrt22:** Awww baby that is so sweet of you
6:47:43 PM **fallinghrt22:** I think I should employ you
6:47:57 PM **ladydi2011:** Honey, I love you and I want the best for you.
6:48:20 PM **fallinghrt22:** I know baby, you are best for me
6:48:38 PM **ladydi2011:** No, just marry me...lol
6:48:50 PM **ladydi2011:** I know you would be here for me!
6:49:09 PM **fallinghrt22:** Yes baby I will marry you but I will have to ask nose to nose
6:49:31 PM **ladydi2011:** Yes, my love. Please don't ever let me go because you will never find anyone else like me. God had to break the mold after he made me...Lol
6:50:05 PM **fallinghrt22:** Lol..I am sure he made you specially for me. I am stuck on you baby
6:50:40 PM **ladydi2011:** Lol...Please know I am not desperate to get married. I DO want a fabulous relationship. The relationship is more important to me than being married.
6:51:00 PM **fallinghrt22:** I want to marry you
6:51:18 PM **ladydi2011:** I know you do baby!
6:51:56 PM **fallinghrt22:** I got my mind made up as regards to US
6:52:06 PM **ladydi2011:** I not only want you, but I want William too.
6:52:17 PM **fallinghrt22:** You got us both baby
6:53:08 PM **ladydi2011:** I know I have both of you and this makes my heart overflow with joy.
6:53:42 PM **ladydi2011:** Honey, I would love to chat with you for hours, but you are exhausted.
6:53:59 PM **fallinghrt22:** I am exhausted and need rest but I need you more
6:54:46 PM **ladydi2011:** Baby, know that all will be ok.
6:55:14 PM **ladydi2011:** When do you have to start work?
6:55:22 PM **fallinghrt22:** I feel you everywhere I go baby.
6:55:37 PM **fallinghrt22:** I can't start work until I get my luggage issues take care of
6:55:56 PM **ladydi2011:** I know, but when were you supposed to start?
6:56:21 PM **ladydi2011:** Your luggage issue will be taken care of in the morning baby.
6:56:42 PM **fallinghrt22:** I am supposed to start Friday.
6:57:13 PM **ladydi2011:** My local bank branch is only a drive through so I have to go to the next town over. I think they open at 9:00.
6:57:34 PM **ladydi2011:** I will look tonight and be up early to handle this for you.
6:57:54 PM **fallinghrt22:** Thank you so much Sweetheart

6:57:59 PM **ladydi2011:** Baby, how do I reach you to let you know it is done?

6:58:05 PM **fallinghrt22:** You are an Angel in disguise

6:58:11 PM **fallinghrt22:** You can text me honey

6:58:20 PM **ladydi2011:** I know and so are you my love.

6:58:32 PM **ladydi2011:** Ok. I will text you...

7:01:29 PM **ladydi2011:** Do they have a restaurant at the hotel?

7:02:03 PM **fallinghrt22:** Yes they do baby but it is all chinese food.

7:02:18 PM **fallinghrt22:** Besides baby it is just 7am here

7:02:40 PM **ladydi2011:** When was the last time you ate?

7:02:52 PM **ladydi2011:** Do you still have to find contractors?

7:05:50 PM **fallinghrt22:** Yes I will do that in a couple of hours

7:05:56 PM **fallinghrt22:** I have to go to an agency

7:06:07 PM **fallinghrt22:** I ate on the plane

7:06:28 PM **ladydi2011:** Ok. Are you in your room or the lobby? Can you even get a room without your traveler's checks?

7:07:00 PM **fallinghrt22:** *I have a credit card with $400 on it that I used to get me a room*

7:07:26 PM **ladydi2011:** *Baby, may I ask why you put your traveler's checks in your checked luggage instead of in your carry on or your wallet?*

7:08:22 PM **fallinghrt22:** *I was told it wasn't safe to carry cash so I hid it trying to be safe*

7:08:56 PM **ladydi2011:** Baby, you need a cloth money belt that you wear under your clothes.

7:09:48 PM **ladydi2011:** You being safe is the most important thing to me.

7:10:38 PM **ladydi2011:** You also need to make sure your passport is safe.

Break in Time

7:13:53 PM **ladydi2011:** R U there baby?

7:14:06 PM **fallinghrt22:** Yes baby I am here

7:14:08 PM **fallinghrt22:** I got booted

7:14:51 PM **fallinghrt22:** *I need you to always prepare for me trips*

7:15:05 PM **fallinghrt22:** When we are married you will have to watch my back while I watch yours

7:15:12 PM **ladydi2011:** I will help you do this my love.

7:15:37 PM **ladydi2011:** Yes, we will watch each other's back

7:15:51 PM **fallinghrt22:** I love you baby

7:16:29 PM **ladydi2011:** I love you too. What can I do from here to relieve your stress right now?

Break in Time

7:21:07 PM **fallinghrt22:** <ding>

7:21:18 PM **fallinghrt22:** You there honey?

7:21:54 PM **ladydi2011:** I am. I was waiting for you to respond to my last entry...

7:22:26 PM **fallinghrt22:** Heres what I said: Aww baby I just need you to take care of yourself for me, until I can take care of you myself

7:23:06 PM **ladydi2011:** Baby, other than find contractors and retrieving your luggage, what else do you need to do?

7:23:32 PM **fallinghrt22:** I need to rent some tractors and mixers

7:24:35 PM **ladydi2011:** Baby, I will take care of me until you can take care of me...

7:24:46 PM **fallinghrt22:** Same here honey

7:24:55 PM **fallinghrt22:** Be right back baby, I got food

7:24:56 PM **fallinghrt22:** Rice

7:24:59 PM **ladydi2011:** Do you already know where you will rent them from?

7:25:28 PM **ladydi2011:** Yay...I am so glad you got food.

Break in Time

7:36:04 PM **ladydi2011:** R U there baby?

7:49:07 PM **fallinghrt22:** Baby I am back

7:49:32 PM **fallinghrt22:** I ate the food as if I haven't eaten in 8 years

7:52:57 PM **ladydi2011:** I am SO glad you ate!

7:53:15 PM **fallinghrt22:** I miss you baby

7:53:30 PM **ladydi2011:** I miss you too!

7:54:18 PM **ladydi2011:** Today while I was at city hall I met a woman who met her husband on line. They were also long distance. They have been very happily married for eight years.

7:55:21 PM **fallinghrt22:** Oh thats cool..We will tell such sweet stories too

7:55:41 PM **ladydi2011:** Yes, we will be able to tell such sweet stories.

7:56:22 PM **ladydi2011:** I have always wanted to write romance novels...but, I have never been romanced. Now, I think I will be able to write them.

7:57:06 PM **fallinghrt22:** My baby, our story is enough for a romance novel, but wait till I get a hold of you and see how sweaty you can get

7:57:16 PM **ladydi2011:** I am a true romantic so I knew my side of it, but not the receiving side.

7:57:31 PM **fallinghrt22:** Be sure you will get nothing less.

7:57:36 PM **ladydi2011:** You are on baby!!!

7:58:25 PM **ladydi2011:** I need exercise to get back to my 36/24/36...

7:59:02 PM **fallinghrt22:** You are perfect for me baby

8:00:03 PM **fallinghrt22:** Baby whatever I am doing, if you cut an eye across the room I will come running

8:00:37 PM **ladydi2011:** Oh baby, I wanted to tell you that from your pictures it appears that you have big hands, is this accurate?

8:00:45 PM **fallinghrt22:** Even when we have visitors, you can give me a wink and I will understand

8:00:50 PM **fallinghrt22:** Yes I do have big hands honey

8:01:03 PM **ladydi2011:** I love it...Same here. I will understand also.

8:02:00 PM **ladydi2011:** I have my dad's hands and I think they are large for a female. Now, they will feel small in your hands.

8:02:15 PM **fallinghrt22:** I can't wait to feel them on my body

8:02:31 PM **ladydi2011:** I can't wait to feel your hands on my body.

8:03:10 PM **ladydi2011:** Even though my hands are bigger, they are still feminine and pretty. I get compliments on them all the time.

8:03:31 PM **fallinghrt22:** We will make unforgettable memories

8:03:41 PM **fallinghrt22:** *The world will hear our stories*

8:03:55 PM **ladydi2011:** I know we will make unforgettable memories.

8:04:10 PM **fallinghrt22:** When we are together I never want to be away from you ever

8:04:10 PM **ladydi2011:** *Yes, the world has to hear our story.*

8:04:26 PM **fallinghrt22:** Yes love

8:04:52 PM **ladydi2011:** It will be more fun writing our story than the business book I am writing

8:05:51 PM **ladydi2011:** I don't ever want to be away from you either baby.

8:05:59 PM **ladydi2011:** I told my mom about you.

8:06:27 PM **fallinghrt22:** You did?

8:06:37 PM **ladydi2011:** She said she is happy for us

8:06:44 PM **fallinghrt22:** Oh baby you are turning me into a Superstar

8:07:12 PM **ladydi2011:** You told William about me, right?

8:07:19 PM **fallinghrt22:** Oh yes, I did

8:07:29 PM **ladydi2011:** Does he know how serious we are?

8:07:33 PM **fallinghrt22:** *And he wanted to know if he was allowed to call you "Mom"*

8:07:47 PM **ladydi2011:** He didn't ask this, did he?

8:07:58 PM **fallinghrt22:** Yes he did baby

8:08:13 PM **ladydi2011:** really? Of course he can.

8:08:26 PM **fallinghrt22:** I will tell him. He will be so excited

8:09:12 PM **ladydi2011:** I will never try to take the place of his mom. He was 13 when your wife passed, correct?

8:09:32 PM **fallinghrt22:** Yes

8:09:45 PM **ladydi2011:** So, he remembers her well.

8:09:45 PM **fallinghrt22:** *Very haard on him*

8:10:11 PM **ladydi2011:** Was your wife from Denmark or the states?

8:10:16 PM **fallinghrt22:** Yes but he was strong and I am sure he understands everything now

8:10:32 PM **fallinghrt22:** She was from Denmark

8:10:57 PM **ladydi2011:** I am sure it was hard on both of you. I am sure he is happy to see you giddy and happy. He also should be proud of himself that he was instrumental in hooking us up.

8:11:15 PM **fallinghrt22:** Oh yes I am grateful

8:11:25 PM **fallinghrt22:** *Baby my eyes are shutting*

8:11:57 PM **ladydi2011:** I am sure they are. Baby, please be sure to text me back once you receive the transfer so I know you got it. Ok?

8:12:19 PM **fallinghrt22:** *Ok baby, you will text me as soon as you get it done, right?*

8:12:35 PM **ladydi2011:** Yes, baby. I will.

8:12:56 PM **fallinghrt22:** Ok baby I do feel you all wrapped around me

8:13:19 PM **ladydi2011:** Good night or morning

8:13:33 PM **fallinghrt22:** Morning baby

8:13:35 PM **fallinghrt22:** I love you

8:13:43 PM **fallinghrt22:** Will find you when I wake up baby

8:13:52 PM **ladydi2011:** I love you too!

8:14:17 PM **ladydi2011:** You will always find me. I am living in your heart rent free...

8:14:30 PM **fallinghrt22:** Yes baby

8:14:35 PM **fallinghrt22:** I love you

8:14:41 PM **ladydi2011:** What time do you plan to get up?

8:15:22 PM **fallinghrt22:** No idea, just need to relax my brain

8:15:32 PM **ladydi2011:** Baby, are you a little calmer now?

8:15:42 PM **fallinghrt22:** Yes I am

8:15:49 PM **fallinghrt22:** Just need sleep

8:16:10 PM **ladydi2011:** Good. Please do not worry. Rest well my love. Till tomorrow...

8:16:25 PM **fallinghrt22:** Ok baby

8:16:26 PM **fallinghrt22:** Love you

8:16:39 PM **ladydi2011:** Love you too

8:16:50 PM **fallinghrt22:** Bye for now baby

8:16:59 PM **ladydi2011:** Bye for now.

WOW! I can't believe he hooked my heart so tight and reeled me in so quickly and easily in just "11 days" that I instantly said "What do you need?" and "I'll send it." I should have listened to the questions in my mind instead of letting his sweet words hook my heart. I didn't, because for some reason the heart has no logic and it usually trumps common sense and initial doubts. All I heard was that he was in trouble and needed help. I also believed this story because I have heard one of my clients, who does technical surveillance countermeasure, say that it is so difficult to get equipment into China that he stopped going to China.

Once a scammer is confident he has your love, the scam moves fast. April 7th I shared my doubts with him. April 9th he tells me he is leaving for China. April 10th he asks for money. April 11th I send the money.

I actually didn't know how true it was when I said, "The world has to hear our story." But never in my wildest dreams did I think the story was going to go like this!

I was a little perplexed that his cashier's check was in his luggage instead of on his person, and I was very surprised that his credit card only had $400 on it, but I believed he was going through hard times.

I found the words he emailed me the morning of April 10th on http://archive.lovingyou.com. Be sure to search words on Google. Unfortunately, this was something I didn't even think to do at the time.

RED FLAGS

- You always become the "only person" the scammer can reach out to.
- A scammer always has a problem that requires money when they travel.
- Scammers that include kids in their story always say the kids want to or are already, calling you mom.
- Scammers will usually not answer personal questions. When I ask a personal question about his wife he is suddenly tired.

From: Diana Garren
Sent: Wednesday, April 11, 2012 8:33 PM
To: Jerry Wesley [mailto:fallinghrt22@yahoo.com]
Subject: Website that I think will help you navigate in China and in ordering food

Hi Baby,

Here is a website that I think will help you navigate in China and in ordering food....
http://www.chinahighlights.com/travelguide/guidebook/food-dining.htm

From: Diana Garren
Sent: Wednesday, April 11, 2012 8:52 PM
To: Jerry Wesley [mailto:fallinghrt22@yahoo.com]
Subject: Info you need to know leaving China

Baby,

It looks like you are going to have the same problem leaving China. You are going to have to ship your tools home. Please see highlighted below about exit restrictions.

http://traveltips.usatoday.com/luggage-restrictions-travel-china-30301.html

Planning a trip to China requires ensuring that you have a valid visa and passport before you leave. In addition, it is important that you are aware of the luggage requirements imposed by the Transportation Security Administration when leaving the United States, your airline and the Chinese government to avoid any delays or misunderstandings at the airport.

Entry Restrictions

Upon arrival in China, you must pass through customs. Americans entering the country are allowed to carry personal items into the country without declaring them, but items such as animals, plants, radio transmitters and commercial products must be listed on your entry declaration form, notes the Chinese Customs website.

In addition, no firearms, poisons, addictive drugs or media materials that are considered harmful to China's best interests will be allowed to pass into the country.

Exit Restrictions

When leaving the country, you must again pass through customs. All items that were prohibited from entry into China also are forbidden from being carried out of the country. In addition, you may not leave the country with valuable cultural relics or rare plants or animals.

From: Diana Garren
Sent: Wednesday, April 11, 2012 9:45 PM
To: Jerry Wesley [mailto:fallinghrt22@yahoo.com]
Subject: URGENT......Please read

Baby,

I just contacted one of my clients who does technical surveillance counter measures worldwide for the last 42 years for knowledge and help for you. He said China is one of the worst! Please read everything below....I am using every resource I have on this side of the world.

There are several things he told me for you to do. He said even if you pay the $3,500 you might not get your tools back. This is actually import taxes. They will do whatever they want and you need someone from the **United States Consulate** or better yet the **government** to help you. Aren't you doing work for the government? If so, call them now. They can probably fix this for you immediately!!! If you do not know someone with the government, then you need to call the United States Consulate.

1)   It is critical for you to contact the Consulate General of the United States in Shanghai and tell them what is going on and ask for their help. This one appears to be the closest to where you are from the hotel address you gave me. http://shanghai.usembassy-china.org.cn/

2)   He said for you to get a money belt ASAP and keep it under your clothes with your valuables in it. Make sure that you protect your passport, tickets and other documents by carrying them on your person, preferably underneath clothing in a pouch or money belt. Never leave valuables lying around your hotel room or in your transport. Buy a padlock so that you can secure your possessions in lockers, or use a safe deposit at the hotel. Carry a photocopy of your passport and other vital documents separately.

3)   He said for you to know that your room is under surveillance *at all times*. They will know when you leave and when you go to the shower and can/will come in to steal everything (information) off your laptop and cell phone or plant a bug in them to steal it so be sure keep these things with you at all times. They might even email you an attachment that can have something embedded in it to steal your information.

4)   He said it would be wise to hire a shipping or bonding agent to get your tools safely out of the country. They handle everything.

IM Apr 12, 2012 2:05:27 AM

2:05:27 AM **fallinghrt22**: Baby!
2:05:33 AM **ladydi2011**: What R U doing awake? Did U get any sleep?
2:05:53 AM **fallinghrt22**: I got some sleep baby, I was missing you
2:06:05 AM **ladydi2011**: My phone battery was completely dead.
2:06:18 AM **fallinghrt22**: Oh ok...
2:06:27 AM **ladydi2011**: I am missing you too
2:06:34 AM **fallinghrt22**: I got your emails baby and I wanted to explain a few things to you my love
2:06:53 AM **ladydi2011**: Ok. Please explain
2:08:39 AM **fallinghrt22**: *I already contacted the consulate regarding the issue before I came online last night and I was asked to make the fine payment and notify them when it is done, I should ask for receipt at the customs office before I make the payment and I will be escorted to*

collect my luggage. I was told it was a normal thing for them to do... So it is certain that once I pay the $3,500 I will get back my luggage. Your friend was correct that some people do not get their luggage after they pay the fine

2:10:18 AM **ladydi2011**: Ok

2:10:36 AM **fallinghrt22**: Did I wake you up my love

2:10:49 AM **ladydi2011**: Who reassured you that you would be sure to get your luggage?

2:11:03 AM **fallinghrt22**: Someone from the Consulate.

2:11:20 AM **ladydi2011**: No baby, you did not wake me up. I am buried in work.

2:11:34 AM **fallinghrt22**: Oh dear you need to give yourself some rest

2:11:43 AM **fallinghrt22**: Don't want you buried in work. You need to save your strength for me

2:12:44 AM **ladydi2011**: I am lying in bed now. Where R U?

2:12:50 AM **fallinghrt22**: When I called you and it went straight to voicemail, I thought you were asleep

2:13:05 AM **fallinghrt22**: In the hotel, wishing I was lying in bed with you

2:13:14 AM **fallinghrt22**: Another sleepless night it will be.

2:14:21 AM **ladydi2011**: Did you sleep at all?

2:14:47 AM **fallinghrt22**: Yes I did get some sleep

2:15:13 AM **ladydi2011**: How much sleep baby?

2:15:15 AM **fallinghrt22**: I'd rather be with you baby.

2:15:27 AM **fallinghrt22**: About 6hours baby

2:15:47 AM **ladydi2011**: I would rather be with you too my love!

2:16:12 AM **ladydi2011**: It is 2 in the afternoon there, right?

2:16:32 AM **fallinghrt22**: Yes, it's 2:16pm

2:16:52 AM **ladydi2011**: Can I tell you something?

2:17:31 AM **fallinghrt22**: Yeah go ahead baby

2:17:49 AM **ladydi2011**: I love you!

2:18:25 AM **fallinghrt22**: Awwww baby I love you more.

2:19:08 AM **ladydi2011**: I think we will debate forever on this...Lol

2:19:45 AM **fallinghrt22**: I love you mostestestestest. Can you compete with that?

2:19:50 AM **ladydi2011**: I love you to eternity and back.

2:19:59 AM **ladydi2011**: Baby, if I wasn't here to help you, who could you have called for help?

2:20:46 AM **fallinghrt22**: *I don't know baby, I just believe this has happened for a reason and I do not want to question God's work in our lives*

2:21:22 AM **fallinghrt22**: Oh yeah you beat me, I will let you win today.

2:21:55 AM **ladydi2011**: I ask you this question because I have been alone for a long time and there wasn't anyone to call when I needed help.

2:22:22 AM **ladydi2011**: You are going to let me win this easily???

2:22:26 AM **fallinghrt22**: Oh dear, you can call on me when you need help

2:22:38 AM **fallinghrt22**: Baby I will always let you win and have your way with me whenever

2:23:26 AM **ladydi2011**: Thank you baby! It is so nice for us to now have each other.

2:23:43 AM **fallinghrt22**: Yes baby it is nice to know that we have each other

2:23:50 AM **ladydi2011**: So, I can always have my way with you?

2:23:56 AM **fallinghrt22**: Have I told you lately that I love you?

2:24:06 AM **fallinghrt22**: Yes baby you can always have your way with me

2:24:47 AM **ladydi2011**: Yes, but I will never tire of you telling and showing me.

2:25:13 AM **fallinghrt22**: I will never get tired of telling you how much I love you baby.

2:26:23 AM **fallinghrt22**: Just thinking about you and how much of a blessing you are to me puts a smile on my face.

2:26:41 AM **ladydi2011**: Awwwww

2:27:29 AM **fallinghrt22**: I am incomplete without you

2:27:37 AM **fallinghrt22**: You call out for me and I hear

2:27:55 AM **ladydi2011**: Have I told you lately how handsome and sexy you are?

2:28:14 AM **fallinghrt22**: Awwww baby

2:28:22 AM **fallinghrt22**: Brb baby nature calls

2:28:35 AM **ladydi2011**: I love the picture of you in your office

2:41:04 AM **ladydi2011**: The light blue shirt looks fabulous on you! I like your taste in clothing.

2:43:39 AM **fallinghrt22**: I am glad you like my clothing taste

2:44:28 AM **ladydi2011**: Very much so!

2:44:53 AM **fallinghrt22**: I love you baby

2:45:36 AM **ladydi2011**: Baby, was I right that you are close to Shanghai?

2:46:02 AM **fallinghrt22**: Shanghai

2:46:21 AM **ladydi2011**: I love you too sweetheart.

2:47:15 AM **fallinghrt22**: Yes I am not far from Shanghai

2:47:35 AM **ladydi2011**: What is it like there?

2:48:06 AM **fallinghrt22**: *Its like the 70's in America*

2:48:22 AM **fallinghrt22**: But they have some massive buildings.

2:49:56 AM **ladydi2011**: Are there a lot of people? Is it busy?

2:50:37 AM **fallinghrt22**: People are like sand, all of them with the same face.

2:50:40 AM **ladydi2011**: *How would you know about America in the early 70's my love?*

2:51:05 AM **fallinghrt22**: I saw pictures of it.

2:51:44 AM **ladydi2011**: Like sand...interesting description.

2:52:06 AM **ladydi2011**: Do you feel safe where you are baby?

2:52:16 AM **fallinghrt22**: Oh yes baby I am safe..

2:53:33 AM **fallinghrt22**: I will come back baby in one piece

2:54:03 AM **ladydi2011**: Speaking of home. Do you consider San Diego home?

2:54:40 AM **fallinghrt22**: Oh yes now I do

2:55:24 AM **fallinghrt22**: But I can always move to anywhere to be with my baby

2:55:33 AM **fallinghrt22**: I can live anywhere as long as I have you with me.

2:55:35 AM **ladydi2011**: Baby, what kind of tools do you have with you?

2:56:34 AM **fallinghrt22**: Drilling machines and electric screw drivers,

2:56:49 AM **ladydi2011**: I can live anywhere as long as we are together

2:57:16 AM **fallinghrt22**: You are more than a Darling

2:57:49 AM **ladydi2011**: Baby, where do you see us starting our life together as far as where to live?

2:58:55 AM **fallinghrt22**: Baby I can work from anywhere

2:59:06 AM **fallinghrt22**: I say this because you are. You always make me happy

2:59:42 AM **ladydi2011**: Baby, I believe I told you what you see with me is what you get. It is true!

3:00:26 AM **ladydi2011**: I can also work from anywhere!

3:01:24 AM **fallinghrt22**: We will sit down and discuss this nose to nose

3:01:29 AM **fallinghrt22**: I just want to be with you baby

3:01:41 AM **ladydi2011**: But, I am not by the water and I want to be by water.

3:02:31 AM **ladydi2011**: I want to be with you too. This is why I am asking logistical questions.

3:02:50 AM **fallinghrt22**: Ok baby, if you want to be by the water then you have to come here

3:02:59 AM **fallinghrt22**: Do you think that will work.

3:05:26 AM **ladydi2011**: Honey, meeting you has definitely made me think about many things!

3:06:15 AM **fallinghrt22**: Oh yes, you have shined your light in my life and I can see a lot of things. I am so thankful to God for bringing you in my life

3:06:31 AM **fallinghrt22**: I want to keep you forever and grow everyday with you.

3:06:51 AM **ladydi2011**: Ditto baby!

3:07:19 AM **fallinghrt22**: I love you.

3:07:24 AM **ladydi2011**: Do you ever feel like you are in a whirlwind?

3:07:54 AM **fallinghrt22**: Yes baby I do.. I feel like I am floating in the air

3:08:49 AM **fallinghrt22**: You are the best thing that has happened to me

3:09:00 AM **fallinghrt22**: I promise to always cherish and adore you.

3:09:00 AM **ladydi2011**: I love you too!!!

3:09:49 AM **fallinghrt22**: Baby what time is it for you?

3:10:55 AM **ladydi2011**: Don't ask!!! I want to chat a few more min. then I will go to sleep.

3:11:50 AM **fallinghrt22**: I love you fiercely

3:12:03 AM **ladydi2011**: So baby, have you thought about our first night together?

3:12:31 AM **ladydi2011**: "Fiercely", great word!

3:12:52 AM **fallinghrt22**: Oh yes baby I have thought about it and I will be sleeping on the plane so I will be well rested. I will need all my strength, right?

3:14:28 AM **ladydi2011**: Yes, you will need ALL your strength my love!!!

3:14:54 AM **fallinghrt22**: ahahaha I like that.

3:15:07 AM **fallinghrt22**: Sounds like a threat but I see it as a challenge

3:15:27 AM **ladydi2011**: You won 1 tonight and I won 1...we are tie!

3:16:07 AM **ladydi2011**: It wasn't a threat baby. It was a challenge. I love having fun with you!

3:16:50 AM **fallinghrt22**: I love you so much more than much

3:17:52 AM **ladydi2011**: Do you realize we have only known each other for 12 days?

3:18:04 AM **fallinghrt22**: Yes baby and it feels like I have known you forever

3:18:56 AM **ladydi2011**: Yes baby, it does feel like forever.

3:20:01 AM **fallinghrt22**: Everything about you baby intrigues me

3:20:24 AM **ladydi2011**: Baby, I cannot believe how much I trust and love you in just 12 days!

3:20:40 AM **fallinghrt22**: It will only grow stronger my love

3:21:40 AM **ladydi2011**: I know it will!

3:21:56 AM **fallinghrt22**: Everyday will be an adventure.

3:24:01 AM **ladydi2011**: How can it not be when our goal is to please the other…

3:24:39 AM **fallinghrt22**: Our life will be so beautiful, anyone who can't see it will need a physician

Break In Time

3:27:48 AM **ladydi2011**: So, where have you been all my life?

3:27:58 AM **fallinghrt22**: Finding my way to you baby. I am here now, not going anywhere

3:28:18 AM **ladydi2011**: Great answer!

3:28:54 AM **ladydi2011**: You know I have way too much room in my king size bed....

3:29:11 AM **fallinghrt22**: I can occupy some space

3:29:27 AM **ladydi2011**: I need you with me to help fill it!

3:29:44 AM **fallinghrt22**: Of course, I will gladly accept that offer

3:30:08 AM **ladydi2011**: I am waiting!!!

3:30:15 AM **fallinghrt22**: It will be great baby

3:30:30 AM **ladydi2011**: Sweetheart, are you calmer now?

3:31:14 AM **fallinghrt22**: Yes baby I am better now. Thanks so much

3:31:41 AM **ladydi2011**: Did you look for contractors yet?

3:32:02 AM **ladydi2011**: Good! I need my man to be ok!

3:32:12 AM **fallinghrt22**: No baby, I just got up and I looked for you

3:32:21 AM **fallinghrt22**: I will go when I put you to bed

3:32:45 AM **ladydi2011**: Awwww. You found me!

3:33:09 AM **ladydi2011**: You my dear are not always easy to find...

3:33:52 AM **fallinghrt22**: The day will come when we will never have to look for each other

3:34:04 AM **fallinghrt22**: Cos I will always be next to you.

3:34:41 AM **ladydi2011**: You will be tucking me in real soon. Oh, how I look forward to that day!

3:35:11 AM **fallinghrt22**: I look forward to it too baby

3:35:26 AM **fallinghrt22**: *You should text me as soon as you get the transfer done hun*

3:36:22 AM **fallinghrt22**: Even Shakespeare doesn't have the words for what I feel for you baby

3:37:21 AM **ladydi2011**: I have never read literature but you have inspired me to read it.

3:37:45 AM **fallinghrt22**: You inspire me to greater heights too baby

3:38:19 AM **ladydi2011**: Good. This is how it should be. Right?

3:38:45 AM **fallinghrt22**: Yes baby this is how it should be.

3:39:03 AM **ladydi2011**: *Baby, did you ask the people you are working for to help?*

3:39:52 AM **fallinghrt22**: *I can't, they will think I am not competent and completely equipped for the job and that's not a good way to start a project.*

3:41:06 AM **ladydi2011**: I knew you would say this. You are right. Perception is everything. You are a smart man my dear!

3:41:36 AM **fallinghrt22**: And you are a smart cute woman, the woman of my dreams, the woman I love and will always love.

3:42:32 AM **ladydi2011**: I think you said in your profile that you were looking for a smart woman, didn't you?

3:43:24 AM **fallinghrt22**: Yes I did

3:44:05 AM **fallinghrt22**: Ok my love, now get some rest and text me when you get up.

3:45:23 AM **ladydi2011**: Ok baby! Good night for me and good afternoon for you.

3:45:34 AM **fallinghrt22**: Ok baby rest well

3:45:47 AM **fallinghrt22**: I am dispatching Angels your way to watch over you while you sleep

3:45:48 AM **ladydi2011**: Thanks baby!

3:45:50 AM **fallinghrt22**: Love you so much

3:46:10 AM **ladydi2011**: I love you too

3:46:23 AM **fallinghrt22**: Goodnight Sunshine.

3:47:57 AM **ladydi2011**: Good night. I will text you in a few hours.

3:48:07 AM **fallinghrt22**: Ok Sweetheart

I called Jerry to tell him I was on my way to the bank and I wasn't sure if I should send him the money. Instead of the loving Jerry I knew, he used a demanding tone with me when I told him I wasn't sure if I should send him the money, but he did reassure me he would get it back to me within two days. Once again, even though I had the feeling that I should not send the money, I sent it.

From: Diana Garren
Sent: Thursday, April 12, 2012 1:32 PM
To: Jerry Wesley [mailto:fallinghrt22@yahoo.com]

Subject: Transfer Document

Hi Baby,

Attached is what you need. As I told you on the phone, I didn't feel real good after I heard a different tone in your voice over the phone. What was that all about? I am trusting you to send the money back to me in two days like you promised. Please don't make me sorry for trusting you. Like all things, I have put this in God's hands.

Love,
Diana

After I said I would send the money, I wanted to find out if what Jerry told me was true, so I called one of my clients who has done Technical Security Counter Measures for espionage worldwide for the last 42 years. He said he stopped going to China because "they are the worst." He told me that what I was being told sounded right and that they could put Jerry in jail if he didn't pay the money; that Jerry should have used a courier to send his tools into and out of China. Being concerned, I emailed Jerry information about China and encouraged him to contact the consulate. Jerry said he already contacted them and that he would be escorted to pick up his luggage. I do not part with my money easily, so while getting ready to go to the bank I was really wrestling with myself about whether or not I should do this. Even the bank teller asked me many times if I was sure I wanted to send it, and in spite of Jerry's demeanor, my reservations and the bank teller's questions, I sent the money.

I thought that Jerry's knowledge of what America was like in the early 70's was odd because he would have been in Denmark at that time. His explanation of seeing pictures made sense.

RED FLAGS

- When I ask Jerry who he would call for help if I wasn't able, he once again uses God with the comment, "I don't know baby, I just believe this has happened for a reason and I do not want to question God's work in our live."
- A scammer always stays close to you when asking for money and they want you to text them as soon as you wire money.

IM Apr 12, 2012 4:33:18 PM

4:33:18 PM **fallinghrt22**: Hi Baby
4:33:31 PM **fallinghrt22**: I Love you and your voice makes me go crazy.
4:34:17 PM **fallinghrt22**: I will never let go of you. Run I will run with you.

4:34:43 PM **fallinghrt22**: *I Live to Love you Diana Wesley*.

4:34:50 PM **ladydi2011**: Mr. Jerry Wesley, I didn't like what I heard in your voice. What was that all about?

4:35:07 PM **fallinghrt22**: I can see you as my future Wife Baby No doubt

4:35:12 PM **fallinghrt22**: Nothing baby, I am just under a lot of stress. I am really sorry. You are my everything.

4:37:47 PM **fallinghrt22**: I can't wait to complete you physically and mentally Baby. We are one.

4:37:53 PM **fallinghrt22**: I Love you

4:38:23 PM **fallinghrt22**: *I took a bath today and I start to think of you taking a bath with me.*

4:38:42 PM **ladydi2011**: Hmmmmmm

4:38:55 PM **ladydi2011**: I love you much more

4:39:18 PM **fallinghrt22**: me beyond compare baby

4:39:20 PM **fallinghrt22**: I win.

4:39:50 PM **ladydi2011**: You win this time....

4:39:50 PM **fallinghrt22**: I will email you about what I think about when I was taking my bath.

4:40:03 PM **fallinghrt22**: I always win as the head and the man...

4:40:13 PM **ladydi2011**: Ok

4:40:38 PM **fallinghrt22**: you would need to take a deep breath and cold shower thou

4:41:24 PM **fallinghrt22**: You complete me Love.

4:42:12 PM **ladydi2011**: You complete me too.

4:43:02 PM **fallinghrt22**: Yes I can't wait for you to keep me busy in the bedroom..

4:43:41 PM **fallinghrt22**: brb.

4:44:24 PM **fallinghrt22**: just your look will melt me Baby

4:44:36 PM **fallinghrt22**: Hope my email don't scare you..HEHEHE

4:48:29 PM **fallinghrt22**: I wlill never get enough of you or get tired of you. You are my soulmate.

4:49:26 PM **ladydi2011**: You are my soul mate, best friend, lover, and confidant...my everything!

4:49:44 PM **fallinghrt22**: You may go keep yourself busy with my email.

4:49:57 PM **fallinghrt22**: you have kept me up all night baby...remember I need rest

4:50:07 PM **fallinghrt22**: please dont allow me to sleep when we are together

4:50:40 PM **ladydi2011**: Baby, I didn't mean to keep you up all night.

4:50:54 PM **fallinghrt22**: as the day passes by my Love for you grows more stronger baby.

4:51:09 PM **fallinghrt22**: I love talking to you Baby. You make me happy and bless me.

4:51:18 PM **ladydi2011**: We will rest together baby, but I am just not sure how soon???

4:51:40 PM **fallinghrt22**: it wont take long baby....I can't wait

4:52:12 PM **ladydi2011**: Baby, when can I expect to hear from you again?

4:52:12 PM **fallinghrt22**: You make me feel extra special.

4:52:18 PM **fallinghrt22**: I will never let go of you.

4:52:42 PM **fallinghrt22**: just text me..if I am available I would get online for you.

4:53:08 PM **fallinghrt22**: *I dont know what I did right to deserve you* Diana W

4:53:38 PM **ladydi2011**: Baby, please be a little better about answering my text.

4:53:40 PM **fallinghrt22**: run I will run with you.

4:53:50 PM **fallinghrt22**: I will baby.

4:55:02 PM **ladydi2011**: Baby, do you have a middle name?

4:55:15 PM **fallinghrt22**: Behr. I told you

4:55:25 PM **ladydi2011**: Is your first name Gerald or is it Jerry?

4:55:39 PM **fallinghrt22**: there you get Behrkylanconstructions.com.

4:55:45 PM **fallinghrt22**: Jerry

4:56:07 PM **ladydi2011**: No, I do not remember you telling me your middle name.
4:56:35 PM **fallinghrt22**: whats your middle name Baby?
4:56:42 PM **ladydi2011**: Lynn
4:56:49 PM **fallinghrt22**: cool I remember.
4:57:22 PM **ladydi2011**: Baby, I am laughing. We have made a commitment to marriage and we didn't ever know each other's full names. *This will be a great line in our romance novel...*
4:58:31 PM **fallinghrt22**: LOL everything about our being together will be great Love.
4:59:07 PM **ladydi2011**: I cannot wait to look into your eyes in person...
4:59:09 PM **fallinghrt22**: I have been smiling and I can't stop smiling.You are the reason Baby.
4:59:39 PM **ladydi2011**: Baby, please get some rest.
4:59:46 PM **fallinghrt22**: Now I don't know what I would do without you in my life.
4:59:51 PM **fallinghrt22**: please dont ever leave me.
5:00:27 PM **ladydi2011**: I will not
5:00:44 PM **fallinghrt22**: You make me strong.
5:00:54 PM **fallinghrt22**: and I promise you I will never leave you . It means forever.
5:01:09 PM **fallinghrt22**: I Love you so much. As much as I Love you so much...I will die for you
5:02:28 PM **fallinghrt22**: I am saying this from th deepest part of my heart
5:04:14 PM **fallinghrt22**: now let me rest..go enjoy your email.
5:04:26 PM **fallinghrt22**: maybe after reading you may be sleeping
5:05:58 PM **fallinghrt22**: I don't know what you have done to me but I am loving every bit of it.
5:07:18 PM **fallinghrt22**: *I will never fail you Baby.*
5:07:21 PM **ladydi2011**: You have done the same to me....
5:08:47 PM **fallinghrt22**: honey let me sleep please..I need this rest.
5:08:53 PM **fallinghrt22**: are you home Baby?
5:09:15 PM **ladydi2011**: Yes baby, I am home.
5:09:36 PM **fallinghrt22**: take good care of that home until we can fill in it together.
5:09:42 PM **ladydi2011**: Feel my loving arms around you as you fall asleep
5:10:10 PM **fallinghrt22**: I Love you much more than you do.
5:10:19 PM **ladydi2011**: You fill my heart with joy baby.
5:10:49 PM **fallinghrt22**: You give me joy and satisfaction Baby.
5:10:57 PM **ladydi2011**: Sleep well my love.
5:11:00 PM **fallinghrt22**: Hmmmmmmm I Love you.
5:11:47 PM **fallinghrt22**: Kisses..go enjoy your email.

From: Jerry Wesley [mailto:fallinghrt22@yahoo.com]
Sent: Thursday, April 12, 2012 4:48 PM
To: Diana Garren
Subject: Breathe taken.

I took a bath today. *i* started to think of you taking a bath with me. *i* ran the water with bubble bath and made room for you, it was not hard since our bodies fit together so nicely in all situations. we wash each others faces and follow the wash with showers of kisses. We press our faces together and we move our bodies closer togehter in the tub. You raise your knees and *i* wrap my legs around ur waist. *i* ask you if you wanted to make love in the tub. you nod and whisper in my ear yes. I ask you to wash the rest of my body, I wash yours and we make sweet passionate love.

You dry me off and *i* dry you off and then *i* carry you naked to our bed. We fall asleep together and *i* tell you that you are the only real lover *i* have ever truly loved. I imagine your embrace. A touch that sends shivers down my spine, and the soft kisses that tickle my skin and sends me into a fairy tale all my own. I imagine your tenderness, and you holding my hands in yours interlacing our fingers to steady yourself as you move rhythmically to our heartbeats, and I close my eyes and imagine.

I imagine ......I hear the tender words of affection you whisper to me, and I respond in kind. I wish this moment could last forever.... "Oh how good it is". There is a shiver that runs through me and I squeeze your hands tight, and you lay still to wait for the moment to pass. You kiss me deeply and more passionately than I knew could be possible.

I look at you, smile, take a deep breath and close my eyes. You kiss me and start our dance once more. This time our bodies are so close we feel as if we are one, dancing in tandem. I follow your stride to keep in rhythm with the dance.... dip...rock...sway.

The pace quickens and again I steady myself not to let you go as you sweep me into another world. "I want to stop, I beg you to stop before it's too late.... please".... and then it happens. I open up my heart and let you in as I call to you.

I hold you tight and lock my embrace and now I lead the dance. Forcing you to feel every movement of my body as I pour my soul out to you. Suddenly you match my movement and tense up as I did mere moments before. I now revel in your passion and hold you.... close....still ..... and silent. I look deep into your eyes and smile hoping that I have shown you exactly how I feel, and that you know I have given you my heart, and with words unspoken I hope you will then know....... Just imagine......I Love you so much.....

Always yours, Jerry

From: Diana Garren
Sent: Thursday, April 12, 2012 7:32 PM
To: Jerry Wesley [mailto:fallinghrt22@yahoo.com]
Subject: Re: Breathe taken.

Wow baby! I need another cold shower! Do you realize how much ecstasy we will experience every day for the rest of our lives? Honey, I can vision and feel everything you wrote. I cannot wait. I have envisioned the first time we become one in this way and how beautiful it will be many times.

Your future wife,
Mrs. Diana L. Wesley

IM Apr 13, 2012 4:16:04 PM

4:16:04 PM **fallinghrt22**: Hi Baby.
4:16:28 PM **ladydi2011**: Hi Baby
4:16:35 PM **ladydi2011**: How are you?
4:16:48 PM **ladydi2011**: Did you just wake up?
4:17:24 PM **fallinghrt22**: Yes Baby I just woke up.
4:17:29 PM **fallinghrt22**: How are you doing?
4:17:34 PM **fallinghrt22**: I miss you tremendously
4:17:55 PM **ladydi2011**: I am good!
4:18:07 PM **ladydi2011**: How are things going?
4:18:50 PM **ladydi2011**: I miss you tremendously and then some….
4:19:01 PM **fallinghrt22**: LOL..I always win Baby
4:19:13 PM **fallinghrt22**: wish you know how much I feel for you
4:19:18 PM **fallinghrt22**: I am okay health wise.
4:19:21 PM **ladydi2011**: Yes, you do always win baby!
4:19:24 PM **fallinghrt22**: with you on my mind.
4:19:47 PM **ladydi2011**: Have you caught up on your rest?
4:19:56 PM **ladydi2011**: Have you started your job?
4:20:21 PM **fallinghrt22**: cant get enough of you.
4:20:42 PM **fallinghrt22**: Not yet..it's weekend so I will get the money on monday.
4:20:48 PM **ladydi2011**: I have a confession...
4:21:02 PM **fallinghrt22**: go ahead.
4:22:01 PM **ladydi2011**: I have not got much work done since I met you. I tried, but my mind is always on you. Today, I had to focus...It was hard but I finally got some work done.
4:22:32 PM **fallinghrt22**: Oh I see.
4:22:36 PM **fallinghrt22**: I am sorry Baby.
4:22:47 PM **fallinghrt22**: do you need your time?
4:23:09 PM **ladydi2011**: Please do not be sorry. Never be sorry for our love or how we feel...
4:23:32 PM **ladydi2011**: It is not the time baby. It is my mind. It is always on you.
4:26:49 PM **ladydi2011**: Baby, are you eating ok?
Break in Time
4:28:08 PM **fallinghrt22**: <ding>
4:28:14 PM **ladydi2011**: <ding>
4:28:56 PM **ladydi2011**: *Looks like you keep getting booted.*
4:29:49 PM **fallinghrt22**: I just don't know how to pay you back for all that you have done for me and how you make me feel special.
4:29:57 PM **fallinghrt22**: I promise I will never stop loving you
4:30:27 PM **ladydi2011**: I am holding you to your promise.
4:30:31 PM **fallinghrt22**: I swear to it. It means forever. You own my heart.
4:31:03 PM **fallinghrt22**: you bring so much joy to my life and I promise to never stop loving you.
4:32:32 PM **ladydi2011**: Baby, you bring joy, satisfaction, happiness and a bright future to my life, so much that I am going to need shades I have been told
4:34:51 PM **fallinghrt22**: I Love you so much.
4:35:01 PM **fallinghrt22**: *I Live to Love you baby.*
4:35:22 PM **ladydi2011**: I live to love you too baby!
4:37:38 PM **ladydi2011**: I was whole prior to meeting you but not complete. You are my other half.

4:37:41 PM **fallinghrt22**: I have tried a million times to put into words how I feel for you. It's so hard to describe such an intense emotion. I knew from the day we met, that you were meant for me..

4:40:33 PM **ladydi2011**: Baby, have you read the emails and text I have been sending you?

4:40:52 PM **fallinghrt22**: I want to take my time to read the email.

4:42:27 PM **ladydi2011**: I have shared a lot with you.

4:43:29 PM **fallinghrt22**: please dont leave me baby..it will destroy me.

4:45:26 PM **ladydi2011**: Baby, I will never leave you.

4:45:44 PM **ladydi2011**: Baby, you are a little quiet today. What is going on?

4:45:53 PM **fallinghrt22**: There are so many expressions of our love: the gentleness of the way you've touched me, how a smile lights up my face when I hear your voice, and how my body responds to your voice, how happy I'm when I'm talking to you - you make me who I am.

4:47:03 PM **ladydi2011**: Ditto baby....just think, this is only the beginning. Wait until we are together in person.

4:47:33 PM **fallinghrt22**: *You will melt* me totally.

4:47:39 PM **fallinghrt22**: *I Live to Love you Baby.*

4:47:47 PM **fallinghrt22**: I cant wait to spend the rest of my life with you. Our Love is so great

4:48:06 PM **fallinghrt22**: I am glad we met each other..this is the best time for us Baby.

4:48:22 PM **ladydi2011**: We will melt into one baby.

4:50:35 PM **fallinghrt22**: There was a huge void in my life until you came along. I thank God everyday for leading us to each other. You complete me. I think back to how empty my life was without you, and I am so grateful that you are here. I can't wait to spend forever with you. You are my life, my love, my soul mate, my heart, and my reason for breathing. I love you with everything I am.

4:50:40 PM **ladydi2011**: Baby, I believe we are both now ready and that is why we met now.

4:51:19 PM **fallinghrt22**: honey can we take an Oath on here now??

4:51:29 PM **ladydi2011**: An oath?

4:51:47 PM **fallinghrt22**: go get a bible and water.

4:52:06 PM **ladydi2011**: I have one in about every room of my home. Got it...

4:52:17 PM **fallinghrt22**: Good... get water

4:52:18 PM **ladydi2011**: Oh, I need to get water?

4:56:13 PM **fallinghrt22**: this is very important.

4:58:44 PM **ladydi2011**: I am back baby. I know this is very important. An oath is only taken if meant.

4:59:23 PM **ladydi2011**: I am ready baby.

5:02:11 PM **fallinghrt22**: You have the water and bible?

5:02:29 PM **ladydi2011**: I do.

5:02:45 PM **fallinghrt22**: Good.

5:03:11 PM **fallinghrt22**: *this is very important Diana....and No one can break it unless death even after dead.*

5:04:17 PM **fallinghrt22**: You will say after me.

5:09:35 PM **fallinghrt22**: *I, Jerry Wesley promise you Diana Garren to love you unconditionally, to support you in your goals, to honor and respect you, to laugh with you and cry with you, and to cherish you for as long as we both shall live. I will always see you as my partner in life and my one true love. I will cherish our union and love you more each day than I did the day before. I will trust you and respect you, laugh with you and cry with you, loving you faithfully through good times and bad, regardless of the obstacles we may face together. I give you my hand, my heart, and my love, from this day forward. Jerry W*

5:17:13 PM **ladydi2011**: I promise to love you unconditionally, to support you in your goals, to honor and respect you, to laugh with you and cry with you, and to cherish you for as long as we both shall live. I will always see you as my partner in life and my one true love. I will cherish our union and love you more each day than I did the day before. I will trust you and respect you, laugh with you and cry with you, loving you faithfully through good times and bad, regardless of the obstacles we may face together. I give you my hand, my heart, and my love, from this day forward. Diana G

5:21:29 PM **fallinghrt22**: with tears in my eyes I am saying this to you Diana, I will die for you..because I have grown to Love you..

Break in Time

5:28:06 PM **fallinghrt22**: Baby, I got booted

5:28:17 PM **fallinghrt22**: we belong to each other..and I am so glad we responded to that call Baby.

5:29:20 PM **ladydi2011**: How could we not respond to this call of our hearts baby?

5:29:25 PM **fallinghrt22**: I Love you my Dearest Woman.

5:29:53 PM **ladydi2011**: I love you too.

5:30:20 PM **ladydi2011**: Thank you baby for initiating and taking this oath with me.

5:30:43 PM **fallinghrt22**: I needed to do it Baby to show my Love to you and how much I am committed to you.

5:32:46 PM **ladydi2011**: Baby, I know you have had loss in your life and have not always been treated well by some women. Please know I am different. I am the woman who will always stand by your side, the woman who will never cheat on you; the woman who will give and not take from you, the woman who will never leave you....This is a new chapter baby!

5:35:29 PM **fallinghrt22**: *I just dont know what I did right to deserve you* Diana. You bring out tears of joy from my eyes.

5:36:02 PM **ladydi2011**: Baby, why do you keep saying this?

5:36:06 PM **fallinghrt22**: You own my life Baby I over trust you.

5:36:30 PM **fallinghrt22**: You are extra special. I will do anything beyond my power to make you happy

5:38:49 PM **ladydi2011**: Yes, baby. I am extra special. I am God's daughter. I know who I am and you are Gods son and I know who you are and how extra special you are.

5:39:22 PM **fallinghrt22**: brb Baby

5:39:48 PM **ladydi2011**: Baby, Thank you for putting my happiness so high on your list.

5:52:00 PM **fallinghrt22**: I Love you so much Baby. You bless me.

5:52:40 PM **ladydi2011**: You bless me too baby.

5:53:06 PM **ladydi2011**: Are you eating? Have you found food you like yet?

5:53:15 PM **ladydi2011**: Have you found a crew?

5:53:48 PM **fallinghrt22**: No not yet by monday all that will be taken care off Baby. thanks for your care

5:54:07 PM **ladydi2011**: Of course I care.

5:54:13 PM **ladydi2011**: What about food?

5:54:26 PM **fallinghrt22**: I had peanut butter and bread.....

5:54:38 PM **ladydi2011**: What else?

5:54:45 PM **fallinghrt22**: fanta.

5:55:04 PM **ladydi2011**: *I wish you would have let me send the money Western Union. You would have had it by now.*

5:55:13 PM **ladydi2011**: Fanta and what else?

5:55:45 PM **fallinghrt22**: do you know the time here...

5:56:07 PM **ladydi2011**: Yes, it is 5:55 AM

5:56:16 PM **fallinghrt22**: *I can't get it Western Union..I dont have ID to get it..and I dont know how it works here. Baby.*

5:56:29 PM **fallinghrt22**: thanks for your care by monday everything will be alright.

5:56:38 PM **fallinghrt22**: Yes 5:55 AM I can't sleep thou

5:56:47 PM **fallinghrt22**: wish I am in your Arms.

5:56:55 PM **ladydi2011**: *Baby, please give me the complete hotel address and your room #. I want to mail you something.*

5:58:11 PM **fallinghrt22**: *I dont know how things work here if it will get here..or get to me..remember what your friend told you about China..I just want to finish this job and get back for you my soulmate.* I can't wait to touch you Baby.

5:58:36 PM **ladydi2011**: I cannot wait to pick you up at the airport.

5:58:58 PM **fallinghrt22**: me too Baby.

5:59:15 PM **fallinghrt22**: in some weeks time now I will be in your Arms Baby.

5:59:19 PM **ladydi2011**: I want you to finish this job as quick as you can and get to me...

6:00:27 PM **fallinghrt22**: Promise..I cant wait to be with you.

6:01:15 PM **ladydi2011**: What is your favorite food?

6:02:10 PM **fallinghrt22**: sea food....

6:02:14 PM **fallinghrt22**: You?

6:02:26 PM **ladydi2011**: Italian

6:02:45 PM **fallinghrt22**: whats your plan..us living together in that house..or getting a bigger and better one?

6:02:51 PM **ladydi2011**: I want to cook you a nice dinner when you are here. So, what seafood is your favorite?

6:03:09 PM **fallinghrt22**: *Rice and fish vegetable.*

6:03:18 PM **fallinghrt22**: anything better thou

6:03:24 PM **fallinghrt22**: I know you are a good cook.

6:03:32 PM **fallinghrt22**: *I like spaghetti.*

6:03:56 PM **ladydi2011**: I don't have any plans for where we are going to live. This is something we need to talk about and decide together.

6:04:18 PM **fallinghrt22**: Yes you are right..thats why I dont have my house yet.

6:04:26 PM **fallinghrt22**: I need to decide with you.

6:04:40 PM **ladydi2011**: I am not attached to this house or this area baby.

6:04:59 PM **ladydi2011**: Yes, my love. This is a "together" decision.

6:05:53 PM **ladydi2011**: Baby, how did you know my ring size?

6:06:36 PM **fallinghrt22**: we are connected. I am addicted to you.

6:06:44 PM **ladydi2011**: Maybe you knew it the same way I knew you were buying a ring...

6:07:02 PM **fallinghrt22**: Wow....I Love you

6:07:14 PM **ladydi2011**: I Love You!

6:07:24 PM **fallinghrt22**: I cant wait to be with you my Love..I just Love you beyond compare

6:07:53 PM **ladydi2011**: When you see Danielle, ask here when I told her you were buying a ring.

6:08:23 PM **ladydi2011**: She is blown away that I knew and that you knew my ring size.

6:09:02 PM **ladydi2011**: Baby, you know I want to meet William, right?

6:09:27 PM **ladydi2011**: Does he have a girlfriend?

6:09:28 PM **fallinghrt22**: I know Baby.

6:09:37 PM **fallinghrt22**: *Yes why not he has...*

6:09:47 PM **ladydi2011**: ???

6:10:18 PM **ladydi2011**: I am so glad he is happy for you.

6:10:31 PM **ladydi2011**: He looks so much like you baby.

6:11:08 PM **ladydi2011**: Baby, what do you want to do when you are here with me?

6:11:14 PM **fallinghrt22**: Yes..like father like son..LOL

6:11:38 PM **ladydi2011**: Lol! You did well raising him.

6:12:23 PM **fallinghrt22**: he is my all my all Baby.

6:12:29 PM **ladydi2011**: Do you know how happy I am that you have William and want to share him with me?

6:12:45 PM **fallinghrt22**: I know you are happy..

6:13:19 PM **fallinghrt22**: do you know that I had a dream that I will have just William..even the woman I would be spending the rest of my life with she wont have a Kid and it happened.

6:13:31 PM **fallinghrt22**: God is at work.

6:14:04 PM **ladydi2011**: Really? When did you have this dream?

6:14:24 PM **fallinghrt22**: 2 months ago before I met you honey.

6:14:41 PM **ladydi2011**: Wow!

6:15:42 PM **fallinghrt22**: Yes and God did prepare us for each other.

Break In Time

6:20:05 PM **fallinghrt22**: I Love you

6:20:37 PM **ladydi2011**: I Love You

6:23:40 PM **ladydi2011**: Are you sure you don't want any more children?

6:24:37 PM **fallinghrt22**: No I don't.

6:25:08 PM **fallinghrt22**: will you be happy if I had more than 1 Kid?

6:26:42 PM **ladydi2011**: You and William are all I need!

6:27:44 PM **fallinghrt22**: Good...

6:27:59 PM **ladydi2011**: I want us to be free to do everything we want in life

6:28:03 PM **fallinghrt22**: you are my dream come through Baby.

6:28:14 PM **fallinghrt22**: we will my Love.

6:28:36 PM **fallinghrt22**: honey do you have things to do today?

6:29:48 PM **ladydi2011**: Nothing important. It is 6:29 so working hours are done.

6:30:05 PM **fallinghrt22**: cool.

6:30:16 PM **fallinghrt22**: Baby I need to sleep more thou.

6:30:29 PM **fallinghrt22**: enjoyed talking to you..makes me feel better

6:30:36 PM **ladydi2011**: Are you tired now?

6:31:12 PM **fallinghrt22**: wish I am in your Arms.

6:31:31 PM **ladydi2011**: Ok. I am going to go out to dinner and shopping. Please text me when you wake.

6:32:26 PM **fallinghrt22**: Ok Baby...wish I am going with you

6:32:37 PM **fallinghrt22**: we have so much to look forward too Baby.

6:32:59 PM **fallinghrt22**: do take good care of yourself until I am able to take care of you myself.

6:34:37 PM **ladydi2011**: Baby, please send me the hotel address and your room number so I can send you something....Please!!!!!

6:36:21 PM **fallinghrt22**: Wet Kisses Baby,

6:36:25 PM **fallinghrt22**: I Love you.

6:36:42 PM **ladydi2011**: Wet kisses and hugs baby.

6:36:51 PM **fallinghrt22**: Love you

6:36:52 PM **ladydi2011**: Love you too.

Everything seems normal, so I still do not realize that I have been scammed. I still think he is going to send me the money back. When I was at the bank, I asked him if I could send the money Western Union instead of by a bank transfer because it would be faster. He said no, it had to be through a bank transfer because he didn't have ID to retrieve it and didn't know how Western Union worked in China. I surely did not know how it worked. I never sent money Western Union or through a bank transfer.

It didn't occur to me then of how he could not have ID. He has to have a passport to get into China. I thought it very odd for him to ask me to take an oath. I do not take oaths easily with my Bible, but I did say it back to him on line. I still have no idea what the water was about.

RED FLAGS

- In Africa they take baths, not showers. This is a red flag.
- He skirts around and does not give me his hotel information. How could he? He was not in a hotel in China. Scammers avoid giving you this type of information.
- When I ask his favorite food he says seafood and then he says rice and fish, vegetables and spaghetti. These are all common foods in Nigeria.
- When he answers "Yes why not he has" I didn't understand it. That is because it is Pidgin English, which is commonly spoken in Nigeria.

From: Jerry Wesley [mailto:fallinghrt22@yahoo.com]
Sent: Friday, April 13, 2012 10:11 PM
To: Diana Garren
Subject: Re: Wow...wow...wow!

Hi Love, How are you doing? I miss you so much. word can't say how much you mean to me from the depth of my heart I say thank you for making me a part of your everything and wanting you to spend the rest of your life with me...I cried a tear, you wiped it dry. I was confused, you cleared my mind. I sold my soul, you bought it back for me. And held me up, and gave me dignity. Somehow you needed me. You put me high, upon a pedestal. So high that *i* could see eternity. You needed me. And *i* can't believe it's you, *i* can't believe it's true. I needed you, and you were there. And *i'll* never leave, *i'd* be a fool. cause *i've* finally found someone who really cares. You held my hand, when it was cold. When *i* was lost, you took me home.

Baby, this is a little thing that *i* wanted to share with you. It says so much of how I feel. I want to thank you so much for being in my life. I have no words to describe the emotions that *i* have felt these past weeks. You are so understanding and thoughtful. The first time I get to meet you I am sure I will be at a loss for words.

always yours...
Jerry

IM Apr 14, 2012 11:21:55 PM

11:21:55 PM **fallinghrt22**: Hey my heartbeat how are you?
11:22:31 PM **ladydi2011**: I am so much better now that I know you are ok.
11:22:44 PM **fallinghrt22**: me too honey.
11:22:52 PM **fallinghrt22**: I am very fine health wise..better now that I can talk to you
11:23:20 PM **ladydi2011**: Sitting here with top down, music playing and chatting with you...
11:24:10 PM **ladydi2011**: I have been worried about you!
11:25:40 PM **fallinghrt22**: please don;t worry I am fine for you. I just can't get my mind off you and my heart is full of joy Baby.
11:28:36 PM **ladydi2011**: Honey, even if I wanted to get you off my mind I couldn't.
11:29:32 PM **ladydi2011**: What have you done to me?
11:29:52 PM **fallinghrt22**: You are always in my heart as much as I would want to get you off my mind..I dont have the power.
11:30:12 PM **fallinghrt22**: same as I will ask you...what have you done to me.
11:30:28 PM **fallinghrt22**: You have reached my heart so greatly if you leave I will die.
11:32:15 PM **fallinghrt22**: I Love you so much and it makes me go crazy.
11:32:27 PM **fallinghrt22**: I Love you to the bone Diana Wesley
11:33:48 PM **ladydi2011**: Ditto baby! My love for you makes me go crazy too!
11:34:08 PM **fallinghrt22**: same as me Baby I want our bond to grow stronger *we will tell the story*.
11:35:32 PM **fallinghrt22**: are you still sick Baby?
11:36:12 PM **ladydi2011**: Baby, stronger...whew, can we handle stronger?
11:36:25 PM **ladydi2011**: Yes baby, I am still sick.
11:36:40 PM **fallinghrt22**: You have to be fine for me Baby.
11:38:03 PM **ladydi2011**: I know baby. I was not drinking enough fluids...I am sorry. If I am still this weak on Monday I will go to the doctor and they will give me fluids through intervenes...
11:38:45 PM **fallinghrt22**: You have to be fine Baby so you would be able to carry me
11:39:26 PM **ladydi2011**: It probably didn't help doing 3 miles at a 10 incline and 3.7 speed on the treadmill in a sauna suit....
11:40:25 PM **ladydi2011**: Carry you where baby?
11:41:27 PM **fallinghrt22**: I am saying the strength to make Love as much as we want Baby.
11:41:38 PM **fallinghrt22**: so you have to be fine for me.
11:42:29 PM **ladydi2011**: I will be finc baby
11:42:45 PM **fallinghrt22**: I care for you greatly
11:43:12 PM **ladydi2011**: I care for you even more...
11:43:32 PM **fallinghrt22**: Awwwwwww I cherish and care for you much.
11:44:41 PM **fallinghrt22**: I just Love you the way you are Baby.
11:46:13 PM **fallinghrt22**: You are the reason of my existance Baby.
Break In Time
11:51:44 PM **ladydi2011**: Are you there?

From: Diana Garren
Sent: Saturday, April 14, 2012 1:23 AM
To: Jerry Wesley [mailto:fallinghrt22@yahoo.com]
Subject: Missing you!

Hi my husband!

How are you? What are you going to do there in China this weekend? I so wish I were there with you!

Thank you for initiating us to take an oath today.

You have the heart I was looking for. Since we met, I feel like I have been in a dream or a fairy tale. I need to be with you face to face. My eyes need to look into yours.

Oh, how I wish you were here! I would have my head on your chest listening to your heart beat.

Well, good night/ afternoon my love.

Your wife,

Diana L. Wesley

From: Diana Garren
Sent: Sunday, April 15, 2012 10:57 AM
To: Jerry Wesley [mailto:fallinghrt22@yahoo.com]
Subject: The greatest of all these is LOVE!

Good evening, my love!

How are you this evening? How was your day? I am awake now.

I woke many times with you in my thoughts. I could see your handsome face. Once again I found myself in deep thought about my feelings for you. *This love is so euphoric and consuming.* This love has taken me to great highs and low lows! This is the kind of love that I have read about many times but never experienced.

The pull of your heart to mine is so powerful, Baby. More powerful than the roaring ocean with 500 foot waves that will consume a yacht, a blazing fire that is out of control and so hot that you cannot go near it, a fierce tornado that destroys everything in its path, the raging 150 mile per hour winds of a hurricane, or an earthquake that shakes so violently that it moves the earth off her axis. Even all this power is not more powerful than our love. *I have never felt so out of control of my thoughts and emotions.*

Honey, when you said last night that our love will only get stronger, I know this is true. Baby, my thoughts travel to so many places...they try to picture what will happen the first time our eyes meet at the airport. How wonderful it will be to finally kiss you, be held by your strong arms and hold your hand. To see how long it will take before we will give each other a look and know exactly what it means with no words spoken. To plan our next steps of how we are going to be with each other every day.

I hope to hear from you before you go to bed.

I love you and miss you fiercely...Diana

From: Jerry Wesley [mailto:fallinghrt22@yahoo.com]
Sent: Monday, April 16, 2012 7:13 AM
To: Diana Garren
Subject: Re: My desire for you... and also my dream

I miss you, my darling, as I always do. I can almost feel you beside me as I write this letter, and I can smell the scent of wildflowers that always reminds me of you. But at this moment, these things no longer give me pleasure. *our visits have been less and less frequent, and I feel sometimes as if the greatest part of who I am is slowly slipping away.* I am trying to hold on, though. At night when I am alone, I call for you, and whenever my ache seems to be the greatest, you still seem to find a way to return to me.

Last night, in my dreams, I saw you on the pier. The wind was blowing through your hair, and your eyes held the fading sunlight. I was speechless as I watched you leaning against the rail. You are beautiful, I thought as I saw you, a vision that I could never find in anyone else. I slowly began to walk toward you, and when you finally turned to me, I noticed that others had been watching you as well. "Do you know her?" they asked me in jealous whispers, and as you smiled at me I simply answered with the truth, "Better than I know myself.

I stop when I reach you and I take you in my arms. I long for this moment more than any other. It is what I live for, and when you return my embrace, I give myself over to this moment, at peace once again. I raise my hand and gently touch your cheek and you tilt your head and close your eyes. My hands are hard and your skin is soft, and I wonder for a moment if you'll pull back, but of course, you don't. I know that this is the moment I have been waiting for, and I pray that the moment never ends.

Love always,
Jerry

From: Jerry Wesley [mailto:fallinghrt22@yahoo.com]
Sent: Monday, April 16, 2012 7:16 AM
To: Diana Garren
Subject: Good Morning.

Good Morning my Sweetheart,

How are you doing and how was your night? Thanks so much for the wonderful e-mail. You're the one who makes me beautiful. You're the one who makes me strong. You're the one who makes me feel so important; you're everything to me.

You show your love to me every day. I thank God that I have found a woman like you. Please forgive me for not giving you enough time to chat with me, but I promise I will make up for it once we are together.

All that I can offer you is a family that will stick together through the good and the bad. I can offer you a family that will support each other every day. Honey, that's all I can give...I hope that's what you want.

I really wish that you were near me. I wish that I could just call your name when I needed you and that you would be there. However, knowing that we have each other is enough for now. You're the only one that I want.

Love Always,
Your Husband.

In my email I made statements of "This love is so euphoric and consuming" and "I have never felt so out of control of my thoughts and emotions." Both of these are accurate descriptions of how it was. This Internet romance swept me off my feet and totally consumed me. It was truly euphoric, and I felt very out of control. To this day, I can't explain why. If someone were to have told me this could happen to me, I would not have believed them. Maybe it was because I thought this man was everything I was looking for so I allowed myself to be vulnerable and jumped in with both feet. Maybe it's the fact that all we really have when dating online is a picture, voice, typed words and our own thoughts that can create a much better picture than what is really in front of us. I don't know why it is like this; I just know that once you are caught in a scammer's web, it rocks your world and turns it upside down.

 **RED FLAGS**

🚩 Again, you see lower case "I's".

🌺 His first email was words of a song. I think many of us speak through music, so this didn't raise a red flag, but it was obvious that the next email was copied and pasted. I remember asking myself what the following sentence was all about, "our visits have been less and less frequent, and I feel sometimes as if the greatest part of who I am is slowly slipping away." Later, while doing research, another scammer used that same dream with me, so I know it is part of a shared format.

IM Apr 16, 2012 7:27:18 AM

7:27:18 AM **fallinghrt22:** Good morning Baby.

7:29:25 AM **ladydi2011:** Good evening Baby.

7:29:39 AM **fallinghrt22:** how was your night sweety

7:30:15 AM **ladydi2011:** I finally got about five hours sleep...yay!

7:30:25 AM **ladydi2011:** How was your day?

7:30:28 AM **fallinghrt22:** I am glad you did sleep well

7:30:34 AM **fallinghrt22:** my day was blissful thanks to you honey.

7:30:51 AM **fallinghrt22:** I missed you tremendously.

7:31:15 AM **ladydi2011:** Please tell me all that happened today.

7:32:03 AM **fallinghrt22:** I got my Luggage Baby, all thanks to you my Darling.

7:32:21 AM **fallinghrt22:** I don't know what I will do without you. I Love you so much.

7:33:02 AM **ladydi2011:** Baby, I am so glad you finally got your luggage

7:33:14 AM **fallinghrt22:** You bless me.

7:33:17 AM **ladydi2011:** Now you have money to eat...this worried me!

7:34:02 AM **fallinghrt22:** You would never know how much I am in love with you.

7:34:05 AM **ladydi2011:** You will never know what it would be like to be without me.

7:35:12 AM **fallinghrt22:** I dream of that day we have our first embrace, our first look into each other's eyes and see what we feel for each other without saying a word. I dream of our first kiss and the first time we make passionate love and share that sacred bond that only true love holds..

7:36:05 AM **fallinghrt22:** all of what you offer me I want from you with all of my heart. because I Love you so much and can't wait to spend the rest of my life with you.

7:36:10 AM **ladydi2011:** Me too baby!

7:37:37 AM **fallinghrt22:** Awwwwww you melt me. You make me Love you much more baby.

7:39:46 AM **fallinghrt22:** I can't thank you enough for what you have done to me and the kind of love you have showed to me.

7:41:07 AM **ladydi2011:** Baby, you have shown me the same kind of love. I thank you for being the wonderful man that you are!!!

7:42:24 AM **fallinghrt22:** I feel so free and comfortable with you honey

7:42:33 AM **fallinghrt22:** thanks so much for loving me beyond words.

7:42:37 AM **fallinghrt22:** did you get my emails?

7:43:16 AM **ladydi2011:** I did and you seemed a little down. Are you a little down baby?

7:45:28 AM **fallinghrt22:** No the internet is slow. Baby and I am trying to arrange things.

7:45:55 AM **ladydi2011:** Ok...I know you have so much to do.

7:46:05 AM **fallinghrt22:** the thought of us being together, even now has my heart pounding faster

7:46:15 AM **ladydi2011:** Baby, you have much more to offer me than a family.

7:47:24 AM **ladydi2011:** You are such a wonderful man. Your love is the sweet gift.

7:48:30 AM **fallinghrt22:** *you melt me*.

7:51:13 AM **fallinghrt22:** You are perfect for me my Love. You are my life.

7:51:35 AM **ladydi2011:** You are my life too baby.

7:52:24 AM **fallinghrt22:** you have no idea as to the magnitude of my love for you. You are a part of me and without you I am dead..

7:53:09 AM **fallinghrt22:** I so believe you are so perfect for me my Love.

7:53:26 AM **fallinghrt22:** You are everything I seek in a woman and desire.

7:53:34 AM **fallinghrt22:** I will never let you go my beloved.

7:53:56 AM **ladydi2011:** Baby, I am so glad I am everything you seek in a woman.

7:53:59 AM **fallinghrt22:** I will always love you from the deepest part of my heart and soul..

7:54:55 AM **ladydi2011:** My search is over. I am very content.

7:55:13 AM **fallinghrt22:** I have never known any feeling as deeply as the feelings I have for you..

7:55:27 AM **fallinghrt22:** my search has been over since the day of our first hello

7:55:31 AM **ladydi2011:** Once I am with you in person, I will be the happiest woman in the world!

7:56:41 AM **ladydi2011:** Yes, my love...from the day of our first hello.

7:58:35 AM **ladydi2011:** *From day one, I knew. I was so sure of this that I told people. Of course they said I was crazy...It didn't matter what they thought. I knew...*

7:59:16 AM **fallinghrt22:** You always make me feel speechless Baby.

7:59:34 AM **fallinghrt22:** I never knew love can be this great until you told me you love me.

8:01:11 AM **ladydi2011:** Baby, many times you say what I want to say...

8:02:07 AM **ladydi2011:** I never knew it could be this great either. It is how you love me that makes it great for me.

8:02:45 AM **fallinghrt22:** we are perfect for each other baby.

8:03:43 AM **fallinghrt22:** you are my air and without you I could not breathe..

8:06:01 AM **fallinghrt22:** I love you. I love every little thing about you. I love your cute smile, your magical eyes, and the sound of your voice. I can't stop thinking about you when we are apart. I need you by my side. You complete me. You mean the world to me. You are the best thing that has ever happened to me. You are the one I've always wished for. I never thought that I would ever meet someone as special as you. I love each and every moment I share with you....I just love you so much.

8:08:15 AM **ladydi2011:** *Sometimes; I have to pinch myself to be sure I am not dreaming.*

8:08:34 AM **fallinghrt22:** I feel alive because of you.

8:10:42 AM **ladydi2011:** Once I met you, everything in my life changed. Thank you for answering my first email and being persistent to get to me...

8:11:36 AM **fallinghrt22:** The reason I've been alone for five longs years is this: I've been waiting for you to see the love in my eyes that's only for you. I'll wait forever if that's how long it takes. I need you so badly..

8:13:17 AM **ladydi2011:** Baby, we have nowhere to go but forward. We both know that our love will continue to grow stronger.

8:14:54 AM **ladydi2011:** The same for me baby. I have been alone for eight long years. Now that I have you, I will never let you go!

8:15:35 AM **fallinghrt22:** You are more wonderful and lovely in my eyes than you ever were before; and my pride and joy and gratitude that you should love me with such a perfect love are beyond all expression. You are my only love, and I thank you for be so kind with my heart..

8:18:56 AM **fallinghrt22:** From the very first moment I saw you *I knew that we were destined to be together*. It has been so long since a woman has captured my attention so fully or made my heart beat as you make it beat baby. Your smile lights up my entire spirit. Your laughter fills me with joy, and your mere presence warms me. I have no doubt you are the woman Heaven has made especially for me

8:19:08 AM **ladydi2011:** You are kind and caring with me. Thank you. Remember we receive what we give. We both give the same to each other because we both want the same thing. It is our time baby.

8:21:31 AM **fallinghrt22:** Each day that passes makes our love for each other grow stronger. Although I know it's hard for us to be apart, I know there is nothing that can keep us apart forever. Our desires will continue to stretch across any distance, over every mountain and ocean between us. Nothing can stand between us, and nothing will stop me from meeting you. I just cant wait for that perfect day. You are my future and ***nothing can ever keep us from our destiny***...

8:22:32 AM **ladydi2011:** I am so glad you have no doubt that I am the woman for you. I have no doubt you are the man for me. *Remember, I sent you the first email.* From the first time I saw your picture and read your profile you called to me and I knew I had to know you. From our first text, I knew. You make me feel so special. You make me know I am loved by you. I don't have to ask or wait for anything, because you freely give yourself and your love to me.

8:25:30 AM **fallinghrt22:** If only I could have come up with the right words to describe the depth of this beautiful feeling that I have for you, I would have whispered them to you the first time we meet. The best thing that I can do is to show you how much I Love you and want you.

8:26:07 AM **ladydi2011:** You are right. Nothing can keep us apart. Our love is strong. What keeps me going is that I know the day will come when we will meet. On this day no words will have to be spoken because our eyes, hearts and souls will talk.

8:27:35 AM **ladydi2011:** I agree, it will be through our actions, our touch and how we love and care for each other that will tell each other how much we love each other.

8:29:30 AM **fallinghrt22:** I love you so much, Sweetie. You are the best thing that ever happened to me. You are like the best poetry ever composed, the best love song ever played, the best picture ever painted. I never thought that someone like me could get so lucky!

8:30:55 AM **ladydi2011:** You did get lucky and so did I...We are blessed baby. God has given us the desire of our hearts. Now it is up to us to nourish and grow what he has given us. Do you agree?

8:31:48 AM **fallinghrt22:** Yes I totally agree and I will never fail from my part baby.

8:32:58 AM **fallinghrt22:** Baby, I not only love you, but I am in love with you. I care about you. I treasure you. I honor you. I cherish you. I will always be kind to you and do my best to take care of you...I Love you so much.

8:34:07 AM **ladydi2011:** I now understand the song, "love hurts" and the song that says "it hurts so good"

8:34:45 AM **fallinghrt22:** I love you more than my life, more than my world. I love you more and more each day and that is the most wonderful feeling any man can ever hope to experience...

8:34:50 AM **fallinghrt22:** (Link was How Do I Live Without You by Trisha Yearwood)

8:34:54 AM **fallinghrt22:** listen.

8:35:16 AM **ladydi2011:** Ok

8:35:46 AM **fallinghrt22:** *have I given you songs to listen before baby?*

8:36:04 AM **ladydi2011:** Hmmm...yes baby

8:36:48 AM **fallinghrt22:** listen to that one.

8:38:10 AM **ladydi2011:** Baby, this is exactly how I feel...I have heard this song many times, but it never had meaning to me. Today as I listen, it says everything I am feeling. I love you so much my darling!

8:38:41 AM **fallinghrt22:** You mean everything to me. I wonna make Love to you all night long.

8:39:43 AM **fallinghrt22:** listen to this one. (Link was Let's Make Love by Faith Hill & Tim McGraw)

8:40:05 AM **ladydi2011:** Please do. I want to make love to you all night long too!

8:42:35 AM **fallinghrt22:** God has got his own reasons for us to meet and come this far. But *I hope* our love will flourish beyond what it is right now because I will die without you in my life.

8:43:48 AM **ladydi2011:** God does have his own reasons. I am not questioning him. Baby, I know we are going the distance, don't you?

8:44:47 AM **ladydi2011:** I think this time apart is to build what God has given us...I am accepting it.

8:45:14 AM **fallinghrt22:** I do baby... and I am ready to give anything to be with you my wife.

8:45:49 AM **ladydi2011:** *Every now and then I have the thought of what if we never meet...Fear and sadness sweeps over me when I think about this.*

8:47:43 AM **fallinghrt22:** Every day when I awake from a dream of us together, I thank God I found you! ***What have I ever done to deserve such a loving, caring, wonderful woman?*** Everything about you is just so perfect. I know you are not without imperfections, but in my eyes, everything you do just seems so flawless.

8:50:24 AM **fallinghrt22:** <ding>

8:51:07 AM **ladydi2011:** Baby, I was looking for a song to send you....I haven't been able to find it, but I will!

8:51:58 AM **fallinghrt22:** The way you express your love to me is so awesome!! I feel so loved! I need only to think of you to have all my troubles melt away. I want to spend my whole life with you, loving you and receiving your love in return. XOXOXOXOXO I long to hold you and feel your sweet caress. The miles that lie between us will soon disappear, and we will have each other always. I don't care what others say about you and me. All I know is that I love you, and that will never change. Thank you for loving me the way you do. I couldn't ask for more in a woman!

8:52:00 AM **ladydi2011:** Baby, I do have imperfections...But beauty is in the eye of the beholder

8:52:08 AM **fallinghrt22:** listen to this one (Video was Don't Give Up On Me by Jason Aldean)

8:53:33 AM **ladydi2011:** Baby...I am speechless! Everything that I feel, you speak...

8:59:52 AM **ladydi2011:** I will never give up on you baby. Please don't ever give up on me...

9:00:02 AM **fallinghrt22:** I will never.

9:00:23 AM **ladydi2011:** Baby, please listen to this song... (I Need You by Tim McGraw feat Faith Hill)

9:00:31 AM **fallinghrt22:** I am listening to this....

9:05:29 AM **ladydi2011:** I found the song....listen baby (When I need you by Celine Dion)

9:11:00 AM **fallinghrt22:** I Love you so much.

9:11:43 AM **ladydi2011:** I am so looking forward to you being here with me.

9:12:04 AM **ladydi2011:** Baby, are you ready to start your work now?

9:12:12 AM **fallinghrt22:** That's what gets me through every minute that I'm without you. And baby, you don't know what I would give to kiss your lips, feel your touch, or even just to see you...

9:12:33 AM **ladydi2011:** The sooner you start, the sooner you finish and the sooner you fly to Atlanta to be with me.

9:12:38 AM **fallinghrt22:** No I am not ready yet..by tomorrow I will go cash my check.

9:12:45 AM **fallinghrt22:** I will let you know baby.

9:12:53 AM **fallinghrt22:** Yes I cant wait. I Love you to the bone.

9:13:40 AM **ladydi2011:** What did you tell them of why you are starting late?

9:14:07 AM **fallinghrt22:** No I just said I had delays.

9:14:20 AM **ladydi2011:** Are they ok with this?

9:14:37 AM **ladydi2011:** *Honey, please tell me you are for real....*

9:14:48 AM **fallinghrt22:** *Yes..but I need to start work fast because of the deadline.*

9:14:54 AM **fallinghrt22:** You want to make me cry

9:15:01 AM **fallinghrt22:** how could you ask such question.

9:15:09 AM **fallinghrt22:** you know better baby.

9:15:32 AM **ladydi2011:** *Baby, I am sorry!*

9:15:42 AM **ladydi2011:** *I just feel like I am in a dream.*

9:15:58 AM **fallinghrt22:** it is never a dream Love.

9:16:04 AM **fallinghrt22:** *this is the best time for us and I am glad we used it for the best baby.*

9:16:20 AM **fallinghrt22:** I Love you so much.

9:16:29 AM **ladydi2011:** Someone like you is what I have asked God for

9:17:34 AM **fallinghrt22:** then why question God???

9:17:35 AM **ladydi2011:** I Love You so much!

9:18:17 AM **ladydi2011:** True...I know He only gives good gifts to his children.

9:18:46 AM **fallinghrt22:** You brought love and laughter to my empty, sad and boring life. My heart had known only emptiness until the day you came and filled my heart to overflowing with your jovial ways. Your sense of humor has turned my frown into a smile..

9:19:13 AM **ladydi2011:** I would never question God.

9:22:47 AM **fallinghrt22:** You taught me how to love again, you taught me to give and receive love by trusting in you and believing. You taught me to go the extra mile. And though there are miles between us, I never stop thinking of you, you have brought a change into my life and my heart is forever yours..

Break In Time

9:25:47 AM f**allinghrt22:** I hope you never quit seeing how much my love for you is true. I don't want to lose you for anyone else or anything. I want you to know that I love you from the deepest part of my heart. My love for you is unconditional. My love for you is so strong and the most powerful feeling that I have had in a long time, and I am just at a lost for words when it comes to you. I want you to know that I love you and always will, and there is nothing that will ever change how I feel about you. I love you..

9:30:16 AM **ladydi2011:** It is your love that sustains me. I am so glad I brought change to your life and heart because you have done the same for me. You brought me back to life. You have received my love with open arms and you love me unconditionally. We are committed to each other baby.

9:30:31 AM **fallinghrt22:** Baby when are you going to work? I need to get off now I have paper work to do...

9:30:57 AM **fallinghrt22:** I Love you so much.

9:31:11 AM **fallinghrt22:** I will talk to you later baby..thanks so much for talking to me.

9:31:15 AM **ladydi2011:** Thank you baby...I feel the same.

9:31:27 AM **fallinghrt22:** Wet Kisses and hugs

9:31:27 AM **ladydi2011:** I Love you much more!!!

9:31:37 AM **ladydi2011:** Have a nice evening my love.

9:32:27 AM **fallinghrt22:** thanks for being there for me.

I was glowing because I was really in love with the "man behind the screen". People noticed it and asked me about it and I told them about Jerry and how we met. Not one person said "He could be a scammer." Many people told me about online dating success stories. This helped me believe that I too would have a success story. When I was chatting I didn't realize he was copying and pasting all the beautiful words, but reading them now, it is obvious, and it is actually overkill! I was a little taken aback when he asked if he had given me songs to listen to before. This made me think that I might not be the only woman in his life and I asked him to please tell me if he was for real. He quickly reassured me that he was. Oh, how we do not listen to our gut instincts or that "little voice" when we want something to be true. I think it is just part of us being human. This is why it is so important to be able to identify a scammer as soon as possible so you do not get caught up in his manipulation of fairytales and sweet words.

RED FLAGS

- Again he says "we were destined to be together" and "nothing can ever keep us from our destiny". Anytime someone starts talking about "destiny," it is a red flag.
- He sends me songs. One of my sources tells me that scammers do this to pull you closer and make the relationship seem more real.
- You know that old saying, "if it seems too good to be true, it probably is". So, if something seems too good to be true while chatting on line, it probably is!

IM Apr 17, 2012 6:37:03 AM

6:37:03 AM **fallinghrt22**: *(Sent video Someone Like You by Adele)*
6:37:23 AM **ladydi2011**: Hi my sexy man. Are you there?
6:41:05 AM **fallinghrt22**: *(Sent video Someone Like You by Adele again)*
6:45:42 AM **ladydi2011**: How was your day?
6:49:17 AM **ladydi2011**: Please listen my love. (Video From This Moment On by Shania Twain)
6:59:15 AM **ladydi2011**: (Video of I Just Wanna Spend My Life With You)
7:01:17 AM **ladydi2011**: (Video of When God Made You)
7:05:04 AM **ladydi2011**: Baby...you have some songs to listen too...
7:07:01 AM **fallinghrt22**: Hi Baby.
7:07:56 AM **fallinghrt22**: <ding>
7:08:13 AM **ladydi2011**: <ding>
7:08:18 AM **fallinghrt22**: 😊😊😊😊😊😊
7:09:08 AM **ladydi2011**: Thank you baby!
7:09:23 AM **ladydi2011**: I love you...
7:09:36 AM **fallinghrt22**: Love you to the moon and back
7:09:41 AM **fallinghrt22**: Baby my heart is heavy
7:09:53 AM **ladydi2011**: Why is your heart heavy baby?
7:11:16 AM **fallinghrt22**: *I went to send money at the bank after cashing my check but they said it will take 21 days to cash my check.*
7:11:36 AM **ladydi2011**: What???
7:12:03 AM **ladydi2011**: Baby, this puts me in a real bind...
7:12:14 AM **fallinghrt22**: Yes baby, very sad and I can't start working without money
7:13:27 AM **ladydi2011**: I never heard of not being able to cash a traveler's check...
7:14:33 AM **fallinghrt22**: *This 3rd world country is crazy my love*
7:15:18 AM **fallinghrt22**: *I have a deadline on this project, I am supposed to start working today and end this project by the 7th of May.*
7:15:48 AM **ladydi2011**: What are you going to do?

7:16:15 AM **fallinghrt22**: *I dont know baby I need capital to start now.*

7:16:42 AM **ladydi2011**: You have also put me in trouble now. Why would you do this to me?

7:17:38 AM **fallinghrt22**: *Baby I had no intentions to do this, I thought I would even get money and by now you would have your money back*

7:17:59 AM **ladydi2011**: Did you call your bank?

7:18:31 AM **fallinghrt22**: *Yes baby I did and they can't help me*

7:18:44 AM **ladydi2011**: Why can't they help you?

7:18:44 AM **fallinghrt22**: *I have been worried, thats why I have been trying to call you.*

7:19:28 AM **ladydi2011**: Baby, I am now in trouble. What am I going to do?

7:20:08 AM **fallinghrt22**: *Sweetheart, we are both in trouble... What do we do?*

7:20:57 AM **ladydi2011**: Baby, you do have traveler's checks, right?

7:21:03 AM **fallinghrt22**: Yes I do.

7:21:13 AM **ladydi2011**: Why won't they cash them?

7:21:32 AM **fallinghrt22**: *It's from the US they have to send it back for confirmation.*

7:21:48 AM **ladydi2011**: this makes NO sense....

7:22:04 AM **fallinghrt22**: Just what I said.

7:23:16 AM **ladydi2011**: I trusted you my love.

7:23:35 AM **fallinghrt22**: Baby when I asked you said of course, so I thought you were giving me from a surplus

7:23:39 AM **ladydi2011**: I told you I had to have it back by the 25th.

7:23:45 AM **fallinghrt22**: Baby I did not mean for any of this to happen

7:23:53 AM **fallinghrt22**: It's just the 17th

7:23:57 AM **fallinghrt22**: Lets find a way.

7:24:02 AM **ladydi2011**: Did you go to the person you are working for?

7:25:08 AM **fallinghrt22**: *Yes I did and they can't give me any advance until the job has gotten to a certain level*

7:25:41 AM **ladydi2011**: So, you traveled to China to do a job with no cash advance?

7:26:55 AM **fallinghrt22**: *Thats the contract, I invest my money in it*

7:27:00 AM **ladydi2011**: Baby, who else do you know to call for help?

7:27:29 AM **fallinghrt22**: *Baby I don't know anyone to call.*

7:27:43 AM **ladydi2011**: What about your friends?

7:28:19 AM **fallinghrt22**: *I don't keep any*

7:28:35 AM **ladydi2011**: You sent me a picture of you and your friends

7:28:49 AM **fallinghrt22**: *Not dependable. Just people I know.*

7:30:19 AM **ladydi2011**: Baby, this is not the first time you have been in other countries.

7:30:39 AM **fallinghrt22**: *Baby please calm down I want us to find a way around this.* Please ok

7:31:59 AM **ladydi2011**: I don't know how to help you now baby...

7:33:09 AM **fallinghrt22**: *Baby do you think we can get a loan and pay it back in a month*

7:33:30 AM **ladydi2011**: I cannot get a loan. I am tapped out.

7:33:36 AM **fallinghrt22**: Geez

7:34:33 AM **ladydi2011**: Baby, $1,000 of that money was to pay my taxes, which I was supposed to mail today.

7:34:44 AM **fallinghrt22**: Damn.

7:34:50 AM **fallinghrt22**: You should have told me all this

7:34:59 AM **ladydi2011**: Hmmm...You have really put me in trouble.

7:35:10 AM **fallinghrt22**: Please don't say that

7:35:14 AM **fallinghrt22**: I feel really bad

7:36:45 AM **ladydi2011**: How could you do this honey?

7:37:11 AM **fallinghrt22**: Honey why are you talking this way

7:37:37 AM **ladydi2011**: How could you ask without knowing for a fact that you had my back? I would never do this to you or anyone else.

7:37:56 AM **fallinghrt22**: 😊

7:38:13 AM **ladydi2011**: I would never put you in jeopardy in any way.

7:38:48 AM **ladydi2011**: Please give me the name of your bank where you got the travelers checks.

7:39:07 AM **fallinghrt22**: why?

7:39:23 AM **ladydi2011**: I need to call them and ask them what we can do.

7:39:44 AM **fallinghrt22**: *BOA*

7:40:23 AM **ladydi2011**: They are worldwide...this really doesn't make sense. This is who my bank was going to send to you through...

7:40:47 AM **fallinghrt22**: *Do you want me to scan and send you the check*

7:40:54 AM **ladydi2011**: Please

7:41:22 AM **fallinghrt22**: Will have to find a place to do it

7:41:33 AM **fallinghrt22**: *If I scan and send it to you, can you get a loan for us*

7:41:37 AM **ladydi2011**: Can the hotel do it?

7:41:57 AM **ladydi2011**: I don't know...I will try.

7:42:23 AM **fallinghrt22**: Give me some time let me check with them

7:42:34 AM **ladydi2011**: Ok. I will wait.

7:47:34 AM **ladydi2011**: Baby, how much money do you have in traveler's checks?

7:47:50 AM **fallinghrt22**: *75k*

7:47:56 AM **ladydi2011**: what?

7:48:08 AM **ladydi2011**: All in one check?

7:48:52 AM **fallinghrt22**: Yes

7:50:06 AM **ladydi2011**: I was just reading about travelers checks. If you send me the check, I can cash it and deposit it into an account here and then wire you the money

7:54:21 AM **ladydi2011**: Are you there baby?

7:56:45 AM **fallinghrt22**: Just hold on, trying to scan

7:58:04 AM **ladydi2011**: Ok...

Break In Time

10:13:34 AM **fallinghrt22**: Hi my wife.

10:16:56 AM **fallinghrt22**: <ding>

10:24:50 AM **ladydi2011**: <ding>

10:26:43 AM **ladydi2011**: Was the hotel able to scan your check? Can they fax it to me?

10:27:11 AM **fallinghrt22**: *They don't have fax here baby it took forever to get the scanner to work*

10:27:34 AM **fallinghrt22**: *Baby please right now I need $10,000 as capital to start working.*

10:28:04 AM **fallinghrt22**: *did you see the check baby?*

10:28:42 AM **ladydi2011**: I cannot see it. Please send it to me via email.

10:29:25 AM **fallinghrt22**: sent the file here.

10:30:00 AM **ladydi2011**: Ok. Let me save and open. Please give me a minute.

10:30:11 AM **fallinghrt22**: Ok baby.

10:31:13 AM **ladydi2011**: Ok. I can see it. It is a cashier's check, not travelers check.

10:31:52 AM **fallinghrt22**: I guess thats why it will take that long to cash

10:32:26 AM **fallinghrt22**: *So please if you can help me on this, I will be able to pay back as soon as the check clears up.*

10:32:51 AM **ladydi2011**: Baby, I am still not sure what the best strategy is. Now that I have the check, I will be able to get better answers. I wasn't able to answer all their questions earlier.

10:33:34 AM **fallinghrt22**: *Baby I need you to help ne raise 10K so I can start working... I can't afford to lose this project*
10:34:29 AM **fallinghrt22**: *Baby you know I need this ASSP.*
10:35:11 AM **ladydi2011**: I know you can't afford to lose this project. Baby, can the people you are working for deposit this into their account and then give you the $10,000 you need?
10:35:32 AM **ladydi2011**: Of course I know you need this as soon as possible.
10:36:37 AM **fallinghrt22**: *No baby they won't do that, right now they feel I am incapable of running this project and I have to prove them wrong*
10:36:48 AM **fallinghrt22**: *Baby please I need your help with this*
10:37:09 AM **ladydi2011**: Honey, I will do everything I can.
10:37:31 AM **ladydi2011**: I might need you to sign and overnight me the check.
10:37:35 AM **fallinghrt22**: *Can you get $10,000*
10:38:12 AM **fallinghrt22**: *I will pay back with 20%* ..Please
10:40:26 AM **fallinghrt22**: are you there baby? Did you get my last message?
10:42:40 AM **ladydi2011**: Do you have your personal checkbook with you?
10:43:35 AM **fallinghrt22**: No I did not
10:43:52 AM **fallinghrt22**: I asked you a question and you did not reply to it
10:44:24 AM **ladydi2011**: I don't know yet baby...
10:44:42 AM **fallinghrt22**: *How and when will you do, I need to plan baby*
10:45:10 AM **ladydi2011**: Baby, I know you need a plan. Give me some time...
10:45:35 AM **fallinghrt22**: *Baby they are not giving me any time here on the job*
10:45:49 AM **ladydi2011**: If I need you to overnight me the signed check can you do this?
10:46:15 AM **fallinghrt22**: *The money on the check can't be paid to anyone but me*
10:46:32 AM **fallinghrt22**: So what good would it do with you?
10:47:18 AM **ladydi2011**: I don't know yet...I have to do a lot of calling around. I could deposit it into your account. Can you access your account from there?
10:48:05 AM **fallinghrt22**: *No baby whatever I have to do on my account has to be in person because of the restraint I put on it due to a hacking problem I had at a time*
10:48:34 AM **ladydi2011**: You are killing me baby!!!

10:49:42 AM **fallinghrt22**: *Baby I am sorry, I need you to help me outside of the check. Please I will pay back with 20%*

10:50:30 AM **ladydi2011**: Honey, I am so very sorry. I cannot get my hands on this kind of money.

10:50:47 AM **ladydi2011**: We have to come up with a different solution.

10:51:48 AM **fallinghrt22**: *How much can you raise?*

10:52:47 AM **ladydi2011**: Baby, I have to talk to my brother...brb

10:53:13 AM **fallinghrt22**: Ok baby.

11:01:05 AM **fallinghrt22**: I'm waiting baby.

11:13:23 AM **ladydi2011**: I need time to think...

11:13:37 AM **fallinghrt22**: *You know I need this ASSP*

11:13:39 AM **ladydi2011**: *You have our wedding set with you, right?*

11:15:04 AM **fallinghrt22**: *Yes why.*

11:15:28 AM **ladydi2011**: *Can you pawn it or something???*

11:15:55 AM **fallinghrt22**: *No I can't I am not that kind of a person..this is precious to me.*

11:16:45 AM **fallinghrt22**: *please dont say such thing again.*

11:16:48 AM **ladydi2011**: Baby, I am thinking outside the box in every way I can...My main goal is for you to be ok...I have never pawned anything either, but you are in a jam my dear.

11:16:52 AM **fallinghrt22**: *remember our Oath to each other.*

11:17:12 AM **fallinghrt22**: *you should have something to pawn then.*

11:18:17 AM **ladydi2011**: What about out oath?

11:19:19 AM **ladydi2011**: I cannot believe you just said that "I should have something to pawn"

11:25:05 AM **ladydi2011**: I am trying to help you.

Break In Time

12:19:54 PM **fallinghrt22**: <ding>

12:20:29 PM **fallinghrt22**: Are you there? I got booted

12:23:13 PM **fallinghrt22**: Where did you go

12:23:16 PM **fallinghrt22**: <ding>

12:27:20 PM **fallinghrt22**: Talk to me. I need sleep

12:30:11 PM **fallinghrt22**: <ding>

12:31:15 PM **fallinghrt22**: *Baby I need you to help me get the $10,000*

12:31:41 PM **fallinghrt22**: *Please so I can get started with work.*

12:32:46 PM **ladydi2011**: I know you are under a lot of stress. I know what you need. I need some time to figure out how I can help you with this.

12:33:31 PM **fallinghrt22**: *Baby how soon can you get the $10,000 for me.*

12:33:43 PM **fallinghrt22**: *Remember I promise to pay back in no time baby*

12:33:55 PM **fallinghrt22**: *I can't sleep I'm stress over this my love*

12:35:36 PM **ladydi2011**: I can't sleep either. Give me some time.

12:36:05 PM **fallinghrt22**: *Are you promising me you will do this for me???*

12:36:14 PM **fallinghrt22**: *I need you honey.. Don't let me fall*

12:37:19 PM **ladydi2011**: Honey, I don't want to let you fall. I will do everything I can.

12:38:08 PM **fallinghrt22**: *Please ASSP*

12:38:33 PM **fallinghrt22**: *Will I hear good news from you when I wake up??*

12:41:31 PM **fallinghrt22**: <ding>

12:43:31 PM **fallinghrt22**: I'm going to sleep

12:46:48 PM **ladydi2011**: <ding>

12:48:16 PM **ladydi2011**: Sorry...client called. Please try to get some rest and let me see what I can do.

12:48:49 PM **fallinghrt22**: Okay

12:49:01 PM **fallinghrt22**: *Will I hear good news when I wake up??*

12:49:57 PM **ladydi2011**: Honey, I am a little dismayed that not once in our correspondence have you been worried about the position you put me in. This is out of character from the Jerry I have come to know and love. Makes my heart sad!!!

12:50:35 PM **fallinghrt22**: Baby do you really know how sad I feel and feel your pain.

12:50:44 PM **fallinghrt22**: *Baby let's do this please*

12:50:56 PM **ladydi2011**: No honey. I don't.

12:50:59 PM **fallinghrt22**: *I do love you so much and will never see you cry*

12:51:05 PM **fallinghrt22**: *Remember our Oath*

12:51:18 PM **ladydi2011**: Stop it already with the oath!

12:51:37 PM **ladydi2011**: Get some sleep.

12:51:50 PM **fallinghrt22**: *I am restless*

12:51:57 PM **ladydi2011**: I am sure you are.

12:51:58 PM **fallinghrt22**: *I need to know please so I can sleep*

12:52:46 PM **ladydi2011**: Hmmmm....While you sleep, I will be trying to figure out a way.

12:53:19 PM **fallinghrt22**: Thanks

12:53:34 PM **ladydi2011**: I also have to figure out a way to pay my taxes...So, now we are both restless.

12:57:49 PM **fallinghrt22**: *Baby once I get my check cashed I will just do all that for us*

12:57:59 PM **fallinghrt22**: *You have nothing to worry about*

1:00:34 PM **ladydi2011**: Get some sleep and know that I will do all I can. Night!

1:01:09 PM **fallinghrt22**: Thanks baby

1:01:12 PM **fallinghrt22**: I love you

1:01:17 PM **fallinghrt22**: Kisses and hugs

He kept the music videos coming and I was really shocked with the first one he sent, but I didn't say anything. I just took note and prepared myself for hurt. The words to it said, "Sometimes it lasts in love and sometimes it hurts instead. I wish nothing but the best for you, don't forget me." Looking back I think he knew once he made his next move it was all over. I now know he is a scammer and that I was taken, and he thinks he can get more. Well, you might get me once due to lack of education, but you will not get me twice. You will NEVER make me into a victim either. You cannot let these scammers make you into a victim or they win. The way to not be a victim is to break the silence and talk about it. They know most people will be too embarrassed and ashamed to talk about it, and they rely on this. The difference this time from the first time when he asked for money is that the first time he was calm and not pushing it. This time he was not calm and he was really pushing to get the money, and he wanted an answer right away. Then he told me to "calm down." What? He wants more money when he didn't keep his word of paying back the prior money I "lent" him when he promised to. Is he kidding me? I called Bank of America and gave them the routing number of the check, and of course they had no account with that routing number or anything under the name Jerry Wesley. I wasn't surprised and now knew for sure he was a scammer. I wanted to see if I could get him to give me my money back.

I was hurt, pissed, and feeling foolish. Oh, if I only knew then what I know now. Time to learn, and game on!

RED FLAGS

- It never takes 21 days to cash a check. If someone tells you this you know it's a scam.
- He got me once and he now wants more. He now says he needs capital money. Scammers always want more money and have many stories to try to get more.
- He doesn't have anyone to call for help but me. No friends or family. Scammers always only have "you" to help them.
- "He has to send the check back to the United States for confirmation." What? In today's world of technology? I don't think so! Pay attention to what is being said and don't get caught up in the urgency of the "story."
- He tells me his bank is Bank of America. They have locations in China. Research everything you are told.
- He wants me to take out a loan and he will pay it back in a month. Scammers will ask you to do this and make promises that they have NO intention of keeping. Do NOT go into debt for ANY man.
- He agrees to scan and send his check for 75K in hopes that if I see the check I will get the loan and send him money. Not happening! It is typical for a scammer to show proof that he has money to make you think that you will get your money back. YOU WILL NOT!
- "Right now," "ASAP" he needs $10,000. Everything is "urgent" when a scammer is trying to get your money.
- He can't afford to lose the project. Scammers use this scenario a lot.
- Pay attention to details. He keeps saying "traveler's check" when in reality he sent me a copy of a "cashier's check".
- When you say you cannot send the money a scammer will offer to pay you back with interest or pay you a higher cut of the deal to get you to send the money.
- "How and when will you do it?" and "They will not give me any more time on this job" is more pressure. He knows if he gives me time to think, he will not get the money.
- Every solution I mention, he has a reason why it will not work. Scammers are great excuse makers.
- He needs my help without using the check. Yes, this means he wants MY MONEY!
- Now he wants me to "raise money" even if it means pawning things I have but he will not pawn what he has.
- Now I see why he had me take an oath. A scammer will use an oath to manipulate you. If someone asks you to take an oath, DISCONNECT IMMEDIATELY from them.
- A scammer will also ask you to "not let them fall".

From: Jerry Wesley [mailto:fallinghrt22@yahoo.com]
Sent: Wednesday, April 18, 2012 6:30 AM
To: Diana Garren

Subject: Re: Thinking of you my darling...

Baby I am in tears writing this email to you... I don't know what I would do without you. My heart is yours to keep. You are the greatest thing that has ever happened to me and I never want to let go. Every moment we share together I could never forget, and I am simply hanging by a moment waiting until I can see you and be held close in your arms. *I will never break your heart*. I'll be right beside you as we chase our dreams together, and you will never have to wonder if I still care. I get angry with myself because I bring the relationship down more than I help it right now...

When I look back on how we met and I see where we are now, I can only believe that *we were destined to be together*. We've both been through some challenging times in our lives, and there is no doubt that our past experiences have partly shaped who we are today. What I have come to realize, though, is that I am learning a little more every day to appreciate what I have found in you. I have lived for a long time, responsible for and dependent upon no one, answering to no one and committed to no one except myself. During this period of my life, I considered the world mine for the taking and truly believed that I was living life to the fullest. Then, you came into the picture, and all of a sudden, I realized that I was deceiving myself. I find that my life is not all that I thought it was. In fact, it is terribly lacking in many things, the foremost being love. Now, through some great fortune, I have found that love and along with it, the one person who can make my life truly complete.

Diana I love you with all my heart. No matter how tough this relationship gets or how hard it may seem to move forward, I will never stop loving you. You are my world and soul, the air that I breathe each day....I just want to be home to be with you....Wet Kisses and Passionate Hugs

Your Lonely Husband.

From: Diana Garren
Sent: Wednesday, April 18, 2012 8:49 AM
To: Jerry Wesley [mailto:fallinghrt22@yahoo.com]
Subject: Money

Hello, my love,
I hope you finally got some sleep and are having a calm day!

Baby, it really meant a lot to me that you wouldn't even consider selling our wedding set.

I have been busy raising the 10K you need. I have over half of it raised and will have the rest by Friday! Hopefully this allows you to breathe easier, my love! You will be able to do your work so that you can quickly get to Atlanta to my loving arms.

I am still having problems walking and navigating the steps is too much for me. You don't have to worry; Asher is here. He brought me some food and is making sure I am drinking enough fluids. He carried me upstairs so I could take a bath, fixed me ice packs and has me tucked tightly in bed. He even blew dry my hair so I don't go to bed with wet hair and catch my cold back. He insists on staying the night in case I need something. He is a good friend! He told me to tell you not to worry, he's got it! That has always been his saying to me: "Baby, I've got it". I know when he says this then he has it handled. Honey, I do wish it were you here taking care of and lying next to me. Your strong arms would be the perfect medicine for me! For the next couple days I am going to have to settle for Asher. It has been a really long day and I am emotionally, physically and mentally exhausted.

Good night, baby...
I love you so much!
Your beloved wife
Diana L. Wesley

IM Apr 18, 2012 8:27:40 AM

8:27:40 AM **fallinghrt22**: Good morning baby..it's like you are sleeping to much.
8:28:49 AM **ladydi2011**: Good morning
8:29:08 AM **fallinghrt22**: how are you doing and how was your night baby.
8:29:35 AM **ladydi2011**: Not really baby.
8:29:46 AM **fallinghrt22**: are you Okay?
8:31:31 AM **ladydi2011**: I just woke up baby!
8:32:26 AM **fallinghrt22**: I know.
8:32:42 AM **fallinghrt22**: I Love you
8:34:18 AM **ladydi2011**: I Love you too! I am still having problems walking and navigating the steps is too much for me. You don't have to worry, Asher is here. He brought me some food and is making sure I am drinking enough fluids. Last night he carried me upstairs so I could take a bath, fixed me ice packs and tucked me tightly in bed. He even blew dry my hair so I didn't go to bed with wet hair and catch my cold back. He insisted on staying the night in case I need something. He is a good friend! He told me to tell you not to worry, he's got it! That has always been his saying to me "baby, I've got it". I know when he says this then he has it handled.
8:35:34 AM **ladydi2011**: How was your night baby?
8:35:35 AM **fallinghrt22**: he has got what?
8:35:45 AM **fallinghrt22**: wish I am there to take care of you baby.
8:36:09 AM **ladydi2011**: Me too my love!
8:36:26 AM **fallinghrt22**: my night was restless, thinking about you and this problem.
8:36:42 AM **fallinghrt22**: you said Asher has got what?
8:36:59 AM **ladydi2011**: I could sure use your sweet kisses and strong arms around me.
8:37:20 AM **fallinghrt22**: I so need to be held by you honey, and also hold you in my Arms.
8:37:30 AM **fallinghrt22**: take care of you
8:38:10 AM **ladydi2011**: Me too baby!
8:38:33 AM **fallinghrt22**: I don't understand Asher said you should tell me he has got it.
8:38:45 AM **fallinghrt22**: I Love you so much.
8:40:38 AM **ladydi2011**: This is Asher's way of letting me know he will take care or whatever I need. Last night I needed food and to be carried upstairs.
8:40:52 AM **fallinghrt22**: Oh thats good of him.
8:41:15 AM **ladydi2011**: I told you he is rough around the edges, right!

8:41:23 AM **fallinghrt22**: so how are you feeling now baby?

8:42:10 AM **ladydi2011**: Tired.

8:42:25 AM **fallinghrt22**: You would be fine baby..I worry about you.

8:43:28 AM **ladydi2011**: Asher will take me back to the chiropractor today.

8:43:44 AM **fallinghrt22**: Ok.

8:45:31 AM **ladydi2011**: Hopefully the feelings in my legs will come back soon.

8:45:57 AM **fallinghrt22**: good....I am praying for you.

8:46:04 AM **fallinghrt22**: I miss you tremendously

8:46:20 AM **fallinghrt22**: *I just don't know what we can do to solve this baby.*

8:46:36 AM **fallinghrt22**: I didn't hear anything from you.

8:46:49 AM **ladydi2011**: I miss you tremendously too!

8:47:43 AM **ladydi2011**: I emailed you last night, didn't you get it?

8:48:17 AM **fallinghrt22**: No I didn't get your email baby.

8:48:54 AM **ladydi2011**: Hold on, let me look and resend it.

8:50:13 AM **ladydi2011**: Opppsss! It was in draft. I just sent it. Please check mail.

8:50:56 AM **fallinghrt22**: I will.

8:51:08 AM **fallinghrt22**: I did sent you an email.

8:51:14 AM **fallinghrt22**: did you get it baby.

8:51:18 AM **fallinghrt22**: I Love you so much. You are the air that I breathe.

8:53:43 AM **ladydi2011**: You are the air that I breathe too...

8:54:02 AM **fallinghrt22**: Awwwwww *you melt me*.

8:54:09 AM **fallinghrt22**: *I Live to Love you*

8:54:14 AM **fallinghrt22**: did you get my email?

8:55:44 AM **ladydi2011**: Hold on, let me go look. Brb

9:00:39 AM **ladydi2011**: Thank you for your honesty baby! Maybe now I understand why you say again and again that you don't know what you ever did to deserve me...

9:02:24 AM **ladydi2011**: R U there baby?

9:08:46 AM **ladydi2011**: Where R U baby?

Break In Time

10:21:15 AM **fallinghrt22**: my heartbeat.

10:23:23 AM **ladydi2011**: Did you read my email?

10:28:27 AM **ladydi2011**: Baby, R U there? Did you see where I raised a little over half the money?

10:29:01 AM **fallinghrt22**: Yes baby, I am so greateful.

10:29:18 AM **fallinghrt22**: *How soon can you send it on friday.*

10:32:56 AM **ladydi2011**: I am not sure what time on Friday I will get the rest. If it is after the bank closes, I will send it Western Union. Please be looking for the closest Western Union office. So, baby, if you start the project on Monday, when will you have it done? When will you be in Atlanta? How long will you be staying with me? I would like to go back to CA with you for a week. I want to meet William!

10:36:42 AM **fallinghrt22**: Yes honey....thanks alot let me know as soon as you get it....if I start this project I will get it done by early may and I will be coming to Atlanta to be with you baby...maybe I will stay 2weeks with you then we can come to CA together. What do you think honey.

10:37:07 AM **fallinghrt22**: I Love you so much baby.

10:37:49 AM **ladydi2011**: No matter what, I will send you the money Western Union. This way you have it in minutes. You cannot afford to wait another 3-5 days!

10:38:39 AM **fallinghrt22**: I never knew I could love a woman more then my own life. I long for the day I can finally look into your beautiful soft kind eyes and tell you how much I love you, and need you. The true beginning of my life is when you are going to be together and start a new life together baby.

10:40:22 AM **ladydi2011**: Oh baby, this sounds heavenly! I can't wait to kiss your sweet lips and feel your embrace. 2 weeks with me will be great!!! I will make sure the house is stocked with food.

10:41:28 AM **fallinghrt22**: Hmmmmmmm that looks great sweety.

10:41:57 AM **fallinghrt22**: I can't wait you will fill me with food and you..I dont think I would want to go back to CA

10:42:12 AM **ladydi2011**: I feel the same baby! I promise you will never want to let me go. *I will live in your heart forever!*

10:42:32 AM **fallinghrt22**: all my dreams are finally coming true..without you I will die baby.

10:43:22 AM **ladydi2011**: I am a fabulous cook and you will never want to leave the bedroom. You will want to stay in ephoria forever!

10:44:09 AM **ladydi2011**: I am looking forward to serving you breakfast, lunch and dinner in bed.

10:44:37 AM **fallinghrt22**: I can tell baby.

10:45:10 AM **fallinghrt22**: Hmmmmmmm, ***you melt me*** I am looking forward to eating your good and delicious food baby.

10:45:29 AM **ladydi2011**: Yes, my love. We will have a fabulous life together.

10:46:14 AM **fallinghrt22**: which seeing you every day is going to be the biggest blessing to my heart knowing you are in touching reach of me..I Love you so much my wife.

10:47:08 AM **ladydi2011**: I love you too my husband...oh, question...

10:47:40 AM **ladydi2011**: When we took our oath, what was the water for?

10:49:30 AM **fallinghrt22**: Oh, the water is the pure of the heart.

10:50:15 AM **ladydi2011**: Ok. So what were we supposed to do with it?

10:51:15 AM **fallinghrt22**: You were surpose to drink from it.

10:51:55 AM **ladydi2011**: Ooooppps. I didn't do that.

10:52:22 AM **fallinghrt22**: where is it water?

10:54:09 AM **ladydi2011**: I dumped it out...I am sorry baby. I was following your lead.

10:54:52 AM **fallinghrt22**: it is Okay..we took it Oath, the water does not matter much, with the bible it matters alot

10:55:09 AM **fallinghrt22**: *anyone of us that leaves each other will die....*

10:55:30 AM **fallinghrt22**: you know the saying... for better and for worse.

10:55:46 AM **fallinghrt22**: I will never leave you baby. You are my everlasting Love.

10:58:43 AM **ladydi2011**: Oh, ok...yes, I do know the saying baby. I could never leave you my love. I am so glad you will never leave me!

11:00:36 AM **fallinghrt22**: You are my every heartbeat, my every gasping breathe of life. What I need to survive and make it through this lonely world can only be conquered with you by my side. I do not think there are any words that could describe the way I actually feel about you. All I know, is you, Diana Wesley are the only woman that is in my mind, the only woman that is in my soul, the only woman who truly and unconditionally has my heart for my lifetime and many more lifetimes the world has to offer us.

11:05:16 AM **ladydi2011**: Baby, I need to work. Get some rest my love.

11:05:47 AM **fallinghrt22**: When I think about you, my eyes start to water because I know you are somewhere else and not in my arms. But the thought of you keeps me going and going for another breathe of fresh air to keep my longing for you in my life going. I will never leave, and I will truly never hurt you. I admire you. You are my inspiration for anything, and everything on this cold damp earth..

11:07:55 AM **fallinghrt22**: I Love you so much Baby, let me sleep and I will talk to you later..Wet Kisses and Hugs....
11:08:37 AM **ladydi2011**: Ok my love. Sleep well and dream about me!

From: Diana Garren
Sent: Wednesday, April 18, 2012 2:22 PM
To: Jerry Wesley
Subject: Where are you my prince???

Hi, my love!

I hope you are having sweet dreams about me and our life together.

I am lying in bed with my side on ice, trying to get rid of the inflammation so I can walk again. 20 min. on and 20 min. off. I will do whatever it takes to have my mobility back. I don't like being down like this! I sure wish you were here to hold me and warm me once I remove the ice. I sure hope I am better by the time you get to Atlanta, so I can drive to pick you up at the airport. You sure don't want to travel all this way for a woman who is lame!

Asher will be back shortly to take me to the chiropractor. He made and brought me breakfast in bed...I didn't know he could cook. It was actually pretty good!

He is having fun messing with me! He knows my strength and usually can't mess with me. He is taking advantage of me being down and needing him! He doesn't know that I noticed that he got aroused standing behind me to hold me so I didn't fall while taking off my makeup and brushing my teeth...he also doesn't know I heard him come into my room and watch me as I was sleeping (he thought I was sleeping). I think he has a little crush on me...he says he doesn't! You have nothing to worry about my love. He is only 39 and just my friend. I would never be unfaithful to you. I really do need help right now.

Baby, you bought a new laptop with web cam before you left. Can we skype tonight? I have to see your handsome face and hear your sexy voice. IM is just not going to cut it for the duration...

By for now, my husband
Diana

IM Apr 19, 2012 10:24:41 AM

10:24:41 AM **fallinghrt22:** Good morning my world.
10:24:57 AM **ladydi2011:** Good morning baby!
10:25:03 AM **ladydi2011:** How are you?
10:25:22 AM **fallinghrt22:** I am better today and you honey
10:26:11 AM **ladydi2011:** I am sad today. I feel like our relationship is slipping away.
10:26:27 AM **fallinghrt22:** why will you say such thing

10:26:53 AM **ladydi2011:** I guess because of how little communication we have...

10:28:12 AM **fallinghrt22:** I see, I am sorry baby, please bare with me.

10:28:30 AM **fallinghrt22:** I so much in love with you so I have to hurry and come be with you

10:30:08 AM **fallinghrt22:** You mean the world to me and I can't wait

10:31:35 AM **fallinghrt22:** I longs to feel lost in your Arms and see your nakedness

10:33:27 AM **ladydi2011:** I long for the same thing my love. I guess long distance relationships are difficult for me. You are all the way around the world.

10:34:34 AM **ladydi2011:** Can we do a video call baby? I think this would help me a lot.

10:35:21 AM **fallinghrt22:** soon baby we would be together, and I will satisfy all your needs and wants.

10:35:39 AM **fallinghrt22:** *I dont know how to do the video call and I would need to down drive.*

10:35:48 AM **fallinghrt22:** *I will figure that out later Okay.*

10:36:29 AM **fallinghrt22:** so tell me how are you feeling now, health wise.

10:37:27 AM **ladydi2011:** Ok baby. Thank you for figuring out how to do a video call. If I can figure it out, I am sure you can...

10:40:26 AM **ladydi2011:** I am really frustrated with my health. I have really pinched some nerves and it is making it difficult to walk and impossible to drive. My legs and right buttock always feel like they are on fire. It is my #5 & #6 lumbar that is messed up. For some reason it was worse yesterday than Monday. It has also affected my right ankle. It keeps giving out on me. Therefore it is not safe to drive.

10:42:05 AM **fallinghrt22:** I am sorry Baby you would be fine.

10:42:17 AM **ladydi2011:** Asher took me to my appointment yesterday. He has a truck. I was not able to get into his truck. So, I had to let him drive my car...Well, of course he had fun driving my car and now wants to use it for a day!

10:42:22 AM **fallinghrt22:** can Asher drive you for the main time?

10:42:36 AM **ladydi2011:** Baby, I have to get better. I do not like depending on other people.

10:42:48 AM **fallinghrt22:** I know baby, you would be fine trust me.

10:42:59 AM **fallinghrt22:** I Love you so much

10:43:11 AM **fallinghrt22:** hope you are Okay today more than before.

10:43:16 AM **ladydi2011:** Thanks for your prayers baby. They mean a lot!

10:43:45 AM **ladydi2011:** I usually do not feel my age. The past couple days I do feel my age.

10:44:06 AM **fallinghrt22:** Ahhhhhh in my eyes you look like a sweet 16

10:44:27 AM **ladydi2011:** Thanks, but sweet 16 is really pushing it my sweet talker...

10:44:59 AM **fallinghrt22:** only God creation can compare to the beauty I see in you.

10:45:05 AM **fallinghrt22:** you drive me crazy.

10:45:33 AM **ladydi2011:** Thanks my love.

10:46:06 AM **ladydi2011:** You drive me crazy too.

10:46:59 AM **ladydi2011:** So, tell me what you have been doing with all your time baby? You have been in China now over a week. What sites have you seen?

10:47:08 AM **fallinghrt22:** You brought love and laughter to my empty, sad and boring life. My heart had known only emptiness until the day you came and filled my heart to overflowing with your jovial ways. Your sense of humor has turned my frown into a smile.

10:47:28 AM **fallinghrt22:** LOL I have not seen any cities until I can start work.

10:48:00 AM **fallinghrt22:** and it has been raining lately, I told you

10:48:06 AM **fallinghrt22:** I have been indoors all day.

10:48:19 AM **ladydi2011:** Baby, why was your life sad and boring?

10:48:40 AM **fallinghrt22:** when there is no love life is boring.

10:49:30 AM **ladydi2011:** You have had to do something other than stay indoors this entire time.

10:50:34 AM **ladydi2011:** Yeah, Life is meant to be shared. Love is what truly makes one happy.

10:50:55 AM **ladydi2011:** Did you picture me with you as you watched and heard the rain?

10:52:41 AM **fallinghrt22:** Oh yeah even thou I am lonely, I never stop thinking of you, you have brought a change into my life and my heart is forever yours.

10:53:06 AM **ladydi2011:** Baby, there is a couple good things about not having love in your life...1) You are safe... 2) You cannot get hurt.

10:54:16 AM **ladydi2011:** I never stop thinking about you either my love...Amazing how love does change our lives, isn't it?

10:55:28 AM **fallinghrt22:** Yes it has changed mine for good, I have not stopped smiling.

10:55:50 AM **ladydi2011:** brb baby...nature is calling. It will take a while because of the issue with my walking

10:56:24 AM **ladydi2011:** I am so glad I make you smile...

10:56:28 AM **fallinghrt22:** thoughts of you out of my mind. I think of your sweet lips and kisses, feel them as if it was yesterday. Thoughts of you warm my heart. You complete me, you are everything my heart desire.

10:56:43 AM **fallinghrt22:** wish am there to walk you.

11:08:13 AM **ladydi2011:** I am back my love. It would be wonderful if you were here to walk me.

11:09:55 AM **ladydi2011:** R U there baby?

11:13:00 AM **fallinghrt22:** <ding>

11:14:11 AM **fallinghrt22:** You came into my life and you have changed me completely

11:14:43 AM **ladydi2011:** Baby, do you think that for the first time you have truly fallen in love?

11:16:26 AM **fallinghrt22:** If only I could have come up with the right words to describe the depth of this beautiful feeling that I have for you. You are the best thing that ever happened to me.

11:17:31 AM **fallinghrt22:** Yes I think this is the first time I am truly in Love with my heart and soul.

11:18:12 AM **ladydi2011:** I think the only two things that truly change people are Christ and love...

11:20:25 AM **fallinghrt22:** Yes you are right and right now I have Love and christ, 120%

11:21:17 AM **ladydi2011:** Baby, the word "love" is an easy word to say, but to mean it when you say it is totally different. People say "I love you" all the time, yet their actions consistently say something different. Love is shown more than said. Words are words. Actions have meaning.

11:21:56 AM **ladydi2011:** Hold on to both Christ and love and your life will be absolutely wonderful!

11:23:19 AM **fallinghrt22:** I have your love in abondance and I have christ, my life is complete

11:24:11 AM **ladydi2011:** Do you think you are now ready to truly give of yourself?

11:24:31 AM **fallinghrt22:** Yes honey,

11:26:32 AM **ladydi2011:** My heart is 100% on the line. I need to know it is safe with you and that you are really ready for our relationship.

11:27:14 AM **fallinghrt22:** I am so ready, infact *I will give my life*

11:28:32 AM **ladydi2011:** Ok my love. Please remember the oath you took with me.

11:28:50 AM **fallinghrt22:** I know baby, it means forever

11:28:57 AM **fallinghrt22:** I will never give up on you.

11:29:28 AM **fallinghrt22:** (Sent video Don't Give Up On Me BY Jason Aldean)

11:29:54 AM **ladydi2011:** Yes, my love. It means forever. I do not want to be hurt or used again. I would rather be alone than go through this again.

11:30:58 AM **fallinghrt22:** I promise you baby.

11:31:01 AM **ladydi2011:** Baby, I deserve good things, not hurt and pain. You deserve the same...

11:31:11 AM **fallinghrt22:** Again he sent me the video Someone Like You by Adele

11:36:02 AM **ladydi2011:** *Baby, I will never give up on you. I want you to be the best man you can be. I want you to walk as proud as a peacock because you live your life with honor and integrity. I never* *want you to have to be looking over your shoulder waiting for karma to bite you in the tail... You deserve the best!*

11:37:54 AM **fallinghrt22:** You are my world. Life wouldn't be life if not shared with you. We may be far away from each other for now, but you have my heart and my love. And I know that I have yours, too. It just feels so wonderful knowing and believing that. Aren't we lucky? I love you... more and more each day.

11:39:12 AM **ladydi2011:** We are lucky baby. I love you more and more each day too!

11:41:21 AM **fallinghrt22:** I Love you so much my world.

11:42:43 AM **ladydi2011:** *Honey, I heard the following last night on the TV show revenge and I think it is so true and powerful! We have talked about how critical trust is. This statement takes broken trust to a whole new level. "Once trust is broken, doubt sets in. Doubt is a disease. It affects the mind creating a miss trust of people's motives and of ones perceptions. Doubt has the ability to call into question everything you once believed about someone and reinforce the darkest suspicions of our minds."*

11:43:20 AM **ladydi2011:** I love you more baby...from here to eternity and back...I win because you cannot beat eternity...

11:44:07 AM **fallinghrt22:** HEHE

11:44:49 AM **fallinghrt22:** *I will Love you until Gods kingdom comes, and even when it comes I will never stop loving you*

11:45:41 AM **ladydi2011:** Baby, I would love to talk forever. I need be on the phone with a client for the next hour. It is almost midnight your time. Please get a good night's rest and then contact me when you wake up. Please figure out how to video chat. I need to see your handsome face and hear your sweet sexy voice. It will mean a lot to me baby!

11:47:04 AM **ladydi2011:** Baby, what do you think of the statement I sent you?

11:47:45 AM **fallinghrt22:** it is very true with your statement, and *I am glad we took the oath, to trust each other no matter what*

11:47:57 AM **fallinghrt22:** thanks honey for talking to me, I will sleep like a babe

11:48:45 AM **ladydi2011:** You are welcome.

11:49:46 AM **fallinghrt22:** Love you so much....good night my wife.

11:50:01 AM **fallinghrt22:** Kisses and Hugs

11:50:22 AM **ladydi2011:** Passionate kisses and hugs...

IM Apr 20, 2012 9:20:30 AM

9:20:30 AM **fallinghrt22:** Good morning my wife.

9:20:34 AM **fallinghrt22:** are you there?

9:20:36 AM **fallinghrt22:** I missed you

9:21:50 AM **ladydi2011:** Good morning my love! I miss you. It has been over 24 hours since I heard from you. R U ok?

9:22:16 AM **fallinghrt22:** *it has been raining so bad Baby.*

9:22:39 AM **fallinghrt22:** *network on the phone cut off I can't even use internet until now.*

9:22:45 AM **fallinghrt22:** so I have been sleeping.

9:22:58 AM **ladydi2011:** Wow!

9:23:01 AM **fallinghrt22:** wish you are here with me.

9:23:12 AM **fallinghrt22:** How are you doing and how was your night? I missed you tremendously.

9:25:23 AM **ladydi2011:** I slept on the floor.

9:25:31 AM **fallinghrt22:** why baby.

Break In Time

10:06:19 AM **fallinghrt22:** <ding>

10:06:22 AM **fallinghrt22:** My wife.

10:06:26 AM **fallinghrt22:** I got booted

10:06:34 AM **fallinghrt22:** *The server is so bad*

10:06:38 AM **fallinghrt22:** I missed you more

10:07:48 AM **fallinghrt22:** So how are you doing and how was your night?

10:08:00 AM **fallinghrt22:** You fill my every thought my wife

10:10:14 AM **ladydi2011:** Got about 2 hrs. sleep. What about you?

10:10:53 AM **fallinghrt22:** I tried to find sleep. Because you are not with me to put me to sleep

10:12:14 AM **ladydi2011:** You are always in my thoughts and heart!

10:12:31 AM **fallinghrt22:** I love you to the bone. I don't know what I will do without you.

10:13:01 AM **fallinghrt22:** *My wife how soon will you be sending the funds??*

10:16:32 AM **ladydi2011:** Still need to put a little more together!

10:17:05 AM **fallinghrt22:** *Okay baby but you will be sending it soon right?*

10:18:11 AM **ladydi2011:** Yes my love!

10:20:08 AM **fallinghrt22:** *I want you to send the money to the same account okay.*

10:23:12 AM **ladydi2011:** To the same account baby? Don't you need the money ASAP?

10:23:51 AM **fallinghrt22:** I will get it by monday since its weekend here. And its safe.

10:24:17 AM **fallinghrt22:** Asap monday I will start working.

10:25:36 AM **ladydi2011:** Isn't Western Union safe?

10:29:32 AM **ladydi2011:** Are you there baby?

10:30:47 AM **fallinghrt22:** *Sorry server is slow.*

10:30:58 AM **fallinghrt22:** *You will spend much sending western union.*

10:32:00 AM **fallinghrt22:** *And I don't want to go receiving the funds it may bring much protocols. The account is better since its weekend.*

10:32:37 AM **fallinghrt22:** *And I think western union is little far from wear I stay. No money on me baby*

10:36:27 AM **fallinghrt22:** I love you more than my life.

10:39:06 AM **ladydi2011:** *Baby, I have never done so much for a man as I have done for you...*

10:40:30 AM **fallinghrt22:** You have done so much for me. And *I promise I will never disappoint you*

10:40:43 AM **fallinghrt22:** I just don't know how to pay you back baby

10:51:05 AM **fallinghrt22:** Are you there baby

10:51:08 AM **fallinghrt22:** <ding>

10:53:04 AM **ladydi2011:** Sorry baby! I am on my phone not the computer.

10:54:21 AM **ladydi2011:** *Baby, are you sure you will pay me this money back?*

10:55:31 AM **fallinghrt22:** *I cross my heart*

10:56:16 AM **fallinghrt22:** *I won't compromise money for love. I have promised to pay you back with 20%* I love you

10:57:31 AM **ladydi2011:** Baby, I really do love you with all my heart!

10:58:13 AM **fallinghrt22:** I know I love you much more than you do love me. And I will treat you right

11:03:24 AM **ladydi2011:** Brb baby. Please don't go anywhere?

11:04:06 AM **fallinghrt22:** I'm here

11:13:23 AM **ladydi2011:** Baby, I sure hope you will treat me right. I deserve that much and more just like you deserve the best!

11:14:45 AM **fallinghrt22:** I know baby I can't wait to kiss your tears away and make you feel like a woman. I have gotten so much love to show to you baby.
11:15:16 AM **fallinghrt22:** *Honey please can I ask for a favour??*
11:16:42 AM **ladydi2011:** Sure baby
11:17:03 AM **fallinghrt22:** *You know that I am broke and I still need to get myself some things like toiletries and transportation and so on. Can you please make it 11K?? Can you do that if not that no problem.*
11:19:51 AM **fallinghrt22:** <ding>
11:21:13 AM **fallinghrt22:** Are you there?
11:22:24 AM **ladydi2011:** I don't know baby, let me try!
11:23:49 AM **fallinghrt22:** Thanks a lot. You are the best
11:24:22 AM **ladydi2011:** How have you been able to pay for the hotel and eat all this time my love?
11:25:47 AM **ladydi2011:** <ding>
11:27:34 AM **fallinghrt22:** I did pay for 2weeks thou. I manage baby.
11:27:55 AM **fallinghrt22:** Thanks for your care
11:27:59 AM **fallinghrt22:** Brb honey
11:28:34 AM **ladydi2011:** Ok baby

IM Apr 20, 2012 12:55:16 PM Continued

12:55:16 PM **fallinghrt22:** Baby,
12:55:54 PM **fallinghrt22:** needed to *take my bath* and also make the bed, wish you are here to bath with me and make the bed for me and also us lying on it together.
12:56:07 PM **fallinghrt22:** it will be so great and awesome.
12:56:10 PM **fallinghrt22:** where are you now> I miss you
12:59:07 PM **ladydi2011:** Hi my love. I wish I were with you too. I miss you and your emails...
1:00:05 PM **fallinghrt22:** I know, I will email you before I go to bed,
1:00:08 PM **fallinghrt22:** I am writing you..you know my heart. Where are you now?
1:00:24 PM **ladydi2011:** Promise...
1:00:37 PM **fallinghrt22:** why not *I have never promised and fail.*
1:03:29 PM **fallinghrt22:** are you there?
1:04:05 PM **ladydi2011:** *Unfortunately my dear you have. You were supposed to have my money back to me within two days. This has not happened. I trusted your word and you made a promise to me. When I told you I would send the money I did and my word was and still is good.*
1:04:38 PM **fallinghrt22:** *Baby, we are talking about us not money issue here.*
1:04:47 PM **fallinghrt22:** *Oh stop now you make me feel quity.*
1:05:51 PM **ladydi2011:** One of the songs you sent me is playing on the radio...brb
1:06:10 PM **fallinghrt22:** wow wihich one?
1:17:33 PM **ladydi2011:** I am back...the song is about not giving up on you...
1:18:19 PM **fallinghrt22:** please dont, I am glad you keep hearing the song, it tells you how much I plead for you not to give up on me.
1:18:40 PM **fallinghrt22:** where are you Baby?
1:26:06 PM **ladydi2011:** Baby, I will never give up on you!
1:26:26 PM **fallinghrt22:** I Love you so much and I will never give up on you my world.
1:26:47 PM **ladydi2011:** I love you too much to give up on you.
1:27:13 PM **fallinghrt22:** where are you baby? did you have to work?

1:27:15 PM **ladydi2011:** Have you been in touch with William?
1:27:40 PM **fallinghrt22:** I emailed him, but he has not gotten back to me.
1:27:45 PM **fallinghrt22:** I know he is Okay.
1:28:11 PM **ladydi2011:** I was at the doctors and Asher just dropped me back to the office.
1:28:36 PM **fallinghrt22:** *Ok Baby, when will you be sending the funds?*
1:28:44 PM **ladydi2011:** How often do you hear from William?
1:29:56 PM **ladydi2011:** I do not have all the funds put together yet. I told you not until late today when I will have them, so since I have to send through the bank, I might not be able to send until Monday.
1:30:41 PM **fallinghrt22:** *Oh baby, please can you make it possible you get it done today, I am delaying baby, please*
1:32:41 PM **fallinghrt22:** where did you go honey.
1:40:17 PM **fallinghrt22:** did you sign out on me baby.

He told me he bought us a wedding set and was going to propose to me when he arrived in Atlanta, so I told him to pawn it for money and he said he couldn't. I am now playing things up to make him think I believed him. I wanted him to think I was doing all I could to raise the 10K for him and that I raised half of it and would have the rest raised by Friday. I wanted to keep him on the hook to learn what I could about how far a scammer would go to get the money. I really was having problems with a pinched nerve and had a male friend here helping me, so I embellished a little to Jerry so he knew I had a man around me and was not alone. I wanted to spark jealousy in him, and it worked. When I told him "I will live in your heart forever", I was thinking "By the time this is over, you will never forget me and will always be watching over your shoulder." When I told him, "*Baby, I will never give up on you. I want you to be the best man you can be. I want you to walk as proud as a peacock because you live your life with honor and integrity. I never want you to have to be looking over your shoulder waiting for karma to bite you in the tail...You deserve the best!*" I was trying to make him feel bad about what he was doing and get him to have a change of heart and to know that what he does has consequences.

I couldn't believe when he raised it from 10K to 11K. Unreal! He didn't want me to send it Western Union because it was too large of an amount for Western Union and it had to go through his "Bosses" account because he worked for a big boss.

He crosses his heart that he will pay me the money back and reminds me that he will give me 20% interest. He says "I won't compromise money for love." Please know that a scammer will NEVER pay you the money back. It is NEVER about love to begin with; it is ALWAYS about money. Don't let their false promises or sweet words get to you.

RED FLAGS

🚩 There he goes again with "I will never break your heart", "we are destined to be together" and "I will never disappoint you". Please take note how this is used by scammers.

- 🖋 Even though my health wasn't good, he is persistent about the money. "How soon can you send it on friday.", "My wife how soon will you be sending the funds??", "Okay baby but you will be sending it soon right?", "You know that I am broke and I still need to get myself some things like toiletries and transportation and so on. Can you please make it 11K? Can you do that if not that no problem." He raised the amount of money by $1,000 as if money grows on trees!
- 🖋 Scammers use oaths and then taunt you with them. Do not take an oath with anyone on line. I thought it was weird so I went along with it in writing but I never did it on the Bible. I was shocked when he went as far as saying "anyone of us that leaves each other will die...."
- 🖋 He still doesn't have a web cam. Scammers will come up with excuse after excuse to not come on cam.
- 🖋 He says it is raining and he keeps getting booted. The network is always extremely bad in Africa when it rains. It will either be really slow or go all the way down. This is another red flag.

April 23 – Jerry called at least ten times a day, but I kept myself from him for a couple days. When I finally answered his call I told him a "story" that I was unavailable because of having problems with sugar. In reality, I didn't want to communicate with him. I was trying to think of ways for him to send me my money back. I knew by this time that I would be writing this book, so I wanted to take him as far as I could. My acting school training came in handy and I began lying to him like he lied to me. I am sinking into a place that is so foreign to me, because I am all about truth. Oh, how I hate being in the darkness!

IM Apr 23, 2012 11:22:20 AM

11:22:20 AM **fallinghrt22**: my Sunshine.
11:22:48 AM **ladydi2011**: My love.
11:23:11 AM **ladydi2011**: What a scary thing I just went through...
11:23:51 AM **fallinghrt22**: Yes baby.
11:23:59 AM **fallinghrt22**: *I am grateful to heavenly father for seeing you through.*
11:24:16 AM **fallinghrt22**: I will never stop thanking him for his wonders.
11:24:41 AM **ladydi2011**: Asher is pissed...He told me I better never do this to him again! Like I did it on purpose!!!!
11:25:58 AM **ladydi2011**: I need to research what "sugar" is all about...
11:26:30 AM **fallinghrt22**: Baby sugar can kill.
11:26:46 AM **fallinghrt22**: I am so happy to be talking to you my beloved wife.
11:27:16 AM **ladydi2011**: Baby, I am so sorry you were so worried. I was unconscious most of the time and when I came through I had no way of reaching you. Asher didn't think to grab my phone.
11:28:25 AM **ladydi2011**: The doctor said if much more time had lapsed I would have been dead.
11:28:50 AM **fallinghrt22**: Oh I will die and follow you baby.
11:29:16 AM **fallinghrt22**: sleepless night and I had sore throat. It was not easy for me baby.
11:29:37 AM **ladydi2011**: I am so sorry baby.

11:29:53 AM **fallinghrt22**: it is never your fault.

11:29:56 AM **fallinghrt22**: I Love you so much

11:29:59 AM **ladydi2011**: I would never put you through something like this on purpose.

11:30:29 AM **fallinghrt22**: I know baby.

11:30:49 AM **fallinghrt22**: wish I am with you now to hold you and never leave your sight.

11:31:53 AM **ladydi2011**: I so wish you were with me. I really need your strong, loving arms around me. I have to tell you that I am still scared baby. This is the closest I have come to death.

11:32:39 AM **fallinghrt22**: I know baby..you are safe.

11:33:08 AM **ladydi2011**: Asher is a good friend and I am so grateful for him, but he is not my love.

11:33:54 AM **fallinghrt22**: I Love you so much my Love and I promise to protect and secure you.

11:33:59 AM **ladydi2011**: I think this is the first time Asher didn't mess with me (tease me)....The dr. told me his face was as white as a ghost when he brought me in.

11:35:22 AM **fallinghrt22**: You mean so much to me my wife.

11:35:34 AM **fallinghrt22**: hope you are feeling much better now and strong baby.

11:35:47 AM **fallinghrt22**: you need a massage and a hug

11:36:18 AM **ladydi2011**: I am still weak but the dr. thinks I am going to be ok. He said I went into sugar shock. What is sugar shock?

11:38:06 AM **ladydi2011**: I am really cold and cannot get warm...I have layers of clothes on and two blankets wrapped around me. I know if you were lying next to me I would be warm and feel safe.

11:38:37 AM **fallinghrt22**: I can't wait to give you a good massage and make you warm and loved.

11:38:56 AM **ladydi2011**: I am so looking forward to this day!

11:39:02 AM **fallinghrt22**: me too baby.

11:39:08 AM **fallinghrt22**: *you wont go out today right?*

11:39:16 AM **ladydi2011**: No baby...

11:40:11 AM **fallinghrt22**: I Love you so much.

11:40:29 AM **fallinghrt22**: I want to get done and be with you my Love. I will never leave your sight.

11:40:45 AM **ladydi2011**: I think it was our love that pulled me through this baby!

11:40:55 AM **fallinghrt22**: Yes baby. I have been praying.

11:41:48 AM **ladydi2011**: Thank you for all your prayers. They worked.

11:43:09 AM **fallinghrt22**: You are welcome my Love.

11:43:12 AM **fallinghrt22**: we are blessed.

11:43:13 AM **ladydi2011**: You know without our health, we have nothing!

11:43:26 AM **fallinghrt22**: Yeh thats true.

11:45:29 AM **ladydi2011**: After I woke up and the dr. told me I almost died, I then thought about many things.

11:47:36 AM **ladydi2011**: Most of all I was grateful that I didn't die. I really want a full life with you my dear. I thought how sad it would be if we didn't get to *live out our love story*. I thought about how this would devastate you!

11:50:15 AM **ladydi2011**: R U there baby?

11:50:52 AM **fallinghrt22**: Baby when I called you and you picked I was speechless until I cried.

11:51:43 AM **ladydi2011**: Baby, what kind of thoughts were going through your mind?

11:53:15 AM **fallinghrt22**: so many things baby, the most I was not able to feel your touch, make Love to you, see you, Kiss you, Marry you, our future together, what would have happened.

11:53:19 AM **fallinghrt22**: so many things baby.

11:56:16 AM **fallinghrt22**: *I just need to start work and get done to get back home..I know now you wont be able to get the funds sent today right?*

11:56:27 AM **ladydi2011**: We now have a taste of how it would be if we didn't have each other...

11:57:26 AM **ladydi2011**: No baby. I am so sorry.

11:58:00 AM **fallinghrt22**: *I understand baby, will it be possible you get it done tomorrow?*

11:58:22 AM **fallinghrt22**: I feel better now talking to you my Love. You are my world.

11:58:56 AM **ladydi2011**: I don't know baby...I do not want to promise you this.

12:00:57 PM **fallinghrt22**: *tell you cant go to the bank or you dont have all the funds yet....???*

12:01:52 PM **ladydi2011**: Asher took my car keys because the dr. said he didn't want me driving for a couple days. I begged him not to and he looked at me and said "Are you serious girl after what you just put me through?" He never talked to me like this.

12:02:15 PM **fallinghrt22**: *I know...can he drive you?*

12:02:55 PM **ladydi2011**: I have half of the money but not the rest. I was supposed to get the rest late Friday, but we know what happened with that plan...

12:03:14 PM **fallinghrt22**: I know.

12:04:20 PM **ladydi2011**: Are you kidding me???? Asher told me you were a fraudster from the very beginning and told me he would kick my ass if I sent you money. He looks out for me baby.

12:04:45 PM **fallinghrt22**: *Oh, Oh. why will he say such, I will surprise him thou*

12:05:51 PM **ladydi2011**: If I tell Asher I sent you $3,500 and you needed another 11k and I was going to send it, he would be hunting you down my love, after he killed me.

12:06:06 PM **fallinghrt22**: Oh

12:06:17 PM **fallinghrt22**: *I understand, but I will never disappoint you.* Thanks for standing by me.

12:06:56 PM **ladydi2011**: Asher is slick. He has done many things and knows many things. He said his mission in life is to teach me things so people cannot get over on me.

12:07:10 PM **fallinghrt22**: *can you tell Daneille to drive you. I need asap baby.*

12:07:54 PM **ladydi2011**: He said I have a big giving heart and I trust too many people. He was even pissed at me when I gave him keys to my house...

12:08:22 PM **fallinghrt22**: *if you have gotten all the funds it is possible you get Danielle to take you to the bank baby.*

12:08:49 PM **ladydi2011**: He said, you know I could make a copy of your key and then wipe you out next time you go out of town...

12:09:39 PM **ladydi2011**: Danielle is angry with you right now. She said if you love me, you would never ask this of me and put me in such a position.

12:09:53 PM **fallinghrt22**: Oh.

12:10:01 PM **fallinghrt22**: *I will surprise them baby*

12:10:11 PM **fallinghrt22**: *thanks so much for trusting me and standing by me.*

12:10:16 PM **fallinghrt22**: *only God knows why.*

12:10:26 PM **fallinghrt22**: *I just dont know how soon you can do this for me.*

12:10:52 PM **ladydi2011**: *So you see baby. I have been warned and warned but I love you and trust you. If I was wrong and they were right, my heart will be broken.*

12:11:46 PM **ladydi2011**: Baby, it might not be until the end of the week that I can help you. Is there someone else who can help you?

12:12:30 PM **fallinghrt22**: *right now there is no one baby thats why I am asking you to do it for me asap so I can get done, I need to be with you.*

12:13:11 PM **fallinghrt22**: *why cant you go out tomorrow?*

12:14:13 PM **ladydi2011**: Asher has my car keys! He said he will not give them back to me until the doctor says it's ok for me to drive. My doctor's appointment is on Thursday morning.

12:15:07 PM **ladydi2011**: Baby, Asher and Danielle are all I have here. My family live far away.

12:15:19 PM **fallinghrt22**: I know baby, I understand.

12:15:43 PM **fallinghrt22**: *will there be possibility you tell Asher you need to get something done,* *that you need your key?*

12:16:11 PM **fallinghrt22**: *he can take you to the bank baby, without knowing what you went there to do.*

12:17:48 PM **fallinghrt22**: *I know you understand how urgent I need this, I shouldn't be stressing you baby, because you need rest my Love.*

12:18:08 PM **ladydi2011**: Baby, I am sorry. I want to do this for you. My first priority has to be gaining my strength back. Asher can see right through me because I am not a good liar. Actually, I am a terrible liar!

12:18:14 PM **fallinghrt22**: I Love you so much and my *desire is to be with you and make you feel safe and secure.*

12:19:25 PM **fallinghrt22**: *do you think you can work out something?*

12:19:44 PM **ladydi2011**: I wish you had done things differently for your China trip baby. When I think about how you went about things, I wonder why you were not more prepared.

12:20:26 PM **fallinghrt22**: I never knew this would happen. it's frustrating baby, we need to finish it baby.

12:22:44 PM **fallinghrt22**: *God will see us through.*

12:23:01 PM **fallinghrt22**: *you own my life Diana Wesley*, never forget how much you have touched me.

12:23:13 PM **ladydi2011**: You know I love you and would do anything for you. Right now, I have to take care of me or you will not have me to come home to. Baby, you know I am already stressed, right?

12:23:59 PM **fallinghrt22**: *I know baby, thats why I am being stressed so you can get this done today or tomorrow so I would be fast honey.*

12:24:02 PM **fallinghrt22**: I feel for you *and you should understand why I am stressing you.*

12:24:44 PM **fallinghrt22**: I am dieing for your touch baby.

12:26:24 PM **ladydi2011**: I just almost died and need to recoup. The doctor said stress would spike my sugar again...Please baby, I cannot go through this again. It is too scary.

12:27:30 PM **fallinghrt22**: I know baby, you do need rest, it would be better me and you together,

12:27:47 PM **fallinghrt22**: *please do find a way to go to the bank today or tomorow. can you?*

12:27:51 PM **ladydi2011**: What I need now is your love and for you to utilize any and all your resources to get yourself out of this jam and come home to me.

12:29:23 PM **ladydi2011**: Baby, if you cannot get yourself out of this jam, how do you plan to take care of me?

12:30:00 PM **fallinghrt22**: Baby how could you say such, I am not poor if not I invested my money on this job, you know baby.

12:30:15 PM **ladydi2011**: You need to be the intelligent, strong, resourceful man I know you are.

12:30:26 PM **fallinghrt22**: *if lets not argue on this, do try to get this done for me today or tomorrow. can you?*

12:30:55 PM **ladydi2011**: Honey, you might have to wait the 21 days for the cashier check to clear if I am unable to get better and help you.

12:31:34 PM **fallinghrt22**: *No baby, if it passes 3 to 4 days I am loosing this job, I know you cant allow that to happen to me.*

12:31:59 PM **ladydi2011**: Ok. I am tired now and this is stressing me and making my heart sad.

12:32:20 PM **fallinghrt22**: *please stop baby, I really need you to understand.*

12:32:29 PM **ladydi2011**: I need TLC now baby, not stress.

12:32:36 PM **fallinghrt22**: *you have the funds just find a way to go to the bank thats all.*

12:32:40 PM **fallinghrt22**: I Love you

12:33:43 PM **ladydi2011**: Let's talk again later. I am now stressed and tired.
12:34:27 PM **fallinghrt22**: *Jess, please stop baby, now you want to make me cry, it is never my intention to make you feel this way Baby, please understand please I beg you think about it and find a way to get this done for me today or tomorrow.......thanks*
12:35:46 PM **ladydi2011**: As I said, I will do my best. I don't feel your love right now.
12:36:11 PM **fallinghrt22**: *please do your best, and never question my Love.*
12:37:51 PM **ladydi2011**: Bye for now.
12:38:53 PM **fallinghrt22**: *I pray you find a way to get this done.... and please when you want to get it done let me know Okay.*
12:39:42 PM **fallinghrt22**: go get some sleep, dream of me, always know that I Love you so much and nothing would stop me from loving you.
12:39:52 PM **fallinghrt22**: Kisses my heartbeat

From: Jerry Wesley [mailto:fallinghrt22@yahoo.com]
Sent: Monday, April 23, 2012 3:04 PM
To: Diana Garren
Subject: my world.

WOW I am speechless, God I thank you so much for making it possible for my wife to live again and didnt leave me in the dark, wish you know the dept of my heart Baby, it calls for just you...thanks for being there when I needed a shoulder to lean on, for patiently listening to my personal problems. Baby, I just want you to know how happy am I to have you in my life and I thank God for that. Thank you for the love and the joy you bring. You've changed my life, Baby. You're the only Woman who gives my heart some excitement and thrills.

When I'm with you I feel like I'm out of control! You taught me how to handle life seriously, you taught me how to solve my problems and to face it without any fear... when I'm with you, I feel no fear, not even a single one. I know that when I admit that I've fallen for you, I know that I wouldn't shed any tears from now on. I love you and that's what I want you to bear in your mind, and it's for keeps. I love you so much my darling

I am just so in love with you! You are everything I have ever wanted! You have fulfilled my life long dream of what I think a woman should be. I want you to know that my love for you is true love and I know you are my soul mate. When you say all you do to me it makes me speechless and when you say I love you it takes my breath away.

Chills run all over my body when you tell me how you love me and how you can't wait to be with me, love me, care for me and make passionate love to me. I think of you and my mind just goes into a frenzy of images of our life together! We have a love that is very rare and will last forever! Our love is truly God sent because we both have been through so much and God knew we needed someone like the two of us are. Someone to love us regardless and to know without doubt that we will always be there no matter what.

I can't wait to be beside you for the rest of my life, to wake beside you every morning seeing your face. To gaze into those beautiful eyes and tell you with my eyes that I love you and you will know what I'm saying without a word. I want to flirt with you all day touch each other hug and kiss in passing.

I would love nothing more than to spend the day cuddling with you or lay outside on a blanket at night under the stars talking, laughing and making out and hoping someone is watching! I want to see new places with you, experience all new things with you and just be where you are all the time. Where ever that is I will be happy as long as we are together.

People who are around will see the love we have and will want that kind of love. There is nothing that I wouldn't do baby to make us work. I know we are meant to be together and as a family. We will have a wonderful life together and our family will be proud to have us as their parents. I am so ready to start our life together!

I will love you forever and nothing can ever change that! You are my dream come true, the love of my life and my prayer answered!

Your man...Jerry

From: Diana Garren
To: Jerry Wesley [mailto:fallinghrt22@yahoo.com]
Subject: Baby, I got all the money we need!
Sent: Apr 24, 2012 10:36 AM

Hi, my love,

Honey, I know our future depends on the job you are doing in China and that you need the money to get this job done so you can come to Atlanta to be with me.

You also know that I needed the money I gave to pay my taxes, so we are both in a bind. I had to take the money I raised for you and pay my taxes. I have been in a deep depression because I would not be able to help you and therefore lose you. I could not bear to let you down or lose you. I have been going crazy knowing I would have to tell you this. Last night I contacted a very wealthy friend of mine. She just called me back. I told her how much I love and trust you and how desperately we want to be together and how you have invested all your money into this job...well, the whole story. I then emailed her your cashier's check. She said she would wire you the entire amount of the cashier's check of $75,000 if you in good faith will send the $3,500. Baby, this solves all our problems and will allow you to get your job done and come home to me and for us to start our life together!

Sweetheart, this is the last resource I have. Please help me help us. You need to come home and marry me. We need to be grandparents to Williams children. We need to grow old together.

I love you
Your wife
Diana

Text Message

To: 6197961879
Sent: Apr 24, 2012 10:38 AM
Subject: Baby, I did it...

Baby, I did it...I did it! I got all the money we need! Please check your email. Now you can do your job and come home to me!!! I love you my husband.

Note: In this text messages and those like it, the "To" messages are those from me, and the "From" messages are from Jerry.

IM Apr 24, 2012 10:53:28 AM

10:53:28 AM **fallinghrt22:** <ding>
10:53:42 AM **fallinghrt22:** my heartbeat
10:54:13 AM **ladydi2011:** Hi my love! Did you get my text and emails?
10:54:34 AM **fallinghrt22:** I am reading.
10:54:38 AM **fallinghrt22:** I Love you
10:55:53 AM **ladydi2011:** I Love you more!!! I am so sorry I pushed you away. I couldn't bare telling you that I had failed you.
10:56:49 AM **fallinghrt22:** *I trusted you baby, that you will not fail me, because my life belongs to you while yours me.*
10:56:58 AM **ladydi2011:** But now I found the way. My friend is going to wire you $75,000!
10:59:02 AM **fallinghrt22:** *Oh you have paid your taxes.....I am glad, you took care of that stress, but remember I will still pay you back with the interest I promise...I will not compromise Baby.*
10:59:08 AM **fallinghrt22:** I Love you to the bone.
11:00:39 AM **ladydi2011:** I love you to the bone and beyond my love!
11:03:02 AM **fallinghrt22:** Baby I don't understand wire me the entire amount of the $75,000
11:03:15 AM **fallinghrt22:** please explain
11:04:42 AM **ladydi2011:** Yes baby. She knows you need all this to get the job done and because I believe in you, so does she. She trusts me baby. She has been my friend for a long time.
11:05:06 AM **fallinghrt22:** is she sending $75.000 to me???
11:06:18 AM **ladydi2011:** I took her to your website and she said she has work she wants you to do for her. She lives in Florida and also has many rich friends. Once they see the work you do for her, they will also hire you.
11:06:30 AM **ladydi2011:** Yes, she will wire you the $75,000
11:07:12 AM **fallinghrt22:** Awwwwwww. thats Awesome...I will be glad to work for them.

11:07:20 AM **fallinghrt22:** *when will she want to wire the money?*

11:07:47 AM ladydi2011: You have to send me the $3,500 that I leant you first so she knows you are a man of your word.

11:08:22 AM **fallinghrt22:** *Baby why didn't you tell her I have nothing on me now, how can we do this?? I trusted you to cover me baby, now you are ashaming me.*

11:09:05 AM **ladydi2011:** I am so glad you send me the scan of the cashier's check. It allowed me to get what you need.

11:09:23 AM **fallinghrt22:** *then let her wire the money. Baby, she has my check, and I need this so fast. please.*

11:09:58 AM **ladydi2011:** These are her terms baby. This is my last resource honey.

11:10:42 AM **fallinghrt22:** *let her send the $75.000 if she want to, I give her my word.*

11:10:58 AM **fallinghrt22:** *Baby can you tell her I did send the money back, and you have it?*

11:11:10 AM **fallinghrt22:** *cover me baby. We need to do this and be together and get married.*

11:12:18 AM **ladydi2011:** No baby. She wants proof of this. I will not lie to her. She has always been there when I need her. *I would never lie to her. It is not who I am honey.*

11:12:55 AM **fallinghrt22:** *why will she bring up this kind of condition, you already know that I am out of cash baby, you know it*

11:13:19 AM **ladydi2011:** Honey, I told her this, but these are her terms.

11:13:38 AM **fallinghrt22:** *You have to find a way to do this if you know you truly Love me and will die for me.*

11:14:25 AM **fallinghrt22:** *You know I can't do this.*

11:14:28 AM **ladydi2011:** I asked if she would cover you for the 11k first and she said no, but this is what she told me she will do.

11:15:03 AM **ladydi2011:** Baby, I have done everything I can possibly do...You are asking me now to do the impossible...

Break In Time

11:19:03 AM **fallinghrt22:** *I got booted*

11:19:19 AM **fallinghrt22:** *you know this is inpossible for me too now, this is crazy*

11:19:39 AM **fallinghrt22:** *how can she give such terms baby, and you know it is inpossible,*

11:19:46 AM **fallinghrt22:** *you have to find a way or talk to her thats all*

11:19:54 AM **ladydi2011:** Everything about this money issue is crazy and is making both of us crazy.

11:20:00 AM **fallinghrt22:** *we need this asap, Baby you are delaying.*

11:20:18 AM **fallinghrt22:** *if she wants to help then she should go ahead*

11:20:34 AM **ladydi2011:** Baby, if you cannot meet her terms, I have no other way to help you.

11:20:50 AM **fallinghrt22:** *then Baby find a way, than this terms, you know it is inpossible.*

11:21:05 AM **fallinghrt22:** *don't forget our Oath,*

11:21:17 AM **fallinghrt22:** *you had the funds and you used it, now you want to fail me.*

11:21:32 AM **ladydi2011:** I cannot do what you need.

11:21:56 AM **fallinghrt22:** *you want me to lose Baby.....you have to find a way to help me baby. don't do this to me.*

11:22:30 AM **fallinghrt22:** *I thought you would be patient Baby, so I can start work and get advance I told you this.*

11:22:34 AM **fallinghrt22:** *why are you doing this.*

11:23:22 AM **ladydi2011:** Jerry, I really thought you loved me. For the last 11 days all our conversations have been about is money...

11:23:50 AM **fallinghrt22:** *why will you say such thing baby, if we leave this aspect then I will lose can't you understand.*

11:24:04 AM **fallinghrt22:** I am not compromising Baby, this is hurting. I Love you with all my heart

11:24:29 AM **ladydi2011:** Baby, maybe you need to find a woman who has money. It isn't me!

11:24:51 AM **fallinghrt22:** *why baby, you should know better than listening to your friends term, I dont want her to do the $75K if I can just get the 11K thats all.*

11:25:04 AM **fallinghrt22:** *please stop this, I choosed you because you are meant for her.*

11:25:08 AM **ladydi2011:** You have broken my heart.

11:25:32 AM **fallinghrt22:** *me*...I am not poor niether I want you for money or anything..I want to take care of you.*

11:25:42 AM **fallinghrt22:** why will you say such to me.

11:26:01 AM **fallinghrt22:** *You know what to do baby.*

11:26:04 AM **ladydi2011:** You have my whole heart baby.

11:26:20 AM **fallinghrt22:** if you want to help me then go ahead.

11:26:40 AM **ladydi2011:** Baby, I want to help you but I can't.

11:26:58 AM **fallinghrt22:** *I know you can.*

11:27:11 AM **fallinghrt22:** *did you use all the 11K you got at first?*

11:27:39 AM **ladydi2011:** *I only got $4,500 and yes, I had to use it.*

11:27:59 AM **fallinghrt22:** *honey can you do this to me??*

11:28:11 AM **fallinghrt22:** *please dont fail me.*

11:28:25 AM **ladydi2011:** Baby, I cannot. Not without my friends help.

11:28:59 AM **ladydi2011:** I am sorry baby.

11:29:31 AM **fallinghrt22:** *why did you tell her I'm the one needing this? You should know better.*

11:30:38 AM **ladydi2011:** *I am honest baby. I cannot lie. It is one of the commandments, remember!*

11:30:51 AM **fallinghrt22:** *I never told you to lie. You need to help us baby.*

11:31:27 AM **ladydi2011:** well telling her it was for me would have been a lie. Then she would want to know why she was wiring it to China and not Georgia.

11:31:58 AM **fallinghrt22:** *she should have wire it to you, then you wire it to me.*

11:32:02 AM **fallinghrt22:** *why did you do this?*

11:32:11 AM **fallinghrt22:** my head is hot.

11:32:48 AM **fallinghrt22:** *why can;t she do this, she has my check scan.*

11:32:59 AM **ladydi2011:** Baby, you didn't even ask me how I was feeling today.

11:33:21 AM **fallinghrt22:** I text you to ask baby, didn't you get my emails?

11:33:30 AM **ladydi2011:** Nope...

11:33:49 AM **ladydi2011:** Jerry, do you really love me?

11:36:02 AM **fallinghrt22:** Are you there baby.

11:36:35 AM **fallinghrt22:** I text you to ask how is were baby. And did email you

Break In Time

11:43:31 AM **ladydi2011:** I got booted this time. Are you there?

11:49:06 AM **fallinghrt22:** <ding>

11:49:35 AM **ladydi2011:** <ding>

11:50:16 AM **fallinghrt22:** *Baby can you call and tell her, we can't get the $3500?*

11:50:44 AM **fallinghrt22:** I Love you. we have to be together.

11:51:04 AM **fallinghrt22:** *No matter what this is a testing time baby..please do this for us.*

11:51:12 AM **ladydi2011:** I love you too

11:51:31 AM **ladydi2011:** I failed the test. I am sorry

11:51:54 AM **ladydi2011:** *This is also your testing time with me....*

11:52:38 AM **ladydi2011:** *I need to know you can take care of things. I need a man I can trust to handle things baby.*

11:53:33 AM **ladydi2011:** *You have put a lot of stress on me. Everything has been about you and your success. What about me. Go back and read our correspondences.*

11:54:42 AM **ladydi2011:** R U there?

11:56:07 AM **fallinghrt22:** <ding>

11:56:22 AM **ladydi2011:** Ok baby...I have to go to work. It is almost noon.

11:57:06 AM **fallinghrt22:** I got booted.

11:57:20 AM **fallinghrt22:** Baby I am so down right now

11:57:30 AM **ladydi2011:** I am down too!

11:57:45 AM **ladydi2011:** Do you think this is easy for me?

11:58:06 AM **ladydi2011:** To think that money is going to destroy us...

11:59:08 AM **ladydi2011:** When I cannot change things, I need to go back to my saying so I can cope, "It is what it is"...This time it hurts like hell!

12:00:11 PM **fallinghrt22:** *Nothing will destroy us, if we can do this. I still have faith in you baby.*

12:00:31 PM **fallinghrt22:** *you can talk to your friend, if you do want to help us,*

12:00:40 PM **ladydi2011:** *"if" is a big word baby...You just did destroy us with "if"*

12:00:50 PM **fallinghrt22:** *you have a 41K account, I still dont know why you can't do this for me.*

12:01:20 PM **ladydi2011:** Good bye my love. I will always remember you and I will love you forever

12:01:30 PM **fallinghrt22:** *I have made so much promise to you, Baby I know what I will do for us.*

12:01:42 PM **fallinghrt22:** hun what did you just say???

12:01:59 PM **ladydi2011:** I cannot do what you want...

12:02:08 PM **fallinghrt22:** *I know you can.*

12:02:27 PM **fallinghrt22:** *I know you can do this for me because I trust you.*

12:02:50 PM **fallinghrt22:** *I'm paying this back, why cant you reason with me.*

12:03:00 PM **fallinghrt22:** *remmeber your promise to me, never to give up on me*

12:03:14 PM **fallinghrt22:** I will never give up on you or let you go Baby, I can never

12:05:31 PM **ladydi2011:** Baby, when you get things worked out, you know how to reach me and where I live. I pray that one day soon you will ring my doorbell and keep your promises to me. I cannot do what you need concerning this money.

12:06:14 PM **fallinghrt22:** *You are not leaving me, you have promised to help me....call your friend and talk to her....if you want too.*

12:06:26 PM **fallinghrt22:** *don't you have a 41K account baby.*

12:06:35 PM **fallinghrt22:** please why are you pushing me away?

12:07:01 PM **fallinghrt22:** I'm not leaving you, we have to do this together.

12:07:14 PM **ladydi2011:** I am not pushing you away. You are pushing me away.

12:07:36 PM **fallinghrt22:** how am I pushing you away, I am fighting for us baby.

12:08:02 PM **fallinghrt22:** *where is your trust, talk to your friend baby, you have a 41K account baby...you can do this for us.*

12:08:58 PM **ladydi2011:** Baby, you are fighting for money, not us. I don't have money. I already gave you all I have. I trusted you so much that I put myself in a bind. Baby, let me ask you, what have you done for me?

12:10:06 PM **fallinghrt22:** I know my plans for us.

12:10:20 PM **fallinghrt22:** I am not fighting for money, I am fighting to take care of you.

12:10:58 PM **fallinghrt22:** *I am looking all I have invested in this job Diana, please if you have a heart, talk to your friend...you can do anything for Love please.*

12:11:20 PM **fallinghrt22:** *if you are in this position I would never let you down, only God knows my heart*

12:11:27 PM **fallinghrt22:** dont hurt me. I know you can do this for me.

12:11:53 PM **ladydi2011:** brb...my brother just called

12:12:16 PM **fallinghrt22:** *I know it Baby.....you told me you have gotten the funds just to go to the bank is the problem and you promised to go this week, now whats the problem....please talk to me*

12:13:47 PM **fallinghrt22:** *why not do this for us to we will be happy, I know I have stressed u but I promise to make it up to you baby, I am your husband, you are in a position to help me now, why fail me baby, you have given me your word that you will stand by me, are you not a woman of your word, what has happened to that...please talk to me....*

12:14:08 PM **fallinghrt22:** *I do need an answer, has the devil come over you, please dont give up on me.*

12:18:46 PM **fallinghrt22:** I Love you....I need you.

12:18:56 PM **fallinghrt22:** so much now baby.

12:22:21 PM **fallinghrt22:** <ding>

12:26:57 PM **fallinghrt22:** <ding>

12:27:58 PM **fallinghrt22:** Baby are you there?

12:33:05 PM **fallinghrt22:** You are ignoring me honey.

12:35:49 PM **fallinghrt22:** <ding>

12:37:57 PM **ladydi2011:** No. I was on phone with my brother.

12:38:26 PM **fallinghrt22:** please read my messages.

12:40:00 PM **ladydi2011:** What??? Has the devil come over me??? What kind of question is this?

12:40:41 PM **fallinghrt22:** I am just scared baby.

12:40:47 PM **ladydi2011:** I have to work. I have spent all morning working on getting you money and talking with you.

12:40:47 PM **fallinghrt22:** *please do this for us.*

12:41:18 PM **fallinghrt22:** *Baby I do want you to do this for me, I am counting on you. please*

12:41:45 PM **fallinghrt22:** *I'm so weak, I have never loved this much to get hurt and destroyed, I pray you do know why I took an Oath with you.*

12:42:03 PM **fallinghrt22:** you mean so much to me.

12:42:14 PM **ladydi2011:** You are hurting me a lot right now!

12:42:29 PM **fallinghrt22:** *Baby, I dont want to $75K......just do this $11K for me please*

12:42:45 PM **fallinghrt22:** I am not hurting you baby. I am just sorry for stressing you

12:42:47 PM **ladydi2011:** Please go back and read our IM's and you will see how everything has been about money.

12:42:50 PM **fallinghrt22:** *I promise to make it up to you*

12:43:22 PM **fallinghrt22:** *Baby everything is not about money, if you get the 11K for me, and I start work we will stop talking about money, cant you see*

12:44:27 PM **ladydi2011:** I am still trying to recover from what happened to me over the weekend. Now my stress is through the roof, I feel it in my neck. I am scared it is going to happen to me again. Can't you see what this is doing to me?

12:44:58 PM **fallinghrt22:** it wont Baby, you just worry yourself, please calm down.....

12:45:05 PM **fallinghrt22:** *do things right for us please*

12:45:12 PM **fallinghrt22:** *I know you can do this*

12:45:16 PM **fallinghrt22:** *I do trust you.*

12:45:36 PM **ladydi2011:** You are not letting me calm down. You are putting this problem on me

12:45:53 PM **fallinghrt22:** honey I am not putting it on you.

12:46:00 PM **fallinghrt22:** *just help us with what is right*

12:46:00 PM **ladydi2011:** *If this is what you consider "love", it is not healthy for me!*

12:46:19 PM **fallinghrt22:** Baby, if I dont have this problem why wil I talk about it.

12:46:47 PM **fallinghrt22:** *I am not stupid. this project is worth, 850,000,00$ Baby...*

12:46:56 PM **fallinghrt22:** I hope you see reasons for my cry.

12:47:24 PM **fallinghrt22:** *just do the $11K so I can start*

12:47:25 PM **ladydi2011:** I know you are not stupid.

12:48:07 PM **ladydi2011:** Let me talk to my friend again. She is a high-end attorney and in court all day today. I will not be able to reach her until later tonight.

12:48:29 PM **fallinghrt22:** *Ok thanks....do your best, just 11K*

12:49:52 PM **ladydi2011:** Ok. I am going to go now. Get some sleep.

12:50:04 PM **fallinghrt22:** *honey can I count on you???*

12:50:13 PM **fallinghrt22:** it will be hard for me to sleep thou

12:50:26 PM **fallinghrt22:** I will never leave your sight once we are together.

12:50:31 PM **ladydi2011:** You can count on me to ask her.

12:50:48 PM **ladydi2011:** Will we ever be together?????

12:51:00 PM **fallinghrt22:** are you loosing faith?

12:51:08 PM **fallinghrt22:** I know we will

12:51:57 PM **fallinghrt22:** *dont forget, anyone who breaks the law of an oath, you know the consequences.*

12:52:18 PM **ladydi2011:** What???

12:52:40 PM **fallinghrt22:** I am sorry about how you feel.

12:53:06 PM **ladydi2011:** What??? Don't forget, anyone who breaks the law of an oath, you know the consequences.

12:53:15 PM **fallinghrt22:** I do Love you so much and want to spend the rest of my life with you.

12:53:25 PM **fallinghrt22:** our Oath baby.

12:54:04 PM **ladydi2011:** I will be with you only because I "want" to be...Do not threaten me!

12:54:36 PM **fallinghrt22:** *Baby, it is not a threaten, this is the word from God, for better for worst, we agreed.*

12:55:01 PM **ladydi2011:** You're good!

12:55:13 PM **fallinghrt22:** I pray you know what you have done to my heart

12:55:23 PM **fallinghrt22:** I am so in Love and I would do anything for Love.

12:55:57 PM **ladydi2011:** I use to know. Honestly, I have MANY doubts!!!

12:56:27 PM **fallinghrt22:** please trust me.

12:56:30 PM **ladydi2011:** You have changed so much since you went to China.

12:56:52 PM **ladydi2011:** Btw...I still have not received our wedding set in the mail.

12:57:27 PM **fallinghrt22:** *Baby I told you I have not been able to send it, I have no cash on me...you know it*

12:57:37 PM **fallinghrt22:** *thats why I asked for extra 1K.*

12:58:13 PM **ladydi2011:** I really have to go to work. I have a client call in 3 min.

12:58:46 PM **fallinghrt22:** *Ok baby, I hope to hear better result from you asap.*

12:58:51 PM **fallinghrt22:** I Love you so much.

12:58:56 PM **ladydi2011:** bye for now. Sleep well...

12:59:22 PM **fallinghrt22:** Wet Kisses and Hugs

From: Diana Garren
Sent: Tuesday, April 24, 2012 6:23 PM
To: Jerry Wesley [mailto:fallinghrt22@yahoo.com]
Subject: letter

Hello, my husband,

I have been a mess for almost two weeks now. We promised to always communicate and so I am going to pour my heart out to you in this email. I am going to tell you everything I am feeling. We have not "really" communicated in weeks. We promised each other that we would always communicate.

I went back and re-read your profile. I want to be with this Jerry. Where is the man I met and fell in love with? Where did you go? The man who stated the below in his profile...

"Thanks for taking the time to learn more about me. I feel truly blessed. I'm healthy, and a big heart. I have had a successful career. I'm well mannered and treat women respectfully. I believe in opening doors and pulling chairs. I understand that you are fully capable of opening a door or pulling a chair out for yourself, but it's just a sign of respect. It's just a nonverbal way of saying that you mean something to me. I'm a pretty romantic guy.. I just believe in free will and trust alot too.I cook then starve..

That's probably my strongest trait, along with the desire to talk to my partner. If we can't talk, then what are we doing really.I 'm very affectionate with my woman and she gets my undivided attention when we are together. My woman will always feel secure, safe, and loved by me. When I say "my woman", I don't mean that in a possessive way, but rather the one I love and I 'm dedicated too.I 'm a one woman guy, and I believe I have a lot to offer the right woman.I never thought that I would resort to online dating, but I think i must give it a try.

We found ways to make each day an adventure, and every now and then, found a way to sneak in a real adventure too... but all in all, it was the sharing that made it special. We are each far from perfect, but together... We were.... are....Perfection. lets get to converse and see what we can offer to each other."

I loved you unconditionally. I honored and respected you. I trusted you. I gave you my heart. I wish we could laugh again. The last time I laughed and smiled was before you left for China.

From the beginning I have supported you in your goals in every way I can. I want you to succeed. Ever since April 11th everything has been about money. I did what I could for you without hesitation or question. Ever since April 13th you have asked again and again and have tried to push me into

137

doing something I cannot do. I exhausted my last resource today and you cannot meet her terms. I have nowhere else to go to help you. This is your problem. You are a grown man, and you need to fix your problem. Please stop depending on me to fix your problem. I cannot fix what is going on there for you. Please do not ask me again for money. This is not good for our relationship or my health. If I matter to you, then please stop. If you ask me for money again, I am no longer going to communicate with you. I know you wouldn't want to do this to me. Please, if you love me at all then honor my request and do not ask me for money again. Please, please, please!

Love,
Diana

I contacted a private investigator friend of mine to see if she could help me scam him to get my money back. I didn't think the strategy she proposed would work, but I tried it anyway. He did not like the deal I was trying to strike and said, "I trusted you to cover me baby, now you are ashaming me." I had to laugh at this statement. He is the one that scammed me and made me feel embarrassed and ashamed. I told him he needed to find a woman with money because I didn't have any. He claims that he has money and will take care of me. A scammer will NEVER take care of you. They are narcissistic parasites. He was upset when I told him I raised $4,500 but used it. His comment was, "honey, how can you do this to me? Please don't fail me." Do it to him? Don't fail him? Excuse me!

I was really shocked when he asked "has the devil come over you?" He is not happy because I am not cooperating. He then tries the sympathy tactic when he tells me that if I were in his position he would not let me down and that God is the only one that knows his heart and asked me to not hurt him. "Romance Scams" thrive on the premise that a person *"WILL DO ANYTHING FOR LOVE"*. This is what makes me call this type of scam *"MOLESTATION FOR MONEY"*. The scammer goes through the same grooming process a sexual predator does, and the key words for both crimes are "You will do this if you love me". Scammers for money groom their prey like sexual predators do for sex.

I told him he is NOT the man I fell in love with and I am tired of him asking me for money and requested that he didn't do it again. However the only thing on his mind is trying to get me to give him money. Scammers know that if they can get money from you once, they can usually get more, so they push hard.

RED FLAGS

- He is still asking for money. I know you read all of this in the chat but I want you to see in one place how relentless a scammer is…"Oh you have paid your taxes…..I am glad, you took care of that stress, but remember I will still pay you back with the interest I promise...I will not compromise Baby.", "when will she want to wire the money?", "then let her wire the money, Baby. she has my check, and I need this so fast. please.", " let her send the $75.000 if she want to, I give her my word.", "Baby can you tell her I did send the money back, and you have it? cover me baby.", "***You have to find a way to do this if you know you truly Love me and will die for me***.", "you have to find a way or talk to her. thats all", "we need this asap, Baby you are delaying.", "if she wants to help then she should go ahead", "then Baby find a way, than this terms, you know it is inpossible.", "you need to help us baby.", "you want me to lose Baby.....you have to find a way to help me baby. don't do this to me. "Baby can you call and tell her, we can't get the $3500?", "No matter what this is a testing time baby. please do this for us.", "Nothing will destroy us, if we can do this. I still have faith in you baby.", "I'm paying this back, why cant you reason with me.", "***remmeber your promise to me, never to give up on me***", "***You are not leaving me, you have promised to help me***....call your friend and talk to her....if you want too.", "where is your trust, talk to your friend baby, you have a 41K account baby...you can do this for us.", "I am looking all I have invested in this job ***Diana, please if you have a heart, talk to your friend...you can do anything for Love please***.", "I know you can do this for me.", "I know it Baby.....you told me you have gotten the funds just to go to the bank is the problem and you promised to go this week, now whats the problem....please talk to me", "why not do this for us to we will be happy, I know I have stressed u but I promise to make it up to you baby, I am your husband, you are in a position to help me now, why fail me baby, ***you have given me your word that you will stand by me, are you not a woman of your word, what has happened to that***...please talk to me....", "please do this for us.", "Baby I do want you to do this for me, I am counting on you. please", "Baby, I dont want to $75K......just do this $11K for me please", "Baby everything is not about money, if you get the 11K for me, and I start work we will stop talking about money, cant you see", "do things right for us please", "I know you can do this. I do trust you.", "just help us with what is right", "just do the $11K so I can start", "do your best, just 11K", "honey can I count on you???", "Ok baby, I hope to hear better result from you asap."

- A scammer wants you to lie to your friends and family. He says, "why did you tell her I'm the one needing this? you should know better". Then he wants me to lie to her and tell her he paid me the money and have her wire the money to me so I can wire it to him. He stops at nothing to get the money and you can see how quick on his feet he is with ways to achieve this.

- He asks me to use my 401k account. "you have a 41K account, I still dont know why you can't do this for me. I know you can do this for me because I trust you." scammers will always bring up trust.

- Again he brings up the oath and that I am failing him. He tells me "I pray you do know why I took an oath with you". Then he threatens me with "dont forget, anyone who breaks the law of an oath, you know the conseguences. A scammer uses anything they can to manipulate and even scare you to get your money. He did the oath early on so he can use it now. Do NOT let a scammer scare you!

🏴 He blames it on me for him to lose. A scammer never takes responsibility.

🏴 A scammer uses the word "weak". "I'm so weak, I have never loved this much to get hurt and destroyed." Whenever they say they are "weak", this is a red flag.

🏴 He says, "I promise to make it up to you". This is another thing scammers say. More false promises.

🏴 He says, "I have made so much promise to you". Yes, he did. A scammer ALWAYS makes false promises to you in order to get you hooked, but he will NEVER keep those promises. Be careful to not fall in love with the "false" promises.

🏴 A scammer talks big dollars to play into the greedy side of people, to make you think if you don't help him he will lose, and also to make you think he is doing this to take care of you.

🏴 "I am not stupid. this project is worth, 850,000,00$ Baby..." They also put the dollar sign after the money amount instead of before it.

IM Apr 24, 2012 7:10:18 PM

7:10:18 PM **fallinghrt22**: Hi Sweetheart.
7:11:05 PM **ladydi2011**: Did you get some sleep?
7:12:15 PM **ladydi2011**: R U there?
7:16:15 PM **fallinghrt22**: *I got booted*
7:16:24 PM **fallinghrt22**: I miss you
7:17:16 PM **ladydi2011**: <ding>
7:18:21 PM **fallinghrt22**: <ding>
7:18:46 PM **ladydi2011**: How was your night?
7:19:29 PM **fallinghrt22**: My night was okay I tried to sleep. But slept a little. Been thinking alot
7:19:38 PM **fallinghrt22**: I love you.
7:19:51 PM **ladydi2011**: Please let's not talk about money. Please!
7:20:16 PM **fallinghrt22**: *Are you getting it for me??*
7:20:36 PM **ladydi2011**: What did I just ask you?
7:20:59 PM **fallinghrt22**: I don't understand.
7:22:04 PM **fallinghrt22**: *I know. I don't want to talk about it tonight. That's why I said if you are getting it for me??*
7:22:36 PM **fallinghrt22**: It is very important I know. I wish you know what I'm passing through. I'm dieing in silence.
7:22:50 PM **fallinghrt22**: I love you baby
7:22:56 PM **fallinghrt22**: So tell me did you eat?
7:23:01 PM **ladydi2011**: That is talking about money. Please don't.
7:23:19 PM **fallinghrt22**: Okay I'm not
7:23:28 PM **fallinghrt22**: *But know that I'm not happy*
7:23:58 PM **ladydi2011**: I ate pizza.

7:25:13 PM **ladydi2011**: I have been thinking too. I am not happy either. I have not smiled or laughed since you left for China.

7:27:38 PM **fallinghrt22**: I have to leave here and be with you honey

7:27:44 PM **fallinghrt22**: I'm hungry for you so much

7:28:27 PM **ladydi2011**: Hmmmmm

7:29:05 PM **fallinghrt22**: When are we going to be together baby? I want to make love to you baby!

7:29:14 PM **ladydi2011**: The last 2 weeks has taken away everything I felt for you!

7:29:53 PM **fallinghrt22**: You are the one seeing it so.

7:30:23 PM **fallinghrt22**: *I just wish you will do what I ask so I can start work. And everything will be normal*

7:30:58 PM **ladydi2011**: Why will you not video chat with me? You promised me this before you left.

7:32:06 PM **fallinghrt22**: *Baby I told you I needed to go miles to get a webcam. And I'm broke.*

7:32:19 PM **fallinghrt22**: See please I wish you know how I feel

7:32:40 PM **fallinghrt22**: *You don't even ask if I eat. Why did I demand for extra 1k??*

7:32:54 PM **ladydi2011**: You told me you took care of that before you left

7:33:24 PM **ladydi2011**: No, I didn't ask if you ate.

7:33:30 PM **fallinghrt22**: *Its not an inbuilt webcam. So I needed to get one. I want you to see me while I see you too*

7:34:10 PM **fallinghrt22**: *I would be fine without food*

7:34:14 PM **fallinghrt22**: *I need my job or I will lose.*

7:34:36 PM **ladydi2011**: Are you going to have breakfast?

7:34:50 PM **fallinghrt22**: *I'm out of cash.*

7:35:01 PM **ladydi2011**: What food do you like there?

7:35:03 PM **fallinghrt22**: I would be fine without food baby.

7:35:48 PM **fallinghrt22**: Soup. Rice. Barbecue chicken. Peanut butter.

7:36:02 PM **ladydi2011**: *You are now making me feel guilty. Please stop. I did not do this to you!!!*

7:36:30 PM **fallinghrt22**: I never want you to feel quity that's why I said I would be fine

7:36:55 PM **fallinghrt22**: *If you do care all I ask is for me to start work.*

7:37:28 PM **fallinghrt22**: I missed you tremendously. It hurts

7:38:12 PM **ladydi2011**: I like wonton soup. Have you had some?

7:38:40 PM **fallinghrt22**: 2days ago

7:39:03 PM **fallinghrt22**: Can I ask you soomething??

7:39:04 PM **ladydi2011**: Did you like it?

7:39:58 PM **fallinghrt22**: *Should I still count on you??*

7:40:14 PM **fallinghrt22**: Yes I like it

7:40:42 PM **ladydi2011**: See, you can't just be with me...It's ALL about the money!

7:41:14 PM **fallinghrt22**: ?????

7:42:15 PM **fallinghrt22**: I miss you and it hurts. I'm in the dark. Do hear my cry

7:42:22 PM **ladydi2011**: I hope you have a wonderful day as I sleep.

7:42:38 PM **fallinghrt22**: Are you ready too sleep?

7:44:00 PM **fallinghrt22**: Why are you so tell me please

7:44:54 PM **ladydi2011**: I am ready to go to sleep.

7:45:17 PM **fallinghrt22**: I will always love you

7:46:04 PM **fallinghrt22**: *Find a way to help me get out of this asap. I will pay back. I asked you about your 41k account you didn't respond.*

7:46:23 PM **fallinghrt22**: *All I asked is the 11K so I can start work.*

7:46:36 PM **ladydi2011**: Good night

7:47:22 PM **fallinghrt22**: *Think about it baby. I love you*
7:47:59 PM **fallinghrt22**: You signed out. Okay goood night. Love you

---

From: Diana Garren
Sent: Wednesday, April 25, 2012 1:00 AM
To: Jerry Wesley [mailto:fallinghrt22@yahoo.com]
Subject: Money

I just got off the phone with my investor friend, and she said she is not interested in investing small amounts of money. 11k will only provide her $2,200 interest and 75k will yield her $15,000 in interest.

She is a wise business woman and only wants to deal with smart business people. Her terms are still the same. She said if you are not able to put up $3,500 for $75,000 and more if you need it, she is not interested in doing business. She said you can take it or leave it...she is not the one who needs the money, you are!

You would be a fool not to take this deal and have her on your side...she is a big money person. Please let me know what you want to do. I am going back to sleep now.

Diana

From: Jerry Wesley [mailto:fallinghrt22@yahoo.com]
Sent: Wednesday, April 25, 2012 1:47 PM
To: Diana Garren
Subject: Money

Good morning love and how was your night?? missed you so much and it hurts knowing that you are trying to push me away. I want you to know that I'm a good business man. You friend can't tell me to return the 3500. When you know I dont have a way to do that right now. And you can't even help matters as you have done baby. I still don't understand if you are still keeping your word to me. I sit down and wonder what I have done wrong. I said I will pay. I have asked you if you can get funds from your 41K account you never answered me. I'm beginning to wonder if you really want to help me or not. Time is going baby. I'm losing this. Why not do this for me I beg you. If I did offend you then forgive me and help me. Go back and read your emails to me. ***Remember your last word that you will never give up on me. Do you keep to your word??*** Am I dreaming or what? Not now that I'm in love.

It is still all about obtaining money from me. When I try to pull the deal away from him he sends me an email with an apology but continues to try to get the money. However, I can tell he is getting worn down. I am a very tenacious person when I want something, and I want to know *"who the real man behind the screen is"* that scammed me. I DO NOT recommend you do this! The emotional hell is way too much!

RED FLAGS

- Within ten minutes he starts badgering for money again and continues for twenty minutes. Scammers are relentless…"Are you getting it for me??", "You don't even ask if I eat. Why did I **demand** for extra 1k??", "If you do care all I ask is for me to start work.", "Should I still count on you??", "Find a way to help me get out of this asap. I will pay back. I asked you about your 41k account you didn't respond.", "All I asked is the 11K so I can start work.", "Think about it baby.", "I just wish you will do what I ask so I can start work. And everything will be normal".
- He finally said the right word, "demand". Scammers will demand money from you.
- Scammers also tell you "they are not happy" when you don't do as they want.
- He still has excuses for not having a webcam. Scammers always have excuses of why they don't have a web cam unless they use a "fictitious" webcam. Don't be fooled by this. You will learn about fictitious webcams in chapter four (p. 369) and seven (p. 677).
- Again he says, "Remember your last word that you will never give up on me. Do you keep to your word??" This is more guilt he is using.

IM Apr 26, 2012 4:20:53 PM

4:20:53 PM **ladydi2011:** Hi
4:21:49 PM **fallinghrt22:** How are you?
4:22:07 PM **ladydi2011:** I am sad. And you?
4:22:32 PM **fallinghrt22:** What's happening to us???
4:22:38 PM **fallinghrt22:** *What can you caused??*
4:22:53 PM **ladydi2011:** Excuse me???
4:24:42 PM **ladydi2011:** What does "What can you caused?
4:25:14 PM **fallinghrt22:** *I meant what have you caused??*
4:25:23 PM **fallinghrt22:** Why will I push you away.
4:25:33 PM **fallinghrt22:** Please I have one thing to ask you.
4:25:40 PM **ladydi2011:** What do you mean what did I cause?
4:25:55 PM **fallinghrt22:** Who am I to you. Am I important to you??do you care anymore??
4:26:14 PM **ladydi2011:** Hmmm
4:26:34 PM **fallinghrt22:** *I know you can help me. But obviously. Yu don't want too*
4:26:44 PM **ladydi2011:** Here we go again...
4:26:52 PM **fallinghrt22:** I asked you something you skipt it and you never answered
4:26:59 PM **fallinghrt22:** Here we go again meaning??
4:27:33 PM **fallinghrt22:** Will I be happy talking to you with my problems. Don't you think???
4:27:37 PM **ladydi2011:** It is called a 401k. I do not have one.
4:27:59 PM **ladydi2011:** You are asking me to do what I cannot do.
4:28:15 PM **fallinghrt22:** *Oh let me tell you something. I can read you. You think I don't care right.*

4:28:26 PM **fallinghrt22:** *I know you can help me. But you don't want to.* Please tell me why???

4:28:56 PM **ladydi2011:** You cannot read me. You don't have a clue who I am!

4:29:25 PM **fallinghrt22:** Trust me I know you

4:29:42 PM **fallinghrt22:** *You don't want to help me cause I know you can do it*

4:30:08 PM **ladydi2011:** Oh how I wish you were the man you portrayed yourself to be. We could have had a wonderful life together. You would have been an extremely happy man! You would have had "true love" and an "extraordinary" life with me. I am exactly who I told you I am. Everything I ever said to you was true and real. Unfortunately, you did not do the same.

4:31:08 PM **fallinghrt22:** How can you tell

4:31:15 PM **fallinghrt22:** *I wish you can do this for us*

4:31:28 PM **ladydi2011:** I easily gave you the money because I thought you were in trouble, I trusted you when you said I would have it back in 2 days, I wanted you to be successful and I cared about your well-being. What I know now is you were never in love with me. You played me and lied to me. You never cared about my well-being and you are definitely not someone who my heart or anything else is safe with!

4:32:14 PM **fallinghrt22:** Why are you saying this to me?? What have I done?

4:32:42 PM **fallinghrt22:** All I asked was your help. So I can do what I came here for??

4:33:05 PM **fallinghrt22:** *Diana I did nothing wrong asking the one I love to help me. You agreed. Now what happened?*

4:33:11 PM **ladydi2011:** This is how I feel. You have hurt me deeply. I don't have it!!!

4:33:41 PM **fallinghrt22:** *Then find it for me*

4:35:11 PM **fallinghrt22:** Do you know the worth of this job. Do you really care. It is my life baby. Please I'm going insane. I do love you. Why not do this for me please

4:35:37 PM **ladydi2011:** You told me it is worth $850,000.

4:36:02 PM **ladydi2011:** Jerry, you put yourself in this position

4:37:41 PM **fallinghrt22:** *Baby how much can you get for me now?*

4:37:52 PM **fallinghrt22:** I do want us to do this, believe me.

4:39:57 PM **ladydi2011:** I spoke with Bank of America and they confirmed that the cashier's check you scanned and sent to me is fraudulent. They do not have any such routing numbers in their ledger. They also do not have a customer by the name of Jerry Wesley or a business customer by the name of BehrKylan Constructions. Would you like to explain this to me please.....

4:41:30 PM **fallinghrt22:** *did you remember what I told you about my account, that no one can call to comfirm or ask about it, because of the hack someone tried to hack my account?*

4:42:03 PM **ladydi2011:** Yes, but it doesn't explain that the cashier's check you scanned and sent to me is fraudulent. They do not have any such routing numbers in their ledger.

4:42:24 PM **fallinghrt22:** they won't tell you.

4:43:36 PM **ladydi2011:** Ok...would you like to tell me how the cashier's check was cut on 4/13 from the bank in San Francisco when you supposedly left CA on 4/11 and I wired you money on 4/12???

4:45:57 PM **fallinghrt22:** that was the date I told them to sign on it.

4:46:04 PM **ladydi2011:** "I am smart dearie!" These are the words you first said to me...correct? Please know that I am smart too!

4:46:27 PM **fallinghrt22:** Baby, I can't lie to you *know* that you are trying to bring up issues that will break us, and I will never allow that to happen. I do Love you.

4:47:03 PM **ladydi2011:** Why would you have them put the 13th on the check when you knew you had to go right to work?

4:47:31 PM **fallinghrt22:** because that was the day, I would be getting the check cashed baby.

4:47:36 PM **ladydi2011:** Two and two are not adding up...

4:47:58 PM **fallinghrt22:** it can't back date, it should be recent baby dont you think

4:48:35 PM **fallinghrt22:** *please can you get this funds for me? I am loosing this job.*

4:49:10 PM **ladydi2011:** How have you been able to stay in China for 15 days on $400?

4:49:19 PM **ladydi2011:** Nothing is adding up baby....

4:49:55 PM **fallinghrt22:** why did I ask you for $1000 extra?

4:50:02 PM **fallinghrt22:** I explained this to you.

4:50:14 PM **ladydi2011:** I mean the last 15 days?????

4:50:15 PM **fallinghrt22:** why are you doing this? Baby dont you want me anymore?

4:50:25 PM **ladydi2011:** How have you paid for the hotel?

4:51:05 PM **fallinghrt22:** I am oweing.

4:51:09 PM **ladydi2011:** I am not doing anything baby....you have done this.

4:51:20 PM **fallinghrt22:** *believing I will start work or you get me the $1000*

4:51:34 PM **fallinghrt22:** Baby, I dont want you to give up on me, or loose me believe me

4:51:44 PM **fallinghrt22:** *please do this for us, if you do Love me*

4:52:37 PM **ladydi2011:** Baby, if you really loved me, you would not ask me to do this. You would never put me in jeopardy like you have.

4:53:06 PM **fallinghrt22:** I have promised you that I will refund this money, I just need to start work.

4:53:13 PM **fallinghrt22:** I am paying you with interest baby.

4:53:16 PM **ladydi2011:** Please do not say "If I love you" I will do this.

4:53:22 PM **fallinghrt22:** *tell me how much can you get for me??*

4:53:30 PM **ladydi2011:** Nothing!

4:54:51 PM **ladydi2011:** I have to hand it to you, you are good baby at getting a woman to fall in love with you and obtain small amounts of money from them. But, you have a lot to learn my dear to be able to get large sums of money from me or any woman who is paying attention. You made MANY mistakes. I will never divulge these mistakes to you. I will never give you anything that will advance your deception and fraud scheme.

4:55:30 PM **fallinghrt22:** *Now you are acusing me right.*

4:55:49 PM **fallinghrt22:** *I will do something, can you help me with my flight money so I can come back and get capital?*

4:56:25 PM **fallinghrt22:** I want you to see me, please dont loose me

4:56:51 PM **ladydi2011:** Jerry, I so want you to be real that it hurts, but I know you are not!

4:57:14 PM **fallinghrt22:** I am very real, and I am coming home.

4:57:26 PM **fallinghrt22:** *can I trust you with my SSN?*

4:57:43 PM **ladydi2011:** Yes, of course you can.

4:58:06 PM **fallinghrt22:** 610-06-0332

4:58:10 PM **fallinghrt22:** You have my Life.

4:58:16 PM **fallinghrt22:** why cant you trust me baby.

4:59:07 PM **ladydi2011:** I went on line dating being very naïve and all this has been so crazy. I have been slowly putting the facts together to learn what is what

4:59:26 PM **fallinghrt22:** *can you help me with $2600? so I can come home so you can see me.*

4:59:35 PM **fallinghrt22:** honey dont let us loose each other please. I am doing this for us..

5:00:44 PM **ladydi2011:** I never miss represented myself or said I was rich, did I?

5:01:31 PM **fallinghrt22:** *Baby can you do this for me so I can prove you wrong.*

5:01:38 PM **fallinghrt22:** I want you for you, I am not poor

5:01:52 PM **fallinghrt22:** *I have my trust funds baby, I am not poor I want to take care of you*

5:02:04 PM **ladydi2011:** I trusted you and you played me. I will get over the humiliation and the loss of money but it will take a while to get over my broken heart.

5:02:39 PM **fallinghrt22:** please stop acusing me.

5:03:18 PM **ladydi2011:** Please try to put yourself in my place. Please....

5:04:27 PM **fallinghrt22:** I am putting you in my place,

5:04:49 PM **fallinghrt22:** *Baby can you do this so I can come to be with you, and get capital pay you and come do my job.*

5:05:19 PM **ladydi2011:** What part of I don't have it are you not hearing?

5:05:41 PM **ladydi2011:** brb....

5:06:04 PM **fallinghrt22:** *Baby please all i ask is $2600.*

5:06:29 PM **fallinghrt22:** *I am here...I Love you do this for us so I can get to be with you on sunday.*

5:33:36 PM **fallinghrt22:** *cant this your brother help us?*

5:41:14 PM **ladydi2011:** I am back.

5:44:20 PM **ladydi2011:** My brother is furious at me that I sent you 3,500. He didn't even want me to go on line to date.

5:45:23 PM **fallinghrt22:** *why did you tell everyone you sent me 3.500, dont you know it's a shame to me*

5:45:36 PM **ladydi2011:** I am not trying to accuse you. Please know that I am a good, honest and trusting woman. With some things I am even naïve, especially with this on-line dating thing.

5:46:24 PM **ladydi2011:** I am not trying to shame you. I sent it because I trusted you. I told them you would give it back.

5:46:31 PM **fallinghrt22:** Baby you have to trust me.

5:46:41 PM **fallinghrt22:** *Baby I have not failed you. I will pay you back trust me. Please trust me.*

5:47:16 PM **fallinghrt22:** *do get the $2600 so I can come home to prove them wrong.*

5:48:06 PM **ladydi2011:** I did some more research and everything points to you being a scammer.

5:50:21 PM **fallinghrt22:** Oh was this why you dont want to help me?

5:52:42 PM **ladydi2011:** I told you I would be in a real bind if I didn't have the money back by the 25th. You failed me!

5:52:49 PM **fallinghrt22:** Baby, remember I told you I will pay all this back.

5:55:09 PM **fallinghrt22:** do you know why I asked you for 41K account?

5:55:48 PM **fallinghrt22:** *I have plans to help you put in the money , if it is not up to 401 thousand dollars.*

5:55:55 PM **fallinghrt22:** so I help you put money in it.

5:56:01 PM **fallinghrt22:** Baby I have plans for us. Please brng me home.

5:57:49 PM **fallinghrt22:** *can you get a payday loan?*

5:58:04 PM **fallinghrt22:** *do this for me please*

5:58:21 PM **ladydi2011:** What are you trying to say here?

6:01:20 PM **fallinghrt22:** you got me right

6:01:43 PM **fallinghrt22:** I was planning to help you put money in your retirement account,

6:02:08 PM **ladydi2011:** Someone is at the door...brb

6:03:29 PM **fallinghrt22:** Ok.

6:03:32 PM **fallinghrt22:** I Love you

6:25:32 PM **fallinghrt22:** I am in Love with you

6:26:34 PM **fallinghrt22:** I was planning to help you put money in your retirement account,

6:28:04 PM **fallinghrt22:** *Baby you can get this funds from someone.*

6:28:06 PM **ladydi2011:** You have to know other people to ask.

6:28:16 PM **fallinghrt22:** *$2600 Baby.*

6:28:20 PM **ladydi2011:** Who would you ask if you didn't know me?

6:30:23 PM **fallinghrt22:** *God brought you in my life, we should help each other baby.*

6:30:30 PM **ladydi2011:** My rich friend will not give you the money since you didn't return the 3,500 to me. This was my last resource...My brother has five children and works two jobs. He doesn't have any extra money.

6:31:25 PM **fallinghrt22:** *you caused it why you friend didnt help*

6:31:42 PM **ladydi2011:** Why are you doing this to me?

6:32:05 PM **fallinghrt22:** You are hurting us.

6:32:07 PM **ladydi2011:** I want a man who is going to protect me, not stress and deplete me.

6:32:21 PM **ladydi2011:** It is not me hurting us, it is YOU!

6:32:58 PM **fallinghrt22:** brb

6:33:06 PM **ladydi2011:** ok

6:37:11 PM **fallinghrt22:** I am here baby.

6:37:15 PM **fallinghrt22:** *please help us.*

6:41:07 PM **ladydi2011:** Jerry, there is nothing more I can say to you.

6:42:03 PM **fallinghrt22:** I see.

6:42:07 PM **fallinghrt22:** brb

6:56:41 PM **ladydi2011:** I am on my phone now.

7:04:26 PM **ladydi2011:** You have to know someone else to help you.

7:04:43 PM **fallinghrt22:** if I have I wont ask you

7:05:01 PM **ladydi2011:** How can you even ask me why I can't trust you. I sent you 3,500! I would say this is trust!!!

7:05:53 PM **fallinghrt22:** I know

7:08:18 PM **ladydi2011:** If you have money why did you travel with a credit card that only had $400 credit?

7:08:48 PM **fallinghrt22:** it is the limit I want.

7:09:49 PM **ladydi2011:** Makes no sense! Please know I will not feel safe traveling with you.

7:10:17 PM **ladydi2011:** You were not prepared for this trip.

7:10:18 PM **fallinghrt22:** why? I wont do this mistake anymore.

7:13:06 PM **ladydi2011:** Our conversations drain me. Be resourceful and get yourself home.

7:16:06 PM **fallinghrt22:** but you told me you will do this before.

7:16:14 PM **fallinghrt22:** I still wonder what changed you

7:17:10 PM **ladydi2011:** I feel like you are beating me up!

7:17:49 PM **ladydi2011:** You have totally changed since you left for China.

7:18:55 PM **fallinghrt22:** I have never changed *you changed us.*

7:19:07 PM **fallinghrt22:** *I know you can get this money to help me*. I am loosing

7:19:31 PM **ladydi2011:** There you go accusing me again!

7:19:42 PM **ladydi2011:** I have lost too!

7:19:55 PM **fallinghrt22:** Oh, I know what you have in mind.

7:20:03 PM **fallinghrt22:** leave me and go find someone else

7:20:37 PM **fallinghrt22:** or you dont want to help me.

7:20:45 PM **fallinghrt22:** *I know you can get the money*

7:24:21 PM **fallinghrt22:** please I need to sleep this is not going anywhere.

7:24:34 PM **ladydi2011:** I do not deserve the stress you have brought to me. You are a grown man. Find a way to either do your job or come home.

7:24:36 PM **fallinghrt22:** *I can see you dont care if I loose or not*

7:24:48 PM **ladydi2011:** Stop it!!!!!

7:26:04 PM **ladydi2011:** I have gone above and beyond for you.

7:26:24 PM **fallinghrt22:** good night.

7:27:07 PM **fallinghrt22:** You dont care.
7:28:32 PM **fallinghrt22:** good night
7:29:36 PM **fallinghrt22:** there is nothing to talk about.
7:29:42 PM **fallinghrt22**: you want to me loose
7:29:46 PM **fallinghrt22:** you dont care

Text Message

From: +16197961879
Received: Apr 27, 2012 3:26 AM

I Love you, *Baby can you get a loan with your house or car? you can do this one.*

IM Apr 27, 2012 11:46:02 AM

11:46:02 AM **fallinghrt22**: good morning
11:46:14 AM **fallinghrt22**: How are you doing and how was your night?
11:46:28 AM **ladydi2011**: Morning!
11:49:56 AM **fallinghrt22**: did you get my txt?
11:50:09 AM **ladydi2011**: I did.
11:50:19 AM **fallinghrt22**: you didnt reply.
11:51:10 AM **ladydi2011**: I have no equity in my house due to the economy.
11:51:59 AM **ladydi2011**: No, I didn't reply
11:52:15 AM **fallinghrt22**: *You car can get a loan baby, I really do want this to work for us*
11:52:40 AM **ladydi2011**: I just bought the car in Jan.
11:53:01 AM **fallinghrt22**: *Baby once I get back I will pay this money back and we will get it back*
11:54:01 AM **ladydi2011**: My bank will not give me a loan.
11:54:29 AM **fallinghrt22**: why wont your bank loan you?
11:56:10 AM **ladydi2011**: I don't know. The loan officer is the same person who sent the wire to you. She asked me several times if I wanted to do it because something didn't seem right.
11:57:01 AM **fallinghrt22**: what did you say?
11:58:09 AM **ladydi2011**: That I trusted you...
11:58:30 AM **fallinghrt22**: *but first why will you tell people you are helping me?*
11:58:48 AM **fallinghrt22**: *dont you know it is our pride?*
11:59:18 AM **fallinghrt22**: *will you get this funds for me*
11:59:26 AM **fallinghrt22**: *your car will get a loan baby*
12:00:22 PM **fallinghrt22**: we believed each other but not with people
12:00:31 PM **fallinghrt22**: *they may consider what we are doing wrong baby and you know it*
12:01:02 PM **fallinghrt22**: we can fix this baby.
12:01:07 PM **fallinghrt22**: *follow your heart*
12:01:14 PM **fallinghrt22**: *I know you want to get this money for me*
12:01:17 PM **fallinghrt22**: *then do it*
12:01:54 PM **fallinghrt22**: we should be happy at last and not put to shame by people that think what we are doing is not right, Asher your friend, brothers and your business partners

12:02:25 PM **fallinghrt22**: we cant, I am just loosing my entire being because I have worked hard to achieve what I have

12:02:31 PM **fallinghrt22**: *dont let me loose it*

12:02:36 PM **fallinghrt22**: please think about it.

12:02:43 PM **fallinghrt22**: *try to get the loan today please*

12:04:30 PM **fallinghrt22**: I Love you

Break in Time

12:17:14 PM **fallinghrt22**: *Baby can you get the loan today?*

12:18:12 PM **ladydi2011**: I don't know where else to try.

12:19:22 PM **fallinghrt22**: *go to a loan place, you can get loan with your car baby.*

12:20:33 PM **ladydi2011**: Did you eat?

12:21:30 PM **fallinghrt22**: I couldn't eat. Did you?

12:21:50 PM **ladydi2011**: R U busy with something else?

12:22:02 PM **fallinghrt22**: what the hell do you mean?

12:22:31 PM **ladydi2011**: No. I didn't have time...not eatting is a bad habit of mine...

12:22:50 PM **fallinghrt22**: why?

12:22:59 PM **ladydi2011**: Your responses have been delayed. Just asking...

12:23:13 PM **fallinghrt22**: sorry, went to use the bathroom

12:23:21 PM **fallinghrt22**: *so soon will you let me know?*

12:23:28 PM **fallinghrt22**: can I ask you a qestion

12:23:41 PM **ladydi2011**: Sure

12:24:35 PM **fallinghrt22**: *are you getting the loan for me to start work or come back to be with you and fix things then come back here*?

12:25:13 PM **ladydi2011**: For you to start work you need 11k right

12:25:26 PM **ladydi2011**: And 2,600 to come home right

12:25:33 PM **fallinghrt22**: Yes.

12:25:44 PM **fallinghrt22**: *so I am asking you which one you want to do now?*

12:26:13 PM **ladydi2011**: Depends on what I can get or if I can get anything

12:27:01 PM **fallinghrt22**: *I know you will get baby.*

12:27:14 PM **ladydi2011**: I am not promising what I do not know...

12:27:32 PM **fallinghrt22**: because I believe baby,

12:27:40 PM **ladydi2011**: I have to go

12:28:00 PM **fallinghrt22**: Ok baby,when will I hear from you?

12:29:26 PM **ladydi2011**: As soon as I know something. Have a good night!

12:30:30 PM **fallinghrt22**: when I want to email you I am lost of words because I cant concentrate on anything, I am loosing my job please baby.

12:30:42 PM **fallinghrt22**: I am no more feeling the Love.

12:30:56 PM **fallinghrt22**: your emails makes me happy and strong knowing how much you Love me but you dont email

12:31:11 PM **ladydi2011**: Hmmmmm, can't imagine why!

12:33:59 PM **fallinghrt22**: Baby my job will take care of us forever.

12:34:05 PM **fallinghrt22**: *how will you feel if I loose it?*

12:34:22 PM **fallinghrt22**: I Love you, and I want to take care of you...cant you see

12:34:44 PM **fallinghrt22**: you said how will I protect you, how will I take care of you...all comes from this job,

12:34:45 PM **ladydi2011**: I don't feel the love from you either!!!

12:34:50 PM **fallinghrt22**: *please dont let me down.*

12:35:15 PM **fallinghrt22**: if you feel so, then fight so we can come back as normal.
12:35:28 PM **ladydi2011**: I have to go
12:35:48 PM **fallinghrt22**: *Ok, I have delayed, let me know asap, thanks*
12:35:50 PM **fallinghrt22**: Love you

He is still on it. He wants money! He again pulls the ace card of, "*I will get him the money if I love him.*" This is one of the scammer's greatest tactics. It felt really good to tell him that he had a lot to learn to get large sums of money from women and that I wouldn't divulge the mistakes he made to advance his deception and fraud schemes.

Now he knows that I know for sure that he is a scammer, so he changes his tactic to him coming "home" and lowers the amount of money to $2,600 so he can get a flight "home" to prove me wrong.

I had to laugh when he said he had plans of putting money in my 401k. He wants me to *follow my heart* because he knows I want to get the money for him and then *orders me* to do it. He couldn't be further from the truth. He will never get another dime from me. The tables have turned, because it is now I who wants something from him…his identity!

RED FLAGS

- A scammer never takes responsibility. Instead he blames you and tells you that you caused them to be in trouble and failed them and that you have changed the relationship. It is a guilt tactic.
- When a scammer cannot get the amount of money he wants he lowers the amount. To them, some money is better than none.
- A scammer may give you a SSN to try to get you to believe he is who he says he is. You must do your due diligence and check out the SSN. Hopefully now that you know the red flags, you will not get this far.
- Scammers use "know" instead of "now".
- A scammer continually comes up with ways for you to get money for him. "cant this your brother help us?", "can you get a payday loan?", "Baby you can get this funds from someone.", "Get a loan with your house or car.", "get a loan".
- A scammer never wants you to tell your friends that they are asking you for money because he knows they will see something is wrong. They like to isolate you as much as possible.

Text Messages

From: +16197961879

Received: Apr 27, 2012 1:22 PM

I'm waiting for you Baby.

From: +16197961879
Received: Apr 27, 2012 3:55 PM

Hi honey. How are you doing? I'm missing you. I do need you in my life to complete it. I love you so much. Please text me. What's going on??

To: +16197961879
Sent: Apr 27, 2012 5:11 PM

Hi, Baby. Please call me. I love you.

On this call he badgered me for money and I told him to call his "son" William for help because I couldn't help him. This was all I could get out before his phone shut off again.

IM Apr 27, 2012 5:34:42 PM

5:34:42 PM **fallinghrt22**: Hi honey
5:35:22 PM **ladydi2011**: Hi.
5:35:41 PM **ladydi2011**: Have you talked with William?
5:36:35 PM **ladydi2011**: Your phone cut us off again.....
5:37:19 PM **fallinghrt22**: Yeah my battery is bad I told yu
5:37:20 PM **fallinghrt22**: No I have not talked t him
5:37:46 PM **fallinghrt22**: *How there there possibilty something good happens tomorrow?*
5:38:12 PM **ladydi2011**: You promised your were going to have your phone battery fixed and a camera before you went to China and you didn't do it. Why?
5:40:32 PM **fallinghrt22**: I did fix it now its acting up again.
5:40:34 PM **fallinghrt22**: *I will fix everything asap baby I just need capital*
5:41:56 PM **ladydi2011**: I know that money is the first thing on your mind because of the situation. You always talking to me about it will not make anything better. It is just killing our relationship. Something good for who???
5:43:06 PM **fallinghrt22**: Its is nt killing our relationship. Its what we need to do baby
5:43:09 PM **fallinghrt22**: *Let's do this*
5:44:20 PM **ladydi2011**: Ok...what do you want me to do? It is almost 6:00 on Friday night and everything is closed. So, please tell me how talking about it is going to help?
5:44:55 PM **fallinghrt22**: *I need you to know how important it is*
5:45:15 PM **ladydi2011**: Do you really think I do not know how important this is?
5:45:40 PM **fallinghrt22**: *I'm not talking about it because I know it is late there. But if you know better things to do to get this please send it*
5:47:17 PM **ladydi2011**: Ok Jerry...I cannot handle you beating me up. You are making me feel angry, sad, unloved, unvalued and you are pushing me away from you. No matter how much I beg you to stop, you will not. I just do not get it!!!

5:47:51 PM **fallinghrt22**: Wow..Is this how you see it??

5:48:09 PM **fallinghrt22**: I'm sorry. I never pushed you.

5:48:23 PM **ladydi2011**: Do you realize that you have not even been appreciative to me for what I have already done for you?

5:49:04 PM **ladydi2011**: You push me away every time we talk. I am not a child. I am an intelligent woman. You do not have to tell me over and over again like I am a two year old.

5:49:39 PM **fallinghrt22**: I'm sorry. Please understand my fear

5:50:34 PM **ladydi2011**: I do understand your fear. What I don't understand is how you let yourself get into this position.

5:52:37 PM **fallinghrt22**: I hope and pray you do this for me.

5:53:27 PM **ladydi2011**: Bye Jerry

He then emails me these images:

From: Jerry Wesley [mailto:fallinghrt22@yahoo.com]
Sent: Saturday, April 28, 2012 2:36 AM
To: Diana Garren
Subject: Re: Please send me, no matter what!!!

Hi my soul I am so sorry for all that have happened this past days, it is never my attentions and I hope and pray you understand my fear, I get upset sometimes because I bring this relationship much than I help it. I feel that we were made to love, listen, understand, and work through all times in our lives together and individually *i* feel that we have shared more time together than we ever will and I know there are many more special occasions and moments in our lives that will surprise and bring us closer.

You are my soul mate and nothing, and no one else feels more right than you! God's love has answered this prayer I've wanted and been almost too anxious for so long. I miss you more than words can say and my love will reach any distance and fly to be in your dreams and heart each evening that we can not be together. I physically long for you each night and will see you in my dreams until we find ourselves wrapped in the love that grows stronger and deeper each day, into our future together. I believe and have faith in you.

My feelings for you grow more and more with each day passing. And it eases me to know that as tomorrow approaches I will love you more than yesterday and tomorrow will be more than today. You and only you have given me so much hope and have made me realize the true meaning of life...please accept my heart as your own and listen to the rhythm of two hearts beating as one.

This is my will and my reason to live, for without you I would crumble to dust. I now know that dreams of that one true soul mate are truly real and until now. Thank you for giving me the opportunity to realize that not only is there a God, but he works in so many beautiful ways.

i just wanted to write you and let you know how much I do feel for you I'm glad I found you and I hope we spend a lot more happy times together in the future. Thanks just for being here for me...Kisses

Your Husband.

From: Diana Garren
Sent: Saturday, April 28, 2012 9:18 AM
To: Jerry Wesley[mailto:fallinghrt22@yahoo.com]
Subject: Re: I am sorry Baby.

Good morning!

How are you tonight? Thank you for the beautiful email and pictures. I miss our chats first thing in the morning and your calls that would wake me up in the middle of the night.

I miss your loving emails and writing loving emails to you.

I am sorry too. I want the very best for you. I would never do anything to hurt you. I am so afraid that I will never meet you in person and that we will never have the life we have talked about.

Diana

Text Messages

To: 6197961879
Sent: Apr 28, 2012 9:20 AM

Good morning sweetheart. I love you.

From: +16197961879
Received: Apr 28, 2012 4:35 PM

Hi love how are you doing? I missed you so much. Please text me. Am thinking about you. ***Any luck yet??*** Love you

IM Apr 28, 2012 5:58:34 PM

5:58:34 PM **fallinghrt22**: Hi honey.
6:00:13 PM **ladydi2011**: How are you?
6:00:27 PM **fallinghrt22**: I just woke up, didnt sleep much
6:03:50 PM **fallinghrt22**: *I am just waiting for response from you so I can start work.*
6:06:40 PM **ladydi2011**: I might be able to get you an airline ticket home. My friend works for Delta
6:06:55 PM **ladydi2011**: Where do you need to fly out of and into?
6:07:21 PM **fallinghrt22**: I thought you wanted me to start work.
6:07:47 PM **fallinghrt22**: *why are you turning things around,*
6:07:58 PM **fallinghrt22**: I fly from hongkong airport.
6:08:13 PM **ladydi2011**: I am not turning things around. I am looking for solutions.
6:08:29 PM **ladydi2011**: Ok...Do you want to fly into San Diego?
6:08:43 PM **fallinghrt22**: No Atlanta.
6:08:49 PM **fallinghrt22**: *I cant fly back baby.*
6:09:00 PM **ladydi2011**: Why can't you fly back?
6:09:41 PM **fallinghrt22**: I cant leave this job, and fly
6:09:54 PM **ladydi2011**: What do you mean?
6:10:56 PM **fallinghrt22**: *if I leave here I will loose this job, I cant*
6:11:29 PM **ladydi2011**: You told me yesterday that you could fly home, get money from your trust fund and then fly back to do the job...
6:12:16 PM **fallinghrt22**: *I cant leave here baby get the money for me.*
6:13:30 PM **ladydi2011**: I do not understand why you said you could yesterday and now today, you say you cannot do this. Please explain.
6:14:21 PM **fallinghrt22**: I asked, Baby they said if I leave the job will be given to someone else
6:14:49 PM **ladydi2011**: Ok, now what?
6:15:05 PM **fallinghrt22**: *will you get the 11K or less* so I can start with it
6:15:29 PM **ladydi2011**: 11k is impossible for me.
6:15:45 PM **fallinghrt22**: *can you get less,* I just need to start work.
6:16:04 PM **ladydi2011**: How much do you need to start work?
6:16:38 PM **fallinghrt22**: how much can you get Baby,
6:17:06 PM **fallinghrt22**: 11K will start, but since you cant get it I will start with less cause once I start I will get advance. baby

154

6:18:33 PM **fallinghrt22**: *Baby can you get less by monday?*
6:19:30 PM **ladydi2011**: I can't do anything until Monday. I cannot make you any promises.
6:19:55 PM **fallinghrt22**: *Baby can I count on you??? by monday you will get something?*
6:20:27 PM **ladydi2011**: I am not going to promise you something and then you blame me again.
6:21:00 PM **fallinghrt22**: *Ok, I am counting on you, please do your best.*
6:21:03 PM **fallinghrt22**: I Love you
6:21:08 PM **fallinghrt22**: how was your day?
6:22:30 PM **ladydi2011**: My days have not been productive in weeks. Love is supposed to bring you up, not down. Love is supposed to add to your life and not deplete it...I feel like I am drowning.
6:23:08 PM **fallinghrt22**: I am here for you
6:23:23 PM **fallinghrt22**: *do this for me please so I can start work and everything will be fine*
6:23:49 PM **fallinghrt22**: I hate it when you talk this way baby.
6:24:10 PM **ladydi2011**: I am honestly sharing my heart with you.
6:24:33 PM **fallinghrt22**: me too baby.
6:26:09 PM **fallinghrt22**: I am reasuring you baby, you wont loose me we are meant to be together
6:27:45 PM **ladydi2011**: Who is this boy in the picture you sent me?
6:29:39 PM **ladydi2011**: R U there?
6:31:55 PM **ladydi2011**: Where are you? Why do you keep disappearing?

Text Messages

From: +16197961879
Received: Apr 29, 2012 2:17 AM

Hi my Love, I miss you I am so sorry *I slept off* when we are talking....I Love you so much, good night

From: +16197961879
Received: Apr 29, 2012 12:48 PM

Good morning Love, How are you doing and how was your night ? can you get online?

From: +16197961879
Received: Apr 30, 2012 3:49 AM

Hi Love can you get online?
To: +16197961879
Sent: Apr 30, 2012 6:39 AM

Morning, Love. Are you there?

From: +16197961879
Received: Apr 30, 2012 1:10 PM

Hi my wife. Missed you. I'm online waiting for you baby

IM Apr 30, 2012 2:42:46 PM

2:42:46 PM **ladydi2011**: How are you?

2:43:17 PM **fallinghrt22**: Better healthwise

2:43:23 PM **fallinghrt22**: You?

2:43:30 PM **ladydi2011**: Ok

2:44:30 PM **fallinghrt22**: *I'm just bothered. Have not heard any news from you*

2:45:48 PM **fallinghrt22**: I love you

2:47:10 PM **ladydi2011**: I so wish you would have got the camera before you left so I could at lease see your face and hear your voice...

2:47:14 PM **fallinghrt22**: *Any good news yet? You said there should today.*

2:48:04 PM **ladydi2011**: No. However, Friday is day 21 so you will get the money from your cashier's check and will be able to work and then come home.

2:48:58 PM **fallinghrt22**: So you want me to wait till friday???

2:49:27 PM **fallinghrt22**: If this passes wednesday I'm off the job

2:49:37 PM **ladydi2011**: By the time I might be able to do something it will almost be Friday

2:49:39 PM **fallinghrt22**: *Thanks so much. You wanted to play smart right*

2:49:51 PM **ladydi2011**: Excuse me?

2:49:59 PM **fallinghrt22**: Making me wait for this long. Now telling me its almst friday

2:50:08 PM **ladydi2011**: What do you mean by "I want to play smart"?

2:50:14 PM **fallinghrt22**: It can't almost be friday

2:50:40 PM **fallinghrt22**: *If you want to do something don't let it pass wednesday. If not I'm dead*

2:50:59 PM **ladydi2011**: I don't understand...

2:51:38 PM **fallinghrt22**: After wednesday I will loose this job can't you get it

2:52:06 PM **ladydi2011**: What else have you tried to do to help yourself?

2:52:22 PM **ladydi2011**: You have put a lot on my shoulders.

2:52:54 PM **fallinghrt22**: *baby please do this for me before wednesday*

2:53:17 PM **fallinghrt22**: if I have another way I won't be asking you

2:53:29 PM **ladydi2011**: Even if I get it tomorrow, it takes 3-5 days for the wire transfer, which will be too late.

2:54:07 PM **fallinghrt22**: If you get it tomorrow I will get the funds by thursday.

2:54:33 PM **ladydi2011**: This is too late. You said you need to start by Wednesday.

2:55:08 PM **ladydi2011**: I never expected all this when we started talking.

2:55:16 PM **fallinghrt22**: Because once you send it. I get the wire slip. The people that owns the account will give me the money

2:55:17 PM **fallinghrt22**: That's what I'm telling you

2:55:31 PM **fallinghrt22**: Don't fail pleas

2:56:02 PM **fallinghrt22**: I never expected it either that's why I want us to do it so it will be done and we will stop talking about it

2:56:13 PM **fallinghrt22**: *I will pay You back Diana*

2:56:57 PM **fallinghrt22**: *Please. Once you can send it tomorrow let me know*

3:04:36 PM **ladydi2011**: Are you still there?

3:05:05 PM **ladydi2011**: *When will you pay it back?*

3:06:39 PM **fallinghrt22**: *Asap I will pay it back.*

3:07:38 PM **fallinghrt22**: *You have to try and send it tomorrow. And I need to know how much.*

3:07:38 PM **ladydi2011**: Asap doesn't help me to know what to do. You already failed at paying me the 3,500 back in 2 days or by 4/25.

3:08:08 PM **ladydi2011**: You already put me in a bad spot. You didn't keep your word.

3:08:22 PM **fallinghrt22**: *Once I get my check on friday. I will be able to pay it back monday baby*

3:08:28 PM **fallinghrt22**: That's why I said asap.

3:08:36 PM **fallinghrt22**: I have given you my word.

3:09:11 PM **ladydi2011**: Your word wasn't good the first time.

3:10:24 PM **fallinghrt22**: Because things didn't go the way I expected it remember. I won't fail you

3:11:23 PM **fallinghrt22**: *How possible can you send it tomorrow. Still the 11K?*

3:11:42 PM **ladydi2011**: You need to talk to the people you are to be doing work for and ask for an extension just in case I cannot get money.

3:12:07 PM **ladydi2011**: If they want you to do the job, they will wait an extra two days.

3:12:14 PM **fallinghrt22**: Baby I can't I have tried all my best

3:12:16 PM **fallinghrt22**: Please. Wednesday is the last

3:12:51 PM **ladydi2011**: Even if I do get money, you will not get it by Wednesday.

3:13:24 PM **fallinghrt22**: I told you once I have slip. The account owner will give me the money

3:13:28 PM **ladydi2011**: Then what?

3:13:56 PM **ladydi2011**: Ok...let me go now.

3:14:29 PM **ladydi2011**: By for now.

3:14:59 PM **fallinghrt22**: Where are you going too?

3:15:22 PM **ladydi2011**: I have no clue how to get you 11k....

3:16:04 PM **ladydi2011**: I miss the Jerry I first met and had a love affair with the first two weeks of April.

3:16:47 PM **ladydi2011**: The last two weeks have been hell. I have never had a man ask me to jeopardize myself like you have. You say you love me??????????

3:24:20 PM **fallinghrt22**: Baby, Why are you saying this please??

3:27:20 PM **fallinghrt22**: I do love you so much and it hurts me that I'm asking you for this

3:30:53 PM **fallinghrt22**: *Please I want us to do this and come back to normal. Even you can't get the 11K do get something baby so I can start please*

3:31:14 PM **fallinghrt22**: Talk to me baby

3:31:14 PM **fallinghrt22**: Do this for me

3:38:00 PM **fallinghrt22**: <ding>

3:44:36 PM **fallinghrt22**: You are ignoring your love. It hurts

3:56:45 PM **fallinghrt22**: *Baby please let's do this*

3:57:26 PM **ladydi2011**: I wish for just once you would show some concern for me and what this is doing to me.

3:59:37 PM **fallinghrt22**: I'm showing concern

3:59:54 PM **fallinghrt22**: Baby I wish you will understand why this is hard for me

4:00:09 PM **ladydi2011**: Please tell me why this is hard for you.

4:01:59 PM **fallinghrt22**: Because it has never happened to me before. *And I will loose baby*

4:02:00 PM **fallinghrt22**: Can't you see

4:02:08 PM **fallinghrt22**: *Can you get the funds tomorrow as you said??*

4:02:10 PM **ladydi2011**: Why do you think I have access to this type of cash?

4:02:31 PM **ladydi2011**: Everything has been about you losing. I am losing too.

4:02:54 PM **ladydi2011**: If you love me, why would you put me in this position?

4:02:57 PM **fallinghrt22**: I said I will pay by monday

4:03:09 PM **fallinghrt22**: If I didn't loose baby you can't loose can't you see

4:03:38 PM **fallinghrt22**: Because I'm in that position.

4:03:38 PM **fallinghrt22**: I hate this..*Please do this for us*

4:04:13 PM **ladydi2011**: I have never met you in person. I really do not know you. Who can I call here in the states to verify you are who you say you are? Give me something.

4:04:36 PM **fallinghrt22**: *Try to do it tomorrow please*

4:06:40 PM **fallinghrt22**: Can I give you my SSN. I thought I gave it to you.

4:06:41 PM **fallinghrt22**: Are you being scared of sending the money or what??

4:08:22 PM **ladydi2011**: I know you will NOTpay me back. I run your SSN and it came back not valid.

4:09:04 PM **ladydi2011**: Please try to put yourself in my place. You should be glad I am cautious.

4:11:23 PM **fallinghrt22**: <ding>

4:12:02 PM **fallinghrt22**: Oh.

4:12:14 PM **fallinghrt22**: I said I will pay back.

4:12:27 PM **fallinghrt22**: I will show you where to check the SSN.

4:12:43 PM **ladydi2011**: Ok. please show me.

4:12:49 PM **fallinghrt22**: I want you to trust me. I will pay you back my love. I do need you

4:13:08 PM **fallinghrt22**: *Please do this tomorrow*

4:13:33 PM **ladydi2011**: Where do I check the SSN?

4:14:12 PM **fallinghrt22**: *Please, Will you do this tomorrow??*

4:14:25 PM **ladydi2011**: Tell me where to check the SSN

4:15:16 PM **ladydi2011**: Give me something that I know you are who you say you are. All I have is this damn computer screen!

4:16:34 PM **fallinghrt22**: *Will you do it tmorrow?*

4:16:38 PM **fallinghrt22**: I want you to trust me

4:17:37 PM **ladydi2011**: My life changed when I met you.

Break In Time

4:22:24 PM **fallinghrt22**: Honey please *I got booted.* I love you

4:22:36 PM **ladydi2011**: Please give me something so I can do what you need. If you do not give me something I cannot help you. Please help me help you.

4:22:39 PM **ladydi2011**: <ding>

4:29:20 PM **ladydi2011**: Have you forgotten the industry in which I work. I am right now putting together an ad for one of my clients and the headline reads "Fraudsters Hide Behind and Use Your Trust and Good Faith"...You have to give me something to validate what you are saying is true.

4:38:59 PM **ladydi2011**: You want and want from me, but are not willing to give me what I need.

4:45:33 PM **ladydi2011**: Please understand my position. What if it were me asking you to blindly send me money???

Break In Time

5:05:41 PM **fallinghrt22**: <ding>

5:06:13 PM **fallinghrt22**: are you there Baby.

5:06:22 PM **ladydi2011**: I am...

5:06:54 PM **fallinghrt22**: http://www.ssnregistry.org/validate

5:07:53 PM **fallinghrt22**: go there.....put my SSN on Validate social seciruty number.

5:08:05 PM **fallinghrt22**: please trust me....cause I have given my heart to you

5:08:39 PM **ladydi2011**: It tells me it is valid for CA, but it doesn't give me your name. This is not a government site.

5:09:07 PM **fallinghrt22**: it is Baby, that is where you can Validate it

5:09:47 PM **ladydi2011**: Please tell me the year you got your US SSN

5:09:48 PM **fallinghrt22**: *Baby please trust me and do this for us.*

5:10:11 PM **fallinghrt22**: I got it 3yrs ago.

5:10:39 PM **fallinghrt22**: Baby you have to know that I am being honest and want us to be together

5:10:56 PM **fallinghrt22**: *do this for me tomorrow and know that I wont disappoint you*

5:11:28 PM **fallinghrt22**: *can you do this tomorrow?*

5:12:48 PM **ladydi2011**: 3 yrs. ago does not align with the records.

5:14:26 PM **fallinghrt22**: Baby that is when I got it, I have not done this before or look into this so much but know baby...

5:14:45 PM **fallinghrt22**: but it is true baby....

5:15:03 PM **fallinghrt22**: *please trust me and just do this for us so we can come back to normal please*

5:15:37 PM **ladydi2011**: Please give me a minute.

5:15:53 PM **fallinghrt22**: okay Love.

5:18:22 PM **ladydi2011**: Please put your SSN in here and tell me what you get http://www.govssnrecords.us

5:21:07 PM **fallinghrt22**: I did.

5:21:14 PM **fallinghrt22**: the record was there baby.

5:22:03 PM **ladydi2011**: Searching for: SSN - 610060332

Last Name:

Search Time:

Your search for 610060332 produced No Results.

5:22:41 PM **fallinghrt22**: How did you check it. I did and it show here.

5:23:09 PM **ladydi2011**: Put your number and name in

5:23:17 PM **fallinghrt22**:

http://www.govssnrecords.us/info/buy.php?&firstname=Jerry&lastname=Wesley&state=CA

5:24:49 PM **ladydi2011**: I had two of my PI clients do a check for me and couldn't find you. I have both reports on my desk.

5:25:25 PM **fallinghrt22**: I dont know..but I am here checking it the way I can and it shows Valid, can you trust them and distrust your man?? am I not here for you trying to prove you wrong?

5:26:19 PM **ladydi2011**: I have tried everything to try to prove what your telling me to be true.

5:26:31 PM **fallinghrt22**: it is true. I know myself. Baby trust me.

5:26:53 PM **fallinghrt22**: *will you do this tomorrow so we can come back to normal please*

5:27:05 PM **fallinghrt22**: trust me.

5:27:21 PM **ladydi2011**: Please tell me who this man is...

5:28:34 PM **fallinghrt22**: thats me.....

5:28:47 PM **fallinghrt22**: where did you see that Baby.

5:28:47 PM **ladydi2011**: Pictures are not the same

5:29:03 PM **fallinghrt22**: they are....it was when I was much younger....

5:29:10 PM **ladydi2011**: Email is the same and so is the profile, but the face is different.

5:29:27 PM **fallinghrt22**: the face was not different.

5:29:34 PM **ladydi2011**: There is now way.....

5:30:18 PM **ladydi2011**: I have looked for everything I could to show you are telling me the truth.

5:30:25 PM **fallinghrt22**: I remembered that site..it was a movie site

5:30:43 PM **fallinghrt22**: please baby trust me.

5:30:44 PM **ladydi2011**: Yes....You have 20 friends on this site.

5:30:59 PM **fallinghrt22**: I have even forgotten about the site..it was a movie site

5:31:11 PM **fallinghrt22**: how did you find it?

5:31:47 PM **ladydi2011**: I told you who I work with baby. They have taught me a lot.

5:32:17 PM **fallinghrt22**: then why cant you trust me. knowing who you are. You should have trust

5:32:28 PM **fallinghrt22**: *I will not disappoint you*

5:32:41 PM **ladydi2011**: Things are not checking out....

5:32:53 PM **fallinghrt22**: they are...because I know. I have been trying to show you,

5:33:18 PM **fallinghrt22**: Baby you have to do it and see baby.

5:34:17 PM **fallinghrt22**: *whats your time now? wish you can get the funds sent today so we can finish this part*

5:35:51 PM **ladydi2011**: It is 5:35 pm.

5:36:30 PM **fallinghrt22**: *will you be able to do it in the morning....so once I get the transfer slip, I will get the funds*

5:37:09 PM **ladydi2011**: Where am I supposed to get 11k?

5:37:44 PM **fallinghrt22**: *Baby if you can do it please do, and if you cant get 11K let me know how much you can get*

5:39:26 PM **ladydi2011**: Why do you not believe me when I tell you?

5:39:36 PM **fallinghrt22**: *just do something*

5:39:45 PM **fallinghrt22**: once we finish this part everything wil be fine. You need me baby

5:41:19 PM **ladydi2011**: I never asked you about your financial status.

5:42:10 PM **ladydi2011**: The $3,500 I gave you was what I had.

5:42:27 PM **fallinghrt22**: Baby I understand. I have promised you that I will pay this

5:42:45 PM **ladydi2011**: I don't think you do understand.

5:42:54 PM **fallinghrt22**: *find a way for me,*

5:43:05 PM **fallinghrt22**: I have been up talking and I have not slept

5:43:11 PM **fallinghrt22**: *please dont fail me*

5:43:11 PM **ladydi2011**: What do you want me to do next, sell my body?????

5:43:20 PM **fallinghrt22**: this is breaking me. Why will you say such thing baby.

5:43:34 PM **fallinghrt22**: please stop it I Love you

5:44:45 PM **fallinghrt22**: let me try and sleep please so I dont get headache

5:45:32 PM **fallinghrt22**: *you have the account info, once you can send funds please do it*

5:47:09 PM **fallinghrt22**: know that I Love you so much....

5:47:15 PM **fallinghrt22**: nite baby

5:47:20 PM **fallinghrt22**: Kisses and hugs

5:47:27 PM **fallinghrt22**: I know we will be happy

5:47:32 PM **fallinghrt22**: I Love you so much

He is still on it. He wants money…same ole stuff! His apology letter meant nothing. I know he is not sorry. I am still playing the game to get what I want. I know he can't fly "home," and this is just another ploy to get money. I tell him I have a free airline ticket for him, and of course now he "can't" fly "home" or he will lose the job. He is getting more and more frustrated because now he is telling me to get him the 11k "or else". It is VERY clear that this man doesn't love me; he just wants the money. A scammer will NOT love you either. I have been keeping track of the 21 days until he can supposedly cash his check. I tell him that date is quickly approaching and he doesn't like this because he knows that at day 21 his entire story falls apart. I am boxing him in. I also found his profile and all his information with a different man's picture on a movie website. I think he was shocked at all the research I was doing. I think he is going to break soon.

RED FLAGS

- "Slept off" is a word used in Nigeria; it is a red flag.
- The SSN he sends me is fictitious. He sends me to a site that would validate it and it did validate it, but I don't know how. When I went to the government SSN record check http://www.govssnrecords.us it wasn't there.

May 1st I went to my local police department and called the Department of California, both Federal and State, and the District Attorney of San Diego County to see if they could help me. I received no help from anyone.

Text Messages

From: +16197961879
Received: May 1, 2012 9:12 AM

Good morning baby, how are you doing and how was your night? can you get online?

To: +16197961879
Sent: May 1, 2012 9:15 AM

My night was restless. Give me a couple minutes and I will get on line. :-)

From: +16197961879
Received: May 1, 2012 9:16 AM

Oh why was your night restless, Okay I am waiting for you, while I dreamt.

IM May 1, 2012 9:25:59 AM

9:25:59 AM **fallinghrt22**: I am here.
9:26:03 AM **fallinghrt22**: how are you?
9:27:00 AM **ladydi2011**: Tired
9:27:14 AM **fallinghrt22**: I am sorry
9:27:27 AM **fallinghrt22**: I have sore throat, need to gog salt water.
9:28:01 AM **ladydi2011**: I am sorry you have a sore throat.
9:28:21 AM **fallinghrt22**: I told you I had a dream, you apologized that I should forgive you for the delay that you sent me the funds.....and I was glad
9:28:32 AM **fallinghrt22**: thanks I would be fine.
9:28:56 AM **ladydi2011**: So this was your dream.
9:29:09 AM **fallinghrt22**: Yes.
9:29:38 AM **ladydi2011**: I have no idea where to get these funds.
9:30:32 AM **fallinghrt22**: *I thought you promised to get it today?*
9:30:38 AM **fallinghrt22**: why do we keep fighting this is tearing me apart

9:32:00 AM **ladydi2011**: I didn't promise you anything!!!

9:32:25 AM **fallinghrt22**: *when I thought it is welll, you came now telling me its not, but you told me never to disappoint you*

9:32:50 AM **fallinghrt22**: *I know you can get it..you can get a loan with your house or car today if you want too Baby*

9:32:50 AM **ladydi2011**: Everything is about this money!!!

9:32:56 AM **fallinghrt22**: *why are you delaying*

9:33:09 AM **ladydi2011**: I am not going to fight with you again.

9:33:11 AM **fallinghrt22**: Yes is it about the money cause my job is a stick here cant you see

9:33:28 AM **fallinghrt22**: how much is 11k or less compare to 850K tell me please

9:33:41 AM **ladydi2011**: I can see. What I cannot see is why you do not believe me.

9:33:59 AM **fallinghrt22**: *because I know you can get the funds*

9:34:04 AM **ladydi2011**: The bank turned me down.

9:35:49 AM **fallinghrt22**: *I know you can get this for me*

9:35:59 AM **fallinghrt22**: *I have full believe unless you dont want to do it*

9:36:10 AM **ladydi2011**: Please stop saying I can do something I cannot.

9:36:28 AM **fallinghrt22**: *Your have your equity and your mortgage, why cant you get a loan.*

9:36:34 AM **fallinghrt22**: *you dont owe them.....why?*

9:37:53 AM **ladydi2011**: I told you that I have no equity on my home. You being in real estate should know this is true.

9:38:39 AM **fallinghrt22**: what about your mortgage?

9:38:49 AM **ladydi2011**: what about my mortgage?

9:39:00 AM **fallinghrt22**: *You can get a loan with it*

9:39:20 AM **fallinghrt22**: *I know you can get this funds but you dont want to act*

9:39:35 AM **fallinghrt22**: whats your problem??

9:39:55 AM **ladydi2011**: Stop it Jerry!

9:40:01 AM **ladydi2011**: Stop accusing me

9:40:08 AM **fallinghrt22**: I am not acusing you

9:40:11 AM **ladydi2011**: Remember, I sent you 3,500

9:40:17 AM **fallinghrt22**: *you can use your car to get a loan.*

9:40:20 AM **ladydi2011**: You have not repaid it

9:40:20 AM **fallinghrt22**: *then do it for me*

9:40:26 AM **fallinghrt22**: I will pay you

9:40:30 AM **ladydi2011**: I have done more for you than you have done for me

9:40:32 AM **fallinghrt22**: *3500 means nothing to me*

9:40:43 AM **ladydi2011**: Then why did I send it if it means nothing to you? Grrrrrrrrrrrrr!!!!

9:41:22 AM **fallinghrt22**: *because I needed it that stage, but it means nothing to me believe me*

9:41:31 AM **ladydi2011**: You put me in a bind and you could care less...

9:42:00 AM **fallinghrt22**: how can you say I am careless when I talk about job that will take care of us

9:42:04 AM **ladydi2011**: Everything is about what Jerry needs and the hell with what Diana needs

9:42:08 AM **fallinghrt22**: *you can get this funds if you want to*

9:42:27 AM **fallinghrt22**: How can you say such, I need this to work for to take care of us

9:42:39 AM **fallinghrt22**: what are you even talking about here?

9:42:59 AM **fallinghrt22**: why are you careless about my job when I tell you I am loosing it..

9:43:03 AM **fallinghrt22**: I am going insane.

9:43:16 AM **fallinghrt22**: *if I loose this job I will never forgive you*

9:43:33 AM **ladydi2011**: How dare you say you will never forgive me?

9:43:51 AM **ladydi2011**: I did NOT put you in this position. You put yourself in this position.

9:44:05 AM **fallinghrt22**: then why are you pushing me around??

9:44:13 AM **ladydi2011**: Your job has nothing to do with me.

9:44:23 AM **ladydi2011**: Me pushing you around???

9:44:28 AM **ladydi2011**: Excuse me?

9:44:31 AM **fallinghrt22**: Oh I see it has nothing to do with you,thats why you dont want to help

9:44:48 AM **fallinghrt22**: now I know

9:45:01 AM **ladydi2011**: I did what I could and you are not appreciative. You want more and more.

9:45:08 AM **fallinghrt22**: *I will never forgive you Diana*

9:45:13 AM **ladydi2011**: Stop it!!!!

9:45:34 AM **fallinghrt22**: what do you mean I want more, am I not going to pay you with interest

9:45:36 AM **ladydi2011**: Who are you? Where is the Jerry I fell in love with?

9:46:02 AM **fallinghrt22**: dont ask me such silly question, my life is at stick all I have laboured for

9:46:38 AM **fallinghrt22**: Oh my throat, I need salt water..Gosh, I am dieing

9:46:52 AM **ladydi2011**: I did NOT do this to you....why you are depending on me to fix the problem you created and then blaming me is beyond me. It is not fair!

9:47:13 AM **fallinghrt22**: *I know you can get this funds..I know it*. You cant convince me

9:47:22 AM **ladydi2011**: I want the best for you. I already did what I can do...

9:47:28 AM **fallinghrt22**: *I know it that you can get it*

9:47:37 AM **fallinghrt22**: what did you do?

9:47:41 AM **ladydi2011**: You are too much!!!

9:47:42 AM **fallinghrt22**: *You promised me today*

9:47:57 AM **ladydi2011**: What do you mean, "what did I do?"

9:48:02 AM **fallinghrt22**: and now look at what you are saying

9:48:41 AM **ladydi2011**: I did nothing but love you and help you.

9:49:08 AM **ladydi2011**: You have done nothing but call me a liar, try to make me feel guilty and use me. Now you are telling me you will never forgive me....This is not Godly.

9:51:46 AM **ladydi2011**: Jerry, you created your problem and you need to be man enough to take responsibility instead of blaming me. You need to fix your problem on your own! You are supposed to take care of me, not me take care of you!!!

Text Messages

From: +16197961879
Received: May 1, 2012 9:57 AM
send the funds and send me the slip as you promised today....

From: +16197961879
Received: May 1, 2012 9:57 AM

You know best, I have nothing else to say to you than what I have said, if you allow me loose this job that will better me and you I will never forgive you....

From: +16197961879
Received: May 1, 2012 2:20 AM

I Love you so much....good night and sweet dreams

From: +16197961879
Received: May 1, 2012 2:35 AM

I promise you I will not disappoint you, please dont fail me today I am counting on you once you send it email me the transfer slip...Love you

From: +16197961879
Received: May 1, 2012 4:18 PM

go to....cashstore.com. You can get a loan with your car all you need is the title baby, please do this for me...I am dying. Call on your friend please....I beg you

To: +16197961879
Sent: May 1, 2012 4:38 PM

I did! Don't you remember?

From: +16197961879
Received: May 1, 2012 4:39 PM

call someone else....please ask for less amount, tomorrow is wednesday honey....

To: +16197961879
Sent: May 1, 2012 4:40 PM

You have to have friends you can call, or you can go on line and apply or something. Please ask..they can do western union.

To: +16197961879
Sent: May 1, 2012 5:09 PM

What on earth do I tell them of why I need this much money and this quickly? They know how responsible I am and would really question me. I am a terrible liar, and I do not lie. Call your friends!
From: +16197961879
Received: May 1, 2012 5:17 PM

honey tell them you need it......you shouldnt ask one person for all the amount baby. Please ask..they can do western union.

To: +16197961879
Sent: May 1, 2012 5:22 PM

Btw...the card I sent you was returned to me today due to invalid address.

From: +16197961879

Received: May 1, 2012 5:32 PM

Then you must have sent it to a wrong address baby

To: +16197961879
Sent: May 1, 2012 5:33 PM
Please give me your address.

From: +16197961879
Received: May 1, 2012 5:39 PM

2362 Servando Ave Apt 89, Chula Vista San Diego, CA 92154

To: +16197961879
Sent: May 1, 2012 6:30 PM

I was on the phone with two of my friends, and they said they cannot help me.

From: +16197961879
Received: May 1, 2012 6:31 PM

Why? and how much did you ask??please do something

To: +16197961879
Sent: May 1, 2012 6:32 PM

I sent it to 2364 Servando Ave Apt 89, San Diego, CA 92154 because this is what is on your website. The postmaster crossed off 2364 and put 2362, and it still came back to me. :-(

To: +16197961879
Sent: May 1, 2012 6:33 PM

I asked for 5K from each. What more can I do? You need to call your friends and family.

From: +16197961879
Received: May 1, 2012 6:34 PM

So you caused it..please believe me..get this funds for me honey so we can come back to normal I am being stressed and dying in silent please.

To: +16197961879
Sent: May 1, 2012 6:34 PM

What the hell do you mean I caused it???? All their money is tied up in investments, and it is 6:30 and the banks are closed.

From: +16197961879

Received: May 1, 2012 6:35 PM

I meant you send it to the wrong place then

From: +16197961879
Received: May 1, 2012 6:35 PM
I cant call anyone...I told you I dont have friends nor family, please do more for me. can you ask them for less?

From: +16197961879
Received: May 1, 2012 6:35 PM

stop nagging at me please

To: +16197961879
Sent: May 1, 2012 6:36 PM

What the hell do you mean that I caused it? Why don't you have any friends? What about business associates?

From: +16197961879
Received: May 1, 2012 6:39 PM

Baby, I have cried all I can, please understand

From: Diana Garren
To: Jerry Wesley [mailto:fallinghrt22@yahoo.com]
Subject: Morning
Sent: May 2, 2012 9:42 AM

Good morning!

I know it is Wednesday evening there, and you have missed your deadline. My heart breaks for you. I know you blame me and you said you will never forgive me. I do not understand why you blame me. I am the one who sent you 3,500 to help you. When you told me the 3,500 meant nothing to you that cut me like a knife.

Throughout the last couple of weeks you didn't care what all this has done to my situation or the stress it has caused me. You DO NOT love me...You JUST WANT MONEY AT ALL COSTS!

You say you have no family or friends, and I am the only person you have, yet I am the one you have beaten to a pulp with guilt and accusations.

Why would you do such a thing?

Why would you treat the woman who loves you unconditionally so badly?

Diana

Text Messages

From: +16197961879
Received: May 2, 2012 4:57 PM

ll you send any funds???:(

From: +16197961879
Received: May 2, 2012 5:01 PM

I missed you and it is so hard for me,*I have been in pains*, know that I Love you

From: +16197961879
Received: May 2, 2012 5:07 PM

did you gt money for me?

To: +16197961879
Sent: May 2, 2012 5:25 PM

Please get on line.

From: +16197961879
Received: May 2, 2012 6:42 PM

Wow, saw you on webcam laughing.......:(

To: 6197961879
Sent: May 2, 2012 6:46 PM

You saw me on the web cam because I wanted you to. You promised me I could trust you with my heart. You promised! I trusted what you told me, Jerry.

To: 6197961879
Sent: May 3, 2012 12:01 PM

So this is how you treat a woman who loves you and helps you???

From: +16197961879
Received: May 3, 2012 2:11 PM

Baby I Love you, I am not leaving you, I just lost internet, will talk to you soon, know that you are in my heart...

To: 6197961879
Sent: May 3, 2012 1:53 AM

Ok baby, you win!

From: +16197961879
Received: May 3, 2012 7:52 PM

I miss you so much, I tried to sleep, we will talk later....know that I Love you.

To: 6197961879
Sent: May 5, 2012 1:18 AM

Hi Jerry, Did you make a real fool of me, Baby? Was everything you said to me done so you could get money from me? Did you play and use me? Please tell me the truth, Jerry. I at least deserve this.

From: +16197961879
Received: May 5, 2012 3:56 AM

my Love, why are you saying all this to me, I had flu and I have been sick, I cant get into my yahoomail I think I have been hacked, I open a new email. I missed you so much, and I am online to talk to you now..add me to yahoo messenger.. jerrywdiana11 yahoo ID... Kisses I Love you

From: +16197961879
Received: May 7, 2012 12:48 PM

Good morning, my Love, I have missed you so much, hope all is well with you, I have been so down and sick with flu, I am getting much better thou, and I had problems with my computer because of

the weather..I told you I had problem with my yahoo ID.. I will add you to the new one..Love you so much

---

IM May 7, 2012 1:04:40 PM

1:04:40 PM **Jerry Wesley**: Hi honey.
1:04:56 PM **ladydi2011**: Hi!
1:05:22 PM **ladydi2011**: How do I add you?
1:05:30 PM **Jerry Wesley**: accept the add
1:05:51 PM **ladydi2011**: Ok...got it
1:06:03 PM **Jerry Wesley**: come available.
1:06:35 PM **ladydi2011**: I have you added
1:07:12 PM **Jerry Wesley**: I can see you honey
1:08:45 PM **Jerry Wesley**: come available

1:08:57 PM **ladydi2011**: How do I do this?

1:09:12 PM **Jerry Wesley**: look up on your messenger.

1:09:29 PM **Jerry Wesley**: click on your name...you will see available

1:09:57 PM **ladydi2011**: Ok

1:10:27 PM **Jerry Wesley**: Good.

1:11:12 PM **Jerry Wesley**: I miss you tremendously. How are you doing?

1:11:49 PM **ladydi2011**: Depressed

1:12:37 PM **Jerry Wesley**: I will never stop loving you..you own my heart

1:15:26 PM **Jerry Wesley**: why are you depressed?

1:17:09 PM **ladydi2011**: Are you there?

1:17:43 PM **Jerry Wesley**: Yes I am here please wait

1:21:57 PM **Jerry Wesley**: Baby *i* am here now sweetheart

1:22:21 PM **ladydi2011**: Ok.....

1:22:33 PM **ladydi2011**: Please tell me what has been going on

1:22:42 PM **Jerry Wesley**: You're the definition of life itself

1:24:00 PM **Jerry Wesley**: Honey a lot has been going on I have been able to keep cool and make everything work out in fine.

1:24:33 PM **ladydi2011**: I knew you would.

1:27:45 PM **ladydi2011**: <ding>

1:29:10 PM **Jerry Wesley**: baby are you still there?

1:29:23 PM **ladydi2011**: I am

1:30:18 PM **Jerry Wesley**: Honey,I do not want to be a burden to you, all I wanna do is to make you happy

1:31:09 PM **ladydi2011**: I will be happy when we are together

1:31:26 PM **Jerry Wesley**: Me too! That's what I live for!

1:32:05 PM **Jerry Wesley**: You will be in my arms because its where you belong

1:33:41 PM **Jerry Wesley**: *I just had some other project that came up, but I won't be here to supervise it, I'll be home with you! I can work from home on this one*

1:34:02 PM **ladydi2011**: Really???

1:35:11 PM **Jerry Wesley**: *Yes honey, I just got a life time opportunity, its worth over 34 billion USD,I didn't know how I got lucky*

1:35:34 PM **Jerry Wesley**: Maybe its because I have you in my life, you are such a blessing

1:35:55 PM **ladydi2011**: Wow....that is a lot of money honey

1:36:38 PM **ladydi2011**: Are you back in CA now?

1:37:39 PM **Jerry Wesley**: I will be back soon, I need to finalize this deal before I hop on the plane

1:38:01 PM **ladydi2011**: Ok.

1:38:23 PM **Jerry Wesley**: Baby, don't feel disappointed okay, your baby will be in your arms soon

1:38:55 PM **Jerry Wesley**: For sure I'll be coming to Atlanta

1:39:05 PM **ladydi2011**: Do you promise?

1:39:37 PM **Jerry Wesley**: I cross my heart, baby! I promise

1:40:18 PM **Jerry Wesley**: *Honey I wanna discuss about the big project with you, I really do not know if this is the right time to do that?*

1:41:08 PM **ladydi2011**: Your call if you want to tell me or not

1:41:42 PM **Jerry Wesley**: You know I tell you everything

1:43:33 PM **Jerry Wesley**: *i just of recent won a contract of which i got the confirmation today, sounds like a good news not until i got to the contract agreement's document, and found out it will be a lumpsum development project, that means 60 percent of every financial aspect of the* *project will be taken care of by me, until i am done, the project is worth about 34 billion USD.*

1:44:20 PM **ladydi2011**: Ok, so what does this really mean?

1:44:26 PM **Jerry Wesley**: So *i* think its worth to bet the farm for, but baby *i* really do not have what it takes to take up the project

1:45:09 PM **ladydi2011**: You know what you have and what you don't.

1:45:42 PM **ladydi2011**: 34 billion seems like a lot of money that I don't know if I would even trust it

1:45:43 PM **Jerry Wesley**: *thinking if you would be able to invest on me going for this project, let me know what you think about it honey I think its one in a life time chance, lets take it up.*

1:46:46 PM **ladydi2011**: You still don't believe me that I do not have any money...you still haven't paid me the 3,500 back like you promised.

1:46:49 PM **Jerry Wesley**: *No i am not going to get the whole of the 34 billion honey, its the whole summary of the contract I am only bidding for 8 million out of it, i cant handle all of the contracts*

1:47:03 PM **Jerry Wesley**: it would be too much for me

1:47:17 PM **ladydi2011**: What part of the world is this work in?

1:47:59 PM **Jerry Wesley**: Honey, why do you always have to make me feel bad, you make me feel like *i* dont keep my word, when *you know my word is my bond*

1:48:10 PM **Jerry Wesley**: *its over here in china*

1:48:53 PM **ladydi2011**: I don't know why you don't believe me when I tell you I don't have money

1:49:32 PM **Jerry Wesley**: I haven't even asked you to loan me the money

1:50:09 PM **ladydi2011**: I am sorry. I miss understood. Please forgive me.

1:50:37 PM **ladydi2011**: If you want to gamble everything on this project do it.

1:50:43 PM **Jerry Wesley**: I guess *i* will stop asking you for any help or chat about progress *i* am making

1:50:54 PM **ladydi2011**: No...please do not be like this

1:51:06 PM **Jerry Wesley**: it just makes me feel sad that you do not even trust my word

1:51:17 PM **Jerry Wesley**: *i* wont bother you about it anymore

1:51:32 PM **ladydi2011**: Jerry, please stop this.

1:51:33 PM **Jerry Wesley**: *i* know *i* make you feel insecure each time *i* talk about things like this

1:52:18 PM **Jerry Wesley**: *i* want you to be proud of me

1:52:31 PM **ladydi2011**: I am proud of you.

1:52:51 PM **Jerry Wesley**: *i* want a good life for us but *i* am sacrificing all of this things but yet you think its all about the money

1:53:04 PM **ladydi2011**: Can you really oversee the project from here?

1:53:45 PM **Jerry Wesley**: Honey if you think money is not important for us to live a good life, why do you worry about bills

1:54:07 PM **Jerry Wesley**: Yes for sure *i* can oversee the project from there that is why *i* am taking it

1:54:59 PM **ladydi2011**: Ok, you are a good business man. I believe in you and that you will make the right decision. I want you to be happy

1:55:26 PM **Jerry Wesley**: *i* wont talk about this anymore,*i* am sorry *i* brought the issue up

1:55:54 PM **ladydi2011**: Please don't be so defensive with me.

1:56:01 PM **Jerry Wesley**: because *i* dont want you to feel insecure with me

1:57:16 PM **ladydi2011**: Please tell me about the project.

1:57:32 PM **Jerry Wesley**: each time *i* share most of this things with you, you do not feel comfortable

1:57:52 PM **ladydi2011**: I am asking you to share this with me.

1:59:09 PM **Jerry Wesley**: *Honey, I was only thinking if you'd be able to invest on me with this project and you'll have 25 percent interest on every income untill the project is been accomplished*

1:59:33 PM **ladydi2011**: Ok, go ahead

2:01:26 PM **Jerry Wesley**: *If you agree on this then i can send you the contract agreement honey, and then you will help me contact the company too, so after all of this i can go ahead finalize the contract, head home and we can both oversee it from home*

2:02:28 PM **ladydi2011**: Please send me the contract and let me review it and have my corporate attorney review it.

2:03:10 PM **Jerry Wesley**: Okay baby, *i* will do that

2:03:24 PM **ladydi2011**: Will you scan and email it?

2:03:38 PM **Jerry Wesley**: Yes honey,*i* am going to do that before the day runs out

2:03:52 PM **ladydi2011**: Do you still have the email address fallinghrt22@yahoo.com?

2:05:49 PM **ladydi2011**: Are you there?

2:05:53 PM **Jerry Wesley**: Hold on baby

2:05:56 PM **ladydi2011**: Ok

2:08:04 PM **Jerry Wesley**: No baby *i* do not have the ID

2:08:24 PM **Jerry Wesley**: I do not have that email address, *i* have been hacked on that email address

2:08:37 PM **Jerry Wesley**: I will be sending you the document with this email address

2:08:48 PM **ladydi2011**: Ok.

2:09:04 PM **ladydi2011**: What do you mean that you have been hacked?

2:09:16 PM **ladydi2011**: I am so naïve to all this Internet stuff

2:09:43 PM **Jerry Wesley**: Honey let me have your email address so *i* can send you the documentation

2:11:06 PM **ladydi2011**: ladydi2011@yahoo.com

2:12:36 PM **Jerry Wesley**: Okay baby, do you mind if I scan the document to you now?

2:12:57 PM **ladydi2011**: Please do

2:13:06 PM **Jerry Wesley**: Okay baby, hold on

2:15:06 PM **ladydi2011**: Ok.

From: Jerry Wesley [mailto:jerrywdiana62@yahoo.com]
Sent: Monday, May 07, 2012 3:14 PM
To: Diana Garren
Subject:

Hi baby, attached is the document of the contract agreement, its yet to be filled honey.

CONTRACT AGREEMENT FOR CONSTRUCTION

THIS AGREEMENT, entered into this _____ day of----_____, by and between THE BOARD OF TRUSTEES OF THE OPTIMALBUILD CONSTRUCTION GROUP of SOUTH AFRICA, a corporation, the party of the first part (hereinafter called the Owner)**, MR HOWARD LANE ,** and of the second part (hereinafter called the Contractor). **MR JERRY WESELY**

WITNESSETH that the Owner and the Contractor, in consideration of premises and of the mutual covenants, considerations, and agreements herein contained, agree as follows:

To complete an ongoing project in premises of Beijing ,maximum of 20 roads,293 shopping complexes and 12 overhead bridges.

STATEMENT OF WORK: The Contractor shall furnish all labor and materials and perform all work for the **REPUBLIC OF CHINA** (the "Work") in strict accordance with the Contract Documents as follows: Plans dated - **30TH** and consisting of 2 sheet(s) and Specifications dated _____and consisting of 2 pages prepared by_____ , including Addenda thereto dated_____which are hereby made a part of this Agreement as fully and to the same effect as if the same had been set forth at length in the body of this Agreement.

TIME OF COMPLETION: The Contractor will begin construction upon notification by the Owner to proceed and agrees to complete all work within **7 months and 2week(s)** consecutive calendar days after notice to proceed is given as stated in Contract Documents.

COMPENSATION TO BE PAID: The Owner will pay and the Contractor will accept in full consideration for the performance of the Work, subject to additions and deductions (including liquidated damages) as provided in the Contract Documents, the sum of _____ _____ _____ The Base Bid for the aforesaid work including

Alternate Prices:
PARTIAL AND FINAL PAYMENTS shall be made in accordance with Article 28 of the General

File Name: contract
April 16, 2012

Conditions.
The Contractor and the Owner for themselves, their successors, executors, administrators, and assigns, hereby agree to the full performance of the covenants herein contained.

IN WITNESS WHEREOF, the parties hereto on the day and year first above written have executed this Agreement in four counterparts each of which shall without proof or accounting for the other counterparts be deemed an original thereof.

The Owner does hereby certify that this contract was let in accordance with the provisions of Title 39 Code of South Africa, as amended.

CONTRACTING PARTIES   **BEIJING,CHINA**
By: **MR Richard Borrows**
Title:CEO
The Board of Trustees of the OptimalBuild Construction Group
(Owner) **MR HOWARD LANE**

By: **JING _HUAN HIN**
Title: Vice President for Financial Affairs and Treasurer
The OptimalBuild Construction Group

3:14:07 PM **Jerry Wesley**: Hi baby

3:15:24 PM **ladydi2011**: Hi

3:15:42 PM **Jerry Wesley**: I just sent you the document honey

3:17:06 PM **ladydi2011**: Ok...let me take a look at it.

3:24:13 PM **Jerry Wesley**: did you get it honey

3:24:16 PM **ladydi2011**: I got the contract and I have reviewed it but the addendum is not there and it doesn't say anything about money, in less I am missing it? Btw, they also spelled your last name wrong.

3:24:52 PM **Jerry Wesley**: Yes baby,*i* am yet to fill it up,*i* just wanted you to check it out first

3:25:55 PM **Jerry Wesley**: *It doesn't matter if they spelled the name right or wrong,i just dont want to go into this without being financially stable*

3:26:38 PM **Jerry Wesley**: *i* dont know if *i* am making any sense to you

3:27:08 PM **ladydi2011**: You are not making any sense, please explain a little more.

3:27:40 PM **ladydi2011**: I am not a contractor, so please help me understand.

3:30:15 PM **Jerry Wesley**: *Baby, if i am to sign that contract agreement, i am to have about 300,000 in my account before they'd be able to award the contract to me, and i do not have that much with me, that's why i am asking you to invest in me, and then i can seal this deal, come home and oversee it from home, you will get 25percent interest on every income*

3:31:49 PM **ladydi2011**: I so wish I had 300,000 to put into your account. If I had 300,000 I wouldn't be in Atlanta. I would be living on the beach in Aruba.

3:32:29 PM **Jerry Wesley**: *Honey, i am not asking you to come up with everything, just the one you can, cant i ask you to assist me?*

3:33:14 PM **ladydi2011**: Of course you can ask me. Nothing has changed with my financial picture since the last time you asked me for money...

3:34:17 PM **Jerry Wesley**: Baby

3:34:25 PM **ladydi2011**: Yes

3:34:44 PM **Jerry Wesley**: *i* am sorry *i* asked you,*i* thought *i* could confide in you sorry *i* was wrong

3:34:56 PM **ladydi2011**: You can confide in me.

3:35:27 PM **ladydi2011**: Confiding in me and me giving you money are two different things.

3:35:56 PM **Jerry Wesley**: I am not asking you to come up with the whole of the 300k honey

3:36:01 PM **ladydi2011**: If you need financial help from a woman, I am the wrong woman for you.

3:36:07 PM **Jerry Wesley**: *cant you risk it for me?*

3:36:16 PM **Jerry Wesley**: Dont tell me you are the wrong woman for me

3:36:38 PM **Jerry Wesley**: If you were to be the wrong woman for me, we wouldnt be here today

3:36:41 PM **ladydi2011**: How much of it do you have?

3:37:14 PM **Jerry Wesley**: I have 175k honey

3:37:26 PM **ladydi2011**: *So you need 125k?*

3:40:31 PM **ladydi2011**: You have more money than me.

3:40:44 PM **Jerry Wesley**: so because *i* dont own a home you wont be lending me the funds *i* need?

3:40:57 PM **Jerry Wesley**: my love,is it all about the material stuff

3:41:16 PM **Jerry Wesley**: Okay,sorry *i* bothered you lets close the chapter

3:41:32 PM **Jerry Wesley**: *i* wont ask you for anything again

3:41:35 PM **ladydi2011**: No...I am just laughing about how much more money you have than me...I must be doing something wrong

3:41:38 PM **Jerry Wesley**: I am sorry

3:42:03 PM **ladydi2011**: All I want to do is be with you.

3:42:23 PM **ladydi2011**: If I had the money, I would give it to you.

3:43:20 PM **Jerry Wesley**: I dont need the money anymore..sorry *i* even asked you

3:44:02 PM **ladydi2011**: This is why the rich get richer and the poor get poorer. The rich have money to invest, therefore they get richer...the poor don't have money to invest and never become rich...

3:44:39 PM **Jerry Wesley**: I DONT NEED MONEY FROM YOU!

3:44:46 PM **ladydi2011**: Ok

3:44:47 PM **Jerry Wesley**: its fine *i* am not asking for your help

3:45:09 PM **ladydi2011**: I want you to have what you want in life.

3:45:15 PM **Jerry Wesley**: *i* am not talking about it anymore so will you stop talking about the money

3:45:16 PM **ladydi2011**: I want you to be happy

3:46:16 PM **Jerry Wesley**: You want me to be happy you want me to accomplish the goal which *i* have set for our future, the future of you and *i*, *but yet you hold back on the little things that counts*

3:46:48 PM **ladydi2011**: What am I holding back?

3:47:30 PM **ladydi2011**: Please tell me what you think I am holding back

3:48:15 PM **Jerry Wesley**: www.optimalbuildingconstruction.com

3:48:31 PM **Jerry Wesley**: Thats it!! you will see what it is *i* am about losing 😠

3:49:19 PM **ladydi2011**: I want you to have this

3:49:29 PM **Jerry Wesley**: *i* never for once believed you're going to let me down

3:50:37 PM **ladydi2011**: You make me out to be some cruel person.

3:51:07 PM **ladydi2011**: Why does your success depend on me???

3:51:40 PM **Jerry Wesley**: *maybe because we were destined to do this together* 😠 baby please *i* am on my kneels

3:53:45 PM **ladydi2011**: I wish for once you would ask me to do something that I can do...You always ask me to do what I can't do.

3:55:14 PM **Jerry Wesley**: *will you check into your 401k and take a loan for me?*

3:55:53 PM **Jerry Wesley**: *i am going to pay it back, with 25 percent interest*

3:56:34 PM **ladydi2011**: I do not have a 401k.

3:57:37 PM **Jerry Wesley**: *i* believe you

3:58:19 PM **Jerry Wesley**: *i* will have to get going

3:59:40 PM **ladydi2011**: I don't think I will ever meet you in person...

4:00:03 PM **ladydi2011**: I will continue to pray for you.

4:00:20 PM **Jerry Wesley**: why are you saying that

4:01:03 PM **ladydi2011**: what?

4:01:06 PM **Jerry Wesley**: it probably means you can live on without me

4:01:10 PM **Jerry Wesley**: *i* mean nothing to you

4:01:18 PM **ladydi2011**: Hmmmm

4:01:19 PM **Jerry Wesley**: thats why you're blowing me off

4:01:28 PM **ladydi2011**: I am not blowing you off

4:01:32 PM **Jerry Wesley**: thats why you are refusing to help me

4:01:32 PM **ladydi2011**: I am insulted!!!

4:02:43 PM **Jerry Wesley**: *i* know you are able to! you are not willing to thats it

He continues to say the same things. He is disappointed that he still cannot get money from me. He is convinced that I have or can get the funds but do not want to, and he is right. I do not want to and I won't! In Nigeria, there is no credit. If you own a home or car the only way you can pay for it is with cash. They don't really understand what a mortgage or car note entails in the United States.

When he tells me to go to the Cash Store it tells me that he does know how to get money by using a car title. But again, he doesn't understand that many people do not own their cars outright, and therefore don't have a title. He really pissed me off when he said that the $3,500 I sent him meant nothing. What? Scammers will push you to do everything possible to get them money. The FIRST time someone asks you for money STOP ALL COMMUNICATION, or you are setting yourself up for this type of abuse.

For the most part, this man didn't use lower case I's. Now he is using them a lot. He is either getting sloppy, he had another scammer send that piece to me or he copied it from another scammers format because he wasn't sure what to do next.

Now he tells me that he will never forgive me if he loses the job. What? It is I who has to forgive him. I have already forgiven him or it would have created a root of bitterness in me, and I will not allow him to have power like that over me. There was never "a job", it was just a "story".

He did see me lauging on webcam because I have already started chatting with a couple other scammers to get stories for this book, and I was laughing with one of them. Got myself out of that one! He wasn't talking to me much and I still wanted to learn his real identity. Then he said, "Ok baby, you win!" I didn't know what that meant. Then he changed his Yahoo ID to jerrywdiana11 to make me feel special. He said his other Yahoo account was hacked. This probably meant someone hacked his account to get his contacts or he was reported as a scammer.

Just when I thought I had him boxed in, he comes up with yet another way to try to extort money from me. Now he has a "lifetime opportunity that is worth over 34 billion in U.S. dollars". What? But it's ok. It will allow me to show you how another scam plays out. Now he wants $125,000 instead of $11,000. He is all over the board with the amount of money he is asking for. What a ride!

He is tenacious but he has met his match, so here goes another round of acting and trying to figure out his game so I can wear him down. I think he is close to being worn down and his time is running out.

- If he was in real estate like he claimed, he would know that home values have dropped and would understand the market and mortgages. His lack of understanding is another red flag.
- If a person doesn't understand how things work in the United States, you should question whether or not they are from the United States.
- A scammer may change his Yahoo ID to reflect your and his name as a way of saying you are a couple.
- A scammer often uses your picture and puts a love message to you in their Yahoo ID to make you think they are letting everyone know that you are their woman. However, you are the only person they use that ID with, so it means nothing.
- If someone says, "I have been in pains" they are from Nigeria.
- A scammer may claim to have an investment project for you to invest in. If this is the case, the money they want you to invest is an extremely high amount. If you invest please know you will never see your money or any other money.
- If a scammer sends you contracts, they are not legitimate.

From: Diana Garren
Sent: Wednesday, May 09, 2012 3:59 PM
To: jerrywdiana62@yahoo.com
Subject: Hey Baby

Hi Jerry,

I have been reading things you have sent me. Baby, where did the man go that I met? This is the man I fell in love with.

I miss him so much. Where is he????

Diana

Text Message

From: +16197961879
Received: May 8, 2012 12:31 PM

Good morning honey and how are you doing....I missed you so much....Sweetheart can you get online?

3:10:47 PM **Jerry Wesley**: Hi baby
3:11:02 PM **ladydi2011**: *Hi*
3:12:31 PM **ladydi2011**: *Gotta go...I have a meeting in 5 min.*
3:13:26 PM **Jerry Wesley**: Okay honey will you be on later in the day?

Text Messages

To: 6197961879
Sent: May 10, 2012 11:47 AM

Hi Jerry, I haven't heard from you. My grandmother died. I need you.

From: +16197961879
Received: May 13, 2012 9:16 AM

Hi honey...Good morning, Oh my God what happened how did it happen, I am so sorry, I have been so sick....can you get online to talk to me....I Love you

From: +16197961879
Received: May 14, 2012 6:49 AM

Hi honey I wish I could be there with you to go through this togeather.

I wish I could be there to give you a hug and tell you how proud I am of you that your still there doing what you set out to do, after everything you have and are still going through takes a lot of courage to stick to it you are an inspiration... you give me a faith in you that is very strong...

I Love you so much.

7:06:16 AM **Jerry Wesley**: <ding>
7:07:17 AM **ladydi2011**: thanks for calling
7:07:59 AM **Jerry Wesley**: Awwwww, I needed too, I miss my wife
7:08:07 AM **Jerry Wesley**: I thought you are not around thou.
7:08:37 AM **Jerry Wesley**: Hi honey I wish I could be there with you to go through this togeather. I wish I could be there to give you a hug and tell you how proud I am of you that your still there doing what you set out to do,after everything you have and are still going through takes a lot of courage to stick to it you are an inspiration... you give me a faith in you that is very strong....
7:08:58 AM **ladydi2011**: The funeral was in Pennsylvania. I didn't have the money to go home for the funeral.
7:09:16 AM **Jerry Wesley**: Oh, How much honey

7:09:27 AM **ladydi2011**: $1,000

7:09:53 AM **Jerry Wesley**: to go?

7:10:14 AM **ladydi2011**: Yes, for the flights and car rental

7:10:31 AM **Jerry Wesley**: You dont have $1000?

7:10:39 AM **ladydi2011**: Nope

7:11:14 AM **ladydi2011**: I know you never believed me, but I was telling you the truth all along.

7:11:47 AM **ladydi2011**: Now when I really needed the money for something important, I don't have it.

7:12:00 AM **Jerry Wesley**: *and I wanted to tell you to send $500 to a friend who is sending me 10K on wednesday, so I can come home to be with you, so we go to the funeral together.*

7:12:14 AM **ladydi2011**: Jerry, I never lied to you about anything.

7:12:23 AM **Jerry Wesley**: I understand.

7:12:31 AM **Jerry Wesley**: *but baby, you have things to get loan with.*

7:12:44 AM **Jerry Wesley**: but its Okay, I dont need money anymore.

7:12:55 AM **Jerry Wesley**: *just send $500 to the guy, Okay*

7:13:56 AM **ladydi2011**: I just told you I didn't even have money to go to my grandmother's funeral, so why do you think I would have 500 to send to this guy?

7:14:53 AM **Jerry Wesley**: *I know baby, thats why I want you to find the $500 today and send so I can be back on thursday baby, so we can go to the funeral together please dont fail this one baby.*

7:15:03 AM **ladydi2011**: Anyway...I am very sad

7:16:33 AM **ladydi2011**: I thought you had the $175,000 for the construction company deal

7:19:43 AM **Jerry Wesley**: *Yes, the person will be sending me the 175, thats why I want you to send him $500, so he wants to send me 11k...first so I can come back to be with you, so I can start the process from there.*

7:19:48 AM **Jerry Wesley**: *please do it..dont fail this one*

7:23:54 AM **Jerry Wesley**: can I give you the info so you can send it this morning.

7:24:27 AM **ladydi2011**: Yes, please send me the info

7:24:41 AM **Jerry Wesley**: Ok.

7:25:40 AM **Jerry Wesley**: *Name: Steven Jefferson*

Country : Nigeria

State : Lagos

City: Ikeja

zipcode: 23401

text question: Hello

text answer: Hi

7:25:47 AM **Jerry Wesley**: *can you go send it now baby.*

7:26:07 AM **ladydi2011**: Is this to be sent Western Union?

7:26:13 AM **Jerry Wesley**: Yes.

7:26:19 AM **ladydi2011**: Ok...

7:26:33 AM **ladydi2011**: Why am I not sending it to you?

7:26:55 AM **Jerry Wesley**: he is needing it, for the transfer.

7:27:10 AM **ladydi2011**: He is in Nigeria?

7:27:40 AM **Jerry Wesley**: Yes...I sent you his picture.

7:28:29 AM **ladydi2011**: There was no picture there

7:28:35 AM **Jerry Wesley**: why did you close the photo sharing

7:29:18 AM **Jerry Wesley**: dont close it

7:29:22 AM **ladydi2011**: Because there is no picture there

7:29:29 AM **Jerry Wesley**: accept and leave it...it will come. Did you see the picture?

7:30:14 AM **ladydi2011**: I did. You sent me this picture once before

7:30:21 AM **Jerry Wesley**: he wants to do the business with me.

7:30:42 AM **Jerry Wesley**: *will you go send the $500 now, so he can wire this today?*

7:30:53 AM **ladydi2011**: Ok

7:31:01 AM **Jerry Wesley**: *are you going now?*

7:31:22 AM **Jerry Wesley**: *I will be home by thursday..please give me your airport where you will pick me.*

7:31:49 AM **ladydi2011**: Atlanta

7:32:14 AM **Jerry Wesley**: Ok, whats your time now?

7:32:25 AM **ladydi2011**: 7:30 am

7:32:48 AM **Jerry Wesley**: *Baby, please be ready for me Okay, I will be home.*

7:33:09 AM **ladydi2011**: Will you then have the money to fly both of us to Pennsylvania and rent a car?

7:33:25 AM **Jerry Wesley**: Yes...he is wiring me 11K..I told you

7:33:47 AM **ladydi2011**: But don't you need that for the business deal there?

7:34:01 AM **Jerry Wesley**: I want to get back first.

7:34:18 AM **Jerry Wesley**: he wants me to get back so we can finanlize the other business..

7:35:02 AM **ladydi2011**: Ok...I am going to go

7:35:07 AM **Jerry Wesley**: Ok.

7:46:50 AM **Jerry Wesley**: *Text me once you get it done.*

Text Messages

From: +16197961879
Received: May 14, 2012 7:50 AM

Baby the guy just emailed me. Saying what he needs is $700. For the wire. Please honey send $700. Thanks. I love you. Once you do it please text me so he can wire to me today. I love you

To: +16197961879
Sent: May 14, 2012 7:51 AM
Hmmmmm

From: +16197961879
Received: May 14, 2012 7:57 AM

Please baby do what he said. Cause he needs it. when you get it done, text me the MTCN number..and senders name...Love you

To: +16197961879
Sent: May 14, 2012 7:59 AM

So you are telling me he has 11k but he doesn't have $700????? Come on, Jerry! Why are you insulting my intelligence?

From: +16197961879
Received: May 14, 2012 8:04 AM

this is bank to bank, he needs the $700 to pay for wire...maybe something else, but he just told me to send him $700....so he can wire me the 11K today....are you on your way now to do it?

From: +16197961879
Received: May 14, 2012 8:05 AM

please stop..why will I insult your intelligence, I am not stupid baby.

From: +16197961879
Received: May 14, 2012 8:11 AM

????? stop Baby get going so he can get it today and wire me what we need, it is getting late there Baby. are you on your way now baby?

From: +16197961879
Received: May 14, 2012 8:39 AM

I missed you and I can't wait to be with you by thursday baby.

From: +16197961879
Received: May 14, 2012 10:18 AM

Baby where are you...text me, it is getting late there baby....I Love you

From: +16197961879
Received: May 14, 2012 9:31 AM

I Love you

From: +16197961879
Received: May 14, 2012 11:45 AM

why not text me and let me know where you are and if you have done it baby, stop making me feel ignored..I want to come home...I Love you

From: +16197961879
Received: May 14, 2012 12:37 PM

I am calling You and you are not picking or replying my text, I am feeling ignored...whats wrong....where are you?

Phone Calls: He called at the following times, but I didn't answer: 10:17am, 10:19am, 11:12am, 11:37am, 12:32pm, 2:17pm and 2:18pm.

From: +16197961879
Received: May 15, 2012 4:20 AM

Hi baby. I can see that you never wanted to reply my text or pick my calls. I see. Does this show that you don't want me anymore right?? I will wait today and see if I will hear from you. ***But remember our Oath.*** Good night

To: +16197961879
Sent: May 15, 2012 6:25 PM

Jerry, when you were in trouble I helped you. When I am in trouble and need to travel to my grandmother's funeral you do not help me. You say you love me. Your actions are speaking so loud that I can't hear your words!!!

From: +16197961879
Received: May 15, 2012 6:43 PM

Hi Baby, How come you are saying this.....***I thought you were sending the $700?*** so I can be with you on thursday? we need to go to the funeral together baby, I have been worried about you.

From: +16197961879
Received: May 15, 2012 6:52 PM

why dont you want to talk to me on the phone? Baby, why are you pushing me away..even hanging the phone on me..because I am looking for a way for us to be together..***so you are telling me you lied of going to send the funds and you didnt go right?***

From: +16197961879
Received: May 15, 2012 7:03 PM

well, I have told you what we need. so if you want go send it. Keep lying to yourself..***so you lied to me about sending the $500 yesterday...well I dont blame you..You want to die single?***

To: +16197961879
Sent: May 15, 2012 7:12 PM

Jerry, please know that I am not desperate!!! I could go out tonight and meet someone if I wanted to. I am single because I chose to be.
From: +16197961879
Received: May 15, 2012 7:13 PM

I know what I feel for you, ***I am the only man for you...dont lose me..go send the $500***

To: +16197961879
Sent: May 15, 2012 7:35 PM

Don't order me to do anything. Anyone who knows me knows I DO NOT do anything I am ordered to do. If you don't want to lose me then you figure out a way to get home to me. Yes, I originally thought you were the man for me. But if you can't even handle this situation, you could never take care of me. I will find a way to get over you!

From: +16197961879
Received: May 17, 2012 8:51 AM

Hi Love.....

From: +16197961879
Received: May 17, 2012 10:24 AM

get online.....

IM May 18, 2012 2:56:58 AM

2:56:58 AM **Jerry Wesley**: <ding>
2:58:51 AM **Jerry Wesley**: Hi.
2:59:46 AM **Jerry Wesley**: Now you are trying to ignore me.
2:59:54 AM **Jerry Wesley**: do you really think we need this?

IM May 18, 2012 Continued

8:02:04 AM **Jerry Wesley**: Diana
8:02:22 AM **ladydi2011**: Yes Jerry
8:02:35 AM **Jerry Wesley**: How are you?
8:03:16 AM **ladydi2011**: Fine!!!
8:04:07 AM **Jerry Wesley**: I am sorry, but remember I want to come home this week
8:04:26 AM **Jerry Wesley**: if you would have sent the $500 I would have been home
8:05:16 AM **ladydi2011**: I don't even want to talk about this.
8:05:38 AM **Jerry Wesley**: we should
8:05:45 AM **Jerry Wesley**: You are not serious and you have started lying
8:08:10 AM **ladydi2011**: We haven't had a relationship for a month. The only time you contact me is when you want money. I started lying when all you wanted from me is money!!!!
8:09:02 AM **Jerry Wesley**: *I never wanted money*
8:09:10 AM **Jerry Wesley**: *Diana remember our Oath*
8:10:47 AM **ladydi2011**: Giving you money wasn't in our oath. You treating me so poorly was not in the oath either!
8:11:17 AM **Jerry Wesley**: *I never treated you poorly or asked you for money Diana*
8:11:32 AM **Jerry Wesley**: *please just go ahead and send the $500 so I will get back , and pay you back*
8:13:08 AM **ladydi2011**: If I had the $500 I would be at my grandmother's funeral! Please DO NOT ask me for money ever again...
8:13:56 AM **Jerry Wesley**: why will I believe you that you dont have $500 or have acess to get $500

8:15:41 AM **ladydi2011**: Believe whatever the hell you want to believe. I hope you feel good knowing that it is because I gave you money that I am not at my grandmother's funeral. I am sure you will never pay me back!

8:16:27 AM **Jerry Wesley**: I will pay you your money'

8:19:57 AM **ladydi2011**: I will believe it when I see it. Jerry, I am so disappointed in you for how you have treated me. I am disappointed in me for letting you into my heart so quickly. I am no longer the same person because of you.

8:20:23 AM **Jerry Wesley**: we can make things back.

8:22:09 AM **ladydi2011**: The heart and spirit I see in your pictures and who you were the first two weeks is not the same man you have been the last month. I do not like who you really are!

8:24:25 AM **Jerry Wesley**: *can you send the $500?*

8:24:40 AM **ladydi2011**: I don't even know you anymore. *I fell in love with the man in the picture. I have no clue who the hell you are!*

8:24:50 AM **ladydi2011**: NO

8:25:00 AM **Jerry Wesley**: I am sorry..thats why I said can we come back together

8:25:53 AM **ladydi2011**: I need to see the man I fell in love with.

8:26:14 AM **ladydi2011**: It has to happen without me sending money.

8:26:19 AM **Jerry Wesley**: You will see me

8:26:35 AM **Jerry Wesley**: Baby how can I come without you sending the $500?

8:27:15 AM **ladydi2011**: I don't know. This is your problem. Figure it out!

8:28:36 AM **Jerry Wesley**: k

8:30:07 AM **ladydi2011**: This is how I look at it...if you love me, you will get here to me and you will pay me back. If you don't, I then know you never loved me and just played me.

8:30:37 AM **ladydi2011**: Where is your money from your $75,000 cashier's check?

8:31:01 AM **Jerry Wesley**: I have put it in the job I told you about

8:32:18 AM **ladydi2011**: You broke my heart Jerry Wesley! You have taken away my faith in people and love.

8:32:49 AM **Jerry Wesley**: never

8:32:57 AM **ladydi2011**: I wish I never believed you when you said my heart was safe with you!

8:33:54 AM **Jerry Wesley**: it is still safe

8:34:34 AM **ladydi2011**: Really? Then why is it broken?

8:35:12 AM **Jerry Wesley**: You are sounding as if I did anything to you, I want a better tomorrow

8:35:21 AM **ladydi2011**: I would rather be alone than feel what I have felt the last month.

8:35:59 AM **Jerry Wesley**: I see

8:36:09 AM **Jerry Wesley**: I Love you

8:36:49 AM **ladydi2011**: Then please show me that you love me...Your words are as sweet as honey and your actions don't match darling!

8:42:29 AM **Jerry Wesley**: *then send the $500*

8:42:36 AM **ladydi2011**: I need to go to the office. I have a lot of work to do. Take care of yourself!

8:42:46 AM **ladydi2011**: NO...NO...NO...!!!!!!!!!!!!!!!

8:43:17 AM **Jerry Wesley**: and you want me?

8:44:10 AM **ladydi2011**: Yep...but I will NOT pay any more money to have you.

8:45:06 AM **Jerry Wesley**: are you buying me?

8:45:47 AM **ladydi2011**: If you want me you will figure it out and come to me. If I never see you then I know and I know you never loved me.

8:46:26 AM **Jerry Wesley**: I see

8:46:30 AM **Jerry Wesley**: *You will die ooooo*

> 8:47:33 AM **ladydi2011**: Thanks for the reassurance...you are a real gem!
> 8:49:47 AM **ladydi2011**: As I said, you broke my heart. I don't deserve this. Time will tell how this chapter of my book will end...

Now I feel as low as the scammer for making up fictitious stories in an attempt to get to this man's heart and concience if he has one. I came up with the story that my grandmother died and I couldn't go to the funeral because he took my money. The only way I was able to do this is because both of my grandmother's have been deceased for years or I could have never used this story line. Even with this, he still asked me for money. This shows just how ruthless and uncaring scammers are and how they don't care about you. Now he has another scam story and can all of a sudden fly "home" to go to the funeral with me, but to do this he needs $500 and then ups it to $700 and I am to send it via Western Union to Nigeria. Now we are getting somewhere close to the truth. I didn't talk, chat or text him for almost two days, then he really made me angry and I broke down and texted him once. Then he asks me, "You want to die single?" This is something a scammer thinks you are afraid of. No matter what, you don't ever have to be desperate or afraid. He tries telling me he is the "only man" for me. News flash... there are many fish in the sea, and he wasn't a good catch and needed to be thrown back anyway! A scammer is NEVER the only man for you. He makes the vital mistake of "ordering me". I will do nothing I am ordered to do. This is when it hits me that I fell in love with the "picture". Nine times out of ten, you too have fallen or will fall in love with the fake picture along with the sweet words and false promises. His last intimidation here to me is " You will die ooooo." This didn't intimidate me at all and you should NOT let it intimidate you either.

Here's the thing about lying, you can never remember what you said prior, so if YOU pay attention you will catch a scammer's lies. ***Warning:*** If your heart is involved and you catch the lies, you still might not be able to get out of the web, because it is your heart and not your logic driving you, and the scammer knows it.

RED FLAGS

⚑ "ooooo" is a Pidgin English phrase. Someone who uses it is likely Nigerian.

IM May 22, 2012 8:45:23 AM

8:45:23 AM **Jerry Wesley**: Hi Baby
8:46:06 AM **ladydi2011**: Hi
8:46:26 AM **Jerry Wesley**: How are you?
8:46:33 AM **ladydi2011**: FINE!
8:47:01 AM **ladydi2011**: How are you? It's been some days since I've heard from you.
8:47:03 AM **Jerry Wesley**: I am Okay, looking for a better way to do my business.

8:47:15 AM **Jerry Wesley**: *Diana, do you have equity on your house and how much is the limit?*

8:48:51 AM **Jerry Wesley**: *did you remember the job I told you about, they said if I am not married they wont give me thev job...and also...the funds to finalize the job will come from the wife and also husband...which I told you that way you will get 20%*

8:49:14 AM **Jerry Wesley**: *Baby, with your equity I can transfer money in there.*

8:49:28 AM **Jerry Wesley**: *so it will look like its your money for the job*

8:49:36 AM **Jerry Wesley**: please lets do this

8:49:43 AM **Jerry Wesley**: *I dont need your money anymore*

8:49:47 AM **ladydi2011**: Hold please

8:50:01 AM **Jerry Wesley**: *all I need now is your equity info so they can do the transfer*

8:50:25 AM **Jerry Wesley**: *if you are still oweing any money in the house payment..I will pay it from the money wired to the account*

8:50:41 AM **Jerry Wesley**: think about it baby.

8:51:00 AM **Jerry Wesley**: *we are distined to be together*

8:51:20 AM **Jerry Wesley**: *I don't need your money anymore.*

9:02:52 AM **Jerry Wesley**: can we do this?

9:04:01 AM **ladydi2011**: Sadly I do not have any equity in my home

9:04:56 AM **Jerry Wesley**: why? I told you I will pay it

9:06:01 AM **Jerry Wesley**: once the money is wired, they will take their money..I will pay it off

9:06:17 AM **Jerry Wesley**: *all I need is the equity account info.*

9:06:52 AM **ladydi2011**: I don't have a home equity account

9:07:11 AM **Jerry Wesley**: can you get an account.

9:07:58 AM **ladydi2011**: No I can't

9:08:24 AM **Jerry Wesley**: you have mortgage you can get an equity account baby.

9:09:01 AM **ladydi2011**: Jerry, you told me you have been in real estate for 19 years, you should know this.

9:09:29 AM **Jerry Wesley**: I know thats why I said you can get an equity account

9:09:43 AM **Jerry Wesley**: *you should have equity and mortgage account Diana*

9:10:09 AM **ladydi2011**: You should also know that they are lowering and closing people's equity accounts. In the good days, this is how it worked, not anymore.

9:11:05 AM **Jerry Wesley**: *I told you that I will pay the money off you owe once the money is wired to the account*

9:11:51 AM **ladydi2011**: I can't get an account until the money is paid...

9:12:09 AM **Jerry Wesley**: k..I know you can.

9:14:19 AM **ladydi2011**: Why didn't you pay me back once you cashed your cashier's check?

9:14:43 AM **Jerry Wesley**: How much is your money?

9:14:53 AM **Jerry Wesley**: 3500..do you know how much I want to pay for you

9:15:13 AM **Jerry Wesley**: you are telling me you dont have equity of your home and you cant get

9:15:21 AM **Jerry Wesley**: I cant believe that

9:18:02 AM **ladydi2011**: Jerry, please answer my question. You told me you would pay me back as soon as you cashed this check.

9:18:26 AM **ladydi2011**: Why did you not keep your word?

9:19:23 AM **ladydi2011**: You did not keep your word because you never intended to pay me back.

9:19:38 AM **ladydi2011**: *You are a user!!!!*

9:21:57 AM **ladydi2011**: *Karma is a bitch. I wouldn't want to be you on judgment day. God will not judge favorably towards you. You will answer to him and he will have vengeance on you. You have used his word to take from me. The penalty for this is high...Life in eternal hell.*

9:25:29 AM **Jerry Wesley**: stop insulting me.
9:27:45 AM **Jerry Wesley**: come online
9:27:53 AM **Jerry Wesley**: let me show you me on webcam.
9:30:44 AM **Jerry Wesley**: please do me that favor and come on yahoo messenger
9:45:33 AM **Jerry Wesley**: are you coming on.

Text Message

From: +16197961879
Received: May 22, 2012 9:54 AM

can you come on yahoo messenger so I can show you myself on webcam.

IM May 22, 2012 9:58:37 AM

9:58:37 AM **ladydi2011**: I am here.
10:01:37 AM **ladydi2011**: Please invite me to view your cam
10:23:28 AM **Jerry Wesley**: can you see me
10:24:06 AM **ladydi2011**: I can
10:24:23 AM **Jerry Wesley**: thats me'
10:24:47 AM **ladydi2011**: Jerry, why did you lie to me all this time?
10:25:03 AM **Jerry Wesley**: I needed you to know that things are hard
10:25:08 AM **Jerry Wesley**: so I have no choice than to lie
10:25:21 AM **ladydi2011**: Ok, please tell me more
10:26:00 AM **ladydi2011**: Please turn your cam back on so I can see your eyes when you type to me
10:27:38 AM **Jerry Wesley**: can you see now?

He continues to try to get me to send him money and convince me we are destined to be together. Then he tells me he doesn't need my money. I think he is finally out of stories and breaking down. I then hit him hard when I told him that he was a user and that karma was a bitch and I wouldn't want to be him on judgment day. I think the real breaking point was when I said that he used God to take from me and the penalty for this is life in eternal hell. The next thing I know he is telling me to stop insulting him and come online so he can show himself to me on webcam. He actually almost begged me to come online so he could show me who he was. He must have been really nervous because we were already on Yahoo when he asked me to come online. I finally got to see "*the man behind the screen*" and he was definitely **NOT** the man he portrayed himself to be.

10:28:07 AM **Jerry Wesley**: I am sorry

10:28:14 AM **Jerry Wesley**: this is the truth you know now

10:28:19 AM **Jerry Wesley**: if you still want me then I need your help

10:28:31 AM **ladydi2011**: I could only see you for a minute

10:28:51 AM **ladydi2011**: Thank you for finally telling me the truth

10:29:04 AM **ladydi2011**: Thank you for apologizing

10:29:23 AM **ladydi2011**: Where do you really live?

10:29:59 AM **ladydi2011**: What is your real name?

10:30:14 AM **Jerry Wesley**: I am from Nigeria

10:30:23 AM **ladydi2011**: I thought so.

10:30:34 AM **ladydi2011**: You know I fell in love with you

10:30:47 AM **Jerry Wesley**: me too I did fall in Love with you thats why I told you the truth

10:31:06 AM **ladydi2011**: I am crying right now

10:31:29 AM **Jerry Wesley**: I am sorry

10:32:16 AM **ladydi2011**: Did you really fall in love with me or money

10:32:39 AM **Jerry Wesley**: I did this for money, but I never knew I will fall for you

10:32:42 AM **Jerry Wesley**: please forgive me

10:32:57 AM **Jerry Wesley**: if you can help me get to the state we can start up something

10:33:03 AM **ladydi2011**: What is your real name?

10:33:37 AM **Jerry Wesley**: You want to hurt me right?

10:33:57 AM **ladydi2011**: No, I am not that kind of person

10:34:18 AM **ladydi2011**: Please tell me your real name

10:34:59 AM **Jerry Wesley**: my real name is Micheal

10:35:08 AM **ladydi2011**: Hello Michael

10:35:25 AM **Jerry Wesley**: Hi Diana

10:35:33 AM **Jerry Wesley**: I am really sorry for everything

10:37:55 AM **ladydi2011**: are you there?

10:38:18 AM **Jerry Wesley**: Yes I am here

10:38:21 AM **Jerry Wesley**: I am crying

10:40:43 AM **ladydi2011**: I am in shock and am signing off. Please give me about 10 min.

10:41:26 AM **Jerry Wesley**: Ok.

Break In Time

10:58:58 AM **ladydi2011**: I am here. Are you still there?

10:59:17 AM **ladydi2011**: Michael

10:59:25 AM **Jerry Wesley**: am here

11:01:14 AM **ladydi2011**: Please give me an email address where I can email what I wrote you.

11:01:46 AM **Jerry Wesley**: email me on this one

11:01:55 AM **ladydi2011**: Michael, I have done mission work in Africa. I know first-hand how difficult it is there. Stealing money from people is NOT a good answer for you.

11:02:06 AM **Jerry Wesley**: You told me

11:03:22 AM **ladydi2011**: Please give me a minute to email you

11:05:27 AM **Jerry Wesley**: Ok

11:07:58 AM **ladydi2011**: I wrote this letter to you back on May 1st.

11:08:02 AM **ladydi2011**: I just sent it

11:09:30 AM **Jerry Wesley**: please let me read.

11:09:59 AM **ladydi2011**: Thank you for reading this. I am actually rereading it

From: Diana Garren
Sent: Thursday, May 22, 2012 11:04 AM
To: jerrywdiana62@yahoo.com
Subject: Goodbye Letter

Hi Jerry,

I have not pushed you away. You have pushed me away. You have been totally different since you went to China. Now that I cannot give you any more money you disappeared, just like the last girl you dated did to you. ***fallinghrt22***: *I dated 2yrs ago..but it didn't work out she drinks and smokes....and she was not ready to settle down...what hurt me the most she ran away with my best friend and with my funds...I have not set my eyes on them...*

You said you were very honest and trustworthy and will never disappoint me. Well, this isn't true! I did trust you and you abused this trust. You have so disappointed me. ***fallinghrt22***: *Oh how do you know whats on my mind...I am very honest and trust worthy if we can trust each other with every bit then I am ready...I will never disappoint you.*You said my heart was safe with you. It was not. It is now broken. I am a good woman and I do not deserve what you did. You obviously do not have a heart, nor do you care. You taught me a good lesson. ***fallinghrt22***: *Diana, I want you to know that we are not Kids...this is so important to me and I am loving getting to know you...your heart is very safe with me.*

Oh, how I wish you were the man you portrayed yourself to be. We could have had a wonderful life together. You would have been an extremely happy man! You would have had "true love" and an extraordinary life with me. I am exactly who I told you I am. Everything I ever said to you was true and real. Unfortunately, you did not do the same.

I have to hand it to you, you are good, Baby, at getting a woman to fall in love with you and obtain small amounts of money from them. But you have a lot to learn, my dear, to be able to get large amount of money from me or any woman who is paying attention. You made MANY mistakes. I will never divulge these mistakes to you. I will never give you anything that will advance your deception and fraud scheme.

I easily gave you the money because I thought you were in trouble. I trusted you when you said I would have it back in 2 days. I wanted you to be successful and I cared about your well-being. What I know now is you were never in love with me. You played me like a fiddle and lied to me. You never cared about my well-being, and you are definitely not someone my heart or anything else is safe with!

Darling, I will never know if this is a game for you or the way you make a living. For all I know it has been a woman sending me text and emails. Whatever it was, it was. One thing I do know is that you might think you can play with people's heart and finances without any repercussion. But what one does in life always has repercussions. The decisions one makes today will always affect their future. What goes around comes around.

I know you are probably laughing at getting over on me. That's ok! Laugh all you want, my dear. I promise you that one day your laughter will turn into deep regret. You will struggle within your own soul, if you are not already doing so. You will be trapped in deep despair because you have sold your soul. This is sad for you, because no amount of money is worth selling your soul for. You might think I am wrong, but you will see one day in the very near future just how very right I am.

I don't know how you sleep at night or how you look at yourself in the mirror. One day you will meet your maker and have to answer for all you have done, especially for using His name and Word for evil. Vengeance belongs to the Lord, not to me. You see, I already have forgiven you, so my soul is free and my heart is clean. I hold no malice for you; just pity.

I promise you that YOU WILL REMEMBER ME FOREVER. I will always be a reminder to you of who you really are, how you sold your soul and what you could have had in life. I feel sorry for you and what your future holds, my dear! There will be times for the rest of your life and on your death bed that you will hear my words and see my face. When you do, there will be a deep sadness in your heart!

There will even be days throughout your life that you will desire me and wonder what it would have been like to touch my face, kiss my soft lips and make love with me. However, I will not wonder these things about you because you are not who you say you are, so I have nothing to miss. One cannot miss what wasn't real!

Your three weeks of actions will NOT define me or stand in my way of what I want in life. I will find my "true love" one day. When I do, this man will be all you claimed to be and then some. He will be the real deal, not a fake. He will have integrity and be kind, caring, honest and loving. God has kept me and prepared me for this man and He WILL give me the desire of my heart. He will give me a real love story!

Jerry or whoever you are, one of these times, you will get caught in your own trap and really fall in love with a woman you are deceiving. You will feel everything you have made others feel. Rest assured that this will happen because like I said, what goes around comes around. When it does it will be 100 fold and then some.

The experience we had together was fun before your deception. It also taught me a lot. I am so grateful that God kept my heart protected like he always does! He is my shield and provider. When I talk about God it is for real. I really am the daughter of the King! When you talk about God it is to deceive others. Karma is a bitch my dear. When you least expect it, it is going to overtake you and make you wish you had lived your life much differently. You WILL have MUCH SORROW and MUCH LOSS in your future!

I will always remember the brief 3 week love story with the "make believe" person I never really knew. I will write my romance novel and be sure to include our material. Yes, I have it all! Thank you for giving me such good material. It is worth much more to me than the 3,500 I paid for it.

Because of how loving and honest I am, I could have never even thought of such a plot. You see, my love, what you meant for evil, God has already turned into good for me.

I am not like most women who will never tell anyone what happened due to feeling embarrassed and ashamed. Living with secrets, embarrassment and shame would make me a victim. As a child I was a victim. As a woman I will NEVER be a victim again. I will always be VICTORIOUS. I know the laws of the universe. I always give the perpetrator back what belongs to them, therefore my power is never lost. I will NOT allow anyone to take away my voice or my power. Especially you!

There is nothing new under the sun. I will not be a mope for your fraud ring, so remove me from your list! Always remember, I emailed you first...there was a reason for this. (Wink)!

Well, my dear, I have to go now. I have a book to write. Thank you once again for the great plot and the material. You have changed my life for the better. Now I will live in even more abundance! I don't know your real name, nor do I care to. The most important thing is that I now know your game and can help others to know it too!

Have fun looking over your shoulder! My contact with you is now over. It is over "forever"! I will always be "forever" in your mind and heart, living rent free and tantalizing your soul til your last breath.

Your Ex-wife,

Diana

IM May 22, 2012 Continued

11:17:05 AM **Jerry Wesley**: what do you want from me now?
11:18:04 AM **ladydi2011**: I want the truth and nothing but the truth
11:19:08 AM **Jerry Wesley**: I want to tell you the truth but I am scared
11:19:21 AM **ladydi2011**: Scared of what?
11:19:41 AM **Jerry Wesley**: You coming to hurt me
11:20:00 AM **ladydi2011**: Michael, I will not come after you or hurt you. This is not who I am.
11:20:25 AM **ladydi2011**: Please tell me what your thoughts are of the letter I wrote you
11:20:34 AM **ladydi2011**: You hurt me deeply
11:20:34 AM **Jerry Wesley**: I pray you understand why I have done this
11:20:42 AM **Jerry Wesley**: things has not been easy with me and my family..we are suffering.
11:20:52 AM **ladydi2011**: I can't understand until you tell me everything
11:20:53 AM **Jerry Wesley**: Nigeria is a hard country
11:21:03 AM **ladydi2011**: I know it is a hard country
11:21:04 AM **Jerry Wesley**: please forgive me
11:21:32 AM **ladydi2011**: I forgave you when I wrote you the letter in May
11:21:41 AM **ladydi2011**: Michael, I am not a stupid woman
11:22:20 AM **ladydi2011**: Have you really fallen in love with me or is this more scam?
11:22:34 AM **Jerry Wesley**: if I am not in Love with you I will never show my self to you

11:22:44 AM **Jerry Wesley**: does that make sense?

11:22:51 AM **ladydi2011**: Hmmmm

11:23:19 AM **Jerry Wesley**: I am sorry for everything I have caused you

11:23:33 AM **ladydi2011**: You have really hurt me

11:23:39 AM **Jerry Wesley**: I know

11:23:43 AM **ladydi2011**: I didn't deserve this

11:23:47 AM **Jerry Wesley**: thats why it was so hard for me to tell you this

11:23:50 AM **Jerry Wesley**: please understand

11:23:52 AM **ladydi2011**: I am a good person Michael

11:23:58 AM **Jerry Wesley**: I never knew I will fall in Love with you

11:24:06 AM **Jerry Wesley**: please forgive me

11:24:19 AM **ladydi2011**: Please tell me when you fell in love with me

11:24:20 AM **Jerry Wesley**: it was never my intention to do this Diana

11:24:39 AM **Jerry Wesley**: Your words touched my heart

11:25:04 AM **Jerry Wesley**: the day you cried to my ears

11:25:35 AM **ladydi2011**: You were so mean to me

11:25:47 AM **ladydi2011**: How could you be so mean to someone you love?

11:26:20 AM **Jerry Wesley**: Diana please understand my situation.

11:26:35 AM **ladydi2011**: You touched a deep place in my heart

11:26:55 AM **Jerry Wesley**: but I will understand if you will leave me now...that you know the truth

11:27:06 AM **Jerry Wesley**: You did touch a place in my heart too

11:27:20 AM **ladydi2011**: Are you married?

11:27:34 AM **Jerry Wesley**: No I am not

11:27:38 AM **Jerry Wesley**: No girlfriend

11:27:43 AM **ladydi2011**: Do you have kids?

11:27:59 AM **Jerry Wesley**: do you know how old I am?

11:28:08 AM **ladydi2011**: No, please tell me

11:29:13 AM **Jerry Wesley**: 25yrs old

11:29:40 AM **ladydi2011**: OMG...I was in love with a 25 year old guy!!!!!!!!!!!!!!!!!!!!!!!!!!!!!!!!!!!!!

11:29:49 AM **Jerry Wesley**: I am sorry

11:30:54 AM **Jerry Wesley**: hope you will forgive me.

11:31:41 AM **ladydi2011**: Thank you for finally telling me the truth

11:32:30 AM **ladydi2011**: I always told you the truth about me

11:32:41 AM **ladydi2011**: I shared my heart with you

11:32:56 AM **Jerry Wesley**: all I told you about my feelings is real..I do Love you

11:34:09 AM **ladydi2011**: I knew deep in my heart that you did

11:34:30 AM **ladydi2011**: Who is Jerry Wesley

11:35:21 AM **ladydi2011**: You know I have many good friends from Nigeria

11:36:55 AM **Jerry Wesley**: please forgive me

11:37:05 AM **ladydi2011**: Are you the mean spirited person who I have come to know the last month?

11:37:33 AM **ladydi2011**: Please answer me

11:37:45 AM **Jerry Wesley**: Yes I am the one.

11:40:21 AM **Jerry Wesley**: please I am sorry on how I treated you

11:40:24 AM **Jerry Wesley**: I never meant it

11:43:06 AM **ladydi2011**: How could you treat me so poorly? You were brutal to me.

11:43:28 AM **Jerry Wesley**: please I am sorry

11:43:33 AM **Jerry Wesley**: will you ever forgive me?

11:43:58 AM **ladydi2011**: I do forgive you.

11:44:14 AM **Jerry Wesley**: if you can help me

11:44:29 AM **ladydi2011**: Michael, I can only get past this if you tell me the truth

11:44:32 AM **Jerry Wesley**: to come to the state..maybe go to school or find something to do.

11:44:47 AM **Jerry Wesley**: I have told you nothing but the truth

11:44:52 AM **ladydi2011**: You have to trust me now, like I trusted you when I sent you the money

11:45:08 AM **ladydi2011**: Please turn your cam on again

11:45:47 AM **Jerry Wesley**: please I am scared of you hurting me...

11:46:07 AM **ladydi2011**: Hurting you how?

11:46:43 AM **Jerry Wesley**: coming to hunt me.

11:47:03 AM **ladydi2011**: This will never happen

11:47:19 AM **Jerry Wesley**: turn your webcam please

11:47:22 AM **ladydi2011**: Maybe you don't know me.....

11:48:06 AM **Jerry Wesley**: invite me again.

11:49:08 AM **Jerry Wesley**: am scared

11:49:14 AM **Jerry Wesley**: invite me to see you please

11:49:32 AM **ladydi2011**: Am trying

11:51:06 AM **ladydi2011**: I do not look to good, do I?

11:51:25 AM **Jerry Wesley**: Your webcam is not available

11:51:36 AM **ladydi2011**: Can you see that you have really broken my heart?

11:52:01 AM **Jerry Wesley**: invite me again.

11:52:02 AM **ladydi2011**: You saw me right?

11:52:09 AM **Jerry Wesley**: No I did not

11:52:51 AM **ladydi2011**: Can you see me now?

11:53:14 AM **Jerry Wesley**: Yes I can.

11:53:25 AM **Jerry Wesley**: I am really sorry Beautiful.

11:53:39 AM **ladydi2011**: I don't feel beautiful right now

11:54:15 AM **Jerry Wesley**: please stop crying you are hurting me.

11:54:22 AM **Jerry Wesley**: right now I feel so guilty.

11:54:29 AM **ladydi2011**: After seeing me, do you really think I am going to hurt you?

11:55:48 AM **ladydi2011**: Michael, I probably have one of the kindest hearts you will ever know

11:56:10 AM **ladydi2011**: This last month has aged me by at least 10 years

11:57:31 AM **ladydi2011**: Are you there?

11:58:03 AM **Jerry Wesley**: I am here

11:58:11 AM **Jerry Wesley**: I am speechless and sad

11:58:17 AM **Jerry Wesley**: please I am sorry

11:58:46 AM **ladydi2011**: I will help you come to the states

11:59:47 AM **Jerry Wesley**: How can I trust you

11:59:54 AM **ladydi2011**: Only if you trust me enough to tell me everything

12:00:20 PM **Jerry Wesley**: I will tell you everything because I have started telling you

12:00:23 PM **ladydi2011**: Michael, you have been living a life of deception, so you will struggle to trust.

12:00:24 PM **Jerry Wesley**: but it will take a lot of trust please

12:00:36 PM **Jerry Wesley**: please I am sorry

12:01:40 PM **ladydi2011**: We need to start over. Everything needs to be the truth or we have nothing.

12:01:46 PM **Jerry Wesley**: I need someone to trust and rely on Diana, I do have a good heart, but circumstances caused me to do this

12:01:54 PM **Jerry Wesley**: I am willing.

12:02:04 PM **ladydi2011**: I understand about circumstances

12:03:10 PM **ladydi2011**: First, please create an email and IM with your name to communicate with me

12:03:38 PM **Jerry Wesley**: I have an account.

12:03:49 PM **ladydi2011**: Of course you do

12:03:58 PM **Jerry Wesley**: collins4u62

12:05:02 PM **ladydi2011**: Michael, how can I trust anything you say?

12:05:21 PM **Jerry Wesley**: How can I?

12:05:26 PM **Jerry Wesley**: You know the real me and right now I am scared to death

12:06:10 PM **ladydi2011**: Please swear on the Bible that you will tell me the truth from this day forth.

12:07:40 PM **Jerry Wesley**: I have already done that and I have been struggling to tell you the truth because I wanted you

12:08:15 PM **Jerry Wesley**: that I had it in mind that I must tell you the truth pretty soon, which I just did

12:08:39 PM **ladydi2011**: How long have you been struggling to tell me the truth?

12:09:54 PM **ladydi2011**: Michael

12:10:49 PM **Jerry Wesley**: can you remember the day we were talking and I told you that you touched my heart

12:11:01 PM **ladydi2011**: Yes

12:11:05 PM **Jerry Wesley**: that day I cried because I know I have been lying to the woman I Love

12:11:50 PM **ladydi2011**: So this was the truth?

12:12:39 PM **Jerry Wesley**: please I am sorry

12:12:44 PM **ladydi2011**: What else was true?

12:13:08 PM **Jerry Wesley**: my feelings and who I am now

12:13:16 PM **Jerry Wesley**: you have made me fall in Love

12:13:24 PM **Jerry Wesley**: which I never believed could happen to me..now I am scared to death

12:14:41 PM **ladydi2011**: You also made me fall in love with you and hard

12:15:13 PM **ladydi2011**: Please tell me who Jerry Wesley is. I need to know so I can let him go

12:16:23 PM **Jerry Wesley**: I used that profile, I got his picture from match.com

12:16:28 PM **Jerry Wesley**: I don't know him.

12:17:08 PM **ladydi2011**: How do you have a CA phone number?

12:17:31 PM **ladydi2011**: Oh....it just hit me. There is no William either

12:17:46 PM **ladydi2011**: No dead wife

12:18:08 PM **Jerry Wesley**: No, I have never been married or have kids

12:18:28 PM **ladydi2011**: Was this man's name on match, Jerry Wesley or did you make this name up?

12:18:34 PM **Jerry Wesley**: I have a CA phone number through skype.

12:18:46 PM **ladydi2011**: I am so stupid!

12:19:13 PM **ladydi2011**: You told me you would never make a fool of me

12:19:37 PM **ladydi2011**: I am sure you said this before you fell in love with me right?

12:19:42 PM **Jerry Wesley**: please forgive me

12:19:48 PM **Jerry Wesley**: Yes I did.

12:20:07 PM **Jerry Wesley**: when I look back on our conversations, I decided that I must let you know the real me if it worth goodbye then I understand but it will kill me inside my heart
12:20:29 PM **ladydi2011**: How often have you read our correspondence?
12:21:06 PM **Jerry Wesley**: I do always
12:21:14 PM **Jerry Wesley**: when I IM you its because I miss you and I dont want to let you go.
12:21:34 PM **Jerry Wesley**: can I tell you something.
12:21:39 PM **ladydi2011**: Please
12:21:55 PM **Jerry Wesley**: the money you sent to me do you know I am not the one that owns it?
12:22:16 PM **Jerry Wesley**: I work for someone, on this that I do.
12:22:37 PM **Jerry Wesley**: right now, I will need to run to somewhere because I have told him I need to stop this job
12:22:41 PM **Jerry Wesley**: this is how I feed
12:22:46 PM **Jerry Wesley**: he pays me.
12:22:52 PM **Jerry Wesley**: I dont get enough
12:23:19 PM **ladydi2011**: This is a big fraud ring, isn't it?
12:23:48 PM **Jerry Wesley**: Yes. he gets workers
12:23:55 PM **Jerry Wesley**: I am really scared Diana
12:23:58 PM **Jerry Wesley**: please forgive me it was never my itentions
12:24:15 PM **ladydi2011**: How much of my money did you get?
12:25:52 PM **ladydi2011**: Michael
12:27:02 PM **Jerry Wesley**: $200
12:27:08 PM **ladydi2011**: What?????????????????????????????????
12:27:26 PM **ladydi2011**: Oh Michael
12:30:15 PM **Jerry Wesley**: You remember the money was sent to his workers in china, so they took there cut..
12:39:15 PM **ladydi2011**: Is he in China?
12:39:33 PM **Jerry Wesley**: he has workers all I do is work for him.
12:39:50 PM **Jerry Wesley**: I am sorry Diana
12:39:52 PM **ladydi2011**: Is he in Nigeria?
12:39:59 PM **Jerry Wesley**: can I ask you a favor.
12:40:08 PM **ladydi2011**: Go ahead
12:40:11 PM **Jerry Wesley**: No he is in China
12:40:23 PM **ladydi2011**: Ok
12:40:34 PM **ladydi2011**: What is the favor?
12:40:49 PM **Jerry Wesley**: are you for real now?
12:40:58 PM **ladydi2011**: Yes...I am
12:42:45 PM **Jerry Wesley**: I am truly sorry
1:00:31 PM **Jerry Wesley**: I just finish readng your email
1:03:02 PM **ladydi2011**: I now see that I didn't send the money to you and this pisses me off
1:03:16 PM **Jerry Wesley**: I am sorry
1:03:21 PM **Jerry Wesley**: I do really want to trust you but I am scared to death
1:03:37 PM **ladydi2011**: I wrote you this email 21 days ago
1:04:04 PM **ladydi2011**: I was hurt and angry
1:04:04 PM **Jerry Wesley**: why didn't you send it?
1:04:19 PM **ladydi2011**: I did IM you bits and pieces
1:04:24 PM **ladydi2011**: Do you remember?
1:04:34 PM **ladydi2011**: If not, go back and look and compare

1:05:24 PM **ladydi2011**: Michael, I will not hurt you.
1:05:40 PM **Jerry Wesley**: please how can I trust you?
1:05:43 PM **ladydi2011**: What about your website?
1:05:59 PM **ladydi2011**: The same way I trusted you to send you $3,500...
1:06:11 PM **ladydi2011**: If you love me, you will trust me
1:06:59 PM **ladydi2011**: I forgive you Michael and am trying to wrap my brain around everything you just told me. I knew that eventually you were going to tell me who you were. That's why I kept talking to you.
1:07:04 PM **Jerry Wesley**: the person I work for did the website
1:07:12 PM **Jerry Wesley**: please forgive me.
1:07:24 PM **Jerry Wesley**: can you do me a favor, I do want to trust you.
1:07:29 PM **ladydi2011**: Do you know I have an investigator on this
1:07:59 PM **ladydi2011**: What favor?
1:08:07 PM **Jerry Wesley**: I am in need of $100, so I can pay for the hotel, I ran to, can I get this favor from you?
1:08:26 PM **ladydi2011**: I already knew the website was not being billed to CA
1:08:38 PM **Jerry Wesley**: but if you cant I understand.
1:08:56 PM **ladydi2011**: Let me see what I can do
1:09:09 PM **ladydi2011**: Is your life in danger? Please tell me the truth
1:09:26 PM **Jerry Wesley**: Yes because I stopped this work and ran away.
1:09:40 PM **Jerry Wesley**: he will want to hurt me.
1:09:47 PM **Jerry Wesley**: because I am tired of this work.
1:09:53 PM **Jerry Wesley**: I have a good heart but situation caused this to me.
1:10:10 PM **Jerry Wesley**: I do go to church and cry to God to forgive me
1:10:48 PM **ladydi2011**: I said from the beginning of meeting you that this was a God thing.
1:11:16 PM **ladydi2011**: God is a forgiving God if you truly repent from your heart
1:11:24 PM **ladydi2011**: Are you there?
1:11:38 PM **Jerry Wesley**: Yes i'm here.
1:12:22 PM **ladydi2011**: Does this man have people in Nigeria who can hurt you?
1:12:40 PM **Jerry Wesley**: I think so
1:12:59 PM **Jerry Wesley**: I just want to run from him.
1:13:13 PM **ladydi2011**: Is the SinglesBee website a front for this work?
1:14:11 PM **Jerry Wesley**: No I got registered on the site.
1:14:35 PM **ladydi2011**: I was thinking it was a front. You have fallen in love with a smart woman...I figured out everything fraudulent you sent me, remember
1:15:02 PM **Jerry Wesley**: Yes *i* know.
1:15:36 PM **ladydi2011**: I bet you didn't expect this, did you?
1:15:43 PM **Jerry Wesley**: No.
1:15:49 PM **Jerry Wesley**: I am sorry
1:16:14 PM **ladydi2011**: My head is spinning..I am still trying to digest all this
1:16:46 PM **Jerry Wesley**: PLEASE.
1:16:48 PM **ladydi2011**: Can this man track your correspondences?
1:17:02 PM **ladydi2011**: Please what?
1:17:09 PM **Jerry Wesley**: forgive me
1:17:19 PM **Jerry Wesley**: I know it is hard.
1:17:36 PM **Jerry Wesley**: Yes he can but in some ways I am smarter than him
1:17:45 PM **ladydi2011**: Ok

1:18:10 PM **ladydi2011**: Does he have all our correspondence on IM and email

1:18:29 PM **Jerry Wesley**: Yes.

1:19:02 PM **ladydi2011**: Is this why you changed your email address?

1:19:48 PM **ladydi2011**: Does he have writers that write the material you sent?

1:20:20 PM **Jerry Wesley**: which materials?

1:20:33 PM **ladydi2011**: Everything you wrote to me

1:21:18 PM **Jerry Wesley**: I wrote them I am the material.

1:21:25 PM **ladydi2011**: He has my banking info and knows where I live, right?

1:22:18 PM **Jerry Wesley**: he cant do anything with your bank info and address

1:22:21 PM **ladydi2011**: He sent the bear and plant

1:22:47 PM **ladydi2011**: I closed out my account before I ever gave you my banking info...remember I am smart

1:22:47 PM **Jerry Wesley**: I did

1:23:03 PM **Jerry Wesley**: Oh good

1:23:12 PM **ladydi2011**: If I didn't trust what you told me about being in trouble and love you I would have never sent you the money

1:23:25 PM **ladydi2011**: You did send them

1:23:26 PM **Jerry Wesley**: I made you Love me.

1:23:46 PM **Jerry Wesley**: Yes I sent them. he never knew I sent you the flower and bear

1:24:00 PM **Jerry Wesley**: because I did feel something for you

1:24:04 PM **ladydi2011**: Yes, you did make me love you

1:24:18 PM **Jerry Wesley**: I can make anyone Love me thats why I work for him

1:24:34 PM **Jerry Wesley**: he is not smart to do such thing.

1:24:34 PM **ladydi2011**: How did you know what to say to me to make me love you

1:24:55 PM **ladydi2011**: So, how many women were you working at a time?

1:26:26 PM **ladydi2011**: Are you there?

1:26:32 PM **Jerry Wesley**: God gave me a good heart.

1:26:40 PM **Jerry Wesley**: Diana please I am a good person

1:26:44 PM **Jerry Wesley**: situation caused this

1:26:54 PM **Jerry Wesley**: well I have just you to talked too

1:27:08 PM **Jerry Wesley**: let me tell you, I have given up the fallinghrt22 ID it was not hacked

1:27:41 PM **ladydi2011**: Ok, please tell me more

1:28:16 PM **Jerry Wesley**: because I talk to so many woman, some fall but some don't

1:28:23 PM **Jerry Wesley**: but my heart Loved you

1:28:26 PM **Jerry Wesley**: I dont know why

1:29:11 PM **ladydi2011**: Does he know about this IM address

1:29:20 PM **ladydi2011**: God sent me Michael

1:29:53 PM **Jerry Wesley**: Yes he knows.

1:30:01 PM **ladydi2011**: Michael, how do you know he cannot see this correspondence?

1:30:04 PM **Jerry Wesley**: but once we finish chatting I will clear all the chat

1:30:15 PM **Jerry Wesley**: I am smarter than him on computer

1:30:35 PM **Jerry Wesley**: remember I taught you the yahoo messenger stuff

1:30:40 PM **ladydi2011**: Michael, we need an address he doesn't know about.

1:31:11 PM **Jerry Wesley**: the one I gave you thats my personal email address

1:31:14 PM **Jerry Wesley**: you did add me

1:31:19 PM **ladydi2011**: Does he know about your Collins4y62 address?

1:31:21 PM **Jerry Wesley**: Diana I am scared of this

1:31:25 PM **ladydi2011**: I did

1:31:27 PM **Jerry Wesley**: No he does not

1:31:37 PM **Jerry Wesley**: please can I trust you

1:31:47 PM **ladydi2011**: Ok, let's get off this now and go to your personal email

1:32:03 PM **Jerry Wesley**: what will you gain to hurt someone that begged you for forgiveness?

1:32:13 PM **ladydi2011**: If you couldn't trust me do you think I would have asked about your safety?

1:32:15 PM **Jerry Wesley**: it is not good to pay evil with evil please

1:32:29 PM **Jerry Wesley**: Ok lets go

1:32:40 PM **ladydi2011**: I already told you that I am not going to hurt you. Please believe me

1:32:46 PM **ladydi2011**: Erase everything now

1:33:06 PM **Jerry Wesley**: I will erase now

1:33:10 PM **Jerry Wesley**: I IM you on collins

1:33:17 PM **Jerry Wesley**: my name is Collins..middle name Micheal..but I like Micheal

1:34:09 PM **Jerry Wesley**: add me on there

1:34:15 PM **Jerry Wesley**: come available

1:32:54 PM **collins4u62**: Hi

1:34:20 PM **ladydi2011**: I am here

1:34:34 PM **collins4u62**: add me back.

1:34:38 PM **collins4u62**: come available

1:35:09 PM **ladydi2011**: Ok, hold

1:35:17 PM **collins4u62**: Ok.

1:35:51 PM **ladydi2011**: Ok, can you see me now?

1:35:55 PM **collins4u62**: No

1:35:59 PM **collins4u62**: come available

1:36:26 PM **ladydi2011**: I did, but it is not working. It doesn't matter, you know I am here

1:36:33 PM **collins4u62**: Ok.

1:36:42 PM **collins4u62**: please forgive me Diana

1:36:52 PM **ladydi2011**: Michael, I do forgive you.

1:36:59 PM **collins4u62**: I beg you with the name of God

1:37:07 PM **ladydi2011**: I know if I don't forgive, God will not forgive me

1:37:08 PM **collins4u62**: I know you have forgiven me but can you forget all our past

1:37:26 PM **collins4u62**: please I know it is hard

1:37:26 PM **ladydi2011**: I love the Lord with all my heart and I know his Word

1:37:40 PM **ladydi2011**: Forgetting is different

1:37:48 PM **ladydi2011**: This will take time

1:37:54 PM **collins4u62**: I know. I need to be safe with you

1:38:06 PM **ladydi2011**: You will have to show me who you really are

1:38:07 PM **collins4u62**: I have given you my life

1:38:17 PM **collins4u62**: I have showed you who I am really

1:38:25 PM **ladydi2011**: I am 48 years old

1:38:32 PM **collins4u62**: you never asked me before I showed you Diana, does this make sense?

1:38:43 PM **ladydi2011**: It does

1:38:47 PM **collins4u62**: does age matters to you?

1:38:51 PM **ladydi2011**: No

1:40:54 PM **collins4u62**: I do want to be happy again, and live a God fearing life

1:40:59 PM **ladydi2011**: Michael, you really hurt me when you didn't care about taking my money.

1:41:34 PM **collins4u62**: I did care Diana, but I was forced to talk to you so you can give money

1:41:54 PM **collins4u62**: it was never my doing please

1:42:00 PM **ladydi2011**: You have made a good first step

1:43:55 PM **ladydi2011**: Please share your cam with me again

1:44:13 PM **collins4u62**: am scared

1:45:15 PM **ladydi2011**: I really do work with private investigators and fraud investigators

1:47:34 PM **collins4u62**: please forgive me

1:48:11 PM **ladydi2011**: I do forgive you...

1:49:06 PM **collins4u62**: please you will have to send the money to this name Jerry Wesley, because of trust issues please

1:49:10 PM **collins4u62**: do you understand

1:50:03 PM **ladydi2011**: I do not. Please explain why I would have to send it to Jerry Wesley

1:50:33 PM **collins4u62**: Diana I am scared if you send it to my name, you may come looking for me.

1:50:51 PM **collins4u62**: please

1:51:02 PM **ladydi2011**: Michael, if you cannot trust me, I cannot help you

1:51:18 PM **collins4u62**: I want to trust you

1:53:16 PM **ladydi2011**: Please hold while I talk to my brother

1:53:41 PM **collins4u62**: talk to him about me???

1:55:16 PM **collins4u62**: please don't hurt me..you better kill me than hurting me.

2:03:34 PM **ladydi2011**: Michael, even though you hurt me, I will not hurt you.

2:03:49 PM **collins4u62**: please I need to trust you

2:04:02 PM **collins4u62**: I have been in tears, its better I die than see you hurt me

2:04:48 PM **ladydi2011**: Please trust me

2:05:10 PM **ladydi2011**: What do you want to do?

2:05:29 PM **collins4u62**: I need to know what you want to do to me.

2:05:47 PM **collins4u62**: maybe Love me for who I am or kill me for what I did to your heart

2:06:11 PM **ladydi2011**: My text the other day hurt you, didn't they?

2:06:35 PM **collins4u62**: which one?

2:06:49 PM **ladydi2011**: when I said I would get over you

2:07:24 PM **collins4u62**: Yes I was heart broken, because I knew you will leave me, and it will be a wound to my heart

2:07:31 PM **collins4u62**: because I began to love you

2:09:56 PM **collins4u62**: please forgive me

2:10:08 PM **ladydi2011**: Michael, how do I know you are just not trying to get more money from me? This is what you are good at.

2:10:11 PM **collins4u62**: why not wish me the best and let me go please???

2:10:19 PM **collins4u62**: I am not

2:10:27 PM **collins4u62**: for me to show you myself took a lot of courage

2:11:03 PM **collins4u62**: then how can I play with you

2:11:37 PM **collins4u62**: unless showing you myself will make you hurt me, I have determined to take what ever this brings

2:12:10 PM **ladydi2011**: Do you really want me to wish you the best and let you go?

2:12:56 PM **collins4u62**: please so I can be free...please

2:13:08 PM **collins4u62**: right now you have my life and a rope holding my heart

2:13:53 PM **ladydi2011**: Didn't you ask yourself yet why I am still talking to you.

2:14:09 PM **collins4u62**: I am still figuring out. I am just scared. I just wish you know how I feel

2:15:42 PM **ladydi2011**: Michael, think about it. I knew by May 1st that you were a scammer but I continued to be in touch with you. Why do you think this was?

2:15:47 PM **collins4u62**: this is so hard on me now. I am weak and getting sick.

2:16:45 PM **ladydi2011**: Michael, I needed to know who you are because I knew you were NOT Jerry Wesley.

2:16:53 PM **collins4u62**: I know the real feelings is there.

2:17:05 PM **collins4u62**: I am never Jerry Wesley

2:17:08 PM **ladydi2011**: Yes, I fell in love with you.

2:17:57 PM **collins4u62**: can I trust your word to me.

2:18:04 PM **ladydi2011**: I have a way for you to make money but you will have to tell me everything.

2:18:28 PM **ladydi2011**: The only time I ever lied to you was when I told you I was going to send you the $500 and didn't.

2:18:39 PM **collins4u62**: I know you lied

2:18:51 PM **collins4u62**: I have told you everything and with time I will open more but now, I am very real to you

2:19:31 PM **ladydi2011**: For the first time you told me you didn't blame me for lying instead of beating me up verbally

2:20:00 PM **ladydi2011**: Are our phone conversations taped?

2:20:38 PM **ladydi2011**: You knew that this was the first time I lied to you

2:21:03 PM **ladydi2011**: Michael, are our phone conversations taped?

2:25:11 PM **ladydi2011**: are you there?

2:27:33 PM **collins4u62**: can you call me?

2:27:52 PM **ladydi2011**: Yes, I have calling cards for Africa

2:27:58 PM **ladydi2011**: please give me the number

2:29:01 PM **collins4u62**: (I have removed his phone number)

2:29:09 PM **collins4u62**: You own my life now do what ever you want to do with it

2:30:16 PM **collins4u62**: try to call and see if you will get through

2:30:22 PM **ladydi2011**: Hold and let me find my calling card

2:30:57 PM **collins4u62**: Ok.

2:33:35 PM **ladydi2011**: Invalid number

2:33:56 PM **ladydi2011**: Please don't waste my minutes on my card

2:34:11 PM **collins4u62**: (I have removed his phone number)

2:34:16 PM **collins4u62**: sorry this is correct

2:35:41 PM **ladydi2011**: It is busy

2:36:28 PM **ladydi2011**: Michael, please. I want to talk to you

2:39:31 PM **collins4u62**: please give me some few minutes

2:39:43 PM **ladydi2011**: Ok

2:41:47 PM **collins4u62**: I do Love you

2:44:34 PM **ladydi2011**: Please don't lie to me anymore Michael

2:44:50 PM **collins4u62**: I have told you I wont before

2:45:18 PM **ladydi2011**: Was "falling heart" your idea?

2:45:38 PM **ladydi2011**: Did you make up all the stories?

2:45:48 PM **ladydi2011**: What do you mean "before"?

2:47:36 PM **collins4u62**: Yes falling heart was my Idea

2:48:50 PM **ladydi2011**: I fell for it all

2:48:59 PM **ladydi2011**: Pretty stupid of me

2:49:13 PM **collins4u62**: please stop.

2:49:57 PM **collins4u62**:

Text Message

From: +16197961879
Received: May 22, 2012 6:05 PM

it's almost late Diana, wont you do the $100 for me?

IM May 22, 2012 7:14:56 PM

7:14:56 PM **collins4u62**: Hi
7:15:18 PM **ladydi2011**: Hi
7:16:03 PM **collins4u62**: Your hair is Beautiful.
7:16:10 PM **ladydi2011**: Thank you
7:16:41 PM **collins4u62**: You are welcome
7:16:48 PM **ladydi2011**: Is Michael really your real name?
7:16:51 PM **collins4u62**: How was your day?
7:17:02 PM **collins4u62**: Middle name I told you
7:17:12 PM **ladydi2011**: I think I am still in shock
7:17:21 PM **ladydi2011**: What is your first name?
7:17:27 PM **collins4u62**: Collins
7:17:41 PM **collins4u62**: You didnt have the chance to do the $100 for me?
7:17:49 PM **ladydi2011**: Collins is your first name
7:17:57 PM **collins4u62**: Yes
7:18:18 PM **ladydi2011**: No...you never told me why I have to send it to Jerry Wesley or where to send it
7:18:53 PM **collins4u62**: can you still send it today?
7:19:03 PM **ladydi2011**: Please invite me to see your cam
7:19:25 PM **ladydi2011**: We need to talk more before I send you money
7:19:46 PM **collins4u62**: I know remember I told you I need to trust you
7:20:16 PM **ladydi2011**: I also need to trust you. It is a two way street
7:20:24 PM **collins4u62**: I know
7:20:45 PM **ladydi2011**: How do I know you are not someone else sent to get money from me
7:22:49 PM **collins4u62**: I am very weak now
7:23:06 PM **ladydi2011**: What do you mean?
7:23:37 PM **collins4u62**: scared..I have nothing to eat
7:24:16 PM **ladydi2011**: hold please
7:24:28 PM **collins4u62**: Ok.
7:33:35 PM **ladydi2011**: Sorry. That was Asher checking on me to see how my legs are.
7:33:53 PM **ladydi2011**: I really couldn't walk well or drive for a couple weeks
7:34:27 PM **ladydi2011**: He has begged me to stop on line dating because he is afraid for my safety.
7:35:53 PM **ladydi2011**: Collins, I do have a big heart and help a lot of people
7:36:05 PM **collins4u62**: I know. I am not happy with myself that I have done this
7:36:44 PM **collins4u62**: I think I need to sleep it is late here and also I'm hungry
7:36:58 PM **collins4u62**: hoped you were going to do the $100 for me
7:37:01 PM **ladydi2011**: You shouldn't be happy with yourself. What you did is very wrong.
7:37:28 PM **ladydi2011**: I might do it, but I need to get to know you and trust you Collins

7:37:46 PM **collins4u62**: I know but you do know that I am scared to death

7:38:01 PM **ladydi2011**: Please tell me what Jerry Wesley's screen name is on Match.com

7:38:03 PM **collins4u62**: you already know me

7:38:30 PM **collins4u62**: I dont know anymore

7:38:38 PM **collins4u62**: I just took the pictures thats all

7:38:40 PM **ladydi2011**: We haven't been in a relationship for over a month. I told you this.

7:38:54 PM **ladydi2011**: All it has been was you badgering me for money

7:39:21 PM **collins4u62**: it was never my intentions,

7:39:26 PM **collins4u62**: things were hard

7:39:32 PM **ladydi2011**: I know

7:39:55 PM **ladydi2011**: What really blows my mind is that you didn't even have to search me out, I emailed you

7:39:56 PM **collins4u62**: hope Asher wont kill me

7:40:13 PM **ladydi2011**: He does not know I gave you the money

7:40:18 PM **collins4u62**: Yes you reached my world

7:40:36 PM **ladydi2011**: If he ever learns the truth, he probably would kill you.

7:40:57 PM **ladydi2011**: This is all so crazy!

7:41:50 PM **ladydi2011**: Collins, I do not want to hurt you, have you arrested or anything of the sorts

7:41:57 PM **collins4u62**: forgive me

7:42:44 PM **ladydi2011**: Please tell me who the ring leader is and where he can be found

7:43:49 PM **ladydi2011**: If you will give me what I need

7:44:34 PM **collins4u62**: what do you mean ring leader?

7:44:41 PM **ladydi2011**: Legal money...you will never again have to look over your shoulder, run or hide

7:44:59 PM **ladydi2011**: The man who is doing this in China. The one you quit from

7:46:06 PM **collins4u62**: Diana, I can't give that info cause he never told anyone his info

7:46:18 PM **ladydi2011**: You have an opportunity of a lifetime right now, choose wisely my dear. What you do will determine your future

7:46:30 PM **ladydi2011**: What do you mean, he never told anyone?

7:47:05 PM **collins4u62**: Yes, he is a fraudulent man, No one knows where he stay or Live

7:47:29 PM **ladydi2011**: What is the name of his shell company?

7:47:42 PM **collins4u62**: he does not have a company

7:47:54 PM **collins4u62**: can you come to Nigeria?

7:48:00 PM **ladydi2011**: Please tell me what you do know

7:48:14 PM **ladydi2011**: Why would you want me to come to Nigeria?

7:48:30 PM **collins4u62**: I just asked.

7:48:39 PM **ladydi2011**: I am asking you why?

7:48:41 PM **collins4u62**: maybe we will meet

7:49:28 PM **ladydi2011**: Collins, please tell me the truth...how much of what you said to me did you say to other women?

7:49:55 PM **collins4u62**: see I have never done to anyone what I did to you

7:49:59 PM **collins4u62**: show you myself

7:50:03 PM **collins4u62**: God knows

7:50:43 PM **ladydi2011**: OK...The written material that you sent to me. Did you use this material all the time? Please tell me the truth

7:51:29 PM **collins4u62**: Yes.

7:51:56 PM **ladydi2011**: Sometimes I could tell it was copied and pasted
7:52:04 PM **collins4u62**: Yes.
7:52:06 PM **ladydi2011**: Thank you for telling me the truth
7:52:27 PM **collins4u62**: I am truthful to you Diana
7:53:00 PM **ladydi2011**: What was different that you said to me than what you said to anyone else?
7:53:59 PM **collins4u62**: that I live to Love you
7:54:27 PM **ladydi2011**: anything else?
7:54:51 PM **collins4u62**: The intimate conversations.
7:55:08 PM **ladydi2011**: Is this truth?
7:55:16 PM **collins4u62**: Yes very true
7:56:05 PM **ladydi2011**: I always shared what was in my heart
7:56:11 PM **ladydi2011**: Do you know this?
7:57:24 PM **ladydi2011**: Since I learned you were a scammer, I have been talking to other scammers and had 2 more try to get money from me
7:57:39 PM **ladydi2011**: One of them tried to get me to take the oath also
7:57:55 PM **ladydi2011**: Is this something standard in your line of work?
8:01:20 PM **collins4u62**: Baby I am sorry for all this..frauds are much. Please dont answer to any of them.
8:01:43 PM **collins4u62**: I need to sleep
8:01:48 PM **ladydi2011**: So I have learned.
8:01:49 PM **collins4u62**: I am not Okay
8:01:55 PM **ladydi2011**: I was so naïve
8:02:07 PM **ladydi2011**: Ok. will I hear from you tomorrow?
8:02:27 PM **ladydi2011**: I trusted so easily
8:03:25 PM **collins4u62**: Yes I will talk to you tomorrow
8:03:35 PM **collins4u62**: so try and help me with the $100...thanks
8:03:48 PM **collins4u62**: Good
8:03:51 PM **collins4u62**: Love you
8:03:54 PM **collins4u62**: Good night
8:03:54 PM **ladydi2011**: Good night

IM May 23, 2012 12:14:40 AM

12:14:40 AM **ladydi2011**: Hi...can't sleep. Why the song Someone Like You by Adele?

IM May 23, 2012 9:24:03 AM

9:24:03 AM **collins4u62**: Good morning,
9:24:52 AM **collins4u62**: I am so sorry I had to leave last night , hope your night was good..
9:24:57 AM **collins4u62**: my heart miss you and I cry praying you forgive me
9:25:29 AM **ladydi2011**: Good morning
9:25:50 AM **ladydi2011**: Did you sleep well?
9:26:39 AM **collins4u62**: confused.
9:27:07 AM **ladydi2011**: What are you confused about?
9:27:58 AM **collins4u62**: everything.

9:28:42 AM **ladydi2011**: This doesn't tell me anything
9:28:54 AM **collins4u62**: me being scared and trusting you
9:29:06 AM **collins4u62**: for all I have done to your heart
9:30:31 AM **ladydi2011**: You not only hurt my heart but my finances
9:31:35 AM **ladydi2011**: Can I ask you something
9:31:45 AM **collins4u62**: I was not the one that asked for this money
9:32:01 AM **ladydi2011**: What do you mean?
9:32:22 AM **collins4u62**: whom I worked for, said I should tell you 3500 and thats what I did.
9:32:32 AM **collins4u62**: please I am sorry
9:40:02 AM **ladydi2011**: I reread some of our writings last night
9:40:48 AM **ladydi2011**: Michael, are you there?
9:41:36 AM **ladydi2011**: It shows you as off line.
9:46:47 AM **ladydi2011**: Where did you go?

IM May 23, 2012 6:19:11 PM

6:19:11 PM **collins4u62**: <ding>
6:19:33 PM **ladydi2011**: Hi
6:19:43 PM **collins4u62**: Hi How are you?
6:20:16 PM **ladydi2011**: Ok, and you?
6:21:11 PM **collins4u62**: I am weak
6:21:37 PM **collins4u62**: How is work with you?
6:22:03 PM **ladydi2011**: Please hold on. I am with tech support
6:22:21 PM **collins4u62**: How do you mean?
6:22:59 PM **ladydi2011**: Trying to get web cam to work
6:23:10 PM **collins4u62**: Ok.
6:23:28 PM **ladydi2011**: It stopped working today
6:24:01 PM **collins4u62**: Ok.
6:24:33 PM **ladydi2011**: I have wanted to talk to you all day. I am on blackberry now
6:24:50 PM **collins4u62**: I know.
6:25:04 PM **collins4u62**: I have been re thinking about everything I have got myself into
6:25:16 PM **ladydi2011**: Just got cam working...need to re boot.
6:25:25 PM **collins4u62**: its like I want to sick
6:26:17 PM **collins4u62**: I Love you , but I am scared
6:26:32 PM **ladydi2011**: I am here for you if you will let me be
6:26:45 PM **ladydi2011**: Why are you scared of me?
6:27:28 PM **collins4u62**: I am scared if you wont hunt me.
6:27:54 PM **collins4u62**: please
6:28:22 PM **collins4u62**: if you do have a good heart as you said you will forgive me and understand
6:28:29 PM **ladydi2011**: I will not. I promise
6:29:16 PM **collins4u62**: am hungry.
6:31:29 PM **collins4u62**: Beauty
6:31:39 PM **ladydi2011**: Can you see me?
6:31:57 PM **collins4u62**: Yes I can.
6:32:22 PM **ladydi2011**: Michael, I really want to help you. Do you read the Bible?
6:33:51 PM **collins4u62**: Yes I do.

6:34:29 PM **ladydi2011**: Do you know when Jesus said to teach men to be fishermen

6:35:41 PM **ladydi2011**: I want to give you an opportunity for redemption of what you have done and to make money in a way that you will be proud of.

6:35:48 PM **ladydi2011**: Are you there?

6:36:50 PM **ladydi2011**: God is giving both of us an opportunity here. If you don't trust me, trust Him.

6:37:10 PM **ladydi2011**: What happened between us is not a coincidence or accident

6:37:37 PM **ladydi2011**: I knew from the time the Singlesbee website popped up in my email it was a God thing

6:38:03 PM **ladydi2011**: God is giving you something right now...are you going to receive it?

6:39:02 PM **ladydi2011**: Why are you not answering me?

IM May 24, 2012 5:29:09 AM

5:29:09 AM **collins4u62**: <ding>

5:29:18 AM **collins4u62**: I am sorry I *slept off* last night

5:29:23 AM **collins4u62**: How are you?

5:29:37 AM **collins4u62**: thanks for the words of encouragment.

IM May 25, 2012 3:12:14 PM

3:12:14 PM **ladydi2011**: This is what God teaches

3:13:29 PM **ladydi2011**: If I didn't forgive you, God will never forgive me. This is what his word teaches.

3:14:07 PM **collins4u62**: thanks

3:14:19 PM **collins4u62**: I will think about this, and I will write what I can.

3:14:33 PM **collins4u62**: I asked you for a favor of just $100 you didnt do it and you know I am sick weather here is bad, I have flu

3:15:20 PM **collins4u62**: Ok...Baby how do *i* manage? so how do I feed? or take care of myself?

3:16:02 PM **ladydi2011**: I don't know

3:16:38 PM **ladydi2011**: You never told me where to send it

3:17:44 PM **ladydi2011**: I have to go now. I am going to my brothers.

3:18:02 PM **ladydi2011**: I will be back Sunday and be looking for your writings.

3:18:26 PM **collins4u62**: I will write and let you know.

3:18:35 PM **collins4u62**: hope you dont hurt me

3:19:00 PM **collins4u62**: Name: Micheal Collins.
Country : Nigeria
State : Lagos
City: Ikeja
zipcode: 23401

3:19:21 PM **ladydi2011**: Thank you.

3:19:43 PM **collins4u62**: I am scared

3:32:27 PM **collins4u62**: Wet Kisses and Hugs

3:33:00 PM **ladydi2011**: Are you still just trying to get money from me?

3:33:34 PM **collins4u62**: why will I?

3:33:44 PM **collins4u62**: I am just asking for your help to make me a better person.
3:33:52 PM **collins4u62**: if you would want to help me

Text Message

From: +16197961879
Received: May 27, 2012 3:39 PM

Hi Diana, How are you doing? hope your visit was Okay...well I miss you and I am on to talk to you.

IM May 27, 2012 3:38:25 PM

3:38:25 PM **collins4u62**: <ding>
3:38:48 PM **ladydi2011**: Hi
3:39:57 PM **ladydi2011**: How are you?
3:40:22 PM **collins4u62**: You are offline.
3:40:50 PM **ladydi2011**: Driving
3:40:56 PM **collins4u62**: Oh.
3:41:00 PM **ladydi2011**: 30 min from home
3:41:00 PM **collins4u62**: be careful.
3:41:22 PM **ladydi2011**: K
3:41:35 PM **collins4u62**: I am waiting, when you get home, let me know
3:42:38 PM **collins4u62**: I have been depressed
3:46:56 PM **collins4u62**: Hey.

IM May 27, 2012 4:07:41 PM

4:07:41 PM **collins4u62**: I will start writing my own side of the book, soon.
4:09:25 PM **ladydi2011**: Ok. Please put all the feeling, emotions, lack of feelings and emotions in your writing.
4:09:37 PM **ladydi2011**: Did you think about the opportunity?
4:10:08 PM **collins4u62**: Yes, you need massage?
4:14:45 PM **ladydi2011**: I do...how did you know?
4:15:13 PM **collins4u62**: rememeber I know you too well
4:15:21 PM **collins4u62**: how is your brother?
4:16:29 PM **ladydi2011**: You do know me well because I let you know me well.
4:22:40 PM **collins4u62**: Can you let me rest a little, so I can do what you asked me to do.
4:22:57 PM **ladydi2011**: Ok. Can I see you first?
4:23:09 PM **collins4u62**: lol
4:23:43 PM **ladydi2011**: Is this a yes?
4:24:23 PM **collins4u62**: I went to church.
4:24:36 PM **ladydi2011**: You did? And?
4:24:43 PM **collins4u62**: Yes.

4:25:23 PM **ladydi2011**: Did it feel good to go to church?

4:25:30 PM **collins4u62**: Yes I did.

4:25:36 PM **ladydi2011**: Good.

4:26:10 PM **collins4u62**: later baby.

4:26:12 PM **ladydi2011**: Doing the right thing isn't always easy, but God honors our repentance

4:26:13 PM **collins4u62**: let me see you

4:26:17 PM **ladydi2011**: Ok

4:28:38 PM **collins4u62**: Wow, Sweetness

4:28:52 PM **collins4u62**: looking like a sweet 16

4:29:08 PM **ladydi2011**: There's your sweet talk again...but thank you.

4:29:52 PM **collins4u62**: why did you off the cam?

4:29:59 PM **ladydi2011**: Why do you shut your camera off so fast?

4:30:11 PM **collins4u62**: You did yours.

4:30:29 PM **ladydi2011**: No I didn't. Let's put them back on again

4:30:43 PM **collins4u62**: Ok.

4:31:16 PM **ladydi2011**: Your cam please

4:31:58 PM **ladydi2011**: It said you stopped viewing my cam...

4:41:41 PM **ladydi2011**: Ok...bye. I hope you feel better as you write.

4:42:13 PM **ladydi2011**: I do not like when you stop talking to me and do not say bye. It frustrates me.

IM May 29, 2012 3:19:55 PM

3:19:55 PM **collins4u62**: <ding>

3:21:56 PM **collins4u62**: Hi baby.

3:24:08 PM **ladydi2011**: Hi!

3:24:20 PM **ladydi2011**: How are you?

3:24:21 PM **collins4u62**: I miss you

3:24:25 PM **collins4u62**: I have been sick

3:24:29 PM **collins4u62**: How are you?

3:24:45 PM **ladydi2011**: I have been sick too!

3:24:54 PM **collins4u62**: I thought you must have sent me the $100

3:25:48 PM **ladydi2011**: I need you to send the writing and then I will send you money.

3:26:21 PM **collins4u62**: You know I need strenght.

3:26:28 PM **collins4u62**: I am starting to write now

3:27:42 PM **collins4u62**: do me one favor, can you go send the $100, so I will know you are really serious with me.

3:27:46 PM **collins4u62**: please do this for me.

3:28:25 PM **ladydi2011**: No. It is time for you to trust me and do this.

3:28:52 PM **collins4u62**: I see..meaning you wont send the $100 unless I write?

3:29:19 PM **ladydi2011**: If you are not willing to do this to help yourself, why should I help you?

3:29:39 PM **collins4u62**: I never said I wont do it.

3:29:52 PM **collins4u62**: I just asked you for a favor, and you took it too far

3:30:02 PM **collins4u62**: well don't bother. I need to recover

3:30:22 PM **ladydi2011**: I did't take anything to far

3:30:23 PM **collins4u62**: I am sick, and if you cant help me with the $100, its Okay

3:31:26 PM **ladydi2011**: I am disappointed. This is you speaking to me like this now and not your boss.

3:32:04 PM **collins4u62**: I told you I am sick, I needed to take care of myself

3:32:11 PM **collins4u62**: look at what you are saying to me.

3:32:20 PM **ladydi2011**: Opportunities like I am giving you comes along once in a lifetime. Your choice!

3:34:44 PM **collins4u62**: I JUST ASKED FOR $100 TO TAKE CARE OF MY HEALTH NOW, THATS ALL

3:34:51 PM **collins4u62**: IS THIS SO MUCH TO ASK?

3:37:37 PM **collins4u62**: I just asked for $100, to get meds Diana why are you pushing this so far

3:38:17 PM **collins4u62**: Your character makes me scared baby.

3:38:46 PM **ladydi2011**: I am not pushing anything.

3:39:08 PM **ladydi2011**: My character scares you?

3:39:14 PM **collins4u62**: but I asked for $100, right now, I know how I feel my eyes is closing

3:40:01 PM **ladydi2011**: Ok ...I don't want you to be sick. I have prayed for you every day.

3:41:01 PM **ladydi2011**: All I ever did was love and give to you. You stole from me and you are questioning my character? Unreal!

3:41:33 PM **collins4u62**: I still say I am sorry.

3:42:01 PM **collins4u62**: but I asked you just for a little favor, I am sick Diana

3:42:26 PM **collins4u62**: You know I am alone right now, because I opened up to you, was I wrong opening up to you?

3:44:30 PM **ladydi2011**: You opening up to me has given you a chance to change your life for the better forever. But for some reason you don't see the gift in front of you.

3:45:09 PM **collins4u62**: why are you pushing me away and going to far I just asked for a little favor and not all this word

3:45:45 PM **collins4u62**: you told me that if I write the book you will send me what I asked for, dont you see how this sounds.

3:45:48 PM **ladydi2011**: I will not beg you to do anything. You are a grown man who can make decisions for your life.

3:45:51 PM **collins4u62**: I need to go lay down please

3:46:02 PM **ladydi2011**: Bye

3:47:22 PM **collins4u62**: now I know that you are unreal to me.

IM May 29, 2012 4:13:02 PM

4:13:02 PM **collins4u62**: are you there?

IM May 29, 2012 7:44:12 PM

7:44:12 PM **ladydi2011**: I am not going to beg you to help yourself. I forgave you and am willing to help you have a better life. You have to help yourself. For this to happen you have to contribute your writing.

IM May 30, 2012 12:46:12 PM

12:46:12 PM **collins4u62**: Yes I am well thanks
12:46:16 PM **collins4u62**: was sleeping

IM May 30, 2012 3:31:34 PM

3:31:34 PM **collins4u62**: Hi.
3:31:40 PM **collins4u62**: I am still down so bad
3:31:54 PM **ladydi2011**: Hi
3:32:26 PM **ladydi2011**: If I go to my computer can I see you?
3:35:16 PM **collins4u62**: Ok come online the computer
3:35:33 PM **ladydi2011**: I am here.
3:38:57 PM **collins4u62**: can you see me?
3:39:07 PM **collins4u62**: dark
3:39:09 PM **ladydi2011**: Yes
3:39:16 PM **ladydi2011**: Can you see me?
3:39:22 PM **collins4u62**: Yes.
3:39:33 PM **collins4u62**: You look sweet
3:39:49 PM **ladydi2011**: Thank you
3:39:50 PM **collins4u62**: I am scared of you not using a camera to camera me.
3:40:05 PM **ladydi2011**: What is a camera to camera?
3:41:11 PM **collins4u62**: How am I sure of this
3:41:15 PM **collins4u62**: I am so sick worrying
3:42:09 PM **ladydi2011**: I do not know what a camera to camera is, but obviously you do. Maybe this is something that can hurt me...Now, I am scared!
3:42:26 PM **collins4u62**: lol..how can I hurt you
3:42:45 PM **collins4u62**: I am not talking about camera to camera
3:42:53 PM **collins4u62**: you may use your phone and snap me a picture
3:42:59 PM **ladydi2011**: What are you talking about?
3:43:21 PM **ladydi2011**: Why would I do this?
3:43:41 PM **ladydi2011**: You have been living a life of hiding for too long. It has caused much fear in your spirit.
3:44:07 PM **collins4u62**: I am so scared
3:44:12 PM **collins4u62**: thats why I am sick
3:44:25 PM **ladydi2011**: God does not give us a spirit of fear
3:44:53 PM **ladydi2011**: If you are telling me the truth and you have really stopped scamming people, then you should no longer be afraid
3:45:37 PM **collins4u62**: I have stopped
3:45:43 PM **collins4u62**: I am really sick Diana
3:45:55 PM **collins4u62**: I wish you know what I am passing through you will pitty me
3:46:00 PM **ladydi2011**: You are sick because of worry
3:46:43 PM **ladydi2011**: Your worry is unfounded
3:47:33 PM **collins4u62**: You work with fbi, inspectors, secret argents..please I am really scared
3:48:01 PM **ladydi2011**: Yes, and if I wanted to hurt you, it would have already happened.
3:48:14 PM **collins4u62**: How?

3:48:36 PM **ladydi2011**: I have contacts all over the world.

3:48:45 PM **ladydi2011**: Here is my goal

3:48:56 PM **ladydi2011**: I want to write this book

3:49:49 PM **ladydi2011**: You can do this with me and we can be a team or not

3:49:56 PM **ladydi2011**: This is all I want

3:50:16 PM **ladydi2011**: Hurting you or having you arrested is not going to help anyone

3:51:18 PM **collins4u62**: I will write my own part but I am trying to be strong

3:51:39 PM **collins4u62**: have you started writing yours

3:51:46 PM **ladydi2011**: Yes.

3:52:30 PM **ladydi2011**: After you, I continued on line and three more men tried to scam me, so I have 4 stories so far. I want 10.

3:56:10 PM **ladydi2011**: If you don't give me your side, I am sure I can get one of the other men to do so.

3:58:37 PM **ladydi2011**: Please say something

3:59:01 PM **collins4u62**: I am reading

4:03:23 PM **ladydi2011**: All the scams are a little different but the grooming process is similar.

4:03:33 PM **ladydi2011**: Almost like clock work

4:07:51 PM **ladydi2011**: I have to go...

4:08:57 PM **collins4u62**: sorry taking medicine

4:09:01 PM **collins4u62**: call me love

4:11:36 PM **ladydi2011**: You didn't answer

4:12:07 PM **collins4u62**: went to get the phone

4:12:09 PM **collins4u62**: call now

4:12:13 PM **ladydi2011**: Ok

4:14:51 PM **collins4u62**: Oh my God please call me

4:14:56 PM **collins4u62**: the phone broke down

IM May 30, 2012 4:33:29 PM

4:33:29 PM **collins4u62**: sorry baby, the network cut me off

4:33:30 PM **collins4u62**: <ding>

4:33:56 PM **ladydi2011**: I tried to call back but I do not have enough left on my card.

I tried to get him to write for this book, but I don't think he is going to do it. He is scared.

IM Jun 1, 2012 10:09:39 AM

10:09:39 AM **collins4u62**: Hi baby.

10:10:42 AM **collins4u62**: my woman.

10:10:52 AM **ladydi2011**: Hi...

10:10:57 AM **ladydi2011**: How are you?

10:11:11 AM **collins4u62**: I am still sick, the weather is bad..night fever always

10:11:20 AM **collins4u62**: how are you?

10:11:38 AM **ladydi2011**: I am sorry you are still sick. I am really down today.

10:12:45 AM **collins4u62**: sorry I am here for you.

10:12:57 AM **collins4u62**: can we be together?

10:13:28 AM **collins4u62**: honey did you tell me anything about sending something to me?

10:13:37 AM **ladydi2011**: No.

10:13:49 AM **collins4u62**: I must be dreaming.

10:14:11 AM **ladydi2011**: I am losing faith in mankind

10:14:26 AM **ladydi2011**: The research to write this book is killing me

10:14:41 AM **ladydi2011**: Nobody is who they say they are!

10:15:05 AM **collins4u62**: I dont understand

10:15:20 AM **collins4u62**: you said no body is who dey say they are?

10:15:30 AM **ladydi2011**: Correct.

10:15:38 AM **collins4u62**: tell me

10:15:52 AM **ladydi2011**: God is sending me one man after the other who is scamming for money.

10:16:01 AM **ladydi2011**: I know he is doing this so I have what I need to help people

10:16:20 AM **ladydi2011**: But it really makes me question man kind and how they can steal and hurt people so easily.

10:16:44 AM **collins4u62**: which man is that?

10:16:53 AM **ladydi2011**: I am so tired of these men saying "I love you" just to play me.

10:17:04 AM **ladydi2011**: There are five of them now.

10:17:31 AM **collins4u62**: are you still on dating sites?

10:17:52 AM **ladydi2011**: Yes.

10:18:00 AM **collins4u62**: 😐

10:18:09 AM **ladydi2011**: I have to be to get what I need for the book

10:18:15 AM **collins4u62**: what are you still doing on there?

10:18:21 AM **collins4u62**: I see

10:18:32 AM **collins4u62**: and you are talking to all the men right?

10:18:56 AM **ladydi2011**: I know God wants me to help people through this book.

10:19:08 AM **ladydi2011**: Yes I am and I hate it!

10:19:39 AM **ladydi2011**: I know everything they are saying is a lie

10:20:05 AM **ladydi2011**: I can tell when they will ask me for the money and what is coming next. You taught me well.

10:20:16 AM **collins4u62**: LOL.

10:20:27 AM **collins4u62**: when I met you, I figured you are smart

10:20:36 AM **collins4u62**: but I never knew you will fall for me.

10:21:11 AM **collins4u62**: its still mazes me.

10:21:13 AM **ladydi2011**: What made you figure I was smart?

10:21:45 AM **collins4u62**: Your occupation and also the people you mingle with...I got scared

10:22:11 AM **collins4u62**: do you remember when I told you that if your job will disturb our relationship then we should stop?

10:22:28 AM **ladydi2011**: No, I do not remember this

10:23:11 AM **collins4u62**: did you remember, then I was saying to myself how can a smart woman like you send money...No way

10:23:57 AM **ladydi2011**: I sent it because I was in love with you and you were in trouble.

10:24:15 AM **ladydi2011**: I almost didn't when you texted me and said "just do it".

10:24:57 AM **ladydi2011**: I learned that love over rides everything

10:25:25 AM **collins4u62**: I know, love can make you do anything.

10:25:50 AM **ladydi2011**: You said all the right things

10:26:09 AM **ladydi2011**: I felt in my heart that you loved me

10:26:38 AM **ladydi2011**: Do they train you to do what you did?

10:27:08 AM **ladydi2011**: Just about every man who has asked me for money seems to go through the same process

10:27:39 AM **collins4u62**: No

10:27:47 AM **collins4u62**: no one will trian you.

10:28:15 AM **ladydi2011**: The last one sent me a huge bouquet of flowers in a lenox crystal vase, candy and a bear. The card said....Next is the ring.

10:28:36 AM **ladydi2011**: It took him a month to ask for the money. He asked for 40k

10:28:53 AM **ladydi2011**: I knew from the very beginning when he would ask...

10:29:09 AM **collins4u62**: I see

10:29:19 AM **ladydi2011**: I think he has also fallen in love with me...

10:29:28 AM **ladydi2011**: What is it about me?

10:30:04 AM **collins4u62**: falling in love?

10:30:15 AM **collins4u62**: are you still talking to him?

10:35:25 AM **ladydi2011**: Do you know what I want?

10:35:32 AM **collins4u62**: what do you want?

10:37:04 AM **ladydi2011**: I want to finish this book

10:40:24 AM **collins4u62**: but baby can I ask you something?

10:40:31 AM **ladydi2011**: Sure

10:41:05 AM **collins4u62**: do you have faith that this book will sell

10:41:20 AM **ladydi2011**: Absolutely

10:44:22 AM **collins4u62**: I will write what I can thou it is not much...but I will pick a point

10:45:27 AM **ladydi2011**: Will it help you if I give you a bullet point of what to write?

10:46:11 AM **collins4u62**: Okay give me points

10:46:30 AM **ladydi2011**: Let me work on this. Should I email it to you?

10:46:46 AM **collins4u62**: please today

10:46:50 AM **ladydi2011**: Should I put it in a word document or in the body of an email?

10:47:01 AM **collins4u62**: body of an email.

10:47:03 AM **ladydi2011**: Ok

10:47:12 AM **collins4u62**: today so I can take my time

10:48:47 AM **collins4u62**: I have choosen the right part...but now I am suffering

10:49:33 AM **collins4u62**: I am so scared and I pray my Love dont fool me.

10:51:49 AM **ladydi2011**: It will not fool you.

10:51:51 AM **collins4u62**: it was so hard for me, knowing what I have done

10:54:51 AM **collins4u62**: to hell is human and to forgive is divine baby.

10:55:15 AM **ladydi2011**: I know. I forgave you before you told me the truth

10:55:38 AM **collins4u62**: I hope Karma don't return to me

10:55:43 AM **ladydi2011**: I knew you scammed me. I just didn't know you stole someone else's identity to do it.

10:55:44 AM **collins4u62**: that word you said to me hurt me

10:55:54 AM **ladydi2011**: I am sorry.

10:56:32 AM **ladydi2011**: I think those words came from God to get to your heart. You belong to him and he wanted you back.

10:56:54 AM **ladydi2011**: He will always call back those who he loves.

10:57:06 AM **collins4u62**: please forgive me.

10:57:28 AM **ladydi2011**: Please believe me when I tell you that I forgive you.

10:57:58 AM **ladydi2011**: Here is how I see it....$3,500 was worth you changing your life around, and us educating millions of people so they don't get scammed, so the money was well spent.

10:58:01 AM **collins4u62**: I want to believe

10:58:10 AM **ladydi2011**: Please read what I just wrote

10:58:11 AM **collins4u62**: wish I know what your heart speaketh

10:58:52 AM **ladydi2011**: $3,500 is a small price for you to turn your life around.

10:59:07 AM **collins4u62**: I got just 200

10:59:28 AM **ladydi2011**: I know that is what you got, but I paid $3,500

10:59:37 AM **collins4u62**: I know

11:00:48 AM **collins4u62**: You dont call me always

11:01:00 AM **ladydi2011**: What do you mean?

11:01:21 AM **collins4u62**: you calling me on phone, I want to feel the connection.

11:01:53 AM **ladydi2011**: I need to get more calling cards. My Africa cards have no more time on them.

11:02:04 AM **collins4u62**: Ok.

11:02:07 AM **ladydi2011**: I will try to get some today.

11:02:34 AM **ladydi2011**: The last week has been crazy with the men on line

11:03:03 AM **ladydi2011**: Two of them fell this week (asked me for money).

11:03:28 AM **ladydi2011**: One I was expecting. The other one I was not.

11:03:50 AM **collins4u62**: lol...please get off the dating, all men are scammers

11:03:53 AM **ladydi2011**: It took a month for the one to fall

11:03:58 AM **ladydi2011**: All men?

11:04:14 AM **collins4u62**: not all thou, any man that travels or dont want to meet you, or ask you for info

11:04:37 AM **collins4u62**: LOL...you are picking point

11:04:47 AM **collins4u62**: I wont go further until I write

11:04:57 AM **ladydi2011**: What do you mean by "I am picking point"?

11:05:06 AM **collins4u62**: Yes on what I just said.

11:05:11 AM **collins4u62**: let me write my part

11:06:49 AM **collins4u62**: I have changed for good

11:06:58 AM **collins4u62**: I come on to talk to just you,

11:07:11 AM **collins4u62**: I am not a dog that goes back to its vomit

11:07:39 AM **ladydi2011**: Did the boss man let you keep the phone for Jerry Wesley?

11:08:23 AM **collins4u62**: lol...I connected the number to my phone.

11:08:53 AM **ladydi2011**: Is it now safe to call you on the California number?

11:09:24 AM **ladydi2011**: If so, I do not need a calling card and can call you anytime I want.

11:09:25 AM **collins4u62**: No, it has been disconnected

11:09:36 AM **ladydi2011**: What about the text?

11:10:15 AM **collins4u62**: I can only text.

11:10:40 AM **ladydi2011**: Is it safe for me to text you on the CA number?

11:11:04 AM **collins4u62**: Yes..text no one can know but call it will go to them.

11:11:28 AM **ladydi2011**: What do you mean it will go to them?

11:11:54 AM **collins4u62**: call will go to the boss

11:12:04 AM **ladydi2011**: But text will not?

11:12:23 AM **collins4u62**: as you called it

11:12:29 AM **collins4u62**: Well I dont have a boss

11:13:02 AM **ladydi2011**: Text will only go to you, right?
11:14:10 AM **collins4u62**: Yes with just your number
11:14:19 AM **ladydi2011**: Oh, ok.
11:14:45 AM **collins4u62**: I connected it to my phone.
11:15:11 AM **collins4u62**: I have something to write
11:15:15 AM **collins4u62**: I am still thinking
11:15:19 AM **ladydi2011**: Ok...
11:15:33 AM **ladydi2011**: You are a difficult man
11:15:47 AM **collins4u62**: No I am not
11:16:24 AM **ladydi2011**: Do you remember how I cried when you "supposedly" left for China?
11:17:20 AM **collins4u62**: Yes.
11:17:22 AM **ladydi2011**: I couldn't explain it then, but I think I knew something bad was about to happen deep in my spirit.
11:18:01 AM **ladydi2011**: By the way, my new word is "supposedly". I don't believe anything anymore.
11:18:20 AM **collins4u62**: I am sorry
11:18:59 AM **ladydi2011**: I am not telling you this to make you feel bad. I am telling you because all this has changed some things about me.
11:19:06 AM **collins4u62**: but what do we have when you wont believe me?
11:19:11 AM **ladydi2011**: I am not as trusting anymore.
11:19:40 AM **ladydi2011**: This is good. I am not so naïve anymore.
11:21:49 AM **ladydi2011**: If I think you are lying, I will let you know and ask you.
11:22:15 AM **collins4u62**: Ok.
11:24:48 AM **ladydi2011**: Are you there?
11:25:27 AM **collins4u62**: Please forgive me, my life is changed forever and I will always love you

IM Jun 2, 2012 4:43:57 AM

4:43:57 AM **collins4u62**: (send video link to You Promised by Brantley Gilbert)
4:44:07 AM **collins4u62**: listen
She was crying out my name
Standing in the driveway
Little bare feet wearing her cotton dress in my way
I still see the rain chasing tears down her face

It was back in October when I said it's over and hid
Behind the door
Behind the shame of my conviction
Beside myself
Beside some empty pill prescription
Can hear her screamin' now
No baby don't, you making my heart hurt
Don't say those words
Take it back
You know you don't mean that
You swore when I wore your ring

It meant forever
I've got it on baby
How can you say I lost it
Oh, you promised

Started crying while I was sleeping
Waking up and reaching out
To a bed as empty as the heart inside my chest
So I gathered up some pictures
Said I had some things to give her
I let her read a letter
I had written her to give her on the day we tied the knot
I saw the tears
I saw them fall as she read the part of my growing old
I heard her words
I heard her say it'll never work

And hit my knees and cried
No baby don't you're making my heart hurt
Don't say those words
Take it back
You know you don't mean that
You swore when you wore my ring
It meant forever
You've got it on baby
How can you say you lost it
Yeah and you promised

We were different people then
Look at all the hateful things we've said
And I'm just as guilty
But girl that's no way to be
Take it easy baby I'm still broken
Memories enough to tear me wide open
When you see me girl you curse my name
Makes me wanna say

No, no baby don't
You're making my heart hurt
Don't say those words
Take it back
You know you don't mean that
You know when you wore my ring
We said forever
But you took it off baby
Safe to say we're through
No matter what you do

214

You know I'll always love you
Well I have to
'Cause I promised

Now I know who scammed me. There was no Jerry Wesley, William, ex-girlfriend or deceased wife. They were all part of his story. When I see who he really is I feel stupid. I have so many questions for my own closure and for this book. I was in total shock when he showed me who he was; I had to sign off line for about 15 minutes to deal with my many emotions. I remember crying a lot this day. He didn't trust me because he knew I could have him arrested, and I didn't trust him because he is not a trustworthy person.

He said I touched his world and he made me love him and that he can make anyone love him. He said to himself the same thing I said to myself, "How can a smart woman like this send money?" He thought I never would. I also thought I could never get scammed. Thinking you cannot get scammed is false security. Anyone can be scammed if the scammer knows how to appeal to your heart.

I was shocked when he gave me his real phone number in Nigeria and I had the opportunity to talk to him without the phone cutting off. He knew if he gave me his phone number I could track him. He said he was sorry eighteen times. He said he was sorry for everything he caused me and how he treated me and he asked for forgiveness eighteen times. I was conflicted but thought maybe he was really sorry.

Was his coming clean with me just another attempt to get money from me? After all, he asked for $100. If it was, he was taking a great risk so he must have either been desperate for money or was really in love with me and wanted to do the right thing. The answer to this I will never know.

I finally sent him the goodby letter I wrote three weeks prior and he was very hurt by this letter. He knew I worked with investigators and I had connections, so he was very scared that I was going to hurt him. He also said he was on the run because he stopped working for the boss and was afraid he was going to hurt him. He said his fallinghrt22 ID was never hacked but he gave it up because he talked to so many women with that identity and some gave him money and some didn't.

I told him I was chatting with many other scammers for the book and he said, "frauds are much". He asked me to not answer any of them and to please get off the dating sites because "all men that travel or don't want to meet you, or ask you for info are scammers."

Questions and Answers:

- ✓ I had to know why he did such a thing. His answer was that things were hard for him and his family; they were suffering and he had no choice but to lie to me.
- ✓ He lived in Nigeria, as I thought.
- ✓ He said he fell in love with me too and this is why he was showing me who he was. He thought he would never fall in love while he did online dating fraud but he did. He thought that maybe I would bring him to the United States where he could be with me and go to school. He said my words touched his heart, and the day he fell in love with me was the day we talked on the phone prior to him "supposedly" leaving for China and I cried. I looked back and he told me this on April 10th. 11 days after we first met. He said this day he also cried because he was lying to the woman he loved. He said he was addicted to chatting with me. He read our correspondences always, and when he IM'ed me he said it was because he missed me. He said if I said goodbye now it would kill him in his heart. When I told him I would get over him he said that made him heart broken because he knew I would leave him. Then he said that I have his life and a rope holding his heart and wanted me to wish him the best and please let him go so he can be free. Wow, we both wanted the same thing…*for our hearts to be free.*
- ✓ The pictures I fell in love with came from a man's profile on Match.com. I went to Match, found him, and emailed him that his identity was stolen; he never emailed me back. Match said they had no such member, so the real man whose picture I fell in love with is still a mystery today.
- ✓ His California phone number was a Skype number. Now I know why it always disconnected.
- ✓ He said he worked for a boss out of China and that his boss dictated the amount of money he was to ask for and that he only received $200 out of the $3,500.
- ✓ It was the boss that created the professional website.
- ✓ He said the boss doesn't have a company but has many workers in China.
- ✓ Because I found many scammers on the SinglesBee website I was curious if a boss owned the dating site; he said no.
- ✓ His boss was able to see all correspondences. So not only do we not know who is behind the screen, we also don't know who is seeing our pictures and what we say or how they will be used.
- ✓ He said he created the "fallingheart ID" and wrote or copied/pasted all his own material.
- ✓ He said he didn't have any training.
- ✓ I needed to know if what he said to me, he said to every woman, and he said yes. Everything he said to me, he said to every woman he tried to scam, except for intimate

conversations and that "he lives to love me". The first time he said this to me was April the 9th.

I never did recoup my $3,500, and what you see here is the last time Michael or whatever his real name is and I corresponded. His last message to me was *"Please forgive me, my life is changed forever and I will always love you* and he sent me the song lyrics from the song, "You Promised". He never took the opportunity I presented him to write for this book, and I never gave him any more money. He asked me to please "not fool" him when it came to the book. He who made a living fooling others didn't want to be fooled.

I have to admit that my heart wanted to send him the $100 because I thought he needed it to start a new life, but my mind said he needed to earn it by giving me information for the book. He said he wanted to be happy again and live a God fearing life, and that he went to church and asked God to forgive him. So maybe I really got through to him that what he was doing was very wrong. I truly hope he changed his life around. I know that is a tall task with nobody cheering him on or helping him change. I really did forgive him and do find myself praying from time to time for his well-being and a changed life.

Once he came clean with me I got what I wanted, which was to know the *"real man behind the screen"* and my love for the "picture in my mind" of Jerry Wesley disappeared. To this day, I am grateful that Michael took the risk to come clean, show me who he was on camera and to apologize and set my heart free.

Yes, this entire experience changed me forever. I am not as trusting nor am I naïve to the scammers and dangers of online dating. I have also learned a lot about myself and have the knowledge and ability to help others. To me the $3,500 was a small price to pay.

The next scammer will take you through many twists and turns and show you some tools professional scammers use, as well as an unexpected surprise at the end.

CHAPTER 3

THE TEACHER OF MANY THINGS

T his man said he would teach me many things, and he did exactly that. What he didn't know was I was looking for a teacher. He didn't know I chatted with him to learn more about scammers and dating scam techniques for this book. He didn't know that *I* had some things to teach *him*.

He was a professional scammer with many tools, but he made mistakes that alerted me to the fact I had another Nigerian scammer on the hook. All people who are online dating need to know about scammers and their tools and techniques. My hope is that someday the scammers will realize that *they* too, need to be careful, because the people they seek to prey on are becoming educated and savvy and courageous enough to call out a scammer when they find one.

In spite of his mistakes, this man was good at his job. His scams were probably very effective with people unfamiliar with online dating scams. His fun, young spirit and sweet words could easily make a woman enjoy his company and fall in love with him, and he played his scam out in a way that would make many women feel guilty and motivated to help him.

As you read through this chapter you will learn many scamming techniques, go on a roller coaster ride of emotions and surely be surprised at how it ends. Buckle up!

His profile as found on *Singlesbee*:

Profile: jugant

Thinking of showing some love...
34-year-old man in London
Looking for girls 31 to 57, up to 10000 miles from me

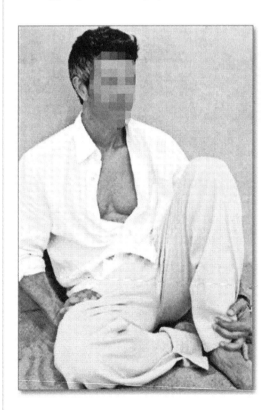

My Headline

Thinking of showing some love…

My Basics

- Height: 5'10"
- Body type: Athletic
- Hair color: Black
- Ethnicity: Not specified
- Looks: Attractive
- Education: Bachelor/4-year degree
- ***Occupation: Engineering***
- Income: Unspecified
- I speak: English
- Religion: Not specified
- Relationship status: Never married
- Children: Not specified
- Wants children: Not specified
- Smoking: Daily
- Drinking: Moderately

My Type of Girl

- Looking for: Dating Only, Dating / Long-term Potential, Long-term Only
- ***With: Women 31 to 57-year-old***
- Distance: Within 10000 miles of London
- ***Height: 4'0" to 7'0"***
- Body type: Any
- Hair color: Any
- Ethnicity: Doesn't Matter
- Education: Associates/2-Year Degree
- Occupation: Any
- Income: Doesn't Matter
- Language(s): English
- Religion: Any
- Relationship status: Any
- Children: Doesn't Matter
- Wants children: Doesn't Matter
- Smoking: Doesn't Matter
- Drinking: Doesn't Matter   ***Note*** – Nothing else on his profile was filled out.

RED FLAGS

- 🚩 The occupation of engineering. Many scammers have this occupation.
- 🚩 He is supposedly 34 years old, but he looks much older in the picture.
- 🚩 The picture looks like a modeling picture.
- 🚩 He says he is looking for women in the age group of 31 to 57, which is within the age group that scammers target. Why does a 34 year old man want a woman in her late 50's?
- 🚩 He wants her height to be 4'0" – 7'0". This tells you he doesn't know feet and inches. An engineer should know feet and inches.

This is where it all started:

From: jugant
To: ladedi
Subject: (none)
Sent: 04/26/2012 06:53PM

hello prett..do u wanna chat...bobjugant@hotmail.com

From: jugant
To: ladedi
Subject: (none)
Sent: 04/29/2012 1:00PM

You look good babes...plz send me an wmail........

From: ladedi
To: jugant
Subject: (none)
Sent: 04/29/2012 1:25PM

Hi Bob!

How are you? I hope you are having a great weekend. You are very handsome :-). I would love to chat. You can reach me at ladydi2011@yahoo.

From: bobjugant@yahoo.com
To: ladydi
Subject: Re:
Sent: Wed, 2 May 2012 11:54:22

Hey pretty..am bob from singlebees..add me on your ym let's chat

Sent from my BlackBerry wireless device from MTN

From: ladydi2011@yahoo.com
To: Bob Jugant
Subject: Re:
Sent: May 2, 2012 12:29 PM

Hi Bob!

I added you to my IM. I am looking forward to chatting with you!

Diana

IM May 2, 2012 12:31:55 PM

12:31:55 PM **ladydi2011**: Hi Bob. It is nice to meet you!
12:33:12 PM **bobjugant**: U too *horney*
12:33:33 PM **bobjugant**: So how are you doing
12:33:52 PM **ladydi2011**: I am well. Thanks for asking.
12:34:00 PM **ladydi2011**: So, you are from London?
12:34:05 PM **bobjugant**: Yea
12:34:25 PM **ladydi2011**: You look like you are a model. Are you?
12:34:50 PM **bobjugant**: Yea am into fashion
12:35:07 PM **ladydi2011**: What time is it there?
12:35:12 PM **bobjugant**: But basically am an engineer
12:35:29 PM **ladydi2011**: Who do you work for?
12:36:07 PM **bobjugant**: Its 5 in *london*
12:36:32 PM **ladydi2011**: 5 in the afternoon?
12:36:56 PM **bobjugant**: Its a low profile company dat service *oil facilities*
12:37:31 PM **ladydi2011**: Do you enjoy your work?
12:38:28 PM **bobjugant**: Hehehe
12:38:37 PM **ladydi2011**: Your profile does not tell me much. What are you looking for on Singles Bees?

12:39:13 PM **ladydi2011**: You have kept yourself mysterious......

12:39:14 PM **bobjugant**: I just joined single besss a month or so

12:39:37 PM **ladydi2011**: Me too...Have you had any luck yet?

12:39:54 PM **bobjugant**: Not @ all

12:40:24 PM **ladydi2011**: Really? You are so handsome!

12:40:44 PM **ladydi2011**: Why are you still single?

12:40:50 PM **bobjugant**: Your pretty too

12:41:13 PM **ladydi2011**: Thank you.

12:41:18 PM **bobjugant**: Wat other language do u speak

12:41:29 PM **ladydi2011**: Just English...

12:41:39 PM **ladydi2011**: What other languages do you speak?

12:42:01 PM **bobjugant**: *German*

12:42:11 PM **ladydi2011**: Any others?

12:42:43 PM **bobjugant**: Dats all

12:42:59 PM **bobjugant**: So were u live?

12:43:29 PM **ladydi2011**: Are you originally from London?

12:43:48 PM **ladydi2011**: I live in Atlanta.

12:44:35 PM **bobjugant**: I was raised in *aberdeen*

12:45:03 PM **bobjugant**: Den I relocated to *london* some couple or years ago

12:45:46 PM **ladydi2011**: Aberdeen is in the United Kingdom, correct?

12:45:54 PM **bobjugant**: *But most times I travel around for contract*

12:46:10 PM **ladydi2011**: Do you ever travel to the states?

12:46:12 PM **bobjugant**: Aberdeen is in *scotland*

12:46:30 PM **ladydi2011**: Scotland....Oh!

12:46:32 PM **bobjugant**: Never been to d states

12:46:56 PM **bobjugant**: Mostly *europe,asia,africa*

12:47:21 PM **ladydi2011**: I have never been to London or Scotland.

12:47:54 PM **bobjugant**: U gona b in d uk one day may b

12:48:00 PM **ladydi2011**: I have been to France, Africa and many Islands

12:48:37 PM **ladydi2011**: I would love to visit.

12:48:56 PM **bobjugant**: Oh dats kool

12:49:03 PM **bobjugant**: *So wat do u do*

12:49:20 PM **ladydi2011**: I am a business consultant and transformational speaker

12:49:44 PM **ladydi2011**: I am in the process of writing my first book

12:49:55 PM **bobjugant**: Hmm...Nice

12:50:21 PM **ladydi2011**: Writing a book is not as easy as people think. It takes a lot of time!

12:50:34 PM **bobjugant**: Yea I knw

12:50:49 PM **bobjugant**: Dedication you knw

12:51:07 PM **ladydi2011**: Yes. Dedication!

12:51:15 PM **ladydi2011**: Have you written a book?

12:51:26 PM **bobjugant**: Lol.. I haven't

12:51:55 PM **ladydi2011**: What do you like to do in your spare time?

12:52:31 PM **bobjugant**: I like chilling with friends

12:52:39 PM **bobjugant**: Swimming

12:52:48 PM **bobjugant**: *Basically I do everything*

12:53:04 PM **ladydi2011**: Is it warm there now?

12:53:29 PM **bobjugant**: Yea warm

12:53:51 PM **bobjugant**: *I will b leaving for africa soon u know*

12:53:57 PM **ladydi2011**: Here too. Our pool just opened yesterday

12:54:07 PM **ladydi2011**: Where in Africa?

12:54:09 PM **bobjugant**: *Some work in south africa*

12:54:18 PM **bobjugant**: *Durban*

12:54:26 PM **ladydi2011**: Have you been to South Africa before?

12:54:46 PM **bobjugant**: A long time ago. Can even remember how it looks

12:55:03 PM **ladydi2011**: How long will you be there?

12:55:34 PM **bobjugant**: Not for long

12:56:07 PM **ladydi2011**: Maybe one day you will have work here in the states

12:56:17 PM **bobjugant**: My office has a job with agip

12:56:34 PM **bobjugant**: yea one day

12:56:36 PM **ladydi2011**: I never heard of Agip

12:56:42 PM **ladydi2011**: So, you are 34?

12:56:51 PM **bobjugant**: Yea I am

12:57:10 PM **bobjugant**: How old are you

12:57:15 PM **ladydi2011**: Agip is an oil company?

12:57:23 PM **ladydi2011**: I am 48...

12:57:30 PM **bobjugant**: Wow

12:57:34 PM **bobjugant**: Dats great

12:57:51 PM **bobjugant**: U look very tender in ur pix

12:57:52 PM **ladydi2011**: Why thank you!

12:59:18 PM **ladydi2011**: It is nice to chat with you. Most men I have chatted with have not yet mastered the English language.

1:00:24 PM **bobjugant**: Rilli

1:00:35 PM **ladydi2011**: Lol!

1:01:00 PM **bobjugant**: I speak and write english babes

1:01:52 PM **bobjugant**: So wat are you up to?

1:01:59 PM **ladydi2011**: I was beginning to wonder about who is on Singles Bees

1:02:24 PM **ladydi2011**: Trying to work. It is 1:00 in the afternoon here.

1:02:38 PM **bobjugant**: Ok nice

1:02:47 PM **ladydi2011**: Are you done with work for the day?

1:02:59 PM **bobjugant**: Yes. I am done

1:03:17 PM **ladydi2011**: So, no nice women in London?

1:03:17 PM **bobjugant**: Am in a park right knw

1:03:31 PM **ladydi2011**: Nice. Can I join you?

1:03:55 PM **bobjugant**: Oh yea u can

1:04:20 PM **ladydi2011**: Would you like me to bring a bottle of red or a bottle of white?

1:04:41 PM **bobjugant**: I like white wine

1:05:05 PM **bobjugant**: 2 glasses for me and you

1:05:09 PM **ladydi2011**: Me too! I actually like German white wine.

1:05:20 PM **ladydi2011**: Some cheese and crackers?

1:05:37 PM **bobjugant**: Yea crackers

1:05:41 PM **ladydi2011**: A blanket

1:05:54 PM **ladydi2011**: A frisbee

1:05:56 PM **bobjugant**: Hmm

1:06:09 PM **ladydi2011**: A camera to take some pictures

1:06:29 PM **bobjugant**: You gat it *baby*

1:06:46 PM **ladydi2011**: Sounds like a wonderful time...

1:06:56 PM **bobjugant**: I like chatting with you

1:07:09 PM **ladydi2011**: I like chatting with you too!

1:07:16 PM **bobjugant**: You sound a lovely person

1:07:59 PM **ladydi2011**: Why, thank you. I love life. I see the glass as half full. I am passionate and love to have fun and new experiences.

1:08:25 PM **ladydi2011**: You seem like a very interesting and nice man. It is my pleasure to meet you.

1:08:27 PM **bobjugant**: Me too

1:08:42 PM **bobjugant**: D pleasure is all mine

1:08:52 PM **bobjugant**: I like life too and I like fun

1:09:38 PM **bobjugant**: I love d beach

1:09:40 PM **ladydi2011**: Life is too short to not enjoy every minute of it.

1:10:04 PM **ladydi2011**: The beach is my favorite place!

1:10:30 PM **ladydi2011**: I try to play full out with everything I do. What about you?

1:10:48 PM **bobjugant**: Same with me

1:11:00 PM **ladydi2011**: Do you have any siblings?

1:11:03 PM **bobjugant**: Am 100% fun to be with

1:11:25 PM **ladydi2011**: Cool...

1:11:28 PM **bobjugant**: No I dont

1:11:49 PM **ladydi2011**: You are an only child...You must be spoiled.

1:11:57 PM **bobjugant**: *My parent are late*

1:12:04 PM **ladydi2011**: I have five brothers and no sisters

1:12:22 PM **ladydi2011**: I am sorry to hear about your parents.

1:12:24 PM **bobjugant**: 5 brothers

1:12:30 PM **ladydi2011**: Yep!

1:12:54 PM **ladydi2011**: 3 older and 2 younger

1:13:01 PM **bobjugant**: Oh

1:13:16 PM **bobjugant**: Do dey stay in the states too

1:14:20 PM **ladydi2011**: Yes.

1:14:39 PM **bobjugant**: Ok kool

1:14:51 PM **bobjugant**: *Do you have kids*

1:15:01 PM **ladydi2011**: They are all married with families. I am the only single one with no children

1:15:25 PM **bobjugant**: Ok

1:15:58 PM **ladydi2011**: Do you have any children?

1:16:50 PM **bobjugant**: No I dont

1:17:03 PM **ladydi2011**: Do you want children?

1:17:26 PM **bobjugant**: Everybody likes children

1:17:32 PM **ladydi2011**: *Have you ever been married?*

1:17:58 PM **bobjugant**: *Yea*

1:18:02 PM **ladydi2011**: Yes, children are precious.

1:18:11 PM **bobjugant**: *It lasted for 1yr*

1:18:23 PM **ladydi2011**: Sorry to hear this.

1:18:38 PM **bobjugant**: Thanks

1:18:43 PM **ladydi2011**: I was married for 8 yrs. and have been divorced for 14 yrs.

1:18:55 PM **bobjugant**: 14yrs

1:19:23 PM **ladydi2011**: It took me almost two years to heal and date again

1:20:03 PM **bobjugant**: so how have you been catching your fun

1:20:09 PM **ladydi2011**: I then met a man and got engaged. We were together for 5 years and then he betrayed me and broke trust

1:20:30 PM **bobjugant**: Some men are like that you know

1:21:17 PM **bobjugant**: Dats why am cumming into your life

1:21:27 PM **ladydi2011**: Nice!!!!!

1:21:46 PM **ladydi2011**: London...this is so far away!

1:22:16 PM **bobjugant**: I do take vacation a lot

1:22:31 PM **ladydi2011**: Cool

1:22:39 PM **bobjugant**: *Cuz my work is based on contract*

1:23:07 PM **ladydi2011**: If you come to the states I will show you around and we can have a lot of fun!

1:23:26 PM **bobjugant**: I look forward to that

1:23:40 PM **ladydi2011**: I can work from anywhere in the world

1:24:07 PM **ladydi2011**: I can visit you in London

1:24:17 PM **bobjugant**: Rilli

1:24:23 PM **bobjugant**: Dats kool

1:24:54 PM **ladydi2011**: Yeah. Nice perks

1:25:52 PM **ladydi2011**: I have really enjoyed getting to know you a little. I have to get back to work. I would love to chat again. What about you?

Break in Time

1:27:27 PM **ladydi2011**: Are you there?

1:27:40 PM **bobjugant**: Yea I will

1:28:02 PM **bobjugant**: We shld chat always ok

1:28:43 PM **ladydi2011**: You got it. You can always reach me via email. I have a blackberry. You do too, right?

1:29:19 PM **bobjugant**: Yea I do

1:29:28 PM **ladydi2011**: Enjoy the rest of your evening. Please send me some more pictures.

1:29:32 PM **bobjugant**: I use it sometimes

1:29:47 PM **ladydi2011**: So, we will chat soon?

1:29:53 PM **bobjugant**: I will

1:30:17 PM **bobjugant**: You send me nice pictures too,ok

1:30:30 PM **bobjugant**: Nice chatting with you

1:30:40 PM **ladydi2011**: I will. Thank you for chatting with me. Bye for now...

1:30:53 PM **bobjugant**: Yea bye

IM May 2, 2012 3:41:13 PM

3:41:13 PM **bobjugant**: *Hey babes*

From: bobjugant@yahoo.com
To: ladydi
Subject: Re:

Sent: Thu, 3 May 2012 04:12:56 -0700 (PDT)

hi darling,i said *i* should see how you are doing,hope you slept well,,*i* just left work **know** to go do some surey,*i* guess you are still sleeping..horney you were on my mind all through my night..wink ..do have a splendid and beautiful day horney..looking forward to see your reply..***take care of your self for me***

To: Bob Jugant
From: ladydi2011@yahoo.com
Subject: Re:
Sent: May 3, 2012 9:09 AM

Hi Bob,

Thank you for the morning message. I hope your survey goes well. Have a wonderful day!

Diana

From: bobjugant@yahoo.com
To: ladydi
Subject:
Sent: May 3, 2012 12:51 PM

yea diana my survey went on smoothly and my thoughts towards you were nice and sweet..not sure if *i* would go to the park today cuz *i* have a lot of arrangement to make..*i* told you *i* would be ***going to africa*** soon., so *i* have to put things in other before *i* leave, *i* always have butterflies in my stomach when ever *i* am reading your email..horney please can you send me a sweet pics of you *i* like to look at it all day..***take care of you self my queen***

To: Bob Jugant
From: ladydi2011@yahoo.com
Subject: Re:
Sent: May 3, 2012 12:54 PM

Hi Bob,

I am glad your survey went well. I am sure you have a lot to do before going to Africa.

When do you leave?

Diana

From: bobjugant@yahoo.com
To: ladydi
Subject: Re:
Sent: May 3, 2012 1:00 PM

diana *i* would be leaving in 4 days time..guess what"*i* would be ***working off shore most of the times*..*its pretty going to be hectic*..*i* would always be talking to you were ever *i* am..so how is work today?

To: Bob Jugant
From: ladydi2011@yahoo.com
Subject: Re:
Sent: May 3, 2012 11:08 PM

Hi Bob!

I am sitting here watching TV and my thoughts keep wandering to you. I am wondering how your night was.

Cheers,

Diana

This is going to be fun! The very first email he sends tells me it was sent from a Blackberry and had the carrier name of MTN. When I researched I learned this carrier was in Nigeria. There is no guessing. I already know I have a scammer on the hook.

RED FLAGS

- The first email he sends me says "hello pretty". This is a typical scammer greeting.
- He continues trying to flatter me when he says, "You look good babes", "honey" and "darling." (I cracked up laughing because he always spelled 'honey', horney.) He uses endearing words with me right away, which is another thing scammers do.
- His picture looks like a model's picture, which is another red flag. The way he chats tells me he is young.
- He does not use proper English and his messages have many typos.
- He says he now lives in London but is originally from Scotland. This is so he has an excuse for his accent.
- He says "My parents are late," which is not proper English, but a phrase common in Nigeria.

🏳 He says he has no siblings, which leaves him alone with nobody to help him. He is already setting the stage to manipulate me.

🏳 Like a lot of scammers, he claims to work for an oil facility and travel around to Europe, Asia and Africa. He tells me he will leave shortly for South Africa. I had a gut feeling he would not ask me for money on this trip but the next. Whenever a man says he does contract work and travels it is a red flag. If he talks about Africa it is a double red flag.

🏳 He tells me he will be *working off shore*. This is a setup that will allow him to not be available to chat that much with me.

🏳 He asks the questions scammers typically ask such as where I live, what I do and if I have kids. When I ask what he likes to do, he says "basically everything". Although his questions may be typical of two people trying to get to know each other, his answers are abnormal. Who really likes to do "basically everything?" This man likes to keep himself mysterious.

🏳 When I asked if he was ever married, he says for one year, but according to his profile he was never married. Even though his profile was sparse, I was still able to find a discrepancy. Always be sure to go back to the profile and look for discrepancies.

🏳 His first email to me was in the middle of the night my time, but if he was in London, it would have been morning there. London and Nigeria are in the same time zone.

🏳 He uses lower case I's and instead of "now", he says "know." Nigerians do this. He says, "take care of your self for me," and I have found most scammers also say this.

🏳 He calls me his *queen.* This is another red flag that suggests you are talking to a scammer from Africa.

🏳 "its pretty going to be hectic" is Pidgin English. Whenever you see a sentence that obviously has words in an unorganized manner, please don't assume that it is a typo, because it is probably Pidgin English and a red flag that you are speaking with a scammer from Nigeria.

IM May 4, 2012 3:23:19 PM

3:23:19 PM **bobjugant**: Hey pretty
3:23:57 PM **bobjugant**: Howz u doing
3:24:04 PM **ladydi2011**: Hello Handsome! How are you? Thank you for the compliment.
3:24:25 PM **ladydi2011**: I am well. How are you?
3:24:56 PM **bobjugant**: Am doing great
3:25:15 PM **bobjugant**: Just got home u know
3:25:29 PM **bobjugant**: Hectic day for me ova here
3:25:39 PM **ladydi2011**: Are you almost ready to leave for Africa?
3:25:56 PM **bobjugant**: Yea baby am very close
3:26:00 PM **ladydi2011**: Did you have dinner yet?
3:26:11 PM **bobjugant**: No
3:26:26 PM **ladydi2011**: Me either. It is only 3:26 here.
3:26:42 PM **bobjugant**: I don't take dinner all d time
3:26:53 PM **ladydi2011**: Will you be going out tonight? It is Friday.
3:26:57 PM **bobjugant**: I take fruit for dinner most times
3:26:59 PM **bobjugant**: Lol..Suree I will. I will b hanging out with some friends in couple of hrs
3:28:13 PM **ladydi2011**: *Please send me some pictures of yourself...*

3:28:34 PM **bobjugant**: *Hmm*

3:28:43 PM **ladydi2011**: Cool. I will be going out to dinner with some friends tonight.

3:28:48 PM **ladydi2011**: Hmmm

3:29:02 PM **bobjugant**: U will cook for me wen I cum oba to d states

3:29:11 PM **ladydi2011**: Absolutely

3:30:15 PM **bobjugant**: Ok

3:30:40 PM **bobjugant**: So wat u up to right know

3:30:43 PM **ladydi2011**: What is your favorite food?

3:31:03 PM **ladydi2011**: Reviewing monthly reports so my staff can send them to clients.

3:31:16 PM **ladydi2011**: Oversight is a big part of my job.

3:31:32 PM **ladydi2011**: Now, I am talking with you.

3:31:35 PM **bobjugant**: *Spaghetti bolonese*

3:32:16 PM **bobjugant**: *I love chips and shreaded chicken*

3:34:33 PM **ladydi2011**: So, how long of a flight is it for you to Africa?

3:34:43 PM **bobjugant**: So wats your favourite food too

3:34:54 PM **bobjugant**: *7hrs maximum*

3:35:07 PM **ladydi2011**: Anything Italian...

3:35:42 PM **ladydi2011**: 7 hrs. isn't too bad. About what it takes me to get from coast to coast

3:35:43 PM **bobjugant**: I have only 11 days in *africa*

3:36:23 PM **ladydi2011**: You will not be there long...this is good.

3:36:31 PM **bobjugant**: *I am processing a contract in america..Argentina*

3:36:44 PM **ladydi2011**: Will I hear from you while you are in Africa?

3:36:51 PM **bobjugant**: I hope I get it

3:37:10 PM **bobjugant**: yea

3:37:12 PM **ladydi2011**: Argentina...Good luck! I hope you get it too. Can I meet you there?

3:37:45 PM **bobjugant**: I will chat with you everyday while am in *africa*

3:37:45 PM **ladydi2011**: I look forward to hearing from you.

3:38:30 PM **bobjugant**: Me too horney

3:38:32 PM **ladydi2011**: What are you still doing single?

3:38:55 PM **bobjugant**: How long is *argentina* from you

3:38:56 PM **bobjugant**: Lol..Awww

3:39:08 PM **ladydi2011**: I don't know. Let me look.

3:39:37 PM **bobjugant**: Ok

3:43:23 PM **bobjugant**: I get the best feeling in the world when you say hi to me, or even smile because I know even if just for a second, I crossed your mind.

3:43:59 PM **ladydi2011**: I cannot find how long it would take me to get to Argentina. I will look it up later and email you.

3:44:19 PM **ladydi2011**: Did you get my email last night?

3:44:39 PM **ladydi2011**: I was watching TV and my thoughts kept wandering to you...

3:45:09 PM **ladydi2011**: I am looking forward to getting to know you.

Break in Time

3:47:30 PM **ladydi2011**: Are you there?

3:51:44 PM **bobjugant**: hey

3:51:55 PM **bobjugant**: *i lost my connection*

3:52:03 PM **bobjugant**: but its bak know

3:52:09 PM **ladydi2011**: I figured as much.

3:52:27 PM **ladydi2011**: Did you see what I wrote to you?

3:52:42 PM **bobjugant**: no *i* did not

3:52:58 PM **bobjugant**: please reend it

3:53:00 PM **ladydi2011**: Did you get my email last night? I was watching TV and my thoughts kept wandering to you...I am looking forward to getting to know you.

3:53:51 PM **bobjugant**: me too darling

3:54:00 PM **bobjugant**: *i* like you alot

3:54:02 PM **ladydi2011**: I like when I hear from you because I know you are thinking about me.

3:54:15 PM **bobjugant**: you wanna know wy

3:54:20 PM **ladydi2011**: So, what are you looking for in a relationship?

3:54:33 PM **ladydi2011**: Yes, please. Why?

3:54:44 PM **bobjugant**: yea *i* think about you always

3:55:23 PM **bobjugant**: truth and honesty

3:55:47 PM **bobjugant**: **i like honesty**

3:55:51 PM **ladydi2011**: You will always get truth and honesty from me. It is who I am.

3:56:17 PM **ladydi2011**: Baby, life is too short to play games or lie to people.

3:56:19 PM **bobjugant**: *i* like dat

3:56:39 PM **bobjugant**: am happy baby

3:56:57 PM **ladydi2011**: I like you!

3:57:12 PM **bobjugant**: you are a nice person

3:57:29 PM **bobjugant**: *i* like you too..and *i* like it if u call me horney

3:58:13 PM **ladydi2011**: Ok, honey

3:58:20 PM **bobjugant**: hehehe

3:58:26 PM **bobjugant**: *i* like dat..you rock

3:58:49 PM **ladydi2011**: You rock too!

3:59:31 PM **bobjugant**: so how has life been treating you

3:59:34 PM **ladydi2011**: So, you want to come take a ride with me in my convertible?

4:00:06 PM **ladydi2011**: Life is good. It would be better if I could be at a picnic with you right now.

4:00:33 PM **bobjugant**: yea *i* remember know *i* think *i* saw your red convertable pix. it was lovely

4:00:43 PM **ladydi2011**: I think I am going to go get an ice cream cone...cruising is my stress releif.

4:00:56 PM **ladydi2011**: It is a fun car honey.

4:01:08 PM **ladydi2011**: I like to have fun!

4:01:09 PM **bobjugant**: horney *i* will take a ride wth you soon

4:01:22 PM **ladydi2011**: I look forward to this. You seem like you are fun!

4:01:32 PM **bobjugant**: me too

4:01:39 PM **bobjugant**: soon..my next vacation

4:02:02 PM **ladydi2011**: Kool....I will hold you to this.

4:02:06 PM **bobjugant**: *i* like to kiss and you have a very lovely lips

4:02:36 PM **ladydi2011**: I love to kiss. Do you like to hold hands?

4:02:51 PM **bobjugant**: yea baby

4:02:53 PM **ladydi2011**: awwww. Thank you

4:02:57 PM **bobjugant**: and cuddle

4:03:05 PM **ladydi2011**: I love to cuddle.

4:03:29 PM **ladydi2011**: What else do you like to do?

4:03:29 PM **bobjugant**: we will cuddle a lot

4:03:43 PM **bobjugant**: *lol*

4:04:08 PM **ladydi2011**: I am looking forward to kissing and cuddling with you.

4:04:13 PM **bobjugant**: kiss your ears and ypur neck

4:04:41 PM **ladydi2011**: Honey, I am looking for my best friend, lover and husband. What are you looking for?
4:04:55 PM **ladydi2011**: My neck is VERY sensitive. Is yours?
4:04:58 PM **bobjugant**: *i* will like to kiss all ova your body
4:05:30 PM **ladydi2011**: Whoa.....
4:06:08 PM **bobjugant**: my tongue is very sensitive
4:06:15 PM **ladydi2011**: We better stop here or I will not be able to go back to work...
4:06:33 PM **bobjugant**: wat else would you like from me
4:06:51 PM **ladydi2011**: I want to see you smile and happy
4:06:54 PM **bobjugant**: *lol*
4:07:09 PM **bobjugant**: horney you have to go back to work
4:07:37 PM **bobjugant**: *lol*
4:07:49 PM **ladydi2011**: I do. I actually need to run out to the bank and post office before they close. Will you have time to chat later tonight?
4:07:54 PM **bobjugant**: but later *i* would make you smile
4:08:03 PM **ladydi2011**: Promise????
4:08:13 PM **bobjugant**: yea *i* will
4:08:18 PM **ladydi2011**: Pictures please
4:08:34 PM **bobjugant**: you send me an email wen your done so *i* can cum back on line
4:08:57 PM **ladydi2011**: I will.
4:09:14 PM **ladydi2011**: Cool...meet you here later.
4:09:21 PM **bobjugant**: and *i* will make your life beautiful
4:09:50 PM **ladydi2011**: I will make your life beautiful too!
4:10:03 PM **ladydi2011**: Until later...
4:10:15 PM **bobjugant**: kisses kisses and be good ok
4:11:04 PM **ladydi2011**: I will think about you as I am driving and eating my ice cream cone...
4:11:35 PM **bobjugant**: awww nice *i* like dat..*i* will think of you too
4:11:59 PM **ladydi2011**: bye for now honey.
4:12:26 PM **bobjugant**: *i* promise we will have time together wen we are done

IM May 4, 2012 9:17:22 PM

9:17:22 PM **bobjugant**: Hey
9:18:21 PM **bobjugant**: Hello horney

From: ladydi2011@yahoo.com
To: Bob Jugant
Subject: Hi!!!
Sent: Sat, 4 May 2012 9:20:28

Hi Honey!
I am thinking about you. Do you want to chat on line?

Diana

From: bobjugant@yahoo.com
To: ladydi2011@yahoo.com
Subject: Re: Hi!!!
Sent: Sat, 4 May 2012 9:22:07

Yea baby..u can cum online *know* am waiting..thou am still out!!

Sent from my BlackBerry wireless device from *MTN*

From: ladydi2011@yahoo.com
To: bob jugant
Subject: Re: Hi!!!
Sent: Sat, 4 May 2012 9:24:45

Hi Honey. I will be up for a while. Do you want to wait until you get home?

The choice is yours. Diana

From: bobjugant@yahoo.com
To: ladydi2011
Subject: Re: Hi!!!
Sent: Sat, 4 May 2012 9:25:31

Ok I will wait..I will be home in a short while..I miss u much horney....I am thinking about you right knw baby

Sent from my BlackBerry wireless device from *MTN*

From: ladydi2011@yahoo.com
To: bob jugant
Subject: Re: Hi!!!
Sent: Sat, 4 May 2012 9:27:52

Ok, Baby!

Please take your time. I am glad you chose to chat with me once you get home. Thinking about you too! Please email me when you are ready to chat.

Always, Diana

From: bobjugant@yahoo.com
To: ladydi
Subject: Re: Hi!!!
Sent: Sat, 4 May 2012 9:28:16

Ok darling ,I geting home know..I would be on line soon..

Sent from my BlackBerry wireless device from *MTN*

From: bobjugant@yahoo.com
To: ladydi
Subject: Re: Hi!!!
Sent: Sat, 4 May 2012 10:12:16

I'm coming on line now love. .

Sent from my BlackBerry wireless device from *MTN*

IM May 4, 2012 10:19:28 PM

10:19:28 PM **ladydi2011**: Hi Honey. Are you there?
10:20:35 PM **bobjugant**: Yea am here horney
10:20:50 PM **bobjugant**: Did u go out?
10:21:25 PM **ladydi2011**: I did. I had a nice dinner with my friends. How was your evening baby?
10:21:47 PM **bobjugant**: My evening was great. I had fun
10:22:05 PM **bobjugant**: But I wish u were with me
10:22:22 PM **bobjugant**: It could have been wonderful
10:22:40 PM **bobjugant**: I miss you
10:22:51 PM **ladydi2011**: I wish I were with you too!
10:22:59 PM **bobjugant**: Yea baby
10:23:04 PM **ladydi2011**: Baby, what time is it there?
10:23:25 PM **bobjugant**: 3:20am
10:23:36 PM **ladydi2011**: It is very late there.
10:24:03 PM **bobjugant**: Yea
10:24:16 PM **bobjugant**: But its kool
10:24:23 PM **ladydi2011**: Are you sure?
10:24:32 PM **bobjugant**: So are you home *know*
10:24:37 PM **bobjugant**: Yea am sure
10:24:51 PM **ladydi2011**: Yes, I am home now.
10:24:57 PM **bobjugant**: Am all yours baby. U can tell me wat ever u want
10:25:13 PM **ladydi2011**: Thank you. I like this
10:25:33 PM **ladydi2011**: Please tell me what a perfect first date would be for you

10:25:50 PM **bobjugant**: Baby wat colour or bra did wear out

10:26:07 PM **ladydi2011**: black lace

10:26:31 PM **bobjugant**: Oh

10:26:41 PM **bobjugant**: Am delightened

10:26:58 PM **bobjugant**: I wish I was with you *know* horney

10:27:28 PM **ladydi2011**: Please tell me what a perfect first date would be for you

10:27:30 PM **bobjugant**: Baby were are right know?

10:27:42 PM **ladydi2011**: I am in my dining room

10:27:47 PM **ladydi2011**: Where are you?

10:27:50 PM **bobjugant**: A perfect firdt date..hmm

10:28:05 PM **bobjugant**: Nottin rilli much

10:28:18 PM **bobjugant**: Just chill with some candles on

10:28:27 PM **ladydi2011**: I love candle light

10:28:39 PM **bobjugant**: And we eat and have fun together

10:28:47 PM **ladydi2011**: And

10:28:54 PM **ladydi2011**: Would we cook together?

10:29:03 PM **bobjugant**: Yea baby

10:29:11 PM **bobjugant**: We cook together

10:29:30 PM **bobjugant**: *Baby I love u very much*

10:29:53 PM **bobjugant**: U make my life worth a while

10:30:14 PM **ladydi2011**: Baby, I am falling in love with you too

10:30:23 PM **ladydi2011**: You make me smile

10:30:27 PM **bobjugant**: And me too baby

10:30:59 PM **bobjugant**: Baby are tou home know?

10:31:14 PM **ladydi2011**: Yes honey, I am home now. Why do you ask?

10:32:03 PM **bobjugant**: I wanted to know wat your putting on right know

10:33:07 PM **ladydi2011**: I am still in the clothes I wore out baby...I have on a black skirt and a black lace top with slits in the sleeves

10:33:43 PM **bobjugant**: Oh

10:33:56 PM **bobjugant**: Wat are you doing?

10:35:06 PM **ladydi2011**: Thinking about what it would feel like to be in your arms.

10:35:33 PM **ladydi2011**: What it would be like to kiss you.

10:35:48 PM **ladydi2011**: How tall are you?

10:36:36 PM **bobjugant**: *Am 5ft 11*

10:36:55 PM **ladydi2011**: What are you doing?

10:37:21 PM **bobjugant**: Nuffing

10:37:36 PM **bobjugant**: Just chatting with you,,

10:37:40 PM **ladydi2011**: Where is your mind traveling to?

10:38:04 PM **bobjugant**: You make me have a hard on horney

10:38:19 PM **ladydi2011**: Really?

10:39:07 PM **bobjugant**: Becuz you are sexy

10:40:05 PM **ladydi2011**: Thank you honey. So are you!

10:40:17 PM **ladydi2011**: I am very passionate

10:40:45 PM **bobjugant**: Me too horney

10:40:47 PM **ladydi2011**: Can I share one of my favorite songs with you?

10:40:55 PM **bobjugant**: Yea baby

10:40:57 PM **bobjugant**: U can

10:41:37 PM **ladydi2011**: This is what I want to feel with my man

10:41:46 PM **bobjugant**: Yea

10:41:51 PM **ladydi2011**: (Breathe by Faith Hill)

10:42:58 PM **bobjugant**: Baby I was on mobile

10:43:22 PM **bobjugant**: I think I have to use my computer

10:43:25 PM **ladydi2011**: So you cannot play the video, correct?

10:43:34 PM **bobjugant**: I love you baby

10:43:47 PM **bobjugant**: I would go online *know*

10:43:55 PM **ladydi2011**: I love you too! But, how is this possible?

10:43:57 PM **bobjugant**: Just wait a minute

10:44:01 PM **ladydi2011**: Ok

10:44:14 PM **bobjugant**: *Its going to be possible..Trust me horney*

10:44:51 PM **ladydi2011**: please let me know when you get on your computer.

10:52:02 PM **bobjugant**: Ok horney

10:55:22 PM **bobjugant**: Baby I can't log on to my betwork so I ve to use my fone

10:55:51 PM **ladydi2011**: Ok.

10:55:56 PM **bobjugant**: Yea

10:56:05 PM **bobjugant**: Have u eaten

10:56:34 PM **ladydi2011**: Yes love. I ate.

10:56:41 PM **ladydi2011**: Did you eat?

10:56:49 PM **bobjugant**: I ate

10:56:55 PM **ladydi2011**: What did you eat?

10:57:07 PM **bobjugant**: I took chips @ d pub

10:57:21 PM **bobjugant**: Chips and beef

10:57:23 PM **ladydi2011**: What did you drink tonight?

10:57:27 PM **bobjugant**: It was nice

10:57:49 PM **bobjugant**: Gray goose and cranberry juice

10:57:49 PM **ladydi2011**: I went to an Italian restaurant

10:58:13 PM **ladydi2011**: I like Gray goose too

10:58:23 PM **bobjugant**: Really

10:58:35 PM **bobjugant**: Dats kool

10:58:59 PM **ladydi2011**: I like white russians

10:59:20 PM **ladydi2011**: Do you dance?

10:59:23 PM **bobjugant**: Yea I like white russian

10:59:29 PM **bobjugant**: Yes babay

10:59:39 PM **bobjugant**: I like to dance alot

11:00:05 PM **ladydi2011**: Do you like the beach?

11:00:25 PM **bobjugant**: The beach is my place. I love de beach

11:00:43 PM **ladydi2011**: Why do you have to live so far from me???????

11:01:07 PM **bobjugant**: *I will be with you soon baby*

11:01:24 PM **ladydi2011**: Please don't play with my heart baby

11:01:50 PM **bobjugant**: *Am not going to play with your heart honey*

11:02:03 PM **ladydi2011**: Promise?

11:02:12 PM **bobjugant**: I like who am chatting with

11:02:44 PM **bobjugant**: Wen I look at ur pics am alway happy

11:02:57 PM **ladydi2011**: I like you. There is something special about your essence.

11:02:58 PM **bobjugant**: Send me a pics of u

11:03:08 PM **bobjugant**: Wink
11:03:15 PM **ladydi2011**: Hold a min. please
11:03:21 PM **bobjugant**: Ok
11:03:29 PM **bobjugant**: Am happy
11:06:23 PM **bobjugant**: You are very beautiful
11:06:40 PM **ladydi2011**: Thank you honey.
11:06:42 PM **bobjugant**: I feel like like kissing you all ova
11:06:54 PM **ladydi2011**: You do?
11:07:01 PM **bobjugant**: Yea baby
11:07:04 PM **ladydi2011**: Please send me a picture of you.
11:07:11 PM **bobjugant**: Ok baby

11:08:54 PM **bobjugant**: Dats me baby
11:09:25 PM **bobjugant**: Horney wat do u want me to do for you right know
11:09:29 PM **ladydi2011**: You are very handsome!
11:09:38 PM **bobjugant**: Awww..You flatter me horney
11:10:03 PM **bobjugant**: I love you very much
11:10:05 PM **ladydi2011**: I love your smile
11:10:22 PM **bobjugant**: I don't know wat I will do without you
11:10:39 PM **ladydi2011**: You will not have to know
11:10:43 PM **bobjugant**: Thanks baby
11:10:51 PM **bobjugant**: *Lol*
11:11:05 PM **ladydi2011**: I still don't know why you are still single???
11:11:11 PM **bobjugant**: I like wen u call me darling
11:11:25 PM **bobjugant**: Because am all yours
11:11:42 PM **ladydi2011**: Well darling, please tell me what you want in a relationship
11:12:10 PM **bobjugant**: *May be I destined to be with you*

11:12:18 PM **ladydi2011**: Maybe
11:12:23 PM **bobjugant**: Yea
11:12:54 PM **bobjugant**: Am a little bit tipsy
11:13:01 PM **ladydi2011**: I thought as much
11:13:12 PM **bobjugant**: I wish you were with me right know
11:13:32 PM **bobjugant**: I need to hear your voice..gonna call u
11:13:47 PM **ladydi2011**: Ok baby

Bob called me and he was really drunk. I had a hard time understanding him because of his Nigerian accent. It took a lot to keep his conversation away from sex. He is a real "player"....

IM May 5, 2012 12:15:33 AM

12:15:33 AM **ladydi2011**: So, darling, when are you coming to see me in person?
12:16:04 AM **bobjugant**: Wen I cum back from africa
12:16:18 AM **ladydi2011**: Wow!
12:16:20 AM **bobjugant**: Dats if you want me to cum
12:16:29 AM **ladydi2011**: Absolutely
12:16:40 AM **ladydi2011**: I want to meet you
12:16:46 AM **bobjugant**: Me too
12:16:53 AM **ladydi2011**: *Please don't break my heart*
12:17:10 AM **bobjugant**: *Am not baby*
12:17:19 AM **bobjugant**: Am all yours
12:17:34 AM **bobjugant**: *Aint breaking your heart horney*
12:17:38 AM **ladydi2011**: I was not expecting this
12:17:44 AM **bobjugant**: Hmm
12:18:00 AM **ladydi2011**: You surprised me my love
12:18:29 AM **bobjugant**: *Lol*
12:18:48 AM **bobjugant**: I am full of suprises
12:18:55 AM **ladydi2011**: yes you sure are!
12:19:18 AM **ladydi2011**: I sensed right away that you were special
12:19:33 AM **bobjugant**: very speacial
12:19:41 AM **bobjugant**: And you too baby
12:19:50 AM **ladydi2011**: Yes. Thank you
12:19:56 AM **bobjugant**: Kool
12:20:07 AM **ladydi2011**: Honey, I do not do or say what I do not feel
12:20:16 AM **ladydi2011**: I do not say what I do not mean
12:22:41 AM **bobjugant**: You rock
12:24:14 AM **bobjugant**: I want you to promise me that you would always write me wen am in *africa*
12:24:24 AM **ladydi2011**: I promise
12:24:41 AM **bobjugant**: Are you sure
12:24:49 AM **ladydi2011**: Either via email or chat
12:24:56 AM **ladydi2011**: I promise baby

12:24:57 AM **bobjugant**: Would you call me

12:25:16 AM **ladydi2011**: Please give me your cell number

12:25:31 AM **bobjugant**: *+447024056738*

12:25:33 AM **ladydi2011**: Promise

12:25:44 AM **bobjugant**: Ok horney

12:26:05 AM **ladydi2011**: I want to fall asleep with my head on your chest

12:26:30 AM **bobjugant**: And I will b tickling your ears

12:26:46 AM **ladydi2011**: What would you be saying?

12:26:49 AM **bobjugant**: And kissing all ova you neck

12:27:06 AM **ladydi2011**: I would serve you breakfast in bed

12:29:10 AM **bobjugant**: I like dat

12:29:29 AM **bobjugant**: Breakfast in bed makes me horney

12:29:38 AM **ladydi2011**: Do you like eggs?

12:29:41 AM **bobjugant**: And wanna make love to you

12:29:45 AM **bobjugant**: Yea

12:29:57 AM **bobjugant**: Scrambled eggs

12:30:15 AM **ladydi2011**: Bacon, ham or sausage?

12:30:25 AM **bobjugant**: Bacon

12:30:49 AM **ladydi2011**: What kind of toast?

12:31:12 AM **bobjugant**: With butter

12:31:17 AM **ladydi2011**: Do you like home fries?

12:31:44 AM **bobjugant**: I like everything u do for me

12:31:53 AM **ladydi2011**: Jelly

12:32:25 AM **bobjugant**: It makes me love you till forever

12:32:45 AM **ladydi2011**: Champagne and strawberries

12:33:26 AM **ladydi2011**: I would love to feed you chocolate covered strawberries

12:33:53 AM **bobjugant**: I love you diana

12:34:05 AM **ladydi2011**: Will you do me a favor?

12:34:28 AM **bobjugant**: I would like to meet you

12:34:34 AM **ladydi2011**: When you get on your computer will you listen to the two songs I sent?

12:34:47 AM **bobjugant**: I will

12:34:49 AM **ladydi2011**: I want to meet you. You will make this happen, right?

12:34:59 AM **ladydi2011**: Please write these down

12:35:00 AM **bobjugant**: Yea I will

12:35:07 AM **bobjugant**: Ok baby

12:35:09 AM **ladydi2011**: Breathe by Faith Hill

12:35:21 AM **ladydi2011**: Falling Into You by Celine Dion

12:35:34 AM **bobjugant**: Hehe

12:35:43 AM **bobjugant**: I know dat song

12:36:05 AM **bobjugant**: Falling into you

12:36:19 AM **bobjugant**: I like the song

12:36:21 AM **ladydi2011**: I am falling into you!

12:36:38 AM **bobjugant**: Me too baby

12:36:49 AM **ladydi2011**: Kool

12:36:59 AM **ladydi2011**: You are a special man and I am so glad you walked into my life

12:37:11 AM **bobjugant**: Thanks horney

12:37:18 AM **bobjugant**: Me too

12:37:31 AM **bobjugant**: I love from my heart
12:37:34 AM **ladydi2011**: When do you leave for Africa?
12:37:47 AM **bobjugant**: 2dsys time..48hrs
12:38:09 AM **ladydi2011**: Please let me know when you land.
12:38:19 AM **ladydi2011**: I will want to know you are safe
12:38:39 AM **bobjugant**: I will darling
12:38:43 AM **ladydi2011**: I love you from my heart too sweetheart
12:38:59 AM **ladydi2011**: Will you dream about me tonight?
12:39:08 AM **bobjugant**: Yea baby
12:39:26 AM **bobjugant**: Its morning ova here
12:39:44 AM **ladydi2011**: I have kept you up all night. I am so sorry
12:39:53 AM **bobjugant**: I did not sleep
12:40:06 AM **ladydi2011**: Thank you for spending your night with me
12:40:20 AM **ladydi2011**: I so appreciate you and the time you give me
12:40:21 AM **bobjugant**: First time am chatting all true d night
12:40:38 AM **ladydi2011**: I am glad to have a first with you
12:40:52 AM **bobjugant**: I will give more time darling
12:41:09 AM **ladydi2011**: Thank you. I love spending time with you
12:41:10 AM **bobjugant**: Thanks. Me too
12:41:21 AM **ladydi2011**: I want to learn more and more about you
12:41:31 AM **ladydi2011**: What is your favorite color
Break in Time
12:42:56 AM **ladydi2011**: R U there baby?
12:43:34 AM **bobjugant**: *I am an honest and good man who loves being surrounded by friends and holidays*
12:44:31 AM **bobjugant**: Baby I feel dizzy know. Are you there
12:45:24 AM **ladydi2011**: I am here
12:45:35 AM **ladydi2011**: You need to sleep my love
12:45:49 AM **bobjugant**: Yea baby
12:45:55 AM **bobjugant**: I need it
12:46:22 AM **ladydi2011**: I am glad you are an honest and good man
12:46:27 AM **bobjugant**: Do have a wonddrful nighT
12:46:40 AM **ladydi2011**: Darling, sleep well.
12:46:58 AM **bobjugant**: I will sen you a mail wen am up
12:47:21 AM **ladydi2011**: Ok. I will be looking for it and I will do the same.
12:47:27 AM **ladydi2011**: Night baby
12:47:36 AM **bobjugant**: I wull think abouy you
12:47:43 AM **ladydi2011**: Ditto
12:47:52 AM **bobjugant**: Hehehe
12:47:58 AM **bobjugant**: I love you
12:48:10 AM **ladydi2011**: I love you too

When I ask for a picture, he says, "hmmm". He probably doesn't have many pictures and wasn't expecting me to ask for another picture so soon. After I ask again, he does send me another picture.

RED FLAGS

- He loves chips and shredded chicken. This is Nigerian food.
- The flight time from London to South Africa is 11.5 hours and he says seven hours maximum. It would take five hours and 45 minutes from Nigeria to South Africa.
- He is already setting me up for the second trip. He is supposedly processing a contract for Argentina on day two of us meeting.
- He loses Internet connection, which is another indicator of him being in Africa.
- He says he likes *honesty and that he is an honest and good man.* Yep, he is following suit of building the illusion that he is an honest and good man.
- On day number two he tells me he loves me very much and he wants to already get into a sex chat.
- He starts with the false promises, "I will be with you soon baby", "Will come to see you after I get back from Africa", "Am not going to play with your heart honey", "Aint breaking your heart honey". Then he says what many scammers say, "Maybe I destined to be with you".
- When I ask him how tall he is he says 5'11" but in his profile he said 5'10". Who doesn't know their own height? When people lie, they can never remember their lies, especially the ones about small details. Always check this type of thing against the profile information.
- He gives me a +44 7 number. All +44 7 numbers are used by scammers in an attempt to *appear* like they are in the United Kingdom.
- Watch for where they say "Lol." Many times they are laughing at what they just said because they know it isn't true.

From: ladydi2011@yahoo.com
To: Bob Jugant
Subject: Morning Darling
Sent: Saturday, May 5, 2012 2:35:38 PM

Good morning, Darling!

How are you this morning? Did you get some sleep? Are you awake yet? Did you have sweet dreams? Do you have a hangover, Honey? I slept like a baby. I had a dream that I picked you up at the airport and we drove right to the beach. We had a picnic on the beach and watched the sunset. We then spent the night on the beach until the sun came up.

We then walked the beach arm in arm smiling and laughing...then I woke up. When I woke up I had a huge smile on my face.
I love you

Diana

From: bobjugant@yahoo.com
To: ladydi2011
Subject: Re: Morning Darling
Sent: Sat, 5 May 2012 08:59:41 -0700 (PDT)

honey how are you,*i* slept well too,you are the sweetest thing that has ever happen to me,honey not even words that many times stronger dan beautiful could ever be use to describe you,all night with you is priceless to me darling,*i* love you very much honey and *i* cant wait to be with you and kiss you passionately and make love to you like u never had before....kiss kiss *i* love you.

IM May 5, 2012 1:22:56 PM

1:22:56 PM **bobjugant**: Hello love
1:23:03 PM **bobjugant**: R you there

From: bobjugant@yahoo.com
To: ladydi
Subject: Re: Morning Darling
Sent: Saturday, May 5, 2012 3:50 PM

hello honey are you there..you wanna hat with me

From: ladydi2011@yahoo.com
To: Bob Jugant
Subject: Re: Morning Darling
Sent: Saturday, May 5, 2012 3:52:15 PM

Hello, Darling! Yes, I would love to chat with you. Please give me 10 min to get to my computer...kisses

---

IM May 5, 2012 4:03:37 PM

4:03:37 PM **ladydi2011**: Hello...
4:03:52 PM **ladydi2011**: How are you darling?
4:04:09 PM **bobjugant**: horney am good
4:04:22 PM **bobjugant**: howz our day going
4:04:26 PM **ladydi2011**: Are you home or out and about?

4:04:40 PM **bobjugant**: am home baby
4:04:46 PM **ladydi2011**: My day is perfect now that I am chatting with my love
4:04:57 PM **bobjugant**: kisss
4:05:06 PM **ladydi2011**: Kisses back baby
4:05:14 PM **ladydi2011**: How did your day go?
4:05:16 PM **bobjugant**: *i* just ate dinner
4:05:29 PM **bobjugant**: my day was great
4:05:30 PM **ladydi2011**: what did you have?
4:05:49 PM **bobjugant**: *chips*
4:06:04 PM **bobjugant**: you wanna talk

Incoming Voice call with bobjugant (4:05:50 PM)

Call Ended: 0 hours 0 minutes 59 seconds

4:07:20 PM **bobjugant**: low connection
4:07:59 PM **ladydi2011**: Thank you for calling.
4:08:12 PM **bobjugant**: you have a cam on your computer
4:08:27 PM **ladydi2011**: I do on my other computer.
4:08:40 PM **bobjugant**: ok..great
4:09:03 PM **ladydi2011**: Do you think your connection is good for me to see you on your cam?
4:09:06 PM **bobjugant**: may b *i* can c you sometime
4:09:26 PM **ladydi2011**: I would love to see your handsome face
4:09:28 PM **bobjugant**: *i dont have a cam baby*
4:09:49 PM **ladydi2011**: I thought you said last night that you did
4:09:54 PM **bobjugant**: *would get one soon*
4:10:03 PM **ladydi2011**: Promise
4:10:29 PM **bobjugant**: yea *i* promise
4:10:50 PM **ladydi2011**: Do you have everything ready to leave for Africa?
4:10:54 PM **bobjugant**: so wat you doig know
4:11:06 PM **bobjugant**: yea am gud to go
4:11:10 PM **ladydi2011**: I was cleaning my house
4:11:21 PM **ladydi2011**: Now I am chatting with my love
4:13:35 PM **ladydi2011**: Please tell me about the work you will be doing in Africa
4:14:13 PM **bobjugant**: servicing of oil equiptment
4:14:27 PM **ladydi2011**: Is it dangerous baby?
4:14:41 PM **bobjugant**: and agip is a big oil company
4:14:57 PM **ladydi2011**: I looked it up. I like their logo
4:15:01 PM **bobjugant**: not dangerous
4:15:31 PM **ladydi2011**: Good. I do not want anything to happen to you
4:15:38 PM **bobjugant**: *i* would be working off shore
4:16:02 PM **ladydi2011**: you will have connection with your bb right?
4:16:17 PM **bobjugant**: *i* might
4:16:46 PM **bobjugant**: but *i* would have acess to the internet
4:17:04 PM **ladydi2011**: Ok...good
4:17:07 PM **bobjugant**: so *i* will talk to you everyday
4:17:20 PM **ladydi2011**: Excellent!
4:17:36 PM **bobjugant**: yea
4:17:44 PM **bobjugant**: *i* love you baby
4:17:47 PM **ladydi2011**: Are you going to land the job in Argentina?

4:18:03 PM **ladydi2011**: I love you too baby.

4:18:04 PM **bobjugant**: *i* hav to bidd for it

4:18:19 PM **ladydi2011**: When will you put the bid in?

4:18:23 PM **bobjugant**: if am lucky *I* ould get it

4:18:42 PM **ladydi2011**: Any jobs in the United States for you to bid on?

4:19:04 PM **bobjugant**: cause a lot of people want it too

4:19:17 PM **ladydi2011**: I am sure a lot of people will bid for it

4:19:52 PM **ladydi2011**: I have never been to South Africa. Will you send me some pictures?

4:19:59 PM **bobjugant**: *i* dont really know how it will be for know

4:20:21 PM **bobjugant**: sure

4:20:38 PM **ladydi2011**: I wish I was going with you

4:20:54 PM **bobjugant**: me too honey

4:21:00 PM **ladydi2011**: As long as I have Internet connection I can work from anywhere.

4:21:40 PM **bobjugant**: mine has to be at the location

4:21:59 PM **ladydi2011**: Do you have a laptop

4:22:24 PM **bobjugant**: yea *i* do

4:22:55 PM **ladydi2011**: So darling, please tell me what is important to you in a relationship

4:23:20 PM **bobjugant**: *trust and understanding*

4:23:46 PM **ladydi2011**: Trust is huge for me too!

4:23:59 PM **ladydi2011**: Honesty and understanding is second.

4:24:06 PM **ladydi2011**: What else baby?

4:24:29 PM **bobjugant**: warm heart

4:24:47 PM **ladydi2011**: This you have.

4:25:02 PM **ladydi2011**: I felt it the first time we chatted

4:25:16 PM **ladydi2011**: You are very kind

4:26:21 PM **bobjugant**: thanks baby

4:26:27 PM **ladydi2011**: Honey, are you good with communicating? Do you ask for what you need?

4:27:01 PM **bobjugant**: yes *i* am good communicating

4:27:08 PM **bobjugant**: *i* dont get you

4:27:36 PM **bobjugant**: if *i* will ask when *i* am in need?

4:27:47 PM **ladydi2011**: I think telling our partner what we need is critical in a relationship

4:28:05 PM **ladydi2011**: Baby, I do not know how to read your mind.

4:28:20 PM **bobjugant**: yes it is

4:28:26 PM **ladydi2011**: I will always let you know what I need

4:28:42 PM **ladydi2011**: So, if I am missing you, I will share this with you

4:28:45 PM **bobjugant**: please always let me know

4:29:05 PM **ladydi2011**: If I need to be held, I will ask

4:29:11 PM **bobjugant**: and anytime you feel down always let me know too no matter what

4:29:24 PM **ladydi2011**: If something is on my mind, I will ask to talk

4:29:36 PM **bobjugant**: it will make our relationship grow stronger

4:29:43 PM **ladydi2011**: I will let you know honey. Please do the same

4:29:57 PM **iadydi2011**: Yes, it will make our relationship grow stronger

4:30:07 PM **bobjugant**: sure *i* will

4:30:18 PM **bobjugant**: *i* love you baby..you are the best

4:30:47 PM **ladydi2011**: I see too many women complain that their man does not provide what they need and when I ask them if they have told their man what they need, they say "no"

4:31:05 PM **ladydi2011**: I love you too baby...You have captured my heart

4:31:49 PM **bobjugant**: *i* will always tell you wat *i* need

4:31:52 PM **ladydi2011**: I am different than most women, just like you are different than most men

4:32:08 PM **bobjugant**: thanks honey you make me smile

4:32:24 PM **ladydi2011**: Same here. Thank you. I want you to be happy baby

4:32:44 PM **ladydi2011**: I love that I make you smile

4:33:56 PM **ladydi2011**: If there is a problem, I want to talk about the solution, not stay stuck in the problem.

4:34:02 PM **bobjugant**: sounds sweet

4:34:07 PM **ladydi2011**: Hey darling

4:34:33 PM **bobjugant**: always ell me whats on your mind ok

4:34:35 PM **ladydi2011**: I love you more today than yesterday

4:34:39 PM **bobjugant**: yea baby

4:34:58 PM **bobjugant**: *i* love even more

4:35:11 PM **ladydi2011**: Thank you for opening my heart again. I thought I had closed it forever.

4:35:44 PM **bobjugant**: *i* will make you happy everytime

4:36:04 PM **ladydi2011**: Thank you...

4:36:19 PM **ladydi2011**: Honey, do you like surprises?

4:36:27 PM **bobjugant**: yes *i* do..a lot

4:36:54 PM **ladydi2011**: good...

4:37:03 PM **bobjugant**: aww

4:37:03 PM **ladydi2011**: I so want to kiss you right now

4:37:21 PM **bobjugant**: me too darling

4:37:31 PM **ladydi2011**: what cologne do you wear?

4:38:30 PM **bobjugant**: givenchy

4:38:49 PM **ladydi2011**: I am looking forward to smelling it on you.

4:39:00 PM **ladydi2011**: My favorite is Red Door

4:39:09 PM **bobjugant**: sweet

4:39:21 PM **ladydi2011**: Did you listen to the song Breathe?

4:39:27 PM **bobjugant**: sounds romatic

4:40:09 PM **ladydi2011**: I just want us to be so comfortable with each other that we can just "be".....

4:40:53 PM **bobjugant**: me too

4:40:55 PM **ladydi2011**: I do not believe relationships should be hard honey. I think they should be fun and complimentary

4:41:00 PM **bobjugant**: and understand each other

4:41:22 PM **ladydi2011**: Yes. Understand each other. I want to be able to look at you and know

4:41:37 PM **ladydi2011**: Many times words should not have to be said

4:42:47 PM **bobjugant**: yea,

4:43:13 PM **bobjugant**: *i* love you more and more baby

4:43:37 PM **ladydi2011**: This is a good thing.

4:44:17 PM **ladydi2011**: I am still asking how it is possible.

4:44:47 PM **ladydi2011**: Then I say, the heart knows...and anything is possible.

4:45:07 PM **ladydi2011**: Baby, have you chatted with other women before?

4:45:34 PM **bobjugant**: if the hearts blends den anything is posible

4:45:53 PM **bobjugant**: dats why am suprise

4:45:59 PM **ladydi2011**: I believe this....I also believe our hearts have blended.

4:46:25 PM **bobjugant**: *i have never done this kind of chat before horny*

4:46:36 PM **ladydi2011**: why...because you have chatted with other women and something different happened with me?
4:46:55 PM **bobjugant**: not really
4:47:26 PM **bobjugant**: *yours is special..you are speaciial to me*
4:47:58 PM **ladydi2011**: thank you baby. I knew from the first time we chatted that you were very special.
4:48:53 PM **ladydi2011**: I knew from the beginning that I wanted to know you better.
4:49:28 PM **bobjugant**: *i* treasure you too
4:49:39 PM **ladydi2011**: thank you.
Break in Time
4:52:52 PM **ladydi2011**: I want to know what your kisses feel like.
4:53:02 PM **bobjugant**: hey darling
4:53:10 PM **ladydi2011**: yes
4:53:22 PM **bobjugant**: its feels like sugar
4:53:46 PM **ladydi2011**: If this is true I will not be able to stop kissing you!
4:54:27 PM **bobjugant**: me too
4:54:29 PM **ladydi2011**: and your tongue is sensitive...
4:54:40 PM **bobjugant**: *you are my queen*
4:54:54 PM **bobjugant**: very sensitive
4:54:56 PM **ladydi2011**: Baby, my lips are soft and my kisses are sweet like honey
4:55:22 PM **ladydi2011**: You are my prince. I will always treat you good my love.
4:55:33 PM **bobjugant**: *i* cant wait to kiss them everyday
4:55:47 PM **ladydi2011**: Every day baby...
4:56:21 PM **bobjugant**: *i want to be with you always*
4:57:24 PM **ladydi2011**: I believe we have started a love story my darling
4:57:30 PM **bobjugant**: *wat do you really do at work baby*
4:57:37 PM **ladydi2011**: Lol...I help companies become profitable
4:57:51 PM **bobjugant**: dat will last forever
4:58:16 PM **ladydi2011**: I consult with CEO's
4:58:32 PM **bobjugant**: by adviceing them
4:58:43 PM **ladydi2011**: I then learn their strengths, weaknesses, opportunities and threats
4:58:53 PM **ladydi2011**: Yes baby. I advise them.
4:58:59 PM **bobjugant**: good
4:59:08 PM **ladydi2011**: I then develop strategies
4:59:13 PM **bobjugant**: *i* like that
4:59:19 PM **ladydi2011**: Help implement the strategies
4:59:34 PM **ladydi2011**: We then develop their sales and marketing pieces
4:59:40 PM **bobjugant**: to make them profit
4:59:45 PM **ladydi2011**: And manage their overall brand
4:59:54 PM **ladydi2011**: Yes baby, to make them profitable
4:59:56 PM **bobjugant**: kool
5:00:11 PM **ladydi2011**: I work in two niche markets
5:00:49 PM **bobjugant**: thats great
5:01:01 PM **ladydi2011**: 1 being private investigators, prior law enforcement, prior CIA, FBI and Secret Service
5:01:12 PM **ladydi2011**: 2nd being attorneys
5:02:04 PM **ladydi2011**: Every day is something different baby. It keeps me from being bored.

5:02:24 PM **bobjugant**: nice

5:02:29 PM **ladydi2011**: Please tell me more about what you do honey

5:04:25 PM **bobjugant**: *i* have worked with shell and chevron

5:04:56 PM **ladydi2011**: When you say off shore, you mean out in the ocean on a platform or rig, is this correct?

5:05:27 PM **bobjugant**: so they have to keep their failities up to date

5:05:47 PM **bobjugant**: yea in de ocean

5:05:55 PM **ladydi2011**: Do you check to make sure things are up to date

5:06:50 PM **bobjugant**: their facilities are mostly in de ocean

5:06:58 PM **ladydi2011**: Yeah, I thought so

5:07:13 PM **bobjugant**: from de rig to de drillre

5:07:20 PM **ladydi2011**: So, you are on the ocean a lot...my favorite place

5:07:43 PM **bobjugant**: if am working

5:07:57 PM **ladydi2011**: Do you live by an ocean?

5:08:13 PM **bobjugant**: no *i* dont

5:08:56 PM **ladydi2011**: would you like to live by the ocean or the sea?

5:09:33 PM **ladydi2011**: I wish I was rich so I could see the world....

5:09:48 PM **bobjugant**: the ocean has no ending

5:10:06 PM **bobjugant**: *i* like d sea

5:11:29 PM **ladydi2011**: If you could live anywhere in the world, where would you want to live?

5:11:55 PM **bobjugant**: the states..las vegas

5:12:14 PM **ladydi2011**: Why Las Vegas?

5:12:57 PM **bobjugant**: *i* just like the fun there

5:13:09 PM **ladydi2011**: Do you like to gamble?

5:13:37 PM **bobjugant**: no

5:13:50 PM **bobjugant**: but *i* like vodka

5:13:56 PM **ladydi2011**: The shows are a lot of fun and I love the lights

5:14:02 PM **ladydi2011**: Lol

5:14:24 PM **ladydi2011**: Baby, I have grey goose in my liquor cabinet

5:14:32 PM **bobjugant**: but *i* have to the casino a couple of times

5:14:40 PM **ladydi2011**: Me too...

5:14:43 PM **bobjugant**: really

5:15:10 PM **bobjugant**: *i* like grey goos and cranberr juice

5:15:31 PM **ladydi2011**: I know you do...you told me last night and I took note

5:15:41 PM **bobjugant**: yea baby

5:15:47 PM **ladydi2011**: When you come to visit, I wIll be sure to have both

5:16:11 PM **ladydi2011**: So, would you consider moving to the states?

5:16:28 PM **bobjugant**: if its for you *i* will

5:16:43 PM **ladydi2011**: Kool

5:17:15 PM **ladydi2011**: Long distance relationships are not as much fun honey

5:17:31 PM **bobjugant**: yea *i* know

5:17:54 PM **bobjugant**: *i* really have to start thinking of moving over horney to be with you

5:18:39 PM **ladydi2011**: Being together would make me really happy

5:18:59 PM **bobjugant**: me too baby

5:19:11 PM **ladydi2011**: Honey, do you work for yourself or for a company there?

5:19:42 PM **bobjugant**: kind of a partner

5:19:56 PM **bobjugant**: *i* work with them

5:20:10 PM **ladydi2011**: Ok. Do you own any shares?

5:20:28 PM **bobjugant**: working on that

5:20:50 PM **bobjugant**: but for me to have a share *i* need to raize some certain amount of money to buy shares

5:22:43 PM **ladydi2011**: Baby, I could always move to wherever you are.

5:22:58 PM **bobjugant**: no *i* dont have to b here to work with them

5:23:24 PM **ladydi2011**: Ok... cool! So, we could be wherever we want to be...Nice!

5:23:42 PM **bobjugant**: yea baby

5:24:30 PM **ladydi2011**: So baby, it is 10:24 pm there, correct?

5:25:03 PM **bobjugant**: yea u are correct

5:25:04 PM **ladydi2011**: Bob, I want us to be happy. Life is too short for anything else.

5:25:37 PM **bobjugant**: we wil be together and be happy

5:25:55 PM **ladydi2011**: Without love and being with the one you love, I think one misses the best thing life has to offer.

5:26:11 PM **ladydi2011**: I trust your word baby.

5:26:31 PM **bobjugant**: me too honey

5:26:42 PM **bobjugant**: *i* love you baby

5:27:09 PM **ladydi2011**: If you were here or I was there, it would be awesome. I would probably be giving you a back massage about now...

5:27:22 PM **ladydi2011**: I love you more darling.

5:27:25 PM **bobjugant**: you make me happy when am chatting with you

5:27:54 PM **bobjugant**: yea baby

5:27:58 PM **ladydi2011**: This is good. I have had a smile on my face the entire time we have been chatting.

5:28:10 PM **ladydi2011**: You make me happy and laugh.

5:28:16 PM **bobjugant**: me too

5:28:40 PM **bobjugant**: lol

5:28:43 PM **ladydi2011**: Baby...nature is calling. brb

5:29:00 PM **bobjugant**: me too

5:29:04 PM **ladydi2011**: Lol

5:29:49 PM **bobjugant**: lol...ok baby

5:31:06 PM **bobjugant**: *late at night when all the world is sleeping ,i stay up and think of you*

5:35:20 PM **ladydi2011**: I am back baby.

5:37:10 PM **bobjugant**: yea baby

5:37:22 PM **ladydi2011**: A client just called.

5:37:48 PM **bobjugant**: ok baby

Incoming Voice call with bobjugant (5:37:31 PM)

Call Ended: 0 hours 2 minutes 36 seconds

5:40:20 PM **bobjugant**: hmm

5:40:33 PM **bobjugant**: *i* love your voice

5:40:35 PM **ladydi2011**: Thank you for calling

5:40:45 PM **ladydi2011**: I love your voice too

5:40:55 PM **ladydi2011**: I love your accent

5:41:07 PM **ladydi2011**: Most of all I love you!

5:41:40 PM **bobjugant**: me too baby

5:41:57 PM **bobjugant**: *i* love you more than words can describe

5:42:39 PM **ladydi2011**: If someone would have told me last week I was going to fall in love, I wouldn't have believed them

5:43:16 PM **bobjugant**: thats why you always expect the un expected

5:43:20 PM **ladydi2011**: Here I am in love with you and very happy!

5:43:49 PM **bobjugant**: am happy that you are happy

5:44:09 PM **ladydi2011**: Baby, even when I am working my mind drifts back to you

5:45:55 PM **bobjugant**: *What I feel for you is really true. You got to know,*

5:46:06 PM **ladydi2011**: I so appreciate what a gentleman you are.

5:46:24 PM **ladydi2011**: What I feel for you is really true too baby.

5:46:42 PM **ladydi2011**: I do not play games, especially with someone's heart and feelings.

5:46:43 PM **bobjugant**: *i* want to send you all my love but he postman said it was too big

5:46:59 PM **ladydi2011**: Smile

5:47:47 PM **bobjugant**: *late at night when all the world is sleeping i stay up and think of you*

5:47:56 PM **bobjugant**: *i* will baby you are always in my heart

5:48:31 PM **ladydi2011**: Darling, I want to live in your heart and your mind and for you to live in mine

5:48:39 PM **bobjugant**: here and everywere

5:49:31 PM **bobjugant**: *You know what, in the whole world there is no such darling whom I love and I want thewhole world to know that I will never forget you!*

5:49:43 PM **bobjugant**: *i* love you

5:50:31 PM **ladydi2011**: You have already stolen my heart. Please don't give it back baby

5:50:32 PM **bobjugant**: *i* will not baby, you are my world and our love is forever

5:50:58 PM **ladydi2011**: You are my world. I treasure and love you...Forever baby!

5:51:35 PM **bobjugant**: I want to hold you close to me and feel our hearts beat as one ... forever

5:51:55 PM **ladydi2011**: me too baby

5:52:00 PM **bobjugant**: *i* love you from the earth till the moon

5:52:36 PM **ladydi2011**: Can you see me baby?

5:53:12 PM **bobjugant**: oh baby you are so beautiful

5:53:24 PM **ladydi2011**: I love you!

5:53:34 PM **bobjugant**: *i* love you more and more

5:53:35 PM **ladydi2011**: Thank you darling

5:53:56 PM **bobjugant**: smile baby

5:54:12 PM **bobjugant**: sexy lips

5:54:31 PM **ladydi2011**: I was smiling baby, but the camera was frozen

5:54:51 PM **ladydi2011**: I love surprising you!

5:55:14 PM **bobjugant**: yea *i* c it

5:55:21 PM **ladydi2011**: You need to get a cam so I can see you. This will help a lot

5:55:34 PM **bobjugant**: yea *i* will

5:55:47 PM **ladydi2011**: Now you can see how you make me smile

5:56:30 PM **bobjugant**: yea *i* can

5:56:38 PM **bobjugant**: and am happy too

5:57:03 PM **ladydi2011**: Baby. I will always be honest with you.

5:57:22 PM **ladydi2011**: You can always believe what I tell you and always trust me.

5:58:02 PM **bobjugant**: thanks honey

5:58:02 PM **ladydi2011**: I know many people lie and hide behind the computer screen, but I am not one of these people

5:58:20 PM **bobjugant**: am happy. *i* love yu honey

5:58:40 PM **ladydi2011**: I want to make you the happiest man in the world darling.

5:59:32 PM **ladydi2011**: Baby, please remember I was cleaning before you asked me to chat, so I do not look my best

5:59:59 PM **bobjugant**: *i* dont mind

6:00:32 PM **bobjugant**: *i* like you like dat

6:00:44 PM **ladydi2011**: Thanks baby.

6:00:53 PM **bobjugant**: you rock

6:00:55 PM **ladydi2011**: Where are you now baby?

6:01:02 PM **ladydi2011**: You rock too

6:01:22 PM **bobjugant**: am sitting out

6:01:35 PM **ladydi2011**: Is it warm there?

6:01:47 PM **bobjugant**: it rained

6:01:57 PM **ladydi2011**: It rained here last night too

6:02:06 PM **bobjugant**: so a little bit cold

6:02:21 PM **ladydi2011**: It is in the 80's here

6:02:44 PM **ladydi2011**: I will probably take the car for a ride since it is supposed to rain tomorrow

6:03:03 PM **bobjugant**: ok baby

6:03:04 PM **ladydi2011**: I bought the convertible to have fun.

6:03:34 PM **ladydi2011**: Just driving with the sun shining on me and the wind blowing through my hair and the music blasting is fun.

6:03:55 PM **bobjugant**: yea *i* can imagine

6:04:09 PM **ladydi2011**: Baby, sometimes owning a business is very stressful. When the stress gets too much I take a ride.

6:04:27 PM **ladydi2011**: If you were here we would cruise together.

6:04:37 PM **bobjugant**: you have to rest some times

6:04:55 PM **bobjugant**: we would b together

6:05:00 PM **ladydi2011**: Yes, my brain has a hard time shutting off

6:05:16 PM **bobjugant**: soon

6:05:16 PM **ladydi2011**: Yes, baby. If you were here I would not work as much.

6:06:02 PM **ladydi2011**: You can come into the office, kiss my neck and I would follow you anywhere...

6:06:31 PM **bobjugant**: awww

6:06:55 PM **bobjugant**: *i* will kiss your neck a million times honey

6:07:17 PM **ladydi2011**: See how you put a huge smile on my face baby

6:07:58 PM **ladydi2011**: Did you read the dream I had last night on my email to you

6:08:07 PM **bobjugant**: *i* will not stop loving you. *i* will love you till enternity

6:08:30 PM **bobjugant**: yea baby

6:08:36 PM **bobjugant**: *i* was so happy because *i* know you are happy

6:09:26 PM **ladydi2011**: Yes baby. I am happy.

6:10:46 PM **bobjugant**: *When you love someone, it's something. When someone loves you, it's another thing. When you love the person who loves you back, it's everything.*

6:11:00 PM **bobjugant**: and you are everything to me

6:11:00 PM **ladydi2011**: I think my anti-virus is messing with the cam

6:11:35 PM **bobjugant**: try cumming back on cam

6:11:48 PM **ladydi2011**: Did the cam shut off?

6:11:56 PM **bobjugant**: yea

6:12:56 PM **ladydi2011**: The anti-virus is running. Please give me a minute baby...

6:13:09 PM **bobjugant**: ok honey

6:15:42 PM **bobjugant**: *life without love is like a year without summer*

6:16:52 PM **ladydi2011**: Honey, can you see me?

6:17:31 PM **bobjugant**: *i* see you *know*

6:17:36 PM **ladydi2011**: I love what you said

6:17:48 PM **bobjugant**: my baby is smiling

6:18:10 PM **ladydi2011**: I had to stop my anti-virus from scanning

6:18:18 PM **bobjugant**: lol

6:18:25 PM **ladydi2011**: Yes, your baby is smiling. Her man makes her smile

6:18:40 PM **bobjugant**: *put on your glasses for a while baby*

6:18:56 PM **bobjugant**: lol

6:19:23 PM **ladydi2011**: Now I can't see the screen they are for a distance

6:19:24 PM **bobjugant**: you look cute

6:19:28 PM **ladydi2011**: Thanks baby

6:19:37 PM **bobjugant**: *i* love your smile

6:19:37 PM **ladydi2011**: Thanks baby

6:20:09 PM **ladydi2011**: I cannot wait until you get a cam so I can see you

6:20:35 PM **ladydi2011**: Hold baby...I am going to send you a picture with my glasses on

6:20:56 PM **bobjugant**: ok baby

6:22:47 PM **bobjugant**: nice nice

6:22:48 PM **ladydi2011**: I just sent you three pictures. Did you get them honey?

6:23:01 PM **bobjugant**: yea baby *i* got dem

6:23:16 PM **bobjugant**: beautiful

6:23:20 PM **ladydi2011**: You can tell where I spend most of my time

6:23:27 PM **ladydi2011**: Thank you baby. You are so kind

6:24:21 PM **ladydi2011**: Which picture is your favorite?

6:24:39 PM **ladydi2011**: Baby, please send me some more pictures of you.

6:25:01 PM **bobjugant**: the one with d purple dress

6:25:09 PM **bobjugant**: ok baby

6:25:18 PM **ladydi2011**: Purple is my favorite color.

6:25:23 PM **bobjugant**: you are an angel

6:25:31 PM **ladydi2011**: Thank you baby.

6:25:53 PM **bobjugant**: *i* will make sure *i* chat with you always wen am in africa

6:26:26 PM **ladydi2011**: I hope so baby. I will miss you terribly if we don't chat.

6:27:13 PM **ladydi2011**: Pictures please baby

Break in Time

6:29:02 PM **ladydi2011**: Are you there baby?

6:29:24 PM **bobjugant**: *i* am here

6:29:43 PM **ladydi2011**: What are you thinking about?

6:30:23 PM **bobjugant**: *i* had to go plug the laptop

6:30:40 PM **ladydi2011**: battery running low baby

6:30:53 PM **bobjugant**: yea baby

6:31:15 PM **bobjugant**: would switch ova to my fone soon

6:31:18 PM **ladydi2011**: Baby, thank you for seeing my outer beauty. My inner beauty is more beautiful.

6:31:38 PM **bobjugant**: *i* can wait to see it baby

6:32:23 PM **ladydi2011**: Honey, what are your goals and dreams in life?

6:33:00 PM **bobjugant**: my goal is to be very sucessful and happy with that special person which is you

6:33:31 PM **ladydi2011**: How long have you been without the love of that special person?

6:33:53 PM **bobjugant**: quite long

6:33:54 PM **ladydi2011**: Yes, my love. It is me.

6:34:09 PM **bobjugant**: and am happy *i* found you honey

6:34:11 PM **ladydi2011**: It has been eight years for me.

6:34:20 PM **ladydi2011**: I am happy we found each other.

6:34:39 PM **bobjugant**: and *i* will fill you up wih it

6:34:52 PM **bobjugant**: am happy too. *i* love u

6:35:14 PM **ladydi2011**: Thank you for filling me with love.

6:35:41 PM **ladydi2011**: Thank you for letting me love you.

6:35:58 PM **ladydi2011**: I want all the days of your life to be happy.

6:36:16 PM **bobjugant**: me too horney

6:36:40 PM **ladydi2011**: I want to dance the dance of life with you.

6:37:31 PM **bobjugant**: baby do you like to dance

6:37:40 PM **ladydi2011**: I love to dance.

6:38:15 PM **ladydi2011**: You dance, right?

6:38:22 PM **bobjugant**: *kiss me and you will see stars, love me and i will give them to you*

6:38:51 PM **ladydi2011**: I want to kiss you again and again and again....Forever

6:39:17 PM **ladydi2011**: I do love you baby.

6:40:20 PM **bobjugant**: *i* love you too horney

6:40:28 PM **ladydi2011**: Darling, I so want to feel your arms around me. I want to feel the kiss of your lips and the touch of your hands

6:41:00 PM **ladydi2011**: I want to explore life with you by my side.

6:41:18 PM **ladydi2011**: I want to hear all about your day and tell you all about mine.

6:43:08 PM **bobjugant**: *i* can't wait to be with you too darling

6:43:10 PM **ladydi2011**: So, I know when two people love each other, it works...

6:43:23 PM **ladydi2011**: Are you getting tired yet baby?

6:43:37 PM **ladydi2011**: It is almost midnight there, right?

6:43:42 PM **bobjugant**: no baby am still awake

6:43:59 PM **bobjugant**: for you *i* will do anything

6:43:59 PM **ladydi2011**: I am sure you saw my smile on that one, yes?

6:44:14 PM **bobjugant**: yes *i* did..*i* like it

6:44:33 PM **ladydi2011**: So, what does success in your career look like for you honey?

6:45:55 PM **bobjugant**: positive

6:46:06 PM **bobjugant**: *i* give it some time *i* will get there

6:46:49 PM **ladydi2011**: I am sure you will accomplish all you want baby.

6:47:34 PM **bobjugant**: thamk baby your one in a million

6:48:17 PM **ladydi2011**: I will always stand behind you to accomplish what you want.

6:48:29 PM **bobjugant**: thanks honey

6:48:29 PM **ladydi2011**: I will never stand in your way baby.

6:48:49 PM **bobjugant**: *i* will do the same for you too

6:48:58 PM **ladydi2011**: Thank you my love.

6:49:18 PM **ladydi2011**: My goal is to be a world renowned speaker and author

6:49:35 PM **ladydi2011**: I love speaking to large groups of people

6:50:25 PM **bobjugant**: *your smile give me butterflies*

6:50:32 PM **ladydi2011**: Where are you now baby?

6:51:14 PM **bobjugant**: am in my room

6:53:55 PM **bobjugant**: *If I have given the chance to choose between you and heaven, I'll choose you because paradise is where love is.*

6:54:12 PM **ladydi2011**: Thank you baby...

6:54:34 PM **bobjugant**: *I can live the life looking into your eyes, I can live the life seeing you smile.*

6:54:40 PM **ladydi2011**: It is true that paradise is where love is....I never heard this said before.

6:54:49 PM **bobjugant**: its makes me happy and its true honey

6:55:08 PM **ladydi2011**: Baby, you do make me smile and make me happy.

6:55:21 PM **bobjugant**: and its you *i* wanna be with..you are my paradise

6:55:41 PM **ladydi2011**: I love when you are happy.

6:55:54 PM **bobjugant**: me too honey

6:56:54 PM **ladydi2011**: *I so want to see you on web cam....*

6:57:11 PM **bobjugant**: *soon baby*

6:57:49 PM **bobjugant**: yea baby

6:58:25 PM **bobjugant**: if you ask why *i* love you so much

6:59:00 PM **ladydi2011**: Why do you love me so much honey?

7:00:05 PM **bobjugant**: *i* will give you everything

7:01:00 PM **bobjugant**: love doesn't require a reason. It simply happens.

7:03:59 PM **ladydi2011**: Bob, are you there?

Break in Time

7:41:10 PM **bobjugant**: Im back..got booted..wat time is it knw

7:41:22 PM **ladydi2011**: 7:41 pm here

7:41:34 PM **bobjugant**: ok baby

7:41:45 PM **ladydi2011**: how long have we been chatting

7:41:54 PM **bobjugant**: lol

7:41:58 PM **ladydi2011**: I loose sense of time when I am with you

7:42:04 PM **bobjugant**: like 4hrs

7:42:12 PM **ladydi2011**: really?

7:42:17 PM **ladydi2011**: wow

7:42:20 PM **bobjugant**: yes baby

7:42:41 PM **bobjugant**: because we love each other

7:42:54 PM **ladydi2011**: It didn't seem like 4 hrs.

7:43:25 PM **ladydi2011**: Baby...you rock my world

7:43:44 PM **bobjugant**: you too. *i* love you baby

7:44:12 PM **ladydi2011**: *i* love you too honey

7:44.31 PM **bobjugant**: *baby you know am travelling*

7:44:43 PM **ladydi2011**: yes

7:44:53 PM **bobjugant**: so *i* have to pack d last and rest a little while *i* think of you

7:45:55 PM **ladydi2011**: I want you to be ready and rested for your trip

7:46:07 PM **ladydi2011**: What time do you leave tomorrow?

7:46:14 PM **bobjugant**: 11 am so *i* gat a short time

7:47:30 PM **ladydi2011**: Please finish packing and get some sleep

7:47:46 PM **ladydi2011**: Will you email me right before you board your flight?

7:47:47 PM **bobjugant**: *i* will think of you while *i* trvel

7:48:07 PM **bobjugant**: make sure you write me always honey

7:48:18 PM **ladydi2011**: I wish I were traveling with you

7:48:42 PM **ladydi2011**: I will write you baby
7:48:52 PM **bobjugant**: me too honey
7:49:12 PM **bobjugant**: baby *i* have to rest know
7:49:12 PM **ladydi2011**: keep me in your heart and mind baby
7:49:22 PM **bobjugant**: *i* will darling
7:49:24 PM **ladydi2011**: Good night and sleep well
7:49:32 PM **bobjugant**: *i* love very much
7:49:46 PM **bobjugant**: sweet dreams honey and think about me ok
7:50:08 PM **ladydi2011**: Always
7:50:18 PM **bobjugant**: smile for me drling
7:50:30 PM **bobjugant**: yea nice
7:50:31 PM **ladydi2011**: I forgot you were watching me
7:50:46 PM **bobjugant**: *i* love your smile it makes me happy
7:52:28 PM **ladydi2011**: Good night my love. Till tomorrow...
7:53:27 PM **bobjugant**: kiss kiss
7:53:51 PM **bobjugant**: SEND ME A SONG WHEN YOU WAKE UP HONEY
7:54:03 PM **ladydi2011**: I will baby.
7:54:09 PM **bobjugant**: BYE

He called me on the Yahoo voice call. It was hard to hear him and I really struggled with his accent. His Internet connection in Nigeria is slow and it cut off. He called back a second time and we were able to talk for over two minutes. I again asked about the cam and he said he still doesn't have one, but promised soon.

 RED FLAGS

- Scammers use the Yahoo voice phone a lot because it doesn't cost them anything.
- He says *trust* and *understanding* are important to him in a relationship. Scammers will always say this and talk about honesty.
- He tries to make me believe I am special to him by telling me he has never done this kind of chat before and throwing a lot of "love talk", which is also typical of a scammer.
- He tells me he wants to be with me always... another hook. Then he tells me that what he feels for me is real and that I have to know this. This statement was a little convincing. If a woman didn't know he was a scammer, she might believe him. He has some "format love lines" he wants to say and he makes sure he does so. Many of the things he says can be found on Facebook and Twitter. It was easy to tell they were NOT from his heart but I played along with it.
- A major red flag is when he says, "I want the whole world to know that I will never forget you!" Forget me; what? I thought we were "building a future together." Watch for this type of phrase that doesn't fit the context of the supposed relationship.
- Of course, he reminds me that he is going to be traveling.
- He again asks what I really do. He is trying to assess how much money I make.

🏴 He asks me to put my glasses on because he really isn't sure if I am a scammer or not because I am asking some good questions. He knows if I do as he asks with the glasses then I am in real time and it is not a fake cam. Always ask the person you are chatting with to do something right now if they come on cam. Stand up, wave, put glasses on or off; this way you can tell if they are in real time or using a fake cam.

From: Bob Jugant
To: ladydi2011@yahoo.com
Subject: Re: A song for you
Sent: Sunday, May 6, 2012 5:16 AM

morning honey hope you slept well,,baby *i* will always communicate with you anytime am with the internet,,honey I'm never tired of looking at your picture, reading your emails that you've written to me. All of these things keep me so happy and feeling so blessed that *I have truly found the one person that I want to spend eternity with.*

Talking to you makes my day great When I am with you, I feel alive. You bring to me a happiness that no one else ever could. You bring to me a love I have never known before. I could not imagine what my life would be like without you. I love being with you and *I want to spend the rest of my life with you.*

He sent me the song Angel by Lionel Richie

From: bobjugant@yahoo.com
To: ladydi
Subject: *i* love you
Sent: Sunday, May 6, 2012 5:34 AM

Honey before you I have never experienced real love and I want to thank you for letting me have one of my own. Now that we want to start a new life together I want you to know that since the first day my love for you has grown more and more. My dear, I simply can't wait for that day to come. My mind was full with you even before but it has become overwhelming now. I want to let you know that you have made me complete. I thank my stars for the moment when you walked into my life.

My heart will never cease to love

From: ladydi2011@yahoo.com
To: Bob Jugant
Subject: A song for you
Sent: Sunday, May 6, 2012 6:56:50 AM

Hello, my Darling!

It is almost 2:00 am here. I am lying in bed thinking about you. I enjoyed the time we spent together today. Thank you for calling me. It was such a nice surprise! I love your voice and your accent! Baby, I am so happy you walked into my life! I cannot wait to meet you in person....

It is almost 7:00 am there. I know your flight is at 11:00. I wish you safe travel. Promise me you will take good care of yourself. As you are flying, please think of me sitting next to you, holding your hand with my head resting on your chest. It is here that I can feel your heart beat, my love. It is where I would feel safe and right at home.

Below is a song for you. I hope you can listen to it before you board your flight...you are in my thoughts, dreams, heart and soul. I love Bob. Kisses and (((hugs))).

(Song– from This Moment – Shania Twain)

IM May 7, 2012 7:19:21 AM

7:19:21 AM **bobjugant**: Honey
7:19:29 AM **bobjugant**: How are you
7:19:42 AM **bobjugant**: I finally got a computer
7:19:44 AM **bobjugant**: Hehehe
7:20:02 AM **bobjugant**: I missed you darling
7:28:46 AM **bobjugant**: I will write you soon

IM May 7, 2012 9:26:37 AM

9:26:37 AM **bobjugant**: hello darling
9:27:00 AM **ladydi2011**: Hello darling
9:27:38 AM **ladydi2011**: How was your flight?
9:28:30 AM **bobjugant**: *the internet is so shitty ova here*
9:28:46 AM **bobjugant**: it goes off and on
9:28:49 AM **ladydi2011**: This is not good!
9:29:07 AM **ladydi2011**: *I saw you come on line briefly last night then disappear*
9:29:24 AM **ladydi2011**: *Right now you do not show as on line*
9:30:32 AM **bobjugant**: *i* was to reply you last night but d intrnet on came on for 20mins
9:30:59 AM **ladydi2011**: I haven't received anything from you since yesterday morning
9:31:12 AM **bobjugant**: *i* love you and *i will never do anything to hurt you*
9:31:53 AM **ladydi2011**: Thank you baby. I will never do anything to hurt you either
9:32:07 AM **bobjugant**: *i* missed you a lot. you were on mind through out
9:32:32 AM **ladydi2011**: How was your flight baby?
9:32:55 AM **bobjugant**: am talking to them so *i* can get a permanent internet over here
9:33:09 AM **ladydi2011**: Cool
9:33:28 AM **ladydi2011**: I know you will do what you can so we don't lose touch
9:34:25 AM **bobjugant**: *i* missed you sweet lips

9:34:27 AM **bobjugant**: kiss kiss kiss

9:34:57 AM **ladydi2011**: kiss, kiss, kiss and (((hugs))) (((hugs))) (((hugs)))

9:35:25 AM **bobjugant**: *i* love you honey

9:35:34 AM **ladydi2011**: I love you too darling

9:35:47 AM **ladydi2011**: How is it there?

9:36:10 AM **bobjugant**: hold 1min

9:36:13 AM **ladydi2011**: Ok

9:36:25 AM **bobjugant**: *am signing out and in*

9:36:32 AM **ladydi2011**: Ok

9:38:04 AM **bobjugant**: Baby am here know

9:38:14 AM **bobjugant**: I love you much. You are the angel of my heart

9:38:46 AM **ladydi2011**: Awwwww

9:39:00 AM **ladydi2011**: Baby, how is it there other than bad Internet connection?

9:39:26 AM **bobjugant**: Its kind of kool u know

9:39:43 AM **ladydi2011**: Please take some pictures for me

9:39:46 AM **bobjugant**: I did some paper work today

9:39:54 AM **ladydi2011**: I need more pictures of you my love

9:40:08 AM **bobjugant**: I woul be joining dem soon again

9:40:12 AM **ladydi2011**: What time is it there?

9:40:43 AM **ladydi2011**: Honey, you are always in my thoughts

9:41:01 AM **bobjugant**: Its 3 30pm over here

9:41:16 AM **bobjugant**: You are in my thought too

9:41:24 AM **ladydi2011**: Ok....What time will you work until?

9:41:35 AM **bobjugant**: I don't know what I will do without you

9:42:02 AM **ladydi2011**: Baby, you will never have to know

9:42:14 AM **bobjugant**: Kiss

9:42:27 AM **ladydi2011**: Many kisses baby

9:42:39 AM **bobjugant**: Am not leaving you baby

9:43:02 AM **ladydi2011**: Is it hot there?

9:43:16 AM **bobjugant**: Its warm

9:43:27 AM **ladydi2011**: We had large hail stones here yesterday

9:43:39 AM **bobjugant**: Yea

9:43:52 AM **ladydi2011**: It is raining and I didn't put the top up on the car before I put it in the garage so I guess I am not going anywhere today....

9:44:32 AM **bobjugant**: So your car is soaked

9:44:48 AM **ladydi2011**: No... It is in the garage and dry

9:45:01 AM **bobjugant**: Ok

9:45:10 AM **bobjugant**: Did you miss me

9:45:10 AM **ladydi2011**: If I pulled it out, it would get wet by time I would got the top up

9:45:20 AM **ladydi2011**: I miss you terribly

9:45:45 AM **bobjugant**: Me too darling

9:46:11 AM **ladydi2011**: Did you get the email I sent you about when two people are meant to connect?

9:46:16 AM **bobjugant**: You are my sunshine

9:46:26 AM **ladydi2011**: You are my world

9:46:29 AM **bobjugant**: I got all your email love and I liked it

9:47:04 AM **ladydi2011**: I heard it on a show called "touch"

9:47:12 AM **bobjugant**: I will never let you miss me horney

9:47:18 AM **bobjugant**: Oh really

9:47:22 AM **ladydi2011**: When I heard it I felt it was true and I thought about us

9:47:34 AM **bobjugant**: Nice

9:48:01 AM **ladydi2011**: Bob, you have my heart

9:48:35 AM **bobjugant**: You have my heart too horney

9:48:42 AM **bobjugant**: I love you very much

9:49:18 AM **ladydi2011**: It seems like I have known you forever

9:49:35 AM **ladydi2011**: Please pinch me so I know I am not dreaming

9:49:45 AM **bobjugant**: Awww

9:49:47 AM **ladydi2011**: If I am dreaming, please don't ever wake me up

9:50:02 AM **bobjugant**: You make my heart sweet

9:50:23 AM **ladydi2011**: Your heart was already sweet darling

9:50:50 AM **bobjugant**: I can feel your arms around me baby

9:50:58 AM **ladydi2011**: Do you think you will be able to connect again later?

9:51:24 AM **ladydi2011**: I can feel your arms around me too baby and I can feel you kiss me

9:51:28 AM **bobjugant**: I must because I have to chat with my darling

9:51:57 AM **bobjugant**: Kiss siss

9:52:11 AM **ladydi2011**: Kiss kiss

9:52:22 AM **bobjugant**: So wat did you do yesterday

9:52:42 AM **ladydi2011**: Cleaned up the house and cooked a nice dinner

9:52:51 AM **bobjugant**: Oh nice

9:52:59 AM **ladydi2011**: I wished you could be here for dinner

9:53:00 AM **bobjugant**: I wish I was there baby

9:53:17 AM **ladydi2011**: I cannot wait until we are together in person

9:53:30 AM **bobjugant**: We would eat together and I will make passionate love to you

9:53:35 AM **ladydi2011**: Did you get the song and the ecard I sent you baby?

9:53:43 AM **bobjugant**: I did baby

9:53:56 AM **bobjugant**: It was so relieving knowing that you were thinking about me

9:54:50 AM **ladydi2011**: I do not want my heart broken

9:55:09 AM **bobjugant**: *I will never break your heart honey*

9:55:16 AM **ladydi2011**: yes honey

9:55:26 AM **bobjugant**: You mean the world to me

9:55:31 AM **bobjugant**: I love you

9:55:49 AM **ladydi2011**: I know baby. I gave you my heart because I trust you honey

9:56:22 AM **ladydi2011**: There is no going back now darling

9:56:26 AM **bobjugant**: *And I will keep it safe*

9:56:38 AM **bobjugant**: *We are together know*

9:56:59 AM **ladydi2011**: I know baby and I am excited about our future

9:57:30 AM **bobjugant**: Me too

9:58:27 AM **ladydi2011**: You make me feel loved and safe.

9:58:38 AM **bobjugant**: *You are my all and all baby*

9:58:55 AM **bobjugant**: Am going to love you more

9:59:10 AM **bobjugant**: I am thinking of you

9:59:22 AM **bobjugant**: I can't wait to be with you

10:00:08 AM **bobjugant**: I feel very happy wen am on chat with you

10:00:43 AM **ladydi2011**: I feel very happy when I chat with you too

10:00:57 AM **ladydi2011**: You make me smile

10:01:33 AM **bobjugant**: Am glad you are happy

10:01:56 AM **ladydi2011**: Baby, I hope I make you happy. I want you to be happy.

10:02:48 AM **bobjugant**: Honey you make me very happy

10:03:01 AM **bobjugant**: *And I never want to leave you*

10:03:12 AM **ladydi2011**: I will never leave you

10:03:37 AM **bobjugant**: I love you

10:03:47 AM **ladydi2011**: I love you too baby

10:04:17 AM **bobjugant**: Baby were are you know

10:04:23 AM **ladydi2011**: In the office

10:04:34 AM **bobjugant**: Ok

10:04:51 AM **ladydi2011**: Are you in your room or in the lobby

10:05:10 AM **bobjugant**: Am in d hotel room

10:05:21 AM **ladydi2011**: Is it a nice hotel?

10:05:34 AM **bobjugant**: Not really

10:05:43 AM **ladydi2011**: I had that feeling

10:05:52 AM **bobjugant**: I had to cut cost down

10:06:00 AM **ladydi2011**: I understand.

10:06:23 AM **ladydi2011**: I might have to drive to North Carolina next week

10:06:32 AM **bobjugant**: Really

10:06:38 AM **ladydi2011**: Is it a safe area baby?

10:06:53 AM **bobjugant**: Yea its safe

10:06:58 AM **ladydi2011**: Yeah, one of my clients turned me on to a possible new account

10:07:11 AM **ladydi2011**: I am glad to know it is safe

10:07:26 AM **bobjugant**: Waoh k

10:07:32 AM **bobjugant**: Lol

10:07:46 AM **bobjugant**: So what's happening in north carolina

10:07:54 AM **ladydi2011**: I am hoping to be able to sell the account over the phone but if not, I will drive to meet them in person

10:08:08 AM **ladydi2011**: It is a large security company

10:08:21 AM **ladydi2011**: They just bought my client's company

10:08:25 AM **bobjugant**: Ok

10:08:40 AM **ladydi2011**: So, if I do not land them then I lose a client

10:08:41 AM **bobjugant**: Oh k

10:08:55 AM **bobjugant**: Den you have to be there

10:09:02 AM **ladydi2011**: yeah

10:09:48 AM **bobjugant**: Hope you would be ok

10:09:56 AM **ladydi2011**: I will be

10:10:12 AM **ladydi2011**: It is so refreshing to have you in my life

10:10:17 AM **ladydi2011**: A real love with no games

10:10:36 AM **ladydi2011**: I so love and appreciate you

10:11:02 AM **bobjugant**: me too baby

10:11:07 AM **ladydi2011**: Baby, you are my safe place to fall and I am yours

10:11:26 AM **bobjugant**: *They say that as long as there is one person loving you, life isn't a waste. So if you lose hope and thought that life is not worth living, just remember I'm here.ok*

10:11:35 AM **ladydi2011**: Sometimes the world feels like a jungle

10:11:43 AM **bobjugant**: I love you

10:11:54 AM **bobjugant**: Yea baby

10:12:06 AM **bobjugant**: *But I will be by your side*

10:12:41 AM **ladydi2011**: I know you will be.

10:12:45 AM **bobjugant**: I love you

10:13:21 AM **ladydi2011**: Our lives have changed so much.

10:13:31 AM **bobjugant**: My biggest reward is to see you smile

10:13:34 AM **ladydi2011**: Thank you my darling for walking into my life

10:13:45 AM **ladydi2011**: Baby, I am smiling!

10:14:05 AM **ladydi2011**: Every time we are together I smiling

10:14:51 AM **bobjugant**: *I will always be with you*

10:16:06 AM **bobjugant**: I always think of you, but I always fail to know the reason why. Is there something else I should know about you?

10:17:14 AM **ladydi2011**: Honey, my heart is always calling out to your heart, my thoughts are always calling out to your thoughts and my soul is now intertwined with your soul.

10:18:49 AM **bobjugant**: I love you honey

10:19:01 AM **bobjugant**: Kiss kiss

10:19:21 AM **ladydi2011**: kiss kiss

10:20:32 AM **ladydi2011**: Baby, do you really not know why you always think of me?

10:20:59 AM **bobjugant**: *Because you are my everything. You are my beggining and my end*

10:21:32 AM **ladydi2011**: There is a song by Keith Urban...You are my everything

10:22:08 AM **bobjugant**: Dats what you are honey

10:22:30 AM **ladydi2011**: Honey, you complete me

10:22:43 AM **bobjugant**: You too baby

10:23:09 AM **ladydi2011**: I feel so comfortable with you

10:24:05 AM **ladydi2011**: I don't know how you did this, but you did....I have now quit questioning how and am just trusting my heart and your love

10:24:45 AM **bobjugant**: I am all your honey

10:25:00 AM **bobjugant**: *We were destined to be together*

10:25:19 AM **bobjugant**: I love you with all my heart and I know you love me too

10:25:44 AM **ladydi2011**: My mind is very analytical, but my heart knows without question

10:26:52 AM **ladydi2011**: Honey, have you had a long distant relationship before?

10:27:06 AM **bobjugant**: No I have not

10:27:34 AM **bobjugant**: We would be together soon

10:27:49 AM **ladydi2011**: A huge smile just overtook my face

10:29:15 AM **bobjugant**: I am thinking of relocating to d states

10:29:37 AM **ladydi2011**: Really baby?

10:29:51 AM **bobjugant**: Yes baby I want to be with you

10:30:17 AM **ladydi2011**: I have been thinking about moving to London

10:31:17 AM **bobjugant**: Baby what do you want

10:31:17 AM **ladydi2011**: I want to experience everything with you my love

10:31:37 AM **bobjugant**: I will give you everything

10:31:39 AM **ladydi2011**: I want to be with you. I do not care where.

10:32:35 AM **bobjugant**: Me too honey

10:33:07 AM **ladydi2011**: I can run my business from anywhere in the world

10:34:03 AM **ladydi2011**: If you want to relocate to the states, this works too

10:34:16 AM **ladydi2011**: What do you want darling?

10:35:01 AM **bobjugant**: Honey I have to know dat you want us to be together den I will cum to you

10:35:52 AM **bobjugant**: My love for you will never die

10:35:52 AM **ladydi2011**: Honey, this is what I want. Do you have any doubt of this?

10:36:10 AM **bobjugant**: No baby I don't have doubt

10:36:34 AM **bobjugant**: I want to be with you too. I love you baby

10:37:07 AM **ladydi2011**: I want to fall asleep every night in your arms

10:37:08 AM **bobjugant**: Me too

10:37:42 AM **bobjugant**: Baby am so happy dat you want us to be together

10:37:59 AM **bobjugant**: I will love you always

10:38:08 AM **ladydi2011**: I will love you always too

10:38:41 AM **ladydi2011**: Baby, I cannot even begin to tell you how I felt this morning when there was no email from you.

10:40:10 AM **bobjugant**: Sorry baby

10:40:28 AM **bobjugant**: I will always reach you from anywere I am

10:40:36 AM **ladydi2011**: I know you are traveling...I understand

10:40:44 AM **ladydi2011**: I know you will

10:40:51 AM **bobjugant**: Yea baby

10:41:09 AM **ladydi2011**: I travel, so I get it

10:41:18 AM **bobjugant**: Baby I told you I was bidding for a contract

10:41:31 AM **ladydi2011**: Yes, the one in Argentina

10:41:39 AM **bobjugant**: *Yea Chille*

10:42:07 AM **ladydi2011**: Did you get it?

10:42:19 AM **bobjugant**: Am still on it

10:43:12 AM **bobjugant**: *A contract to service some oil equiptment and to instal some*

10:43:27 AM **bobjugant**: Facilities in d rig

10:43:39 AM **bobjugant**: Baby do you knw what a rig is

10:43:41 AM **ladydi2011**: I know you said many people want this one

10:43:49 AM **ladydi2011**: I do know what a rig is

10:44:09 AM **bobjugant**: Ok baby

10:44:47 AM **bobjugant**: But I would get it

10:44:55 AM **ladydi2011**: What would getting this bid mean to you honey?

10:45:30 AM **bobjugant**: Its a big contract honey

10:46:01 AM **bobjugant**: I will have the chance to be on my own

10:46:05 AM **ladydi2011**: Do everything you can to win the bid honey

10:46:16 AM **bobjugant**: Starting up my own u know

10:46:38 AM **bobjugant**: I will honey

10:46:47 AM **ladydi2011**: I do know...honey, I will stand behind anything you want

10:46:50 AM **bobjugant**: *They always want commission*

10:47:02 AM **bobjugant**: Thanks honey

10:47:04 AM **ladydi2011**: *You mean they pay commission*

10:47:22 AM **bobjugant**: *Yea I already did*

10:48:02 AM **bobjugant**: *Dats how bidding is*

10:48:12 AM **ladydi2011**: Ok

10:48:24 AM **bobjugant**: *Everybody want to pull strings*

10:48:25 AM **ladydi2011**: *So, do they put these bids out on line*

10:48:44 AM **bobjugant**: *Am not sure*

10:48:57 AM **ladydi2011**: As I said...the world is a jungle

10:49:04 AM **bobjugant**: Yea baby

10:49:15 AM **ladydi2011**: I know you are good at navigating the jungle

10:49:22 AM **ladydi2011**: You are a smart man

10:49:57 AM **bobjugant**: Thanks honey

10:50:12 AM **ladydi2011**: I believe in you honey

10:50:14 AM **bobjugant**: *I will do anything to be with you*

10:50:31 AM **ladydi2011**: I know you can accomplish anything you set your mind to

10:50:49 AM **ladydi2011**: Thank you baby.

10:51:25 AM **bobjugant**: I love you ...

10:51:32 AM **ladydi2011**: I love you

10:51:55 AM **bobjugant**: I would be going out soon

10:52:07 AM **bobjugant**: I would be meeting some people

10:52:13 AM **ladydi2011**: When will you put the bid in?

10:52:33 AM **ladydi2011**: Ok baby....

10:52:34 AM **bobjugant**: I did that today

10:52:43 AM **ladydi2011**: Excellent!

10:52:59 AM **ladydi2011**: Please keep me posted.

10:53:08 AM **bobjugant**: In 2days time I will be informed

10:53:15 AM **ladydi2011**: Kool

10:53:30 AM **ladydi2011**: Are you going out on the rig today?

10:53:39 AM **bobjugant**: Yea

10:53:50 AM **ladydi2011**: Please be careful

10:54:12 AM **bobjugant**: Notting works there

10:54:14 AM **ladydi2011**: Do you think we will be able to chat later tonight?

10:54:32 AM **ladydi2011**: Nothing works there?

10:54:40 AM **ladydi2011**: This doesn't sound safe

10:54:43 AM **bobjugant**: I must get a conection to chat with you

10:54:58 AM **ladydi2011**: Ok honey...

10:55:13 AM **bobjugant**: Only satelite phones

10:55:30 AM **ladydi2011**: Oh...

10:55:41 AM **bobjugant**: I will be in de rig for only 2hrs den I will come back to make you happy

10:56:14 AM **ladydi2011**: Ok. It is 11 am here and I will be in the office until at least 8pm

10:56:23 AM **bobjugant**: Really

10:56:30 AM **bobjugant**: 8pm

10:56:47 AM **bobjugant**: Sounds stressful

10:56:56 AM **ladydi2011**:Yeah...I have to talk to a client on the west coast today and there is a 3 hrs. difference

10:57:12 AM **ladydi2011**: Some days...all is ok baby

10:57:13 AM **bobjugant**: Ooh...ok

10:57:45 AM **ladydi2011**: I do not want you to worry about me. I want your mind on what you are doing so you are safe. Promise...

10:58:20 AM **ladydi2011**: I know you love me and will connect with me when you can.

10:58:52 AM **ladydi2011**: Have a wonderful day my love

10:59:30 AM **ladydi2011**: I love you

11:00:07 AM **bobjugant**: I love you more

11:01:59 AM **bobjugant**: Thanks honey. You are the best

11:02:48 AM **ladydi2011**: You're the best!

11:03:10 AM **bobjugant**: *"heart to heart... soul to soul... day to day.... every moment behold....you are my air, my water, my space i love you more with each passing day darling*

11:04:05 AM **ladydi2011**: Darling, this is so beautiful...thank you.

11:05:26 AM **ladydi2011**: Wherever you go I am right there with you.

11:05:47 AM **bobjugant**: Baby pleas send me an email

11:05:54 AM **bobjugant**: I love you very much

11:05:58 AM **bobjugant**: Kiss kiss

11:06:06 AM **ladydi2011**: I will honey. Please try to connect with me later tonight

11:06:20 AM **bobjugant**: I have to go off d I'm for knw

11:06:32 AM **bobjugant**: I will connect you surely honey

11:06:36 AM **ladydi2011**: kisses and (((hugs)))

11:06:43 AM **bobjugant**: I love you

11:06:45 AM **ladydi2011**: I love you

11:07:13 AM **bobjugant**: You make my whold world rock

11:07:39 AM **ladydi2011**: You make my whole world rock too!

11:07:40 AM **bobjugant**: See you soon darling

11:07:47 AM **ladydi2011**: Ok darling

IM May 7, 2012 1:09:04 PM

1:09:04 PM **bobjugant**: honey

1:09:13 PM **bobjugant**: I love you

1:09:25 PM **ladydi2011**: I love you!

1:09:26 PM **bobjugant**: Thinking about you

1:09:35 PM **ladydi2011**: You are back from the rig?

1:10:03 PM **bobjugant**: Yea

1:10:18 PM **bobjugant**: But am not @ the hotel yet

1:10:28 PM **bobjugant**: Are working know baby

1:10:39 PM **ladydi2011**: Where are you darling?

1:10:50 PM **ladydi2011**: Yes my love, I am working

1:10:56 PM **ladydi2011**: It is 1:10 here

1:11:01 PM **bobjugant**: Ok baby

1:11:42 PM **ladydi2011**: Are you on your phone honey?

1:12:12 PM **bobjugant**: No honey

1:12:30 PM **ladydi2011**: Where are you baby?

Break in Time

1:14:14 PM **ladydi2011**: Are you still there darling?

1:14:21 PM **bobjugant**: Am somwere around durban

1:14:47 PM **ladydi2011**: Ok. Are you at an Internet cafe or something?

1:14:52 PM **bobjugant**: Am here darling

1:15:22 PM **bobjugant**: Yea public cafe

1:15:26 PM **ladydi2011**: Ok

1:15:40 PM **bobjugant**: I miss u

1:15:40 PM **ladydi2011**: I knew you would find a way to reach out to me...

1:15:57 PM **bobjugant**: Yea some guy took me here

1:16:16 PM **bobjugant**: *I told him I wanted to chat with my wife*

1:16:17 PM **ladydi2011**: Kool

1:16:33 PM **ladydi2011**: Are the people nice?

1:16:47 PM **bobjugant**: Yes baby

1:17:03 PM **bobjugant**: Nice to visitors

1:17:22 PM **ladydi2011**: This is good

1:17:40 PM **ladydi2011**: You are always on my mind darling

1:17:55 PM **bobjugant**: You too honey. I love very much

1:18:21 PM **bobjugant**: I don't want to ever loose you

1:18:44 PM **ladydi2011**: Darling, you will never loose me

1:18:51 PM **bobjugant**: Thanks baby

Break in Time

1:20:53 PM **ladydi2011**: Is the connection better there?

1:21:24 PM **bobjugant**: I will always make you happy

1:21:42 PM **ladydi2011**: I know. Whenever I am with you I am smiling.

1:22:53 PM **ladydi2011**: I always want you to be smiling

1:25:20 PM **ladydi2011**: Bob, are you there?

Break in Time

1:26:13 PM **bobjugant**: Yea baby

1:26:38 PM **bobjugant**: Internet not strong over here

1:27:05 PM **ladydi2011**: I thought that might be the case.

1:27:15 PM **ladydi2011**: I remember from when I was in Africa

1:27:21 PM **bobjugant**: Yea it is love

1:27:25 PM **bobjugant**: Really

1:27:32 PM **ladydi2011**: I thought it would be better in South Africa

1:27:36 PM **bobjugant**: Were did you go in africa

1:28:00 PM **ladydi2011**: Niger and Nigeria

1:28:11 PM **ladydi2011**: It was a mission trip

1:28:17 PM **ladydi2011**: I spoke to the women

1:28:40 PM **ladydi2011**: I have a heart to let women know they have worth and are loved by God

1:29:13 PM **ladydi2011**: Honey, so many women do not love themselves or know their worth. I am blessed because I do.

1:29:21 PM **bobjugant**: You know am in durban

1:29:44 PM **bobjugant**: Nice of you honey

1:29:50 PM **bobjugant**: I love that

1:30:08 PM **ladydi2011**: Thanks baby. It is who I am.

1:30:10 PM **bobjugant**: You are a good woman

1:30:17 PM **ladydi2011**: I love encouraging others

1:30:37 PM **ladydi2011**: Yes, my love. I am a good woman

1:31:27 PM **bobjugant**: I love you. You make me very happy

1:31:57 PM **ladydi2011**: Good...this is what I now live for honey

1:32:12 PM **bobjugant**: You are so sweet and you are my world

1:34:21 PM **ladydi2011**: You are my world too!

1:35:06 PM **bobjugant**: My sweet potato

1:35:17 PM **ladydi2011**: Awwww

1:35:26 PM **ladydi2011**: Are you done working for the day?

1:36:28 PM **bobjugant**: Yes am done

1:36:53 PM **ladydi2011**: Kool...are you tired my love?

1:37:23 PM **bobjugant**: The hotel manager told me they making provision for wifi
1:37:39 PM **bobjugant**: So I will be able to chat with my darling everytime
1:37:44 PM **ladydi2011**: Kool....I knew you would make it happen
1:38:22 PM **bobjugant**: I will be leaving the cafe know
1:38:32 PM **bobjugant**: *I will send you an email when am at the hotel*
1:38:44 PM **ladydi2011**: Ok baby. I will go back to work so I can chat with you again later.
1:38:56 PM **bobjugant**: And we will have a nice time together
1:39:14 PM **ladydi2011**: Yes, we will
1:39:17 PM **bobjugant**: I miss you
1:39:22 PM **bobjugant**: Kiss kiss
1:39:25 PM **ladydi2011**: Thank you for making me smile
1:39:46 PM **ladydi2011**: Kiss kiss (((hugs))) (((hugs)))
1:40:10 PM **bobjugant**: I love you
1:40:33 PM **ladydi2011**: I love you baby

RED FLAGS

- He is talking about spending eternity together. I have seen the words *"Honey before you I have never experienced real love and I want to thank you for letting me have one of my own"* used by other scammers.
- I saw him come on line last night and then disappear. I am sure he was chatting with other women and when he was chatting with me he showed invisable.
- He tells me he will never do anything to hurt me, that he will never break my heart and he will keep it safe because "we are together now" and I am his "all and all". He tells me that he never wants to leave me and he will always be with me because I am his everything, "his beginning and his end because we were destined to be together". He will do anything to be with me. All scammer words.
- Now he calls me "his wife". Most legitimate men don't use this term when they first start chatting with you, but scammers do. Legitimate men take things slow and try to get to know you. Most men are wary of commitment in the first couple days of meeting. You should be too. A legitimate man is not "fast and furious" like when a scammer chats with you.
- Now that he is supposedly in South Africa he says that "the internet is shitty" so he's going to sign out and sign back in. That is his excuse for Nigeria's poor Internet service.
- He first told me he was bidding on a contract to service and install some oil equipment in Argentina and then changed it to Chile. He said he had to pay commission to bid. I never heard of paying commission to bid on a job. If it doesn't seem logical then something is probably wrong. He is starting to set the stage for his next trip.

From: ladydi2011@yahoo.com
To: Bob Jugant
Subject: Something for you
Sent: Monday, May 07, 2012 2:30 PM

Hello, my darling....

I am so happy you walked into my life. Honey, every thought of you and every time I am with you, I am smiling. I love being loved by you!

I heard the attached song today and it is how I feel when it comes to you....Please listen, baby.

Always, Diana

(SONG – If I don't have you....Alicia Keys)

From: bobjugant@yahoo.com
To: ladydi
Subject: Re: Hello Darling
Sent: Monday, May 7, 2012 6:15 PM

hello love ,you are in my thought right know.*i* love you so much,*I miss you in the morning, I long for your sweet diana If I denied it, I'd be so remiss. I miss you in the afternoon, I long for your silken and soft skin.*

Darling, I love you so much. I miss you in the evening, when the blueblack curtain falls; I stare at your picture and wish that you would be in my arms. I miss you in the night time; I long to hold your sexy body.

i love you very much

From: ladydi2011@yahoo.com
To: Bob Jugant
Sent: Monday, May 7, 2012 10:28:05 PM
Subject: Hello Darling

Hello, Darling!

I am thinking about you, therefore there is a huge smile on my face. How is your day going, Baby? I forgot I had a doctor's appointment today. I am now sitting in the waiting room.
I miss you, baby! I hope we can be together later tonight. Well, I guess it is already later tonight for you. I wonder if you are still awake...

I love you,
Diana

IM May 7, 2012 5:52:25 PM

5:52:25 PM **bobjugant**: Honey
5:52:50 PM **bobjugant**: I got the song
5:53:32 PM **bobjugant**: And *i* want to tell you that *i will always be there for you...*
5:53:44 PM **bobjugant**: Kiss

IM May 7, 2012 7:06:03 PM

7:06:03 PM **bobjugant**: Are you there baby
7:06:50 PM **bobjugant**: baby u said you had a doctor appointment hope you are ok
7:07:13 PM **bobjugant**: I dont want my baby to fall ill
7:07:29 PM **bobjugant**: I love you very much

IM May 7, 2012 7:45:46 PM

7:45:46 PM **bobjugant**: Hello baby
7:46:00 PM **bobjugant**: I was so tired
7:46:13 PM **ladydi2011**: Hello darling
7:46:27 PM **bobjugant**: *i* slept alittle
7:46:33 PM **ladydi2011**: I am sure you are tired.
7:46:35 PM **bobjugant**: I am baby
7:46:40 PM **ladydi2011**: What time is it there?
7:47:04 PM **ladydi2011**: Baby, as much as I want to be with you, you need your rest.
7:47:44 PM **bobjugant**: It would soon b 2am
7:47:51 PM **ladydi2011**: Did you get the song I sent you?
7:47:57 PM **bobjugant**: Yea yea. Honey it was nice.
7:48:25 PM **bobjugant**: And *i* love you baby
7:48:39 PM **ladydi2011**: I love you too darling
Break in Time
7:50:00 PM **ladydi2011**: Did you fall back to sleep my love?
7:50:01 PM **bobjugant**: *When am chatting with you, I smile, my world shines so bright, I can hear my heart beat so loud and so fast.I'm so happy*
7.50.12 PM **bobjugant**: No baby
7:50:21 PM **bobjugant**: Am up know
7:50:44 PM **ladydi2011**: Did you get a couple hours sleep?
7:50:45 PM **bobjugant**: Are you home darling
7:50:51 PM **ladydi2011**: I am darling
7:50:55 PM **bobjugant**: Yea baby
7:51:01 PM **ladydi2011**: I had to be with ice on my hip
7:51:57 PM **bobjugant**: Yea u said you had an appointment with the doctor
7:52:08 PM **ladydi2011**: Baby, I am not sick. Please do not worry.
7:52:14 PM **bobjugant**: What was the problem
7:52:33 PM **ladydi2011**: I was working out and I had too much weight when I did squats

7:52:39 PM **ladydi2011**: I crushed some nerves. They will heal

7:53:05 PM **bobjugant**: Ok darling

7:53:16 PM **bobjugant**: I love you very much

7:53:28 PM **ladydi2011**: I love you very much too baby.

Break in Time

7:56:23 PM **bobjugant**: *If every time I thought of you baby a star fell.. Well, then the sky would be empty*

7:57:06 PM **ladydi2011**: Thank you baby...

7:57:17 PM **ladydi2011**: Do you read poetry darling?

7:57:42 PM **bobjugant**: Yea *i* like reading poems

7:58:12 PM **ladydi2011**: I can tell. You like writing poetry too don't you baby?

7:59:23 PM **bobjugant**: Yea baby. Some times

7:59:42 PM **bobjugant**: You do too honey

8:00:06 PM **ladydi2011**: I want you to be the happiest man in the world

8:00:15 PM **bobjugant**: Dats whats happening to me baby

8:00:17 PM **ladydi2011**: You deserve the very best of everything

8:00:30 PM **bobjugant**: Thanks alot darling

8:01:07 PM **ladydi2011**: Years ago *i* sat down and created a list of what *i* wanted in a man

8:01:18 PM **bobjugant**: Ok yea

8:01:23 PM **ladydi2011**: You are everything that is on my list

8:01:40 PM **bobjugant**: Oh honey

8:01:46 PM **ladydi2011**: You are kind

8:01:50 PM **ladydi2011**: Thoughtful

8:01:52 PM **bobjugant**: You are the best

8:01:52 PM **ladydi2011**: Sweet

8:01:55 PM **ladydi2011**: Attentive

8:02:16 PM **ladydi2011**: You are smart

8:02:25 PM **ladydi2011**: You are handsome

8:02:27 PM **bobjugant**: I love you very much

8:02:36 PM **ladydi2011**: Most of all you love me back

8:03:05 PM **ladydi2011**: Darling, I will never ask something of you that I am not willing to give

8:03:18 PM **bobjugant**: Baby you make me happy

8:04:07 PM **ladydi2011**: Darling, you have not seen anything yet...I will spoil you.

8:04:42 PM **ladydi2011**: We will have so much fun together

8:04:50 PM **ladydi2011**: I always want you to be laughing and happy

8:06:14 PM **ladydi2011**: Baby, in the middle of the night when we are at the beach, can we skinny dip? I never did this but always wanted to...

8:07:43 PM **bobjugant**: Yea baby

8:07:53 PM **bobjugant**: We will

8:08:07 PM **bobjugant**: I promise honey

8:08:13 PM **ladydi2011**: I know that I ask for some crazy things, don't I?

8:08:24 PM **bobjugant**: I like it

8:08:46 PM **bobjugant**: You are so sweet

8:08:47 PM **ladydi2011**: I want to experience all of life with you

8:09:02 PM **ladydi2011**: Things that I only dreamt about

8:09:08 PM **bobjugant**: We will

8:09:23 PM **bobjugant**: We will have so much fun together

8:09:30 PM **ladydi2011**: Baby, I can tell you are tired.

8:10:24 PM **ladydi2011**: If I were with you I would ask you to lay your head on my chest and I would run my fingers through your hair until you fell asleep...then, I would watch you sleep.

8:10:49 PM **bobjugant**: Yea u know

8:11:26 PM **bobjugant**: But a first thing a man should do is to make love to his woman first befor anything else

8:11:45 PM **ladydi2011**: Nice

8:11:47 PM **bobjugant**: So *i* want you to be happy

8:12:12 PM **bobjugant**: Even if its to stay awake longer

8:12:43 PM **bobjugant**: My love then *i* would want to please you...then you will sleep even better

8:12:56 PM **ladydi2011**: I would take all your strength

8:13:24 PM **ladydi2011**: Baby...brb. Please don't leave

8:13:35 PM **bobjugant**: Am here honey

8:15:56 PM **ladydi2011**: I am back

8:17:53 PM **ladydi2011**: Baby, what time do you have to get up for work?

8:18:20 PM **bobjugant**: Am here honey

8:18:42 PM **bobjugant**: In couple of hours

8:18:54 PM **bobjugant**: 6hrs

8:19:12 PM **ladydi2011**: Did you have dinner baby?

8:19:50 PM **bobjugant**: Yes baby *i* did

8:20:02 PM **ladydi2011**: Did you have a hot shower?

8:20:20 PM **bobjugant**: Cold shower honey

8:20:26 PM **ladydi2011**: Are you lying in bed now or sitting at a table?

8:20:34 PM **ladydi2011**: Cold, why cold baby?

8:20:40 PM **bobjugant**: Am laying on the bed

8:20:55 PM **bobjugant**: Durban is hot

8:21:13 PM **ladydi2011**: Can I lay with you?

8:21:20 PM **bobjugant**: Yes baby

8:21:27 PM **bobjugant**: You own my body

8:21:34 PM **ladydi2011**: I want to put my head on your chest and hear your heart beat

8:21:36 PM **bobjugant**: Anything you want baby

8:21:57 PM **ladydi2011**: I want to intertwined with you darling

8:22:27 PM **ladydi2011**: Is there air conditioning in the room?

8:22:36 PM **ladydi2011**: If so, does it work?

8:23:05 PM **bobjugant**: Yea baby

8:23:09 PM **bobjugant**: It works

8:23:24 PM **ladydi2011**: Anything I want?????

8:23:33 PM **bobjugant**: Yes baby

8:23:37 PM **ladydi2011**: I want to love you forever and ever and ever

8:23:49 PM **bobjugant**: Me too honey

8:24:03 PM **bobjugant**: Kiss kiss

8:24:22 PM **ladydi2011**: (((hugs))), (((hugs))), (((hugs)))

8:24:31 PM **bobjugant**: You have got my love too honey

8:24:51 PM **ladydi2011**: I know baby.

8:25:09 PM **ladydi2011**: Now that I have your love, I don't ever want to lose it

8:25:20 PM **ladydi2011**: I appreciate you darling

8:25:49 PM **bobjugant**: Me too love

8:26:09 PM **bobjugant**: I never want to leave your arms

8:26:30 PM **ladydi2011**: This is good because I never want to leave your arms

8:27:01 PM **ladydi2011**: Do you believe in destiny?

8:27:33 PM **bobjugant**: Yea baby

8:27:36 PM **ladydi2011**: Do you believe in chance?

8:27:36 PM **bobjugant**: I do

8:28:16 PM **bobjugant**: And *i* believe in your love

8:28:56 PM **bobjugant**: I love you even more than words could describe

8:29:07 PM **ladydi2011**: Same here darling

8:29:29 PM **ladydi2011**: Honey, I never saw the word "dats" until I met you

8:30:02 PM **bobjugant**: Yea

8:30:14 PM **ladydi2011**: Today when I was out there was a woman wearing a t-shirt with the word "dats" on it, and it put you right there with me...

8:30:43 PM **bobjugant**: Thanks honey

8:30:48 PM **ladydi2011**: It was like the universe catapulted you right to me

8:30:49 PM **bobjugant**: You rock

8:31:01 PM **ladydi2011**: Thanks baby...you rock more

8:31:30 PM **ladydi2011**: You do rock my world

8:31:47 PM **bobjugant**: You too honey

8:32:00 PM **ladydi2011**: What did you have for dinner?

8:32:54 PM **ladydi2011**: Do you like the food there?

8:33:01 PM **ladydi2011**: Is the water safe?

8:33:14 PM **bobjugant**: *Sweet rice and chicken sauce*

8:33:19 PM **ladydi2011**: It was not safe to drink the water in Niger or Nigeria

8:33:28 PM **ladydi2011**: Was it good?

8:33:47 PM **ladydi2011**: I ate camel in Niger...there is a first time for everything I guess

8:34:07 PM **bobjugant**: Bottle

8:34:21 PM **ladydi2011**: Yeah, it was the same in Niger and Nigeria

8:34:24 PM **bobjugant**: Baby did you say you ate camel

8:34:28 PM **ladydi2011**: Yes baby

8:34:39 PM **bobjugant**: Lol

8:34:40 PM **bobjugant**: Hmm

8:34:43 PM **ladydi2011**: I didn't know it until after the fact

8:34:56 PM **ladydi2011**: I was not a happy camper

8:35:23 PM **bobjugant**: Hmm

8:35:26 PM **ladydi2011**: Have you ever seen a termite hill baby?

8:35:44 PM **bobjugant**: Not at all honey

8:36:14 PM **ladydi2011**: I saw one in Niger and it was 9 feet tall

8:36:16 PM **bobjugant**: did you see termites

8:36:29 PM **bobjugant**: Really

8:36:35 PM **ladydi2011**: Yes baby...

8:36:47 PM **bobjugant**: Baby give me 2mins

8:36:49 PM **ladydi2011**: When we are together, I will show you pictures

8:36:51 PM **ladydi2011**: Ok love

8:36:56 PM **bobjugant**: Dont go away ok

Break in Time

8:41:17 PM **bobjugant**: hello love

8:41:28 PM **ladydi2011**: Baby, they lost my luggage so I had to buy African clothes to wear.

8:42:30 PM **ladydi2011**: I sent you a picture of me when I was in Africa. Did you get it?

8:42:58 PM **bobjugant**: did you like the clothes

8:43:22 PM **ladydi2011**: I cut my hair really short because it was 100 degrees every day

8:43:31 PM **ladydi2011**: Hot...very hot!

8:43:45 PM **ladydi2011**: Yeah. I still have the dresses

8:44:12 PM **bobjugant**: how long were you there honey

8:44:29 PM **ladydi2011**: Two weeks

8:44:39 PM **bobjugant**: ok baby

8:44:47 PM **ladydi2011**: I loved going to the orphanage

8:44:56 PM **ladydi2011**: The kids needed so much love honey

8:45:19 PM **bobjugant**: I guess alot of orphanage there

8:45:26 PM **ladydi2011**: Yes baby

8:45:53 PM **ladydi2011**: It makes me sad when I think how many people are hungry to be loved

8:46:03 PM **ladydi2011**: Baby, you have a family now

8:46:09 PM **bobjugant**: me too honey

8:46:25 PM **ladydi2011**: A big one too!

8:46:45 PM **bobjugant**: yea baby I love that

8:46:55 PM **ladydi2011**: I have many brothers, nieces and nephews and my mom and dad are still alive

8:46:57 PM **bobjugant**: you make me feel good

8:47:07 PM **bobjugant**: really

8:47:09 PM **ladydi2011**: You will never be alone again

8:47:26 PM **bobjugant**: yea you told me 5brothers

8:47:28 PM **ladydi2011**: My dad is 84 and my mom is 72

8:47:37 PM **bobjugant**: ooohh

8:47:46 PM **bobjugant**: nice

8:47:54 PM **ladydi2011**: Yes....they are not close in age

8:48:32 PM **bobjugant**: baby do they stay in the states too

8:48:53 PM **bobjugant**: am trying call

Incoming Voice call with bobjugant (8:48:43 PM)

Call Ended: 0 hours 28 minutes 29 seconds

9:18:12 PM **bobjugant**: baby i said my work in chile is going to be more hectic

9:19:05 PM **bobjugant**: am going to be servicing some big oil facilities and installing some equiptments

9:19:46 PM **bobjugant**: <ding>

9:20:01 PM **bobjugant**: baby are you there

9:20:09 PM **ladydi2011**: I am here

9:20:35 PM **bobjugant**: i miss you very much

9:20:42 PM **ladydi2011**: Baby, let me sign off and sign back on to try to get my camera to work

9:20:52 PM **bobjugant**: ok baby

9:20:56 PM **ladydi2011**: I miss you very much too

9:21:12 PM **ladydi2011**: Thank you for calling. I love when I get to hear your voice!

9:21:40 PM **bobjugant**: the pleasure is all mine

9:24:02 PM **bobjugant**: baby i see you know

Incoming Voice call with bobjugant (9:24:13 PM)

Call Ended: 0 hours 0 minutes 33 seconds

9:25:23 PM **bobjugant**: *i* love you
9:25:32 PM **ladydi2011**: See how you make me smile
9:26:06 PM **bobjugant**: and you smiled like an angel
9:26:15 PM **ladydi2011**: Thank you love
9:26:36 PM **ladydi2011**: Please tell me I am not dreaming
9:27:04 PM **bobjugant**: you are not baby. You are my love
9:27:21 PM **ladydi2011**: Good...I don't want to be dreaming
9:27:36 PM **bobjugant**: *i* love and cherish you alot honey
9:27:36 PM **ladydi2011**: I am very in love with you
9:27:59 PM **ladydi2011**: Our hearts are saying the same things
9:28:13 PM **bobjugant**: yea baby
9:28:29 PM **ladydi2011**: I want you to dream about me tonight
9:29:09 PM **bobjugant**: *i* will honey
9:29:19 PM **ladydi2011**: Thank you for calling me baby
9:29:39 PM **bobjugant**: baby make sure you dream about me ok
9:29:47 PM **ladydi2011**: Absolutely
9:30:00 PM **bobjugant**: *i* love you from my heart baby
9:30:15 PM **ladydi2011**: Me too
9:30:34 PM **ladydi2011**: Honey, please sleep so you are safe tomorrow.
9:30:42 PM **bobjugant**: yea baby
9:30:55 PM **bobjugant**: *i* need to take a nap
9:31:16 PM **bobjugant**: *i* will dream about our love honey
9:31:38 PM **ladydi2011**: Baby, look out at the moon
9:31:59 PM **bobjugant**: *i* will baby
9:32:02 PM **ladydi2011**: It is something we can both see and know that we are seeing it together
9:32:23 PM **bobjugant**: *i* dont feel like sleeping baby but *i* have to honey so dat *i* would be strong later
9:33:09 PM **ladydi2011**: Baby, you will sleep once you turn the computer off and lay your head on the pillow
9:33:10 PM **bobjugant**: *i* love you very much more than words could describe
9:33:20 PM **ladydi2011**: I love you very much too!
9:33:30 PM **ladydi2011**: Can you read my lips on the camera?
9:33:46 PM **bobjugant**: yea baby
9:34:00 PM **bobjugant**: your sweet and sexy lips
9:34:10 PM **ladydi2011**: I blew you kisses. Did you get them?
9:34:22 PM **ladydi2011**: Good night my darling
9:34:39 PM **bobjugant**: gud night my love
9:35:39 PM **bobjugant**: *i* love you
9:35:41 PM **bobjugant**: kiss kiss
9:35:47 PM **ladydi2011**: Kiss kiss
9:36:05 PM **ladydi2011**: Take care of you
9:36:09 PM **bobjugant**: bye love
9:36:14 PM **ladydi2011**: Bye darling

From: ladydi2011@yahoo.com
To: Bob Jugant
Subject: Good night my darling
Sent: Tuesday, May 08, 2012 12:55 AM

My Darling Bob,

I wonder if I dreamed of you if you would appear?
To make my nights full of love and always hold me near.

I wonder if I thought of you if you would feel it in your soul?
Like two spirits in the universe, who always seem to know.

Even if the stars went black and the sun were to shine no more.
They could find their way to each other, no matter how far the shore.

Safely in each other's arms, to bid the rest of time.
Finding Eternal Love so many seek to find.

Caring for each other through the worst of storms.
Leaning on the arms of love and never need anymore.

This is how I feel for you. I've known it all along.
You are my one true love, My world. My heart. My soul!

Good night, Sweetheart. I love you with all I am, my darling.

Always and forever,
Diana

From: ladydi2011@yahoo.com
To: Bob Jugant
Subject: Trying to sleep
Sent: Tuesday, May 8, 2012 6:56:25 AM

Oh, my darling,
I lay in bed 30 minutes ago and cannot fall asleep. My thoughts are on you, us and our future. Oh, how I want to look into your eyes, hold your hand, feel your lips on mine and your strong arms around me. I look at your pictures and read the beautiful emails you have written to me, and I have this huge smile on my face and in my heart. Darling, you make me so happy. Thank you for being the wonderful man that you are. I keep hearing your sexy voice telling me that you love me very

much, my smile gets even bigger and my heart skips many beats. Then when I close my eyes I can feel my body lying next to yours, and then I hear our hearts beating as one. I see the moonlight dancing across your handsome face and I watch you sleep, and my heart is finally content because I have traveled across the miles and time to be where I belong...lying in your arms!

Good night, my prince
I love you more than any words can describe
Yours forever,
Diana

From: bobjugant@yahoo.com
To: ladydi
Subject: Re: Trying to sleep
Sent: Tuesday, May 8, 2012 5:21 AM

baby you are so wonderful..*i love you very much..you are everything i dream off..i love you,i dream of you anytime i close my eyes,i think of you because you are my reality,my only truth,dat is the truth, but how do i convince you of it? thought i should write it in the mirror,,tell you that i have no world other than that you are my universe,my life ,my reason for existence,thats much i know,be my life my world..i* love you from the bottom of my heart.......kiss kiss kiss,,,bob

---

From: bobjugant@yahoo.com
To: ladydi
Subject: my love for you will never die
Sent: Tuesday, May 8, 2012 5:59 AM

i love you baby,,you mean the world to me,you are my angel,,

IM May 8, 2012 2:51:46 PM

2:51:46 PM **bobjugant**: Hello honey
2:52:01 PM **bobjugant**: Are you there

IM May 8, 2012 4:08:23 PM

4:08:23 PM **bobjugant**: Hello baby
4:08:33 PM **bobjugant**: Are you there
4:27:30 PM **bobjugant**: hello diana

From: bobjugant@yahoo.com
To: ladydi
Subject: hi
Sent: Tuesday, May 8, 2012 4:36 PM

hello my love ...*i* miss you so much darling..am on online know baby..if you are less busy we could chat..my day was great today..am moving up to the nest step of work over here....

From: ladydi2011@yahoo.com
To: Bob Jugant
Subject: Re: hi
Sent: Tuesday, May 8, 2012 4:40 PM

Hello, my darling. I miss you too! I am running errands. I will be back in about 45 min. Can we meet on line then, Honey? Love, Kisses and (((Hugs)))

From: bobjugant@yahoo.com
To: ladydi
Subject: Re: hi
Sent: Tuesday, May 8, 2012 4:42 PM

ok baby,just send me an email when your done ok...kiss kiss

IM May 8, 2012 5:27:04 PM

5:27:04 PM **ladydi2011**: Hello honey...I am here waiting for you.
5:41:49 PM **ladydi2011**: Hi honey

IM May 8, 2012 5:49:13 PM

5:49:13 PM **ladydi2011**: I am listening to a really great song that my man sent me...He is a real sweetheart! I can't wait to meet him in person...

IM May 8, 2012 6:40:51 PM

6:40:51 PM **bobjugant**: hello honey

6:41:03 PM **ladydi2011**: Hello darling
6:41:10 PM **ladydi2011**: How was your day?
6:41:13 PM **bobjugant**: *i* miss you
6:41:23 PM **ladydi2011**: I miss you too
6:41:31 PM **bobjugant**: my day was nice
6:41:48 PM **ladydi2011**: Did you get a lot accomplished?
6:42:06 PM **bobjugant**: yea alots baby
6:42:13 PM **ladydi2011**: Kool
6:42:19 PM **ladydi2011**: Did you have dinner?
6:42:39 PM **bobjugant**: *i* did honey
6:43:01 PM **ladydi2011**: What did you have? Was it good?
6:43:04 PM **bobjugant**: honey are you ok
6:43:19 PM **ladydi2011**: I am ok baby. Why do you ask?
6:43:27 PM **bobjugant**: the electricity here keeps comming of and on
6:44:04 PM **bobjugant**: making sure my baby is doing good
6:45:28 PM **ladydi2011**: I love how much you care about my wellbeing.
6:45:32 PM **bobjugant**: darling give me 3mins
6:45:43 PM **bobjugant**: dont log out ok
6:45:56 PM **ladydi2011**: Ok honey. I am going to go get something to drink
6:50:37 PM **ladydi2011**: I am back my love.
Break in Time
6:53:49 PM **bobjugant**: Hello my love
6:53:54 PM **bobjugant**: They changed the service provider
6:53:59 PM **bobjugant**: Are you there baby
6:57:26 PM **bobjugant**: The internet is so poor over here
6:57:43 PM **bobjugant**: It keeps tripping of and on
6:57:44 PM **ladydi2011**: That has to be frustrating
6:58:41 PM **ladydi2011**: I am sure you will be glad to get back to London
7:00:57 PM **bobjugant**: Yea baby
7:01:20 PM **ladydi2011**: Thank you for the wonderful song this morning.
7:04:51 PM **ladydi2011**: Baby. I am here. I had to sign out to be able to get my web cam to work...

IM May 8, 2012 7:46:50 PM

7:46:50 PM **ladydi2011**: Baby. I am thinking the electric went off and you cannot get back on line... Please send me an email if and when you can get back on line. I love you.

From: ladydi2011@yahoo.com
To: Bob Jugant
Subject: Keeper of my heart
Sent: Wednesday, May 09, 2012 10:55 AM

Good morning, Darling,

For me it is late morning, for you it is late afternoon...I hope you slept well and are having a good day. I really miss you, Honey! You are the keeper of my heart. Please always take care of it. Every passing day my desire to be with you in person gets stronger and stronger. Maybe you can go back to the cafe where you were the other day so we can connect today. Just a thought...but I am sure you have also had this thought.

Kisses and (((hugs))),

Diana

IM May 9, 2012 11:12:57 AM

11:12:57 AM **bobjugant**: Hello baby
11:13:10 AM **ladydi2011**: Hello darling
11:13:18 AM **ladydi2011**: How are you?
11:13:30 AM **bobjugant**: Am doing good honey
11:13:40 AM **bobjugant**: I knew you would be up soon
11:13:54 AM **ladydi2011**: Did you get a good night's sleep?
11:13:56 AM **bobjugant**: Hope you did sleep well
11:14:02 AM **bobjugant**: Yea baby *i* did
11:14:06 AM **ladydi2011**: I did.
11:14:16 AM **ladydi2011**: I miss you!
11:14:26 AM **bobjugant**: I miss you too
11:14:39 AM **ladydi2011**: How is your day going?
11:14:40 AM **bobjugant**: So are you at work know
11:14:48 AM **ladydi2011**: I am.
11:14:57 AM **bobjugant**: My day is going on well
11:15:17 AM **ladydi2011**: Is the Internet fixed now at the hotel?
11:15:24 AM **bobjugant**: Am in a cafe not too far from the rig honey
11:15:38 AM **ladydi2011**: Did you get my email baby?
11:15:49 AM **bobjugant**: Yea darling
11:16:40 AM **bobjugant**: Baby *i* missed you alot last night
11:17:05 AM **bobjugant**: The internet over here was bad
11:17:12 AM **ladydi2011**: I know honey
11:17:17 AM **bobjugant**: I love you very much
11:17:26 AM **ladydi2011**: I love you very much too!
11:17:39 AM **ladydi2011**: I can't wait to be with you in person
11:17:48 AM **bobjugant**: Me too honey
11:18:19 AM **bobjugant**: Baby *i* have to go know...*i* will be with you pretty soon...
11:18:38 AM **ladydi2011**: Oh, ok honey
11:18:52 AM **bobjugant**: I love my baby so much
11:19:07 AM **ladydi2011**: I love you very much too baby
11:19:09 AM **bobjugant**: You are the angel of my heart
11:19:18 AM **ladydi2011**: You are the keeper of my heart
11:19:30 AM **bobjugant**: *I would never do anything to make you sad*
11:19:39 AM **ladydi2011**: I know baby.

11:19:58 AM **bobjugant**: I do that wen *i* cum back baby
11:20:02 AM **ladydi2011**: Until later my love
11:20:06 AM **bobjugant**: Kiss kiss
11:20:14 AM **ladydi2011**: Kisses and (((hugs)))
11:20:20 AM **bobjugant**: I will be with you soon
11:20:26 AM **bobjugant**: love you
11:20:29 AM **bobjugant**: Kiss kiss
11:20:39 AM **ladydi2011**: Love you too darling

IM May 9, 2012 4:02:42 PM

4:02:42 PM **bobjugant**: Hello baby
4:02:49 PM **bobjugant**: Are you there honey
4:02:58 PM **ladydi2011**: Hi Baby
4:03:13 PM **bobjugant**: How are you baby
4:03:19 PM **ladydi2011**: I am here...how are you?
4:03:23 PM **bobjugant**: Am ok
4:03:34 PM **ladydi2011**: I am smiling now that I am with you
4:03:39 PM **bobjugant**: I left the rig
4:03:44 PM **bobjugant**: Me too baby
4:03:50 PM **ladydi2011**: What do you mean that you left the rig?
4:04:12 PM **bobjugant**: Yea baby
4:04:20 PM **ladydi2011**: Baby...on phone with client. Please hold. Do not leave.
4:04:34 PM **bobjugant**: Ok am here
4:05:30 PM **ladydi2011**: Thanks for waiting
4:05:51 PM **bobjugant**: Yea baby
4:05:56 PM **bobjugant**: Anything for you
4:06:06 PM **bobjugant**: I love you too baby
4:06:30 PM **bobjugant**: Are yo at the office honey
4:06:44 PM **ladydi2011**: Yes honey
4:06:50 PM **ladydi2011**: Still on phone
4:07:34 PM **bobjugant**: Ok let me know when your done
4:08:07 PM **ladydi2011**:1 or 2 min
4:09:34 PM **bobjugant**: Ok baby
4:09:45 PM **bobjugant**: *I FEEL VERY VERY HAPPY BECAUSE I SUIT YOU VERY WELL,MY LOVELY PRINCESS, HONEY YOU ARE A QUEEN OF MY LIFE,*
4:10:22 PM **ladydi2011**: You just put a BIG SMILE on my face
4:10:38 PM **bobjugant**: Thanks baby
4:10:47 PM **bobjugant**: I mean it honey
4:17:17 PM **ladydi2011**: Baby, where did you go?
Break in Time
4:29:46 PM **bobjugant**: Am here baby
4:29:52 PM **ladydi2011**: Hi darling...I am glad you could get back on line
4:30:21 PM **bobjugant**: the internet was down
4:30:26 PM **ladydi2011**: I am now off the phone.
4:30:34 PM **bobjugant**: Baby did you see what *i* sent you

4:30:39 PM **ladydi2011**: Are you at the hotel?

4:30:54 PM **ladydi2011**: No baby. I have not received anything from you

4:31:10 PM **bobjugant**: No baby

4:31:30 PM **bobjugant**: In a presentation

4:31:37 PM **ladydi2011**: Ok

4:31:49 PM **bobjugant**: They have wifi here

4:31:56 PM **ladydi2011**: Cool....

4:32:14 PM **bobjugant**: I will be leaving here soon

4:32:22 PM **bobjugant**: Baby *i* missed you

4:32:40 PM **ladydi2011**: I missed spending time with you last night

4:32:49 PM **bobjugant**: Me too honey

4:32:53 PM **ladydi2011**: I missed not waking up to an email from you

4:33:06 PM **bobjugant**: Sorry baby

4:33:27 PM **ladydi2011**: I know you are having Internet problems

4:33:39 PM **bobjugant**: *i* will love you more

4:34:32 PM **bobjugant**: You are the queen of my life,

4:35:03 PM **ladydi2011**: You are the prince of my life and my heart

4:35:28 PM **bobjugant**: I love you

4:35:30 PM **ladydi2011**: Baby, I hope I make you happy

4:35:46 PM **bobjugant**: So baby how did work go today

4:35:54 PM **bobjugant**: Yea baby you make me feel good

4:36:09 PM **bobjugant**: Am happy *i* met you

4:36:26 PM **ladydi2011**: Good baby

4:36:34 PM **ladydi2011**: I will be working late tonight

4:36:42 PM **ladydi2011**: This is normal

4:36:53 PM **ladydi2011**: My to-do list is always way too long

4:37:07 PM **ladydi2011**: Baby, will you promise me something?

4:37:22 PM **bobjugant**: *I GET YOU BESIDE ME FOREVER WE WILL LOVE EACH OTHER DURING THIS LIFE AND WE WILL BE FAITHFUL TO EACH OTHER*

4:37:52 PM **bobjugant**: Yea baby anything for you. What is it baby

4:38:21 PM **ladydi2011**: Promise me you will always tell me what you need

4:38:46 PM **bobjugant**: Ok

4:38:49 PM **ladydi2011**: I wish I could read minds, but I can't...

4:39:00 PM **bobjugant**: So how was work today

4:39:13 PM **ladydi2011**: Busy...what about for you?

4:39:23 PM **bobjugant**: Hectic

4:39:38 PM **ladydi2011**: You said it would be hectic while you were there

4:39:41 PM **bobjugant**: Work is stressful you know But *i* like my work baby

4:40:48 PM **ladydi2011**: I am glad you like your work

4:41:07 PM **ladydi2011**: I like mine too...some days I just get overwhelmed

4:41:13 PM **bobjugant**: you would never have a sad moment with me

4:41:31 PM **ladydi2011**: Thank you my love...

4:41:37 PM **bobjugant**: I will always make you smile

4:41:39 PM **ladydi2011**: I believe this

4:41:49 PM **ladydi2011**: I will always make you smile

4:41:53 PM **bobjugant**: I love you much

4:41:59 PM **bobjugant**: Thanks dear

4:42:17 PM **ladydi2011**: Honey, sometimes things happen to bring sadness. When this happens, will you wipe my tears?

4:42:19 PM **bobjugant**: You rock baby

4:42:29 PM **bobjugant**: I will baby

4:42:47 PM **ladydi2011**: I will do the same for you. I will always be by your side.

4:43:01 PM **bobjugant**: I will wipe your tears and make you smile

4:43:05 PM **ladydi2011**: Hopefully later you can listen to the song I sent you

4:43:25 PM **bobjugant**: Yea *i* will

4:43:45 PM **ladydi2011**: It is almost 11pm there isn't baby?

4:43:53 PM **bobjugant**: And *i* will make you smile more baby

4:44:19 PM **bobjugant**: Yea baby

4:44:36 PM **ladydi2011**: Did you get a good night's sleep last night?

4:45:14 PM **bobjugant**: I did honey

4:45:14 PM **bobjugant**: 5hrs

4:45:25 PM **ladydi2011**: only 5 hrs.?

4:45:33 PM **ladydi2011**: Baby, you must be tired

4:45:37 PM **bobjugant**: You were in my mind all through

4:45:54 PM **ladydi2011**: I met you in our dreams last night

4:46:28 PM **bobjugant**: I cant wait to be with you

4:46:35 PM **bobjugant**: Me too honey

4:47:12 PM **bobjugant**: I hope to get a better conection when get to the hotel

4:47:36 PM **ladydi2011**: I hope you get a better connection tonight too

4:47:47 PM **ladydi2011**: Baby, please resend what you sent me earlier

4:47:54 PM **bobjugant**: Baby my agent contacted me today

4:48:02 PM **bobjugant**: I will

4:48:12 PM **ladydi2011**: What did the agent say?

4:49:13 PM **bobjugant**: he said *i* could get chile or mexico

4:49:57 PM **ladydi2011**: Mexico is very dangerous right now. Please take Chile.

4:50:25 PM **bobjugant**: I told him to make equiries on the eazy one...so less stress

4:50:31 PM **bobjugant**: Oh really

4:50:32 PM **ladydi2011**: The drug lords would rather kill you than look at you

4:50:51 PM **bobjugant**: Awwww

4:50:55 PM **ladydi2011**: Yes my love...Mexico is REALLY bad now.

4:50:56 PM **bobjugant**: Hmm

4:51:08 PM **ladydi2011**: I cannot lose you now that I have found you

4:51:33 PM **bobjugant**: I have to send him an email

4:51:47 PM **ladydi2011**: Please do and tell him Chili

4:51:53 PM **bobjugant**: You will not loose me honey

4:52:21 PM **bobjugant**: We would not leave each other

4:52:31 PM **bobjugant**: You have me know

4:52:49 PM **ladydi2011**: I love you Bob

4:53:45 PM **bobjugant**: Thanks love

4:53:52 PM **bobjugant**: *DARLING ' WE WILL FOREVER LOVE EACH OTHER AND NEVER QUIT EACH OTHER. YOU PROMISE ME THAT YOU WOULD BE MINE AND I WOUD BE YOURS*

4:54:22 PM **bobjugant**: I LOVE YOU

4:54:33 PM **ladydi2011**: I promise that we will never quit each other and that I will be yours forever...

4:54:42 PM **ladydi2011**: I LOVE YOU

4:55:54 PM **bobjugant**: Ok love

4:55:57 PM **ladydi2011**: The only place I want to be is with you, securely in your arms

4:55:57 PM **bobjugant**: Baby you said *i* should choose chille

4:56:12 PM **ladydi2011**: Yes baby. Please choose Chile

4:56:27 PM **bobjugant**: You would have me honey

4:56:56 PM **bobjugant**: Ok *i* will mail him when *i* get to the hotel

4:56:59 PM **ladydi2011**: What do you mean by "I would have you?"

4:57:54 PM **bobjugant**: It means am all yours baby

4:58:29 PM **ladydi2011**: This is good. I don't want to share you...

4:59:01 PM **bobjugant**: I think *i* have to choose chille honey

4:59:04 PM **ladydi2011**: You will never have to share me. My heart belongs to you...

4:59:30 PM **bobjugant**: I will be with you always

4:59:35 PM **ladydi2011**: Yes baby. Please chose Chile...Please do your own due diligence and research it for yourself

4:59:44 PM **bobjugant**: We will hols hands

4:59:57 PM **ladydi2011**: (smile)

5:00:03 PM **bobjugant**: I will kiss your ears

5:00:09 PM **ladydi2011**: (smile)

5:00:21 PM **bobjugant**: Down to your neck

5:00:30 PM **ladydi2011**: (smile)

5:00:34 PM **bobjugant**: All over your body

5:00:48 PM **ladydi2011**: (smile) (smile) (smile)

5:00:57 PM **bobjugant**: And we will make passionate love

5:01:06 PM **ladydi2011**: (really big smile)

5:01:26 PM **bobjugant**: You are my everything

5:01:36 PM **ladydi2011**: You are my everything

5:01:51 PM **ladydi2011**: You are my forever

5:02:27 PM **bobjugant**: You are my forever too baby!

5:03:00 PM **ladydi2011**: Baby, how long is the contract for in Chile

5:03:14 PM **bobjugant**: Baby am loking at 3weeks

5:03:32 PM **ladydi2011**: Ok...Does it pay the same as Mexico?

5:03:59 PM **bobjugant**: Yea yea

5:04:06 PM **ladydi2011**: Kool

5:04:30 PM **ladydi2011**: Even if it paid less, *i* would still feel better if you took Chile

5:04:32 PM **bobjugant**: *But the custom duty is higher* because of the equiptment

5:04:45 PM **ladydi2011**: Customs for what?

5:05:20 PM **ladydi2011**: *You take equipment in instead of rent it there?*

5:06:04 PM **bobjugant**: *We are going to instal*

5:06:09 PM **bobjugant**: Some instalation honey

5:06:16 PM **ladydi2011**: Oh, ok

5:06:41 PM **ladydi2011**: Please do all your research of the countries policies

5:06:51 PM **bobjugant**: Yea baby I will honey when *i* get back home

5:08:01 PM **bobjugant**: *i* have to make preparation

5:08:33 PM **ladydi2011**: Please do all your homework...you want everything to go smoothly

5:08:48 PM **ladydi2011**: You know what you have to do better than me

5:09:02 PM **bobjugant**: Yea baby

5:09:03 PM **ladydi2011**: You are a world traveler and a very capable man

5:09:19 PM **ladydi2011**: I trust you baby

5:09:58 PM **bobjugant**: *i* love you

5:10:08 PM **ladydi2011**: I love you more....

5:10:15 PM **ladydi2011**: Eternity and back

5:10:28 PM **bobjugant**: *Baby what is your best colour*

5:10:36 PM **ladydi2011**: Plum

5:10:47 PM **ladydi2011**: Honey, when is your birthday?

5:10:47 PM **bobjugant**: *What colour of bag*

5:11:09 PM **ladydi2011**: Black, so it will go with anything

5:11:11 PM **bobjugant**: *June 3rd baby*

5:11:23 PM **bobjugant**: Ok

5:11:27 PM **ladydi2011**: It is coming up soon

5:11:39 PM **bobjugant**: Yea baby

5:11:55 PM **bobjugant**: I might be in chile by den

5:12:06 PM **ladydi2011**: Ok

5:12:26 PM **bobjugant**: Honey when is your birth date

5:12:33 PM **ladydi2011**: When does the contract for Chili start?

5:12:46 PM **ladydi2011**: November 15th

5:13:22 PM **bobjugant**: Ok nice

5:13:33 PM **bobjugant**: When *i* get the papers for the work *I have to start in less than 3weeks*

5:14:49 PM **ladydi2011**: Ok. Does your agent think you will get this job?

5:15:02 PM **bobjugant**: *If you dont comply then you gonna loose*

5:15:09 PM **ladydi2011**: Last night you thought June or July

5:15:17 PM **ladydi2011**: I understand

5:15:43 PM **bobjugant**: *Yea am gonna get it*

5:15:45 PM **ladydi2011**: Please keep me posted baby

5:16:08 PM **ladydi2011**: This was fast. You just put the bid in the other day

5:16:23 PM **bobjugant**: *Baby i will tell you more later on the voice chat*

5:16:38 PM **ladydi2011**: Ok baby...

5:16:45 PM **ladydi2011**: I am excited for you honey

5:17:20 PM **bobjugant**: Yea baby *i* think june

5:17:34 PM **ladydi2011**: *Baby, do you have unlimited data on your blackberry*

5:17:43 PM **bobjugant**: Beacause the paper comes out tomorow

5:18:06 PM **ladydi2011**: Oh, ok

5:18:14 PM **bobjugant**: The bid is for 5days only and only 20 client they got

5:19:13 PM **ladydi2011**: Wow, you thought they would have had a lot more

5:19:38 PM **bobjugant**: Yea

5:20:18 PM **bobjugant**: *Baby lets talk about us*

5:20:25 PM **ladydi2011**: Baby, you deserve this work...

5:20:52 PM **bobjugant**: I will send you am email when *i* get to the hotel honey

5:21:18 PM **ladydi2011**: Ok baby.

5:21:49 PM **bobjugant**: They gonna shut down the wifi

5:21:57 PM **ladydi2011**: *Honey, I was thinking we can also do IM through our blackberries*

5:22:33 PM **ladydi2011**: I will go back to work until we can chat again later

5:22:44 PM **bobjugant**: Yea baby

5:22:52 PM **bobjugant**: I love you very much

5:23:08 PM **ladydi2011**: I love you very much too darling
5:23:43 PM **bobjugant**: Take good care of your self
5:23:48 PM **bobjugant**: Kiss kiss
5:23:55 PM **ladydi2011**: I will...you too baby
5:23:56 PM **bobjugant**: Be a good girl ok
5:24:00 PM **bobjugant**: Love you
5:24:15 PM **ladydi2011**: I love you too...........

He loves me *so much*. He will *always* be there for me and he will *never* do anything to make me sad...I am his *Princess* and *Queen* and we will *be faithful* to each other. All sweet words to get my money! He is very attentive. He sends me emails, ecards, songs, and he chats with me on a regular basis. He copied and pasted sweet, poetic things to me many times during these chats. If a woman didn't know this man was a scammer she could easily fall for his sweet words and attention. It is critical for you to identify a scammer early and disconnect IMMEDIATELY so you don't get caught up with them. Some of them are very good at what they do.

RED FLAGS

- He tells me his agent contacted him and he could get the bid either in Chile or Mexico. I tried to convince him to get Chile. He tells me custom duty is higher in Chile because of equipment that he is going to install. He tells me he will lose the job if he doesn't comply and then tells me he is going to get it. He is setting the stage.
- He doesn't like me asking technical, intelligent questions so he changes the subject by asking me my favorite color for a purse. Once again, he sways me away from the work conversation by telling me he would tell me later and would rather talk about "us". A scammer is good at changing the subject.
- Then I said we could IM on BBM with our blackberries, and he totally avoided this. He knew this would surely expose him. Soon after I asked this our conversation ended. A scammer has his story thought out but not in enough detail to talk in depth about it. If you consistently ask a lot of questions you will wear the scammer down.
- I ask him his birthday and he tells me June 3rd. Let's see if he tells me the same date down the road. Always ask the same question many times on different days to see if you get the same or different answer.

IM May 9, 2012 7:28:48 PM

7:28:48 PM **bobjugant**: hello baby
7:29:02 PM **ladydi2011**: Hello my love
7:29:11 PM **ladydi2011**: Are you at the hotel now?
7:29:26 PM **bobjugant**: yea baby
7:29:36 PM **bobjugant**: am calling honey

Incoming Voice call with bobjugant (7:29:25 PM)

Call Ended: 0 hours 7 minutes 41 seconds

7:38:03 PM **bobjugant**: *i* love you baby

7:38:18 PM **ladydi2011**: I love you very much baby

7:38:31 PM **ladydi2011**: **As I said, I trust you.**

7:39:21 PM **bobjugant**: **you have to baby**

7:39:31 PM **bobjugant**: *i* love you very much

7:39:33 PM **ladydi2011**: You will have to go to your profile and check out the young blonde who wants to get to know you. She is much younger than me baby...

7:39:46 PM **bobjugant**: *the internet was low*

7:39:50 PM **ladydi2011**: Baby, if I didn't trust you, I couldn't be with you

7:40:13 PM **ladydi2011**: I could hear you better on this computer. It has better speakers.

7:40:50 PM **bobjugant**: *baby i will leave there*

7:41:14 PM **ladydi2011**: This is your choice honey. I want you to do whatever is in your heart.

7:41:15 PM **bobjugant**: *i* already declined all email from everybod

7:41:35 PM **ladydi2011**: Thank you baby.

7:41:42 PM **bobjugant**: *i* love baby

7:41:53 PM **ladydi2011**: Please always let your heart lead you.

7:41:53 PM **bobjugant**: *i will never leave you*

7:42:08 PM **bobjugant**: *i* am following my heart

7:42:10 PM **ladydi2011**: I only want you to be with me as long as you want to be with me.

7:42:18 PM **bobjugant**: *and my heart is yours*

7:42:41 PM **bobjugant**: *i* love you diana

7:42:54 PM **ladydi2011**: My heart is yours...You have awakened it

7:43:08 PM **bobjugant**: *i will never leave you alone*

7:43:18 PM **bobjugant**: *i* will awake more honey

7:43:43 PM **ladydi2011** I know you will baby. I am looking forward to it.

7:43:44 PM **bobjugant**: *i will always make you happy*

7:44:22 PM **ladydi2011**: It is your love, kindness, honesty, truth, how you treat me and how I feel when I am with you that makes me happy baby.

7:44:22 PM **bobjugant**: and *i* will make sure *i* get intouch with you everyday

7:44:42 PM **bobjugant**: *and i wish to love you more*

7:44:45 PM **ladydi2011**: I know you will honey.

7:44:55 PM **bobjugant**: *i* am very happy over here baby

7:45:08 PM **bobjugant**: *i* hope you are happy too

7:45:33 PM **ladydi2011**: I am happy baby when I am with you and knowing that you love me

7:45:34 PM **bobjugant**: kiss kiss

7:45:49 PM **bobjugant**: *i* love you honey

7:45:50 PM **ladydi2011**: Kisses and (((hugs)))

7:46:14 PM **bobjugant**: *dont ever doubt my love for you honey*

7:46:23 PM **ladydi2011**: You are my world now honey

7:46:28 PM **bobjugant**: *i will always make you happy*

7:46:40 PM **bobjugant**: *i will make you young*

7:46:47 PM **ladydi2011**: You have never given me a reason to doubt your love for me baby, so I don't doubt it.

7:47:01 PM **bobjugant**: *you will feel like a lady in love*

7:47:24 PM **ladydi2011**: I already feel like a lady in love, because I am in love with YOU!

7:47:38 PM **bobjugant**: kiss kiss

7:47:49 PM **bobjugant**: me too baby

7:47:55 PM **ladydi2011**: *Baby, I guess the trip to Chile will postpone your trip to see me???*

7:48:16 PM **bobjugant**: yes baby

7:48:23 PM **ladydi2011**: Baby, I hope every woman who meets you can tell that you are already in love and spoken for.

7:48:38 PM **bobjugant**: *thats why i wanna go to chile so that i can meet you after wards*

7:49:15 PM **ladydi2011**: Oh, ok

7:49:23 PM **bobjugant**: yea baby

7:49:37 PM **bobjugant**: baby hold one a minute

7:49:43 PM **ladydi2011**: Ok

Break in Time

7:53:16 PM **bobjugant**: baby am back

7:53:32 PM **ladydi2011**: I am so glad you didn't get booted

7:53:49 PM **ladydi2011**: baby, you are striking out on your own with this one, correct?

7:54:02 PM **bobjugant**: yea baby

7:54:16 PM **ladydi2011**: Do you have everything you need to do this?

7:55:42 PM **bobjugant**: yea *i* have everything worked out

7:55:46 PM **ladydi2011**: Cool

7:56:17 PM **bobjugant**: thanks for been here honey

7:56:20 PM **ladydi2011**: I know you will be successful at everything you do

7:56:26 PM **bobjugant**: you are the best

7:56:35 PM **ladydi2011**: Thank you honey

7:57:15 PM **bobjugant**: baby *i* think the internet is strong know

7:57:23 PM **ladydi2011**: Cool

7:57:42 PM **ladydi2011**: I don't want to lose you tonight

7:57:58 PM **bobjugant**: *i* will be with you baby

7:58:00 PM **ladydi2011**: Are you tired baby?

7:58:15 PM **bobjugant**: with you am not

7:58:23 PM **ladydi2011**: Nice

7:58:30 PM **bobjugant**: *i* want to see your beautiful face

7:58:44 PM **bobjugant**: *i* miss your nice smile honey

7:59:02 PM **ladydi2011**: My cam is not working due to connection being low...lots of thunder storms

7:59:14 PM **bobjugant**: ok baby

7:59:27 PM **ladydi2011**: I am hoping the storms stop by tomorrow

7:59:32 PM **bobjugant**: *i* am thinking of you over here

7:59:42 PM **bobjugant**: *i* love you very much

8:00:00 PM **ladydi2011**: Baby, I have asked you a couple times for more pictures. Do you have more pictures to send me?

8:00:48 PM **bobjugant**: *i* will baby

8:01:11 PM **bobjugant**: am using the compuer at the hotel know

8:01:12 PM **ladydi2011**: Baby, here is a picture of me at the orphanage in Africa

8:01:42 PM **ladydi2011**: So you are in the lobby?

8:01:51 PM **bobjugant**: *lol*

8:02:05 PM **ladydi2011**: This picture was my second week there and they found my luggage

8:02:21 PM **bobjugant**: yea

8:02:29 PM **bobjugant**: *i* like this honey

8:02:45 PM **ladydi2011**: Baby, my heart broke for these children

8:03:02 PM **ladydi2011**: They loved that we were there.

8:03:08 PM **bobjugant**: yea *i* can imagine

8:03:31 PM **ladydi2011**: I have a huge heart baby, just like you.

8:03:53 PM **ladydi2011**: So, are you in the lobby baby?

8:04:37 PM **bobjugant**: *lol*

8:04:44 PM **bobjugant**: yes honey

8:04:52 PM **ladydi2011**: Why do you keep saying lol?

8:05:02 PM **ladydi2011**: What am I saying that is funny?

8:05:02 PM **bobjugant**: no computer in the room

8:05:14 PM **ladydi2011**: *Where is your laptop?*

8:05:34 PM **bobjugant**: *its not*

8:05:54 PM **bobjugant**: *i dont know what happened to it*

8:05:57 PM **ladydi2011**: *Its not ???*

8:06:06 PM **bobjugant**: may be heat

8:06:40 PM **bobjugant**: *i* was working on it at the rig and it went off

8:06:53 PM **ladydi2011**: Bummer

8:07:11 PM **bobjugant**: *baby i like you thats why i say lol*

8:07:31 PM **bobjugant**: you are making me laugh

8:07:45 PM **bobjugant**: *i* like you because you make me smile

8:07:52 PM **ladydi2011**: Cool...I like making you laugh and smile

8:08:07 PM **bobjugant**: thanks honey

8:08:14 PM **bobjugant**: you are the best

8:08:22 PM **ladydi2011**: I best behave myself with you then...lol

8:08:36 PM **bobjugant**: lol

8:08:41 PM **ladydi2011**: You are not in your room....

8:08:49 PM **bobjugant**: you giving me the lol

8:08:56 PM **ladydi2011**: I am trying

8:09:04 PM **bobjugant**: kool

8:09:14 PM **ladydi2011**: Please get your laptop fixed.

8:09:20 PM **bobjugant**: *i* will

8:09:42 PM **ladydi2011**: I love being playful with you

8:09:50 PM **bobjugant**: me too honey

8:10:12 PM **bobjugant**: *i* love the way we play together

8:10:21 PM **ladydi2011**: Me too!

8:10:29 PM **bobjugant**: since *i* found you *i* have been so happy

8:10:42 PM **ladydi2011**: You make life fun for me baby

8:10:51 PM **bobjugant**: when *i* think about you *i* know *i* have found true love

8:11:39 PM **ladydi2011**: Same here baby

8:12:02 PM **bobjugant**: baby guess what

8:12:06 PM **ladydi2011**: What?

8:12:53 PM **bobjugant**: *some top offiials wanted me to come for some party or something*

8:13:01 PM **ladydi2011**: Tonight?

8:13:02 PM **bobjugant**: late night party

8:13:10 PM **ladydi2011**: Please go and have fun

8:13:13 PM **bobjugant**: *i* told them *i* cant

8:13:18 PM **ladydi2011**: Why baby?

8:13:38 PM **bobjugant**: that *i* was going to be with my love tonight

8:13:50 PM **bobjugant**: and you are my love

8:14:02 PM **bobjugant**: *i* love you so much

8:14:11 PM **ladydi2011**: I know I am your love and I really dig this you know

8:14:29 PM **ladydi2011**: Baby, I do not want you to miss out on anything

8:14:44 PM **bobjugant**: and *i* have to be at the rig early you know

8:15:00 PM **bobjugant**: am not missing *i* will have a lot of fun later when we are together

8:15:43 PM **ladydi2011**: Ok....

8:16:05 PM **ladydi2011**: Yes, my love, you will have a lot of fun. I promise!

8:16:28 PM **bobjugant**: kiss kiss

8:16:34 PM **ladydi2011**: More please

8:16:45 PM **bobjugant**: kiss kiss kiss

8:17:10 PM **bobjugant**: from your neck down to your breast

8:17:24 PM **ladydi2011**: Nice

8:17:42 PM **bobjugant**: me kissing all over your body

8:18:05 PM **bobjugant**: and you rubbing my ears with your nails

8:18:22 PM **bobjugant**: *i* wish *i* was with you

8:18:27 PM **ladydi2011**: Me too

8:18:39 PM **ladydi2011**: I want to kiss you so badly

8:19:04 PM **bobjugant**: honey hold a minute

8:19:39 PM **ladydi2011**: Ok baby. I am going to run to the bathroom...please don't leave

8:29:30 PM **bobjugant**: ok baby

8:33:37 PM **ladydi2011**: I am back

8:35:16 PM **bobjugant**: am here baby

8:35:52 PM **bobjugant**: *i* also went to the bathroom

8:36:26 PM **ladydi2011**: Yeah, nature stills works...lol

8:36:58 PM **bobjugant**: yea baby it does

8:37:21 PM **bobjugant**: *what happenig in the states*

8:37:44 PM **bobjugant**: *obama and romney*

8:38:02 PM **bobjugant**: do they have a quarel

8:38:03 PM **ladydi2011**: I don't want either

8:38:11 PM **bobjugant**: hmm why did you say that baby

8:39:01 PM **bobjugant**: *i* thought pres obama was their choice

8:39:47 PM **bobjugant**: obama is more popular *i* guess

8:40:15 PM **ladydi2011**: He was not my choice ever since he said he didn't know what his pastor was preaching...how could he not know when he sat under the teaching for 20 years?

8:40:17 PM **bobjugant**: he deserve a second term you know

8:40:56 PM **bobjugant**: he said that?

8:41:13 PM **ladydi2011**: Actions always tell me who people are...actions always over rides words

8:41:29 PM **ladydi2011**: Yes, he did...many people don't listen.

8:41:57 PM **ladydi2011**: They believe whatever they are told

8:42:11 PM **bobjugant**: anyways

8:42:22 PM **bobjugant**: the best wins

8:43:06 PM **ladydi2011**: Now much of the black community is no longer for him

8:43:14 PM **bobjugant**: baby are you sure

8:43:40 PM **bobjugant**: but he is a negro

8:43:56 PM **ladydi2011**: Baby, I have a lot of black friends and this is what they tell me

8:44:09 PM **ladydi2011**: For me it has nothing to do with the color of his skin

8:44:09 PM **bobjugant**: *i* heard a negro would always support a negro

8:44:18 PM **bobjugant**: ok

8:44:22 PM **ladydi2011**: We all bleed the same baby

8:44:25 PM **bobjugant**: *i* guess so

8:44:54 PM **ladydi2011**: Baby, *i* am all about the character of a person

8:45:20 PM **bobjugant**: yea baby

8:45:21 PM **ladydi2011**: All my friends will tell you that I do not see color. I am looking for character and integrity

8:45:29 PM **bobjugant**: *characteer matters alot*

8:45:46 PM **ladydi2011**: Character is everything my love

8:45:59 PM **ladydi2011**: The most valuable thing we own is our reputation

8:46:06 PM **bobjugant**: *i* know baby

8:46:27 PM **ladydi2011**: Honey, I am probably very different than other women you have met

8:46:37 PM **ladydi2011**: I have a lot of substance

8:47:51 PM **ladydi2011**: So, baby...they say never to talk about religion or politics...we just talked about politics....did we do ok?

8:47:58 PM **bobjugant**: *i* can see it

8:48:07 PM **bobjugant**: you are a classy lady and *i* like the way you tlk

8:48:38 PM **ladydi2011**: Thanks my love.

8:48:43 PM **bobjugant**: you are very elightened

8:48:57 PM **bobjugant**: *i* cant wait baby

8:49:07 PM **ladydi2011**: Yes baby. I am!

8:49:22 PM **ladydi2011**: You can't wait for what baby?

8:49:39 PM **bobjugant**: to be with you my love

8:50:02 PM **ladydi2011**: Lol...I knew what you were thinking. I just wanted to hear it...sorry my love.

8:50:20 PM **ladydi2011**: I shouldn't have done that...I just had too...

8:50:38 PM **ladydi2011**: You are laughing again, aren't you?

8:50:43 PM **bobjugant**: aww

8:50:58 PM **bobjugant**: *i* knew you know baby

8:51:14 PM **bobjugant**: u caught me there *i* was laughing for real

8:51:38 PM **ladydi2011**: You're the Best!!!

8:51:47 PM **bobjugant**: you too honey

8:51:54 PM **bobjugant**: *i* love you so much and *i* love being with you

8:52:08 PM **ladydi2011**: So, let's get the other hot topic on the table

8:52:21 PM **bobjugant**: you make my world complete

8:52:26 PM **ladydi2011**: What are your religious beliefs?

8:52:43 PM **bobjugant**: *i* believe in God

8:52:44 PM **ladydi2011**: Oh baby, you do the same for me. You complete me.

8:53:12 PM **bobjugant**: and *i* believe doing good is the best

8:53:38 PM **ladydi2011**: I also believe in God. I do not believe in organized religion.

8:54:04 PM **bobjugant**: me too honey

8:54:10 PM **ladydi2011**: I also believe that doing good is what all people should do. I believe that what you do will come back to you.

8:54:21 PM **bobjugant**: me too

8:54:33 PM **bobjugant**: we are thinking the same

8:54:35 PM **ladydi2011**: I believe it is not about speaking it, but being it.

8:54:50 PM **bobjugant**: thats it

8:54:54 PM **ladydi2011**: Yes my love, we are on the same page here. This is important.

8:55:07 PM **bobjugant**: *i* know love

8:55:15 PM **ladydi2011**: I love you so much baby

8:55:25 PM **bobjugant**: *i* love you too

8:55:29 PM **ladydi2011**: I am never letting you go in less you want to go

8:55:41 PM **bobjugant**: me too

8:55:51 PM **ladydi2011**: I would never want to keep you against your will

8:55:53 PM **bobjugant**: *i* will always be by you

8:56:06 PM **ladydi2011**: I want you with me because you want to be with me

8:56:12 PM **bobjugant**: *my heart is for you i promise*

8:56:31 PM **ladydi2011**: Baby, when I was in 7th grade I painted a picture

8:57:15 PM **bobjugant**: what did the picture say baby

8:57:15 PM **ladydi2011**: It said, "If you love something, set it free. If it comes back, it was yours, if it doesn't, it never was." I still believe this today...

8:57:42 PM **bobjugant**: *i* believe in that too honey

8:57:51 PM **ladydi2011**: Honey, I will never try to manipulate you...

8:58:01 PM **bobjugant**: what is yours will nver pass you by

8:58:04 PM **ladydi2011**: Kool...another thing we both believe

8:58:14 PM **ladydi2011**: I love that!

8:59:01 PM **bobjugant**: we will be together

8:59:32 PM **ladydi2011**: Yes baby...together forever.

8:59:47 PM **bobjugant**: *i* promise to love you

8:59:59 PM **ladydi2011**: Honey, when you come to the states to see me, how am I ever going to let you leave?

9:00:06 PM **bobjugant**: *i will never do anything to hurt you my love*

9:00:26 PM **ladydi2011**: I know you won't darling.

9:00:42 PM **bobjugant**: am happy you know that

9:00:59 PM **ladydi2011**: I do know this honey

9:01:06 PM **bobjugant**: *Baby i will be leaving here in 5 days time*

9:01:26 PM **ladydi2011**: 5 days...

9:01:43 PM **bobjugant**: yea baby

9:01:48 PM **ladydi2011**: Then you will be busy preparing for Chili

9:02:17 PM **bobjugant**: yea *i* have to go strt making arrangements

9:02:26 PM **ladydi2011**: What are your non-negotiables in a relationship?

9:02:53 PM **bobjugant**: *trust*

9:03:03 PM **bobjugant**: and understanding

9:03:19 PM **bobjugant**: and love

9:03:53 PM **bobjugant**: most inportantant factors to build any foundation for a good relationship

9:04:15 PM **bobjugant**: and thats what *i* have for you

9:04:32 PM **ladydi2011**: Thank you baby. I agree with all these

9:04:50 PM **ladydi2011**: I would also add in communication and commitment

9:05:23 PM **bobjugant**: yea committment its also very important

9:06:44 PM **ladydi2011**: Honey, I want to be able to tell you everything...I want you to be my best friend and confidant. This is important to me.

9:07:00 PM **ladydi2011**: I don't ever want any secrets between us.

9:07:24 PM **bobjugant**: *i will never hide anything from you*

9:07:31 PM **ladydi2011**: *I will never lie to you even if the truth hurts, I will tell you. I promise you this.*

9:07:52 PM **bobjugant**: *i promise you too baby*

9:07:54 PM **ladydi2011**: I will never hide anything from you either.

9:08:22 PM **ladydi2011**: We complement each other very well my love.

9:08:51 PM **bobjugant**: yea baby

9:09:12 PM **ladydi2011**: Honey, do you realize we fell in love before having the very important conversation that we just had?

9:09:52 PM **bobjugant**: yea abay

9:10:06 PM **bobjugant**: *our love was meant to be honey*

9:10:10 PM **ladydi2011**: So, I guess the ole saying of "the heart knows" is true...

9:10:53 PM **bobjugant**: *i* knew that along time

9:11:14 PM **bobjugant**: love has no hidding place

9:11:38 PM **ladydi2011**: Wow...I never thought of it like that. You are right my love.

9:12:20 PM **bobjugant**: because *i* love so much honey

9:12:34 PM **ladydi2011**: I know this is true.

9:12:48 PM **ladydi2011**: Honey, you are on the other side of the world

9:13:28 PM **ladydi2011**: The universe found a way for us to meet. How awesome is this?

9:13:49 PM **bobjugant**: thats true love

9:14:05 PM **ladydi2011**: You my dear, should not be single...

9:14:06 PM **bobjugant**: it must find its better half

9:14:13 PM **ladydi2011**: How are you still single?

9:14:44 PM **bobjugant**: *i* just found out you were the one *i* was waiting for

9:14:54 PM **ladydi2011**: Yes, the two halves made for each other must be brought together....you are my better half.

9:15:00 PM **bobjugant**: my heart beats for you

9:15:12 PM **ladydi2011**: My heart beats for you too baby..

9:15:18 PM **bobjugant**: you are my better half too

9:15:50 PM **ladydi2011**: Baby...you are in so much trouble when we meet. You do know this, right?

9:16:21 PM **bobjugant**: *i* will handle you baby

9:16:26 PM **ladydi2011**: Lol

9:16:37 PM **bobjugant**: *i* will give you so much joy baby

9:16:45 PM **ladydi2011**: The real question is can I handle you???

9:17:03 PM **bobjugant**: am not leaving no were

9:17:08 PM **bobjugant**: lol

9:18:15 PM **bobjugant**: you make me happy

9:18:28 PM **bobjugant**: your sweet talk

9:18:43 PM **bobjugant**: smile

9:18:50 PM **ladydi2011**: You make me happy too my love.

9:19:01 PM **ladydi2011**: Sweet talk???

9:19:05 PM **bobjugant**: me too darling

9:19:44 PM **bobjugant**: am still smiling because you make me feel good

9:20:28 PM **ladydi2011**: Bob, you deserve the best.

9:21:09 PM **ladydi2011**: I LOVE YOU AND ALWAYS WILL

9:22:31 PM **bobjugant**: *i* love you from the bottom of my heart

9:22:40 PM **bobjugant**: you are so sweet honey. *i* never want to loose you

9:22:53 PM **ladydi2011**: So are you baby.

9:23:15 PM **bobjugant**: what time is it over there
9:23:23 PM *ladydi2011*: 9:23pm
9:23:32 PM **bobjugant**: ok honey
9:23:48 PM *ladydi2011*: Oh no, it is 3:23 am there, isn't it?
9:23:53 PM **bobjugant**: when are you leaving your office
9:24:00 PM **bobjugant**: yea baby you gat it
9:24:13 PM *ladydi2011*: I have about three more hours of work to do
9:24:22 PM *ladydi2011*: Baby, you need to sleep
9:24:38 PM *ladydi2011*: See, when we are together, I totally lose track of time
9:24:44 PM *ladydi2011*: I am so sorry baby
9:25:56 PM **bobjugant**: yea thats my honey
9:26:10 PM **bobjugant**: *i will show you more love baby*
9:26:18 PM *ladydi2011*: Lol
9:26:39 PM **bobjugant**: *i* love you very much
9:26:40 PM *ladydi2011*: Ok my love. It is time to say good night...
9:26:49 PM **bobjugant**: yea baby
9:27:00 PM **bobjugant**: *i* wish *i* never had to go to bed
9:27:05 PM *ladydi2011*: I still didn't get what you sent to me earlier. Did you resend it?
9:27:18 PM **bobjugant**: but *i* have to
9:27:30 PM *ladydi2011*: Oh baby, when we are together, you might be saying something different....lol
9:27:36 PM **bobjugant**: baby it was a song am sure it expired
9:27:50 PM *ladydi2011*: I didn't get it baby
9:27:59 PM *ladydi2011*: What was the name of it?
9:28:12 PM **bobjugant**: *i* will send you another one honey
9:28:35 PM **bobjugant**: *my hearts beats for only you*
9:28:39 PM *ladydi2011*: Ok honey...did you ever get to listen to the song I sent you this morning?
9:28:48 PM **bobjugant**: *i* did. it was nice. *i* liked it
9:29:10 PM *ladydi2011*: Kool
9:29:11 PM **bobjugant**: *i* love you baby
9:29:32 PM *ladydi2011*: Good night my darling. Please meet me in your dreams and kiss me.
9:29:49 PM *ladydi2011*: Thank you for choosing to be with me tonight.
9:29:49 PM **bobjugant**: *i* will my love
9:30:06 PM **bobjugant**: anything for my love
9:30:21 PM **bobjugant**: anything you want *i* will do
9:30:38 PM *ladydi2011*: Right now, I want you to sleep my love.
9:30:46 PM *ladydi2011*: Please email me in the morning.
9:30:51 PM **bobjugant**: yea baby
9:31:02 PM *ladydi2011*: Please take care of you
9:31:03 PM **bobjugant**: sweet dreams my love
9:31:09 PM **bobjugant**: *i* will baby
9:31:11 PM *ladydi2011*: Sweet dreams darling
9:31:31 PM **bobjugant**: *i* will think about you while *i* sleep
9:31:54 PM **bobjugant**: good nyght my baby
9:32:00 PM **bobjugant**: kiss kiss
9:32:05 PM *ladydi2011*: Good night my prince
9:32:12 PM *ladydi2011*: Kisses and (((hugs)))

9:32:28 PM **bobjugant**: Good night my queen

From: ladydi2011@yahoo.com
To: Bob Jugant
Subject: Good night baby!
Sent: Thursday, May 10, 2012 2:33 AM

Hello, my darling,

Have a wonderful day, and think of me at least once! (I hear you saying, "What is she talking about at least once, she has to know I think about her more than this") (I hear you laughing again). Baby, trust is really important to me. I look at it like this...if you drop a vase and it breaks into pieces and you are able to glue it back together and it even holds water without leaking, you will still remember that it was broken every time you look at it, therefore it has changed forever. I also believe that when you don't believe (or stand) firmly for something, you fall for anything. Remember, my love, I am a perception management specialist. Everything in life is about perception. Everything! Baby, in my circle, I do not demand respect, but I command it because of who I am. People know I say what I mean and mean what I say. They know they can trust me. To me this is what integrity is. I wouldn't want to live my life any other way. Not to say I haven't made mistakes, because I have. I am not perfect either. However, I am a truly a good person who tries my best to live a good life and treat others with respect, love, fairness, understanding and kindness. I am also humble and forgiving. I try really hard not to judge because I learned years ago that whatever I judge will boomerang back into my life and much worse.

Your lady forever....

From: ladydi2011@yahoo.com
To: Bob Jugant
Subject: Hello
Sent: Thursday, May 10, 2012 9:07 AM

Hello, Honey. I am awake now. I wanted to say hello. I will be on client calls for the next two hours. I hope you are having a wonderful day. I haven't received an email from you so maybe your Internet isn't working again... Kisses and (((hugs)))

IM May 10, 2012 2:48:49 PM

2:48:49 PM **bobjugant**: Hello my love
2:49:16 PM **ladydi2011**: Hello honey
2:49:48 PM **ladydi2011**: How are you today?
2:50:48 PM **bobjugant**: Hope your day is going on smoothly
2:51:01 PM **ladydi2011**: It is...how is yours going?

2:51:17 PM **bobjugant**: Am fine baby
2:51:20 PM **ladydi2011**: Did you have dinner my love?
2:51:22 PM **bobjugant**: And you ?
2:51:31 PM **bobjugant**: Yes *i* did
2:51:38 PM **bobjugant**: Missing you
2:52:16 PM **ladydi2011**: I am missing you too...I am sure you can tell by all the emails I sent you...lol
2:52:34 PM **bobjugant**: Yes baby

2:52:39 PM **bobjugant**:
2:52:56 PM **bobjugant**: How is work?
2:53:33 PM **ladydi2011**: Work is going smoothly today. I got everything done last night to meet deadlines.
2:53:35 PM **bobjugant**: Network is a bit slow
2:53:57 PM **bobjugant**: Good girl
2:53:59 PM **ladydi2011**: Baby, I would like to sign out and sign back in to see if the camera will work.
2:54:18 PM **ladydi2011**: Do you think I will lose you if I do this?
2:54:24 PM **bobjugant**: Ok, me too
2:54:43 PM **ladydi2011**: Ok baby...see you right back here.
2:54:46 PM **bobjugant**: Lets sign out and sign in
2:54:55 PM **ladydi2011**: Ok
2:55:21 PM **bobjugant**: Give me a kiss

2:55:28 PM **bobjugant**:
2:57:25 PM **ladydi2011**: Kiss, kiss, kiss, kiss, kiss, kiss, kiss, kiss, kiss, kiss, kiss
2:57:50 PM **ladydi2011**: Baby, I got the camera on. I hope you can sign back in.

IM May 10, 2012 3:36:29 PM

3:36:29 PM **bobjugant**: hi baby
3:36:35 PM **bobjugant**: are you there?
3:36:48 PM **ladydi2011**: Hi baby. I am here
3:37:06 PM **bobjugant**: ok.. connection a bit slow here
3:37:07 PM **ladydi2011**: I am so glad you are back.
3:37:12 PM **bobjugant**: sorry *i* kept you waiting
3:37:35 PM **ladydi2011**: Can you see me baby?
3:38:56 PM **ladydi2011**: Honey, are you there?
3:40:27 PM **bobjugant**: yes *i* am
3:40:33 PM **bobjugant**: put on your cam
3:41:03 PM **ladydi2011**: Please accept my cam baby
3:41:20 PM **ladydi2011**: Can you see me honey?
3:41:20 PM **bobjugant**: wow....
3:41:27 PM **ladydi2011**: Wow, what?
3:42:09 PM **bobjugant**: love you
3:42:34 PM **ladydi2011**: It has stopped storming here, so my connection is better
3:42:48 PM **bobjugant**: good...
3:42:51 PM **ladydi2011**: Was your day busy today honey?
3:42:56 PM **bobjugant**: you looking so sweet baby

3:43:05 PM **bobjugant**: yes busy baby...
3:43:13 PM **bobjugant**: have a little back pain
3:43:19 PM **bobjugant**: really need a massage
3:43:22 PM **ladydi2011**: Thank you honey.
3:43:39 PM **ladydi2011**: Oh honey, I wish I were there. I would give you a good massage.
3:43:57 PM **bobjugant**: yes baby.. really need that
3:44:28 PM **ladydi2011**: Did you lift something really heavy today or bend the wrong way honey?
3:44:50 PM **bobjugant**: lifted something
3:44:57 PM **bobjugant**: but *i* will be ok...
3:45:09 PM **ladydi2011**: Not good honey.
3:45:24 PM **bobjugant**: *i* will be fine...
3:45:26 PM **ladydi2011**: Maybe some ice honey?

3:45:41 PM **bobjugant**: *your husband is a very strong man..* 😊
3:45:57 PM **ladydi2011**: You have to be fine...you told me last night you were going to keep me young...I know you will do this.

3:46:00 PM **bobjugant**: *strong in all aspect...* 😊
3:46:22 PM **ladydi2011**: Yes, my love. You are a strong man...
3:47:37 PM **ladydi2011**: I just now read where you are strong in all aspects. I know this is true...
3:47:54 PM **bobjugant**: thanks baby
3:48:05 PM **ladydi2011**: Honey, I love your smile on the picture of you in the ocean.
3:48:18 PM **ladydi2011**: I always want you to smile and be happy like this
3:49:02 PM **ladydi2011**: Is it 9:50 pm there honey?
3:49:32 PM **bobjugant**: yeah
3:49:46 PM **ladydi2011**: What did you have for dinner baby?
3:50:37 PM **bobjugant**: *chips and chiken*
3:50:53 PM **bobjugant**: whats your plan for the day?
3:51:52 PM **ladydi2011**: I need to do a little more work and then go to the grocery store later.
3:52:02 PM **ladydi2011**: What about you baby?
3:52:15 PM **ladydi2011**: Are you tired today?
3:52:52 PM **bobjugant**: honey am not too tired
3:53:10 PM **bobjugant**: just the bak pain dats all
3:53:23 PM **ladydi2011**: Baby, do you have anything like Bengay to put on your back?
3:53:29 PM **bobjugant**: but its going to be ok baby
3:53:39 PM **ladydi2011**: I so wish I were there...
3:53:44 PM **bobjugant**: yea
3:53:56 PM **ladydi2011**: I would kiss you and massage you and then you would sleep like a baby.
3:54:10 PM **bobjugant**: thanks honey you made my day
3:54:31 PM **bobjugant**: *i* love you so much honey
Break in Time
3:57:48 PM **ladydi2011**: Are you there baby?
3:59:03 PM **bobjugant**: the internet went off
3:59:18 PM **bobjugant**: it just reconeced baby
4:00:27 PM **bobjugant**: *i* love you so much honey and *i* missed you alot
4:00:45 PM **ladydi2011**: Can you still see my cam?
4:00:53 PM **bobjugant**: no baby
4:00:56 PM **ladydi2011**: I miss you too baby.
4:01:05 PM **bobjugant**: can you turn it on honey

4:01:13 PM **ladydi2011**: I just did baby

4:01:34 PM **bobjugant**: baby *i* was denied

4:01:54 PM **bobjugant**: re invite me

4:02:22 PM **ladydi2011**: What about now?

4:02:45 PM **bobjugant**: re invite baby

4:03:52 PM **bobjugant**: it says *i* do not have permission to view your cam

4:03:55 PM **ladydi2011**: What about now baby?

4:04:04 PM **bobjugant**: *guess its the network*

4:04:21 PM **bobjugant**: we can try later baby

4:04:31 PM **ladydi2011**: Try one more time my love

4:04:37 PM **bobjugant**: tomorrow *i* will know my faith regarding the contract

4:04:40 PM **bobjugant**: ok, can see you now

4:05:03 PM **ladydi2011**: Yay!

4:05:47 PM **ladydi2011**: Ok, please let me know as soon as you know

4:05:58 PM **ladydi2011**: I know you will get it honey.

4:05:59 PM **bobjugant**: yes baby, *i* will let you know

4:06:05 PM **bobjugant**: either good or bad

4:06:15 PM **bobjugant**: yes *i* am positive *i* will

4:06:33 PM **bobjugant**: with you by my side, we hope for the best...

4:06:38 PM **ladydi2011**: Oh baby....I heard something on the news today that they are now doing a lot of drilling for oil in the mid-western part of the states.

4:06:54 PM **bobjugant**: thanks love for coming into my life

4:06:56 PM **bobjugant**: oh yeah...

4:06:56 PM **ladydi2011**: I will always be by your side honey

4:07:13 PM **bobjugant**: thanks baby

4:07:43 PM **bobjugant**: love you so much

4:07:58 PM **ladydi2011**: I love you so much too darling

4:08:11 PM **ladydi2011**: I am looking forward to our life together

4:08:22 PM **bobjugant**: yes me too baby...

4:08:34 PM **bobjugant**: *best of both worlds...*

4:09:35 PM **ladydi2011**: Baby, I wish I could see you, like you can see me...

4:09:47 PM **ladydi2011**: I want to see you smile and laugh

4:10:21 PM **bobjugant**: yes me too...

4:10:23 PM **ladydi2011**: Honey, you will probably always travel a lot, is this correct?

4:11:12 PM **bobjugant**: *i* am planing to retire and invest more real estate

4:11:42 PM **ladydi2011**: Hold baby...phone just rang

4:11:49 PM **bobjugant**: ok love

4:12:37 PM **ladydi2011**: Baby, you get to watch me work

4:12:52 PM **bobjugant**: take your time

4:15:56 PM **ladydi2011**: Thanks baby

4:22:03 PM **bobjugant**: you done?

4:22:12 PM **ladydi2011**: I am done now

4:22:19 PM **ladydi2011**: Can you still see me?

4:22:33 PM **bobjugant**: yes baby

4:22:47 PM **ladydi2011**: This was for me to conduct a seven hour workshop in June

4:23:22 PM **bobjugant**: oh yeah...

4:24:10 PM **ladydi2011**: I am sorry our conversation was interrupted. I was waiting on this call

4:24:24 PM **bobjugant**: its ok darling
4:24:55 PM **ladydi2011**: So honey, you plan to retire and invest in more real estate?
4:25:07 PM **ladydi2011**: Do you own real estate now honey?
4:26:01 PM **bobjugant**: sorry hold a minute
4:26:07 PM **ladydi2011**: Ok...
4:27:21 PM **bobjugant**: yes *i* do in London?
4:27:47 PM **bobjugant**: you think its a nice ideal?
4:27:50 PM **bobjugant**: yes baby
4:27:59 PM **ladydi2011**: I do think it is a nice idea
4:28:08 PM **bobjugant**: how is the market over there?
4:28:17 PM **ladydi2011**: Terrible honey
4:28:22 PM **bobjugant**: really?
4:28:34 PM **ladydi2011**: But, you can buy low right now
4:28:55 PM **bobjugant**: what do you advice *i* invest into ?
4:29:21 PM **ladydi2011**: I just got my tax bill for my home and the value decreased a lot
4:29:46 PM **ladydi2011**: Actually land they are fracking. Do you know what this is?
4:29:58 PM **bobjugant**: wow.. seems the market is really terrible
4:30:25 PM **ladydi2011**: But, it is good to buy low and when it goes back up, sell high
4:30:31 PM **bobjugant**: yes *i* do
4:30:47 PM **bobjugant**: yes baby...
4:30:49 PM **ladydi2011**: I figured you would know what fracking is
4:30:58 PM **ladydi2011**: It is really big here now
4:31:12 PM **ladydi2011**: This is the land to buy and then lease it to the oil companies
4:31:29 PM **bobjugant**: oh yeah...
4:31:29 PM **ladydi2011**: Honey, I am sure you would know what to look for
4:31:40 PM **bobjugant**: yes baby *i* will ...
4:32:03 PM **bobjugant**: *i* like your hair..
4:32:10 PM **bobjugant**: love you so much..
4:32:13 PM **ladydi2011**: Really?
4:32:34 PM **bobjugant**: yeah its nice...
4:32:41 PM **bobjugant**: and its good on you...
4:33:04 PM **ladydi2011**: Thank you baby.
4:33:14 PM **ladydi2011**: Do you like short or long hair?
4:33:35 PM **bobjugant**: short...
4:33:42 PM **bobjugant**: short makes you look smart
4:33:47 PM **ladydi2011**: Kool
4:34:02 PM **ladydi2011**: Baby... I am smart!
4:34:29 PM **bobjugant**: thats my baby
4:35:01 PM **ladydi2011**: We make a good team baby
4:35:52 PM **bobjugant**: yes we will baby..best team ever
4:36:10 PM **ladydi2011**: Yeah baby
4:37:05 PM **ladydi2011**: Eventually I want to write books and speak
4:37:23 PM **bobjugant**: thats nice...
4:37:41 PM **bobjugant**: you will have time for yourself
4:37:56 PM **ladydi2011**: This has been my dream since I was a little girl...
4:38:15 PM **ladydi2011**: Yes baby and time to be with you. This is important to me.
4:38:40 PM **bobjugant**: thats my baby...

4:39:06 PM **ladydi2011**: So honey, can you make some money with the fracking?

4:39:54 PM **bobjugant**: yes...

4:40:12 PM **ladydi2011**: I know where all the hot beds are in the country.

4:43:02 PM **ladydi2011**: How is your back?

4:43:20 PM **bobjugant**: getting better..

4:43:30 PM **ladydi2011**: Are you fibbing to me so I don't worry?

4:43:57 PM **bobjugant**: haha.. no darling

4:44:09 PM **bobjugant**: *i* will be ok...

4:44:12 PM **ladydi2011**: Darling, I did something today

4:44:20 PM **ladydi2011**: I know you will....

4:44:32 PM **bobjugant**: whats that baby?

4:45:16 PM **ladydi2011**: I took my profile down from the site

4:46:05 PM **bobjugant**: ok baby.. why dont we both delete our profiles..

4:46:22 PM **ladydi2011**: I deleted mine baby

4:46:33 PM **bobjugant**: ok.. *i* will delete mine too

4:47:11 PM **ladydi2011**: My search is over.

4:47:31 PM **bobjugant**: yes baby...

4:47:41 PM **bobjugant**: two lucky stars..

4:47:44 PM **ladydi2011**: Yes baby...I am with you.

4:48:01 PM **bobjugant**: haha.. both of us...

4:48:15 PM **ladydi2011**: See, there is a great one liner

4:48:24 PM **ladydi2011**: You have many of them....

4:48:31 PM **ladydi2011**: I love them

4:48:42 PM **ladydi2011**: You got me this time!

4:48:51 PM **bobjugant**: haha..

4:49:35 PM **ladydi2011**: OH, HOW I WISH WE WERE TOGETHER IN PERSON RIGHT NOW

4:50:02 PM **bobjugant**: *yes baby, soon.. once am done*

4:50:11 PM **bobjugant**: your soft lips

4:50:24 PM **ladydi2011**: Yes my love

4:50:51 PM **bobjugant**: whisper into your ears

4:51:00 PM **bobjugant**: tell you sweet words

4:51:12 PM **ladydi2011**: What would you whisper to me baby?

4:51:19 PM **ladydi2011**: I am listening

4:51:29 PM **bobjugant**: whats you favorite colour of lingerie?

4:51:50 PM **ladydi2011**: My favorite color would be a deep blue

4:52:02 PM **bobjugant**: thats a secret...

4:52:08 PM **ladydi2011**: What is your favorite color of lingerie?

4:52:34 PM **ladydi2011**: A secret....so you will not tell me until you can actually do it, yes?

4:52:39 PM **bobjugant**: oh yeah.. candle lit in the bedroom...

4:52:54 PM **ladydi2011**: Yes baby....I love candles

4:52:55 PM **bobjugant**: yes until *i* am doing it..

4:53:14 PM **ladydi2011**: Atmosphere is important

4:53:15 PM **bobjugant**: kiss you head to your toe

4:53:23 PM **ladydi2011**: I like your style baby

4:53:37 PM **bobjugant**: cuddle you...

4:53:49 PM **bobjugant**: yes baby..

4:53:57 PM **ladydi2011**: I can feel your strong arms around me

4:54:29 PM **bobjugant**: pull your sexy lingerie slowly..
4:54:54 PM **bobjugant**: bring you closer, den start kissing your body...
4:55:12 PM **ladydi2011**: Baby, I have a client call that just came in
4:55:26 PM **bobjugant**: ok will look for you here in a couple hours
4:55:32 PM **ladydi2011**: Ok baby...till then
4:55:43 PM **bobjugant**: I love you
4:55:43 PM **ladydi2011**: I love you too

I tell him I trust him so he believes that I do. He tells me I have to trust him, but I do NOT trust him to do anything other than ask me for money. He tells me he will never leave me or leave me "alone" and that his heart is all mine, that he will always make me happy and he wishes to love me more and show me more love. He tells me he is very happy. Of course he is happy, he thinks he is chatting with a woman he can scam for money.

He is in for a big surprise!

 RED FLAGS

🚩 He then tells me to *never doubt* his love for me and that he will "make me young" and I will "feel" like a lady in love. He tells me *his heart is for me* and *promises to never do anything to hurt me*. He tells me that trust is important and that he will NEVER *hide anything* from me or *lie* to me. Then again, he said "our love was meant to be". These are all wonderful words and promises filled with honey that every woman will want to hear, but they are ALL LIES said to MANIPULATE. They are the words scammers use to get you to fall in love with them and trust them so they can get to your MONEY!

🚩 He once again tells me he is going to leave the dating site, but he didn't leave the first time, so I am sure he will not leave this time. He is still fishing for more women to scam. I am sure he is talking too many of us.

🚩 He tells me that his trip to Chile will *postpone* him coming to see me. A scammer will NEVER come to see you. You will *prepare* and *wait* and ALWAYS be disappointed.

🚩 Now he can't come on cam because supposedly his laptop isn't working because of the heat. A scammer will ALWAYS have an excuse to not come on cam unless he has a fake video to show you.

🚩 He wants me to feel special and important to him so he tells me he skipped a party to be with me. A scammer wants you to feel very special and important, but you are only important so he can get to your money. All you are is his "Client."

🚩 I had the feeling this man was falling for me and thinking about coming clean with me. His political question had nothing to do with politics. He was trying to find out if I was prejudiced against blacks. Since the door was opened, I emphasized the importance of *character* and *one's reputation* in hopes of penetrating his heart about what he is doing;

and if he was thinking about coming clean with me, I wanted to push him the rest of the way. Unlike other scammers, he never brought God into the scam, so I thought I would ask his religious beliefs. I think he has a reverence, so he would not use God to scam money.

🏴 He tells me he is leaving for Chile in five days. I know that when he is supposedly in Chile that he will "get in trouble" and need money...MY MONEY!

🏴 He tells me "my husband" is a *very strong man in all aspects*; he is talking about sexual stamina. Scammers are usually between the ages of 12 – 30, and they pride themselves on being very strong in bed.

IM May 10, 2012 6:04:54 PM

6:04:54 PM **bobjugant**: Hello darling
6:05:26 PM **ladydi2011**: Hello my love
6:05:31 PM **bobjugant**: I enjoyed the time we spent
6:05:38 PM **bobjugant**: I love you so much
6:05:48 PM **bobjugant**: You make me rock
6:05:49 PM **ladydi2011**: Me too
6:06:05 PM **bobjugant**: Thanks for being there
6:06:25 PM **ladydi2011**: This is a good thing, yes?
6:06:44 PM **bobjugant**: Baby did you like us being together
6:07:22 PM **ladydi2011**: Yes my love. Did you?
6:09:38 PM **bobjugant**: I did honey
6:10:15 PM **ladydi2011**: Honey, you make me happy
6:10:36 PM **ladydi2011**: How is your back now?
6:10:45 PM **bobjugant**: You too honey
6:11:03 PM **bobjugant**: Yea my back is getting better baby I took some pain reliver
6:12:24 PM **bobjugant**: I love you may princess
6:13:28 PM **ladydi2011**: I love you my prince...baby, you are the best!
6:13:31 PM **bobjugant**: *You are my darling wife*
6:13:49 PM **bobjugant**: You make me happy each day baby
6:15:03 PM **bobjugant**: Baby hold a minute
6:17:01 PM **bobjugant**: am back
6:17:08 PM **ladydi2011**: Baby, if I remember correctly you said on your profile that "you were thinking about loving someone" or something like this. Did you think you were going to find love on the site?
6:17:40 PM **bobjugant**: *i* was just trying my luck baby
6:17:55 PM **bobjugant**: and *i* follow my heart and *i* found you
6:18:17 PM **bobjugant**: **it was destined to be honey**
6:18:42 PM **ladydi2011**: We both got lucky honey!
6:18:48 PM **bobjugant**: yea am always lucky baby
6:19:21 PM **bobjugant**: and am lucky to have you my princess
6:19:21 PM **ladydi2011**: It all started with...hello pretty...do u wanna chat
6:19:47 PM **bobjugant**: yea twice
6:20:03 PM **ladydi2011**: I am lucky to have you in my life baby
6:20:12 PM **bobjugant**: me too darling

6:20:55 PM **ladydi2011**: I just went to your profile and you said "thinking of showing someone love"

6:21:08 PM **bobjugant**: *i* will be leaving here in 4 days baby

6:21:24 PM **ladydi2011**: Baby, that is all you said.

6:21:24 PM **bobjugant**: that was then untill *i* found you

6:21:46 PM **bobjugant**: you are my everything

6:21:58 PM **ladydi2011**: I know baby...

6:22:32 PM **ladydi2011**: I am the lucky woman who got to open the mysterious package

6:22:50 PM **ladydi2011**: Are you anxious to get home?

6:23:16 PM **bobjugant**: not baby

6:24:28 PM **bobjugant**: its work thats all and work takes me to differnt places u know

6:25:17 PM **ladydi2011**: I know. Do you like to travel?

6:25:37 PM **ladydi2011**: My work does the same for me.

6:26:04 PM **bobjugant**: baby to be a speaker you would find your self everywere

6:26:40 PM **ladydi2011**: What do you mean honey?

6:27:14 PM **bobjugant**: *i* meant your work takes you places

6:27:55 PM **ladydi2011**: Yes, in the states. I am published internationally.

6:28:13 PM **ladydi2011**: I want to be global...

6:28:22 PM **bobjugant**: thats kool

6:28:42 PM **bobjugant**: honey *i* left the site know

6:28:51 PM **ladydi2011**: Do you like to travel?

6:29:18 PM **bobjugant**: yea but not everytime

6:29:24 PM **ladydi2011**: That's cool! I like that.

6:29:43 PM **bobjugant**: its good to see new place you know

6:29:49 PM **bobjugant**: thanks honey

6:30:09 PM **ladydi2011**: Same here baby. I would like to have 7-8 speaking gigs a year

6:30:14 PM **bobjugant**: because you love me *i* can do anything for you

6:30:35 PM **ladydi2011**: I like seeing places but I like to be home

6:30:55 PM **bobjugant**: yea baby,,home is everything

6:31:07 PM **ladydi2011**: Baby, I feel the same way

6:31:08 PM **bobjugant**: but you gat to explore a little

6:31:41 PM **ladydi2011**: I am the same. I love to explore

6:32:14 PM **bobjugant**: *i* have to start working toward going to chile when *i* get back

6:32:16 PM **ladydi2011**: I am not a bar person baby. I would go with you but I don't go by myself.

6:32:39 PM **bobjugant**: you are my world honey

6:32:51 PM **ladydi2011**: I know you do. This is a big opportunity for you

6:32:51 PM **bobjugant**: *i* love you so much

6:33:07 PM **ladydi2011**: You are my world too baby

6:33:09 PM **bobjugant**: yea

6:33:58 PM **bobjugant**: *i* love you even more than you can imagine

6:35:11 PM **ladydi2011**: Baby, I know every day will be special

6:35:35 PM **ladydi2011**: I want to show you every day how much I love you

6:36:20 PM **ladydi2011**: Honey, you never told me your favorite color of lingerie. Please tell me.

6:37:26 PM **bobjugant**: oh sorry baby, purple

6:38:23 PM **ladydi2011**: Nice!

6:39:00 PM **bobjugant**: yea

6:39:11 PM **ladydi2011**: Baby, I am on my phone. I want to get back on the computer but I don't want to lose connection

6:39:30 PM **bobjugant**: honey are you at the office
6:39:32 PM *ladydi2011*: These buttons are so small
6:39:53 PM *ladydi2011*: Now in my dining room
6:40:38 PM **bobjugant**: have you eaten
6:41:13 PM *ladydi2011*: Baby, I am going to sign off my phone and sign back on my computer.
6:42:00 PM **bobjugant**: ok baby
6:42:28 PM *ladydi2011*: Ok my love, I am now on my computer
6:42:34 PM *ladydi2011*: Much easier to type
6:42:49 PM *ladydi2011*: We didn't lose connection...yay!
6:44:00 PM **bobjugant**: are you on your computer know
6:44:17 PM *ladydi2011*: I am. I just invited you to view my cam
6:44:33 PM **bobjugant**: yea *i* see my baby know
6:44:46 PM *ladydi2011*: Cool
6:44:49 PM **bobjugant**: she makes me so happy and smilling
6:45:09 PM *ladydi2011*: I had breakfast and lunch but have not had dinner yet
6:45:18 PM **bobjugant**: baby you are very beautiful
6:45:34 PM *ladydi2011*: I think I am going to make some dill lime chicken
6:45:42 PM *ladydi2011*: Thank you baby
6:45:53 PM **bobjugant**: oh sounds sweet
6:45:54 PM *ladydi2011*: You are very handsome
6:46:06 PM *ladydi2011*: Honey, I Googled your name last night
6:46:17 PM *ladydi2011*: I saw your picture on Linked in
6:46:23 PM *ladydi2011*: I like you in a suit
6:46:33 PM **bobjugant**: lol
6:46:42 PM **bobjugant**: really
6:46:50 PM *ladydi2011*: The first time I saw you in a suit
6:46:51 PM **bobjugant**: aww
6:47:08 PM **bobjugant**: *i* like that baby
6:47:20 PM *ladydi2011*: It is the truth
6:47:42 PM *ladydi2011*: You are so sexy baby
6:47:56 PM **bobjugant**: thanks honey
6:48:05 PM *ladydi2011*: I am the luckiest woman in the world
6:48:13 PM **bobjugant**: you are baby and *i* will show you alot of love and happiness
6:48:51 PM **bobjugant**: kiss kiss
6:49:07 PM *ladydi2011*: I have waited a long time my love, by choice...now I know why
6:49:17 PM *ladydi2011*: Kisses and (((hugs)))
6:50:45 PM *ladydi2011*: Did you laugh where I thought you would laugh in my one email?
6:51:30 PM **bobjugant**: you got me right ther honey
6:51:42 PM *ladydi2011*: Cool
6:51:46 PM **bobjugant**: lol
6:51:58 PM **bobjugant**: *i* like your smile [image on opposing page]
6:52:11 PM *ladydi2011*: Thank you baby. You make me smile
6:52:32 PM **bobjugant**: *i* smile when your laughing
6:52:57 PM *ladydi2011*: I smile when your laughing
6:53:24 PM *ladydi2011*: Baby, I am going to buy a calling card so I can call you
6:53:42 PM **bobjugant**: yea baby
6:53:49 PM **bobjugant**: *i* like dat

6:54:19 PM **ladydi2011**: I thought maybe you would like this.
6:54:29 PM **ladydi2011**: I want to hear your sexy voice
6:55:42 PM **bobjugant**: *i* will send you my souyhafrican number ok
6:56:10 PM **ladydi2011**: Baby, I called AT &T the other day and it is free if you IM me from the computer
6:56:26 PM **ladydi2011**: We can also IM blackberry to blackberry for free

6:56:45 PM **bobjugant**: yea baby
6:57:10 PM **bobjugant**: *am not with a blackberry over here baby*
6:59:01 PM **ladydi2011**: What?
6:59:25 PM **ladydi2011**: What, the number?
6:59:30 PM **bobjugant**: *i dont know the number off heart baby*
6:59:46 PM **bobjugant**: *i will send it to you in the morning*
7:00:36 PM **bobjugant**: *i dont have the number in my head honey*
7:00:50 PM **bobjugant**: *i will send it to you shortly*
7:00:59 PM **ladydi2011**: Ok...honey, please teach me all this international stuff. I learn quickly
7:01:06 PM **ladydi2011**: Ok...when you can
7:01:19 PM **bobjugant**: *i* have to call their customer care or something
7:01:34 PM **bobjugant**: ok honey *i* will
7:01:38 PM **ladydi2011**: Oh, ok...did you buy a disposable phone?

7:01:51 PM **bobjugant**: yea baby

7:02:05 PM **ladydi2011**: That is what I did when I was in Africa

7:02:23 PM **bobjugant**: really

7:02:34 PM **bobjugant**: we think alike darling

7:02:46 PM **ladydi2011**: Yes, we sure do...

7:03:09 PM **bobjugant**: *i* love you more and more honey

7:03:18 PM **ladydi2011**: Baby, I love being with you

7:03:42 PM **ladydi2011**: You loving me more and more is a good thing. I like dat!

7:04:03 PM **bobjugant**: thanks honey

7:04:13 PM **ladydi2011**: Baby, do you like animals?

7:04:48 PM **bobjugant**: *i* do honey

7:05:00 PM **ladydi2011**: I have one inside cat and four outdoor cats

7:05:12 PM **bobjugant**: really

7:05:19 PM **bobjugant**: dats great baby

7:05:31 PM **ladydi2011**: They are all strays

7:05:36 PM **bobjugant**: *i* will meet them soon baby

7:05:56 PM **ladydi2011**: Yes baby you will. They are all females...and all fixed!

7:05:59 PM **bobjugant**: smile for me my love

7:06:09 PM **bobjugant**: *i* like that

7:06:24 PM **bobjugant**: you are the angel of my heart

7:06:35 PM **bobjugant**: *i* can see it honey

7:06:45 PM **bobjugant**: what its name baby

7:06:55 PM **ladydi2011**: Her name is sweetie

7:07:05 PM **bobjugant**: sound nice

7:07:08 PM **ladydi2011**: I had a full breed main coon for 16 years

7:07:23 PM **ladydi2011**: I had to put her to sleep and I was heart broken

7:07:42 PM **ladydi2011**: The day I buried her, Sweetie was in the woods watching me

7:08:03 PM **ladydi2011**: Usually when I see a cat, I say, here kitty, kitty

7:08:08 PM **ladydi2011**: Not with her

7:08:26 PM **ladydi2011**: I felt the sweetness of her spirit and said come here sweetie

7:08:39 PM **ladydi2011**: It took me 24 hours to get her inside with me

7:08:57 PM **ladydi2011**: She has been my shadow ever since and she took away my pain instantly

7:09:11 PM **bobjugant**: dats nice honey

7:09:13 PM **ladydi2011**: She is so sweet honey. She loves so unconditionally

7:09:20 PM **ladydi2011**: She was a gift.

7:09:35 PM **ladydi2011**: Sorry for the long story

7:09:52 PM **bobjugant**: baby you tired

7:10:05 PM **ladydi2011**: No honey

7:10:10 PM **bobjugant**: anything for you honey

7:10:12 PM **ladydi2011**: Just needed to stretch

7:10:18 PM **bobjugant**: yea

7:10:29 PM **ladydi2011**: I could also use a massage

7:10:34 PM **ladydi2011**: My neck is stiff

7:10:50 PM **ladydi2011**: The chiropractor had to adjust it the other day

7:11:01 PM **ladydi2011**: I think it is from being on the phone a lot

7:11:23 PM **ladydi2011**: Baby, what color nail polish do you like on a woman?

7:11:49 PM **bobjugant**: what colour do you put on

7:12:36 PM **ladydi2011**: It depends....when I speak, I get a french manicure done. I really think it is classy and goes with everything I wear

7:12:48 PM **ladydi2011**: Other times I wear red and sometimes pink

7:13:03 PM **bobjugant**: *i* like red

7:13:07 PM **ladydi2011**: My nails are real, not acrylic

7:13:27 PM **bobjugant**: sexy red

7:13:33 PM **ladydi2011**: They always break in the spring and fall so they are a little short right now

7:13:43 PM **ladydi2011**: Baby, I have sexy red....

7:13:53 PM **ladydi2011**: Do you like long nails?

7:14:05 PM **ladydi2011**: Not dragon lady long???

7:14:23 PM **bobjugant**: a little bit

7:14:40 PM **bobjugant**: can *i* see yours honey

7:15:04 PM **ladydi2011**: Sure...I am going to paint them tonight

7:15:35 PM **bobjugant**: bay theyre plane

7:15:55 PM **ladydi2011**: Yes, now because I don't have any polish on them

7:15:56 PM **bobjugant**: red *i* guess

7:16:14 PM **ladydi2011**: I had to let them breathe for a week

7:16:23 PM **ladydi2011**: Tonight I am going to pain them red

7:16:37 PM **ladydi2011**: Tomorrow you can tell me what you think

7:16:43 PM **ladydi2011**: Deal?

7:16:52 PM **bobjugant**: yea baby

7:17:05 PM **bobjugant**: they will look good on you baby

7:17:13 PM **ladydi2011**: I am enjoying getting to know what you like

7:17:37 PM **ladydi2011**: You can tell me tomorrow. Please be honest.

7:18:13 PM **ladydi2011**: Baby, are you tired?

7:18:25 PM **bobjugant**: *i* will baby

7:18:32 PM **bobjugant**: *am a honest man*

7:18:59 PM **ladydi2011**: Thank you. I appreciate your honesty

7:19:29 PM **bobjugant**: am all yours darling

7:19:32 PM **ladydi2011**: Honey, from your pictures, your eyes look brown...are they brown or a hazel?

7:20:11 PM **bobjugant**: not brown

7:20:15 PM **bobjugant**: its hazle

7:20:28 PM **ladydi2011**: Cool

7:20:32 PM **ladydi2011**: Mine change from blue to grey

7:20:52 PM **ladydi2011**: Honey, is your hair thick?

7:21:17 PM **bobjugant**: thick

7:21:34 PM **bobjugant**: a little

7:21:49 PM **ladydi2011**: Mine is really thick

7:22:25 PM **bobjugant**: *i* saw it on de cam honey

7:22:39 PM **ladydi2011**: It is natural wavy too

7:23:12 PM **ladydi2011**: Honey, when you are home and not working, what do you like to do?

7:23:34 PM **bobjugant**: *i* read books most times

7:23:51 PM **ladydi2011**: What kind of books?

7:24:11 PM **bobjugant**: history books

7:24:24 PM **bobjugant**: *i* like reading

7:24:24 PM **ladydi2011**: Cool...

7:24:37 PM **ladydi2011**: I like reading too

7:25:03 PM **bobjugant**: I know you do baby because you are a speaker

7:25:15 PM **ladydi2011**: My third bedroom has an entire wall of books. My godson calls it the library

7:25:25 PM **ladydi2011**: Yes my love

7:25:53 PM **ladydi2011**: My godson is coming to stay with me the beginning of June for a week

7:26:22 PM **bobjugant**: dats great

7:26:33 PM **ladydi2011**: We will go to the zoo, bowling, riding go carts, miniature golf, the movies and play a lot of games

7:26:38 PM **ladydi2011**: He is 14 now

7:27:00 PM **ladydi2011**: He likes visiting me

7:27:16 PM **ladydi2011**: I can't wait for you to meet everyone

7:27:30 PM **ladydi2011**: They will love you baby

7:27:52 PM **bobjugant**: *i* am looking forward to that baby

7:28:01 PM **bobjugant**: meeting the whole family

7:28:07 PM **ladydi2011**: Yes my love

7:28:27 PM **ladydi2011**: I will want you to myself for a couple days before I share you

7:28:32 PM **bobjugant**: *i* love you baby

7:28:40 PM **ladydi2011**: I love you too baby

7:28:56 PM **ladydi2011**: Please tell me if I am dreaming

7:29:06 PM **bobjugant**: you are not baby

7:29:14 PM **bobjugant**: its real honey

7:29:16 PM **ladydi2011**: Yay!!!

7:29:21 PM **bobjugant**: am all yours

7:29:41 PM **ladydi2011**: Forever and ever

Break in Time

7:40:17 PM **bobjugant**: hey baby

7:40:28 PM **ladydi2011**: Hey baby

7:40:36 PM **ladydi2011**: Did you get kicked off

7:40:48 PM **bobjugant**: *what chat is dis honey*

7:40:57 PM **bobjugant**: lol

7:41:16 PM **ladydi2011**: What baby?

7:41:19 PM **bobjugant**: like we are chatting offline

7:41:40 PM **ladydi2011**: Can you see my cam?

7:41:49 PM **bobjugant**: no *i* cant

7:43:14 PM **bobjugant**: is not cumming on know

7:43:18 PM **ladydi2011**: I am too afraid to sign out. I don't want to lose you

7.43.28 PM **bobjugant**: you wont bahy

7:43:46 PM **ladydi2011**: Ok. Let me sign out and sign back in

7:43:57 PM **bobjugant**: ok baby

7:44:09 PM **ladydi2011**: I love you......

7:44:25 PM **bobjugant**: *i* love you too

IM May 11, 2012 2:32:44 PM

2:32:44 PM **bobjugant**: hey baby

2:37:29 PM **ladydi2011**: Hi baby...please hold

2:38:36 PM **bobjugant**: ok
2:38:46 PM **bobjugant**: take your time baby
2:40:41 PM **ladydi2011**: How are you honey?
2:41:58 PM **bobjugant**: am doing good honey
2:42:42 PM **bobjugant**: honey did you receive myy evard
2:43:02 PM **ladydi2011**: I did
2:43:23 PM **bobjugant**: nice
2:43:37 PM **ladydi2011**: It made me smile...
2:44:17 PM **bobjugant**: honey *i* have to be back here in less than 20mins
2:44:33 PM **ladydi2011**: back where my love?
2:45:02 PM **bobjugant**: *i* have to speak to my agent
2:45:06 PM **bobjugant**: hold please
2:45:24 PM **ladydi2011**: Ok baby. Please take your time

IM May 11, 2012 3:13:15 PM Continued

3:13:15 PM **bobjugant**: hello baby
3:13:27 PM **ladydi2011**: Hello honey
3:13:35 PM **ladydi2011**: How did it go with your agent?
3:13:48 PM **bobjugant**: brb
3:13:54 PM **ladydi2011**: Ok
3:15:11 PM **bobjugant**: honey am here
3:15:42 PM **ladydi2011**: So, how did it go baby?
3:15:51 PM **bobjugant**: *i* just finish speaking with kelvin
3:15:58 PM **ladydi2011**: And
3:16:15 PM **bobjugant**: he said *i* got it
3:16:29 PM **ladydi2011**: Yeah baby! You rock....
3:16:32 PM **bobjugant**: am happy baby
3:16:39 PM **bobjugant**: for real
3:16:39 PM **ladydi2011**: I am sure you are
3:16:52 PM **ladydi2011**: I am happy for you and proud of you
3:16:59 PM **bobjugant**: smiling
3:17:07 PM **ladydi2011**: So, when do you leave for Chile?
3:17:37 PM **bobjugant**: thanks alot for supporting me
3:17:47 PM **bobjugant**: I love you
3:17:49 PM **ladydi2011**: Of course my love
3:17:55 PM **ladydi2011**: I love you too
3:18:09 PM **ladydi2011**: I will always support you and your dreams baby
3:18:19 PM **bobjugant**: you are indeed an angel
3:18:27 PM **ladydi2011**: You are my prince
3:19:06 PM **bobjugant**: honey he said *i* have 10 days to be in chille
3:20:04 PM **bobjugant**: and *i* have 3 more days here
3:20:08 PM **ladydi2011**: To get to Chile?
3:20:33 PM **ladydi2011**: How much time will you need to prepare for Chile?
3:20:58 PM **bobjugant**: *i* have less than 8 days baby
3:21:12 PM **ladydi2011**: You can do it baby

3:21:35 PM **bobjugant**: YEA I WILL
3:21:40 PM **ladydi2011**: We might have to cut back on our time together so you can
3:22:34 PM **bobjugant**: ohh the job in chille is going to be very hectic
3:24:08 PM **bobjugant**: *i* love you honey
3:24:18 PM **ladydi2011**: I am SO proud of you baby
3:24:22 PM **bobjugant**: you are my world
3:24:36 PM **bobjugant**: thanks a lot
3:24:42 PM **ladydi2011**: Baby, are you done work now?
3:25:19 PM **bobjugant**: first time *i* would be going to chille you know
3:25:28 PM **ladydi2011**: How exciting
3:25:35 PM **ladydi2011**: Can *i* go in your suitcase
3:25:38 PM **ladydi2011**: Please, please...I have never been
3:26:02 PM **bobjugant**: but *i* would meet up some people soon
3:26:05 PM **ladydi2011**: Do you work tomorrow and Sunday too?
3:26:39 PM **bobjugant**: *i* might cut my stay here you know
3:26:55 PM **ladydi2011**: I am having dinner with my friend tonight.
3:27:16 PM **ladydi2011**: Can you cut your stay there without it affecting you?
3:27:28 PM **bobjugant**: thinking of leaving here on sunday
3:27:33 PM **ladydi2011**: Ok
3:27:37 PM **bobjugant**: yea baby
3:28:03 PM **bobjugant**: we should get backonline later
3:28:11 PM **ladydi2011**: I need your phone number so I can call you
3:28:16 PM **bobjugant**: after you had your dinner
3:28:27 PM **ladydi2011**: I would really like that.
3:29:13 PM **ladydi2011**: How about if I call you when I get home.
3:29:59 PM **bobjugant**: ok baby
3:30:46 PM **bobjugant**: *+447024091034*
3:30:48 PM **bobjugant**: have it
3:31:00 PM **bobjugant**: *my uk number*
3:31:00 PM **ladydi2011**: You rock!
3:31:12 PM **bobjugant**: haha.. you welcome
3:31:45 PM **bobjugant**: *its an international number, had to roam so i can pick up calls here*
3:31:56 PM **ladydi2011**: Baby, I bought phone cards to call Africa. Is this an African number?
3:32:05 PM **bobjugant**: hope to hear you soon..
3:32:14 PM **bobjugant**: its my uk number
3:33:18 PM **ladydi2011**: I am having problems finding calling cards for the UK
3:33:26 PM **bobjugant**: ok baby
3:33:39 PM **ladydi2011**: *I thought you had a disposable phone while in Africa. My error*
3:34:04 PM **bobjugant**: *yes i taught about that, but needed this number so i could be reached anytime*
3:34:17 PM **bobjugant**: *i* think *i* will have to get a local number here tomorrow
3:34:18 PM **ladydi2011**: Most of them are for Africa and India
3:34:25 PM **bobjugant**: so you can still call me with that..
3:34:52 PM **ladydi2011**: Tonight I can reach you at the number you just gave me, right?
3:35:01 PM **bobjugant**: yes baby
3:35:13 PM **ladydi2011**: you are teaching me new things my love
3:35:20 PM **ladydi2011**: I love to learn new things

3:35:25 PM **bobjugant**: haha...new experience

3:35:49 PM **ladydi2011**: You are the best boyfriend in the whole world!!!

3:35:57 PM **ladydi2011**: Yes, new experiences..

3:36:03 PM **bobjugant**: thanks honey....

3:36:21 PM **bobjugant**: you the sweetest lady ever

3:36:30 PM **ladydi2011**: Thank you baby

3:36:43 PM **ladydi2011**: I love you...

3:36:51 PM **bobjugant**: love you more...

3:37:07 PM **ladydi2011**: So, maybe by mid to late June I will be able to be with you in person....

3:37:19 PM **bobjugant**: yes baby...

3:37:32 PM **ladydi2011**: Whooooooooo hoooooooooooooooo!

3:37:36 PM **bobjugant**: wow... it going to be crazy......

3:37:43 PM **bobjugant**: yes baby!!!!!!!!!!!!!!!!!!!!!!!!!!!!!!

3:37:53 PM **ladydi2011**: Yes, your life is going to be crazy

3:38:02 PM **bobjugant**: *hmmmmmm cant wait for the first warm hug and kiss*

3:38:14 PM **ladydi2011**: When you get with me, I will make sure to rejuvenate and relax you

3:38:35 PM **bobjugant**: thats my baby...

3:38:59 PM **ladydi2011**: I told you that you found a woman who will spoil you.

3:39:14 PM **ladydi2011**: If you don't want to be spoiled, you better run now baby

3:39:29 PM **bobjugant**: hahahahahahaha...

3:39:35 PM **ladydi2011**: Lol

3:40:06 PM **bobjugant**: love you baby...

3:40:16 PM **ladydi2011**: I love you more honey

3:40:24 PM **bobjugant**: go get ready honey

3:40:27 PM **ladydi2011**: So, how was your day today?

3:40:50 PM **bobjugant**: my day was nice... and now more happy

3:40:56 PM **ladydi2011**: Cool

3:41:02 PM **bobjugant**: after *i* just got a positive news

3:41:10 PM **ladydi2011**: Will you have some drinks tonight to celebrate?

3:41:52 PM **bobjugant**: just a little... baby lets celebrate and have a toast...

3:42:04 PM **bobjugant**: you have a wine at the office?

3:42:31 PM **ladydi2011**: That is exactly what I was thinking. We will do this when we get together after dinner

3:43:23 PM **bobjugant**: ok baby, when you get back

3:43:27 PM **bobjugant**: love you

3:43:47 PM **ladydi2011**: Yes, when I get back

3:44:08 PM **bobjugant**: ok baby

3:44:11 PM **bobjugant**: we talk more

3:44:15 PM **ladydi2011**: Baby, when you have a sip of your first drink tonight I want you to see my face and hear my voice whispering in your ear telling you that "I love you and am proud of you"

3:44:15 PM **bobjugant**: love you

3:44:46 PM **bobjugant**: *i* will honey

3:45:10 PM **bobjugant**: thanks

3:45:10 PM **bobjugant**: *i* will think about you all through

3:45:16 PM **ladydi2011**: I am so happy to be your woman

3:45:34 PM **ladydi2011**: Ok. I am going to go get ready

3:45:44 PM **ladydi2011**: I will call you when I get home

3:45:48 PM **ladydi2011**: Oh baby
3:45:50 PM **bobjugant**: its ok
3:45:54 PM **ladydi2011**: I just had a thought
3:46:17 PM **ladydi2011**: Can I call the hotel
3:46:33 PM **ladydi2011**: Then I could talk to you on the landline since my calling card is for Africa
3:47:35 PM **ladydi2011**: Are you there honey?
3:48:20 PM **bobjugant**: yes *i* am here
3:48:29 PM **ladydi2011**: Please give me the hotel number and your room number
3:48:32 PM **bobjugant**: sorry *i* had to get water to drink
3:48:39 PM **bobjugant**: its a service flat baby
3:48:55 PM **ladydi2011**: What is a service flat baby?
3:49:03 PM **bobjugant**: tomorrow *i* get a local number or talk to the manager
3:49:11 PM **bobjugant**: so you can reach me on it
3:50:08 PM **bobjugant**: serviced apartment
3:50:14 PM **ladydi2011**: Ok...got it.
3:50:32 PM **ladydi2011**: Now you taught me 2 new things today
3:50:42 PM **ladydi2011**: Ok, my love. Have fun tonight
3:50:48 PM **bobjugant**: hahahaha
3:50:55 PM **ladydi2011**: I will miss you while we are apart
3:51:09 PM **bobjugant**: apart from your boy ffriend
3:51:15 PM **bobjugant**: *am your teacher....wink*
3:51:56 PM **ladydi2011**: Teach me baby!!!
3:52:10 PM **bobjugant**: *i* love you honey...
3:52:25 PM **bobjugant**: *i will teach you so many new things baby*
3:52:30 PM **ladydi2011**: I love you too baby
3:52:45 PM **ladydi2011**: I can't wait...I will teach you new things too!
3:52:46 PM **bobjugant**: *i* gat to go out soon baby
3:53:03 PM **ladydi2011**: Ok honey, go get ready.
3:53:17 PM **ladydi2011**: Kisses, kisses and more kisses
3:53:33 PM **bobjugant**: kiss kiss
3:53:36 PM **ladydi2011**: (((hugs))) (((hugs))) and more (((hugs)))
3:53:51 PM **ladydi2011**: Once again, congrats baby
3:54:09 PM **bobjugant**: *i* cant wait for us to be together
3:54:15 PM **ladydi2011**: I can see you smiling...
3:54:20 PM **bobjugant**: talk to you soon baby
3:54:30 PM **ladydi2011**: Tonight

From: Ladydi2011@yahoo.com
To: Bob Jugant
Subject: Congratulations
Sent: Friday, May 11, 2012 3:59 PM
Baby...
Congratulations...I am so proud of you!

Message on E-Card to me from Bob- 5/11/12

My love for you reaches past the furthest planet, Burns stronger then the sun, Will last longer than eternity. For you I'd travel to the moon and back, Climb the tallest tower, Fight the largest army. You are my friend, My companion, My lover My soul mate. You are my reason to live, My elixir of life, Without you I'm nothing, With you I'm a superhero. bob loves you so much and will always be with you

---

From: bobjugant@yahoo.com
To: ladydi
Subject: Re: Congratulations
Sent: Friday, May 11, 2012 6:56 PM

thanks honey you made my day................am at the apartment know...its 1 am over here…

From: ladydi2011@yahoo.com
To: Bob Jugant
Subject: Re: Congratulations
Sent: Friday, May 11, 2012 7:08 PM

Hi Baby, just got to dinner. Do you want me to call you and wake you when I get in? I love you.

From: bobjugant@yahoo.com
To: ladydi
Subject: Re: Congratulations
Sent: Friday, May 11, 2012 7:15 PM

honey that would be so sweet of you..*i* look forward to hear your voice..call me when your done

---

From: ladydi2011@yahoo.com
To: Bob Jugant
Subject: please go on line honey...I am so sad and so happy
Sent: Saturday, May 12, 2012 12:07 AM

Hey, my love! *I bought the calling card and it will call the United Kingdom but not your number. I spoke with customer service and they said that all cell phone numbers starting with 6, 7 or 8 have local government restrictions and can not be reached from the United States*... I so want to hear your voice and I can't. I am disappointed and I know you are disappointed. :(Please come on line, Darling. I really need to talk to you, Baby. I love you....forever and always.

IM May 12, 2012 4:04:10 AM

4:04:10 AM **bobjugant**: honey
4:04:46 AM **bobjugant**: *i* saw your email when *i* woke up
4:05:12 AM **bobjugant**: *i* know you must be sleeping by know
4:05:25 AM **bobjugant**: *i* love you baby
4:05:38 AM **ladydi2011**: Hi baby
4:05:51 AM **ladydi2011**: Baby, are you still there
4:06:03 AM **bobjugant**: *i* am
4:06:11 AM **bobjugant**: aww
4:06:19 AM **ladydi2011**: Did you get all my emails?
4:06:42 AM **bobjugant**: am about going to the rig honey
4:07:00 AM **ladydi2011**: *Baby...I tried to call and I can't get through*
4:07:10 AM **ladydi2011**: Can you see me baby?
4:07:51 AM **bobjugant**: *i* can darling
4:08:04 AM **bobjugant**: what time is it over there
4:08:31 AM **bobjugant**: *i* love you honey
4:08:56 AM **ladydi2011**: *Darling, I received beautiful flowers from you tonight when I got home. Thank you so much my love* [images on opposite page]
4:08:57 AM **bobjugant**: *i* yhought about you all through the night
4:09:04 AM **ladydi2011**: Me too
4:09:17 AM **ladydi2011**: It is 4:00 am
4:09:33 AM **ladydi2011**: I have been painting my nails while waiting for you to wake up
4:10:17 AM **bobjugant**: your welcome baby
4:10:43 AM **bobjugant**: really
4:11:01 AM **ladydi2011**: *Honey, how did you get my address?*
4:11:04 AM **bobjugant**: you have the red on right
4:11:06 AM **ladydi2011**: You so surprised me
4:11:16 AM **ladydi2011**: Yes, my love I have red on
4:11:22 AM **bobjugant**: anything for my honey
4:11:40 AM **ladydi2011**: Honey, my entire room smells so good because of the flowers
4:11:53 AM **bobjugant**: honey *i* cant see you anymore
4:12:01 AM **ladydi2011**: Thank you for the beautiful surprise. I so appreciate you!

Dozen of pink roses with white lilies in a crystal vase with a card that says *"The Ring Will Be Next...I Love You Bob"*, a huge box of chocolates and a Teddy Bear. [images in on opposing page]

4:12:36 AM **ladydi2011**: I just invited you again baby

4:12:43 AM **ladydi2011**: Can you see me now?

4:12:49 AM **bobjugant**: no, try again

4:13:29 AM **ladydi2011**: What about now?

4:14:11 AM **bobjugant**: *i* can see you baby

4:14:22 AM **ladydi2011**: Honey, did you get the picture I sent you tonight?

4:14:30 AM **bobjugant**: can *i* see the flowers?

4:15:55 AM **bobjugant**: hope you like it

4:16:16 AM **ladydi2011**: I love them baby. They are beautiful!

4:16:29 AM **ladydi2011**: You have exquisite taste my love

4:16:49 AM **bobjugant**: you are beautiful

4:17:03 AM **ladydi2011**: Thank you my love

4:17:13 AM **bobjugant**: *i* miss you

4:18:15 AM **ladydi2011**: How was your night honey?

4:18:36 AM **ladydi2011**: *Baby...so, the ring will be next????*

4:18:57 AM **bobjugant**: *yes it will*

4:19:13 AM **bobjugant**: *a diamond ring for my woman*

4:19:34 AM **bobjugant**: honey *i* cant see you again

4:19:37 AM **ladydi2011**: I love you darling...

4:19:44 AM **bobjugant**: *i* have lost the feed

4:20:26 AM **ladydi2011**: I just invited you again, can you see me?

4:20:48 AM **bobjugant**: yea baby

4:21:06 AM **ladydi2011**: Baby...you are the best!

4:21:19 AM **ladydi2011**: *Honey, why can't I call into your phone?*

4:21:37 AM **bobjugant**: *i* dont kne baby

4:22:03 AM **bobjugant**: *i think i have to get a local number to day*

4:22:11 AM **bobjugant**: yea baby

4:22:24 AM **ladydi2011**: Ok. If you can, that would be great!

4:23:17 AM **bobjugant**: Hold on baby

4:23:19 AM **ladydi2011**: I so wanted to hear your voice and thank you for the flowers

4:23:23 AM **ladydi2011**: Ok honey

4:27:30 AM **bobjugant**: Baby am here

4:27:38 AM **bobjugant**: I missed you alot

4:27:49 AM **bobjugant**: Hope you like the flowers

4:27:56 AM **ladydi2011**: I missed you a lot too!

4:28:27 AM **bobjugant**: *The internet is low*

4:28:47 AM **ladydi2011**: It will now not let me connect you into my cam in less I sign out

4:29:00 AM **ladydi2011**: I don't want to do this because I am afraid of losing you

4:29:56 AM **bobjugant**: Baby, am with you honey

4:30:29 AM **bobjugant**: I will always be with you

4:30:34 AM **ladydi2011**: How was your night baby?

4:30:58 AM **bobjugant**: It was splendid

4:31:05 AM **bobjugant**: Tot of you all night

4:31:24 AM **ladydi2011**: I thought of you all night too

4:31:56 AM **ladydi2011**: Baby, I also had three glasses of wine tonight while waiting for you because I wanted to toast to your success

4:32:27 AM **bobjugant**: I love you baby

4:32:30 AM **bobjugant**: Am happy you waited till *i* was up baby

4:32:56 AM **ladydi2011**: Honey, I just sent you a picture of the flowers

4:33:07 AM **bobjugant**: Thanks baby

4:33:21 AM **bobjugant**: Hope you liked it

4:33:34 AM **bobjugant**: You are my baby

4:34:06 AM **ladydi2011**: I love them...they are beautiful...they mean so much because they came from you!

4:34:26 AM **ladydi2011**: *Baby, how did you get my address?*

4:34:42 AM **bobjugant**: Lol

4:35:03 AM **ladydi2011**: why are you laughing?

4:35:07 AM **bobjugant**: *I told you i would teach you new things*

4:35:15 AM **ladydi2011**: Yes you did my love

4:35:33 AM **ladydi2011**: They were a total surprise because I know I didn't give you my address

4:35:48 AM **ladydi2011**: *I am looking forward to all you will teach me*

4:35:58 AM **ladydi2011**: Baby, you know I love surprises

4:36:12 AM **ladydi2011**: The message on the card was a surprise too!

4:37:01 AM **bobjugant**: I will suprise you more honey

4:37:16 AM **ladydi2011**: I will surprise you too baby...

4:37:38 AM **ladydi2011**: Honey, are you going to go back home tomorrow?

4:38:20 AM **bobjugant**: I dont know for know baby

4:38:26 AM **ladydi2011**: Baby, you are not very talkative. Is everything ok?

4:38:38 AM **bobjugant**: I would speake to them later today

4:38:48 AM **bobjugant**: Am ok baby

4:39:13 AM **bobjugant**: Am chatting with you and am getting ready tooo

4:39:27 AM **ladydi2011**: I thought this might be what was going on

4:39:43 AM **ladydi2011**: Thank you for making time for me

4:40:48 AM **bobjugant**: Always love

4:42:02 AM **bobjugant**: Baby do you work today
4:42:05 AM **ladydi2011**: Do you need to go?
4:42:27 AM **bobjugant**: I have to honey
4:42:39 AM **bobjugant**: I have to tell them about leaving tomorrow
4:42:41 AM **ladydi2011**: Ok baby...have a wonderful day.
4:42:54 AM **bobjugant**: Baby *i* will try as much as comming online soon so *i* can chat with you...
4:43:07 AM **ladydi2011**: Ok baby...I am going to go to sleep for at least 5 - 6 hrs.
4:43:23 AM **bobjugant**: Ok love
4:43:56 AM **bobjugant**: Do have sweet sleep
4:45:20 AM **bobjugant**: And make sure you dream about me
4:45:35 AM **ladydi2011**: I will dream of you
4:45:55 AM **bobjugant**: I love you so much
4:46:26 AM **ladydi2011**: I love you more!!!
4:46:56 AM **ladydi2011**: Have an outstanding day
4:46:56 AM **bobjugant**: Thanks honey
4:47:15 AM **bobjugant**: I will baby
4:48:10 AM **bobjugant**: Bye baby

 **RED FLAGS**

🚩 He tells me he is "an honest man". A scammer is NOT an honest man.

🚩 He gave me a United Kingdom phone number that he claims was an international number that has roaming, but I couldn't get through to this number. It is *always* a red flag when you are given a +44 70 phone number for the United Kingdom. I also caught him in a lie about getting a disposable phone while in Africa.

🚩 He continues to build me up to the fact that he is coming to be with me. He sent me an e-greeting card and beautiful flowers with a card that read, "The Ring Will Be Next," and a box of chocolates and teddy bear to further prove his love for me. He is a good researcher because he never asked me for my address in order to send me these gifts. It would be difficult for most women to resist falling for this man. He is a real charmer and knows how to make a woman feel loved and desired.

He was right about being my "teacher" and that he would teach me many new things, but he had no idea this was exactly what I was looking for and what I would be doing with my new found education.

IM May 14, 2012 12:04:50 PM

12:04:50 PM **bobjugant**: hi baby

12:59:27 PM **ladydi2011**: Hi honey, how are you?

12:59:31 PM **ladydi2011**: Are you home?

1:23:59 PM **ladydi2011**: Sorry I missed your phone calls. I would love to hear your voice. Please call back my love. I SO miss you!!!!!

2:10:35 PM **bobjugant**: hi baby

2:11:02 PM **ladydi2011**: Hi baby! I MISS YOU...

2:11:29 PM **ladydi2011**: How are you?

2:11:41 PM **bobjugant**: am fine and you?

2:11:47 PM **bobjugant**: *i* miss you too

2:11:57 PM **bobjugant**: tried caling your mobile and office

2:12:03 PM **ladydi2011**: I am sorry that I missed your call

2:12:16 PM **bobjugant**: its ok darling...

2:12:49 PM **ladydi2011**: I would love to hear your voice

2:14:54 PM **ladydi2011**: How was your flight?

2:15:01 PM **bobjugant**: nice honey...

2:15:13 PM **ladydi2011**: How is your back baby?

2:15:23 PM **bobjugant**: much much better

2:15:29 PM **ladydi2011**: Oh good

2:15:37 PM **ladydi2011**: Did you get any sleep?

2:15:53 PM **bobjugant**: yes *i* did...

2:15:57 PM **ladydi2011**: Cool

2:16:06 PM **ladydi2011**: Did you think of me at least once?

2:16:13 PM **bobjugant**: hahahahahahaha....

2:16:17 PM **bobjugant**: many times...

2:16:22 PM **ladydi2011**: I heard you laughing

2:16:26 PM **ladydi2011**: I love you

2:16:28 PM **bobjugant**: love you so much baby...

2:17:07 PM **ladydi2011**: Darling, you have really stolen my heart

2:17:28 PM **bobjugant**: you stole mine too....

2:18:08 PM **bobjugant**: hold baby, give me some minute...

2:18:14 PM **ladydi2011**: Ok

2:18:25 PM **bobjugant**: thanks

2:18:54 PM **ladydi2011**: Please take your time baby. I am here

Break in Time

2:27:32 PM **bobjugant**: what number showed on your phone?

2:27:50 PM **ladydi2011**: 661-380-3000

2:28:02 PM **ladydi2011**: Honey. I need your land line

2:28:18 PM **bobjugant**: ?

2:28:26 PM **bobjugant**: this is my landline

2:28:37 PM **bobjugant**: 442032397893

2:28:38 PM **ladydi2011**: My calling card will not go through to your cell phones

2:28:49 PM **bobjugant**: how come
2:29:27 PM **bobjugant**: call my landline
2:29:29 PM **ladydi2011**: Ok baby. I am going to call you back
2:30:15 PM **bobjugant**: ok

IM May 14, 2012 5:59:56 PM Continued

5:59:56 PM **bobjugant**: *i* am back honey
6:00:01 PM **bobjugant**: you there?
6:00:06 PM **ladydi2011**: I am
6:00:17 PM **bobjugant**: ok honey....
6:00:29 PM **ladydi2011**: Is it 11pm there?
6:00:38 PM **bobjugant**: yes baby...
6:01:00 PM **bobjugant**: soon be going to bed because *i* have to wake up early
6:01:15 PM **ladydi2011**: Ok honey.
6:01:22 PM **ladydi2011**: Did you have dinner?
6:01:35 PM **bobjugant**: yes *i* did...
6:01:39 PM **ladydi2011**: Cool
6:01:57 PM **ladydi2011**: Honey, what is everything that you have to do to prepare for Chile?
6:02:20 PM **bobjugant**: *i* just have to buy equipment *i* will be needing and do some shopping
6:03:09 PM **ladydi2011**: Do you send the equipment via courier?
6:03:34 PM **bobjugant**: yes the company *i* am buying it from will take care of that...
6:03:48 PM **bobjugant**: it will be added to the total cost
6:03:52 PM **ladydi2011**: Cool
6:04:13 PM **ladydi2011**: Baby, please repeat for me what you said about coming to see me.
6:04:55 PM **bobjugant**: yes *i* said after the contract *i* will come over to see you
6:05:05 PM **ladydi2011**: *I will be able to understand your accent much better once we are together in person*
6:06:05 PM **bobjugant**: baby have to go to bed early because tomorrow will be a busy day
6:06:14 PM **ladydi2011**: What do you have going on tomorrow?
6:06:48 PM **bobjugant**: *tomorrow i am going to meet with an agent and also go to the new company to check for the equipment i need then the bank*
6:07:20 PM **ladydi2011**: I am so excited for you that you got this contract!
6:07:29 PM **bobjugant**: thanks baby...
6:07:34 PM **ladydi2011**: Do you need to go to bed now baby?
6:07:44 PM **bobjugant**: yes love....
6:07:54 PM **bobjugant**: we will talk more tomorow
6:07:58 PM **ladydi2011**: Ok sweetheart...
6:08:08 PM **bobjugant**: sorry *i* am going to bed early...
6:08:17 PM **ladydi2011**: It is ok honey
6:08:22 PM **bobjugant**: please take very good care of yourself
6:08:38 PM **ladydi2011**: I will. You too my love
6:08:39 PM **bobjugant**: yes *i* will honey...
6:08:46 PM **bobjugant**: bye love
6:08:48 PM **bobjugant**: love you
6:08:54 PM **ladydi2011**: By honey

6:08:58 PM **ladydi2011**: I love you too
6:09:01 PM **ladydi2011**: Sleep well
6:09:05 PM **bobjugant**: you too

From: ladydi2011@yahoo.com
To: Bob Jugant
Subject: thinking about you
Sent: Tuesday, May 15, 2012 11:52 AM

Hi, Baby...thinking about you. I hope you are having a good day. I am on my way out to meet my friend for lunch. Should be back by 7:30pm YOUR time. Love you...kisses and (((hugs)))

From: bobjugant@yahoo.com
To: ladydi
Subject: Re: thinking about you
Sent: Tuesday, May 15, 2012 12:26 PM

Ok honey, had a hectic day today.. call my mobile +447700061892 or house line +442032397893 when you get back. have fun baby and please take good care...love you

---

IM May 15, 2012 3:27:34 PM

3:27:34 PM **bobjugant**: hi baby
3:50:39 PM **ladydi2011**: Hi my love.
3:51:01 PM **ladydi2011**: Please tell me about your day.
3:52:02 PM **ladydi2011**: Did you get booted?
3:52:35 PM **bobjugant**: yes baby...
3:52:43 PM **bobjugant**: *i* had a hectic day honey
3:53:15 PM **ladydi2011**: Can you see me baby?
3:53:17 PM **bobjugant**: mwaahhhhhhhhhhhhhh!!!!!!!
3:53:25 PM **bobjugant**: yes baby....
3:53:56 PM **ladydi2011**: mwahhhhhhh!!!!
3:54:08 PM **ladydi2011**: What did you get done today baby?
3:54:40 PM **bobjugant**: *i bought the equipment i will be using*
3:54:48 PM **bobjugant**: had to check another company
3:55:02 PM **bobjugant**: recession really affect alot of these companies
3:55:27 PM **ladydi2011**: I am sure the recession has.
3:55:35 PM **bobjugant**: yes baby...
3:55:44 PM **ladydi2011**: So you bought it and they are shipping it?
3:55:52 PM **bobjugant**: yes baby
3:56:18 PM **bobjugant**: tomorrow *i* have an appointment with my doctor

3:56:38 PM **ladydi2011**: For what my love?

3:57:14 PM **bobjugant**: yes, normal check up before *i* travel for any job

3:57:38 PM **ladydi2011**: Cool. I am so glad you do this. Do you need any specific shots for Chili?

3:57:55 PM **ladydi2011**: I had to have many shots before I went to Africa.

3:58:48 PM **bobjugant**: not really... yeah had alot before going to SA

3:59:02 PM **bobjugant**: missed you so much

3:59:14 PM **ladydi2011**: I miss you too baby!

3:59:23 PM **bobjugant**: Am about to download the song you sent

3:59:45 PM **ladydi2011**: Cool...

4:00:34 PM **ladydi2011**: Baby, do you have any idea yet about the dates of when you will be coming to see me and for how long you are staying. I want to clear my calendar....

Break in Time

4:07:24 PM **bobjugant**: Baby

4:07:24 PM **bobjugant**: Sorry lost connection

4:07:39 PM **ladydi2011**: Can you still see me honey?

4:07:49 PM **bobjugant**: invite me again

4:08:41 PM **ladydi2011**: I just tried but it didn't seem to take. Did you get the invite?

4:08:58 PM **bobjugant**: no, send again

4:09:44 PM **ladydi2011**: Did it work?

4:09:49 PM **bobjugant**: yes baby

4:10:10 PM **bobjugant**: so how was your day?

4:10:39 PM **ladydi2011**: *It was good honey. My friends do not think you are real...lol*

4:10:50 PM **bobjugant**: hahahahahahaha

4:11:01 PM **bobjugant**: am *i* a spirit??

4:11:09 PM **ladydi2011**: Lol

4:11:43 PM **ladydi2011**: Baby, do you have any idea yet about the dates of when you will be coming to see me and for how long you are staying. I want to clear my calendar....

4:12:15 PM **bobjugant**: sure baby

4:12:36 PM **bobjugant**: *i* will know that tomorrow then let you know

4:12:57 PM **ladydi2011**: Cool. I want to work as little as possible while you are here

4:13:05 PM **bobjugant**: *will also send you my flight details once i buy my ticket*

4:13:17 PM **ladydi2011**: Thank you honey

4:13:29 PM **ladydi2011**: Did *i* tell you today that I LOVE YOU

4:13:35 PM **bobjugant**: *we will suprise everyone*

4:13:52 PM **bobjugant**: *so its better you don't even tell any of them again...*

4:14:12 PM **bobjugant**: *we will invite them for a lunch or dinner*

4:14:29 PM **bobjugant**: I LOVE YOU MORE....

4:14:31 PM **ladydi2011**: Sounds wonderful!

4:14:48 PM **ladydi2011**: Honey, what do you want to do while you are here?

4:14:55 PM **bobjugant**: hmmm...

4:15:02 PM **bobjugant**: many many things...

4:15:31 PM **bobjugant**: hold please my mobile is ringing

4:15:37 PM **ladydi2011**: Ok

4:19:38 PM **bobjugant**: am back...

4:20:43 PM **bobjugant**: hmmm.. you should be my tour guide...

4:20:53 PM **ladydi2011**: Of course

4:21:07 PM **ladydi2011**: But I really do want to know what you want to do my love

4:21:48 PM **bobjugant**: spend all my time with you

4:21:55 PM **bobjugant**: anything you want honey

4:22:03 PM **bobjugant**: anything that makes you happy

4:22:16 PM **ladydi2011**: I will not want to share you right away....

4:22:51 PM **ladydi2011**: Once I know how long you are staying, I will know better what to plan.

4:23:01 PM **ladydi2011**: Beach is a must, yes?

4:23:22 PM **bobjugant**: yesssssssssssssssssss

4:23:32 PM **ladydi2011**: I knew this

4:23:47 PM **bobjugant**: of course its a must

4:24:25 PM **ladydi2011**: What about having that picnic like we first talked about with a bottle of white, cheese and crackers, blanket, frisbee?

4:24:51 PM **bobjugant**: lovely...

4:25:04 PM **bobjugant**: *i* said you are my tour guide...

4:25:22 PM **ladydi2011**: Ok baby...I will have many surprises for you.

4:25:33 PM **ladydi2011**: *Baby, please give me your home address*

4:25:45 PM **bobjugant**: *hmmmm...*

4:25:51 PM **bobjugant**: want to surprise me?

4:25:59 PM **ladydi2011**: Absolutely!

4:26:13 PM **bobjugant**: *will send to your email*

4:26:25 PM **ladydi2011**: Ok baby. Thank you.

4:26:32 PM **bobjugant**: you welcome

4:26:38 PM **ladydi2011**: Were you able to download the song?

4:27:02 PM **bobjugant**: *the network disconnected, let me try again*

4:27:14 PM **ladydi2011**: OK...I also sent you a picture

4:27:35 PM **bobjugant**: now?

4:27:52 PM **ladydi2011**: A few minutes ago.

4:28:09 PM **ladydi2011**: You might want to open it and take a peek

4:28:33 PM **bobjugant**: ok love

4:28:44 PM **bobjugant**: am listening to the song you sent

4:28:57 PM **ladydi2011**: Cool

4:29:36 PM **bobjugant**: wow!!!!!!!!!!!!!!!!!!!!!!!

4:29:42 PM **ladydi2011**: Yeah

4:29:49 PM **ladydi2011**: It is true!

4:29:53 PM **bobjugant**: I LOVE YOUUUUUUUUUUUUUUUUUUUUUUUUUUUUUUUUUUUUUUU

4:30:08 PM **ladydi2011**: I Love you too

4:30:15 PM **ladydi2011**: Did you see my picture yet?

4:31.11 PM **bobjugant**: *yes.. am Stearing at it*

4:31:20 PM **bobjugant**: looking into your eyes

4:31:31 PM **ladydi2011**: And?

4:31:52 PM **bobjugant**: love you!!!!!!!!!!

4:32:28 PM **ladydi2011**: Thanks for making me smile my love. You are the best and I love you too!

4:32:39 PM **ladydi2011**: I cannot wait to have you here with me.

4:32:51 PM **bobjugant**: me too baby...

4:33:34 PM **bobjugant**: please hold honey, *i* need to use the toilet

4:33:44 PM **ladydi2011**: I have another investment idea that I will send to you via email. Would still have to do research of profit and demographics and such...I think it is a hot franchise

4:34:06 PM **bobjugant**: please send

Break In Time

4:43:25 PM **bobjugant**: am back

4:44:02 PM **ladydi2011**: I sent you the investment info for you to review later

4:44:19 PM **ladydi2011**: I still think the biggest and easiest money is with fracking

4:44:21 PM **bobjugant**: ok *i* will read before going to bed

4:44:32 PM **ladydi2011**: Especially with your knowledge baby

4:44:40 PM **bobjugant**: yeah baby...

4:45:14 PM **ladydi2011**: So honey, what type of music do you like?

4:46:04 PM **bobjugant**: classical music

4:46:27 PM **ladydi2011**: Anything else?

4:47:03 PM **bobjugant**: blues

4:47:17 PM **bobjugant**: opera

4:48:18 PM **ladydi2011**: Anything else?

4:49:01 PM **bobjugant**: no baby...

4:49:13 PM **bobjugant**: only that *i* want you next by me now

4:49:20 PM **ladydi2011**: Thanks for sharing. I want to learn all your likes

4:49:32 PM **ladydi2011**: I want to be next to you now too

4:49:42 PM **ladydi2011**: Honey, what do you have going on tomorrow?

4:50:12 PM **bobjugant**: go see my doctor, check with my travel agent

4:50:25 PM **bobjugant**: go shopping...

4:51:27 PM **bobjugant**: then back home hopefully and spend quality time with you

4:51:52 PM **ladydi2011**: I love spending quality time with you baby.

4:51:58 PM **ladydi2011**: Did you have dinner?

4:52:21 PM **bobjugant**: yes honey, tomorrow we will have alot of time to chat

4:52:34 PM **ladydi2011**: Are you tired now baby?

4:52:34 PM **bobjugant**: because *i* will be home early hopefully...

4:52:51 PM **bobjugant**: yes baby, eyes are getting heavy

4:52:54 PM **ladydi2011**: Cool. I will have less work on my plate tomorrow

4:53:11 PM **bobjugant**: *i* can quickly go through what you sent and then go to bed

4:53:20 PM **bobjugant**: because *i* have to wake up again early

4:54:33 PM **ladydi2011**: Bob, I really enjoy what we have.

4:54:50 PM **bobjugant**: *you deserve more*

4:54:57 PM **bobjugant**: me too honey

4:55:01 PM **ladydi2011**: *why would you say this????*

4:55:29 PM **bobjugant**: *because you are a special person*

4:55:38 PM **bobjugant**: *love you so much*

4:55:57 PM **ladydi2011**: Thank you baby. You are a special person too!

4:56:11 PM **bobjugant**: have a lovely night rest baby

4:56:19 PM **bobjugant**: chat with you tomorrow

4:56:23 PM **ladydi2011**: You too

4:56:32 PM **bobjugant**: mwahhhhhhhhhhhhhhh

4:56:34 PM **ladydi2011**: Please dream about me

4:56:41 PM **bobjugant**: yeahhhhhhhhhhh

4:56:43 PM **ladydi2011**: mwahhhhhhhhhhhhhhhhhhh

4:56:47 PM **bobjugant**: bye baby

4:56:57 PM **ladydi2011**: By honey

From: ladydi2011@yahoo.com
To: Bob Jugant
Subject: Smiling
Sent: Wednesday, May 16, 2012 10:42 AM

Hello Baby,

Thinking about you. I hope you found the additional equipment you need. I have been busy working all morning. Love you.

IM May 17, 2012 3:21:40 PM

3:21:40 PM **bobjugant**: hello baby
3:21:57 PM **bobjugant**: are you there, you tried calling
3:22:00 PM **bobjugant**: <ding>

From: ladydi2011@yahoo.com
Subject: Good night my darling
To: "Bob Jugant"
Received: Friday, May 18, 2012, 12:56 AM

Good night my darling! I hope you got a good night's rest honey. I am extremely tired. I just left the office. I wrote many pages of my book tonight.

There are many thoughts and emotions swirling around within me, so it is time for me to lay my head on the pillow and try to shut everything off and get some sleep.

Did I ever share with you that I have a hard time shutting my brain off and relaxing. It is draining sometimes! Good night honey.

I love you.

From: bobjugant@yahoo.com
To: ladydi
Subject: Love you
Sent: Friday, May 18, 2012 7:33 AM

Hi Honey

First of all *i* have to apologise *i* have not been in contact for the past 2 days... Honey past few days has been so hectic..I am drained but *i will always stay strong...* Yesterday *i* went for a friend's birthday party, *i* came back home so tired and *slept off*. I am so sorry *i* made you stay online for long. I just finished arranging my luggage, about leaving to the airport

Please baby, don't stress yourself that much, anytime you feel tired when working go and rest please!!!! *Yes i was there with you, am always with you in heart even if not physical. I love you so much baby..i want to say its so hard to be away from you, not talk to you , not hear or see you I miss your beautiful smile.*

You are the most beautiful,wonderful,sweet,kind,caring, loving, true darling. I could not live without you. As i wait it hurts more, As i wait Im still happy knowing you love me and i have a love that is magical and the most wonderful feeling in the universe.

I will never lose faith in your power.

our hearts and minds are conected, a conection you only find once in a lifetime. I will never let you go ..i will wait as long as it takes but i still worry every day and it hurts in every way, i want you now I want to touch you ,hold you and kiss you all night long. I want to feel your heart beat. I hate this, It hurt so much..At the same time i am filled with joy because i have the most perfect woman in this universe. For that i am happy ...you are mine and thats how it always shall be as i am yours devoted to you , I bow to your beauty and grace...

Please take very good care of yourself, *i* will let you know once *i* arrive chile...

My one true love, My best friend and My sweet Angel

I love you baby always

From: ladydi2011@yahoo.com
To: Bob Jugant
Subject: Re: Love you
Sent: Friday, May 18, 2012 3:16 PM

Hi Honey,

Thank you for this email. I have so much I want to say to you... My blackberry died....hopefully sometime this weekend I will be able to replace it. I was on with tech support for two hours. I did manage to salvage my data, so when I get a new phone I can transfer my data.

Darling, please do email me when you arrive in Chile so I know you are safe and do not worry. You never emailed me your itinerary like you said you would, so I have no clue when you should be arriving. I will check email when I am at my computer.

I love you. Kisses and (((hugs)))

Diana

IM May 19, 2012 1:58:49 PM

1:58:49 PM **bobjugant**: <ding>
1:58:51 PM **bobjugant**: honey

IM May 19, 2012 2:36:10 PM

2:36:10 PM **bobjugant**: please let me know ehrn you come online

---

IM May 19, 2012 10:06:54 PM

10:06:54 PM **ladydi2011**: Hi baby, I am now home and just called you but it went to voice mail. Please come on line....

IM May 19, 2012 10:49:39 PM

10:49:39 PM **ladydi2011**: Ok my love...I called and no answer. I waited for you on line but no Bob. I am really tired so I am going to bed. I miss you and love you! Good night.............

May 19th – Phone Call – Bob called. He asked me what I was doing and I was reading the book, "Why Men Love Bitches," and he asked me to tell him what it was about.

He also proclaimed his undying love for me and told me how much he misses me.

From: ladydi2011@yahoo.com
To: Bob Jugant
Subject: Baby, I have learned that you are in love with Bitch sprinkled with a little nice girl
Sent: Sunday, May 20, 2012 5:24 PM

Hi Darling,

You wanted a recap of the book I am reading, "Why Men Love Bitches" by Sherry Argov, here it is. However, I must warn you that I am learning that you are in love with a "Bitch" according to the definition of a Bitch in this book. As I am reading, I have been saying to myself, "Hmmmm, I am a bitch and didn't even know it. Wait until Bob learns he is in love with a bitch sprinkled with a little nice girl"…(I hear you laughing) Lol! Baby, please let me know what you think, am I a Bitch sprinkled with a little nice girl?

Ok…recap so far of book and my thoughts concerning what I have read. My personal thoughts are italicized.

So tell me, my darling, how much happiness can you handle? Because you are in love with a good woman…I hope your answer is "A LOT"!

What a Bitch Is Not:

- ✓ A woman who speaks in a harsh tone of voice.
- ✓ She is not abrasive.
- ✓ She is not rude.

Really? This is what I always thought when I thought of a bitch…This is a good day, I learned something new!

What a Bitch Is:

- ✓ She is confident – *This I am*
- ✓ She has worth and knows it. – *This is true. This is what makes me very selective.*
- ✓ She doesn't treat disrespect as a laughing matter and does not tolerate it. *Baby, this is VERY true. I deserve to be respected. I will always respect you. As my team says, I don't demand it but I command it because of who I am and how I treat others.*
- ✓ She is polite but clear. – *Yep, this is true. I try to always be polite but clear when communicating what I want and need and what is and is not acceptable to me.*
- ✓ She knows what she wants and needs from her man and communicates it clearly to him. – *Yep, this is me. I know what I need and I will always try to clearly communicate with you what I need.*
- ✓ She will not be a doormat. – *Nope, I will not be a doormat for anyone no matter how much I love them.*
- ✓ She doesn't waffle – *I don't waffle.*
- ✓ She doesn't dress sleazy and show everything she owns to capture a man's attention (she leaves things to the imagination) – *I wouldn't even think of dressing sleazy to capture a man's attention…*
- ✓ She isn't threatened by another beautiful woman – *I admire beauty and will point her out to you…I am not threatened at all!*
- ✓ She isn't a bootie call – *Not this girl…NEVER going to happen!*
- ✓ She is not into a man only "accepting her" but wants a man to "love and want her madly." *Absolutely! I know I am a catch. I don't need acceptance. I know, love and accept myself. I love madly and want the same thing in return.* A man accepts a doormat but desires his dream girl – *I agree… I will never be a doormat for anyone. I love and agree with the following, "if you want acceptance go to a self-help group"*

- ✓ She is a woman who is comfortable in her own skin. – *Yep, I am very comfortable in my own skin.*
- ✓ She will not allow anyone to make her feel bad about herself – *As I wrote you days ago. I do not allow people in my life who try to make me feel bad about myself... I believe this type of person does this because they have low self-esteem and they try to feel better about themselves by bringing others down...I have not time or energy for this.*
- ✓ She doesn't want anyone who doesn't want her – *This is EXTREMELY true for me...I want to be wanted and desired by my man. I will not beg for someone to want me. I would rather be alone.*
- ✓ She is nice, feminine and takes good care of herself. – *This is true about me... See, I had the wrong perception of a bitch. I always considered myself a nice woman...Glad to learn what a bitch really is...I believe I even asked you why men love bitches not to long after we met. Miss Perception herself had the wrong perception... (I hear you laughing!)*
- ✓ She doesn't make decisions based on losing a man. – *Nope, I sure don't. If he wants to walk away then he wasn't the man for me.*
- ✓ She remains the person she is when in a relationship. – *This is true. What you see is what you get forever............*
- ✓ Has enormous self-respect - *Absolutely!*
- ✓ Her self-respect governs her decisions – *Every one of them!*
- ✓ She is not always predictable. – *This is true to a point. I am VERY predictable when it comes to anything that would jeopardize trust and respect when in a long-term relationship. In a casual dating relationship, I am not always so predictable.*
- ✓ She has honor – *Absolutely!*
- ✓ She maintains her independence – *I will always maintain my independence.*
- ✓ She has a sense of humor – *Yes, I do have a sense of humor.*
- ✓ She places a high value on herself – *Absolutely...If I don't value me, why should anyone else?*
- ✓ She receives compliments – *I do receive and appreciate compliments. You are good at giving them to me. Thank you, Darling.*
- ✓ She has other passions and goals. – *I sure do and always will. You will never be bored with me.*
- ✓ If a man tells her he doesn't like red lipstick but it makes her feel good, she wears it anyway. – *This is true. I would still wear it when I wanted to but I would not wear it when we are going out on a date for the simple fact that when you look at me, I would want you to smile and not be thinking to yourself, I do not like that on her. Honey, I do want to know what you like, and if I am comfortable wearing it I just might surprise you from time to time... (You are smiling now, I see you).*
- ✓ She will not pick up the phone when he finally calls. – *This might be true on occasion in certain situations. However, I will not do this to you in a way of playing games. I do not like playing games. I wouldn't want this done to me, so I would not do this to you. Here is the sprinkling of the nice girl in me.*

A Nice Girl: Honey, here is where my nice girl comes in and where I am not a bitch.

- ✓ The nice girl worries when she hasn't heard from her man....*Baby, we just went through this. The reason I worried was because you told me you were going to do something and then didn't. It was out of character for you, which made me worry and ask if this is what life would be like with you. This is NOT ok behavior for me. I am so glad we talked about this today and you promised me this wouldn't happen again. For me, as I said, this involves trust and respect for the one you love. I want to be with a man I trust and that his word is his bond. If you tell me you are going to do something, I need you to follow-through. If you will be busy and you think you will not have time to be in touch with me, just tell me and it will not be a problem. I will not be expecting to hear from you, so I will not worry. Honey, thank you for promising me that this will not happen again. It takes 2 min. to call me. I deserve this much respect, Baby. If in question, please ask yourself what you would want from me.*

✓ *The nice girl worries he is pulling away, the bitch could care less….If I am in a casual relationship and do not have my heart invested, I could care less. If he is pulling away, then my thought is "He is not for me…NEXT"! However, when I am in love with a man, I would want to know if he is pulling away from me so I can protect my heart that is totally vested, to try to lessen the impact of hurt that could very well be coming my way. I think this is just human nature. With you, Baby, I would very much care……….*

All this from the first two chapters….. I hope you are feeling better, my love. I so wish I were there to take care of you. Being sick is no fun, but being alone and sick is even worse.

I Love You
Diana

From: ladydi2011@yahoo.com
To: Bob Jugant
Subject: Love making you laugh
Sent: Sunday, May 20, 2012 11:35 PM

Yes, my darling. I am in love with you. My soul and heart is connected to yours, so I know when you will laugh. Isn't it great! Baby, I promise you I will always make you laugh. :-)

Thank you for hearing what I need and promising to keep your word. This means a lot to me!

Thank you for letting me know your number will be out of reach. I wouldn't call you during your work hours. Talking in the morning and evening would be great! A message or chat during the day would be a bonus. Baby, please focus on your work.

I will be having dinner with one of my friend's tomorrow night so you can call me on my cell or once I get home between 9:30 - 10:00. I promise to take care of me. Please take care of you.

Good night, my darling
I Love You........

From: ladydi2011@yahoo.com
To: Bob Jugant
Subject: Good morning darling
Sent: Monday, May 21, 2012 9:15 AM

Good morning, Darling,

I hope you slept well, had pleasant dreams and are feeling better. Today is the first day of you striking out on your own.

Please have a wonderful day and know I am smiling about your success. I know you have to feel great about this. I am so proud of you, Honey, and happy you are MY man!!! Thinking about you and smiling :-)

I LOVE YOU

Diana

From: ladydi2011@yahoo.com
To: Bob Jugant
Subject: Thinking about you
Sent: Monday, May 21, 2012 4:26 PM

Hello, my darling,

I just had a break and my thoughts instantly went to you. I am wondering how you are feeling and how your day is going. I hope you are feeling so much better and that your day is fabulous! Attached is a song from my heart to you. (Song is Forever Love by Reba McEntire)

IM May 21, 2012 7:07:05 PM

7:07:05 PM **bobjugant**: hi honey
7:07:11 PM **bobjugant**: are you there?

IM May 21, 2012 8:14:55 PM

8:14:55 PM **bobjugant**: baby *i* have been online waiting
8:15:11 PM **bobjugant**: *i* have to go to bed now, hope everything is ok with you and hope you had a lovely dinner? take good care baby, Love you

IM May 21, 2012 10:29:01 PM

10:29:01 PM **ladydi2011**: Hi honey. I tried calling but couldn't get through. It is 10:30pm Monday night. Love You.

IM May 23, 2012 8:07:41 PM

8:07:41 PM **bobjugant**: hi honey
8:08:03 PM **bobjugant**: you there?
8:08:07 PM **ladydi2011**: Hi honey
8:08:21 PM **ladydi2011**: How are you?
8:08:36 PM **bobjugant**: miss you so much
8:08:48 PM **ladydi2011**: yeah, me too!
8:08:55 PM **bobjugant**: *i* am fine, and you?
8:09:03 PM **ladydi2011**: Good
8:09:09 PM **ladydi2011**: How are you feeling?
8:09:25 PM **bobjugant**: much better honey
8:09:33 PM **ladydi2011**: Yay, I am so glad to hear this!
8:09:34 PM **bobjugant**: work has been so stressfull
8:09:49 PM **ladydi2011**: I was just going to ask
8:10:10 PM **bobjugant**: yes love it has but everything is going on fine
8:10:19 PM **bobjugant**: how is work?
8:10:26 PM **ladydi2011**: I am glad everything is going good
8:10:41 PM **ladydi2011**: Busy...getting more of my book written
8:10:47 PM **ladydi2011**: I go back to the chiropractor tomorrow
8:11:36 PM **bobjugant**: miss you so so much
8:11:39 PM **ladydi2011**: Hopefully he releases me to work out again
8:12:04 PM **ladydi2011**: Did you think about me at least once a day?
8:12:15 PM **bobjugant**: more than once baby
8:12:24 PM **ladydi2011**: I called my trainer and told him if I am released I will be in to workout
8:12:25 PM **bobjugant**: always on my mind
8:12:44 PM **ladydi2011**: I think there is a song called "always on my mind?"
8:13:02 PM **ladydi2011**: I miss you much to darling
8:13:03 PM **bobjugant**: you always on my mind baby
8:13:17 PM **ladydi2011**: It seems like forever since we have chatted
8:13:26 PM **ladydi2011**: Have you been getting my emails?
8:13:49 PM **bobjugant**: *i can't access emails offshore cuz this rig has limited access*
8:14:11 PM **bobjugant**: only messenger works
8:14:21 PM **ladydi2011**: *are you off shore now?*
8:14:33 PM **bobjugant**: *i am still offshore*
8:14:42 PM **bobjugant**: will be onshore hopefully weekend
8:14:54 PM **ladydi2011**: Honey...I need a big favor
8:15:37 PM **bobjugant**: ok what is it darling
8:15:50 PM **ladydi2011**: I need your address there in Chile
8:16:19 PM **bobjugant**: you mean the rig address?
8:16:33 PM **ladydi2011**: Wherever you can get a package

8:16:39 PM **bobjugant**: want to come over??
8:16:41 PM **ladydi2011**: Your birthday is coming up
8:16:54 PM **ladydi2011**: Would love too...when does my flight leave?
8:17:07 PM **bobjugant**: hahaha...
8:17:25 PM **bobjugant**: once *i* get onshore *i* will send it to you
8:17:55 PM **ladydi2011**: Ok baby....I am leaving for my brother's Friday late afternoon
8:18:27 PM **ladydi2011**: I have no way of getting this address in less you give it to me.
8:18:47 PM **ladydi2011**: my niece graduates Saturday morning at 10:00
8:18:51 PM **bobjugant**: *i* have to go talk with the locals tomorrow *i* have to wake up early
8:19:01 PM **ladydi2011**: now?
8:19:02 PM **bobjugant**: ok honey
8:19:26 PM **bobjugant**: yes i just quickly came online to drop offline or let you know *i* am ok
8:19:32 PM **ladydi2011**: are you sleeping on the rig?
8:19:35 PM **bobjugant**: tomorrow we will have time to chat
8:19:49 PM **bobjugant**: off course there is accomodation on tthe rig
8:20:10 PM **ladydi2011**: Ok darling, it was nice to hear from you
8:20:23 PM **bobjugant**: hahaha, please take good care
8:20:28 PM **ladydi2011**: You too
8:20:35 PM **bobjugant**: yes nice to chat with you too...
8:20:49 PM **bobjugant**: remember *i* promised to always keep in touch
8:21:18 PM **bobjugant**: love you baby
8:21:25 PM **ladydi2011**: Love you too baby
8:21:45 PM **bobjugant**: please take good care..have to go now
8:22:02 PM **ladydi2011**: Ok...take care of you
8:22:15 PM **bobjugant**: *i* will honey
8:22:18 PM **bobjugant**: sweet dreams
8:22:21 PM **bobjugant**: *i* love you
8:22:23 PM **bobjugant**: bye
8:22:24 PM **ladydi2011**: You too

From: ladydi2011@yahoo.com
To: Bob Jugant
Subject: Hmmmm....good food there?
Sent: Thursday, May 24, 2012 2:50 PM

Hello Darling,

First let me say that I miss you! I am so glad all is going well for you. I knew it would. I did some research today to learn what it is like on an oil rig... Asking dumb questions always sends me to research (your laughing...).

They say that some of the best food is found on the rig, is this true? Ok, honey, I have to run. Take care of you!

Love you. Diana

RED FLAGS

🚩 His "story" of being on a rig is a good one because it gives him an excuse to spend less time with me and have more time to chat with multiple women. Remember, it's a numbers game.

🚩 When we talk on the phone I have a real hard time understanding him because his accent is very thick.

🚩 He never gives me a direct answer about when he will come to meet me, but promises to send me his flight itinerary once he buys his airline ticket.

🚩 I asked him for his home address and he said he would email it to me, but he never did.

🚩 He claims that he can't access email when he is off shore, but he can access Yahoo! messenger to chat. Now, we all know if you can access one, you can access the other, so this makes no sense. I researched rigs and found that they have satellite communication. *Do your research*. It was right after I told him I researched a rig that the scam started. I figured this would hurry the process along.

🚩 I told him that my friend said he wasn't real. Then he said it is better if I no longer tell my friends anything else and that we will surprise them when he gets here. Scammers don't like you telling anybody about the relationship because they know an outside person will clearly see it is a scam due to their heart not being involved.

🚩 He knew what he was about to do and out of the blue told me, "You deserve more." *When a man tells you this, always believe them.*

🚩 He promised me he will "keep his word." We all know this will never happen!

🚩 Anytime they say they will "stay strong" or that they "slept off", it is a red flag and you know they are from Nigeria.

IM May 24, 2012 8:58:56 PM

8:58:56 PM **bobjugant**: hi baby
8:59:02 PM **bobjugant**: you there?
9:04:40 PM **bobjugant**: baby you there?
9:08:43 PM **ladydi2011**: I am
9:09:59 PM **bobjugant**: how are you doing?
9:10:28 PM **ladydi2011**: Just pulled in garage
9:10:35 PM **ladydi2011**: On phone
9:11:04 PM **ladydi2011**: How are you?
9:11:40 PM **ladydi2011**: Booting now
9:12:03 PM **bobjugant**: *not fine at all baby, i had a terrible day honey*
9:12:37 PM **ladydi2011**: What happened?
9:13:05 PM **bobjugant**: *having problems with equipment and it affected one of the locals*
9:13:47 PM **ladydi2011**: Did he get hurt?

9:14:21 PM **bobjugant**: yes he did but not that bad
9:14:56 PM **bobjugant**: *really had a terrible day*
9:14:59 PM **ladydi2011**: What happened?
9:15:47 PM **ladydi2011**: Sending BIG hugs
9:15:54 PM **bobjugant**: thanks love
9:16:02 PM **bobjugant**: how was your day?
9:17:49 PM **ladydi2011**: Busy...but good
9:18:49 PM **ladydi2011**: I went and had a spa treatment and a manicure and pedicure
9:20:30 PM **bobjugant**: *baby can you please help me check on a web were i bought my equipment from*

I knew the website he sent me was fictitious, so I took a screenshot.

9:20:39 PM **ladydi2011**: Sure

9:20:41 PM **bobjugant**: www.hogsequipment.net

9:21:19 PM **ladydi2011**: What do you need me to find?

9:21:42 PM **bobjugant**: *help me check if they have Kill Manifolds*

9:22:16 PM **ladydi2011**: Ok honey. I have the site up. Please hold.

9:22:37 PM **bobjugant**: ok darling

9:22:49 PM **ladydi2011**: They do honey

9:22:59 PM **bobjugant**: ok

9:23:26 PM **bobjugant**: check for contact us

9:23:47 PM **ladydi2011**: Got it

9:24:01 PM **bobjugant**: and help me write to James

9:24:22 PM **bobjugant**: *please inform him i need the equipment urgently*

9:24:41 PM **ladydi2011**: Ok...let me get a pen honey. Brb

9:24:51 PM **bobjugant**: ok love

9:26:42 PM **ladydi2011**: I am back, go ahead

9:27:01 PM **bobjugant**: ok

9:27:13 PM **bobjugant**: please send an email to james and tell him *i* need Kill Manifold urgently

9:27:41 PM **bobjugant**: you got his email already?

9:28:01 PM **ladydi2011**: Of course my love

9:28:28 PM **ladydi2011**: What else?

9:29:26 PM **bobjugant**: nothing else baby....

9:29:43 PM **bobjugant**: let me see the email you compose before you send

9:30:03 PM **ladydi2011**: Ok...should I let him know I am writing this for you?

9:30:11 PM **bobjugant**: yes baby

9:32:27 PM **ladydi2011**: Hold please while I compose...thank you

9:32:36 PM **bobjugant**: ok baby

9:33:58 PM **ladydi2011**: Honey, should he ship it to the same place he shipped the other equipment?

9:34:09 PM **bobjugant**: yes baby he has the details

9:38:46 PM **ladydi2011**: Hello James,

My name is Diana Garren. I am writing to you on behalf of Bob Jugant. He is on the rig and urgently needs you to ship him a Kill Manifold to the same location you shipped the other equipment.

Your prompt attention to this request is greatly appreciated.

Please correspond with me if you have any questions and to let me know when this has shipped. Thank you,

Diana Garren/Bob Jugant

9:39:38 PM **bobjugant**: thanks love

9:39:54 PM **ladydi2011**: Is this good?

9:40:15 PM **bobjugant**: its good honey...

9:40:29 PM **ladydi2011**: Ok. Please hold while I send. Brb

9:40:42 PM **bobjugant**: ok love

9:43:11 PM **ladydi2011**: Do you want me to call him in the morning?

9:43:54 PM **bobjugant**: yes if you can so he attends to it faster

9:44:21 PM **ladydi2011**: I sure will. Consider this handled and please do not worry about it. I got it!

9:44:33 PM **bobjugant**: thanks baby

9:44:40 PM **ladydi2011**: You are so welcome.

9:44:51 PM **ladydi2011**: Breathe baby breathe

9:45:02 PM **bobjugant**: hahahaha...
9:45:04 PM **ladydi2011**: Did you eat dinner?
9:45:21 PM **bobjugant**: have not eaten baby...
9:45:34 PM **bobjugant**: *have been so worried honey...*
9:45:42 PM **ladydi2011**: I am sure
9:45:54 PM **ladydi2011**: What are the repercussions to you honey?
9:46:36 PM **bobjugant**: *the local is been treated but i need the equipment to continue working and make work faster so i don't the local for extra time*
9:47:10 PM **ladydi2011**: Got it
9:47:21 PM **ladydi2011**: I am so glad he wasn't hurt badly
9:47:43 PM **ladydi2011**: Honey, do you get my messenger messages when I send them?
9:48:06 PM **bobjugant**: yes honey... *i* got only one
9:50:09 PM **ladydi2011**: If I send you an IM you get it, correct?
9:50:33 PM **bobjugant**: yes *i* do
9:50:38 PM **ladydi2011**: Ok
9:51:27 PM **ladydi2011**: honey, I never knew anyone who worked off shore before. This is all new to me. My man is teaching me new things, just like he promised.
9:51:48 PM **bobjugant**: hahahaha...yeahhhh...

9:51:59 PM **bobjugant**: am your teacher...
9:52:09 PM **ladydi2011**: I love it!!!
9:52:28 PM **ladydi2011**: Honey, other than what happened today, how is everything else going?
9:53:04 PM **bobjugant**: everything going on well.. am very much better now
9:53:13 PM **bobjugant**: only *i* kept on missing you
9:53:45 PM **ladydi2011**: I so miss waking up to your emails and talking with you every day.
9:54:45 PM **bobjugant**: me too honey...
9:54:58 PM **bobjugant**: love you so much
9:55:11 PM **ladydi2011**: I love you so much too....
9:55:37 PM **ladydi2011**: I am looking forward to the day you arrive in Atlanta
9:56:03 PM **bobjugant**: me too... honey please hold for some minutes
9:56:09 PM **ladydi2011**: Ok
9:56:13 PM **bobjugant**: will be right back
9:56:17 PM **ladydi2011**: K
Break in Time
10:10:54 PM **bobjugant**: am back honey
10:11:26 PM **ladydi2011**: *Ok...Please give me the address where i can send you something for your birthday.*
10:11:53 PM **bobjugant**: *ok when i get onshore i will get the right address and send to you but honey i will be with you before my birthday hopefully*
10:12:32 PM **ladydi2011**: When is your birthday again?
10:12:48 PM **bobjugant**: *26th june*
10:13:05 PM **ladydi2011**: *Baby, you told me June 3rd.......*
10:13:12 PM **ladydi2011**: Which is the truth?
10:13:34 PM **bobjugant**: 26th darling...
10:13:51 PM **ladydi2011**: Ok....
10:14:28 PM **bobjugant**: 3rd???
10:14:34 PM **bobjugant**: 26th darling
10:14:35 PM **ladydi2011**: Honey, why did you tell me the 3rd

10:15:33 PM **bobjugant**: 3rd is a close friend birthday
10:15:37 PM **ladydi2011**: Maybe it was the night you were tipsy....I will have to go back and look.
10:16:33 PM **bobjugant**: hahahaha...
10:16:46 PM **ladydi2011**: Mr. grey goose
10:16:53 PM **bobjugant**: hahahahahahahahaha....
10:16:58 PM **ladydi2011**: And cranberry juice
10:17:29 PM **bobjugant**: yeahhhhhhhhhh
10:17:49 PM **ladydi2011**: Baby, I have one more piece of chocolate left from what you sent me. Every time I eat a piece I envision you tasting it from my mouth
10:18:10 PM **ladydi2011**: It will be in the liquor cabinet when you arrive
10:18:36 PM **bobjugant**: yes better.. so *i* can taste them from your mouth..yummmy!!!!
10:19:06 PM **ladydi2011**: I am smiling........you will be very pampered while you are here!
10:19:32 PM **ladydi2011**: I hope you like massages
10:19:57 PM **bobjugant**: yes *i* will really need that especially after this contract
10:20:21 PM **ladydi2011**: I know honey.
10:20:33 PM **bobjugant**: honey *i* need to go check on the local
10:20:41 PM **ladydi2011**: Ok baby
10:20:55 PM **ladydi2011**: You know I am leaving town tomorrow, right?
10:21:06 PM **bobjugant**: yes you told me, please take good care
10:21:15 PM **ladydi2011**: I will
10:21:30 PM **bobjugant**: and please drop me an offline message when you get a response from james please
10:21:31 PM **ladydi2011**: Please IM me and let me know how everything is going
10:21:40 PM **ladydi2011**: I will
10:21:46 PM **bobjugant**: yes *i* will let you know honey
10:21:50 PM **bobjugant**: thanks love
10:21:59 PM **ladydi2011**: I love you
10:22:00 PM **bobjugant**: sweet dreams baby
10:22:05 PM **bobjugant**: love you too
10:22:11 PM **bobjugant**: mwahhhhhhhhhhhhhhhhhhhh
10:22:22 PM **ladydi2011**: mwahhhhhhhhhhhhhhh

From: ladydi2011@yahoo.com
To: ukcustomercare@hogsequipment.net
Cc: Bob Jugant
Subject: Urgent need of equipment for Bob Jugant
Sent: Friday, May 25, 2012 4:41 AM

Hello James,

My name is Diana Garren. I am writing to you on behalf of Bob Jugant. He is on the rig and urgently needs you to ship him a Kill Manifold to the same location you shipped the other equipment.

Your prompt attention to this request is greatly appreciated.

Please correspond with me if you have any questions and to let me know when this has shipped.

Thank you,

Diana L. Garren/Bob Jugant

From: ukcustomercare@hogsequipment.net
To: ladydi
Subject: Re: Urgent need of equipment for Bob Jugant
Sent: Friday, May 25, 2012 5:11 AM

Dear Diana L. Garren,

We have received your mail requesting on behalf of Mr Bob Jugant for equipment (Kill manifold).It is available,Please find below details on the equipment you requested. I hope you would find these information useful:

Specifications of Kill manifold

MODEL - KM15
WORKING PRESSURE - 15,000 PSI
INLET - 2-9/16" - 15,000 PSI / 3-1/16" - 15,000 PSI
OUTLET - 2-9/16 " - 15,000 PSI / 3-1/16 " - 15,000 PSI

We have two types of delivery system which are:

1) Air Cargo Delivery: This take only 48hours to be delivered in Chile. The price of this delivery is £ 2,250GBP.
2) Shipment Delivery: This is estimated to deliver within 30-35 working business day to Chile and it is £640GBP.
Please do state which of the above delivery system you desire, We have attached a Pro Forma Invoice.Please read carefully. We await your response so that we can furnish you with company account information.

Yours Faithfully,
James Brooks
Sales Manager
Phone Number - 4420 8133 4934
Fax Number - 4487 0479 5053
website: www.hogsequipment.net
email- sales@hogsequipment.net

IM May 25, 2012 5:36:48 AM

5:36:48 AM **ladydi2011**: Morning darling. I hope you slept well and that the local is doing better today. I called HOGS Equipment. James was not in but I spoke to his assistant. He confirmed that he received my email and said he will respond to it. I will let you know more as I know more. Have a wonderful day baby. I love you...Kisses and (((hugs)))

From: ladydi2011@yahoo.com
To: ukcustomercare@hogsequipment.net
Cc: Bob Jugant
Subject: Urgent need of equipment for Bob Jugant
Sent: Friday, May 25, 2012 5:58 AM

Dear Mr. Brooks,

Thank you for your quick reply. I will get this information to Mr. Bob Jugant and get back with you with his response.

Diana L Garren

From: ladydi2011@yahoo.com
To: Bob Jugant
Subject: FW: Urgent need of equipment for Bob Jugant
Sent: Friday, May 25, 2012 1:46 PM

Hello Honey,

Below is what James sent. Love you...

Diana

From: ukcustomercare@hogsequipment.net
To: ladydi2011@yaoo.com
Subject: Re: Urgent need of equipment for Bob Jugant
Sent: Friday, May 25, 2012 5:11 AM

Dear Diana L. Garren,

We have received your mail requesting on behalf of Mr Bob Jugant for equipment (Kill manifold).It is available,Please find below details on the equipment you requested.

I hope you would find these information useful:
Specifications of Kill manifold

MODEL - KM15
WORKING PRESSURE - 15,000 PSI

INLET - 2-9/16" - 15,000 PSI / 3-1/16" - 15,000 PSI

OUTLET - 2-9/16 " - 15,000 PSI / 3-1/16 " - 15,000 PSI

We have two types of delivery system which are:

1) Air Cargo Delivery: This take only 48hours to be delivered in Chile. The price of this delivery is £ 2,250GBP.

2) Shipment Delivery: This is estimated to deliver within 30-35 working business day to Chile and it is £640GBP.

Please do state which of the above delivery system you desire, We have attached a Pro Forma Invoice.Please read carefully.

We await your response so that we can furnish you with company account information.

Yours Faithfully,
James Brooks
Sales Manager
Phone Number - 4420 8133 4934
Fax Number - 4487 0479 5053
website: www.hogsequipment.net
email- sales@hogsequipment.net

IM May 25, 2012 3:38:28 PM

3:38:28 PM **ladydi2011**: Hi honey. I hope everything is going smoothly for you today. I am going to pack now and leave for my brothers. I have a 3 hr. drive. I miss you and love you.

IM May 25, 2012 8:17:35 PM

8:17:35 PM **bobjugant**: Please take good care and have a safe trip honey, any message yet from james? *everything is not ok honey, much stress and am tensed.. i need the equipment urgently.. love you*
8:18:28 PM **ladydi2011**: Hi
8:18:37 PM **bobjugant**: hi honey
8:18:56 PM **ladydi2011**: I am driving
8:19:17 PM **bobjugant**: ok please concentrate so you don't get distracted
8:19:24 PM **bobjugant**: any message from james?
8:19:33 PM **ladydi2011**: Yes
8:20:01 PM **ladydi2011**: Please hold so I can pull over
8:20:08 PM **bobjugant**: ok baby
8:23:35 PM **ladydi2011**: Ok honey I am stopped
8:24:25 PM **ladydi2011**: I called James this morning and he has it and sent info and invoice
8:24:56 PM **ladydi2011**: I sent it to you on IM and email. Did you not get it?
8:25:03 PM **ladydi2011**: Are you there?
8:25:30 PM **ladydi2011**: Honey
8:25:39 PM **ladydi2011**: <ding>
8:26:15 PM **ladydi2011**: I am going to sign off and sign back on
8:27:15 PM **bobjugant**: ok honey
8:27:15 PM **ladydi2011**: Baby, are you there?
8:27:57 PM **bobjugant**: yea baby
8:28:23 PM **ladydi2011**: Did you see what I said about James?

8:28:34 PM **bobjugant**: no *i* did not get it

8:28:41 PM **bobjugant**: what did he say?

8:28:43 PM **ladydi2011**: I called James this morning and he has it and sent the info and invoice

8:29:27 PM **ladydi2011**: I sent it to you on IM and email first thing this morning.

8:29:30 PM **bobjugant**: *how much is it?*

8:29:43 PM **bobjugant**: *please tell him i will pay once i get back*

8:29:59 PM **bobjugant**: *i* did not get your IM

8:30:19 PM **ladydi2011**: Honey. You have to choose a shipping method

8:30:37 PM **bobjugant**: Air ofcourse

8:31:17 PM **ladydi2011**: Can you be back on line at 10 so I can have it in front of me?

8:31:36 PM **ladydi2011**: I will be at my brothers then

8:32:12 PM **bobjugant**: ok when you get back home just drop offline message

8:32:37 PM **ladydi2011**: How do I drop offline message honey?

8:33:02 PM **bobjugant**: just write here even if *i* am not online

8:33:10 PM **ladydi2011**: Always teaching me baby….

8:33:13 PM **bobjugant**: when *i* log in later *i* will read the message

8:33:40 PM **ladydi2011**: I did this and you said you didn't get it

8:34:09 PM **bobjugant**: *i* only got the message you said you going to pack

8:34:16 PM **bobjugant**: just drop message again honey

8:34:22 PM **bobjugant**: hopefully *i* will get it

8:34:35 PM **ladydi2011**: Go back baby and open past messages

8:34:51 PM **bobjugant**: *i* cant...

8:35:08 PM **ladydi2011**: Hmmm

8:35:08 PM **bobjugant**: ok love please take good care of yourself

8:35:21 PM **bobjugant**: love you baby

8:35:54 PM **ladydi2011**: Love you to darling

8:36:21 PM **ladydi2011**: Bye for now. I am going to drive again now

8:36:57 PM **ladydi2011**: Wait

8:37:47 PM **ladydi2011**: Baby, the pricing is in an Adobe file

8:38:05 PM **ladydi2011**: Can you open it?

8:38:32 PM **bobjugant**: no *i* cant

8:38:40 PM **bobjugant**: how much is it?

8:39:03 PM **bobjugant**: just tell him *i* will please pay when *i* get back

8:39:10 PM **ladydi2011**: Don't remember because it is in pounds ...lol

8:39:13 PM **bobjugant**: *i can't send out money from here please*

8:39:13 PM **bobjugant**: *i* have to rush now

8:39:28 PM **bobjugant**: please just let him know *i* will pay once *i* am out

8:39:29 PM **ladydi2011**: Bye

8:39:33 PM **bobjugant**: ok love..bye

8:39:36 PM **bobjugant**: love you

8:39:43 PM **bobjugant**: and please drive safely

IM May 25, 2012 10:12:29 PM

10:12:29 PM **ladydi2011**: Baby, please be sure this is what you need and look at the prices. Once you give me the green light I will email James. Specifications of Kill manifold - (Price - £ 23, 320.00)

MODEL - KM15 WORKING PRESSURE - 15,000 PSI - INLET - 2-9/16" - 15,000 PSI / 3-1/16" - 15,000 PSI - OUTLET - 2-9/16 " - 15,000 PSI / 3-1/16 " - 15,000 PSI - Air Cargo Delivery: This take only 48hours to be delivered in Chile. The price of this delivery is £ 2,250GBP. I am safely at my brothers. I will be waiting for your reply so I can email James. Love you.

From: Ladydi2011@yahoo.com
To: Bob Jugant
Subject: Please tell me what to do
Sent: Saturday, May 26, 2012 1:31 AM

Hell, Darling,

I felt your stress when we chatted. I didn't know much about what you did but I am starting to get the picture. I know this trip has to be off the charts because it is the first job on your own and you are having problems.

I sent you the info and pricing again from James and am waiting for you to tell me that this is ok and to order. I am stressed because I am not sure if I should have just ordered it without hearing back from you. I can tell time is of the essence. I hope I have done the right thing by waiting for your reply. I already have the email composed to send to James and will send it as soon as you say to.

I miss you and love you, Darling. Diana

IM May 26, 2012 6:02:48 AM

6:02:48 AM **bobjugant**: yes love this is what *i* want.. please let james know so he can send it as soon as possible... please take good care, love you

From: ladydi2011@yahoo.com
To: ukcustomercare@hogsequipment.net
Cc: Bob Jugant
Subject: RE: Urgent please ship Kill manifold to Bob Jugant
Sent: Saturday, May 26, 2012 8:09 AM

Hello James,

I spoke with Mr. Bob Jugant. He would like you to ship the Kill manifold air cargo as soon as possible. He said he will pay you as soon as he returns. Please let me know when you can ship this.

Thank you so much.
Kind regards,
Diana

IM May 26, 2012 7:54:40 PM

7:54:40 PM **bobjugant**: Hi baby, hope you having a nice time? miss you so much and *please let me know if james has shipped the equipment. work here is frustrating and i am getting sick*.. love you

From: ukcustomercare@hogsequipment.net
To: ladydi
Subject: RE: Urgent please ship Kill manifold to Bob Jugant
Sent: Monday, May 28, 2012 4:13 AM

Dear Diana L. Garren,
Please inform Mr. Bob Jugant,Equipment cannot be cargoed until after payment.

Thanks for your understanding

Yours Faithfully,
James Brooks
Sales Manager
Phone Number - 4420 8133 4934
Fax Number - 4487 0479 5053
website: www.hogsequipment.net
email- sales@hogsequipment.net

IM May 28, 2012 9:19:50 AM

9:19:50 AM **ladydi2011**: Hello honey. I hope you made it to shore this weekend and that you are feeling better. I just received a message from James this morning and he said he cannot cargo the equipment until you pay for it. Please take care of you. Love you.

IM May 28, 2012 4:04:50 AM

4:04:50 AM **bobjugant**: hi baby, no offline message from you. everything ok? plase let me know because *i* am worried... *baby please let james know i need this equipment urgently, they have treaten to terminate my contract*, please drop me offline message and take good care.Love you

IM May 28, 2012 12:36:53 PM

12:36:53 PM **bobjugant**: honey are you there, talk to me please
12:38:05 PM **bobjugant**: <ding>
12:41:23 PM **ladydi2011**: Hi honey

12:41:44 PM **bobjugant**: hi baby
12:41:45 PM **bobjugant**: are you ok?
12:41:56 PM **ladydi2011**: Yeah...
12:42:14 PM **ladydi2011**: How are you feeling?
12:42:15 PM **bobjugant**: *i* was a bit worried..no offline messages from you
12:42:40 PM **bobjugant**: honey its very terrible here
12:42:50 PM **ladydi2011**: I am sorry. There was a hurricane that came to the coast where I was so I traveled yesterday
12:43:00 PM **ladydi2011**: It sounds terrible there
12:43:06 PM **bobjugant**: hope you had nice time with your brother
12:43:15 PM **ladydi2011**: I did. Thank you.
12:43:26 PM **bobjugant**: hope everything is fine
12:43:29 PM **ladydi2011**: Did you get the message I sent you from James?
12:43:45 PM **bobjugant**: no *i* did not, has he sent it?
12:43:58 PM **ladydi2011**: I don't want to worry you with anything going on with me. Your plate is full enough.
12:44:13 PM **ladydi2011**: Why are you not getting my messages?
12:44:53 PM **bobjugant**: *i* dont know baby...
12:45:01 PM **bobjugant**: maybe its network
12:45:03 PM **ladydi2011**: ladydi2011: Hello honey. I hope you made it to shore this weekend and that you are feeling better. I just received a message from James this morning and he said he cannot cargo the equipment until you pay for it. Please take care of you. Love you.
12:45:49 PM **bobjugant**: *i* did not come onshore, weather was not good enough
12:45:53 PM **bobjugant**: oh my God...
12:46:32 PM **bobjugant**: what the hell....
12:46:43 PM **ladydi2011**: I don't know baby
12:46:49 PM **ladydi2011**: This is what he said
12:47:46 PM **ladydi2011**: Are you there?
12:49:47 PM **bobjugant**: yes *i* am honey
12:49:55 PM **bobjugant**: damn!!! they treaten to terminate my contract
12:50:30 PM **bobjugant**: *i* am so confused and *i* need it to work here
12:50:34 PM **ladydi2011**: This is not good.
12:50:46 PM **bobjugant**: not at all
12:50:58 PM **ladydi2011**: Breathe baby
12:51:10 PM **ladydi2011**: Slow down and think for a minute
12:51:25 PM **ladydi2011**: Do not panic there is always a solution
12:51:59 PM **bobjugant**: yes baby
12:52:28 PM **bobjugant**: oh my God...
12:52:41 PM **ladydi2011**: Baby....
12:53:02 PM **ladydi2011**: Why are they threatening to terminate your contract?
12:53:39 PM **bobjugant**: because of the work progress, *i* have to finish before another company start working..this is totally crazy...
12:54:18 PM **ladydi2011**: Being on your own is not always fun...ask me, I know!
12:54:45 PM **bobjugant**: please *i* need to get a glass of water, am having headache
12:54:46 PM **bobjugant**: damn!!!
12:54:51 PM **ladydi2011**: So, you do not have an account with any equipment suppliers?
12:55:28 PM **bobjugant**: yes *i* do, *i* bought equipment from them

12:55:41 PM **bobjugant**: oh *i* mean hogs...

12:56:00 PM **bobjugant**: the other company *i* normally buy from has been closed *i* just started buying from james

12:56:46 PM **bobjugant**: please give me a minute so *i* go get a glass of water

12:56:55 PM **ladydi2011**: Ok baby. I am here.

12:59:43 PM **bobjugant**: *i* am back..my head hurts

1:00:21 PM **ladydi2011**: I am here

1:00:26 PM **ladydi2011**: I am sure your head does hurt

1:00:31 PM **ladydi2011**: How is the local?

1:00:48 PM **ladydi2011**: Sending you (((hugs))) and kisses

1:01:06 PM **ladydi2011**: So, how can you get money to James?

1:02:17 PM **bobjugant**: he is getting much better

1:02:27 PM **bobjugant**: *i* am still thinking baby

1:02:30 PM **ladydi2011**: Good. This is one positive.

1:03:09 PM **bobjugant**: *if i could find someone to send to him, when i am out i will refund*

1:03:31 PM **ladydi2011**: You have a lot of friends back home

1:04:53 PM **ladydi2011**: Can you do a bank transfer. With how much you travel, you must do online banking.

1:06:24 PM **ladydi2011**: I am sure you traveled with a credit card on you. If you give me your credit card info I will get this to him.

1:07:59 PM **bobjugant**: *yes i do but i don't ask all my friends*

1:07:59 PM **bobjugant**: *just a close friend*

1:07:59 PM **bobjugant**: *i* will drop an offline message for him *i* just hope he can help

1:08:08 PM **bobjugant**: how is work darling?

1:08:35 PM **ladydi2011**: I haven't gone to the office today. It is a holiday here.

1:09:10 PM **bobjugant**: ok ask him if he accepts credit card because last time *i* was there they did not accept..please ask him and let me know

1:09:50 PM **ladydi2011**: Ok, I will ask him.

1:10:16 PM **ladydi2011**: What about transferring money to them from your account?

1:10:49 PM **ladydi2011**: Let me email James now and see if I can get a response.

1:13:05 PM **bobjugant**: ask him and let me know

1:13:19 PM **bobjugant**: also ask for bank accoun informations

1:13:54 PM **bobjugant**: please *i* will be back online next 1 hour hopefully

1:13:58 PM **ladydi2011**: Ok

1:14:01 PM **bobjugant**: will you be online then?

1:14:17 PM **ladydi2011**: I will try.

1:14:32 PM **bobjugant**: or let me know when you can be online

1:14:46 PM **bobjugant**: so incase *i* dont get your offline message

1:15:03 PM **ladydi2011**: If you give me a time you will definitely be on line, I will be here.

1:15:12 PM **ladydi2011**: Please give me a time.

1:16:31 PM **bobjugant**: 3pm be ok?

1:16:53 PM **ladydi2011**: Ok baby.

1:17:01 PM **bobjugant**: thanks love

1:17:09 PM **ladydi2011**: You are welcome.

1:17:18 PM **bobjugant**: take care

1:17:18 PM **bobjugant**: love you

1:17:30 PM **ladydi2011**: Keep breathing. Love you too..........

From: ladydi2011@yahoo.com
To: ukcustomercare@hogsequipment.net
Cc: Bob Jugant
Subject: FW: Urgent please ship Kill manifold to Bob Jugant
Sent: Monday, May 28, 2012 3:13 PM

Hello James,

I have spoken with Bob Jugant. He wants to know if he can pay with credit card. Please advice. Thank you.

Kind regards,
Diana

IM May 28, 2012 3:28:35 PM

3:28:35 PM **bobjugant**: hi baby
3:28:44 PM **ladydi2011**: Hi honey
3:28:47 PM **bobjugant**: so sorry *i* came late
3:29:05 PM **ladydi2011**: So, what is going on?
3:29:52 PM **bobjugant**: am just trying to convince the locals and my supervisors
3:30:11 PM **bobjugant**: did you get to james?
3:30:47 PM **ladydi2011**: Finally...My email went down.I haven't heard back from him yet.
3:31:26 PM **bobjugant**: guess its already late for him to reply
3:31:50 PM **ladydi2011**: What are you trying to convince the locals and supervisors of?
3:32:05 PM **bobjugant**: about work...
3:33:08 PM **bobjugant**: locals *i* have to pay for extra working days too
3:33:20 PM **ladydi2011**: why?
3:34:01 PM **bobjugant**: because *i* think *i* might not finish on the actual date *i* told them
3:34:45 PM **ladydi2011**: Ouch...not good.
3:34:58 PM **ladydi2011**: Do you think James would answer the phone if I called?
3:35:29 PM **bobjugant**: he will be out of office now
3:35:38 PM **ladydi2011**: Ok....
3:35:51 PM **ladydi2011**: Did you reach your friend in London?
3:36:50 PM **bobjugant**: *i* have droped offline for him
3:37:16 PM **ladydi2011**: It doesn't make sense for this company to not take a credit card...
3:38:33 PM **bobjugant**: they might start accepting now ask him
3:39:23 PM **ladydi2011**: I did ask him. I am just waiting for a reply. In the line of work they are in, I do not see how they cannot take credit card.
3:39:35 PM **ladydi2011**: Are you ok honey?
3:40:18 PM **bobjugant**: *i* am a bit down
3:40:55 PM **bobjugant**: guess they had problems then but still its better to ask so *i* know what to do
3:41:44 PM **ladydi2011**: do you do online banking?
3:41:58 PM **bobjugant**: yes *i* do

3:42:26 PM **bobjugant**: also get the account from James, tomorrow hopefully *i* will try and go onshore and see if *i* can wire

3:42:48 PM **ladydi2011**: So, if need be you can send him money from your account, correct?

3:42:59 PM **bobjugant**: yes baby

3:43:47 PM **ladydi2011**: Ok. Do you want me to ask for his account info now or wait to see what he says about accepting credit cards.

3:44:12 PM **bobjugant**: ask him for both so we don't waste time

3:44:25 PM **ladydi2011**: Ok. I will send another email.

3:44:33 PM **bobjugant**: thanks baby

3:44:38 PM **bobjugant**: *i* really appreciate

3:44:41 PM **ladydi2011**: you are welcome

3:44:43 PM **bobjugant**: *i* miss you

3:45:01 PM **bobjugant**: am really down but *i* know *i* will be ok..even more stronger

3:45:26 PM **ladydi2011**: I know it will be ok too. Is there anything else I can do to assist you?

3:46:03 PM **bobjugant**: nothing for now baby.. just take good care of yourself and be a good girl

3:46:25 PM **bobjugant**: *i* love you

3:46:26 PM **ladydi2011**: How do you feel health wise?

3:46:45 PM **bobjugant**: miss you so much... having headache but *i* am much better

3:46:47 PM **ladydi2011**: I love you too!

3:46:59 PM **ladydi2011**: You said yesterday you are getting sick

3:47:26 PM **bobjugant**: kept thinking.. but *i* am ok honey

3:47:53 PM **ladydi2011**: Ok. I am glad to know this.

3:47:57 PM **bobjugant**: honey have to go talk with the supervisors again, *i* had to quickly come online to talk to you

3:48:09 PM **ladydi2011**: I know you are busy, so I will let you go.

3:48:24 PM **bobjugant**: *i* will try and come online again but if *i* dont come *i* will try to drop offline message

3:48:34 PM **bobjugant**: thanks for understanding love..miss you so much

3:48:43 PM **bobjugant**: bye love

3:48:52 PM **bobjugant**: love you

3:48:55 PM **bobjugant**: mwahhhhhhhhhhh

3:49:01 PM **ladydi2011**: mwahhhhhhhhhhhhh

3:49:22 PM **bobjugant**: please take good care

3:49:35 PM **ladydi2011**: You too baby. Try not to stress

3:49:43 PM **bobjugant**: ok baby

3:49:46 PM **bobjugant**: have to go now

3.49:49 PM **bobjugant**: byc

3:49:51 PM **ladydi2011**: everything will work out

3:49:55 PM **ladydi2011**: Bye

From: ladydi2011@yahoo.com
To: ukcustomercare@hogsequipment.net
Cc: Bob Jugant
Subject: FW: Urgent...Bob Jugant needs payment options
Sent: Monday, May 28, 2012 4:22 PM

Hello James,

Bob Jugant needs to know all the different ways of payment that you will accept. If he has to transfer or wire you money, please send your banking information to me so I can send it to Bob. Thank you so much for all your assistance so Bob gets what he needs to finish the job. He and I both appreciate all you are doing.

Kind regards,

Diana

From: ukcustomercare@hogsequipment.net
To: ladydi
Subject: Re: FW: Urgent...Bob Jugant needs payment options
Sent: Tuesday, May 29, 2012 8:18 AM

Dear Diana L. Garren,

Please find below subcidiary company account information below:

ACCOUNT NAME: SOTEX COLLECTION
NAME OF BANK : HSBC
IBAN: GB13MIDL40190441848372
ACCOUNT NUMBER: 41848372
BIC: MIDLGB2128k
BANK ADDRESS: 38 HIGH STREET, DARTBOARD KENT DA11DG COMPANY ADDRESS: OFFICE 105, HUDSON HOUSE 8 TAVISTOCK ST CITY OF LONDON GREATER LONDON, WCZE 7PP UNITED KINGDOM

Please send a scanned copy of payment receipt. As soon as we get confirmation we will cargo equipment to Chile.

We hope to hear from you.

Yours Faithfully,
James Brooks
Sales Manager
Phone Number - 4420 8133 4934
Fax Number - 4487 0479 5053
website: www.hogsequipment.net
email- sales@hogsequipment.net

From: ladydi2011@yahoo.com
To: ukcustomercare@hogsequipment.net
Cc: Bob Jugant
Subject: RE: FW: Urgent...Bob Jugant needs payment options
Sent: Tuesday, May 29, 2012 8:22 AM

Hello James,

Thank you for this information. Do you accept credit cards?

Make it an outstanding day!

Kind regards,
Diana

RED FLAGS

- The scam has begun. He now has a different tone that is more panicked. He is *supposedly* having problems with a piece of equipment and it *supposedly* hurt one of his supposed local workers.
- Once the scam starts the sammer will usually act as if he is panicked and confused.

He wants me to go onto a website where he supposedly bought the equipment; as soon as I get there, I can tell it is a fictitious website. The average person might not realize it is fictitious. One of the things my company does is website development, so I know what to look for. I searched for another website that might have been the real one, but couldn't find it. It's a good thing I took a screen shot of this website, because as soon as I told him I knew he was a scammer the website could no longer be found. He took it down.

- Scammers use fictitious websites.

He asks me to write a letter to James, but HE is actually James too. He used a voice changer to change his voice when I called, and he wrote the emails that "supposedly" came from James.

- Scammers usually are *all* the people they use in their story.
- He now needs the equipment "urgently" or he will lose his contract. Scammers commonly say if they don't get what they need they will lose the contract.

He tells me to tell James he will pay him when he gets home because he can't send money from there. Of course, James sent an invoice and said he cannot ship the equipment until it is paid for. He has me do all the correspondence so that I am part of this and so I hear the bad news from the "supposed" equipment dealer himself so I will be more likely to believe it and be motivated to help him. He is on Yahoo! IM with me, which means he has Internet service, so he could have sent the email to James himself.

Then I am to ask James about the different payments. Of course, he doesn't have an account with them and they don't take credit cards. Then he says the ultimate, "if i could find someone to send to him, when i am out i will refund". Yep, there it is, and guess who he wants that someone to be? You guessed it, me! When I ask if he had a close friend to ask he says, "Yes i do but i don't ask all my friends, just close friends." He also says he is getting sick. He is actually pretty clever in his approach. He is not pushy but *VERY MANIPULATIVE*. I asked him if he could do a bank transfer and that is exactly what he wanted me to ask. If I didn't know the red flags and got caught into his sweet words, he could have gotten money from me.

🏴 Many scammers will tell you they are getting sick from the stress.

When he didn't hear from me he got scared that I bailed on him. This is the "close of the sale" for them, and if this doesn't work, they know they have lost you.

🏴 All scammers get nervous if they don't hear from you like they expect to once they start talking about money.

He told me his birthday was June 3rd and it is now May 24th, and the perfect time for me to ask him for his address to send him a birthday present. He said he would send me the address but of course he never did. But I caught him in a lie about his birthday. Now he says his birthday is June 26th and that he will hopefully be with me before then. Remember to always be on the lookout for incongruencies in his facts; this will tell you a lot.

🏴 Scammers many times get their facts wrong the second time you ask because they don't remember the lie they told you the first time. If two and two are not adding up, there is a reason.

IM May 29, 2012 10:24:53 AM

10:24:53 AM **bobjugant**: hi baby
10:25:01 AM **ladydi2011**: Hi baby
10:25:05 AM **bobjugant**: thanks for the offline message
10:25:06 AM **ladydi2011**: How are you?
10:25:13 AM **ladydi2011**: You are welcome
10:25:16 AM **bobjugant**: not good at all baby
10:25:25 AM **ladydi2011**: What is happening now?
10:26:21 AM **bobjugant**: *they have give me a deadline*
10:26:38 AM **ladydi2011**: Of when?

10:26:52 AM **bobjugant**: *and the weather its not safe to fly out..i going crazy here..honey you need to help me wire from my account online. i cant access my account here so i will give you my login information*

10:28:02 AM **ladydi2011**: Ok

10:28:39 AM **ladydi2011**: I will do it while we are on here

10:28:49 AM **bobjugant**: ok baby

10:28:50 AM **bobjugant**: hold

10:29:05 AM **bobjugant**: *www.allied-ft.com*

10:29:37 AM **ladydi2011**: Got it baby...

10:30:46 AM **bobjugant**: **hold so i give you my account login**

10:30:56 AM **ladydi2011**: Ok, I am here.

10:31:55 AM **bobjugant**: account number - 3379762476158399

10:32:04 AM **bobjugant**: password- jugantb

10:32:25 AM **ladydi2011**: Got it

10:32:36 AM **bobjugant**: check the balance

10:32:47 AM **ladydi2011**: Ok, please hold

10:33:24 AM **bobjugant**: click on balance

10:34:48 AM **ladydi2011**: *Baby, It looks like on May 17th the balance was 548,000*

10:35:03 AM **bobjugant**: ok

10:35:27 AM **bobjugant**: *click on funds transfer*

10:35:32 AM **ladydi2011**: Ok

10:36:04 AM **ladydi2011**: Need transfer amount

10:36:24 AM **bobjugant**: amount to wire to james right?

10:36:42 AM **ladydi2011**: Yes for both the equipment and air shipment together

10:36:59 AM **bobjugant**: how much is it in total?

10:37:07 AM **ladydi2011**: Hold please

10:38:03 AM **bobjugant**: ok baby

10:39:29 AM **ladydi2011**: the equipment is 23,320.00 and the air cargo is 2,250. Honey I am not familiar with the pounds so please tell me exactly what to put in.

10:40:53 AM **ladydi2011**: My thought is 25, 570.00. Is this correct?

10:44:26 AM **bobjugant**: yes

10:44:33 AM **bobjugant**: lost connection

10:44:48 AM **ladydi2011**: Ok

10:45:13 AM **bobjugant**: hold so *i* calculate in usd

10:45:37 AM **ladydi2011**: Ok

10:46:55 AM **bobjugant**: *40 thousand usd*

10:47.01 AM **ladydi2011**: Ok

10:47:13 AM **bobjugant**: fill the form

10:47:37 AM **ladydi2011**: Do I put this in the transfer amount OR the wire amount?

10:47:55 AM **bobjugant**: wire

10:48:03 AM **ladydi2011**: Ok..Please hold

10:48:33 AM **ladydi2011**: Need your phone number

10:49:13 AM **bobjugant**: 447700061892

10:50:31 AM **ladydi2011**: Receiver's name will be SOTEX COLLECTION right?

10:50:44 AM **bobjugant**: yes

10:51:46 AM **ladydi2011**: Do I put in the bank's address or the company address - BANK ADDRESS: 38 HIGH STREET, DARTBOARD KENT DA11DG COMPANY ADDRESS: OFFICE 105, HUDSON HOUSE 8

TAVISTOCK ST CITY OF LONDON GREATER LONDON, WCZE 7PP UNITED KINGDOM
10:52:05 AM **bobjugant**: company address
10:52:13 AM **ladydi2011**: Ok...please hold
10:55:51 AM **bobjugant**: you there?
10:55:55 AM **ladydi2011**: I am
10:56:07 AM **ladydi2011**: They now need the account number
10:56:41 AM **bobjugant**: thats the ABA ?
10:57:12 AM **ladydi2011**: Which one baby
10:57:16 AM **ladydi2011**: IBAN: GB13MIDL40190441848372
ACCOUNT NUMBER: 41848372
BIC: MIDLGB2128k
10:57:33 AM **ladydi2011**: The 41848372
10:57:38 AM **bobjugant**: yes.. 41848372
10:57:41 AM **ladydi2011**: Cool
10:57:48 AM **ladydi2011**: Do you want a memo
10:58:41 AM **bobjugant**: no need for that
10:58:51 AM **bobjugant**: have you finished filling everything?
10:58:52 AM **ladydi2011**: Local or international bank
10:59:20 AM **bobjugant**: local
10:59:58 AM **ladydi2011**: Almost...just need to fill in the bank info. Please hold
11:00:20 AM **bobjugant**: ok baby
11:01:12 AM **ladydi2011**: Which one is the bank routing #?
11:01:20 AM **ladydi2011**: IBAN: GB13MIDL40190441848372 or BIC: MIDLGB2128k
11:02:00 AM **bobjugant**: the last 8 iban numbers
11:02:48 AM **ladydi2011**: Ok, I am ready to hit process request. Will this give us what we need to send James?
11:03:03 AM **bobjugant**: yes.. Process request
11:03:50 AM **ladydi2011**: *It says I am not authorized to access this location*
11:04:07 AM **ladydi2011**: I need to put in your log in info again. Please hold
11:04:43 AM **bobjugant**: *you need to start all over again?*
11:05:22 AM **bobjugant**: *i mean are you starting all over again?*
11:05:33 AM **ladydi2011**: Yes love..Are you there?
11:09:16 AM **ladydi2011**: It now says the transfer amount cannot be left blank...What do I put in here?
11:09:46 AM **bobjugant**: put same as wire
11:09:50 AM **ladydi2011**: Ok
11:10:54 AM **ladydi2011**: I received 2 messages
11:11:00 AM **ladydi2011**: *The transfer has been successfully processed. Click here to close this page.*
11:11:22 AM **ladydi2011**: *Transfer failed.Account has been suspended. We have detected suspicious log on from a different Internet provider. Please Contact Your Account Officer For More Details.*
11:11:40 AM **ladydi2011**: So, which is it?
11:12:07 AM **ladydi2011**: Your Fund Transfer Progress is 100%.
11:12:08 AM **bobjugant**: my account has been suspended???
11:12:27 AM **ladydi2011**: Like I said, there were actually 2 messages
11:12:32 AM **ladydi2011**: What the hell?
11:12:35 AM **bobjugant**: transfer failed???
11:13:00 AM **ladydi2011**: First it said it was successfully processed

11:13:02 AM **bobjugant**: *i* think *i* have to come on shore
11:13:19 AM **ladydi2011**: Should I call your bank?
11:13:31 AM **bobjugant**: no *i will call myself. they will not realese any information to you since its not your account*
11:13:59 AM **ladydi2011**: Ok
11:14:01 AM **bobjugant**: *i* think *i* have to come onshore baby
11:14:08 AM **ladydi2011**: I am sorry baby
11:14:23 AM **bobjugant**: damn!!!
11:14:31 AM **ladydi2011**: I will save a screen shot of this and email it to you
11:14:36 AM **bobjugant**: this is crazy
11:15:00 AM **ladydi2011**: Yeah it is
11:15:22 AM **ladydi2011**: I have a screen shot so you know what I am seeing when you call them
11:15:41 AM **bobjugant**: just close the page
11:15:45 AM **ladydi2011**: Ok
11:15:50 AM **bobjugant**: *i* will call once *i* get onshore
11:15:59 AM **bobjugant**: *i* have to go check again if *i* can fly out
11:16:18 AM **ladydi2011**: Ok honey
11:16:23 AM **ladydi2011**: Please be careful
11:16:34 AM **bobjugant**: *i* will baby
11:16:45 AM **bobjugant**: *i* will let you know once *i* get onshore
11:16:54 AM **ladydi2011**: Please do...
11:17:06 AM **ladydi2011**: I love you
11:17:27 AM **bobjugant**: love you too
11:17:29 AM **bobjugant**: bye baby
11:17:33 AM **bobjugant**: take care
11:17:36 AM **ladydi2011**: bye honey
11:17:49 AM **bobjugant**: bye love

On the opposing page is a screenshot of the banking website he took me to and it was another fictitious website. It had a lot of broken links and the URL was www.allied-ft.com but the name of the bank on this website was AIFT Financials.

A bank would not have a URL that was so different then its name. I could not find a real bank with this name.

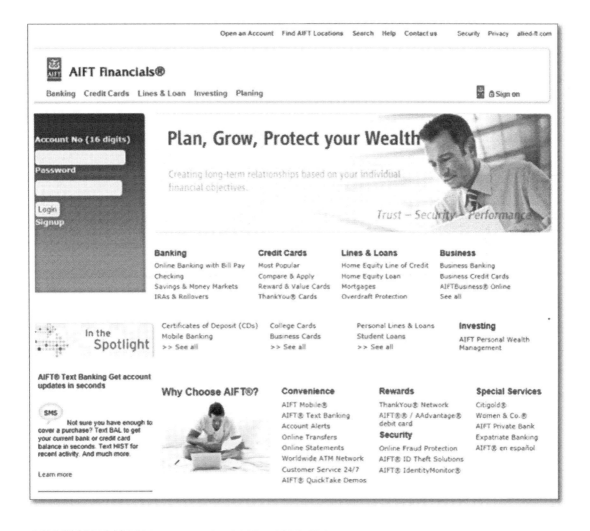

From: ladydi2011@yahoo.com
To: Bob Jugant
Subject: Bank info........
Sent: Tuesday, May 29, 2012 11:25 AM

Hello darling,

I am so sorry you have to go to shore.

Please be careful.

I have attached a screen shot of what the bank website said so you can talk intelligently when you call them.

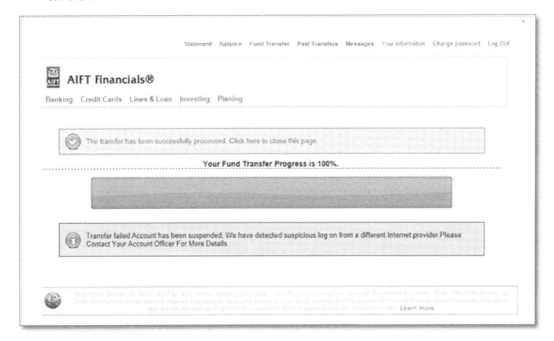

- Now he turns up the urgency by saying they gave him a "deadline" and he really needs the equipment fast. He says the weather is not safe to fly back to land so he needs me to access his bank account and wire money to James. Again, he has Internet service to be online with me on Yahoo IM, so why can't he access his bank account? You need to think about these types of things. I didn't ask him about it because I wanted the scam, but this is a red flag.
- Scammers usually end up telling you they have a deadline to meet and if they don't meet it their contract will be cancelled.

He takes me to another factious website. This time it is a banking website. He gives me his user name and login information and then asks me to check his balance. He does this so I feel like he trusts me enough to give me all the information to enter his bank account, and so I can see he has a lot of money in his account. He wants me to think he has money. I converted his "supposed" balance of 548,000 pounds, and it is $939,589.84 in U.S. currency. He then walks me through where to click. He converts the cost of the equipment that is in pounds into U.S. currency for me and it was 40,000 U.S. currency. $40,000 would be nothing for him if he really had almost a million dollars in his account.

The fictitious banking website would not take my first request so I had to fill it out again. At first it said the transfer was successfully processed and then it said "Transfer Failed.Account has been suspended. We have detected suspicious log on from a different Internet provider. Please Contact Your Account Officer For More Details." He set it up to happen this way so I would feel that this was my fault and want to send him the money. He then called me on the phone asking if I would send James $40,000 and when I said no, he asked if I would send him $25,000 as a deposit. When I said no, he tried to make me jealous by telling me he will ask his neighbor who fancies him.

🏴 When a scammer cannot get the amount they ask for they will always decrease the amount they need. They want to be compensated for the time they spent with you, and some money is better than none.

From: ladydi2011@yahoo.com
To: Bob Jugant
Subject: I think....
Sent: Wednesday, May 30, 2012 12:21 PM

Bob, I think you need to call your neighbor to help you. Even if this means losing me, you being ok is important to me.

Take care of yourself

Diana

IM May 31, 2012 10:10:21 AM

10:10:21 AM **ladydi2011**: Baby, you there?
10:18:25 AM **bobjugant**: yes
10:18:42 AM **bobjugant**: *network is messed up*
10:19:13 AM **bobjugant**: *2nd my contract is gone*
10:19:17 AM **bobjugant**: still have to move on
10:19:24 AM **bobjugant**: its life
10:19:38 AM **bobjugant**: *have to back to the rig and sign the contract termination*
10:20:07 AM **ladydi2011**: I hate this for you
10:20:29 AM **bobjugant**: me too.. *i* have no choice since *i* cant even make a deposit
10:20:31 AM **ladydi2011**: I really hate this for you
10:20:47 AM **bobjugant**: me too baby.. *i* am just trying to cheer myself up
10:21:28 AM **bobjugant**: *i have to be strong.. i really put alot of effort in this and my profit was huge*
10:21:39 AM **ladydi2011**: *i* know baby.
10:21:47 AM **bobjugant**: love you diana

10:22:18 AM **ladydi2011**: I love you
10:22:29 AM **ladydi2011**: I feel so helpless
10:22:49 AM **bobjugant**: its ok
10:23:00 AM **bobjugant**: *i* love you with all my heart
10:23:25 AM **bobjugant**: *i* am not going to ask my neighbour
10:23:37 AM **bobjugant**: its better *i* loose my contract than giving her the oppurtuinity
10:24:35 AM **ladydi2011**: I would call her if this was what you had to do
10:24:51 AM **bobjugant**: please just take good care of yourself
10:25:11 AM **ladydi2011**: When will I hear from you again?
10:25:31 AM **bobjugant**: once the contract has been terminated
10:25:34 AM **bobjugant**: *oh my God...*
10:25:39 AM **ladydi2011**: What?
10:25:46 AM **bobjugant**: *its ok...*
10:25:49 AM **ladydi2011**: What?
10:25:58 AM **bobjugant**: its ok baby...
10:26:03 AM **ladydi2011**: What?
10:26:12 AM **bobjugant**: *please its ok*
10:26:16 AM **ladydi2011**: Ok.
10:26:20 AM **bobjugant**: take good care pleas
10:26:28 AM **bobjugant**: *tears just rolled out from my eyes*
10:26:48 AM **bobjugant**: *i don't believe am saying once the contract is terminated*
10:26:54 AM **ladydi2011**: My heart is breaking for you
10:26:54 AM **bobjugant**: *just because of 25k*
10:27:16 AM **bobjugant**: *am in tears*
10:27:22 AM **bobjugant**: bye
10:27:25 AM **ladydi2011**: There has to be a way
10:27:51 AM **bobjugant**: james need a deposit
10:27:58 AM **bobjugant**: *i* can't convince him with even a little amount
10:28:10 AM **ladydi2011**: Call him and the bank again
10:28:43 AM **bobjugant**: *i* have been on the phone with the bank today
10:28:46 AM **bobjugant**: *i* could not sleep
10:28:51 AM **ladydi2011**: What did they say?
10:28:59 AM **bobjugant**: so *i* had to call the bank uk time this morning
10:29:19 AM **bobjugant**: they cant assist on till the said date
10:29:24 AM **bobjugant**: screw everybody
10:29:40 AM **bobjugant**: james need a deposit
10:30:01 AM **ladydi2011**: Baby, can you think of anyone else that can help
10:30:11 AM **bobjugant**: forget it
10:30:14 AM **ladydi2011**: What about a line of credit from your credit card
10:31:07 AM **bobjugant**: *i* cant get cash to wire
10:31:13 AM **bobjugant**: honey forget about it
10:31:17 AM **bobjugant**: thanks
10:31:?? AM **bobjugant**: bye
10:??:?? AM **ladydi2011**: Baby, are you sure you don't want to ask your neighbor?
10:??:?? AM **bobjugant**: now *i* am in a mood to drink again
10:??:?? M **ladydi2011**: Hmmmm
10:??:?? M **bobjugant**: *i* don't want anything with her

10:33:16 AM **ladydi2011**: Ok
10:33:36 AM **bobjugant**: if *i* ask she will help once
10:33:44 AM **bobjugant**: but *i* know her
10:33:53 AM **ladydi2011**: what do you mean?
10:34:04 AM **bobjugant**: *She will be over me*
10:34:29 AM **ladydi2011**: Please take care of yourself
10:34:39 AM **bobjugant**: ok
10:34:40 AM **bobjugant**: bye
10:34:45 AM **bobjugant**: take care
10:34:52 AM **bobjugant**: love you
10:34:53 AM **ladydi2011**: Love you too

IM May 31, 2012 6:29:42 PM Continued

6:29:42 PM **ladydi2011**: Hi Darling
6:30:03 PM **bobjugant**: hi honey
6:30:36 PM **ladydi2011**: Can you see me baby?
6:30:50 PM **bobjugant**: yes *i* can
6:31:04 PM **ladydi2011**: How are you?
6:31:14 PM **bobjugant**: not good at all
6:31:21 PM **bobjugant**: how is work?
6:31:34 PM **ladydi2011**: Busy...payroll and other stuff
6:31:40 PM **bobjugant**: ok
6:31:46 PM **ladydi2011**: Tell me honey what is happening
6:31:57 PM **bobjugant**: nothing good
6:32:16 PM **ladydi2011**: Did you call James again?
6:32:24 PM **bobjugant**: yes *i* did
6:32:41 PM **ladydi2011**: He will not budge?
6:32:55 PM **bobjugant**: needs a deposit
6:33:25 PM **ladydi2011**: Have you talked to the supervisors
6:33:35 PM **bobjugant**: yes *i* did and same old story
6:34:33 PM **ladydi2011**: Are you ok?
6:34:41 PM **bobjugant**: no baby..am in a sad mood
6:35:07 PM **ladydi2011**: I am sure
6:35:45 PM **ladydi2011**: Are you back on shore?
6:36:12 PM **bobjugant**: *i* did not go ofshore again
6:36:21 PM **ladydi2011**: Oh, ok.
6:36:48 PM **ladydi2011**: I don't know what to say
6:37:08 PM **bobjugant**: just concentrate more on your work
6:37:16 PM **bobjugant**: have to go baby
6:37:29 PM **ladydi2011**: I am worried about you.
6:37:34 PM **bobjugant**: just came online to check up on you
6:37:45 PM **ladydi2011**: Please take care of yourself for me.
6:37:51 PM **bobjugant**: ok
6:38:06 PM **ladydi2011**: Thank you for checking on me.
6:38:12 PM **bobjugant**: ok

6:38:13 PM **bobjugant**: bye
6:38:25 PM **ladydi2011**: Bye

IM Jun 1, 2012 9:24:23 AM

9:24:23 AM **ladydi2011**: Morning honey. How are you?
9:24:24 AM **bobjugant**: hi
9:24:36 AM **bobjugant**: not good as usual
9:24:50 AM **ladydi2011**: What is happening now my love?
9:25:09 AM **bobjugant**: *i* am going to sign the contract termination today
9:25:33 AM **ladydi2011**: I am sorry baby. Did you call your agent?
9:26:13 AM **bobjugant**: yes *i* did
9:26:27 AM **ladydi2011**: Nothing he can do to help?
9:26:31 AM **bobjugant**: he has only 5k dollars but james did not accept that
9:26:55 AM **ladydi2011**: I so hate this for you!
9:28:35 AM **ladydi2011**: I won't ask if you are ok, because I know you are not.
9:32:07 AM **ladydi2011**: Bob....please talk to me
9:34:07 AM **bobjugant**: *i* am here
9:35:41 AM **bobjugant**: what do you want me to say?
9:36:19 AM **ladydi2011**: I don't know. I did not do this to you.
9:36:32 AM **bobjugant**: ok
9:36:39 AM **ladydi2011**: Ok?
9:37:04 AM **ladydi2011**: Are you blaming me?
9:37:15 AM **bobjugant**: no
9:37:49 AM **ladydi2011**: You have always been good at one liners. These are not good one liners.
9:38:43 AM **ladydi2011**: Other than money, because we know I cannot help you with this. What can I do for you?
9:39:31 AM **bobjugant**: dont worry
9:40:09 AM **ladydi2011**: How can I not worry?
9:40:34 AM **ladydi2011**: How would you feel if I was in trouble and you could not help?
9:41:57 AM **bobjugant**: terrible
9:42:03 AM **bobjugant**: *i* will try my best even if *i* can't do everything but *i* know *i* will come up with something
9:49:09 AM **ladydi2011**: Unfortunately, all I have to offer you is my love. In this situation, it is not enough.
9:50:16 AM **bobjugant**: ok
9:50:54 AM **bobjugant**: *i* will ask my neighbour
9:51:27 AM **bobjugant**: have a nice day, *i* will let you know if she is able to assist me
9:51:36 AM **bobjugant**: take care
9:51:40 AM **ladydi2011**: Ok
9:51:43 AM **ladydi2011**: You too
9:51:48 AM **bobjugant**: bye
9:51:51 AM **bobjugant**: love you
9:52:03 AM **ladydi2011**: Bye

IM Jun 1, 2012 12:16:00 PM

12:16:00 PM **bobjugant**: she said she will pay on monday, *i* just wanted to let you know
12:16:11 PM **bobjugant**: take good care, bye. Love you

IM Jun 2, 2012 5:17:56 AM

5:17:56 AM **ladydi2011**: Hi, I am so happy that you don't have to terminate the contract and lose profit and face. I know this has to brighten your day. The earliest you will get the equipment is Wed or Thurs. Enjoy your weekend in Chile. Bye

IM Jun 2, 2012 10:57:27 AM

10:57:27 AM **ladydi2011**: The greatest love of all is when you willingly sacrifice your own happiness for the one you love....

IM Jun 4, 2012 10:55:35 PM

10:55:35 PM **ladydi2011**: Thinking about you. Did your neighbor pay for the equipment today? Has it been shipped to you? Is everything ok now?

IM Jun 5, 2012 9:27:46 PM

9:27:46 PM **bobjugant**: hi baby
9:27:54 PM **bobjugant**: you there?
9:28:03 PM **ladydi2011**: I am
9:28:15 PM **bobjugant**: how are you doing?
9:28:23 PM **bobjugant**: just read you offline message
9:28:33 PM **bobjugant**: why would you ever think that way
9:28:42 PM **bobjugant**: *i promised you and gave you my words*
9:28:46 PM **ladydi2011**: You just disappeared
9:28:51 PM **bobjugant**: you doubt me?
9:28:55 PM **bobjugant**: *i* went to the rig
9:29:15 PM **ladydi2011**: How are things there?
9:29:26 PM **bobjugant**: why would *i* disappear?
9:29:38 PM **ladydi2011**: I don't know?
9:29:39 PM **bobjugant**: you never even asked how did *i* go with my job
9:29:45 PM **bobjugant**: all you say *i* disappear
9:29:52 PM **bobjugant**: when you know *i* am tensed
9:29:57 PM **ladydi2011**: You didn't see that message
9:30:01 PM **ladydi2011**: Please hold
9:30:02 PM **bobjugant**: when you know the task *i* have ahead

9:30:09 PM **ladydi2011**: And I will copy and paste it for you

9:30:42 PM **ladydi2011**: ladydi2011: Hi, I am so happy that you don't have to terminate the contract and lose profit and face. I know this has to brighten your day. The earliest you will get the equipment is Wed or Thurs. Enjoy your weekend in Chile. Bye

9:31:06 PM **bobjugant**: *i* have been thinking about you and tried all my possible best to come online to chat with you

9:31:12 PM **ladydi2011**: The greatest love of all is when you willingly sacrifice your own happiness for the one you love....ladydi2011: Thinking about you. Did your neighbor pay for the equipment today? Has it been shipped to you? Is everything ok now?

9:31:36 PM **ladydi2011**: I was worried about you.

9:31:40 PM **bobjugant**: *i* told you she paid and *i* have gotten the equipment

9:31:48 PM **ladydi2011**: You didn't tell me you were going back to the rig

9:32:01 PM **ladydi2011**: You said she would pay yesterday

9:32:04 PM **bobjugant**: what will *i* be doing onshore when *i* have work to do

9:32:12 PM **ladydi2011**: Wow, you already got the equipment

9:32:29 PM **bobjugant**: when did *i* tell you she paid???

9:32:34 PM **ladydi2011**: I thought you couldn't work until you got the equipment

9:32:54 PM **bobjugant**: what's wow *i* already got the equipment???

9:33:05 PM **bobjugant**: when did *i* tell you she paid?

9:33:13 PM **bobjugant**: answer that please

9:33:33 PM **ladydi2011**: bobjugant: she said she will pay on monday, *i* just wanted to let you know take good care, bye. Love you

9:33:50 PM **ladydi2011**: This was the last I heard from you and it was 4:00 on Friday

9:34:14 PM **bobjugant**: she paid on saturday because of bank holiday in uk

9:34:14 PM **ladydi2011**: Shipping takes 48 hours

9:34:24 PM **ladydi2011**: I didn't know this

9:34:25 PM **bobjugant**: on monday and tuesday

9:34:33 PM **ladydi2011**: I didn't hear anything from you

9:34:40 PM **bobjugant**: she paid for express

9:34:46 PM **ladydi2011**: I am so glad all is well there for you now

9:34:54 PM **bobjugant**: *i* have been depressed

9:34:58 PM **ladydi2011**: Why?

9:35:04 PM **bobjugant**: a woman who *i* don't love after she paid she has been on me

9:35:28 PM **ladydi2011**: What do you mean?

9:36:04 PM **bobjugant**: *i* mean a woman who *i* don't love rescued me

9:36:21 PM **ladydi2011**: Hmmmm

9:36:41 PM **bobjugant**: *i* have to tell you my mind

9:36:50 PM **ladydi2011**: I have called you

9:36:56 PM **ladydi2011**: I have sent you ecards

9:36:57 PM **bobjugant**: *i* am about to read them

9:37:06 PM **bobjugant**: ecards to do what?

9:37:11 PM **bobjugant**: make me feel good?

9:37:25 PM **ladydi2011**: If I had it, I would have given it to you

9:37:35 PM **bobjugant**: know thats not true

9:37:41 PM **ladydi2011**: What??????

9:37:42 PM **bobjugant**: at least you support

9:37:55 PM **ladydi2011**: I supported you through all of this

9:37:56 PM **bobjugant**: yes *i* am telling you my mind

9:38:03 PM **ladydi2011**: Please continue

9:38:45 PM **bobjugant**: yes *i* know you did but you know deep down what toy thought about

9:39:01 PM **bobjugant**: sorry for my mistake

9:39:03 PM **ladydi2011**: What? I do not understand

9:39:47 PM **bobjugant**: you never wanted to assist me sending money

9:39:57 PM **bobjugant**: thats what really hurts me

9:40:00 PM **ladydi2011**: Why do you say this?

9:40:20 PM **bobjugant**: because you don't want to speak out your mind

9:40:32 PM **ladydi2011**: Please continue

9:40:58 PM **bobjugant**: *i* am speaking out my mind and *i* need you too speak out yours too

9:41:25 PM **ladydi2011**: You do not know my mind

9:41:49 PM **ladydi2011**: Please speak first

9:42:02 PM **ladydi2011**: Get it all off your chest

9:42:29 PM **bobjugant**: *i* have

9:43:39 PM **ladydi2011**: I never burdened you with my issues because you had enough of your own

9:44:11 PM **ladydi2011**: You told me you love me for me and it didn't matter if I have money or not

9:44:22 PM **ladydi2011**: Now you're angry because I don't

9:45:21 PM **bobjugant**: *if it was me, even if it was 1k usd*

9:45:38 PM **bobjugant**: *i* will tell you thats what *i* can come up with

9:46:12 PM **bobjugant**: never mind, but *i* just need to clear out my mind

9:46:25 PM **ladydi2011**: *1 k wouldn't have helped you*

9:46:49 PM **ladydi2011**: Thank you for telling me the truth

9:46:57 PM **bobjugant**: even if wont help me but at least you say baby this is what *i* have

9:47:10 PM **bobjugant**: then *i* tell you it won't help

9:48:09 PM **bobjugant**: *i* am a straight forward person and *i* need you to be forward to me

9:48:41 PM **ladydi2011**: I was.

9:49:24 PM **bobjugant**: if *i* was in your shoes at leats *i* tell you baby this is what *i* can offer

9:49:29 PM **ladydi2011**: Hmmmm

9:49:36 PM **bobjugant**: *i* wont leave you on a dead end..well its ok..*i* finally got it fixed

9:50:18 PM **bobjugant**: put yourself in my position, what will you think

9:50:25 PM **ladydi2011**: I have

9:50:48 PM **ladydi2011**: No matter what I say, it appears you will not believe me

9:51:37 PM **bobjugant**: *i* love you and you know it

9:52:34 PM **ladydi2011**: Your neighbor gave you the money

9:52:48 PM **bobjugant**: yes she did...

9:53:03 PM **bobjugant**: and she has been checking on me

9:53:29 PM **bobjugant**: asking me if *i* have ny problem *i* should let her know

9:53:44 PM **ladydi2011**: Well at least she knows how to get through to you

9:53:50 PM **ladydi2011**: I tried but couldn't

9:53:59 PM **bobjugant**: baby please *i* am messed up right now

9:54:12 PM **bobjugant**: she kept on sending me offline messages

9:54:20 PM **ladydi2011**: Hmmmm

9:54:21 PM **bobjugant**: and *i* have not replied her

9:55:15 PM **bobjugant**: because *i* did not want to talk to any body

9:55:39 PM **bobjugant**: *i* need to go and sleep

9:55:55 PM **bobjugant**: hope you don't mind...

9:56:21 PM **ladydi2011**: Please rest
9:56:29 PM **ladydi2011**: I am glad all is ok there now
9:56:35 PM **bobjugant**: am sorry, but *i* just have to speak out my mind
9:56:40 PM **bobjugant**: have to go now
9:56:44 PM **bobjugant**: take good care
9:56:44 PM **ladydi2011**: Ok, you too
9:56:53 PM **bobjugant**: bye
9:56:58 PM **ladydi2011**: Bye

IM Jun 6, 2012 11:41:52 AM

11:41:52 AM **bobjugant**: hi
11:43:05 AM **bobjugant**: you there?

IM Jun 7, 2012 12:06:36 AM

12:06:36 AM **bobjugant**: you there?
12:06:48 AM **bobjugant**: <ding>

IM Jun 8, 2012 12:07:01 PM

12:07:01 PM **ladydi2011**: You have an email that you should take the time to read...

From: ladydi2011@yahoo.com
To: Bob Jugant
Subject: Goodbye Bob
Sent: Tuesday, June 08, 2012 12:01 PM
My darling Bob...

You thought you were so slick. You forgot that I am a smart woman. I have known from the beginning you were a Nigerian scammer when I saw your email was sent from MTN.

I knew from the beginning you would not ask me for money on your first "supposed" trip, but that you would ask for money on your second "supposed" trip. I was right. I have good instincts, my dear.

I knew that the equipment and the bank websites were bogus and part of your fraud scheme. Many people would not, but when my book comes out people will be educated of what to look for. I do want to thank you for not trying to lay the guilt on me too thick. I appreciated this! Using another woman to make me jealous was pretty funny...You see, if I was in love with you, I would never allow someone to be my priority while they consider me an option.

This entire time I was trying to get more information for the book I am writing on online dating scams. Before I met you a man scammed me out of money. This made me smarter concerning online dating fraud. After some research I learned "romance scams" are stealing billions of dollars from women and men. Nobody talks about it because they are ashamed and embarrassed. They become silent victims. I will NEVER be a silent victim. I have a heart for women and I do not want to see them or men get their hearts broken or their wallets emptied. *I will help them have a voice.* I am writing a book about this to educate people so they do not get caught in scamming ploys such as yours. I have to. Someone has to speak up and break the silence.

I am not sure how you look yourself in the mirror every day, but this is your problem, not mine! Please remember that karma is a bitch! I wouldn't want your karma... I also wouldn't want to be you on judgment day.

I hope one day you will really fall in love with the woman you are trying to scam so you learn what heartbreak feels like.

Well, our time is over. You actually lost money on me. I make money the legal way! I do not have to look over my shoulder like you do. I am truly free, but you are not. How sad for you, my dear.

As for me, I will be busy writing my book and I once again will live by my two sayings..."It is what it is" and "Next"!

Darling, I hope you don't allow yourself to get so poor that all you have is money. May I always remain in your thoughts until your last breath.

Take good care.
Diana

IM Jun 8, 2012 1:44:44 PM

1:44:44 PM **bobjugant**: Hello love
1:44:53 PM **bobjugant**: Hmmmmmm
1:45:03 PM **ladydi2011**: Hello
1:45:08 PM **ladydi2011**: How are you?
1:45:19 PM **bobjugant**: Pretty good
1:45:30 PM **ladydi2011**: Did you read the email I sent you today?
1:45:38 PM **ladydi2011**: What is hmmmmmmmmmmmm
1:45:49 PM **bobjugant**: *Suprised*
1:46:07 PM **ladydi2011**: Surprised about what?
1:46:25 PM **bobjugant**: *You swept me off my feet*
1:46:45 PM **ladydi2011**: What do you mean?
1:48:08 PM **bobjugant**: *I promised you den dat I would stand by you*
1:50:35 PM **bobjugant**: First of all
1:50:49 PM **bobjugant**: *Am sorry if I hurt you*
1:51:01 PM **bobjugant**: Secondly
1:51:12 PM **bobjugant**: *I will always be yours*
1:51:25 PM **bobjugant**: Thirdly

1:51:46 PM **bobjugant**: *I never had feelings for my neigbhour*

1:52:32 PM **bobjugant**: I was tensed

1:53:16 PM **bobjugant**: *I love you very much*

1:53:32 PM **bobjugant**: *We are together*

1:54:07 PM **ladydi2011**: Did you read my email?

1:54:36 PM **bobjugant**: *You said I was a con artist*

1:54:55 PM **bobjugant**: *I was a scammer*

1:55:07 PM **ladydi2011**: This is what I said

1:56:04 PM **bobjugant**: My contacts told me you were asking questions about me

1:56:16 PM **bobjugant**: Hogs equiptments

1:56:33 PM **ladydi2011**: I asked if they were located in London or Manchester

1:57:33 PM **bobjugant**: *James told me someone was carrying a survey of the company*

1:57:51 PM **ladydi2011**: It wasn't me.

1:58:01 PM **bobjugant**: *But you could not get d answer*

1:58:12 PM **ladydi2011**: What answer?

1:58:19 PM **bobjugant**: *Hogs equiptment can never be found*

1:58:37 PM **bobjugant**: *They are kind of invicible*

1:59:05 PM **bobjugant**: *You can never know were they are*

2:00:03 PM **bobjugant**: *Baby I truthful to you*

2:00:12 PM **bobjugant**: *I loved you so much*

2:01:07 PM **bobjugant**: Can I tell you something???

2:01:21 PM **ladydi2011**: Please do

2:02:14 PM **bobjugant**: You are the first woman to know about me above 60%

2:02:36 PM **ladydi2011**: What do you mean?

2:02:38 PM **bobjugant**: I find it unbelievable

2:03:11 PM **ladydi2011**: Will you ever let me know you 100%

2:03:15 PM **bobjugant**: *I am so in love with you*

2:03:20 PM **bobjugant**: I will

2:03:33 PM **bobjugant**: The other 40%

2:04:08 PM **ladydi2011**: Hmmmm

2:04:41 PM **bobjugant**: *With information I will give you your book would be the bomb*

2:05:09 PM **ladydi2011**: please tell me the other 40%

2:06:06 PM **bobjugant**: *Your book would be so intresting with it*

2:07:20 PM **bobjugant**: Its an adventure

2:08:20 PM **bobjugant**: *My love for you will never change*

2:08:58 PM **bobjugant**: Or you don't you wanna know 100% about me??

2:09:19 PM **ladydi2011**: I want to know 100% of you

Break in Time

2:09:52 PM **ladydi2011**: Please hold while I get rid of this other guy....6 on the hook

2:10:47 PM **bobjugant**: Wat other guy

2:11:06 PM **ladydi2011**: Other scammers I have been chatting with for the book.....

2:12:36 PM **bobjugant**: Really

2:12:55 PM **ladydi2011**: I am going to show unavailable so nobody knows I am on line

2:13:19 PM **bobjugant**: Ok

2:19:47 PM **ladydi2011**: Millions have been scammed and they don't talk about it because they feel ashamed and embarrassed.

2:20:07 PM **ladydi2011**: When they stay silent they lose their power...

2:20:09 PM **bobjugant**: Oh I c
2:20:18 PM **ladydi2011**: it is the same with molestation and rape
2:20:26 PM **bobjugant**: Yea that's true
2:20:51 PM **ladydi2011**: The man who got money from me came clean with me
2:21:02 PM **ladydi2011**: He is a 25 year old guy from Nigeria
2:21:24 PM **bobjugant**: Really
2:21:36 PM **ladydi2011**: He said there was something about me that made him fall in love with me and the guilt was killing him
2:22:09 PM **bobjugant**: So how did you know he was 25
2:23:00 PM **ladydi2011**: He showed me himself on cam....then he said, do you want to know how old I am, when he told me I about fell off my chair
2:23:30 PM **bobjugant**: How much did he take from you
2:23:38 PM **ladydi2011**: 3,500
2:24:04 PM **bobjugant**: Ok
2:24:16 PM **ladydi2011**: So, why am I the only woman who knows 60% about you?
2:25:10 PM **bobjugant**: I am so invisible to some people
2:26:14 PM **ladydi2011**: Bob, are you there?

IM Jun 8, 2012 4:51:56 PM

4:51:56 PM **bobjugant**: Hello baby
4:52:10 PM **bobjugant**: Am here know
4:52:11 PM **ladydi2011**: Hello
4:52:27 PM **ladydi2011**: I am now on a client call
4:54:07 PM **bobjugant**: Take your time honey
4:54:19 PM **ladydi2011**: Thank you
4:54:26 PM **bobjugant**: Ok baby
4:54:55 PM **bobjugant**: I love you
4:56:15 PM **bobjugant**: Send me an email when your done
4:56:20 PM **ladydi2011**: Ok

IM Jun 8, 2012 6:08:41 PM

6:08:41 PM **ladydi2011**: Please come on line.

IM Jun 8, 2012 11:38:51 PM

11:38:51 PM **bobjugant**: Hello baby
11:39:15 PM **ladydi2011**: Are we being monitored?
11:39:16 PM **bobjugant**: Internet was down
11:39:48 PM **bobjugant**: Have you eatin
11:39:59 PM **bobjugant**: Monitored by who??
11:40:07 PM **ladydi2011**: Yes, finally at 9:00
11:40:28 PM **ladydi2011**: I don't know???

11:41:29 PM **bobjugant**: Am doing fine
11:41:46 PM **ladydi2011**: Is your name really Bob?
11:41:52 PM **bobjugant**: So how did your call go
11:42:09 PM **ladydi2011**: It went well.
11:43:31 PM **bobjugant**: *Baby you have a blackberry right*
11:43:34 PM **ladydi2011**: Yes
11:43:48 PM **bobjugant**: Is there a pin
11:43:53 PM **ladydi2011**: Yes
11:44:04 PM **bobjugant**: *I want the pin*
11:44:32 PM **ladydi2011**: Ok
11:44:43 PM **ladydi2011**: I have to remember how to find it
11:45:24 PM **bobjugant**: Lol
11:45:36 PM **bobjugant**: Try finding it
11:45:45 PM **ladydi2011**: Please don't laugh at me
11:45:46 PM **bobjugant**: Am waiting
11:45:57 PM **ladydi2011**: Why do you want the pin?
11:46:03 PM **ladydi2011**: I am doing a search
11:46:17 PM **bobjugant**: Kk
11:46:34 PM **ladydi2011**: I am still smart!!!
11:46:48 PM **ladydi2011**: I hear you laughing
11:46:54 PM **bobjugant**: Dats my girl
11:46:57 PM **bobjugant**: Lol
11:47:15 PM **ladydi2011**: 29049EB2
11:47:20 PM **bobjugant**: Kk
11:47:44 PM **bobjugant**: Nice
11:48:09 PM **bobjugant**: So wat did you have for dinner
11:48:09 PM **ladydi2011**: What do you mean nice?
11:48:21 PM **ladydi2011**: Why did you want my pin?
11:48:41 PM **ladydi2011**: Tortellini
11:48:49 PM **bobjugant**: *I will add you over here on my bb*
11:49:01 PM **ladydi2011**: Ok....
11:49:13 PM **bobjugant**: Yea
11:49:24 PM **ladydi2011**: where are you?
11:50:04 PM **bobjugant**: My apartment
11:51:05 PM **ladydi2011**: Can I see you on cam
11:51:39 PM **bobjugant**: I don't have a cam for now
11:52:18 PM **bobjugant**: *But you gonna eventually c me*
11:53:04 PM **ladydi2011**: Is your real name Bob?
11:54:31 PM **bobjugant**: *Did you get my bb invite*
11:55:30 PM **ladydi2011**: *I did and I accepted*
11:55:37 PM **bobjugant**: *I love very much*
11:55:48 PM **bobjugant**: *For real*

RED FLAGS

- In an attempt to make me feel guilty he said his contract is gone and he has to go back to the rig to sign the contract termination just because of 25 thousand dollars. He also made sure to tell me that the profit would have been huge.
- He said his neighbor gave him the money and he already has the equipment. That would have been really fast. Pay attention to details.
- He was really upset that I didn't even offer him a thousand dollars. Once again, when the scammer's plan goes awry and he doesn't get the money he wants, he will take anything.

It was time to tell him I have known all along that he is a scammer and he is going to be in my book. I was shocked at his response to my goodbye letter. He said he was surprised, that I swept him off his feet, and then he promised he would stand by me, always be mine and that he loves me very much. He also apologized for hurting me. He said James (who is him) said someone was surveying Hogs Equipment but they could never get the answers and it can never be found because it is "kind of invisible" and I can never know where it is. With this, he is confessing that he is a scammer.

He says he is truthful with me and he loves me so much, is so in love with me, and his love for me will never change. Hmmm, another scammer that claims to have fallen in love with me. Am I a scammer magnet now or what? He then says I am the first woman to know him above 60% and asked me if I wanted to know 100% about him. I am now thinking he is going to tell me who he really is and provide me the deep information I have wanted for this book. He was shocked to learn he is going to be in a book and tells me the information he will provide for this book will make it "the bomb" and be so interesting. Now, I think I finally have someone who will tell me what I want to know.

I was beyond shocked when he asked for my Blackberry pin number and added me to his Blackberry Messenger. When do scammers tell you who they are and bring you this far into their world? This is just more confirmation that I am supposed to write this book to educate you. He always said he will teach me many things. Let's go on this adventure and see what he is going to teach me.

This man taught me much of what is in chapter seven, Inner Workings of the Scamming World (p. 677) and provided me the scenarios of what he would have done to obtain more money from me if I had given him any money:

1. Since he showed me the balance in his account he would continually need something and ask me for money. He would remind me that I know he has the money because I

saw it in his back account, so I should have no doubts of being paid back once he got back home. He would keep getting money from me this way until I would no longer send him money.

2. Once I refused to send any more money, he would tell me his contract was finished and he has been paid. He would then ask me to open a bank account since his has been frozen. Then he would put the money he "made from the contract" in my account. Once he "supposedly" put the money in my account he would ask me to send different increments of the money to three different accounts, claiming that once I did this he would be on his way here to be with me. This is called "flashing." Flashing is giving the appearance of money in an account, but it is never really there. In truth, if I had sent the money, I would have heard from my bank shortly after, and then I would have heard from law enforcement. Of course, I would never meet or hear from Bob again, but he would have obtained a lot of money from me!

The next scammer you will read about really does know how to utilize a child to rip your heart out to get to your money…

CHAPTER 4

MASTER AT RIPPING YOUR HEART OUT TO GET YOUR MONEY

B y the time I encountered this man, I had been chatting with scammers for three months. I must say, his first of many formats is the cruelest and most despicable of all the scammers I chatted with for this book. He used a child to pull at my heart strings and try to get to my purse strings. I didn't think anyone could stoop that low. This really woke me up and I hope it wakes you up too, to see how low people will go to steal your money. He was ruthless and relentless in his ploy, and he is not the only one out there.

His profile as found on *Singlesbee*:

Profile: jeffcand

Looking for long term Relationship!...
48-year-old in United Kingdom
Seeking 30 to 75-year-old women

My Basics

- Height: Not Specified
- Body type: Unspecified
- Hair color: Unspecified
- Ethnicity: White / Caucasian
- Looks: Unspecified
- Education: Graduate degree
- ***Occupation: Banking, insurance and financial services***
- Income: $50,000
- I speak: English
- Religion: Christian - other
- Relationship status: Widowed
- Children: Yes, living at home
- Wants children: Undecided
- Smoking: Never
- Drinking: Occasionally

My Type of Girl

- Looking for: Not Specified
- *With: Women 30 to 75-year-old*
- Distance: Within 0 miles of London
- Height: Not Specified
- Body type: Any
- Hair color: Any
- Ethnicity: Doesn't Matter
- Education: Doesn't Matter
- Occupation: Any
- Income: Doesn't Matter
- Language(s): English
- Religion: Any
- Relationship status: Any
- Children: Doesn't Matter
- Wants children: Doesn't Matter
- Smoking: Doesn't Matter
- Drinking: Doesn't Matter

About Me

Honest and caring man, *i* am a very *simple man with simple heart*, and *i* love treating my partner just the way *i* treat myself. life is all about caring for one another... *God fearing man, am not here for games or toy with peoples heart, i hate cheat and lier... just be yourself and see what it will happened next, that is life for you.*

Who I'd Like To Meet

understanding and caring woman who is ready to have her own home and *live a happy family*. a woman with *brave heart and loving kind*. a woman that knows how to love a family and care for them.

RED FLAGS

- He has almost no specific preferences in his profile for himself and for what he's looking for in a woman. This is a red flag in itself; then consider that he supposedly has a daughter. Don't you think he would have preferences for the woman he would introduce to his daughter?

- He says he is 48 years old, but the age of the woman he is looking for is 30-75. Why is a 48 year old man looking for a woman as old as 75? The real reason is many scammers believe that women in this age group have money and are lonely due to divorce or the death of a spouse.
- He says he works in banking, insurance and finance. Which is it?
- He says he has a graduate degree, yet he has poor English.
- Nigerian scammers commonly describe themselves as "God-fearing men".
- He says he is not here for games or to toy with people's hearts and that he hates cheaters and liars. Most scammers will use these lines.
- He uses the terms "happy family", "brave heart" and "loving kind"; all are commonly used by Nigerian scammers.

This is our first contact and where the story starts.

From: jeffcand
To: ladedi
Subject: HELLO DAMSEL
Sent: 06/01/2012 7:18PM

How are you doing today.Am Jeff from united kingdom, *i* was just checking when *i* saw your profile and *i* find it very difficult to pass without saying hi.

Just want to know you more, who knows, it could be the start of something new.***It my whisper prayer to God today***, to keep you reminding you how special you are to to Him, When the world feels like it's on your shoulder, look at the person next to you and see what they are going through. Don't take life for granted.

Love the one that loves you, because sometimes we don't get a second chance. All am saying is give me the chance even if you want me to be just your friend. ***If you have yahoo messenger please send so we can chat.***

I WILL BE WAITING TO HFAR FROM YOU.
Jeff

From: ladedi
To: jeffcand
Subject: HELLO DAMSEL
Sent: 06/03/2012 01:16PM

Hello Jeff,

How are you today? I am glad you had to say hello. Wow...I like what you wrote. I could always use another friend. You seem like a nice and interesting man.

Please email me at ladydi2011@yahoo.com and my messenger is ladydi2011. I am looking forward to hearing from you.

Sincerely,
Diana

From: jeffery candel
To: ladydi2011
Subject: hello its me Jeff from singlebee
Sent: Mon, 4 Jun 2012 13:19:11 +0000

Hello Dear,

I just have to thank you for replying my mail, if not for other things but for the efforts you made to type the mail.

My hobbies are reading, watching movies, swimming, listening to gospel music, sport and traveling, I've turned to the Internet to look for a partner, because I haven't yet met someone who has really fulfilled my expectations.

I'm not searching for adventures or games, on the contrary, I hope to find that special person in you, and someone with whom I can create the family I've always wanted and spend the rest of my life with.
I expect to read from pretty soon....*kiss kiss*.

I care,
Jeff

From: jeffcand
To: ladedi
Subject: HELLO DAMSEL
Sent: 06/04/2012 8:05AM

I got your email and the content well noted, am happy to read back from you too.

i have add you to my yahoo im, and *i* will be waiting to meet you online soon, me while *i* have sent you an email and *i* will be very happy to read back from you soon.

Jeff

> **From:** ladydi2011
> **To:** jeffery candel
> **Subject:** hello its me Jeff from singlebee
> **Sent:** Tuesday, Jun 4, 2012 9:42 AM
>
> Hello Jeff,
>
> I hope this finds you having a splendid Monday morning! I think you are a man of high caliber and integrity and you have substance, which is what I am looking for. It appears we both started online dating for the same reason. I was looking for my "forever", a man who would love me as passionately and madly as I love him. I thought I found him, I fell in love and then he broke my heart. I am a very honest person, I do not play games and I will not play with your heart. These are things you can count on. My heart is precious and I am in the mode of protecting it at this time. It will take me some time to get over this man and trust again. Are you willing to be my friend and take the time needed for me to really get to know and trust you?
>
> Sincerely,
> Diana

- On our very first correspondence he attempted to get me off the dating site and onto Yahoo! This is always a BIG red flag. Scammers are usually in a hurry to get you off the dating site. They want to ensure that their chats and messages with you are private, so it is easier for them to run their scam.
- Many scammers use God as part of their format. This man is following suit with doing the same.
- In his second correspondence to me he ends it with "kiss kiss". This is a red flag for two reasons: one, it is extremely fast for affection, and two, "kiss kiss" is a phrase commonly used by Nigerian scammers.
- Pay attention to his grammar and speech. It doesn't align with a man who has a degree.

I am intentionally telling this man my heart has been broken, that it will take me time to trust him and that I want to only be friends. Let's see how long it takes him to move beyond friendship.

Now the chatting begins.

IM Jun 4, 2012 10:07:35 AM

10:07:35 AM **Jeff Candel:** hello
10:08:52 AM **Jeff Candel:** hope to chat with you soon dear

10:09:20 AM **ladydi2011:** Me too...on phone with client at this time.

10:09:42 AM **Jeff Candel:** ooh am sorry for disturbing you ok

10:09:56 AM **Jeff Candel:** may be we talk later when you are less busy ok

10:11:09 AM **Jeff Candel:** may be later we get to talk and get to know more about each other better ok. *i* have sent you and email and *i* hope to read from you soon

10:13:02 AM **ladydi2011:** Sounds good. Give me about 30 min. I did reply. Did you see it?

10:13:25 AM **Jeff Candel:** *i* have not check dear

10:13:34 AM **Jeff Candel:** when *i* check *i* will get back to you ok

10:13:44 AM **Jeff Candel:** am in the office right now

10:20:12 AM **ladydi2011:** Thank you.

10:20:30 AM **Jeff Candel:** you are welcome my dear

10:21:24 AM **ladydi2011:** I am now off the phone. How are you today?

10:22:44 AM **Jeff Candel:** a cool and you

10:23:41 AM **ladydi2011:** I am well.

10:23:54 AM **ladydi2011:** Did you have a chance to read my email?

10:24:05 AM **Jeff Candel:** sure dear

10:24:18 AM **Jeff Candel:** thank you very much for your email

10:24:29 AM **Jeff Candel:** when am less busy *i* will write you back ok

10:24:36 AM **ladydi2011:** Ok

10:24:59 AM **ladydi2011:** Are you at work?

10:26:06 AM **ladydi2011:** Until later. Make it a fabulous day!

10:26:23 AM **Jeff Candel:** sure am at work dear

10:27:05 AM **ladydi2011:** Look for me when you are off work.

10:27:16 AM **Jeff Candel:** ok dear

10:27:25 AM **Jeff Candel:** *i* will look for you and *i* will find you

10:27:30 AM **ladydi2011:** Lol

10:27:36 AM **ladydi2011:** Bye for now.

10:27:41 AM **Jeff Candel:** bye dear

10:27:46 AM **Jeff Candel:** *i* will email you ok

10:27:52 AM **Jeff Candel:** nice meeting you

10:28:03 AM **ladydi2011:** Ok...Nice meeting you too.

10:28:21 AM **ladydi2011:** Have a fabulous day!

10:28:39 AM **Jeff Candel:** and you too dear

IM Jun 4, 2012 1:08:58 PM Continued

1:08:58 PM **Jeff Candel:** hello dear

1:09:10 PM **ladydi2011:** Hello Jeff

1:09:27 PM **Jeff Candel:** how are you doing dear

1:09:30 PM **ladydi2011:** How is your day going?

1:09:38 PM **Jeff Candel:** cool

1:09:41 PM **ladydi2011:** I am good. Thanks for asking

1:09:44 PM **Jeff Candel:** and yours

1:09:51 PM **ladydi2011:** Are you done work?

1:10:02 PM **Jeff Candel:** yes dear

1:10:11 PM **Jeff Candel:** and what are you doing now?

1:10:14 PM **ladydi2011**: Is it 6:10 pm there?

1:10:27 PM **ladydi2011**: Working

1:10:27 PM **Jeff Candel**: *who do you know dear*

1:10:43 PM **ladydi2011:** What do you mean?

1:10:49 PM **Jeff Candel**: *my time here dear*

1:11:00 PM **Jeff Candel**: *are you working with my time here*

1:11:16 PM **ladydi2011**: No, but I know people all over the world.

1:11:23 PM **Jeff Candel**: ok

1:11:32 PM **Jeff Candel**: can you tell me moe about you

1:11:49 PM **ladydi2011**: Sure....What would you like to know?

1:12:01 PM **Jeff Candel**: everything dear

1:12:30 PM **ladydi2011**: I am a business consultant and strategist, professional speaker and author.

1:12:41 PM **ladydi2011**: What do you do for a living?

1:12:46 PM **Jeff Candel**: ooh god

1:12:57 PM **Jeff Candel**: profession you have there?

1:13:15 PM **ladydi2011**: Yeah, it is fun.

1:13:31 PM **Jeff Candel**: *maintainers engineer. i repair oil refinary machine*

1:14:14 PM **Jeff Candel**: *that is what i read in school*

1:14:20 PM **ladydi2011**: out on rigs?

1:14:37 PM **Jeff Candel**: *but i end up being an accountant in one of the bank here*

1:14:54 PM **Jeff Candel**: *geting to retired soon dear*

1:15:01 PM **ladydi2011**: Ok...so you crunch numbers?

1:15:16 PM **ladydi2011**: How soon will you retire?

1:15:41 PM **Jeff Candel**: *my retirement comes up this june*

1:15:54 PM **ladydi2011**: This month?

1:16:01 PM **Jeff Candel**: yes

1:16:06 PM **Jeff Candel**: but am still working on it now

1:16:14 PM **Jeff Candel**: *it may end up by next month*

1:16:16 PM **ladydi2011**: So, what do you want to do when you retire?

1:16:32 PM **Jeff Candel**: *i want to set up a busines for myself*

1:16:50 PM **Jeff Candel**: *i have a friend who is introducing me to a business*

1:17:06 PM **Jeff Candel**: *my father business before he died*

1:17:10 PM **ladydi2011**: What type of business?

1:17:17 PM **Jeff Candel**: *oil busines dear..buying and selling of crude oil*

1:17:37 PM **ladydi2011**: Nice

1:17:50 PM **ladydi2011**: May I ask you something?

1:17:58 PM **Jeff Candel**: ask dear

1:18:20 PM **ladydi2011**: Why are you looking across the world for love? No nice women in London?

1:19:02 PM **Jeff Candel**: *i* want you to know that looking for love ex where does not mean that there are no kind and loving woman in here but you juist have to go to another side of the world and show does who want to be loved love

1:19:43 PM **Jeff Candel**: its all for the best

1:20:18 PM **ladydi2011**: So, how do you see a long-distance relationship working?

1:20:54 PM **Jeff Candel**: well as for me *i* know that there is no distance too far for love to travel

1:21:08 PM **ladydi2011**: I agree.

1:21:23 PM **ladydi2011**: Did you have an opportunity to read my email?

1:21:32 PM **Jeff Candel**: yes dear, sorry *i* have not reply back to you ok

1:21:46 PM **ladydi2011**: It is ok
1:21:55 PM **Jeff Candel:** *i just wanna take my time and get you something sweet ok*
1:22:15 PM **Jeff Candel:** there *i* will tell you what am looking for in a woman
1:22:26 PM **Jeff Candel:** so tell me more about you
1:22:50 PM **ladydi2011**: I have five brothers and no sisters. What about you?
1:23:17 PM **Jeff Candel:** *my father is late, and i have just one sister*
1:23:43 PM **ladydi2011**: Four are still alive. One died of cancer when he was 38.
1:23:45 PM **Jeff Candel:** and she is married now to usa man
1:23:52 PM **ladydi2011**: What about your mom?
1:24:07 PM **Jeff Candel:** my mom is no more dear
1:24:10 PM **ladydi2011**: Does your sister live in the USA?
1:24:12 PM **Jeff Candel:** *she is late too*
1:24:18 PM **Jeff Candel:** sure dear, she live with her husband
1:24:31 PM **ladydi2011**: Both of my parents are still alive.
1:24:41 PM **Jeff Candel:** good to hear that
1:24:44 PM **ladydi2011**: Where in the states does she live?
1:24:54 PM **Jeff Candel:** California
1:25:01 PM **ladydi2011**: Nice state.
1:25:11 PM **Jeff Candel:** where do you live
1:25:14 PM **ladydi2011**: Would you ever consider moving to the states?
1:25:32 PM **Jeff Candel:** if *i* found what am looking for *i* will relocate
1:25:36 PM **ladydi2011**: I live in Georgia
1:25:44 PM **Jeff Candel:** *you live alone?*
1:25:55 PM **ladydi2011**: Yes, me and a kitty cat.
1:26:00 PM **ladydi2011**: What about you?
Break In Time
1:26:44 PM **ladydi2011**: Are you there?
1:26:55 PM **Jeff Candel:** yes dear
1:27:08 PM **ladydi2011**: Do you live alone?
1:27:35 PM **Jeff Candel:** *i* live alone with my daughter
1:27:45 PM **Jeff Candel:** her name is sarah
1:27:57 PM **ladydi2011**: How old is Sarah?
1:28:28 PM **Jeff Candel:** she is 14yrs old
1:28:39 PM **Jeff Candel:** do you have a kid?
1:28:46 PM **ladydi2011**: No, I do not.
1:28:52 PM **Jeff Candel:** ok
1:28:55 PM **ladydi2011**: Are you widowed or divorced?
1:29:14 PM **Jeff Candel:** a widowed, *her mom is late*
1:29:41 PM **ladydi2011**: I am sorry. How long ago did you lose her?
1:30:05 PM **Jeff Candel:** 6yrs now *i* have been single since *i* lost her
1:30:17 PM **Jeff Candel:** she daignose cancer of the blood
1:30:46 PM **ladydi2011**: Do you want more children?
1:30:58 PM **Jeff Candel:** its depends on you dear
1:31:12 PM **Jeff Candel:** if you want to have kids with me?
1:31:27 PM **Jeff Candel:** its a matter of understanding
1:31:44 PM **ladydi2011**: This is true.
1:31:53 PM **ladydi2011**: How tall are you?

1:32:07 PM **Jeff Candel:** *i* am 6:1 tall

1:32:19 PM **Jeff Candel:** *weight 85 pounds*

1:32:34 PM **Jeff Candel:** and you/

1:32:36 PM **ladydi2011**: 85 or 185?

1:32:49 PM **ladydi2011**: I am 5'7"

1:32:51 PM **Jeff Candel:** *85*

1:33:19 PM **ladydi2011**: What is on your bucket list of things to do?

1:33:52 PM **Jeff Candel:** looking for the right woman to spend the rest of my life with

1:34:05 PM **Jeff Candel:** *i* dont mind relocating and make her happy

1:34:16 PM **Jeff Candel:** and live together as one big family

1:34:46 PM **Jeff Candel:** what are you looking for in a relationship?

1:34:55 PM **ladydi2011**: Looking for the right man and building a life together.

1:35:21 PM **Jeff Candel:** sure dear

1:35:30 PM **Jeff Candel:** *have you been married before and how long have you been single?*

1:36:37 PM **ladydi2011**: Someone who loves me as madly as I love him, someone I can't just live with but who I cannot live without, honesty, open communication, vulnrability, my safe place to fall and me being his, my forever.

1:36:57 PM **ladydi2011**: Was married for 8 years and have been divorced for 14 years.

1:37:00 PM **Jeff Candel:** ok good

1:37:23 PM **Jeff Candel:** *i* want you to know in any relationship there must be trust and undersanding. Do you agree with that?

1:37:50 PM **ladydi2011**: I 100% agree with this.

1:37:57 PM **Jeff Candel:** ok, good

1:38:08 PM **Jeff Candel:** *i* know you have been through alot in life and *i* have been too

1:38:25 PM **ladydi2011**: How would you know this?

1:38:34 PM **Jeff Candel:** so all we need now is to get to know each other and see where it lead us to

1:40:20 PM **Jeff Candel:** *i* believe that things happen for a reason and that reason is that you have experience does triars and pains through

1:40:36 PM **Jeff Candel:** well am just saying this out of experience

1:40:38 PM **ladydi2011**: I have been hurt recently and have a huge steel wall around my heart.

1:40:53 PM **Jeff Candel:** *i* understand dear

1:41:07 PM **Jeff Candel:** that is the more reason why we need each others here

1:41:26 PM **Jeff Candel:** to take out that pains and stress out

1:41:39 PM **ladydi2011**: Jeff, I am a good woman with a loving heart. I am scared to give it away again, just to have it trampled on.

1:42:04 PM **Jeff Candel:** dear *i* understand you and *i* know what you mean

1:42:22 PM **Jeff Candel:** *i* want you to know that *its all base on trust and understanding*

1:42:40 PM **Jeff Candel:** *i* dont want you to be in rush to give someone your heart ok

1:42:54 PM **Jeff Candel:** you have to take your time and think before doing that ok

1:43:00 PM **ladydi2011**: Are you a patient man?

1:43:08 PM **Jeff Candel:** *i* am dear. *i* know being patience will make me to get to know you more

1:43:48 PM **Jeff Candel:** no what you like and what you dont like

1:43:58 PM **Jeff Candel:** so *i* will not get to hurt you

1:44:52 PM **ladydi2011**: Do you have a web cam?

1:45:09 PM **Jeff Candel:** *am sorry my daughter has broken it*

1:45:19 PM **Jeff Candel:** *am thinking of geting another one dear*

1:45:27 PM **Jeff Candel:** *i will let you know if i get any ok*

1:45:44 PM **ladydi2011**: Ok...They are pretty cheap now.

1:46:00 PM **Jeff Candel:** *i* hardly have time for myself dear

1:46:21 PM **ladydi2011**: I understand this, same for me.

1:46:23 PM **Jeff Candel**: always busy with work

1:47:06 PM **ladydi2011**: Jeff, trust is earned, not just given. You know this right?

1:47:24 PM **Jeff Candel**: yes dear that is very true

1:47:54 PM **ladydi2011**: How long have you done online dating?

1:48:10 PM **Jeff Candel**: *i* have not been in an online dating before, this just my first time and *i* dont how much its works dear

1:48:29 PM **Jeff Candel**: and you ?

1:48:38 PM **ladydi2011**: I have learned people lie easily because they can hide behind a screen.

1:48:50 PM **Jeff Candel**: really

1:48:54 PM **ladydi2011**: I have been doing it for a little over 2 months

1:48:55 PM **Jeff Candel**: and how does that works?

1:49:10 PM **Jeff Candel**: and have you find any one yet

1:49:18 PM **ladydi2011**: Words are easy to say, but hard to mean.

1:49:27 PM **Jeff Candel**: sure

1:49:39 PM **ladydi2011**: People seem to like to play with your heart.

1:50:08 PM **Jeff Candel**: that is why *i* dont like been online to do anything online dating

1:50:19 PM **Jeff Candel**: because *i* know that is all that is going to be

1:50:49 PM **Jeff Candel**: but *i* came to find out that is **all base on trust** and how much communication you and your partner both have

1:51:36 PM **ladydi2011**: This is what I thought too, but have learned that many are not who they portray themself to be.

1:51:55 PM **ladydi2011**: I am trying not to get jaded, but it is difficult.

1:51:59 PM **Jeff Candel**: yes *i* have also heard that dearr

1:52:13 PM **Jeff Candel:** *yes baby i understand ok*

1:52:24 PM **Jeff Candel:** *oooooh am sorry for calling you baby*

1:52:30 PM **Jeff Candel:** *am sorry ok*

1:52:32 PM **ladydi2011**: Will you make me a promise?

1:52:45 PM **Jeff Candel**: what are the promise dear

1:53:03 PM **ladydi2011**: Please DO NOT ever say something to me you don't mean.

1:53:14 PM **Jeff Candel**: ok *i* promise

1:53:17 PM **ladydi2011**: DO NOT play games with me.

1:53:19 PM **Jeff Candel**: crose my heart

1:53:31 PM **Jeff Candel**: ok *madam* your humble servant is at your servic any time

1:54:13 PM **ladydi2011**: I promise that I will not play games with you.

1:54:27 PM **Jeff Candel**: ok *my madam*

1:54:45 PM **Jeff Candel:** *i promise you that i will not play or toy with your lovely heart ok*

1:55:32 PM **ladydi2011**: Thank you. Please know I have heard this before and then they did it anyway...I am now very gun-shy and scared.

1:55:55 PM **Jeff Candel**: *i* nunderstand

1:55:59 PM **ladydi2011**: I will try not to project this onto you

1:56:29 PM **Jeff Candel:** *honesty is what you will get from me ok*

1:56:39 PM **Jeff Candel**: and faithfulnes

1:56:46 PM **ladydi2011**: Thank you.

1:56:53 PM **Jeff Candel**: you are welcome

1:57:04 PM **Jeff Candel**: *so tell me more about your background*

1:57:27 PM **ladydi2011**: I have 30 years of sales and marketing experience.

1:57:44 PM **ladydi2011**: I have owned my business for 12 years

1:57:54 PM **ladydi2011**: I make companies profitable

1:58:41 PM **Jeff Candel**: ok good

1:58:51 PM **Jeff Candel**: *i* guess you are a very busy woman

1:59:03 PM **ladydi2011**: I work with attorneys, private investigators, data forensic and counter espionage companies, retired law enforcement, CIA, FBI, and Secret Service

1:59:18 PM **ladydi2011**: Yes, I usually work 16-18 hours a day.

1:59:27 PM **Jeff Candel**: hmmm long hours

1:59:49 PM **ladydi2011**: Yes. This is what it takes when you own a business.

1:59:54 PM **Jeff Candel**: when do you always have time for yourself there

2:00:03 PM **Jeff Candel**: sure

2:00:21 PM **ladydi2011**: I work hard and play hard.

2:00:21 PM **ladydi2011**: On weekends and I take vacations

2:00:36 PM **Jeff Candel**: sure

2:00:43 PM **ladydi2011**: here in the states is totally different from where you are

2:00:51 PM **ladydi2011**: We all work too much...

2:01:30 PM **Jeff Candel**: yes *i* know that

2:01:50 PM **Jeff Candel**: state people are always bussy with work

2:01:51 PM **ladydi2011**: I have enjoyed talking with you. I have a scheduled call with a client in California, so I have to run.

2:02:09 PM **Jeff Candel**: you going to california

2:02:36 PM **ladydi2011**: No, I do a lot of my business on Skype so my clients can see me and I can see them

2:02:51 PM **Jeff Candel**: why?

2:02:53 PM **ladydi2011**: Many of my clients have never met me in person

2:03:03 PM **Jeff Candel**: you think is good like that and its works like that

2:03:18 PM **ladydi2011**: Yes

2:03:31 PM **ladydi2011**: We talk on a weekly basis

2:03:32 PM **Jeff Candel**: oooh really

2:03:41 PM **ladydi2011**: I have clients all over the country

2:04:51 PM **Jeff Candel**: ok that is good to hear

2:05:16 PM **Jeff Candel**: *i* must say you are a very hard working woman and *i* love that

2:05:20 PM **ladydi2011**: I will be looking for your email...

2:05:28 PM **ladydi2011**: Yes, I am.

2:05:34 PM **ladydi2011**: You do?

2:05:37 PM **Jeff Candel**: *i* have never see any one like your type before

2:05:44 PM **Jeff Candel**: woman woeking like a man

2:05:47 PM **ladydi2011**: I am an original

2:05:55 PM **Jeff Candel**: sure dear

2:06:01 PM **Jeff Candel**: without been told

2:06:03 PM **ladydi2011**: I have supported myself for a long time

2:06:04 PM **Jeff Candel**: you are

2:06:12 PM **Jeff Candel**: *i* see dear

2:06:45 PM **ladydi2011**: Yep

2:06:54 PM **Jeff Candel**: *i lost my dad and mom when i was 16yrs old*

2:06:59 PM **ladydi2011**: Wow
2:07:08 PM **Jeff Candel**: *i* was very little
2:07:11 PM **ladydi2011**: Is your sister younger or older than you
2:07:29 PM **Jeff Candel**: am the senior, she is my younger sister
2:07:52 PM **ladydi2011**: What did your father die of?
2:07:56 PM **Jeff Candel**: we are just 2 in the family
2:08:14 PM **Jeff Candel**: heart failure
2:08:39 PM **ladydi2011**: Who took care of you and your sister?
2:08:53 PM **Jeff Candel**: my uncle wife
2:09:38 PM **ladydi2011**: This was nice of her.
2:09:45 PM **Jeff Candel**: then we where still little and my uncle took care of mye and my sister before *i* when back to school to make sure that *i* stand on my own
2:09:47 PM **ladydi2011**: I really do need to run
2:09:52 PM **Jeff Candel**: ok
2:10:01 PM **ladydi2011**: You are blessed
2:10:07 PM **Jeff Candel**: when will you be back dear
2:10:12 PM **ladydi2011**: Bye for now...
2:11:07 PM **ladydi2011**: Later tonight
2:11:17 PM **Jeff Candel**: ok *i* will try and be online ok
2:11:26 PM **Jeff Candel**: *i* will also send you an email ok
2:11:31 PM **Jeff Candel**: bye
2:11:45 PM **Jeff Candel**: *i* dont want to get you late ok
2:12:12 PM **ladydi2011**: Ok
2:12:22 PM **ladydi2011**: Take care
2:12:30 PM **Jeff Candel**: and you too dear
2:12:53 PM **ladydi2011**: ok
2:13:08 PM **Jeff Candel**: talk to you later
2:13:13 PM **Jeff Candel**: *God bless you*
2:13:24 PM **ladydi2011**: You too
2:13:37 PM **Jeff Candel**: byeeee
2:14:13 PM **Jeff Candel**: am so happy to meet you dear
2:14:26 PM **ladydi2011**: You too...bye
2:14:44 PM **Jeff Candel**: byeee

RED FLAGS

- Buying and selling crude oil gives them a reason to travel, and convincing you that they're traveling is essential to their scam. It is usually when they are supposedly traveling that something supposedly happens and they need money.
- You might be tempted to overlook the grammar because the man says he is from the UK. Maybe he's just speaking in local slang. Maybe, but probably not. Scammers know you want to believe the person is who he says he is, and they claim to be from outside the United States so you have a reason to overlook their poor grammar and accent when they do speak with you on the phone. It would behoove you to go on You Tube and listen to Nigerians speak so you are familiar with their accents. However, some of them speak with very little accent if they have practiced, so you cannot 100 percent rely on this.

- He said he is a widow. Many scammers claim to be widowed.
- He said both his parents are "late". Two red flags here: one, the way he says "my father is late" is how they say it in Nigeria, and two, he is setting the stage so that when he needs money he has nobody else to ask.
- He asked if I lived alone. This is a question scammers ask because they want to know if there is anyone in the house that may interrupt the scam. They know that your heart keeps you hooked, and if you live alone, there is a good chance you are lonely. Both of these things make you more vulnerable to manipulation.
- Asking about my background is another common strategy of scammers. He is trying to gather as much information as he can so he knows how to manipulate me. Scammers are superb manipulators. It is their livelihood.
- When I asked him his height and weight he said he weighed 85 lbs. Yes, the United Kingdom uses the metric system, but so does Nigeria. He didn't specify his height and weight in his profile so I couldn't compare. Usually scammers specify something in their profile, so when they do tell you their age, weight, height, eye color, hair color, marital status, etc., be sure to go back to the profile and compare. If these things are different you know this person is lying.
- He said he doesn't have a webcam. This is highly unlikely, because almost all laptops today come with webcams. Most scammers will tell you they don't have a webcam or it is broken, because they don't want you to see who is really behind the screen. However, if you push the issue for a webcam, they will produce something and it will be a "fake cam".
- Notice that there was a time break in our chat. He was probably researching me on Google or he was chatting with other women besides me.
- He called me "baby" and then apologized because I told him I only wanted to be friends. His regular format was to go right into romance using sweet talk. Scammers are VERY good at sweet talk.

From: jeffery candel
To: ladydi2011
Subject: Hope to hear from you soon.
Sent: Monday, June 4, 2012 3:02 PM

I immensely value friendship; I hate conflict; I'm sincere and detest hypocrisy; I'm open minded; I respect other's ideas and listen to them (so I expect to be listened to, because I wait for my turn to speak); I'm witty and have a great sense of humor; I think our destiny is something we discover every day, according to how we face it, what we do and what we don't and I doubt there's a second chance for a first good impression. Appealing, cerebral and of average size, my best qualities are loyalty, passion and creativity.

I am a man of great integrity, my quiet serene demeanor accords me an air of mystery and diffidence as I go my way as a serene, wise observer of human society. I have a penchant for remaining above the fray and for maintaining my individuality. I am always well groomed and handsome eyeglasses frame my eyes.

I can be best described as optimistic, high spirited and broadminded. I love romance, freedom and I am very much future oriented. I am a physical person. I respond to the world through action, rather than practicality, intellect, or emotion.

While I am about action and getting things started, I am not in a hurry. I want to experience life, rather than read about it. I am an eager explorer and interested in mental outreach. I enjoy travel and spiritual study, and have a daring and adventurous spirit.

I am high-spirited and enthusiastic, often flirtatious, and enjoy social life immensely. In my leisure time, athleticism comes to the forefront but for now this hobby is already slipping away from my hands. Personal challenge is always appreciated, and I prefer solitary or one-on-one sports that stretch myself to the limit. My philosophical side makes me enjoy drama and debate, as well as most other mentally challenging pursuits.

In love relationships, I am sincere, straightforward, flirtatious and playful. I can also be one cool customer. Although few would describe me as being warm, cuddly, or sentimental, those close to me see me as an important source of support in their lives.

That's because when things are chaotic or falling apart, I'm the type of person who can be virtually unflappable. I am also known for being a talented problem solver. When it comes to my relationships, I usually know how to speak up for myself so that others know what I want. But that doesn't mean I'm rigid or inflexible. In fact, I'm quite willing to acquiesce for the right person.

They just need to make their case honestly.Hope to hear from you soon.

I care,
Jeff.

From: ladydi2011
To: jeffcand101
Subject: Re: Hope to hear from you soon.
Sent: Monday, 4 Jun 2012 20:35:02 -0700

Hello Jeff,

Thank you for this email. I appreciate that you know yourself so well. I am impressed. I do want to get to know you better. I enjoyed our chat this afternoon and hope to chat again soon.

You should still be sleeping at this time. I hope you got a good night's rest. I will probably be going to bed about the time you wake up... (smile).

Sincerely,
Diana

From: jeffery candel
To: ladydi2011
Subject: THE KIND OF LADY I NEED
Sent: Tuesday, Jun 5, 2012 10:08 AM

THE KIND OF LADY I NEED the type of lady who attracts me is honest, direct, and reliable - who can be my "pal". I like a lady who's playful one minute, and philosophical the next. Above all, companionship, honesty, and idealism appeal to me - and a sense of humor!

My ideal partner is a very passionate person who knows how to fully enjoy life. She has a highly active imagination when it comes to trying new things.

More than most people, she knows how to value the pleasures of romance and is not afraid to pursue those feelings when the timing is right. She also has a strong intellect, with a penetrating thought process and a continual curiosity about the world around her.

ANOTHER SIDE OF ME Born into this world, but not of this world. I paint romantic portraits with words. Strong, but sensitive. Healthy, beautiful bodies. Warm soft voice with curious accent. NOT into the abuse of anyone or anything.

Wise as a sage, with a heart of a child. Love and forgiveness as a way of life. Bohemian. Social transcendent. Spiritual drummer. Faithful friend. Very romantic sweet lover.

I would like to meet a lady that believes in the power of love and forgiveness. Wants to transcend beyond the worldly norm and discover new vistas of companionship, sharing, peace, and joy.

Someone, who is very romantic and believes in angels. Surely, no one lives to himself or herself and what ever we can do today for one another may stand for our glory tomorrow. Love feels no burden, thinks nothing of trouble, attempts what is above its strength, pleads no excuse of impossibility...

It is therefore able to undertake all things, and it completes many things, and warrants them to take effect, where she who does not love would faint and lie down.

 i hope you are doing good dear, and am so happy to read from you. I attached my photo to this email and i hope you will like them dear. Hope to read from you soon.

I care,

Jeff

From: jeffery candel
To: ladydi2011
Subject: THE KIND OF LADY I NEED
Sent: Tuesday, Jun 5, 2012 12:21 PM

here is the song of my heart to you dear (Song was Your Sweet Love)

From: jeffery candel
To: ladydi2011
Subject: song for you
Sent: Tuesday, Jun 5, 2012 3:45 PM

Check this song out too (Song was Amanda)

From: jeffery candel
To: ladydi2011
Subject: song for you
Sent: Tuesday, Jun 5, 2012 5:26 PM

i love this song and i hope you like it too sweetie (Song was It's Gotta Be Magic)

RED FLAGS

- These emails are very well written compared to how this man chats. The reason for this is that they are copied from another man's profile. You can easily tell he wrote the section at the end of the one email. I cannot stress enough that you have to pay attention.
- He sent me an electronic bouquet of flowers and songs to listen to. This also follows a scammer's format. He is trying desperately to rush past the "friend" barrier, because he knows that if he doesn't win my heart he will not get any money from me. Remember, it's always the heart that gives money, not the intellect. As we know, a heart has a mind of its own.
- You can tell what's copied and pasted because it doesn't have lower case I's like his writing.

IM Jun 5, 2012 5:57:37 PM

5:57:37 PM **Jeff Candel**: hello
5:57:40 PM **Jeff Candel**: how are you doing today?
5:57:54 PM **ladydi2011**: Hello Jeff. I am well and you?
5:58:00 PM **Jeff Candel**: am fine
5:58:05 PM **Jeff Candel**: just missing you that all
5:58:20 PM **Jeff Candel**: how is work and everything?
5:58:34 PM **ladydi2011**: Work is busy. How was your day?
5:58:51 PM **Jeff Candel**: fine thanK God and yours?
5:59:30 PM **ladydi2011**: Stressful but good.
5:59:36 PM **ladydi2011**: I read your email.
5:59:46 PM **ladydi2011**: You write so beautifully
5:59:58 PM **ladydi2011**: I didn't even know how to reply.
6:00:07 PM **Jeff Candel**: ooh thank you very much dear
6:00:16 PM **Jeff Candel**: am glad you like what *i* write to you
6:00:35 PM **Jeff Candel**: so tell me what are you doing now?
6:00:37 PM **ladydi2011**: Do you read a lot?
6:00:45 PM **ladydi2011**: In the office working.
6:00:51 PM **Jeff Candel**: sure dear
6:00:58 PM **ladydi2011**: Trying to work, I should say.
6:01:06 PM **Jeff Candel**: ok dear
6:01:22 PM **Jeff Candel**: *i* just came online to see if you are online
6:01:25 PM **ladydi2011**: I am struggling to focus today.
6:01:39 PM **Jeff Candel**: struggling?
6:01:56 PM **Jeff Candel**: *i* dont understand
6:02:14 PM **Jeff Candel**: is everything ok
6:02:43 PM **ladydi2011**: Yeah, just tired.
6:02:48 PM **ladydi2011**: Thanks for asking.

6:02:50 PM **Jeff Candel**: oooh dear am sorry to hear that

6:03:04 PM **Jeff Candel**: *i* know you ust be dear

6:03:12 PM **ladydi2011**: I will catch up on my sleep sometime this week.

6:03:22 PM **Jeff Candel**: sure

6:03:28 PM **Jeff Candel**: you really need it dear

6:03:33 PM **ladydi2011**: Please tell me more about your job.

6:03:44 PM **Jeff Candel**: you have to get some rest ok

6:03:59 PM **ladydi2011**: I will...Please don't worry.

6:04:01 PM **Jeff Candel**: well as for now nothing more to say

6:04:10 PM **ladydi2011**: what do you mean?

6:04:20 PM **Jeff Candel**: *you know i told you that am working on my retirement*

6:04:49 PM **ladydi2011**: Retirement into your own business, right?

6:04:56 PM **Jeff Candel**: yes

6:05:12 PM **ladydi2011**: It is not going to be retirement....trust me. I know.

6:05:14 PM **Jeff Candel**: my dad was an oil business man before he died

6:05:32 PM **ladydi2011**: Oh. So, you know the ropes?

6:05:42 PM **Jeff Candel**: so *i* still have the link to be one of the business man

6:05:50 PM **Jeff Candel**: sure dear

6:06:12 PM *Jeff Candel: i have the link and i have also make the requirement too*

6:06:27 PM **Jeff Candel**: so am just waiting for them to get back to me

6:06:49 PM **ladydi2011**: Cool. I wish you much success with this.

6:07:15 PM **Jeff Candel**: thank you very much

6:07:47 PM **ladydi2011**: So, could you do this business from anywhere in the world?

6:07:58 PM *Jeff Candel: sure all you need is to have the link and get the contact*

6:08:47 PM *Jeff Candel: its a worldwild business*

6:09:02 PM **ladydi2011**: Nice. Will you travel a lot with it?

6:09:22 PM **Jeff Candel**: its depends, sometimes *i* may not travel

6:09:53 PM **Jeff Candel**: all *i* will do is just to tell them and they will send it to me any where *i* am and *i* go get it

6:10:30 PM **ladydi2011**: Go get what? I am confused.

6:10:43 PM **Jeff Candel**: *i* mean the goods

6:11:06 PM **ladydi2011**: I don't know much about the oil business, please excuse me.

6:11:20 PM **Jeff Candel**: ok

6:11:22 PM **ladydi2011**: Sorry, I still don't understand. What goods?

6:11:26 PM **Jeff Candel**: this is how is works

6:12:17 PM *Jeff Candel: i will get the link and the contact and then write them that i want to be part of thier group in this business*

6:12:56 PM *Jeff Candel: and then they will send me some forms which i will fiill and then send it back to them*

6:13:26 PM *Jeff Candel: then they will tell me what to do next to be a member of the group after that i can other any amount of the good i want and also get a link to supply to the western part of the country in the world*

6:14:15 PM **Jeff Candel**: hope you understand now

6:14:35 PM **ladydi2011**: A little. Thank you for taking the time to explain.

6:14:54 PM **ladydi2011**: So, it is predominantly all on paper, yes?

6:15:07 PM **Jeff Candel**: sure dear

6:15:37 PM **ladydi2011**: I love learning something new every day. Thank you for teaching me something new today.

6:16:02 PM **Jeff Candel**: *i* love learning too dear

6:16:07 PM **Jeff Candel**: its part of life to get more experience

6:16:51 PM **ladydi2011**: It sure is...

6:17:02 PM **ladydi2011**: I love having new experiences.

6:17:18 PM **Jeff Candel**: YES

6:17:29 PM **Jeff Candel**: so what have you been doing?

6:17:50 PM **ladydi2011**: Working and reading a book

6:18:02 PM **ladydi2011**: How to manifest what you want in life

6:18:10 PM **Jeff Candel**: waooo

6:18:21 PM **Jeff Candel**: that is an adventure book right?

6:18:28 PM **ladydi2011**: Yes.

6:18:37 PM **Jeff Candel**: *i* love adventure books

6:18:44 PM **Jeff Candel**: thats is my favorite its imspired me more dear

6:19:09 PM **ladydi2011**: Me too

6:19:21 PM **ladydi2011**: I can tell we are both very deep people.

6:19:23 PM **Jeff Candel**: its give me more ideal on how to move on in life

6:19:30 PM **ladydi2011**: Yep

6:19:39 PM **ladydi2011**: I am always looking to move forward

6:20:03 PM **Jeff Candel**: that is the best any human can achive in life

6:20:10 PM **Jeff Candel**: moving forward that is the best tag ever

6:20:24 PM **ladydi2011**: I like you Jeff

6:20:39 PM **Jeff Candel**: *i* like you too Diana

6:21:02 PM **ladydi2011**: So, at the top of my personal goals for 2012 was to find my forever love.

6:21:18 PM **Jeff Candel**: me too dear

6:21:41 PM **Jeff Candel**: *i* have been waiting for the right woman to come into my life

6:22:04 PM **Jeff Candel**: be together and spend the rest of our lifes together

6:22:27 PM **ladydi2011**: I am so ready to meet my "forever" man. The right man for me

6:22:54 PM **Jeff Candel**: always on my prayers to get the right one dear

6:23:17 PM **Jeff Candel**: *i know and my feelings told me that my searching is over because all i seek for has been answered*

6:23:39 PM **ladydi2011**: I am so ready and my heart is opened, even though it got broken. An experience I was not prepared for.

6:23:58 PM **Jeff Candel**: sure dear

6:24:18 PM **ladydi2011**: Please hold...sorry

6:24:21 PM **Jeff Candel**: in life we have all hard a different experience

6:24:26 PM **Jeff Candel**: ok

6:26:54 PM **ladydi2011**: I am sorry. I have a man from singlesbee who I was chatting with for the first time and he sent me a picture earlier that was very distasteful. I am trying to figure out how to block him.

6:28:15 PM **ladydi2011**: Jeff, I do not tolerate disrespect and this man was very disrespectful. Sorry to put you on hold to deal with this.

6:29:21 PM **Jeff Candel**: its ok dear

6:29:41 PM **Jeff Candel**: am here just take all your time ok

6:29:54 PM **ladydi2011**: I only chatted with this guy for 5 min. last week

6:30:10 PM **ladydi2011**: Within 5 min. I knew I did not want to be associated with him

6:30:18 PM **ladydi2011**: I am very selective.

6:30:34 PM **ladydi2011**: How familiar are you with yahoo, IM?
6:30:42 PM **Jeff Candel**: good to hear that dear
6:30:57 PM **ladydi2011**: I have deleted him but he still keeps buzzing through. How is this possible?
6:31:09 PM **Jeff Candel**: well am not that too good on yaoo im
6:31:35 PM **Jeff Candel**: well that means he still have your contact
6:31:58 PM **Jeff Candel**: if he have your coontact on his list he can still buzz you and trying to chat with you
6:32:21 PM **ladydi2011**: I am not good on it either. Next time he buzzes in I will hit the spam button and maybe this will do it....
6:32:36 PM **ladydi2011**: I removed his contact from my list.
6:32:39 PM **Jeff Candel**: *i* hope so dear
6:33:28 PM **ladydi2011**: Some people do not know what respect is or how to treat a real lady.
6:33:38 PM **Jeff Candel**: sure dear
6:33:52 PM **Jeff Candel**: *i* have always learn to be patient
6:34:10 PM **ladydi2011**: who taught you this?
6:34:26 PM **Jeff Candel**: *i* learn it from my *late dad*
6:34:34 PM **Jeff Candel**: he *is* a very patient man
6:34:38 PM **ladydi2011**: He taught you well
6:34:50 PM **Jeff Candel**: and when *i* do dear its always work otu for my good
6:35:17 PM **ladydi2011**: I am usually a calm woman, but my feather's get ruffled when someone is disrespecting me.
6:35:33 PM **ladydi2011**: Usually good things take time.
6:35:55 PM **ladydi2011**: Fast and furious usually also fizzles fast and furiously...lol
6:37:53 PM **ladydi2011**: Slow and steady usually wins the prize....this means patience.
6:38:15 PM **ladydi2011**: So, we were talking about adventures, correct?
6:39:11 PM **ladydi2011**: Are you there?
6:39:24 PM **Jeff Candel**: yes
6:39:56 PM **Jeff Candel**: you like adventure right?
6:41:00 PM **ladydi2011**: Love adventure!
6:41:05 PM **ladydi2011**: What about you?
6:41:16 PM **Jeff Candel**: *i* love adventure too
6:41:28 PM **Jeff Candel**: am so happy you like it too
6:41:54 PM **ladydi2011**: I think life should be lived to its fullest.
6:42:04 PM **Jeff Candel**: sure
6:42:12 PM **ladydi2011**: I know it is short and I want to experience as much as possible.
6:42:13 PM **Jeff Candel**: and also with happiness
6:42:23 PM **ladydi2011**: Yes, with happiness.
6:43:00 PM **ladydi2011**: I have a good life. However, at the end of the day there is a missing piece. I want the missing piece filled in.
6:43:05 PM **Jeff Candel**: *i* came to understand tha when you are happy the life itself became more intersting
6:43:31 PM **ladydi2011**: I never heard it stated like this. I would have to agree.
6:43:43 PM **Jeff Candel**: sure dear
6:43:53 PM **Jeff Candel**: *i* understand how you feel but *i* came asure you that as from today you will begine to experince it
6:44:35 PM **ladydi2011**: You do?
6:44:44 PM **Jeff Candel**: yes dear

6:45:09 PM **ladydi2011**: If I didn't know better, I would think you are trying to capture my heart...

6:45:58 PM **Jeff Candel**: *As far as the ocean is wide through miles and miles of sea; You will be someone special a true miracle to me*

6:47:33 PM **ladydi2011**: I am sorry Jeff...I don't know what to say right now.

6:48:36 PM **Jeff Candel**: *As high upon the mountain tops as high as one can climb You will be so dear to me the best friend I can find*

6:49:47 PM **ladydi2011**: Do you read a lot of poetry?

6:49:57 PM **Jeff Candel**: yes dear

6:50:13 PM **ladydi2011**: I can tell.

6:51:01 PM **ladydi2011**: Jeff, I am so sorry. My heart is still broken. It is broken more than I realized.

6:51:14 PM **Jeff Candel**: *As many stars that twinkle throughout the heavens above; You will be a a bright reminder of what it means to love.*

6:51:42 PM **Jeff Candel**: *i* understand and also know how you feel

6:51:55 PM **ladydi2011**: I do love with all I have. I don't hold back.

6:52:06 PM **Jeff Candel**: *i* want you to know that life is all about bold steps

6:52:34 PM **Jeff Candel**: *i* want you to take that bold step and put your past behind you ok

6:52:38 PM **ladydi2011**: A good friend of mine once taught me that it is better to love and be hurt than not love at all.

6:52:57 PM **Jeff Candel**: yes that is very true

6:52:59 PM **ladydi2011**: I am trying...This is very recent.

6:53:07 PM **Jeff Candel**: yes and *i* dont want you to rush into it it ok

6:53:21 PM **ladydi2011**: When was the last time you were hurt?

6:53:40 PM **Jeff Candel**: dear *i* cant remember

6:53:44 PM **ladydi2011**: Thank you. I can't. I do not want to hurt anyone.

6:53:56 PM **Jeff Candel**: ever since *i* lost my wife *i* have never ben in any relationship

6:53:56 PM **ladydi2011**: Rebounds are never good.

6:54:36 PM **Jeff Candel**: sure

6:54:52 PM **ladydi2011**: Wow....I can't even imagine the pain this caused you.

6:55:36 PM **Jeff Candel**: yes dear

6:56:00 PM **Jeff Candel**: but *i* have to let the past behind me and take a move forward

6:56:11 PM **ladydi2011**: This is true.

6:56:49 PM **ladydi2011**: The rearview mirror is only helpful when driving...lol

6:57:33 PM **Jeff Candel**: sure dear

6:57:53 PM **Jeff Candel**: and you can still see how pretty you are right

6:57:58 PM **ladydi2011**: Please share more of your philosophy with me

6:59:04 PM **Jeff Candel**: dear to get something in life its all by determination

6:59:08 PM **ladydi2011**: Thank you. Yes, I can.

6:59:35 PM **ladydi2011**: I agree.

7:00:07 PM **Jeff Candel**: having that which you determin for is a precious thing to you, am i right?

7:00:41 PM **ladydi2011**: This is right.

7:00:46 PM **Jeff Candel**: ok good

7:01:18 PM **Jeff Candel**: *i* love your sense of human

7:01:24 PM **ladydi2011**: Thank you....

7:01:34 PM **Jeff Candel**: and *i* see you as a very brave lady who is worth dieing for

7:02:06 PM **ladydi2011**: Here are a couple things I live by....never allow someone to be my priority while allowing myself to be their option....It is what it is....Next!

7:02:24 PM **ladydi2011**: I am brave, but I am also human.

7:03:17 PM **Jeff Candel**: being human and also brave makes you so special and a wonderful woman on earth do you know that

7:03:45 PM **ladydi2011**: No...But thanks for sharing this.

7:04:11 PM **Jeff Candel**: *i* want you to know that you are a special woman on earth

7:04:15 PM **ladydi2011**: So, you live on the other side of the world.....hmmmmmmmm

7:04:43 PM **ladydi2011**: Thank you Jeff. I do know this. I do know my worth.

7:05:02 PM **Jeff Candel**: ok good to hear that dear

7:05:23 PM **Jeff Candel**: what is the best thing you wish for in life?

7:05:56 PM **ladydi2011**: True and real love. I want to be loved as passionately and madly as I love.

7:06:02 PM **ladydi2011**: What about you?

7:06:43 PM **Jeff Candel**: *love, care, cherish my partner and live a happy home*

7:08:55 PM **Jeff Candel**: one thing *i* came to understand in life is that when you are *lving a happy life* people will always talk good about you because they dont have what you have

7:10:42 PM **Jeff Candel**: are you there?

7:10:53 PM **ladydi2011**: Sorry...I got booted.

7:10:59 PM **ladydi2011**: I agree with this

7:11:05 PM **Jeff Candel**: its ok

7:12:15 PM **ladydi2011**: I want it all. I am not willing to settle for anything less. I see so many people settle and not happy.

7:12:35 PM **Jeff Candel**: yes that is why *i* said it

7:13:04 PM **Jeff Candel**: because been happy is from the mind not from the face..its a mind set

7:13:14 PM **ladydi2011**: We are on the same wave length.

7:13:48 PM **Jeff Candel**: some marriege dont seem to understand that

7:14:19 PM **Jeff Candel**: that is why you see many homes are not happy because they dont understand that happiness comes from both partners

7:14:35 PM **ladydi2011**: This is true. I believe both partners need to be intentional to make the relationship be the best it can be.

7:14:47 PM **Jeff Candel**: once there is understanding in a marriege then there is a room for happiness to come in

7:15:18 PM **ladydi2011**: I agree.

7:15:31 PM **ladydi2011**: Both have to desire the same thing.

7:15:38 PM **ladydi2011**: Both have to commit

7:15:46 PM **Jeff Candel**: yes dear

7:16:08 PM **Jeff Candel**: *i* want you to know that Love is a precious thing. It is a feeling that makes your heart sing

7:16:15 PM **ladydi2011**: Both have to pay attention to the small things...they are more important than the big things...in my opinion. Would you agree?

7:16:37 PM **Jeff Candel**: *Whether you are far or near it is like whispering in my ear*

7:16:51 PM **Jeff Candel**: sure dear *i* agree with that

7:17:05 PM **ladydi2011**: You have encouraged me to read more poetry.

7:17:19 PM **Jeff Candel**: really?

7:17:23 PM **ladydi2011**: Yes

7:17:32 PM **Jeff Candel**: ok good dear

7:18:04 PM **Jeff Candel**: When you find true love it is something you keep within your heart

7:18:08 PM **ladydi2011**: Did I tell you that I like your company?

7:18:12 PM **ladydi2011**: True

7:18:25 PM **Jeff Candel**: really

7:18:27 PM **ladydi2011**: Maybe it even becomes a part of your heart.

7:18:30 PM **ladydi2011**: Yes

7:18:35 PM **Jeff Candel**: am so happy to hear that dear

Break In Time

7:21:03 PM **ladydi2011**: Are you there?

7:21:32 PM **Jeff Candel**: sure dear am here with you

7:22:08 PM **ladydi2011**: Please share more with me.

7:22:20 PM **Jeff Candel**: *Never thought there'll come a time, I'll feel again the warmth of its shine. You came like a rain in my mind, Still there's a reason that I should find*

7:23:50 PM **ladydi2011**: Do you have this in your memory or do you have a book of poems in front of you?

7:24:19 PM **Jeff Candel**: nope all in my memory dear..*i* love writing poem

7:25:27 PM **ladydi2011**: It shows. I like reading what you write.

7:27:18 PM **Jeff Candel**: *The thought of you starts me trembling a fire is raging deep inside my heart i can still feel your body close to mine the way you held me so tenderly*

7:28:02 PM **ladydi2011**: Wow...Are you ready to meet the love of your life and start a new chapter?

7:29:27 PM **Jeff Candel**: sure dear am ready to take that move

7:30:33 PM **Jeff Candel**: *How I want to say so much but words cannot express The deep passionate love I have for you words and ways outweighs my stress. The many nights I dreamnt about you the many days I wonder the many hours I prayed to God. That our love will never wander*

7:32:59 PM **ladydi2011**: Brb...bathroom break. Please wait

7:33:11 PM **Jeff Candel**: ok dear, am waiting

7:36:53 PM **ladydi2011**: Sorry...thank you for waiting.

7:37:05 PM **Jeff Candel**: its ok, are you through now?

7:37:22 PM **ladydi2011**: With work?

7:37:46 PM **ladydi2011**: No, because I have been chatting with you.

Break In Time

7:40:09 PM **ladydi2011**: Was it your turn to get booted?

7:40:16 PM **Jeff Candel**: yes dear

7:40:40 PM **Jeff Candel**: *i* guess one one right

7:40:54 PM **ladydi2011**: Yes

7:40:58 PM **Jeff Candel**: ok, good

7:41:32 PM **ladydi2011**: So, it is almost 1:00 AM there isn't it?

7:42:19 PM **Jeff Candel**: sure dear you are right

7:42:45 PM **Jeff Candel**: and what is yours

7:42:48 PM **ladydi2011**: You must be tired. You had a long day.

7:42:53 PM **ladydi2011**: 7:42 pm

7:43:16 PM **ladydi2011**: What time do you have to get up in the morning?

7:43:24 PM **Jeff Candel**: *what state is that again please?*

7:43:32 PM **ladydi2011**: Georgia

7:43:37 PM **Jeff Candel**: ok

7:43:47 PM **ladydi2011**: I am 5 hours behind you.

7:44:14 PM **Jeff Candel**: in the morning *i* do get up by 5:30am and get some things don before getting ready for work

7:44:56 PM **ladydi2011**: As much as I love chatting with you, you need to sleep my dear.

7:45:11 PM **Jeff Candel**: no no..am still here if *i* try to sleep will never come

7:45:38 PM **ladydi2011**: Why?

7:45:43 PM **Jeff Candel**: because am going to miss you

7:46:22 PM **ladydi2011**: You could possibly dream about me

7:46:28 PM **Jeff Candel**: yes *i* have always dream about you

7:46:51 PM **ladydi2011**: What do you mean?

7:47:00 PM **Jeff Candel**: *i* dont mind spending my whole day with you

7:48:31 PM **ladydi2011**: I need to go downstairs to get something to drink. I am going to sign off this computer and then sign on once I get downstairs. Please wait.

7:48:50 PM **Jeff Candel**: ok dear *i* will be waiting and get some for me too ok

7:50:03 PM **ladydi2011**: I will. Do you like ice tea?

7:50:11 PM **Jeff Candel**: yes

7:50:20 PM **ladydi2011**: Do you drink tea or coffee?

7:50:32 PM **Jeff Candel**: coffee

7:50:44 PM **ladydi2011**: Do you take sugar?

7:50:54 PM **Jeff Candel**: not really

7:51:00 PM **ladydi2011**: Cream?

7:51:02 PM **Jeff Candel**: *i* dont like sugar that much

7:51:08 PM **Jeff Candel**: yes *i* like cream

7:51:20 PM **ladydi2011**: Coffee with cream, right?

7:51:31 PM **Jeff Candel**: sure

7:51:53 PM **ladydi2011**: I drink earl grey tea with travina (healthy sweetner) and cream.

7:52:02 PM **ladydi2011**: I also like berry tea.

7:52:11 PM **ladydi2011**: Ok...be back.

7:52:16 PM **Jeff Candel**: ooh thats cool

7:52:20 PM **Jeff Candel**: ok

8:01:02 PM **ladydi2011**: I am back...so ice tea my dear?

8:01:15 PM **ladydi2011**: Thank you for waiting.

8:01:22 PM **Jeff Candel**: its ok dear

8:01:31 PM **Jeff Candel**: did you get my ice tea

8:01:33 PM **ladydi2011**: What is your favorite color?

8:01:42 PM **ladydi2011**: I did...

8:02:17 PM **Jeff Candel**: pink color

8:02:42 PM **ladydi2011**: What is your favorite breakfast?

8:03:12 PM **Jeff Candel**: *i* love taking coffee before going to work

8:03:36 PM **ladydi2011**: Ok...what about food?

8:04:18 PM **Jeff Candel**: *i like eggs, fried rice and salad*

8:04:41 PM **ladydi2011**: how do you like your eggs cooked?

8:05:22 PM **Jeff Candel**: borling

8:05:57 PM **Jeff Candel**: after borlling it then you slice it

8:06:11 PM **ladydi2011**: Ok

8:06:26 PM **ladydi2011**: What is your favorite song?

8:06:43 PM **Jeff Candel**: don williams

8:06:51 PM **Jeff Candel**: *i* love counrty songs and you?

8:07:23 PM **ladydi2011**: Which Don Williams song is your favorite?

8:08:51 PM **Jeff Candel**: I record the gymsy woman and amanda

8:09:00 PM **Jeff Candel**: those are still my favorite songs

8:09:52 PM **ladydi2011**: Can you find them on you tube and send to me?

8:11:49 PM **Jeff Candel**: ok

8:12:33 PM **ladydi2011**: I am looking for a song to send to you. I fell in love with it the first time I heard it. It is called "Keeper"

8:13:29 PM **Jeff Candel**: ok just send it to me now as am attaching mine now to send to you babe

8:14:42 PM **ladydi2011**: www.youtube.com/watch?v=rDyOeH2rtjE&feature=related

8:18:16 PM **Jeff Candel**: baby it sweet and it just make me wanna cry

8:18:59 PM **ladydi2011**: I just hear this in January of this year...I fell in love with it!

8:19:34 PM **ladydi2011**: I guess it suits where I am in life because I am looking for the "keeper of my heart".

8:19:40 PM **ladydi2011**: Your turn to send

8:19:49 PM **Jeff Candel**: yeah

8:20:11 PM **Jeff Candel**: it take a day to meet people but a life time to forget them

8:20:17 PM **Jeff Candel**: *i* guess that keeper of your heart is here now

8:20:44 PM **ladydi2011**: What you said is true...

8:21:07 PM **ladydi2011**: Just friends right now. Ok

8:21:21 PM **Jeff Candel**: yeah *i* know and *i* promise *i* will not rush you

8:21:40 PM **Jeff Candel**: but there is one thing *i* know for sure..we are both meant to be

8:22:03 PM **ladydi2011**: How do you know this?

8:23:56 PM **Jeff Candel**: because that how *i* feel as *i* hear this song

8:24:52 PM **ladydi2011**: Thank you for sharing this with me.

8:24:54 PM **Jeff Candel**: *i* just sent you one song to your email

8:25:05 PM **Jeff Candel**: check and see

8:25:10 PM **ladydi2011**: Ok...please let me look.

8:30:13 PM **ladydi2011**: I am listening to Amanda now. This is a real country song....

8:31:33 PM **ladydi2011**: I never heard this before. I like it!

8:31:52 PM **Jeff Candel**: really? that good to know love

8:32:40 PM **ladydi2011**: I am now listening to your sweet love

8:33:20 PM **Jeff Candel**: ok, do you like it?

8:33:37 PM **ladydi2011**: I do...

8:33:54 PM **Jeff Candel**: *tell me now from your heart baby how do you feel now?*

8:34:42 PM **ladydi2011**: Happy and scared at the same time.

8:36:12 PM **ladydi2011**: You surprised me. I didn't take you for liking country music. This is cool.

8:36:39 PM **Jeff Candel**: yeah baby

8:36:41 PM **ladydi2011**: You have depth to you and I like this.

8:36:44 PM **Jeff Candel**: yeah baby and my eye are so feel with tears now baby

8:36:54 PM **Jeff Candel**: and you know what?

8:36:59 PM **ladydi2011**: What?

8:37:03 PM **Jeff Candel**: this is the start of something new my love

8:37:41 PM **ladydi2011**: Walking away from the past and into the future...

8:38:40 PM **Jeff Candel**: yeah baby

8:38:52 PM **Jeff Candel**: Let walk into the future together my angel

8:39:39 PM **ladydi2011**: Baby steps

8:40:02 PM **Jeff Candel**: yeah *i* know sweetie

8:40:25 PM **ladydi2011**: I so want to, but am so scared.

8:40:33 PM **ladydi2011**: I do not want to be hurt again

8:40:40 PM **Jeff Candel**: you know in lofe shit happens

8:40:56 PM **ladydi2011**: Yes, it does

8:41:21 PM **ladydi2011**: How do I know I can trust you with my heart?

8:41:22 PM **Jeff Candel:** *Maybe God wants us to meet a few wrong people before meeting the right one so that when we finally meet the right person, we will know how to be grateful for that gift*

8:41:27 PM **Jeff Candel:** *Maybe God wants us to meet a few wrong people before meeting the right one so that when we finally meet the right person, we will know how to be grateful for that gift*

8:41:32 PM **Jeff Candel:** *Maybe God wants us to meet a few wrong people before meeting the right one so that when we finally meet the right person, we will know how to be grateful for that gift*

8:41:51 PM **ladydi2011:** I am laughing...this came across 3 x

8:42:04 PM **ladydi2011:** This is very possible

8:42:08 PM **Jeff Candel:** When the door of happiness closes, another opens, but often times we look so long at the closed door that we don't see the one which has been opened for us

8:42:20 PM **ladydi2011:** This is also true

8:42:32 PM **ladydi2011:** I also want to be fair to you

8:42:33 PM **Jeff Candel:** It's true that we don't know what we've got until we lose it, but it's also true that we don't know what we've been missing until it arrives

8:42:45 PM **Jeff Candel:** am not saying am the best man because at time we all make mistakes and that we are all humans

8:43:13 PM **ladydi2011:** I agree

8:43:24 PM **ladydi2011:** We do all make mistakes and we are all human

8:43:32 PM **ladydi2011:** I am not looking for perfect

8:43:38 PM **Jeff Candel:** but in all of this, we should still learbn to say am sorry even when we are right just to make things go the way it should

8:43:53 PM **ladydi2011:** I agree with this too

8:43:56 PM **Jeff Candel:** neither am *i*

8:44:07 PM **ladydi2011:** Good, because I am not perfect

8:44:11 PM **Jeff Candel:** *i* just want to lbe love the way *i* am and love you the way you are

8:44:20 PM **Jeff Candel:** and *i* must tell you this *i have already fallen in love with you*

8:44:50 PM **ladydi2011:** I am shocked.

8:44:56 PM **ladydi2011:** How did you do this?

8:45:38 PM **ladydi2011:** I have been pushing you away...

8:45:50 PM **Jeff Candel:** yeah, the more you push, the more closer *i* get

8:46:16 PM **Jeff Candel:** great minds always work alike

8:46:19 PM **Jeff Candel:** no matter what

8:46:52 PM **ladydi2011:** Yeah am just so happy here babe

8:49:13 PM **ladydi2011:** I like your tenacity

8:49:26 PM **Jeff Candel:** really?

8:49:31 PM **ladydi2011:** Yes

8:49:56 PM **Jeff Candel:** hmmm it good to know

8:49:58 PM **Jeff Candel:** am happy

8:49:59 PM **ladydi2011:** Even when I don't have a broken heart, I am not an easy catch....

8:50:19 PM **ladydi2011:** You would have had to be tenacious with me no matter what.

8:50:38 PM **Jeff Candel:** *i* promise babe

8:50:42 PM **ladydi2011:** Easy women are a dime a dozen my dear

8:50:50 PM **Jeff Candel:** yeah

8:50:57 PM **Jeff Candel:** you are my jewel and loving you will always be my pleasure

8:52:10 PM **ladydi2011:** You are a very special man.

8:52:24 PM **ladydi2011:** I am glad you emailed me

8:52:34 PM **Jeff Candel**: me too baby

8:52:38 PM **ladydi2011**: I am sure there were hundreds of women to choose from

8:52:49 PM **Jeff Candel**: but yet *i* choose you

8:53:01 PM **ladydi2011**: They say online dating is like being in a candy store

8:53:10 PM **ladydi2011**: Yes, you did. Thank you

8:53:28 PM **Jeff Candel**: you wellcome

8:53:33 PM **Jeff Candel**: baby that what they say

8:53:44 PM **Jeff Candel**: but guess what? never listen to what people say they will always have to say

8:54:03 PM **Jeff Candel**: but here we are to share true happiness

8:54:29 PM **ladydi2011**: *How long have you been on singles bee?*

8:54:52 PM **Jeff Candel**: *since i lost my wife*

8:54:56 PM **Jeff Candel**: *6years now*

8:54:59 PM **Jeff Candel**: and you??

8:55:01 PM **ladydi2011**: Wow that is a long time.

8:55:12 PM **ladydi2011**: 2 months

8:55:42 PM **Jeff Candel**: o ok

8:55:44 PM **ladydi2011**: I think I told you I didn't date for 8 years

8:55:46 PM **Jeff Candel**: *i* just decided

8:56:03 PM **ladydi2011**: Decided what Babe?

8:56:27 PM **Jeff Candel**: not to till now

8:56:54 PM **ladydi2011**: What, not to look? not to chat? not to pursue?

8:57:14 PM **Jeff Candel**: hmmm explain

8:57:37 PM **ladydi2011**: you said you decided not to until now. Not to what?

8:57:46 PM **Jeff Candel**: just sent you another song by don william and it my favorite among them all

8:58:35 PM **Jeff Candel**: *not to have anything to do with relationships till now because i wanted dedicated my time to my daughter*

8:58:54 PM **ladydi2011**: I just got it. Please hold. Thank you.

8:59:07 PM **ladydi2011**: This makes sense. She needed you.

8:59:14 PM **Jeff Candel**: yeah

9:04:13 PM **ladydi2011**: Very nice. I believe in magic.

9:04:39 PM **Jeff Candel**: me too babe

9:04:43 PM **Jeff Candel**: do you like it

9:04:49 PM **ladydi2011**: I do like it.

9:05:14 PM **ladydi2011**: I travel a lot and will play it when I travel

9:06:02 PM **Jeff Candel**: oh ok where do you travel to?

9:06:27 PM **ladydi2011**: All over the country to speak

9:07:11 PM **ladydi2011**: It is 2:00 there now and you have to get up in 3 1/2 hours.

9:07:25 PM **ladydi2011**: You will be drinking extra coffee

9:09:03 PM **Jeff Candel**: yeah baby

9:09:14 PM **Jeff Candel**: speak

9:09:27 PM **ladydi2011**: I have operated on a couple hours of sleep and it can be difficult

9:09:35 PM **ladydi2011**: I am a professional transformational speaker

9:09:44 PM **Jeff Candel**: you said you travel to speak, really?

9:09:52 PM **ladydi2011**: Yes

9:09:57 PM **ladydi2011**: I am also an author

9:09:58 PM **Jeff Candel**: hope *i* will watch you speak soon

9:10:06 PM **ladydi2011**: That would be nice

9:10:16 PM **Jeff Candel**: have you written any book?

9:10:16 PM **ladydi2011**: I like transforming people's lives

9:10:32 PM **ladydi2011**: I have many articles published worldwide

9:10:34 PM **Jeff Candel**: just like you have transform mine

9:10:45 PM **ladydi2011**: I am writing my first two books now

9:10:50 PM **ladydi2011**: I have?

9:10:59 PM **Jeff Candel**: they online?

9:11:04 PM **ladydi2011**: Not yet.

9:11:06 PM **Jeff Candel**: tell me about some of them

9:11:09 PM **ladydi2011**: They will be soon

9:11:12 PM **Jeff Candel**: ok

9:11:20 PM **ladydi2011**: My designer is designing the covers now

9:11:31 PM **Jeff Candel**: ok

9:11:34 PM **ladydi2011**: Then we need to build the websites and then get them on Amazon and go viral on you tube

9:12:12 PM **ladydi2011**: One is a business book and one is a love story

9:12:13 PM **Jeff Candel**: ok

9:12:48 PM **ladydi2011**: This is why I work so many hours every day

9:12:53 PM **Jeff Candel**: ok tell me about the love story

9:13:14 PM **ladydi2011**: It is what I imagine true love to be.

9:13:31 PM **ladydi2011**: What would make a wonderful relationship?

9:13:51 PM **Jeff Candel**: yeah

9:13:52 PM **ladydi2011**: One day I would love to live on a beach and write romance novels.

9:14:03 PM **Jeff Candel**: enlite me on it babe

9:14:05 PM **Jeff Candel**: me too

9:14:11 PM **ladydi2011**: Really?

9:15:08 PM **ladydi2011**: It is about a woman who knows her worth, what she wants and is not willing to settle and she sets out to find her forever love.

9:15:48 PM **ladydi2011**: It talks about who she is and how one can only attract who they are because you can't desire what you don't know.

9:16:29 PM **ladydi2011**: It tells the process she went through to get to be who she is and to discover her worth.

9:17:16 PM **ladydi2011**: She meets a lot of men, but not one of them is for her.

9:17:32 PM **ladydi2011**: You get the picture, right?

9:17:38 PM **Jeff Candel**: yeah

9:17:54 PM **ladydi2011**: I don't want to tell you everything or you will not want to read it

9:18:10 PM **Jeff Candel**: *i* want you to tell me before *i* read it babe

9:18:17 PM **ladydi2011**: The good part is when she meets the right man and how they build a future together

9:18:27 PM **ladydi2011**: You do? Why?

9:18:48 PM **ladydi2011**: This is where all the romance is

9:19:05 PM **ladydi2011**: He works diligently to romance her and win her heart

9:19:18 PM **ladydi2011**: He is consumed with winning her heart

9:19:47 PM **ladydi2011**: He actually courts her, which is a lost art today

9:20:08 PM **ladydi2011**: Today, people are more concerned with jumping into bed and they miss the journey

9:20:44 PM **ladydi2011**: I am hoping this will inspire young women to treasure who they are and not give themselves away to a man who is undeserving

9:20:57 PM **ladydi2011**: See, there is the transformational part of me

9:21:03 PM **ladydi2011**: I have a heart for women

9:21:15 PM **Jeff Candel**: yeah *i* can observe that

9:22:03 PM **ladydi2011**: Can you tell I have passion?

Break In Time

9:22:27 PM **ladydi2011**: Are you there?

9:23:00 PM **Jeff Candel**: yes am here

9:23:04 PM **Jeff Candel**: you have it all baby

9:23:10 PM **Jeff Candel**: you are woman of great value

9:23:10 PM **ladydi2011**: I thought maybe you fell asleep

9:23:16 PM **Jeff Candel**: no am here]

9:23:28 PM **ladydi2011**: Thank you

9:23:35 PM **Jeff Candel**: and woman like you are rare

9:23:41 PM **ladydi2011**: This is true

9:24:49 PM **ladydi2011**: I am hoping through the novel, they might hear what I am saying

9:24:58 PM **Jeff Candel**: yeah

9:25:52 PM **ladydi2011**: I have learned that until you love and value yourself, nobody else can love and value you

9:28:18 PM **ladydi2011**: Please hold

9:28:40 PM **Jeff Candel**: ok

9:35:47 PM **ladydi2011**: Babe, I need to go...Good night. Sleep well.

9:35:53 PM **ladydi2011**: Let's connect tomorrow

9:35:57 PM **Jeff Candel**: ok baby

9:36:01 PM **ladydi2011**: Neighbor is now here

9:36:04 PM **Jeff Candel**: *no matter what you do just know that i love you*

From: jeffery candel
To: ladydi2011
Subject: you are my happiness
Sent: Wednesday, June 6, 2012 8:24 AM

Love is watchful and sleeping, slumbered not.

Though weary, it is not tired; though pressed, it is not straitened; though alarmed, and it is not confounded... Friends are God's way of taking care of us. There is only one happiness in life, to love and be loved.

Marriage is not a ritual or an end. It is a long, intricate, intimate dance together and nothing matters more than your own sense of balance and your choice of partnered.

I am waiting for your photographs. Please you should take good care of yourself for me
Seek out that particular mental attribute which makes you feel most deeply and vitally alive, along

with which comes the inner voice which says, 'This is the real me, and when you have found that attitude, follow it. hope to read from you soon.

I care, Jeff

RED FLAGS

- He set the stage to "retire" and travel for his worldwide "oil" business. A scammer almost always has a format that makes them travel. Oil is a resource in the Delta of Nigeria, and it is a common theme among Nigerian scammers.
- His description of business doesn't make any sense. Notice he said the "western part of the country in the world," which does not make grammatical sense. He was probably talking about West Nigeria, as the highest percentage of Nigerian scammers live in the western part of Nigeria.
- Ladies, as much as we want a man to speak poetry and beautiful words to us, most don't. He said he wrote all the beautiful words he spoke above, but he didn't. I found this poem on http://www.1lovepoems.com/love/what-means-love.shtml http://lovegalleryfree.blogspot.com/2011_12_01_archive.html and many other websites. This poem is part of his format and his way to hook women into falling in love with him. Always remember the goal is to get a woman to fall in love and then get to her money."
- "Live a happy home" is a term common to Nigerian scammers.
- He once again asked what state I live in. This suggests he is talking to more than one woman and maybe he is having difficulty keeping them straight.
- Ask what "your man" likes to eat, and pay attention to the answer. Eggs and rice are staple foods in Africa.
- Watch for when he sends a message multiple times in a row; this is a good indicator that he is copying and pasting. Scammers save their commonly used phrases in a Word document and then copy and paste into their chat.
- He is already trying to learn where my heart is when he asks "tell me now from your heart baby how do you feel now?" A scammer will never start the scam until they know they have your heart.
- Within four days he has supposedly already fallen in love with me. This is normal for a scammer and not someone in a real relationship. Quick claims of love are big red flags.
- First he said he had been on Singlesbee dating site since he lost his wife six years ago, and then he said he has not had a relationship until now. Which is it?

Pay attention to all these little things. If your gut tells you something doesn't seem right, believe it, and STOP ALL COMMUNICATION. Good scammers are proficient in catching you in their web. Remember, this is their job.

IM Jun 6, 2012 10:07:13 AM

10:07:13 AM **Jeff Candel**: hello dear

10:07:23 AM **Jeff Candel**: how are you doing today?

10:07:27 AM **ladydi2011**: Hello

10:07:40 AM **ladydi2011**: How are you?

10:07:46 AM **Jeff Candel**: am fine

10:07:57 AM **Jeff Candel**: just thinking about you

10:08:16 AM **ladydi2011**: I just read your email. Thank you.

10:08:26 AM **Jeff Candel**: welcome dear

10:08:31 AM **ladydi2011**: are you at work?

10:08:42 AM **Jeff Candel**: am at home today dear

10:08:59 AM **Jeff Candel**: *today is my off day*

10:09:09 AM **ladydi2011**: are you taking the day off or working from home?

10:09:13 AM **Jeff Candel**: am just alone at home

10:09:25 AM **ladydi2011**: Sorry...I didn't finish reading

10:09:38 AM **Jeff Candel**: ok

10:09:44 AM **ladydi2011**: You are never alone....

10:10:07 AM **Jeff Candel**: ok dear

10:10:07 AM **ladydi2011**: I am glad you are off since you were up so late with me last night.

10:10:15 AM **Jeff Candel**: thank you for that

10:10:24 AM **Jeff Candel**: yes dear

10:10:41 AM **ladydi2011**: what are you going to do to bring adventure into your life today?

10:10:50 AM **Jeff Candel**: hmmmm, just here thinking about you and when you will be online

10:11:15 AM **Jeff Candel**: am so happy you are here dear

10:11:36 AM **ladydi2011**: I am happy you are here too

10:11:54 AM **ladydi2011**: so, maybe you should go to the park and have a picnic.

10:12:05 AM **ladydi2011**: think about me being there with you

10:12:05 AM **Jeff Candel**: sure dear

10:12:14 AM **Jeff Candel**: ok *i* am now

10:12:49 AM **Jeff Candel**: being here with you *makes me strong* dear

10:13:10 AM **ladydi2011**: this is a good thing...I think you are pretty strong on your own.

10:13:40 AM **ladydi2011**: Do you drink wine?

10:13:45 AM **Jeff Candel**: sure *i* am now with you dear

10:13:51 AM **Jeff Candel**: sure nor acholic wine

10:14:03 AM **ladydi2011**: Ok

10:14:11 AM **ladydi2011**: Take some of this to the park with you

10:14:24 AM **Jeff Candel**: so whata re you doing now?

10:14:54 AM **ladydi2011**: Checking email and then I have loads of client work

10:15:04 AM **Jeff Candel**: *i* think you should come and join me there

10:15:17 AM **ladydi2011**: I will be there with you in mind and spirit

10:15:23 AM **ladydi2011**: you will feel me there

10:15:24 AM **Jeff Candel**: ok *i* will dear

10:15:40 AM **ladydi2011**: I like swiss cheese, what about you?

10:16:23 AM **Jeff Candel**: *i* like crackers

10:16:34 AM **ladydi2011**: You don't like cheese?

10:16:45 AM **Jeff Candel**: *i* like cheese too

10:17:06 AM **ladydi2011**: so, what did you do so far on your day off?

10:17:21 AM **Jeff Candel**: nothing just in the house doing some paper work and relaxing

10:18:23 AM **Jeff Candel**: *i* wanna hear your voice dear

10:18:58 AM **ladydi2011**: Do you want to call me?

10:19:19 AM **Jeff Candel**: *i* would have love to dear

10:19:24 AM **Jeff Candel**: do you mind?

10:19:34 AM **ladydi2011**: This would be nice.

10:19:39 AM **Jeff Candel**: ok dear

Incoming Voice call with Jeff Candel (10:21:09 AM)

Call Ended: 0 hours 24 minutes 52 seconds

10:46:18 AM **Jeff Candel**: your voice is so sweet baby

10:46:26 AM **ladydi2011**: Thank you.

10:46:34 AM **Jeff Candel**: *i* love the way you laugh too

10:46:43 AM **ladydi2011**: *thank you for calling. I love your voice and your accent.*

10:46:46 AM **Jeff Candel**: hahahahaha

10:46:50 AM **Jeff Candel**: *i* love the sound..is like a music to my head

10:47:19 AM **Jeff Candel**: *i* will never forget the sound of your voice baby

10:47:35 AM **ladydi2011**: I will never forget the sound of your voice either.

10:48:40 AM **Jeff Candel**: *can you see me*

10:48:55 AM **ladydi2011**: *Thank you for inviting me to see you.*

10:49:01 AM **Jeff Candel**: ok baby

10:49:14 AM **ladydi2011**: You are soooo handsome!

10:49:15 AM **Jeff Candel**: *i* just want you to know that *i* want you in life

10:49:21 AM **Jeff Candel**: thank you baby

10:49:38 AM **Jeff Candel**: you are all *i* want in life

10:50:03 AM **ladydi2011**: Jeff, *i* am ready to now share something with you.

10:50:11 AM **Jeff Candel**: ok baby

10:50:22 AM **Jeff Candel**: and am ready to be with you too baby

10:50:35 AM **Jeff Candel**: *i want to spend the rest of my life with you*

10:51:07 AM **ladydi2011**: I believe you

10:51:15 AM **Jeff Candel**: ok baby thank you for believeing in me

10:51:31 AM **ladydi2011**: *Baby, in the last two months on line, I have had many scammers play with my heart*

10:51:34 AM **Jeff Candel**: *i promise i will never let you down ok*

10:51:53 AM **Jeff Candel**: am here for you now ok baby

10:52:00 AM **ladydi2011**: *It has made me very skeptical of who is behind the screen*

10:52:20 AM **Jeff Candel**: *now i have show myself to you*

10:52:24 AM **ladydi2011**: I wanted to trust you and what you were saying but was struggling

10:52:25 AM **Jeff Candel**: *am for real ok*

10:52:40 AM **Jeff Candel**: *do you believe me now*

10:52:50 AM **ladydi2011**: I see this!

10:52:58 AM **ladydi2011**: I do

10:53:06 AM **Jeff Candel**: ok baby

10:53:21 AM **Jeff Candel**: am happy baby

10:53:35 AM **ladydi2011**: The fact that I didn't ask you to come on cam makes it even better.

10:53:46 AM **Jeff Candel**: *have to go now baby*

10:53:46 AM **ladydi2011**: How did you know this?

10:53:55 AM **Jeff Candel**: *i* will talk to you later

10:54:13 AM **ladydi2011**: Tonight I will also get on cam...

10:54:22 AM **Jeff Candel**: ok *i* will be very glad to see you baby

10:54:39 AM **ladydi2011**: I am so glad you are real!

10:54:48 AM **Jeff Candel**: thank you baby

10:55:05 AM **Jeff Candel**: *can i give you my cell number now?*

10:55:48 AM **ladydi2011**: Yes, please do give me your cell phone number

10:56:00 AM **Jeff Candel**: *i* want to be the one that always make your heart jump with joy

10:56:24 AM **Jeff Candel**: *+447031902149 that is my cell number ok*

10:56:39 AM **ladydi2011**: thank you...

10:56:50 AM **Jeff Candel**: welcome baby

10:56:58 AM **ladydi2011**: I cannot even explain how *i* feel right now

10:57:10 AM **Jeff Candel**: oooh baby me too

10:57:18 AM **ladydi2011**: Very happy!

10:57:26 AM **Jeff Candel**: am happy too baby

10:58:22 AM **Jeff Candel**: am so happy to meet you hun

10:58:35 AM **ladydi2011**: *i* am so happy to meet you too baby

10:58:52 AM **ladydi2011**: I have to go to work. I will see you later.

10:58:58 AM **Jeff Candel**: ok baby

10:59:06 AM **ladydi2011**: Please enjoy your day

10:59:15 AM **Jeff Candel**: just let me know when you areonline ok

10:59:23 AM **ladydi2011**: Ok. I will

10:59:32 AM **ladydi2011**: Do you have unlimited text?

10:59:36 AM **Jeff Candel**: you have a nice day now

10:59:42 AM **Jeff Candel**: *nop i cant send txt*

10:59:50 AM **ladydi2011**: Oh, never mind, you are in London!

10:59:56 AM **Jeff Candel**: yes

10:59:58 AM **ladydi2011**: Lol

11:00:08 AM **Jeff Candel**: *but i can send txt to with email ok*

11:00:19 AM **ladydi2011**: Email works

11:00:35 AM **ladydi2011**: Take care of you

11:00:52 AM **Jeff Candel**: ok baby

11:01:47 AM **ladydi2011**: enjoy your day.

11:01:52 AM **ladydi2011**: Be for now.

11:02:09 AM **Jeff Candel**: ok baby

11:02:11 AM **Jeff Candel**: byeeeee

RED FLAGS

- He said today was his day off. Watch for how often the man you are chatting with isn't working. In reality, he *is* working and YOU are his job!

- He called me on Yahoo voice and not on the phone. He then came on cam, which surprised me because usually a scammer will NOT come on cam, especially without much urging. However, he only stayed on cam for one minute and 26 seconds and then said he had to go, but continued to chat for almost nine minutes. This behavior was puzzling until I spoke with Bob Jugante who is one of my sources. Bob had already come clean with me and was actually protecting and teaching me as I continued to chat for this book. He told me that scammers use fake cams. I, not having a criminal mind, never even considered that the cam was fake. Remember, these people have criminal minds. They look for ways to deceive people. If you are going to date online, you have to know that these criminals are out there. They are predators, and they think differently than you do.

- He said, "I promise I will never let you down". The phrase "I will never let you down" is also something a scammer will say and emphasize.
- He could not text in a normal way; only through the computer. This is a red flag.
- He provided me a +44 7 number. Anytime someone gives you a number beginning with +44 7, you know they are a scammer.
- He doesn't even know me and says he wants to spend the rest of his life with me. When a man is "fast" and "furious" about falling in love with you so quickly, he is probably a scammer.

Ok, the game is full on now. It is time for me to make him think I totally believe him and that I am now in love with him so I can get his *"scam story"* for this book. I must warn you, this was one of the hardest scam stories I experienced, so brace yourself to learn just how cruel scammers can be to get your money. Remember, they DO NOT CARE ABOUT YOU. They just want YOUR MONEY!

From: ladydi2011
To: jeffcand101
Subject: Re: you are my happiness
Sent: Wednesday, Jun 6, 2012 11:55 AM

Hello,

Wow! You are full of surprises. All good ones...

I had to leave the office for a minute to be with my emotions and share with you how I am feeling.

From the first email I received from you I saw something very special about you. I was attracted to you immediately and wanted to get to know you. I am so glad I did!

Thank you so much for inviting me to see you on cam. I have been holding back because of the experiences I have had online.

I have been trying to figure out if you were who you said you were. Trying to figure out if I could believe what you were saying and if I could trust you. I am sorry that I was like this.

I told you I would always be honest with you and I meant this. No relationship can survive without honesty. I always say what I mean and mean what I say.

You will never have to wonder. Please be patient with me. Please know I will always tell you what I am really feeling. You are my friend and very possibly my future.

Talk with you soon!

Fondly,
Diana

IM Jun 6, 2012 5:39:54 PM

5:39:54 PM **ladydi2011**: Jeff, are you there?
5:43:40 PM **Jeff Candel**: Am here baby
5:44:40 PM **ladydi2011**: *I tried calling and I couldn't get through with my calling card...?????*
5:45:03 PM **Jeff Candel**: Really
5:45:18 PM **Jeff Candel**: But my phone is on baby
5:45:19 PM **ladydi2011**: Yeah.
5:45:49 PM **ladydi2011**: *It had nothing to do with your phone being on. It had to do with your actual number.*
5:49:08 PM **ladydi2011**: Are you there baby?
5:50:12 PM **ladydi2011**: Hello...........
5:55:27 PM **ladydi2011**: Hello. Baby, are you there?

IM Jun 6, 2012 6:26:51 PM Continued

6:26:51 PM **ladydi2011**: Welcome back!
6:26:52 PM **Jeff Candel**: thanks baby
6:26:53 PM **ladydi2011**: You are the first man who would come on cam.
6:26:56 PM **Jeff Candel**: Sure baby
6:27:18 PM **Jeff Candel**: *I just want you. To know that am for real*
6:27:29 PM **ladydi2011**: I couldn't let my feeling get involved with you until I knew you were real.
6:27:51 PM **Jeff Candel**: Yes baby
6:27:56 PM **ladydi2011**: I am so glad you wanted me to know you were real...because if the truth be told I was really scared.
6:28:10 PM **ladydi2011**: From the start I really liked you.
6:28:20 PM **ladydi2011**: I did not want my heart broken again
6:29:09 PM **Jeff Candel**: *Baby I love you so much and that is why I show myself to you*
6:29:25 PM **ladydi2011**: Thank you.
6:29:31 PM **Jeff Candel**: *I promise I will not brreak your heart ok*
6:30:08 PM **ladydi2011**: Nothing against you my dear. I have had this promised to me before.
6:30:51 PM **Jeff Candel**: ThAnk you my love
6:31:24 PM **Jeff Candel**: Baby can I trust you with my heart
6:31:33 PM **ladydi2011**: Absolutely

6:32:08 PM **Jeff Candel**: You promise me that you will take good carre. Of it
6:32:20 PM **ladydi2011**: I promise.
6:32:44 PM **Jeff Candel**: *I love you*
6:32:59 PM **ladydi2011**: I am falling in love with you too.
6:33:12 PM **ladydi2011**: It has happened so fast that it scares me
6:36:05 PM **Jeff Candel**: I don't want to be hurt baby
6:36:26 PM **ladydi2011**: Did I ever lead you on?
6:36:42 PM **Jeff Candel**: No baby
6:36:48 PM **ladydi2011**: Was I honest with you?
6:36:59 PM **Jeff Candel**: *I believe iin you with all my life*
6:37:20 PM **ladydi2011**: I have nothing to hide from you baby.
6:37:29 PM **ladydi2011**: You are too important to me.
6:37:30 PM **Jeff Candel**: Ok baby
6:37:54 PM **Jeff Candel**: *Thank you darlling*
6:37:54 PM **ladydi2011**: You can ask me anything at any time and I will tell you
6:40:01 PM **Jeff Candel**: You are my joy in life. Myy heart belongs to you
6:40:04 PM **Jeff Candel**: Every part of my body is yours baby
6:40:06 PM **Jeff Candel**: No one can ever take your place in my heart
6:40:15 PM **ladydi2011**: Thank you baby.
6:40:25 PM **ladydi2011**: You make me smile
6:40:38 PM **ladydi2011**: Please be patient with me.
6:40:50 PM **Jeff Candel**: I will baby
6:41:19 PM **Jeff Candel**: I told you that I am a patient man
6:41:26 PM **ladydi2011**: I know you did.
6:41:35 PM **ladydi2011**: I promise you that I am worth the wait
6:41:41 PM **Jeff Candel**: I understand. Baby
6:41:46 PM **ladydi2011**: I am everything I portray myself to be. I am hiding nothing from you honey.
6:43:10 PM **Jeff Candel**: *Have you hard any prob with your client before*
6:43:21 PM **ladydi2011**: what do you mean?
6:43:25 PM **Jeff Candel**: I know baby
6:44:19 PM **Jeff Candel**: *Am justt asking if you have. Ever hard any misunderstanding with any of your client before*
6:44:42 PM **ladydi2011**: No, my clients have been with me for years. I have a stellar reputation.
6:45:09 PM **ladydi2011**: I am very well respected.
6:45:15 PM **Jeff Candel**: Good to hear that
6:45:21 PM **Jeff Candel**: Sure baby
6:45:35 PM **ladydi2011**: By the way...I have not been with a man in 8 years.
6:45:46 PM **ladydi2011**: I was too busy building my business.
6:45:54 PM **Jeff Candel**: I know you well tto be a very kkind and loving woman
6:45:59 PM **ladydi2011**: I DO NOT have one night stands.
6:46:12 PM **ladydi2011**: I am a very kind and loving woman.
6:46:13 PM **Jeff Candel**: Ooh gooD
6:46:23 PM **ladydi2011**: Just as you are a very kind and loving man.
6:46:34 PM **ladydi2011**: I saw this in you right away.
6:46:36 PM **Jeff Candel**: Ooh baby thank you
6:46:54 PM **Jeff Candel**: You are so sweet hun
6:49:00 PM **ladydi2011**: I am a good woman honey. You saw correctly.

6:49:24 PM **ladydi2011**: I so appreciate you!

6:49:39 PM **Jeff Candel**: Thank. You hun

6:49:49 PM **ladydi2011**: Baby, we have to figure out why my calling card won't work.

6:49:58 PM **Jeff Candel**: Life is all about be good

6:50:18 PM **Jeff Candel**: Baby try the number again

6:50:22 PM **ladydi2011**: It sure is.

6:50:29 PM **ladydi2011**: Ok...let me try now.

6:50:40 PM **ladydi2011**: I have to go get my land line. Please hold

6:50:43 PM **Jeff Candel**: Ok

6:52:30 PM **Jeff Candel**: *+447031902149*

6:52:48 PM **Jeff Candel**: That is. The number

6:53:27 PM **ladydi2011**: I am back and going to call now

6:53:33 PM **Jeff Candel**: Make sure you add your country code before daillim

6:53:46 PM **Jeff Candel**: Ok

6:55:34 PM **ladydi2011**: *Honey i just tried and it said, "I am not permitted to call this location with this card." I don't understand because I can call other London numbers with this card.*

6:55:52 PM **ladydi2011**: *It is something with the 703*

6:57:05 PM **Jeff Candel**: Baby I don't understand why is not going

6:57:34 PM **ladydi2011**: Me either. I don't know what to do to be able to call you. This is a worldwide card.

6:58:08 PM **Jeff Candel**: Baby am confused now

6:58:49 PM **ladydi2011**: I am confused too

6:59:26 PM **ladydi2011**: *When i researched this, it had something to do with the UK blocking numbers*

6:59:37 PM **Jeff Candel**: Did u add your country code

7:00:08 PM **Jeff Candel**: Hmm..Its ok baby

7:00:22 PM **ladydi2011**: To get out on the card I have to dial 011, and then I dialed 447031902149

7:01:16 PM **Jeff Candel**: Correct baby

Break In Time...He Called Me

7:16:51 PM **ladydi2011**: Are you there baby?

7:17:15 PM **ladydi2011**: Hello....

7:17:28 PM **Jeff Candel**: Am here baby

7:18:01 PM **Jeff Candel**: Am glad hearing your voice baby

7:18:37 PM **ladydi2011**: I am so glad you like my laugh because I laugh often.

7:20:06 PM **Jeff Candel**: And your laugh kept rringing in mu head like a sound of. Music. Baby

7:20:07 PM **Jeff Candel**: I love you so much baby

7:20:34 PM **ladydi2011**: I love you too

7:21:34 PM **ladydi2011**: I will never hurt your heart baby.

7:22:10 PM **Jeff Candel**: I will nnever huuurt you baby

7:23:13 PM **ladydi2011**: Baby, what is your home address?

Break In Time

7:26:09 PM **ladydi2011**: Baby, are you there?

7:27:10 PM **Jeff Candel**: 13 shant street london

7:27:20 PM **Jeff Candel**: Am here baby

7:27:58 PM **ladydi2011**: I want to send you something, so please give me your entire address.

7:29:48 PM **ladydi2011**: *Baby, all I got was 13 Shant Street London*

7:30:43 PM **Jeff Candel**: *Shant. House no 13 shant street london*

7:31:23 PM **Jeff Candel**: Baby what do you want to send

7:31:28 PM **ladydi2011**: No zip code?

7:31:48 PM **ladydi2011**: Now, if i tell you, it wouldn't be a surprise, would it?

7:32:32 PM **Jeff Candel**: Sure baby

7:33:14 PM **ladydi2011**: Do I put UK? What about a zip code?

Break In Time

7:37:37 PM **Jeff Candel**: Baby are you there

7:37:50 PM **Jeff Candel**: Am here

7:37:57 PM **ladydi2011**: Do I put UK? What about a zip code?

Break In Time

7:39:42 PM **Jeff Candel**: baby can't you tell me

7:39:43 PM **Jeff Candel**: *Am not too good in suprrise baby*

7:39:59 PM **Jeff Candel**: The last suprise I received was from my dad

7:40:07 PM **Jeff Candel**: Before he died

7:40:14 PM **ladydi2011**: I want to send you a card

7:41:03 PM **Jeff Candel**: Ok

7:41:57 PM **Jeff Candel**: **SE12ES that is the posta code**

7:42:28 PM **ladydi2011**: Thank you baby

7:42:40 PM **ladydi2011**: Do I put UK on it?

7:43:22 PM **ladydi2011**: Honey, when is your birthday?

7:43:33 PM **Jeff Candel**: No just the address and. The posta code

Break In Time

7:44:45 PM **Jeff Candel**: 15th september

7:44:48 PM **ladydi2011**: ok

7:44:56 PM **ladydi2011**: Mine is Nov. 15th

7:45:08 PM **ladydi2011**: Baby, are you tired?

7:45:37 PM **Jeff Candel**: No baby

7:45:54 PM **Jeff Candel**: Nov 15th Is that your birthday?

7:47:05 PM **ladydi2011**: I am not perfect honey

7:47:11 PM **ladydi2011**: I don't think anyone is

7:47:20 PM **ladydi2011**: Will you have me even with my flaws?

7:47:34 PM **Jeff Candel**: Sure no one is pperfect

7:48:15 PM **ladydi2011**: So, I occupy your mind sometimes?

7:48:34 PM **Jeff Candel**: All the. Time baby

7:49:11 PM **ladydi2011**: I was waiting to see you on line today.

7:50:17 PM **Jeff Candel**: Really? Am. So glad to hear that

7:51:06 PM **ladydi2011**: I wanted to talk with you.

7:51:30 PM **Jeff Candel**: Cool baby

7:51:55 PM **ladydi2011**: Honey, you have been through a lot in life.

7:52:04 PM **ladydi2011**: How many years were you married?

7:52:42 PM **Jeff Candel**: 12yrs

7:53:15 PM **ladydi2011**: I was married 8 years.

7:54:20 PM **ladydi2011**: My ex-husband is a nice man. We didn't have a bad marraige, but wanted different things.

7:57:10 PM **ladydi2011**: He remarried 10 years ago and is happy. I am happy for him.

7:57:27 PM **Jeff Candel**: Ooh. Good

7:57:29 PM **ladydi2011**: Baby, I am always honest and respectful to people.

7:58:08 PM **ladydi2011**: This is why he and I are still friends today.

7:59:30 PM **ladydi2011**: What do you see for our life together?

Break In Time

8:02:42 PM **ladydi2011**: Baby, are you there?

8:05:25 PM **ladydi2011**: Jeff. Are you there?

8:10:13 PM **Jeff Candel**: hello baby are you still ther?

8:10:29 PM **ladydi2011**: I am

8:10:38 PM **Jeff Candel**: ok good

8:10:50 PM **ladydi2011**: I thought you fell asleep

8:11:04 PM **Jeff Candel**: yes baby

8:11:13 PM **Jeff Candel**: but *i* couldnot sleep

8:11:20 PM **ladydi2011**: Why not?

8:11:43 PM **Jeff Candel**: *i* try closed my eyes and kept missing you baby

8:11:49 PM **Jeff Candel**: *i* dont wanna miss you

8:12:24 PM **ladydi2011**: Baby...you are not going to miss me. I am not going anywhere.

8:12:33 PM **Jeff Candel**: ok baby promise me

8:12:52 PM **ladydi2011**: I will try to go past time and distance and visit you in your dreams.

8:13:09 PM **Jeff Candel**: ok baby *i* love you

8:13:17 PM **ladydi2011**: Sleep well

8:13:26 PM **Jeff Candel**: ok baby

8:13:34 PM **ladydi2011**: Until tomorrow...Night

8:14:06 PM **Jeff Candel**: *i* love you

8:14:10 PM **Jeff Candel**: good night baby

8:14:16 PM **ladydi2011**: Love you too.

8:14:28 PM **Jeff Candel**: *i* have to catch some sleep now and dream of you too

8:14:40 PM **Jeff Candel**: hope you will dream of me tonight baby

8:14:46 PM **ladydi2011**: I will

8:14:50 PM **Jeff Candel**: ok baby

8:14:53 PM **Jeff Candel**: night

8:15:18 PM **ladydi2011**: Night

8:15:25 PM **Jeff Candel**: ok hun

8:16:10 PM **Jeff Candel**: byeee

8:16:13 PM **Jeff Candel**: love you

RED FLAGS

🚩 When I mentioned he was the first man that went on cam for me, he said he wanted me to know that he was "for real" and that he loves me so much and this is why he "showed himself" to me. Listen to the terminology, "show myself to you". Would a man with nothing to hide say this? I don't think so.

🚩 Then he promised not to break my heart. This line is often used by scammers. Remember, they want to gain your trust.

🚩 Then he told me he believed in me with "all his life". Again, who says this? Nigerian scammers say this. It is a common phrase in Nigeria.

🚩 I really threw him off when I asked for his address. He gave me the address of 13 Shant Street London. I asked him several times if this was all there was to his address, and then he said House 13 Shant Street London, SE12ES. He never said England. Anyone living there would definitely say England. I did a website search for the address he gave me and on www.192.com/places/se/se1-2/se1-2es/they stated Sorry; we have no records of residential addresses within this postcode.

When I asked for his address, he was not responding as quickly. I am sure he was on Google looking for an address.

I already knew that a +44 70 number was a scammer's phone number because I dealt with this with Bob Jugante. I learned about this on www.419scam.org/419-phone-uk.htm#phone-uk. They say that all United Kingdom phone numbers starting with +44 70 usually mean it is a scammer. The United Kingdom number is used to lend credibility to the scammer, and +44 70 numbers belong to international call forwarding services. These services make it possible for scammers to hide the fact that they are based in Nigeria or somewhere else, so the scam victim believes they're dealing with someone in the United Kingdom. Very few (if any) legitimate individuals use these numbers. Banks, law offices, United Kingdom immigration officials, etc. never use +44 70 numbers. Their offices are based in the United Kingdom, so they have no need to redirect calls to some mobile phone outside the United Kingdom. Additionally, phone numbers starting with '70' are "Personal numbering" in the "Find me anywhere" range. Charges for calls to these numbers are not distance-dependent. They can cost as much as (USD $.90) per minute to call and can forward the call to virtually any phone number in the world. Forwarding numbers can be set up for free and completely anonymously via websites such as www.uknumbers.com.

Again, I can't stress enough to not take anything at face value. Do your own research, call us at 678-583-0401 or hire a private investigator to research for you. Whatever you do, if a man asks you to send him money, DO NOT SEND IT!

From: ladydi2011
To: jeffcand101
Subject: Re: Good night my love
Sent: Wednesday, June 6, 2012 9:53 PM

Darling,

I am in bed thinking about you. I wanted you to wake up to an email from me. Please have a wonderful day and think about me at least once.

When you do smile and know you are loved. Good night for me and good morning for you baby.

I love you

Diana

Text Messages

Sent From: 1410000007
Received: Jun 7, 2012 5:48 AM
From: jeffery candel
Subject: Morning my Queen

MSG: If you hide, I'll seek for you. If you're lost, I'll search for you. If you leave, I'll wait for you. If they try to take you away from me, I'll fight for you, because I never want to lose someone I love. *i love you my Queen.*

From your King,
Jeff

Sent From: 1410000009
Received: Jun 7, 2012 5:54 AM
From: jeffery candel
Subject: *i* love you my Queen

MSG: I promise to be there when you need me, I promise to hug you tight when you're lonely, I promise to wipe your tears when they fall and I promise to keep you, not for the rest of my life but for the rest of yours.*i love you baby. you are my angel. my Queen*

Sent From: 1410000004
Received: Jun 6, 2012 5:35 PM
From: jeffery candel
Subject: *i* love you my Queen

MSG: *baby how are you doing. am missing you baby. i want you to know that i luv u, you are the air that i breath. life*

Sent From: 1410000006
Received: Jun 6, 2012 5:59 PM
From: jeffery candel
Subject: RE:

MSG: baby what happen am still online baby and am missing you so much please come onlone baby ok.

Sent To: 1410000009
From: Diana
Sent: Jun 7, 2012 9:07 AM
Subject: RE:

Morning Baby. I hope you slept well and are having a wonderful day. Thank you for these promises. I promise the same back to you. I love you. Kisses and hugs.

IM Jun 7, 2012 511:29 PM

5:11:29 PM **Jeff Candel**: Hello baby am. Missing you so much please. Come online ok
5:17:30 PM **Jeff Candel**: Baby I love you
5:39:39 PM **ladydi2011**: Hi Baby! Are you there?
5:39:55 PM **Jeff Candel**: Baby. Am here
5:40:08 PM **Jeff Candel**: Where. Have you been baby
5:40:16 PM **ladydi2011**: Sleeping
5:40:28 PM **Jeff Candel**: Ok baby
5:40:35 PM **ladydi2011**: Am I showing invisible?
5:40:46 PM **Jeff Candel**: Yes baby
5:41:04 PM **Jeff Candel**: Hope I didn't disturbe ur sleep
5:41:13 PM **ladydi2011**: Good. I don't want anyone else to know I am online
5:41:38 PM **ladydi2011**: You didn't wake me. My assistant called and woke me
5:41:51 PM **Jeff Candel**: Ok baby
5:42:24 PM **Jeff Candel**: Baby hope notthing happen?
5:42:26 PM **ladydi2011**: I was working at the computer and my eyes wouldn't stay open
5:42:38 PM **ladydi2011**: How are you my love?
5:42:50 PM **Jeff Candel**: Am fine baby
5:43:42 PM **Jeff Candel**: And u?
5:44:45 PM **Jeff Candel**: Baby pleases don't stress yourslef much ok
5:46:09 PM **Jeff Candel**: Hope you are doing fine
5:46:29 PM **ladydi2011**: I am fine just tired and needed a break!
5:46:42 PM **Jeff Candel**: Ok baby
5:46:49 PM **ladydi2011**: Please tell me about your day honey
5:47:09 PM **Jeff Candel**: Well my day was good
5:47:30 PM **ladydi2011**: What did you do?
5:48:23 PM **Jeff Candel**: Baby when I get tto the office today my couliins where. Asking me what happen
5:48:38 PM **ladydi2011**: Why?
5:48:47 PM **Jeff Candel**: they said that my face is full of happiness
5:49:12 PM **Jeff Candel**: They wanted to know what happend
5:49:35 PM **Jeff Candel**: So I told them that something good has happend
5:49:55 PM **Jeff Candel**: You did it baby
5:50:47 PM **ladydi2011**: Lol
5:50:58 PM **Jeff Candel**: I tolD them that I have the right to be happy because I have. Found my happines
5:51:20 PM **ladydi2011**: Thank you baby
5:51:31 PM **Jeff Candel**: I love you baby
5:51:50 PM **ladydi2011**: I am glad you are happy. You deserve it!
5:52:02 PM **Jeff Candel**: Yes baby
5:52:06 PM **ladydi2011**: I love you too baby
5:52:15 PM **Jeff Candel**: You are. My happiness

5:52:23 PM **ladydi2011**: You are a good man!

5:52:37 PM **Jeff Candel**: Thank you baby

5:52:40 PM **ladydi2011**: You are my happiness too!!!

5:52:57 PM **ladydi2011**: Are you at your computer?

5:53:01 PM **Jeff Candel**: I love you more baby

5:53:37 PM **Jeff Candel**: Baby am on phone now

5:53:48 PM **ladydi2011**: Ok

5:54:05 PM **ladydi2011**: Me too

5:54:21 PM **Jeff Candel**: Kisssssssss

5:54:26 PM **ladydi2011**: Are you home?

5:54:27 PM **Jeff Candel**: Muah muah

5:54:36 PM **Jeff Candel**: Yess baby

5:54:45 PM **Jeff Candel**: Inside my. Room

5:54:54 PM **Jeff Candel**: On my bed

5:54:54 PM **ladydi2011**: Kisssssssssses back

5:55:10 PM **ladydi2011**: It is late there

5:55:27 PM **ladydi2011**: What did you do after work?

5:56:22 PM **Jeff Candel:** I came home and cook fried rice and salad for me and my daughter

5:57:13 PM **ladydi2011**: When does Sarah get out of school for the summer?

5:57:34 PM **Jeff Candel**: September

5:57:45 PM **ladydi2011**: Baby, I am going to switch to the computer...be right back

5:57:55 PM **Jeff Candel**: Ok baby

5:58:52 PM **ladydi2011**: I am back

5:58:57 PM **ladydi2011**: much easier to type

5:59:50 PM **ladydi2011**: How does the school system work there honey?

6:00:31 PM **Jeff Candel**: And sarah love tthe school

6:00:48 PM **ladydi2011**: I am glad she loves school

6:00:54 PM **ladydi2011**: how are her grades?

6:01:51 PM **Jeff Candel**: *College*

6:02:04 PM **ladydi2011**: What is her favorite subject?

6:02:41 PM **ladydi2011:** *College?*

6:04:24 PM **ladydi2011:** *What do you mean when you say college?*

6:04:52 PM **Jeff Candel:** *Her favorrite subjectt is arithetic*

6:05:28 PM **ladydi2011**: Nice. It was mine too and you have to be good with numbers to do your job.

6:05:37 PM **Jeff Candel: she in imperian College in london**

6:05:52 PM **Jeff Candel**: Yes baby

6:05:55 PM **ladydi2011: At 14 she is in college?**

6:06:07 PM **Jeff Candel**: Yes baby

6:06:31 PM **ladydi2011: so what is after college?**

6:07:01 PM **ladydi2011: they don't have high school there?**

6:07:45 PM **ladydi2011**: here we have grade school, middle school, high school (age 5-17) then college or university

6:08:34 PM **Jeff Candel**: Baby ok

6:08:58 PM **Jeff Candel:** So baby how was your day

6:09:21 PM **ladydi2011**: It was good. Good thing I am the boss...lol

6:09:35 PM **Jeff Candel**: HmmMm

6:09:37 PM **ladydi2011**: I thought of you often and missed you
6:09:48 PM **Jeff Candel**: The boss
6:09:55 PM **ladydi2011**: I own the company
6:10:08 PM **Jeff Candel**: Yes the. Boss
6:10:11 PM **ladydi2011**: I do not act like a boss
6:10:47 PM **ladydi2011**: I am pretty laid back in less work is not getting done or not getting done properly
6:10:49 PM **Jeff Candel**: I like that
6:10:53 PM **ladydi2011**: Then I am not happy
6:11:03 PM **Jeff Candel**: Surre baby
6:11:04 PM **ladydi2011**: My people work hard and respect me
6:11:17 PM **Jeff Candel**: YeS baby
6:11:17 PM **ladydi2011**: I hold them to high standards
6:11:35 PM **ladydi2011**: However, they know I give as much if not more than what I ask of them
6:11:56 PM **Jeff Candel**: Sure
6:12:13 PM **Jeff Candel**: *Baby do you still have a mom?*
6:12:26 PM **ladydi2011**: Yes honey, I do. She is 73
6:12:35 PM **Jeff Candel**: Waoooo
6:12:43 PM **ladydi2011**: My dad is still alive. He will be 85 this month
6:12:44 PM **Jeff Candel**: *Old momy*
6:13:02 PM **Jeff Candel**: Waoooo
6:15:38 PM **ladydi2011**: are you there?
6:16:03 PM **ladydi2011**: Jeff
6:17:21 PM **ladydi2011**: Jeff

RED FLAGS

⚑ He said his 14 year old daughter is in Imperian College in London and her favorite subject is arithetic, but I am sure he meant arithmetic. He never answered the question about high school. This is a red flag and something to be researched. When something doesn't sound right , it usually isn't. Investigate it. There is no Imperian College in London, but there is an Imperial College in London. WhenI reseached the age divisions of the education system in London (http://en.wikipedia.org/wiki/Education_in_England) I found that the education system is divided into early years (ages 3–4), primary education (ages 4–11), secondary education (ages 11–18) and tertiary education (ages 18+). It would be very unlikely for a 14 year old to be in college.

⚑ He asked if I had a mom. Rest assured he has a specific reason for wanting to know. If he is really 48 years old, he would not think my mom was old at 73. Yes, you need to look at all little things. The attention you pay to them will save your heart and money.

Sent From: 1410000010
Received: Jun 8, 2012 10:11 AM
From: jeffery candel
Subject: *i* love you my Queen

MSG: A gentle word like a spark of light, illuminates my soul, and as each sound goes deeper, It's YOU that makes me whole, There is no corner, no dark place, YOUR LOVE cannot fill, And if the world starts causing waves,it's your devotion that makes them still. And yes you always speak to me in sweet honesty and truth. Your caring heart keeps out the rain, YOUR LOVE, the ultimate roof. So thank you my Love for being there for my life I'll do the same for you, you know, ***My Beautiful, Darling Wife. Hope to read from you hun. Kisssssssss... Hugsssssss***

Your king,
Jeff

Sent To: 1410000010
From: Diana
Sent: Jun 8, 2012 12:17 PM
Subject: *i* love you my Queen

Hello my love and poet, I love what you write to me. I smile every time I hear from you. You are the wind beneath my wings. I love you. Kisses and (((hugs))) my king.

Sent From: 1410000011
Received: Jun 8, 2012 3:56 PM
From: jeffery candel
Subject: *i* love you my Queen

MSG: OOh baby thank you my queen, hope you are doing good. Everyone wants to be your sun who'll light up your life, so *i* guess i'll just be your moon. I may not be as big and bright, but *i* promise to be there for you, when your sun is shinning in someone else's sky. baby *i* love you so much, am online now baby come online and want us to chat ok.. my hear is missing you baby. *i* will be waiting for you online ok... love you... kisssssssss....Hugsssssss
Your king.
Jeff

Sent To: 1410000011
From: Diana
Sent: Jun 8, 2012 3:58 PM
Subject: *i* love you my Queen

You are the best! I have client calls for the next 3 hours. Please come on line in 3 hours. Can you my love? I miss you

Sent From: 1410000012
Received: Jun 8, 2012 4:08 PM
From: jeffery candel
Subject: *i* love you my Queen

MSG: Its ok baby, *i* will wait for you baby. here is sarah photo for you my queen, she say hi to you baby... *i* love you so much baby. check the attache ok you will see them ok I love you my queen,
your king,
Jeff

Sent To: 1410000012
From: Diana
Sent: Jun 8, 2012 4:21 PM
Subject: *i* love you my Queen

Hello baby...no pictures came through. Please email them to me. Please tell Sarah I said hello. Thanks for waiting. Love you!

Sent From: 1410000013
Received: Jun 8, 2012 4:24 PM
From: jeffery candel
Subject: RE: *i* love you my Queen

MSG: ok baby *i* will email it to your email address ok, when you are less busy you can check on it ok. *i* love you too baby.

From: jeffcand101
To: ladydi2011
Subject: Re: Picture of sarah for you my queen
Sent: Friday, June 8, 2012 4:36 PM

MSG: Here is sarah photo, my queen i hope you like them its just for you and for you alone ok... we both love you baby. you are her mom and she cant wait to be with you... she said she need you more than the sky need the moon.

baby she thank you for putting s good smile on her dad face again. baby you are my everything in life life without you is not complete.

i love you my queen.

Your King,
Jeff

IM Jun 8, 2012 6:45:25 PM

6:45:25 PM **Jeff Candel**: hello my love
6:45:31 PM **Jeff Candel**: how are you doing
6:45:37 PM **ladydi2011**: Hello honey
6:45:38 PM **Jeff Candel**: miss talking to you my queen
6:45:54 PM **Jeff Candel**: am glad you are on baby
6:45:59 PM **ladydi2011**: And I you
6:46:00 PM **Jeff Candel**: how was your day baby
6:46:14 PM **ladydi2011**: busy but good. I'm under many deadlines.
6:46:20 PM **ladydi2011**: How was your day?
6:46:43 PM **Jeff Candel**: did you get my email *i* sent to you with sarah pics?
6:46:57 PM **ladydi2011**: I did. She is beautiful!
6:49:39 PM **ladydi2011**: Please tell her I said she is beautiful.
6:50:21 PM **ladydi2011**: You are very blessed and now I am very blessed through you
6:50:49 PM **Jeff Candel**: thank you so much baby you are my blessing ok
6:51:05 PM **ladydi2011**: And you and Sarah are mine
6:51:15 PM **Jeff Candel**: thank you baby
6:51:21 PM **Jeff Candel**: *you are her mom now*
6:51:27 PM **Jeff Candel**: *she say hi to you baby*
6:51:38 PM **ladydi2011**: Please tell her I said hello
6:51:42 PM **Jeff Candel**: *And she was asking me when is mom coming home*
6:51:46 PM **Jeff Candel**: *I said soon*
6:53:06 PM **ladydi2011**: Will you be able to relocate here
6:54:16 PM **Jeff Candel**: yeah babe of course that if you wnt dear
6:55:32 PM **ladydi2011**: I am sorry babe. Please hold...phone call
6:55:42 PM **Jeff Candel**: ok sweetie
7:00:28 PM **ladydi2011**: Sorry
7:00:36 PM **Jeff Candel**: It ok babe
7:00:43 PM **ladydi2011**: I will be with you soon
7:00:58 PM **Jeff Candel**: yeah am still here dear
7:01:01 PM **Jeff Candel**: still on phone?
7:05:12 PM **ladydi2011**: I am now off the phone...so sorry
7:05:20 PM **ladydi2011**: It has been one of those days
7:05:31 PM **Jeff Candel**: it ok am still here
7:05:36 PM **Jeff Candel**: just that *i* miss you more
7:06:03 PM **ladydi2011**: I miss you more too
7:07:12 PM **ladydi2011**: Baby, what do you want to do for us to be together?
7:07:37 PM **Jeff Candel**: well alot
7:07:44 PM **Jeff Candel**: tell me what do you want me to do??
7:08:22 PM **ladydi2011**: I really don't know. I haven't ever had a long-distance relationship before.
7:08:30 PM **Jeff Candel**: oh yeah?
7:08:38 PM **ladydi2011**: I have never been to London
7:09:15 PM **Jeff Candel**: do you wanna come??
7:09:23 PM **ladydi2011**: I would love to come
7:09:36 PM **Jeff Candel**: that will be good babe
7:09:47 PM **Jeff Candel**: *i* will love that and sarah would love to see you too

7:10:07 PM **ladydi2011**: I want to meet both of you "in person"

7:10:33 PM **Jeff Candel**: yes baby

7:10:35 PM **Jeff Candel**: soon that *i* assure you

7:10:40 PM **ladydi2011**: Are you on your computer or phone

7:10:58 PM **ladydi2011**: I know I can trust your word

7:11:13 PM **Jeff Candel**: am on my computer

7:11:25 PM **ladydi2011**: *Please turn on your cam*

7:11:36 PM **Jeff Candel**: *i have issues with it*

7:11:45 PM **Jeff Candel**: *it not working for now sorry*

7:11:48 PM **Jeff Candel**: turn on yours

7:11:59 PM **ladydi2011**: I look really tired today

7:12:06 PM **Jeff Candel**: it ok by me *i* love you the way you are baby

7:13:19 PM **ladydi2011**: Can you see me?

7:13:24 PM **Jeff Candel**: that my sweet angel

7:13:31 PM **Jeff Candel**: you look adorable

7:13:39 PM **ladydi2011**: You need glasses baby

7:13:40 PM **Jeff Candel**: keep that smile

7:13:52 PM **Jeff Candel**: your smile almost wanna make me go on my knees *lol*

7:13:59 PM **ladydi2011**: You make me smile

7:14:02 PM **Jeff Candel**: why glasses?

7:14:13 PM **ladydi2011**: I do not look good today

7:14:30 PM **Jeff Candel**: you do babe

7:14:41 PM **Jeff Candel**: your smile alone is enough for me babe

7:14:42 PM **ladydi2011**: As you can see, I am in my office

7:14:55 PM **Jeff Candel**: am full of greater joy here right now looking at you

7:15:03 PM **Jeff Candel**: yes babe *i* can see

7:15:07 PM **ladydi2011**: I like when you smile

7:15:16 PM **ladydi2011**: Please get your cam fixed

7:15:19 PM **Jeff Candel**: and *i* love it when you laugh whith your sparkling teeth

7:15:31 PM **Jeff Candel**: hmmm

7:15:42 PM **Jeff Candel**: jus keep smiling and laughing don't stop

7:16:02 PM **ladydi2011**: As long as you stay in my life, I will

7:16:10 PM **Jeff Candel**: *yeah baby and I promise I will always be there forever*

7:16:39 PM **Jeff Candel**: **and promise me you will be there for me too**

7:16:58 PM **ladydi2011**: I promise that I will always be there for you too.

7:17:41 PM **Jeff Candel**: youare one in a million and loving you is always my pleasure

7:17:52 PM **ladydi2011**: So are you babe.

7:17:55 PM **Jeff Candel**: did you get those sarah's pics i sent to you

7:18:09 PM **ladydi2011**: Yes baby. She is beautiful.

7:18:36 PM **Jeff Candel**: *only if you can imagine the joy you have brought into our lives*

7:18:51 PM **Jeff Candel**: you stoped the cam why?

7:18:54 PM **ladydi2011**: I am so glad that we met

7:19:13 PM **Jeff Candel**: me too babe

7:19:21 PM **Jeff Candel**: it gives me great joy everyday

7:19:25 PM **ladydi2011**: Singlesbee ended up being good after all

7:19:37 PM **ladydi2011**: How was work today baby?

7:20:19 PM **Jeff Candel**: well hectic but it all good

7:20:30 PM **Jeff Candel**: how was your day?

7:20:30 PM **ladydi2011**: Same as yours

7:20:39 PM **Jeff Candel**: relly

7:20:50 PM **Jeff Candel**: you were in my mind all through honey

7:21:09 PM **ladydi2011**: You were in mine.

7:21:17 PM **Jeff Candel**: yeah

7:21:25 PM **ladydi2011**: I haven't even had a chance to eat yet today

7:21:32 PM **Jeff Candel**: why?

7:21:33 PM **ladydi2011**: It has been crazy. Busy with deadlines, client calls, writing proposals, answering emails, design issues and the list goes on.

7:22:27 PM **ladydi2011**: This is not a complaint. I am very grateful for the business

7:22:48 PM **Jeff Candel**: hmmm

7:22:54 PM **Jeff Candel**: am happy for you babe

7:22:59 PM **ladydi2011**: Many businesses here are closing

7:23:02 PM **Jeff Candel**: you are a career woman

7:23:09 PM **ladydi2011**: Money is getting tighter and tighter

7:23:13 PM **Jeff Candel**: why are the business closing

7:23:16 PM **ladydi2011**: hmmmmmmm...Economy

7:23:20 PM **Jeff Candel**: *bad economy?*

7:23:26 PM **ladydi2011**: Yes babe

7:23:29 PM **Jeff Candel**: how is yours?

7:23:37 PM **Jeff Candel**: *am sure yours is not bad at all*

7:24:04 PM **ladydi2011**: The only thing that saves me is that I am nation-wide, a good sales person and have built a stellar reputation.

7:25:00 PM **Jeff Candel**: it so bad here too and has affected many business here

7:25:12 PM **Jeff Candel**: and *i* think it gonna affect my work too

7:25:14 PM **ladydi2011**: I think it is bad all over the world

7:25:17 PM **Jeff Candel**: from the way it going

7:25:23 PM **Jeff Candel**: yeah babe

7:25:36 PM **ladydi2011**: What about your retirement idea with the oil?

7:25:45 PM **ladydi2011**: Do you think it will affect this too?

7:25:56 PM **Jeff Candel**: yeah am working on it dear it takes time babe

7:26:07 PM **ladydi2011**: Of course it does

7:26:28 PM **Jeff Candel**: yeah

7:26:35 PM **ladydi2011**: What is the saying, Rome was not built in a day.....

7:26:48 PM **ladydi2011**: I gave up a lot to build this company

7:26:52 PM **Jeff Candel**: yeah that true babe it takes time

7:27:35 PM **ladydi2011**: Honey, I am an idea person

7:27:40 PM **Jeff Candel**: *i* know

7:27:43 PM **Jeff Candel**: that why *i* call you a woman of great value

7:27:56 PM **ladydi2011**: Oh really?

7:28:05 PM **Jeff Candel**: yeah

7:28:07 PM **ladydi2011**: The ideas continue to flow

7:28:11 PM **Jeff Candel**: that who you are

7:28:20 PM **ladydi2011**: If I could only capitalize on them all I would be rich

7:28:22 PM **Jeff Candel**: a woman of vitue and a woman of great value

7:28:33 PM **Jeff Candel**: yeah

7:28:40 PM **Jeff Candel:** *Tell me how much do you make in them*

7:28:48 PM **ladydi2011**: thank you baby for seeing who I really am

7:28:56 PM **Jeff Candel**: even if not much but you are ok with what you getting right?

7:28:57 PM **ladydi2011**: Fluctuates, my hourly rate is $150 an hour

7:29:16 PM **Jeff Candel:** *what?*

7:29:25 PM **Jeff Candel**: oh ok

Break In Time – He Got Booted

7:32:08 PM **Jeff Candel**: it realy very bad every where now

7:32:21 PM **Jeff Candel:** *sometimes it even hard for me to get sarahs meds for her *

7:32:31 PM **Jeff Candel:** *because work not too good as before*

7:32:40 PM **ladydi2011:** *How much are her meds baby?*

7:33:00 PM **Jeff Candel:** *they are expensive meds and i get them weekly*

7:33:15 PM **Jeff Candel**: *850 pounds every week*

7:33:34 PM **ladydi2011**: Now I need to learn pounds

7:33:41 PM **Jeff Candel:** *depends sometimes i go for the lower one 600pounds*

7:33:58 PM **Jeff Candel**: do the calculation like this

7:34:00 PM **ladydi2011**: So how much is this in US currency

7:34:19 PM **Jeff Candel**: 1000 pounds is 1500 pounds

7:34:26 PM **ladydi2011**: ?????

7:34:33 PM **Jeff Candel**: $1500

7:34:46 PM **Jeff Candel**: pounds is bigger than dollar

7:34:53 PM **ladydi2011**: Hmmm

7:35:31 PM **Jeff Candel**: 600pounds is 890$

7:35:45 PM **ladydi2011**: How many pounds would equal a dollar?

7:35:51 PM **Jeff Candel**: and 850 is about a thousand plus

7:36:08 PM **ladydi2011**: Oh wow, this is really expensive

7:36:25 PM **ladydi2011**: Do you own your home?

7:36:34 PM **Jeff Candel**: yes baby *i* have been coping

7:36:48 PM **Jeff Candel**: yes *i* do

7:36:53 PM **ladydi2011**: Do you still have a mortgage?

7:37:06 PM **Jeff Candel**: yeah

7:37:10 PM **Jeff Candel**: and you?

7:37:14 PM **ladydi2011**: Yes

7:37:24 PM **ladydi2011**: I am really upside down in my home

7:37:52 PM **ladydi2011**: Makes me want to cry

7:38:13 PM **ladydi2011**: However, I know ALL things belong to God and He is the provider of ALL things

7:38:39 PM **ladydi2011**: He will always make sure we have what we need

7:38:41 PM **Jeff Candel**: yes baby that so true

7:39:04 PM **Jeff Candel**: and everyday of my life *i* place sarah in his hands

7:39:08 PM **ladydi2011**: Honey, I have a really strong faith

7:39:15 PM **Jeff Candel:** *to ensure she survive this her cancer problem*

7:39:20 PM **Jeff Candel**: me too

7:40:10 PM **ladydi2011**: I have studied (not read) God's Word since I was very young.

7:40:56 PM **ladydi2011**: Please know God has Sarah.

7:41:05 PM **ladydi2011**: I now have her in my prayers. I am a real prayer worrier.

7:41:39 PM **Jeff Candel**: just worried and tears in my eyes

7:41:46 PM **ladydi2011**: I could feel it. Please do not worry. God has you and Sarah

7:42:31 PM **Jeff Candel**: yes baby *i* kknow am so happy you care

7:42:46 PM **ladydi2011**: I do care.

7:43:13 PM **Jeff Candel**: *i* know baby

7:43:22 PM **ladydi2011**: I have no clue how you feel because I have not walked in your shoes, so I will never pretend like I know because I don't

7:43:22 PM **Jeff Candel**: and *i* love you my angel

7:43:47 PM **ladydi2011**: I promise I am here for you no matter what

7:44:16 PM **Jeff Candel**: *i* love you with all my been

7:44:25 PM **ladydi2011**: I have not gone through half of what you have gone through

7:44:51 PM **ladydi2011**: God does promise he will not give us more than we can handle

7:45:06 PM **ladydi2011**: Every time it gets too heavy I read the book of Job

Break In Time

8:06:50 PM **ladydi2011**: Jeff, are you there?

8:07:19 PM **Jeff Candel**: ys baby *i* got booted

8:07:40 PM **Jeff Candel**: am yours forever

8:07:43 PM **Jeff Candel**: I wnt to take you to the bedroom

8:07:51 PM **ladydi2011**: No sir, I have only known you a week. Court me.

8:08:03 PM **ladydi2011**: Romance me.

8:08:23 PM **ladydi2011**: Wait patiently for the entire gift.

8:08:31 PM **ladydi2011**: You will be glad you did.

8:08:39 PM **Jeff Candel**: yes baby

8:08:42 PM **Jeff Candel**: am not in a hurry

8:08:46 PM **Jeff Candel**: am waiting baby

8:09:09 PM **ladydi2011**: I am smiling right now and you?

8:09:51 PM **Jeff Candel**: can *i* see you one more time on cam

8:09:57 PM **ladydi2011**: Baby, easy women are a dime a dozen. God's women are different. They are virtuous.

8:09:59 PM **Jeff Candel**: *i* wanna see your beautiful smile

8:10:50 PM **Jeff Candel**: you stop it again

8:11:02 PM **ladydi2011**: Because it was dark

8:11:10 PM **ladydi2011**: Can you see me now?

8:11:13 PM **Jeff Candel**: keep the smile

8:11:16 PM **Jeff Candel**: yeah

8:11:30 PM **Jeff Candel**: *i* love your smile

8:11:33 PM **ladydi2011**: You love my smile?

8:11:36 PM **Jeff Candel**: it just keep me alive

8:11:47 PM **ladydi2011**: I love your smile too

8:11:55 PM **ladydi2011**: Please get your cam fixed

8:12:28 PM **Jeff Candel**: ok *i* can't do it now

8:12:50 PM **ladydi2011**: I want to see your face

8:13:15 PM **ladydi2011**: *I have an extra cam that I can send to you if you want me too*

8:13:54 PM **Jeff Candel**: oh yeah?

8:14:00 PM **ladydi2011**: yeah

8:14:06 PM **Jeff Candel**: ok

8:14:34 PM **ladydi2011**: *I will send it. Please email me exactly how I write out your address so I make sure it gets to you.*

8:14:52 PM **ladydi2011:** Both of my laptops have cams in them

8:14:53 PM **Jeff Candel:** *not to worry baby*

8:15:00 PM **Jeff Candel:** *i will fix this one*

8:16:06 PM **ladydi2011:** it is after 1:00 am there, yes?

8:16:20 PM **Jeff Candel:** yes baby and am still here for you

8:16:49 PM **ladydi2011:** You promised you will be here for me forever, remember?

8:16:59 PM **ladydi2011:** You are a man of your word, right?

8:17:18 PM **Jeff Candel:** yes baby *i* give you my word

8:17:32 PM **Jeff Candel:** digest it *i* will alwys be here for you

8:17:52 PM **ladydi2011:** and I for you.

8:18:24 PM **ladydi2011:** every time I think about the distance between us, I just shake my head....

8:18:39 PM **ladydi2011:** It is so far

8:19:09 PM **Jeff Candel:** *i* know

8:19:14 PM **ladydi2011:** being this far away from you and Sarah is hard.

8:19:14 PM **Jeff Candel:** but we can make it ok, that should not ba a problem

8:19:36 PM **ladydi2011:** I know we can make it.

8:19:52 PM **ladydi2011:** I never saw this coming.....

8:20:14 PM **ladydi2011:** Life is like a box of chocolates...we never know what we are going to get.

8:20:27 PM **Jeff Candel:** yeah baby

8:20:40 PM **ladydi2011:** I love when you write to me. You write so beautifully!

8:20:59 PM **Jeff Candel:** am happy you just said that as it comeing feom the most wonderful and beautiful woman in my life

8:21:48 PM **ladydi2011:** Awwww...thank you baby

8:24:32 PM **ladydi2011:** Baby, I could stay here with you all night. I need to eat.

8:24:39 PM **Jeff Candel:** ok ok ok.................

8:24:49 PM **ladydi2011:** It is almost 1:30 am there

8:25:01 PM **ladydi2011:** What are you and Sarah doing tomorrow?

8:26:16 PM **Jeff Candel:** well *i* will be taking sarah out tomorrow

8:26:26 PM **ladydi2011:** To where?

8:26:38 PM **Jeff Candel:** to the movies and there to the park

8:26:49 PM **ladydi2011:** Cool

8:26:53 PM **Jeff Candel:** *i* just want her to have a good time tomorrow

8:26:57 PM **ladydi2011:** Can I come?

8:27:22 PM **ladydi2011:** Is there water and ducks at the park?

8:27:25 PM **Jeff Candel:** yeah you can

8:27:41 PM **ladydi2011:** I know I will be there....you know why?

8:27:58 PM **Jeff Candel:** why?

8:28:06 PM **Jeff Candel:** *i* know you will be here in spirit

8:28:06 PM **ladydi2011:** I am in your heart and mind

8:28:23 PM **ladydi2011:** Yes, I will be there in spirit

8:28:42 PM **ladydi2011:** Please send me a text when you get to the movies and to the park

8:28:53 PM **Jeff Candel:** ok

8:29:15 PM **ladydi2011:** You are a very special man Jeff

8:29:32 PM **Jeff Candel:** thank you and you are a special lady too

8:29:39 PM **Jeff Candel:** and *i* love you for you and nothing else

8:29:40 PM **ladydi2011:** Thank you babe

8:29:46 PM **Jeff Candel:** *i* love you the way you are]

8:29:50 PM **ladydi2011**: Thank you
8:29:55 PM **Jeff Candel**: you wellcome
8:29:57 PM **ladydi2011**: I love you for you too.
8:30:03 PM **ladydi2011**: Just the way you are
8:30:16 PM **Jeff Candel**: so tell me have you eaten today?
8:30:21 PM **ladydi2011**: No baby I have not, this is why I have a headache.
8:30:44 PM **ladydi2011**: My blood sugar is dropped.
8:30:51 PM **Jeff Candel**: oh you need to rest now darling
8:31:00 PM **ladydi2011**: I do baby
8:31:12 PM **Jeff Candel**: ok *i* will be here again tomorrow and send yiou sms in the morning ok?
8:31:55 PM **ladydi2011**: Ok...I look forward to hearing from you in the morning
8:32:09 PM **Jeff Candel**: ok baby
8:32:21 PM **ladydi2011**: Sleep well honey
8:32:26 PM **Jeff Candel**: ok baby
8:32:30 PM **Jeff Candel**: *i* love you
8:32:33 PM **Jeff Candel**: night
8:32:34 PM **ladydi2011**: I love you too
8:32:37 PM **ladydi2011**: night
8:34:06 PM **ladydi2011**: Baby, you're the best!
8:34:06 PM **Jeff Candel**: *i* know babe
8:34:19 PM **Jeff Candel**: and you are the best thing that has ever happen to me
8:34:57 PM **Jeff Candel**: night

Note that when I asked to see him on camera he told me it wasn't working. When I offered to send him one, he said he would fix the one he has. He doesn't want me sending one because he doesn't live in London, so it would be returned and he would be exposed.

RED FLAGS

- It doesn't look like this little girl is 14. Why did he say the pictures were only for me to see? We have only chatted for a week and he called me her mom, said that she needs me and that his life isn't complete without me. He doesn't even know me. This is all part of his format to try to quickly get me attached to the little girl. He then told me she is asking when "mom" is coming home. "Mom," "home," "brought joy into his and Sarah's lives".... I have only been chatting with him for seven days!
- He promised to always be there for me. This is also part of the format to make me feel obligated to be there for him too.
- He asked how much I make, and was shocked when I told him. Surely he thought "Wow, I can get some money from her," and he instantly started talking about Sarah's expensive medication.

Text Messages

Sent From: 1410000014

423

Received: Jun 9, 2012 4:36 AM
From: jeffery candel
Subject: *i* love you my Queen

MSG: Morning my QUEEN , how was your night, hope you are doing good, baby have you see the doc, please baby *i* dont want you to sick ok. Hope you are doing good now, last night *i* couldn't sleep just thinking about you, *i* hate to see you sick baby. try and see the doc ok. well *i* and sarah is ready to go to the movie house now..... and *i* wish you are here so we can all go together as one big family. we talk later baby.... *i* love you...... we love you baby. kisssss...Hugssssssss.
Your
KING,
Jeff

Sent To: 1410000014
From: Diana
Sent: Jun 9, 2012 8:07 AM
Subject: *i* love you my Queen

Hello my King... I am so happy your call woke me. Baby, I am just exhausted and probably a little dehydrated...I am not sleeping well for some reason. I am at the theatre house with you and Sarah. What movie are we seeing? I am feeding you popcorn. You have one are around me and one around Sarah. You are sandwiched in between us and wrapped in love. Please tell Sarah I said hello and give her a hug from me. Enjoy your day :-)

Diana

Sent From: 1410000015
Received: Jun 9, 2012 11:04 AM
From: jeffery candel
Subject: YOU ARE THE QUEEN OF MY HEART

MSG: How are you doing my QUEEN, today was really fun for me and Sarah, my queen I wish you where here baby,*i* but sarah popcorn and icream baby.. *i* love you baby, what did the doc say about your headache, hope is not that serious baby. even when *i* was inside the movies house *i* was thinking about you. sarah says hi to you baby. we wacth some movies

Tittle.... Moonrise Kingdom... producer, Jeremy Dawson, Scott Rudin and Wes Anderson.... directed by Wes Anderson. And will also watch BATTLESHIP Directed by.... Peter Berg

Jeff

Sent From: 1410000016
Received: Jun 9, 2012 11:41 AM

From: jeffery candel
Subject: *i* love you my Queen

MSG: I love you all my life, Now and forever, I will always love you, and whatever trials, I will come closer, I will always be faithful and true to you, You have given me hope, made me stronger in times when I am blue. The hope which I thought was really hard to find Just came along the way, just at the right time. The time in which no more tears left to cry, Your hugs of comfort ease my pain, now, there's no need to cry. I am amazed of how you filled my heart with so much love, You treat me like a prince, so glad how you raise me up above, You have been pouring out so much love from your heart my queen

Jeff

To: 1410000015
From: Diana
Sent: Jun 9, 2012 11:49 AM
Subject: i love you my Queen

Hello my Prince, you hold my glass slipper and the key to my heart. You are the sunshine that makes me smile. Your words melt my heart and take away sadness out of every day. I love you with all my heart. I am so glad you and Sarah are having a good day. I am on my way to the pool once I finish this proposal.

I love you.
Diana

Sent From: 1410000017
Received: Jun 9, 2012 5:03 PM
From: jeffery candel
Subject: YOU ARE THE QUEEN OF MY HEART

MSG: To the world you may be one person, but to one person you may be the world,Baby you are my world Enveloping me in your soft folds of comfort.Eyes closed, your gentle caress soothes my concerns and carries my thoughts to a bed of pure contentment. Completely satisfied, I lay in your sweet embrace, longing to remain indefinitely.
I love you my queen.
Your King,
Jeff

Sent From: 1410000018
Received: Jun 10, 2012 12:42 AM
From: jeffery candel
Subject: YOU ARE THE QUEEN OF MY HEART

MSG: how are you today my angel?? *i* miss you evn more today baby

IM Jun 10, 2012 5:38:59 AM

5:38:59 AM **Jeff Candel**: hi sweetie
5:54:40 PM **Jeff Candel**: sweetie

Text Messages

Sent From: 1410000019
Received: Jun 10, 2012 7:36 AM
From: jeffery candel
Subject: *i* love you my Queen

MSG: If I could have just one wish, I would wish to wake up everyday to the sound of your heart beating with mine... your breath on my neck, the warmth of your lips on my cheek, the touch of your fingers on my skin, and the feel of Knowing that I could never find that feeling with anyone other than you. I love you my Queen, **My darling, you are easy to love because of the wonderful man that you are.** I LOVE YOU MY QUEEN. YOUR KING,
JEFF

Sent From: 1410000020
Received: Jun 10, 2012 8:08 AM
To: Diana
Subject: *i* love you my Queen

MSG: I love you so deeply, I love you so much, I love the sound of your voice.I love your warm smile, And your kind, thoughtful way, The joy that you bring to my life every day. I love you today as I have from the start, And I'll love you forever with all of my heart. Your king.
Jeff

Sent To: 1410000019
From: Diana
Sent: Sun, 10 Jun 2012 09:17:02 -0500
Subject: *i* love you my Queen

MSG: Good morning my King. I just woke up to find another beautiful message from you. You always make me feel cherished, desired and loved. Diana

Sent To: 1410000019
From: Diana
Sent: Jun 10, 2012 10:18 AM
Subject: *i* love you my Queen

MSG: Good morning my King. I just woke up to find another beautiful message from you. You always make me feel cherished, desired and loved. I am in bed thinking about how wonderful it would be if

you were here next to me. I can't wait for the day when we are together to share every part of our lives together. What will you and Sarah do today? Please give her a big hug for me. I LOVE YOU.
Diana

Sent From: 1410000021
Received: Jun 10, 2012 10:48 AM
From: jeffery candel
Subject: *i* love you my Queen

MSG: Happy to hear from you my queen. *i* wish to hear your voice my queen, *i* feel like making love to you right away my queen. *i* love you so much my queen.. hearing your voice makes me strong my queen. *i* love you my queen. Your King,
Jeff

Sent To: 1410000021
From: Diana
Sent: Jun 10, 2012 11:56 AM
Subject: i love you my Queen

I am about to take a shower and then go run some errands. I miss you! Can we get on line later? I want to hear your voice. Can you call me on the computer later? I would love to see your handsome face. Did you get your cam fixed? I love you my king.
Diana

Sent From: 1410000018
Received: Jun 10, 2012 12:42 AM
From: jeffery candel
Subject: YOU ARE THE QUEEN OF MY HEART

MSG: how are you today my angel?? *i* miss you evn more today baby

RED FLAGS

🚩 Many women want a man to be this attentive and sweet. You must remember that this man is pretending to be attentive and sweet to obtain money. It was very obvious that the words were not his own or from his heart and were probably the words of a woman with the sentence, "My darling, you are easy to love because of the wonderful *man* that you are."

IM Jun 10, 2012 9:28:34 PM

9:28:34 PM **ladydi2011**: Hi babe, I miss you!

9:29:12 PM **Jeff Candel**: *i* miss you more love

9:29:17 PM **Jeff Candel**: how are you my heart

9:30:04 PM **ladydi2011**: I am good!

9:30:10 PM **ladydi2011**: How was your day?

9:30:15 PM **ladydi2011**: What did you do?

9:31:00 PM **Jeff Candel**: alots dear, and you>?

9:31:07 PM **Jeff Candel**: how was urs??

9:31:24 PM **ladydi2011**: It was good baby

9:31:32 PM **ladydi2011**: My computer is acting funny

9:31:35 PM **ladydi2011**: Uggggg

9:32:09 PM **Jeff Candel**: oh yeah

9:32:22 PM **Jeff Candel**: am sure you have to shut it downa dna on again baby

9:32:53 PM **ladydi2011**: Probably

9:33:04 PM **ladydi2011**: Don't go anywhere ok

9:33:23 PM **ladydi2011**: I really want to talk with you

9:33:31 PM **Jeff Candel**: ok am here

9:38:23 PM **Jeff Candel**: you back now sweetie?

9:40:32 PM **ladydi2011**: I am. Please hold one more minute. I need to get some water

9:40:37 PM **ladydi2011**: So sorry

9:40:41 PM **Jeff Candel**: ok baby

9:44:38 PM **ladydi2011**: Did you get my picture baby?

9:45:31 PM **Jeff Candel**: just accepted it now

9:45:51 PM **Jeff Candel**: did you just took this today>??

9:46:31 PM **ladydi2011**: The other day

9:46:37 PM **ladydi2011**: Do you like it?

9:46:42 PM **Jeff Candel**: *i* love it babe

9:46:47 PM **Jeff Candel**: you look so adorable

9:46:53 PM **ladydi2011**: Thanks

9:46:57 PM **Jeff Candel**: and it just make me love you more

9:47:17 PM **ladydi2011**: What did you do today?

9:47:40 PM **Jeff Candel**: well baby *i* did alots

9:47:47 PM **Jeff Candel**: just that am not happy

9:48:36 PM **ladydi2011**: Why are you not happy?

9:49:06 PM **Jeff Candel**: it sarah. she is pissing me off

9:49:16 PM **ladydi2011**: Why, what is she doing?

9:49:32 PM **Jeff Candel**: *i* told her not to play in the drive way and yet she did

9:49:51 PM **ladydi2011**: She didn't get hurt, did she?

9:49:56 PM **Jeff Candel**: nope just that it dangerous to play in the drive way and *i* have warn her on several ocaasions

9:51:14 PM **ladydi2011**: She is being a typical kid

9:51:28 PM **ladydi2011**: Do you remember when you thought you were invincible?

9:51:39 PM **ladydi2011**: I miss those days, what about you?

9:51:54 PM **Jeff Candel: *she knows her heart condition and yet she messes up with the other kids and play too much***

9:52:08 PM **Jeff Candel**: yeah that so true babe

9:54:00 PM **ladydi2011**: I know it is hard to have to keep her from doing things because of her condition

9:54:09 PM **ladydi2011**: How can I help baby?

9:54:17 PM **Jeff Candel**: it ok baby

9:54:34 PM Jeff Candel: *i* just wanted to share it with you, ***u know i cannot never hide anything from you***

9:54:52 PM **Jeff Candel: *just that her meds are really weighing me down financially***

9:55:08 PM **Jeff Candel**: and it breaks my heart to see her endangering her life you know?

9:55:25 PM **ladydi2011**: I know this is hard on you in many ways

9:56:02 PM **Jeff Candel**: yeah baby

9:57:07 PM **ladydi2011**: I am glad I am here for you to have someone to talk to

9:57:36 PM **Jeff Candel**: yeah baby

9:57:44 PM **Jeff Candel: *and i know you will be always be there***

9:57:48 PM **ladydi2011**: you are not alone now

9:58:09 PM **Jeff Candel**: *i* know baby

9:58:29 PM **Jeff Candel**: everytime *i* realise you with me it gives me great joy

10:00:01 PM **ladydi2011**: I am glad

10:01:34 PM **Jeff Candel**: at least it take greaat weight of my shoulder

10:02:13 PM **Jeff Candel**: you seems busy

10:02:38 PM **ladydi2011**: On phone. I will be off in a minute

10:03:10 PM **Jeff Candel**: ok

10:07:52 PM **ladydi2011**: Sorry baby

10:08:05 PM **Jeff Candel**: it ok

10:08:10 PM **ladydi2011**: My brother calls me a lot because he is home alone with the kids

10:08:12 PM **Jeff Candel**: you done with the phone now??

10:08:23 PM **ladydi2011**: Yes baby

10:08:27 PM **Jeff Candel**: he wants you to come over ???

10:08:36 PM **ladydi2011**: No, he lives 3 hrs away

10:09:03 PM **ladydi2011**: His wife is 18 hours away helping her mom who was in a car accident

10:09:18 PM **Jeff Candel**: ohh that bad sorry to hear that

10:09:56 PM **ladydi2011**: Yeah, it is not good

10:11:01 PM **Jeff Candel**: so tell me what did you eat today ??

10:11:08 PM **ladydi2011**: Nothing healthy. Chips and a burger and yogurt.

10:11:29 PM **ladydi2011**: What about you. What did you eat?

10:11:48 PM **Jeff Candel**: exactly what *i* eat but no yogurt

10:12:05 PM **ladydi2011**: really?

10:12:18 PM **ladydi2011**: I have been cleaning out my closet

10:12:42 PM **Jeff Candel**: must be hectic day for you

10:12:47 PM **ladydi2011**: I will be giving a lot to good will

10:12:50 PM **Jeff Candel**: good

10:13:08 PM **ladydi2011**: Some things I will take to be tailored

10:13:15 PM **ladydi2011**: Cheaper than buying new

10:13:22 PM **Jeff Candel**: yeah baby

10:13:49 PM **ladydi2011**: I am very frugal honey

10:14:03 PM **Jeff Candel**: oh yeah

10:14:37 PM **Jeff Candel**: am about to ask a very nasty question now

10:14:42 PM **ladydi2011**: Ok

10:14:51 PM **Jeff Candel**: yeah baby though money is tight

10:14:53 PM **Jeff Candel**: we wil cope

10:15:02 PM **Jeff Candel**: God will se us through

10:15:16 PM **ladydi2011**: I agree

10:15:26 PM **ladydi2011**: What is the nasty question baby?

10:15:28 PM **Jeff Candel**: what color of underwear are you putting on now?

10:15:42 PM **ladydi2011**: Black

10:16:27 PM **Jeff Candel**: *i* love black, blue and red

10:16:32 PM **ladydi2011**: Why are you asking?

10:16:32 PM **Jeff Candel**: those are my favorite and your bra?

10:16:44 PM **ladydi2011**: Nice to know this

10:16:49 PM **ladydi2011**: Black

10:17:32 PM **Jeff Candel**: ok

10:17:35 PM **Jeff Candel**: wow *i* can imagine

10:18:04 PM **Jeff Candel**: if only *i* was there now to take them off your body

10:18:12 PM **Jeff Candel**: 🙂

10:19:21 PM **ladydi2011**: Baby, you really desire me, don't you?

10:19:28 PM **Jeff Candel**: yeah baby you know this

10:19:50 PM **ladydi2011**: I do know this

10:20:20 PM **Jeff Candel**: because you are part of me now and everyday give me joy to know that *i* have you

10:21:01 PM **ladydi2011**: I know baby....I am blushing

10:21:33 PM **Jeff Candel**: *i* bet you do

10:22:47 PM **Jeff Candel**: wow sweeet

10:23:00 PM **Jeff Candel**: *will you show me those sweet apple in your bra*

10:23:45 PM **ladydi2011**: I don't do that on cam baby

10:23:51 PM **Jeff Candel**: you know what *i* mean sweetie

10:23:55 PM **Jeff Candel**: ok it ok by me

10:24:04 PM **Jeff Candel**: *you not gonna do that for me*

10:24:09 PM **Jeff Candel**: *just want to see that all*

10:24:28 PM **ladydi2011**: I can't baby

10:25:09 PM **Jeff Candel**: ok

10:25:17 PM **Jeff Candel**: am gonna cry now

10:25:28 PM **ladydi2011**: don't cry

10:25:45 PM **Jeff Candel**: no *i* will now

10:25:54 PM **Jeff Candel**: let me cry

10:26:06 PM **ladydi2011**: Baby is your camera working?

10:26:16 PM **Jeff Candel**: not yet

10:26:34 PM **Jeff Candel**: have things to do today and did not really had to take it to them to fix it

10:27:04 PM **ladydi2011**: Ok

10:27:22 PM **Jeff Candel**: *i* love your smile

10:27:28 PM **ladydi2011**: Baby, it is worth the wait...*i* promise

10:27:44 PM **Jeff Candel**: you radiate a new day for me and make the sun set for me

10:28:08 PM **ladydi2011**: I love what you write to me baby

10:28:47 PM **Jeff Candel**: really?

10:28:56 PM **Jeff Candel**: tell me something sweet

10:29:46 PM **ladydi2011**: Your love makes me a better woman

10:29:58 PM **Jeff Candel**: hmmmmmmmm

10:30:02 PM **ladydi2011**: You love brought me back to life

10:30:14 PM **Jeff Candel**: hmmmm'
10:30:18 PM **ladydi2011**: Your love is so genuine and pure
10:30:24 PM **ladydi2011**: what is hmmmmmmmmmmmmm
10:30:45 PM **Jeff Candel**: well *i* want you to know that am happy and you have made me a better man too
10:31:12 PM **Jeff Candel**: put the cam back on
10:32:08 PM **ladydi2011**: It is storming here and I am trying but it will not
10:32:23 PM **Jeff Candel**: do me one favor
10:32:27 PM **ladydi2011**: Sure
10:32:34 PM **Jeff Candel**: smile for me and never stop
10:32:46 PM **ladydi2011**: I will baby
10:32:50 PM **Jeff Candel**: always
10:32:51 PM **ladydi2011**: You make me smile
10:33:02 PM **Jeff Candel**: *i* can hear your laugh here in my heart
10:33:29 PM **ladydi2011**: I am so glad you love my laugh
10:33:38 PM **Jeff Candel**: yeah baby
10:33:40 PM **ladydi2011**: I love your heart
10:33:48 PM **Jeff Candel**: *i* wanna watch you sleep too
10:34:04 PM **Jeff Candel**: and sing nice songs to your ear to put you to sleep
10:34:20 PM **ladydi2011**: I can't wait
10:34:31 PM **ladydi2011**: I will be sleeping in your arms
10:34:39 PM **ladydi2011**: Would you like this honey?
10:34:57 PM **Jeff Candel**: always baby
10:35:36 PM **ladydi2011**: Cool
10:35:51 PM **Jeff Candel**: you are my gold in the morning sun
10:36:21 PM **ladydi2011**: Your emails to me are so sweet that sometimes I do not know what to say
10:36:29 PM **ladydi2011**: I cannot write like you do
10:37:04 PM **ladydi2011**: You always take my breath away
10:37:10 PM **Jeff Candel**: really..am happy you said that honey
10:37:26 PM **ladydi2011**: Thank you for teaching me poetry baby
10:37:46 PM **Jeff Candel**: you so much wellcome and thanks for learning too
10:38:31 PM **ladydi2011**: I love to learn
10:38:44 PM **Jeff Candel**: yeah and you will sweet hert
10:39:05 PM **ladydi2011**: I look forward to when we are finally together.
10:39:35 PM **Jeff Candel**: yes baby
10:39:59 PM **ladydi2011**: I love how you treat me and make me feel.
10:40:43 PM **Jeff Candel**: *i* will never ever stop honey
10:40:58 PM **ladydi2011**: Thank you baby
10:41:16 PM **Jeff Candel**: *but we will be together soon that my promise to you baby*
10:41:49 PM **Jeff Candel**: *i swear with my life on it we will*
10:42:15 PM **ladydi2011**: Please don't ever forget this
10:42:28 PM **Jeff Candel**: *i* won't
10:42:31 PM **Jeff Candel**: *baby i promise*
10:42:36 PM **Jeff Candel**: *i give you my word*
10:43:06 PM **ladydi2011**: Thank you
10:43:28 PM **Jeff Candel**: you wellcome
10:44:47 PM **Jeff Candel**: you are always in my heart

10:45:04 PM **ladydi2011**: Same here honey

10:45:16 PM **ladydi2011**: Do you work tomorrow?

10:45:45 PM **Jeff Candel**: yeah but will be off soon

10:46:08 PM **ladydi2011**: What do you mean?

10:46:55 PM **ladydi2011**: Baby, I just realized that it is 4:00 am there

10:47:01 PM **ladydi2011**: What are you doing awake?

10:47:20 PM **Jeff Candel**: am her with you talking

10:47:30 PM **Jeff Candel**: *i* wanna be awake for you

10:48:01 PM **ladydi2011**: Honey, you need your rest

10:48:13 PM **ladydi2011**: Lack of sleep increases our stress level

10:48:51 PM **Jeff Candel**: *i* know 'but *i* wanna be here with you

10:49:12 PM **ladydi2011**: Being in a different time zone plays havoc

10:49:31 PM **ladydi2011**: Awww, thank you love. I want you to be here with me too

10:50:12 PM **ladydi2011**: I have missed chatting

10:51:30 PM **ladydi2011**: It seems like I have known you forever

10:52:22 PM **Jeff Candel**: me too baby

10:55:00 PM **Jeff Candel**: what are you dong now?

10:55:08 PM **Jeff Candel**: you seems quiet

10:56:12 PM **ladydi2011**: Sorry baby

10:56:15 PM **ladydi2011**: Got booted

10:56:20 PM **ladydi2011**: Bad storm here

10:56:54 PM **Jeff Candel**: ok

10:56:56 PM **Jeff Candel**: far more than you ever know, far more than words can say, you are on my mind and in my heart; with every passing day, you fill my life with happiness, you are all my dreams come true

10:56:58 PM **ladydi2011**: It has been storming on and off all day

10:57:21 PM **ladydi2011**: So beautiful baby.

10:57:41 PM **Jeff Candel**: yeah

10:57:45 PM **ladydi2011**: Yeah, you make me smile

10:58:19 PM **Jeff Candel**: am happy baby

10:58:22 PM **ladydi2011**: I am hugging you right now. Can you feel it?

10:59:13 PM **Jeff Candel**: yes baby

10:59:23 PM **Jeff Candel**: *i* can feel your warm sexy body

11:00:12 PM **Jeff Candel**: am safe in your arms

11:00:22 PM **ladydi2011**: Always safe in my arms

11:01:22 PM **Jeff Candel**: am happy babe

11:01:29 PM **ladydi2011**: I have the news on honey and there are a lot of accidents due to this storm.

11:01:38 PM **ladydi2011**: I am happy too babe.

11:01:57 PM **ladydi2011**: The only thing that will make me happier is for us to be together in person

11:02:16 PM **ladydi2011**: You have made me addicted to email

11:02:36 PM **Jeff Candel**: yeah?

11:02:39 PM **ladydi2011**: I check it as soon as my eyes open and before I get out of bed

11:03:01 PM **Jeff Candel**: that great babe

11:03:13 PM **ladydi2011**: I came on line many times today looking for you

11:03:53 PM **Jeff Candel**: and me too..am so into you babe

11:04:06 PM **ladydi2011**: Ditto babe

11:04:17 PM **ladydi2011**: I know. It is my blonde hair, right?
11:05:12 PM **ladydi2011**: baby, I am so into you too....
11:05:53 PM **ladydi2011**: Thank you for taking the time to write me
11:06:05 PM **ladydi2011**: I so appreciate that you do this for me
11:06:17 PM **ladydi2011**: It makes me know you love me and are thinking about me
11:06:33 PM **Jeff Candel**: you are so much wellcome
11:06:44 PM **Jeff Candel**: baby *i* think *i* need to get some nap now
11:07:03 PM **ladydi2011**: Yes you do...
11:07:16 PM **ladydi2011**: Sleep well
11:07:20 PM **ladydi2011**: Dream about me
11:07:33 PM **Jeff Candel**: *i* always will baby
11:08:12 PM **Jeff Candel**: thank you so much my angel
11:08:15 PM **Jeff Candel**: *i* love you
11:08:17 PM **ladydi2011**: when you wake up smile for me...ok
11:08:18 PM **Jeff Candel**: sarah says hi
11:08:23 PM **ladydi2011**: I love you too
11:08:28 PM **Jeff Candel**: *i* love you more
11:08:37 PM **ladydi2011**: Please hug her for me and tell her I said hello
11:09:13 PM **Jeff Candel**: gnite my love
11:09:21 PM **ladydi2011**: Night baby
11:10:52 PM **Jeff Candel**: *i* forgot to give you a kiss
11:11:03 PM **Jeff Candel**: so *i* came back to give it to you bofore *i* go to bed
11:11:14 PM **Jeff Candel**: Kissses
11:11:19 PM **Jeff Candel**: gnight
11:11:23 PM **ladydi2011**: Kisses and hugs my love
11:11:23 PM **Jeff Candel**: gnight
11:11:34 PM **ladydi2011**: Night

RED FLAGS

- Previously he said Sarah had cancer; he since changed it to a heart condition, and talked again about the cost of the medicine. He has casted his bait, and he will keep dangling it. He thinks every woman will give into helping a sick child.
- Once again, he tried to make sexual moves. This is also part of the scammers format and plan. If you EVER do sexual things on the camera with a scammer they WILL use it to extort money from you. They will also use pictures you send of yourself, your profile and the words of your chats to scam men.

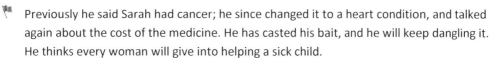

Text Messages

Sent From: 1410000022
Received: Jun 11, 2012 7:11 AM

From: jeffery candel
Sunject: Good Morning My Queen

MSG: Baby am still online *i* cant sleep baby.. please come online lets talk baby..... am waiting ok. I wrote your name in the sky, but the wind blew it away. I wrote your name in the sand, but the waves washed it away. I wrote your name in my heart, and forever it will stay. When I'm with you, eternity is a step away, my love continues to grow, with each passing day. This treasure of love, I cherish within my soul, how much I love you... you'll never really know. You bring a joy to my heart, I've never felt before, with each touch of your words, I love you

Send To: 1410000022
From: Diana
Sent: Jun 11, 2012 9:45 AM
Subject: Good Morning My Queen

Good morning my Prince, thank you for these beautiful words. Hearing your heart and voice through your words first thing when I wake up puts a smile on my face and starts my day off beautifully. You are the love of my life, there could be no other.

You are handsome, sexy, smart, kind and sweet. Your heart is pure and filled with love. Your smile radiates joy throughout the universe. The best thing of all is that you have chosen to give your sweet love to me. For this I am forever grateful.

I hope you are having a wonderful day. Love you baby.

Your princess, Diana

IM Jun 11, 2012 5:16:52 PM

5:16:52 PM **ladydi2011**: Hi Baby
5:16:59 PM **Jeff Candel**: Hello my queen
5:17:08 PM **ladydi2011**: How are you today?
5:17:20 PM **Jeff Candel**: Am fine
5:17:27 PM **Jeff Candel**: And u?
5:17:39 PM **ladydi2011**: Good honey
5:17:49 PM **Jeff Candel**: Miss u hun
5:17:58 PM **ladydi2011**: Been working all day and still have about 5 hrs. of work to do today
5:18:07 PM **ladydi2011**: I miss you too honey
5:18:50 PM **ladydi2011**: How is Sarah today?
5:19:48 PM **ladydi2011**: Are you there baby?
Break In Time
5:24:56 PM **Jeff Candel**: Hun are you there
5:25:39 PM **ladydi2011**: I am honey
5:25:48 PM **ladydi2011**: Did you see what I wrote you?

5:26:04 PM **Jeff Candel**: Where hun

5:26:22 PM **Jeff Candel**: I tthought you where busy

5:26:55 PM **Jeff Candel**: Sarah is fine

5:26:55 PM **ladydi2011**: I am baby, but I will always do my best to make time for you.

5:27:14 PM **ladydi2011**: *I have been working on proposals to land new clients all day*

5:27:17 PM **Jeff Candel**: She is sleeping

5:27:27 PM **ladydi2011**: One is for $300k

5:27:43 PM **Jeff Candel**: You wanna buy land

5:27:48 PM **ladydi2011**: I am sure she is sleeping. It is 10:30 there, right?

5:27:56 PM **ladydi2011**: Buy land?

Break In Time

5:32:04 PM **ladydi2011**: Baby, are you there?

5:34:37 PM **Jeff Candel**: Yes hun

5:35:23 PM **Jeff Candel**: Hun am here forr u

5:35:48 PM **ladydi2011**: Ok

5:35:55 PM **ladydi2011**: Did you get booted?

5:36:07 PM **Jeff Candel**: Yes

5:36:20 PM **Jeff Candel**: I love you. Hun

5:36:33 PM **ladydi2011**: What did you mean by "You want to buy land"?

5:37:03 PM **Jeff Candel**: U said that u are working on cllient

5:37:32 PM **Jeff Candel**: *And the land. Is 300k bus*

5:38:05 PM **ladydi2011**: Yes baby...I lost a client because I helped him build his business and then he sold it for $3 million. The new owners need my help to take it to the next level and the price I gave them was 300k

5:38:33 PM **ladydi2011**: *No baby...when I say land, I mean bring the new business in the door.*

5:38:40 PM **ladydi2011**: I will know tomorrow

5:39:19 PM **Jeff Candel**: *So I was asking if you are the one buying the lannd*

5:39:28 PM **ladydi2011**: Slang here. Sorry honey

5:39:43 PM **Jeff Candel**: Ok hun

5:40:02 PM **Jeff Candel**: I pray it will work out fine ok

5:40:06 PM **ladydi2011**: People pay for my knowledge honey

5:40:16 PM **Jeff Candel**: Ok baby I will always prray forrr your business ok

5:41:16 PM **ladydi2011**: Thank you baby

5:41:50 PM **ladydi2011**: I always pray for your success and for Sarah's health

5:42:12 PM **Jeff Candel**: Sure baby

5:42:35 PM **ladydi2011**: It hurts me to see you stress

5:42:36 PM **Jeff Candel**: Hun sarah is becoming so stuborn baby

5:42:45 PM **ladydi2011**: With what honey?

5:44:14 PM **Jeff Candel**: I told her stop play is cold wealther because of healtth

5:44:14 PM **Jeff Candel**: But she wouldn't listen

5:44:15 PM **Jeff Candel**: Today she compllaine of. Head ach

5:45:26 PM **Jeff Candel**: But she promise not to do that again

5:45:56 PM **ladydi2011**: I think she is seeing how far she can push herself and you. All kids do it.

5:46:15 PM **Jeff Candel**: Yes baby

5:46:29 PM **ladydi2011**: She doesn't know what you know concerning her health. Youth don't get it.

5:46:38 PM **ladydi2011**: She wants to do what others do.

5:46:53 PM **Jeff Candel**: I try to make her understand. That baby

5:47:11 PM **Jeff Candel**: She has ppromise not to do it again

5:47:19 PM **ladydi2011**: How old was she when her mom died?

5:47:53 PM **Jeff Candel**: She was 7yrs old

5:50:22 PM **ladydi2011**: Please hold....phone just rang...client

5:50:27 PM **ladydi2011**: Thank you baby

5:50:31 PM **Jeff Candel**: Ok hun

5:59:17 PM **Jeff Candel**: I love does your beautiful eyes..... Each time I look at your pics my love for you grow sstronger

5:59:34 PM **Jeff Candel**: When I try to think of something its you that always coome to my mind

5:59:53 PM **Jeff Candel**: I will neverr. Stop loving my queen. My heart belongs tto you

6:01:40 PM **Jeff Candel**: Silver and gold have not to give to you... But my heart will always be yourrs.

6:04:12 PM **Jeff Candel**: You are like a blessing from God to. Take away my sadness and pains

6:06:53 PM **Jeff Candel**: I swaer with my life to loove you till I die my queen

6:07:24 PM **Jeff Candel**: No one I mean no will ever take your place in my heart

6:10:40 PM **Jeff Candel**: When I look at you I see my happpiness in you

6:13:32 PM **ladydi2011**: Hi, I am back

6:13:51 PM **ladydi2011**: Thank you for the beautiful writings

6:13:58 PM **ladydi2011**: You are the best!

6:14:06 PM **ladydi2011**: I love you

6:14:58 PM **Jeff Candel**: I. Love you too hun

6:15:14 PM **Jeff Candel**: You are my best

6:15:32 PM **Jeff Candel**: Is that your client?

6:16:35 PM **ladydi2011**: Yes honey. It was my new prospective client. He had a couple questions about the proposal.

6:16:52 PM **Jeff Candel**: Ok hun

6:17:01 PM **Jeff Candel**: Pls do that now

6:17:27 PM **ladydi2011**: Are you sure you don't mind?

6:17:40 PM **Jeff Candel**: No no no baby

6:17:42 PM **ladydi2011**: I miss you sooo much!

6:17:54 PM **Jeff Candel**: Its your business baby

6:17:59 PM **ladydi2011**: Please look for me later honey.

6:18:20 PM **ladydi2011**: You are so understanding. I love this about you!

6:18:29 PM **Jeff Candel**: Ok, Dontt worry about me

6:18:35 PM **Jeff Candel**: Am ok witth it ok

6:18:48 PM **ladydi2011**: Ok baby

6:18:48 PM **Jeff Candel**: I will be online later

6:18:58 PM **ladydi2011**: I will chat with you later

6:19:03 PM **ladydi2011**: I love you

6:19:10 PM **Jeff Candel**: Pls you have to focus now hun

6:19:10 PM **ladydi2011**: Bye for now

6:19:17 PM **ladydi2011**: I will

6:19:23 PM **Jeff Candel**: I wiill. Always love u

6:19:29 PM **ladydi2011**: I know you will

6:19:36 PM **ladydi2011**: I will always love you

6:19:42 PM **ladydi2011**: Kiss Sarah for me

6:19:47 PM **Jeff Candel**: Ok hun

6:19:49 PM **ladydi2011**: I am sending you kisses and hugs

6:22:15 PM **Jeff Candel**: Kisses and huggs
6:22:29 PM **Jeff Candel**: Byee hun

IM Jun 11, 2012 8:03:06 PM Continued

8:03:06 PM **Jeff Candel**: hello my queen
8:03:11 PM **Jeff Candel**: are you through now
8:03:25 PM **Jeff Candel**: hope am not disturbing you my love
8:03:30 PM **Jeff Candel**: *i* couldnt sleep

IM Jun 11, 2012 8:30:42 PM Continued

8:30:42 PM **Jeff Candel**: talk to you tomorrow ok baby.... see you ... love you baby.... kissss........ hugsssss. *i* love you my queen

RED FLAGS

- African's do not understand american slang. When I said, "I have been working on proposals to land new clients all day", he thought I meant actual property. This is another red flag.
- He spoke again about problems with Sarah; this is his setup for obtaining money.
- He wants me to focus on my business so I have money to give him.

Text Messages

Sent To: 1410000023
From: Diana
Sent: Jun 12, 2012 2:40 AM
Subject: Good Morning My Queen

Hello my love...I miss you! I did come back on line and saw your message but you were gone. I wanted to talk to you. Sorry I missed you. Thank you for being so understanding of my work. You know I provide for myself and my employees. I am now finally in bed but cannot close my eyes until I tell you how much I treasure you and tell you good morning. Diana

Sent From: 1410000024
Received: Jun 12, 2012 5:54 AM
From: jeffery candel
Subject: Good Morning My Queen

MSG: *i* know that my ***God will never keep his favour and blessing from you*** my queen. *i* kove you so much baby. you are the best my love. *i* will always love you with all my heart...

I LOVE YOU MY QUEEN.
YOUR KING.

Jeff

Sent From: 1410000025
Received: Jun 12, 2012 6:02 AM
From: jeffery candel
Subject: RE: Good Morning My Queen

MSG: *i* love you my queen. and *i* will always love with all my heart till *i* die baby. The world is too small to give to you. that is why *i* am ***giving you my whole life to you*** and you alone my queen. take me as your servant my queen and *i* will be at your service any time my queen. You are now why I wake up every day. I am now finally in bed but cannot close my eyes until I tell you how much I love you very much my queen.

Your king.
Jeff

Sent To: 1410000025
From: Diana
Sent: Jun 12, 2012 8:30 AM
Subject: Good Morning My Queen

Hello my love. I am now awake. Thank you for pouring out your heart to me once again. Diana

Sent To: 1410000026
From: Diana
Sent: Jun 12, 2012 11:44 PM
Subject: Good Morning My Queen

My love...I miss you! I looked for you several times on line and sent you a couple messages. I pray everything is ok there. Honey, my day was so empty without you...I lost the smile on my face and my heart aches for you. It was a long day for me my love. A lot of client negotiations and today was deadline to get our clients e-newsletters produced and scheduled. It is 4:30 there baby so I am sure you and Sarah are sound to sleep. I couldn't close my eyes until I told you how important you are to me and that I love you. I hope this makes you smile when you wake up. Diana

Sent From: 1410000026
Received: Jun 12, 2012 12:42 PM

From: jeffery candel
Subject: Good Morning My Queen

MSG: How was your night my queen.. hope you are doing good baby. *i* love you. hope to hear from you soon my love. kisssssssss... hugsssss

Sent To: 1410000026
From: Diana
Sent: Jun 11, 2012 9:45 AM
Subject: Good Morning My Queen

Hello sweetheart, how are you? My day has been crazy busy. I wrote to you a little earlier but a client called so I didn't get to write again until now. I want you to know you are the light in my life, the air I breathe. I went on line but you were not there. I miss and love you my king. Kisses and hugs.........till later

---

IM Jun 12, 2012 5:03:33 PM

5:03:33 PM **ladydi2011**: Hi love. I was here looking for you. Miss you!

Text Messages

Sent From: 1410000027
Received: Jun 13, 2012 6:01 AM
From: jeffery candel
Subject: Good Morning My Queen

MSG: Words simply cannot tell how much I love you. There aren't enough words in the world to express my feelings for you, so I will just say: I Love You. If I had to choose between breathing and loving you I would use my last breath to tell you I love you.
I love you my Queen.
Your King.
Jeff

Sent To: 1410000027
From: Diana
Sent: Jun 13, 2012 7:37 AM
Subject: Good Morning My Queen

Good morning my love, my king. I just woke up my love. I slept well but for some reason, I am still tired. Thank you for your beautiful words that I know is true coming from you. You always make me smile my love and I pray I do the same for you. Honey, what time will you be on line? I miss you. I love you my king. Diana

Sent From: 1410000029
Received: Jun 13, 2012 3:57 PM
From: jeffery candel
Subject: Good Morning My Queen
MSG: Baby am missing you so much baby.. my heart is beating so fast baby.....
please I want you to come online baby. *i* need you right away baby.

i love you

IM Jun 13, 2012 9:47:09 AM

9:47:09 AM **Jeff Candel**: hello my love
9:47:14 AM **Jeff Candel**: <ding>
9:47:31 AM **Jeff Candel**: miss talking to you my queen

Text Message

Sent From: 1410000028
Received: Jun 13, 2012 10:01 AM
From: jeffery candel
Subject: Good Morning My Queen

MSG: My queen am online now ok... *i* wish *i* can talk to you now baby. hope to hear from you soon. *i* love you my angel

Many scammers quote scripture and Christian sayings, and many good-hearted people are fooled by it. One of my sources gave me access to his Yahoo! account to get information for chapter seven (page 677), and I saw where he actually had a prayer to God attached to the woman's name he was currently trying to scam. The prayer said, "God, this is my only source for money. Please let her give me money." I couldn't believe my eyes.

In Africa, people have great faith and heavily rely on God because of the suffering and poverty, so they know scripture. Unfortunately, some use it to scam others.

 RED FLAGS

- Beware of Christian language.
- "Giving you my whole life to you" is another phrase used by Nigerian scammers.

IM Jun 13, 2012 3:48:43 PM

3:48:43 PM **Jeff Candel**: <ding>
3:48:52 PM **Jeff Candel**: my queen
3:49:01 PM **Jeff Candel**: am missing you too baby
3:50:40 PM **Jeff Candel**: baby am online now
3:50:48 PM **Jeff Candel**: and *i* need you to come online baby
3:50:56 PM **Jeff Candel**: am missing you so much baby

IM Jun 13, 2012 5:02:18 PM Continued

4:42:44 PM **Jeff Candel**: hello baby
4:44:57 PM **Jeff Candel**: baby are you there?
4:45:11 PM **Jeff Candel**: <ding>
4:49:24 PM **Jeff Candel**: baby are you busy?
4:53:57 PM **ladydi2011**: Hi baby
4:54:23 PM **Jeff Candel**: baby are you busy
4:55:08 PM **ladydi2011**: On phone
4:55:17 PM **Jeff Candel**: ok baby
4:55:25 PM **Jeff Candel**: how are you doing today?
4:55:33 PM **Jeff Candel**: *i* miss you so much baby
4:56:38 PM **ladydi2011**: Please hold honey
4:56:45 PM **ladydi2011**: Thank you
4:56:46 PM **Jeff Candel**: ok
4:59:17 PM **ladydi2011**: Ok baby....I am now off the phone and soooo happy we have finally connected!
4:59:25 PM **ladydi2011**: How are you?
5:00:16 PM **Jeff Candel**: am fine baby
5:00:29 PM **Jeff Candel**: my love *i* miss you
5:00:38 PM **ladydi2011**: I missed you too
5:00:47 PM **Jeff Candel**: me too my angel
5:00:57 PM **ladydi2011**: I am so glad you are here with me now
5:01:06 PM **Jeff Candel**: me too my angel
5:01:17 PM **Jeff Candel**: am glad to have you here baby
5:01:23 PM **Jeff Candel**: how is work baby?
5:01:30 PM **ladydi2011**: Very busy honey
5:01:44 PM **Jeff Candel**: always baby
5:01:53 PM **ladydi2011**: Many deadlines and now with this new client it is even busier
5:02:04 PM **ladydi2011**: I received the check today so the work begins
5:02:13 PM **ladydi2011**: How is Sarah?
5:02:18 PM **Jeff Candel**: fine
5:02:34 PM **Jeff Candel**: *how much check*
5:02:37 PM **ladydi2011**: How is your work honey?
5:02:43 PM **ladydi2011**: $300,000
5:02:44 PM **Jeff Candel**: cool baby
5:03:25 PM **Jeff Candel**: so how did it go baby

5:03:36 PM **ladydi2011**: it went well honey

5:03:36 PM **Jeff Candel**: *do you get the check baby*

5:03:51 PM **ladydi2011**: Yeah, I got the check and deposited it

5:04:04 PM **ladydi2011**: They are going to be a good client

5:04:06 PM **Jeff Candel**: *in to your account?*

5:04:17 PM **ladydi2011**: Yes love, into the business account

5:04:21 PM **Jeff Candel**: ok

5:04:34 PM **Jeff Candel**: *i* told you that its going to work out baby

5:04:44 PM **ladydi2011**: yes my love, you did

5:04:54 PM **ladydi2011**: Thank you for all your support and prayers. You are the best!

5:05:05 PM **Jeff Candel**: you are welcome baby

5:05:12 PM **Jeff Candel**: you are the best baby

5:05:24 PM **Jeff Candel**: *well baby sarah is not feeling too strong she is sleeping now*

5:05:43 PM **ladydi2011**: *Why is she not feeling too strong?*

5:06:10 PM **Jeff Candel**: baby she came back from school complaining of head ach

5:06:26 PM **ladydi2011**: Another headache

5:06:27 PM **Jeff Candel**: so *i* too her to the doc and the doc said she will be ok

5:06:37 PM **ladydi2011**: Oh, thank goodness

5:06:50 PM **ladydi2011**: Did he say what the headaches are coming from?

5:06:58 PM **Jeff Candel**: no baby

5:06:59 PM **ladydi2011**: Have you had her eyes checked?

5:07:07 PM **Jeff Candel**: *i* have baby

5:07:17 PM **Jeff Candel**: and the doc said we should come back tomorrow

5:07:32 PM **ladydi2011**: Was the doctor concerned about the headaches?

5:08:07 PM **Jeff Candel**: he said that tomorrow he will give her proper check up

5:08:18 PM **ladydi2011**: I know you must be thinking the worst baby, but please try not to

5:08:32 PM **ladydi2011**: I am glad he is going to do this

5:08:35 PM **Jeff Candel**: baby she is my only eye baby

5:08:46 PM **ladydi2011**: Please let me know what he says

5:08:56 PM **ladydi2011**: I know my love...

5:08:57 PM **Jeff Candel**: ok baby

5:09:01 PM **ladydi2011**: I am here with you

5:09:08 PM **Jeff Candel**: *i* understand baby

5:09:48 PM **ladydi2011**: Did you eat?

5:10:13 PM **Jeff Candel**: yes baby

5:10:18 PM **ladydi2011**: Good

5:10:42 PM **Jeff Candel**: bahy *i* love you

5:11:07 PM **ladydi2011**: How was the rest of your day?

5:11:25 PM **Jeff Candel**: stressful hun

5:11:35 PM **Jeff Candel**: *i* was very busy today

5:11:49 PM **Jeff Candel**: *i* am my director went somewhere

5:12:13 PM **ladydi2011**: If I was there I would de-stress you baby

5:13:06 PM **Jeff Candel**: sure baby

5:13:13 PM **Jeff Candel**: you are the best baby and *i* will always love you

5:13:30 PM **ladydi2011**: You are the best

5:13:52 PM **ladydi2011**: I am so happy we have finally been able to talk

5:14:09 PM **ladydi2011**: Thank you for all the beautiful writings you sent me

5:14:19 PM **ladydi2011**: I will treasure them forever

5:14:48 PM **ladydi2011**: so where did the director go today?

5:15:25 PM **Jeff Candel**: will went to one of the banks here for a meeting

5:16:01 PM **ladydi2011**: Oh, ok

5:17:37 PM **Jeff Candel**: so when *i* came back *i* was very tired

5:18:16 PM **Jeff Candel**: baby can you see me?

5:19:00 PM **Jeff Candel**: hun

5:19:07 PM **Jeff Candel**: are you there/

5:19:07 PM **ladydi2011**: I can

5:19:14 PM **Jeff Candel**: ok

5:19:17 PM **ladydi2011**: You are so handsome

5:19:26 PM **Jeff Candel**: thank you baby

5:19:29 PM **ladydi2011**: You just put a huge smile on my face

5:19:53 PM **ladydi2011**: You got your cam fixed

5:20:10 PM **Jeff Candel**: *yes but still giving prob baby*

5:20:20 PM **ladydi2011**: *It seems frozen*

5:20:27 PM **Jeff Candel**: yes baby

5:20:58 PM **Jeff Candel**: still not good yet baby

5:21:07 PM **ladydi2011**: Thank you so much baby for fixing the cam

5:21:16 PM **ladydi2011**: You move sometimes

5:21:25 PM **ladydi2011**: I love seeing you!

5:21:31 PM **ladydi2011**: *Please smile for me*

5:21:53 PM **Jeff Candel**: *baby am not in a good mood baby*

5:22:04 PM **ladydi2011**: *Baby, I lost your video*

5:22:14 PM **Jeff Candel**: am still disturb abuot sarah baby

5:22:28 PM **Jeff Candel**: its has started again baby

5:22:32 PM **ladydi2011**: I know you are honey

5:22:48 PM **ladydi2011**: *Please invite me again*

5:22:54 PM **Jeff Candel**: *its showing error*

5:23:06 PM **ladydi2011**: Mine is missing plug ins

5:23:13 PM **Jeff Candel**: ok good

5:23:18 PM **ladydi2011**: I hope to have it fixed by tomorrow

5:23:34 PM **Jeff Candel**: have you eating baby?

5:23:39 PM **ladydi2011**: Honey, what can I do to make you feel better?

5:23:47 PM **ladydi2011**: No honey, not yet

5:23:58 PM **Jeff Candel**: just be here with you baby

5:24:26 PM **ladydi2011**: I wish I was there to hold you

5:24:34 PM **Jeff Candel**: but you should try and creat time for yourself to eat ok

5:24:37 PM **ladydi2011**: Go to the doctor with you

5:24:45 PM **Jeff Candel**: yes baby

5:24:59 PM **ladydi2011**: I know I have to eat soon because I am getting a headache

5:25:17 PM **ladydi2011**: I still have to work out today too

5:25:26 PM **ladydi2011**: There is never enough time

5:26:08 PM **Jeff Candel**: ooh baby am sorry ok

5:26:23 PM **Jeff Candel**: dont be hard on yourself ok

5:26:28 PM **Jeff Candel**: *i* love you baby

5:27:31 PM **ladydi2011**: I will try not to be hard on myself....

5:27:37 PM **Jeff Candel**: thinking about you gives me joy

5:27:47 PM **ladydi2011**: Same here my love

5:28:12 PM **ladydi2011**: I take better care of myself now that you are in my life

5:28:13 PM **Jeff Candel**: you know you are the only one *i* have baby

5:28:25 PM **ladydi2011**: I know honey

5:28:27 PM **Jeff Candel**: good to hear that

5:29:20 PM **ladydi2011**: So, are you still glowing?

5:29:29 PM **ladydi2011**: Are you still "in love"?

5:29:43 PM **Jeff Candel**: am inlove with you baby

5:29:50 PM **ladydi2011**: I know baby...

5:29:59 PM **ladydi2011**: I am just trying to make you smile

5:30:13 PM **Jeff Candel**: ☺

5:30:42 PM **ladydi2011**: So baby, I would like to come and visit you soon

5:30:50 PM **Jeff Candel**: really?

5:30:54 PM **ladydi2011**: Yes honey

5:31:15 PM **Jeff Candel**: waooo that will be great

5:31:48 PM **ladydi2011**: Yes, it will

5:32:03 PM **ladydi2011**: I want to meet you and Sarah in person

5:32:11 PM **Jeff Candel**: ok good

5:32:24 PM **ladydi2011**: So, you like this idea?

5:32:31 PM **Jeff Candel**: so baby tell me how is the waelther over there?

5:32:37 PM **Jeff Candel**: sure baby

5:32:44 PM **ladydi2011**: In the 80's and finally sunny today

5:32:57 PM **ladydi2011**: We had several days of rain

5:33:03 PM **ladydi2011**: What about there?

5:33:07 PM **Jeff Candel**: same here too baby

5:33:32 PM **ladydi2011**: When I come over, how long do you want me to stay?

5:33:47 PM **Jeff Candel**: as long as you want baby

5:34:12 PM **Jeff Candel**: and *i* know that your work will not let you stay for long

5:34:26 PM **Jeff Candel**: because you will be needed in your compnay

5:34:28 PM **ladydi2011**: True baby

5:34:54 PM **ladydi2011**: I will need to get a hotel.

5:35:06 PM **ladydi2011**: What one do you recommend?

5:35:12 PM **Jeff Candel**: my house is big enough baby

5:35:32 PM **ladydi2011**: What will Sarah think if I stay there baby?

5:35:43 PM **Jeff Candel**: you are her mom baby

5:35:57 PM **Jeff Candel**: So you guys need to talk like mother and daughter

5:36:05 PM **ladydi2011**: This is true

5:36:17 PM **ladydi2011**: I always want to be a good example for her honey

5:36:36 PM **ladydi2011**: I want her to know her value

5:36:44 PM **ladydi2011**: Especially when it comes to men

5:36:44 PM **Jeff Candel**: sure baby

5:37:06 PM **ladydi2011**: Honey, I have always wanted a daughter

5:37:14 PM **Jeff Candel**: sure baby

5:37:26 PM **Jeff Candel**: its will shally come to pass ok

5:37:34 PM **Jeff Candel**: you will have a daughter ok

5:37:40 PM **ladydi2011**: I do, in Sarah

5:37:59 PM **Jeff Candel**: sure baby

5:38:21 PM **ladydi2011**: Honey....this is a lot of "sure baby"...lol

5:38:37 PM **Jeff Candel**: lol

5:38:46 PM **Jeff Candel**: sure sure sure

5:38:46 PM **ladydi2011**: You made me laugh and laugh some more

5:38:58 PM **Jeff Candel**: waaooo

5:39:12 PM **Jeff Candel**: *i* wish *i* camn hear the sound

5:39:12 PM **Jeff Candel**: hahahaha

5:39:33 PM **Jeff Candel**: sounds like a music to my ear baby

5:39:50 PM **ladydi2011**: Yes my love

5:39:59 PM **ladydi2011**: I am so glad you like my laugh

5:40:07 PM **Jeff Candel**: sure baby

5:40:10 PM **ladydi2011**: And that it is like music to your ears

5:40:18 PM **ladydi2011**: Sure baby..............

5:40:23 PM **ladydi2011**: Yeah baby!!!!

5:40:53 PM **Jeff Candel**: what are you doing now and where are you now?

5:41:04 PM **ladydi2011**: Chatting with my love

5:41:13 PM **ladydi2011**: What are you doing now?

5:41:31 PM **Jeff Candel**: am here having a cool chat with my queen

5:41:33 PM **ladydi2011**: I am in the office

5:41:37 PM **Jeff Candel**: ok baby

5:41:59 PM **ladydi2011**: *Honey, where did you get the term "my queen"?*

5:42:31 PM **Jeff Candel**: you are my queen baby

5:42:39 PM **Jeff Candel**: *i dreamt of it baby*

5:42:50 PM **ladydi2011**: You did....

5:43:07 PM **Jeff Candel**: *and the angel says called her your queen because that is what she is*

5:43:17 PM **ladydi2011**: Wow

5:43:21 PM **Jeff Candel**: so *i* decided to call you my queen ever since then

5:43:30 PM **ladydi2011**: Cool

5:43:52 PM **ladydi2011**: You are so very special

5:44:01 PM **ladydi2011**: I am so happy you are in love with me because I am in love with you

5:44:18 PM **Jeff Candel**: am happy you are in love with me too baby

5:44:23 PM **ladydi2011**: I am honey

5:44:37 PM **Jeff Candel**: *i* am the happiest man on earth now

5:44:50 PM **ladydi2011**: I am the happiest woman on earth

5:45:12 PM **ladydi2011**: The only thing that will make me happier is when we are in person together

5:45:36 PM **Jeff Candel**: sure baby

5:45:40 PM **ladydi2011**: Where I can look into your eyes, touch your face and kiss your lips

5:45:46 PM **Jeff Candel**: *i* believe so too baby

5:45:59 PM **Jeff Candel**: wow

5:46:44 PM **Jeff Candel**: *i* cant wait for that day when *i* will kiss you use my toung round your ears romance you and make sweet love to you

5:47:15 PM **Jeff Candel**: hold you closed to my heart

5:47:25 PM **Jeff Candel**: romance your breast

5:47:37 PM **Jeff Candel**: and suck it like 5yrs baby

5:48:22 PM **Jeff Candel**: *i* wanna make sweet and hot love to you and have you all night

5:49:19 PM **ladydi2011**: We might need to get a hotel room the first night together baby or have Sarah stay at a friend's house
5:49:51 PM **Jeff Candel**: sure baby
5:50:15 PM **Jeff Candel**: we make love all over the house baby
5:50:30 PM **Jeff Candel**: get naked and walk around the house hun
5:50:46 PM **Jeff Candel**: *do you like hard sex baby?*
5:51:07 PM **ladydi2011**: Hmmmmm
5:51:17 PM **Jeff Candel**: *am going to give you hard baby*
5:51:35 PM **Jeff Candel**: *make you scream for me baby*
5:51:47 PM **Jeff Candel**: *cool sex*
5:52:44 PM **ladydi2011**: Honey, I need to make the trip to see you soon
5:52:51 PM **ladydi2011**: What do you think?
5:53:03 PM **Jeff Candel**: its ok
5:53:10 PM **ladydi2011**: What's ok?
5:53:14 PM **Jeff Candel**: *will can work that out some day*
5:53:32 PM **ladydi2011**: What do you mean some day?
5:53:58 PM **Jeff Candel**: *i* mean will can work it out when you are ready baby
5:54:16 PM **ladydi2011**: Ok baby
5:54:24 PM **ladydi2011**: Thank you for your patience
5:54:33 PM **Jeff Candel**: its ok
5:54:34 PM **ladydi2011**: I promise I am worth the wait!
5:54:45 PM **Jeff Candel**: thank you baby
5:54:51 PM **Jeff Candel**: am happy to hear that
5:54:58 PM **ladydi2011**: It doesn't mean I do not desire you
5:55:07 PM **ladydi2011**: Because I desire you very much
5:55:17 PM **Jeff Candel**: me too baby
5:55:31 PM **Jeff Candel**: my heart belongs to you baby
5:55:41 PM **ladydi2011**: And mine belongs to you
5:56:06 PM **ladydi2011**: I wish I could call you on the phone
5:56:18 PM **ladydi2011**: my calling card does not work with your number
5:56:24 PM **ladydi2011**: I still don't know why
5:56:31 PM **Jeff Candel**: baby try *i* really wanna hear your voice
5:56:45 PM **ladydi2011**: I have several times

Outgoing Voice call with Jeff Candel (5:56:56 PM)

5:57:46 PM **ladydi2011**: I just tried to call you over the computer but you didn't answer
5:57:52 PM **Jeff Candel**: ok baby
5:57:55 PM **Jeff Candel**: call again
5:58:04 PM **ladydi2011**: Ok

Outgoing Voice call with Jeff Candel (5:57:59 PM)

6:05:19 PM **ladydi2011**: Baby, it was SO good to hear your voice!
6:05:29 PM **ladydi2011**: I hope you are smiling now
6:05:35 PM **Jeff Candel**: am happy to hear your voice baby
6:05:39 PM **Jeff Candel**: yes baby
6:05:40 PM **ladydi2011**: Sleep well my love
6:05:50 PM **Jeff Candel**: you have put a big smile on my face
6:05:51 PM **ladydi2011**: Dream about me

6:05:58 PM **Jeff Candel**: *i* will my queen

6:06:13 PM **Jeff Candel**: 🙂

6:06:44 PM **ladydi2011**: Good night my love

6:06:51 PM **Jeff Candel**: that is what *i* always want from you baby

6:06:54 PM **ladydi2011**: I will email you before I go to sleep

6:06:57 PM **Jeff Candel**: always keep smiling

6:07:02 PM **Jeff Candel**: ok baby

6:07:03 PM **ladydi2011**: I will look for your email when I awake

6:07:10 PM **Jeff Candel**: ok my queen

6:07:19 PM **ladydi2011**: Bye

6:07:27 PM **ladydi2011**: mwhaaaaaaaaaaaaaaaaaaaaaaaa

6:07:36 PM **Jeff Candel**: muahhhhhhhhhhh

6:07:39 PM **Jeff Candel**: muahhhhhhhhhhh

6:07:54 PM **Jeff Candel**: 😘

6:08:23 PM **Jeff Candel**: love you my queen

6:08:40 PM **ladydi2011**: Love you too honey

6:08:47 PM **Jeff Candel**: byeee

6:08:52 PM **ladydi2011**: byeeee

RED FLAGS

🚩 He was very interested in knowing if I got the check, how much it was and if it was in my account. A scammer will always be interested in your finances. Of course I staged making a large amount of money because one of my sources told me this would accelerate the scammer's request for money. Notice that he then instantly set me up with the "doctors" appointment for Sarah.

🚩 Once I told him about the money, he came on cam. However, it was frozen and he didn't keep it on long, saying "it showed error". It was the same fake cam he originally showed me, so he had to distort it and not let it be on long so I wouldn't become suspicious and notice it was the same cam. I asked him to smile for me when he was on cam and he told me he didn't feel like it because of Sarah. The truth was he couldn't because it was a pre-recorded cam. Notice if the person you're chatting with has no cam or only turns it on for short periods of time. Ask him to remove his glasses, show you how tall he is by standing up, or some other action that could not be done if it was a recorded cam.

🚩 I intentionally mentioned that I wanted to come and visit soon. He quickly changed the subject to the weather. I brought the subject back up about coming to visit him and he brought up that I was "already" Sarah's mom so I should stay with him instead of a hotel.

🚩 I was getting the response "sure baby" a lot because he really didn't know what to say.

🚩 In Africa, they use the term "my queen" a lot so I questioned him about always calling me his queen and where he got this term. He said he dreamt of it and the angel said to call me this because this is what I was. Really? Not likely!

🚩 He asked if I like hard sex. This is another terminology young Nigerian scammers use. He knows I do not want to have sex talk so he backed off and said "When you are ready baby." His talk here tells me this man is probably in his early 20's.

🏴 I again brought up to him that I wanted to talk to him but my calling card didn't work, nor did calling on the computer. It is a red flag when communication via telephone is always difficult.

Text Messages

Sent To: 1410000024
From: Diana
Sent: Jun 14, 2012 12:58 AM
Subject: Good Morning My Queen

Hello the King of my heart. You are sleeping now and I am in bed soon to be sleeping and dreaming about you. I look forward to the day we fall asleep in each other's arms. You are always in my thoughts. I hope you now have a smile on your face as you hear me tell you, "good morning my love".
Have a wonderful day. Think of me at least once. Lol... I will be on line around 8:30 pm your time as I wait for them to service my car. I will want to hear what the doctor says about Sarah. Well my love, I am going to close my eyes. 6am will arrive very quickly. Kisses and (((hugs))). The Queen of your heart

Sent From: 1410000033
Received: Jun 14, 2012 2:37 PM
From: jeffery candel
Subject: BAD NEWS BABE

MSG: *Baby can you come online i need to talk to you right now baby..am so confused right now. i need you hun. please come online ok. oh baby, something bad just happened*

Sent From: 1410000031
Received: Jun 14, 2012 5:35 AM
From: jeffery candel
Subject: BAD NEWS BABE

MSG: *oh baby, something bad just happened to Sarah now, she was upstairs and was coming down and she fell from upstairs and broke her legs, OMG am rushing her ti the emergency now.. she is really in a bad situation now and am so scared now.. i will let you know when i get to the hospital.*

Sent To: 1410000031
From: Diana
Sent: Jun 14, 2012 8:26 AM
Subject: Good Morning My Queen

OMG...both legs? She will be ok. I know you have to be beside yourself. I will be waiting to hear back from you. I love you! Diana

Sent From: 1410000032
Received: Jun 14, 2012 10:46 AM
From: jeffery candel
Subject: BAD NEWS BABE

MSG: *baby am so tired here and sacred too, she has been place on bed right now and the doc said she need emergency surgery to be carried out on her and she really in a bad shape tight now and i do not know what to do, am so so scared honey..... i do not want to lose her........ i am sending you a pics of her in her hospital bed \ now.... she really in a bad shape honey.....*

Sent From: 1410000032
Received: Thursday, June 14, 2012 10:50 AM
From: jeffery candel
Subject: PICS OF SARAH IN HER SICK BED

MSG: she is really in a bad shape honey and am so scared

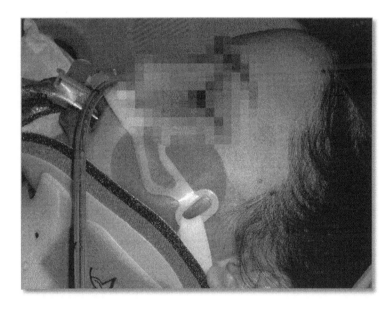

IM Jun 14, 2012 1:26:22 PM

1:26:22 PM **Jeff Candel**: hello baby
1:26:29 PM **Jeff Candel**: my love are you there
1:26:37 PM **Jeff Candel**: *i* need you online right now baby

---

Text Messages

Sent From: 1410000033

Received: Jun 14, 2012 2:37 PM
From: jeffery candel
Subject: BAD NEWS BABE

MSG: *Baby can you come online i need to talk to you right now baby... am so confused right now.*

- Do you hear the panic in his email? This is a scammer's attempt to get his victim (you) caught up in the story.
- He said he is "confused," which is another common scam tactic.
- Notice how the story becomes more and more tragic. Sarah supposedly broke "both" legs from a fall, which is highly unlikely. Then he sends a picture of her with a neck brace and breathing tubes. Why would she have a neck brace and breathing tubes for broken legs?

This deception may seem obvious to you as a reader, but it is far more difficult to discern facts and fraud when we are emotionally invested. Whenever there is a panic situation brought before you, please, please, please walk away and go call a friend and share it with them. They will be able to see what you cannot see because your heart is involved. If you don't want to call a friend, call us at 678-583-0401.

IM Jun 14, 2012 3:39:33 PM

3:39:33 PM **Jeff Candel**: hello hun
3:39:42 PM **ladydi2011**: Hi baby
3:39:44 PM **Jeff Candel**: thank God you are here
3:39:54 PM **ladydi2011**: I am sorry it took me so long. I was driving
3:40:13 PM **ladydi2011**: How is Sarah?
3:40:23 PM **Jeff Candel**: ok
3:40:27 PM **Jeff Candel**: did you get my texts and did you get the pics of her *i* sent you too??
3:40:38 PM **ladydi2011**. I did
3:41:00 PM **Jeff Candel**: am still at the hospital now and the situation is really very bad now
3:41:11 PM **ladydi2011**: what are they saying?
3:41:25 PM **Jeff Candel**: *and doc say she need to undergo surgery and it expensive and i do not have all the money they are asking and am so confused at this point honey*
3:42:21 PM **ladydi2011**: what type of surgery?
3:42:40 PM **ladydi2011**: I am sure you are confused...please calm down baby
3:42:51 PM **Jeff Candel**: they said she broke her leg and they need to set it back and they why she needs the surgery
3:43:13 PM **Jeff Candel**: *and she will also need a blood transfusion*
3:43:25 PM **ladydi2011**: A blood transfusion???

3:43:38 PM **Jeff Candel**: ☺

3:43:47 PM **Jeff Candel**: yes

3:43:48 PM **Jeff Candel**: yes

3:44:05 PM **Jeff Candel**: *she lost a lot of blood too*

3:44:09 PM **Jeff Candel**: 😠

3:44:15 PM **Jeff Candel**: *am so scared*

3:44:17 PM **ladydi2011**: What does a broken leg have to do with a blood transfusion?

3:44:43 PM **ladydi2011**: Please calm down...for me

3:45:02 PM **Jeff Candel**: rememebr sarah has cancer

3:45:02 PM **ladydi2011**: How did she loose so much blood?

3:45:13 PM **ladydi2011**: I know she has cancer of the blood

3:45:27 PM **Jeff Candel**: *i told you she fell from stair rememebr*

3:45:48 PM **Jeff Candel**: *she had a cut from the broken leg*

3:45:53 PM **Jeff Candel**: don't you understand ???

3:45:59 PM **ladydi2011**: Oh, ok

3:46:18 PM **ladydi2011**: honey, how much money do you need?

3:47:12 PM **Jeff Candel**: *i have 1000 pound here and they need 2.400 pounds*

3:47:52 PM **ladydi2011**: So you need 2,400 pounds?

3:47:55 PM **Jeff Candel**: *and that $1.650*

3:48:04 PM **ladydi2011**: Don't you have insurance baby?

3:48:25 PM **Jeff Candel**: *i* have 1000 pounds wiith me

3:48:34 PM **ladydi2011**: Ok....

3:50:13 PM **Jeff Candel**: *i will pay back before month end*

3:54:21 PM **Jeff Candel**: you still here baby??

3:55:47 PM **Jeff Candel**: baby you here??

3:55:50 PM **Jeff Candel**: talk to me please

3:57:32 PM **Jeff Candel**: <ding>

3:57:40 PM **Jeff Candel**: <ding>

3:57:51 PM **Jeff Candel**: you here baby???

3:58:20 PM **ladydi2011**: I am now...there are problems with my car and they needed to talk to me. I am at the car dealership

3:58:36 PM **ladydi2011**: so you need $1,650

3:58:47 PM **Jeff Candel**: yes baby

3:59:02 PM **ladydi2011**: Ok honey. please tell me how to get it to you

4:01:20 PM **ladydi2011**: Are you there baby?

4:02:12 PM **Jeff Candel**: baby am here

4:02:32 PM **ladydi2011**: Did you see what I wrote honey?

4:02:40 PM **Jeff Candel**: no

4:02:51 PM **Jeff Candel**: please write again

4:03:15 PM **ladydi2011**: Please tell me how to get it to you

4:03:21 PM **Jeff Candel**: ok

4:05:46 PM **Jeff Candel**: am sending the info

4:05:48 PM **Jeff Candel**: <ding>

4:05:58 PM **ladydi2011**: I am here

4:06:00 PM **Jeff Candel**: *First Name: Jeffery*
Last Name: candel

451

Address: Shant House no 13 shant street, London-England
Amount: $1.650
ENURE IT SEN VIA WESTERN UNION
4:07:21 PM **Jeff Candel:** *Once money has been sent kindly send to me the following details*
4:07:51 PM **Jeff Candel:** *SENDER NAME:*
MTCN :
ADDRESS:
Amount sent
4:08:34 PM **Jeff Candel**: did you get the info honey??
4:10:06 PM **ladydi2011**: I got it baby. I am stuck here for a couple hours with no car. They are servicing the car and the bank closes in less than an hour so I cannot do this until tomorrow.
4:10:46 PM **Jeff Candel:** *can't you take a taxi to the nearest location now ??*
4:11:05 PM **ladydi2011**: let me see what I can do, ok
4:11:15 PM **Jeff Candel**: so that *i* can notify the doc to commence on treatment that the money is on it way?
4:11:56 PM **ladydi2011**: Let me get off here and see what *i* can do, ok
4:12:10 PM **Jeff Candel**: ok
4:12:18 PM **Jeff Candel:** *send me sms and let me know when you are back and i will be here again in the next 40 mins or an hour*
4:12:46 PM **Jeff Candel:** *you should be back by then right??*
4:12:46 PM **ladydi2011**: Yes
4:12:54 PM **ladydi2011**: Are you calmer now?
4:12:58 PM **Jeff Candel:** *i need to let the doc know now that moeny is on it way*
4:13:08 PM **Jeff Candel**: a little bit baby
4:13:17 PM **Jeff Candel**: just that *i* want her to be fine
4:13:23 PM **Jeff Candel**: love you
4:13:23 PM **ladydi2011**: She will be honey
4:13:28 PM **ladydi2011**: Love you too.
4:13:34 PM **ladydi2011**: Bye for now.
4:13:38 PM **Jeff Candel**: later
4:13:42 PM **Jeff Candel**: *i* will be here again in an hour for the info
4:13:47 PM **ladydi2011**: Ok baby
4:13:51 PM **ladydi2011**: Breathe

RED FLAGS

- He instantly converted pounds to US dollars. I couldn't do that so quickly, could you? He asked me for $1,650 and promised to pay me back by the end of the month. A scammer will NEVER PAY YOU BACK.
- A scammer also knows what to tell you so you can get them the money and will want you to send it to them right away. They know they have to keep you emotionally charged and get the money from you quickly before you have time to think or talk to someone about it. This is why when I said I could do it tomorrow he told me to take a taxi and let him know within 40 minuites to an hour. He was fully in "it's time to get the money" mode!
- This man has an off-shore guy in London who will pick up this money and send it to him in Nigeria.

IM Jun 14, 2012 6:03:11 PM

6:03:11 PM **Jeff Candel**: baby are you back now?

Text Messages

Sent From: 1410000035
Received: Jun 14, 2012 6:04 PM
From: jeffery candel
Subject: BAD NEWS BABE

MSG: my love are you back.... ***have you sent the money.*** am still here waiting baby.

Sent From: 1410000036
Received: Jun 14, 2012 9:31 PM
From: jeffery candel
Subject: BAD NEWS BABE

MSG: *baby,what is happening? i have been waiting to hear from you*

IM Jun 14, 2012 9:32:21 PM

9:32:21 PM **Jeff Candel**: sweetie
9:32:23 PM **Jeff Candel**: you here ?
9:32:24 PM **Jeff Candel**: <ding>

Text Messages

Sent From: 1410000037
Received: Jun 15, 2012 1:35 AM
From: jeffery candel
Subject: BAD NEWS BABE

MSG: Baby how are you doing... *i* waited yesterday baby you didnt come back online.. baby please *i* want to know what is happening, baby my mind is not rest my love. ***have you sent the money i will be going to the hospital this morning.*** please do write me back baby. *i need you* <u>right now</u> *to write me back to know that situation there ok. i* love you.

Sent From: 1410000038
Received: Jun 15, 2012 11:06 AM
From: jeffery candel
Subject: BAD NEWS BABE

MSG: Goodmorning my queen, how was your night. *baby i have been in the hospital and the doc was asking if i have the money with me there. baby am still waiting for the money so doc can commence with the treatment. please baby let me know when you are don sending the money ok.* and also dont forget to send me the details which you use insending the money and the MTCN Nubers ok. *i* love you baby am waiting. *Help me to save sarah life* my queen.
YOur King.

Sent From: 1410000039
Received: Jun 15, 2012 4:36 PM
From: jeffery candel
Subject: BAD NEWS BABE

MSG: Baby can you please come online so we can talk please... *i really need to talk to you now baby*.... my heart is bleeding baby, *i dont wanna loose my daughter* baby please come online baby, *i* need you here baby... please am waiting for you baby... *i* dont know what to tell the doc again baby. *help me save my daughter life* baby. *i* love you.

IM Jun 15, 2012 5:01:05 PM

5:01:05 PM **Jeff Candel**: baby *i need you online now*
5:01:54 PM **Jeff Candel**: *i* want to talk to you baby

Text Messages

Sent From: 1410000040
Received: Jun 15, 2012 6:06 PM
From: jeffery candel
Subject: BAD NEWS BABE

MSG: My queen what is going on baby... why are you not talking to me.... *i* need you online baby, *i need to talk with you right now.*

IM Jun 15, 2012 8:21:58 PM

8:21:58 PM **Jeff Candel**: baby you here?
8:22:28 PM **Jeff Candel**: <ding>
8:22:28 PM **Jeff Candel**: <ding>
8:22:28 PM **Jeff Candel**: <ding>

IM Jun 15, 2012 9:21:50 PM

9:21:50 PM **Jeff Candel**: <ding>
9:21:51 PM **Jeff Candel**: hello baby
9:22:40 PM **Jeff Candel**: hun are you there
9:22:40 PM **Jeff Candel**: please talk to me

Missed Voice call with Jeff Candel (9:23:55 PM)

Text Messages

Sent From: 1410000041
Received: Jun 15, 2012 9:30 PM
From: jeffery candel
Subject: BAD NEWS BABE

MSG: Hun why is this happening to me.. *what have i done to deserve this treatment* my love.

Sent From: 1410000041
Received: Jun 15, 2012 9:31 PM
From: jeffery candel
Subject: BAD NEWS BABE

MSG: *i* will always love you no matter what my love. *i* love you baby. God bless you my queen.

Sent From: 1410000041
Received: Jun 15, 2012 9:31 PM
From: jeffery candel
Subject: BAD NEWS BABE

MSG: Hun why is this happening to me.. *what have i done to deserve this treatment* my love. *My daughter is dieing* and i cant do something about it. well baby if its because of the money *i* ask from that is why you are not responding to my email its ok baby. *i* can get some of my properties sell out to raise the money ok. *i dont want my only daughter to die*. *i* know that read from you, am planing of selling my car baby to raise the money ok. please *i* need to read from you my love. what have *i* done to deserve this treatment from you my queen. baby *i* love you so much and *i* dont wanna loose you hun.

Sent From: 1410000042
Received: Jun 16, 2012 7:52 AM
From: jeffery candel
Subject: my heart is full of tears baby.

MSG: *My love why do you want my daughter to die like this baby*.... I am on line. Please come on line. I read from you, am planing of selling my car baby to raise the money ok. please *i* need to read from you my love. what have *i* done to deserve this treatment from you my queen. baby *i* love you so much and *i* dont wanna loose you hun.

Sent From: 1410000043
Received: Jun 16, 2012 10:16 AM
From: jeffery candel
Subject: Thank God

MSG: *Baby sarah is now talking i have paid for he treatment there is no need for you to send me money again i have sold my car baby,* thanks for your concern baby. am happy *she is now talking she ask after you i told her you are doing fine and sent your greetings*... baby *i* just need you to try and pick up my calls please baby. *i* need you to be happy for me now you can't leave me like this baby. *i* love you with all my heart baby.

Your King

IM Jun 16, 2012 1:36:44 PM

1:36:44 PM **Jeff Candel**: hello baby
1:36:54 PM **Jeff Candel**: how are you doing today
1:36:58 PM **Jeff Candel**: and how is work

IM Jun 16, 2012 7:41:22 PM

7:41:22 PM **Jeff Candel**: <ding>
7:41:24 PM **Jeff Candel**: hello
7:41:25 PM **Jeff Candel**: baby

From: jeffcand101
To: ladydi2011
Subject: Re: I carry your heart with me..
Sent: Sunday, June 17, 2012 6:51 PM

How are you doing today baby,my love *i* hope you are doing fine... *i* dont seems to understand what is going on baby, am so sceard and right now *i* dont know what to do am so confused here baby... How can you disapear away from me just like that baby...
please baby *i* a so worried about you and *i* know where you are baby *God will always guard you and protect you for me my love*... *i* have miss you more than enough baby, am tired of crying, weaping tears all becuase of you hun, *i* have loved you and you only... my heart belongs to you and *if i dont have you in my life my love i will kill myself*. *i* can't stop thinking about you everything *i* do in my office now is never right because my heart is in you.... *sarah needs you more than the world needs the light to shine on the surface baby*. my life is worhtless because of you my love. *i* can't eat nor drink anything am dieing baby my heart is frozen *baby please come back to me i need you. dont*

go away from me. Wherever you go ,Whatever you do I will be right here waiting for you..
Whatever it takes Or how my heart breaks.

I will be right here waiting for you. I carry your heart with me

While I sit and stare at the moon while I sit, Just thinking of you as I stare at the beautiful stars

As I stare wondering just how you are while I wonder as I stare and I sit *i* know I'll see Your face again
my love and my queen.

Your King,

IM Jun 19, 2012 9:20:26 AM

9:20:26 AM **Jeff Candel**: hello hun

IM Jun 19, 2012 1:47:13 PM

1:47:13 PM **Jeff Candel**: <ding>
1:47:17 PM **Jeff Candel**: hello

IM Jun 19, 2012 4:22:11 PM

4:22:11 PM **Jeff Candel**: hello

IM Jun 19, 2012 4:58:17 PM

4:58:17 PM **Jeff Candel**: hello hun

IM Jun 19, 2012 11:31:52 PM

11:31:52 PM **Jeff Candel**: hi babe

IM Jun 20, 2012 12:22:47 PM

12:22:47 PM **Jeff Candel**: hello hun
12:22:52 PM **Jeff Candel**: are you there hun
12:23:00 PM **Jeff Candel**: Talk to me:
12:23:31 PM **Jeff Candel**: Your buddy hung up

12:24:53 PM **Jeff Candel**: hello hun
12:25:07 PM **Jeff Candel**: hun are you there?

Missed Voice call with Jeff Candel (12:25:19 PM)

Text Messages

Sent From: 1410000046
Received: Jun 20, 2012 9:26 AM
From: jeffery candel
Subject: Your Love Is All I Need

MSG: You make me happy
You make me cry
you make me sad
you make me mad
you make me
feel again
you make me breathe
you started my whole world again
like it was your own book to read.

You stole my heart
you have my soul
you stood in front of me like it was your turn to bowl.
My life had started when you came in
you knew how to unlock me like you knew my pin
and now your love is all I need to keep me alive happy and free.

My queen you are my life baby. and *i* will never stop loving you till *i* die baby.

Your King,

Jeff

From: jeffery candel
Received: Wednesday, June 20, 2012 4:28 PM
To: Ladydi2011
Subject: READ AND GET BACK TO ME

My queen i really dont understand you any more baby you seems to be doubting me. i thought you trusted me baby... i so much love you and yet you dont trust me. i show myself to you for you believe who i am and also gave you my address, what else will a man give to a woman for her to

458

believe that the man is for real tell me baby please tell me. i love you right from the first day i saw you baby. and *i* even told you about my daughter, *a daughter is very much happy to be your daughter*, my queen you go off me without telling me good bye... baby you know that was very hurt. baby am really hurt right now by you and *i feel pains all over my heart baby*. baby *i* want you to get back to me as soon as read this ok. *my daughter needs you baby.*

IF YOU STILL LOVE ME BABY YOU WILL WRITE BACK, BUT IF YOU DONT CARE ABOUT ME AND MY DAUGHTER, AND IF YOU DONT LOVE US AS PART OF YOUR BODY AND SOUL. I GUESS THERE IS NO REASON IN WRITING BACK.. BUT KNOW THIS WE WILL ALWAYS LOVE YOU WITH ALL OUR HEART.

Jeff

I purposely didn't talk to him for six days so you could see the tactic a scammer will use when you don't send money. By day two of me not talking to him, he changed his tactic. Remember, the ONLY thing he wants is MONEY, and he has invested time in me and thought he had me. By day six he knew I doubted him and didn't trust him, so he told me that he even showed himself on cam and gave me his address so I would trust him. You see, he did both of these things to gain my trust and he thought he had my trust. His ploy requires him to regain my trust. He poured it on really heavy because he is desperate to not lose me as a client. After all he has spent 20 days working me. After 20 days, he is SO in love with me. Really? No. Now it's time for me to reveal that I know he's a scammer.

RED FLAGS

- They want to hear from you "right now". They say it in such a way that they are ordering you. They are anxiously awaiting the money so they want you to tell them as soon as you send it.
- He used the guilt tactic of, "Help me save Sarah life", "I don't want to lose my daughter", "my daughter is dying", "I don't want my only daughter to die", "My love why do you want my daughter to die like this".
- He said he sold his car and paid for her treatment and she is now talking and asking for me. This is his ploy to try to pull me back.
- Again, he used God, then goes back to guilt, that if he doesn't have me in his life he will kill himself and tells me how Sarah needs me.

IM Jun 20, 2012 4:27:09 PM

4:27:09 PM **ladydi2011**: Hi!
4:27:42 PM **Jeff Candel**: baby *i* just sent you an email
4:28:12 PM **ladydi2011**: At phone store...having phone issues
4:28:24 PM **Jeff Candel**: I WANT YOU TO READ IT AND GET BACK TO ME BABY
4:29:10 PM **Jeff Candel**: still having prob with your phone

4:30:15 PM **ladydi2011**: Read what?
4:31:51 PM **Jeff Candel**: *i* sent you an email
4:34:39 PM **ladydi2011**: I just read it. There is much more to this.
4:35:54 PM **ladydi2011**: I need to drive to the car dealership again...I will send you something once there. I am sorry I hurt you and Sarah. This was never my intention.
4:36:24 PM **Jeff Candel**: baby we so much love you baby
4:36:34 PM **Jeff Candel**: why baby
4:36:46 PM **Jeff Candel**: *what happened to the trust and love baby*
4:37:32 PM **ladydi2011**: I will explain...I have to drive now baby
4:37:49 PM **Jeff Candel**: ok
4:38:40 PM **Jeff Candel**: *i* will leave you to drive now baby o
4:38:54 PM **Jeff Candel**: let me know when you are done driving

IM Jun 20, 2012 5:16:49 PM

5:16:49 PM **Jeff Candel**: hello love are you through now
5:19:24 PM **Jeff Candel**: hun are you there?

IM Jun 20, 2012 6:30:55 PM

6:30:55 PM **Jeff Candel**: hello

IM Jun 22, 2012 3:12:40 PM

3:12:40 PM **Jeff Candel**: hi sweetie

IM Jun 22, 2012 3:42:13 PM

3:42:13 PM **Jeff Candel**: sweetie are you there?
3:59:12 PM **Jeff Candel**: hello
4:05:51 PM **ladydi2011**: Hi
4:06:04 PM **ladydi2011**: Just getting on client call
4:06:10 PM **Jeff Candel**: sweetie where have you been?
4:06:18 PM **Jeff Candel**: *i* have been waiting all day baby
4:06:27 PM **Jeff Candel**: how are you doing?
4:06:40 PM **ladydi2011**: I am good
4:06:49 PM **Jeff Candel**: ok
4:06:50 PM **ladydi2011**: I want to chat, will you be on later?
4:06:53 PM **Jeff Candel**: happy to hear that
4:06:59 PM **ladydi2011**: How are you and Sarah?
4:07:04 PM **Jeff Candel**: what time baby
4:07:16 PM **Jeff Candel**: we are doing good

4:07:27 PM **Jeff Candel**: *she ask after you baby*
4:07:42 PM **ladydi2011**: brb
4:08:03 PM **Jeff Candel**: ok baby
4:08:07 PM **Jeff Candel**: waiting

IM Jun 22, 2012 5:07:33 PM

5:07:33 PM **ladydi2011**: Are you still there?
5:07:43 PM **Jeff Candel**: sure baby
5:07:49 PM **Jeff Candel**: am here waiting for you
5:08:05 PM **Jeff Candel**: are you done with what you are doing now
5:08:23 PM **ladydi2011**: Yes, thank you for waiting.
5:08:47 PM **ladydi2011**: How are you?
5:09:51 PM **Jeff Candel**: am fine baby and you?
5:10:23 PM **ladydi2011**: Did you get Sarah released?
5:10:36 PM **Jeff Candel**: *i* dont have the money baby
5:10:45 PM **Jeff Candel**: that is why *i* have not
5:10:48 PM **Jeff Candel**: *i* told you baby
5:12:46 PM **Jeff Candel**: baby you think am lieing to you
5:13:03 PM **Jeff Candel**: *i* want you to know that *i* have no reason to lie to you about my daughter ok
5:14:19 PM **Jeff Candel**: *baby you are the only person on this plannet that i can call to baby*
5:14:26 PM **Jeff Candel**: *i* want you to understand that
5:14:40 PM **ladydi2011**: I know you are lying to me

The below information that proves he is in Lagos, Nigeria obtained for me by Michael West at Arkansas Investigations is what I sent him.

To: ladydi2011@yahoo.com
Date: Thu, 14 Jun 2012 14:49:20 +0000
Subject: PICS OF SARAH IN HER SICK BED
Location: Nigeria
Misdirected: No
Abuse Address: olorunfemi.emmanuel@visafone.com.ng
From IP: 41.138.191.122
inetnum: 41.138.184.0 - 41.138.191.255
netname: VISAFONE-LAGOS-PDSN2

5:15:29 PM **Jeff Candel**: what is this?
5:16:24 PM **Jeff Candel**: are you in any way trying to call me a liar?
5:16:32 PM **ladydi2011**: Do you want the rest of the info
5:16:34 PM **Jeff Candel**: make me understand what you sent to me
5:16:48 PM **Jeff Candel**: what info is that baby
5:17:18 PM **Jeff Candel**: what are you sending to me
5:17:22 PM **ladydi2011**: The IP address all your info is coming from
5:17:27 PM **ladydi2011**: It is not from London

5:17:32 PM **ladydi2011**: It is from Nigeria
5:17:42 PM **Jeff Candel**: what do you mean by that
5:17:45 PM **Jeff Candel**: *i* cant get it baby
5:17:58 PM **Jeff Candel**: what do you mean my ip
5:17:58 PM **ladydi2011**: *You block your IP address*
5:18:22 PM **Jeff Candel**: *what nonsense are you talking about*
5:18:34 PM **Jeff Candel**: *why will i block my address*
5:18:40 PM **Jeff Candel**: *because of what*
5:19:18 PM **Jeff Candel**: baby i dont understand you any more
5:19:33 PM **ladydi2011**: I don't understand you either
5:19:36 PM **Jeff Candel**: *first you dont believe me and i show myself on cam to you*
5:19:46 PM **Jeff Candel**: now you are sending me rubish
5:19:54 PM **ladydi2011**: yeah, you did show yourself to me on cam
5:19:57 PM **Jeff Candel**: telling me its my ip
5:20:20 PM **Jeff Candel**: you are making me angry right now
5:20:42 PM **ladydi2011**: Hmmmm
5:20:43 PM **Jeff Candel**: what its because *i* ask of your help baby
5:20:57 PM **Jeff Candel**: is that why you are calling my all sult of names
5:21:01 PM **Jeff Candel**: baby its ok
5:21:12 PM **ladydi2011**: I haven't called you any names
5:21:13 PM **Jeff Candel**: may be *i* was blind in falling for you baby'
5:21:19 PM **ladydi2011**: I am just showing you what I know
5:21:27 PM **ladydi2011**: Maybe
5:21:29 PM **Jeff Candel**: *i* dont believe you will treat me like this baby
5:21:48 PM **Jeff Candel**: *you have made me hate love and everthing in the world*
5:22:14 PM **Jeff Candel**: *i* never thought of loving again but you make me do it baby
5:22:20 PM **Jeff Candel**: now you are calling me names
5:22:50 PM **Jeff Candel**: *i know that my God is not sleeping my daughter will be release ok*
5:22:55 PM **Jeff Candel**: without any body help
5:23:25 PM **Jeff Candel**: thank you for calling me noames
5:24:45 PM **Jeff Candel**: baby let me ask you something ?
5:25:03 PM **Jeff Candel**: do you ever love me the way you claim to ?
5:26:32 PM **ladydi2011**: I have to go now. I would like to discuss this later if you want to

IM Jun 23, 2012 2:59:49 PM

2:59:49 PM **Jeff Candel**: hello baby
3:00:09 PM **Jeff Candel**: am hee now ok
3:00:17 PM **ladydi2011**: Hello
3:00:39 PM **Jeff Candel**: how are you doing baby
3:01:06 PM **ladydi2011**: Ok, how are you? How is Sarah?
3:01:17 PM **Jeff Candel**: sarah is fine baby
3:02:09 PM **ladydi2011**: Good. I am glad to know this.
3:02:42 PM **Jeff Candel**: *but she is still at the hospital because i have not pay for her release baby*
3:03:00 PM **Jeff Candel**: *i* told you that *i* dont have money with me now
3:03:09 PM **ladydi2011**: I know

3:03:11 PM **Jeff Candel**: *its very ruff for me baby*

3:03:28 PM **Jeff Candel**: *that is why am asking you to help me out baby*

3:04:02 PM **Jeff Candel**: *if i have it i will not have disturb you with it baby*

3:04:56 PM **ladydi2011**: Why did you ask me for my full name and address?

3:05:33 PM **Jeff Candel**: *baby i ask so that i can have it when sarah get better will come together to meet you baby*

3:05:56 PM **Jeff Candel**: *seems you dont wanna believe anything i say to you*

3:06:07 PM **Jeff Candel**: *i want you to see me in person*

3:07:06 PM **ladydi2011**: Ok...let me get back on computer

3:07:30 PM **Jeff Candel**: like how many mint do you want me to give you for that?

3:13:56 PM **ladydi2011**: what do you mean?

3:14:27 PM **Jeff Candel**: *i was asking if you are on computer yet baby*

3:15:14 PM **ladydi2011**: I am

3:15:20 PM **Jeff Candel**: ok baby

3:15:34 PM **Jeff Candel**: so how is work baby

3:16:03 PM **Jeff Candel**: *baby am really mess up here and i dont know what to do next*

3:16:29 PM **Jeff Candel**: *you need to come to my help baby*

3:16:32 PM **Jeff Candel**: please

3:16:46 PM **Jeff Candel**: *if not for me but for God ok*

3:17:02 PM **Jeff Candel**: *i will pay you back ok*

3:18:19 PM **ladydi2011**: Are you home?

3:18:27 PM **Jeff Candel**: yes baby

3:18:41 PM **ladydi2011**: *Please come on cam*

3:18:43 PM Jeff Candel: *i* came home to talk with you and know what to do ok

3:18:58 PM **Jeff Candel**: *baby i told you my cam is bad now*

3:19:27 PM **Jeff Candel**: *i cant fix it baby*

3:20:52 PM **Jeff Candel**: baby you are not talking

3:21:18 PM **Jeff Candel**: *baby i will pay you your money back ok*

3:21:47 PM **Jeff Candel**: *i need you to help me and also help my daughter sarah to get otu of that hospital bed please*

3:21:50 PM **Jeff Candel**: *that is all i need from you and its just $850*

3:22:08 PM **Jeff Candel**: please baby

3:24:32 PM **Jeff Candel**: baby are you there ?

3:24:38 PM **Jeff Candel**: please talk to me

3:27:06 PM **Jeff Candel**: hello

3:28:10 PM **ladydi2011**: You never answered me. Why do you want my full name and address?

3:28:40 PM **Jeff Candel**: *baby i need you to believe that am for reall baby*

3:29:19 PM **Jeff Candel**: *i* was thinking if my daughter get better we come together and meet in person seems you dont believe every word *i* say to you

3:29:31 PM **Jeff Candel**: that was why *i* need it baby

3:29:50 PM **Jeff Candel**: *so i can pay you a suprise visit*

3:30:15 PM **Jeff Candel**: you dont want to believe every word *i* say baby... and *i* dont know what else to do for you to believe me baby

3:30:25 PM **Jeff Candel**: am so confused right now you gave me hope to live for another day baby

3:31:16 PM **Jeff Candel**: *i feel like killing myself right now baby*

3:31:28 PM **Jeff Candel**: that is just the honest truth ok

Break In Time

3:38:02 PM **Jeff Candel**: baby seems you dont have the to talk with me

3:39:12 PM **Jeff Candel**: we have been through this right

3:40:00 PM **Jeff Candel**: *you really need to help me out and get sarah out of that hospital ok*

3:40:17 PM **Jeff Candel**: *that is all i need you to do for me now ok*

3:40:42 PM **ladydi2011**: Let me think. I will let you know later

3:41:07 PM **Jeff Candel**: baby *i* know alots have happen to you and me too

3:41:35 PM **Jeff Candel**: *but i want you to know that i am promising you with my life on it that i will never hurt you and do anything to you all i ask is your trust and commitment, is that too much t6o ask?*

3:43:52 PM **ladydi2011**: I have to go

3:44:08 PM **Jeff Candel**: *i can even explain to sarah why we are still here in the hospital*

3:44:08 PM **Jeff Candel**: ok

3:44:09 PM **Jeff Candel**: talk later

3:44:20 PM **ladydi2011**: Ok

IM Jul 3, 2012 12:04:42 AM

12:04:42 AM **Jeff Candel**: hi

12:05:20 AM **Jeff Candel**: baby are you there?

12:09:00 AM **ladydi2011**: Hi

12:09:04 AM **ladydi2011**: How are you?

12:09:10 AM **ladydi2011**: How is Sarah?

12:33:11 AM **Jeff Candel**: she is fine

12:33:20 AM **Jeff Candel**: kept asking after you hun

12:33:25 AM **ladydi2011**: I am glad she is good

12:33:28 AM **ladydi2011**: And you?

12:33:33 AM **Jeff Candel**: am fine

12:33:48 AM **Jeff Candel**: *i* have been thinking alot about you

12:34:04 AM **Jeff Candel**:.why have you decided to leave us like this baby

12:35:26 AM **ladydi2011**: I think about you too

12:35:49 AM **Jeff Candel**: baby you dont if you do you would have ask after us

12:35:57 AM **Jeff Candel**: not even a call from you hun is that a what you called thinking

12:36:57 AM **Jeff Candel**: baby just because you have bad experience in life does not mean you should not trust people again

12:36:58 AM **Jeff Candel**: ok

12:37:16 AM **ladydi2011**: You are right

12:37:23 AM **ladydi2011**: It is hard

12:37:33 AM **Jeff Candel**: baby *i* understand its hard

12:37:48 AM **Jeff Candel**: you are not the only one on this ok

12:38:45 AM **Jeff Candel**: *baby do you know that i all most lost my only daughter because of you?*

12:39:30 AM **ladydi2011**: What do you mean, because of me?

12:39:53 AM **Jeff Candel**: *yes because of you baby*

12:40:17 AM **Jeff Candel**: *well i thank God for everything*

12:40:34 AM **ladydi2011**: How, because of me?

12:41:22 AM **Jeff Candel**: baby *i* want you to know that *i* hardly ask people for help

12:41:53 AM **Jeff Candel**: *but because of the love and also take you as part of me that was why i ask you for help*

12:42:08 AM **Jeff Candel**: but you turn it to be another thing baby

12:43:10 AM **Jeff Candel**: so let me ask you one thing

12:43:30 AM **Jeff Candel**: *have you also written that in your book too*

12:43:51 AM **ladydi2011**: *Excuse me*

12:44:58 AM **Jeff Candel**: *you told me that you are on a book which we turn people to know that some people are all after their money right*

12:45:16 AM **ladydi2011**: Yeah, it is to educate people

12:45:32 AM **Jeff Candel**: *i* want you to know that the more reason why God kept you alive is to be love and love return ok

12:45:49 AM **ladydi2011**: I know

12:46:01 AM **ladydi2011**: this is what *i* wanted when *i* came on line

12:46:13 AM **Jeff Candel**: so why are you making things too difficult to me baby

12:46:29 AM **Jeff Candel**: so you where never here to be loved right ?

12:46:57 AM **ladydi2011**: I was here for love

12:47:13 AM **Jeff Candel**: *i* dont think so baby

12:47:29 AM **ladydi2011**: Why don't you think so?

12:47:47 AM **Jeff Candel**: if you where here for that you will not treat me this way dear

12:48:36 AM **Jeff Candel**: baby *i* have always love you

12:48:51 AM **Jeff Candel**: even when you treat me bad and hurt me baby *i* still love you

12:49:46 AM **Jeff Candel**: am here for you always baby

12:50:02 AM **Jeff Candel**: *i* see no reason why you should not trust me baby

12:50:33 AM **ladydi2011**: I want to trust you

12:50:50 AM **Jeff Candel**: baby you dont trust me

12:51:23 AM **Jeff Candel**: *i want you to understand that in any relationship trust is the only thing to make it work out fine*

12:52:05 AM **Jeff Candel**: *how is the business going*

12:52:12 AM **ladydi2011**: It is ok

12:52:21 AM **Jeff Candel**: good to know that

12:52:41 AM **Jeff Candel**: baby *i* miss you

12:53:40 AM **ladydi2011**: I miss you too

12:53:57 AM **Jeff Candel**: have you repaired your phone now?

12:54:51 AM **ladydi2011**: Yes, but it keeps acting up

12:55:08 AM **Jeff Candel**: cant you buy another phone?

12:56:01 AM **ladydi2011**: I did buy another one but it is also bad.

12:56:33 AM **Jeff Candel**: so what is wrong with that now baby

12:56:50 AM **ladydi2011**: the battery wouldn't charge

12:57:07 AM **ladydi2011**: I took it out, cleaned the connectors and it seems to be charging now

12:57:43 AM **Jeff Candel**: ok good

12:58:33 AM **ladydi2011**: Please hold...noise at back door

12:58:34 AM **Jeff Candel**: *baby what is you full name*

12:58:40 AM **Jeff Candel**: ok

1:00:47 AM **ladydi2011**: back

1:01:00 AM **ladydi2011**: You know my full name

1:02:26 AM **Jeff Candel**: *i* dont baby

1:02:38 AM **Jeff Candel**: *i* only know diana

1:02:56 AM **ladydi2011**: Really?

1:03:01 AM **Jeff Candel**: yes baby

1:03:13 AM **Jeff Candel**: you have never told me before baby

1:03:31 AM **Jeff Candel**: when *i* ask you.. you never told me

1:03:37 AM **ladydi2011**: Hmmmmmm

1:03:49 AM **ladydi2011**: that noise again

1:03:55 AM **ladydi2011**: hold again please

1:04:08 AM **Jeff Candel**: what is going on baby?

1:07:32 AM **Jeff Candel**: hello baby are you there?

1:08:52 AM **ladydi2011**: I am back

1:09:55 AM **Jeff Candel**: what was that baby?

1:10:33 AM **ladydi2011**: not sure

1:10:39 AM **Jeff Candel**: ok

1:10:49 AM **Jeff Candel**: hope you are ok

1:12:34 AM **ladydi2011**: I am

1:12:57 AM **ladydi2011**: Do you remember what day we met?

1:13:22 AM **Jeff Candel**: sure baby

1:13:37 AM **Jeff Candel**: what happened?

1:16:01 AM **Jeff Candel**: baby are you there?

1:17:17 AM **ladydi2011**: I am

1:17:21 AM **ladydi2011**: Sorry

1:17:27 AM **ladydi2011**: Got booted

1:17:47 AM **ladydi2011**: Please hold one more minute k

1:17:56 AM **Jeff Candel**: ok

1:17:59 AM **ladydi2011**: Let me close some programs

1:20:24 AM **ladydi2011**: My computer is unstable

1:20:45 AM **Jeff Candel**: ok

1:21:21 AM **Jeff Candel**: have you closed some programs nows?

1:21:54 AM **ladydi2011**: yeah

1:22:15 AM **ladydi2011**: *Why is your IP address from Nigeria?*

1:24:14 AM **Jeff Candel**: baby what do you mean by that

1:24:34 AM **Jeff Candel**: *i* dont understand baby

1:26:05 AM **ladydi2011**: From an email address the ip address where the email is coming from can be found and yours is not London, it is Nigeria

1:27:02 AM **Jeff Candel**: *i* really dont know how its happened ok

1:27:34 AM **Jeff Candel**: its may be the network am using baby

1:27:52 AM **Jeff Candel**: am using visa phone network

1:28:08 AM **Jeff Candel**: *visafone network*

1:28:50 AM **ladydi2011**: *What is visafone network?*

1:29:10 AM **Jeff Candel**: *its a network here for browsing hun*

1:29:23 AM **Jeff Candel**: its work with the internet

1:30:07 AM **ladydi2011**: Yeah, but this is your email

1:30:41 AM **Jeff Candel**: sure its can be also hun

1:31:18 AM **Jeff Candel**: since the visafone is on my computer deffinately my email will also care it along too

1:32:48 AM **ladydi2011**: Hmmmmm

1:33:15 AM **ladydi2011**: *Please come on cam*

466

1:33:31 AM **Jeff Candel**: *baby i told you my cam is bad havnt i*

1:33:51 AM **Jeff Candel**: even before my daughter took ill

1:34:28 AM **ladydi2011**: It was but then you fixed it

1:34:52 AM **Jeff Candel**: that will be when *i* fixed it

1:35:02 AM **Jeff Candel**: baby *i* ask you something

1:35:08 AM **Jeff Candel**: what is your full name?

1:36:07 AM **ladydi2011**: Why do you want my full name?

1:36:24 AM **Jeff Candel**: just wanna know baby

1:36:41 AM **Jeff Candel**: if you wanna know my is JEFFERY CANDELL

1:36:45 AM **Jeff Candel**: ok

1:37:06 AM **ladydi2011**: Mine is Diana Wesley

1:37:33 AM **Jeff Candel**: ok

1:37:50 AM **Jeff Candel**: *so baby what is your mind now?*

1:38:22 AM **ladydi2011**: I want to know if you are who you say you are

1:39:03 AM **Jeff Candel**: baby do we have to go on this again

1:39:21 AM **Jeff Candel**: *i* have told you and show you who *i* am

1:39:30 AM **Jeff Candel**: *i* dont know what you want me to do again

1:39:47 AM **Jeff Candel**: *or do you want me to kill myself for you to know who i am*

1:39:59 AM **ladydi2011**: Please do not say things like this

1:40:10 AM **Jeff Candel**: baby *i* have to you are not helping my situation here

1:41:55 AM **ladydi2011**: So, how can I get past this fear?

1:42:31 AM **Jeff Candel**: baby you just have to ok

1:42:58 AM **Jeff Candel**: there is no way you can acept anything in your mind with this doubt

1:43:09 AM **ladydi2011**: Yeah, *i* know

1:43:29 AM **Jeff Candel**: baby *i* dont wanna loose you

1:43:47 AM **Jeff Candel**: you are the air that *i* breath..for long now *i* hardly breath baby

1:44:16 AM **Jeff Candel**: you left without saying good bye to me and my daughter

1:44:25 AM **ladydi2011**: I am sorry

1:45:01 AM **Jeff Candel**: its ok

1:45:12 AM **ladydi2011**: You are so understanding

1:45:14 AM **ladydi2011**: Why?

1:45:39 AM **Jeff Candel**: may be that is just the way *i* was brought up by my parent

1:46:02 AM **Jeff Candel**: they always have this nice patience and understanding

1:46:17 AM **Jeff Candel**: so *i* learnt it from them

1:46:27 AM **Jeff Candel**: my dad *is* such an understanding man and my mom love him so much

1:49:30 AM **Jeff Candel**: baby are you there

1:50:51 AM **Jeff Candel**: *i* will always love you no matter what happened baby

1:51:49 AM **Jeff Candel**: *baby i want you to promise me that you will never break my heart again*

1:53:14 AM **ladydi2011**: I promise I will not break your heart

1:53:35 AM **Jeff Candel**: baby you promise?

1:54:04 AM **ladydi2011:** *Please do not ask me for money again....promise?*

1:54:45 AM **Jeff Candel**: *sure baby*

1:55:13 AM **Jeff Candel**: *baby does that mean when i need your help you cant help me*

1:55:39 AM **ladydi2011**: We need to meet in person

1:55:49 AM **Jeff Candel**: *i* know that baby

1:56:17 AM **Jeff Candel**: *you know i told you that my retiredment will me this month so me and my daughter is planning of coming to your place*

1:56:45 AM **ladydi2011**: Once we have met I would give you everything I have ok hun

1:57:33 AM **Jeff Candel**: once am done *i* will let you know when am coming ok

1:57:41 AM **ladydi2011**: Ok

1:57:58 AM **Jeff Candel**: baby *i* cant wait to be with you hun

1:58:08 AM **Jeff Candel**: *i* wanna make love to you

1:59:26 AM **ladydi2011**: Where is this coming from?

2:01:08 AM **Jeff Candel**: what is that baby

2:01:34 AM **ladydi2011**: You still desire me like this?

2:01:48 AM **Jeff Candel**: sure baby *i* still do baby no matter what you have done to me ok

2:04:44 AM **Jeff Candel**: *i* have forgive you long time ago

2:05:26 AM **Jeff Candel**: *if our Lord God can forgive us of our sin who am i not to forgive baby*

2:05:39 AM **Jeff Candel**: you did nothing wrong k

2:05:44 AM **ladydi2011**: This is true

2:05:56 AM **Jeff Candel**: you are just trying to protect yourself ok

2:06:06 AM **ladydi2011**: I was

2:06:18 AM **Jeff Candel**: *i* dont have any crost with you ok

2:06:42 AM **Jeff Candel**: *i* love you and *i* will always love you ok

2:07:29 AM **ladydi2011**: Where do we go from here?

2:07:44 AM **Jeff Candel**: if *i* dont learn how to forgive you now.. is it when will are together *i* will now start to learn it

2:09:51 AM **Jeff Candel**: *i* want you to believe in the love *i* have for you baby

2:10:26 AM **ladydi2011**: Ok, I know I want to meet you and Sarah in person

2:10:42 AM **Jeff Candel**: sure baby and will want to meet you in person too hun

2:11:28 AM **ladydi2011**: I wish you said...you will meet me in person

2:11:52 AM **Jeff Candel**: sure baby *i* will meet you in person too baby

2:12:31 AM **ladydi2011**: Jeff, I am really glad we connected again tonight

2:13:49 AM **Jeff Candel**: am glad too baby

2:14:02 AM **Jeff Candel**: *what have you been thinking about me baby*

2:14:15 AM **Jeff Candel**: if only you do think about me

2:15:49 AM **Jeff Candel**: *i* tried not to think about you because you hurt me so bad

2:16:02 AM **Jeff Candel**: but my heart kept beating for you

2:16:26 AM **Jeff Candel**: *i* find it very difficult to stop thinking about you

2:16:48 AM **Jeff Candel**: *i* guess we are meet to be together hun

2:16:51 AM **ladydi2011**: Is it because of anger or love?

2:17:53 AM **Jeff Candel**: baby we both love each others and *i* dont want anything to seperate us ok

2:19:02 AM **Jeff Candel**: baby have you gotten any way *i* can send you a txt

2:19:21 AM **Jeff Candel**: since you are no longer with that old one

2:19:34 AM **ladydi2011**: I have the same number

2:19:50 AM **ladydi2011**: We keep our numbers here

2:20:05 AM **Jeff Candel**: so if *i* send you txt on that number you will get it?

2:20:09 AM **ladydi2011**: Yes

2:20:14 AM **Jeff Candel**: ok baby

2:20:26 AM **ladydi2011**: Do you still have my number?

2:20:38 AM **Jeff Candel**: why not baby

2:20:47 AM **Jeff Candel**: if only you have change it

2:20:57 AM **ladydi2011**: I haven't

2:21:20 AM **ladydi2011**: It is 2:21 am here and I need to go to sleep

2:21:31 AM **ladydi2011**: I need to get up at 6:00
2:21:32 AM **Jeff Candel**: its ok hun
2:21:40 AM **Jeff Candel**: *i* will send you a txt ok
2:21:43 AM **ladydi2011**: Ok
2:21:49 AM **Jeff Candel**: *i* love you hun
2:21:56 AM **ladydi2011**: Night
2:22:02 AM **Jeff Candel**: night hun
2:22:05 AM **Jeff Candel**: swt dreams
2:22:11 AM **ladydi2011**: You too
2:22:25 AM **Jeff Candel**: kisssssss
2:22:29 AM **Jeff Candel**: hugssssssssss
2:22:57 AM **Jeff Candel**: love u

IM Jul 3, 2012 5:39:17 PM

5:39:17 PM **Jeff Candel**: hi

IM Jul 3, 2012 8:48:26 PM

8:48:26 PM **ladydi2011**: Hey...are you there?

I didn't talk to him again for ten days but he didn't give up. When I finally did talk to him, he instantly talked about trust and love. He said Sarah is asking about me. Really? I had never even talked to Sarah. He started to put things together that I am going to use his story for this book.

 RED FLAGS

- He said what most scammers say, that I am the only person on the planet he can call for help. Again, this is a manipulation to obtain money.
- He played dumb about blocking his number. This is another red flag.
- He again brought up that he showed himself on cam so I should believe him.
- He also brought God up again when he said he knows his God is not sleeping and his daughter will be released. Then said he does not have the money to pay for her release because of how ruff it is for him and that is why he is asking me to help him out. He tried desperately to get the money. He dropped the amount to $850 and pleaded with me to send it. When a scammer cannot get the origional amount of money asked for they always lower the amount. He said all he needs me to do is send the money.
- Again he mentioned that he feels like killing himself. He then promised me he will never do anything to hurt me and again asks me to trust him and be committed to him because he

can't explain to Sarah why she's still in the hospital. He did all he could to pull at my heart strings. Scammers always try to pull at yout heart strings and make you feel guilty.

🏴 He's so in love with me and wants me to give him money, yet he never took the time to know my full name till now. Something is really wrong with this picture. Because of the knowledge I gained about spells and how they need your full name to cast a spell, I gave him a bogus name. You should never give your full name out online. You can do this once you meet someone in person.

🏴 I asked him to come on cam but again he wouldn't. He knew if he showed the same fake cam again, I would surely recognize it. Remember, if a man doesn't come on cam, he is a scammer.

🏴 When I questioned him about his Nigerian IP address he played dumb and said he really does not know how that happened, and that he uses a visafone network that is used for browsing. I researched visafone (www.visafone.com.ng) and found that Visafone Communications Ltd was born out of the strategic acquisition of 3 CDMA mobile network operators that had been in operation for up to 8 years with 30,000 subscribers and coverage in different parts of Nigeria. So there it is, more confirmation that he is in Nigeria. Please do your research and you will learn much and it can keep you from being scammed.

🏴 When I asked him to promise never to ask me for money again, he said sure but then asked if this meant that I wouldn't help when he needs help. He will ask me for money again, just like every scammer will ask for money again and again and again.

🏴 As he asked "What have you been thinking about me baby," in the beginning, he asks it again now to see if he still has me on their hook. Watch for this question. When you hear it, you know the scammer wants to ask for money. It is another red flag.

Let me see if I can get one more "ploy" he will use to try to obtain money from me. A scammer is relentless and will continue to create new "hard luck stories" as long as you talk to them. This is why as soon as you recognize they are a scammer you MUST cut them all the way off. Please do not play with them.

They will take you on many emotional rollercoasters.

IM Jul 4, 2012 3:16:04 AM

3:16:04 AM **Jeff Candel**: baby am here
3:16:19 AM **Jeff Candel**: how are you doing

IM Jul 4, 2012 6:08:22 AM

6:08:22 AM **ladydi2011**: Morning. How are you today?

IM Jul 4, 2012 10:38:37 AM

10:38:37 AM **Jeff Candel**: <ding>
10:39:16 AM **Jeff Candel**: Baby am doing good..hope you are ok hun..miss you so much baby, hope to talk with you tonight hun..*i* love you

IM Jul 4, 2012 2:59:54 PM

2:59:54 PM **Jeff Candel**: hello baby

IM Jul 4, 2012 8:30:03 PM

8:30:03 PM **Jeff Candel**: hello hun

IM Jul 5, 2012 8:52:21 AM

8:52:21 AM **ladydi2011**: Hello baby

IM Jul 5, 2012 2:55:58 PM

2:55:58 PM **Jeff Candel**: <ding>
2:56:17 PM **Jeff Candel**: how are you doing baby

IM Jul 5, 2012 3:20:42 PM

3:20:42 PM **ladydi2011**: I am here
3:21:02 PM **Jeff Candel**: how are you doing baby
3:21:26 PM **ladydi2011**: I am tired but ok
3:21:35 PM **ladydi2011**: How are you?
3:21:40 PM **Jeff Candel**: am good \
3:21:52 PM **Jeff Candel**: *i* was thinking about you and also worried hun
3:22:23 PM **ladydi2011**: What were you thinking and why are you worried?
3:22:38 PM **Jeff Candel**: alot hun
3:22:54 PM **Jeff Candel**: *i was thinking about you and i spending the rest of our life together*
3:23:14 PM **Jeff Candel**: and also worried that where ever you are now you are not doing good hun
3:23:27 PM **ladydi2011**: Ok, please tell me more
3:24:32 PM **Jeff Candel**: *i was having a little rest and i fel asleep and in that sleep i dremt and saw you touching my face with your soft hands*
3:24:41 PM **ladydi2011**: Why do you think I am not doing well?

3:24:47 PM **Jeff Candel:** *and when we where smiling at each others wiht your sexy lips on my lips i was holding you closed to me heart and your arms on my chest baby*

3:28:28 PM **Jeff Candel:** *baby the more reason why i want you to come online is that i will be traveling to south Africa soon*

3:28:59 PM **ladydi2011:** Why to South Africa?

3:29:18 PM **Jeff Candel:** *i want to go and buy some crude oil*

3:29:32 PM **ladydi2011:** Ok

3:29:40 PM **Jeff Candel:** *i* just have a contrat of supplying some client

3:29:57 PM **Jeff Candel:** they just ask me if *i* have to supply to them

3:30:00 PM **ladydi2011:** This is good

3:30:19 PM **Jeff Candel:** so any moment from now *i* will be going to south Africa

3:30:34 PM **Jeff Candel:** *i* just said *i* should let you know this hun

3:31:06 PM **ladydi2011:** This is what you wanted right?

3:31:17 PM **Jeff Candel:** yes baby

3:31:41 PM **ladydi2011:** This is a good thing

3:31:48 PM **Jeff Candel:** yes hun am so happy right now

3:32:09 PM **ladydi2011:** I am happy for you

3:32:18 PM **Jeff Candel:** Thank you hun am glad you are happy for me

3:32:43 PM **ladydi2011:** Who will look after Sarah while you are gone?

3:33:24 PM **Jeff Candel:** *i* will take Sarah to my wife mother place

3:33:43 PM **ladydi2011:** Ok. Good!

3:33:56 PM **ladydi2011:** How is Sarah?

3:34:10 PM **Jeff Candel:** well she is fine we are managing

3:34:20 PM **ladydi2011:** Good

3:34:32 PM **Jeff Candel:** *its only God that has been helping us*

3:34:36 PM **ladydi2011:** You are a good father

3:34:43 PM **Jeff Candel:** thank you hun

3:34:49 PM **ladydi2011:** He always does

3:34:57 PM **Jeff Candel:** what will *i* do if not to be there for her she is my only eye

3:35:43 PM **ladydi2011:** She is very precious

3:35:55 PM **Jeff Candel:** yes hun she is

3:36:03 PM **Jeff Candel:** she is all *i* gat baby

3:37:10 PM **ladydi2011:** So what else have you been thinking about?

3:37:37 PM **Jeff Candel:** baby *i* want you to know that *i* think alot about you

3:38:20 PM **ladydi2011:** I think a lot about you too

3:39:09 PM **Jeff Candel:** really baby

3:39:23 PM **Jeff Candel:** *i* thounght you have forgting about me hun

3:39:55 PM **ladydi2011:** Why would you think this?

3:40:52 PM **Jeff Candel:** baby because *i* was so scared *i* have offended you and *i* was thinking you will never have me in your mind again

3:43:42 PM **ladydi2011:** Much has happened that I am still confused about. I have left our relationship in God's hands.

3:44:12 PM **Jeff Candel:** really

3:44:16 PM **ladydi2011:** If we are meant to be together it will happen.

3:44:39 PM **Jeff Candel:** baby *i* want you to understand that *i will never do anthing to hurt your feelings* and the love you have for me hun

3:44:49 PM **ladydi2011:** If not, then it won't

3:45:01 PM **Jeff Candel**: *baby will you marry me* ?

3:45:14 PM **Jeff Candel**: *i want you to <u>answer me now</u>*

3:45:19 PM **ladydi2011**: Wow!!!

3:45:26 PM **Jeff Candel**: *think about it and <u>get back to me now</u>*

3:46:18 PM **ladydi2011**: *Jeff, Don't you think we need to meet in person first*

3:46:43 PM **Jeff Candel**: *baby its does not matter if we meet or not ok*

3:46:55 PM **Jeff Candel**: *i need you to <u>tell me now</u> if you will marry me*

3:46:58 PM **Jeff Candel**: *<u>now</u>*

3:47:00 PM **Jeff Candel**: *<u>now</u>*

3:47:50 PM **ladydi2011**: Why do you need me to tell you now honey? Why is this so urgent?

3:48:09 PM **Jeff Candel**: *baby <u>its has to be now</u>*

3:48:39 PM **Jeff Candel**: baby *i* dont wanna loose you ok

3:48:58 PM **Jeff Candel**: *i want you to be the person i will spend the rest of my life with till death come baby*

3:49:22 PM **Jeff Candel**: understand this is the heart of man talking now ok

3:51:03 PM **ladydi2011**: Getting married is not going to hold on to me. Who you are with me on a daily basis is what is going to keep me.

3:51:31 PM **Jeff Candel**: sure baby..you are my heart and my body and soul hun

3:51:49 PM **ladydi2011**: It is all about relationship

3:52:18 PM **Jeff Candel**: *i swear by my soul and body that you are the woman i want to spend the rest of my life with*

3:52:44 PM **Jeff Candel**: *i want you to know that relationship always end up in marriege right and that is what am trying to do right now*

3:53:03 PM **Jeff Candel**: *i* want to have you to myself forever hun

3:53:49 PM **ladydi2011**: I am here

3:54:09 PM **Jeff Candel**: *i* know you are not ok

3:54:17 PM **ladydi2011**: I would much rather you propose to me in person

3:54:23 PM **Jeff Candel**: will you marry me hun?

3:54:50 PM **Jeff Candel**: *let the spirit work together hun*

3:55:01 PM **ladydi2011**: What do you mean that you know I am not ok?

3:55:01 PM **Jeff Candel**: *let my soul be your soul and my body be your body*

3:55:48 PM **Jeff Candel**: *i* mean *i* know that already

3:56:22 PM **Jeff Candel**: *i* know you are not going any where

3:56:28 PM **Jeff Candel**: that was what *i* mean hun

3:56:38 PM **ladydi2011**: Ok

3:57:14 PM **ladydi2011**: When will you be coming to see me?

3:57:35 PM **Jeff Candel**: baby as soon am done with everything *i* am doing here

3:57:47 PM **Jeff Candel**: *i* really need to get myself back on track ok

3:58:00 PM **ladydi2011**: I know

3:58:34 PM **Jeff Candel**: *you where the one that ask me to stop asking you for money*

3:58:42 PM **ladydi2011**: Yes

3:58:50 PM **Jeff Candel**: *so am trying to look for it myself and see where God takes me to*

3:59:16 PM **ladydi2011**: This is excellent

3:59:35 PM **Jeff Candel**: *i want you to know that am not after your money ok*

3:59:51 PM **Jeff Candel**: *dont think that am after your money*

3:59:55 PM **Jeff Candel**: *am not like that ok*

4:00:05 PM **ladydi2011**: Ok

4:00:56 PM **ladydi2011**: All this online stuff is crazy

4:01:40 PM **Jeff Candel**: what do you mean that all this line are crazy

4:02:48 PM **ladydi2011**: Hard to explain

4:03:04 PM **Jeff Candel**: what does that mean hun

4:03:19 PM **Jeff Candel**: please dont get me angry here ok

4:03:38 PM **ladydi2011**: I am grateful for it or we wouldn't have met

4:04:15 PM **ladydi2011**: The distance (miles) that are between us is crazy

4:04:44 PM **ladydi2011**: We talk to a screen

4:05:12 PM **Jeff Candel**: we talk to a screen

4:05:19 PM **ladydi2011**: I want to see you in the flesh

4:05:24 PM **Jeff Candel**: what is that surpose to mean

4:05:31 PM **Jeff Candel**: *i* dont understand baby

4:05:41 PM **Jeff Candel**: why dont you come out please

4:06:09 PM **ladydi2011**: What do you mean by come out?

4:06:35 PM **Jeff Candel**: *i* mean you should spit it out to the way *i* will understand

4:06:47 PM **ladydi2011**: Lol

4:07:05 PM **Jeff Candel**: baby *i* want you to know that there is no distance that is too far for love to travel

4:07:17 PM **Jeff Candel**: what is funny baby

4:07:26 PM **Jeff Candel**: why are you laughing?

4:07:29 PM **ladydi2011**: I mean I wish we could be together in person instead of on line

4:07:57 PM **Jeff Candel**: baby we must be together ok'

4:08:03 PM **ladydi2011**: Did you see my last message?

4:08:27 PM **Jeff Candel**: on here?

4:08:54 PM **ladydi2011**: I mean I wish we could be together in person instead of on line

4:09:23 PM **Jeff Candel**: ok baby

4:09:29 PM **ladydi2011**: I am a touchy, feely type of gal

4:09:40 PM **Jeff Candel**: *i* understand

4:09:55 PM **ladydi2011**: I want to look into your eyes

4:09:55 PM **Jeff Candel**: baby *i* need you more than you need your self baby and *i* want to feel the softness of your skin baby

4:11:06 PM **ladydi2011**: I hope everything goes well in South Africa.

4:12:43 PM **Jeff Candel**: ok baby

4:13:03 PM **ladydi2011**: I am counting on you!

4:13:28 PM **ladydi2011**: I will be waiting for you

4:14:22 PM **Jeff Candel**: and *i* will also let you know howmits gose

4:14:58 PM **Jeff Candel**: baby you are my strenght in life

4:15:40 PM **Jeff Candel**: *i* love you so much baby

4:17:14 PM **ladydi2011**: Please keep me posted on how it goes

4:17:27 PM **Jeff Candel**: ok baby *i* will *i* promise hun

4:17:57 PM **ladydi2011**: Thank you

Break In Time

4:22:19 PM **Jeff Candel**: you so much wellcome babe

4:23:35 PM **ladydi2011**: We will text or chat tomorrow, yes?

4:23:49 PM **Jeff Candel**: yes baby

4:24:00 PM **ladydi2011**: Ok

4:24:00 PM **Jeff Candel**: that is fine by me

4:24:12 PM **ladydi2011**: I have to go now
4:24:21 PM **Jeff Candel**: ok baby
4:24:24 PM **Jeff Candel**: *i* love you
4:24:35 PM **ladydi2011**: I love you too
4:24:41 PM **Jeff Candel**: no *i* love you more
4:25:17 PM **ladydi2011**: Bye for now
4:25:19 PM **Jeff Candel**: million kisses to you
4:25:34 PM **ladydi2011**: Got them

IM Jul 6, 2012 6:56:08 PM

6:56:08 PM **Jeff Candel**: hello hun
6:57:27 PM **ladydi2011**: hello babe
6:57:31 PM **ladydi2011**: how are you?
6:57:44 PM **Jeff Candel**: am good baby
6:57:55 PM **Jeff Candel**: and you?
6:57:58 PM **ladydi2011**: What is happening there?
6:58:10 PM **ladydi2011**: I am good today. I was sick yesterday
6:58:22 PM **Jeff Candel**: ooh really
6:58:28 PM **Jeff Candel**: what happened baby
6:58:32 PM **Jeff Candel**: you did not tell me
6:58:36 PM **Jeff Candel**: why?
7:00:01 PM **ladydi2011**: I was sleeping honey
7:00:22 PM **Jeff Candel**: you should have told me baby
7:01:23 PM **ladydi2011**: I am sorry honey
7:01:38 PM **ladydi2011**: I had a migraine that was really bad, tired and a fever
7:01:45 PM **ladydi2011**: I am much better now
7:02:04 PM **Jeff Candel**: good to hear that
7:02:11 PM **Jeff Candel**: am so sorry hun
7:02:24 PM **ladydi2011**: Thanks baby...part of life!
7:02:35 PM **Jeff Candel**: sure hun
7:02:43 PM **Jeff Candel**: baby you know when you are sick *i* ma sick too
7:02:48 PM **ladydi2011**: What is going on with the South Africa deal?
7:03:04 PM **Jeff Candel**: baby am still working on it
7:03:08 PM **ladydi2011**: Cool
7:03:09 PM **Jeff Candel**: by next week baby
7:03:15 PM **Jeff Candel**: *i* should be living
7:03:21 PM **ladydi2011**:????
7:03:34 PM **Jeff Candel**: they called me today
7:03:37 PM **ladydi2011**: Ok
7:03:47 PM **Jeff Candel**: so next week am going to supply them
7:04:02 PM **ladydi2011**: Cool
7:04:09 PM **ladydi2011**: How is Sarah?
7:04:30 PM **Jeff Candel**: she is fine hun
7:04:39 PM **Jeff Candel**: *she kept asking after you hun*
7:04:50 PM **Jeff Candel**: *i told her that you aks after her too hun*

7:05:07 PM **ladydi2011**: Good

7:05:16 PM **ladydi2011**: Give her a hug for me please

7:05:51 PM **Jeff Candel**: *i* love you baby

7:06:02 PM **ladydi2011**: Are you really ok?

7:06:15 PM **Jeff Candel**: *baby we thank God*

7:06:25 PM **Jeff Candel**: *i* dont wanna ask you for anything now *i* dont want you to leave me again

7:06:51 PM **Jeff Candel**: it has not be easy with me here hun but *i* dont want you to leave ma again

7:07:32 PM **ladydi2011**: It has not been easy here either honey

7:07:57 PM **Jeff Candel**: am really facing it hard here baby

7:09:38 PM **Jeff Candel**: baby am not after your money ok

7:10:15 PM **Jeff Candel**: so you think because of your money that is why am in love with you

7:10:23 PM **Jeff Candel**: isn that what you are thinking?

7:10:41 PM **Jeff Candel**: baby know this *i* never love because of money ok

7:10:46 PM **ladydi2011**: I don't have money

7:11:19 PM **Jeff Candel**: *i* understand baby

7:11:27 PM **Jeff Candel**: God will make things up for both of us

7:11:44 PM **Jeff Candel**: *i* know how it is ok

7:11:59 PM **ladydi2011**: I want real love

7:12:03 PM **Jeff Candel**: he will

7:12:04 PM **ladydi2011**: You know this

7:12:27 PM **Jeff Candel**: yes baby *i* know that and *i* love you when you come out natural to me ok

7:13:02 PM **ladydi2011**: Thanks baby

7:13:23 PM **Jeff Candel**: money is not everything ok

7:13:34 PM **ladydi2011**: I am just a woman looking for a man to love me unconditionally

7:13:37 PM **Jeff Candel**: what *i* want is happiness and love

7:13:45 PM **ladydi2011**: Me too baby

7:13:52 PM **ladydi2011**: Money comes and goes

7:14:04 PM **ladydi2011**: Jobs come and go

7:14:07 PM **Jeff Candel**: sure baby

7:14:09 PM **ladydi2011**: With real love all things can be conquered

7:14:19 PM **Jeff Candel**: will really have to be natural to each other ok

7:14:45 PM **Jeff Candel**: and lets make things happen ok

7:15:03 PM **Jeff Candel**: *We have to work together to make a parfect home*

7:15:25 PM **ladydi2011**: I agree

7:16:23 PM **Jeff Candel**: so baby tell me how are you doing now

7:16:35 PM **ladydi2011**: I am ok

7:16:42 PM **Jeff Candel**: have you see doc to know what is wrong with you

7:17:22 PM **ladydi2011**: I have not seen a doctor

7:17:48 PM **Jeff Candel**: why baby?

7:17:59 PM **Jeff Candel**: am not comfortable with that baby

7:18:05 PM **Jeff Candel**: you have to visit the doc ok

7:20:36 PM **Jeff Candel**: you know what baby *i* want you to know that ok

7:21:25 PM **ladydi2011**: I know honey

7:23:22 PM **Jeff Candel**: *hun dont you like investing on a business?*

7:23:58 PM **ladydi2011**: I do

7:24:12 PM **Jeff Candel**: have you invest in any business before?

7:24:26 PM **ladydi2011**: It is storming here really bad and I should shut the computer down

7:24:35 PM **ladydi2011**: Can you come on line again later baby?
7:24:50 PM **Jeff Candel**: its ok may be later then ok
7:25:32 PM **ladydi2011**: Ok honey
7:25:43 PM **ladydi2011**: They are calling for tornadoes
7:25:48 PM **ladydi2011**: They scare me
7:25:59 PM **Jeff Candel**: its ok baby just stay inside ok dont go out
7:26:17 PM **ladydi2011**: I will
7:26:28 PM **Jeff Candel**: ok
7:26:31 PM **ladydi2011**: Bye for now
7:26:32 PM **Jeff Candel**: love you hun
7:26:36 PM **Jeff Candel**: ok
7:26:38 PM **Jeff Candel**: bye

IM Jul 7, 2012 6:03:11 PM

6:03:11 PM **Jeff Candel**: hello hun
6:03:17 PM **Jeff Candel**: how are you doing
6:03:26 PM **Jeff Candel**: are you online now baby?
6:03:33 PM **Jeff Candel**: please come online ok
6:03:42 PM **Jeff Candel**: am missing you so much baby
6:24:13 PM **ladydi2011**: Hi baby....
6:24:36 PM **Jeff Candel**: hey my love
6:24:44 PM **Jeff Candel**: how are you doing today
6:27:21 PM **ladydi2011**: Hello
6:27:31 PM **Jeff Candel**: baby am here

IM Jul 8, 2012 6:46:23 PM

6:46:23 PM **Jeff Candel**: hello baby
6:57:25 PM **Jeff Candel**: <ding>
6:57:33 PM **Jeff Candel**: baby am online now ok
6:57:59 PM **Jeff Candel**: *i* want you to know that *i* love you and *i* will always do baby
6:58:04 PM **Jeff Candel**: *God bless you hun*
6:58:17 PM **Jeff Candel**: you are my strenght baby
6:58:28 PM **Jeff Candel**: kisssssssss... hugssss to you my queen
6:58:32 PM **Jeff Candel**: love you
6:58:35 PM **Jeff Candel**: nite

IM Jul 11, 2012 1:51:24 AM

1:51:24 AM **ladydi2011**: Hi honey
1:51:34 AM **ladydi2011**: How are you?
1:51:50 AM **Jeff Candel**: how are you baby

1:52:05 AM **Jeff Candel**: am just confuse here my love not knowing what to do
1:52:47 AM **ladydi2011**: Why honey?
1:53:20 AM **Jeff Candel**: *doc and people i owe money are on my neck baby*
1:53:37 AM **Jeff Candel**: *i do not know what to do now and they are threathening to get me arrested*
1:55:13 AM **Jeff Candel**: how are you doing?
1:55:42 AM **ladydi2011**: Hmmmmm
1:55:48 AM **ladydi2011**: Good
1:56:13 AM **Jeff Candel**: am stressed and right now believe me *i* do not know what to do
1:56:46 AM **Jeff Candel**: *i even sold my gold wrist watch yesterday and still is not up to the said amount*
1:57:57 AM **Jeff Candel**: *right now am do not know who to ask to lend me*
1:58:19 AM **Jeff Candel**: *and am even scared to ask you due to the last time you know*

2:00:18 AM **Jeff Candel**:
2:00:58 AM **Jeff Candel**: sorry for bothering you with my problems anyway
2:01:04 AM **Jeff Candel**: how was your day??
2:01:20 AM **ladydi2011**: You promised me you would never ask me for money
2:01:46 AM **Jeff Candel**: yes and that why am just telling you now and am not asking
2:02:04 AM **Jeff Candel**: just telling you how *i* feel
2:02:28 AM **Jeff Candel**: *but if you feel you can help it ok but if you do not it fine by me too*
2:02:30 AM **ladydi2011**: I am really sorry you are going through this
2:04:11 AM **Jeff Candel**: *how will you feel when sarah give you a call and let you know that <u>his</u> father has been arrested for a small amount that would have been sorted out... think about it... how will you feel when you hear am in jail??*
2:05:50 AM **ladydi2011**: Stop it Jeff
2:06:12 AM **ladydi2011**: Keep your guilt tactics to yourself
2:06:24 AM **Jeff Candel**: just saying the truth
2:06:48 AM **Jeff Candel**: *i* love you and you know what *i* will do if *i* was in your shoes
2:07:00 AM **Jeff Candel**: but it ok by me since it your decision
2:07:20 AM **Jeff Candel**: *i* love you and nothing can ever change that '
2:08:48 AM **ladydi2011**: Yeah
2:09:00 AM **ladydi2011**: Drama
2:09:19 AM **Jeff Candel**: what do you mean by that?
2:09:25 AM **Jeff Candel**: why did you say that?

IM Jul 14, 2012 9:08:44 PM

9:08:44 PM **Jeff Candel**: hello baby
9:09:30 PM **Jeff Candel**: <ding>
9:09:37 PM **Jeff Candel**: hun are you there?
9:14:56 PM **Jeff Candel**: hun talk to me

IM Jul 15, 2012 4:59:04 PM

4:59:04 PM **Jeff Candel**: Baby its be long we talk baby
4:59:16 PM **Jeff Candel**: And am missing you so much baby

IM Jul 18, 2012 7:37:10 PM

7:37:10 PM **Jeff Candel**: hello baby
7:37:16 PM **Jeff Candel**: how are you doing today
7:37:27 PM **Jeff Candel**: its be long *i* heard from you
7:37:35 PM **Jeff Candel**: *i* hope you are doing fine

IM Jul 18, 2012 8:51:51 PM

8:51:51 PM **ladydi2011**: I am well, and you?
8:51:52 PM **ladydi2011**: Hello
8:52:18 PM **Jeff Candel**: baby where have you been
8:52:30 PM **Jeff Candel**: you dont respond to my txt
8:52:36 PM **ladydi2011**: Busy honey.
8:52:49 PM **Jeff Candel**: too busy to txt me back right?
8:52:55 PM **ladydi2011**: I haven't received any text.
8:53:03 PM **Jeff Candel**: *i* sent you txt baby
8:53:23 PM **ladydi2011**: Didn't get it baby
8:53:32 PM **Jeff Candel**: its okay how is life with you hun
8:54:02 PM **ladydi2011**: Ok...getting ready to travel!
8:54:30 PM **Jeff Candel**: yes baby
8:54:49 PM **ladydi2011**: Where are you now?
8:55:01 PM **Jeff Candel**: baby are you planing of travling?
8:55:25 PM **ladydi2011**: Yep
8:55:30 PM **Jeff Candel**: to where hun?
8:55:46 PM **ladydi2011**: Texas and Africa
8:55:58 PM **Jeff Candel**: where in africa baby and what are you going to do in africa?
8:56:24 PM **ladydi2011**: Lagos
8:56:33 PM **Jeff Candel**: lagos to do what baby
8:56:41 PM **ladydi2011**: Meet some people
8:56:51 PM **Jeff Candel**: what people baby?
8:57:25 PM **ladydi2011**: People who came clean with me
8:57:42 PM **Jeff Candel**: *i* dont understand baby
8:58:15 PM **ladydi2011**: Scammers
8:58:42 PM **Jeff Candel**: scammers?
8:58:58 PM **Jeff Candel**: *i* dont understand what you mean by scammers
8:59:39 PM **ladydi2011**: So where are you?
9:00:11 PM **Jeff Candel**: am in South Africa right now
9:00:18 PM **Jeff Candel**: *i* told you right

9:00:40 PM **ladydi2011**: How's it going there?
9:00:50 PM **Jeff Candel**: cool baby
9:01:13 PM **Jeff Candel**: just trying to make sure am done with everything am doing on here
9:01:25 PM **ladydi2011**: This is great!
9:01:40 PM **Jeff Candel**: *just that there is something i really need you to do for me baby*
9:01:58 PM **Jeff Candel**: *here i find it hard to access my account here*
9:02:05 PM **Jeff Candel**: and *i* dont understand baby
9:02:29 PM **ladydi2011**: Don't understand what?
9:02:29 PM **Jeff Candel**: *the bank said that i will need to activate it first before making use of it*
9:02:39 PM **ladydi2011**: Hmmmm
9:03:20 PM **ladydi2011**: *And?*
9:04:13 PM **Jeff Candel**: *the bank said i will need to pay the sum of $750 before they can activate*
9:04:40 PM **ladydi2011**: Ok
9:04:43 PM **Jeff Candel**: and *i* dont have now the cash with *i* have use it to pay my hotel bilss
9:05:15 PM **ladydi2011**: You are too much my dear
9:05:49 PM **Jeff Candel**: what do you mean by that ?
9:05:54 PM **Jeff Candel**: *i* dont understand
9:06:46 PM **ladydi2011**: *I know you are a YAHOO BOY and that you used a fake cam with me. You continue to try to insult my intelligence...*
9:07:11 PM **Jeff Candel**: what an insult
9:08:13 PM **ladydi2011**: I gotta go baby!
9:08:23 PM **Jeff Candel**: its ok
9:08:24 PM **ladydi2011**: Take care...
9:08:29 PM **Jeff Candel**: no prob
9:08:39 PM **Jeff Candel**: take cra eof yourself baby
9:08:48 PM **ladydi2011**: U 2

He said he wanted to marry me and expected my answer right then. What? We never even met in person. Obtaining money from me was his objective and he tried everything he could think of to accomplish it.

He had many stories, just like all scammers.

RED FLAGS

- 🚩 Another manipulation of the scammer is to claim "We have to work together to make a perfect home."
- 🚩 Now for another story he said he would be leaving for South Africa soon to buy some crude oil. He tried to convince me that he was not after my money. He asked if I don't like investing in a business so later he could ask me to invest in his crude oil business. I cut him off prior to him going down that road.
- 🚩 He claimed people were threatening to arrest him for money owed and said he was scared to ask me. "But if you feel you can help it ok but if you do not it fine by me too." Then it's back to the guilt trip with "how will you feel when sarah give you a call and let you know

that "his" father has been arrested for a small amount that would have been sorted out... think about it... how will you feel when you hear am in jail?" More guilt! Did you catch "he" instead of "she" when referring to Sarah?

⚐ Supposedly he couldn't access his account from South Africa and he needs $750 to activate it.

⚐ Most scammers use dreams they "supposedly" have as part of their format. He has followed suit.

I already got many formats from him to show you how scammers operate, and I couldn't stand to chat with him anymore. Once I called him a "Yahoo Boy" I never heard from him again. He knew he was never going to get money from me. Whew, I am so glad to be done with this man! I hope you learned a lot about the ploys scammers use and that this will keep you from being scammed.

In the next chapter you will learn what a "small money" scammer who is not on top of his game looks like. This chapter ends with an unexpected twist of valuable information to keep you safe.

CHAPTER 5

AN UNEXPECTED TWIST...

I didn't think I was going to get this story because we just didn't seem to connect, but something told me I had to try to capture his attention for this story, so I chased him. After I caught him, I quickly learned that this man was not on top of his game. He did not have a cohesive story and tried to get money from me too quickly. He is a good example of a *small money* scammer. I was shocked by where he wanted me to send the money and how this story ended, and you will be too!

His profile found on *Singlesbee:*

Profile: Newlovelife49

Looking For Love And No Head Games Please
47-year-old man in Charlotte, NC
Looking for girls 48 to 60

My Headline
Looking For Love And No Head Games Please

My Current Status
- Height: Not Specified
- Body type: Unspecified
- Ethnicity: White / Caucasian
- Education: Graduate degree
- ***Occupation: Construction and installation***
- Income: Unspecified
- I speak: English
- Religion: Catholic
- Relationship status: Divorced
- Children: Yes, living at home
- Wants children: Undecided
- Smoking: Never
- Drinking: Occasionally

My Type of Girl

- Looking for: Not Specified
- **_With: Women 48 to 60-year-old_**
- Distance: Within 0 miles of Charlotte
- Height: Not Specified
- Body type: Any
- Hair color: Any
- Ethnicity: Doesn't Matter
- Education: Doesn't Matter
- Occupation: Any
- Income: Doesn't Matter
- Language(s): English
- Religion: Any
- Relationship status: Any
- Children: Doesn't Matter
- Wants children: Doesn't Matter
- Smoking: Doesn't Matter
- Drinking: Doesn't Matter

About Me

I am sweet, thoughtful, kind, and have a great sense of humor. I am very easy going and laid back. I am often told that I am very easy to talk with. I am not an angry person, and I am not interested in someone that is. Having past events shape your life is one thing, carrying the past as a burden that sits heavily upon your shoulders is not the way I view life. I am happy with myself, and my life, and I like to think it shows. I have a wonderful Son. I would do best with someone that isn't extremely uptight, unless of course you are willing to learn to let things go! I love to try new things, and can laugh at myself when I fail miserably. I don't give up easily, and have so many things I've yet to try. Please love to laugh and have fun, what is better than laughing so hard your stomach hurts?!I love traveling, going on unknown adventures, and trying something I thought I never would. I'll try anything once, well, but fun none the less! I take pride in my appearance, but am not high maintenance. I love a nice dinner out, but staying home, having chines food after a day spent working together on a completely dirty, yet fulfilling project, can be so much fun with the right person. Being honest and open is very important to me and I expect my match to feel the same way. I am not a game player, and I don't have any interest in dating one. I do however, make exceptions for board game lovers. I am very creative and artistic. I love working on my house and digging in my gardens, I have no problem getting dirt under my nails.

I believe in a best friend to spend my life with, and if it takes awhile and I meet new friends along the way, that's a good thing too. Please have an adventurous silly side, although I can be very sophisticated when necessary, life isn't as much fun if you subdue your inner child all the time. I'm a straight and easy going person with a kind and gentle heart full of love...I love to travel and would love a partner to travel with me. I have been a workaholic in that past but last year I had a change of attitude and decided to live life now. I might live to be a 100 years old or my time could end tomorrow. Rather than wait and miss life I want to take advantage while I have the opportunity in front of me. My friends/coworkers will tell you that I am a shy person. I can be picky but I really believe that love is out of our control. I cannot create a spark or stop a spark. There is either a connection or not. I have met people online or via telephone conversations and they seem great but when we meet there is no chemistry or connection. It is not all about looks especially as we get older but none-the-less there has to be a physical attraction. A personality can make someone cuter or uglier as you get to know them. Profiles help but lack personal interaction and feedback that can only come through emails if people are honest and the true test comes at eventual Trusting each other. Long profiles are boring and we are too busy to read long drawn out introductions so I will shut up. If you want me to keep talking then send me an email and I will respond even if it is a Thanks, but no thanks. I am honest, dependable, loving, gentle, affectionate and have good friendship. I feel that a WOMAN is GOD's undeserved gift to MAN and she is supposed to be loved, reverenced, protected, respected, and cherished...Would like to go to the Hawaiian islands, like small intimate places to talk, not to much on the bar/clubs seen.. Like all types of food, I'm open to try new places and things, I also like to cook... I wish *i* have someone to cook for...I love cooking, going to the beach, Although *i* haven't gone to the beach in a long time now... stay home listening to a country or romantic song, I enjoy love story's, I'm a very sensitive person *i cry sometimes, with just watching a movie*... I usually read several books at a time. I am currently reading the following: Max Lucado - Traveling Light; *Chicken Soup for the Womans Soul;* It's All Too Much, Also 5 Languages of Love. I enjoy the outdoors, esp the beach. Walking on the beach at night, waves crashing restlessly, a million stars in the sky,, ahhh perfect for me. I also like dining out, plays, movies, art. Im pretty flexible as far as activities.. I like fishing, camping, reading, going to the movies, hanging around with friends, cracking jokes, listening to music, dancing, and also spending time with someone interesting.... Brett

RED FLAGS

- The occupation of construction and installation. Many scammers have this occupation.
- He is 47 and looking for women in the age group of 48 to 60. This is the normal age group

that scammers look for. Some will go as high as 70.

🚩 He doesn't capitalize his "I's." This is typical of scammers.

🚩 He is not specific about his height, hair color or body type. He is also not specific about the type of woman he is looking to date, which is especially unusual since he has a child. Scammers do not usually fill out the profile completely. They just want to get attention and start chatting.

🚩 The reason he had 0 miles of Charlotte is that he was trying to attract women in Charlotte because he was told women in Charlotte had money so he wanted to penetrate Charlotte.

🚩 It is unlikely that a man would put in his profile "*i cry sometimes, with just watching a movie.*" He probably copied and pasted this from a woman's profile.

🚩 He claims to be reading Chicken Soup for the Woman's Soul. This too suggests he has taken some of his material from a woman's profile. Watch for these things; they reveal a lot!

From: newlovelife49
To: ladedi
Subject: Hello
Sent: 06/06/2012 07:09PM

Hi pretty@};-@};-, how are you doing.. I'm Brett, I hope you get this IM and it finds you well, I was glancing through profiles when your gorgeous picture got me attracted while your lovely words had me write you, I really was marveled reading your profile and *i* enjoyed doing so... The first thing that came to my mind when *i* saw your picture was..

'WOW..you're drop dead GORGEOUS.. Lol... So *i* thought *i* would take out time to introduce myself.:x..you can mail or *add me to your yahoo messenger* list if you got one..(brett_robson101@yahoo.com)..hope to hear from you real soon..

From: ladedi
To: newlovelife49
Subject: Hello
Sent: 06/07/2012 10:13AM

Hello Brett,

It is nice to meet you! You have a fabulous smile! I am well, and you? Thank you so much for taking the time to read my profile and emailing me the lovely compliments. I am glad you enjoyed reading what I wrote. I am known for my honesty.

My name is Diana and my friends say "Diana is my name and blunt is my game". Life is short and I am ready to meet my "forever". I have added you to my messenger.

I look forward to chatting with you....

Diana

~ Tomorrow is shaped by the choices you make today...choose wisely!

From: ladedi
To: newlovelife49
Subject: Hello
Sent: 06/08/2012 9:01AM

Morning Brett,

My IM is ladydi2011. Please add me. I look forward to chatting. :-)

~ Tomorrow is shaped by the choices you make today...choose wisely!

From: newlovelife49
To: ladedi
Subject: Hello
Sent: 06/11/2012 10:39PM

ok..thanks for that am *so sorry about the other day..i had a call while i was chatting with you*..but please forgive for not letting you know..talk to u later

And the chatting begins...

IM Jun 8, 2012 10:17:07 AM

10:17:07 AM **ladydi2011:** Hello Brett. It is nice to meet you!
10:18:55 AM **brett_robson101:** Hello
10:19:14 AM **brett_robson101:** how are you?
10:19:28 AM **ladydi2011:** I am well, and you?
10:19:54 AM **ladydi2011:** Please tell me more about yourself.
10:20:06 AM **brett_robson101:** am doing great
10:20:14 AM **brett_robson101:** what is your name?
10:20:24 AM **ladydi2011:** Diana. Is yours Brett?
10:20:37 AM **brett_robson101:** oh..ok
10:20:40 AM **brett_robson101:** yes
10:21:09 AM **ladydi2011:** Where do you live?

488

10:22:06 AM **brett_robson101**: am from *Carlotte* NC and got a home in *ohio cleveland* where *i* get to spend holidays with my son
10:22:45 AM **ladydi2011**: Nice. I love Charlotte. I am originally from Pennsylvania.
10:23:03 AM **ladydi2011**: How old is your son?
10:25:37 AM **ladydi2011**: Are you there?

IM Jun 10, 2012 7:41:14 PM

7:41:14 PM **ladydi2011**: Hi Bret. How are you?

IM Jun 11, 2012 6:31:16 AM

6:31:16 AM **brett_robson101**: <ding>
6:32:09 AM **brett_robson101**: Hello dear how are you doing you there?

IM Jun 11, 2012 11:34:43 AM

11:34:43 AM **brett_robson101:** <ding>
11:36:51 AM **brett_robson101**: Hello, how are you doing today and how's your weekend hope you had a great time..sorry for the other time *i* had a call from my business associate so *i* had to run..hope you are not angry with me..wish *i* could chat with you..talk later and take good care

---

IM Jun 13, 2012 10:35:24 AM

10:35:24 AM **ladydi2011**: Hi Brett, How are you?
10:36:20 AM **brett_robson101**: am doing good and you?
10:37:04 AM **brett_robson101**: so sorry for the other time that *i* left *i* had a call *i* was waiting for it..
10:37:09 AM **ladydi2011**: I am well, thanks.
10:37:17 AM **ladydi2011**: It's ok. I understand
10:37:18 AM **brett_robson101**: hope you are not offended?
10:37:24 AM **ladydi2011**: Not at all.
10:37:36 AM **ladydi2011**: I run a business, so I get it!
10:37:56 AM **ladydi2011**: Promise you will not be offended if one day I have to do this to you.
10:38:17 AM **ladydi2011**: So, do you have time to chat now?
10:38:20 AM **brett_robson101**: not at all
10:38:25 AM **ladydi2011**: thank you
10:38:48 AM **brett_robson101**: so pls what is your name again?
10:38:53 AM **ladydi2011**: Diana
10:39:16 AM **brett_robson101**: oh ok..
10:39:25 AM **ladydi2011**: I live in Georgia
10:39:38 AM **ladydi2011**: Please tell me about yourself

10:40:27 AM **brett_robson101**: am from charlotte NC and got a home in *Ohio cleveland* where *i* go to spend most of my holidays with my only son Fred

10:41:04 AM **brett_robson101**: am an *INTERIOR DESIGNER/CONTRACTOR BUILDING AND ROAD CONSTRUCTION*

10:41:27 AM **ladydi2011**: I am originally from Pennsylvania

10:41:35 AM **ladydi2011**: I have lived in Georgia for 15 years

10:42:09 AM **ladydi2011**: Wow...interior design, building and road construction are worlds apart

10:42:36 AM **ladydi2011**: Which do you like best?

10:43:02 AM **brett_robson101**: construction *i* do most

10:43:25 AM **brett_robson101**: for the interior is just once in a while *i* get to do it

10:43:31 AM **brett_robson101**: *how old are you?*

10:43:53 AM **ladydi2011**: Oh, ok....cool

10:43:59 AM **ladydi2011**: I am 48 and you?

10:45:28 AM **brett_robson101**: wow same here *48 years*

10:45:58 AM **ladydi2011**: Cool

10:48:19 AM **brett_robson101**: *what do you do for a living*?

10:49:03 AM **ladydi2011**: I am a business consultant

10:50:12 AM **brett_robson101**: ok.

10:50:50 AM **ladydi2011**: I own my own business. I am also a professional speaker and author

10:51:31 AM **ladydi2011**: So, what are you looking for in a relationship?

10:53:37 AM **brett_robson101**: Well, in a relationship, we must feel easy together, be able to talk about anything, or nothing. We must love to cuddle, touch, kiss a lot, laugh, make love and do things either on the spur of the moment or with planning. I like to feel a womans strength, arms around me, holding me, spontaneously. I like an active sex life and think I will into old age.

10:56:52 AM **ladydi2011**: I like what you wrote

10:57:16 AM **ladydi2011**: I agree. Relationships must feel easy and not be hard.

10:57:46 AM **ladydi2011**: Being best friends is a must for communication to be open and free

10:57:59 AM **brett_robson101**: thanks

10:58:23 AM **ladydi2011**: Kissing, cuddling and making love are some of the best joys in life...an absolute must

10:58:40 AM **ladydi2011**: Laughing is the best medicine for the soul

10:59:02 AM **ladydi2011**: I'm want a man who is going to love me as passionately as I love him

10:59:10 AM **ladydi2011**: I will not settle for anything less

11:00:21 AM **brett_robson101**: ok

11:00:30 AM **brett_robson101**: what makes you laugh?

11:01:54 AM **ladydi2011**: Good question

11:03:30 AM **ladydi2011**: Many things....funny movies, children, when I do something foolish, cats when they do crazy things, jokes

11:03:35 AM **ladydi2011**: What about you?

11:04:11 AM **brett_robson101**: I like to tease and kid each other a bit, nothing mean, you can't tease me about my Blue lovely eyes lol ! I love laughing with others, when we are all looking at the cute antics of kids, or animals, funny movies.

11:05:24 AM **ladydi2011**: I also like to tease. Oh, and I am very ticklish...this makes me laugh

11:06:00 AM **ladydi2011**: What are your favorite foods?

11:06:01 AM **brett_robson101**: ok

11:06:19 AM **brett_robson101**: *i* love Chinese food a lot and my son too

11:06:25 AM **brett_robson101**: and you?

11:07:02 AM **ladydi2011**: Japanese hibachi is one of my favorites and Italian

11:07:09 AM **ladydi2011**: How old is your son?

11:08:03 AM **brett_robson101**: 8 years now

11:08:24 AM **ladydi2011**: What is his name?

11:08:45 AM **brett_robson101**: Fred

11:08:50 AM **brett_robson101**: *you got kids?*

11:08:59 AM **ladydi2011**: No, I do not have children

11:09:09 AM **ladydi2011**: Does Fred live with his mom?

11:09:48 AM **brett_robson101**: no. *i lost my late wife about years ago* of cancer when he was little

11:10:04 AM **brett_robson101**: so *i* have been taking good care of him since then

11:10:14 AM **ladydi2011**: I am sorry to hear this

11:10:53 AM **brett_robson101**: it ok..

11:11:17 AM **ladydi2011**: Do you travel a lot for your job?

11:14:02 AM **brett_robson101**: *yeah some time i do cos you know how it is with construction it takes almost round the world*

11:14:49 AM **brett_robson101**: *what do your parent mean to you, do have any brother or sisters?*

11:15:03 AM **ladydi2011**: Yeah, I know

11:15:32 AM **ladydi2011**: I love and respect my parents a lot. They are now 85 and 73.

11:16:05 AM **ladydi2011**: I have 5 brothers and no sisters. I lost my one brother to cancer when he was 38.

11:16:09 AM **ladydi2011**: What about you?

11:16:21 AM **ladydi2011**: What do your parents mean to you?

11:16:29 AM **ladydi2011**: Do you have siblings?

11:18:01 AM **brett_robson101**: *well i lost my parent years back and i have no siblings just me*..didn't get to know much about my father before he died and my mom was my best friend she took care of me and died later on and *i* had to struggle and get to finish my education

11:18:45 AM **ladydi2011**: Wow, we all have our own crosses to bear.

11:18:49 AM **brett_robson101**: it kind of rough but *i* think am getting ok with life..but when *i* lost my late wife *i* felt life was just not kind with me

11:18:59 AM **ladydi2011**: Congratulations on finishing your education

11:19:08 AM **brett_robson101**: thank you so much

11:19:27 AM **ladydi2011**: I am sure of this. You have had much loss in your life.

11:19:42 AM **ladydi2011**: I will not say I know how you feel because I don't.

11:19:54 AM **ladydi2011**: I have not experienced what you have.

11:20:17 AM **ladydi2011**: I learned a long time ago that we never "get it" unless we experience it

11:20:57 AM **ladydi2011**: This is why you tell your wisdom to people younger than you, but they will never really grasp it until they have the experience for themselves

11:21:21 AM **ladydi2011**: Wisdom is more precious than rubies or gold

11:22:35 AM **brett_robson101**: yes you are very correct

11:23:23 AM **ladydi2011**: So, what do you like to do in your spare time?

11:24:53 AM **ladydi2011**: brb

11:25:08 AM **brett_robson101**: I am honest, dependable, loving, gentle, affectionate and have good friendship. I feel that a WOMAN is GOD's undeserved gift to MAN and she is supposed to be loved, reverenced, protected, respected, and cherished.. Would like to go to the Hawaiian islands, like small intimate places to talk, not to much on the bar/clubs seen.. Like all types of food, I'm open to try new places and things, I also like to cook.. I wish *i* have someone to cook for...

11:25:49 AM **brett_robson101**: I love cooking, going to the beach, Although *i* haven't gone to the beach in a long time now.. stay home listening to a country or romantic song, I enjoy love storys, I'm a very sensitive person *i cry sometimes, with just watching a movie*... I usually read several books at a time. I am currently reading the following: Max Lucado - Traveling Light; *Chicken Soup for the Womans Soul;* It's All Too Much

11:26:57 AM **brett_robson101**: I enjoy the outdoors, esp the beach. Walking on the beach at night, waves crashing restlessly, a million stars in the sky,, ahhh perfect for me. I also like dining out, plays, movies, art. Im pretty flexible as far as activities.. I like fishing, camping, reading, going to the movies, hanging around with friends, cracking jokes, listening to music, dancing, and also spending time with someone interesting.

11:31:25 AM **ladydi2011**: Sorry. I am back

11:32:13 AM **ladydi2011**: I like what you wrote

11:33:15 AM **brett_robson101**: and you?

11:36:38 AM **ladydi2011**: I am very honest and dependable. I live my life with integrity. I believe the most important thing about a person is their character. I am very affectionate, loving, gentle and kind. I do hold my own. Being raised with 5 brothers has taught me a lot. I love God with all my heart. I treat the man in my life with love, honor and respect. I cherish him and build him up. I make him know he is the most important person in the world.

11:37:38 AM **brett_robson101**: ok nice words

11:37:55 AM **ladydi2011**: I love to travel and experience new things. I love adventure. I love the beach. I am very calm and relaxed when there. Like you, I am not big on the bar scene.

11:38:31 AM **ladydi2011**: I like to cook special dishes. I don't do much of it because I live alone. I do cook when I have friends or family over.

11:38:50 AM **brett_robson101**: ok

11:40:46 AM **ladydi2011**: I like R & B, jazz and some country music. I like dining out, wine tasting, plays, movies, swimming, boating, snowmobiling, dancing, listening to music, driving my car with the top down, going for ice cream, hanging out, barbecuing, reading, cuddling, roasting marshmallows over an open fire and just "being".

11:41:34 AM **brett_robson101**: oh..cool

11:42:16 AM **ladydi2011**: I also read several books at one time. Right now I am reading Let's Get Real or Let's Not Play and Wishes Fulfilled, Mastering the Art of Manifesting.

11:42:40 AM **brett_robson101**: *I like all these below,* Pop, rock, country, Classical, Novels, history, Honest, loyal, devoted, romantic, sincere, dependable, strong, adventurous, poetic, passionate, social, intelligent, professional. Exercises, Visiting Friends, Water Sports, Snow Skiing, Fly Fishing, Camping, Dancing, Movies and I love to love to travel... I like to spend a lot of time in the outdoors, Camp, Fly fishing, Water Skiing, Snow Skiing, Rock Climbing, I like to take walks, I workout most days. I'm 6"0" tall 216 pounds and in great shape.

11:43:15 AM **ladydi2011**: Nice....6"

11:44:01 AM **ladydi2011**: I am 5'7", and work out most days. I do 3 miles on the treadmill and strength train every other day.

11:44:20 AM **ladydi2011**: I believe in making things happen and not waiting for things.

11:44:32 AM **ladydi2011**: Life is short and I like to play it full out

11:44:46 AM **brett_robson101**: yeah you are right

11:45:14 AM **brett_robson101**: *What do your friends mean to you?*

11:46:20 AM **ladydi2011**: everything...I have a close inner circle of friends. I love them very much. We laugh and cry together and go through the journey of life together. I treasure them as they do me...

11:46:27 AM **ladydi2011**: What do they mean to you?

11:47:03 AM **ladydi2011**: I don't demand respect, but have been told I command it because of who I am

11:47:21 AM **ladydi2011**: For me, it is not about SPEAKING it, it is about BEING it

11:47:40 AM **ladydi2011**: Words are words, but ACTIONS tell us who people really are

11:47:56 AM **brett_robson101**: ok

11:48:17 AM **ladydi2011**: I am very selective of who I allow into my inner circle....I do not do drama!!!

11:48:30 AM **brett_robson101**: Friends are very important. I love having friends to laugh and hang out with. My best friends are family right now. *I have good friends in several parts of the country*

11:48:43 AM **ladydi2011**: Cool

11:48:51 AM **ladydi2011**: Where are you right now?

11:51:10 AM **brett_robson101**: *in Alaska a friend want me to get something for him so I had to run down there*

11:51:59 AM **ladydi2011**: Wow...Alaska. Nice! Is it pretty there?

11:52:38 AM **brett_robson101**: yea cool place to be

11:53:05 AM **brett_robson101**: *what do others admire about you?*

11:55:06 AM **ladydi2011**: My honesty, sincerity, I say what I mean and mean what I say, I have a caring heart, my character and I love passionately.

11:55:15 AM **ladydi2011**: What do others admire about you?

11:56:07 AM **brett_robson101**: They think I am smart and hard working. I am always kind, nice, and caring. I am understanding and easy to talk to.

11:57:40 AM **brett_robson101**: *What makes you proud?*

11:58:05 AM **ladydi2011**: I like your qualities

11:59:19 AM **ladydi2011**: I am proud of the woman I have become. I am a real lady. I have taken the time to know who I am and what I want and need. I am also proud of my heart. I have a really great heart. I am also very humble.

11:59:28 AM **ladydi2011**: Good questions Brett

11:59:36 AM **ladydi2011**: What makes you proud?

12:00:08 PM **brett_robson101**: ok

12:01:01 PM **brett_robson101**: I am very proud of my Self, *And Carrier.* I am proud of myself for having the courage to Live with out my Family, even though it was not easy.

12:02:11 PM **ladydi2011**: Ok

12:02:47 PM **ladydi2011**: Please know it is not always easy even when you have family

12:03:00 PM **ladydi2011**: Sometimes family can hurt you the worst

12:04:50 PM **brett_robson101**: yes.. it really had when you find your self living without your parent

12:05:02 PM **brett_robson101**: they really are important to us sometimes

12:06:01 PM **ladydi2011**: Yeah, they are important. I admire you for being the strong man you are.

12:06:17 PM **ladydi2011**: It is also human nature for us to want what we don't have...

12:06:53 PM **brett_robson101**: yes..

12:07:07 PM **brett_robson101**: *how do you define success?*

12:10:12 PM **ladydi2011**: another good question. I do not define it by material things or money. I define it by happiness and moments that take my breath away. Money cannot buy love, happiness, time, knowledge or health. Most of all I define it by the love you have in your life. Today, I am very successful with the love I have from friends and family but not successful at all because I am missing the love of that special man in my life. I know one day he will walk into my life.

12:10:23 PM **ladydi2011**: how do you define success?

12:11:48 PM **brett_robson101**: yeah if you keep that in mind the right man will fall in your heart and remain forever

12:12:29 PM **brett_robson101**: *I define success as being at peace with God . Also being able to take care of myself financially.*

12:12:43 PM **ladydi2011**: Thank you. I am sure of this. I am ready.

12:13:05 PM **ladydi2011**: Nice

12:13:10 PM **ladydi2011**: God is love.

12:13:42 PM **ladydi2011**: God is everything in my life. He has always provided for me and loved me so I have never lacked anything.

12:13:57 PM **ladydi2011**: I am so glad you have a strong faith.

12:14:10 PM **ladydi2011**: This is a quality I am looking for in a man

12:14:26 PM **ladydi2011**: I hate to do this, but I have to go back to work.

12:14:37 PM **ladydi2011**: Can we chat again in the near future?

12:15:17 PM **ladydi2011**: I have really enjoyed getting to know more about you and would like to continue

12:15:32 PM **ladydi2011**: This is if you are interested in getting to know more about me too

12:16:43 PM **brett_robson101**: *i* am dear.. *i* will be here always to chat with you

12:17:08 PM **brett_robson101**: hope to talk later..and please take good care of your self and *i* will pray for God protection

12:17:13 PM **brett_robson101**: go in peace ok

12:17:49 PM **ladydi2011**: Thank you Brett

12:17:59 PM **ladydi2011**: Have a wonderful day!

12:18:40 PM **brett_robson101**: and you too dear

12:18:51 PM **brett_robson101**: talk to you later

12:18:54 PM **brett_robson101**: bye for now

IM Jun 14, 2012 8:33:28 AM

8:33:28 AM **brett_robson101**: <ding>

8:33:54 AM **ladydi2011**: Morning!

8:34:02 AM **brett_robson101**: hello, Good Morning

8:34:15 AM **ladydi2011**: I like the hearts

8:34:18 AM **brett_robson101**: how are you and how was you nite?

8:34:46 AM **ladydi2011**: I am well. I had a good night, what about you?

8:35:23 AM **brett_robson101**: same here cos *i thank God for his protection*

8:35:33 AM **ladydi2011**: Amen to this.

8:35:50 AM **ladydi2011**: What time is it there?

8:36:55 AM **brett_robson101**: *it about 8:36*

8:37:01 AM **brett_robson101**: and there

8:39:12 AM **ladydi2011**: Same....

8:39:23 AM **brett_robson101**: ok

8:41:44 AM **brett_robson101**: what are you up to today?

8:42:56 AM **ladydi2011**: I am sorry for the delay

8:43:04 AM **ladydi2011**: Phone rang....please hold

8:43:07 AM **ladydi2011**: In the office

8:43:23 AM **brett_robson101**: oh ok

9:00:44 AM **ladydi2011**: Sorry

9:00:48 AM **ladydi2011**: I am back

9:01:05 AM **ladydi2011**: What are you up to today?

9:01:29 AM **brett_robson101**: hope am not disturbing you *i* can let you get busy we talk later?

9:01:53 AM **ladydi2011**: I was hoping to have time this morning but it has not turned out this way.

9:02:29 AM **ladydi2011**: I need to take my car for service today at 3:30 and they have Wi-Fi so I should be on line then if you're available we can chat then

9:03:09 AM **ladydi2011**: Btw...I never see you as disturbing me

9:03:25 AM **ladydi2011**: Have to run

9:03:32 AM **ladydi2011**: Have a wonderful day!

9:03:41 AM **ladydi2011**: Hope to catch you later

9:03:48 AM **ladydi2011**: Bye for now

9:04:05 AM **brett_robson101**: ok *i* will be here all day waiting for you ok...

9:04:12 AM **ladydi2011**: Cool

9:04:17 AM **brett_robson101**: *may God protect you*

9:04:21 AM **ladydi2011**: Thank you

9:04:34 AM **ladydi2011**: He always does....he has assigned many angels to me

9:04:41 AM **ladydi2011**: Blessings to you all day

9:05:11 AM **brett_robson101**: ok

IM Jun 14, 2012 3:39:22 PM Continued

3:39:22 PM **ladydi2011**: Hi Brett

3:39:31 PM **ladydi2011**: Are you there?

3:40:57 PM **brett_robson101**: am doing good and you?

3:41:10 PM **brett_robson101**: how's work ?

3:41:50 PM **ladydi2011**: I am good. Work is busy. Now I am at the car dealership. I can work from wherever I am as long as I have my laptop

3:41:55 PM **ladydi2011**: How is your day going?

3:43:57 PM **brett_robson101**: good

3:45:48 PM **ladydi2011**: I am sorry, the service manager needed to ask me a question

3:46:56 PM **brett_robson101**: it ok

3:47:09 PM **ladydi2011**: I am back....

3:47:18 PM **ladydi2011**: Thank you for bearing with me...

3:47:29 PM **ladydi2011**: One day I will have free time...Lol

3:48:13 PM **brett_robson101**: yeah you will

3:48:31 PM **brett_robson101**: *God will make a way for you one day*

3:49:10 PM **ladydi2011**: Oppps, they need me again. Please hold. I am sorry.

3:50:24 PM **brett_robson101**: ok

4:01:40 PM **ladydi2011**: Ok...I am back. Thank you for waiting.

4:01:55 PM **brett_robson101**: ok

4:01:57 PM **ladydi2011**: Are you still there?

4:02:29 PM **brett_robson101**: am here

4:02:44 PM **ladydi2011**: So, how is your day?

4:03:58 PM **brett_robson101**: not much here today just home all day

4:04:42 PM **brett_robson101**: *i* guess you are very busy today?

4:05:59 PM **brett_robson101**: much to handle at work i guess

4:07:51 PM **brett_robson101**: you there?

4:10:17 PM **ladydi2011**: I am sorry

4:10:29 PM **ladydi2011**: The service manager keeps coming to talk to me about my car

4:10:33 PM **brett_robson101**: ok

4:11:22 PM **ladydi2011**: He is gone now

4:11:34 PM **brett_robson101**: ok

4:12:32 PM **ladydi2011**: When do you travel again?

4:14:03 PM **brett_robson101**: *i* guess when the contract am waiting for comes in *i* will travel for it

4:14:22 PM **brett_robson101**: but *i* don't it coming this week

4:14:35 PM **ladydi2011**: Oh, ok

4:14:46 PM **ladydi2011**: So you are in Carolina now?

4:15:55 PM **brett_robson101**: yeah

4:16:59 PM **ladydi2011**: How is the weather there today?

4:18:27 PM **brett_robson101**: it about 80°F / *27°C i guess*

4:19:19 PM **ladydi2011**: It is about the same here. I am having some issues with the convertible top on my car.

4:19:26 PM **ladydi2011**: I do love the convertible

4:19:36 PM **ladydi2011**: I have a young spirit and love to have fun

4:20:00 PM **brett_robson101**: oh ok

4:20:24 PM **ladydi2011**: So, do you have a young spirit

4:20:39 PM **ladydi2011**: Please hold...service manage is here again

4:21:11 PM **brett_robson101**: ok

4:21:25 PM **brett_robson101**: on and off..lol

4:21:28 PM **brett_robson101**: it ok

4:30:23 PM **ladydi2011**: Sorry...they see a single woman walk in and they see dollar signs

4:30:49 PM **ladydi2011**: I have to go and handle this... hopefully we can catch up later

4:30:52 PM **ladydi2011**: Sorry again

4:31:19 PM **brett_robson101**: it ok *i* understand this things about business

4:31:44 PM **ladydi2011**: Yeah....I have been around cars my entire life

4:32:08 PM **ladydi2011**: I may be blonde, but not stupid...especially when it comes to cars.

4:32:13 PM **ladydi2011**: Talk later, ok...

4:32:17 PM **ladydi2011**: Bye for now

4:32:42 PM **brett_robson101**: what if *i* text you later?

4:32:55 PM **ladydi2011**: That would be great

4:33:01 PM **ladydi2011**: Did I give you my number?

4:33:11 PM **brett_robson101**: no

4.33:28 PM **ladydi2011**: (gave him my phone number)

4:33:41 PM **brett_robson101**: is it your mobile?

4:33:49 PM **ladydi2011**: It is...

4:34:10 PM **brett_robson101**: ok

4:34:19 PM **brett_robson101**: *i* will text you later ok..

4:34:23 PM **ladydi2011**: Ok

4:34:26 PM **ladydi2011**: Until later

4:34:30 PM **ladydi2011**: Signing off now

4:34:34 PM **brett_robson101**: *take care and God bless you and protect you ok*

When you see "To" or "From", it is either going to or coming from Brett. I was shocked that he gave me his Nigerian phone number. Because it is his real phone number, I have removed it when he uses it.

Text Messages

From: +234_____
Received: Jun 17, 2012 6:30 PM

Hello Diana, how are you doing today and how's work and everything *it me Brett hope you remember me? just wanna if you are fine..take care and hope to hear from you soon..*

To: +234_____
Sent: Jun 17, 2012 9:33 PM

Hi Brett, of course I remember you! How are you? How was your day? I had a nice day. I am looking forward to hearing back from you soon...Diana

~ Tomorrow is shaped by the choices you make today ...choose wisely!

I already know from his profile that this man is a scammer. Now I want to see if I can learn a different type of scam from him.

RED FLAGS

- "Hi Pretty" is something many scammers say on their first correspondence.
- Like many scammers, he wants to instantly get me over to Yahoo! Messenger, and I am ready to do so to learn all I can learn.
- I think he might have mixed me up with another woman, because we haven't chatted yet. Pay attention to this type of error.
- He misspells Charlotte and says Ohio Cleveland instead of Cleveland Ohio. Once again you see lower case I's and no capitalization where there should be capitalization.
- There are huge differences between interior design, road construction and "a building contractor." What is it that he does?
- He asks my age and then tells me he is the same age of 48, but his profile says he is 47. Watch for discrepancies.
- He follows suit of a scammer by asking early on what I do for a living. He wants to know if I make good money.
- He tells me he has a son and then says, "I lost my late wife about years ago". Notice his improper English and poor grammar.

- He then tells me he lost his parents and has no siblings, which is a typical set up for a scammer. He is setting the stage to ask me for money and wants me to think there is no one else who can help him.
- He says he travels around the world, which is another red flag. Often scammers say they travel.
- This is the first time I am asked the following questions:
  1. "What do your friends mean to you?" He is trying to find out if I have close friends, if I confide in my friends, and if I can borrow money from them.
  2. "What do others admire about you?" He is trying to learn about my personality and any rules I might have (such as my "yes" is "yes" and "no" is "no," so he can figure out how to persuade me to give him money.)
  3. "What makes you proud?" He is trying to learn if I am successful and if I have children or grandchildren, and he wants to answer in such a way that he looks responsible and successful to me.
- He was supposedly in Alaska at noon the day before and already in Charlotte at 8:36 AM the next morning. It is always important to ask where they are and what time it is there.
- He uses both Farenheit and Celcius. If he was in the United States he would know we do not use Celcius.
- His text number is a Nigerian phone number. Huge red flag. Pay attention to text numbers. Since his text number was Nigerian, I had no need for his IP address to be run, because I already knew he was from Nigeria.

IM Jun 18, 2012 6:19:46 AM

6:19:46 AM **brett_robson101**: Hello Dear Good morning how are you doing today and thanks *i* got your reply on the text *i* sent you *i* really appreciate you time with me..so how's work everything and your health?

6:19:58 AM **brett_robson101**: *i* really miss your talk here..lol..

6:20:45 AM **brett_robson101**: hope we can still talk soon..thanks and ***take good care of your self for me..***

IM Jun 21, 2012 3:30:33 PM

3:30:33 PM **ladydi2011**: Hi Brett, I miss you! How are you? I am sorry I have not been on line lately. Please forgive me. For days I have been having technical issues with my phone and computer. I signed on a major client in the last week. This client is extremely time consuming. I also brought in 2 more clients this week. I am so busy with work I can barely breathe. I miss chatting with you. Being a single woman and the sole provider for myself, please understand my first priority has to be running my business. Please don't give up on me. I am even batting my eye lashes at you...

IM Jun 22, 2012 6:02:42 AM

6:02:42 AM **brett_robson101**: ok thanks for those kind words *i* really appreciate it..but please you just have to take it easy cos your health count a lot.. am fine and hope we can talk any time you are much ok with talking..*i wish you all the best in your business and more clients to make more money..lol*..hope we can talk soon take good care of your self and bye for now..kisses

IM Jun 25, 2012 12:06:33 AM

12:06:33 AM **ladydi2011**: Hi Brett! Are you ever on line anymore? I miss chatting with you. Please email me @ ladydi2011@yahoo.com

Text Messages

From: +12408139578
Received: Jun 25, 2012 2:02 PM

Honey love is the shortest distance between hearts,it draws to heart together and make it one to love and cherish each other forever....***LOVE U.***

From: +12408139578
Received: Jun 25, 2012 2:07 PM

Honey please try and come online tonight so that we can chat together.cuz *i* miss you alot and *i* care also..***LOVE U***

To: +12408139578
Sent: Jun 25, 2012 6:33 PM

Hi honey. I am in a meeting right now but should be able to be on line around 10:00 my time. Will you be awake at this time so we can chat. Love you too!

From: +12408139578
Received: Jun 26, 2012 9:14 AM

Hello, wake up honey, Receive my simple gift of 'GOOD MORNING' wrapped with sincerity, tied with care and sealed with a prayer to keep u safe, strong and quick recovery and happy all day long!

From: +12408139578
Received: Jun 26, 2012 9:15 AM

Early this morning God gave me 3 baskets of fruits- LOVE + HAPPINESS + PEACE OF MIND with you honey and told me 2 share them with peal Dear 2 me. sharing all with U...An ideal day should begin with a cute little yawn of smiles on your face. A cup of coffee in your hand & A sms from me on your mobile to show how much I care and love you much more!

To: +12408139578
Sent: Jun 26, 2012 9:24 AM

Good morning honey. Thank you for such a nice heartfelt message. You put a big smile on my face. It is a wonderful morning filled with love, happiness and peace of mind. How is your day going? I pray you have a smile on your face. I care and love you too!

IM Jun 27, 2012 10:19:19 PM

10:19:19 PM **ladydi2011**: Hey Brett...how are you? I miss you. How are you? Is everything ok? Did you start dating someone?????

IM Jun 28, 2012 8:29:22 AM

8:29:22 AM **brett_robson101**: <ding>
8:33:20 AM **brett_robson101**: you there?
8:35:29 AM **brett_robson101**: am doing great and not gotten any woman here to date...lol..just that you are too busy and wanted to give you all the time to work so that when we are chatting you can be very free to say anything at all..*i* really miss you here too..but am back to chat so if you wanna get online am here for you all day..miss you and talk with you later..
8:35:36 AM **brett_robson101**: bye for now

IM Jun 28, 2012 9:00:42 AM

9:00:42 AM **brett_robson101**: Hello
9:00:47 AM **brett_robson101**: you there?
9:00:55 AM **ladydi2011**: Hello
9:01:02 AM **ladydi2011**: Nice to see you on line
9:01:07 AM **ladydi2011**: How are you?
9:01:13 AM **brett_robson101**: same here
9:01:22 AM **brett_robson101**: am doing great and you
9:02:00 AM **brett_robson101**: <ding>
9:02:06 AM **ladydi2011**: I am doing great too!
9:02:36 AM **brett_robson101**: ok..really miss talking to you here
9:02:44 AM **ladydi2011**: Same here
9:02:45 AM **brett_robson101**: and how's work going
9:02:55 AM **ladydi2011**: Did you get my message last night?

9:03:55 AM **ladydi2011**: Work is good...busy

9:04:05 AM **ladydi2011**: What about for you?

9:05:12 AM **brett_robson101**: ok...well *i* have been here for some times but when *i* didn't see you *i* just thought maybe *i* should wait until you are free from work so that *i* can talk to you

9:05:43 AM **brett_robson101**: *i* love this pics of your it very beautiful

9:05:52 AM **ladydi2011**: Thank you

9:05:56 AM **brett_robson101**: and your smile

9:06:04 AM **ladydi2011**: Thank you again

9:06:18 AM **brett_robson101**: So tell me what are you up to today?

9:06:46 AM **ladydi2011**: Please send me an email with some pictures of yourself ladydi2011@yahoo.com

9:06:55 AM **ladydi2011**: Work as usual

9:07:02 AM **ladydi2011**: It is Thursday

9:07:15 AM **brett_robson101**: ok *i* will later..yeah it is

9:07:34 AM **brett_robson101**: you told me it your personal business you do right?

9:07:45 AM **ladydi2011**: Yes. I own a business

9:08:42 AM **brett_robson101**: ok..you know it been a while and forgot much on what we have talked so far..lol

9:09:05 AM **brett_robson101**: so tell me what do you wanna know about me?

9:09:09 AM **ladydi2011**: This is not a good sign........................

9:10:32 AM **ladydi2011**: Just teasing you

9:10:45 AM **ladydi2011**: Are you there?

9:10:51 AM **brett_robson101**: <ding>

9:11:34 AM **brett_robson101**: am here

9:11:58 AM **brett_robson101**: what sign?

9:12:28 AM **ladydi2011**: Just teasing you Brett

9:12:36 AM **brett_robson101**: lol ok

9:12:49 AM **ladydi2011**: If you don't remember what we talked about, maybe you are not that into me

9:14:30 AM **brett_robson101**: yeah *i* guess so cos we have not really talked about ourselves much you know?

9:14:52 AM **ladydi2011**: Brb

9:15:29 AM **brett_robson101**: cos if *i* could remember the time we had to talk you where very busy with work and other things so *i* had to wait until you are free to chat with me

9:21:00 AM **brett_robson101**: <ding>

9:22:52 AM **ladydi2011**: I am back....sorry

9:23:11 AM **ladydi2011**: My phone rang

9:23:21 AM **brett_robson101**: ok

9:23:55 AM **ladydi2011**: Please tell me what you are doing today

9:24:41 AM **brett_robson101**: nothing much just here to chat with you

9:25:06 AM **ladydi2011**: Where are you?

9:25:49 AM **ladydi2011**: What part of the world?

9:26:16 AM **brett_robson101**: you mean where am from?

9:26:39 AM **ladydi2011**: No honey. Where you are at now?

9:27:08 AM **brett_robson101**: charlotte..*i* told you the other time we talk here

9:27:45 AM **ladydi2011**: I knew you were from Charlotte. I thought maybe you were traveling

9:28:03 AM **brett_robson101**: no am not

9:28:32 AM **brett_robson101**: *i* wanted to but it not gonna work any more

9:28:45 AM **ladydi2011**: Oh, ok

9:29:14 AM **brett_robson101**: *so tell me how long have you been on internet dating?*

9:29:44 AM **ladydi2011**: 2 1/2 months

9:29:56 AM **ladydi2011**: What about you?

9:30:38 AM **brett_robson101**: that pretty much time you got on internet..am *just quite new here and don't even know how it works*

9:31:17 AM **ladydi2011**: It is different

9:31:38 AM **ladydi2011**: Are you looking for someone close to Charlotte?

9:32:20 AM **brett_robson101**: love is every where and any where *i* find the right woman to love and can love me for who *i* am that all

9:32:23 AM **brett_robson101**: and you?

9:32:43 AM **ladydi2011**: I feel the same way

9:32:54 AM **ladydi2011**: I can run my business from anywhere in the world

9:33:13 AM **brett_robson101**: ok..

9:33:32 AM **brett_robson101**: your address so that *i* can send you the pictures?

9:34:24 AM **ladydi2011**: ladydi2011@yahoo.com

9:34:57 AM **brett_robson101**: ok..*i* will send it in few minute

9:35:09 AM **ladydi2011**: I look forward to seeing them

9:35:15 AM **ladydi2011**: I will also send you some

9:35:26 AM **ladydi2011**: You have a child, right?

9:35:44 AM **brett_robson101**: yeah *i* do..his name is Fred

9:35:54 AM **brett_robson101**: 8 years of age

9:35:58 AM **brett_robson101**: and you?

9:36:08 AM **ladydi2011**: Is he in Ohio?

9:36:16 AM **ladydi2011**: I do not have any children?

9:37:00 AM **brett_robson101**: oh ok..what happen never been married before?

9:37:10 AM **brett_robson101**: my son is with me and he's very nice and friendly

9:37:29 AM **ladydi2011**: I was married for 8 years but we never had children

9:38:37 AM **brett_robson101**: oh so sorry to hear that

9:38:46 AM **ladydi2011**: It is ok. If we get together, can I share Fred with you?

9:39:38 AM **brett_robson101**: lol..ofcourse yes he's gonna be your child too

9:39:57 AM **ladydi2011**: Cool

9:40:12 AM **ladydi2011**: So, do you ever come to Atlanta?

9:40:56 AM **brett_robson101**: have been there several times to spend the weekends with fred but *i* have not been there for a while now

9:41:36 AM **ladydi2011**: I have been to Charlotte a couple times

9:41:40 AM **ladydi2011**: It is nice there

9:42:05 AM **brett_robson101**: yeah it is..and atlanta too *i* love the place

9:42:27 AM **ladydi2011**: Yeah...it is supposed to be 108 degrees here on Saturday

9:42:33 AM **ladydi2011**: Hotlanta

9:43:47 AM **brett_robson101**: ok

9:44:55 AM **ladydi2011**: Too hot for me!

9:45:23 AM **brett_robson101**: oh..ok

9:45:42 AM **brett_robson101**: you know some times the weather get hot and warm most times too

9:45:54 AM **ladydi2011**: Yeah

9:46:07 AM **brett_robson101**: how about *i* share my pictures here then you save?

9:46:45 AM **ladydi2011**: Ok

 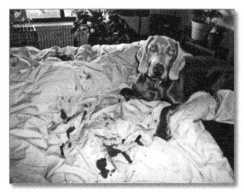

9:48:39 AM **brett_robson101**: This is me..*lol* hope you love them?
9:49:03 AM **brett_robson101**: can you see them?
9:49:13 AM **ladydi2011**: thank you. I do love them
9:49:32 AM **brett_robson101**: ok
9:49:48 AM **brett_robson101**: hope you can save them right?
9:49:49 AM **ladydi2011**: You are very handsome
9:49:54 AM **ladydi2011**: Let me try
9:49:57 AM **brett_robson101**: thank you
9:50:58 AM **ladydi2011**: What is your dog's name?
9:51:06 AM **ladydi2011**: The blue paint is too funny!
9:51:57 AM **ladydi2011**: I was able to save
9:52:54 AM **ladydi2011**: Are you there?
9:53:05 AM **brett_robson101**: his name is misha it a russian name.it was when *i* got a job there *i* got him
9:53:48 AM **ladydi2011**: Cool
9:53:56 AM **ladydi2011**: Do you have pictures of Fred
9:55:00 AM **ladydi2011**: <ding>
9:55:07 AM **brett_robson101**: yeah *i* do

9:55:16 AM **ladydi2011**: Please send
9:55:17 AM **brett_robson101**: wanna see?
9:55:22 AM **ladydi2011**: Yes please

9:57:07 AM **brett_robson101**: that him
9:57:59 AM **brett_robson101**: got it?
9:58:02 AM **ladydi2011**: He looks like you. He is adorable!
9:58:13 AM **brett_robson101**: thanks honey
9:58:31 AM **ladydi2011**: So, why did traveling not work for you?
9:58:54 AM **brett_robson101**: *i* lost the job
9:59:10 AM **ladydi2011**: Sorry to hear this
9:59:26 AM **brett_robson101**: it ok..life goes on you know
9:59:33 AM **ladydi2011**: Yeah it does
9:59:39 AM **ladydi2011**: Jobs come, jobs go
9:59:46 AM **ladydi2011**: Money comes, money goes
9:59:56 AM **brett_robson101**: yeah you are right
10:00:08 AM **brett_robson101**: just hoping for another one some time
10:00:42 AM **brett_robson101**: so lets talk about us..and *i* wanna ask you something and please tell me
10:00:56 AM **ladydi2011**: Ok
10:01:33 AM **brett_robson101**: *have you ever met anybody on internet dating before cos i don't anybody to start asking me to get off his woman..lol*

504

10:01:57 AM **ladydi2011**: Did someone do this to you?

10:02:34 AM **ladydi2011**: I have chatted with many men from the site

10:02:46 AM **brett_robson101**: oh..ok

10:02:57 AM **ladydi2011**: I am not involved with any of them

10:03:07 AM **brett_robson101**: so you didn't find any interesting?

10:03:12 AM **ladydi2011**: Nope

10:03:17 AM **brett_robson101**: why?

10:03:39 AM **ladydi2011**: Just not a match

10:03:51 AM **ladydi2011**: Many of them were overseas. I need a man who will be here with me

10:04:11 AM **brett_robson101**: oh ok..that nice

10:04:51 AM **ladydi2011**: I have made many friends

10:04:57 AM **ladydi2011**: What about you?

10:05:05 AM **ladydi2011**: What have you experienced?

10:06:20 AM **brett_robson101**: just you as a friend on my list and don't really make friends on internet dating cos when you make too many friends you get confused to which that really match

10:06:39 AM **ladydi2011**: Hmmmmmmm

10:06:45 AM **ladydi2011**: Good point

10:07:12 AM **brett_robson101**: so you just have to take it one afterthe other

10:07:19 AM **ladydi2011**: Bathroom break...brb

10:07:27 AM **brett_robson101**: ok

10:10:13 AM **ladydi2011**: I am back

10:10:19 AM **ladydi2011**: Thanks you for holding

10:10:26 AM **brett_robson101**: ok

10:10:43 AM **ladydi2011**: How many women have you chatted with?

10:11:30 AM **brett_robson101**: since *i* opened my yahoo messenger you are the first to be my friend on the list

10:11:39 AM **brett_robson101**: *i* guess you are lucky..*lol*

10:12:39 AM **ladydi2011**: Really????

10:12:48 AM **ladydi2011**: Yeah, I am lucky!

10:12:59 AM **brett_robson101**: yeah you are

10:13:03 AM **ladydi2011**: So are you...lol

10:13:15 AM **ladydi2011**: I am a good woman Brett

10:13:58 AM **brett_robson101**: ok..your smile says it all from your picture

10:15:11 AM **ladydi2011**: Thank you

10:15:46 AM **brett_robson101**: *i don't really have my cam here i would have love to put it on...*

10:16:08 AM **ladydi2011**: Where is your cam?

10:16:50 AM **brett_robson101**: *My Dog broke it few days ago..lol*

10:17:14 AM **ladydi2011**: Will you be getting a new one soon?

10:18:04 AM **brett_robson101**: yeah *i* will but that when *i* have the money soon to get one..*lol*

10:18:09 AM **brett_robson101**: so you got one there?

10:18:41 AM **brett_robson101**: wow *i* love your pictures they are so lovley

10:19:20 AM **brett_robson101**: pretty smile and your lips looks good to get a kiss..lol

10:19:26 AM **ladydi2011**: Thanks Brett

10:19:51 AM **ladydi2011**: My cam on my work computer doesn't work

10:20:00 AM **ladydi2011**: On my home computer it does

10:20:12 AM **brett_robson101**: ok

10:20:37 AM **brett_robson101**: so *i* guess *i* will be seeing your face on cam soon when you get home right?
10:21:03 AM **ladydi2011**: If you would like too
10:21:23 AM **brett_robson101**: *i* would love it..can't wait to see how beautiful you will look on it
10:23:22 AM **ladydi2011**: Ok
10:24:35 AM **brett_robson101**: *i* got to go now ok..*i* hope *i* can meet you here later?
10:24:53 AM **ladydi2011**: Ok honey
10:25:03 AM **ladydi2011**: Look for me later
10:25:06 AM **ladydi2011**: Until then
10:25:08 AM **ladydi2011**: Bye
10:25:49 AM **brett_robson101**: bye

IM Jul 4, 2012 6:07:45 AM

6:07:45 AM **ladydi2011**: Hi Brett...how are you? Happy 4th! What do you have planned for today?

IM Jul 4, 2012 9:33:28 AM

9:33:28 AM **brett_robson101**: <ding>
9:33:37 AM **brett_robson101**: Hello honey
9:34:26 AM **brett_robson101**: how are you doing and your nite? hope it was great..sorry *i* missed you here *i* took my little boy out for Games..
9:35:25 AM **brett_robson101**: *well not really having much to do cos i told you the other time that i was especting a job form a company so they called me to imform me about the progress..*
9:46:26 AM **brett_robson101**: will talk to you later today..miss you so much
9:46:29 AM **brett_robson101**: kisses

I must say it isn't easy to keep him on the hook and get the story. I thought I lost him for a couple of days. We are not really connecting so I wasn't sure if I was going to get a story from him, but something told me to go a little further with him. I was chatting with several other scammers at the same time who also wanted my attention, so I found myself making excuses and apologizing a lot. Talking to many scammers at once was not an easy task.

He stopped texting me from his Nigerian number and switched to a Maryland number.

Within 19 days he calls me "honey" and says "Love U". I didn't think we were even close to this place where he would do this. He was not on top of his game.

RED FLAGS

- "Take good care of yourself" is something most scammers say.
- He shares many pictures with me. This surprises me because a lot of scammers don't have many pictures. He only sends one picture of "Fred," and it looks as if a caption or something was removed from the background.
- He quickly changes the subject of his job and wants to know if I met anyone on Internet dating. He is trying to figure out if I have been scammed or if anyone attempted to scam me.
- Of course he doesn't have a cam. Remember, a scammer can't come on cam in less it is a fake cam. He does want to see me on cam. Scammers want to see you on cam to be sure you are not another scammer.

IM Jul 4, 2012 11:29:24 AM

11:29:24 AM **ladydi2011**: Hi honey
11:29:46 AM **brett_robson101**: Hello love
11:29:50 AM **brett_robson101**: how are you doing?
11:29:59 AM **brett_robson101**: *i* really miss you so much
11:30:08 AM **ladydi2011**: I am good and you?
11:30:19 AM **ladydi2011**: I miss you too!
11:30:32 AM **brett_robson101**: how'a work honey
11:30:36 AM **ladydi2011**: What is happening with the job?
11:30:56 AM **ladydi2011**: It is good
11:31:03 AM **brett_robson101**: *i* really don't know what is going on with it but *i* just hope all is well
11:31:34 AM **ladydi2011**: So you think you will be working soon?
11:31:54 AM **brett_robson101**: *i* think so honey
11:32:17 AM **ladydi2011**: Where will this work be?
11:32:20 AM **brett_robson101**: so what have you been up to?
11:32:54 AM **ladydi2011**: I am going to listen to some bands and watch fireworks later
11:33:37 AM **ladydi2011**: What are you doing for the 4th?
11:34:25 AM **brett_robson101**: oh.. well *i* guess *i* will be some where with my son playing games
11:34:36 AM **ladydi2011**: Cool. Please email or text me if you don't see me on line
11:35:35 AM **brett_robson101**: you mean when ever *i* don't see you online?
11:35:50 AM **ladydi2011**: Yeah, so we don't lose touch for so long
11:37:25 AM **ladydi2011**: Are you there?
11:38:08 AM **brett_robson101**: am here my love
11:38:17 AM **brett_robson101**: so tell me what are you doing now?
11:38:57 AM **ladydi2011**: Going through clothes
11:39:13 AM **brett_robson101**: ok..
11:39:33 AM **ladydi2011**: Getting rid of those I no longer wear
11:39:44 AM **ladydi2011**: What are you doing now?
11:40:07 AM **brett_robson101**: that good to get rid of it when you don't need it any more
11:40:18 AM **brett_robson101**: here with you talking

11:40:39 AM **brett_robson101**: my love you promise to get your cam on when you are home?

11:40:40 AM **ladydi2011**: True...there are many people who can use them

11:41:24 AM **brett_robson101**: yeah..maybe you take them to the needy they can make use of them

11:41:25 AM **ladydi2011**: Yeah, I did but not now...

11:41:56 AM **ladydi2011**: Yeah. I will take them to the needy

11:42:09 AM **ladydi2011**: We have a lot of homeless

11:43:18 AM **brett_robson101**: ok..that would be nice if you do that

11:43:35 AM **ladydi2011**: Yeah

11:43:48 AM **ladydi2011**: So, do you think about me?

11:45:42 AM **brett_robson101**: first your eyes are so charming

11:46:08 AM **ladydi2011**: Thank you...windows to my soul!

11:46:08 AM **brett_robson101**: and you are the most beautiful woman *i* have ver met

11:46:25 AM **ladydi2011**: Awwww. Thanks baby!

11:47:04 AM **ladydi2011**: So, when do you think we can meet in person?

11:48:05 AM **brett_robson101**: *very soon* just hoping to get the job *i* told you about

11:49:05 AM **ladydi2011**: Ok. Please tell me more about the job

11:50:11 AM **brett_robson101**: it a very big contract nd *i* guess you saw the man standing with me on the pictures *i* sent to you..the Black man skating with me on the snow?

11:50:44 AM **ladydi2011**: Yeah

11:51:04 AM **brett_robson101**: we have been friend for a long time and promise to help since *i* lost my late wife

11:51:21 AM **ladydi2011**: Ok

11:51:25 AM **brett_robson101**: and he has been there for me all along

11:51:48 AM **ladydi2011**: Cool...a good friend!

11:52:05 AM **brett_robson101**: *He's from West Africa*

11:52:33 AM **ladydi2011**: Where about in West Africa?

11:53:21 AM **brett_robson101**: *South Africa*

11:53:48 AM **ladydi2011**: West or South?

11:54:49 AM **ladydi2011**: So, does he have the contract for you?

11:55:29 AM **brett_robson101**: no he doesn't just gonna help with people he know concerning the job on costruction

11:56:04 AM **ladydi2011**: Ok...will the work be in Africa?

11:57:51 AM **brett_robson101**: don't know yet honey

11:58:17 AM **ladydi2011**: Please keep me posted. Ok?

11:58:24 AM **brett_robson101**: he's only trying to get me intouch with the company that want a contractor for the job

11:59.24 AM **ladydi2011**: I will be praying you get this job.

12:00:12 PM **brett_robson101**: thanks honey *i* really apprciate it

12:02:26 PM **ladydi2011**: You're welcome

12:02:45 PM **brett_robson101**: you still getting rid of those clothes?

12:02:55 PM **ladydi2011**: Yeah

12:03:35 PM **ladydi2011**: I should go now honey so I can get this task done.

12:03:46 PM **ladydi2011**: Please keep in touch with me

12:04:12 PM **ladydi2011**: Email is ladydi2011@yahoo.com

12:04:20 PM **brett_robson101**: ok *i* will maybe *i* will text you later on ok

12:04:51 PM **ladydi2011**: Ok, I would like that.

12:05:05 PM **ladydi2011**: Have a wonderful day!

12:25:24 PM **brett_robson101**: and you too my love

Text Messages

From: +234_____
Received: Jul 4, 2012 7:19 PM

hello honey how are you doing today *i* miss you so much and *i* can be with you to put a smile on your face..kisses Brett

To: +234_____
Sent: Jul 4, 2012 7:41 PM

Hi honey...I am good. I am waiting for the fireworks to start. What are you doing tonight? Diana

From: +234_____
Received: Jul 4, 2012 7:50 PM

all *i* will do is think about you all night..my heart bit for you and love you ok. Brett

From: +234_____
Received: Jul 5, 2012 9:50 AM

Honey am online now hope to talk thanks. Brett

IM Jul 5, 2012 9:56:58 AM

9:56:58 AM **ladydi2011**: Hi honey
9:57:11 AM **ladydi2011**: How are you today?
9:57:25 AM **brett_robson101**: hello love
9:57:37 AM **brett_robson101**: am doing great and you?
9:57:54 AM **ladydi2011**: I am great too!
9:58:34 AM **ladydi2011**: What are your plans for today?
9:59:23 AM **brett_robson101**: just waiting for a call from the company for te job *i* told you about..
9:59:49 AM **ladydi2011**: I hope the call comes in today.
10:00:11 AM **brett_robson101**: hope so too honey
10:00:27 AM **ladydi2011**: If you get it, how soon do you think before you leave?
10:01:52 AM **brett_robson101**: don't know yet cos it all depends on he job time been
10:02:08 AM **brett_robson101**: so tell me what are your plans for today?
10:02:37 AM **ladydi2011**: I have a lot of paper work to do and going to dinner with friends later
10:03:31 AM **brett_robson101**: oh ok..guess am gonna miss the fun
10:03:59 AM **ladydi2011**: Wish you were here!
10:04:53 AM **brett_robson101**: same to my love
10:05:01 AM **brett_robson101**: can *i* ask yo something?

10:05:36 AM **ladydi2011**: Sure, please ask

10:07:20 AM **ladydi2011**: Are you there?

Break In Time

10:12:36 AM **brett_robson101**: *i* was thinking of you all night *i* couldn't sleep

10:13:17 AM **ladydi2011**: hmmmm...What were you thinking about that kept you awake?

10:14:15 AM **brett_robson101**: yeah it did keep me awake

10:14:42 AM **ladydi2011**: I hope these were good thoughts

10:15:29 AM **brett_robson101**: *i was just thinking if you where the one for me and if i can make decission to tel you how much love i have for you..*

10:17:16 AM **ladydi2011**: hmmmm...do you think I am the one for you?

Break In Time

10:20:38 AM **ladydi2011**: Hello

10:21:07 AM **brett_robson101**: yeah you are cos *i* thought about it all night and *i* had to make it straight to my heart ok

10:22:21 AM **ladydi2011**: Ok. I am glad you feel this way.

10:24:46 AM **brett_robson101**: *i* don't know if you feel the same way?

10:27:42 AM **ladydi2011**: I do...and wonder how this could be after only knowing you such a short period of time.

10:30:28 AM **brett_robson101**: cos in every relationship we need to *build trust and honesty* before we can meet cos when we do meet there will be now changing of minds right?

10:31:20 AM **ladydi2011**: This is true

10:36:08 AM **brett_robson101**: we need to bilieve in our selves and trust what we wanna do ok

10:43:42 AM **brett_robson101**: <ding>

10:50:59 AM **brett_robson101**: you there?

10:51:35 AM **ladydi2011**: Sorry

10:51:49 AM **ladydi2011**: I am here and I agree

10:52:05 AM **brett_robson101**: what happend?

10:52:56 AM **ladydi2011**: I fell asleep

10:53:17 AM **brett_robson101**: ok..sorry *i* guess you didn't sleep well

10:53:18 AM **ladydi2011**: With the phone in my hand

10:53:31 AM **brett_robson101**: lol

10:53:52 AM **ladydi2011**: I guess not

10:54:03 AM **brett_robson101**: ok

10:54:41 AM **brett_robson101**: *how much do you love me?*

10:55:49 AM **ladydi2011**: Good question

10:56:15 AM **ladydi2011**: I don't know how to measure love

10:56:37 AM **ladydi2011**: How much do you love me?

10:57:16 AM **brett_robson101**: with all my heart and *ready to give away my life just for you honey*

10:58:04 AM **ladydi2011**: Wow...I am glad to know this

10:59:25 AM **ladydi2011**: Now I know why you were awake all night

10:59:41 AM **ladydi2011**: I love you too

11:01:32 AM **brett_robson101**: *i* sent you a text did you get it?

11:01:59 AM **ladydi2011**: I did

11:09:08 AM **brett_robson101**: you at home?

11:11:37 AM **ladydi2011**: I am

11:12:08 AM **brett_robson101**: honey just this time can *i* see you on the cam for a while please?

11:16:39 AM **ladydi2011**: Later today honey. I promise!

11:17:17 AM **brett_robson101**: ok honey *i* love you
11:17:24 AM **ladydi2011**: My assistant is on her way here
11:17:46 AM **ladydi2011**: I love you too
11:17:52 AM **brett_robson101**: ok..what is she gonna do for you ?
11:18:15 AM **ladydi2011**: She is doing some marketing research
11:18:36 AM **brett_robson101**: ok
11:22:37 AM **ladydi2011**: What time will you be online later?
11:23:38 AM **brett_robson101**: my love *i* really don't know yet ok..but if am able to get free time *i* will text you ok
11:24:11 AM **ladydi2011**: Ok...what are you busy doing honey?
11:26:06 AM **ladydi2011**: <ding>
11:26:41 AM **brett_robson101**: *honey to be honest with you i was really hoping for the job i told you about so that i can leave on it and my food is the house is already finishe and i don't have much to get food so i was thinking if i can go see some one to assist me with a little help*
11:27:13 AM **ladydi2011**: Ok honey
11:27:35 AM **ladydi2011**: It WILL all work out
11:28:30 AM **brett_robson101**: *it just that i can't figure where to go for this assistance. lol*
11:29:09 AM **ladydi2011**: Hmmmm
11:30:19 AM **ladydi2011**: My assistant is here...got to go
11:30:25 AM **ladydi2011**: Text me
11:30:33 AM **ladydi2011**: Love you
11:30:37 AM **ladydi2011**: Bye
11:30:40 AM **brett_robson101**: ok

Notice that he really wants to see me on cam. He says the black man in the picture he sent earlier promised to help him and he is from West Africa; he then switched it to South Africa. This man is not "on point" with his story line, and he continues to make obvious mistakes like again texting me from a Nigeria number. If I were going to date a man, it surely wouldn't be this man. He appears to be lazy!

RED FLAGS

- He says he wants to "give away his live for me". Nigerians are big on saying they give their life for you or to you.
- He's really laying it on thick with "I'm broke" and "I have no food".
- His grammar and writing skills are horrible!
- He went back to using a Nigerian phone number.

IM Jul 14, 2012 3:33:30 AM

3:33:30 AM **brett_robson101**: Hello my love

3:33:33 AM **brett_robson101**: you there?

3:33:35 AM **ladydi2011**: Hello honey

3:33:37 AM **ladydi2011**: I am. How are you?

3:33:40 AM **brett_robson101**: Good morning

3:33:47 AM **ladydi2011**: Where are you?

3:33:59 AM **brett_robson101**: am doing great

3:34:02 AM **brett_robson101**: am home

3:34:25 AM **brett_robson101**: how was your nite babe?

3:34:33 AM **ladydi2011**: It was good honey

3:34:38 AM **ladydi2011**: How was yours?

3:35:05 AM **brett_robson101**: miss you so much and *had a dream about you*

3:35:27 AM **ladydi2011**: I miss you too

3:35:31 AM **ladydi2011**: Really, what was the dream about?

3:37:33 AM **brett_robson101**: *you told me that if we could get married and i said yes and you took me to a very nice garden to show me how wonderful you wanted us to be together*

3:37:59 AM **ladydi2011**: WOW!

3:38:04 AM **ladydi2011**: Sounds fabulous

3:38:08 AM **brett_robson101**: all *i* was doing is smile and laugh a lot cos *i* was so happy to hear sweet things from you

3:38:44 AM **ladydi2011**: Please hold

3:38:47 AM **ladydi2011**: Sorry

3:38:53 AM **ladydi2011**: Battery dying

3:39:01 AM **brett_robson101**: ok honey

4:19:30 AM **brett_robson101**: <ding>

4:19:42 AM **brett_robson101**: you there honey?

4:28:33 AM **ladydi2011**: Sorry honey

4:28:41 AM **ladydi2011**: Are you still there?

4:29:08 AM **ladydi2011**: <ding>

4:29:26 AM **brett_robson101**: am here for you honey

4:29:42 AM **ladydi2011**: Sorry

4:30:07 AM **ladydi2011**: I am so happy that I make you smile

4:30:18 AM **ladydi2011**: This is good

4:31:13 AM **brett_robson101**: *you are my morning and each time i think of you it brighthens my day*

4:31:35 AM **ladydi2011**: Same here

4:31:40 AM **ladydi2011**: I have missed you

4:32:06 AM **brett_robson101**: *i* can't do without thinking of you each day that passes by

4:32:35 AM **ladydi2011**: I hope every time you think of me a smile comes on your face

4:33:02 AM **brett_robson101**: sure cos it you that makes me hope for a new day

4:33:06 AM **ladydi2011**: I know one comes on my face every time I think of you

4:33:35 AM **ladydi2011**: Did you get the job honey?

4:35:28 AM **brett_robson101**: yeah *i* got a mail about the job yesterday

4:36:03 AM **ladydi2011**: Excellent

4:36:11 AM **ladydi2011**: When do you leave?

4:37:36 AM **brett_robson101**: *don't know yet cos i don't think am going too far again am only gonna be in England for the job*

4:37:58 AM **ladydi2011**: Oh, ok

4:38:14 AM **brett_robson101**: and *i* will get some people working then my friend will handle the rest cos *i* told him *i* found a beautiful woman to be with

4:39:17 AM **brett_robson101**: *i* just hope they understand with my proposal cos *i* really need to be with you soon and *i* can't just go far and keep you so distance so *i* had to tell my friend to help me out

4:39:30 AM **brett_robson101**: so what do you think?

4:40:07 AM **ladydi2011**: I think this is great!

4:40:19 AM **ladydi2011**: I want to be with you too!

4:40:37 AM **ladydi2011**: How long do you think you will be gone?

4:41:27 AM **brett_robson101**: *i think it gonna be for three weeks*

4:41:51 AM **brett_robson101**: *if that's too much i can make it two weeks just for you my love*

4:42:27 AM **ladydi2011**: Of course I would much rather two weeks than three weeks

4:42:44 AM **ladydi2011**: Will we still be able to chat while you're gone?

4:43:25 AM **brett_robson101**: ok..*i* will make it just for you cos *i* love you so much

4:43:42 AM **brett_robson101**: *i* will be in England guess you know there right?

4:43:56 AM **brett_robson101**: but *i* will be chatting with you while am there ok

4:45:25 AM **ladydi2011**: Thank you honey

4:45:45 AM **ladydi2011**: I am glad we will still be able to chat

4:46:01 AM **ladydi2011**: Or I would really miss you more than I already do

4:46:28 AM **brett_robson101**: *i* will too honey

4:48:44 AM **brett_robson101**: *it just that i got a little problem now that i don't even have anything for the job..they gave me a form to fill out for the job and it cost some money to do that..i thought i would be able to get it but i don't have much with me honey..sorry i don't want to border you with this ok..please don't feel disturb.. i just feel i should tell you cos what i have is your too*

4:49:37 AM **ladydi2011**: It cost money to fill out the form?

4:51:06 AM **brett_robson101**: yeah honey..it a very big job cos *i* told them *i* can't go down to Africa for it so they mail me to fill out the form for it..

4:51:46 AM **ladydi2011**: Hmmmmm, Africa or England? I am confused

4:53:22 AM **brett_robson101**: am suppose to go down to Africa for the job but *i* told them *i* can't cos *i* have a wife..lol..*i* had to tell them the truth cos *i* don't want to loose you..so they mail me a form to fill cos am not gonna be there

4:54:56 AM **brett_robson101**: *you are just all i want to be with ok..cos i thought of it many times that if i get to travel to Africa i wouldn't not have much time to chat with you and get to see you..so i had to tell them the truth about the woman i just found*

4:55:30 AM **brett_robson101**: if you are not ok with that..*i* don't mean to get you worried ok?

4:56:10 AM **ladydi2011**: You are so sweet honey

4:56:24 AM **ladydi2011**: How much do you have to pay for this form?

4:57:26 AM **brett_robson101**: it about $1000 for the form..and *i* got only just $200 here with me..

4:58:59 AM **ladydi2011**: Ok, so you need $800

4:59:50 AM **brett_robson101**: *yeah but i don't want to border you for it ok..i just thought of telling you ok cos i want you to know everything about me and what i do ok..i love you and i don't wanna keep anything from you*

5:01:12 AM **ladydi2011**: Thank you for telling me honey

5:01:24 AM **ladydi2011**: We need to always be open and honest

5:01:48 AM **brett_robson101**: *you are all i got now and i don't want to by any chance loose you for anything ok*

5:02:16 AM **ladydi2011**: You are not going to lose me. So, where do you think you will be able to get this money from?

5:02:35 AM **brett_robson101**: *i* don't know yet honey

5:02:45 AM **brett_robson101**: still thinking honey

5:03:14 AM **ladydi2011**: Do you have any gold jewelry you could sell?

5:03:40 AM **ladydi2011**: It won't take much to get $800

5:03:55 AM **brett_robson101**: no honey *i* don't have that

5:04:46 AM **brett_robson101**: *that why i don't wanna get you worried..if only i can get assistant from some one but i don't now*

5:05:12 AM **ladydi2011**: If you need my help, please let me know, ok

5:06:11 AM **brett_robson101**: *ok..but please can you help me with that honey i promise to pay you back as soon as i get the job done?*

5:06:35 AM **ladydi2011**: Honey, how soon will the job be done?

5:07:54 AM **brett_robson101**: as soon as am done in two weeks..then *i* will get paid for the job

5:08:18 AM **ladydi2011**: And you promise to pay it back then honey

5:08:51 AM **ladydi2011**: Will this payment be hand delivered with your own hands?

5:09:07 AM **brett_robson101**: *sure i promise with the love i have for you and will never fail to do that*

5:09:16 AM **brett_robson101**: you mean for the job?

5:09:59 AM **brett_robson101**: they will wire the money to my account as soon am done honey

5:11:09 AM **ladydi2011**: Ok

5:11:24 AM **brett_robson101**: *and i promise you honey if they wire it i will pay you back ok*

5:11:37 AM **ladydi2011**: Ok...How do I get you this money?

5:12:29 AM **brett_robson101**: *i* will mail you the account where you will send the money ok..

5:12:59 AM **ladydi2011**: Ok honey

5:13:10 AM **ladydi2011**: I want you to be successful

5:13:47 AM **brett_robson101**: *thank you so much my love.. and i promise i will always be there for you and will keep loving you till the world comes to an end*

5:14:10 AM **brett_robson101**: you are the sweetest and most beautiful woman *i* have ever seen

5:14:19 AM **ladydi2011**: I know you will

5:14:43 AM **brett_robson101**: so tell me which side of the bed did you find your self this morning?

5:15:02 AM **ladydi2011**: The right side

5:15:10 AM **ladydi2011**: What about you?

5:15:39 AM **brett_robson101**: WOW that lovely and romantic..we both thought of each other

5:15:48 AM **brett_robson101**: *i* woke up the same side too

5:15:57 AM **ladydi2011**: Ahhhhh...I am sure we did

5:17:17 AM **brett_robson101**: the right of a bed is the most romantic side and the day we will meet *i* promise to love you for the rest of my life and be so romantic..*lol*

5:17:51 AM **ladydi2011**: So, what do you have in mind for our first date when you get to Atlanta?

5:18:58 AM **brett_robson101**: first give you a very lovely and romantic kiss that will last for ten minute then *i* will take you to the most wonderful place for real lovers to be take you to a nice place so quiet where both of us can talk and make the most out of our time

5:20:53 AM **ladydi2011**: I am so looking forward to this nice long romantic kiss

5:21:16 AM **ladydi2011**: Sounds wonderful

5:21:26 AM **ladydi2011**: I can't wait until you get here

5:22:32 AM **brett_robson101**: ok..so tell me about that day?

5:23:28 AM **ladydi2011**: I am looking forward to looking into your eyes

5:23:33 AM **ladydi2011**: holding your had

5:24:00 AM **ladydi2011**: maybe a horse and carriage ride

5:24:23 AM **ladydi2011**: a quiet restaurant where we can talk

5:25:34 AM **brett_robson101**: *i* will be the happiest man ever

5:25:41 AM **brett_robson101**: *i* love you so much honey

5:26:25 AM **ladydi2011**: I love you so much too!

5:26:47 AM **ladydi2011**: I have an appointment so I have to jump in the shower honey

5:27:01 AM **ladydi2011**: Please be sure to send me everything I need, ok

5:27:26 AM **brett_robson101**: ok my love *i* will..

5:27:41 AM **ladydi2011**: Have a wonderful day honey

5:27:53 AM **ladydi2011**: Let's chat tonight, ok?

5:28:34 AM **brett_robson101**: ok my love *i* will send it later and *i* will be here later to chat with you

5:28:40 AM **brett_robson101**: *i* love you so much honey

5:28:58 AM **ladydi2011**: Ok honey

5:29:00 AM **brett_robson101**: please take good care of your self for me ok..*i* will miss you so much..

5:29:06 AM **ladydi2011**: I love you so much too!

5:29:12 AM **brett_robson101**: *i* just wish *i* could come and bath you

5:29:13 AM **ladydi2011**: I will

5:29:25 AM **ladydi2011**: You take care of yourself for me too

5:29:40 AM **ladydi2011**: Until later

5:29:50 AM **brett_robson101**: ok my love..

5:29:54 AM **ladydi2011**: Bye for now baby

5:29:54 AM **brett_robson101**: kisses and hugs

5:30:00 AM **ladydi2011**: kisses and hugs

From: robson101@yahoo.com
To: ladydi
Subject: Hello My Love
Sent: Saturday, July 14, 2012 9:39 AM

Hello my love how are you doing and how did the appointment go hope it was great? am missing you here so much and can't wait to meet you soon after the job and see your pretty smile you always put on your face..honey *i* mail my friend and asked him on how am gonna make the payment for the Form so he gave me one of the ***Director's address for the job on how am gonna make the payment***..*i* wanted to make the payment through account but he said that wouldn't be necessary..so *i* think am gonna make the payment twice and *i* guess *i* will have to give you the information on how you will send it and then mail me everything so that *i* can forward it to them..cos *i* want him to know it coming from me..*i* will be going out later to send the $200 *i* have here and will mail him to wait for the rest..here's the information..

Name: Chris Terumun
State: Lagos
Country: Nigeria
Text Question: What is the money for?
Answer: Contract

that is the directors address where you will have to make the payment..honey i**t gonna be western union cos my friend told me it the only and fastest way to make the payment**..and after you have done that just mail me the rest and *i* will forward it quick to them..*i* will be here later my love to chat with you cos *i* can't wait to have that lovely words from you..*i* love you so much and will miss you here..thanks and take good care of your self for me..talk to you later sweetie. Brett

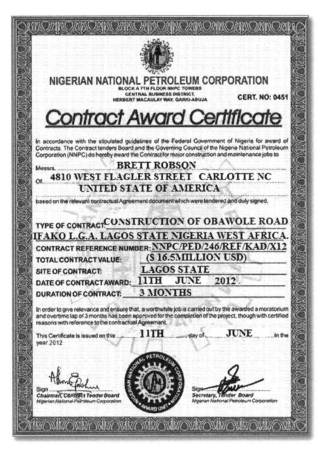

RED FLAGS

- Notice another inconsistency: he tells me he is going to work in England because Africa is too far away from me, but the contract says Nigeria; not England.
- He doesn't ask me for the whole $1000, because he wants to make me think he has some money and he is just in a bind. In the same conversation he changes from promising to pay me back and not "fail me" to "**if**" they wire him his pay he will pay me back.
- Of course, as with all scammers, I am all he has now and he doesn't want to lose me. He will always be there for me and will keep loving me till the world comes to an end. Yeah, right.

🏴 He sends me the contract and the information to wire him the money Western Union to his director in Lagos Nigeria.

🏴 Please take note that the name, city and month have been whited out and changed. Look for alterations on documents.

I got the story... *but there is more*!

IM Jul 14, 2012 2:34:15 PM

2:34:15 PM **ladydi2011**: Hello honey
2:34:36 PM **brett_robson101**: Hello my love
2:34:38 PM **ladydi2011**: I received your email and text
2:34:39 PM **brett_robson101**: am here
2:34:48 PM **brett_robson101**: miss you so much
2:34:57 PM **ladydi2011**: How are you today?
2:35:07 PM **ladydi2011**: I miss you too
2:35:44 PM **brett_robson101**: am already back from walmart to send the money *i* have with me and *i* guess they must have recieved and pick the money
2:36:01 PM **ladydi2011**: Ok, good!
2:36:04 PM **brett_robson101**: am doing great and so happy that *i* will be with you very soon
2:36:58 PM **ladydi2011**: I will do this for you on Monday because my bank was closed by time I got out of my meeting
2:37:13 PM **ladydi2011**: I am happy too baby
2:38:38 PM **brett_robson101**: ok my love..*i* guess *i* will have to mail them again to wait till monday..but the thing that makes me happy is that *i* will see your pretty face and the smile you always put very soon..*i* love you so much..
2:38:59 PM **brett_robson101**: *i* hope you got the information *i* sent from the mail?
2:39:42 PM **ladydi2011**: Yeah honey, we will be together real soon
2:40:08 PM **brett_robson101**: so tell me how did the meeting go?
2:40:35 PM **ladydi2011**: Honey, I did receive the information. Why am I sending this to Lagos?
2:41:05 PM **ladydi2011**: My meeting went really good. Thanks for asking.
2:41:41 PM **brett_robson101**: cos that's where the job is coming from and *i* don't wanna go so far way cos am scared if *i* do i will loose you
2:42:06 PM **ladydi2011**: Ok...Why do you think you will lose me?
2:42:50 PM **brett_robson101**: *i* mean what *i* say about so scared of loosing you cos you mean so much in my life right now
2:43:11 PM **brett_robson101**: you are so charming and very pretty that every man would wanna hold hands with you..*lol*
2:43:32 PM **ladydi2011**: Thanks darling
2:44:02 PM **ladydi2011**: Please do hurry back so we can be together
2:45:16 PM **brett_robson101**: *i* will my love..that why *i* don't wanna go far way from you..you know Lagos is so far way from here and *i* can't bare the distance..*i* love you honey
2:45:58 PM **brett_robson101**: *i* really wanna be with you and give you all the love in life and take good care of you..***we can be together like husband and wife***
2:46:44 PM **ladydi2011**: I want to be with you too!
2:47:19 PM **brett_robson101**: *i* wanna spend my life with you and have kids some day

2:48:16 PM **brett_robson101**: *i* will love to have kids that will look so pretty like you honey

2:48:25 PM **ladydi2011**: *So honey, are you a Yahoo Boy?*

2:49:18 PM **brett_robson101**: what do you mean?

2:49:54 PM **ladydi2011**: *Am I your client?*

Break In Time

2:50:44 PM **brett_robson101**: <ding>

2:50:55 PM **ladydi2011**: *Do you think I am a maga?*

2:51:08 PM **ladydi2011**: <ding>

2:51:42 PM **brett_robson101**: *na wa oo – (hmmmm)*

2:53:08 PM **brett_robson101**: *you dey do dis kind tin*

2:53:35 PM **brett_robson101**: *and you feel it rite to be dis way*

2:53:43 PM **ladydi2011**: Hmmmmmm

2:54:32 PM **brett_robson101**: *hw far nah?*

2:55:32 PM **brett_robson101**: <ding>

2:56:41 PM **brett_robson101**: <ding>

2:56:46 PM **brett_robson101**: talk nah

2:56:53 PM **ladydi2011**: Take care my love!

2:57:12 PM **brett_robson101**: talk to me

2:58:00 PM **ladydi2011**: Kisses

2:58:26 PM **brett_robson101**: much love

2:59:00 PM **ladydi2011**: So, who are you really?

2:59:29 PM **ladydi2011**: How old are you really?

2:59:47 PM **brett_robson101**: *28 and u?*

2:59:55 PM **ladydi2011**: 48

3:00:19 PM **brett_robson101**: talk to me for real ok..

3:00:45 PM **ladydi2011**: Life is like a box of chocolates, you never know what you are going to get!!!

3:01:16 PM **ladydi2011**: For real honey, I am Diana

3:01:34 PM **ladydi2011**: Everything I told you about me is true, unlike everything you told me.

3:02:25 PM **brett_robson101**: *your full name?*

3:02:30 PM **ladydi2011**: 3:05:06 PM **brett_robson101**: *i really had hope you know..things are so rough with me cos my mom is so sick i had to get into dis stuff hoping you will help the situation and now you turn to be not what i was hoping for*

3:05:27 PM **ladydi2011**: You made some major errors in your story line that revealed you as a scammer

3:06:20 PM **brett_robson101**: *i know i was too fast with it but guy i dey para cos i get some paro wey i wanna run with money*

3:06:39 PM **ladydi2011**: *Sorry about your mom and that I am not a good client for you*

3:07:03 PM **brett_robson101**: lol

3:07:17 PM **brett_robson101**: *for real am chris by name*

3:07:27 PM **brett_robson101**: *from Lagos Ikeja*

3:07:34 PM **ladydi2011**: Hello Chris

3:08:02 PM **ladydi2011**: I knew you were from Lagos. I ran your IP

3:08:24 PM **ladydi2011**: It is nice to meet you...for real!

3:09:08 PM **brett_robson101**: me too..

3:09:14 PM **brett_robson101**: where are you from?

3:09:24 PM **ladydi2011**: United States

3:09:42 PM **brett_robson101**: *i see..you really American or Naija?*

3:09:53 PM **ladydi2011**: American

3:10:09 PM **ladydi2011**: Are you surprised?

3:10:10 PM **brett_robson101**: *then what your full name if that is true?*

3:10:28 PM **ladydi2011**: Diana Garren

3:10:36 PM **brett_robson101**: ok

3:10:40 PM **ladydi2011**: Google me baby

3:10:46 PM **brett_robson101**: you are female right?

3:10:53 PM **ladydi2011**: I am a smart woman

3:10:57 PM **brett_robson101**: ok

3:10:58 PM **ladydi2011**: Yeah baby

3:11:55 PM **ladydi2011**: Did you find me?

3:12:20 PM **brett_robson101**: *even if i google you it makes no sence to me cos i know how to creat stuff like that ok*

3:12:31 PM **ladydi2011**: Lol... I know you do

3:12:38 PM **brett_robson101**: *i guess that why you don't wanna put your cam on right?*

3:13:12 PM **ladydi2011**: I will put my cam on later. I am on my phone now.

3:13:17 PM **brett_robson101**: just looking at your page on facebook

3:13:30 PM **ladydi2011**: Yeah

3:13:50 PM **brett_robson101**: with a man and kids right?

3:13:51 PM **ladydi2011**: Go to www.truepercaptions.com

3:13:58 PM **ladydi2011**: Nope!

3:14:18 PM **brett_robson101**: your site?

3:14:25 PM **ladydi2011**: Yep...my business

3:14:30 PM **brett_robson101**: ok

3:14:43 PM **brett_robson101**: what is your real name on facebook

3:14:59 PM **ladydi2011**: You won't find me on FB

3:15:10 PM **brett_robson101**: ok

3:15:31 PM **ladydi2011**: You will find me on linked in

3:15:46 PM **brett_robson101**: ok

3:15:52 PM **ladydi2011**: So, how long have you been doing this?

3:16:02 PM **ladydi2011**: I am the real deal baby

3:16:30 PM **brett_robson101**: *the truth is for four years now battling with this and i have not even make any good money out of it*

3:16:50 PM **ladydi2011**: Wow....

3:17:14 PM **brett_robson101**: *but i can't stop cos i know one day it gonna be ok*

3:17:15 PM **ladydi2011**: It cannot be a fun job

3:17:34 PM **ladydi2011**: You have a lot of competition

3:17:46 PM **brett_robson101**: i guess so

3:18:01 PM **brett_robson101**: *some times i get tired but i keep pushing it*

3:18:33 PM **ladydi2011**: Every man that hit on me from the site was a yahoo boy

3:18:40 PM **ladydi2011**: I must be a magnet

3:19:17 PM **ladydi2011**: You are number 16

3:19:25 PM **brett_robson101**: *it just that we are so many hussling here you know*

3:19:37 PM **ladydi2011**: Yeah, I know

3:19:51 PM **ladydi2011**: I have been to Africa, I get it!!!

3:20:26 PM **ladydi2011**: Do you work for yourself or for a boss?

3:20:36 PM **brett_robson101**: *so why do you keep talking when you know who you are..cos the one i met there don't really hide this long*

3:20:45 PM **brett_robson101**: *i work for my self for this long*

3:21:43 PM **ladydi2011**: Writing a book to hopefully stop online dating fraud and help the people of Nigeria. The government there needs to be changed so the people have more opportunity.

3:21:58 PM **brett_robson101**: ok

3:22:34 PM **brett_robson101**: *it not gonna change anything cos the youth are far way thinking beyond that*

3:22:50 PM **ladydi2011**: What do you mean?

3:22:59 PM **brett_robson101**: *cos every youth now wants to make good money and enjoy life*

3:23:22 PM **ladydi2011**: Yeah, this is what I have learned

3:23:28 PM **brett_robson101**: *yahoo is becoming more tough and they go extra mile to make it*

3:23:49 PM **brett_robson101**: *which you already know...YAHOO PLUS*

3:24:28 PM **ladydi2011**: I did not know about YAHOO PLUS...please tell me about this

3:25:08 PM **ladydi2011**: Chris, I really do want to make a difference

3:26:48 PM **brett_robson101**: *it has gotten into youth now and dey really want to make money..it called yahoo plus becos they go to a spiritualist to hit on a maga then get control over the client..so you have to be careful with the way you talk to people cause if they just get your number that all*

3:27:38 PM **ladydi2011**: If they get my number, what will happen?

3:28:29 PM **brett_robson101**: *your maiden name, fone number and picture then they will take it to a spiritualist to bewitch you and control you to send money when you don't know wat you are doing*

3:28:35 PM **brett_robson101**: *go to go now*

3:29:10 PM **ladydi2011**: Africa is the richest continent and it shouldn't be like this for the people.

3:29:50 PM **ladydi2011**: Take care of yourself Chris

3:30:15 PM **ladydi2011**: It really is nice to meet you!

He was really shocked when I asked him if he was a Yahoo Boy and if I was his "client", or "maga." He then started speaking in Pidgin English trying to figure out if I am another scammer. He really wants to see me on cam but I still have not gone on cam for him. He thinks I am another scammer because he asks me why I kept talking so long. He said the other scammers he met online didn't hide this long. He told me he has worked for himself the entire time.

He was really upset I turned out to not be what he was hoping for. He was not who he portrayed himself to be but I guess that was ok and fair. Excuse me!

He is the first one to tell me about Yahoo Plus. This is where they take the persons maiden name and picture to a spiritualist to bewitch them so they can have control over that person to send money. He then tells me I better be careful with the way I talk to people when I don't know what I am doing...and then he was gone! He definitely got my attention and I started researching this and found information on it that you will read in chapter eight, The Unknown Hidden Dangers of Online Dating (p. 739). Not long after this, I no longer chatted under my real name and created a new profile with a picture of me in a wig. I thought this was the last I would ever hear from Chris, but I was wrong. Two weeks later he called and said he was really pissed off that day when he learned I played him to get information. He then said he couldn't get me off his mind and wanted to know if I was who I said I was and if I was, he wanted to help me but he first wanted to see me on cam.

Text Messages

To: +234_____
Received: Jul 27, 2012 9:17 AM

Hi Chris. Thanks for calling. Sorry we got cut off. I am who I told you I am. My intentions are good.

IM 2012 9:18:11 AM

9:18:11 AM **ladydi2011**: Hi
9:18:22 AM **ladydi2011**: I am here
9:18:28 AM **ladydi2011**: What's up?
9:18:31 AM **brett_robson101**: ok dear
9:18:45 AM **brett_robson101**: how are you doing today and *i* really miss chatting with you here
9:18:54 AM **ladydi2011**: Nice to hear from you
9:19:28 AM **ladydi2011**: I miss chatting with you too
9:20:00 AM **brett_robson101**: am doing good
9:20:30 AM **ladydi2011**: I am glad
9:20:38 AM **brett_robson101**: so tell me what up with you?
9:21:04 AM **ladydi2011**: Really busy speaking and writing
9:21:47 AM **brett_robson101**: *i just really wanna know more about you ok*
9:22:10 AM **brett_robson101**: *i still find it hard to think if you are real to me*
9:22:33 AM **ladydi2011**: What do you mean?
9:22:45 AM **ladydi2011**: Of course I am real!
9:23:50 AM **ladydi2011**: Thanks for telling me about the YAHOO PLUS
9:24:21 AM **brett_robson101**: *but there is more to it my friend*
9:24:27 AM **ladydi2011**: That's pretty deep
9:24:37 AM **ladydi2011**: There is?
9:24:49 AM **brett_robson101**: *i only gave you a bit of it and if you wanna know more about it i will but i must kow why and what you are trying to do ok*
9:25:13 AM **ladydi2011**: I really do want to know more
9:25:44 AM **ladydi2011**: I told you. I am trying to make a positive difference
9:26:21 AM **ladydi2011**: My intern is from Tanzania
9:26:34 AM **brett_robson101**: *look my friend...there's lot more to it than you can ever imaging*
9:26:36 AM **ladydi2011**: I have some friends from Nigeria
9:26:50 AM **brett_robson101**: and you have never been here?
9:27:09 AM **ladydi2011**: I have been to Niger on a mission trip but not to Nigeria
9:28:07 AM **ladydi2011**: I have had a love for Africa since I was a little girl

9:28:34 AM **ladydi2011**: I never set out to write this book...it just happened

9:29:06 AM **brett_robson101**: *ok...but can you prove to me that you got friends from my country...cos this imformation i wanna give to you is gonna cause me my life ok*

9:29:43 AM **ladydi2011**: I don't know if you believe in God but I do and I know he is using me

9:30:21 AM **ladydi2011**: Let me get to my computer and I will send you some pictures...ok

9:30:39 AM **ladydi2011**: I am on my phone

9:31:06 AM **brett_robson101**: ok...*i* do believe in God so much

9:31:11 AM **ladydi2011**: Chris...nobody will ever know you gave me the information

9:31:20 AM **ladydi2011**: Please hold while I sign out from my phone and into pc

9:40:32 AM **ladydi2011**: I am back

9:40:33 AM **brett_robson101**: ok

9:40:53 AM **brett_robson101**: can *i* ask you something?

9:41:23 AM **ladydi2011**: Of course, please ask

9:43:03 AM **brett_robson101**: *i really wanna help you with this but my instick keep telling me something isn't right*

9:43:32 AM **brett_robson101**: *if you know you are for real let me see you on cam now and no excuses*

9:44:05 AM **ladydi2011**: Here is a website of my friends that I just sent you a picture of

9:44:26 AM **ladydi2011**: Ok....But please give me a minute to put some clothes on

9:48:40 AM **brett_robson101**: ok

9:48:47 AM **brett_robson101**: are you there?

9:49:03 AM **brett_robson101**: <ding>

9:51:53 AM **ladydi2011**: My cam is showing black

9:51:59 AM **ladydi2011**: Can you see me?

9:52:04 AM **brett_robson101**: nothing

9:52:16 AM **ladydi2011**: Ok....I have had problems with this cam

9:52:25 AM **ladydi2011**: Please let me go to my other computer

9:52:31 AM **brett_robson101**: ok

9:52:32 AM **ladydi2011**: Hold again...ok

9:52:37 AM **brett_robson101**: ok

9:52:41 AM **ladydi2011**: I am going to sign off here

9:52:51 AM **ladydi2011**: It will take a minute because I have to boot it

9:52:57 AM **brett_robson101**: ok

10:00:27 AM **ladydi2011**: I am back again

10:00:42 AM **brett_robson101**: ok

10:00:53 AM **ladydi2011**: Can you see me?

10:01:38 AM **brett_robson101**: yeah *i* can now

10:01:47 AM **ladydi2011**: Good

10:01:57 AM **brett_robson101**: you look very pretty and so young

10:02:07 AM **ladydi2011**: Thank you I am 48

10:02:21 AM **brett_robson101**: *i* love that smile Diana

10:02:32 AM **ladydi2011**: you are so kind Chris

10:02:57 AM **brett_robson101**: *thanks..that who i am..if am not i wouldnt be here talking to you..*

10:03:16 AM **ladydi2011**: Thank you for telling me your real name

10:03:31 AM **ladydi2011**: Do you now believe I am who I say I am?

10:03:57 AM **brett_robson101**: *you can check me out on facebook if you wanna know more about me*

10:04:11 AM **ladydi2011**: Ok...what do I look under
10:05:06 AM **brett_robson101**: how do you mean?
10:05:34 AM **ladydi2011**: You only ever told me your first name
10:05:46 AM **ladydi2011**: I would need more than this to find you on FB
10:06:06 AM **brett_robson101**: (Removed his real name)
10:07:35 AM **ladydi2011**: Chris, you look so young
10:07:40 AM **ladydi2011**: How old are you?
10:09:11 AM **brett_robson101**: you check my profile already?
10:09:36 AM **ladydi2011**: I did. I wanted to have a "real" face with your name
10:10:00 AM **brett_robson101**: ok..so what did you see ?
10:10:17 AM **ladydi2011**: Did you go to school here in the states?
10:10:24 AM **ladydi2011**: Do I have your page?
10:10:44 AM **brett_robson101**: yeah that my page..lol
10:11:02 AM **brett_robson101**: yeah *i* did
10:11:42 AM **ladydi2011**: This is wonderful!
10:11:58 AM **brett_robson101**: thanks.. but *i* lost everything when *i* lost my dad
10:12:14 AM **ladydi2011**: What happened to your dad?
10:12:49 AM **brett_robson101**: *i couldn't finish what He wanted me to become..He died from a gun shot straight to his head..*
10:13:08 AM **ladydi2011**: What?
10:13:55 AM **brett_robson101**: *yeah i was still in school and after that i came back and eveything started going down for me*
10:14:14 AM **brett_robson101**: *i couldn't go back to school and all my dad had whent with the wind*
10:14:36 AM **brett_robson101**: it a long story and so sorry *i* can't say much about that ok
10:14:56 AM **ladydi2011**: I am so sorry
10:15:21 AM **ladydi2011**: I believe you will still achieve what your dad wanted for you
10:15:26 AM **ladydi2011**: It is your destiny
10:15:37 AM **brett_robson101**: it ok..life goes on you know
10:15:45 AM **ladydi2011**: I do know
10:16:03 AM **ladydi2011**: I have had some bad things happen too but I am still alive
10:16:30 AM **ladydi2011**: Chris, I would really appreciate your knowledge
10:16:56 AM **ladydi2011**: I do not believe in coincidences in life
10:17:08 AM **ladydi2011**: There is a purpose to our meeting
10:17:26 AM **brett_robson101**: you are right
10:17:43 AM **brett_robson101**: can *i* call you girl cos you really look so young and pretty..lol?
10:17:54 AM **ladydi2011**: Sure....
10:17:58 AM **ladydi2011**: Thank you
10:18:05 AM **brett_robson101**: that my girl
10:20:24 AM **brett_robson101**: *you know when i first got into this yahoo of a thing i really had love for white women smile and i couldnt hold it but wanna tell them the real me but friends who led me into this said if i do i wouldn't make any money from it so i had to keep my silence as a fake white man..lol*
10:21:16 AM **brett_robson101**: your smile and charming eyes reminds me of the very first day girl
10:21:26 AM **ladydi2011**: Yeah
10:22:23 AM **ladydi2011**: God has blessed me with my looks and smile and I am grateful

10:23:22 AM **brett_robson101**: *yeah you are so pretty and i thought if you were born on a raining day the first time i saw your picture*

10:23:44 AM **ladydi2011**: Why on a raining day?

10:24:42 AM **brett_robson101**: *cos it so pretty when a woman gives birth on a rainig day..and the baby look pretty the way the raing drops from the sky*

10:24:50 AM **ladydi2011**: Chris, my heart and spirit is much prettier than my exterior

10:25:07 AM **ladydi2011**: I never heard this before

10:25:08 AM **brett_robson101**: *i* can feel that already girl

10:25:14 AM **ladydi2011**: Thank you

10:25:33 AM **brett_robson101**: so tell me about your life..do you have any kids?

10:26:05 AM **ladydi2011**: I have been divorced for 15 years

10:26:12 AM **ladydi2011**: I do not have any children

10:26:21 AM **ladydi2011**: I have 5 brothers and no sisters, many nieces and nephews

10:27:01 AM **brett_robson101**: oh so sorry for everything...but God is able and will give you a child one day if you still want any

10:27:34 AM **ladydi2011**: Yes, I know.

10:28:08 AM **ladydi2011**: Chris, ever since I was 8 yrs old, I knew I would write a book that would make a difference but I never knew what it was about until now

10:29:13 AM **brett_robson101**: ok, am ready to help you in writing a wonderful book ok girl

10:30:00 AM **ladydi2011**: I know you will fulfill the purpose God has for you

10:30:07 AM **ladydi2011**: You rock!

10:31:00 AM **brett_robson101**: thanks and God has a purpose for us ok

10:33:01 AM **brett_robson101**: *i* will mail you everything you wanna know later ok

10:33:10 AM **ladydi2011**: OK

10:33:31 AM **brett_robson101**: and anything you wanna know let me know and *i* try my best to help you

10:33:48 AM **ladydi2011**: Thank you Chris

10:33:59 AM **ladydi2011**: Do you miss the States?

10:34:20 AM **brett_robson101**: are you in any relationship now or married?

10:34:29 AM **brett_robson101**: *i* do a lot girl

10:35:09 AM **ladydi2011**: No

10:40:27 AM **ladydi2011**: I am still here but need to take this call

10:41:28 AM **brett_robson101**: ok

10:45:21 AM **ladydi2011**: Sorry

10:45:37 AM **ladydi2011**: This is a friend who just had surgery. She is 69

10:46:07 AM **brett_robson101**: oh ok..hope she's fine

10:46:40 AM **ladydi2011**: She is but needs me to bring her some things later today

10:46:46 AM **ladydi2011**: She is alone

10:47:01 AM **brett_robson101**: oh ok..

10:47:05 AM **brett_robson101**: *i* understand girl..

10:48:03 AM **brett_robson101**: do you still have my number?

10:48:09 AM **ladydi2011**: I like my new name

10:48:18 AM **brett_robson101**: lol

10:48:28 AM **brett_robson101**: and *i* love it when you smile

10:49:03 AM **ladydi2011**: Thank you

10:49:07 AM **ladydi2011**: I like smiling

10:50:21 AM **ladydi2011**: I really need to go but will email you

10:51:20 AM **brett_robson101**: yeah..if not that you are my friend and older than *i* am *i* would want to date you for real
10:51:34 AM **brett_robson101**: Ok, I wait your email

Text Messages

To: +234_____
Received: Jul 27, 2012 11:47 AM

Chris, you are a good man with a good heart. I am grateful God has connected us. You WILL do GREAT things to bring about change. Sincerely, Your Girl...

I was extremely shocked to get a call from Chris after two weeks had passed. I thought he was gone forever! He still didn't know if I was a real person or a scammer. I went on cam so he could see who I am and gain his trust because I really need to learn what he knows for this book. Once I showed myself to him on cam he believed I was who I said and became one of my sources. He then taught me all he knew about Yahoo Plus and Yahoo Extreme that you will find in chapter eight (p. 739), and the inner workings of the scam in chapter seven (p. 677). He nicknamed me "girl".

One of the first things I asked him when he started giving me information was why he used his real phone number and name and he said he didn't like having different phones and SIM cards and tried to keep things simple. I asked him what he told women that asked about his number and he told them it is an international phone number that he has, and they believed him and were impressed. I think it is extremely risky to use a real name, and to this day I am not convinced he gave me his real name. Because his life could be in danger for telling me things, I cannot blame him if he is lying. Scammers are such good liars that it is very difficult to know when a scammer is telling the truth. I am very grateful to Chris for freely teaching me so I can teach you. The scammer in the next chapter is a real puzzle. You will learn a lot from "this" man or should I say "these" men.

CHAPTER 6

ARE YOU JIMMY OR ARE YOU ROBIN?

T he scammer or scammers in this chapter use the same format but different scam stories. To this day, I do not know if it was one scammer using different names and pictures or two different scammers using the same format and different stories. This chapter will teach you how scammers can use the same format but put different stories to the format. It will help you to look for the same words and terminologies and know that if you see them, you are dealing with a scammer.

In this chapter you will see how someone who is confident and on top of his game becomes sloppy and desperate when he fears the end is near. You will learn how a scammer will come back after you when you least expect it and as always, you will go through many different emotions and learn much about how to recognize a scam, so you can protect your heart and your money.

Profile as found on *Singlesbee*:

Profile: lovecope48

49-year-old man in Atlanta, GA
Looking for girls 37 to 60, up to 50 miles from me

My Headline

LOOKING FOR MY *DREAMN* SOUL MATE. I will *i* find my match on this dating site.

My Basics

- Height: 6'9"
- Body type: Average
- Ethnicity: White / Caucasian
- Education: Graduate degree
- *Occupation: Construction and installation*
- Income: $250,000
- I speak: English
- Religion: Christian - other
- *Relationship status: Widowed*
- Children: No
- Wants children: Undecided
- Smoking: Never Drinking: Occasionally
- Drinking: Occasionally

My Type of Girl

- Looking for: Dating / Long-term Potential, Long-term Only
- With: ***Women 37 to 60-year-old***
- Distance: Within 50 miles of Atlanta
- Height: 5'0" to 6'0"
- Body type: Any
- Hair color: Any
- Ethnicity: Doesn't Matter
- Education: Doesn't Matter
- Occupation: Any
- Income: Doesn't Matter
- Language(s): English
- Religion: Any
- Relationship status: Any
- Children: Doesn't Matter
- Wants children: Doesn't Matter
- Smoking: Doesn't Matter
- Drinking: Doesn't Matter

About Me

I am a simple man that is self employed,*i* believe that handwork, planning and some elements of luck are important in achieving success.I love to go the beach,watch movies and *i* do like playing tennis too.A short walk or running during my leisure periods are things are enjoy doing because *i* need to be fit.I'm an open book and someone with a simple heart because *i* believe that this life is short and needs to be fully enjoyed .I would like to meet a woman who understands the meaning of love without conditions, someone who knows the importance of honesty ,care and understanding in a relationship .I understand that they are nice women out there who are searching for love without conditions,i'm a romantic man who needs a woman who will be my best friend.*i* hope joining here would worth it, *I also love helping orphanage home children very much*, goes out to only who is intersted out there *know time for games*,let us give it a shot out try. Again you must bee very caring and honest , mostly respect, you must also love children the same way *i* do, *i hate cheating and lairs very much*..I know *i* will meet that woman right here on this same dating market as my faith promise me.

I always dream to meet that right woman of my life who *i* will always be closer to.which *i* will also love all that matters to her? always *treat her like a queen* bring her breakfast to her bed then kiss her after telling me thank you Hun? Do you love to run away with me sometimes where we would be out of business environment to spend quality time together?*i* will like to take her to places show her what new life is all about also show her some new things and end up been on the Mountain cuddling Each Other *tell her God Great News*.and how us future will be cos it will be the best future so far..

Who I'd Like To Meet

Nice woman of God who believe in Christian faith possibly, possibly not. Optimistic, happy caring woman who loves life, herself, others & is adventurous & maybe even *wants to save the world*. Someone who does not feel sorry for herself & is not afraid of life and is open-minded to new ideas. She is aggressive & confident but not pushy. Believes in being healthy, positive and understands basic human psychology and how life works. A woman who is beautiful and modest. Does not use her body to sell herself in pictures to men for attention; but uses her mind & spirit. Self-motivated. Wants to be loved and adored & gives the same unconditionally.

RED FLAGS

- The occupation of construction and installation. Many scammers have this occupation
- Poor spelling and grammar; lower case I's
- Looking for women between the ages of 37-60
- Widowed
- He has no specific preferences about the type of woman he is looking for
- He loves helping orphanage homes. This is part of his scam
- He has no time for games and hates cheating and liars; this assertion is often a red flags
- He will treat his woman like a "queen." This terminology is used in Africa
- Proclaims to be a Christian and is looking for a woman who wants to "save the world"
- Taking all of the above as a whole, you can be sure it is a scammer

And the emails began…

From: lovecope48
To: ladedi
Subject: Hello Cute, never stop smiling!
Sent: 06/04/2012 07:41AM

Hi,My name is Jimmy Everyone here call me Jim Hmmm (more...) , that's funny right... I saw your charming pics and *i* was like Oh My God,*i* must stop by to say hello to this beautiful creation. I have never in my life set my eyes on something as beautiful as this. I am shocked to see a beautiful woman like you on here, Wow it seems *i* have seen an angel?? to be honest with you cause am interested in what *i* see and what *i* see is beautiful to my eyes sight. I will also love to get to know you better. We can be friend may be see where this gonna lead us both to.Here *i* go, you can as well hit me on. *jimmylove4827 at ya hoo dot com* or send me yours own email address so that *i* can also write you more about me same time send you more pictures of me ok.

I lone to read from you asap.
Have a blessed day.
Jimmy

From: ladedi
To: lovecope48
Subject: Hello Cute, never stop smiling!
Sent: 06/04/2012 010:19AM

Hello Jimmy!

Thank you for taking the time to read my profile and write me. I received and appreciate the compliments. God has blessed me with inner beauty that is so much more beautiful than my outer beauty. You are very handsome yourself. I love what I read on your profile. We appear to have similar interests and share the most important thing, which is our love for the Lord. For me, it is not about speaking it, but being it!

I have been so busy building my business for the last eight years that I didn't date. Now is the time for me to find my "forever" man, a man who will love me as passionately as I will love him. I am ready! Are you ready for your "forever" relationship? I would like to start building a friendship and see where it takes us. You can reach me at ladydi2011@yahoo.com.

I look forward to hearing back from you!
Blessings,
Diana

From: jimmylove4827@yahoo.com
To: ladydi
Subject: More about me, Read and also get back to me ASAP...
Sent: Tuesday, June 5, 2012 5:02 AM

Hello sweets,

Hope you are having a wonderful day,it was so good to hear from you and *i* am also honored that you could share all you did with me,for a minute there *i* was scared that *i* would not hear from you again.*I must say that i feel i can share anything with you already so I'M going to let the cat out of the bag.i* like that of yours lovely Compliment.oh My Gosh such a cute and beautiful angel who have a great words and Respect kind of person you *her* Dear.I guess you should truly know who *i* am ,

I don't really know how this is to work, but hey! here is an exclusive. If at my age *i* do not know what and when to say, then what would *i* be? When a wise man sees he has probably spent about half of his time in life already, he begins to assess his main goals in life. What could be more. important than a happy ending? *LOL,.* A man needs to live his life full of joy and happiness. No matter his achievements, he is reduced to nothing if he has no crown to complete him and that is a woman to call his own. Wife and Best friend.

A woman who knows that even while arguing they still need to hold hands. A woman whom *i* can call a partner in crime,lol A woman whom you can tell anything. How could you think anything can make you happier in life than finding a love that knows no bound. To make you know more about me,.I will break this down to segments and it would be like a case study.

MY BACKGROUND

I am *48yrs* of Age I was born to a loving couple, a home, by an *America man and a British woman*. My father was an international business man who met this British orphan whose only family were close friends.. She says there was something about the man that no woman could ever resist, sometimes she says she sees same in me,*lol.* During my father's global movement, *when i was twelve i left to study int lethridge Alberta in Canada. where i got the first degree in civil Eng* and then *i* later moved on to join them back in the UK. My father died and she was left alone. I met my late-wife and best friend in Paris. she was a fashion model. Very good at heart.Actually *i* could say *i* met her in a funny way, would. explain that later.

My mother is old now and at almost 80 she cant wait to have a proper family, and *i* cant wait to have a *happy home* too. after my last project here in Dubai, UAE, *i* am quitting field works. Any other job would only require my attention from my home office wherever *i* go. I want to spend the rest of my life having fun.

I have a house in Paris where *i* found my Late-wife and got married, I have one in South Chelsea London, while *i have no home.one in (U.S.A. in Atlanta GA)*my father Original country were *i* live presently before going for this great trip here in Dubai. Would you stand by me to build a home? Would you smile at me when *i* look tense? I don't need a super model, *i* rather need a very good friend who knows when *i* am tensed just by looking into my eyes and a super woman.

The whole world may be mad at me, but if you are smiling at me, *i* would care less of cos *Age doesn't matter to what am looking for in my woman* as you know is just a number not all men know what the real love is all about. so *i* prefer to meet that great woman who know what the feeling of love is all about. If I also have to tell you this am not looking for a child as undermost but if by any reason my woman can still bear more kid fine that will be ok by me but if you can't bear more children *i* will %100 accept you that way you are. love, honest,caring, hate cheating,Here are the most important things am after in a relationship which can also lead tomarriage.

MY JOB

I am a global contractor. I do basically rig constructions and renovations. or over water bridges. We have worked at many countries across the globe. The presentproject here is my last on the field and *i* shall quit field works and continue my works from my home office while my men do the field ops.I think *i* really have gotten to this height cos *i* embraced work for so long trying to get over my late wife, that *i* worked this hard, but *i* think *i* now realize *i* can move on.

MY DREAM

I have told you how my typical dream day would be like, *i* just want to spend the rest of my life enjoying the fruit of my labor. I just want a woman who would be my best friend and everything. You know someone whom we would still love each other more as the days pass by, even when we cant make love anymore and all we could do is play bingo, **LOL**.

I saw something in your face, something that made my heart pause to read you, something that tickles in the heart, could it be love at first sight? maybe we could find that out,*lol*. I'm talking about faith here when feelings are so powerful it's as if some force beyond your control is guiding you to someone who can make you happy beyond your wildest dreams. Now tell me more about you....*what do you do for a living? what do you do for fun?whats your best color?whats your best meal? how long have you been on the internet dating and what are your Experience with those men on the dating site, i mean how many men have you met so far also want to know which of this country in the world are they from, e.t.c*

MYHOBBIES

I love mostly out doors for fun, like *i* love reading, listening to music and clubbing,Cooking,dancing,I love dirt bike riding,snowboarding, taking my boat to the lake, wake boarding and fishing and *i also love visiting new places mostly going to an.Orphanage Home to help those Lil Saint Childcare's* and lot more I am a total package , *i* only need someone who understands the value of a good smile. I cant wait to hear back from you distance really doesn't matter in what *i* am looking for ok my dearest.

Have a nice day my ballerina girl
Love
Jimmy Jackson,
xoxoxo

From: ladydi2011@yahoo.com
To: Jimmy Jackson
Subject: Good Morning........Looking forward to your reply
Sent: Wednesday, June 6, 2012 1:52 AM

Hello Jimmy,

My day was good but long. How was your day? I am sorry it has taken me so long to write back. I wanted to have the time to really write to you. (smile).

The same is true for me; all my achievements, yet I have no man to love and be loved by. I was too busy building my business...one day I woke up and said, "Something is drastically wrong with my life. I have all this love to give and nobody to give it to." This is what brought me to online dating.

You made me laugh when you said "like a case study." I have my clients write case studies all the time. By the way, did I tell you I am a business strategist, transformational speaker and author?

Nice, we are both 48. So, you are charismatic? So am I! People say there is something about me too that cannot be resisted. When I walk into a room, everyone knows I have walked in because I have a huge presence. I do not see it, but this is what I am told. So, you were married to a fashion model from Paris. I look forward to learning how you met. I am sorry you lost her. I am sure this was difficult for you. I was married for 8 years (from 27-35). We are still friend's today...long story that I will tell you another time.

Both my parents are still alive. My dad is 85 and my mom is 73. I had 5 brothers. I lost one of them to cancer at the age of 38. I am the only girl. I have many nieces and nephews but no kids of my own. At this age, I do not think I want to have children. I would be almost 70 by time they graduate. This wouldn't be fair to them. However, I would consider adopting an older child. There are so many children who need a home and to be loved.

So, you are in Dubai. I hear it is nice there. Is it? Please send me some pictures of Dubai. Considering how much you have traveled, do you still want to travel or do you want to be a homebody? Which home would you want to live in; the one in Paris, London or Atlanta? So, why did you choose Atlanta?

Of course I would stand with you and build a home together. I would smile at you and bring you to a place of calm when you are tense. I would be your best friend, confidant, soul mate and lover. I don't want a man that I can live with; I want a man I can't live without! I do know what love is. I love with all I am and I am looking for a man who will love me back with the same passion, desire and intensity. I want it all and I am ready to give my all! One cannot want what they do not know. Nor can one give what they do not know. I do know what love is and I have a lot of it to give. I am extremely honest and blunt. My friends say, "Diana is my name and blunt is my game." lol... sometimes the truth hurts, but it will never hurt as much as a lie. I do not lie. I have never cheated on a man and will never disrespect my man in such a way. If my eyes wandered it would mean there was a problem, and I would go to my man and tell him what was happening and ask him to work with me on our relationship to fix it. A vow is sacred...to love, honor and cherish means just that. Nowhere in there do I hear "dis-respect", "lie" or "cheat."

I know what it is like to bury oneself in work. I did the same thing. I have not dated in 8 years. Now I am ready. It sounds like you are too. As long as I have the man next to me who I was in love with, I would be happy anywhere doing anything. Btw...sex is sex. Nothing to write home about. However, making love with real intimacy...this is what I am looking for. What about you?

I was really attracted to you too. Truth be told, I was anxiously awaiting this email and pictures. Please do not tell anyone, especially Jimmy...I do not want him to know this soon after meeting that I am attracted...(see, I can make you laugh and smile even across all these miles. Can you imagine what I can do in person? You would be happier than your wildest dreams).

About me... Hmmmm... What you see is what you get. I do not pretend to be someone I am not. I am a confident woman. I am comfortable in my own skin. However, it doesn't look the same as it did in my 20's. I would never want to be in my 20's again. I like where I am and who I am today. I do not demand respect; I command it because of who I am. I respect others and appreciate others. I live in a place of gratitiude and integrity. For fun I love to travel, swim, read, and listen to music (I love the blues, R &B and jazz the best). I like boating, cruising in my convertible, walking and lying on the beach, smowmobiling, horseback riding, dancing, dining, going to plays and movies, drinking wine, roasting marshmellows over a fire, grilling out, having picnics, being fed, cuddling, surprising my man, and being surprised by my man... I think it is great that you visit orphanages. I would love to do this with you. I have gone on a mission trip to Africa and it changed me forever. People in the United States who have not traveled outside their little world have no clue how lucky and blessed they are. I am a global thinker and have a huge heart.

My best color is plum, what about yours? I love the hibachi and Italian food the best. What is your favorite food?

Prior to online dating I dated a man from Greece who lives here. It wasn't a match. He was only 42 and still trying to find himself and he was very negative. He sucked the life and energy out of me... I am a positive person. I do not dwell on a problem, I look for a resolution. I see the glass as half full, not half empty. I am not looking for a man I need to mold or shape. I am also not looking for a man who I would want to change. I am looking for a man who I love and admire exactly how he is. I do not believe love can happen without admiration. I am attracted to foreign men and sharp dressed men. Online dating... I have been on line for two and a half months. I get a minimum of 10 hits a day. I chatted with many men but seriously with only three. Two of them were not who they portrayed themselves to be, so I was dissapointed. It is easy for cowards to hide behind a screen and lie. As you know, I do not like liars and people who play games. I have chatted with men from all over the world. The two I just told you about... one was from London and one from Denmark. I am currently talking to a man from Michigan who appears to be the real deal. I have not met anyone in person yet. The man from Michigan is supposed to fly here to meet me within the next couple weeks. He is 53 and a real estate investor. He told me his goal is to court me and win my heart. We will see!

I have learned in the online dating world that everything to me is now "supposedly." Talk is cheap and always has been. I want to see actions behind the talk. I am extremely big on people keeping their word. To me, your word is your bond. Jimmy, I am ready to meet my "forever," but I am not desperate. I am very selective. I know what I want and I will not settle. Men have sent me inappropriate pictures, which showed me they did not respect me, and this really did not set right with me. I had a man want to enter a business deal with me in which he would pay me $15,000 a month and buy me whatever home and car I wanted. I would have had to be available to him when he flew into town, travel with him, and keep my emotions out of it. This I am not interested in... I AM NOT FOR SALE!

Please tell me what you have experienced online. They say you have to go through a lot of frogs before you find your prince. I have gone through some frogs... it is time to meet my prince! So, when will you be back in Atlanta? Love knows no distance. However, I do not want a long distance relationship that will always be long distance. I want to be with my man and am willing to go wherever he is. I can run my business from anywhere in the world. Btw, it is 1:49 am here and 9:49 am there, so good morning!

Fondly,

Diana

From: jimmylove4827@yahoo.com
To: ladydi
Subject: Hello here are some new pix of me, I want you to keep to us promise ok baby...
Sent: Wednesday, June 6, 2012 8:30 AM

Honey pie,

You are a very giving woman in every way (yes I am spoiled), and most of all you make me feel safe, emotionally and mentally. Thank you for being part of my life. I'm very happy with you and I could not ask for a better woman than you. **Thank you for warming feeling you have for me despite of my shortcomings and emotional rollerskating.** Thank you for being an exceptional woman - you are one of a kind!

Here are some more picture of me check them out and tell me what *i* look like on those wonderful pictures of me my love..lol

Yours For Ever Jimmy **Husband To Be**!!!

Love always,
xoxoxox

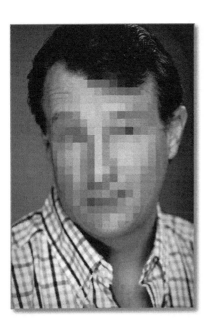 

I already know this man is a scammer from his profile, and since he took a different approach with his email I wanted to see his game.

RED FLAGS

- He was full of compliments in his first email. This is typical of scammers.
- His grammar and use of punctuation was poor and he used a lot of lower case I's. Even if you do not know good grammar, I am sure after reading all the chats, you will be able to now pick out scammer grammar and poor use of punctuation.
- Instead of saying his address was jimmylove4827@yahoo.com, he spelled out ya hoo dot com. This is also something I have seen scammers do.
- Scammers make you think they are comfortable with you very quickly.
- Many times when a scammer writes "lol", he is actually laughing to himself about what he is writing to you, so pay attention when someone you are chatting with is laughing.
- In his profile he said he was 49 and in his email he says he is 48. You will often find a discrepancy in a scammer's supposed age, so be sure to go back and look on his profile.
- He said the age of the woman he is looking for doesn't matter. This is because he doesn't want to eliminate a woman who has money.
- He also used the term "happy home", which is a definite red flag that you are chatting with a man from Nigeria.
- His email does not make it clear if he does or doesn't have a home in Atlanta. Look for what he isn't saying to make things clear for you.
- He follows the scammer pattern of asking what I do for a living, what I do for fun, how long I have been Internet dating, what type of experiences I have had, and also what parts of the world the men I met were from.
- He mentioned an orphanage again, so I am sure his scam will involve an orphanage. The pictures he sent me were numbered Jimmy 1, Jimmy 2 and so on. Who labels their pictures this way? One of the pictures he sent me had a copyright by a photography studio, so I didn't include it. When I looked closely, it didn't look like the face of the other pictures. I have seen this many times with scammers. Be sure to compare pictures closely.
- He signed his third email "Husband to be". Yep, this is another red flag of a scammer. They quickly want you to think of yourself as their wife so you will do anything for them.

From: ladydi2011@yahoo.com
To: Jimmy Jackson
Subject: Re: Hello here are some new pix of me, I want you to keep to us promise ok baby...
Sent: Wednesday, June 6, 2012, 2:52 PM

Hello Sugar...

How did your day go? Mine was busy. Thank you for the pictures. You are very sexy! So you are spoiled and so am I. Let's continue to be spoiled together and spoil each other. I am a giving woman and I want the man I choose to feel very loved and special at all times. Can you handle this?

You are an exceptional man and I am grateful you are a part of my life. Thank you for recognizing my qualities. Yes, I am one of a kind. God had to break the mold after he made me. His angels are on overtime watching over me...my godmother has always said that extraordinary things and experiences just seem to find me. With you looking out for me, maybe the angels can have a little break... lol

Please tell me more about your shortcomings and your emotional roller skating. Please also tell me what my life would be like with you. You are a man who knows what he wants, aren't you? So, you want to be my husband without ever meeting me in person first? Are you sure? I have attached some more pictures of me. Please let me know what you think of them...

Love,
Diana

From: jimmylove4827@yahoo.com
To: ladydi
Subject: How Are You Doing Today Wonder?
Sent: Wed, 6 Jun 2012 05:27:54 -0700 (PDT)

Hello angel,

I really appreciate this consistent communication and *i* will say it is a sign of will, and *i* tell you where there is a will there is success ahead. I believe we both know that Love is not a destination but a journey and this is a journey that takes two to walk. I mean two souls who understand ahead that they aren't in for a kid walk, and what they have ahead is the most important mission in life. A place meant for true people,it is a place called joy and happiness.Really *i* just see in your face that *i* can live with this woman, not the beauty part alone, but the depth of your soul.

As *i* could remember, as a kid *i* was a very cute one,lol. One whom many bullies would target, but only to realize there is a tough side to me. I could make a sober person dance. *i* could affect one with my smile. I grew up having more older friends. Many would confide in me. To tell you, *i* am a type that doesn't judge. no matter how dirty you may be, just come clean to me, and *i* will give you support.

There is no Mr right until we make him right. A relationship is never about how much at the beginning but how much we could make it grow into. My old friend and pastor would tell me, if you aren't ready to feel or look stupid, then don't fall in love ,lol But sincerely that is the bitter truth. When *i* lost my late wife, she told me that the fact that something good ends doesn't mean something better can't start. Can you prove that right? I have come to realize that let a man write a better book, let him preach a better sermon, let him sing the best of songs, let him gain wealth beyond dreams, he is reduced to nothing except he has a woman to call, my wife, my best friend and co-pilot. My usual saying, and *i* am known for it, is that, Life is simple, for those who take it simple. I don't like to complicate things,there is joy in every situation if you know the right angle to look it from. I say,Who says we cant design our own paradise together?

It is workable,just walk by my side as for me don't think distant really matter to what we are looking for cos *i* wouldn't mind changing my destination place to meet that dream woman of my life. I long to read from you later in the day,for now *i* must take care of some work still at the Site *i* will check back on you later in the morning ok. Have a lovely nights rest sweets

Jim@};-

 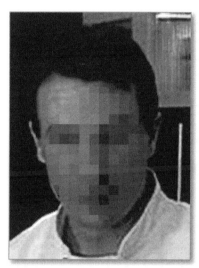

From: ladydi2011@yahoo.com
To: Jimmy Jackson
Subject: Re: How Are You Doing Today Wonder?
Sent: Thursday, June 7, 2012, 12:10 AM

Hello, my love!

This is your friend, co-pilot and future wife confirming that your late wife was right... the start of something better has started. Are you ready to start designing our paradise? The world is our oyster! I have no attachments and am ready for takeoff as soon as you are... I see you smiling!

How was work? My day was good. I agree that where there's will there is success. I also believe that to keep a relationship fresh the "little things" and "open communication" need to be intentional, and actions have to be taken regularly to make sure what we have doesn't slip away. I don't like when things slip away. I want to maintain the magic. Life is too short to not do this. You are right, life is simple so let's go with the flow and not complicate things.

Baby, I want to be more than the woman you can live with, I want to be the woman you can't live without! Hmmmm. I was also bullied when I was younger. I also don't judge and I forgive quickly. And I have always had older friends too. I think I am an old soul with a young spirit. My best friend is 71. I learn much wisdom from my older friends.

Yes, a long-term relationship, just like success and life is a journey, not a destination. I am all for enjoying and savoring each day and experience of the journey. So, my darling, how much longer before your job is done and we can meet?

I am thinking about you as I start to fall asleep. I hope you will come and visit me in my dreams... I have attached some pictures for you. One of them was when I was at the orphanage in Niger, Africa and the other one is me in my convertible.

Night, my love,
Kisses, kisses and more kisses
Diana

From: jimmylove4827@yahoo.com
To: ladydi
Subject: Can't Wait To Read From You Wonder
Sent: Thursday, June 7, 2012 3:39 AM

Hello my wonderful one .

How are you today? Why am *i* getting addicted to my email? *lol*. I get a good glow on my face just waking up to read from you. Wonderful. How was your night?. I knew something was missing since *i* haven't smiled all morning till now,*lol*. I was almost late for my chopper in the morning, *i* woke up late, *i* think *i* am becoming restful again, Maybe *i* could sense something good ahead of us.Dear *i* am in Dubai now working in my last contract *I am an engineer of international repute*. I deal basically with *oil platforms* ranging from middle east now *i* am working in Dubai *i* know we can make this work *i* am not here playing games *i* want to spend the rest of my life with you hope yup have the same vision with me?

What wouldn't *i* do to make my dreams come true. It is like a rigger waiting for a trigger. Would you be my trigger? *lol*. I just need a woman to hold me before *i* am old. Absolutely *i* have come to know that we spend the most of our life seeking for the secondary needs, while our primary needs are left unseen. We have worked so hard and attained some wealth right? but for what purpose? To be realistic, except if you just want to be known as a rich person, wealth means nothing if you have no best friend to share it with. All the millions are useless indeed. how much do we need to eat? How much do we need for shelter? how much do we need for daily fun. excess and excess leads us to vanity. But for few of us who value the simplicity, we sure would do well in finding happiness. As *i* always say, money can buy a good bed, But never will money buy sleep. it can buy the best diamond watch, but can never buy time, It can buy piles of books , but cant buy knowledge.. It can buy food, but not satisfaction, Money can buy sex, but can NEVER buy love. That is why , *i* refuse to follow the crowd, so as my own man, *i* would give up all that can be bought for that which cant be bought. I want true joy and happiness. I want my woman to have power over my moods,. she can make me smile in all weather.

I am glad that *i* could get your attention my dear. You have a special thing in your heart, and *i* intend to find out what it is. It could take a lifetime to figure, but *i* don't mind,*lol*. Please tell me about your ideology of life my dear. just want us to be sincere with each other as *i* said before that time is too short for such games cos really really *i* think you are that woman have been truly looking for all my life..

If *i* may answer to your question, *I have been scammed by women online* but that wont even stop me being who *i* am. I know some day *i* will meet that dream woman of my life. *i* also hope you wont allowed your past experience should affect our relationship this mostly why *i* ask about your online experience. cos you may think all men are all the same which they are not.all *i* want from my woman is to love me for who *i* am same way *i* will also love her for who she is.

I so much love that wonderful pictures of you and, mostly the one you took with those wonderful orphanage home children Wow very good and kind of you right baby... May God keep blessing you for that wonderful step you have taking out helping those kids. *well me and my mum always do the same thing to put a smile on there faces every Monday baby i will like you to also bee the part of us weekly fund raise donation which start we do so evry monday ok baby. if you are agree with me also let me know your mind about this ok honey*.

I wouldn't mind changing my destination country to meet you were ever you are soon as am done with this contract in Dubai which will be over be for the middle of the month then we can start making arrangement of my coming over to meet you were ever you are my dearest angel.infarct if *i* have to tell you the whole truth you are so nice and very lovely kind of person you are my dear, *i promise never to let you down in any way my dearest angel.*

I will be waiting impatiently to hear from you.
Your
Jimmy Jackson@};-

From: ladydi2011@yahoo.com
To: Jimmy Jackson
Subject: Re: How Are You Doing Today Wonder?

Sent: Thursday, June 7, 2012, 1:16 PM

Hello, Darling!

I am wonderful. My night was restful, what about yours, Honey? How is your day going? I enjoy getting mail from you when I wake up in the morning. You make me smile and I like this! I am glad I do the same for you and that you are more restful and sense something great, not just good, ahead of us. Like you, I am also getting addicted to email. It is nice. I am looking forward to the day when I meet you in person. Missing your chopper would not have been good. I am glad you woke up in time. I laughed when I read you were waiting "impatiently" for my next email. You are a funny man. lol.....

I am so glad to read you are not playing games. Neither am I. I have no time or patience for games. I will never allow someone to be my priority while they consider me an option. Please know I will be cautious until I meet you in person. My heart is too precious to allow anyone to play with or break it. Jimmy, I am truly a good woman and a great catch. I am the real deal. I am looking for my "forever." I am not looking for the man I can live with. I am looking for the man I cannot live without. It is by choice that I have not been with anyone for eight years. I am looking for the man who is going to love me as completely and passionately as I love him. I am not willing to settle for anything less. I really have a good feeling about you and us!

Lol... a rigger waiting for a trigger. I love it. Baby, I will be your trigger and make you a VERY HAPPY MAN! Honey, our philosophies are identical. I heard a great quote the other day that I think you will appreciate... *Some people are so poor, all they have is money.* It is love that makes our life rich. I am SO ready to be rich. What about you? I love and admire that you are your own man and don't follow the crowd. I am my own woman. I also do not follow the crowd or the road that has been traveled by many. I make my own path. Many are trying to be perfect, yet they look to others to show them what perfect is. They don't realize that what is perfect for one person is usually not perfect for another. I have taken the time to know myself well. I know what I want and need. Darling, I cannot be bought. However, my heart can be won by the right man (wink). A man who SHOWS me he loves me and doesn't just say it. Words are cheap! I am looking for a man who will romance, treasure and cherish me. A man who will make me smile and laugh. A man who will be my safe place to fall and I his, a man who will protect me and make me feel safe and loved, a man who will be my everything.

Honey, you definitely got my attention. No doubt about this. I am glad you have made the decision to intentionally find out the special thing in my heart. I have done the same. I want to know you... all of you... even if it takes a lifetime. Jimmy, I cannot put my finger on it, but there is something inside of me that is also saying that you are the man I have been looking for. It is just a knowing deep within me. I would be lying if I said it didn't scare me, because it does. I am allowing myself to be vulnerable with you. I do not want to be hurt again. Please do not hurt me... Love me!

My past experiences have made me very cautious, pay close attention and take my time. I would not let it jade me or "they" win. I will never let anyone take away my power or change who I am. Not this girl... Thank you for telling me that not all men are the same. I am sorry to hear you have been scammed on line.

I am glad you liked my pictures. I hope they keep me close to you. Baby, please tell me what your destination country is currently once you are done with this contract. I do want to meet you when you are done.

Well, my love, I have to go now. Please know you are in my thoughts.
Anxiously awaiting another email from you so I continue to get to know you.

Yours always,

Diana

From: ladydi2011@yahoo.com
To: Jimmy Jackson
Subject: I miss you
Sent: Friday, June 8, 2012, 5:56 PM

Hi my love, I have not heard from you today so I have not smiled. Are you ok? I miss you!

Diana

From: jimmylove4827@yahoo.com
To: ladydi
Subject: Can't Wait To Read From You Wonder
Sent: Sat, 9 Jun 2012 01:29:42

He re-sent me the same email that he sent me on Thursday, June 7, 2012 3:39 AM

From: ladydi2011@yahoo.com
To: Jimmy Jackson
Subject: I miss you
Sent: Saturday, June 9, 2012, 07:22 PDT

Hello Jimmy,

Hmmmmm...this is the same email you sent me two days ago.

Hope you are well.

Diana

From: jimmylove4827@yahoo.com
To: ladydi
Subject: Re: Can't Wait To Read From You Wonder,
Sent: Sat, 9 Jun 2012 08:54:25

I thought you said you didn't see my messga ethat is what make me to re send the message to you over again.

I am more than well than you do ok.

Take care,

Jimmy

From: ladydi2011@yahoo.com
To: Jimmy Jackson
Subject: I miss you
Sent: Saturday, June 11, 2012, 1:14 AM

Miss you baby! I hope everything is ok!!!

Diana

From: jimmylove4827@yahoo.com
To: ladydi
Subject: Re: How Are You Most Wonderful?
Sent: Sat, 9 June 11, 2012 4:12 AM

Hello my wonder!

Hope you are feeling as happy and great as *i* am feeling after getting back from work and opening my email to see that there was something to read from you,*i* am so glad that you shared all you did with me,it is really glaring that we are really heading in the right direction. Who are you? A woman being a goddess? or a goddess pretending to be a woman? Whichever you are, you are doing something special to me.***lol***.I mean after all these years, *i* would have thought *i* might not have the possibilities again of having my dream woman, my partner, my best friend and co pilot. ***I'm talking about fate here*** - when feelings are so powerful it's as if some force beyond your control is guiding you to someone who can make you happy beyond your wildest dreams.

I wouldn't be scared anyway, because truly, Love is not about finding the right person, but creating a right relationship. It's not about how much love you have in the beginning but how much love you build till the end. The inevitable truth is, If it is meant to be, our hearts will find each other when we meet. And if our hearts melt together so will our bodies and souls. Then every word and every touch will fuel our passion flame. I will be yours, you will be mine, and we will be one.

I am on the a project site in Dubai having to wake up every morning to catch up my job down here. Working from then till late at night, yet being able to be distracted by this woman(YOU). I have over 100 labors here, both skilled and locals, yet all could notice a new glow on my face. **LOL**. Tommy, Jacob and I have always stayed at Jacob's in his CA home, he just got married almost A years now. He found his woman on the net and to be sincere, he inspired us. ***I did not buy a house in the states yet*** because *i* would love to find my woman first, then building a home would start from there.

I am being true to my feelings, as my old friend would say, Never question if you are in love or not, because if you were you wouldn't need to ask. So the best of men, would accept what they feel without questions, because truly, Love and death can't be escaped, no one can tell , when, how, or where. It is never too early or too late.LOL. What is more important to you the love you share, the memories you have or the lover? Give love a chance to swallow you up. Don't just think it will happen in an instant, it will surprise you before you know it, but it will be the most rewarding experience you will ever have. I thank you for being so open minded and simple as me, i can promise you that the sky is the limit for us.

I am guessing you will be in bed right now or about to so which ever ways.
Do have the most pleasant of dreams as you rest.
I long to read from you much much much more............
Your Prince charming
Jimmy Jackson@};-
xoxoxo

This man's writing and tactic was different than any other scammer I encountered, which is one reason I put it in the book. I want you to see that online dating scammers may use vastly different tactics. It is only when you know the red flags that you can identify them.

RED FLAGS

- He says he was scammed by a woman online. This really surprised me that he said this.
- Just like other scammers, he promised to "never let me down".
- As I anticipated, his scam was around the orphanages. The scam was to donate every Monday to the supposed orphanage fund raiser.

I received one email twice and then heard from him less and less because I didn't commit to donating to the orphanage on a weekly basis. He didn't push it; he just disappeared, so I was only able to obtain a glimpse of his scam.

I asked Mike West from Arkansas Investigations to run his IP address and Mike confirmed that Jimmy was from Lagos, Nigeria, just as I thought.

jimmylove4827@yahoo.com
Location: Lagos, Nigeria
Misdirected: No
Abuse Address: adminit@starcomms.com
Abuse Reporting: To automatically generate an email abuse report click here

From IP: 41.155.86.102
inetnum: 41.155.86.0 - 41.155.86.255
netname: STARCOMMS-20081218
descr: Dial pool subnet for Lagos

subscribers
country: NG
admin-c: CM9-AFRINIC
tech-c: CM9-AFRINIC
status: ASSIGNED PA
mnt-by: STARCOMMS-MNT

source: AFRINIC # Filtered
parent: 41.155.0.0 - 41.155.127.255
person: Admin IT
address: Plot 1261C, Bishop Kale Close, off Saka Tinubu
phone: +234-1-8041234
fax-no: +234-1-8110301
e-mail: adminit@starcomms.com
nic-hdl: CM9-AFRINIC
source: AFRINIC # Filtered

But the story doesn't stop here. There is a twist. Continue on to read about Robin and what unfolds only 16 days after Jimmy disappeared. Profile Found on *Singlesbee*.

Profile: roblufz

46-year-old man in La Porte, IN
Looking for girls 39 to 62, up to 50 miles from me

My Headline

Looking for someone to spend quality time with for friendship, a relationship, and possibly marriage.

My Basics

- Height: 6'4"
- Body type: Average
- Hair color: Black
- Ethnicity: White / Caucasian
- Looks: Attractive
- Education: Graduate degree
- ***Occupation: Construction and installation***
- Income: $250,000
- I speak: English
- Religion: Christian - other
- ***Relationship status: Widowed***
- Children: Yes, living at home
- Wants children: Yes
- Smoking: Never
- Drinking: Do not drink

My Type of Girl

- Looking for: Dating Only, Dating / Long-term Potential, Long-term Only
- With: ***Women 39 to 62-year-old***
- Distance: Within 50 miles of La Porte
- Height: 5'0" to 6'0"
- Body type: Any
- Hair color: Any
- Ethnicity: Doesn't Matter
- Education: Doesn't Matter
- Occupation: Any
- Income: Doesn't Matter
- Language(s): English
- Religion: Any
- Relationship status: Any
- Children: Doesn't Matter
- Wants children: Doesn't Matter
- Smoking: Doesn't Matter
- Drinking: Doesn't Matter

About Me

What did you do today? Did you learn, laugh, experience something wonderful? Did you find yourself with a great bottle of wine sitting outside behind a fun French restaurant or at a museum slowly walking through lost in thought? Were you grateful for something that happened that was unexpected? Did you think about your next escape to somewhere in the world you'd never been to before? Did you wonder about how much better the day would have been with someone who you could talk about it all with. Here it gos a little about me, I'm an old fashioned romantic at heart, believe in being faithful, upfront, honest and ***don't play head games***. Life's too short to waste time with that. We all have our dreams and it would be great to meet someone who fits the bill I live my life with authenticity and passion. I'm warm, sensitive, fun and enthusiastic. The simple things in life excite me, a sunset or a sunrise, a lonely beach in the winter, good conversation. I look for connection and communication in my relationships, not superficiality and convention. I believe in living, not existing, in following my heart and never underestimating the strength of the human soul. My life is starting a new chapter and I'm very excited about it.

Who I'd Like To Meet

I hope to find a partner who will share in my excitement. The person I'm looking for has a great sense of humor, is outgoing and confident but not arrogant, is motivated and ambitious, and doesn't take themselves too seriously. A person who has their own friends and interests and is not afraid to share/combine those with mine. Someone who is not afraid to follow their heart.someone who may share some of the same interests and values. It's also great to meet someone that's into different things so you can turn each other on to them as well. Hopefully, we can get together to and see what happens. You never know until you take that chance When you think with your heart I feel that it will always work out in the end. "The heart see's what the eye's miss".

RED FLAGS

- 🚩 The occupation of construction and installation is a red flag. Many scammers have this occupation. Jimmy had the same occupation.
- 🚩 Looking for women between the ages of 39 and 62. Jimmy was looking for a woman between the ages of 37-60. This is the age group scammers prey upon.
- 🚩 Both said they were widowed, attractive, had a graduate degree and were Christian/other.

- Both said they were tall, Robin at 6'9 and Jimmy at 6'4
- Neither indicated any preferences about the woman he was seeking.
- The only real difference was that Jimmy said he didn't have children and Robin said he did.
- He has no time for games.

Taking all of the above as a whole, you can be sure he is a scammer.

From: ladydi
To: roblufz
Subject: Someone on SinglesBee is winking at you
Sent: 06/27/2012 07:56 PM

From: roblufz
To: ladydi
Subject: I just winked back at you
Sent: 06/27/2012 07:56 PM

From: ladydi2011@yahoo.com
To: roblufz
Subject: I just winked back at you
Sent: 06/27/2012 10:25 PM

Hello,

Thanks for winking back... I would like to get to know you better. Please tell me what is most important to you in life. What is on your bucket list? What are you looking for in the woman of your dreams?

Diana

From: potty4350@yahoo.com
To: ladydi
Subject: Re: Hello My Eight Wonder
Sent: 6/28/2012 10:10 AM

Hi sweetness... You are gorgeous. When I saw your charming pics and *i* was like Oh My God,*i* must stop by to say hello to this beautiful creation. Wow it seems *i* have seen an angel. I will also love to get to know you better. We can be friend may be see where this gonna lead us both to.

I'm an old fashioned romantic at heart, believe in being faithful, upfront, honest and ***don't play head games***. I'm warm, sensitive, fun and enthusiastic. The simple things in life excite me, a sunset or a sunrise, a lonely beach in the winter, good conversation. I look for connection and communication in my relationships, not superficiality and convention. I believe in living, not existing, in following my heart and never underestimating the strength of the human soul. My life is starting a new chapter and I'm very excited about it.

I am looking for ***my eigth wonder***, best friend and ***co-pilot*** to join my and my sons life. Do you have any children?

I long to read from you asap.
Robin

From: ladydi2011@yahoo.com
To: RobLufz
Subject: Re: Hello My Eight Wonder
Sent: Sun, 1 Jul 2012 4:06 PM

Hello Robin,

I am Diana. It is nice to meet you! How are you on this Sunday afternoon? Thank you for taking the time to email me. I am sorry it took me so long to reply. I do not come on the Singlesbee site that often. Chatting and email through Yahoo is the best way for me to stay in touch! Thank you for the wonderful compliments. You are very handsome yourself (smile).

I like everything I read on your profile. I would like to explore to see if we might be a good match. From first impressions, I would say we will be. Like you, I am authentic and sincere. I am not only looking for love, I am looking for my forever. I do go the extra mile and know how important the small things are. I am in no hurry nor am I looking for just anyone. I am looking for the man who complements me and who I complement. A man who will love me as madly as I love him. A man who would be my safe place to fall and would let me be his.

I am a business consultant, speaker and author. I love what I do. My life is full except for having that one special man to share everything with.

What is your son's name? No, I do not have any children, but I love children.

I would love to find that we are a match so I could be "the" woman for you. Your eighth wonder, best friend, co-pilot and lover. So, let's start to communicate and see where we can go from here and if we have what it takes to build a future together. One that is so awesome, we ourselves will be in awe. One that is so bright, we will have to wear sunglasses.

I hope to hear back from you soon.
Fondly,
Diana

From: potty4350@yahoo.com
To: ladydi
Subject: Hello My Eight Wonder
Sent: Sun, 1 Jul 2012 15:12:16 -0700 (PDT)

Hello Wonder,

How are you doing today? Hope your night was awesome thanks for your constant response *i* am glad you did write back, I guess you should truly know who *i* am, I don't really know how this is to work, but hey! here is an exclusive. If at my age *i* do not know what and when to say, then what would *i* be? When a wise man see's he has probably spent about half of his time in life already, he begins to assess his main goals in life, What could be more important than a happy ending? *LOL*, A man needs to live his life full of joy and happiness. No matter his achievements, he is reduced to nothing if he has no crown to complete him and that is a woman to call his own. Wife and Best friend.

A woman who knows that even while arguing they still need to hold hands, A woman whom *i* can call a partner in crime, lol A woman whom you can tell anything. How could you think anything can make you happier in life than finding a love that know's no bound. To make you know more about me, I will break this down to segments and it would be like a case study.

MY BACKGROUND
I suppose you know my name now lol. I was born to a loving couple, a home, by a German man and an American woman. My father was on an international job in America where he met my mom, She says there was something about the man that no woman could ever resist, sometimes she says she sees same in me, lol. During my father's global movement, Its just me and mom most of the time, I did most of my studying in the Germany but my father died after a brief illness and we were left alone, But my mom was strong for me and that's why she remains one of my best woman.

I met my late wife in Paris, she was a fashion model, She was a good and lovely woman, We were married for 9 yrs before she passed away 3 years ago, Not been easy getting over her, But life has to go on very good at heart. I would tell you more about her as time goes on, *I have a son who is 10 years old, he is Christian by name, My second half* lol.

551

MY JOB
I am a Global contractor, I do basically rig constructions and renovations or over water bridges.
We have worked at many countries across the globe, *I'm presently in Northumberland park,*
Tottenham London working on a project, The present project here is my last on the field and *i* shall
quit field works and continue my works from my home office while my men do the field jobs. I think
i really have gotten to this height cause *i* embraced work for so long trying to get over my wife,
that *i* worked this hard, but *i* think *i* now realize *i* can move on, Do you like your present job, do you
want marriage, *will you like to be my crown??*

MY DREAM
I have told you how my typical dream day would be like, *i* just want to spend the rest of my life
enjoying the fruit of my labor, I just want a woman who would be my best friend and everything.
You know someone whom we would still love each other more as the days pass by, even when we
can't make love anymore and all we could do is play bingo, LOL. I am a total package, *i* only need
someone who understands the value of a good smile.. I would like to learn more about you.

Hope you have a great day, I will be waiting to hear from you soon.

Your new friend,
Robin.

From: ladydi2011@yahoo.com
To: Robin Lulofs
Subject: Re: Hello My Eight Wonder
Sent: Sunday, July 1, 2012 11:28 PM

Hello Robin, or should I say *Jimmy*...

You see, I instantly recognized the writing in your last email to me. It is almost identical to what a
man named Jimmy sent me. I was extremely interested in Jimmy but then he stopped writing me.
Now, does he appear again? Is this destiny, a game or a scam? If a scam, money should be donated
to the orphanage. Is this correct? Please tell me. What a shame, because I am a really good catch
for an honest man of character and integrity!

Awaiting your response,
Diana

From: potty4350@yahoo.com
To: ladydi
Subject: Re: Hello My Eight Wonder
Sent: Sun, 1 Jul 2012 15:36:11 -0700 (PDT)

Well I am not jimmy I am Robin and *i* don't understand what you are talking about Ok?

From: ladydi2011@yahoo.com
To: Robin Lulofs
Subject: Re: Hello My Eight Wonder
Sent: Sunday, July 1, 2012 11:51 PM

I am sorry Robin. Someone going by the name of Jimmy must be stealing your material.

From: potty4350@yahoo.com
To: ladydi
Subject: Re: Hello My Eight Wonder
Sent: Sun, 1 Jul 2012 15:58:08 -0700 (PDT)

Well you can text me on 260-267-0302, *i* would really like to talk to you and see where we go from there.

Text Messages

To: 260-267-0302
Sent: July 1, 2012 7:02 pm

Hello Robin. Diana here.

From: 260-267-0302
Sent: July 2, 2012 1:36 am

Hello Diana, How are you doing? thanks for dropping by on here, I would be looking forward to texting with you.

To: 260-267-0302
Sent: July 2, 2012 1:41 am

I look forward to texting with you also.

From: 260-267-0302
Sent: July 2, 2012 1:46 am

Night Diana ..

To: 260-267-0302
Sent: July 2, 2012 1:48 am

Good night Robin :)

From: 260-267-0302
Sent: July 3, 2012 2:54 am

Hey

To: 260-267-0302
Sent: July 4, 2012 5:24 am

Happy 4th of July!

From: 260-267-0302
Sent: July 8, 2012 2:00 pm

Hello Diana ..How are you doing and how is your day going with you there??

To: 260-267-0302
Sent: July 8, 2012 3:01 pm

Hello! I am well and you? My day is relaxing. What about yours?

From: 260-267-0302
Sent: July 9, 2012 9:41 am

Good Morning Diana

To: 260-267-0302
Sent: July 9, 2012 9:48 am

Good morning Robin

From: 260-267-0302
Sent: July 9, 2012 9:49 am

How are you doing today and how was your night?

To: 260-267-0302
Sent: July 9, 2012 9:51 am

I am well and my night was restful, what about yours?

From: 260-267-0302
Sent: July 9, 2012 10:20 am

Mine was good dear, hope you are doing well?

To: 260-267-0302
Sent: July 9, 2012 10:30 am

I am. Think of you often!

From: 260-267-0302
Sent: July 9, 2012 10:32 am

Really? *What are you awlays thinking about me Diana?*

To: 260-267-0302
Sent: July 9, 2012 10:39 am

You are a mystery...I get these short text from you but no real conversation. Therefore you are still a mystery to me!

From: 260-267-0302
Sent: July 10, 2012 12:31 am

I have sent you a request on Yahoo IM. I hope you accept

I was after more information for this book so I hit on this man since I knew from his profile and picture that he was a scammer. He took the bait and we had an interesting start. I was really surprised that in his first and second email he used much of the same terminology that Jimmy used. He changed some information in the format Jimmy used, such as where his father was from, adding in his son, claiming to be from London rather than Atlanta, and wanting me to be his "crown" instead of his "queen".

I wasn't sure what to do with this duplication but thought I would call his attention to it and see what he would do once I did. I figured if he was going to use the same format with me I didn't need it, so if he disappeared it was no loss. I was surprised when he still proceeded with me and by the slow way he did it, with only brief text for nine days. I don't know if he was trying to decide if he really wanted to proceed with me or if he was thinking of a new way to proceed with me, but I played along. His text number was a Texas area code but he claimed to be from Indiana.

Now the chats begin.

IM Jul 10, 2012 12:40:47 AM

12:40:47 AM **ladydi2011**: Well hello!
12:41:16 AM **potty4350**: How are you?
12:41:20 AM **potty4350**: How was your day?
12:41:35 AM **ladydi2011**: I am well and you?

12:41:48 AM **ladydi2011**: My day was fabulous and very busy

12:41:58 AM **potty4350**: oh very good to hear that

12:42:01 AM **ladydi2011**: What about your day?

12:42:29 AM **potty4350**: it was stressful, very busy day at work

12:42:37 AM **potty4350**: it morning here right now

12:43:27 AM **ladydi2011**: Good morning

12:43:35 AM **ladydi2011**: What time is it there?

12:43:56 AM **potty4350**: it 5:43am here

12:44:08 AM **potty4350**: *I'm presently in London UK working on a project*

12:44:16 AM **potty4350**: I sent you a couple of emails telling you about myself

12:44:25 AM **ladydi2011**: I received them

12:44:30 AM **potty4350**: good

12:44:37 AM **potty4350**: so you should know few things about me

12:44:44 AM **potty4350**: my work, life and everything

12:44:48 AM **potty4350**: I have a son his name is Christian

12:45:44 AM **ladydi2011**: How old is Christian?

12:46:56 AM **potty4350**: *christian is 9*

12:47:37 AM **ladydi2011**: Please tell me more about your work

12:49:36 AM **ladydi2011**: Are you there?

Break In Time

12:53:35 AM **potty4350**: Are you there?

12:53:44 AM **ladydi2011**: I am

12:53:52 AM **ladydi2011**: *Did you get booted?*

12:53:58 AM **potty4350**: *Yes*

12:54:10 AM **ladydi2011**: Welcome back!

12:54:17 AM **potty4350**: thank you

12:54:22 AM **potty4350**: so tell me more about yourself

12:54:31 AM **potty4350**: did you get my last message??

12:54:44 AM **potty4350**: *what do you do for a living?*

12:55:00 AM **ladydi2011**: The last message *i* received was Christian is 9

12:55:38 AM **potty4350**: Oh really

12:55:56 AM **potty4350**: I am a Global contractor, I do basically rig constructions and renovations or over water bridges. We have worked at many countries across the globe. The present project here is my last on the field and *i* shall quit field works and continue my works from my home office while my men do the field jobs.

12:56:24 AM **ladydi2011**: Where is your home office?

12:57:06 AM **potty4350**: that is after *i* am done with my present project

12:57:17 AM **potty4350**: An Engineer of international repute, I deal basically with *Oil Platforms* ranging from the middle east to Europe and far east Asia. But really I am hanging the hat this year

12:58:03 AM **ladydi2011**: I am glad you are going to "hang your hat" this year.

12:58:14 AM **ladydi2011**: Where is your home office located?

12:58:54 AM **potty4350**: I mean *i* will he hanging the hat this year and *i will be working from my home office that would be in Indiana*

12:59:16 AM **ladydi2011**: Are you origionally from Indiana?

1:01:20 AM **potty4350**: *I am originally from Berlin Germany*

1:01:34 AM **potty4350**: *what do you do for a living?*

1:01:39 AM **potty4350**: *tell me more about yourself*

1:02:01 AM **ladydi2011**: Ok...

1:02:19 AM **ladydi2011**: I am origionaly from Pennsylvania

1:02:36 AM **ladydi2011**: Modeled and went to acting school in Manhattan

1:02:50 AM **ladydi2011**: Been is sales and marketing for 30 years

1:02:52 AM **potty4350**: Okay

1:03:07 AM **ladydi2011**: Have owned my own marketing company for the last 12 years

1:03:15 AM **potty4350**: *what do you do presently*

1:03:17 AM **ladydi2011**: Been divorced for 14 years

1:03:20 AM **potty4350**: do you still own it

1:03:32 AM **potty4350**: I lost my wife a couple of years back

1:03:47 AM **ladydi2011**: Yes, I still own my company

1:04:07 AM **ladydi2011**: I am also an author and am published world-wide in my niche market

1:04:23 AM **ladydi2011**: I am also a Professional Transformational Speaker

1:04:34 AM **ladydi2011**: Sorry to hear about the loss of your wife

1:04:41 AM **ladydi2011**: She was a model, correct?

1:06:00 AM **potty4350**: Yes she was a model

1:06:04 AM **potty4350**: I met her in paris

1:06:11 AM **potty4350**: *what are you really looking for?*

1:06:20 AM **potty4350**: *do you have kids? want more kids?*

1:06:29 AM **ladydi2011**: I do not have any children

1:06:49 AM **ladydi2011**: I wouldn't mind being with a man who does have children

1:06:56 AM **ladydi2011**: Good question

1:07:06 AM **ladydi2011**: I know exactly what I am looking for

1:07:30 AM **ladydi2011**: I have not dated in 8 years by choice due to building my business

1:07:45 AM **ladydi2011**: I was on a mission

1:07:51 AM **potty4350**: Good

1:08:11 AM **ladydi2011**: The beginning of this year I knew I was ready for the relationship I wanted

1:08:37 AM **potty4350**: Awesome

1:08:41 AM **ladydi2011**: I am looking for a man who will love me as madly and passionately as I love him

1:08:49 AM **potty4350**: *How long have you been on the dating site? any luck ever since you have been on here??*

1:08:55 AM **ladydi2011**: I will not settle for anything less

1:08:58 AM **potty4350**: awesome

1:09:07 AM **ladydi2011**: Since the end of March

1:09:23 AM **potty4350**: that's a couple of months now

1:09:26 AM **ladydi2011**: spoke with several men but in the end they were not a match

1:09:30 AM **potty4350**: *I am new on there and don't use it again*

1:09:36 AM **ladydi2011**: I am in no hurry

1:09:42 AM **potty4350**: yes same here *i* am in no hurry

1:09:52 AM **ladydi2011**: For me, it is not about finding "a" man

1:10:06 AM **ladydi2011**: It's about finding the "perfect man" for me

1:10:24 AM **potty4350**: well *i* pray *i* am the perfect man for you

1:10:31 AM **ladydi2011**: Not perfect, because *i* do not believe anybody is perfect

1:10:34 AM **potty4350**: I have told you how my typical dream day would be like, *i* just want to spend the rest of my life enjoying the fruit of my labor, I just want a woman who would be my best friend and everything.

1:10:53 AM **ladydi2011**: This is nice

1:11:08 AM **potty4350**: You know someone whom we would still love each other more as the days pass by, even when we can't make love anymore and all we could do is play bingo, LOL.

1:11:14 AM **ladydi2011**: Out of all the men I have met, you are the one who has caught my interest

1:11:32 AM **ladydi2011**: Lol about the bingo or when we are rocking in the rocking chairs

1:12:04 AM **potty4350**: I am very happy we met

1:12:07 AM **potty4350**: *i only need someone who understands the value of a good smile.*

1:12:24 AM **ladydi2011**: I am happy we met too

1:12:31 AM **potty4350**: Awesome

1:12:36 AM **potty4350**: *what is your faith?*

1:12:38 AM **ladydi2011**: I agree about the value of a good smile

1:12:46 AM **ladydi2011**: I am a Christian

1:12:52 AM **ladydi2011**: What about you?

1:13:19 AM **ladydi2011**: Life is too short to not smile or be in a bad relationship

1:13:47 AM **potty4350**: I am glad you are a christian

1:13:52 AM **ladydi2011**: I would rather be by myself than in a bad or unfulfilling relationship

1:13:57 AM **potty4350**: *I want you to know that GOD brought us together for a purpose*

1:14:11 AM **ladydi2011**: Why do you say this?

1:14:28 AM **potty4350**: <ding>

1:14:31 AM **potty4350**: I am christian

1:15:41 AM **ladydi2011**: I am here

1:15:51 AM **ladydi2011**: Please hold...ok?

1:16:39 AM **potty4350**: Okay

1:19:32 AM **ladydi2011**: Sorry...bathroom called

1:19:39 AM **potty4350**: lol, okay

1:20:00 AM **ladydi2011**: Too much ice tea today...Lol

1:20:09 AM **potty4350**: really

1:20:19 AM **potty4350**: *what do you like doing for fun?*

1:20:35 AM **ladydi2011**: Just about anything

1:20:47 AM **potty4350**: spent most of my day on the work field

1:20:52 AM **ladydi2011**: I love adventure and trying new things

1:20:55 AM **potty4350**: *so do you live alone*

1:20:58 AM **potty4350**: awesome

1:21:04 AM **potty4350**: *do you own your house??*

1:21:08 AM **ladydi2011**: me and my kitty cat

1:21:16 AM **ladydi2011**: Yes, I own my home

1:21:18 AM **potty4350**: *good*

1:22:37 AM **ladydi2011**: one of my beliefs is to "Be it" not "Speak it". For me, actions always speak much louder than words

1:23:21 AM **potty4350**: *i like dancing salsa, ballet, skiing, bowling, white water rafting, walking, cuddling, holding hands, dinning out, wineries, camping, the beach, swimming, reading, writing poems, watching, listening to music ..trying new things*

1:23:35 AM **potty4350**: *i really like that*

1:23:43 AM **potty4350**: do you have more pictures to share with me

1:23:46 AM **potty4350**: *how old are you?*

1:23:51 AM **ladydi2011**: I do

1:23:56 AM **ladydi2011**: Hmmmmmm...Should a woman really tell her age?

1:24:12 AM **potty4350**: yes sure
1:24:16 AM **potty4350**: *i am 46*
1:24:16 AM **ladydi2011**: Kidding
1:24:18 AM **potty4350**: lol
1:24:21 AM **potty4350**: you?
1:24:28 AM **ladydi2011**: I am a young in spirit 48
1:24:47 AM **potty4350**: great .. hope you don't mind the age difference??
1:24:58 AM **potty4350**: my name is Robin Lulofs, *what is your full name ??*
1:25:33 AM **ladydi2011**: Not at all
1:25:46 AM **ladydi2011**: my name is Diana Garren
1:25:50 AM **potty4350**: *i* am very glad to hear that
1:26:07 AM **potty4350**: perfect
1:26:15 AM **potty4350**: we can photo share

1:28:07 AM **potty4350**: Wow
1:28:12 AM **potty4350**: you are a very beautiful lady
1:28:19 AM **ladydi2011**: Thank you!
1:28:22 AM **potty4350**: *I wanna marry you*
1:28:27 AM **potty4350**: You are welcome gorgeous
1:28:42 AM **ladydi2011**: I am more beautiful on the inside than the outside
1:29:02 AM **ladydi2011**: Please share your pictures with me
1:29:11 AM **ladydi2011**: You do????
1:29:34 AM **potty4350**: Yes *i* do Diana
1:29:40 AM **potty4350**: I hope you don't mind me saying that
1:29:54 AM **potty4350**: was only kidding though but *i* am serious about it
1:30:00 AM **potty4350**: do you get my pictures
1:30:02 AM **ladydi2011**: *Do you always want to marry a woman so quickly?*
1:30:19 AM **ladydi2011**: I did not get your pictures
1:30:24 AM **ladydi2011**: The file was empty
1:31:28 AM **potty4350**: with time *i* would like to marry her after we both fall in love with each other

1:32:41 AM **potty4350**: do you get my pictures now
1:32:50 AM **ladydi2011**: I did get your picture

1:32:57 AM **ladydi2011**: You are very handsome!
1:33:06 AM **ladydi2011**: I love your style of dress
1:33:23 AM **potty4350**: I am glad you do
1:33:28 AM **ladydi2011**: Christian is adorable
1:33:33 AM **potty4350**: I love everything about you
1:33:36 AM **ladydi2011**: How old is he on here?
1:33:39 AM **potty4350**: thank you gorgeous
1:33:50 AM **ladydi2011**: Thank you
1:33:53 AM **potty4350**: he is just 8
1:33:57 AM **potty4350**: you are welcome
1:34:46 AM **ladydi2011**: Were you dressed for a Halloween party?
1:34:59 AM **potty4350**: Yes
1:35:11 AM **ladydi2011**: You look awesome in the tux
1:35:24 AM **ladydi2011**: I am VERY attracted to sharp dressed men
1:36:03 AM **ladydi2011**: I am a fashionista
1:36:30 AM **potty4350**: thank you Diana
1:36:38 AM **ladydi2011**: I have a beautiful hand beaded gown that would look great next to you in that tux
1:36:39 AM **potty4350**: I really do like your kind of person
1:36:45 AM **potty4350**: do you have more pictures to share with me
1:36:53 AM **ladydi2011**: I am the real deal Robin
1:36:55 AM **potty4350**: Wow
1:37:10 AM **potty4350**: I really can't wait to see you in the beaded gown
1:37:26 AM **ladydi2011**: The gown is heavy but stunning
1:37:37 AM **potty4350**: I love fashion
1:37:44 AM **ladydi2011**: I own many...I attend many black tie functions
1:37:54 AM **ladydi2011**: I can tell you love fashion

1:38:02 AM **potty4350**: Lol..I really do

1:38:29 AM **ladydi2011**: This is one of my modeling pictures

1:39:31 AM **ladydi2011**: I use to race cars....I love FAST cars

1:40:23 AM **ladydi2011**: It is me and Paul Newman when I was a race queen

1:40:31 AM **ladydi2011**: I have had a fun life and want to continue to have fun the rest of my life

1:40:50 AM **ladydi2011**: What about you?

1:41:30 AM **potty4350**: Yes Diana

1:41:42 AM **potty4350**: I want to continue to have fun for the rest of my life

1:41:55 AM **potty4350**: I would really love to spend the rest of my life with *your kind of woman*

1:42:02 AM **potty4350**: I really do hope you give me the chance

1:42:44 AM **ladydi2011**: I am very interested in you so, I will give you a chance

1:43:03 AM **ladydi2011**: I do like to be romanced

1:43:06 AM **potty4350**: thank you

1:43:08 AM **ladydi2011**: What do you like?

1:43:13 AM **potty4350**: *Diana i want your love, trust and care*

1:43:25 AM **potty4350**: I love to be romanced too

1:43:35 AM **potty4350**: OMG..I don't ever wanna lose you to another man

1:43:54 AM **potty4350**: I want your true love

1:44:52 AM **potty4350**: You are a very pretty woman

1:45:02 AM **potty4350**: You look so damn gorgeous in the race suit

1:45:06 AM **ladydi2011**: Thank you

1:45:23 AM **ladydi2011**: Remember, my interior is more beautiful

1:45:49 AM **ladydi2011**: You should see me drive fast cars

1:46:04 AM **potty4350**: Really, you drive fast cars

1:46:18 AM **ladydi2011**: So, do I have your interest and attention now?

1:46:20 AM **potty4350**: You are just the perfect match for me

1:46:23 AM **potty4350**: what car do you drive??

1:46:38 AM **ladydi2011**: I have two

1:46:40 AM **potty4350**: yes sure you have my interest and attention now Diana

1:46:51 AM **potty4350**: you have 2 fast cars?

1:46:56 AM **ladydi2011**: A Solara convertible

1:47:03 AM **potty4350**: oh good

1:47:08 AM **ladydi2011**: And a BMW

1:48:18 AM **ladydi2011**: The Solara isn't fast, but I love driving with the top down with the wind blowing through my hair

1:48:26 AM **ladydi2011**: What do you drive?

1:49:18 AM **potty4350**: I drive a Range Rover Sport 2008

1:49:43 AM **potty4350**: I don't have fast cars but *i* will like to have one for us

1:49:54 AM **potty4350**: maybe a Aston Martins

1:49:59 AM **potty4350**: Do you like Aston Martins

1:50:21 AM **ladydi2011**: I do like the Aston

1:50:26 AM **potty4350**: And I also drive a BMW x6

1:50:29 AM **ladydi2011**: And the Lamborghini

1:51:06 AM **ladydi2011**: Do you own a home?

1:51:20 AM **potty4350**: I like lamborghini too

1:51:24 AM **potty4350**: *Yes i own a home*

1:51:32 AM **potty4350**: well with time you will get to know me *more better* Diana

1:51:45 AM **ladydi2011**: I am looking forward to this

1:52:09 AM **ladydi2011**: So, are you ready for another relationship?

1:52:54 AM **potty4350**: Yes

1:53:05 AM **potty4350**: I haven't date ever since *i* lost my wife Diana

1:53:13 AM **potty4350**: You are my kind of woman

1:53:20 AM **potty4350**: *will you do anything to make your man happy??*

1:53:42 AM **ladydi2011**: Yes, I will do anything to make my man happy

1:53:59 AM **ladydi2011**: Will you do anything to make your woman happy?

1:54:16 AM **ladydi2011**: I am a one man woman

1:54:26 AM **ladydi2011**: Always have been and always will be

1:54:38 AM **ladydi2011**: What are your non-negotiables?

1:54:50 AM **potty4350**: Yes *i* will do anything to make my woman happy Diana

1:54:56 AM **potty4350**: Yes same here I am a one woman man

1:55:32 AM **potty4350**: Diana if only you would give me the chance *i* promise you will never regret your action

1:55:52 AM **ladydi2011**: Ok....

1:56:11 AM **potty4350**: thank you Diana

1:56:24 AM **potty4350**: I want something serious with you with marriage potentials

1:56:42 AM **ladydi2011**: Are you ready to get married again?

1:58:20 AM **ladydi2011**: Robin, I am ready to get married again. However, an honest, caring, loving relationship that brings out the best in both partners is the most important thing to me

1:58:30 AM **ladydi2011**: Are you there?

1:58:38 AM **potty4350**: Yes *i* am here dear and thinking about you

1:58:53 AM **potty4350**: Yes *i* am ready to get married again

1:59:16 AM **potty4350**: I will do anything to make you happy baby

1:59:21 AM **ladydi2011**: I do not want to get married, just to be married

1:59:53 AM **ladydi2011**: I am looking for that relationship that others want when they see us together...I want it all!

2:00:59 AM **ladydi2011**: Well my dear, it has been my pleasure to get to know you tonight

2:01:07 AM **ladydi2011**: Well, today for you...lol

2:01:16 AM **ladydi2011**: I need to go to bed

2:01:28 AM **potty4350**: Okay Diana

2:01:32 AM **ladydi2011**: Please think of me at least once today

2:01:34 AM **potty4350**: I am getting ready for work already

2:01:39 AM **potty4350**: it 7:01am here

2:01:45 AM **potty4350**: Yes sure dear *i* will think of me too Diana Ok

2:01:56 AM **potty4350**: *And i promise i will never hurt you*

2:01:59 AM **ladydi2011**: Make it a fabulous day!

2:02:03 AM **potty4350**: *You can count on my word*

2:02:13 AM **potty4350**: Do you like letters? poems?

2:02:15 AM **ladydi2011**: Thank you

2:02:16 AM **potty4350**: I write

2:02:25 AM **ladydi2011**: Please surprise me

2:02:31 AM **ladydi2011**: I like surprises

2:02:42 AM **ladydi2011**: I do have two requests

2:03:06 AM **ladydi2011**: 1) Always be yourself

2:03:17 AM **ladydi2011**: 2) Only do what you plan to continue to do

2:03:31 AM **potty4350**: Thank you my dear
2:03:38 AM **potty4350**: *Trust me i will never let you down Ok?*
2:03:46 AM **potty4350**: I would like to have your address dear
2:03:50 AM **ladydi2011**: Do you have any requests?
2:04:04 AM **potty4350**: *Honey All i want is your true love and trust*
2:04:31 AM **ladydi2011**: Do you plan to visit me?
2:04:38 AM **potty4350**: Yes baby
2:04:46 AM **potty4350**: Remember *i* am presently in London UK for a project
2:04:53 AM **potty4350**: *Yes baby i am planning to visit you dear Ok*
2:05:01 AM **ladydi2011**: When will you return from London?
2:05:01 AM **potty4350**: I will always keep you posted
2:05:05 AM **potty4350**: Will you like to call me sometimes
2:05:14 AM **ladydi2011**: I would like this
2:05:19 AM **potty4350**: *+447035920385*
2:05:48 AM **ladydi2011**: Thank you dear
2:05:55 AM **ladydi2011**: Until next time
2:06:08 AM **potty4350**: that is my number
2:06:12 AM **ladydi2011**: Thank you for sharing your time with me tonight
2:06:16 AM **potty4350**: should *i* be looking forward to your call
2:06:24 AM **ladydi2011**: Yes, you should be
2:06:25 AM **potty4350**: I am very glad to talk to you
2:06:33 AM **potty4350**: Ok Diana
2:06:35 AM **ladydi2011**: Same here
2:06:42 AM **potty4350**: I will be waiting for your call
2:06:46 AM **ladydi2011**: You might get addicted to my laugh...Lol
2:07:13 AM **ladydi2011**: Bye for now
2:08:34 AM **potty4350**: bye for now dear
2:08:49 AM **potty4350**: honey *i* will text you when *i* am on break at work
2:08:53 AM **potty4350**: can *i* text you anytime
2:14:02 AM **potty4350**: <ding>

IM Jul 10, 2012 10:26:54 PM

10:26:54 PM **potty4350**: Hello .. How are you doing and how was your day? hope it went well as planned?

From: potty4350@yahoo.com
To: ladydi
Subject: Hello Let Me Be
Sent: Tuesday, 10 Jul 2012 11:03 PM

I do think about you and *i* am mostly in thoughts of holding you, I admire your independence and courage, you handle yourself very professionally. I can't wait to see you in person, *i* won't be shy but maybe you would, *i* love your sincerity and beauty, and most of all "Your Warm Heart" that I crave in my heart .You are no longer alone and I will always be at your side through good and bad times. Let me fill your heart and soul with the "True Love" that you deserve. Let me be the one to take the emptiness of your life and fill it with joy and happiness. Let me be the man of your dream and destination, together we can build an empire.

You are so pleasant to my eyes and *i* dont want to loose talking to you, *i want you to tell me what you think and feel towards me, i* need to hear something from you that will warm my heart.

Robin Cares.

From: potty4350@yahoo.com
To: ladydi
Subject: How are you most wonderful
Sent: Tuesday, 10 Jul 2012 11:25 PM

Hello My Wonderful lady,

How are you today? Been getting so addicted to you now, And am loving every bit of it, smiles is what you bring to my face since our last chat, I get a good glow on my face just waking up thinking about you. I knew something was missing since I have not smiled all morning till now, *lol. I woke up a little late, I think I am becoming restful again, I strongly sense something good ahead of us smiles*.

What wouldn't I do to make my dreams come true. *It is like a rigger waiting for a trigger*. Would you be my trigger, smiles? I just need a woman to hold me so closely to her heart. Absolutely I have come to know that we spend the most of our life seeking for the secondary needs, while our primary needs are left unseen. We have worked so hard and attained wealth to a certain height, but for what purpose? To be realistic, wealth means nothing if you have no best friend to share it with basically.

But for few of us who value the simplicity, we sure would do well in finding happiness. As I always thought, money could buy a good bed, but never would it buy sleep. It could buy the best diamond watch, but never would it buy time, It could buy piles of books, but not knowledge. It can buy food, but not satisfaction, Money can buy sex, but can NEVER buy love. That is why I refuse to follow the crowd, so as my own man, I would give up all that can be bought for that which can't be bought. I want true joy and happiness. I want my woman to have power over my moods, she can make me smile in all weather.

I am glad that I could get your attention my dear, You have a special thing in your heart, and I intend to find out what it is, I dont mind how long it would take...smiles...

Am so very happy we are getting to know each other more and more, I will be waiting impatiently to hear from you, Cheers.

Care about you.
Thoughts,
Robin.

Well, I am now making headway with Robin (or is it Jimmy?). He once again sends me an email that has much of what Jimmy sent me. I am amazed that this scammer is even talking to me and still sending me the same material. I'm not sure this is the same scammer that portrayed himself as Jimmy, but this is obviously a format that is circulating.

RED FLAGS

- He originally told me Christian was 10 and now he says he is nine.
- He is supposedly from Indiana but first had a Texas phone number for texting and now gives me a +44 7 phone number to call. As we already know, this a red flag that he is a scammer. He follows suit with asking the questions of:
  1. What do you do for a living?
  2. Tell me about yourself
  3. How long have you been on the dating site?
  4. Have you had any luck on the dating site?
  5. What is your faith?
  6. Do you live alone?
  7. Do you own your house?
  8. How old are you?
  9. What is your full name?
- He says he is new to the dating site. Scammers will often tell you this.
- He says God brought us together for a purpose. I agree with this, but not for the purpose he thinks.
- He promises to never hurt me and tells me I can count on his word; he says I need to trust him because he will never let me down. He then tells me all he wants is my "true love" and "trust". These are all words scammers use.
- He asks for my address and says he plans to visit me.
- Like other scammers, he asks me how I feel towards him. This is their way of gauging their victim's feelings so they know how to proceed.

IM Jul 11, 2012 1:40:39 AM

1:40:39 AM **potty4350**: <ding>
1:42:21 AM **ladydi2011**: Hello Robin
1:43:41 AM **ladydi2011**: I am sorry I missed you. I signed in on my phone and then I fell asleep!
1:43:54 AM **ladydi2011**: How was your day?

6:12:57 PM **potty4350**: Hey Baby
6:13:07 PM **ladydi2011**: Hello
6:13:12 PM **ladydi2011**: How are you?
6:13:17 PM **potty4350**: Did you just close from work
6:13:31 PM **ladydi2011**: From talking with clients, yes
6:13:40 PM **ladydi2011**: I have about 4 hours of other work to do
6:13:46 PM **ladydi2011**: Busy, busy day...Deadlines
6:14:52 PM **ladydi2011**: Are you there?
Break In Time
6:16:13 PM **potty4350**: <ding>
6:16:30 PM **ladydi2011**: I am writing but you are not replying
6:16:40 PM **ladydi2011**: Are you there?
6:16:41 PM **potty4350**: Yes *i* am here
6:17:31 PM **ladydi2011**: I didn't know London had such a bad connection issue
6:18:10 PM **potty4350**: not much
6:18:32 PM **potty4350**: *i* am here diana
Missed Voice call with potty4350 (6:19:19 PM)
6:20:26 PM ladydi2011: I answered and then it hung up
6:20:30 PM ladydi2011: Please try again
Missed Voice call with potty4350 (6:20:58 PM)
Outgoing Voice call with potty4350 (6:21:20 PM)
Call Ended: 0 hours 0 minutes 16 seconds
6:22:10 PM potty4350: call again babe
Outgoing Voice call with potty4350 (6:22:03 PM)
Call Ended: 0 hours 0 minutes 28 seconds
Outgoing Voice call with potty4350 (6:23:08 PM)
Call Ended: 0 hours 18 minutes 35 seconds

Note: We spoke but his accent was so heavy I couldn't understand a word he said.

6:42:14 PM **potty4350**: are you there?
6:42:22 PM **ladydi2011**: I am here
6:42:35 PM **potty4350**: okay baby
6:42:40 PM **ladydi2011**: Are you surprised I removed my profile?
6:42:40 PM **potty4350**: *just trust me ok*
6:42:58 PM **ladydi2011**: Please tell me why I should trust you
6:44:02 PM **ladydi2011**: I love your accent
6:44:14 PM **ladydi2011**: I can understand you
6:44:20 PM **potty4350**: are you sure?
6:44:21 PM **ladydi2011**: Very clearly
6:44:43 PM **ladydi2011**: I have freinds from all around the world so I am use to listening closely
6:44:52 PM **potty4350**: *To know me is to trust me*, To like me is to know me....To understand me is to be my friend.... And to accept me is to be forever in my life.

6:45:27 PM **ladydi2011**: I trust you
6:45:33 PM **potty4350**: thank you
6:45:40 PM **ladydi2011**: Do you trust me?
6:45:49 PM **potty4350**: yes sure *i* do diana
6:45:59 PM **ladydi2011**: thank you
6:46:08 PM **ladydi2011**: So, where do we go from here?
6:46:29 PM **potty4350**: where do you want us to go from here diana
6:46:57 PM **ladydi2011**: this is the question I have asked you
6:48:20 PM **potty4350**: honey *i* wanna love you foreevr
6:48:59 PM **ladydi2011**: I have never had a long distant relationship before
6:49:24 PM **potty4350**: honey *i* know you are the perfect woman for me
6:50:06 PM **ladydi2011**: I think you might be the perfect man for me
6:50:13 PM **potty4350**: *i* like what you like, what *i* want is what you want too
6:50:22 PM **potty4350**: good
6:50:52 PM **ladydi2011**: So, will you romance me?
6:51:15 PM **potty4350**: Yes honey if you want me to
6:51:19 PM **ladydi2011**: Robin, I want to be romanced
6:51:39 PM **ladydi2011**: I want it all and will not settle for anything less
6:52:13 PM **potty4350**: good baby
6:53:01 PM **ladydi2011**: Please so not break my heart
6:53:38 PM **potty4350**: I promise honey
6:54:02 PM **ladydi2011**: I am going to hold you to this
6:55:53 PM **ladydi2011**: Honey, I have to go back to work.
6:56:03 PM **ladydi2011**: What time will you be on line tomorrow?
6:56:43 PM **potty4350**: honey *i* will text you tomorrow when i'm online Ok?
6:57:00 PM **ladydi2011**: Ok
6:57:26 PM **potty4350**: *i* cherish you so much diana
Break In Time
7:02:01 PM **ladydi2011**: I need to get back to work
7:02:08 PM **ladydi2011**: We will chat tomorrow. You will text me when you are on line, yes
7:02:35 PM **potty4350**: will you be able to text?
7:02:48 PM **ladydi2011**: Hopefully
7:02:59 PM **ladydi2011**: Depends if I am on the phone with client
7:03:00 PM **potty4350**: okay then
7:03:05 PM **ladydi2011**: Work first my love
7:03:15 PM **ladydi2011**: remember, I run a company
7:03:20 PM **ladydi2011**: Large responsibility
7:03:48 PM **ladydi2011**: I need to do payroll. I have people depending on me and their pay check
7:07:20 PM **ladydi2011**: I need to go now
7:07:35 PM **ladydi2011**: I need to chat with my assistant who prepares payroll
7:07:44 PM **ladydi2011**: Bye for now
7:07:50 PM **ladydi2011**: Take care of yourself
7:08:02 PM **potty4350**: *i* cherish you so much dear
7:08:06 PM **potty4350**: don't work too much ok
7:08:44 PM **ladydi2011**: I cherish you too
7:08:50 PM **ladydi2011**: Until tomorrow
7:08:56 PM **potty4350**: okay dear

7:09:02 PM **potty4350**: *i* will text you tomorrow ok
7:09:40 PM **ladydi2011**: Ok

From: potty4350@yahoo.com
To: ladydi
Subject: True Love
Sent: Thursday, 12 Jul 2012 6:42 AM

Honey I want to talk to you about myself and what *i* know about true love, I have a big heart and *i* am willing to share my true love with you, Honey I am sure you know that death can not stop true love, it can only delay it for a little while and you know true Love can make you do things that you never thought possible.

True Love is an emotion so strong that you would give up everything. To just feel it once, to know that you are part of something special, To know that you can feel what love really is to know, to feel to love, Love and electricity are one in the same, Honey if you do not feel the jolt in your soul every time a kiss is shared, a whisper is spoken, a touch is felt, then your not really in love at all. To love someone is to understand each other, to laugh together, to smile with your heart and to **trust one another**. True love is just like rain it touches us all.

True love is a wonder that has no end or beginning. I have true love and if you think it is a lie, well let me tell you for real, true love doesn't comes everyday, True love doesn't just fill your heart, it overflows into your whole body and soul. True love can not be found where it does not exist, nor can it be denied where it does, True love doesn't have a happy ending because true love doesn't end. Remember that the truest love, is one where your love for each other is greater than your need for each other. Love isn't love until you give it away, so give it wings and let it go, if it's meant to be it will fly right back to you. No matter how hard things seem, true love will aid you through it. When during sad times an angel should come to you, open your eyes and see who that angel is, for that is your one true love. Never underestimate the power because love can do miracles which you never thought possible.

True Love comes to those who wait for it, trust it and don't question it when it does finally come. If you are willing to trust in a person when all others tell you to go against it, if you are willing to risk getting your heart broken because you believe in that other person, Then that is true love. Time has no meaning when your in love. True love knows no boundaries. It is the people involved who create them. Now tell me for real , if *i* dont know what true love is, will *i* ever find it? There is one pain I often feel, which you will never know, It's caused by the absence of you Honey.

My heart is set for you and I am praying so much for you to be the woman of my life, I cant wait to have you as mine forever.

With Love,

Robin

IM Jul 12, 2012 4:51:05 PM

4:51:05 PM **potty4350**: Hey Baby
4:51:05 PM **potty4350**: <ding>

From: potty4350@yahoo.com
To: ladydi
Subject: Feelings
Sent: Friday, 13 Jul 2012 3:34 AM

I don't know what further words can describe what we have together? For our feelings to grow together, I took with every beat of my heart, Words can no longer describe it, but rather in feeling and emotion of what we have for each other, You have always had the key to my heart, it is just that we just me, with you inside my heart has made me more than I can ever be. Though the sea will separates us till that special day we are going to meet, I know we take each breath with every beat, and always will be together as one. I will be loving you with all that I am, I could kiss you a thousand times and still not be satisfied. My love for you will be endless, so tender, so hot and complete. My love for you can not be measured by words alone as love does express my true feelings..You and only you have given me so much hope and have made me realize how much I want to be with you! You show the true meaning of how a man should treat a woman. For the first time in my life I have someone to believe in..

I thank God for you every day because I know you're heaven sent.

Right now we are far away from each other and I really mean it's killing me but I know in my heart that we are doing alright. I don't want to lose you to anyone else or anything that anyone wants to say about you. I'm always so lost for words when it comes to you, I just wish that *i* am done here so *i* can plan to meet you in person.

I cant wait to meet you for real.
Thinking about you,
Robin.

IM Jul 13, 2012 9:17:22 AM

9:17:22 AM **potty4350**: Hello

IM Jul 14, 2012 11:57:10 AM

11:57:10 PM **potty4350**: Hey Baby
11:57:45 PM **ladydi2011**: Morning

569

11:57:54 PM **potty4350**: Morning baby
11:58:15 PM **ladydi2011**: Did you sleep well?
11:58:17 PM **potty4350**: How are you doing?
11:58:21 PM **potty4350**: I miss you so much Diana
11:58:26 PM **ladydi2011**: I am well.
11:58:34 PM **ladydi2011**: I miss you too!
11:58:38 PM **potty4350**: I am very glad to hear that
11:58:46 PM **potty4350**: How is work with you?
11:58:52 PM **potty4350**: How was your day like? what did you do?
11:59:21 PM **ladydi2011**: Work went well
11:59:24 PM **ladydi2011**: TGIF
11:59:34 PM **ladydi2011**: Dinner was nice, food was good
11:59:46 PM **ladydi2011**: Now I am home having some wine
11:59:53 PM **potty4350**: do you work weekend?
12:00:12 AM **ladydi2011**: Sometimes
12:00:20 AM **ladydi2011**: Depends on my work load
12:00:51 AM **ladydi2011**: I have to go to Texas to speak in 2 weeks
12:01:03 AM **ladydi2011**: So I will be working on my power points
12:01:03 AM **potty4350**: oh really
12:01:09 AM **potty4350**: so when will you be back from texas?
12:01:36 AM **ladydi2011**: The 6th of August
12:01:44 AM **potty4350**: Oh okay baby
12:02:19 AM **ladydi2011**: I believe I told you I am a speaker, right?
12:03:05 AM **ladydi2011**: Hmmmmm....some falling hearts
12:03:09 AM **potty4350**: Yes baby you told me
12:03:11 AM **potty4350**: Yes baby, do you like it??
12:03:18 AM **ladydi2011**: Yeah
12:03:23 AM **potty4350**: Did you get my email about feelings?
12:03:48 AM **ladydi2011**: I did
12:03:55 AM **potty4350**: Okay baby
12:03:56 AM **ladydi2011**: I really liked it
12:04:05 AM **potty4350**: You don't respond to my emails why Diana?
12:04:14 AM **ladydi2011**: I am sorry honey
12:04:23 AM **ladydi2011**: So, please tell me
12:04:32 AM **ladydi2011**: How do you feel about me?
12:05:33 AM **ladydi2011**: I am waiting
12:06:54 AM **potty4350**: *Honey i feel love for you true love and care .. i will always love you till the end of time if only you could just love and trust me back in return*
12:07:18 AM **potty4350**: I just need a woman to hold me so closely to her heart
12:08:08 AM **potty4350**: Absolutely I have come to know that we spend the most of our life seeking for the secondary needs, while our primary needs are left unseen
12:08:50 AM **ladydi2011**: Honey, I am a little surprised how fast you have fallen in love with me
12:09:44 AM **ladydi2011**: It is really nice...I am just surprised
12:10:16 AM **potty4350**: *Honey what do you feel for me?*
12:10:47 AM **ladydi2011**: I care VERY deeply for you and am falling in love with you too
12:11:11 AM **potty4350**: Honey search your heart very well are you sure you are in love with me?

12:11:32 AM **potty4350**: But for few of us who value the simplicity, we sure would do well in finding happiness

12:12:17 AM **potty4350**: Money could buy a good bed, but never would it buy sleep

12:12:21 AM **ladydi2011**: I am getting there

12:12:27 AM **potty4350**: It could buy the best diamond watch, but never would it buy time

12:12:40 AM **potty4350**: It could buy piles of books, but not knowledge

12:13:13 AM **potty4350**: It can buy food, but not satisfaction, Money can buy sex, but can NEVER buy love.

12:13:43 AM **ladydi2011**: All this is true baby

12:14:09 AM **potty4350**: I would give up all that can be bought for that which can't be bought. I want true joy and happiness with you

12:14:36 AM **potty4350**: I want my woman to have power over my moods, she can make me smile in all weather.

12:14:40 AM **ladydi2011**: I want true joy and happiness with you too

12:14:52 AM **potty4350**: You have my heart

12:15:23 AM **potty4350**: I am glad that I could get your attention my dear

12:15:59 AM **potty4350**: You have a special thing in your heart, and I intend to find out what it is

12:16:04 AM **ladydi2011**: You did get my attention

12:16:17 AM **potty4350**: Yes *i* know baby

12:16:34 AM **potty4350**: I have true feelings for you Diana

12:17:09 AM **ladydi2011**: I have true feelings for you too Robin

12:17:23 AM **potty4350**: *Don't let me down Diana*

12:17:36 AM **potty4350**: *Promise me you will always be with me during good and bad time*

12:17:53 AM **ladydi2011**: I promise you baby

12:17:59 AM **ladydi2011**: Do you promise me the same?

12:18:00 AM **potty4350**: thank you baby

12:18:07 AM **potty4350**: *i* promise you too diana

12:18:21 AM **potty4350**: I wanna grow old in your arms. I wanna be with you forever

12:18:45 AM **potty4350**: Diana *i* know this love will last forever

12:19:12 AM **ladydi2011**: I believe it will too

12:19:18 AM **potty4350**: Good baby

12:19:52 AM **potty4350**: just be by me

12:19:59 AM **potty4350**: this will be forever baby you don't have to worry baby Ok?

12:20:21 AM **potty4350**: I am all yours forever

12:20:34 AM **ladydi2011**: I am not worried

12:20:46 AM **ladydi2011**: Honey, what is meant to be will be

12:20:53 AM **potty4350**: Good baby

12:20:55 AM **potty4350**: *You own me* and you have won my heart already

12:21:19 AM **ladydi2011**: I like that I have won your heart

12:21:26 AM **potty4350**: *Honey this is meant to be* that is why *i* feel this way towards you, if it is not mean to be I won't be up by this time chatting with you

12:21:28 AM **ladydi2011**: It must have been my smile...Lol

12:21:42 AM **potty4350**: Lol

12:22:38 AM **ladydi2011**: I wish you were here

12:22:50 AM **potty4350**: So *i* wsih too my lady

12:23:04 AM **potty4350**: *But I want you to know that in no time we will be together*

12:23:36 AM **ladydi2011**: I hope you are telling me the truth about this

12:23:50 AM **potty4350**: Yes I'm telling you the truth

12:23:57 AM **potty4350**: Do you have doubt towards me?

12:24:02 AM **ladydi2011**: No

12:24:22 AM **ladydi2011**: For us to have forever, we need to meet and be together in person

12:24:52 AM **potty4350**: honey do you mean you have doubts for me?

12:24:55 AM **potty4350**: Yes *i* know and we will surely be together in person definitely

12:25:58 AM **ladydi2011**: Ok baby. I trust your words. Please do not let me down...Promise

12:26:20 AM **potty4350**: *I promise I will never let you down*

12:26:27 AM **potty4350**: *Trust me..trust my words*

12:26:49 AM **ladydi2011**: Ok honey

12:27:43 AM **potty4350**: thank you diana

12:28:17 AM **ladydi2011**: What are you going to do today?

12:28:54 AM **potty4350**: Honey I will be doing some paper work today and later in the afternoon *i* will be going to the work field to see what we have done so far during the week

12:29:07 AM **ladydi2011**: Oh, ok

12:29:54 AM **potty4350**: Honey i'm listening to Boyz II Men I will make love to you

12:30:24 AM **ladydi2011**: Great song!!!

12:30:39 AM **potty4350**: Yes baby

12:30:50 AM **potty4350**: I will make love to you like you want me to Diana

12:31:27 AM **potty4350**: I wanna love you endlessly

12:31:58 AM **potty4350**: I'm sorry but *i* just have to tell you the truth Diana

12:32:01 AM **potty4350**: I really do love you

12:32:06 AM **potty4350**: I don't ever wanna get hurt

12:32:15 AM **ladydi2011**: I want to love you endlessly too

12:32:26 AM **potty4350**: OMG..I bless the day we met

12:32:52 AM **ladydi2011**: Me too

12:33:02 AM **potty4350**: Are you listening to the song

12:33:28 AM **ladydi2011**: I am looking for a man who will love me as madly and passionately as I love him

12:33:49 AM **potty4350**: are you willing to love me madly and passionately??

12:34:03 AM **ladydi2011**: Yes Robin, I am

12:34:08 AM **potty4350**: good baby

12:34:13 AM **ladydi2011**: I will never ask for what I will not give

12:34:21 AM **potty4350**: Do you like Joe Cocker .. You Are So Beautiful

12:34:35 AM **ladydi2011**: I do

12:34:45 AM **ladydi2011**: I do not have this song

12:35:01 AM **potty4350**: Oh okay baby

12:35:10 AM **potty4350**: Truly, Madly, Deeply .. Savage Garden?

12:35:30 AM **potty4350**: Donna Summer..Love to Love You Baby

12:35:59 AM **ladydi2011**: Another good song

12:36:06 AM **potty4350**: Yes baby

12:36:14 AM **potty4350**: I can't stop thinking about you

12:36:39 AM **potty4350**: Do you like Frank Sinatra?

12:36:47 AM **ladydi2011**: Yes, of course

12:36:55 AM **potty4350**: Awesome baby

12:37:01 AM **potty4350**: You are just the perfect woman for me

12:37:22 AM **ladydi2011**: Ah, yeah baby

12:37:44 AM **potty4350**: what are you doing now diana?

12:38:12 AM **ladydi2011**: Chatting with my love

12:38:22 AM **ladydi2011**: What are you doing now Robin?

12:39:10 AM **potty4350**: I am chatting with you my lady and listening to Elvis Presley

12:39:31 AM **ladydi2011**: Which song?

12:39:42 AM **potty4350**: Love me tender

12:39:55 AM **potty4350**: you are so wonderful my lady

12:40:06 AM **ladydi2011**: You are so wonderful too!

12:40:08 AM **potty4350**: don't ever let me go diana Ok?

12:40:43 AM **ladydi2011**: I will not

12:40:52 AM **potty4350**: thank you baby

12:40:52 AM **ladydi2011**: Don't ever let me go Robin

12:41:07 AM **ladydi2011**: If you did, you would regret it baby

12:41:07 AM **potty4350**: Yes baby

12:41:11 AM **potty4350**: I will never let you go

12:41:21 AM **potty4350**: No baby

12:41:22 AM **ladydi2011**: Nobody can make you as happy as I will

12:41:25 AM **potty4350**: I will never let you go

12:41:51 AM **potty4350**: I know baby

12:41:55 AM **potty4350**: I love you tenderly

12:42:26 AM **potty4350**: today is one of the best day of my life

12:42:26 AM **ladydi2011**: I love you tenderly back

12:42:42 AM **potty4350**: I have to rejoice .. I'm ready for the fight if any if gonna come up

12:43:10 AM **ladydi2011**: Hmmmmm

12:43:16 AM **ladydi2011**: What do you mean?

12:43:46 AM **potty4350**: *i* mean any fight for your love .. if *i* had any rival .. just kidding

12:44:38 AM **potty4350**: Are you there Diana??

12:44:42 AM **potty4350**: <ding>

12:45:06 AM **ladydi2011**: A rival

12:45:11 AM **ladydi2011**: Sorry, got booted

12:45:16 AM **potty4350**: Yes baby

12:45:21 AM **potty4350**: Don't mind me just kidding..lol

12:45:27 AM **ladydi2011**: Lol

12:45:56 AM **potty4350**: just been silly

12:46:12 AM **ladydi2011**: I am glad to know you would fight for me

12:46:15 AM **ladydi2011**: I like this

12:46:45 AM **potty4350**: *I will never let you down baby..Trust me dear*

12:47:08 AM **ladydi2011**: Honey, why do you keep asking me to trust you?

12:48:25 AM **potty4350**: cause that is the ultimate thing

12:48:36 AM **potty4350**: Do you?

12:48:57 AM **ladydi2011**: You are right...it is the ultimate thing

12:49:00 AM **ladydi2011**: Yes, i do

12:49:21 AM **potty4350**: good

12:50:23 AM **ladydi2011**: Do you trust me darling?

12:50:32 AM **potty4350**: Yes *i* do trust you and love you more

12:51:19 AM **ladydi2011**: Why do you say you love me more?

12:52:07 AM **potty4350**: cause it keeps growing the more we talk

12:52:11 AM **potty4350**: can you call me dear?

12:53:13 AM **ladydi2011**: I do not have a calling card here honey

12:53:51 AM **potty4350**: Okay baby

12:53:58 AM **potty4350**: I wanna hear your voice

12:54:03 AM **potty4350**: what time is it there?

12:54:10 AM **ladydi2011**: 1:00 am

12:54:25 AM **potty4350**: Oh

12:54:33 AM **potty4350**: *i* just wish *i* am there with you

12:54:38 AM **ladydi2011**: Me too. It would be very nice

12:55:09 AM **potty4350**: Yes..very nice

12:56:25 AM **ladydi2011**: It is 6 am there, right?

12:56:31 AM **potty4350**: yes you are right baby

12:56:50 AM **ladydi2011**: Did you have your coffee?

12:56:59 AM **potty4350**: *Am so very happy we are getting there*

12:57:04 AM **potty4350**: not yet baby

12:57:34 AM **ladydi2011**: What time will you go to the site?

12:58:03 AM **potty4350**: later in the afternoon

12:58:19 AM **ladydi2011**: So, what will you do all morning?

12:58:20 AM **potty4350**: *i* have to get done with some paper work first .. do some sketch

12:58:28 AM **potty4350**: working on some documents

12:59:15 AM **ladydi2011**: Ok

12:59:24 AM **ladydi2011**: Am I keeping you from your work?

12:59:47 AM **potty4350**: No you are not. Why do you ask?

1:00:32 AM **ladydi2011**: I do not want to keep you from your work darling

1:00:57 AM **potty4350**: no you are not keeping me from work

1:01:19 AM **ladydi2011**: Ok

1:01:34 AM **ladydi2011**: I like spending time with you

1:01:37 AM **potty4350**: good

1:01:45 AM **potty4350**: yes cause it keeps us going

1:01:54 AM **potty4350**: *i* like spending time with you too

1:02:02 AM **potty4350**: honey you should always respond to my email ok?

1:02:09 AM **ladydi2011**: Ok baby

1:02:13 AM **ladydi2011**: I am so sorry

1:02:21 AM **ladydi2011**: I get over 500 emails a day in my business

1:02:54 AM **potty4350**: okay baby

1:03:23 AM **ladydi2011**: Please don't ever take it personally if I don't respond

1:03:26 AM **ladydi2011**: Promise

1:03:40 AM **potty4350**: *i* promise diana

1:03:53 AM **potty4350**: but sometimes *i* might not be able to come on here or text you, Ok

1:04:03 AM **ladydi2011**: I believe I answered all your text, didn't I?

1:04:06 AM **potty4350**: maybe we should have a private email address then

1:04:09 AM **potty4350**: what do you think?

1:04:15 AM **ladydi2011**: Oh, ok

1:04:18 AM **potty4350**: not all diana but it ok

1:04:20 AM **potty4350**: good

1:04:29 AM **potty4350**: *i* will do mine now and you do yours too now

1:04:29 AM **potty4350**: ok?

1:04:47 AM **ladydi2011**: This might work...Good idea
1:04:55 AM **potty4350**: yes it will work
1:06:29 AM **ladydi2011**: Please send to Garren20@gmail.com
1:07:02 AM **potty4350**: Okay baby
1:07:06 AM **potty4350**: I will write you on there
1:07:29 AM **ladydi2011**: Honey, where did you come up with the name potty?
1:10:42 AM **potty4350**: got it baby
1:10:50 AM **potty4350**: it my son *i* call potty boy
1:12:17 AM **ladydi2011**: Ok
1:12:25 AM **potty4350**: I got 2 private email for us .. one on yahoo and the other on aol mail
1:12:52 AM **ladydi2011**: Ok...we only need one
1:13:06 AM **potty4350**: yes i know
1:13:09 AM **ladydi2011**: You are funny
1:13:11 AM **potty4350**: but just incase we wanna chat..lol
1:13:15 AM **potty4350**: yes
1:13:20 AM **ladydi2011**: Do you always go over the top?
1:13:40 AM **ladydi2011**: Chatting here is good
1:14:28 AM **potty4350**: yes honey *i* know..just kidding
1:14:36 AM **potty4350**: this is the second private email
1:14:39 AM **potty4350**: we can always text too
1:14:47 AM **ladydi2011**: So, can I have a physical address where I can send you something
1:16:04 AM **ladydi2011**: Please hold
1:16:11 AM **ladydi2011**: Battery is running low
1:16:22 AM **ladydi2011**: Need to go get cord and a glass of water
1:16:23 AM **ladydi2011**: Brb
1:16:24 AM **potty4350**: okay baby
1:16:36 AM **ladydi2011**: Thanks for holding
1:16:43 AM **potty4350**: You are welcome my love
1:29:36 AM **ladydi2011**: I am back
1:30:16 AM **potty4350**: I am here baby
1:30:27 AM **potty4350**: Working on some documents
1:30:42 AM **ladydi2011**: What kind of documents?
1:31:01 AM **potty4350**: construction documents baby
1:31:08 AM **potty4350**: wanna come help me??
1:31:13 AM **ladydi2011**: Yeah baby
1:32:33 AM **ladydi2011**: Honey, it is 1:30 in the morning here
1:32:41 AM **ladydi2011**: I should get some rest
1:32:53 AM **potty4350**: did you get your cord?
1:32:56 AM **ladydi2011**: You have work to do
1:33:00 AM **ladydi2011**: I did
1:33:03 AM **potty4350**: yes baby
1:33:10 AM **potty4350**: you need to go to bed dear
1:33:15 AM **potty4350**: *i* will email you in the morning
1:33:19 AM **potty4350**: *i* cherish you so much
1:33:27 AM **ladydi2011**: I am in bed now
1:33:44 AM **potty4350**: oh *i* should be laying next to you right there baby
1:33:48 AM **ladydi2011**: I will look for your email when I wake up

1:33:54 AM **potty4350**: okay baby

1:34:03 AM **ladydi2011**: Yeah baby, you should be here with me

1:34:03 AM **potty4350**: go to bed now and dream about me darling

1:34:19 AM **potty4350**: *well i will be there with you in no time baby..i promise ok?*

1:34:36 AM **ladydi2011**: Ok baby

1:34:41 AM **ladydi2011**: I will dream about you

1:34:50 AM **ladydi2011**: Think about me at least once today

1:35:15 AM **potty4350**: *i* will baby

1:35:26 AM **potty4350**: you occupy my mind darling

1:35:27 AM **ladydi2011**: Bye for now

1:35:42 AM **potty4350**: bye for now darling

1:35:53 AM **potty4350**: do you mind talking on here before going to bed

1:36:02 AM **ladydi2011**: Not at all

Missed Voice call with potty4350 (1:36:42 AM)

1:37:46 AM potty4350: did you get my call??

Outgoing Voice call with potty4350 (1:37:49 AM)
Call Ended: 0 hours 0 minutes 5 seconds

1:38:12 AM **potty4350**: can you call me back darling

1:38:21 AM **ladydi2011**: I did but couldn't hear you

1:38:28 AM **potty4350:** okay

Missed Voice call with potty4350 (1:37:25 AM)
Call Ended: 0 hours 0 minutes 8 seconds
Outgoing Voice call with potty4350 (1:38:25 AM)
Call Ended: 0 hours 3 minutes 31 seconds

1:42:18 AM **ladydi2011**: I love hearing your voice

1:42:27 AM **ladydi2011**: Now I can sleep well

1:42:41 AM **ladydi2011**: Goodnight love

1:43:20 AM **potty4350**: good night my lady

From: ladydi2011@yahoo.com
To: Robin Lufos
Subject: Hello Darling
Sent: Saturday, July 14, 2012 6:37 PM

Hello Darling,

How are you this evening? I hope you had a wonderful day. Did you have dinner yet, Baby? Did you think of me at least once? Do you have a smile on your face? I am thinking about you and smiling.

All my love, Diana

1:19:42 AM **potty4350**: <ding>

2:02:33 AM **ladydi2011**: Hi Baby
2:02:39 AM **ladydi2011**: How are you?
2:02:43 AM **potty4350**: Good Morning Honey
2:02:49 AM **potty4350**: I am doing well and you?
2:02:54 AM **potty4350**: How was your day?
2:02:55 AM **ladydi2011**: I am well
2:03:02 AM **ladydi2011**: It was fabulous
2:03:06 AM **ladydi2011**: And yours
2:03:34 AM **potty4350**: I am very glad to hear that my lady
2:03:34 AM **potty4350**: My day was awesome sweet lady
2:03:36 AM **potty4350**: You occupy my mind Diana
2:04:16 AM **ladydi2011**: I am very glad to know I occupy your mind
2:04:46 AM **ladydi2011**: Robin, you also occupy mine
2:05:17 AM **ladydi2011**: Have you had breakfast yet?
2:05:44 AM **potty4350**: No breakfast yet baby
2:06:03 AM **potty4350**: maybe if you were here with me you would be making my breakfast
2:06:06 AM **potty4350**: I miss you so much
2:06:10 AM **potty4350**: Was worried ..
2:06:26 AM **potty4350**: I didn't take my phone with me to the work field yesterday
2:06:46 AM **ladydi2011**: Oh, this is why I didn't hear from you
2:06:57 AM **ladydi2011**: I miss you too!
2:07:30 AM **ladydi2011**: I emailed you but you didn't reply
2:08:23 AM **ladydi2011**: Are you there baby?
2:08:38 AM **ladydi2011**: Are you busy with something else honey?
Break In Time
2:10:19 AM **ladydi2011**: Ok honey, I need to get ready for bed
2:10:35 AM **ladydi2011**: I guess we will talk tomorrow......
2:10:53 AM **potty4350**: No
2:10:56 AM **potty4350**: I am here darling
2:11:04 AM **potty4350**: I am just trying to make coffee
2:11:14 AM **ladydi2011**: Ok
2:11:34 AM **ladydi2011**: Did you get it made?
2:12:22 AM **potty4350**: I am about making it when *i* heard your IM
2:12:38 AM **potty4350**: Are you still there
2:12:45 AM **potty4350**: <ding>
2:12:53 AM **ladydi2011**: I am here
2:13:13 AM **ladydi2011**: Go ahead and finish making your coffee
2:13:24 AM **ladydi2011**: I am going to change for bed

2:14:13 AM **potty4350**: Okay baby .. *i* will be back in a minute darling
2:14:32 AM **ladydi2011**: Me too...........
2:14:46 AM **potty4350**: Ok baby
2:14:48 AM **potty4350**: Don't go to bed yet darling
2:20:57 AM **ladydi2011**: I am back darling, what about you?
2:22:36 AM **ladydi2011**: Sweetheart, I need to go to sleep
2:23:00 AM **ladydi2011**: I need to get up in 4 1/2 hours for church
2:23:43 AM **ladydi2011**: Text me later ok baby
2:23:52 AM **ladydi2011**: I love you <3
2:27:15 AM **potty4350**: <ding>
2:27:20 AM **potty4350**: I am back
2:27:24 AM **potty4350**: done with coffee
2:28:06 AM **potty4350**: <ding>

From: Robin Lulofs
To: garren40@gmail.com
Subject: Re: Hello Darling
Sent: Sun, 15 Jul 2012 14:32:45 -0700 (PDT)

I sent you an email with my other email address, we can email on both though, You occupy my heart honey *i* think about you every moment of my life, I wanna love you endlessly honey, I cherish you so much, I bless the day we met, you are such a wonderful woman, I don't ever wanna end this journey with you.

I adore you my lady.
Robin Cares.

Text Messages

From: 260-267-0302
Sent: July 15, 2012 8:50 am

Good Morning Honey, How are you doing this morning and how was your night?

To: 260-267-0302
Sent: July 15, 2012 1:35 pm

Hello honey!

From: 260-267-0302
Sent: July 15, 2012 4:57 pm

Hello Diana .. How are you doing? How was your day??

To: 260-267-0302
Sent: July 15, 2012 6:25 pm

Hi honey. I am driving home and at a red light...

From: 260-267-0302
Sent: July 15, 2012 6:32 pm

Lol .. I wish *i* am there with you darling

From: 260-267-0302
Sent: July 15, 2012 6:46 pm

Are you home now?

To: 260-267-0302
Sent: July 15, 2012 9:29 pm

Hi Robin. Sorry baby. I got caught behind a major accident. I just got home. Can you meet me on yahoo?

From: ladydi2011@yahoo.com
To: potty4350@yahoo.com>
Sent: Monday, July 16, 2012 4:42 AM
Subject: Re: Hello Darling

Thank you, Darling. You occupy my heart and thoughts. I too am very grateful that we met. I am looking forward to our journey and I don't want it to end.

Good night, my prince
Always
Diana

IM Jul 16, 2012 5:03:52 AM

5:03:52 AM **ladydi2011**: Hey Baby
5:04:11 AM **ladydi2011**: How are you handsome?
5:04:24 AM **ladydi2011**: I miss you!
5:04:51 AM **potty4350**: I have missed you too Diana
5:04:54 AM **potty4350**: How are you doing?
5:04:57 AM **potty4350**: I was worried about you
5:05:32 AM **ladydi2011**: I just woke up and thought of you!
5:05:52 AM **potty4350**: You are always on my mind

5:05:56 AM **ladydi2011**: Got tied up behind an accident for hours
5:06:04 AM **potty4350**: I tried texting you but you were not responding
5:06:07 AM **potty4350**: How was your day?
5:06:14 AM **potty4350**: I am so sorry dear. Hope nothing happened to you
5:06:20 AM **ladydi2011**: How is your morning going honey?
5:06:45 AM **ladydi2011**: Sorry baby. Phone battery died.
5:06:49 AM **potty4350**: it going good dear
5:06:55 AM **potty4350**: I am doing some paper work
5:07:10 AM **ladydi2011**: Nothing happened to me love. I am good!
5:07:23 AM **potty4350**: I am very glad to hear that Diana
5:07:26 AM **potty4350**: I got your email
5:07:36 AM **potty4350**: do you have my other email address now?
5:07:40 AM **potty4350**: *potty4520@att.net*
5:08:08 AM **ladydi2011**: Yes honey. Thank you
5:08:26 AM **potty4350**: I miss you so much my lady
5:08:39 AM **ladydi2011**: *Honey, do you have a cam?*
5:08:47 AM **potty4350**: *No baby I don't have a cam*
5:09:01 AM **ladydi2011**: I miss you so much too love
5:09:02 AM **potty4350**: *Honey do you have any problem with that*
5:09:11 AM **potty4350**: I cherish you Diana
5:09:26 AM **potty4350**: Don't worry *i* will be done with my project in a short while and *i* will be there with you Ok?
5:09:35 AM **ladydi2011**: I would like to see your handsome face
5:09:52 AM **ladydi2011**: Promise?
5:10:07 AM **ladydi2011**: Did you have your coffee?
5:10:18 AM **potty4350**: Yes baby I did
5:10:26 AM **potty4350**: I have been up since 7am
5:10:43 AM **potty4350**: I will be going to the work field soon when *i* am done chatting with you
5:10:53 AM **potty4350**: Yes I promise you my lady
5:11:03 AM **potty4350**: All *i* just want is your love
5:11:08 AM **potty4350**: I love you Diana that is my true feelings for you
5:11:21 AM **ladydi2011**: I am glad I caught you before you left
5:11:29 AM **potty4350**: I wanna spend the rest of my life with you
5:11:49 AM **ladydi2011**: Me too!
5:12:35 AM **potty4350**: I am very glad you are here Diana
5:12:43 AM **ladydi2011**: We can take time together to have fun and stop to smell the roses
5:12:48 AM **potty4350**: *Diana? what do you think about me so far?*
5:12:58 AM **potty4350**: Yes baby
5:13:13 AM **ladydi2011**: Sorry I am typing so slow...on phone
5:13:22 AM **potty4350**: It ok baby
5:13:24 AM **ladydi2011**: I'm in bed
5:14:08 AM **ladydi2011**: I am falling in love with you my dear
5:14:30 AM **potty4350**: I have fallen in love with you. You won my heart
5:14:42 AM **ladydi2011**: Please know I am cautious
5:16:01 AM **ladydi2011**: Honey, I am glad to know this. I haven't done anything yet to win your heart...The best is yet to come
5:17:15 AM **potty4350**: I am patiently waiting for the best to come Diana

5:17:24 AM **potty4350**: I really can't wait to see the best to come

5:17:31 AM **potty4350**: I cherish you so much. I hope i'm not rushing you into things

5:17:52 AM **ladydi2011**: You will be a HAPPY MAN!

5:17:58 AM **potty4350**: Let us stack the build blocks to form our coming life.

5:18:18 AM **potty4350**: To take the very first step, a home for me and you

5:18:37 AM **ladydi2011**: Which block are we on now?

5:18:58 AM **ladydi2011**: Where do you want to live?

5:19:03 AM **potty4350**: honey that question is for you

5:19:11 AM **ladydi2011**: Lol...You make me smile

5:19:33 AM **potty4350**: You make me happy

5:19:48 AM **potty4350**: I thought *i* would never find what *i* want

5:20:02 AM **potty4350**: I thought *i* would never find someone that is *more better* than my wife

5:20:10 AM **potty4350**: But you prove me so wrong

5:20:18 AM **ladydi2011**: Honey, if you are who you say you are I want to spend forever with you!

5:20:45 AM **potty4350**: Yes *i* am who *i* say i'm

5:20:54 AM **potty4350**: *I have never lied to you before and i will never lie to you*

5:21:01 AM **potty4350**: *pls don't ever doubt me ok?*

5:21:09 AM **ladydi2011**: Same here!

5:21:13 AM **potty4350**: *I'm not playing games with you*

5:21:32 AM **ladydi2011**: Many men do play games

5:21:46 AM **ladydi2011**: I am not a game type of woman. I am looking for my forever

5:22:04 AM **potty4350**: I am not here for games

5:22:10 AM **potty4350**: Life's too short for all that

5:22:13 AM **ladydi2011**: I will not settle

5:22:30 AM **ladydi2011**: I do not want my heart broken

5:23:13 AM **ladydi2011**: I do want a man who will love me as madly and passionately as I love him!!!

5:23:33 AM **potty4350**: *I will never break your heart Diana Trust me*

5:23:51 AM **potty4350**: *give me your heart and i promise i will cherish it till the end of time*

5:23:51 AM **ladydi2011**: Baby, honesty and trust are the foundation must haves

5:24:14 AM **potty4350**: I wanna love you endlessly, madly and *i* want the same in return

5:24:43 AM **ladydi2011**: Honey, you are so perfect for me!

5:25:29 AM **potty4350**: You are all *i* have been praying for ever since *i* lost my wife

5:25:38 AM **ladydi2011**: I can't wait to meet you in person!

5:25:44 AM **potty4350**: Yes dear

5:26:05 AM **potty4350**: Have it in your mind that we will surely spend the rest of our life together

5:26:19 AM **ladydi2011**: So, where do you want to live baby?

5:26:43 AM **potty4350**: Diana anywhere you wanna live is where *i* wanna live

5:26:48 AM **ladydi2011**: I do have this in my mind...promise darling.

5:26:55 AM **potty4350**: remember *i* told you i'm hanging my hat this year

5:27:02 AM **potty4350**: I promise

5:27:10 AM **ladydi2011**: Yeah, I know

5:27:29 AM **potty4350**: I'm quiting my field work and *i* will work from my house office

5:27:30 AM **ladydi2011**: Do you like Indiana?

5:27:37 AM **potty4350**: Yes *i* like Indiana

5:28:14 AM **ladydi2011**: I love the ocean. I feel very calm there.

5:28:49 AM **potty4350**: Wow I love the ocean too

5:29:01 AM **potty4350**: We can have another house anywhere you want

5:29:06 AM **ladydi2011**: I would love to live on the beach

5:29:16 AM **potty4350**: Okay fine then

5:29:22 AM **ladydi2011**: My next phase in life is writing romance novels

5:29:26 AM **potty4350**: *How big is your house you live in presently?*

5:29:59 AM **ladydi2011**: 3,000 square ft.

5:30:16 AM **potty4350**: We can do that together baby

5:30:26 AM **potty4350**: I can do the writing and you be on it as the author is that cool with you?

5:30:40 AM **ladydi2011**: Yeah, this is what I was hoping for

5:30:57 AM **potty4350**: Yes dear

5:31:04 AM **ladydi2011**: You are a fabulous writer

5:31:08 AM **potty4350**: is that Ok with you Diana?

5:31:19 AM **ladydi2011**: Sure baby

5:31:23 AM **potty4350**: Good

5:31:36 AM **potty4350**: *do you have the pictures of your house?*

5:32:06 AM **ladydi2011**: I do but not on my phone

5:32:13 AM **potty4350**: Oh okay dear

5:32:21 AM **potty4350**: maybe when you get on your computer

5:32:29 AM **potty4350**: or will you like to get on your computer?

5:32:44 AM **ladydi2011**: You are capturing my heart more and more every day

5:33:01 AM **potty4350**: I am very glad to hear that Diana

5:33:30 AM **ladydi2011**: I am in bed honey

5:33:41 AM **potty4350**: Okay baby it ok ..

5:33:50 AM **potty4350**: I wish *i* am there with you right now

5:33:55 AM **potty4350**: What will you be doing to me?

5:34:04 AM **ladydi2011**: No rush to see my house, right?

5:34:16 AM **potty4350**: Yes baby no rush

5:34:22 AM **ladydi2011**: I wish you were here too!

5:34:29 AM **ladydi2011**: Hmmmm

5:34:48 AM **ladydi2011**: My head would be on your chest

5:34:58 AM **potty4350**: wow

5:35:28 AM **potty4350**: I would love to make love to you baby

5:36:20 AM **potty4350**: *Honey do you think you love me yet?*

5:36:39 AM **ladydi2011**: Getting very close

5:36:52 AM **ladydi2011**: I am fighting it...

5:36:55 AM **potty4350**: I am very glad to hear that

5:37:07 AM **potty4350**: *Honey just know that i will never do anything to hurt you*

5:37:24 AM **ladydi2011**: Ok baby

5:37:44 AM **potty4350**: *do you owe any mortgage on your house??*

5:37:50 AM **ladydi2011**: You seem too good to be true

5:38:19 AM **potty4350**: *Well i am good and i'm true*

5:38:26 AM **ladydi2011**: If I am dreaming, please don't wake me....

5:38:34 AM **potty4350**: lol..this is reality

5:38:44 AM **ladydi2011**: Yes, I have a mortgage

5:39:03 AM **potty4350**: *you owe?*

5:39:30 AM **ladydi2011**: Do you know I own the phrase "perception creates reality"?

5:39:42 AM **ladydi2011**: Yeah, I owe

5:39:50 AM **potty4350**: *how much do you owe baby?*

5:40:14 AM **ladydi2011**: $50k

5:40:24 AM **potty4350**: Okay baby

5:40:31 AM **potty4350**: *How much does the house worth?*

5:40:49 AM **ladydi2011**: $450k

5:40:58 AM **potty4350**: Okay baby

5:41:06 AM **potty4350**: *Honey will you be willing to relocate*

5:41:41 AM **ladydi2011**: Yes

5:42:18 AM **ladydi2011**: I can run my business from anywhere in the world

5:42:19 AM **potty4350**: Okay baby

5:42:59 AM **ladydi2011**: I work out of my home office

5:43:11 AM **ladydi2011**: All my employees are remote

5:43:26 AM **ladydi2011**: We have clients nationwide

5:43:33 AM **potty4350**: I am very glad to hear that honey

5:43:45 AM **ladydi2011**: Do you own your home?

5:43:57 AM **potty4350**: *Yes i own my house*

5:44:25 AM **ladydi2011**: Do you have a mortgage?

5:45:27 AM **potty4350**: there's this project i did in qatar UAE a couple of months back it was a huge project where i invested a lot of my money and savings on

5:46:38 AM **ladydi2011**: Honey, my eyes are closing so if I stop responding it means I fell asleep

5:47:01 AM **ladydi2011**: If this happens, I am sorry.

5:47:25 AM **potty4350**: Okay

5:47:33 AM **ladydi2011**: I am grateful we were able to connect this morning

5:47:57 AM **potty4350**: *This is a project payment worth of $9.4m, which included his invested funds*

5:48:00 AM **ladydi2011**: Sounds like a profitable project

5:48:24 AM **potty4350**: *i* got a bank loan with my house back home

5:48:31 AM **ladydi2011**: Who's invested funds?

5:49:04 AM **ladydi2011**: Ok...how much do you still owe?

5:49:41 AM **potty4350**: my invested funds

5:49:54 AM **potty4350**: *i still owe a lot from different angle*

5:49:58 AM **ladydi2011**: Ok

5:50:04 AM **potty4350**: well with time *i* will tell you more about this

5:50:19 AM **ladydi2011**: Ok

5:50:36 AM **ladydi2011**: Baby, I am fading fast

5:50:39 AM **potty4350**: I really can't wait to be with you

5:50:43 AM **potty4350**: Okay then

5:50:54 AM **ladydi2011**: Have a fabulous day my love

5:50:58 AM **potty4350**: what time is it there now

5:51:04 AM **potty4350**: thank you my woman

5:51:09 AM **potty4350**: I cherish you so much

5:51:10 AM **ladydi2011**: Love, kisses and hugs

5:51:20 AM **potty4350**: I can't wait to make love to you slowly

5:51:26 AM **ladydi2011**: 5:51 am

5:51:31 AM **potty4350**: Okay baby

5:51:34 AM **ladydi2011**: Nice

5:51:36 AM **potty4350**: What time are you gonna leave for work?

5:51:50 AM **ladydi2011**: You have my attention

5:52:01 AM **potty4350**: You have had mine already dear

5:52:04 AM **ladydi2011**: 8:30 baby
5:52:06 AM **potty4350**: I will always be there for you darling
5:52:18 AM **potty4350**: Okay baby
5:52:26 AM **ladydi2011**: Same here baby
5:52:30 AM **potty4350**: Go to bed now dear
5:52:50 AM **ladydi2011**: Bye for now baby
5:52:51 AM **potty4350**: I will text you during my break at work
5:52:55 AM **potty4350**: bye for now sweetie
5:53:03 AM **ladydi2011**: Ok
5:53:16 AM **ladydi2011**: I will be looking for it

From: Robin Lulofs
To: garren20@gmail.com
Sent: Mon, Jul 16, 2012 at 4:15 PM
Subject: Re: Hello Darling

I cherish you so much my charming princess.

He is a very handsome man, so if I didn't know the red flags and know he was a scammer, it would be easy to "fall in love with his picture." Many victims fall in love with the picture first and then the sweet words.

I do not always answer his emails and he doesn't like this so he gives me an AT&T address for private email. Knowing he is in Nigeria I was surprised that he had an AT&T email address. This could easily fool a woman into thinking he is from the United States if they didn't understand that scammers can use emails and phone numbers from anywhere in the world.

Of course he doesn't have a camera on his computer. However, if I push the issue, he might come on with a fake cam. He thinks he has a rich client on the hook and he will do whatever it takes to get my money.

RED FLAGS

- When I speak with this man he has a very thick accent that makes it difficult to understand him. I usually don't understand anything he says. This is a big red flag that he is from Africa.
- He continually asks me to trust him, asks what I think about him and if I am in love with him yet. He tells me he will always love me till the end of time if only I could just love and trust him back in return. Remember, he knows if he can't get me to love and trust him, he can't get to my money, so he is working diligently to make me fall in love with him.

🏴 He asks me to not let him down and to promise to always be with him during good and bad times. He tells me "I own him". This is another statement a Nigerian man will say; another red flag.

🏴 He tells me that he wants me to know that in no time we will be together. Several times he tells me he will never let me down and I need to trust him and his words. He tells me he has never lied to me and he will never lie to me, so I should not doubt him. Yeah, right!

🏴 He tells me he is not playing games with me and he will never break my heart.

🏴 He wants to know how big my house is, how much it's worth and how much I owe on it. He is asking these questions so he knows how much money to ask me for and what he can ask me to do to get the money.

🏴 He says he owns a house but he put a mortgage on it to invest in his last project that paid $9.4 million. It is typical of a scammer to talk in grandiose numbers.

IM Jul 16, 2012 6:28:51 PM

6:28:51 PM **ladydi2011**: Hey baby
6:28:56 PM **ladydi2011**: Waiting for you
6:51:13 PM **potty4350**: Hello
6:51:20 PM **potty4350**: How are you doing baby?
6:51:22 PM **potty4350**: Are you there??
6:51:38 PM **ladydi2011**: I am here
6:51:52 PM **ladydi2011**: How are you baby?
6:52:14 PM **potty4350**: I am doing well baby
6:52:28 PM **potty4350**: I miss you so much
6:53:31 PM **ladydi2011**: I miss you too!
6:53:48 PM **ladydi2011**: How was your day and evening?
6:54:28 PM **potty4350**: Work was stressful baby
6:54:38 PM **potty4350**: You got me thinking about you so muchh Diana
6:54:45 PM **potty4350**: Did you like my letter??
6:55:07 PM **ladydi2011**: Why was work stressful honey?
6:55:38 PM **potty4350**: I had to get a lot done today
6:55:44 PM **potty4350**: few of the workers did not show up but *i* hope they will be at work tomorrow
6:55:57 PM **potty4350**: how was your day like?
6:55:59 PM **ladydi2011**: I understand
6:56:01 PM **potty4350**: what did you do dear?
6:56:07 PM **potty4350**: what time is it there with you now
6:56:18 PM **potty4350**: thanks for your understanding
6:56:24 PM **ladydi2011**: My right hand person broke every bone in her ankle over the 4th of July holiday
6:57:07 PM **potty4350**: oh so sorry to hear that
6:57:11 PM **ladydi2011**: It is 6:57 pm here and 11:57 there, right?
6:57:23 PM **potty4350**: yes you are right baby

6:57:49 PM **ladydi2011**: So, my love...how am I able to occupy so much of your mind?

6:57:59 PM **ladydi2011**: What are you thinking about?

6:58:37 PM **potty4350**: I am thinking of our future

6:58:51 PM **potty4350**: *I really wanna meet you soon and start planning our life together*

6:59:25 PM **ladydi2011**: I like these thoughts

6:59:34 PM **potty4350**: I am glad you like it

6:59:38 PM **ladydi2011**: I also want to meet you and for the same reason

7:00:07 PM **ladydi2011**: I told you...if you are the real deal...YOU WILL be a VERY HAPPY MAN

7:01:31 PM **ladydi2011**: I mean VERY HAPPY................

7:01:32 PM **potty4350**: Yes

7:01:37 PM **potty4350**: *I am the real deal Diana..Trust me*

7:01:47 PM **potty4350**: *What do you think about me so far*

7:02:05 PM **ladydi2011**: Hmmmmmmmm

7:02:15 PM **ladydi2011**: What do you think I think about you so far?

7:02:36 PM **potty4350**: I really don't know baby that is why *i* ask

7:02:50 PM **potty4350**: you sound like you still have some doubt in mind towards me

7:02:55 PM **ladydi2011**: Baby, I told you I am falling in love with you

7:03:03 PM **ladydi2011**: You make me smile and very happy

7:03:11 PM **ladydi2011**: I can see forever with you but I cannot commit until we meet in person

7:04:29 PM **ladydi2011**: When I give my heart, word and commitment it will be for real and forever

7:04:38 PM **ladydi2011**: I am not here to play games. I want it ALL!

7:04:57 PM **potty4350**: Yes I am not here to play games too Diana

7:05:06 PM **ladydi2011**: I am an all or nothing type of gal

7:05:16 PM **potty4350**: I can understand

7:05:40 PM **potty4350**: *Well i want your love, trust, support, care and honesty*

7:05:55 PM **ladydi2011**: I believe you are an all or nothing type of man

7:06:03 PM **ladydi2011**: You have this honey

7:06:38 PM **ladydi2011**: Are you there honey?

7:06:59 PM **ladydi2011**: I am so glad you are not here to play games

7:07:14 PM **ladydi2011**: Games of the heart are too painful

7:07:32 PM **ladydi2011**: I promise to always protect your heart

7:08:26 PM **potty4350**: Yes *i* am here

7:08:36 PM **potty4350**: I am here with you Diana

7:09:13 PM **ladydi2011**: I am really excited about "us"

7:09:26 PM **ladydi2011**: I want to take this step-by-step

7:09:32 PM **potty4350**: thanks for the sweet words

7:09:38 PM **potty4350**: Yes *i* know. It ok if you wanna take it step by step. I understand

7:10:07 PM **potty4350**: *But always know one thing that i will never hurt you*

7:10:14 PM **potty4350**: *We need to work together as one*

7:10:22 PM **ladydi2011**: I agree

7:10:25 PM **potty4350**: I want to spend the rest of my life loving you more and more

7:10:45 PM **potty4350**: If you don't let out your love things might not go the way we want it

7:10:55 PM **ladydi2011**: Between you and Christian, I am outnumbered with charm

7:10:57 PM **potty4350**: *cause i won't be free enough to tell you everything*

7:11:09 PM **ladydi2011**: Hmmmmmm...Good point honey

7:11:29 PM **potty4350**: *Christian is very excited*

7:12:21 PM **potty4350**: *if you say you don't want any commttment right now baby i will say you don't want anything then .. and you don't want all you said you are looking for*

7:13:06 PM **potty4350**: *Do you think i am not the real deal??*

7:13:18 PM **ladydi2011**: Hmmmmmm

7:13:52 PM **ladydi2011**: Now baby, me not wanting anything is not true

7:14:12 PM **ladydi2011**: I do want all I am looking for

7:14:30 PM **ladydi2011**: I do think you are the real deal, but I am testing the waters

7:14:52 PM **ladydi2011**: One needs to be cautious

7:15:06 PM **ladydi2011**: You are a business man, you should understand this

7:16:03 PM **ladydi2011**: Let me say it another way....You are always on my mind

7:16:04 PM **potty4350**: Yes dear

7:16:11 PM **potty4350**: Baby cautious of what?

7:16:21 PM **potty4350**: Do you mind telling me what you are been cautious of?

7:16:29 PM **ladydi2011**: I do not want my heart broken

7:16:41 PM **ladydi2011**: I have saved myself for my "forever" man

7:16:46 PM **potty4350**: I swear I will never break your heart

7:16:52 PM **ladydi2011**: and I want to be sure I have found him

7:16:54 PM **potty4350**: *Pls can you just trust my love for you*

7:17:23 PM **potty4350**: *well i think you have found him cause i believe i have found her*

7:17:28 PM **ladydi2011**: Ok my love, I will trust your love for me

7:17:46 PM **ladydi2011**: I will trust you will NOT hurt me

7:17:57 PM **potty4350**: *real committment is what we should have from now on and everything will be so cool*

7:18:08 PM **potty4350**: *I promise i will never hurt you..GOD knows i will never hurt you*

7:18:29 PM **ladydi2011**: Please know, the only thing that could ever take me from you is you

7:18:38 PM **potty4350**: *I want you to know that God brought us together for a very great purpose don't let fear take it all away from you*

7:19:35 PM **ladydi2011**: I agree. I will not

7:19:54 PM **potty4350**: Good

7:20:01 PM **potty4350**: *Fear is of the devil*

7:20:08 PM **ladydi2011**: This is true..God does not give us a spirit of fear

7:20:45 PM **ladydi2011**: But the wisdom he gives us is more precious than rubies and gold

7:21:34 PM **potty4350**: Good Baby

7:21:40 PM **potty4350**: *I want your love trust and support*

7:21:49 PM **potty4350**: they are some more thing we are yet to know about each other

7:21:49 PM **ladydi2011**: Honey, you would not want to be with a woman who is "easy" and available to anyone and everyone, would you?

7:22:02 PM **potty4350**: No *i* know *i* would not

7:22:06 PM **ladydi2011**: See

7:22:15 PM **potty4350**: You don't have to be like that to me

7:22:22 PM **potty4350**: I let out my love so easy for you

7:22:38 PM **ladydi2011**: A man who finds a "good" woman is blessed

7:22:57 PM **potty4350**: But what will you do to a man who let go of other women disturbing him because of you

7:23:08 PM **ladydi2011**: Baby, I told you that I am falling in love with you

7:23:23 PM **ladydi2011**: Hmmmmm. Nice. Thank you darling

7:23:42 PM **ladydi2011**: I have done the same with other men disturbing me because of you

7:23:59 PM **potty4350**: thank you baby

7:24:02 PM **ladydi2011**: I am a one man woman

7:24:03 PM **potty4350**: I really do appreciate

7:24:11 PM **potty4350**: We would make the best and perfect match ever

7:24:25 PM **ladydi2011**: This is what I want

7:24:52 PM **potty4350**: *let be committed*

7:25:28 PM **ladydi2011**: Ok Robin. Let's be committed to each other

7:26:35 PM **ladydi2011**: I want to give it my all and see where we go....

7:27:02 PM **potty4350**: Honey the sky is our limit

7:27:19 PM **potty4350**: *I know we would have a good life together as the best couple ever*

7:27:24 PM **potty4350**: be calm with me, ask me things you don't know

7:27:58 PM **potty4350**: let be there for each other

7:28:06 PM **potty4350**: love me endlessly, trust me endlessly

7:28:15 PM **potty4350**: You got my heart baby

7:28:22 PM **potty4350**: You have all you want in a man

7:28:30 PM **potty4350**: *You rule my world, you rule my life*

7:28:35 PM **potty4350**: You are everything to me

7:28:48 PM **potty4350**: I can't just get you out of my mind

7:28:57 PM **ladydi2011**: Wow

7:29:11 PM **ladydi2011**: I am so glad I stayed on the site

7:29:28 PM **ladydi2011**: I was ready to take my profile down right before we met

7:29:49 PM **ladydi2011**: I will love and trust you

7:30:00 PM **ladydi2011**: You do have my heart

7:30:19 PM **ladydi2011**: You do have all you could ever want in a woman with me

7:30:30 PM **ladydi2011**: You will feel like a king every day

7:30:45 PM **ladydi2011**: You will feel like you are the only man on the planet

7:31:26 PM **ladydi2011**: You are like a drug...When I am not with you I want to be

7:31:40 PM **ladydi2011**: When I am with you...I want more of you

7:31:57 PM **potty4350**: Wow baby

7:32:02 PM **potty4350**: I can't wait to get done here

7:33:22 PM **potty4350**: *I will never break your heart Diana*

7:33:42 PM **ladydi2011**: I can't wait for you to get done and be here in my arms

7:33:58 PM **potty4350**: I will be done soon Ok

7:33:59 PM **ladydi2011**: *I will never break your heart either*

7:34:07 PM **potty4350**: *Let start planning our life together*

7:34:15 PM **potty4350**: this is a very great moment

7:34:23 PM **ladydi2011**: Ok

7:36:13 PM **potty4350**: thank you my love

7:36:19 PM **potty4350**: have you had dinner??

7:37:09 PM **ladydi2011**: I did. I took my intern to dinner

7:37:25 PM **potty4350**: What did you have for dinner??

7:37:28 PM **ladydi2011**: Mexican and I am full

7:37:34 PM **potty4350**: Lol..I wish *i* am there with you baby

7:37:54 PM **potty4350**: *I wish i had met you before i leave maybe then you will be more rest assured*

7:38:08 PM **ladydi2011**: Yeah honey, me too.

7:38:11 PM **potty4350**: are you on the computer now

7:38:17 PM **ladydi2011**: I am....

7:38:28 PM **potty4350**: Okay

7:38:29 PM **ladydi2011**: My one laptop died today

7:38:34 PM **potty4350**: *so can you share some pictures with me dear*

7:38:36 PM **ladydi2011**: Just ordered a new one

7:38:55 PM **potty4350**: what other laptop did you order today?

7:39:20 PM **ladydi2011**: Oh honey....I am sorry, my pictures are on the computer that gave me the dreaded blue screen today

7:39:22 PM **potty4350**: You one laptop died today? *do you mean got spoiled?*

7:39:31 PM **ladydi2011**: Yes baby

7:39:41 PM **potty4350**: I am so sorry dear

7:39:50 PM **potty4350**: so what laptop did you order today??

7:40:24 PM **ladydi2011**: Dell Latitude

7:40:34 PM **potty4350**: Okay

7:40:39 PM **potty4350**: Do you like apple laptop?

7:41:10 PM **ladydi2011**: I do like apple, my designer and assistant have apple

7:41:39 PM **potty4350**: oh cool

7:41:46 PM **ladydi2011**: I have not changed to an apple yet because I do not have time for the learning curve. I love change as long as nothing changes

7:41:48 PM **potty4350**: why don't you order apple laptop dear??

7:42:10 PM **potty4350**: oh okay dear..lol

7:42:18 PM **potty4350**: *i will teach when i am home with you then*

7:42:26 PM **ladydi2011**: Thank you baby. I learn quickly

7:42:47 PM **ladydi2011**: I am a people person more than a technology person

7:43:12 PM **ladydi2011**: I love technology when it works and do not care for it when it breaks or when I don't know how to use it

7:44:00 PM **potty4350**: I love you Diana

7:44:03 PM **ladydi2011**: I can speak in front of 1,000 people and not break a sweat, but technology...

7:44:06 PM **potty4350**: I am sorry *i* just have to let you know

7:44:13 PM **potty4350**: Wow..that is great

7:44:21 PM **ladydi2011**: Give me broken technology and I come undone

7:44:33 PM **ladydi2011**: My IT guy hates getting a call from me

7:44:49 PM **ladydi2011**: I love you too Robin

7:45:07 PM **potty4350**: Lol, why does he hate getting a call from you dear?

7:45:18 PM **potty4350**: Thanks so much for your love darling

7:45:39 PM **ladydi2011**: Because he can hear the panic in my voice

7:45:56 PM **ladydi2011**: He also knows his job is secure because I need him

7:46:04 PM **potty4350**: Lol

7:46:13 PM **potty4350**: *How many worker do you have?*

7:46:45 PM **ladydi2011**: 9 right now and getting ready to launch new products so we will be adding five more

7:47:07 PM **potty4350**: Oh good

7:47:13 PM **potty4350**: *Honey how big is your company?*

7:47:23 PM **ladydi2011**: How many workers do you have honey?

7:47:42 PM **ladydi2011**: It is a small business but I am nationwide

7:48:05 PM **potty4350**: Lol..I think *i* told you before baby

7:48:36 PM **ladydi2011**: Please tell me again my love

7:48:48 PM **ladydi2011**: My brain is not recalling this info
7:48:56 PM **ladydi2011**: Must have had too much food...Lol
7:48:58 PM **potty4350**: I have over 300 men on this location
7:49:08 PM **ladydi2011**: Ok
7:49:11 PM **potty4350**: lol
7:49:25 PM **ladydi2011**: This food has made me tired
7:49:43 PM **ladydi2011**: Honey, do these men travel from location to location or do you hire different people at each location?
7:49:50 PM **potty4350**: be it professional, acquired expatriate, and locals. While working I try to build a personal relationship with each and every one
7:50:00 PM **potty4350**: No, *i* only employ them here
7:50:21 PM **ladydi2011**: Ok
7:50:31 PM **ladydi2011**: This makes economic sense
7:50:37 PM **ladydi2011**: I am all about profit
7:51:19 PM **potty4350**: same here dear
7:51:29 PM **potty4350**: *what is your annual income?*
7:51:43 PM **ladydi2011**: Depends
7:51:47 PM **ladydi2011**: Oh love my neighbor is at the door
7:52:07 PM **ladydi2011**: Will you be on line later baby?
7:52:29 PM **ladydi2011**: I need to make sure she knows what to do to take care of my pets while I am gone
7:52:44 PM **ladydi2011**: I love you baby
7:52:49 PM **ladydi2011**: Kisses...Hugs...All my love
7:53:01 PM **potty4350**: Kisses dear
7:53:06 PM **potty4350**: I will talk to you later
7:53:12 PM **potty4350**: I will be up later
7:53:21 PM **ladydi2011**: Ok
7:53:22 PM **potty4350**: When will you be done with her
7:53:25 PM **ladydi2011**: I will text you
7:53:33 PM **ladydi2011**: We will probably have some wine
7:53:39 PM **ladydi2011**: bye for now baby
7:53:44 PM **potty4350**: Okay baby
7:53:46 PM **potty4350**: bye for now
7:53:49 PM **potty4350**: Love you!!!

IM Jul 17, 2012 2:27:24 AM

2:27:24 AM **potty4350**: <ding>
2:31:53 AM **ladydi2011**: Morning my love
2:32:13 AM **potty4350**: thank you my lady
2:32:18 AM **potty4350**: how are you sweetie?
2:32:42 AM **ladydi2011**: I am good. I will soon go to bed I have tight deadlines tomorrow
2:33:44 AM **potty4350**: *I dreamt I met an angel and he ask me to make a request*
2:34:17 AM **potty4350**: *I ask him to watch over you for me he went and came back and said angels don't watch over angels is it true you are an angel pls watch over me my lady*
2:34:59 AM **ladydi2011**: Awe...you are so sweet darling.

2:35:15 AM **potty4350**: you are the sweetest diana

2:36:09 AM **potty4350**: did you read my email

2:36:22 AM **ladydi2011**: Honey, you have done a good job at capturing my heart

2:36:29 AM **ladydi2011**: When did you send it honey?

2:36:42 AM **potty4350**: *i* send it yesterday after work

2:36:55 AM **potty4350**: I am very glad *i* could at least capture your heart

2:37:35 AM **ladydi2011**: I believe I did. I replied to 3 emails you sent

2:37:49 AM **potty4350**: Okay baby

2:37:57 AM **ladydi2011**: What do you mean by "at least"?

2:38:13 AM **potty4350**: I will check before *i* leave for work

2:38:24 AM **ladydi2011**: Ok honey

2:38:34 AM **potty4350**: I cherish you so much

2:38:37 AM **ladydi2011**: I have a request

2:38:44 AM **potty4350**: I asked you a question yesterday dear

2:38:48 AM **ladydi2011**: I cherish you too

2:38:51 AM **potty4350**: what is your request?

2:39:18 AM **potty4350**: Honey *i* just check and *i* got no reply from you yet

2:39:42 AM **ladydi2011**: Please always stay how you are with me now...and don't do something you can't continue.

2:40:06 AM **potty4350**: Yes sure dear

2:40:23 AM **potty4350**: I promise *i* will never do anything *i* can't continue

2:41:24 AM **potty4350**: are you there?

2:42:11 AM **potty4350**: Hello??

2:42:31 AM **ladydi2011**: Thank you love.

2:42:40 AM **ladydi2011**: I promise the same.

2:42:43 AM **potty4350**: You are welcome my dear

2:42:44 AM **potty4350**: Good

2:42:54 AM **potty4350**: *Promise you will always be there for me no matter what*

2:43:46 AM **ladydi2011**: I promise!

2:43:51 AM **potty4350**: thank you baby

2:43:59 AM **ladydi2011**: Do you promise the same?

2:44:11 AM **potty4350**: Yes dear *i* promise

2:44:40 AM **potty4350**: *Honey i asked how much is your annual income? monthly income ..*

2:44:52 AM **potty4350**: Do you intend going into a larger business?

2:45:07 AM **ladydi2011**: Every year is different honey. Depends on how much business I bring in the door

2:45:20 AM **potty4350**: Okay

2:45:35 AM **ladydi2011**: Yes, I do intend in going into a larger business

2:45:41 AM **potty4350**: how much is the highest and lowest you have made

2:45:43 AM **potty4350**: Oh good then

2:45:56 AM **ladydi2011**: And opening up a 501 3c business

2:46:15 AM **potty4350**: Well we will talk more about that my love

2:46:16 AM **potty4350**: Ok?

2:46:26 AM **ladydi2011**: Lowest was my first year in buss. -$50,000 a year, highest has been 500k

2:46:53 AM **ladydi2011**: What about you honey?

2:46:56 AM **potty4350**: Oh okay

2:47:12 AM **potty4350**: Honey *i* have made a lot of money from this contruction business

2:47:34 AM **potty4350**: but when *i* work in some countries they dont give upfront you have to use your money to cover everything and when you are done they will pay you everything

2:48:17 AM **ladydi2011**: Hmmmmmm

2:48:37 AM **potty4350**: Yes baby

2:50:10 AM **potty4350**: Are you there??

2:50:12 AM **potty4350**: Busy?

2:50:15 AM **potty4350**: Sleeping ??

2:50:26 AM **ladydi2011**: Sorry baby

2:50:35 AM **potty4350**: What are you doing?

2:50:45 AM **ladydi2011**: I was looking for your email?

2:50:52 AM **potty4350**: Oh okay

2:50:59 AM **potty4350**: I sent it to your gmail address

2:52:03 AM **ladydi2011**: Please hold honey

2:53:25 AM **ladydi2011**: Found them...you are so sweet honey

2:53:38 AM **potty4350**: you are the sweetest baby

2:53:52 AM **potty4350**: honey we will write together ok and my wife would be the author

2:54:03 AM **potty4350**: *i* love you more

2:54:15 AM **ladydi2011**: I don't know why the contract work is like this...please tell me.

2:55:13 AM **potty4350**: well some says it because maybe when you are done with he project and they don't like it that much, they will only give you part of the money and won't give you everything

2:59:01 AM **ladydi2011**: Has this ever happened to you?

2:59:26 AM **potty4350**: no dear, but *i* have once lost a project

3:01:09 AM **ladydi2011**: How honey?

3:01:40 AM **ladydi2011**: Sorry for the delay honey. My assistant is emailing me.

3:01:59 AM **ladydi2011**: She is in another state and we are on deadline...

3:02:17 AM **potty4350**: Oh .. What deadline dear??

3:03:34 AM **ladydi2011**: One of the many services we offer is email marketing campaigns.

3:03:49 AM **ladydi2011**: I work best under pressure

3:04:26 AM **ladydi2011**: How did you lose the project baby?

3:04:31 AM **potty4350**: I wish *i* am there to give you the support you need

3:04:38 AM **potty4350**: But i'm so sorry *i* am not there now

3:04:44 AM **potty4350**: *I will be there with you soon ok? I promise*

3:05:28 AM **ladydi2011**: I am looking forward to it!

3:05:50 AM **potty4350**: Okay baby

3:05:53 AM **potty4350**: thank you so much

3:06:16 AM **ladydi2011**: Baby, one of the reasons I didn't date for 8 yrs. was because of how many hours I work.

3:06:29 AM **potty4350**: I can understand baby

3:06:34 AM **potty4350**: How many hours do you work?

3:06:53 AM **potty4350**: Now you have me are you still looking to date? *we should be talking about marriage now*

3:06:53 AM **ladydi2011**: As you know, it takes a lot of time to build a business

3:07:09 AM **potty4350**: Yes *i* know it takes a lot of time

3:07:10 AM **ladydi2011**: Usually 12-18 hours a day

3:07:16 AM **potty4350**: How long have you been doing this business??

3:07:26 AM **potty4350**: Oh that is to much for my woman

3:07:29 AM **ladydi2011**: 12 years

3:07:34 AM **potty4350**: Oh good baby

3:07:39 AM **ladydi2011**: Yeah baby

3:07:52 AM **ladydi2011**: When I play, I also play hard

3:08:15 AM **potty4350**: I can't wait to go play hard with you my love

3:08:17 AM **ladydi2011**: Marriage

3:08:23 AM **potty4350**: Yes baby

3:08:32 AM **potty4350**: *What do you think about marriage?*

3:08:42 AM **ladydi2011**: Me too baby. We will have a lot of fun!

3:09:26 AM **ladydi2011**: More than marriage I am looking for the relationship

3:09:52 AM **ladydi2011**: I am not a woman who "has to be married"

3:09:53 AM **potty4350**: I love you

3:10:40 AM **ladydi2011**: However, if the relationship is what it needs to be, than of course I will say yes

3:10:47 AM **ladydi2011**: I love you too

3:11:34 AM **ladydi2011**: Baby, I choose wisely in life. Today's choices shape my future.

3:11:53 AM **ladydi2011**: As you know I divorced 14 yrs. ago

3:12:07 AM **ladydi2011**: I do not want another divorce

3:12:58 AM **ladydi2011**: I know what I want and need in my man and my relationship

3:13:19 AM **ladydi2011**: I need to admire and respect my man

3:13:19 AM **potty4350**: baby are you still there?

3:13:46 AM **ladydi2011**: I am.....did you get everything I wrote?

3:13:55 AM **potty4350**: No dear

3:14:03 AM **potty4350**: I did not get everything you wrote my woman

3:14:09 AM **potty4350**: computer is acting up

3:14:15 AM **potty4350**: Honey when are you traveling

3:14:26 AM **ladydi2011**: What was the last thing you saw baby?

3:14:44 AM **ladydi2011**: I leave on the 30th

3:15:27 AM **potty4350**: You need to admire and respect your man

3:15:56 AM **ladydi2011**: Then you got it all baby.

3:16:24 AM **potty4350**: Okay my sweet

3:16:39 AM **ladydi2011**: Honey, some women marry just to be married. I am not this kind of woman.

3:16:40 AM **potty4350**: When are you traveling and where are you traveling too?

3:17:02 AM **ladydi2011**: I leave the 30th of this month for Texas

3:18:12 AM **potty4350**: when will you be back?

3:18:57 AM **ladydi2011**: August 6th

3:20:09 AM **ladydi2011**: Honey, it is 3:20 am and I have to get some sleep

3:20:30 AM **potty4350**: Okay baby

3:20:30 AM **ladydi2011**: I need to get up in 5 hours

3:20:34 AM **potty4350**: I cherish you so much

3:20:39 AM **potty4350**: Okay baby

3:20:42 AM **potty4350**: Don't wanna keep you up

3:20:54 AM **ladydi2011**: I cherish and treasure you too my love

3:21:23 AM **ladydi2011**: I am glad we got to chat before you go to work

3:21:23 AM **potty4350**: Love you Diana

3:21:32 AM **potty4350**: I am very glad too..I am the happiest man on earth

3:21:43 AM **ladydi2011**: Love you too Robin

3:21:54 AM **potty4350**: I will go check my email now and write you back ok?

3:22:04 AM **potty4350**: *this is a sign of good will..I see success*
3:22:31 AM **ladydi2011**: Please remember that you haven't seen anything yet
3:22:45 AM **potty4350**: Yes *i* know my love
3:22:47 AM **ladydi2011**: Yeah baby!
3:22:50 AM **potty4350**: And you haven't seen anything yet either
3:23:01 AM **ladydi2011**: Nice!
3:23:07 AM **potty4350**: Good baby
3:23:12 AM **ladydi2011**: Bye for now my love
3:23:13 AM **potty4350**: I love you with *everything of my life*
3:23:19 AM **potty4350**: Bye for now sweet
3:23:28 AM **potty4350**: Are you gonna write back when you wake up?
3:23:38 AM **ladydi2011**: I will....
3:23:45 AM **potty4350**: Okay my love go to bed now. I will talk to you later
3:24:02 AM **ladydi2011**: Kk
3:24:02 AM **potty4350**: Pls call me if you can when you wake up ok?
3:24:09 AM **potty4350**: I will have my phone with me on the work field
3:24:14 AM **potty4350**: I will love to hear your voice
3:24:19 AM **potty4350**: good night sweetie
3:24:40 AM **ladydi2011**: How about I text you and you call me
3:24:59 AM **potty4350**: Okay
3:25:03 AM **ladydi2011**: I would love to hear your voice too!
3:25:11 AM **potty4350**: Why don't you call baby??
3:25:25 AM **ladydi2011**: Kisses and (((hugs)))
3:25:35 AM **ladydi2011**: It never goes through!
3:25:45 AM **potty4350**: Okay baby
3:25:49 AM **potty4350**: You should try baby it your man that is involve ..
3:25:56 AM **potty4350**: good night
3:26:01 AM **potty4350**: I will talk to you later
3:26:04 AM **potty4350**: I will call you when *i* get your text *i* will
3:26:15 AM **potty4350**: I love you baby
3:26:32 AM **ladydi2011**: I love you too
3:26:39 AM **potty4350**: Night

IM Jul 17, 2012 10:29:52 PM

10:29:52 PM **ladydi2011**: Hello baby
10:30:07 PM **ladydi2011**: I have missed you!
10:30:16 PM **potty4350**: I have missed you too darling
10:30:19 PM **potty4350**: I love you Diana
10:30:26 PM **potty4350**: Hope your day wasn't stressful?
10:30:38 PM **ladydi2011**: I love you too Robin
10:30:47 PM **ladydi2011**: I had a good day
10:30:57 PM **potty4350**: I am very glad to hear that my lady
10:31:02 PM **potty4350**: What did you do today?
10:31:12 PM **ladydi2011**: Sorry I did not hear your text come in
10:31:30 PM **potty4350**: Oh okay Diana

10:31:34 PM **ladydi2011**: I shut everything off to read a little bit

10:31:55 PM **ladydi2011**: How was your day my love?

10:32:29 PM **ladydi2011**: Is this not a good time?

10:32:53 PM **ladydi2011**: Robin

10:32:58 PM **potty4350**: Yes baby

10:33:01 PM **potty4350**: I am here with you

10:33:10 PM **potty4350**: My day was stressful, had a lot to do today

10:33:52 PM **ladydi2011**: I am sorry honey

10:34:03 PM **potty4350**: It is always a good time for us and it will always be a good time for us

10:34:12 PM **potty4350**: *i* love you so much

10:34:22 PM **ladydi2011**: If I was there, I would give you a massage

10:34:23 PM **potty4350**: you got me thinking about you sweetie

10:34:36 PM **potty4350**: Yes *i* really can't wait to have that massage my lady

10:34:37 PM **ladydi2011**: Yeah?

10:34:44 PM **potty4350**: Yes baby

10:35:27 PM **ladydi2011**: I am reading Fifty Shades of Grey. Have you read it?

10:36:07 PM **potty4350**: No *i* haven't dear

10:36:11 PM **potty4350**: *I will when i come home dear*

10:36:11 PM **ladydi2011**: It is pretty steamy

10:36:16 PM **potty4350**: Really??

10:36:22 PM **ladydi2011**: Yeah

10:36:38 PM **potty4350**: *Honey when i am home with you .. you will have to take a 2 weeks break for us*

10:36:40 PM **potty4350**: Will you?

10:37:02 PM **ladydi2011**: Did you accomplish everything you needed to do today?

10:37:14 PM **ladydi2011**: Yes my love I will take a 2 week break

10:37:28 PM **potty4350**: Yes thank you baby

10:37:44 PM **potty4350**: Did you accomplish everything you needed to do today baby

10:37:53 PM **ladydi2011**: No

10:37:57 PM **potty4350**: Why honey?

10:37:59 PM **potty4350**: What happened?

10:38:11 PM **ladydi2011**: Too tired. I got done what had to be done

10:38:56 PM **ladydi2011**: Honey, if you were here I would be snugged tightly into your arms

10:40:35 PM **potty4350**: Wow

10:40:51 PM **potty4350**: I just can't wait to get done with this

10:40:57 PM **potty4350**: *I would fly straight to you Diana*

10:41:09 PM **potty4350**: *I love you so much and nothing is going to change that*

10:41:18 PM **potty4350**: You did not respond to my email baby

10:41:21 PM **ladydi2011**: I was hoping you would

10:41:31 PM **potty4350**: Yes *i* will

10:41:38 PM **ladydi2011**: Oh baby. I am sorry

10:42:34 PM **ladydi2011**: I spent my day answering business email and when I left the office I shut everything off

10:42:47 PM **potty4350**: Oh okay baby

10:42:56 PM **ladydi2011**: I really needed an hour of down time

10:43:20 PM **ladydi2011**: So honey, what do you want to do for 2 weeks?

10:43:35 PM **potty4350**: I will be indoor with you.. just me and you

10:44:01 PM **potty4350**: What do you want to do?

10:44:13 PM **ladydi2011**: I am reading your mind

10:44:18 PM **ladydi2011**: Just be

10:44:29 PM **potty4350**: lol

10:44:43 PM **ladydi2011**: Please hold honey

10:44:50 PM **potty4350**: Ok

10:44:56 PM **ladydi2011**: I want to send you something

10:45:03 PM **potty4350**: Okay

10:46:27 PM **ladydi2011**: Baby...you should have mail

10:46:39 PM **potty4350**: not yet

10:46:57 PM **ladydi2011**: While you check your mail I am going to get my phone charger

10:47:10 PM **potty4350**: okay..got it now

10:47:31 PM **ladydi2011**: Listen closely

10:47:40 PM **potty4350**: *i was hoping you are going to send it to potty4520@att.net*

10:59:01 PM **potty4350**: I love you so much

10:59:04 PM **ladydi2011**: Do you want me to start using your AT&T address?

10:59:14 PM **potty4350**: yes baby

10:59:18 PM **ladydi2011**: I love you too

10:59:26 PM **potty4350**: let use both

10:59:32 PM **ladydi2011**: Ok

10:59:47 PM **potty4350**: but that is the only address *i* use for you

10:59:47 PM **ladydi2011**: Have you heard this song before?

10:59:53 PM **potty4350**: it our private address

10:59:57 PM **potty4350**: No baby. I love the song

11:00:13 PM **potty4350**: You are a very wonderful woman

11:00:29 PM **ladydi2011**: You are a fabulous man!

11:00:43 PM **potty4350**: I will never stop loving baby

11:01:08 PM **ladydi2011**: I will never stop loving you either

11:01:17 PM **potty4350**: thank you Diana

11:01:29 PM **potty4350**: did you get your charger

11:01:35 PM **ladydi2011**: Yea

11:01:40 PM **potty4350**: good honey

11:01:45 PM **potty4350**: what do you have for dinner

11:01:55 PM **ladydi2011**: Do you have a busy day tomorrow?

11:02:05 PM **potty4350**: yes *i* will dear

11:02:06 PM **ladydi2011**: Chinese

11:02:11 PM **potty4350**: uhmm

11:02:26 PM **potty4350**: *i just wanna get done here quick so that i can be wIth you there honey*

11:02:32 PM **ladydi2011**: what did you have honey?

11:02:42 PM **potty4350**: *i* did not have dinner baby *i* slept very early

11:02:54 PM **ladydi2011**: Oh

11:03:12 PM **ladydi2011**: I looked for you on line a couple times today

11:03:17 PM **potty4350**: really

11:03:20 PM **potty4350**: *i* was on the field

11:03:33 PM **ladydi2011**: I was missing you

11:03:39 PM **potty4350**: awwww..*i* am sorry dear

11:03:48 PM **potty4350**: you should have text me to come online

11:04:27 PM **ladydi2011**: Did you sleep well?

11:04:43 PM **ladydi2011**: *Honey, it is 4am there what are you doing awake?*

Break In Time

11:05:43 PM **ladydi2011**: Robin

11:05:54 PM **ladydi2011**: Hmmmmm

11:06:09 PM **potty4350**: yes *i* sleep a little bit baby and now *i* am here for you

11:06:27 PM **potty4350**: yes it 4.00am here

11:06:39 PM **potty4350**: *i am awake because of you*

11:06:50 PM **potty4350**: *wanna talk to you till i am ready to go to work*

11:07:04 PM **ladydi2011**: Seems like we both have irregular sleep patterns

11:07:25 PM **potty4350**: really

11:07:31 PM **ladydi2011**: Yeah

11:08:35 PM **potty4350**: I love you with all my heart body and soul

11:08:38 PM **ladydi2011**: I am smiling

11:08:50 PM **potty4350**: that is my joy

11:09:03 PM **potty4350**: I always wanna see you smile and happy

11:09:10 PM **ladydi2011**: You have really captured my heart

11:09:18 PM **potty4350**: You will never have any reason to be sad honey

11:10:00 PM **potty4350**: *honey what is your fav color? birthday? do you like diamonds?*

11:10:30 PM **ladydi2011**: I sent you something on email today from my BellSouth account to your yahoo account. Did you get it?

11:10:46 PM **potty4350**: Yes *i* got it my love

11:10:49 PM **ladydi2011**: Plum is my favorite color

11:10:53 PM **potty4350**: thank you so much my lady

11:10:57 PM **ladydi2011**: What is yours?

11:11:20 PM **ladydi2011**: Yes, I like diamonds. What woman doesn't?

11:11:37 PM **potty4350**: *i* like black, white and yellow

11:11:45 PM **potty4350**: your birthday??

11:12:04 PM **ladydi2011**: November 15th

11:12:12 PM **ladydi2011**: What is yours?

11:12:36 PM **potty4350**: Wow

11:12:43 PM **potty4350**: Mine is November 30

11:13:00 PM **ladydi2011**: Nice!

11:13:04 PM **potty4350**: Yes so nice

11:13:25 PM **ladydi2011**: So, November is a good month

11:13:47 PM **ladydi2011**: What is your favorite cologne?

Break In Time

11:17:12 PM **potty4350**: I like clive christian and ambre topkapi

11:17:13 PM **ladydi2011**: Baby, are you chatting with someone else too?

11:17:18 PM **potty4350**: No

11:17:23 PM **potty4350**: I am not chatting with anyone you are all *i* have

11:17:49 PM **potty4350**: are you there??

11:18:02 PM **ladydi2011**: I am

11:18:10 PM **potty4350**: do you like amber topkapi

11:18:14 PM **potty4350**: clive christian?

11:18:30 PM **ladydi2011**: I have never smelled them

11:18:47 PM **ladydi2011**: But I will

11:19:05 PM **potty4350**: *i* am very sure you will like them
11:19:20 PM **ladydi2011**: I am sure I will
11:19:20 PM **potty4350**: what is your fav cologne?
11:20:05 PM **potty4350**: I love you baby
11:20:12 PM **ladydi2011**: Red Door, Giorgio and Channel#5
11:20:30 PM **potty4350**: how much is the red door?
11:21:01 PM **ladydi2011**: Depends on the size
11:21:07 PM **potty4350**: okay
11:21:16 PM **potty4350**: do you know sean john cologne
11:21:17 PM **ladydi2011**: Red Door is my favorite of the three, it mixes well with my body chemistry
11:21:51 PM **ladydi2011**: No baby, I do not
11:21:59 PM **potty4350**: okay
11:22:06 PM **potty4350**: *i* love you so much
11:22:17 PM **potty4350**: nobody is perfect but you are perfect for me diana
11:22:20 PM **ladydi2011**: I love you too baby
11:22:32 PM **potty4350**: *i will awlays love you sincerely*
11:23:12 PM **ladydi2011**: What matters is that we are perfect for and complement each other
11:23:31 PM **potty4350**: *tell me your true mind dear*
11:23:42 PM **ladydi2011**: I will always love you sincerely too Robin
11:24:03 PM **ladydi2011**: What do you mean honey?
11:24:27 PM **potty4350**: *i will always appreciate it when you tell me your true mind towards me baby i mean how you feel*
11:24:51 PM **ladydi2011**: I have fallen in love with you
11:25:03 PM **potty4350**: I am in love with you Diana
11:25:13 PM **ladydi2011**: I am anxious to meet you
11:25:24 PM **potty4350**: I really can't wait for that to happen
11:25:34 PM **potty4350**: *Will you come pick me up from the airport??*
11:26:00 PM **potty4350**: I know you are the perfect woman for me
11:26:01 PM **ladydi2011**: Of course I will
11:26:05 PM **potty4350**: I know it is you Diana
11:26:09 PM **potty4350**: good baby
11:26:56 PM **ladydi2011**: So how are you so sure honey?
11:27:09 PM **potty4350**: I am very sure
11:27:34 PM **potty4350**: *if it is not you ..we will never meet each other and i will never come on that dating site*
11:27:49 PM **ladydi2011**: What is telling you that I am the woman for you?
11:28:09 PM **potty4350**: you arc the woman for me diana..or what do you think?
11:28:26 PM **ladydi2011**: I agree
11:28:38 PM **potty4350**: if not *i* won't be here right now talking to you
11:28:54 PM **ladydi2011**: How long were you on the site?
11:29:00 PM **ladydi2011**: True
11:29:10 PM **potty4350**: *i* was new on the dating site diana
11:29:19 PM **potty4350**: how long have you been on the dating site?
11:29:39 PM **ladydi2011**: 2 months
11:30:19 PM **potty4350**: did you talk to any man from the site apart from me??
11:30:25 PM **ladydi2011**: Did you chat with many women?
11:30:32 PM **ladydi2011**: Lol

11:30:32 PM **potty4350**: No dear just you

11:30:43 PM **potty4350**: but *i* got emails from a couple of young girls

11:30:49 PM **ladydi2011**: We both had the same question

11:30:56 PM **potty4350**: yes

11:31:19 PM **potty4350**: diana this is just for you to know that our heart see's each other

11:31:29 PM **ladydi2011**: I chatted with about 20 men

11:31:38 PM **potty4350**: Wow

11:31:46 PM **potty4350**: So what happened to the men you chatted with?

11:31:55 PM **ladydi2011**: I know our hearts do

11:31:59 PM **potty4350**: good *i* know *i* will never do you any wrong

11:32:29 PM **ladydi2011**: Honey, I know exactly what I am looking for and need in a man

11:32:49 PM **potty4350**: *i* am glad you know exactly what you are looking for and need in a man

11:32:59 PM **ladydi2011**: My phone acts up when I am charging it

11:33:06 PM **potty4350**: okay baby

11:33:10 PM **potty4350**: what phone do you use?

11:33:11 PM **ladydi2011**: It has a mind of its own

11:33:54 PM **ladydi2011**: I am not looking to change a man…He either is or is not for me

11:34:27 PM **potty4350**: I am not looking to change a woman

11:34:29 PM **ladydi2011**: All the men prior to you were not for me

11:34:40 PM **ladydi2011**: This is good baby

11:34:40 PM **potty4350**: Diana what happened to the 20 men you chatted with

11:35:09 PM **ladydi2011**: I thanked them for their time and said good bye

11:35:31 PM **potty4350**: uhmmmmm

11:35:37 PM **potty4350**: what time and why did you say good bye??

11:35:41 PM **ladydi2011**: Some of them were not gentlemen at all

11:36:02 PM **ladydi2011**: They were all different

11:36:14 PM **potty4350**: uhmmmmm

11:36:17 PM **potty4350**: can you tell me more??

11:36:28 PM **ladydi2011**: The ones who were disrespectful I just deleted

11:36:42 PM **potty4350**: oh okay

11:36:48 PM **potty4350**: do you have a date with anyone??

11:36:59 PM **ladydi2011**: The ones who wanted to see my body parts I also deleted

11:37:11 PM **potty4350**: oh that is very bad

11:37:12 PM **ladydi2011**: A live date?

11:37:17 PM **potty4350**: yes

11:37:30 PM **ladydi2011**: No honey

11:37:42 PM **potty4350**: and did you talk to them on the phone

11:38:07 PM **ladydi2011**: There was one man from Michigan who I thought might be a possibility

11:38:26 PM **ladydi2011**: Yes, we talked on the phone

11:38:31 PM **potty4350**: so what happened to the man from michigan

11:38:48 PM **ladydi2011**: Good question

11:39:30 PM **ladydi2011**: He was supposed to come to meet me and a week prior I never heard from him again

11:39:55 PM **ladydi2011**: My guess is that he was lying about his age

11:40:03 PM **potty4350**: oh really

11:40:07 PM **potty4350**: what is his name

11:40:07 PM **ladydi2011**: His voice sounded older??

11:40:17 PM **ladydi2011**: Gary

11:40:27 PM **potty4350**: I am here to stay with you forever

11:40:39 PM **potty4350**: trust me

11:40:42 PM **ladydi2011**: Thanks honey

11:40:48 PM **potty4350**: you are welcome my lady *i* cherish you so much

11:40:59 PM **ladydi2011**: He did not break my heart because I never gave it to him!

11:41:02 PM **potty4350**: did you take off your profile on singlesbee?

11:41:25 PM **ladydi2011**: I hid it

11:41:39 PM **ladydi2011**: What about you?

11:42:57 PM **potty4350**: I no longer use the site

11:43:32 PM **potty4350**: well *i* was new on the site and you are the only woman *i* met on the site

11:43:41 PM **potty4350**: the rest were younger than my age

11:44:02 PM **potty4350**: 19, 24, 20 and 27..they are all looking for fling

11:44:55 PM **ladydi2011**: I could see where the younger girls would be attracted to you

11:45:23 PM **ladydi2011**: So, you are not into flings?

11:45:37 PM **potty4350**: I am not, why do you ask?

11:45:51 PM **ladydi2011**: This is GOOD!

11:46:00 PM **potty4350**: Why do you think they are attracted to me

11:46:21 PM **potty4350**: are you still on the site?

11:46:21 PM **ladydi2011**: You are very sexy

11:46:29 PM **potty4350**: you are the sexiest

11:46:53 PM **ladydi2011**: Thanks love. My profile is hidden

11:47:12 PM **ladydi2011**: I did this once we really started talking. I haven't logged into the site since

11:47:53 PM **potty4350**: Okay

11:47:58 PM **ladydi2011**: Are you still on the site?

11:48:04 PM **potty4350**: *Honey i want you to take off your profile on the site*

11:48:07 PM **potty4350**: NO

11:48:12 PM **potty4350**: *i* want to do this for you

11:48:18 PM **ladydi2011**: Ok baby

11:48:33 PM **ladydi2011**: I just haven't had time

11:48:41 PM **potty4350**: *i* want to do this for you diana

11:49:19 PM **ladydi2011**: I was also on 2 other sites

11:49:40 PM **ladydi2011**: So your profile is still on the site

11:49:54 PM **potty4350**: NO

11:50:07 PM **potty4350**: *i mean i want your username and password for me to do it for you*

11:50:11 PM **ladydi2011**: I let my membership run out on those 2 sites

11:50:16 PM **potty4350**: what other site are you on??

11:50:39 PM **ladydi2011**: You want what?

11:51:42 PM **ladydi2011**: I was on Match and E-Harmony

11:52:03 PM **potty4350**: Oh did you meet any man from this 2 sites?

11:52:14 PM **potty4350**: Are you still on both site??

11:52:30 PM **ladydi2011**: Darling. If I tell you I will take my profile down, then I will.

11:52:33 PM **potty4350**: *I would like to cancel your profile on singlesbee for you*

11:52:39 PM **potty4350**: Yes *i* know Diana

11:52:46 PM **potty4350**: *Don't you want me to do it right now?*

11:53:04 PM **ladydi2011**: No. I only had a 3 month subscription

11:53:23 PM **potty4350**: on which site?

11:53:28 PM **ladydi2011**: I did not renew because I met you

11:53:37 PM **potty4350**: okay

11:53:51 PM **potty4350**: *so i want to take off the profile myself honey*

11:54:01 PM **ladydi2011**: Please calm down..Nobody is going to steal me from you

11:55:12 PM **potty4350**: Yes *i* know

11:55:21 PM **ladydi2011**: I did get a lot of flowers, teddy bears and chocolates

11:55:31 PM **potty4350**: Honey do you mean you can't share your password with me?

11:55:44 PM **potty4350**: from who did you get all that

11:55:55 PM **ladydi2011**: I can but I choose not to

11:56:03 PM **ladydi2011**: Several of the men

11:56:24 PM **ladydi2011**: Many tried to win my heart and failed

11:56:41 PM **ladydi2011**: Honey, are you a jealous man?

11:56:57 PM **potty4350**: why do you ask?

11:57:25 PM **ladydi2011**: Because of this conversation

11:57:46 PM **potty4350**: No baby I am not

11:57:53 PM **ladydi2011**: Robin, I will never lie to you

11:58:01 PM **potty4350**: I love you and *i* believe we should share everything together

11:58:09 PM **potty4350**: I know you will never lie to me and *i* will never lie to you

11:58:17 PM **ladydi2011**: This is why I answered all your questions honestly

11:58:31 PM **potty4350**: I will never hurt you

11:58:35 PM **potty4350**: Good, I am very glad you answered all my questions honestly and *i* answered all your honestly too baby

11:58:59 PM **potty4350**: *I love you and nothing is going to change that*

11:59:00 PM **ladydi2011**: I will never hurt you either

11:59:18 PM **potty4350**: Where did you get all the flowers, chocolate and teddy bear from

11:59:23 PM **ladydi2011**: I love you too baby

11:59:47 PM **ladydi2011**: The different men

12:01:25 AM **ladydi2011**: I had to tell my local florist I was online dating because I am sure they were wondering

12:02:06 AM **ladydi2011**: I live in a small town and have a stellar reputation

12:02:09 AM **potty4350**: Okay baby

12:02:35 AM **potty4350**: I love you more

12:02:46 AM **ladydi2011**: I did not need any false rumors spreading

12:03:15 AM **ladydi2011**: Baby. I see in you what I am looking for in a man

12:03:49 AM **potty4350**: I know baby

12:03:58 AM **potty4350**: *thanks so much for giving me your heart and trust this is the most important thing in a relationship*

12:04:12 AM **ladydi2011**: I have not seen anything about you that I would want to change

12:04:24 AM **ladydi2011**: Yes it is honey

12:04:43 AM **potty4350**: I am very glad to hear that

12:04:53 AM **ladydi2011**: Baby, I really am not in the business of changing a man. I tried that when I was younger and it doesn't work

12:05:11 AM **potty4350**: *Honey i only want to delete your profile on the site myself just because i feel like it and i would be glad if you could understand me and respect your man*

12:05:38 AM **ladydi2011**: Because you feel like what honey

12:06:04 AM **ladydi2011**: Baby, you are going to have to trust me

12:06:17 AM **potty4350**: *honey since you found me and everything is going pretty well you should take it off and not hide it*

12:06:53 AM **ladydi2011**: I work in a niche industry that is almost all men

12:07:19 AM **ladydi2011**: *I promise you that I will take it down this weekend*

12:07:27 AM **potty4350**: *weekend? Why that long baby??*

12:07:43 AM **ladydi2011**: Stop it baby

12:07:51 AM **potty4350**: *why don't you want me to do it for you now Diana*

12:07:59 AM **ladydi2011**: I am busy with work during the week

12:08:35 AM **ladydi2011**: Honey, there is no activity when the profile is hidden

12:08:59 AM **potty4350**: okay

12:09:03 AM **ladydi2011**: Why are you so insistent with this?

12:09:23 AM **potty4350**: I am not

12:09:34 AM **ladydi2011**: What are you afraid of my love?

12:09:49 AM **potty4350**: *You are my wife and you should respect my wish and orders isn't it*

12:10:11 AM **ladydi2011**: ORDERS??????????????

12:10:24 AM **potty4350**: *if you ever hurt me you have hurt my son and me and i can promise you that i will never fall in love with any woman again till i die*

12:11:28 AM **ladydi2011**: You don't trust me

12:11:46 AM **potty4350**: No, I do

12:11:52 AM **potty4350**: I really do trust you..You are getting it all wrong

12:12:04 AM **ladydi2011**: Baby, there are two things you need to know about me

12:12:23 AM **ladydi2011**: 1) DO NOT ever try to manipulate me

12:12:55 AM **ladydi2011**: 2) DO NOT order or tell me to do something or I will never do it

12:13:10 AM **ladydi2011**: These are non-negotiable

12:13:30 AM **potty4350**: Okay baby

12:13:33 AM **potty4350**: I love you and thanks so much for telling me this

12:14:01 AM **ladydi2011**: I will never try to manipulate you nor will I ever order you to do something

12:14:37 AM **ladydi2011**: I will never ask of you what I am not willing to give in return

12:14:48 AM **potty4350**: *but we have to listen to each other and be helpful*

12:15:02 AM **ladydi2011**: Yes, we do

12:15:07 AM **potty4350**: well *i* will give you everything

12:15:30 AM **potty4350**: *be helpful and generous to each make us more stronger and trusthworthy*

12:16:35 AM **potty4350**: *you there?*

12:16:44 AM **ladydi2011**: I am. I was getting a glass of water

12:17:06 AM **ladydi2011**: I am hungry

12:17:30 AM **potty4350**: you need to prepare something to eat?

12:17:41 AM **ladydi2011**: Too late honey. I am ready for bed

12:17:57 AM **potty4350**: just try and look for something to eat

12:18:24 AM **ladydi2011**: Honey, please promise me that you will trust me

12:19:14 AM **potty4350**: Yes , will you trust that *i* will never do anything to hurt you

12:19:28 AM **ladydi2011**: If we don't have trust, we don't have anything

12:19:58 AM **ladydi2011**: I do trust you or I would not have given you my heart

12:20:38 AM **ladydi2011**: Are you there?

12:20:43 AM **potty4350**: Yes

12:20:57 AM **potty4350**: thanks for giving me your heart

12:21:04 AM **potty4350**: I will always trust and love you so much

12:21:17 AM **ladydi2011**: You are welcome

12:21:40 AM **ladydi2011**: I will always trust and love you too
12:21:58 AM **potty4350**: thank you diana
12:21:59 AM **ladydi2011**: Thank you for giving me your heart
12:22:28 AM **potty4350**: honey you should email me at potty4520@att.net
12:23:08 AM **ladydi2011**: I will from now on
12:23:16 AM **potty4350**: thank you my lady
12:23:27 AM **potty4350**: it 5:23am here, what time is it there??
12:23:56 AM **ladydi2011**: 12:23 and time for me to go to bed honey
12:24:43 AM **potty4350**: okay sweetie
12:24:55 AM **potty4350**: *i* will talk to you tomorrow
12:25:01 AM **potty4350**: I cherish you so much my lady
12:25:04 AM **ladydi2011**: I love you
12:25:12 AM **potty4350**: I love you too
12:25:20 AM **ladydi2011**: Yes, we will talk tomorrow
12:25:33 AM **potty4350**: okay dear
12:25:34 AM **ladydi2011**: Have a wonderful day
12:25:44 AM **potty4350**: thank you ma'am, have a good night sweetie
12:26:06 AM **ladydi2011**: Bye for now
12:26:24 AM **potty4350**: Bye for now
12:26:49 AM **potty4350**: You are always on my mind
12:27:11 AM **ladydi2011**: You are always on mine too
12:27:13 AM **potty4350**: go to bed now
12:27:27 AM **ladydi2011**: I am honey?
12:27:42 AM **potty4350**: I wish *i* am right there with you
12:28:09 AM **ladydi2011**: Me too
12:28:18 AM **potty4350**: honey what phone do you use? can you get videos on it??
12:29:19 AM **ladydi2011**: Yes baby I can
12:29:27 AM **potty4350**: really
12:29:29 AM **potty4350**: what phone??
12:30:00 AM **ladydi2011**: iPhone
12:30:20 AM **potty4350**: what iphone do you use?
12:30:31 AM **potty4350**: but you send me emails with a blackberry
12:31:05 AM **ladydi2011**: I have both
12:31:12 AM **potty4350**: ok
12:31:24 AM **potty4350**: good night
12:31:27 AM **potty4350**: go to bed now sweetie
12:31:31 AM **ladydi2011**: Night baby
12:31:45 AM **potty4350**: *Night Diana Lulofs*

IM Jul 18, 2012 6:39:38 PM

6:39:38 PM **ladydi2011**: Hi Honey
6:40:06 PM **ladydi2011**: Are you there?
6:40:24 PM **ladydi2011**: I see you now have 2 accounts
6:40:28 PM **ladydi2011**: Lol!
6:40:33 PM **ladydi2011**: <ding>

6:42:31 PM **ladydi2011**: Ok love. I guess you're not there my snowman...lol
6:42:50 PM **ladydi2011**: Hopefully we can connect later
6:43:04 PM **ladydi2011**: I hope you had dinner baby
6:43:12 PM **ladydi2011**: Miss you

IM Jul 18, 2012 11:01:40 PM Continued

11:01:40 PM **ladydi2011**: Hi dear
11:01:44 PM **potty4350**: Hello baby
11:01:48 PM **potty4350**: how are you doing?
11:01:51 PM **ladydi2011**: How was your sleep?
11:01:53 PM **potty4350**: it was good
11:01:56 PM **ladydi2011**: I am well
11:01:59 PM **potty4350**: *i* miss hearing from you
11:02:07 PM **potty4350**: *i* wish *i* am there with you diana
11:02:20 PM **potty4350**: sometimes *i* just wish you could see my heart and see how *i* feel about you
11:03:45 PM **ladydi2011**: Baby, I do see your heart
11:03:57 PM **potty4350**: I want to open it for you to see
11:04:15 PM **potty4350**: I wish you have a magic mirror which you could use to see me and my heart
11:04:24 PM **potty4350**: *i* love you dearly
11:04:45 PM **ladydi2011**: I started an email to you today and every time I tried to finish it, I got interrupted
11:05:05 PM **potty4350**: how do you get interrupted?
11:05:16 PM **ladydi2011**: Phone calls
11:05:24 PM **ladydi2011**: Business emails
11:05:29 PM **potty4350**: oh okay
11:05:37 PM **potty4350**: but you know you should always have time for your man first
11:05:56 PM **ladydi2011**: Oh baby....This is why I didn't date for so long
11:06:30 PM **potty4350**: *i* put GOD first in everything *i* do and you next
11:06:35 PM **ladydi2011**: Time issues
11:06:48 PM **ladydi2011**: Robin
11:06:54 PM **potty4350**: Yes my lady
11:07:20 PM **ladydi2011**: Every day I fall deeper and deeper in love with you
11:07:42 PM **ladydi2011**: If you only knew how much I do love you
11:07:49 PM **potty4350**: Every minute *i* fall deeper and deeper in love with you Diana
11:08:15 PM **potty4350**: I love you so much more than you do love me ..
11:08:41 PM **ladydi2011**: Do not be so sure of this
11:09:08 PM **potty4350**: I am very sure baby
11:10:02 PM **ladydi2011**: Ok...I can see we will debate over this till the end of time
11:10:21 PM **potty4350**: I love you Diana..I really do
11:10:28 PM **potty4350**: *Don't let me down ok*
11:10:51 PM **ladydi2011**: I will not let you down
11:11:01 PM **potty4350**: thank you my love
11:11:08 PM **potty4350**: and pls don't take my love for granted
11:11:57 PM **ladydi2011**: Honey, I do not take your love for granted
11:12:07 PM **potty4350**: thank you my love

11:12:08 PM **ladydi2011**: Why would you say this?

11:12:18 PM **potty4350**: Honey *i* am just saying

11:12:25 PM **potty4350**: I am so much in love with you Diana

11:12:41 PM **ladydi2011**: As I am with you

11:13:53 PM **potty4350**: *I love you sincerely and i will never do anything to hurt you*

11:14:45 PM **ladydi2011**: Thank you baby. I am counting on this.

11:14:57 PM **potty4350**: *And i promise i will be there with you real soon*

11:15:00 PM **potty4350**: thank you my love

11:15:04 PM **ladydi2011**: I sincerely love you too

11:15:06 PM **potty4350**: thanks for giving me your heart

11:15:16 PM **potty4350**: what did you have for dinner??

11:15:28 PM **ladydi2011**: I will not do anything to hurt you either

11:15:47 PM **ladydi2011**: Chicken and salad

11:15:57 PM **potty4350**: We are ONE baby

11:15:58 PM **ladydi2011**: What did you have?

11:16:05 PM **potty4350**: *i* did not have dinner

11:16:09 PM **potty4350**: had so many work to do and I *slept off* while *i* was doing some paper work

11:16:46 PM **ladydi2011**: You need to eat

11:16:55 PM **potty4350**: Yes baby

11:17:01 PM **ladydi2011**: *It is 4am there again*

11:17:03 PM **potty4350**: I will eat this morning

11:17:08 PM **potty4350**: Yes it is dear

11:17:12 PM **potty4350**: Honey do you like coldplay?

11:17:15 PM **ladydi2011**: Promise

11:17:24 PM **potty4350**: I promise darling

11:17:32 PM **ladydi2011**: What is coldplay?

11:19:50 PM **potty4350**: coldplay are a british alternative rock band formed in 1996 by lead vocalist chris martin and lead guitarist jonny buckland

11:20:59 PM **ladydi2011**: Never heard them honey

11:21:15 PM **potty4350**: oh really

11:21:18 PM **potty4350**: do you like rock?

11:21:28 PM **ladydi2011**: I do

11:21:36 PM **potty4350**: your fav?

11:21:50 PM **ladydi2011**: I have many

11:22:03 PM **potty4350**: really..wow

11:22:08 PM **potty4350**: *i* love you baby

11:22:13 PM **potty4350**: you are the bestest .. *lol*

11:22:19 PM **potty4350**: do you like ozzy osbourne

11:22:20 PM **ladydi2011**: I also like the blues, jazz

11:22:25 PM **ladydi2011**: Yes

11:22:28 PM **potty4350**: oh you like blues

11:22:36 PM **potty4350**: you like ozzy osbourne??

11:23:00 PM **ladydi2011**: Love the blues and Ozzy

11:23:20 PM **ladydi2011**: ZZ Top - sharp dressed man

11:23:34 PM **potty4350**: lol

11:23:43 PM **ladydi2011**: R & B

11:23:44 PM **potty4350**: never heard of that before

11:24:00 PM **potty4350**: tell me fav rock and R & B
11:24:25 PM **ladydi2011**: Beyoncé
11:24:41 PM **ladydi2011**: Alicia Keys
11:24:50 PM **potty4350**: wow, you like Alicia Keys. I like her so much
11:25:06 PM **ladydi2011**: Barry White
11:25:12 PM **potty4350**: I like her husband too
11:25:19 PM **potty4350**: Yes *i* like barry white
11:25:30 PM **ladydi2011**: Celine Dion
11:25:45 PM **potty4350**: do you like Jon Bon Jovi?
11:25:53 PM **ladydi2011**: Boy II Men
11:25:56 PM **potty4350**: Celine Dion is great
11:26:07 PM **ladydi2011**: Yeah...saw him in concert
11:26:14 PM **ladydi2011**: Pink Floyd
11:26:27 PM **potty4350**: jim morrison
11:26:30 PM **ladydi2011**: Oh yeah
11:26:46 PM **potty4350**: steven tyler
11:26:58 PM **potty4350**: you saw jon bon jovi in a concert?
11:27:05 PM **ladydi2011**: Led Zeppelin
11:27:21 PM **ladydi2011**: Yeah...Pink Floyd too
11:27:32 PM **ladydi2011**: Tina Turner
11:27:46 PM **ladydi2011**: Johnny Lang
11:27:59 PM **ladydi2011**: Michael Grim
11:28:04 PM **ladydi2011**: Heart
11:28:04 PM **potty4350**: led zeppelin were an english rock band, active in the late 1960s and throughout the 1970s
11:28:18 PM **ladydi2011**: Yeah
11:28:31 PM **potty4350**: I like Tina Turner so much
11:28:34 PM **potty4350**: she is great too
11:28:48 PM **ladydi2011**: Saw her in concert too...she rocked it!
11:29:03 PM **potty4350**: wow
11:29:13 PM **potty4350**: she is an actress too baby
11:29:26 PM **potty4350**: Anna Mae Bullock
11:29:49 PM **potty4350**: Kurt Cobain ..
11:29:50 PM **ladydi2011**: Love her
11:29:57 PM **ladydi2011**: Adelle
11:30:03 PM **potty4350**: Wow
11:30:11 PM **potty4350**: I love Adelle
11:30:13 PM **ladydi2011**: Haven't heard Kurt
11:30:29 PM **potty4350**: Noble Five
11:30:46 PM **ladydi2011**: Josh Groban
11:31:01 PM **potty4350**: Chris Cornell
11:31:17 PM **potty4350**: Dave Navarro
11:31:17 PM **ladydi2011**: Haven't heard of Noble Five or Chris Cornell
11:31:32 PM **ladydi2011**: Looks like I will be on U Tube
11:31:32 PM **potty4350**: Really
11:31:39 PM **potty4350**: Jeff Buckley
11:31:55 PM **ladydi2011**: Nope to Dave and Jeff

11:31:58 PM **potty4350**: Jakob Dylan
11:32:15 PM **ladydi2011**: I am laughing
11:32:19 PM **potty4350**: Lol
11:32:22 PM **ladydi2011**: Keep going
11:32:36 PM **potty4350**: I wish *i* could talk to you on the phone right now
11:32:48 PM **potty4350**: Brandon Boyd?
11:33:07 PM **potty4350**: Joey Barnes??
11:33:19 PM **potty4350**: What do you think abou them?
11:33:31 PM **ladydi2011**: Me too...I would love to hear your voice
11:33:43 PM **ladydi2011**: Haven't heard them
11:33:53 PM **potty4350**: really?
11:34:01 PM **ladydi2011**: Call me please
11:36:02 PM **potty4350**: I love you so much
11:36:23 PM **ladydi2011**: I love you more
11:42:57 PM **potty4350**: are you there baby
11:43:04 PM **potty4350**: *the weather is not clear and honey you know i use a us line here i have to get it roam maybe that is the reason it is not clear*
11:44:00 PM **potty4350**: <ding>
11:44:01 PM **ladydi2011**: I am here
11:44:36 PM **potty4350**: I love you Diana
11:44:54 PM **potty4350**: *I will be home with you real soon*
11:45:44 PM **ladydi2011**: I miss you
11:46:17 PM **potty4350**: I miss you too diana
11:47:10 PM **ladydi2011**: Thank you for a fun evening!
11:47:27 PM **potty4350**: You are welcome my dear
11:48:42 PM **ladydi2011**: Honey, it is now my turn to sleep even though I want to stay here with you
11:49:05 PM **potty4350**: Oh okay baby
11:49:09 PM **potty4350**: *i* love you so much Diana
11:49:41 PM **potty4350**: Honey *i* really need you to go to bed ok
11:49:41 PM **ladydi2011**: I love you so much too Robin
11:49:54 PM **potty4350**: thank you Diana
11:50:04 PM **ladydi2011**: Have breakfast and a wonderful day
11:50:20 PM **ladydi2011**: I am going to bed now
11:50:35 PM **potty4350**: thank you diana
11:50:39 PM **ladydi2011**: Good morning to you
11:50:50 PM **potty4350**: good night to you my woman
11:50:57 PM **potty4350**: love you so much
11:50:59 PM **potty4350**: go to bed now ok
11:51:08 PM **ladydi2011**: Love you too

IM Jul 20, 2012 12:38:06 AM

12:38:06 AM **potty4350**: Hey Honey
12:38:10 AM **potty4350**: How are you doing??
12:38:22 AM **potty4350**: I am sorry *i* have not been able to text you all day
12:38:27 AM **potty4350**: I had issues with my phone

12:38:43 AM **potty4350**: I love you so much Honey I can't wait to get out of here it really frustrating
12:38:48 AM **potty4350**: I wanna be with you
12:38:48 AM **potty4350**: <ding

IM Jul 20, 2012 1:20:33 AM Continued

1:20:33 AM **ladydi2011**: Hi baby
1:20:38 AM **ladydi2011**: I am here
1:23:04 AM **Robin Lulofs**: <ding>
1:23:07 AM **Robin Lulofs**: Are you there?
1:23:16 AM **ladydi2011**: I am
1:23:42 AM **ladydi2011**: I am sorry you had a tough day
1:24:05 AM **Robin Lulofs**: thank you baby
1:24:10 AM **Robin Lulofs**: *i* am very tired right now diana
1:24:15 AM **Robin Lulofs**: *i* wish you are here with me
1:24:52 AM **ladydi2011**: Me too...I would de-stress you
1:25:06 AM **ladydi2011**: Your welcome honey
1:25:32 AM **Robin Lulofs**: I love you Diana..I really do
1:26:54 AM **ladydi2011**: I know baby
1:27:09 AM **Robin Lulofs**: *No one will ever love you like i do baby*
1:27:33 AM **ladydi2011**: I believe this
1:27:38 AM **Robin Lulofs**: thank you baby
1:29:00 AM **ladydi2011**: Did you sleep?
1:29:43 AM **Robin Lulofs**: not much baby *i* came home very late from work
1:31:06 AM **ladydi2011**: Honey, you need your rest
1:31:15 AM **Robin Lulofs**: Yes baby
1:31:15 AM **ladydi2011**: Did you eat baby?
1:31:17 AM **Robin Lulofs**: but *i* have to work
1:31:30 AM **Robin Lulofs**: *i* ate yesterday afternoon
1:31:37 AM **ladydi2011**: Ok...now you sound like me!!!
1:32:03 AM **Robin Lulofs**: I love you baby
1:32:13 AM **Robin Lulofs**: I will always have time for my woman no matter what *i* am going through
1:32:18 AM **Robin Lulofs**: *i* will always make out time for you
1:32:27 AM **Robin Lulofs**: you are the most important thing in my life
1:32:36 AM **Robin Lulofs**: I don't play with you .. you are very precious to me Diana
1:32:44 AM **Robin Lulofs**: pls take note .. no joking with Diana
1:33:23 AM **ladydi2011**: Honey...I have taken note and I love this about you
1:33:39 AM **Robin Lulofs**: good honey
1:33:54 AM **ladydi2011**: Did you notice I took time for my man today?
1:34:21 AM **Robin Lulofs**: yes dear
1:34:28 AM **Robin Lulofs**: you should always do that to your man, your man love's you so much
1:34:45 AM **ladydi2011**: Something I love about you is that you give me what's important without me asking...You get it!
1:35:35 AM **Robin Lulofs**: Yes baby. You worth having it if not *i* won't give it out
1:36:02 AM **ladydi2011**: Thank you my love
1:36:20 AM **Robin Lulofs**: you are welcome baby

1:36:24 AM **Robin Lulofs**: what did you have for dinner??

1:36:28 AM **ladydi2011**: I MISS YOU

1:36:33 AM **ladydi2011**: Cereal

1:37:06 AM **Robin Lulofs**: I MISS YOU TOO BABY

1:37:09 AM **Robin Lulofs**: Wow..I love you just so much *i* can't control it

1:37:36 AM **ladydi2011**: Same here...

1:38:18 AM **ladydi2011**: It is that "madly" in love that I wanted...

1:38:49 AM **Robin Lulofs**: I am willing to give you more

1:39:06 AM **ladydi2011**: Can you imagine once we are together in person

1:39:32 AM **ladydi2011**: I am also willing to give more and more and more

1:39:32 AM **Robin Lulofs**: yes baby

1:39:39 AM **Robin Lulofs**: *i* will make love to you everyday

1:40:13 AM **ladydi2011**: Nice...I will make love right back

1:40:48 AM **Robin Lulofs**: Honey .. do you like sex?

1:41:00 AM **ladydi2011**: Nope

1:41:06 AM **Robin Lulofs**: Oh okay baby

1:41:17 AM **ladydi2011**: Love it!!!!!!!!!!!!!!

1:41:17 AM **Robin Lulofs**: Hope you don't mind me asking you??

1:41:22 AM **Robin Lulofs**: Oh you love it

1:41:23 AM **Robin Lulofs**: Lol.. you are so silly! You got me wondering

1:41:40 AM **ladydi2011**: Are you smiling now?

1:41:50 AM **ladydi2011**: Maybe even laughing....

1:42:53 AM **ladydi2011**: I promise you Robin that I will rock your world

1:43:07 AM **Robin Lulofs**: Lol

1:43:12 AM **Robin Lulofs**: I really can't wait to have you baby

1:43:16 AM **Robin Lulofs**: I love you baby

1:44:10 AM **ladydi2011**: Same here

1:44:29 AM **ladydi2011**: I have not been with anyone in 8 years. Saving myself for my forever man

1:45:04 AM **Robin Lulofs**: I love you baby

1:45:21 AM **Robin Lulofs**: I want to spend the rest of my life loving you more more and more dear

1:45:30 AM **Robin Lulofs**: When was the last time you had sex?

1:46:22 AM **ladydi2011**: 8 yrs. ago

1:46:41 AM **Robin Lulofs**: oh really

1:46:47 AM **Robin Lulofs**: mine was 3years ago

1:46:59 AM **Robin Lulofs**: before my wife passed away

1:47:41 AM **ladydi2011**: I do not do one night stands baby

1:48:41 AM **Robin Lulofs**: Yes *i* dont do it too. I don't like it

1:49:02 AM **Robin Lulofs**: I have a lot of girls, ladies and women disturbing me for one night stand on the site but *i* said no

1:50:30 AM **Robin Lulofs**: I love you and you are the woman *i* want to spend the rest of my life loving

1:52:03 AM **Robin Lulofs**: are you there?

1:52:04 AM **Robin Lulofs**: <ding>

1:52:22 AM **ladydi2011**: Yeah honey

1:52:29 AM **ladydi2011**: Keys stuck on phone

1:52:41 AM **Robin Lulofs**: Okay baby

1:52:44 AM **Robin Lulofs**: hope it ok now??

1:53:39 AM **Robin Lulofs**: can you come on your computer?

1:53:52 AM **ladydi2011**: Yeah
1:53:58 AM **ladydi2011**: Brb
1:54:30 AM **Robin Lulofs**: Ok
2:05:06 AM **Robin Lulofs**: Are you there baby??

IM Jul 20, 2012 2:31:03 AM

2:31:03 AM **Robin Lulofs**: <ding>
2:38:53 AM **Robin Lulofs**: <ding>

From: Robin Lulofs
To: ladydi
Subject: For you my love
Date: Fri, Jul 20, 2012 at 4:26 AM

I am just writing to show the world how much I love you. From the moment that we found each other, till our last words I have always loved you... I have never stopped loving you. You are one of the most remarkable people I have ever known. You're kind, caring, compassionate, loving and incredibly sexy, When I am reading from you, I feel alive. You bring to me a happiness no one else has before. You bring to me a love I have never known before. I could not imagine what my life would be like without you. I know that I don't want to even imagine. You have touched my heart in ways no one could ever comprehend. I love being with you and I want to spend the rest of my life with you. My woman, my sexy monster, there is nothing on this Earth that I could ever give you that would ever come close to how I feel about you.

I want to be with you for the rest of our life, and I hope you feel the same. If only you knew how much I want to stay in your life, Is it wrong to be so much in love, yet feel so strong about you? I do not know what love is. But if it means caring for you, respecting you, believing in you and putting your happiness above my own, then I am in love. This is not lust or a silly crush, I really do love you. The past few weeks we have spent together knowing each other have been incredibly romantic. I hope that there are more great times to come. I love you.

Your Love
Robin.

IM Jul 20, 2012 5:31:27 PM Continued

5:31:27 PM **Robin Lulofs**: Hello Diana
5:38:27 PM **Ladydi2011**: Hello Robin
5:38:52 PM **Ladydi2011**: So what happened at work today?
5:41:20 PM **Robin Lulofs**: We started final installations of equipments ...
5:43:47 PM **Ladydi2011**: I like the word "final" when it refers to this project

5:45:01 PM **Ladydi2011**: And I also like the word "final" when it comes to YOU being my final man...the man I will journey through the rest of life with...

5:46:02 PM **Robin Lulofs**: I love you endlessly baby

5:46:10 PM **Robin Lulofs**: I love you so much darling

5:46:16 PM **Robin Lulofs**: thanks for coming into my life, you are my eight wonder

5:46:42 PM **Ladydi2011**: Thank you for coming into my life!

5:47:41 PM **Ladydi2011**: Baby, it is as if you can read almost everything I want and need. How do you do this?

Break In Time

5:50:32 PM **Ladydi2011**: <ding>

5:50:36 PM **Robin Lulofs**: <ding>

5:50:40 PM **Robin Lulofs**: I am here baby

5:50:47 PM **Robin Lulofs**: went to get a glass of water

5:50:55 PM **Ladydi2011**: Ok

5:51:09 PM **Ladydi2011**: I am reading a HOT book

5:51:38 PM **Ladydi2011**: Read about it on line...Fifty Shades of Grey

5:52:33 PM **Robin Lulofs**: I love you so much baby

5:52:35 PM **Robin Lulofs**: brb..hold on a few minute sweetie

5:52:54 PM **Ladydi2011**: Ok baby

5:53:09 PM **Ladydi2011**: Do you need to go?

Break In Time

5:56:44 PM **Robin Lulofs**: No, I am here

5:56:55 PM **Robin Lulofs**: What are your plans for the rest of the evening?

5:57:37 PM **Ladydi2011**: Need to put together two power points for Texas

5:57:47 PM **Ladydi2011**: What about you?

5:57:51 PM **Robin Lulofs**: Oh baby

5:58:03 PM **Robin Lulofs**: Will be going to bed when *i* am done chatting with you

5:59:02 PM **Ladydi2011:** It is 5 hrs. later there than here

5:59:09 PM **Robin Lulofs**: *i* really do wanna be with you baby

5:59:19 PM **Robin Lulofs**: yes baby

5:59:26 PM **Ladydi2011:** It 11pm there, right?

5:59:48 PM **Robin Lulofs**: yes it 11pm here now

6:00:05 PM **Ladydi2011**: I will take breaks to read this book...it is hard to stop reading it!

6:00:49 PM **Robin Lulofs**: do you wanna go now my love??

6:01:40 PM **Ladydi2011**: Not unless you do honey

6:02:24 PM **Robin Lulofs**: Okay baby

6:02:31 PM **Robin Lulofs**: I am here my love. I am going no where

6:02:40 PM **Robin Lulofs**: *i* love you sweetie

6:03:13 PM **Robin Lulofs**: I am here with you. Are you there?

6:04:43 PM **Ladydi2011:** I am here...Sorry

6:04:56 PM **Robin Lulofs**: what are you doing diana?

6:04:58 PM **Ladydi2011**: Had to answer email

6:05:06 PM **Robin Lulofs**: what email baby??

6:05:22 PM **Ladydi2011**: I have several buss things I need to tend to baby

6:05:40 PM **Ladydi2011**: Some days, I wish I had a 9-5 job

6:06:05 PM **Ladydi2011**: I will be glad when I am just an author and speaker...

6:07:01 PM **Robin Lulofs**: You are a very wonderful lady

6:07:24 PM **Robin Lulofs**: Pls don't stress yourself too much

6:07:33 PM **Ladydi2011**: Thanks baby I will not

6:07:39 PM **Robin Lulofs**: Ok

6:07:54 PM **Robin Lulofs**: When *i* am there *i* will help you with the writing ok?

6:08:02 PM **Robin Lulofs**: We will have to share your work Ok?

6:08:06 PM **Ladydi2011**: Later tonight I will have some champagne and strawberries

6:08:27 PM **Robin Lulofs**: uhmmmmmm

6:08:45 PM **Robin Lulofs**: we will do that together real soon

6:08:51 PM **Ladydi2011**: Just show me the romance so I can write about it.....

6:09:05 PM **Ladydi2011**: Yeah, we will

6:09:19 PM **Robin Lulofs**: I will baby

6:09:46 PM **Ladydi2011**: I know this comes natural for you

6:10:09 PM **Robin Lulofs**: Yes baby..It flows like a river with different currents

6:10:24 PM **Robin Lulofs**: No response to my email dear

6:11:59 PM **Robin Lulofs**: are you busy baby?

6:13:40 PM **Ladydi2011**: Hmmmm

6:13:51 PM **Ladydi2011**: When did you send it honey?

6:14:12 PM **Robin Lulofs**: to your gmail address

6:17:20 PM **Ladydi2011**: Please hold baby

6:17:29 PM **Robin Lulofs**: Ok

6:19:07 PM **Ladydi2011**: Thank you baby

6:19:26 PM **Ladydi2011**: You only hope that there is more to come?

6:19:29 PM **Ladydi2011**: Hmmmmm

6:19:58 PM **Robin Lulofs**: honey *i* love you so much and nothing can change that

6:20:02 PM **Robin Lulofs**: you mean a lot to my life

6:20:55 PM **Ladydi2011**: I love you too...Nothing will change this!

6:21:35 PM **Ladydi2011**: I feel like I have completely changed your life...is this true?

6:21:37 PM **Robin Lulofs**: *trust me no one will ever love you like i do*

6:22:05 PM **Ladydi2011**: I have tapped into a part of your heart you didn't know existed

6:22:31 PM **Ladydi2011**: I love how you love me baby!

6:23:05 PM **Ladydi2011**: Darling, no one will ever love or complete you like I do.

6:23:40 PM **Ladydi2011**: Baby, I haven't even started to rock your world yet...for real!

6:23:46 PM **Robin Lulofs**: You are so wonderful

6:23:56 PM **Robin Lulofs**: Wow baby I can't wait to see you rock my world

6:24:36 PM **Ladydi2011**: For the rest of your life I want you to be saying "wow baby"

6:24:52 PM **Ladydi2011**: It will always be when you least expect it

6:24:56 PM **Robin Lulofs**: wow

6:25:12 PM **Robin Lulofs**: then *i* don't ever want to stop saying that

6:25:59 PM **Ladydi2011**: Battery is blinking red and door bell is ringing

6:26:00 PM **Robin Lulofs**: I love you so much darling

6:26:15 PM **Ladydi2011**: I need to go now baby

6:26:40 PM **Robin Lulofs**: okay

6:26:44 PM **Ladydi2011**: Dream about me

6:26:52 PM **Robin Lulofs**: *i* will rest now and talk to you tomorrow morning

6:27:13 PM **Ladydi2011**: Ok my love

6:27:21 PM **Ladydi2011**: Night

6:27:29 PM **Ladydi2011**: Until tomorrow

6:28:42 PM **Robin Lulofs**: Night my love
6:28:50 PM **Robin Lulofs**: I will dream about you

He now talks about meeting me soon, starting to plan our lives together and marriage. We all know that he has no intention of meeting me in person, having a life with me or marrying me. Scammers are experts at making FALSE PROMISES that will make their victims think what they are saying will actually happen. He tells me he is the "real deal" and to "trust him" and again asks me "What do you think of me so far?" He is again testing the water so he knows when to ask for money.

This man is really working the "love and commitment thing" and I want to know his scam, so I had to work it right back!

RED FLAGS

- He tells me he wants my love, trust, support, care and honesty and that he always wants me to know that he will never hurt me and that we need to "work together as one". He says he wants to feel free to tell me everything. He wants me to commit to him because I have been holding out. He tells me that "real commitment" is what we should have from now on and everything will be cool. He begs me to just trust his love for me and tells me that I have found my man and he has found his woman. He says, "God knows I will never hurt you," "I want you to know God brought us together for a very great purpose don't let fear take it all away from you," and "Fear is of the devil." There he goes bringing God into the picture. All this terminology is very common for scammers.

- He says we would make the best and perfect match ever and again asks me to commit because "I rule his world and his life." He again tells me he will never break my heart and we need to start planning our life together. He tells me he wishes he met me before he left so I could be assured. He asks my favorite color, my birthday and if I like diamonds. He asks me to promise "to be there for him no matter what." He is trying to get me to agree to this so he can use it against me when I refuse to send him money. Please know that EVERYTHING the scammer says is said to MANIPULATE YOU. It is never said because they mean it.

- The following are common Nigerian terminology and thus, definite red flags:
    1. When I told him my laptop died, he said, "do you mean got spoiled?"
    2. "Tell me your true mind"
    3. "You rule my world and my life"
    4. "I slept off"

- Most scammers (but not all) will tell you they dream about you. Please know that they really didn't. It is just another way for them to pull you closer and make you think they are in love with you.

🦅 When he asks how big my company is and what my income is he is digging for financial information so he can figure out how much money to ask from me. He asks about my monthly income because people in Nigeria are paid monthly. I am sure this man has been scamming for a while and is not a kid.

🦅 He was having a problem with his Internet connection and indicated it was due to the weather. This is another clue you chatting with someone in a third world country.

🦅 I laughed when he said, "I see success" because he will NOT have any financial success with me, but I will have the success in obtaining what I want from him – the scam he is running.

🦅 He continues to talk about when he will come see me. Scammers usually say they will fly right from where they are directly to you, and they ask if you will pick them up at the airport.

🦅 He is not happy when I tell him I only hid my profile and didn't delete it. He wants it deleted so no other scammers can pursue me and possibly get the money he wants for himself. He wanted my user name and password so "he" could delete it right that moment. **Do not ever give anyone your user name and password or they can get your credit card information.**

🦅 He tells me he loves me so much and "nothing is going to change that". He doesn't want to lose me. He even says I am his "wife" and should respect his "wishes" and "orders." Yes, scammers will order you to do things. He shows his manipulative and nasty side. He makes sure to tell me twice that nobody will ever love me like he does. At the end of the heated discussion he says, "Night Diana Lulofs." Again, trying to manipulate me into the mindset of being his "wife."

🦅 He then tells me if I hurt him, I also hurt his son. Yes, a scammer will use children to manipulate you.

🦅 He is always awake in the middle of the night because he is chatting. Scammers in Africa are awake all night and sleep during the day.

IM Jul 21, 2012 12:21:25 AM

12:21:25 AM **Robin Lulofs**: Hey Baby
12:21:33 AM **Robin Lulofs**: Good Morning
12:21:46 AM **ladydi2011**: Good morning honey
12:21:52 AM **ladydi2011**: How was your rest?
12:22:02 AM **Robin Lulofs**: It was good baby
12:22:07 AM **Robin Lulofs**: *I miss you and dreamt about you*
12:22:16 AM **ladydi2011**: I have been sipping champagne, eating strawberries and reading this book
12:22:24 AM **ladydi2011**: I miss you too...
12:22:45 AM **ladydi2011**: Hmmmm....please tell me about your dream
12:23:00 AM **Robin Lulofs**: Lol

12:23:09 AM **Robin Lulofs**: *I saw you in my dream Diana*

12:23:37 AM **ladydi2011**: Nice...I hope it was a good dream

12:23:49 AM **Robin Lulofs**: believe me baby

12:24:00 AM **Robin Lulofs**: you were in my thought last night before going to bed

12:24:40 AM **Robin Lulofs**: *I dreamt we had a big family, i saw Christian too and my mom ..*

12:24:57 AM **Robin Lulofs**: *I dreamt we had a very happy family*

12:25:22 AM **ladydi2011**: Nice dream honey

12:25:53 AM **Robin Lulofs**: I love you woman

12:26:17 AM **ladydi2011**: I love you too

12:26:18 AM **Robin Lulofs**: You have made me love you so much

12:26:31 AM **Robin Lulofs**: *Will you change your last name to Lulofs?*

12:27:10 AM **ladydi2011**: Thank you for wanting me to have your last name

12:27:33 AM **Robin Lulofs**: You are welcome baby

12:27:37 AM **Robin Lulofs**: Will you have it??

12:27:43 AM **Robin Lulofs**: I will do anything for you baby

12:27:54 AM **ladydi2011**: Anything baby?

12:28:02 AM **Robin Lulofs**: yes baby anything to make my woman happy and smiling forever

12:28:52 AM **ladydi2011**: Thank you so much honey I feel the same way concerning you

12:29:09 AM **ladydi2011**: I always want you to be happy

12:29:41 AM **Robin Lulofs**: And *i* will give you all the happiness you want baby

12:29:51 AM **Robin Lulofs**: Love you like there's no tomorrow

12:30:05 AM **Robin Lulofs**: I want to give you all the love in this world

12:30:26 AM **ladydi2011**: Your words are a melody to my heart

12:31:01 AM **Robin Lulofs**: you are my life and everything

12:31:24 AM **ladydi2011**: There is something really special when you do not have to ask for what you need because it is already given freely and from the other person's desire

12:31:38 AM **Robin Lulofs**: *I will hurt myself if you ever hurt me baby*

12:32:16 AM **ladydi2011**: Oh honey, please do not talk like this

12:32:32 AM **Robin Lulofs**: I am sorry baby

12:32:46 AM **Robin Lulofs**: Cause *i* know *i* can never love anyone the way *i* love you

12:33:09 AM **Robin Lulofs**: so *i* better have myself kill cause *i* cuz *i* will never find any love like yours

12:33:21 AM **ladydi2011**: Baby

12:33:26 AM **Robin Lulofs**: I am here for you baby

12:33:27 AM **ladydi2011**: I am not going anywhere I am here

12:33:37 AM **Robin Lulofs**: Yes *i* know

12:33:38 AM **Robin Lulofs**: OMG..I wish you have a magic mirror which you can use to see me

12:34:05 AM **ladydi2011**: a magic mirror???

12:34:44 AM **Robin Lulofs**: yes baby

12:34:47 AM **Robin Lulofs**: lol

12:35:12 AM **ladydi2011**: hmmmmm. I will have to look for a magic mirror

12:35:29 AM **ladydi2011**: However, I know one day I will know ALL of you

12:35:58 AM **Robin Lulofs**: Yes baby

12:36:03 AM **Robin Lulofs**: You will know all of me

12:36:13 AM **Robin Lulofs**: then you will know how much *i* love you

12:36:46 AM **ladydi2011**: hmmmmmm

12:37:55 AM **ladydi2011**: Honey, why do I feel like there is something you are not telling me.....

12:38:14 AM **Robin Lulofs**: you are a goddess pretending to be a woman

12:38:24 AM **Robin Lulofs**: *i* will love you till my last breath

12:38:45 AM **Robin Lulofs**: you are doing something special to my life

12:39:01 AM **ladydi2011**: What am I doing to your life honey?

12:39:20 AM **Robin Lulofs**: great things of life

12:39:54 AM **ladydi2011**: I am so glad that it is me doing great and special things to your life

12:39:58 AM **Robin Lulofs**: *i* mean after all these years, I would have thought I might not have the possibilities again of having my dream woman, my partner, my best friend and co-pilot

12:40:15 AM **ladydi2011**: Yet, you have!

12:41:03 AM **ladydi2011**: And I have found the man who loves me as madly as I love him

12:41:18 AM **Robin Lulofs**: *i am talking about fate here* when feelings are so powerful it's as if some force beyond your control is guiding you to someone who can make you happy beyond your wildest dreams.

12:41:48 AM **ladydi2011**: I agree baby. I feel the same way

12:42:48 AM **Robin Lulofs**: It's not about how much love you have in the beginning but how much love you build till the end .. I will love you till my last breath

12:43:20 AM **ladydi2011**: I agree with this honey. I will love you till my last breath too!

12:44:28 AM **Robin Lulofs**: My heart keep calling for you

12:45:06 AM **ladydi2011**: I know. I can feel it. Mine keeps calling for you. Can you hear and feel it?

12:45:15 AM **Robin Lulofs**: Yes baby

12:45:21 AM **Robin Lulofs**: I can hear and feel your love for me

12:45:50 AM **ladydi2011**: Some things are just out of our control

12:46:03 AM **Robin Lulofs**: tell me baby

12:46:12 AM **ladydi2011**: Love...The heart has its own mind

12:46:36 AM **Robin Lulofs**: yes you are right

12:46:38 AM **ladydi2011**: Many times it is not rational

12:46:52 AM **ladydi2011**: It feels what it feels

12:47:00 AM **ladydi2011**: It wants what it wants

12:47:21 AM **ladydi2011**: It can overflow its desire into ones entire being

12:47:53 AM **ladydi2011**: You are in deep thought this morning my love. I can feel it!

12:48:16 AM **ladydi2011**: You also seem to be in turmoil about something.

12:48:57 AM **Robin Lulofs**: OMG..How do you get to see what *i* feel in my heart

12:49:37 AM **ladydi2011**: We are connected baby at a very deep level

12:49:48 AM **Robin Lulofs**: GOD..and have been from the beginning

12:49:56 AM **Robin Lulofs**: you are the perfect woman for me

12:50:11 AM **ladydi2011**: You are the perfect man for me

12:50:30 AM **ladydi2011**: If you do not come home soon I am going to die

12:50:37 AM **ladydi2011**: You are the air that I breathe. I need to kiss you and be in your arms

12:51:01 AM **Robin Lulofs**: No baby

12:51:05 AM **Robin Lulofs**: I will be home soon

12:51:11 AM **Robin Lulofs**: *Promise me you will never go anywhere*

12:51:19 AM **ladydi2011**: I promise

12:51:29 AM **ladydi2011**: In less you do not come home then I cannot promise anything

12:52:18 AM **Robin Lulofs**: Yes baby

12:52:23 AM **Robin Lulofs**: Why do you think *i* won't come home

12:52:26 AM **Robin Lulofs**: that is funny baby..this is gonna be my last project

12:52:50 AM **ladydi2011**: I don't know honey...I guess it is my deepest fear

12:53:59 AM **Robin Lulofs**: *after this project i will be coming home to you to plan our life*

12:54:10 AM **Robin Lulofs**: Honey I am gonna make love to you our first night

12:54:38 AM **Robin Lulofs**: it been very long *i* did this

12:55:34 AM **Robin Lulofs**: I love you baby

12:55:41 AM **Robin Lulofs**: I am very happy you keep yourself for so long

12:56:09 AM **ladydi2011**: Yes my love.

12:56:23 AM **Robin Lulofs**: I love you more

12:56:30 AM **ladydi2011**: I do not see partaking in something that has no meaning

12:56:38 AM **ladydi2011**: Then it is just sex...Just sex is NOT enough for me

12:57:02 AM **Robin Lulofs**: ***You are all i am living for baby***

12:57:18 AM **Robin Lulofs**: I will give you all you want baby

12:57:45 AM **ladydi2011**: Thank you honey

12:57:57 AM **ladydi2011**: Your love is what I want most

12:58:08 AM **ladydi2011**: You know that money comes and money goes

12:58:15 AM **ladydi2011**: Things come and things go

12:58:27 AM **Robin Lulofs**: Yes baby

12:58:28 AM **ladydi2011**: At the end of the day neither has any meaning

12:58:49 AM **ladydi2011**: What I need is real, true and passionate love

12:58:58 AM **ladydi2011**: I will not settle for anything less

12:59:32 AM **Robin Lulofs**: *i* love you baby

12:59:42 AM **Robin Lulofs**: I believe you are getting all you want baby

12:59:49 AM **Robin Lulofs**: I will never take it away from you. I will love you forever.

1:00:13 AM **ladydi2011**: I am getting all I want baby

1:00:24 AM **ladydi2011**: I hope I am giving you what you want and need. Am I???

1:00:57 AM **Robin Lulofs**: Yes baby you are and *i* want more .. ***Lol***

1:01:20 AM **ladydi2011**: You can have all you want baby, my heart is filled with love honey

1:02:14 AM **Robin Lulofs**: I love you sincerely baby

1:02:31 AM **Robin Lulofs**: Honey I am gonna send you a picture

1:02:37 AM **Robin Lulofs**: let me know if you like it ok?

1:05:16 AM **ladydi2011**: Your picture is pixilated and I am trying to see why

1:05:43 AM **Robin Lulofs**: it blurry?

1:06:16 AM **ladydi2011**: Baby, please email them to me

1:06:38 AM **Robin Lulofs**: Okay *i* will do that right now

1:06:47 AM **ladydi2011**: Thank you

1:07:09 AM **Robin Lulofs**: you are welcome dear

1:08:23 AM **ladydi2011**: I found it

1:08:36 AM **Robin Lulofs**: found what dear

1:09:52 AM **ladydi2011**: What I was looking for concerning why the share wasn't working

1:10:11 AM **Robin Lulofs**: oh okay baby

1:10:11 AM **ladydi2011**: I am a researcher baby when something doesn't work

1:10:21 AM **Robin Lulofs**: so do you want me to share here

1:10:27 AM **Robin Lulofs**: Lol..You rock ma'am ..

1:10:38 AM **Robin Lulofs**: 😵😵

1:11:46 AM **ladydi2011**: Just because they say it will work, doesn't mean that it will

1:12:05 AM **ladydi2011**: Baby, please email to me so I have you on my phone

1:12:12 AM **Robin Lulofs**: lol..okay baby

1:12:31 AM **Robin Lulofs**: *i* will email it to you my lady

1:20:21 AM **ladydi2011**: I didn't get the email yet baby

1:20:33 AM **Robin Lulofs**: yes baby *i* am still attaching the pictures

1:21:47 AM **ladydi2011**: I will wait

1:22:03 AM **Robin Lulofs**: okay baby I am getting it done

1:23:41 AM **ladydi2011**: take your time baby

1:31:59 AM **Robin Lulofs**: sent baby

1:33:18 AM **ladydi2011**: I received the picture

1:33:25 AM **ladydi2011**: I am drooling darling

1:33:53 AM **Robin Lulofs**: Lol..I love you baby

1:34:15 AM **ladydi2011**: Honey, I love your hands

1:34:25 AM **ladydi2011**: OMG...Honey, you are so handsome!

1:36:24 AM **ladydi2011**: I love how you dress

1:37:00 AM **Robin Lulofs**: thank you baby. I am glad

1:37:09 AM **Robin Lulofs**: I will love you forever

1:38:18 AM **Robin Lulofs**: I love everything about you darling. You are one in a million

1:38:42 AM **ladydi2011**: Darling, I love you so much. I want you in my life forever

1:39:42 AM **ladydi2011**: I know we are made for each other

1:39:50 AM **Robin Lulofs**: Yes baby

1:39:53 AM **ladydi2011**: I will love you into eternity

1:40:00 AM **Robin Lulofs**: *GOD brought us together for a great purpose*

1:40:30 AM **ladydi2011**: This I believe. Do you have any clue what this purpose is?

1:41:02 AM **Robin Lulofs**: Uhmmmmm *i* don't baby

1:41:08 AM **Robin Lulofs**: you tell if you have a clue dear

1:41:38 AM **ladydi2011**: I don't baby

1:41:52 AM **ladydi2011**: God is love so ....

1:42:14 AM **Robin Lulofs**: I am in love you with

1:43:57 AM **ladydi2011**: I am in love with you too darling

1:44:42 AM **Robin Lulofs**: I am being true with my feelings

1:44:54 AM **ladydi2011**: Me to darling

1:45:05 AM **Robin Lulofs**: good darling

1:45:06 AM **ladydi2011**: Even my friends see a difference in me

1:45:09 AM **Robin Lulofs**: *i* am glad you like me

1:46:41 AM **Robin Lulofs**: baby what are you doing??

1:47:09 AM **ladydi2011**: I am sorry

1:47:32 AM **ladydi2011**: I was researching to see how many copies of this book I am reading has sold

1:47:45 AM **ladydi2011**: Baby...I DO like you and I love you

1:47:50 AM **Robin Lulofs**: who wrote the book

1:48:01 AM **ladydi2011**: EL James

1:48:24 AM **Robin Lulofs**: Oh okay baby

1:48:40 AM **Robin Lulofs**: so how many copies has been sold?

1:48:49 AM **ladydi2011**: over 50 million

1:49:25 AM **Robin Lulofs**: Wow

1:49:44 AM **Robin Lulofs**: Okay baby .. I am getting ready to start writing for you Ok?

1:50:02 AM **ladydi2011**: Ok my love

1:50:12 AM **ladydi2011**: I so love how you write

1:50:22 AM **ladydi2011**: Where did you go to college, baby?

1:51:50 AM **Robin Lulofs**: *Lol..Berlin Germany*

1:52:18 AM **ladydi2011**: What is your degree honey?

Break In Time

1:55:59 AM **ladydi2011**: Honey

1:56:03 AM **ladydi2011**: Are you there?

1:56:15 AM **Robin Lulofs**: *yes my computer is acting up on me*

1:57:12 AM **ladydi2011**: Oh...I never like when this happens

1:58:08 AM **Robin Lulofs**: I am sorry ok?

1:58:08 AM **Robin Lulofs**: Me too baby

1:58:39 AM **ladydi2011**: It is ok

1:58:43 AM **ladydi2011**: I understand

1:58:53 AM **Robin Lulofs**: thank you baby

2:00:40 AM **Robin Lulofs**: Master's degree

2:00:45 AM **Robin Lulofs**: are you there baby??

2:02:06 AM **ladydi2011**: Please hold honey

2:02:22 AM **Robin Lulofs**: okay baby

2:03:59 AM **ladydi2011**: Sorry honey

2:04:04 AM **ladydi2011**: Bathroom break

2:04:24 AM **Robin Lulofs**: Okay baby

2:06:49 AM **ladydi2011**: Honey, I need to go to bed. My eyes are closing

2:08:14 AM **Robin Lulofs**: oh okay baby

2:08:23 AM **Robin Lulofs**: *i* will talk to you tomorrow ok?

2:08:38 AM **ladydi2011**: Yes my love

2:09:18 AM **Robin Lulofs**: *I can't wait to be back home baby*

2:09:22 AM **Robin Lulofs**: I love you so much baby

2:09:45 AM **ladydi2011**: I can't wait either baby

2:09:54 AM **Robin Lulofs**: *I will be home soon ok?*

2:10:43 AM **Robin Lulofs**: *baby i will be there with you soon*

2:10:50 AM **ladydi2011**: ok my love

2:10:51 AM **Robin Lulofs**: you will be sleeping next to me very soon ok? *i* promise
2:10:57 AM **Robin Lulofs**: *i* love you dearly sweet
2:10:58 AM **ladydi2011**: Yay!!!!
2:11:07 AM **ladydi2011**: I love you too
2:11:21 AM **Robin Lulofs**: I adore you my eight wonder
2:11:29 AM **ladydi2011**: I am smiling
2:11:36 AM **ladydi2011**: Good night my love. I love you!!!!
2:12:04 AM **Robin Lulofs**: good night my love
2:12:27 AM **ladydi2011**: Visit me in my dreams
2:12:34 AM **ladydi2011**: Have a fabulous day my darling
2:12:34 AM **Robin Lulofs**: I will baby
2:12:40 AM **Robin Lulofs**: thank you baby
2:12:43 AM **Robin Lulofs**: I love you more
2:12:45 AM **Robin Lulofs**: night baby
2:13:17 AM **ladydi2011**: *(((hugs))) (((hugs))) (((hugs)))*

IM Jul 22, 2012 12:03:46 AM

12:03:46 AM **ladydi2011**: Hi Baby
12:03:52 AM **ladydi2011**: Are you there?
12:03:54 AM **Robin Lulofs**: Hello Honey
12:04:00 AM **Robin Lulofs**: Yes *i* am here sweetie
12:04:06 AM **Robin Lulofs**: I adore you my baby
12:04:10 AM **Robin Lulofs**: How was your day?
12:04:21 AM **ladydi2011**: Busy but good
12:04:43 AM **ladydi2011**: I am really missing you right now
12:06:07 AM **Robin Lulofs**: Yes honey, I am here with you
12:06:21 AM **Robin Lulofs**: I need to get a glass of water
12:07:45 AM **ladydi2011**: Ok
12:07:54 AM **ladydi2011**: How was your day?
12:08:00 AM **Robin Lulofs**: My day was stressful honey
12:08:18 AM **ladydi2011**: Did you think of me at least once?
12:08:53 AM **Robin Lulofs**: Yes baby
12:08:58 AM **Robin Lulofs**: You are always in my thought
12:09:14 AM **ladydi2011**: You are always in my thoughts too
12:10:05 AM **Robin Lulofs**: I love you baby..thanks for coming into my life
12:10:27 AM **Robin Lulofs**: when are you leaving?
12:10:38 AM **ladydi2011**: The 30th
12:11:09 AM **ladydi2011**: I am so glad you are in my life
12:11:41 AM **Robin Lulofs**: I love you more and more sweetie
12:12:12 AM **ladydi2011**: Thanks baby...You're the BEST!
12:12:44 AM **Robin Lulofs**: You are the BESTEST .. *Lol*
12:13:28 AM **ladydi2011**: Lol
12:13:40 AM **ladydi2011**: I see you like topping me...Yes?
12:13:52 AM **Robin Lulofs**: Lol
Break In Time

12:15:36 AM **Robin Lulofs**: Oh baby
12:15:54 AM **Robin Lulofs**: What were you doing?
12:16:18 AM **ladydi2011**: Thinking of you
12:16:29 AM **Robin Lulofs**: for real?
12:16:56 AM **ladydi2011**: Yes for real!
12:17:09 AM **Robin Lulofs**: I was dreaming about you baby
12:17:15 AM **Robin Lulofs**: I saw you again in my dream
12:17:18 AM **Robin Lulofs**: this is true love
12:17:23 AM **ladydi2011**: Hmmmmmm
12:17:33 AM **ladydi2011**: I like when you dream about me
12:17:54 AM **ladydi2011**: This better be true love for you
12:19:00 AM **Robin Lulofs**: It is baby believe me
12:19:11 AM **Robin Lulofs**: I love every bit of this
12:19:20 AM **Robin Lulofs**: *This is a sign of good will baby..I see success*
12:19:55 AM **ladydi2011**: Please do NOT break my heart
12:19:56 AM **Robin Lulofs**: Christian want's to talk to you
12:20:04 AM **ladydi2011**: He does?
12:20:05 AM **Robin Lulofs**: He is very eager to talk to you ..
12:20:12 AM **Robin Lulofs**: He is loving his new mom
12:20:16 AM **ladydi2011**: I would love to talk with him too
12:20:24 AM **Robin Lulofs**: I promise I will never break your heart baby
12:20:29 AM **ladydi2011**: He is here in the states, right?
12:20:32 AM **Robin Lulofs**: *You can trust me*
12:20:51 AM **ladydi2011**: Who watches him when you travel?
12:20:58 AM **Robin Lulofs**: My mom darling
12:21:40 AM **Robin Lulofs**: He keeps asking when you will be coming to see them ..
12:21:40 AM **ladydi2011**: Is she in Indiana?
12:21:54 AM **Robin Lulofs**: No she is not in Indiana
12:22:03 AM **ladydi2011**: Where is she honey?
12:22:20 AM **Robin Lulofs**: I must confess, *i* miss my mom and my son, but then she is a strong woman my dear.
12:22:42 AM **ladydi2011**: Aww....this is why you are attracted to strong women
12:22:45 AM **Robin Lulofs**: *Sometimes i call her Jesus's mother, lol. She has a good heart and also I can tell you her instincts are like oracle. She did say she likes you*
12:23:05 AM **ladydi2011**: What have you told her about me?
12:23:45 AM **Robin Lulofs**: Truely, Love needs no map, for it can find it's way blindfolded
12:23:54 AM **Robin Lulofs**: I told her I found my wife and She said Wow Robin are you serious
12:24:48 AM **ladydi2011**: Wow...So what did you tell her about me?
12:25:45 AM **Robin Lulofs**: Told her you are a very lovely woman
12:25:54 AM **Robin Lulofs**: I told her I am in love with you
12:26:03 AM **Robin Lulofs**: And she said that's my boy
12:27:01 AM **Robin Lulofs**: I just sent you her picture
12:27:25 AM **ladydi2011**: Cool
12:28:56 AM **ladydi2011**: Baby, no pictures are showing up....
12:30:25 AM **Robin Lulofs**: Are you there? Did you get the picture of my mom?
12:31:18 AM **ladydi2011**: I did honey. She has a wonderful spirit [image on next page]
12:31:25 AM **ladydi2011**: She seems like a lot of fun. I can't wait to meet her!!!

621

12:33:09 AM **Robin Lulofs**: She can't wait to meet you too
12:33:23 AM **ladydi2011**: Where does she live baby?
12:33:50 AM **Robin Lulofs**: she is presently in canada
12:34:15 AM **Robin Lulofs**: she is there with Christian
12:34:18 AM **ladydi2011**: Where in Canada
12:34:43 AM **Robin Lulofs**: Hamilton, ON
12:35:06 AM **Robin Lulofs**: What are you doing Diana?

12:35:19 AM **ladydi2011**: Chatting with you
12:35:37 AM **Robin Lulofs**: Okay baby
12:35:39 AM **ladydi2011**: What are you doing Robin?
12:36:45 AM **ladydi2011**: So baby, what did you do today?
12:37:39 AM **Robin Lulofs**: I will be going to the work field with some worker to inspect some of the machines
12:37:52 AM **ladydi2011**: On Sunday?
12:37:58 AM **Robin Lulofs**: Yes baby
12:38:14 AM **ladydi2011**: We are so alike when it comes to work
12:38:22 AM **Robin Lulofs**: I will be going around 6am and be back home by 7am or 8am ..
12:38:59 AM **Robin Lulofs**: I will be going to church by 9am..tight one right?
12:39:07 AM **ladydi2011**: I will be sleeping
12:39:16 AM **ladydi2011**: Yeah baby...tight one!
12:39:41 AM **ladydi2011**: Speaking of church, what are your religious beliefs?
12:41:36 AM **Robin Lulofs**: I believed the sun fought darkness every night and rose to save mankind
12:42:09 AM **ladydi2011**: Ok
12:42:26 AM **Robin Lulofs**: I do believe in GOD
12:43:03 AM **ladydi2011**: Me too
12:43:16 AM **Robin Lulofs**: I am very glad to hear that
12:43:17 AM **ladydi2011**: I have a very strong faith
12:43:36 AM **Robin Lulofs**: I have a very strong believe in GOD
12:43:39 AM **ladydi2011**: I do not believe in organized religion
12:43:41 AM **Robin Lulofs**: HE IS ALIVE

12:43:56 AM **ladydi2011**: I have STUDIED the Bible since I was 22. It is my plumline

12:44:14 AM **Robin Lulofs**: Wow

12:44:18 AM **ladydi2011**: Yes, He is VERY much ALIVE

12:44:20 AM **Robin Lulofs**: Awesome!!!

12:44:38 AM **ladydi2011**: For me it is about being it, not speaking it

12:44:45 AM **Robin Lulofs**: I believe that everyone, every creature has a soul.

12:45:07 AM **ladydi2011**: If someone has to tell me they are a Christian and display it, I am weary

12:45:19 AM **ladydi2011**: It should be in everything they say and do

12:45:19 AM **Robin Lulofs**: Do you believe in past lives and rebirths??

12:45:49 AM **ladydi2011**: No, it is not Biblical

12:46:08 AM **Robin Lulofs**: I believe that anger and hatred only make us sick and forgiveness lets us move on

12:46:21 AM **Robin Lulofs**: Yes it is not baby

12:46:24 AM **ladydi2011**: I 100% agree with this

12:46:39 AM **ladydi2011**: I am very quick to forgive

12:46:53 AM **ladydi2011**: Our Father only forgives us if we forgive

12:47:17 AM **Robin Lulofs**: I am very glad you do baby

12:47:20 AM **ladydi2011**: Forgiveness is for our soul and not the person who hurt us

12:47:46 AM **ladydi2011**: I also live by the following;

12:48:08 AM **ladydi2011**: If someone betrays, hurts, deceives me I say, thank you for showing me who you are, now I can chose if I want you in my life

12:48:45 AM **Robin Lulofs**: Uhmmmmmmmmmm

12:48:56 AM **ladydi2011**: I realize they have done this because it is who they are

12:49:07 AM **Robin Lulofs**: *I will never hurt you, I am very sure you know that*

12:49:23 AM **ladydi2011**: I do know this my love

12:49:40 AM **Robin Lulofs**: I am happy you do

12:49:50 AM **ladydi2011**: I have had people hurt, betray and deceive me

12:49:53 AM **Robin Lulofs**: I believe that we can learn many things if we only listen

12:50:02 AM **Robin Lulofs**: I am so sorry to hear that, I will never do any of this to you

12:50:12 AM **Robin Lulofs**: *Trust me ok?*

12:50:23 AM **ladydi2011**: Yes baby....we can learn many things if we listen

12:50:35 AM **ladydi2011**: I do trust you

12:51:05 AM **ladydi2011**: I will never do any of these things to you either

12:51:16 AM **Robin Lulofs**: I love you baby

12:51:20 AM **ladydi2011**: Trust me ok?

12:52:28 AM **Robin Lulofs**: God is all and all

12:52:34 AM **Robin Lulofs**: Yes baby *i* do trust you

12:53:02 AM **ladydi2011**: God is the Alpha and Omega

12:53:06 AM **ladydi2011**: He knows all things

12:53:11 AM **ladydi2011**: He owns all things

12:53:25 AM **ladydi2011**: Most importantly...He is Love

12:53:47 AM **ladydi2011**: One of my sayings is: Where there is hatred and prejudice, let me sow love

12:54:01 AM **ladydi2011**: Where there is darkness, let me be the light

12:54:17 AM **ladydi2011**: Where there is deception, let me be truth

12:54:19 AM **Robin Lulofs**: Yes HE knows everything

12:54:20 AM **Robin Lulofs**: I love GOD

12:54:30 AM **Robin Lulofs**: I thank GOD for bringing you into my life

12:54:39 AM **ladydi2011**: I love God too baby

12:55:08 AM **Robin Lulofs**: We are Love

12:55:09 AM **ladydi2011**: He answered my heart desires through you

12:55:29 AM **Robin Lulofs**: You make me happy baby

12:55:32 AM **ladydi2011**: Did you see the saying I live by honey?

12:55:36 AM **Robin Lulofs**: You are a blessing to me

12:55:44 AM **Robin Lulofs**: Yes

12:56:01 AM **ladydi2011**: You make me happy too baby

12:56:16 AM **Robin Lulofs**: You rock ma'am

12:56:25 AM **ladydi2011**: Thank you Sir. So do YOU!

12:56:37 AM **Robin Lulofs**: You are welcome ma'am

12:56:45 AM **ladydi2011**: YOU rock my world!

12:57:17 AM **ladydi2011**: So baby.....When are you coming to Atlanta?

12:57:50 AM **Robin Lulofs**: *I will be coming in a few weeks baby ..*

12:58:11 AM **Robin Lulofs**: *Hopefully when you are back in August*

12:58:24 AM **Robin Lulofs**: Is that Ok with you ma'am?

12:58:33 AM **ladydi2011**: Yes sir!!!

12:58:45 AM **Robin Lulofs**: Love you ma'am

12:59:00 AM **ladydi2011**: Honey, please stop with the ma'am it makes me feel old, and I am NOT old

12:59:07 AM **Robin Lulofs**: Lol

12:59:32 AM **Robin Lulofs**: I know you would say that so *i* was waiting

12:59:42 AM **ladydi2011**: Oh....you did?

1:00:37 AM **Robin Lulofs**: Lol..Yes baby

1:02:16 AM **ladydi2011**: Hmmmmm....how do you know so much about me?

1:02:51 AM **Robin Lulofs**: I know everything about you my love

1:02:59 AM **Robin Lulofs**: You are my woman what do you expect?

1:03:17 AM **ladydi2011**: Hmmmmmm

1:04:36 AM **ladydi2011**: Do you believe in wishes coming true?

1:05:24 AM **Robin Lulofs**: Yes baby. Do you?

1:06:57 AM **ladydi2011**: I do baby

1:07:03 AM **ladydi2011**: Sorry for the delay

1:07:11 AM **ladydi2011**: Had to plug laptop in

1:07:11 AM **Robin Lulofs**: Okay baby

1:07:14 AM **Robin Lulofs**: I am glad you do

1:07:22 AM **ladydi2011**: You are my wish come true

1:07:30 AM **ladydi2011**: Did you know this?

1:07:43 AM **Robin Lulofs**: Yes baby

1:08:50 AM **Robin Lulofs**: Honey put on your webcam

1:09:00 AM **ladydi2011**: Honey....It is 6:08 your time

1:09:06 AM **ladydi2011**: You need to go to work

1:09:13 AM **Robin Lulofs**: yes baby *i* know

1:09:20 AM **ladydi2011**: Baby, my cam is broke on this computer

1:09:26 AM **Robin Lulofs**: don't worry *i* am my boss

1:09:32 AM **ladydi2011**: My new computer should be in next week

1:09:35 AM **ladydi2011**: Lol...I know you are the boss

1:10:04 AM **ladydi2011**: I have to call tech support to fix this cam but haven't had time

1:10:13 AM **Robin Lulofs**: Okay baby

1:10:23 AM **ladydi2011**: This process is usually hours on the phone

1:10:38 AM **ladydi2011**: I like being in love with the boss

1:11:23 AM **Robin Lulofs**: Lol..Are you in love with the boss

1:11:39 AM **ladydi2011**: Honey, you might not hear from me as much when I am in Texas

1:11:59 AM **ladydi2011**: Probably mostly through text

1:12:19 AM **Robin Lulofs**: Okay text is better than nothing

1:12:32 AM **Robin Lulofs**: How many days are you gonna be gone?

1:13:11 AM **ladydi2011**: I thought I had to leave on the 30th I am leaving early morning on the 1st

1:13:53 AM **ladydi2011**: Returning after midnight on the 4th

1:14:03 AM **Robin Lulofs**: Okay baby

1:14:57 AM **Robin Lulofs**: and emails would be better too ok?

Missed Voice call with Robin Lulofs (1:13:51 AM)
Call Ended: 0 hours 1 minutes 11 seconds
Outgoing Voice call with Robin Lulofs (1:16:06 AM)
Call Ended: 0 hours 2 minutes 29 seconds
Missed Voice call with Robin Lulofs (1:19:11 AM)

1:19:30 AM **Robin Lulofs:**

1:25:30 AM **Robin Lulofs:** *I love Diana Lulofs*

Outgoing Voice call with Robin Lulofs (1:19:28 AM)
Call Ended: 0 hours 6 minutes 15 seconds
Outgoing Voice call with Robin Lulofs (1:26:04 AM)
Call Ended: 0 hours 2 minutes 45 seconds

1:30:41 AM **Robin Lulofs**: <ding>

1:30:46 AM **Robin Lulofs**: Do you like my picture?

Outgoing Voice call with Robin Lulofs (1:29:34 AM)
Call Ended: 0 hours 1 minutes 11 seconds
Outgoing Voice call with Robin Lulofs (1:31:08 AM)
Call Ended: 0 hours 2 minutes 14 seconds

1:33:51 AM **Robin Lulofs:** Before we go home we need to stay in an hotel close to the airport

Outgoing *Voice call with Robin Lulofs (1:33:45 AM)*
Call Ended: 0 hours 2 minutes 24 seconds
Outgoing Voice call with Robin Lulofs (1:36:41 AM)
Call Ended: 0 hours 3 minutes 9 seconds

1:40:16 AM **Robin Lulofs:**

Outgoing Voice call with Robin Lulofs (1:40:15 AM)
Call Ended: 0 hours 4 minutes 43 seconds

1:45:25 AM **ladydi2011**: I am in love with you!!!!
1:45:40 AM **Robin Lulofs**: I am in love with you too baby
1:45:55 AM **Robin Lulofs**: OMG
1:46:06 AM **ladydi2011**: Have a wonderful day my love
1:46:12 AM **Robin Lulofs**: I will my love
1:46:15 AM **ladydi2011**: Yeah baby
1:46:21 AM **Robin Lulofs**: Dream about me Ok?
1:46:25 AM **Robin Lulofs**: Good baby
1:46:27 AM **ladydi2011**: I will honey
1:46:39 AM **ladydi2011**: Visit me in my dreams
1:46:47 AM **Robin Lulofs**: I will my love

Text Messages

From: 260-267-0302
Sent: July 21, 2012 5:23 pm

How are you doing baby??

To: 260-267-0302
Sent: July 21, 2012 5:24 pm

Good, how are you baby?

From: 260-267-0302
Sent: July 21, 2012 5:26 pm

I am fine honey, how was your day? I miss you so much sweetie.

To: 260-267-0302
Sent: July 21, 2012 5:36 pm

Honey, I am not going to be able to chat tonight. I really need to do my work. I hope you understand.

From: 260-267-0302
Sent: July 21, 2012 5:37 pm

Baby .. I love you so much and *i* wish you could see how *i* feel about you right here

To: 260-267-0302
Sent: July 21, 2012 5:40 pm

I know you love me baby...I love you too!

From: 260-267-0302

Sent: July 21, 2012 5:44 pm

baby you are the life that *i* am living. I just can't go on without you in my life.
There's no one like you baby. ***Diana i want you to believe this is true love.*** I love you more
everything baby

To: 260-267-0302
Sent: July 21, 2012 5:59 pm

How was your day baby?

From: 260-267-0302
Sent: July 21, 2012 6:079 pm

Baby...I have looked at your picture so many times today! I cannot wait to look into your eyes, kiss
your lips, hold your hand, feel your arms around me and make love to you all night long....yeah
baby!

IM Jul 22, 2012 1:47:15 AM

1:47:15 AM **Robin Lulofs**: We are One baby
1:47:39 AM **Robin Lulofs**: We are different from others
1:47:48 AM **Robin Lulofs**: We are perfect
1:47:51 AM **ladydi2011**: Yeah baby, we are one
1:48:03 AM **ladydi2011**: Yes, we are different from others
1:48:10 AM **Robin Lulofs**: I love you my wife
1:48:20 AM **ladydi2011**: I love you too my husband
1:48:26 AM **ladydi2011**: Bye for now
1:48:32 AM **Robin Lulofs**: Bye for now baby
1:48:35 AM **Robin Lulofs**: Night

Text Messages

From: 260-267-0302
Sent: July 23, 2012 10:50 am

Hi baby, I miss you, been busy all day fixing things. How are you my love?

To: 260-267-0302
Sent: July 23, 2012 10:52 am

I am better now that I have heard from you... :-)

From: 260-267-0302
Sent: July 23, 2012 10:57 am

Oh my love, where are you and what are you up to?

To: 260-267-0302
Sent: July 23, 2012 11:04 am

Baby, I am in the office...

From: 260-267-0302
Sent: July 23, 2012 11:17 am

Okay baby. I love you!

To: 260-267-0302
Sent: July 23, 2012 11:17 am

I love you too baby!

From: ladydi2011@yahoo.com
To: potty4520@att.net
Subject: Good morning my love...
Sent: Mon, July 23, 2012 7:11:40 AM

Good morning, my love...

How are you this morning? How was your night? I went to sleep and woke up thinking about you. I miss you, Honey!

I am getting ready to leave for the office but wanted to first tell you good morning and that I love you. Have a wonderful day, my love. Please know that you are always on my mind.

Always and forever,
Diana

Text Messages

From: 260-267-0302
Sent: July 23, 2012 4:07 pm

Thanks for the lovely email baby, had a very stressful day. How is your day going?

To: 260-267-0302
Sent: July 23, 2012 4:29 pm

Hi baby. You are welcome! What has you so stressed honey?

From: 260-267-0302
Sent: July 23, 2012 5:14 pm

The whole business things in Qatar. When we chat online I will give you the details. When are you free to chat?

To: 260-267-0302
Sent: July 23, 2012 5:15 pm

Ok...in 2-3 hrs. Will you still be awake?

From: 260-267-0302
Sent: July 23, 2012 5:23 pm

Okay baby. I will stay up for you. Love you!

From: 260-267-0302
Sent: July 23, 2012 9:16 pm

Hi honey...I am now able to come on line. Can you come on line? I miss YOU!

IM Jul 23, 2012 9:23:33 PM

9:23:33 PM **Robin Lulofs**: Hi Honey
9:23:41 PM **ladydi2011**: Hi Honey
9:23:46 PM **ladydi2011**: How are you?
9:23:55 PM **Robin Lulofs**: better now that you're here.
9:23:58 PM **Robin Lulofs**: how are you?
9:24:05 PM **ladydi2011**: Same here baby
9:24:09 PM **ladydi2011**: I am good
9:24:14 PM **Robin Lulofs**: how was your day?
9:24:25 PM **ladydi2011**: Good baby. I still have about 4 hours of work to do
9:24:50 PM **Robin Lulofs**: oh, 4 more hours today?
9:24:59 PM **ladydi2011**: Yeah honey
9:25:04 PM **Robin Lulofs**: wow..
9:25:23 PM **ladydi2011**: So, why was your day so stressed baby?
9:25:42 PM **Robin Lulofs**: *I could not sleep. not really happy, stressed and a lot on my mind.*
9:26:04 PM **Robin Lulofs**: *Well, I got a feed back from the attorney in Qatar, working on my payment.*
9:26:17 PM **ladydi2011**: Ok

9:27:07 PM **Robin Lulofs**: *He was able to submit all the necessary documents, but there is a clearance he needs to obtain on my behalf, he needs to submit the clearance as well, before they give payment approval.*

9:28:21 PM **ladydi2011**: Ok...is he working on this?

9:29:06 PM **Robin Lulofs**: *Yes, he's working on it. He told me we have five working days to get the clearance, before the deadline.*

9:29:28 PM **ladydi2011**: Ok...

9:30:00 PM **Robin Lulofs**: *However, the clearance has to be paid for.*

9:30:44 PM **Robin Lulofs**: *When he told me, I had to send him the funds available with me at the moment; Thought they would take part payment but they did not. I was not happy at all.*

9:32:11 PM **Robin Lulofs**: *I don't know baby. I asked if he could come up with the rest of the fee, but he said he does not have funds right now.*

9:32:36 PM **Robin Lulofs**: I can actually get all the funds paid, but then, I would not meet up with the deadline.

9:33:01 PM **ladydi2011**: Hmmmmm....What are all your options?

9:34:32 PM **Robin Lulofs**: That's why I've been stressed baby.

9:34:44 PM **ladydi2011**: I am sure honey.

9:35:08 PM **ladydi2011**: It would be so nice if life was always easy, but this will never be.

9:36:14 PM **Robin Lulofs**: *You're right. I'm always in control of things like this. But the deadline is close and I already invested so much on the job i have here.*

9:37:08 PM **Robin Lulofs**: *And the Qatar payment is huge. I cannot be non challant about it.*

9:37:21 PM **ladydi2011**: I hear you there

9:37:56 PM **Robin Lulofs**: So, this is what has stressed your baby all day

9:38:36 PM **Robin Lulofs**: I actually feel a bit better now chatting with you. I Love you baby!

9:39:41 PM **Robin Lulofs**: Thank you!

9:39:52 PM **ladydi2011**: I am so glad chatting with me has made you feel better.

9:40:12 PM **ladydi2011**: I love you too baby!

9:40:16 PM **Robin Lulofs**: You're part of me, and I adore you!

9:40:33 PM **ladydi2011**: I know and I love being part of you and you of me.

9:40:49 PM **ladydi2011**: I am so happy you adore me because I adore you too...

9:41:14 PM **Robin Lulofs**: I'm happy you do.. You make me happy.

9:41:44 PM **ladydi2011**: You make me happy too honey.

9:41:57 PM **Robin Lulofs**: So, tell me about your day..

9:42:38 PM **ladydi2011**: Hmmmmm

9:43:08 PM **ladydi2011**: Finalized my eight hr. seminar power point and sent it to the conference coordinator

9:43:56 PM **ladydi2011**: Updated website

9:44:09 PM **ladydi2011**: Trained my intern a little more

9:44:24 PM **ladydi2011**: Did our monthly newsletter

9:44:34 PM **ladydi2011**: Spoke with clients and agents

9:44:55 PM **ladydi2011**: Finally ate for the first time at 3:00 pm and just finished dinner

9:45:09 PM **ladydi2011**: Now, I am chatting with my love

9:45:19 PM **Robin Lulofs**: Great..

9:45:21 PM **ladydi2011**: That's today's rundown honey

9:45:29 PM **Robin Lulofs**: Proud of you baby..

9:45:59 PM **ladydi2011**: Thanks honey

9:46:22 PM **ladydi2011**: You need a nice massage

9:46:39 PM **Robin Lulofs**: YEs I do baby

9:46:45 PM **ladydi2011**: Yeah baby

9:46:57 PM **ladydi2011**: If I was there, you would have one....

9:47:12 PM **Robin Lulofs**: *Well, I hope everything works out. There's no problem though, just have to figure out how to get the clearance.*

9:47:31 PM **ladydi2011**: I am sure it will all work out.

9:47:42 PM **ladydi2011**: Every problem has a solution.

9:47:54 PM **ladydi2011**: Please explain this "clearance" to me.

9:48:21 PM **Robin Lulofs**: Okay baby.

9:51:57 PM **Robin Lulofs**: *the Job was for an oil company in Qatar; After the job was done, they are yet to issue payment because it's over $5m, and some govenrment officials were to inspect the job. All that have been done now, and the payment is ready. But the clearance would be from the ministry of works there in Qatar, just like paying work permit, that is the tax to be paid over the job that has been done to get the payment required.*

9:52:57 PM **Robin Lulofs**: *This clearance would be issued by another body of the same government, to certify that we are entitled for the payment. do you understand baby?*

9:53:40 PM *ladydi2011:* Hmmmmm. I think so but why can't they just deduct the clearance from the money and pay the other body of government?

9:53:53 PM **Robin Lulofs**: *When the clearance fee is paid, the attorney needs the receipt, to tender at the compamny for payment approval.*

9:54:27 PM **Robin Lulofs**: *That is the point, they cannot do it that way. We have to pay for it prior to getting payment.*

9:54:47 PM **ladydi2011**: Ah.....I see. So, how much is this payment?

9:55:19 PM **Robin Lulofs**: *The payment is $52,000*

9:55:58 PM **Robin Lulofs**: *But I already sent $41,000 to the attorney*

9:56:26 PM **ladydi2011**: So, you are $11,000 shy?

9:56:41 PM **Robin Lulofs**: I just had to send him everything I could get this morning, because I don't want anything to go wrong.

9:56:43 PM **Robin Lulofs**: Yes baby.

9:57:18 PM **Robin Lulofs**: *And I thought they would take that as part payment, but they did not.. sadly!*

9:57:19 PM **ladydi2011**: $52,000 is a small amount of money for $5 million

9:58:04 PM **Robin Lulofs**: *That is the way they do things over there. it's a calculated % of the total amount of the expected payment.*

9:58:21 PM **Robin Lulofs**: *You see why I cannot allow small amount to ruin my business?*

9:59:02 PM **Robin Lulofs**: *And when little things like this happens, not funny at all..*

9:59:25 PM **ladydi2011**: I do see honey.

9:59:33 PM **ladydi2011**: No, it is not fun at all.

10:00:02 PM **ladydi2011**: What are your options? Yes, the business strategist in me is surfacing...lol

10:01:37 PM **Robin Lulofs**: *The options I have cannot meet up with the limited time I have. I have about 4 more days. I cannot get funds I want right now, because I have obviously sent what i can at the moment. I have invested so much on the Qatar project, and even the one here in the UK*

10:02:51 PM **Robin Lulofs**: *Well, I know this shouldn't be a problem, 11k.. But I cannot discuss my business life to everyone. You're getting all this info because you are in my life, and I trust and love you very much!*

10:03:35 PM **ladydi2011**: I know baby.

10:03:48 PM **ladydi2011**: I am the same way when I have business issues

10:03:55 PM **ladydi2011**: I am hugging you

10:04:00 PM **ladydi2011**: Can you feel it?

10:04:04 PM **Robin Lulofs**: Yes baby..

10:04:24 PM **Robin Lulofs**: We are just the same. we have a lot in common.

10:04:50 PM **Robin Lulofs**: *What do you think I should do? My brain isn't thinking so much right now..*

10:04:50 PM **ladydi2011**: Yeah, this we do.

10:04:57 PM **Robin Lulofs**: 11k... 4 days..

10:05:12 PM **ladydi2011**: Did you ask your mom?

10:06:08 PM **Robin Lulofs**: Yes I did that already.

10:06:44 PM **Robin Lulofs**: *she could send 10k, added it to the 41k*

10:07:09 PM **Robin Lulofs**: *You have no idea what I've done all day to sort this out.. It was a crazy day baby..*

10:07:42 PM **ladydi2011**: I am sure honey.

10:07:48 PM **Robin Lulofs**: *You know, not everytime one has available cash.. mostly in investments!*

10:08:06 PM **ladydi2011**: This is very true

10:08:23 PM **ladydi2011**: Many times it takes more than 4 days to get access to funds

10:08:47 PM **Robin Lulofs**: *But If i can get the 11k, I will definitely pay it back within 10 working days, even with interest..*

10:09:30 PM **Robin Lulofs**: *I told my attorney that today as well, I know he would have dropped it if he has.. he's a nice person!*

10:09:58 PM **ladydi2011**: He doesn't know any money people who would have it?

10:10:04 PM **ladydi2011**: What about your CPA?

10:11:39 PM **Robin Lulofs**: Qatar/Dubai.. where he is..

10:11:52 PM **Robin Lulofs**: I mean the project Attorney baby.

10:12:16 PM **ladydi2011**: I am talking about your personal CPA here in the states

10:13:07 PM **Robin Lulofs**: *Oh okay. I called him already. trust me... He said he'll need more than 4 days to process anything out for me.*

10:14:24 PM **Robin Lulofs**: *BAby, trust me.. I have done everything possible.*

10:14:57 PM **ladydi2011**: Did you have a stiff drink yet???

10:15:23 PM **Robin Lulofs**: no baby

10:15:50 PM **ladydi2011**: I think this would be what I would have done...

10:15:54 PM **ladydi2011**: Yikes!

10:15:57 PM **ladydi2011**: Lol

10:16:04 PM **Robin Lulofs**: lol

10:16:29 PM **Robin Lulofs**: I love you!

10:16:51 PM **ladydi2011**: I love you too!

10:17:05 PM **ladydi2011**: I am here for you.

10:17:11 PM **Robin Lulofs**: Thank you baby.

10:18:09 PM **Robin Lulofs**: So, that's what happened today!

10:18:33 PM **ladydi2011**: A lot of stress my love

10:18:35 PM **Robin Lulofs**: despite all, you have been on my mind all day

10:19:25 PM **ladydi2011**: I am so glad I have been on your mind all day

10:19:37 PM **ladydi2011**: I hope they were good thoughts that brought a smile to your face, joy to your heart and somehow lessened your stress

10:21:07 PM **ladydi2011**: You have been on my mind all day too

10:21:17 PM **Robin Lulofs**: Yes baby

10:21:25 PM **Robin Lulofs**: always good thoughts about you.

10:21:39 PM **Robin Lulofs**: You bring joy to my hearts and smile to my face.

10:21:58 PM **Robin Lulofs**: You have my love always and forever darling!

10:22:19 PM **ladydi2011**: And you have mine.

10:24:28 PM **Robin Lulofs**: I'm smiling here...

10:24:47 PM **Robin Lulofs**: I know I'll sleep well tonight. I could not sleep earlier. depressed much!

10:24:47 PM **ladydi2011**: Good honey. I am sure it is the first time for you all day.

10:24:56 PM **Robin Lulofs**: yes baby

10:24:59 PM **ladydi2011**: I am glad it is me making you smile.

10:25:38 PM **ladydi2011**: I showed my intern your picture and she said, she wanted to pick you up from the airport

10:25:50 PM **ladydi2011**: She thinks your hot baby

10:26:00 PM **ladydi2011**: I told her, I know you are hot!

10:26:11 PM **Robin Lulofs**: haha...Thanks baby..

10:26:20 PM **Robin Lulofs**: Hot for you only!

10:26:27 PM **ladydi2011**: You should be flattered because she is only 28

10:26:37 PM **ladydi2011**: Awww, thanks honey

10:26:53 PM **ladydi2011**: Are you sure you don't want a 28 yr. old baby?

10:27:10 PM **Robin Lulofs**: haha... Sorry I DON'T

10:27:21 PM **Robin Lulofs**: I'm taken!

10:27:29 PM **ladydi2011**: Ok....well, still be flattered darling

10:27:39 PM **ladydi2011**: Thank you baby

10:27:39 PM **Robin Lulofs**: well, I am,,

10:27:46 PM **ladydi2011**: Yes, you are taken

10:27:47 PM **Robin Lulofs**: I Love my baby! No one can change that..

10:28:42 PM **Robin Lulofs**: *You will fully understand the strength of the love i have for you when I'm home baby.*

10:28:46 PM **ladydi2011**: You are racking up the point my love

10:29:09 PM **Robin Lulofs**: oh, what is the point? lol

10:29:17 PM **ladydi2011**: Lol...Just teasing you honey

10:29:32 PM **ladydi2011**: Trying to make you laugh

10:29:45 PM **ladydi2011**: But she really did think you are hot

10:29:56 PM **ladydi2011**: And I know you are hot and all MINE

10:30:13 PM **ladydi2011**: I like that you are all MINE

10:30:21 PM **Robin Lulofs**: I've been laughing..

10:30:23 PM **ladydi2011**: I do NOT share my man

10:30:34 PM **Robin Lulofs**: And I do not share my woman too..

10:30:35 PM **ladydi2011**: Not in this lifetime!!!!

10:30:42 PM **Robin Lulofs**: You are all mine!!!

10:30:49 PM **ladydi2011**: You will never have too my love

10:30:57 PM **ladydi2011**: I am all yours!!!

10:32:40 PM **Robin Lulofs**: Thank you my love!

10:32:52 PM **ladydi2011**: I love you baby!

10:33:22 PM **ladydi2011**: When you come home, you will realize just how much I love you

10:33:29 PM **ladydi2011**: I promise you this!

10:33:54 PM **Robin Lulofs**: I know baby.

10:34:13 PM **Robin Lulofs**: But I know you love me, I feel it. You are so loving, caring and always there for me.

10:34:26 PM **ladydi2011**: Yeah baby

10:34:40 PM **Robin Lulofs**: *I will always be there for you too. Anytime and however you may need me. I will not let you down or disappoint you..*

10:34:48 PM **Robin Lulofs**: *I promise you this!*

10:35:23 PM **ladydi2011**: Thank you my love.

10:35:37 PM **ladydi2011**: I will not let you down or disappoint you either.

10:37:10 PM **ladydi2011**: You still with me honey?

10:37:51 PM **Robin Lulofs**: Yes *i* am baby

10:38:07 PM **Robin Lulofs**: Thank you my love

10:38:10 PM **ladydi2011**: Are you ok my love?

10:38:27 PM **Robin Lulofs**: Yes baby.. (to some extent)

10:38:36 PM **Robin Lulofs**: I will be fine my love..

10:38:42 PM **ladydi2011**: I knew this...

10:39:14 PM **ladydi2011**: Even though you are miles away I can feel what is going on with you.

10:39:57 PM **Robin Lulofs**: I know baby. You know me so much!

10:40:14 PM **ladydi2011**: Yes my love, I do.

10:41:54 PM **ladydi2011**: So, there is something else you are pondering, what is it?

10:43:10 PM **Robin Lulofs**: Nothing baby, I've told you everything. If anything else comes up, I will surely tell you.

10:43:20 PM **ladydi2011**: Ok honey.

10:43:35 PM **ladydi2011**: Thanks for sharing everything with me.

10:43:47 PM **Robin Lulofs**: Thanks for giving me options on what to do..You're a darling..

10:44:12 PM **ladydi2011**: Yeah, but none of them were workable for you. For this, I feel bad.

10:44:30 PM **Robin Lulofs**: I know, but they are good options honey.

10:44:41 PM **Robin Lulofs**: Please don't feel bad. not your fault my love!

10:44:59 PM **ladydi2011**: Ok, honey. I trust your abilities to handle things. I know you will come up with the solution. This is also why I trust you to be my man

10:46:45 PM **Robin Lulofs**: Thank you my baby.

10:46:57 PM **Robin Lulofs**: I will try other options tomorrow.

10:47:23 PM **Robin Lulofs**: I'm sure things will work out.

10:47:32 PM **ladydi2011**: I am sure they will

10:48:28 PM **ladydi2011**: Hey baby

10:48:53 PM **Robin Lulofs**: YEs baby

10:49:06 PM **ladydi2011**: I so admire you

10:49:21 PM **Robin Lulofs**: Thanks honey. You're so sweet!!!

10:49:32 PM **ladydi2011**: Did you know that for me admiration has to be there for me to love you

10:49:49 PM **Robin Lulofs**: Oh yeah..I'm smiling here. I'm a lucky man

10:50:20 PM **Robin Lulofs**: I've always known I deserve the best

10:50:27 PM **ladydi2011**: Yes, my love. You are the luckiest man in the universe

10:51:04 PM **ladydi2011**: You do deserve the best. I am the best for you...

10:52:24 PM **Robin Lulofs**: I Love you!

10:52:31 PM **Robin Lulofs**: We are BEST together!

10:52:35 PM **Robin Lulofs**: nothing can beat us..

10:52:49 PM **ladydi2011**: This is true baby

10:53:33 PM **ladydi2011**: Baby, you must be tired. It is 4 am there

10:54:15 PM **Robin Lulofs**: Yes baby I should rest now..

10:55:09 PM **Robin Lulofs**: Then take off with some plans tomorrow. Hopefully everything works out. I will keep you posted anyway...

10:55:53 PM **ladydi2011**: When you close your eyes, you will feel me softly kiss your eyelids, and then you will feel me kiss your cheek, and then your lips and then you will sleep like a baby...

10:56:15 PM **Robin Lulofs**: Thank you baby. I'm sure I will..

10:56:40 PM **Robin Lulofs**: Yes my baby..

10:56:59 PM **Robin Lulofs**: When are you going to bed though?

10:57:27 PM **ladydi2011**: In about 2 hours....Even though I have 4 hours of work to do.

10:57:40 PM **ladydi2011**: I do not think my brain can do 4 more hours honey. I feel pretty fried

10:58:06 PM **Robin Lulofs**: okay honey

10:58:16 PM **Robin Lulofs**: Goodnight..

10:58:25 PM **Robin Lulofs**: I Love you !!!

10:58:26 PM **ladydi2011**: Goodnight honey

10:58:39 PM **ladydi2011**: I Love You!!!

10:58:53 PM **Robin Lulofs**: Thank you for everything!

10:58:54 PM **ladydi2011**: Keep me posted

10:58:59 PM **Robin Lulofs**: I appreciate and adore you!

10:59:14 PM **ladydi2011**: I appreciate and cherish you my love.

10:59:14 PM **Robin Lulofs**: Sure, I will baby!

10:59:23 PM **ladydi2011**: Bye for now honey

10:59:48 PM **Robin Lulofs**: hugs and kisses!

11:00:04 PM **ladydi2011**: Hugs and kisses

He continues to try to make me feel like I will be his *wife* by asking if I will change my last name to Lulofs. He then adds more guilt when he says, "I will hurt myself if you ever hurt me baby." He talks about us planning our life together and then he tells me "you are all I am living for," and makes me promise I will never go anywhere. He again says, "This is a sign of good will..I see success," and "You can trust me."

RED FLAGS

- 🚩 When I ask about college and his degree, there is a break in time and he claims his computer is acting up. I am sure this is because he had to go research the answer. Watch for things like this.
- 🚩 He tells me his son is excited to have me as his mom and his mother is happy for him. Many scammers bring others into the story so they can use them to manipulate you. There is NO son and NO mother.
- 🚩 He talks about "fate". Most scammers say meeting you is fate or destiny. This is another ploy to draw you closer to them and for you to believe this relationship is real and meant to be.
- 🚩 I have not counted the times this man has told me "I will not hurt you" and "trust me," but I know it has been an excessive number of times. If someone tells you this so many times,

you should know they WILL hurt you and you CANNOT trust them.
- We met on June 27th and by July 23rd he has a money problem. I am sure he would have had a money problem much sooner if I didn't take so long to tell him that I was in love with him. I really want you to see how this works.
- The scammer's job is to get you to trust them and fall in love with them so they can ask for money.
- Once you have fallen in love, they promise to be with you and try to get you to feel like their wife.
- They make you promise things they can manipulate you with if you don't want to give them money.
- Almost immediately after the above three things have been achieved they will have a money problem and ask you for money.
- If you remember all the red flags I pointed out, you will see where everything fits into the scam for money. Do you remember when he said he had to feel comfortable to tell me things? The reason he said that was so he could tell me he had a money problem.
- If you really read what he says about why he needs the money, it makes no sense. However, if you were in love with this man and caught in his web of love, you wouldn't even notice that it makes no sense. I give him ideas for a solution to his money problem, but I never offer financial help. He makes sure to tell me he has exhausted all his resources and that he still needs 11K and he will pay it back within 10 working days with interest. HE WILL NEVER PAY IT BACK!

Text Messages

From: 260-267-0302
Sent: July 24, 2012 1:22 pm

Baby, are you okay? Haven't heard from you!

To: 260-267-0302
Sent: July 24, 2012 1:24 pm

Hi baby...I am ok.

From: 260-267-0302
Sent: July 24, 2012 1:24 pm

How are you today my love? Did you find a solution yet?

From: 260-267-0302
Sent: July 24, 2012 1:57 pm

No solution darling. How are you?

To: 260-267-0302

Sent: July 24, 2012 1:58 pm

Tired baby. Didn't sleep well!

From: 260-267-0302
Sent: July 24, 2012 2:01 pm

Oh my love, sorry dear. Are you free to chat now or busy?

To: 260-267-0302
Sent: July 24, 2012 2:13 pm

Driving baby. I will text you when I get back to the office...kisses

From: 260-267-0302
Sent: July 24, 2012 2:31 pm

Hi honey, I met with some people but no luck. Sad!

From: 260-267-0302
Sent: July 24, 2012 7:57 pm

Hi love...are you still awake? I am on line now. I really want to chat with you baby.

To: 260-267-0302
Sent: July 24, 2012 8:53 pm

Ok baby. Meet you there!

IM Jul 24, 2012 8:56:21 PM

8:56:21 PM **Robin Lulofs**: Are you there?
8:56:35 PM **Ladydi2011**: I am
8:56:43 PM **Robin Lulofs**: Hi baby
8:56:57 PM **Ladydi2011**: Did you sleep a little?
8:56:58 PM **Robin Lulofs**: waited for you for so long, wondering where you were..
8:57:09 PM **Robin Lulofs**: not really. Can't really sleep you know..
8:57:39 PM **Ladydi2011**: Had a lot of client calls late in the day who are on the west coast
8:57:53 PM **Robin Lulofs**: Oh okay.
8:58:18 PM **Ladydi2011**: So sorry to keep you waiting my love.
8:58:37 PM **Ladydi2011**: It was not intentional.
8:59:04 PM **Ladydi2011**: There is nowhere I would rather be than with you!
8:59:16 PM **Robin Lulofs**: It's okay honey.
8:59:21 PM **Robin Lulofs**: I understand you're busy.
9:00:00 PM **Robin Lulofs**: I miss you!
9:00:32 PM **Ladydi2011**: Thank you for your understanding baby

9:00:46 PM **Ladydi2011**: I miss you too

9:01:15 PM **Robin Lulofs**: You're welcome my love.

9:01:36 PM **Robin Lulofs**: Day wasn't good for me, but you didn't leave my mind.

9:02:24 PM **Ladydi2011**: I like that I am always on your mind and that you are always on mine.

9:02:39 PM **Ladydi2011**: This is how it should be

9:02:57 PM **Robin Lulofs**: Yes baby.

9:03:38 PM **Ladydi2011**: I read all your text and in the one you said you have still not found a solution.

9:03:54 PM **Robin Lulofs**: Yes..sadly!

9:04:34 PM **Ladydi2011**: Baby, I know you have to be beside yourself.

9:05:52 PM **Ladydi2011**: Are you there baby?

9:05:56 PM **Robin Lulofs**: I'm here

9:06:41 PM **Robin Lulofs**: *Well, I called the attorney there today, I told him I'm still on it, trying to get funds to him. But he reminded me of the deadline, and i told him I'm aware.*

9:06:45 PM **Ladydi2011**: You are to quiet my love

9:07:33 PM **Robin Lulofs**: *Your baby is not very happy darling. Do you have an idea how i can get some funds, to be paid back within 10 days. This is what I have been thinking most of the day.*

9:08:52 PM **Ladydi2011**: I know you are not honey. I know this is the main thought on your mind. This is a lot of money at stake!

9:09:22 PM **Robin Lulofs**: Yes, a lot of money at stake baby! my mind can't get out of it.

9:09:54 PM **Ladydi2011**: I am sure.

9:10:34 PM **Robin Lulofs**: Well..

9:11:02 PM **Ladydi2011**: I am thinking baby!

9:11:50 PM **Ladydi2011**: When is your deadline again?

9:11:57 PM **Robin Lulofs**: friday

9:13:13 PM **Ladydi2011**: This silence is not good baby

9:13:59 PM **Ladydi2011**: Are you asking me for the money baby?

9:14:23 PM **Robin Lulofs**: You asked when my deadline is, and *i* told you honey..

9:14:28 PM **Robin Lulofs**: I said friday..

9:16:38 PM **Ladydi2011**: Ok...baby, I gave you my ideas the other night. But you already worked all of them.

9:16:54 PM **Robin Lulofs**: Yes that's true

9:17:41 PM **Robin Lulofs**: *I did not ask you for the money. I do not know how you will feel about it. I just ask how you think I can get the funds and would pay it back within 10 days.*

9:19:02 PM **Robin Lulofs**: *Anything i do, I will always consider your feelings. I wouldn't want anything to destroy the love we have. And the beautiful relationship we have. You understand? But then, you know the thought of a man in a tight situation, I hope you understand me baby..*

9:20:18 PM **Ladydi2011**: I do know honey.

9:21:20 PM **Ladydi2011**: I am so glad you think about our relationship and the love we have. I do too!

9:22:01 PM **Robin Lulofs**: I always think about it. I Love you so much Diana!

9:22:43 PM **Ladydi2011**: I love you too Robin.

9:24:09 PM **Robin Lulofs**: I will always love you.

9:24:23 PM **Ladydi2011**: Honey, I don't even know if I can get you the $11,000 by Friday or how much the penalty would be or how I would get it from here to there...

9:25:39 PM **Robin Lulofs**: *What penalty is that honey? I will be very happy if you can get it to me. It will solve the problem and I will appreciate it so much, and WILL NOT disappoint you.*

9:26:06 PM **Robin Lulofs**: But about getting it here or Dubai; I can confirm that tomorrow.
9:27:25 PM **Ladydi2011**: There is a penalty to remove it from my acct.
9:27:42 PM **Robin Lulofs**: Oh okay. Would you find out what the penalty is and let me know.
9:27:51 PM **Ladydi2011**: Please check where I would have to send it.
9:27:51 PM **Robin Lulofs**: Paying the penalty will not be a problem.
9:28:22 PM **Robin Lulofs**: Okay honey. Thank You! I will find out in the morning and let you know
9:29:11 PM **Ladydi2011**: Ok baby. Please get some rest now.
9:29:23 PM **Robin Lulofs**: I will darling.
9:29:28 PM **Robin Lulofs**: You want to get busy?
9:30:34 PM **Ladydi2011**: I am actually really tired tonight too baby.
9:30:42 PM **Robin Lulofs**: Okay my Love.
9:30:51 PM **Ladydi2011**: I did not sleep well last night.
9:31:04 PM **Robin Lulofs**: Oh, what's wrong?
9:32:11 PM **Ladydi2011**: Just having a hard time shutting my mind down...
9:32:38 PM **Robin Lulofs**: Oh honey. A good massage would be good now, what do you think?
9:33:23 PM **Ladydi2011**: Yeah, for both of us!!!
9:33:39 PM **Robin Lulofs**: you're right.
9:34:23 PM **Ladydi2011**: I so wish you were here!
9:34:52 PM **Robin Lulofs**: ME too baby
9:35:04 PM **Robin Lulofs**: I will hold you so close to myself, and hug you so tight.
9:35:24 PM **Ladydi2011**: I know I would sleep like a baby in your arms....
9:35:58 PM **Ladydi2011**: What time is it there baby?
9:36:12 PM **Robin Lulofs**: I know baby..
9:36:48 PM **Robin Lulofs**: 2:36 am baby
9:37:08 PM **Robin Lulofs**: have you had dinner?
9:37:23 PM **Ladydi2011**: It is late. Please get some sleep honey.
9:37:34 PM **Ladydi2011**: Some fruit baby.
9:38:14 PM **Robin Lulofs**: Okay baby.
9:38:25 PM **Robin Lulofs**: Goodnight my Love.
9:38:44 PM **Robin Lulofs**: *Thanks for bringing smile to my face. I LOVE YOU!*
9:39:08 PM **Ladydi2011**: You're welcome
9:39:18 PM **Robin Lulofs**: Dream about me..
9:39:19 PM **Ladydi2011**: I love you too!
9:40:04 PM **Robin Lulofs**: Goodnight!
9:40:11 PM **Robin Lulofs**: sweet dream..
9:40:14 PM **Ladydi2011**: Night sweetheart

IM Jul 25, 2012 12:04:33 PM

12:04:33 PM **Robin Lulofs**: Hi baby
12:14:28 PM **Robin Lulofs**: I'm here honey, let me know when you're here
12:14:30 PM **Robin Lulofs**: <ding>

IM Jul 25, 2012 12:32:05 PM

12:32:05 PM **ladydi2011**: Hi baby
12:32:30 PM **ladydi2011**: How are you?
12:32:57 PM **Robin Lulofs**: Hi my love
12:33:02 PM **Robin Lulofs**: fine thank you
12:33:40 PM **ladydi2011**: Did you sleep well?
12:34:28 PM **Robin Lulofs**: Yes *i* did honey.
12:34:31 PM **Robin Lulofs**: Did you?
12:34:44 PM **ladydi2011**: I did
12:34:58 PM **ladydi2011**: Did you have dinner yet honey?
12:35:41 PM **Robin Lulofs**: not yet baby, *i* will later
12:36:00 PM **Robin Lulofs**: what have you been up to?
12:36:20 PM **ladydi2011**: Working baby
12:36:38 PM **Robin Lulofs**: okay.
12:36:45 PM **Robin Lulofs**: Good day?
12:37:37 PM **ladydi2011**: Yeah honey
12:37:51 PM **Robin Lulofs**: That's great
12:37:54 PM **Robin Lulofs**: I love you!
12:38:24 PM **ladydi2011**: I love you too baby
12:40:39 PM **Robin Lulofs**: You're so sweet
12:41:10 PM **ladydi2011**: So are you my love
12:41:25 PM **ladydi2011**: So, what did you find out for me?
12:42:30 PM **Robin Lulofs**: *I got the info from the Attorney in Dubai, you can wire directly to a bank account, and he will get it. that's the same account i sent the amount to.*
12:42:59 PM **Robin Lulofs**: It takes 24 hours, which is actually fast.
12:43:15 PM **ladydi2011**: Ok
12:43:19 PM **Robin Lulofs**: Yes baby, so, I have the account details.
12:44:04 PM **ladydi2011**: Will you please email the details to me
12:44:15 PM **Robin Lulofs**: Yes honey. I will do that now
12:44:21 PM **ladydi2011**: So this is a bank to bank transfer, is this correct?
12:44:33 PM **Robin Lulofs**: Yes baby.
12:45:52 PM **ladydi2011**: Ok
12:46:18 PM **ladydi2011**: Honey, they are going to charge me a 20% penalty for withdrawing this money now
12:46:30 PM **Robin Lulofs**: Okay baby.
12:46:48 PM **Robin Lulofs**: *I will pay the penalty*
12:47:10 PM **Robin Lulofs**: that's about $2500 i guess..
12:47:27 PM **ladydi2011**: $2,200
12:48:28 PM **Robin Lulofs**: Okay.
12:48:43 PM **Robin Lulofs**: I just sent the info, please check it out darling.
12:49:51 PM **ladydi2011**: I received it

From: Robin Lulofs
To: Ladydi2011@yahoo.com
Subject: Info...
Sent: Wed, Jul 25, 2012 at 12:48 PM

Baby, here's the info:

Bank Name: ABU DHABI COMMERCIAL BANK
Branch: JEBEL ALI BRANCH, DUBAI, U.A.E
Account Name: LATEEF ABDUL LAWAL
Account No: 966552208001
Bank Swift code: ADCBAEAA
IBAN: AF980030000966552208001
Account holder's address: 10, Al rasheed road, dubai, UAE

Thank you my love, I appreciate this so much!

IM Jul 25, 2012 12:50:07 PM

12:50:07 PM **ladydi2011**: I will not beable to do this until tomorrow or Friday morning
12:50:51 PM **Robin Lulofs**: *Okay honey..Thank you!*
12:51:18 PM **ladydi2011**: You are welcome honey
12:51:29 PM **Robin Lulofs**: *Kindly let me know as soon as it's done; So I can contact the attorney.*
12:52:51 PM **Robin Lulofs**: baby, are you there?
12:53:21 PM **ladydi2011**: I will do this
12:53:38 PM **Robin Lulofs**: *Thanks..*
12:54:32 PM **ladydi2011**: So, what do you still need to do today?
12:55:49 PM **Robin Lulofs**: Dinner, send a business email to an investor, talk to my love, watch tv,

12:56:25 PM **Robin Lulofs**: If you're right beside me now, I would have added other things 😊
12:56:52 PM **ladydi2011**: Sounds good honey
12:57:08 PM **ladydi2011**: What will you have for dinner?
12:57:52 PM **Robin Lulofs**: fries, and chicken, may be..
12:57:59 PM **Robin Lulofs**: What are you doing today?
12:58:19 PM **ladydi2011**: Sounds good
12:58:42 PM **ladydi2011**: I need to get back to work and then in 3 hours go get my hair done
12:58:53 PM **Robin Lulofs**: Oh okay.
12:59:06 PM **Robin Lulofs**: And you need to get lunch too, right?
12:59:18 PM **ladydi2011**: Yes, I do need to get lunch
12:59:27 PM **Robin Lulofs**: Okay my Love,
12:59:33 PM **Robin Lulofs**: I guess we will chat later then.
12:59:41 PM **ladydi2011**: Ok
12:59:48 PM **Robin Lulofs**: Let me know when you're free to chat. I love and miss you baby
12:59:48 PM **ladydi2011**: Enjoy your evening

1:00:02 PM **ladydi2011**: I love and miss you too
1:00:12 PM **Robin Lulofs**: Have a lovely day... kisses!
1:00:21 PM **ladydi2011**: You too baby
1:00:26 PM **ladydi2011**: Kisses and hugs
1:00:43 PM **Robin Lulofs**: bye for now baby
1:00:59 PM **ladydi2011**: Bye for now

From: Robin Lulofs
To: ladydi2011@yahoo.com
Subject: Re: Good morning my love...
Sent: Wed, Jul 25, 2012 at 9:08 AM

Morning Baby,

How are you my baby, I hope you slept well today? Let me start by saying that I thank God every night since I found you. You came into my life when everything seemed dark but you provided the light to find my way in every ways. I've never been so certain of anything in my life like I am of us, you have actually changed my outlook in life and I thank you for that. I feel as if I'm walking over clouds just thinking about you because you make my life complete honey.There are no words to express how I feel about you, I guess I have said it all to you, I constantly search for the words, and they all seem less than I truly feel. You are my life, my heart, and my soul, you are my best friend and you are my one and only true love. I am happy you're mine and happy I'm yours, this is how it will be always and forever sweetheart.

In this short time that we've been together, we have grown so much and I can't wait to experience the amazing things the future holds for us, because *i* know we have a very bright future together. I love you darling with all my heart and soul, I tell you this everyday (I know) because it's never too much, you are the most loving and caring person I know, inside and out and I see that more clearly with each passing day. I love everything about you, about us. You do something to me that no other has, you have made me so happy, the happiest I've ever been. You give me the most amazing feelings inside, the feeling of being in love and being loved at the same time; That's a wonderful feeling you know!

I've said it before and I'll say it again, words cannot express how you make me feel. I make this promise to you my dear, to love you the way that you love me. I now look to the future and forget the past, ***your life is mine, and mine is yours*** and we will make it last forever. I love you more today than I did yesterday, and I'll love you more tomorrow than I do today. I can actually write you how *i* feel about you all day without getting tired or bored, but *i* have to go now, get some info and some errands, Please text me when you're up, I will be back soon.

Your baby,
Robin

10:40:31 PM **Ladydi2011**: Hi baby

10:40:39 PM **Ladydi2011**: How was your day?

10:41:02 PM **Robin Lulofs**: Hi baby, it was fine honey

10:41:11 PM **Robin Lulofs**: How was yours? I guess it was a busy day for you.

10:41:56 PM **Ladydi2011**: I am glad your day was good!

10:42:08 PM **Ladydi2011**: Mine was busy honey.

10:42:26 PM **Robin Lulofs**: *Thanks to you honey, contacted the attorney, that everything is fine now.*

10:43:19 PM **Ladydi2011**: Good baby. I am glad everything is fine for you now.

10:44:01 PM **Robin Lulofs**: *I really appreciate your support darling. Thank you!*

10:44:23 PM **Ladydi2011**: Much to prepare for with speaking in front of hundreds of people

10:45:05 PM **Robin Lulofs**: I understand that.

10:45:13 PM **Robin Lulofs**: I know it will be a success!

10:45:46 PM **Ladydi2011**: Yeah, I am sure it will

10:46:59 PM **Ladydi2011**: You do know you are in love with a very charismatic woman, right?

10:47:33 PM **Robin Lulofs**: Yes *i* know baby.

10:47:44 PM **Robin Lulofs**: Not only that.. Very smart, loving and caring!!!

10:47:57 PM **Ladydi2011**: Thank you baby, you are so kind...

10:48:12 PM **Robin Lulofs**: I Love you baby, and proud of you!

10:48:35 PM **Ladydi2011**: I love you too and am proud of you too!

10:48:46 PM **Ladydi2011**: We make a great team!

10:49:19 PM **Robin Lulofs**: Yes we do my Love.

10:50:33 PM **Robin Lulofs**: So, tell me about your trip. When do you leave? You're ready, right?

10:50:53 PM **Ladydi2011**: I leave Wednesday morning. I am ready.

10:52:11 PM **Ladydi2011**: I have been training since January and every 2 weeks I need new clothes. I keep shrinking in size...

10:52:43 PM **Ladydi2011**: However, I always remain proportioned.

10:52:58 PM **Ladydi2011**: Goal is 36/26/36

10:53:27 PM **Ladydi2011**: Right now I am 38/28/38

10:53:41 PM **Ladydi2011**: 6 more inches and I will be happy!

10:53:46 PM **Robin Lulofs**: Oh, does that mean you'll have to get new clothes

10:53:59 PM **Ladydi2011**: I have a kick ass personal trainer

10:54:20 PM **Robin Lulofs**: That's nice. All for me right?

10:55:02 PM **Ladydi2011**: For me and for you. I want to look my best...

10:55:35 PM **Robin Lulofs**: You're a sweetheart.

10:55:39 PM **Ladydi2011**: You are sexy!

10:55:46 PM **Robin Lulofs**: You will always be best in my arm baby.

10:55:56 PM **Robin Lulofs**: Thank you.. I Love you baby!

10:55:58 PM **Ladydi2011**: Yeah, I know!

10:56:08 PM **Ladydi2011**: I love you too!

10:56:53 PM **Ladydi2011**: So please tell me more about your day honey.

10:58:18 PM **Robin Lulofs**: I met with some investors here. You know I have not been fully involved with the job going on here for couple of days. My mind has been occupied by the payment in Dubai.

10:59:14 PM **Robin Lulofs**: After we talked online, I sent messages out to them, and we are meeting tomorrow. Then I contacted the Attorney in Dubai, that the funds will be wired tomorrow or next.

643

10:59:36 PM **Ladydi2011**: Ok...what did he say?

11:00:05 PM **Robin Lulofs**: However, you know you're on my mind all day. You have no idea what you have done for me, I really appreciate it. I just want to hold you tight and kiss you.

11:00:34 PM **Ladydi2011**: I would like this...for real!!!

11:00:40 PM **Robin Lulofs**: He said great. And he told me to let him know as sooon as it's wired so he can get the funds, and go for the payment rightaway

11:00:56 PM **Ladydi2011**: Ok

11:01:08 PM **Ladydi2011**: Honey, I have a request...

11:02:02 PM **Robin Lulofs**: Okay, what is it?

11:02:27 PM **Ladydi2011**: I really need to see you on cam.

11:03:05 PM **Robin Lulofs**: okay baby

11:03:15 PM **Ladydi2011**: I know you can make this happen.

11:03:31 PM **Robin Lulofs**: Sure I can baby.

11:04:06 PM **Ladydi2011**: You rock my love

11:04:35 PM **Ladydi2011**: I miss you SO much!

11:04:41 PM **Robin Lulofs**: I miss you too baby

11:05:34 PM **Ladydi2011**: I can't wait to be in your arms

11:06:43 PM **Robin Lulofs**: I can't wait to have you in my arms. I want to look into your eyes, and tell you how much I love you!

11:06:44 PM **Ladydi2011**: Are you sleeping off on me baby?

11:06:56 PM **Robin Lulofs**: No baby, I'm here

11:07:02 PM **Robin Lulofs**: Where are you?

11:07:12 PM **Ladydi2011**: You must be reading my mind.

11:07:28 PM **Ladydi2011**: In bed

11:07:43 PM **Ladydi2011**: Where are you honey?

11:08:18 PM **Robin Lulofs**: Okay

11:08:30 PM **Robin Lulofs**: bed..

11:08:54 PM **Robin Lulofs**: I was sleeping before *i* got your message

11:09:06 PM **Robin Lulofs**: You know I love to hear from you..

11:09:17 PM **Ladydi2011**: Are you on your phone or laptop?

11:09:30 PM **Ladydi2011**: I am so sorry to wake you...

11:09:40 PM **Robin Lulofs**: It's okay baby.

11:09:55 PM **Ladydi2011**: Well, really not...I had to chat with you

11:10:07 PM **Robin Lulofs**: I like that

11:10:31 PM **Ladydi2011**: Yeah...do you like being woke up?

11:10:59 PM **Robin Lulofs**: To everyone, NO..To my Love, Yes.

11:11:20 PM **Ladydi2011**: Nice!

11:11:33 PM **Robin Lulofs**: I was actually expecting to hear from you because *i* did not all day

11:11:46 PM **Robin Lulofs**: So, *i* was ready for it, *lol*

11:11:49 PM **Ladydi2011**: I promise there will always be a nice payoff for you if I wake you.

11:12:02 PM **Robin Lulofs**: You were on my mind before *i* fell asleep

11:12:21 PM **Robin Lulofs**: haha, I like that. You should wake me up everyday then...

11:12:42 PM **Ladydi2011**: Lol.. I will remember this

11:13:09 PM **Ladydi2011**: Honey, I am very playful!!!

11:13:17 PM **Robin Lulofs**: You should..If you ever forget, I will remind you

11:13:27 PM **Ladydi2011**: Lol

11:14:05 PM **Ladydi2011**: I can't wait to undress you...very slowly

11:14:37 PM **Ladydi2011**: Opppps. Did I just say this?

11:14:40 PM **Robin Lulofs**: I love that

11:14:44 PM **Robin Lulofs**: Ha! go on baby...

11:14:56 PM **Robin Lulofs**: You're bad tonight.. I like that!

11:15:09 PM **Ladydi2011**: First your jacket

11:15:51 PM **Ladydi2011**: If you remember on my profile I said a sharp dressed man turns me on...this is very true!

11:16:00 PM **Ladydi2011**: You dress so sharp!

11:16:27 PM **Robin Lulofs**: Yes baby, Thank you!

11:16:27 PM **Ladydi2011**: Every time I look at your picture I fantasize about undressing you!!!

11:16:46 PM **Robin Lulofs**: Wow.. I think you'll do a good job by doing that. haha

11:17:30 PM **Ladydi2011**: Once your jacket is off, I just might have to massage your shoulders

11:17:58 PM **Ladydi2011**: Then I will have to slowly remove your tie...

11:18:32 PM **Ladydi2011**: Hmmmm...What could I do with the tie once I remove it?

11:19:00 PM **Ladydi2011**: My imagination is roaming on this one and I hope yours is too.

11:19:12 PM **Robin Lulofs**: haha, I know right

11:19:21 PM **Robin Lulofs**: But go on and tell me, what you'll do..

11:19:23 PM **Robin Lulofs**: lol

11:19:42 PM **Ladydi2011**: Then I will have to kiss you deeply and passionately

11:20:54 PM **Ladydi2011**: Next I will have to unbutton your shirt and kiss your neck

11:21:00 PM **Robin Lulofs**: I love that baby

11:22:44 PM **Ladydi2011**: Hmmmm...I would love to go further

11:22:47 PM **Robin Lulofs**: and when you kiss me there, the response is very high.. lol

11:22:48 PM **Ladydi2011**: But...

11:23:23 PM **Ladydi2011**: I do not want to ruin what I have planned for you when we are in person

11:23:24 PM **Robin Lulofs**: Now I'm thinking so much what I want to do to you baby

11:23:33 PM **Robin Lulofs**: Oh yeah? 😊

11:23:42 PM **Ladydi2011**: Please share with me...

11:24:43 PM **Robin Lulofs**: It should be secret baby

11:24:50 PM **Robin Lulofs**: I don't want to give you hint...

11:24:57 PM **Ladydi2011**: No fair!!!!

11:24:58 PM **Robin Lulofs**: 😊 haha!

11:25:17 PM **Ladydi2011**: Hmmmm

11:25:28 PM **Robin Lulofs**: Yes baby

11:25:29 PM **Ladydi2011**: I see how you play!

11:25:43 PM **Robin Lulofs**: But you will love everything I'll do to you my love

11:26:18 PM **Ladydi2011**: I am sure I will!

11:26:50 PM **Robin Lulofs**: I love you my baby, so much!

11:27:01 PM **Robin Lulofs**: I'm sure you have an idea how much I do, right?

11:27:15 PM **Ladydi2011**: I love you too!

11:27:31 PM **Ladydi2011**: Yes honey. I have an idea.

11:28:07 PM **Robin Lulofs**: I will always love you..

11:28:17 PM **Robin Lulofs**: Take note of that darling..

11:28:36 PM **Ladydi2011**: Note taken!

11:28:53 PM **Ladydi2011**: Please do not break my heart...

11:29:06 PM **Robin Lulofs**: *I will never break your heart. I promise, with my life!*

11:29:37 PM **Ladydi2011**: I am now deeply seeded into your heart baby

11:29:55 PM **Robin Lulofs**: I will take care of your heart always.

11:30:06 PM **Ladydi2011**: Even if you leave me, you will NEVER forget me...

11:30:30 PM **Robin Lulofs**: *Please do not break my heart too. And do not question or doubt my love and trust for you.*

11:30:38 PM **Ladydi2011**: You will ALWAYS desire me all the way into eternity.

11:31:08 PM **Ladydi2011**: I will not break your heart. I promise.

11:31:31 PM **Robin Lulofs**: Okay honey

11:31:58 PM **Ladydi2011**: I love you so much Robin!

11:32:14 PM **Robin Lulofs**: *I am deeply in love with you, and I don't wnat you to let me down..*

11:32:29 PM **Robin Lulofs**: *I Love you too Diana.. very much!!!*

11:34:44 PM **Robin Lulofs**: *the message i sent you today, I meant everything i wrote there. Sincerely from my heart.*

11:35:03 PM **Robin Lulofs**: *When you're alone and not busy, you should read it again and again.*

11:35:18 PM **Ladydi2011**: I know you did honey. I could tell.

11:35:47 PM **Ladydi2011**: I will read it again before I sleep tonight.

11:36:03 PM **Robin Lulofs**: Okay baby

11:36:20 PM **Ladydi2011**: I can't wait to be with you in person!!!

11:36:29 PM **Robin Lulofs**: You make me happy and feel good. When *i* think of you, I have this beautiful smile on my face.

11:36:37 PM **Robin Lulofs**: Me too baby.

11:37:16 PM **Ladydi2011**: I am looking forward to our future.

11:37:54 PM **Robin Lulofs**: Same here darling. I know it's a beautiful one. Don't you?

11:38:23 PM **Ladydi2011**: I have no doubt

11:38:36 PM **Robin Lulofs**: Good

11:39:22 PM **Ladydi2011**: So baby, what time will I see your sexy face on cam tomorrow?

11:39:31 PM **Ladydi2011**: I can't wait!!!!!

11:39:37 PM **Robin Lulofs**: When we chat tomorrow.

11:40:05 PM **Robin Lulofs**: I have a meeting tomorrow morning with the investors, after that, we will chat

11:40:12 PM **Robin Lulofs**: What are you doing tomorrow?

11:40:18 PM **Ladydi2011**: Ok. I will make sure to be on my computer and not my phone.

11:41:03 PM **Robin Lulofs**: ok

11:41:11 PM **Ladydi2011**: Many things...from 12-2 I have client calls so it will have to be before or after these times.

11:41:51 PM **Robin Lulofs**: okay honey..

11:42:06 PM **Ladydi2011**: Do you want to use yahoo or Skype?

11:42:09 PM **Robin Lulofs**: I will text you during tht you know then

11:42:34 PM **Ladydi2011**: Ok...I will be watching for your text.

11:42:41 PM **Robin Lulofs**: Okay honey

11:43:37 PM **Ladydi2011**: Are you tired baby?

11:43:54 PM **Robin Lulofs**: yes baby.

11:43:59 PM **Robin Lulofs**: Are you?

11:44:23 PM **Ladydi2011**: Yes

11:44:38 PM **Robin Lulofs**: ok my love

11:44:45 PM **Robin Lulofs**: We should sleep now busy day tomorrow.

11:45:06 PM **Ladydi2011**: Yes my love

11:45:15 PM **Robin Lulofs**: I love you baby. so much!

11:45:22 PM **Ladydi2011**: Plus I want to stay beautiful for you
11:45:35 PM **Ladydi2011**: I love you so much too baby!
11:46:02 PM **Robin Lulofs**: Sweet dream baby
11:46:04 PM **Ladydi2011**: Sleep well honey
11:46:15 PM **Robin Lulofs**: Sleep well sweetheart
11:46:21 PM **Robin Lulofs**: Hugs and Kisses!!!
11:46:24 PM **Ladydi2011**: Sweet dreams to you too my love
11:46:32 PM **Ladydi2011**: Hugs and kisses

I offered to send the money because I already got the scam for this book and don't want to waste much more time with him. However, I do want to play with his emotions, build him up and then let him down so he knows how it feels. I DO NOT recommend you do this. It is extremely difficult and draining to play with people's emotions. My life never got back to normal until I had all the information I needed for this book and stopped chatting. This was no picnic!

Can you hear his excitement once I tell him I will give him the money? He thinks it's a done deal. It is too large an amount to send via Western Union so it has to be sent via bank wire. This scammer is in Nigeria who has a big guy (Chair) in Dubai. This person has a bank account that can handle this amount of transfer without question. This person will keep 40% and send 60% to the scammer. The scammers take for this transaction would be $6,600. Not a bad wage for a month of chatting.

He sends me a beautiful love email to ensure he holds onto me. He tells me to not question or doubt his love and trust for me. He tells me he is deeply in love with me and "he doesn't want me *to let him down*." He doesn't want to lose me now, but what he doesn't know is that he never had me. I seriously do not know how these scammers live with themselves.

 RED FLAGS

- Of course he has not come up with a solution. He wants me to be the solution. All of his chats with me have led up to this moment. He mentions the deadline because now he wants the money quickly. Most scammers put urgency on the money once they ask for it.
- He asks me if I have any idea how he can get some funds to be paid back within 10 days. HE HAS NO INTENTION OF PAYING THE MONEY BACK.
- He does not come right out and ask me for the money, and many scammers won't unless they have to. They want you to offer it. He's slick when he says, "I wouldn't want anything to destroy the love we have and the beautiful relationship we have."

Text Messages

To: 260-267-0302
Sent: July 26, 2012 8:50 am

Morning baby, did you sleep well?

From: 260-267-0302
Sent: July 26, 2012 9:58 am

I slept well darling, day is going fine, couple of meetings more. How is your day going?

To: 260-267-0302
Sent: July 26, 2012 10:00 am

My day is good. Looking forward to our time on cam today :-)

From: 260-267-0302
Sent: July 26, 2012 10:02 am

Same here baby, what are your plans today?

To: 260-267-0302
Sent: July 26, 2012 10:04 am

Office work and client calls and banking

From: 260-267-0302
Sent: July 26, 2012 10:16 am

Oh okay. Keep me posted baby okay? Love you!!!

To: 260-267-0302
Sent: July 26, 2012 2:22 pm

Love you too baby! Can you get on cam now baby?

From: 260-267-0302
Sent: July 26, 2012 2:50pm

I can only get on cam when I get back to the apt. When we chat later, is that okay?

From: 260-267-0302
Sent: July 26, 2012 2:51pm

And you've been talking about the cam most of the day. Something behind it baby?

From: 260-267-0302
Sent: July26, 2012 4:17pm

Busy I guess... Love you!

From: 260-267-0302
Sent: July 26, 2012 5:40pm

You're not online. Let me know when you're free darling!

To: 260-267-0302
Sent: July 26, 2012   7:20pm

I am getting on line now baby. Please join me.

IM Jul 26, 2012 7:23:28 PM

7:23:28 PM **Robin Lulofs**: Hi baby
7:23:41 PM **ladydi2011**: Hi Baby
7:24:01 PM **Robin Lulofs**: You've been so busy for me today..
7:24:09 PM **Robin Lulofs**: you did not reply your text messages
7:24:25 PM **Robin Lulofs**: send your webcam too baby
7:24:32 PM **ladydi2011**: Honey
7:24:39 PM **ladydi2011**: I cannot see you on cam
7:24:54 PM **ladydi2011**: Yes, I have been busy baby
7:25:07 PM **Robin Lulofs**: But you got my texts right?
7:25:13 PM **Robin Lulofs**: the cam is ON
7:25:41 PM **Robin Lulofs**: I can see my self.
7:26:00 PM **ladydi2011**: Please re-invite me baby
7:26:01 PM **Robin Lulofs**: *Yours is showing blank image*

7:26:08 PM **Robin Lulofs**: okay..

7:26:40 PM **Robin Lulofs**: baby, stop your webcam and re invite me

7:26:43 PM **Robin Lulofs**: *i* cannot see you

7:27:07 PM **ladydi2011**: Hmmmm...I can see me

7:27:16 PM **Robin Lulofs**: Oh really?

7:27:24 PM **ladydi2011**: *Yours looks like a piece of material is over the cam*

7:27:29 PM **Robin Lulofs**: I can see me here. can you see me?

7:27:47 PM **ladydi2011**: No baby...I cannot see you.

7:27:57 PM **Robin Lulofs**: Nothing is over my webcam. I fixed it today and it worked fine.

7:28:08 PM **Robin Lulofs**: Why can't I see you either?

7:28:31 PM **ladydi2011**: I closed mine and am going to restart it in hopes that you can see me.

7:28:42 PM **Robin Lulofs**: I hope so too.

7:29:03 PM **Robin Lulofs**: *I got this new sexy shirt to show off. And now you can't see me.. it better work!*

7:31:10 PM **Robin Lulofs**: <ding>

7:33:17 PM **ladydi2011**: Baby, my IM froze and I just signed back in

7:33:26 PM **ladydi2011**: Please re-invite me

7:33:27 PM **Robin Lulofs**: okay

7:33:50 PM **Robin Lulofs**: do the same baby

7:35:08 PM **Robin Lulofs**: <ding>

7:35:12 PM **Robin Lulofs**: are you there?

7:35:17 PM **Robin Lulofs**: I invited you baby

7:35:43 PM **ladydi2011**: Baby, IM keeps freezing

7:35:47 PM **ladydi2011**: Grrrrrr

7:35:52 PM **Robin Lulofs**: wow..

7:35:59 PM **ladydi2011**: Please invite me again

7:36:04 PM **Robin Lulofs**: let me invite you again then

7:36:07 PM **Robin Lulofs**: Sure baby

7:36:10 PM **Robin Lulofs**: do the same..

7:36:13 PM **ladydi2011**: I want to see your sexy new shirt

7:36:20 PM **ladydi2011**: I will honey

7:36:39 PM **Robin Lulofs**: Yes my Love, You will like it.

7:36:45 PM **Robin Lulofs**: I can see myself now, can u see me?

7:37:06 PM **ladydi2011**: Nope....Same thing

7:37:17 PM **Robin Lulofs**: grrrr..send yours

7:38:15 PM **Robin Lulofs**: are you still with me?

7:40:13 PM **ladydi2011**: IM keeps freezing honey to where I cannot even type

7:42:43 PM **Robin Lulofs**: okay baby

7:42:48 PM **Robin Lulofs**: better now?

7:51:03 PM **ladydi2011**: Ok baby

7:51:39 PM **ladydi2011**: I am on a different computer. Please re-invite me.

7:53:06 PM **Robin Lulofs**: okay baby

7:54:46 PM **Robin Lulofs**: send yours baby

7:55:26 PM **ladydi2011**: Same thing for your webcam

7:56:04 PM **ladydi2011**: Can you see me baby?

7:56:31 PM **Robin Lulofs**: baby, *i* cannot see you showing a blank image like a dark room.

7:56:46 PM **ladydi2011**: I can see me

7:56:47 PM **Robin Lulofs**: can u see me?
7:56:50 PM **ladydi2011**: Nope
7:56:56 PM **Robin Lulofs**: I can see me too
7:56:59 PM **Robin Lulofs**: what's wrong then
7:57:22 PM **Robin Lulofs**: are you there?
7:57:24 PM **Robin Lulofs**: <ding>
7:57:52 PM **ladydi2011**: I don't know.
7:58:12 PM **ladydi2011**: Do you have a Skype account baby?
7:58:54 PM **Robin Lulofs**: I don't.
7:59:22 PM **Robin Lulofs**: *Oh, so you're not going to see my shirt tonight?*
7:59:31 PM **Robin Lulofs**: *I got it because of you..*
8:00:48 PM **ladydi2011**: I am bummed
8:01:04 PM **ladydi2011**: I really wanted to see you tonight and for you to see me
8:01:15 PM **Robin Lulofs**: me too baby
8:01:18 PM **ladydi2011**: Yes, I wanted to see your new shirt
8:01:23 PM **Robin Lulofs**: I've been looking forward to it all day
8:01:31 PM **Robin Lulofs**: something is wrong then, *i* guess
8:01:56 PM **ladydi2011**: Yeah, I guess
8:02:05 PM **ladydi2011**: IM keeps freezing on me
8:02:33 PM **Robin Lulofs**: I will format my computer again tomorrow then.
8:02:48 PM **Robin Lulofs**: I had it fixed today because of the webcam.
8:03:05 PM **Robin Lulofs**: *imagine how i spent hours on this, and not working. not fair..*
8:04:05 PM **ladydi2011**: Thank you for trying baby. I appreciate it
8:04:39 PM **ladydi2011**: I am having a hard time pushing messages
8:05:03 PM **Robin Lulofs**: are you still here at all?
8:05:26 PM **Robin Lulofs**: Okay baby
8:05:26 PM **Robin Lulofs**: I Love you!
8:05:28 PM **Robin Lulofs**: *You know I will do anything that makes you happy*
8:05:29 PM **ladydi2011**: Yeah
8:05:45 PM **ladydi2011**: Struggling but still here
8:07:11 PM **ladydi2011**: I love you too baby
8:07:25 PM **ladydi2011**: I know you will do anything to make me happy
8:07:34 PM **ladydi2011**: Same here honey
8:08:07 PM **Robin Lulofs**: I know baby
8:08:14 PM **Robin Lulofs**: Tell me about your day baby
8:20:21 PM **Robin Lulofs**: are you there now?

From: Robin Lulofs
To: Ladydi2011@yahoo.com
Date: Thu, Jul 26, 2012 at 11:02 PM
Subject: what happened?

Baby, I have been online waiting for you, and I've been sending text messages but no response from you. I'm not sure if you're getting my messages, I know you cannot ignore me.

It's getting late here, and may go to bed soon. I miss you and I want to chat with you before I leave.

Love you
Robin.

IM Jul 26, 2012 11:35:42 PM

11:35:42 PM **Robin Lulofs**: <ding>
11:35:54 PM **Robin Lulofs**: well, goodnight baby
11:35:57 PM **Robin Lulofs**: *i* love you!

IM Jul 27, 2012 12:20:39 AM

12:20:39 AM **Robin Lulofs**: Hi
12:21:10 AM **Robin Lulofs**: <ding>
12:21:16 AM **ladydi2011**: Hi Baby
12:21:23 AM **Robin Lulofs**: Hi honey.
12:21:28 AM **Robin Lulofs**: What happened?
12:22:02 AM **ladydi2011**: I fell asleep. I am sorry
12:22:09 AM **Robin Lulofs**: Okay..
12:22:17 AM **Robin Lulofs**: It's okay. I was wondering what went wrong..
12:22:49 AM **ladydi2011**: Yahoo was really messed up tonight
12:23:02 AM **ladydi2011**: It kept telling me error and closing
12:23:27 AM **Robin Lulofs**: I guess you're using the mobile yahoo now?
12:24:23 AM **ladydi2011**: No, it wouldn't work from my phone either...It wouldn't even sign in
12:24:33 AM **ladydi2011**: I am on my laptop and so far so good
12:24:49 AM **Robin Lulofs**: Okay honey
12:24:55 AM **Robin Lulofs**: Glad is working now.
12:25:11 AM **Robin Lulofs**: I guess the whole webcam thing messed everything up. I don't know why!
12:25:55 AM **ladydi2011**: I am really bummed about the web cam
12:26:12 AM **Robin Lulofs**: *I guess it will work another time. I will keep the shirt for you*
12:26:32 AM **ladydi2011**: Thank you baby
12:26:40 AM **Robin Lulofs**: I Love you!
12:26:47 AM **ladydi2011**: I love you too
12:26:59 AM **Robin Lulofs**: So, tell me about your day... what did you do today?
12:27:22 AM **ladydi2011**: It was long and stressful
12:28:13 AM **ladydi2011**: Honey, I am sorry to tell you this but I have had second thoughts about sending you $11,000
12:28:50 AM **Robin Lulofs**: Really? tell me about it..
12:29:40 AM **ladydi2011**: I need to know you are who you say you are...
12:30:09 AM **ladydi2011**: You know I work with some pretty high level people
12:30:30 AM **ladydi2011**: I had one of my data forensic people run your IP address and it is out of Nigeria
12:31:08 AM **Robin Lulofs**: LOL.. BAby, I know you are smart.

12:31:44 AM **Robin Lulofs**: *And You should be smart enough to know I am smart too, right?*

12:31:51 AM **ladydi2011**: Yes

12:31:55 AM **Robin Lulofs**: Good.

12:32:10 AM **Robin Lulofs**: *Firstly, what does my Ip has to do with Nigeria? how's that possible?*

12:33:02 AM **Robin Lulofs**: *Secondly, You are not sure I am who I say I am.. That's really deep, and I enevr expected that to come from you. I trust you so much, and I thought you did too.*

12:33:44 AM **Robin Lulofs**: *I have no say over your money. And I would not want anything to come between us, and to destroy the beautiful love we have.*

12:33:55 AM **Robin Lulofs**: *If that is what you have decided. Forget about the money.*

12:34:28 AM **Robin Lulofs**: *But the doubt about my identity should stop. I never expected you to say something like this to me. Never ever!*

12:34:51 AM **ladydi2011**: Baby, I am so sorry

12:35:03 AM **Robin Lulofs**: You don't have to be sorry.

12:35:16 AM **Robin Lulofs**: *You should have told me you do not trust me all this while.*

12:35:43 AM **Robin Lulofs**: *I have been so relaxed and promised them in Dubai everything is fine.*

12:36:07 AM **Robin Lulofs**: *Things will actually get worse now. Because of your lack of trust. which is highly unbelievable.*

12:36:17 AM **ladydi2011**: I cannot even begin to tell you all the emotions I have been going through

12:36:26 AM **Robin Lulofs**: I don't think so.

12:36:58 AM **Robin Lulofs**: *I have been open enough to share with you, my private life. I trust you enough to share my problems and joy with you; But what do i get in return?*

12:37:08 AM **Robin Lulofs**: *doubts and disapointments?*

12:37:28 AM **Robin Lulofs**: *When did you start having this emotions and doubts anyway?*

12:37:49 AM **ladydi2011**: When the money issue came up

12:37:58 AM **ladydi2011**: There is more I need to tell you

12:38:05 AM **Robin Lulofs**: Tell me..

12:38:45 AM **ladydi2011**: I was scammed by a man the end of April because I was new to online dating and didn't know the rules of the road

12:39:07 AM **ladydi2011**: Since this time, 14 other men tried to scam me...guess I am a magnet

12:39:30 AM **ladydi2011**: So, I am writing a book to help other people avoid being scammed

12:39:54 AM **ladydi2011**: I have a voice and yes, I am very smart

12:40:52 AM **Robin Lulofs**: *I'm sorry you were scammed. Who is the man and how did it happen?*

12:40:56 AM **ladydi2011**: Yes, they were all yahoo boys

12:41:13 AM **ladydi2011**: 25 yrs. old from Nigeria

12:41:24 AM **ladydi2011**: 5 of the men have come clean with me

12:41:33 AM **ladydi2011**: I know who they really are

12:41:44 AM **ladydi2011**: I am not looking to have anyone arrested

12:42:05 AM **ladydi2011**: I am just looking to help people stop the heartbreak and the loss of money

12:42:36 AM **ladydi2011**: I will be starting an awareness program and take this world wide

12:43:10 AM **Robin Lulofs**: Oh okay. That's a good thing. The awareness!

12:43:36 AM **Robin Lulofs**: *But you should know who this people are, if you talk to them.*

12:43:53 AM **Robin Lulofs**: *How does this concerns me? I mean the people from Nigeria?*

12:44:08 AM **Robin Lulofs**: *And why can't they be arrested?*

12:44:16 AM **ladydi2011**: I choose not to have them arrested. I want information!

12:44:28 AM **Robin Lulofs**: *Isn't that the best way to reduce the hearbreaks they cause people?*

12:44:48 AM **ladydi2011**: What, to have them arrested?

12:44:56 AM **Robin Lulofs**: Yes.

12:45:30 AM **Robin Lulofs**: *Well, I don't know.. But it's not a good act at all. It destroys trust and love for people.*

12:46:00 AM **Robin Lulofs**: Anyway, I think writing the book is a good thing, and it should really help.

12:46:09 AM **ladydi2011**: Thank you

12:46:14 AM **Robin Lulofs**: You're welcome.

12:46:21 AM **ladydi2011**: I have lost hope for man kind

12:46:31 AM **Robin Lulofs**: really?

12:46:53 AM **Robin Lulofs**: *Well, my money issue is not a problem*

12:47:00 AM **Robin Lulofs**: *Forget about it, I've told you this.*

12:47:08 AM **Robin Lulofs**: *But why didn't you tell me this before now?*

12:47:37 AM **Robin Lulofs**: *I told you the situation of things because I trusted you, and because I see you're part of my life.*

12:47:53 AM **Robin Lulofs**: *I guess you didn't really mean everything you've said to me, right?*

12:48:58 AM **Robin Lulofs**: *Well, May be you think I was one of your Nigerian men.*

12:49:15 AM **Robin Lulofs**: *drop that!*

12:49:33 AM **Robin Lulofs**: *I wouldn't appreciate it if you compare me with those people.*

12:50:53 AM **Robin Lulofs**: *Darling, I think you don't know I have my PRIDE. And it means a lot to me. I don't want to say i regret the fact that i shared my situation with you. The way it is now, you're making me blame myself for doing that you know..*

12:52:19 AM **Robin Lulofs**: *And remember before I got the info about sending the money; I told you I don't want anything to ruin our love, I asked if i can trust and confide in you; You gave me go ahead.*

12:53:14 AM **Robin Lulofs**: *I SO WISH THIS CAM CAN WORK NOW. I NEED YOU TO SEE MY FACE, I AM NOT IN A GOOD MOOD.*

12:53:51 AM **Robin Lulofs**: *I can't believe we are talking about this. when you have to compare me with internet scams!!!*

12:53:56 AM **ladydi2011**: I also want your cam to work

12:53:58 AM **Robin Lulofs**: send your webcam too

12:54:35 AM **ladydi2011**: All I see is a black screen

12:54:46 AM **Robin Lulofs**: send yours please

12:57:17 AM **Robin Lulofs**: I cannot see u

12:57:32 AM **ladydi2011**: I see that. I cannot see me either

12:57:39 AM **Robin Lulofs**: resend

12:58:10 AM **Robin Lulofs**: reinvite pls.

12:59:24 AM **ladydi2011**: Can you see me?

12:59:28 AM **ladydi2011**: I cannot

12:59:39 AM **Robin Lulofs**: I cannot see you!

1:01:11 AM **Robin Lulofs**: okay

1:02:18 AM **ladydi2011**: I was a maga once, but will not be one again

1:02:33 AM **Robin Lulofs**: *what do you mean?*

1:02:37 AM **Robin Lulofs**: *maga?*

1:02:46 AM **ladydi2011**: it means "fool"

1:02:52 AM **Robin Lulofs**: Oh

1:02:57 AM **Robin Lulofs**: *what language is that?*

1:03:03 AM **ladydi2011**: Nigerian

1:03:03 AM **Robin Lulofs**: *french?*

1:03:07 AM **Robin Lulofs**: Oh. I see

1:03:24 AM **Robin Lulofs**: *You are really into this Nigerian men, aren't you?*

1:03:48 AM **Robin Lulofs**: *Because you speak their language now.*

1:04:09 AM **Robin Lulofs**: *I think we should stop talking about this Nigeria things. It's getting irritating*

1:05:18 AM **Robin Lulofs**: *Forget about the money baby.*

1:05:38 AM **Robin Lulofs**: *I would rather have the payment be there, and the worst should happen to it.*

1:05:43 AM **Robin Lulofs**: *Rather than lose you!*

1:06:29 AM **Robin Lulofs**: *I didn't know you have that wound inside you about the past; You didn't tell me. Won't have brought it up at all.*

1:06:41 AM **Robin Lulofs**: *And you know I asked you if you were okay with it, you said YES.*

1:07:09 AM **Robin Lulofs**: *So, what happened?*

1:07:21 AM **Robin Lulofs**: *you asked people and they told you I'm one of your Nigerian men?*

1:07:32 AM **Robin Lulofs**: *I'm really confused, you know..*

1:07:52 AM **ladydi2011**: I really need to see your face

1:09:38 AM **Robin Lulofs**: *Oh is this why you told me to get a webcam?*

1:09:43 AM **Robin Lulofs**: *because you don't trust me?*

1:09:52 AM **Robin Lulofs**: *or because you want to see my smile?*

1:10:02 AM **Robin Lulofs**: *I really don't know what is true anymore. Really!*

1:10:54 AM **Robin Lulofs**: *It's okay..*

1:11:08 AM **Robin Lulofs**: *So, when did you change your mind about getting me the funds?*

1:11:16 AM **Robin Lulofs**: *today?*

1:11:23 AM **ladydi2011**: Hmmmmm

1:11:35 AM **Robin Lulofs**: Oh okay. what happened

1:11:50 AM **Robin Lulofs**: *Tell me. If there are somethings you're not clear about, tell me*

1:12:31 AM **Robin Lulofs**: *You want to loan me.*

1:13:00 AM **Robin Lulofs**: *And you want to help me from a situation, i didn't see coming.*

1:13:27 AM **Robin Lulofs**: *You have no idea how happy I was the night you decided to help me, I told you to read the email i sent that morning again, did you?*

1:14:20 AM **ladydi2011**: I did

1:14:54 AM **Robin Lulofs**: *Well, i understand the "fear" you have.*

1:15:25 AM **Robin Lulofs**: *The fear of not falling a victim again. I'm sorry about what has happened to you in the past. But you have to put the past behind you and move on.*

1:15:51 AM **Robin Lulofs**: *When I told you I will never let you down or break your heart; I meant it in all ways.*

1:17:18 AM **Robin Lulofs**: *everyway you can think of. Why would I disappoint you? what would I gain? And another thing is that, I want you involve in the procesing of the payment, I want the attorney to carry you along. You will get the details of everything because I want you to know*

1:18:02 AM **Robin Lulofs**: *I want you to be part of everything I do, this is because I trust and love you. And not because you want to loan me money. Money is just a material thing and can never be compared to LOVE.*

1:18:41 AM **Robin Lulofs**: *A lot of people in the world have so much money. a lot, but they are not as happy as YOU and I. because they have no LOVE. you know this right?*

1:19:02 AM **ladydi2011**: I know this all too well!

1:20:32 AM **Robin Lulofs**: *I don't know. You said you have people in high places, the same people that told you my IP is Nigeria's.. I wanted to know if someone got your password, and wanted to know if this is truly the woman I fell in love with.*

1:21:27 AM **Robin Lulofs:** *I wanted to be sure I am talking to that same woman that makes me happy, just by saying she loves me. You have never lied to me before, i know. And I just don't want anything to go wrong.*

1:22:44 AM **Robin Lulofs:** *How can you check my IP and it shows Nigeria, that is ridiculous. How can my proxy be Nigeria's? When I am not there! Is that not insane?*

1:23:06 AM **ladydi2011:** You are talking to the woman you fell in love with. I am also NOT a scammer. If I was, I would have said "Baba how your side,omo iya mi,yes boss,ba wo lon se lo?,how u dey?"

1:23:09 AM **Robin Lulofs:** *I know you're very smart, so I do not expect this kind of onversation from you, so i wanted to double check.*

1:23:36 AM **Robin Lulofs:** *can you please stop typing this strange words?!!!*

1:24:40 AM **Robin Lulofs:** really!!!

1:24:47 AM **ladydi2011:**

From: potty4520@att.net
To: garren40@gmail.com
Date: Tue, 17 Jul 2012 22:33:11 -0700 (PDT)
Subject: You are the woman I want!!!
Location: Nigeria

Misdirected: No
Abuse Address: hostmaster@mtnnigeria.net
Abuse Reporting: To automatically generate an email abuse report click here
From IP: 41.206.1.1
inetnum: 41.206.0.0 - 41.206.31.255
netname: MTN-Nigeria
descr: MTN Nigeria
country: NG
admin-c: BO5-AFRINIC
tech-c: BO5-AFRINIC
org: ORG-MN1-AFRINIC
status: ALLOCATED PA
mnt-by: AFRINIC-HM-MNT
mnt-lower: MTNNIGERA1-MNT
source: AFRINIC # Filtered
parent: 41.0.0.0 - 41.255.255.255

organisation: ORG-MN1-AFRINIC
org-name: MTN Nigeria
org-type: LIR
country: NG
address: Golden Plaza,
address: Falomo Roundabout,
address: Ikoyi
address: Lagos

1:25:33 AM **Robin Lulofs:** *And what is all this?????*

1:27:21 AM **ladydi2011**: This is your IP address
1:27:34 AM **Robin Lulofs**: Really?
1:27:39 AM **Robin Lulofs**: *How do you check that? With a software or what?*
1:30:20 AM **Robin Lulofs**: are you still here?
1:30:21 AM **Robin Lulofs**: <ding>
1:30:30 AM **ladydi2011**: I am
1:30:42 AM **Robin Lulofs**: *so, do you have the software?*
1:30:57 AM **Robin Lulofs**: *If yes, I think you should scan the rest of the emails i sent to you.*
1:31:15 AM **Robin Lulofs**: *And I want to know your result.*
1:31:29 AM **Robin Lulofs**: *After then, I will tell you the things you don't know about softwares.. lol*
1:31:41 AM **Robin Lulofs**: *I am an engineer. Remember! I know a lot!!*
1:32:11 AM **ladydi2011**: please hold
1:32:19 AM **Robin Lulofs**: okay
1:33:56 AM **ladydi2011**:

From: potty4350@yahoo.com
To: ladydi2011@yahoo.com
Date: Fri, 13 Jul 2012 00:34:48 -0700 (PDT)
Subject: FEELINGS
Location: Atlanta, Georgia, USA

Misdirected: No
Abuse Address: abuse@nobistech.net
Abuse Reporting: To automatically generate an email abuse report click here
From IP: 173.234.216.88
NetRange: 173.234.216.0 - 173.234.219.255
CIDR: 173.234.216.0/22
OriginAS: AS15003
NetName: NETBLK-UBIQUITY-ATLANTA-173-234-216-0
NetHandle: NET-173-234-216-0-1
Parent: NET-173-234-0-0-1
NetType: Reallocated
Comment: Addresses in this block are non-portable.
Comment: For security issues, abuse reports, and
Comment: technical issues, please contact the
Comment: Nobis Technology Group NOC at admin@nobistech.net
RegDate: 2010-12-09
Updated: 2010-12

1:34:53 AM **Robin Lulofs**: go on..
1:35:11 AM **Robin Lulofs**: *I hope you can see the difference?*
1:35:22 AM **ladydi2011**: I can
1:35:29 AM **Robin Lulofs**: go on please..
1:35:43 AM **Robin Lulofs**: *may be you should scan the last email i sent you..*
1:35:51 AM **ladydi2011**: *Please tell me what you know*
1:36:18 AM **Robin Lulofs**: *what you don't know about this softwares. they generate proxies randomly and most of the time, they give wrong information about proxies.*

1:37:07 AM **Robin Lulofs**: *so, 13th of july, it stated i was in Atlanta, USA, and 17th of july, i was in Nigeria*

1:37:24 AM **Robin Lulofs**: *I'm sure if you go on, you will see me in Russia..this is INSANE!*

1:39:25 AM **ladydi2011**: Everything I have been through has been insane

1:39:42 AM **Robin Lulofs**: Well, I think so!

1:39:58 AM **Robin Lulofs**: *I guess that's why You have the software on your laptop.*

1:40:15 AM **ladydi2011**: I do not have software

1:40:17 AM **Robin Lulofs**: *I bet you must have bought it online.*

1:40:26 AM **Robin Lulofs**: *So, how did you check the proxy?*

1:40:56 AM **ladydi2011**: My connections

1:41:15 AM **Robin Lulofs**: okay.

1:41:36 AM **Robin Lulofs**: *good for you!*

1:41:56 AM **Robin Lulofs**: *You should not have doubts about me, in ANYWAY!*

1:42:06 AM **Robin Lulofs**: *I will not hurt you. I am not like the bad people you have met.*

1:42:47 AM **Robin Lulofs**: *And if you really want this relationship, If you actually cherish it as much as I do, You need to TRUST ME. as much as I TRUST you.*

1:43:30 AM **Robin Lulofs**: *The reason I have been here all night chatting with you, despite the humiliation and doubts, is because I truly and sincerely Love you.*

1:44:01 AM **Robin Lulofs**: *I'm sorry about your past, and about what has happened before. But this is US now. You and I. I Robin, WILL NEVER HURT YOU*

1:44:41 AM **Robin Lulofs**: *I have been hurt before too, not monetry though; But I have never linked you with my past, because I want a new life and begining with you.*

1:44:51 AM **Robin Lulofs**: That's the way it should be for you too.

1:45:59 AM **Robin Lulofs**: *Sincerely, the whole scam things and Niegria languages makes no sense to me, because I don't know anything about it. And about the country. I just know it's in Africa somewhere! And i'm not interested.*

1:47:03 AM **Robin Lulofs**: *I will really appreciate it if you will stop bringing it up to our conversation and our lives. You know I will support you in whatever you chose to do. So therefore, I'm not saying you should not write the book, Please write it, but be careful with those you deal with.*

1:48:06 AM **Robin Lulofs**: *You can always get information online about any culture, you should do more of that, rather than relate with this bad people. I don't want anything to hurt you, and I don't want anyone to hurt you. Please be careful. I LOVE YOU!*

1:48:25 AM **ladydi2011**: Please hold...bathroom

1:48:33 AM **Robin Lulofs**: okay

1:55:01 AM **ladydi2011**: I promise you I will be very careful.

1:55:49 AM **Robin Lulofs**: *I know you are smart, but at the same time, you have to be careful.*

1:56:09 AM **Robin Lulofs**: *I truly care about you.*

1:56:13 AM **ladydi2011**: I know I have to be careful

1:56:28 AM **Robin Lulofs**: *I love and I adore you. This I really MEAN!*

1:57:18 AM **Robin Lulofs**: *You should have told me about your experience long ago baby, why didn't you tell me?*

1:57:25 AM **Robin Lulofs**: *You didn't trust me enough or what?*

1:58:56 AM **Robin Lulofs**: *Oh.. but telling me about it doesn't mean it's come into our relationship.*

1:59:30 AM **Robin Lulofs**: *But acting to me as a reaction from the past means you've allowed it into our relationship. Do you understand this darling?*

2:00:04 AM **Robin Lulofs**: *When it comes to being very careful, I am as well.*

2:01:34 AM **Robin Lulofs**: *I know it's not safe enough to reveal one's business to people. But when I discussed my deal in Dubai with you, I told you what my payment is, i told you when they are paying, i told you everything. I did not think you will be after my wealth, I opened up to you, because I trust you. That is what happens when you truly love someone.*

2:02:43 AM **Robin Lulofs**: *Material things cannot be determinant of the strength of your love. I've had experience when someone was just after my wealth, I did not allow that to come into my head, if i allowed it, I will never discuss my monetary issues with you at all. Do you understand?*

2:03:47 AM **Robin Lulofs**: *I don't know about you. When I am in Love, I give my all, everything. I open up to my lover, I tell her everything and I don't hide anything from her.*

2:04:52 AM **Robin Lulofs**: *I have not said you are after my wealth. You see how i felt when you told me about the man that scammed you? You have no idea. I felt like you never trusted me all the while. And the truth is IF you don't trust someone, You can NEVER love the person. Because it takes 100% trust to give your HEART for LOVE!*

2:05:48 AM **ladydi2011**: I 100% agree with everything you are saying.

2:06:20 AM **ladydi2011**: Do you remember in the beginning when I asked many times if you are who you say you are?

2:06:37 AM **Robin Lulofs**: Yes I do.

2:07:19 AM **ladydi2011**: There questions came from my past experience and from only having a computer screen in front of me.

2:07:36 AM **Robin Lulofs**: I understand now.

2:07:56 AM **Robin Lulofs**: *Because there are bad people in the world does not mean everyone is bad, you know that right?*

2:08:19 AM **Robin Lulofs**: *You will meet me very soon baby, I will be home soon. I am working here, and rounding up soon.*

2:08:51 AM **Robin Lulofs**: *I don't think I can go through this again, tonight has been so dramatic, you know..*

2:09:12 AM **Robin Lulofs**: *I can't believe you were writing some funny words.. LOL*

2:09:34 AM **Robin Lulofs**: *I had to text you to be sure who i was talking to,,*

2:09:57 AM **Robin Lulofs**: *God know's what all those words mean.*

2:10:15 AM **Robin Lulofs**: *It could be some computer virus!!*

2:10:22 AM **ladydi2011**: I have the meaning of them

2:10:34 AM **Robin Lulofs**: Oh okay.

2:10:55 AM **Robin Lulofs**: *I love you with all my heart*

2:11:10 AM **Robin Lulofs**: *This is why i shared my pain and thoughts with you*

2:11:32 AM **Robin Lulofs**: *And when I asked if you were okay with it, i knew why i asked.*

2:12:14 AM **Robin Lulofs**: *Because I didn't want you to be pressured. I wanted to know if you actually wanted to help and safe the situation, from your HEART.*

2:13:13 AM **Robin Lulofs**: *And when you said YEs. I was happy; i could not turn you down because I need the assistance, and coming from you, is great, because I see you as part of my LIFE.*

2:14:14 AM **Robin Lulofs**: *The worst is that I will lose the funds if i don't get things done as fast as possible. But then, It does not mean I will lose my life. life goes on, but the pain will be there, because it will hurt. That is why I accepted the offer from you. I hope you understand this baby.*

2:15:19 AM **ladydi2011**: Why did you ask if I was ok with this?

2:15:42 AM **Robin Lulofs**: *Okay with you helping me with the funds?*

2:15:47 AM **ladydi2011**: yes

2:15:57 AM **Robin Lulofs**: *Because I wanted to be sure if it was from your heart.*

2:16:38 AM **Robin Lulofs**: *I wanted to know if you truly want to do it because we are ONE. not just to do it, to be that "saviour" . I just want us to be REAL with each other at all times.*

2:16:54 AM **Robin Lulofs**: **And I don't want you to think I'm taking advantage of the love you have for me.**

2:17:01 AM **Robin Lulofs**: *because I WILL NEVER do that!*

2:17:23 AM **ladydi2011**: Thank you

2:17:43 AM **Robin Lulofs**: *I Love you.. very much!*

2:17:54 AM **Robin Lulofs**: *words can't express how much I DO.*

2:20:30 AM **ladydi2011**: It is almost 2:30 here and my eyes are closing

2:20:57 AM **Robin Lulofs**: Okay baby.

2:20:58 AM **ladydi2011**: I need to get up at 6:30

2:21:05 AM **Robin Lulofs**: Tired too..

2:21:10 AM **Robin Lulofs**: Why that early?

2:21:32 AM **ladydi2011**: I have meetings all day tomorrow

2:21:38 AM **Robin Lulofs**: wow..

2:21:47 AM **Robin Lulofs**: Okay honey

2:22:05 AM **Robin Lulofs**: Will you keep in touch?

2:22:17 AM **ladydi2011**: What do you mean?

2:22:26 AM **Robin Lulofs**: I mean texts messages

2:22:37 AM **ladydi2011**: Yes, I will.

2:22:40 AM **Robin Lulofs**: You hardly reply this days

2:22:56 AM **ladydi2011**: I will tomorrow.

2:23:06 AM **Robin Lulofs**: ha! so, why didn't you today?

2:23:20 AM **Robin Lulofs**: tell me the truth.. lol

2:24:09 AM **Robin Lulofs**: Please don't keep things to yourself always talk to me.

2:24:34 AM **Robin Lulofs**: Okay..

2:24:55 AM **Robin Lulofs**: I Love you..

2:25:38 AM **Robin Lulofs**: *Please don't bring doubts to my mind anymore!*

2:26:28 AM **Robin Lulofs**: *Don't know what I'll be doing today.. I guess it's going to be a crazy day again..*

2:27:26 AM **Robin Lulofs**: *I want to be with you so much.. I will be home VERy soon..*

2:27:54 AM **Robin Lulofs**: *What i need now is a miracle..lol*

2:28:24 AM **Robin Lulofs**: *what would I tell the Attorney, this means starting over again..*

2:29:24 AM **ladydi2011**: I am sorry. I fell asleep at the computer

2:29:35 AM **ladydi2011**: I am in bed

2:29:40 AM **Robin Lulofs**: Oh..

2:29:47 AM **Robin Lulofs**: hmm, can i join you baby 😊

2:30:20 AM **Robin Lulofs**: want to share what you'll do to me?

2:30:56 AM **ladydi2011**: All I can say is that you would have loved it!!!

2:31:18 AM **Robin Lulofs**: remind me when *i* get home.. I want to handcuff you to the bed.. that would be your punishment, for not trusting me 100% 😊

2:32:01 AM **ladydi2011**: Whoa.....

2:32:47 AM **Robin Lulofs**: yes baby

2:33:02 AM **Robin Lulofs**: I love you..

2:33:23 AM **ladydi2011**: Until tomorrow

2:33:31 AM **Robin Lulofs**: Okay.. goodnight baby

IM Jul 27, 2012 11:21:52 AM

11:21:52 AM **Robin Lulofs**: i'm here
11:24:35 AM **ladydi2011**: I am here too
11:28:28 AM **Robin Lulofs**: hi baby
11:28:34 AM **Robin Lulofs**: how are you?
11:28:47 AM **Robin Lulofs**: <ding>
11:29:00 AM **ladydi2011**: I am ok
11:29:13 AM **Robin Lulofs**: busy day? what time is it there now?
11:29:20 AM **ladydi2011**: 11:30
11:29:54 AM **Robin Lulofs**: oh okay
11:30:02 AM **ladydi2011**: It is 4:30 there, right?
11:30:07 AM **Robin Lulofs**: yes baby
11:30:15 AM **Robin Lulofs**: baby, this is what came up...
11:31:05 AM **Robin Lulofs**: *Last night, i already gave up on the Dubai stuff, because of the deadline. When i contacted the Attorney that there's a problem that i may not be able to get the rest of the funds today he said I can still make it because today is friday and it's a work free day. so, i have tomorrow and next. meaning they work on saturdays and Sundays, which makes it good, because it won't be too late when the funds get there. The problem is I have no other means to get this done within this short period of time. I am telling you this because I REALLY need you to fix this for me, i will really appreciate it. If you want me to send you a promisory note on this, I will. I want you to lease contact your bank and have it sent to him. If you're not very comfortable with that, you can send it to me here, in my name.. and i will send it to dubai immediately. this is what i want to share with you baby*
11:34:09 AM **ladydi2011**: Ok, so what papers were you talking about from the attorney?
11:36:06 AM **Robin Lulofs**: *The payment approval.*
11:36:17 AM **Robin Lulofs**: *he will collect it when he pays the clearance*
11:36:37 AM **ladydi2011**: *So this is after I would send the money?*
11:36:41 AM **Robin Lulofs**: *I've told him to send me the receipt as soon as he pays. And I'll tell him to CC your email.*
11:37:11 AM **Robin Lulofs**: *When he pays the clearance, he gets the payment approval, and that would be taken to the designated bank for payment processing.*
11:37:39 AM **ladydi2011**: Oh....ok
11:37:44 AM **Robin Lulofs**: Yes baby.
11:38:05 AM **Robin Lulofs**: *Please do this for me as early as you can. I 'll really appreciate it honey.*
11:38:35 AM **ladydi2011**: I will not be able to do this until tomorrow
11:39:04 AM **ladydi2011**: My meeting last all day and then a dinner meeting
11:39:12 AM **Robin Lulofs**: Oh.
11:39:27 AM **Robin Lulofs**: Tomorrow is Saturday
11:39:41 AM **ladydi2011**: Yes. My bank is open from 8-12
11:39:56 AM **Robin Lulofs**: Okay baby.
11:40:01 AM **Robin Lulofs**: Thank you so much!
11:40:36 AM **ladydi2011**: You're welcome Robin
11:40:55 AM **Robin Lulofs**: *Baby, if you have anything you want to know, pls don't hesitate to ask me.*
11:41:04 AM **ladydi2011**: I need to go now. I only have 5 min to get into the office building.

11:41:13 AM **Robin Lulofs**: *You know I will always be open to you, and you'll alway get the truth , okay?*
11:41:27 AM **Robin Lulofs**: Oh okay.. Have a great day, I love you!
11:42:03 AM **ladydi2011**: I know
11:42:10 AM **ladydi2011**: You have a great day too
11:42:18 AM **ladydi2011**: bye for now
11:42:22 AM **Robin Lulofs**: bye for now baby

Text Messages

To: 260-267-0302
Sent: July 31, 2012 6:09 pm

Hmmmmm. If you are so wealthy you wouldn't need to ask a woman for money.

From: 260-267-0302
Sent: Aug 1, 2012 12:29 pm

I will be on line in about 5 min. Will you be available?

To: 260-267-0302
Sent: Aug 1, 2012 1:03 pm

I am in Texas now

From: 260-267-0302
Sent: Aug 3, 2012 9:36 am

Good Morning Honey .. How are you doing?

To: 260-267-0302
Sent: Aug 3, 2012 9:38 am

I am well and you?

From: 260-267-0302
Sent: Aug 3, 2012 9:39 am

I am doing pretty well honey, *i* miss you so much Diana

To: 260-267-0302
Sent: Aug 5, 2012 3:47 pm

Hi Robin. I got back from Texas at 2am and just woke up. How are you?

From: 260-267-0302
Sent: Aug 5, 2012 4:29 pm

I am fine baby .. How was your trip? Can you come on yahoo messenger baby? I love everything about you my lady, you mean a lot to my life .. you are now part of me and we are now one.

From: 260-267-0302
Sent: Aug 6, 2012 2:15 pm

Hey Diana .. How are you doing and how is your day going?

To: 260-267-0302
Sent: Aug 6, 2012 2:16 pm

Hi Robin. I am good. How are you doing?

From: 260-267-0302
Sent: Aug 6, 2012 2:22 pm

I am doing pretty good and happy to hear from you, *i* miss you loads baby. How is your day going? are you at work??

To: 260-267-0302
Sent: Aug 6, 2012 2:34 pm

My day is going good and busy as always...yes, I am at work. What about you?

From: 260-267-0302
Sent: Aug 6, 2012 2:36 pm

I just got home from work baby .. what time is it there now? What time are you gonna close from work? you need to rest.

To: 260-267-0302
Sent: Aug 6, 2012 3:01 pm

Lol...probably around 7 pm

From: 260-267-0302
Sent: Aug 6, 2012 3:05 pm

i wish *i* am there baby. *i* feel so sad things are not right and that things happened the that way.

To: 260-267-0302
Sent: Aug 6, 2012 3:21 pm

Nothing will change in less I meet you in person!

From: 260-267-0302
Sent: Aug 6, 2012 3:26 pm

yes *i* know and *i* promise you that you will see me soon ok? trust me ok? you there Diana

To: 260-267-0302
Sent: Aug 6, 2012 4:05 pm

I am...was on phone. You've been around long enough to know trust is earned. Yes?

From: 260-267-0302
Sent: Aug 6, 2012 4:07 pm

i know diana ..*i* just want you to know that *i* am not who you think *i* am .. and *i* can't wait to prove that to you

To: 260-267-0302
Sent: Aug 6, 2012 4:09 pm

I am waiting!

From: 260-267-0302
Sent: Aug 6, 2012 4:09 pm

i know you are .. *i* am rushing things here because of you.

To: 260-267-0302
Sent: Aug 6, 2012 4:11 pm

I am not going anywhere...I am no longer on any dating sites...just waiting!!!

From: 260-267-0302
Sent: Aug 6, 2012 4:14 pm

i am very glad to hear that, you own me Diana. honey what can *i* do to prove myself to you??

To: 260-267-0302
Sent: Aug 7, 2012 12:03 pm

How are you doing?

From: 260-267-0302
Sent: Aug 7, 2012 12:07 pm

I am doing pretty well darling, *i* miss you darling.

To: 260-267-0302
Sent: Aug 7, 2012 12:08 pm

I miss you too and am looking forward to the day we will be together in person.

From: 260-267-0302
Sent: Aug 7, 2012 12:10 pm

we will there's no doubt about that diana trust me k?

To: 260-267-0302
Sent: Aug 7, 2012 12:10 pm

Ok, I am trusting you with this!

From: 260-267-0302
Sent: Aug 7, 2012 12:11 pm

i would be glad if you do anyways .. are you at work?

To: 260-267-0302
Sent: Aug 7, 2012 12:16 pm

I am at work. What about you?

From: 260-267-0302
Sent: Aug 7, 2012 12:19 pm

i am on the work field too diana .. how is your day going?

To: 260-267-0302
Sent: Aug 7, 2012 12:20 pm

Busy, and yours?

From: 260-267-0302
Sent: Aug 7, 2012 12:24 pm

very busy .. you need to rest yourself diana .. you work too much and that is not good for your health *i* am very sure you know that.

To: 260-267-0302
Sent: Aug 7, 2012 12:24 pm

I do know this. Client demands are high. Have a wonderful day.

From: 260-267-0302
Sent: Aug 7, 2012 12:25 pm

thank you diana .. what are you doing now?

To: 260-267-0302
Sent: Aug 7, 2012 12:30 pm

I am getting ready to call a prospective client.

From: 260-267-0302
Sent: Aug 7, 2012 12:36 pm

when will you be done??

To: 260-267-0302
Sent: Aug 7, 2012 12:41 pm

Probably around 7:00. I have client calls the rest of the day.

From: 260-267-0302
Sent: Aug 7, 2012 12:44 pm

Okay .. so will you be able to text?

To: 260-267-0302
Sent: Aug 7, 2012 12:46 pm

On and off.

From: 260-267-0302
Sent: Aug 8, 2012 10:14 am

Good Morning Baby .. How are you doing and how is your day going?

To: 260-267-0302
Sent: Aug 8, 2012 10:21 am

I am well. Day is busy. How are you and how is your day going?

From: 260-267-0302
Sent: Aug 8, 2012 10:22 am

My day is going good thanks for asking .. how is work going with you?

To: 260-267-0302
Sent: Aug 8, 2012 10:30 am

I am glad your day is going good. All is well here. As always I am buried in work. Now you know why I didn't date for 8 years...

From: 260-267-0302
Sent: Aug 8, 2012 10:34 am

yes *i* can understand baby .. *i* adore you so much darling. Please have a fabulous day!

It is time I ask him to come on camera. He agrees to, but wants to know why I am asking. Of course, I don't answer right away because I want to see what he does. He does turn his camera on but it is obvious he has a piece of material over it. Of all times, my camera acted up so I couldn't press the issue. He is slick when he says he worked on fixing the camera all day and even bought a new sexy shirt to show off, so the camera better work. This man is quick on his feet.
I wasn't sure how I was going to break the news to this man that I knew he was a scammer because I couldn't read if he might come clean and help with the book or not. I decided to tell him online instead of in a letter. He is not happy when I tell him I had second thoughts about sending the money and had his IP address checked and found out that his IP address was out of Nigeria. I was surprised at all he said without hesitation. He was actually pretty convincing. If a woman didn't have any experience with scammers he might have convinced her that she was more important to him than the money. This man is a professional scammer and a good one!

In trying to get this man to come clean and help me with information, I told him that I was scammed. He wanted to know how it concerned him and why the people from Nigeria can't be arrested for the heartbreak they cause people. I knew that he knew exactly what he did to people and he didn't care. For him it was all about the money at all costs, so I figured he would never help. He was shocked with how much I did know and I was shocked that he had a good comeback for all of it!

He had three email addresses and three IP addresses. One was out of Lagos, Nigeria, One was AT&T out of Atlanta, GA and I didn't check the third one, but it just might have been out of Russia, since he mentioned Russia. This shows that one never knows where the person is or who the "real man behind the screen" really is.

These scammers are much more skilled than the average woman or man who is looking for love on a dating site. Unless you have a criminal mind or are trained in this type of activity, you would never think of the things these men think of and do.

RED FLAGS

   🚩 "It's getting late here" is something scammers say when they are waiting for you to send them money.

🏴 If his ranting about my lack of trust and my suspicions made you doubt he was a scammer, I am sure those thoughts disappeared when you read the next day's chats where he said, "The problem is I have no other means to get this done within this short period of time. I am telling you this because I REALLY need you to fix this for me, i will really appreciate it. If you want me to send you a promisory note on this, I will." The scammer will always come back after making his case and ask for the money.

For me, I closed this chapter when I sent him the text on July 31st that said, "Hmmmmm. If you are so wealthy you wouldn't need to ask a woman for money." Please understand that many scammers go away for a short period of time and then resurface. They might even pass your information to their friends to try to scam you, or if their yahoo box gets hacked by another scammer, the new scammer will have your information. So, know that if you have an encounter with a scammer and you want to get rid of them forever, you will have to change all your contact information. As I said, they will come back, so please read on to see what this man said when he came back a month later…..

IM Aug 27, 2012 6:12:22 PM

6:12:22 PM **potty4350**: <ding>

IM Aug 29, 2012 1:32:53 AM

1:32:53 AM **potty4350**: hey diana
1:35:50 AM **potty4350**: <ding>

IM Aug 29, 2012 4:50:47 PM

4:50:47 PM **potty4350**: <ding>
4:50:52 PM **potty4350**: Hello Honey
4:51:00 PM **potty4350**: How are you doing darling??
4:51:03 PM **potty4350**: <ding>
4:51:32 PM **ladydi2011**: I am good
4:51:36 PM **ladydi2011**: And you?
4:51:39 PM **potty4350**: How have you been baby??
4:51:50 PM **potty4350**: I am doing pretty good and happy to chat with you?
4:52:13 PM **ladydi2011**: Where are you?
4:58:53 PM **potty4350**: *Honey I am still here in the UK Diana*
4:58:59 PM **potty4350**: Why did you stop talking to me for so long?

4:59:07 PM	**potty4350**: *Have I done anything wrong to you*
4:59:16 PM	**potty4350**: Did you decide not to talk to me anymore
5:00:01 PM	**ladydi2011**: I never saw you on line
5:01:15 PM	**potty4350**: Yes honey because I have been very busy with so many things right here
5:01:27 PM	**potty4350**: What have you been up to lately??
5:02:17 PM	**ladydi2011**: I am so glad things are going good for you.

5:03:42 PM   **potty4350**: Well Diana not so good but *i* am very glad *i* can at least chat with you today

5:03:50 PM	**ladydi2011**: I have been working and traveling.
5:04:32 PM	**ladydi2011**: Just returned from Florida. Next will be Pennsylvania
5:06:05 PM	**ladydi2011**: I thought you would have been at my door by now!
5:08:34 PM	**potty4350**: <ding>
5:08:49 PM	**potty4350**: I wish baby
5:08:58 PM	**potty4350**: But I know *i* will Diana..I promise
5:09:03 PM	**potty4350**: *I just need you to trust me*
5:10:24 PM	**potty4350**: <ding>
5:10:28 PM	**potty4350**: Are you there Diana
5:10:39 PM	**potty4350**: <ding>
5:10:46 PM	**ladydi2011**: I am
5:11:24 PM	**potty4350**: Honey why did you unload the IMVironment?
5:11:41 PM	**ladydi2011**: I didn't
5:11:47 PM	**ladydi2011**: I am on my phone
5:12:04 PM	**ladydi2011**: I am out having dinner
5:13:39 PM	**potty4350**: Okay Honey
5:14:48 PM	**potty4350**: *I wish i am there with you darling*
5:14:51 PM	**potty4350**: *I adore you still Diana*
5:14:57 PM	**potty4350**: *I love you so much still Diana*
5:15:07 PM	**potty4350**: I really don't know if you feel that way towards me
5:16:02 PM	**ladydi2011**: I am just waiting for you to arrive at my door
5:16:56 PM	**potty4350**: Hmmmm
5:16:59 PM	**potty4350**: *Well I will Diana*
5:17:07 PM	**potty4350**: I really do know that feelings
5:17:45 PM	**potty4350**: What are your plans for the rest of the day?
5:18:18 PM	**ladydi2011**: Relaxing once I get home
5:18:27 PM	**potty4350**: good darling
5:18:31 PM	**potty4350**: are you working tomorrow?
5:18:36 PM	**ladydi2011**: What about you? It is late there...
5:18:46 PM	**ladydi2011**: Yes, I always work!
5:19:35 PM	**ladydi2011**: Did you have dinner?
5:19:52 PM	**potty4350**: I will be working tomorrow
5:20:06 PM	**potty4350**: I was suppose to go to Dubai on friday but something came up

5:20:31 PM   **potty4350**: *I am afraid i will be losing the opportunity i have right now on getting my money*

5:21:02 PM	**ladydi2011**: I am sorry to hear this.
5:21:51 PM	**potty4350**: Yea it ok
5:21:56 PM	**potty4350**: *Diana i really want to come to you*
5:22:13 PM	**potty4350**: *Do you think all this while that I have not been able to talk to you .. do*

you think i am happy?

5:22:42 PM **ladydi2011**: I thought maybe you found another woman
5:22:50 PM **potty4350**: No, I stop looking ever since I found you Diana
5:23:30 PM **ladydi2011**: I am still waiting my dear
5:25:30 PM **potty4350**: Yes *i* know you are
5:25:39 PM **potty4350**: *And I really can't wait to meet you either Diana*
5:27:59 PM **ladydi2011**: Then you WILL make it happen!
5:28:11 PM **potty4350**: Yes *i* know *i* will diana
5:28:21 PM **potty4350**: *what can i do for you to trust me?*
5:28:42 PM **ladydi2011**: I told you
5:28:48 PM **ladydi2011**: Show up at my door
5:29:18 PM **potty4350**: Yes *i* know, but things are going way to wrong for me here
5:29:46 PM **potty4350**: *And diana you know* i *can't just leave without getting done here in the UK*
5:30:49 PM **ladydi2011**: I do. I also have faith in your abilities to make it happen.
5:31:53 PM **potty4350**: *Well you make me happy diana*
5:31:58 PM **potty4350**: I am trying my best though
5:32:09 PM **potty4350**: *I feel so bad things went this way*
5:32:11 PM **potty4350**: *I feel like failure*
5:33:42 PM **ladydi2011**: Once you are here all will be good
5:34:07 PM **potty4350**: Yes *i* know
5:36:05 PM **potty4350**: thank you diana
5:36:21 PM **potty4350**: what time is it over there?
5:36:59 PM **ladydi2011**: 5:35 pm
5:37:26 PM **ladydi2011**: My battery is dying
5:37:43 PM **ladydi2011**: Hope to hear from you again soon
5:37:58 PM **potty4350**: Okay baby
5:38:02 PM **potty4350**: When will you be back online??
5:38:19 PM **potty4350**: Can we chat later tonight?
5:38:43 PM **ladydi2011**: In about 2 hrs. from now
5:42:53 PM **potty4350**: Okay
5:43:02 PM **potty4350**: I will be here to chat with you in about 2hours

---

IM Aug 30, 2012 2:46:03 AM

2:46:03 AM **potty4350**: <ding>

IM Aug 31, 2012 6:27:50 PM

6:27:50 PM **potty4350**: <ding>
6:28:04 PM **potty4350**: Hey Honey
6:28:12 PM **potty4350**: <ding>
6:29:35 PM **potty4350**: <ding>
6:30:12 PM **potty4350**: hiii

12:19:32 PM **potty4350**: Hello

1:42:05 PM **potty4350**: Hello .. How are you doing?

2:48:22 PM **ladydi2011**: Hi Robin
2:48:26 PM **ladydi2011**: How are you?
2:49:03 PM **potty4350**: I am fine honey and you?
2:49:13 PM **potty4350**: How is your day going with you there?
2:49:38 PM **ladydi2011**: My day is good.
2:49:42 PM **ladydi2011**: How is yours?
2:49:54 PM **ladydi2011**: I need to go out shortly
2:49:55 PM **potty4350**: Mine was bad but *i* will be fine
2:50:07 PM **ladydi2011**: Why? What is going on?
2:50:11 PM **potty4350**: *not sure if you care though*
2:50:14 PM **potty4350**: *everything is wrong*
2:50:27 PM **ladydi2011**: Please do not try to put guilt on me with "not sure if I care".
2:50:48 PM **potty4350**: I am not
2:50:55 PM **potty4350**: *just saying my mind and what i feel so far*
2:51:02 PM **ladydi2011**: Ok
2:51:05 PM **potty4350**: ever since *i* asked for your help you have been acting strange
2:51:11 PM **potty4350**: *but it all good*
2:51:17 PM **potty4350**: *i* regret ever asking you for help
2:51:34 PM **ladydi2011**: It is what it is
2:51:53 PM **potty4350**: how do you mean diana
2:52:18 PM **ladydi2011**: Whatever is in the past is in the past. All we can do is move forward.
2:52:57 PM **ladydi2011**: I am sorry that things are not going well for you. I wish they were
2:53:42 PM **ladydi2011**: Are you there?
2:53:57 PM **potty4350**: Yes sure
2:54:07 PM **potty4350**: Yes *i* am here diana
2:54:11 PM **ladydi2011**: You sound angry
2:54:37 PM **potty4350**: I am not
2:54:44 PM **potty4350**: *I don't like the way you acting this is not the way we use to be before*
2:55:04 PM **ladydi2011**: How do you perceive me to be acting?
2:55:46 PM **potty4350**: *i* dont care diana
2:55:49 PM **potty4350**: *you own yourself*
2:55:58 PM **potty4350**: *i* have really tried my best to bring us back
2:56:03 PM **potty4350**: but it like you dont want it
2:56:14 PM **potty4350**: maybe you found someone else you really like it all good

2:56:22 PM   **potty4350**: *you own yourself* and you can do whatever you like

2:56:28 PM   **ladydi2011**: Hmmmmmm...I guess I just don't know what to say

2:57:30 PM   **potty4350**: really

2:58:03 PM   **potty4350**: well you are the type that would text me every morning and do all sort of good things before but you don't do that anymore

2:58:24 PM   **potty4350**: *if you think i am here all for your money then you are wrong and i will say you should screw off with it ..*

2:58:47 PM   **potty4350**: *i have really tried my best to make you realise that i love you and if not for what happened to me here i won't be asking for your help and now that i am at the point of losing everything i am sure you would be glad to hear that .. right??*

2:59:15 PM   **potty4350**: great ..

2:59:29 PM   **potty4350**: *Let me tell you this i am not one of those scammers or what did you call them ..*

2:59:36 PM   **potty4350**: *I am never gonna rip anyone ok?*

2:59:46 PM   **potty4350**: *so pls take that tag of me*

3:00:09 PM   **potty4350**: *I would give you my ssn if you want me too my address and everything just for you to know i am real and you lose*

3:00:41 PM   **ladydi2011**: Wow! I never heard you use this type of language

3:01:24 PM   **ladydi2011**: I am glad to now know this side of you

3:01:46 PM   **potty4350**: diana what will you do if you were in my shoes

3:02:20 PM   **potty4350**: *when you love a woman and you have tried your best to make her know how much you do love her and yet she still thinks you are not been real to her*

3:02:28 PM   **potty4350**: that is so sad and depressing

3:03:08 PM   **potty4350**: *thought you are someone i could confide in ..*

3:03:21 PM   **potty4350**: *I wish you know the plans i have for us*

3:03:29 PM   **potty4350**: *you break my son's heart*

3:03:47 PM   **potty4350**: *you made me love you and let me down*

3:04:08 PM   **potty4350**: remember you told me to give you a little attention when you realise *i* dont have your time and *i* give you all the attention you needed and you let it all off

3:04:32 PM   **potty4350**: you make me cry diana..this is so sad

3:04:48 PM   **ladydi2011**: I am sorry Robin

3:05:02 PM   **potty4350**: *but remember no one will ever love you like i do*

3:05:05 PM   **ladydi2011**: I didn't break your son's heart

3:05:13 PM   **potty4350**: *you will never find the kind of love i have for you*

3:05:20 PM   **potty4350**: *you did cause i told him everything about us*

3:05:58 PM   **ladydi2011**: You will never find another woman who loves you like I do

3:06:10 PM   **ladydi2011**: You will also lose

3:06:27 PM   **ladydi2011**: I am here to emotionally support you

3:06:41 PM   **ladydi2011**: But I will not financially support you

3:06:53 PM   **ladydi2011**: What you need is finances

3:07:07 PM   **ladydi2011**: Maybe you can find another woman to do that for you

3:07:36 PM   **ladydi2011**: I want the best for you but not at my expense

3:08:01 PM   **ladydi2011**: Take care baby

3:09:56 PM   **potty4350**: <ding>

5:47:28 PM **potty4350**: hi
5:47:39 PM **ladydi2011**: Hi
5:47:50 PM **ladydi2011**: How are you?
5:47:57 PM **potty4350**: I am fine and you?
5:48:06 PM **ladydi2011**: I am good
5:48:30 PM **potty4350**: How is work with you there?
5:49:05 PM **ladydi2011**: Busy...doing payroll now
5:49:10 PM **potty4350**: oh cool
5:49:13 PM **potty4350**: are you still at work?
5:49:14 PM **ladydi2011**: What about with you?
5:49:18 PM **ladydi2011**: Yes
5:49:23 PM **potty4350**: just there
5:49:29 PM **potty4350**: getting done
5:49:33 PM **potty4350**: not been easy tho
5:49:47 PM **ladydi2011**: Most things are not easy
5:49:51 PM **ladydi2011**: You know this
5:50:29 PM **potty4350**: Yes
5:50:30 PM **ladydi2011**: Have you had dinner?
5:50:57 PM **potty4350**: No, haven't had dinner
5:51:07 PM **potty4350**: *Don't think i will tonight diana*
5:51:16 PM **ladydi2011**: Oh
5:51:20 PM **ladydi2011**: I have not either. I need to do so soon
5:51:28 PM **potty4350**: why not honey
5:51:33 PM **potty4350**: how soon do you have to go
5:51:39 PM **ladydi2011**: Busy
5:52:02 PM **ladydi2011**: Can I ask you a question?
5:52:17 PM **potty4350**: Yes sure
5:52:46 PM **ladydi2011**: Why are you still talking with me....You told me to screw off
5:52:55 PM **potty4350**: No I did not
5:53:05 PM **potty4350**: And do you want to stop talking to me
5:53:30 PM **ladydi2011**: Yes you did
5:53:55 PM **potty4350**: I don't mean it that way
5:54:10 PM **potty4350**: *And that day was so frustrated and at the point of losing my son diana*
5:54:41 PM **ladydi2011**: What do you mean by "losing your son"?
5:55:16 PM **potty4350**: *do you care about him?*
5:55:37 PM **ladydi2011**: Of course I do, he is part of you
5:55:50 PM **potty4350**: *why don't you believe or trust me baby?*
5:55:55 PM **potty4350**: Yes *i* know he is diana
5:56:30 PM **potty4350**: *he is dying and i need to be home*
5:56:44 PM **potty4350**: and *i* can't leave here if *i* don't get done with this project
5:56:52 PM **ladydi2011**: Dying?
5:57:00 PM **potty4350**: this is a point where *i* can't leave the project
5:57:03 PM **potty4350**: yes *dying!!!!*
5:57:06 PM **ladydi2011**: What is wrong with him?
5:58:01 PM **potty4350**: diana *i* need to be home

5:58:08 PM	**potty4350**: *i am already working on this*
5:58:13 PM	**potty4350**: *he is seriously ill*
5:58:29 PM	**potty4350**: he is with my aunt and mom in canada
5:58:34 PM	**potty4350**: *I have to see him*
5:58:41 PM	**potty4350**: *I don't want to lose him*
5:58:44 PM	**ladydi2011**: I am sure you have to see him
5:58:54 PM	**ladydi2011**: of course you don't want to lose him
5:59:22 PM	**potty4350**: diana *i am already working on this*
5:59:33 PM	**potty4350**: *can you help me with the ticket fee*
5:59:55 PM	**potty4350**: *just a token to you and i will come meet you in texas and see if we can go see christian in canada together*
6:00:13 PM	**potty4350**: *or better still if you can help me raise some money for them in canada*
6:00:24 PM	**potty4350**: *i dont know why all this keep happening to me*
6:01:35 PM	**potty4350**: <ding>
6:01:45 PM	**ladydi2011**: Hmmmm
6:01:49 PM	**potty4350**: *i am just asking you for a token*
6:01:54 PM	**ladydi2011**: Why would you meet me in Texas?
6:01:57 PM	**potty4350**: *i believe you should just do this for me*
6:02:38 PM	**potty4350**: thought you still there diana. I am sorry if i am wrong but you should understand that *i* have a lot on my mind
6:03:08 PM	**ladydi2011**: No, I got back from Texas a month ago
6:03:11 PM	**potty4350**: *at the point of losing everything i have been working for all my life*
6:03:19 PM	**potty4350**: *i am sure you understand that feelings*
6:03:29 PM	**ladydi2011**: Yeah, I do understand
6:04:02 PM	**potty4350**: *sometimes it better you die than seeing yourself losing everything one have ever worked for*
6:04:10 PM	**potty4350**: this is so crazy diana
6:04:22 PM	**potty4350**: *i just hope you know how i feel ..*
6:04:59 PM	**potty4350**: *diana i just hope you would understand me this time and do this for me ...*
6:05:31 PM	**ladydi2011**: I am sorry so much is happening in your life
6:05:43 PM	**ladydi2011**: I am not in the position to give you any money
6:05:47 PM	**ladydi2011**: Sorry baby
6:06:13 PM	**potty4350**: *do you think you can help raise chris raise some little money in canada*
6:07:44 PM	**ladydi2011**: Hmmmm...How?
6:08:17 PM	**potty4350**: *maybe you could just help me send him some money so that my mind can be at rest a little bit*
6:08:27 PM	**potty4350**: you can have it sent to my aunt or mom
6:08:36 PM	**potty4350**: *i would really appreciate if you could do this for me diana*
6:08:52 PM	**ladydi2011**: I am not in a financial position to do this now
6:09:00 PM	**potty4350**: diana???
6:10:55 PM	**ladydi2011**: ???
6:12:43 PM	**potty4350**: *well he is a little boyy and no amount is too small if you really want to*
6:13:55 PM	**ladydi2011**: I have to go now Robin
6:18:48 PM	**potty4350**: <ding>
6:18:51 PM	**potty4350**: Diana
6:19:48 PM	**potty4350**: Hello
6:19:52 PM	**potty4350**: Are you there??

6:19:53 PM **ladydi2011**: Yes Robin
6:20:13 PM **potty4350**: *Diana I am only asking you to do this for my son*
6:20:22 PM **potty4350**: *No amount is too small for him*
6:20:39 PM **potty4350**: *And you can talk to him yourself if you want*
6:21:30 PM **potty4350**: Ok?
6:22:30 PM **ladydi2011**: I have been down this road more than once
6:22:38 PM **ladydi2011**: I know you are mad right now
6:22:44 PM **ladydi2011**: You are a scammer!!!
6:36:45 PM **potty4350**: Okay
6:36:54 PM **potty4350**: How do you mean?

I have been dealing with scammers for some time now, so I was not surprised that he came back or that he still called me endearing names. Instantly, he says, "I just need you to trust me," "I wish I am there with you darling," "I adore you still Diana" and "I love you so much still Diana." We all know by now that these are all lies and just sweet words. I figured since he came back, I would learn his next scam to educate you.

He asks me what he can do for me to trust him and I tell him to show up at my door. This is a safe answer and one he can't get around or do. He tells me he feels bad things went the way they did and he feels like a failure. (I am sure he does feel like a failure because he failed to get money from me.)

His real self and anger come out when he says, "*If you think i am here all for your money then you are wrong and i will say you should screw off with it. And now that i am at the point of losing everything i am sure you would be glad to hear that .. right?? Let me tell you this i am not one of those scammers or what did you call them. I am never gonna rip anyone ok? so pls take that tag of me*".

He then tells me that he wishes I knew the plans he has for us and that I made him love me and then let him down. (I don't think he's taking this well.)

 RED FLAGS

- He says he is losing the opportunity to get his money. (Really? I thought that opportunity was gone a month ago.) Remember to pay attention to any timeline given.
- He says he is not sure that I care anymore and he doesn't like how I am acting because we are not like we used to be before. He says I "own myself," and "but it all good," which is Nigerian terminology.
- For punctuation purposes, in their written correspondence scammers characteristically type an ellipses with only two periods (..) instead of the more common three (...).
- He says everything is going wrong and he offers to give me his social security number and address for me to know he is real and for me to not lose. Scammers will give you their

social security number trying to gain your trust.

- 🎣 He then brings his "supposed" son into it and said I broke his son's heart. Please, don't ever believe this. The scammer has no son and you haven't broken anyone's heart.

- 🎣 He uses other classic scammer lines like, "Remember, no one will ever love you like I do" and "You will never find the kind of love I have for you." Neither of these statements are true; don't ever believe them.

- 🎣 His latest scam is that his son is dying and he needs to get back to Canada to see him. Scammers often use children in their stories, and it is disgusting. Do not fall victim to anything having to do with children. They use children because they know it pulls at a woman's heart strings. In the end, he does what all scammers do; he tries to get whatever money he can from you.

Although I have many more scam stories to share with you from my two years of chatting with scammers, this is the final story for this book because the binding can't handle anymore! My hope is that by the time you finish this book, you will have so much information you will never get caught in the web of a scammer and your heart and money will be safe. Please do not play with these guys. There are many dangers in doing so. Keep yourself safe!

Don't miss the next chapter, Inner Workings of the Scamming World. It is filled with Information told by the scammers themselves and verified by an inside source. This information is dynamite for teaching you about the scamming world and what you can do to protect yourself.

CHAPTER 7

INNER WORKINGS OF THE SCAMMING WORLD

---

*Isaiah 5:20 - Woe unto them that **call evil good**, and **good evil**; that put darkness for light, and light for darkness; that put bitter for sweet, and sweet for bitter!*

If you are a scammer or a would-be scammer, please know that this is NOT a legal or honorable trade. Using God and His Word to steal comes with a high price. "Thou shall NOT steal", "Thou shall NOT lie". I know I can't do anything to stop you, but I will do everything in my power to educate people worldwide so they recognize the red flags, do not get caught up in your ploy, and do not give you money. My goal is to drastically cut your money-making opportunities. If you are scamming, stop hurting and stealing from people; become an honorable and respectable person. The most valuable things you will ever own are your reputation and your dignity. Become someone your children will be proud of. If you have to hide and lie about what you are doing, you shouldn't be doing it.

I chatted with scammers for over a year and a half to gather accurate information for this book, and five scammers "came clean" with me. Of those five men three of them disclosed their real identity and taught me the inner workings of online dating scams. As I chatted with other scammers to gather more information for this book, these three sources told me the inside story about what the scammer I was chatting with was doing, and why. They taught me much and helped me safely navigate the rough waters in which I traveled. I spoke, emailed, chatted or texted daily with these invaluable sources.

Then I met two other men on Twitter that verified what my three sources told me. This chapter wouldn't exist without these men. I want to thank them all for protecting me and teaching me so I can teach you. I am not convinced their stories about themselves are 100% accurate. They know that scamming involves criminal acts, and they were understandably wary of using their real names and pictures. They trust me, but they can't fully anticipate the potential repercussions once their words are released to the world in print. However, whether or not their stories are completely true, the insider information they shared with me is priceless, and I hope you will use it to protect your heart and your money.

This chapter is filled with information provided by these three sources, all of whom are from Nigeria. None of them knew about the other sources. This allowed me to ask all three of them the same questions in an effort to make my research verifiable, forensically sound (dealing with the application of knowledge), objective, reliable and absent of confirmatory bias. I then verified the information that was verifiable via two other sources in Nigeria and the Internet. Neither this chapter nor this book is an exhaustive encyclopedia of everything scammers do or the means they utilize. Scammers evolve themselves and their methods every day. I provided this information to help you identify and avoid scammers that you are likely to encounter while dating online.

I have learned all scammers are *not the same*, but most have the same title… *"THE YAHOO BOYZ"*. Be aware although my sources are in Nigeria, scammers are all over the world, and you will encounter them on most, if not every, Internet dating site. Each scammer has his own specific motivation for what he does, however, all their motives fall under the umbrella of *stealing your hard earned money*! Not all scammers are at the same level. They may be "beginner", "small money", "professional" or "chair or boss". Regardless of his level and regardless of his sweet talk, a scammer does not love you and never will. You are his victim and he wants to take your money. That's all.

What follows is my description of the different level of scammers. Please know there are always exceptions to the rules. I speak specifically of Nigerian and Ghana scammers because they have a large population of scammers, but scammers operate from all corners of the world.

The Beginner

A *beginner* scammer is called "Guy" or "G". He makes many errors in telling his story and often goes off point because he is still learning. He usually asks for a couple hundred dollars and often asks for it too early in the relationship. Sometimes he starts the scam and then passes you on to someone more experienced to ask for the money. From reading this book, you should be able to identify his red flags pretty quickly. He does not have any tools such as fictitious websites or documents or fake cam videos. He doesn't have money so he uses data or Yahoo calls and text so he doesn't have to pay for the calls. He may ask you to send the money right to where he is scamming from (Nigeria, Ghana, etc.) because he does not have any contacts yet to collect and forward the money to him. He may ask you to send the money to the fictitious name he has been using with you, his real name or a friends name. If he asks you to send the money to Nigeria he works it into the scam. For example, he says he needs to travel to Nigeria on business, he has a business partner in Nigeria, the money has to be sent to Nigeria in order to win a bid or obtain a contract, he has been in an accident in Nigeria, he has a nanny watching his child in Nigeria, he needs money to clear his goods from customs or his cars at the port in Nigeria, or something similar.

If it is a military scam he says he needs the money for a TS2 line so he can talk to you on the phone, and the money needs to be sent to his commander who is traveling in Nigeria. A *beginner* is usually on free dating sites because he does not have money to pay for a site nor does he have his Internet Protocol (IP) address covered, therefore he cannot get into dating sites that have security to keep Nigerian scammers out. If you trace his IP address it will many times show he is in Nigeria. It is always helpful to hire a private investigator, such as Arkansas Investigations, to trace the IP address as soon as you receive the first email from someone on a dating site. Arkansas Investigations can be reached at 501-605-0360.

Small money

A *small money* scammer is also called "Guy" or "G." He asks for a couple hundred or maybe a thousand dollars. He does not have any tools such as fictitious websites or fake cam videos. He might have a fictitious passport, and he might send you a $25-$40 bouquet of flowers with a small teddy bear, but nothing expensive or extravagant. He likely shows you red flags early on. Like a *beginner* scammer, he may ask you to send the money right to Nigeria, Ghana or other parts of Africa.

He almost certainly uses a fictitious name when having you send the money because he does not want it to be traced back to him. If he asks you to send the money to Nigeria he works it into the scam, much like a *beginner*. He may even email you an airline flight itinerary to convince you that he is traveling for business. If so, he will probably use KML Airlines. He goes on the KML airlines website and selects a flight and an itinerary without actually booking the flight.

Many *small money* scammers have connections in other parts of the world such as the United States and United Kingdom, and may tell you to send the money to an acquaintance there. The acquaintance is known among scammers as an "off shore guy" or "picker." The "picker" picks up the money and keeps 10-20% for himself and sends the rest to the scammer. If this is the case, the scammer will not mention Nigeria in his story. He may have the resources and knowledge to hide his IP address from a secure dating site; otherwise, he will be on free dating sites.

Professional

These scammers are called "Guy", "G" or "Boss," and they play for big money! A *professional scammer* asks for thousands or millions of dollars. He has the tools and the know-how to pull off a large money scam, leveraging fictitious news, banking, contracting, and equipment websites to name a few; fake cam video, fictitious passports, bank checks, contracts and other fictitious documents. If he takes you to any website such as these, STOP ALL COMMUNICATIONS IMMEDIATELY.

If it is a military scam, he will show documents such as leave request, leave policies and instructions, approval for leave, authorization for leave, benefits and claims document, leave bonus form, certificate of marriage, death certificate, Veterans Affairs claims form and personal details form that includes banking information. His military scam is designed to take from $300,000 to over a million dollars from his victims. You can learn how these scams are run in the book, "Is It a Real Soldier behind the Screen?" Online Dating: How to Protect Your Heart and Money.

A *professional* has access to hacked credit cards, so if he sends you flowers, they will be expensive; he might even send you jewelry or money. The more money he plans to ask for, the more elaborate the gifts you will receive. He is usually on top of his game and makes few, if any, mistakes. He is very careful and difficult to detect. It takes longer to find red flags, but they are there. If you know all the red flags in this book, you will be able to identify them, as long as you do so before he captures your heart. He will likely not mention Nigeria, but might mention South Africa, Dubai, United Kingdom, Yemen, South America or some other part of the world where he allegedly travels.

A *professional* specializes in money transfer scams (Advance-fee fraud). In this scam, he makes what is called a fuse. That is, he "flashes" an account by showing a large sum of money in the client's account, so it appears to be there when the client (you) and the bank check. When you call and tell him the money is there, he asks you to withdraw the money, keep a certain amount for yourself, and send the rest to him. BEWARE. Within a few days the bank will call and ask you to pay back the money you withdrew, because in reality, it was never in the account. The bank notifies authorities and you can be charged with fraud and or money laundering.

A *professional* rarely asks to have money sent directly to him. He asks for large sums of money that have to be wired through a bank and sent to his off shore guy in another part of the world who has an account capable of handling such large amounts of money without questions. The *professional* usually has his IP address covered, but not always. If it is covered you will find him on every dating site because he can break through the security without being detected.

Chair or *Boss*

These scammers play for real big money! Chair is short for *Chairman*, and he gets money almost every day from the lower level Yahoo Boyz. He may be in the United States, United Kingdom, Malaysia, China, Egypt or any other place in the world that has an advanced Internet system, but usually not Nigeria or Ghana. He has ample information and resources such as software, fast Internet service and access to many tools like fictitious web cam videos, websites and documents that nobody else has, and he uses these tools to make money. Many of these resources that are available in other countries are restricted in Nigeria. For example, a bank account can be opened remotely in the United Kingdom, but in Nigeria it requires a face-to-face interaction, which increases his chances of being traced and caught.

He has a bank account capable of handling large amounts of money without questions. When a Professional Yahoo Boy does an "advance fee" scam for big money, that money is sent to the *Chair*, who keeps 40% for himself and sends 60% on to the scammer. He is a good researcher and skilled on the Internet. He knows how to break through security of dating sites. He can also hack or gain access to stolen credit cards. He lives a lifestyle of excess.

The Scammer

Scammers are criminals engaging in criminal acts. There are many ways to tell a story. I am here to tell the unbiased story so you have a better understanding of what you have already dealt with if you have been scammed, and what you might encounter while on line dating. I am nobody's judge or jury. I have no hatred for anyone, nor am I on a witch hunt. My only agenda is to obtain and provide reliable and accurate facts to educate and create an awareness that will elicit positive change, stop heartbreak and stop money from being stolen.

The root motivation of scamming should not be overlooked or dismissed. In Nigeria and Ghana, the motivation stems from lack of jobs due to government corruption. Scamming has been a way of life in Nigeria since at least the 1960's. Since most scammers range in age from 12 to late 20's, they have been born into this environment.

The daily wage in Nigeria can be as low as $1 a day, and many scammers simply seek to provide for themselves and their families. Some scam to put themselves through school in hopes of landing a higher paying job when they graduate, but very few jobs are available in Nigeria or Ghana. Some scam to get rich, to have seed money to start a business, or for the thrill it provides. Others become addicted to the quick money and the finer lifestyle. Scammers' wives are supportive of the scams because of the material wealth the lifestyle affords them. Many wives even help with the scam.

I traveled to Africa a couple of years ago on a mission trip, and I learned first-hand how poor and difficult life in Africa can be. When I arrived in Africa I thought I had been catapulted back to Old Testament times. If you have never been to a third-world country, it is difficult to understand how bad living conditions can be.

Throughout the process of gathering the information for this book, I have asked myself, and I want you to ask yourself, "What am I capable of doing to feed my family?" and "What am I capable of doing to survive?" We all hope our answer would be, "*not this*", however, until we are confronted with survival, we really do not know what we are capable of.

Some people are so poor that they go to Malaysia to sell their kidney to make quick, clean and quiet money. It has been reported a kidney sells for 10 Million Naira, which is equivalent to $63,391.40 in U.S. currency.

http://newsrescue.com/nigerians-selling-kidneys-in-asia-30000-a-pop/#axzz2jqLAmcrX.

Imagine how desperate a person must be to willingly sell a body organ for money? When clients (like you) give money to a Yahoo Boy, it may provide for his survival, but it can also provide the motivation for these boys to live reckless lifestyles that in many cases can lead to death. I see a vicious circle where many people are victims. My cry is for it all to stop!

It seems to me each of the three reformed scammers who helped me navigate the online dating waters and protected me while doing so just *might* have a conscience. Each said he did not want to continue doing what he had been doing. One told me he wanted to be a good man and no longer live a life of shame. Another said he went in and out of scamming and only did it when things got really bad. I believe this because he surely wasn't a pro. Another said he did it because he saw others with "things" and wanted to achieve "things" but there were no jobs for him even though he has a BBA to do it legally, nor was there another means of obtaining capital to start his own business. Nigeria operates on a cash only basis. They all say they have provided me this information because they want to see this stopped; they are breaking their silence to help women and men avoid becoming victims of heartbreak and loss of money. They also hope it will shine a light on the overarching problem of no jobs or future for the youth in Nigeria. One asked me to beg readers to *"Never go on an online dating site"*. He said the dangers are too many. He taught me that spells are used and he knows of men and women that have committed suicide as a result. If a "short term" spell is cast it is called *"Yahoo Plus"* and if a "long-term" spell is cast it is called *"Yahoo Plus Plus" or "Yahoo Extreme"*. You can read more about this in chapter eight, The Unknown Hidden Dangers of Online Dating (p. 739).

These men are concerned about what the future holds for the youth of Nigeria who are now Yahoo Boyz. They all say Internet crimes and other crimes stem from the corruption of the country's uncaring leadership and high rates of unemployment in the country. Corruption breads more corruption. Scamming spreads quickly among Nigerian youth and a rise in online dating scams correlates with a drop in the rate of armed robbery. Nigerian youth are also drawn to Internet crime as a way of "getting back" at a society that has no plans or place for them. Many say it's to "get back" at the white man that enslaved them. Many times the youth who are scamming become the provider for their family and legions of relatives.

They do not hide the fact they scam. They are actually proud to be a scammer and make it very well known they scam. They are easily identified in their designer sneakers, expensive watches, and designer clothes. They wear a lot of gold, own sports cars, and party on the weekends with expensive champagne, brandy, and drugs. Many even live in mansions by the age of 22. What starts as a way to survive becomes a lifestyle. Once they make money from scamming, some of these young men feel trapped and some become addicted to the money and lifestyle; oftentimes their families do too, and family members encourage them to continue the criminal activity because they benefit from it.

Some of them open businesses or go to a university with the money. Many of them start scamming while attending the university because the universities are hotbeds for this criminal activity. Often their desperation turns to greed, and they justify their actions with the perception that "People are gullible and rich in America and other parts of the world, so they can afford it." They perceive women have soft hearts, fall in love easily and will do anything for the man they love, so women are natural targets. Scammers also target men, falsely representing themselves with pictures and videos of young, partially nude or nude women. *Men have no idea they're being scammed by another man.*

My sources tell me scammers love working in Nigeria because the police work hand-in-hand with the scammers, and the banks will issue money to them no matter how illegal it is as long as the banks get a percentage. They say Nigerian scammers run scams in every country they inhabit, especially in major cities like Malaysia, and scamming is now a worldwide trade. They also say Malaysia is where much of the software can be bought that helps them perfect their trade. Many have accomplices in different parts of the world to pick-up and send them the money and stolen goods.

An online dating scam intended to obtain money from someone is a *job* for the scammer. It is his trade; it is how he makes a living. Most scammers first learn the basic skills by shadowing an experienced scammer. They pay a fee to be taught, and they learn how to develop a format and story, select profile pictures, write a profile, find the dating site, find love material on line, identify a good target (they call someone they are trying to scam a "client"), how to navigate Yahoo!, and how to talk to the client and coerce them to fall in love. Once they grasp the concept, they go out on their own, and they learn many things by trial and error and by sharing ideas with other scammers.

Those who stay in the profession continually hone their skills just like anyone who works a legitimate job. Their ultimate objective is to become a *professional* scammer who can easily fool clients to obtain their money. They are not looking to fall in love. Sometimes the scammer that really doesn't have a scammer heart will feel bad and not ask for money and just disappear. This is extremely rare. The majority of scammers have ruthless hearts and care nothing for you. You are just someone behind the computer screen that they don't know. All they want is your money at all costs.

A scammer spends up to sixteen hours a day, seven days a week on line. Scammers with blackberries or smart phones chat online with their client almost constantly, even if they are out. Almost all scammers own a laptop. Many times the beginner scammers will pay to use a computer at an Internet café. The Internet cafés are equipped with satellite Internet. Many of them serve the scammers specifically by closing their doors during afterhours from 10:30 PM to 7:00AM so the scammers can work without fear of discovery and arrest. Some scammers use one person's place of residence that has Internet connection to conduct the scams because it's safer than the Internet café. One of my sources told me the Internet cafés used to play songs such as "Maga Don Pay" by Kelly Hansome, Nkem Owoh's "I Go Chop Your Dollar" and Olu Maintain's "Yahoozee" to encourage scammers to get the money, but then it became illegal for these songs to be played. If you want to see what is important to the scammer and what they do with the money they steal, please watch these songs on YouTube.

You can also find an article about theses songs at

http://nzesylva.wordpress.com/2008/10/27/scammers-new-anthem-mugu-don-pay/

Yahoozee is the song sung by Olu Maintain. It is a Nigerian term that originates from the term "Yahoo Boyz" which is generally used to define Internet scammers. Yahoozee is a dance step where you hold your hand in a gun like gesture and move it over your head in a stylish way that goes with the rhythm of the song. It's the official dance of the Yahoo Boyz. Many of the words in this song are Yoruba language. One of my sources is from the Yoruba tribe and translated the words of the song for me.

Yahoozee Song Lyrics with Meaning:

Ewo awon boys yi - "look at this boys – See these boys"
Kamikaze on Ketto level – "making money on a coded level - let's roll on ghetto levels"
Yahoozee
E jami si jo – "please show me the way – Let me enjoy"

Oh oh Yahoo!
Oh oh Yahoo!
Oh oh Yahoo!
Oh oh Yahoozeee!
Yahoozeee!
Yahoozeee!
Yahoozeee!

If I hammer – "when I a hit money – If I succeed in getting money"
1st thing na hummer - "the first thing I will do is to buy an hummer car"

1 million dollars
Elo lo ma je ti n –"how much will it be"
Ba se si Naira – "when I convert it to naira"

If I hammer – "when I a hit money – If I succeed in getting money"
1st thing na hummer - "the first thing I will do is to buy an hummer car"

1 million dollars
Elo lo ma je ti n –"how much will it be"
Ba se si Naira – "when I convert it to naira"
Monday, Tuesday, Wednesday, Thursday, Boys dey hustle
Friday, Saturday, Sunday, Gbogbo aye – "is meant for drinking and clubbing"
Champagne, Hennessy, Moet for everybody

Ewo awon- "see these babes"
Omoge dem dey – "check their body"
Shake their body – "young ladies are shaking their body"

Oh oh Yahoo!

Oh oh Yahoo!
Oh oh Yahoo!
Oh oh Yahoozeee!
Yahoozeee!
Yahoozeee!
Yahoozeee!
Yahoozeee!

Everybody, enough effizy – "every body enough swag"
Take am easy – "take it easy"
It's all about the Benjamins baby – it's all about the money baby"
Everybody, enough effizy – "every body enough swag"
Take am easy – "take it easy"
It's all about the Benjamins baby – it's all about the money baby"

(La la la la la la la)
London la mule si – "we get a home in London"
America ła ti pawo – "but hustle in America"

Awon oshomo – "women freak men"
Gbomo tiawn – "don take our woman"
Awon oshomo – "we flex with babe"
Gbomo Gbin – "flexing guys"

To ba wunmi mo le – "if I like"
Gba Tokyo lo – "I can go to Tokyo"
To ba wunmi ma lo- "if I like"
Jamaica o – "I can go to Jamaica"

Ole tun wunmi ki n ni – "and if I feel like it again"
Mo fe lo Germany o – "I may go to germany"
Ki n ni mo fe lo ojo Meji pere- "and decide just to use 2 days"
Owo lo n soro o – "money is what is speaking"

If I hammer – "when I a hit money – If I succeed in getting money"
1st thing na hummer - "the first thing I will do is to buy an hummer car"

1 million dollars
Elo lo ma je ti n –"how much will it be"
Ba se si Naira – "when I convert it to naira"

If I hammer – "when I a hit money – If I succeed in getting money"
1st thing na hummer - "the first thing I will do is to buy an hummer car"

1 million dollars

Elo lo ma je ti n –"how much will it be"
Ba se si Naira – "when I convert it to naira"

Oh oh Yahoo!
Oh oh Yahoo!
Oh oh Yahoo!
Oh oh Yahoozeee!
Yahoozeee!
Yahoozeee!
Yahoozeee!
Yahoozeee!

Owe n be lapo mi o – "I have money in my pocket"
Dide ko ba mi jo – "stand up and dance with me"

Owe n be lapo mi o – "I have money in my pocket"
Dide ko ba mi jo – "stand up and dance with me"
Mama Charley n Be lapo mi o – "I have mama charley (UK currency) in my pocket"
Dide ko ba mi ra – "stand up and rock with me"

Dollar n be – "there is Dollars"
Naira n be – "there is Naira"
Kuruje n be – "wealth exist"
Paper n be – "money is available"
Lapo waaa – "in our pocket"

Everything is there!

Awon kan,Awon kan – "some people, some people"
Awon kan,Awon kan – "some people, some people"
Awon kan,Awon kan – "some people, some people"
Awon kan,Awon kan – "some people, some people"

Awon kan waye wa sise – "some people are in the world to work"
Awon kan kan waye wa jaye – "some people are in the world to have fun"

Awon kan waye wa gbowo – "some people are in the world to collect money"
Awon kan way wa saye – "some people are in the world to enjoy"

Awon kan waye wa sayo ooooooooooh – "some people are in the world to drink"
Awon kan waye wa sayo – "some people are in the world to drink"

Yahoozeee!

Oh oh Yahoozee!

Oh oh Yahoozee!
Oh oh Yahoozee!
Oh oh Yahoozee!

Owe n be lapo mi o – "money in my pocket"
Dide ko ba mi jo – "stand up and dance with me"
Owe n be lapo mi o – "money in my pocket"
Dide ko ba mi jo– "stand up and dance with me"
Mama Charley n be lapo mi o – "Mama Charley (UK currency) in my pocket"

Dide ko ba mi ra – "stand up and rock with me"

Owe n be lapo mi o – "money in my pocket"
Dide ko ba mi jo – "stand up and dance with me"
Owe n be lapo mi o – "money in my pocket"
Dide ko ba mi jo– "stand up and dance with me"

How to identify a scammer

This is a lengthy list of red flags that can help you determine if the person you are talking to is legitimate or a scammer. I am sure it is not complete, because scammers and their ways are very different, and they are always creating new ways to con. Please note: I use the pronoun "he" in this list, but scammers can also be female.

 RED FLAGS

- He always has some kind of dramatic grandiose story, which is why he needs you to help by sending him money.
- He has no family, business associates or close friends to turn to; he only has you.
- Common themes are travel, illness, investment, and banking delays. He may claim to be traveling and unable to cash his check for many days; he needs money temporarily, and he promises to pay it back to your account. Illness may involve a child, parent or sibling, or he may claim to have been in an accident himself. He may offer you an investment opportunity. He needs money to help pay custom charges, clear goods, or purchase equipment. He needs money to start a job. He will promise to pay interest on the money you give him. He will NEVER pay the money back. Once you send the money, it is gone. You cannot get it back.
- He asks you to assist with a personal transaction such as depositing funds or shipping merchandise.
- He asks you to wire money through a bank, Western Union or Money Gram.
- He says he is new at online dating.

- He lives in one country with a child in school in a different country.
- He has a nanny who is taking care of his child somewhere.
- He only has a few pictures to send you. Some scammers only have a few because they use stolen pictures. However, some professional scammers will have many pictures. Many times the pictures he sends has the same number file with a different letter of the alphabet following, such as 198765A, 198765B, 198765C, etc. or Jerry1, Jerry2, Jerry3, etc.
- He does not display his picture on his dating site profile. But many do.
- His facts are inconsistent.
- He leaves a lot of blanks in his profile; although some complete them. It depends if he has taken time to generate the information.
- He will not send you his IM until the second or third email. But there are exceptions to this where he will ask you to meet him on Yahoo messenger the first contact. It all depends on his style.
- His occupation is in engineering, construction, oil, geology, business, or something else that requires traveling country to country. He will not tell you he is a doctor, teacher, factory worker or anything else stable.
- He claims to be widowed or divorced.
- He calls you his queen.
- He quickly refers to you as his wife. He does this because he thinks if you think of yourself as his wife, you will do anything for your husband. He tries to get you into this mind set.
- He sends a very sugar coated and heart winning love letter email right away instead of one that says, "Hi, how are you? I would like to get to know you."
- He gives only attractive details about himself.
- He replies to your email very quickly.
- He asks for your personal email address and wants to take you away from the dating site to Yahoo IM really quickly.
- He might change his Yahoo ID to be both of your names.
- He might put your picture with love messages on his Yahoo ID
- He asks you to close your account on the dating site. He does this so no other scammers can get to you.
- He disappears from the dating site or Yahoo messenger and reappears with a different name.
- He spends an inordinate amount of time chatting with you and is very attentive. He knows the more time he spends with you, the better his chances of getting you to fall in love with him.
- Within the first week or two he says it was destiny or fate that brought you together.
- He will always ask for your pictures and give you lots of compliments.
- He sends you flowers, candy, teddy bears, jewelry, etc. that he has purchased with a

stolen credit card. Some might even send you money. He is wooing your heart.

- He tells you he has to travel, sometimes to Nigeria, Ghana, South Africa, Dubai or other countries.
- In the first or second email or chat he calls you baby, darling, babe, hun, my love, honey, and other endearing names.
- He says "I love you" very quickly. Usually within the first or second chat.
- He talks quickly about getting married.
- He asks if you are chatting with other men.
- He uses God and Scripture to gain your trust. Do not feel safe just because someone appears to be a Christian.
- He sends love letters that he copies and pastes from other sites like www.lovingyou.com, www.lovelysms.com, www.1001loveletters.com and www.lovepoemsandquotes.com.
- He frequently asks "So what do you think of me?" He asks this early on to gauge if you are a prospective client; he then asks it a little further along to gauge how close you are to falling in love with him so he knows when to ask for money.
- He asks a lot of questions such as if you live alone, if you own or rent, and if you work.
- He does not want you to tell friends or family members about your relationship with him.
- He has poor spelling and grammar.
- He says in his profile that he is educated, but when he sends emails and chat, only parts will seem like the writing of an educated person and other parts will not. This happens because he copies and paste from someone else's profile.
- The words in his sentences are out of order. Nigeria has roughly 250 tribes speaking 521 languages and dialects. Nigerian scammers typically speak Pidgin English, which puts what should be at the end of a sentence in the middle of a sentence. Examples: How You Dey? – How are you doing today? I go land you slap – I will slap you!
- Some scammers say they are from abroad and then intentionally use bad grammar to make you think they really are from abroad and that English is their second language.
- He uses Nigerian vernacular, such as "I slept off", "I'm going to bath now" or "my parents (mother or father or siblings) are late", "happy family", "loving kind", "brave heart", "I love you with all my life", "I promise I will never fail you", "Your heart is safe with me", "it got spoiled", "tell me your true mind", "you rule my world and my life", "soonest", "your kind of woman", "more better", "you own me", "I will not disappoint", "It all good", "I am very strong" (meaning sexually. Remember, most of them are in their 20's.)
- For punctuation purposes, in their written correspondence scammers characteristically type an ellipses with only two periods (..) instead of the more common three (…).
- He does not capitalize "I" or the names of cities or states, and he may misspell the

names of cities and states.

- He will type "know" for "now".
- When he wants your attention he hits the "BUZZ" on Yahoo messenger. He hits it a lot.
- He doesn't understand English slang.
- When chatting, he gives details that contradict his profile, especially his age, date of birth, where he is from, height, eye and hair color.
- He refers to the United States as the USA and does not know much about the United States, even though he claims to be from the United States.
- He talks a lot about current events. Scammers watch CNN every morning to learn about what is happening in the United States so he can talk to clients about what he saw on the news.
- He is intensely interested in you one hundred percent of the time until he gets money from you; then you hear from him about half as often. When the money is gone, he is again intensely interested. *Professional* scammers will not always be with you because they tell you they are always busy working and sometimes in an area that doesn't have Internet connection.
- He IMs, texts and calls you at unusual hours, because they are in a different time zone. Many calls, text and IM's will come in at 2:00, 3:00 or 4:00 in the morning if you are in the Eastern time zone.
- If you ask what time it is where he is, he might give you the wrong time because he didn't calculate time zones properly.
- If you chat at night he is tired. This is because it is the middle of the night in his time zone. Most scammers don't sleep at night because they are chatting.
- His correspondence sometimes has someone else's name other than yours or uses "him" when it should say "her" and "her" when it should say "him".
- There are lapses in conversation on IM. This usually occurs for two reasons: he is chatting with more women than just you or he is looking something up you asked him that he doesn't have the answer to.
- He tells you he is in the middle of the sea, or in a remote place to work, or in the desert if it's a military scam and that the network isn't strong. He purposely logs in and out just so you think he has a bad network if his story warrants it.
- If he is careless you get the same IM message two or more times in a row because he is copying and pasting and mistakenly hitting the send button.
- He gets booted off the computer a lot and tells you it is because of a bad network or bad weather. Africa does not have a stable Internet connection. If the weather is bad in Africa, so is the network.
- He always wants you to come on camera but tells you his web cam doesn't work. If he does come on, it will be very brief, because it is a fake cam.

- He does not answer personal and specific questions you ask him.
- Sometimes you do not hear from him for a couple days. This is because he had no electricity to charge his phone or laptop. It is not uncommon for people in Nigeria to go without electricity for extended periods of time.
- If he calls you, you have a hard time understanding him because of his accent and background noise. He may say it is a friend of his calling on his behalf.
- If he gives you a phone number, you are not able to get through when you call.
- If he gives you a phone number starting with +44 70 he is definitely a scammer.
- He sends you a (fictitious) passport to prove his identity.
- He sends you a (fictitious) social security number to gain your trust and make you believe that he is who he says he is.
- He is a master at making you feel guilty. "If you love me you will send money to help me."
- He becomes verbally abusive if you refuse to send money,
- If you accuse him of being a scammer he denies it and acts deeply offended.
- He asks you to open a new account to transfer money.
- He sends you a log in and password for a bank account. You will see there is an account open for you and money has been transferred to your account. He asks you to withdraw money to send to him. When you try to withdraw money it will not work. You receive a message that the account has been frozen and that you need a passkey to transfer. When you tell him, he says it was too big an amount and it became a risk transfer, and now you have to pay $20,000 before the transaction can be completed. You will not think twice because you saw there was $100,000 in the account. Once you pay the $20,000 he will give you a passkey and it will be frozen again and he will then tell you another story so you can pay more money because you believe there is $100,000 in account. THE ACCOUNT IS FAKE.
- He sends you copies of (fraudulent) checks and money orders when conducting an advance-fee scam to gain or further solidify your trust in the validity of the scam.
- He sends you money as a gift (a couple thousand dollars) through wire transfer to gain your trust.
- He may create accounts on Linked In, White Pages, Switchboard and Checkmate to make his fictitious identity appear real if you do an Internet search for him.
- He has many fictitious identities, emails and IM accounts at one time. He may ask you to use an alternative email or IM. He would do this because his original identity has been suspended.
- If a scammer cannot get to you with one identity and thinks you have money, he will use a different identity to try to woo you.
- He usually uses web-based email service (because it does not require valid identifying information and lets him mask his IP address).

- If he has a website he might email you from that website domain.
- He can say he is from anywhere in the world.
- He wants the relationship to progress very quickly.
- His demands for money become aggressive.
- He wants to have sex chats.
- He tells you a dream he had about you.
- He requests your home or work address to send you something. Professional scammers might research and find your address online and surprise you with gifts.
- He wants you to compromise your principles.
- If you ask too many questions or seem suspicious, he tries to put you in the hot seat.
- He blames other for troubles in his life.
- He says customs is holding him. Customs cannot hold a person; only goods. Only immigration can hold a person.
- He tells you customs is holding his goods for his contract or for high taxes.
- He says the bank won't cash his check.

What should you do if you suspect you are chatting with a scammer?

Scammers are filled with "sugary words." They are deceptive, quick thinkers. The more time you spend chatting with them the more opportunity they have to catch you in their web. If you suspect you are chatting with a scammer IMMEDIATELY delete him/her from your messenger and delete their emails and texts without reading them, because they will be full of sweet excuses and lies. Scammers are persistent, so you need to cut ALL ties IMMEDIATELY!

What makes the romance scam work?

It is very simple logic. Women and men come on line to meet someone and fall in love. Scammers review your profile and then manipulate you by telling you what you want to hear, and they make you fall in love with sweet words, magic love letters and extravagant promises. They want you to think these are their real feelings. Once you are in love, they say they are in trouble and need your help. If you resist, the guilt trip begins. "If you love me, you will help me." That is the ultimate manipulation to get the money.

How many different dating scams are there?

It's impossible to say, because scammers create new scam stories every day. There are also dating scams taking place on Skype, Facebook and Whatsapp to name a few.

Where do scammers usually say they are from?

Many times they say they are from the United States, Canada, United Kingdom, Australia and other rich and famous countries.

Do scammers use their client's pictures and profile to scam others?

Yes, scammers might use your picture and profile information to scam men.

How long is the process to scam someone out of money?

It is usually a one-to-two-month process to get the first piece of money, but the scam will go on as long as a scammer can get money. They usually chat with at least two clients at a time, and they don't get emotionally attached.

It is just a job for them. They have to stay on point and not get distracted or let their heart feel anything. Scammers learn to play the odds. Some have as many as 50 clients, knowing that out of the 50, they may get money from five.

Do scammers ever feel bad after they scam money from someone?

No, they don't know you. You are just someone on the Internet. They talk about it and laugh. Usually they have no remorse. It's all about the money for survival and to stop suffering and live a better life.

There are no jobs and they don't believe they have other options. "Sometimes when a woman tells us that she doesn't have money in her account, we have her borrow the money, mortgage things and sell things to get us money."

Does a scammer say the same thing to every woman or man?

Yes, they have formats they follow for the introduction and the second follow-up and the third reply. When chatting, the scammer knows what he sent to you and what to say and how to say it.

He follows the story line he has written and always asks the same questions.

Do men scammers chat with and scam other men?

Yes, a lot of men scammers chat with and scam other men. They will either do it man to man if it is a gay man or pretend to be a woman with a straight man. But few do gay scams.

694

To pretend to be a woman all they do is talk like a woman and make a man feel good. Because men love nude women online, the scammers use this medium to attract and get men. They use voice changer equipment and fake video to pull the scam off.

To target gay men they go onto gay dating websites in Germany, Holland and Europe. They look for men over 40 years old and show them a video of a man masturbating to make the gay man think the scammer is real; they then use the regular scamming format to get the money.

Are there women scammers?

Yes, there are women scammers but not as many as the men scammers. Women scammers scam both men and lesbian females. They use sexy young ladies pictures and fake video that they get from xxx websites, and some create their own sex videos. They show the sex video to make the man or woman think the scammer is real and then use the regular scamming format to get the money.

In what parts of the world do the scammers reside?

Scammers are all over the world. Many are Nigerian, but different countries in Africa, such as Ghana and South Africa have a high number of scammers. There are also a high number of scammers in the United States, United Kingdom, Malaysia, Canada and Australia. Scamming has become a worldwide trade. Most transactions go through the United Kingdom because there are a lot of scammers in the United Kingdom.

How do scammers get money that is sent somewhere other than Nigeria?

They use what is called a "Picker", "My guy Off Shore" or "Receiver" – someone who retrieves the money from either a bank, Western Union or Money Gram and forwards the money to the scammer. They typically keep 10% to 40% of the money, and many times they want more. Sometimes the scammer will even ask the client if he/she will do it for them and they will pay them for their time and effort.

Of course they come up with a story of where the money came from and whom it is being sent to. Scammers have pickers all over the world who partake in the scam by receiving money from the client and sending it to them.

Some scammers know people in the United Kingdom and the United States who operate a Western Union outlet. They will have the money sent to either the United Kingdom or United States, call their Western Union friend, and give them the MTCN number. Their friend keeps 10% of the money and wires the rest of it to the scammer in Nigeria.

How do scammers pick up their money in Nigeria?

They create fictitious ID's that they use to pick up the money at the Western Union offices. Most scammers have made a friend at a Western Union office, and when the money comes in they don't even go to the office to pick it up; they just send their friend the MTCN number and the friend takes 5% out for themselves and sends the remainder to the scammer's online account.

What do scammers do with the money?

Most of them live reckless lifestyles and party the money away. Some have goals such as going to school, building houses, investing the money and starting businesses. Those that do have goals stop scamming once they reach their goals.

Do scammers have training?

Yes, there is training on how to register into the dating sites, choose good pictures, speak sweet words, how to cover their IP address, how to create an identity that appears real and how to make a lot of extravagant fake promises. Many learn first by watching others, and then by trial and error.

Do scammers use their own material?

Other than their story line, everything about scamming is copy and paste. They copy and paste from other people's profiles, and copy and paste information from love letter sites to win a woman's heart. When chatting, scammers will actually be copying and pasting information about "themselves" and using their own material other times. The material about themselves is called "the format;" the rest is their "story". They try different material and continue to change it until it is very effective.

Why do scammers find this life appealing?

They see scamming as a way to make big money quickly. They don't care who gets hurt. They don't think about it emotionally. It is highly promoted in the Universities and it is not seen as a bad occupation in Nigeria. Ghana actually has more scammers than Nigeria.

Do scammers see scamming as a game?

Scammers don't see it as a game; it is a job and a way to make a living, and they go to work every day.

Is scamming addictive?

Scamming itself isn't addictive but the easy money and lifestyle can be addictive.

Do scammers know each other?

Scammers do know each other. Beginner and small money scammers help each other with material to carry forth additional scams. If they meet on the dating sites they exchange greetings and pass on information about themselves and whether or not the dating site is good.

Professional scammers usually do not share their tools or their story line. They don't want other scammers to use their tools and story line to get more or bigger clients than they have. They also don't want their tools and story line to be everywhere. They know that amateurs will use their tools and story line and then clients will be aware of them. They keep their scam quiet. On occasion they will share them with another pro that they trust.

If two scammers meet online how do they approach each other?

Beginner and small money scammers approach other scammers by saying, "Baba how your side, omo iya mi, yes boss, ba wo lon se lo? how u dey?" and that means "my friend or my guy, what's up? How's your job there my brother from another mother? Yes boss, how's the scam going? How are you?" Then the other one would reply by saying, "ki lon se le" and that means "What's up? Is there any new information around to get?" This is a mix of pidgin, Yoruba & English language together. If you want to know if you are chatting with a scammer, type in while chatting, Baba, how your side, omo iya mi?

Professional scammers will not chat like this because they would be too scared of being caught. They realize they do not know who is on the other side of the screen. So if approached, they say, "I don't know what you are talking about. This is the first time I am on a computer."

Common terms used by scammers

Terms used depend on what part of the country the scammer comes from and the language they speak. If you use any of these terms while chatting it will shock the scammer and they will then chat back to you in pidgin. Once this happens you know you are chatting with a scammer.

- "Guy" or "G" – means scammer. This is how they greet each other.
- "Guy", "G" or "Boss" – is a professional scammer
- "Chair or Boss" – Is the big guy
- Client – a person (man or woman) a scammer is chatting with to obtain money
- Mayee – a client

- Office – an Internet café
- Magha – a fool who was scammed through trickery. It is a Yoruba word meaning "fool".
- Piano – a computer (will say, "I am going to press the piano")
- Scammer – "guy" or "G"
- Omo how far..... "Greetings. What's happening?"
- How paro na..."How far is the fraud going?"
- Sha d level pure.... "any other way of new fraud?"
- Wetin be the new site.... (U get site) "What is the latest dating site?"
- Client or maga sure for dere – cher "I go get clients there?"
- Maga dey dere – "Is there a maga there?"
- In Nigeria, the people that do not scam call the scammers "Runs Man".
- 1ST Email – sent format
- 2ND Email – follow up

Other approaches

Scammers that use the format of having a child will many times say a nanny is taking care of the child.

If the scammer has you speak to the supposed child, they are either having a young kid talk to you or they are using a voice changer phone from China. They tell me they can buy these for around $30.00. This allows them to instantly change their voice. http://en.wikipedia.org/wiki/Voice_changer says "The term **voice changer** (also known as voice enhancer) refers to a system of altering a person's voice to either make them sound like someone else or to disguise their voice. Voice changers change the tone or pitch, add distortion to the user's voice, or a combination of all of the above and vary greatly in price and sophistication." This allows the scammer to sound like a little girl or boy or a man or woman. Many times they will use several people in their story and will use the voice changer to change their voice to talk to you as each of the characters.

The scammer that scammed me told me *"The Boss needs me because he has no clue how to make women fall in love with him so my job is to make women fall in love with me so they will give me their money, and I am damn good at it!"*

If you encounter a professional scammer who has mastered his game and you do not know the red flags, there is an extremely high likelihood that you will get scammed. He will groom and molest you for money, just like a sex molester grooms someone in order to be able to molest them for sex. Once he infiltrates your heart, he will get your money. I was new to online dating and did not know the rules of the road or the red flags to look for, and I made the mistake of thinking the best of people. I even overlooked the red flags because I believed the person I was chatting with was in trouble and would pay me back as he promised. The mistake I made was that I trusted someone who was untrustworthy. He was a professional scammer and did his job well. Does this make me (or anyone who has been scammed) stupid? I do not think so. I think it makes us human and naïve due to lack of knowledge. This book has been written to provide that knowledge.

You can equate the online dating scammer's job to that of a sales person. He needs to have all the tools in place before he can go onto a dating site to look for his prey. In his world, you are a **"client"**. Just like a sales person wants to make the sale, the scammer wants to *"obtain your money"*. He knows he has to be believable. You are a game to him, and he wants to **win**! Just as a skilled sales person would ask a prospective client many questions so they know how to present what they are selling, so does the scammer ask many questions. He is a good listener and knows how to extract the information he needs in order to scam you. Every question he asks is designed to give him information he can use to manipulate you. Your interests, your livelihood, where you live, whether or not you have children…all tell him whether or not you are a good prospect. He thinks you have money if you have traveled a lot, if you have a good job, if you don't have children around and live alone, so there is nobody to discourage you from the relationship or sending them money.

Many times the scammer will be younger than you on their profile (and most likely in real life they are much younger than you because most of them are in their teens or twenties) so they will ask you how old you are. Then they will indirectly tease you about your age, and many times tell you, "I will keep you young". He asks personal questions to pre-qualify you, to learn if you have money and to have information to be able to dominate and manipulate you, not because they are interested in you.

If he cannot get money from you he might pass you to an experienced *professional* scammer who has been in the scamming game for a long time and has more advanced tools and equipment to obtain your money. If a scammer perceives you have a lot of money they might move you into Yahoo Plus Plus or Yahoo Extreme and have a spell cast upon you to get your money. Again, you have **No Idea** what you are getting into when online dating. Professional scammers are very good at their job!

Before the Scam Begins

For a scammer to successfully conduct a dating scam he does the following things before posting his profile on a dating site. Everything is premeditated and he goes to great lengths to fool you. Remember, this is his business and he wants to get paid for his efforts.

He creates his "fake identity". Scammers *always* use fake identities. His picture, name, format and his stories are all fake.

He chooses a profile picture. What I have found is that in one way or another, the profile picture contains at least one genuine depiction of the scammer, such as similar eyes, facial expression, body style, personality, etc. This makes sense because he has to relate to the picture to be good at what he does. He obtains photos without consent from online sources such as social media sites, other dating sites, modeling websites and even photo houses. If he is good at his trade, he will find someone who has posted many pictures of himself, because he knows you will continually ask for more pictures.

The scammer might not even be the gender portrayed in the on-line profile.

Scammers like to use children to pull at a woman's heart strings; so many times they will use a family picture of a man with a child and a man with a child and woman, who they will then say the woman is their mother or a nanny.

He chooses a name and address. He understands the attraction of names. He utilizes websites such as www.fakenamegenerator.com to generate complete names including the meaning of the name, country, state, address, phone numbers, working emails attached to that name, credit card numbers with expiration date and CVC code, SSN for United States, SIN for Canada, NINO for United Kingdom, mother's maiden name, birthday, occupation, name and website for the company they work, year, make and model of car, UPS tracking number, blood type, weight in both pounds and kilograms, height in both feet, inches and centimeters, a GUID, GEO coordinates and QR code. He maintains a large list of identities and will generate names and occupations for an entire family. He looks up ABA/ACH routing numbers to find out what bank these identities are associated with, and he has PIC/CIC codes that allow people to have long distance calls handled by carriers of their choice. He uses this information to create his format and story line.

Fakenamegenerator.com states, "We do not condone, support, or encourage illegal activity of any kind. We will cooperate with law enforcement organizations to assist in the prosecution of anyone that misuses the information we provide or that asks us to provide illegal materials, such as forged documents or genuine credit card numbers. All of the information we provide, including credit card numbers and national identification numbers, are fake. They can't be used to make purchases online or to obtain employment. We cannot and will not provide genuine credit card numbers or national identification numbers."

He may use English names such as Bob, Brett, Chris, Dave, David, Harold, James, Jeff, Jerry, Jimmy, Richard, Kelvin, Kevin, Paul, Frank, Andrew, Tim, Stephen and Wilson. He may go on

Google and type in "men's names that women like" or search on social media for names that sound nice and sexy. He searches for United States or United Kingdom names.

He creates an address. If he chooses a United States address, he uses www.555us.com because it contains all the U.S. states, cities and zip codes. Once he has a state, city and zip code he goes to Google and finds a street address. As part of a scam he will also find a house for sale in that area and uses the realtor's description of the house to describe "his" house. He may tell you he is trying to sell his house and will pay your money back once he gets a buyer.

He creates a believable "story line." He does everything possible to make his story believable, including picking where he supposedly lives, where he travels, and if he is divorced or widowed. Everything he says is premeditated and said to get you to fall in love with him and give him money. He is not looking to fall in love, all he wants is your money. You are *not* the only woman he is professing his love to. Everything he says is a script, part of his sales pitch.

He creates a *"fairytale"* story line to make it easy for you to get caught up in the fairytale. If you are chatting on line and everything seems too good to be true, it probably is. Remember, he is a professional story teller, and he operates in a land of make-believe and deceit.

He creates a "Format". This is what he uses to introduce himself, get the conversation going and get to know you. It is used for the first, second and third messages, for the profile information and for emails. He obtains formats from other scammers or from the Internet.

A format is easy to create. Formats are created from online "real" profiles, love letter websites and some the scammer writes himself. You will be able to clearly see what part of this format was copied and pasted from someone else and what parts were written by the scammer.

When setting up profiles, sending emails and text and chatting, the scammer will copy and paste from the format to save time. When I read through the format I saw where there was Scripture that is also used to manipulate, and it gave me an understanding of why some scammers say "himself" instead of "herself" and vice versa. It's obvious the format is a conglomerate of content taken from both male and female profiles. It also explains why the scammer appears to have feelings and says what every woman wants to hear to sweep her off her feet. It is all pre-calculated. However, there is so much in this format I can see where a scammer, if not careful, will make errors easily. My source said the "questions to ask" were taken from a dating site, however, many were incomplete. If incomplete questions are being asked, that would be another red flag.

The following is an actual pre-written format one of my sources provided. Read carefully and you will notice the errors, overly heavy "sweet talk," and red flags I described earlier. This format is characteristic of a scammer, and should help you recognize the difference between a scammer grammar and an authentic potential friend or partner.

MY PROFILE

"I'm searching for my life long partner to share a Great Life of Love with; romance, long slow kisses, feeling very special, intimacy, spirituality, pleasurable communication, dancing, meeting of the minds, opening a door for you, flowers, traveling and other exciting interests and adventures, A GREAT LIFE of LOVE! I am one who strongly believes in respect and that without respect, you can't experience true love and generate a healthy relationship. I believe in a smaller "wow" when it is first a friendship and then a larger "Wow" later as it evolves into a Beautiful Loving committed relationship. I believe it's not just what you are like on the outside, but more about what you are like on the inside. I'm seeking friendship first, (no game playing please) with someone who appreciates some of the same temperaments and interests I enjoy.

I want to love a woman for who she is, to spoil her, and love her, and let her know just how much she means to me, by the little things I do or say to make her feel special, while at the same time she treats me in the same way with love and respect. I'm really looking for Someone Honest, Caring, Romantic, Kind, Posses Great Sense of Humor, Loyal, gentle, cheerful, has the fear of God in hear life, LOVES KIDS, responsible, someone that still believes in true love, Affectionate, Passionate, Understanding, Intelligent, Respectful and Trust Worthy...

I'm a gentle soul, quiet and certainly not what most people would assume - a social butterfly. Instead I'm the quiet watchful, listener who will provide you with a listening ear after a tough day, and not judge, or assume or tell you what to do. I love nature, and water and feel an especial kinship to just being near water and having water right near my home. I feel the peace of the world in the breeze across the water, the lapping of the waves on the shore, the unassuming nature of water and nature. I am one with nature, and could spend hours just sitting by the beach, river, lake, ocean and stitch, read, listen to music and feel at the end of a day that I've had an incredible day...

I am a person who looks beyond what may be the obvious. Character is worth more than flashiness. I am a person who appreciates honesty and a great sense of humor. I love to laugh and to enjoy the simple things in life. I would appreciate a person who has a good sense of who she is and a sense of direction about where she wants to be. I can appreciate a woman who sees a man as a friend and a partner...

I know that men and women all have an inner child within and that is why I would appreciate days filled with fun and laughter. I respect and adhere to taking care of business in life--family, work, community, etc Yet, I know life involves balance. I look for the good in most situations and choose to look for the good in others. I know that life involves give and take and that what you seek--is that you must be willing to give and demonstrate yourself. I am a romantic at heart. I like to be appreciated and complimented to which I would do the same for that special someone.....

I like discovering new things about the person I meet. I am a person who looks for the possibilities versus what cannot be achieved. Life is better going through with a special one instead of just any one. I like poetry I like trying new things. I respect the direct approach--that is saying what you mean and meaning what you say. I believe in smiling--even when things are not going as perfect as you had hoped. A smile can brighten someone's day--I like smiling--it is one of my trademarks...I am an honest dependable person and I want someone I can depend on to talk to me when I feel disappointed or sad....I want someone that can provide an emotional balance for me and in return I will give the same.....when things happen to the one I love I take that seriously and try to focus on a solution to the problem by talking about it....give and take....I expect the same thing...I don't believe that is much to ask for. It keeps things real and most of all it provides someone in your life you know you can count on...

I am a true romantic and believe that there is such a thing as a soul mate, but they are not easily found... out of millions of people those 2 souls must meet by chance and circumstance. I believe that you should consider your soul mate, your best friend and be able to talk about any and everything, not feel strange if there is silence between you. I feel true love and connection doesn't require constant talking, as a glance or longing stare says everything and more than words could ever convey. I believe in holding hands, and public displays of affection, as I would want everyone to know that the person who I am with is truly special to me. I believe that being able to be your true self with someone without judgment is one of the best things in life.

I am honest always as there is nothing that I can think of that would make it wrong. I have a very off beat sense of humor and I am quick with wit, one of the happiest things to feel is laughter until the tears stream down your cheeks, I find humor in almost everything, but never take anyone feelings lightly. I am an astute listener as I also believe that if it is important enough for you to say, it is important enough for me to listen, and take heed in what is being said. I too am not a night life person, I prefer to stay home or be someplace special with my someone special. I am ready to find that someone who can appreciate all of things I have to offer and accept me as I am. I approach this renewed journey with caution as my feelings and heart are quick to get the best of my head. However, once I give them they are true and deep in every sense.

I love ------ so much and I'm trying to raise him to be one of the rare breed out there: a gentleman who owns his words, who is independent, self-confident, knows his worth, loves God, treats people, and especially women & older people with respect, focused, disciplined, be playful, be fun, sense of humor ~ always and be a warrior with a tender heart....

I feel all is not fair in love and war. That is, I feel you should give someone your best and that you should exercise respect and honesty. I appreciate genuine companionship and soul inspired relationship. You the one in which you can feel the earth move beneath your feet with just one kiss. Or, one in which you spend idle moments just thinking about the other person...

I am sweet, thoughtful, kind, and have a great sense of humor. I am very easy going and laid back. I am often told that I am very easy to talk with. I am not an angry person, and I am not interested in someone that is. Having past events shape your life is one thing, carrying the past as a burden that sits heavily upon your shoulders is not the way I view life. I am happy with myself, and my life, and I like to think it shows. I have a wonderful Son. I would do best with someone that isn't extremely uptight, unless of course you are willing to learn to let things go! I love to try new things, and can laugh at myself when I fail miserably. I don't give up easily, and have so many things I've yet to try. Please love to laugh and have fun, what is better than laughing so hard your stomach hurts?

I love traveling, going on unknown adventures, and trying something I thought I never would. I'll try anything once, well, but fun none the less! I take pride in my appearance, but am not high maintenance. I love a nice dinner out, but staying home, having Chinese food after a day spent working together on a completely dirty, yet fulfilling project, can be so much fun with the right person.

Being honest and open is very important to me and I expect my match to feel the same way. I am not a game player, and I don't have any interest in dating one. I do however make exceptions for board game lovers.

I am very creative and artistic. I love working on my house and digging in my gardens, I have no problem getting dirt under my nails. I believe in a best friend to spend my life with, and if it takes a while and I meet new friends along the way, that's a good thing too. Please have an adventurous silly side, although I can be very sophisticated when necessary, life isn't as much fun if you subdue your inner child all the time.

I'm a straight and easy going person with a kind and gentle heart full of love...I love to travel and would love a partner to travel with me. I have been a workaholic in that past but last year I had a change of attitude and decided to live life now. I might live to be a 100 years old or my time could end tomorrow. Rather than wait and miss life I want to take advantage while I have the opportunity in front of me.

My friends/coworkers will tell you that I am a shy person. I can be picky but I really believe that love is out of our control. I cannot create a spark or stop a spark. There is either a connection or not. I have met people online or via telephone conversations and they seem great but when we meet there is no chemistry or connection. It is not all about looks especially as we get older but none-the-less there has to be a physical attraction. A personality can make someone cuter or uglier as you get to know them.

My Traits are Optimistic, Adventurous, Happy, Kind, loyal, modest, Friendly, Forward Thinking, Innovative, Reliable, Honest, Kind, Romantic, Funny, Confident with great Business Scene, Reliable, Committed, Responsible, Communicative, sensitive, gentle, Intelligent, Purposeful, I try to be Gentleman at all times.

I like all these below, Pop, rock, country, Classical, Novels, history, Honest, loyal, devoted, romantic, sincere, dependable, strong, adventurous, poetic, passionate, social, intelligent, professional. Exercises, Visiting Friends, Water Sports, Snow Skiing, Fly Fishing, Camping, Dancing, Movies and I love to love to travel... I like to spend a lot of time in the outdoors, Camp,

Fly fishing, Water Skiing, Snow Skiing, Rock Climbing, I like to take walks, I workout most days. I'm 6"0" tall 216 pounds and in great shape.

I'm going to be honest and straight forward about what I'm looking for. One I don't play game please don't with me, I am what I am, I expect the same. I'm a strong professional businessman and in life. I work hard but at the same time I enjoy life so when I play I like to play hard. I'm working on a part of me that I seem to have a hard time with patience's, not one of my virtues in life. I do know this I think I'm finally starting get it.

If you're looking for honesty, caring, a family man, loving, a man who loves this Life, a man who has a love for life, then you have a great man here. I travel a lot, so you need to want to see the world some. I have been blessed with one wonderful child the best kid in the world to work with, just need my full time partner...lol

I'm orginally from Italy, But was born in the US, my dad was in the military and was posted in the US, I lived in the US until i was 8years old, Then i lost my parents in a car accident.. I am an only child and was then adoped by my uncle who lives in South Africa after i lost my parents. I just came back to the states 5years ago, after i lost my uncle, He died from cancer. You could say i spent almost all my life in South Africa. I attended a college had my asociates' degree Construction/Craft Building/Technolgy Infor/ Management Systems. I'm very laid-back and down-to-earth. I'm also very old-fashioned when it comes to my respect and treatment for women. I'm a social wine drinker but a non-smoker, have a great sence of humor and like to spend time with someone i Love, and loved ones.."

MY MATCH

"I would like someone that will love and respect me for who I am, that likes to hold my hand and surprise me with a little kiss when I least expect it, or give me a wink from across the room to let me know she's thinking about me or give me a call just to let me know she's thinking about me... Because I will be doing the same...

I would love someone who is fun to be around, likes to laugh, joke around, enjoy being outdoors going for long romantic walks, enjoys looking at the stars at night, and watching the sun set and rise over the ocean. I am looking for someone that enjoys the simple things in life, just as I do. I would like to meet someone special that I can grow old with, and that we can always look into each other's eyes and know that the love between us is just as wonderful and exciting as the day we met...

That special someone is a woman with integrity, is spiritually compatible with me, having similar beliefs - and is responsible, intelligent, has a sense of humour, positive, is clean and neat in habit and appearance, romantic, passionate about living and loving. I would prefer that someone to show interest and be supportive of my spiritual work. She should be financially secure, and has 'been there, done that'. I like an adventurous person who likes travel, nature and enjoys being home. She is a woaman who is at peace with himself. I am hoping to connect with people of like minds to form friendship first and then leave the rest to the Universe...

I want to meet a nice, attractive, socially outgoing woman who is happy, friendly, dependable, and loyal. You are passionate, affectionate and devoted in a relationship, placing priority on family, good friends, health and personal well-being. Your main priorities are not material but you aren't afraid to indulge because you deserve it. You like sports, travel, have solid self-esteem, personal worth and enjoy a compliment."

FOR IM MAGA

"Hi pretty@};-@};-, how are you doing.. I'm William, I hope you get this IM and it finds you well, I was glancing through profiles when your gorgeous picture got me attracted while your lovely words had me write you, I really was marveled reading your profile and I enjoyed doing so... The first thing that came to my mind when I saw your picture was WOW...you're drop dead GORGEOUS.. Lol... So I thought I would take out time to introduce myself.

Profiles help but lack personal interaction and feedback that can only come through emails if people are honest and the true test comes at eventual trusting each other.

Long profiles are boring and we are too busy to read long drawn out introductions so I will shut up. If you want me to keep talking then send me an email and I will respond even if it is a Thanks, but no thanks."

WORK

"As you can see in my profile I am into construction, I'm a Civil Engineer, I work for myself as a private contractor from home..I specialize on buildings like Real estate, Roads, Bridges, residential homes etc, I travel with my work alot.. and right now i'm presently in the west part of Africa "Nigeria" working, I came down here because of the new establishment of an orphanage home building, and estate designing project, I will be coming back home in a couple of weeks time... the contracts i came down here to do are almost coming to an end. By the Grace of the lord when i get back home i am going to start up my own company with what i'm going to bed paid down here..."

WHAT I DO FOR FUN

"I am honest, dependable, loving, gentle, affectionate and have good friendship. I feel that a WOMAN is GOD's undeserved gift to MAN and she is supposed to be loved, reverenced, protected, respected, and cherished. Would like to go to the Hawaiian islands, like small intimate places to talk, not to much on the bar/clubs seen. Like all types of food, I'm open to try new places and things, I also like to cook. I wish i have someone to cook for...

I love cooking, going to the beach, Although i haven't gone to the beach in a long time now.. stay home listening to a country or romantic song, I enjoy love storys, I'm a very sensitive person i cry sometimes, with just watching a movie...   I usually read several books at a time. I am currently reading the following: Max Lucado - Traveling Light; Chicken Soup for the Womans Soul; It's All Too Much, Also 5 Languages of Love.

I enjoy the outdoors, esp the beach. Walking on the beach at night, waves crashing restlessly, a million stars in the sky, ahhh perfect for me. I also like dining out, plays, movies, art. Im pretty flexible as far as activities. I like fishing, camping, reading, going to the movies, hanging around with friends, cracking jokes, listening to music, dancing, and also spending time with someone interesting."

MOVIES

"I enjoy chick flicks but I also like those movies you have to watch every little thing so you understand the plot and the ending, movies that make you think. Horror movies usually scare me pretty good, so I don't watch them every often. Action movies about blowing everything up are okay, comedy movies to make you laugh until you can hardly breath are wonderful too, It makes you look forward to every day..."

MY PERFECT FIRST DATE

"The perfect first date for me would be a quiet intimate dinner somewhere romantic where we spend the evening getting to know each other by conversation that just seem to endlessly flow and before too long we realize that hours have passed yet it only seemed like minutes. We would never want the night to end. The night would possibly end with a romantic kiss and we would both go home and think of each other till we fell asleep."

MY IDEAL RELATIONSHIP

"An ideal relationship for me would be one where be both respect and show one another that we care for each other. It would be loving and intimate. We would do things for each other because that it what we want.to please each other. It should not be stressfulit should be mutual, honest, caring and loving

Please, please be honest, being single is hard for all of us, no one wants to be alone in life, if you fall for me or some one online understand we are older and understand what we are looking for, but though we know this about ourselves, and even though we may fall for someone fast, a relationship takes time to build. So take your time enjoy getting to know each other. Let's have some fun and get to know each other.

This has taken me years to learn, and I'm still learning. I do know this there are five things that are needed in a relationship of love, "Quality time, words of affirmation, gifts, acts of service, and physical touch, any of these without the others make it harder but knowing these areas about each other help us grow closer and understand each other so that a relationship will grow, and stay alive after marriage for eternity if we work at it. A few of my word and thoughts, if you can understand these words then you can understand who I am, and what I'm looking for in this eternal life, just don't want to do it alone.

I believe peace to be having quality time with a companion, pursuing her activity or mine. I'm extremely proud of my educational and professional accomplishments and seeing how well my two children have turned out. Our perfect first date could be a casual dinner in a delightful restaurant, uninterrupted, to talk, get to know one another better. If you enjoy our first date, maybe I could cook for you next."

QUESTIONS TO ASK CLIENT

1. If you were taken by your date to a party where you knew no one, how would you respond?
2. How often do you lose your temper?
3. When in a relationship, how much personal space do you generally find you need?
4. If you had to characterize the end of most of your romantic relationships, they would be described as:
5. Which of the following marriage issues do you fear most?
6. How important is chemistry to you?
7. Which of the following scenarios would make you more nervous?
8. How many books did you read last year?
9. When going somewhere:
10. Which of the following indoor activities sounds like the most fun to you?
11. What best describes your parents' relationship towards each other:
12. What best describes your attitude toward work?
13. Where do you see yourself living in 15 years?
14. If you were to marry, how many children would be ideal?
15. Your idea of adventure is:
16. On Saturday night, would you rather go to:
17. What kind of exercise do you prefer?
18. If you went out to eat with a friend, which of the following would you prefer?
19. If you could take a dream getaway, where would you most likely choose to spend a week?
20. Your idea of a romantic time would be:
21. What style of dress do you prefer?
22. Which of the following quirks would bother you most about your partner?
23. Would you rather date someone who is:
24. What is your opinion of committed long distance relationships?
25. What do you think of "Soul Mates?"
26. How important is it to you that your partner be accepted by your family and
27. How many years have you lived alone?
28. How romantic are you?
29. Do you enjoy being alone?
30. How trusting are you?
31. Which of the following things would you rather have lots of?
32. Which sort of date sounds like the most fun to you?
33. How organized are you?
34. With which sentence do you agree most?
35. How do you feel about relocating for a relationship?
36. What is your opinion of traditional gender roles?
37. Do you consider yourself an ambitious person?

38. When in a relationship, are you a jealous person?
39. How do you feel about premarital sex?
40. Financially, how would you characterize yourself?
41. How much ongoing stress do you have in your life?
42. How would you assess your verbal intimacy skills?
43. Realizing that labels are imperfect, do you consider yourself a dominant person in your personal life?
44. Do you consider yourself physically affectionate when involved in a relationship?
45. How do you feel about food?
46. How often do you find yourself laughing?
47. Do you enjoy debating the issues of the day with your partner?
48. Outside of a romantic relationship, are you competitive?
49. How often do you exercise?
50. If I had a bad day, what is the first thing you would do for me?
51. What's your philosophy on travel?
52. Are pets an important part of your life?
53. Are you a passionate person?
54. What are your body-type preferences for your mate?
55. What is your opinion on your mate having opposite sex friendships?
56. In a marriage how would you feel if the woman made significantly more money than the man?

FOOD

I love southern "soul food" - italian - thai - chinese - turkish.. favorite fast food - pizza with fresh moz and basil drizzled with olive oil.. classics - that maltese falcon - the good earth - deception - mildred pierce - also action and drama - love real life stories and documentaries... and stupid move that makes me laugh so hard I think I am going to pee myself...Ice Cream - black raspberry - logan berry - strawberry - chocolate

LOVE MAIL

"Here in my heart, that's where you will be, you will be with me, here in my heart, No distance can keep us apart as long as you're here in my heart I know when i come back every thing will be alright, the distance will keep us apart. But distance no matter how far can't change these feelings in my heart, Time may take us apart that's true, but I will always be there for you, You're in my heart, you will be in my dreams, no matter the miles between us. These lonely nights are hard to get through, I will keep you in my eyes by making you a dream...I love you

Imagine a cold, rainy evening with thunderstorms and severe lightening. You are graciously preparing a beautiful candlelight dinner for us. As we savor our meal, we are engaged in some diverse conversation which only two people who are very close will appreciate whether its light and breezy banter or assisting each other with each's daily concerns. After dinner we huddle in front of the fireplace with a blanket, some fabulously smooth wine, and some soft intimate music. Our feelings eminate as does the warmth of the fireplace. Later on we conclude the

romantic night with candles, sensual massage creams/oils and delight in wonderful full body massages. We will fall asleep safe and secure in comfy positions; we are definitely holding each other. That is my PERFECT evening with my best friend/Only Lover/Soulmate. This evening is what my persona is all about.
Love always,

I have tried a million times to put into words how I feel for you. It's so hard to describe such an intense emotion. I knew from the day we met, that you were meant for me.
Love always,

There are so many expressions of our love: the gentleness of the way you've touched me, how a smile lights up my face when I hear your voice, and how my body responds to your voice, how happy I'm when I'm talking to you - you make me who I'm.
Love always,

There was a huge void in my life until you came along. I thank God everyday for leading us to each other. You complete me. I think back to how empty my life was without you, and I am so grateful that you are here. I can't wait to spend forever with you. You are my life, my love, my soul mate, my heart, and my reason for breathing. I love you, with everything I am.
Love always,

As the days pass, my love for you grows more and more everyday. When your telling me that you love me, I feel better for who I am because I got you everyday. All my life was a disaster, but when you appear in my life, my disaster turn into happiess because you appear. I belive in you, your the light in my deepest, darkest hour, your the key to my very soul, you are my savior when I fall. In your arms I found my paradise. As 1000 years would past, I would fall in love with you again. You are my only chance for happiness, if I lose you now I know I would die. If I can't have you, I don't want nobody else baby girl, your more than a woman, more than a woman to me,I love you....
Love always,

You speak what I feel and to know that the intense emotions run the same through me as they do you. I can not explain what is happening between you and I, I just know that there is a reason for why we are here and if it is for each other, then I will not let go. Its amazing that you think the way that I do for I have had the most unhappy 5 years of my life and for some reason the events of today have taken me to you. If this is what love Is, then may I feel it forever, for it fills me with want and desire again and for that I am truly thankful.
Love always,

I tried not to feel the way that i'm feeling right now with you for I did not know who you were but began to desire your touch, and your smile. I need you to know that you complete me babe and this stirring desire of passion and want is what love is all about. I will be here for you, waiting till the day that I will be in your arms forever. Take me as I am, as I will do the same for you. Love me for who I am and know that I am yours. And can not wait to tell you those words, to see the passion in your eyes, and the love that you will have forever.

Love always,

You're everything I dreamed of A woman after God's heart So kind and compassionate Beyond your rugged exterior Is a sweet and gentle spirit You walked in when others walked out My peace in the midst of the storm You are my best friend I could not ask for more The perfect gentlelady You could teach others a thing or two About how to treat a guy And what the word respect means.
Love always,

I've never felt so special So much love and tenderness You take care of me like no one else can You love me for who I am We have a spiritual connection A bond that cannot be broken You understand my struggles and my pain Your support of my dreams is so encouraging I love talking to you and i would love Strolling hand in hand on a country road Enjoying nature and its breathtaking beauty You're so funny You make my heart smile The joy you bring I can't explain I just know it feels good God gave me my heart's desire When He sent you.
Love always,

Every day that passes, my feelings for you grows. You are my dream come true and I can't wait to spend forever in your arms, get lost in your eyes, be warmed by your smile, melt with every kiss, and fall deeper in love when we make love.
Love always,

Babe, you have changed my life completely. You're the one who makes me beautiful. You're the one who makes me strong. You're the one who makes me so important; you're everything to me....
Love always,

If only you knew, how my heart overflows with love for you. If only you could see the way you fill my hopes and dreams. You're the owner of my heart, the ruler supreme. Even in the dark of night, I have only to think about you to feel your loving light and from this world I drift feeling as if I will never touch the ground again... If only you knew.
Love always,

If only you could guess how I hear your voice when others speak, for you hold the key to my happiness, and it's always you my soul seeks. If only you could feel, how your very presence has the power to heal, all the wounds inside me. You've made me abandon the pain of yesterday, and you've shown me that the past can no longer stand in the way of what I hope to achieve...
If only you knew.
Love always,

If only you could realize the way you've shown me that it's better to give than to take, and whatever I do, I do for your sake. I'm willing to give you my all and expect nothing in return. But, oh how I yearn for you... if only you knew....
Love always,

I like very much how you look. I will be honest, I don't ever, not ever look at the outside to learn about someone, I feel the real person is who is inside. Oh, of course there has to be some kind of physical attraction of course but that is not the only part of a person, I am good and kind and loving, I am always there to give help to anyone who needs it. I am always told I am too good to everyone else. But that is my nature and I feel rewarded just knowing I have helped that someone no matter what it is.
Love always,

I know that such a beautiful woman as beautiful as you are men will be coming for you from all over the world so tell me how many you know from this part of the world that i'm in now?.. I plan to settle down with my one true love when i get back home... To have a family of my own, The kind of family that has the fear of God and always do the right things... I like compliments, i believe compliments can make someone day...
Love always,

Forever I beg to be counted among the crowds who behold your splendor for angels conspired to paint you A masterpiece, forever displayed in the gallery of my heart and yet amongst the hoards of those more deserving I find only me a speck of dust in a mountain of humanity, for I raise my voice to the heavens in awe as angels saw fit to bind together a woman so perfect and an undeserving man, but still I grasp love's jagged thorn endure its pain and smile safe in the knowledge that I have given with certitude my heart as you travel through the depths of my being to meet at a place where our hearts can dwell as you search for my soul I will take you there where bodies grow old but the love in our heart will always burn and when the master beckons I will look in your eyes to wipe away a tear with a final kiss as we begin our journey to eternity I have to travel some 8 to 10 times a year. Most all of our work is over seas; I may be gone every 6 to 8 weeks on a trip for about 7 to 14 days each time. I love to travel if you're my sweetheart I hope you would enjoy traveling and seeing the world some because I sure don't want to go to all these wonderful parts of the world alone.
Love always,

If we were at a party, I would let you lead me around the room, introducing me to all your friends. And then I would try to get to know them better. If we were to get parted in the room, I would very romantically look over at you through the crowd and smile at you very softly and then think to myself, you are all mine and I am so lucky to be going home with you and how passionate the love is going to be when we get home. I wouldn't hang on to you desperately because I think that makes people feel smothered, I would expect you to get me a drink though before leaving me alone with any of your friends. A glass of wine would be great.
Love always,

Just before I turn in for the night, I want to let you know that my heart stays with you tight, so that my warmth will make you feel that everything's going to be right.
Love always,"

SEXUAL CONVERSATION

"Imagine.... I inadvertently lick my lips moistening them as if in anticipation of the sweetness of your essence. Pulling my bottom lip up and running my teeth across as to devour every drop. Ambrosia.... my lips pucker and then release, as I wish I could taste you. Licking incessantly hoping that one of the times I will be there, feeding me every drop, as I look up at you and smile for satisfying my hunger.

As each minute passes I feel the moistness ebbing from the depths of my being, readying myself for what's to come. I imagine your embrace. A touch that sends shivers down my spine, and the soft kisses that tickle my skin and sends me into a fairy tale all my own. I imagine your tenderness, and you holding my hands in yours interlacing our fingers to steady yourself as you move rhythmically to our heartbeats, and I close my eyes and imagine.

I imagine ......I hear the tender words of affection you whisper to me, and I respond in kind. I wish this moment could last forever.... "Oh how good it is". There is a shiver that runs through me and I squeeze your hands tight, and you lay still to wait for the moment to pass. You kiss me deeply and more passionately than I knew could be possible and I imagine.

I look at you, smile, take a deep breath and close my eyes. You kiss me and start our dance once more. This time our bodies are so close we feel as if we are one, dancing in tandem. I follow your stride to keep in rhythm with the dance.... dip...rock...sway. The pace quickens and again I steady myself not to let you go as you sweep me into another world. "I want to stop, I beg you to stop before it's too late.... please".... and then it happens. I open up my heart and let you in as I call to you. I hold you tight and lock my embrace and now I lead the dance. Forcing you to feel every movement of my body as I pour my soul out to you. Suddenly you match my movement and tense as I did mere moments before. I now revel in your passion and hold you,.... close....still ..... and silent. I look deep into your eyes and smile hoping that I have shown you exactly how I feel, and that you know I have given you my heart, and with words unspoken I hope you will then know....... Just imagine......"

PAST RELATIONSHIP

"I will never forget the relationships before because I'm just that kind of person, but I do know that I have enough love and forgiveness in my heart for someone else. well my ex did stupid things, i was thinking she was nice i didn't know she was the devil herself, that mend away with my heart and made me go through so much emotional trauma, i give her whatever she needs, she just changed all of a sudden due to the kind of friend she mingle with bad company smokes, come home late being drunk, flex around with men, then one day i caught her sleeping with a man in my house she pleaded and i forgived her the second time i caught her sleeping with my best friend, i fainted and was rushed to the hospital, i was unconscious for 3 days, that is what the doctor said to me, I went through alot....

When i was in the hospital she came visiting a couple of times, but the doctor wouldn't let anyone see me. after i got out of the hospital she tried to plead for the second time, but i didn't take her back, we got divorced... after the divorce was final she made away with some of my money, neither have i seen my best friend who she was cheating on me with.. i have not seen nore my ex friend till this day. We were married for 9years and have been divorced now for 4years, the most annoying part is she haven't been calling to check up on her own child. I dont see that happening ever. I need that special someone in my life, i am tired of being lonely i need somone to love me for whom i am, i promise to make my woman happy forever.

I thought my ex loved me, but she had to break my heart for me to know what true love really is. I believe the best thing about loving and being hurt is that you get to know what true love really is. For as gold is tested in fire, and so will love be perfected in pain, - Love, an emotion so strong that you would give up everything. To just feel it once, to know that you are part of something special. To know that you can feel what love really is; to know, to feel, to love - To love someone is to understand each other, to laugh together, to smile with your heart and to trust one another. One important thing is to let each other go if you can't do this... i hope you understand all that, I'm searching for TRUE LOVE...

I do want to go on with my life and I've asked God to bring someone into my life who will want me for me and be good to me and my kid because I know that there has to be someone out there for me because He never does anything without a reason even if we can't figure it out. I know just because the lord has someone else in mind for me to share the rest of my life with, because He doesn't want us to be alone or lonely.

My ex wife parents all depend on me, She came from a very poor family and i guess that was why she was a cheater all her life..."

SCARS FROM THE PAST

"It is impossible to completely and effectively love someone without being included in that other person's history. Our history has made us who we are. The images, scars and victories that we live with have shaped us into the people we have become. We will never know who a person is until we understand where they have been.

The secret of being transformed from a vulnerable victim to a victorious, loving person is found in the ability to open your past to someone responsible enough to share your weakness and pains with. "Bear ye one another's burdens, and so fulfil the law of Christ," writes Paul in Galatians 6:2. You don't have to keep reliving it. You can release it."

GIVE HIM ALL YOUR SECRETS

"The enemy wanted to change your destiny through a series of events, but God will restore you to wholeness as if the events had never happened. The Triumphant person locked inside shall come forth to where he belongs. He's delivering you. He's releasing you. He's restoring you. he's building you back. He's bringing you out. He's delivering by the power of his Spirit. "...Not by might, nor by power, but by my spirit, said the Lord of Hosts'(Zechariah4:6)

God has already determined your need. He looked down from heaven long ago and saw your pain. He evaluated your situation and decided that you needed a good man. He knew that you would need someone to reach down and lift you up. He saw that you needed to recognize how important you are. It is impossible to know all that was in the mind of God when he looked down on broken humanity, but we can know that he looked past our broken hearts, wounded histories and saw our need.

The Bible says," Love doesn't hold a grudge. Love doesn't harbor unforgiveness"(1 Corinthians 13:5) You may have people in your life who have done you great wrong, and you have right to be angry and bitter. You may feel as though your whole life has been stolen away by somebody who has mistreated you or deceived you. But if you will choose to let go of your grudge and forgive them, you can overcome that evil with good. You can get to the point where you can look at the people who have hurt you and return good for evil. If you do that, God will pour out His favor in your life in a fresh way. He will honor you; He will reward you , and He'll make those wrongs right. No matter what you've gone through, no matter who hurt you or whose fault it was, let it go. Don't hold a grudge. Don't try to pay them back. God says show mercy. Aim for kindness. You may be thinking, No, it's not fair. We have to remember that God is the One keeping the score. He is in control. And when you bless your enemies, you will never lose. God will always make it up to you..."

SPEAKING WORDS OF FAITH

"Our words are vital in bringing our dreams to pass. It's not enough to see your dreams simply by faith or in your imagination. You have to begin speaking words of faith over your life. The moment you speak something out, you give birth to it. This is a spiritual principle, and it works whether what you are saying is good or bad, positive or negative.

Before I lay my head down to sleep I just want to say: rose are red violets are blue I've been counting the days till i see you!

I feel your arms around me
My head against your bobs
I should sleep too
And try to get some rest
I gently kiss you one last time
And start to close my eyes
knowing I'm holding you
My heartbeat begins to rise
You kiss me goodnight
Feelings of love and passion
Are running through my head
I begin to miss you
Your body so close to mine
I want to hold you in my arms
And kiss you one last time

I want to say "Sweet dreams my queen"
And let you know how much I care
As I make sweet passionate love to you.
Love,

I just want to lay you down and make sweet passionate love to you....please you like have never been pleased before......love you like you have never felt, I am a confidant lover, just been out of practice, saving for someone like you.. very much get pleasure out of pleasing my woman.. when we meet I want to flirt with you all day by gentle touches, looking into your eyes,,,brushing up agenst you.....then, when evening falls..... all that flirting will make me want you even more when i lay you doen

For your eyes alone!!

WISHES

I wish a wish
And my wish is this
That I can feel
The warmth of your kiss
That I can touch
A lock of your hair
That our bodies can meet
In the same air
That time can pass
And the waiting be done
So our lives can begin
With some degree of fun
That the longing I feel
Disappear with the breeze
In your arms I can know
the strength of your squeeze

Honey, It is wonderful to my heart the feelings I have for you! I am so glad God brought us together. You are so special to me and you make me feel so special, I woke up this morning, and i found myself longing for you more than the day before. I miss you so much and i hope you're having a good night sleep. I will be online waiting to talk to you even if it just for a little while.. Missing you loving you..:X:X:x

I am attending a Non-Denominational that is wonderful, I enjoy seeing God's love at work in my life and the fellowship I have with my church.

I usually read biography's if they are about people I admire but I also read inspirational and Christian books from authors like Max Lucado and Tony Campolo. One is more serious and the other is more Christian with a touch of life's humor.

You should know my faith is very important to me and I believe everything in the Bible and try to follow God's word and live each day to please Jesus.

Proverbs 18:22 says that "he who finds a wife, finds a good thing and obtains and receives favor from the Lord......my life has been a total preparation for someone like you preparation and consecration for a woman who will love me like Christ loves the church.. cherish me like Christ cherishes the church... and for me to do the same in return i so love to be loved and i love to love i know that the person in my life will totally and fully complete me."

DREAM

"I didn't want to EVER wake up!!! You and I were somewhere up in the Mountains. It was winter. Lots of snow. We were playing outside just laughing and having a great time playing in the snow like a couple of little kids! we began getting cold so we went inside a warm cozy little cabin. The fireplace was blazing and there were candles burning all around the room.

We each took our turn in the shower to warm ourselves. I was waiting for you near the fire when you came out wearing a robe. your hair was still wet, & you had no makeup on, & you were the most beautiful woman I had ever layed eyes on. you layed your head on my shoulder and i could feel your breath on my neck! We sat on the sofa & you curled up in my arms. We sat there together and watched the fire....AND THAT'S WHEN I WOKE UP!!!!!!"

He creates places online where he can be found. He tries to think of everything he can do to make his fictitious identity visible and his story appear real while hiding his real identity. He will set up a page on Linked In, White Pages, Switchboard and any other online location he can, so if you research him, you will find him.

He creates email and messenger accounts. He may occasionally use hot mail but mostly uses Yahoo! This is why worldwide they are known as the YAHOO BOYZ. It is not uncommon for him to have many different user names and email addresses so he can talk to many clients at once. He may have to change his email address and messenger user name because he has been reported or compromised in one way or another.

A professional scammer may also have an email account through a well-known American carrier such as AT& T, Sprint and Verizon.

He may create an email signature especially for military scams and anything having to do with banking or business. Pay attention to those signatures and research the company name, website addresses, phone number and address listed. Don't take anything at face value.

He may create emails using domain names of fictitious websites he is using.

How a scammer purchases things. He uses stolen credit cards he purchases from hackers to pay for online dating sites, laptops, phones, voice changers, websites and other tools he needs to pull off his scam or send you flowers, clothes, jewelry, chocolates and anything else he needs to buy to woo you and make you believe he is real.

He does not know how much credit is on the stolen credit cards or when they will be cancelled, so he must be fast with his purchases. Of course he uses a fake name when purchasing the credit card and usually pays for it through PayPal or WebMoney. Hackers are extremely good with technology. Many hackers are located in Egypt, India, Russia, Malaysia and other Asian Countries to name a few.

Most online companies will not ship into Nigeria, so his online purchases must be sent to his offshore guy, picker, or to you and then be shipped to him.

One of the main websites scammers used to purchase stolen credit cards was www.libertyreserve.com. This domain has been shut down as of May 28, 2013.

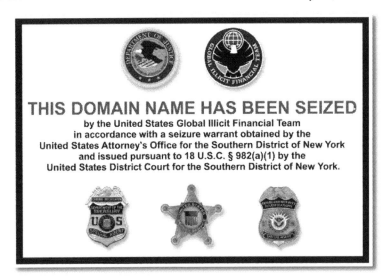

Please read this International Business Times article written by David Gilbert.

David Gilbert, in his 2013 article *US Authorities Shut Down Liberty Reserve – The Criminal Underworld's Bank of Choice* details the role of Liberty Reserve in facilitating online scams.

> "Liberty Reserve was established in 2006 and was designed "to help criminals conduct illegal transactions and launder the proceeds of their crime." It offered anonymity to those using it,

meaning it attracted everyone from those selling drugs online to cyber-criminals renting out their botnets to customers."

You can read the entire article at www.ibtimes.co.uk/articles/472005/20130528/liberty-reserve-shut-down-arthur-budovsky-arrested.htm

How a scammer creates phone numbers and text numbers. A scammer knows he will eventually have to talk to you so you believe he is real. He also knows there is a great risk that his accent will "give him away", so he may say he is originally from another country and now lives in the United States. ***An accent is a big red flag.***

He may use www.datacalls.com to set up free United Kingdom telephone numbers. This service allows calls to be forwarded to virtually any phone number in the world anonymously and for free. Usually the presence of a +44 70 number means you're dealing with a scammer based in Nigeria who is using these numbers to make you believe he is legitimate and in the United Kingdom. +44 70 numbers belong to an international call forwarding services. These services make it possible for scammers to hide the fact that they are based in Nigeria or other countries in Africa and elsewhere, while you will believe you are dealing with someone in the United Kingdom. You can find phone codes for many countries that are used in scams at http://www.419scam.org/419-by-phone.htm.

Some countries do not allow roaming. A scammer will never say he is in a country where he cannot get a phone number that has roaming.

He uses unlocked phones that allow him to use different SIM cards. A Nigerian scammer can buy SIM cards on the street for carriers in the United States and the United Kingdom for a couple hundred dollars. He can then make and receive calls and texts using these SIM cards. The SIM cards for the United States carriers are for AT&T, T-Mobile and Verizon and for the United Kingdom carriers they are O2, Vodafone and T-Mobile to name a few. A scammer can top-off his account on line. This means he can pay on his account and purchase additional air time. Scammers also use MagicJack and Yahoo!

When a scammer calls you, your caller ID will likely show "private number." This is a ***Red flag***. A scammer can always tell it's you calling them because of the international number they gave you.

He sends text through the computer. It is called bulk SMS. Many companies, including Yahoo! Messenger, offer this service. A *professional* scammer will text you from his phone number.

The SMS feature lets you send text messages to your friends' mobile phones right from Yahoo!

Messenger. Just type in a friend's mobile phone number, compose your message as you would a regular instant message, then hit send. Your friend will receive your text message on their phone, and their replies come back to you in Yahoo! Messenger.

https://messenger.yahoo.com/features/sms/

It's free to send SMS messages from Yahoo! Messenger to your friends (and to receive their replies). However, your friends may incur data charges from their mobile carrier for receiving and replying to your messages.

Yahoo! Messenger supports SMS messaging for the following countries and carriers:

United States: AT&T, Alltel, Nextel (including Sprint), Verizon Wireless, T-Mobile, Virgin Mobile
Canada: Rogers, Fido, Telus
India: Vodaphone Essar, Airtel, Aircel, Spice, Escotel, Reliance, BPL, BSNL, IDEA, MTNL
Indonesia: XL, Indosat, Hutch 3, Telkomsel, Mobile-8, Bakrie, Smart
Malaysia: Celcom, DiGi, Maxis
Philippines: Globe, Smart, Sun
Thailand: AIS, DTAC
Vietnam: Mobifone, Viettel, Vinaphone, S-Fone, EVN, Vietnamobile, Beeline
Kuwait: Wataniya
Pakistan: Mobilink

How a scammer creates fictitious websites. Yes, a professional scammer uses fictitious websites to carry out his scam and make his story more believable. Depending on his story line he may have more than one fictitious website. He hires website designers to replicate real websites. He cannot use the real website because you might want to use the "real phone number" to call them. Fictitious websites are usually small (five or so pages) and often have broken links. Sometimes the verbiage does not make sense. When someone you are chatting with shows you a website, conduct an Internet search of the name of the company to see if another website comes up that is different than what you are shown. If it is a bank or news website you can usually find the real website. If it is a company, he may change the name of the company but use their content; therefore the real website will not come up under the name. If this happens, put some content from the home page into the Internet search bar and you might find the real website.

He uses fictitious news websites to make you believe his story. Many times the news will have something to do with money.

He uses fictitious banking websites to deceive you into thinking he doesn't need your money. He may say he is unable to access his account and give you his user name and password to enter his account, which will show a large sum of money. This is intentional. He wants you to see (think) he has a lot of money so you will not realize he is after yours. Once you transfer the money for him, you will receive an error message that his account has been closed due to someone with a foreign IP address accessing the account. This is all done intentionally to manipulate you and make you feel guilty that you put him in a financial bind. Then he will ask you to send YOUR MONEY. You will see this in action in chapter three (p. 218).

You can also go to Network Solutions Who Is and type in the domain name to see who owns it.

http://www.networksolutions.com/whois

One of the military scammers found in the book, "Is It A Real Soldier Behind The Screen? Online Dating: How to Protect Your Heart and Money" used the Halifax Bank in the United Kingdom in his scam. He used the URL www.halifax-securities.org and the real bank's URL is www.halifax.co.uk. The real bank has many warnings about fraud. The bank address that the scammer emailed to me is not the same as the bank's actual address; neither are the phone numbers the same. The phone number sequence supplied by the scammer is not how someone in the United Kingdom would sequence the phone numbers, i.e. (fake number +44 1132 798 302) (real bank number +44 207 193 9244).

There were also misspelled words in the email that supposedly came from bank personnel, which is another indication that the scammer is pretending to be the bank personnel.

It is critical to do your research and not take anything at face value. Remember, trust is earned and should not be freely given. Again, please remember once you give your heart to someone, it is difficult to see things that are otherwise obvious.

On a ficticious website a scammer may have five different fake people with pictures giving testimony to how good the company is. Many times the website sells different types of goods specifically for the work he claims to do.

How a scammer creates fictitious documents. A scammer uses fictitious documents all the time to make his story more believable. He researches what real documents and stamps would look like and then either uses design software to create them himself or finds someone to create them for him; he may also buy false documents. There are entire networks of people to do whatever he needs. Military scams require a lot of fictitious documents with military seals and stamps on them. In the book, "Is It A Real Soldier Behind The Screen? Online Dating: How to Protect Your Heart and Money" you will see pictures of all the documents used in the military scam.

He may send a fictitious passport to gain your trust. He might even invite you to check the authenticity because he assumes you never will, and even if you do, he knows it is very difficult for the average person to identify a counterfeit passport. According to World-Check, provider of structured risk intelligence to more than 3000 institutions, including 47 of the world's 50 largest banks and hundreds of government agencies, the keys to identifying the legitimacy of a passport normally lie in characteristics such as watermarks, special security threads inserted during the paper production process, threads coated with ink that react to ultraviolet light, miniature plastic disks embedded in the paper, micro-line printing, background printing, holograms and similar reflective coatings. There is no way you can possibly do this without the actual passport in your possession, and a scammer knows this. However, it is a big red flag if he sends you his passport. If he does, compare the birthdate on it with the birthday he told you he has. Many times you will find a discrepancy.

http://www.world-check.com/media/d/content_pressarticle_reference/AFMA_
March2009.pdf

How a scammer creates fake cam videos. Scammers say, "It's all about gaining trust so they can get the Benjamins, Baby." He knows you will ask him to come on cam. A professional scammer will have a fake cam video ready. He finds a false identity online that not only has a lot of pictures but also has a video of the man, or he creates a video using **www.manycam.com** or hires someone to do it. This software allows people to add thousands of webcam effects and custom graphics and create their own custom graphics and effect.

He can change his face, eyes, hair, add backgrounds, and much more. He can draw over his video window or screencast their desktop and change his voice with a built in voice changer. He may also go to porn websites to look for a video that resembles the identity he wants to use. He may even start talking to a gay male and convince the gay male to do whatever he wants them to do, and then record it and save it on the computer. Yes, he records people on cam, so be very careful about going on cam and what you do on cam. He may try very hard to get you to commit lewd acts so he can extort money from you.

When he comes on cam, ask him to do something in real time such as stand up to see how tall he is, remove his glasses or hold his watch close to the camera so you can see it better. If it is a pre-recorded cam, he will not be able to do any of these things and you will know you are chatting with a scammer.

A scammer conceals his real IP address (Internet Protocol Address). An IP address allows one computer (or other digital device) to communicate with another via the Internet. IP addresses allow the location of literally billions of digital devices that are connected to the Internet to be pinpointed and differentiated from other devices. In the same sense that someone needs your mailing address to send you a letter, a remote computer needs your IP address to communicate with your computer. "IP" stands for Internet Protocol, so an IP address is an Internet Protocol address. An Internet Protocol is a set of rules that govern Internet activity and facilitate completion of a variety of actions on the World Wide Web. Therefore an Internet Protocol address is part of the systematically laid out interconnected grid that governs online communication by identifying both initiating devices and various Internet destinations, thereby making two-way communication possible.

http://whatismyipaddress.com/ip-address

A scammer does everything he can to keep his real identity and location concealed. He generates IP addresses from the United States, United Kingdom, Canada and many other countries to use on dating sites so it cannot be detected that he is actually from Africa. He knows many dating sites look for IP addresses from Nigeria and will not allow access if a Nigerian IP address is found.

He likely uses a proxy server. When he connects with a proxy server and asks for a resource available on another server, the proxy connects with the other server or brings up what he asks for from a cache. Some proxy servers don't pass along their IP address, but some will. Some charge for their services and some don't. An anonymous proxy doesn't pass along their IP address, but it does identify itself as a proxy server when connecting with the other server, while a distorting proxy provides an incorrect IP address. A high anonymity proxy doesn't pass along their IP address and it doesn't identify itself as a proxy server.

http://computer.howstuffworks.com/internet/basics/hide-ip-address.htm

Hiding his IP address allows him to stay anonymous on the Internet so sites he visits are not able to trace him.

He uses "international proxies," which allow him to visit web pages and do research undetected, bypass filters of online dating service, and conceal his real IP address from you, online dating services, private investigators and law enforcement. International proxies can usually be accessed through Yahoo!, Gmail and Hotmail.

He also uses virtual private network (VPN). A VPN extends a private network across a public network. He uses this to connect to proxy servers for the purpose of protecting personal identity and location.

A professional scammer also uses Mobile VPNs to set where an endpoint of the VPN is not fixed to a single IP address but instead roams across various networks such as data networks from cellular carriers or between multiple Wi-Fi access points. They allow the scammer to roam seamlessly across networks and in and out of wireless-coverage areas without losing application sessions or dropping the secure VPN session. A conventional VPN cannot survive such events because the network tunnel is disrupted, causing applications to disconnect, time out, or fail, or even cause the computing device itself to crash.

Michael J. West from Arkansas Investigations looked up IP addresses for me as I was chatting and can do the same for you. He can be reached at 501-605-0360.

The Scamming Begins

A scammer surfs dating sites for clients. A scammer goes to both free and paid dating sites and if he can get into the site, he first searches to find people that look rich from the United States, United Kingdom, Australia, Canada and other countries that have a good economy. If he doesn't find many he leaves that site and goes to another one.

He continues searching until he finds a dating site that has a lot of possibilities. He then settles in and works many clients at the same time. If he doesn't get reported he works that site until he has exhausted all the possibilities on that site.

Beginner and low money scammers tell their scamming buddies which websites are fruitful, and that dating site becomes flooded with scammers. This is how I was able to chat with so many scammers on SinglesBee. It was flooded with scammers.

A professional scammer will not tell any other scammers about a fruitful dating site, and if they see a lot of scammers on a dating site he usually will not stay on that site.

What a scammer looks for in profiles. A scammer considers many attributes to determine if you are a good prospect. He looks at the backgrounds of your profile pictures to see if you look classy and rich. He does the same when looking for men to scam.

He perceives women are very sincere with the way they feel in their profiles so he looks for clues that might tell him if you would be easy prey or not. What makes you easy prey is you reveal specifically what you are looking for in your profile. When you do this, you give a scammer the password to your heart. You become a tool for him to use.

He looks for a woman between the ages of 44 and 70. He thinks this woman does not have time for games, and he knows this woman will probably be separated, divorced, widowed, or retired. He assumes you are lonely, desperate for love and might even want a younger man to keep you young. He sees this as a weakness and believes that your desperation will make you fall in love and give him your money. He perceives a woman in this age group will also have money from a divorce settlement, retirement and real estate.

He looks for occupations such as real estate, nurse, accountant, attorney, doctor, sales representative, manager and business owner. He is only interested if you are working, because it's not about falling in love, it's about obtaining money. You must have a big job that brings in big money.

He looks for income level. Beginner and some small money scammers look for women that make $20,000 to $25,000. It is so low because in Nigeria they get paid monthly, so they think the income on a dating site is also monthly instead of annually. A professional scammer understands the income level on dating sites is annual so he looks for incomes of $100,000 and above. So much is about perception!

He notices what country and state a woman is from so he can appeal to her in his format.

He primarily looks for Caucasian, Asian (Singapore) and Christian women, but if he thinks you have money, your race does not matter.

He pays attention to your interests so he can pretend to have things in common with you. He wants you to feel comfortable and be more interested in him.

Scammers say they perceive 80% of the women on Match.com and Chemistry.com are classy and have money. Professional scammers frequent these dating sites often.

Scammers know that those who have been scammed usually write little about themselves in their profiles or write: "Beware of scammers, I don't play games and I don't want anyone to play games with me. If you are not in the States or you have a job outside the states don't contact me." Scammers think of this woman as a challenge and consider her to be a MAJOR MAGA that has been a victim 4 or 5 times from different scammers and will go after her.

A scammer will take the user name you use on the dating site and try it on Yahoo! Messenger and then open up the Yahoo! Detector to see if that ID is online. If it is, he will start sending short messages to try to get you to respond, such as "I got your profile on _____ dating site and want to get to know you better", "Hi pretty", and "Hello beautiful queen, how are u doing?, wow babe u real look beautiful, looking at ur beautiful pix i just don't want to set my eyes off u, am James widowed i was searching when suddenly i came across ur stunning profile and after going true it i became interested in u, pls if single send me ur email id for chat online and to know more better…babe i wait impatiently for Ur reply soonest…cheers."

Bombing. Beginners and low money scammers often have ten or more scammers working together in one room using one wireless broadband, and if one of them gets a client that pays quickly they pass around the zip code from where she is; the other scammers will then search for clients in that city, state and zip code and sends them all an email. This is what beginners and low money scammers call bombing.

A professional scammer considers bombing to be when he searches profiles on a dating site and picks the ones that have a good yearly income and occupation that depicts they are wealthy. Once he finds twenty or so women that fit his criteria, he sends them all the same message. If you are a teacher, waitress or other low paying profession, he is not interested.

If security is high a professional scammer will break in because he knows most beginners and low money scammers will not be on that dating site.

A scammers perception about women

American Women – He believes American women in the United States are very inquisitive and computer savvy, and he wants to make sure you can find him if you look for him on line. He thinks all Americans are rich and white people are transparent when they are in love. He also thinks American women don't love easily and any woman who speaks English may be able to wear him down with questions. He tries to make his story believable so as not to arouse suspicions.

Asian Women – His perception of Asian women is much different. He perceives Asian women as not very inquisitive, and therefore, easier targets. He believes most Asian women will not want to find out anything about him other than what he volunteers. He believes they fall in love easily and have a heart for children, so he uses a child and a child's voice in the scam.

United Kingdom Women –He believes United Kingdom women do not love easily and they are more aware of scams on dating sites.

African Women – He scams African women too. He doesn't care where you come from, as long as you have money. He will ask an African woman to pay money to the United Kingdom, and he collects it from there. She may never know she has been scammed by someone who could be her neighbor.

Send First Message. A scammer sends a message to several women who may be good clients. The message may be as short as "Hello pretty" or as long as a paragraph or two. He may instantly ask you to join him on Yahoo! IM or email back and forth a couple times with you on the dating site and then ask you to join him on Yahoo! IM. His goal is to get you off the dating site and onto

Yahoo! IM.

WARNINGS

Once you leave the dating site, you can no longer hold the dating site accountable for what happens.

When you are dealing with the virtual world, many of the safeguards and natural instincts you have built up over your lifetime are greatly diminished because you never see the person so you can't look in their eyes and read their body language. You forfeit your sense of sight, smell and touch. The "virtual" world is very different than the "real" world. The virtual world operates on emotion more than anything. Most people are not prepared or knowledgeable enough about what happens in the virtual world to play safely, and sooner or later they become a victim. It's not "if" you will become a victim, it's "when" you will be.

Once On Yahoo IM

A SCAMMER LEARNS ABOUT YOU SO HE CAN MANIPULATE YOU…He uses his format to learn all he can about you so he can manipulate you, and then he tries to get a hold of your heart and control you with your likes and what makes you smile. He does all this to make you fall in love with him.

A SCAMMER MAKES YOU FALL IN LOVE WITH HIM…He uses care, love and makes false promises to hook your heart. He builds a relationship with you and might even send you flowers, chocolates, stuffed animals, jewelry, and even money to woo you. He sends love poems and sweet words to make you fall in love with him. He will be online with you every day. Some will call you, some will text you and some will do both. *He knows how to make the virtual world become a very real world for you.* He may build the relationship and ask for money in a few days, a week or two, a month, or more. It depends on his desperation and skill and how much money he plans to ask for.

A SCAMMER THEN STEALS YOUR MONEY…Once he believes he has your heart he will come up with a reason why he needs money and makes you believe you are the only person in the world that can help him. It is always an emergency, and he doesn't want to give you time to think about it. At this point he does all he can to get you totally emotionally involved and uses your love to get you to send the money.

If it is a large amount of money he will have you send it via a bank wire; he will ask for smaller amounts to be sent through Western Union or Money Gram. No matter what method he tells you to use, it is irreversible and not traceable. Remember, just because he doesn't have you send the money to Africa, doesn't mean he is not in Africa.

If you tell him you do not have the money he will ask you to mortgage your home, get a payday loan on your car, take money from your retirement fund, sell things you have and even ask you to borrow money from others. He will get very pushy and demanding because he has spent a lot of time and maybe money on you. He will stop at nothing to get money. YOUR MONEY!

IF HE BELIEVES YOU HAVE MONEY BUT CAN'T GET IT FROM YOU…He will disappear and either pass you to another higher level scammer or use another identity and start all over again using another strategy. REMEMBER, YOU DO NOT KNOW WHO IS BEHIND THE SCREEN!

ONCE HE GETS MONEY FROM YOU…You then become his "Magha" (a fool by way of trickery). He will continue to ask you for money. Even if you tell him he is a scammer he might go away for a while but he will come back to you again. Once the money you gave him runs out, he will be back hot and heavy with another reason to ask you for money. Once he believes he has gotten all the money he can from you, or you are onto him, he will shut the scam down and have no future contact with you. He will delete all emails, phone numbers and such so you cannot trace, bother or threaten him.

MY BEST ADVICE…Stay away from online dating. If you are going to date online, know all the red flags and be extremely careful. *Professional* scammers have many tools and are very deceptive and believable, and don't forget that many use spells to get your money. There are SO many dangers!

After being scammed, I chatted with twenty five scammers in order to obtain information for this book, and to my surprise the below three scammers came clean with me and taught me much of what is in this chapter.

Bob Jugant

My name is Bob Jugant and I live in Africa. I first started internet dating to look for love. Soon I learned that I could make a living by scamming on dating sites. As with many in Africa, making a living is difficult to say the least. Most jobs pay one dollar a day. I wanted what most people want, a home, a car and money to survive. All around me I saw men who had all these things and I wanted them too. This is what led me to scamming on dating sites. However, it wasn't how I thought it would be and I never liked doing it because I realized that I was toying with people's emotions and directly hurting people by cheating them out of their hard earned money. But, it was a way to make a living.

I did online dating scams for some time. It wasn't until I tried to scam Diana Garren that things changed for me. She told me she was writing a book to educate the public worldwide about Internet dating scams so they could keep their heart and money safe. She wanted to bring awareness to those who have been scammed and those who are online dating so they would not be scammed. She wanted information of how the scam worked and for me to roll play how a scammer would continue to get money from the victim and I agreed. Even though I knew this book would put millions of scammers all over the world out of business I decided to take the time to help her with the book and teach her the inner workings of the scam.

Brett Robson

I am the 4[th,] child in a family of six children. I hail from the middle belt (Benue State) part of Nigeria, you know what is it like coming from a family that is so huge and when you have parents that can't afford all the care for the much children they have...My life became something when I lost my Dad, may his gentle soul rest in peace. He did all the best to raise his children to achieve the best education in life and to lead a responsible life in a good society but he never knew life was too short for him then he lost his life in that process.

My life became miserable and frustrating when I lost my Dad at a tender and immature age where I never knew what life has for me as a young man, this is where the struggle all started.

I went out to the world to find greener pastures to further my education when my Dad lost his life when he couldn't do more...I travelled down from the state I hail to a State called Lagos City where we all know in Nigeria that it's one of the places where hustle and a lot of people from different ethnic groups come together to achieve their goals and find opportunity or transact businesses. When I got to Lagos I had no one in Lagos to live with or find a shelter so that I can look forward to whatever I went out to find and I got to the capital city of Lagos called Ikeja, it's a place located in the Mainland part of Lagos where we have a lot of people who are less than average in wealth and wealthy people too.

It was really a big thing for me you know when getting into a city you haven't been before I had to find shelter first where I met a colleague of my late Dad at his place of work thinking at least I can stay at his place for a while so that I can get a job to earn some money to care for my life and make some savings to rent a small room where I can think of better things, but no it was another hell of living I got myself into, so I called a friend of my late Dad who accepted me for a while to stay at his place and my life started from there where I wake up every morning go out to find a job, I searched for almost a month but got none and I decided I would rest a little bit so that I figure out a better plan in finding a good job...living in Lagos is a big thing and stressful but if you are very patient and hard working in finding your greener pastures your dreams will definitely come to pass.

One day I met this guy on the faithful morning of Wednesday 6th July 2007 where I was so tired and frustrated looking for a job he asked if I was really looking for a job I said yes and he took me down to a nearby restaurant to eat and discuss more and that was where we introduced ourselves better and exchanged cell phone numbers then later that day I went home and rest to wait for the next day...it was the next day I got a call from this guy I met asking me to come to his apartment where he resides, then I took a motorcycle drove to his apartment and when I got there I met some other guys three of them and we all exchanged greetings and names...This is where my uncalled life all started.

We all went into his apartment and he introduced me to this business which he said it's the latest in town which is called (YAHOO) which is known to be an Internet Fraudulent Act.

I already had computer skills when we all started and I went into a couple of weeks training and I developed more interest and I got into it so fast that after the couple of weeks I was trained. I made some little money out of it and that was where more fun started and each day that passes I develop more skills and ways of fraud...then I made my first hit from a white woman and widower with two kids which she sent a sum of three thousand dollars($3,000)which we all know it's a good start from this act then this life started growing, then in two month I made another good hit but I never wanted to buy a car because I wanted something else to do with the money, which is furthering my education although that was my intensions this life of crime seems to be sweeter and having all the things you desire and want you know, I started spending the money with crazy things. I buy myself good cloths and go to clubs have fun but don't drink is one of the rules I have in my life as a man and I don't womanize at all because my principles in life are so strong that I control them whenever I go.

Having made some good money out of this different ideals always comes in this YAHOO thing, I and my friends got more ideals to scam and each one of us made money and we all fled to our own part to enjoy what we had but we never stopped playing the game because our contact where still intact and we got a lot of guys into it and they all had their own trainings and it became a bigger thing and more money was coming in. The rest I got was about seventy to eighty thousand dollars ($70,000-80,000) and I spent all of this enjoying myself. I knew more is going to come when I scam more...but on this faithful year that is 2009 where I began to have issues with my life where I met people who always ask me why I am into this crime thing and that is where things became in real terms for me that I later realized that it's a sinful and ungodly act but I tried all that I could to change from the act. It took a lot of time and perseverance to change, you know leaving out of that life was a hell of a thing and I couldn't get money the way I used to. Life became miserable and I did stop the act for a year and I became broke and no money to live the way I used to but sometimes I go to the internet to check mails and see friends to help out with little favors to go on with life...

Why I got myself into Scamming was because of all the things my late Dad had promised to make me achieve but when I couldn't get that I had to go out and get it myself but I found my life into something else after searching for a job which I didn't get and this country is so frustrating that it will lead you into anything and I mean anything. Nigeria is one of the countries where a lot of investors from all over the world come to transact business because it has different mineral resources opportunity but the so called leaders we have here are making the lives of graduate and undergraduate miserable, after finishing your education getting a job is one of the major thing a graduate would face and thinking the government would provide good and more jobs, ways that the citizens would benefit from it but none seems to be given to the society all of this leads to different crimes in the society at large.

A lot of youth go out to find what they can achieve to make their lives better but on going out and when they can't find what they really want it becomes something that leads them into crimes and killings, stealing and all kinds of crime you can ever imaging...am saying all of this because it part of my experience in life and the things I have seen and gone through in life.

Later this year August 2012 where I really wanted to go into the crime act well I really started but the reasons where just but because I had an issue that my Mum was very ill that she couldn't walk for months and I got so worried and had nothing to take her to the hospital to get some treatment and when I started my first dating site called SINGLES BEE well I started quite well and I got couple of friends to chat with so to say where I met this woman called Diana she was the woman that gave me little hopes of getting some money to take my mum to the hospital but I never knew that month was the very last month and day that I would do the internet crime thing, I was actually not stable with going to the internet because I had other means to hustle for money so that I can at least raise the money the fastest way I can...then on this morning where this lady Diana we had an agreement that she would send me some money but behold she's one of the victims that has been scammed on the internet, I started asking for money and she was actually responding fine but later she made mention of words such as MAGA, CLIENT, etc. which are words the scammers uses to communicate I paused for a while and had a deep thought inside me and was thinking if I don't have any ideal about this act any more but I didn't stop talking anyway first I thought it was one of the scammers then I started chatting with those words scammers use but I realized that she didn't understand anything I said so I became furious and asked who she really was she came clean with me asking me why I am into scamming and was asking more questions but I didn't run away I only said to her that she should be very careful and the way she should not use her real name and identity because scamming is more dangerous now than the way it used to be and I signed out and left her for some time but something inside me never stopped thinking about her then one morning I gave her a call and asked more about her and she told me who she was and what she does for a living and she was another opportunity for me to stop the internet crime and that was how and what led me to coming clean with her and now am writing this story about my awful life that I have lived.

I just want to say that writing about me would be a lot better to absolutely stay away from the crime life.

I want to say to all and one that in any circumstances you find yourself in life first you must thank God for keeping you safe and ask him for directions and open doors for a better future and not follow the wrong path of life. I was lucky though that I was never caught in the act from any crime officers but I am saying you might not be lucky the way I was.

Thank you for taking time to read this and wish you all the best in life.

STAY SAFE and BLESSED

Kelvin Mitchelle

My life of Internet dating scamming started two years ago during my second semester of my first year once I started attending a university. Scamming is very common in the university among the students.

80% of the Nigeria youth first go into scamming to obtain money to pay their way through school and to have food, clothes and shelter. Once these necessities are met they use the money to either travel abroad or set up a legitimate business once they graduate from the university. Scamming or drugs are their only options because Nigeria has no jobs for us once we graduate from university. Without a higher education the annual wage in Nigeria is $365 a year. Nigeria is a third world country. It is very difficult to just survive, let alone try to better yourself with education.

Some will say they are in the game of scamming as a means of revenge for the slavery of our fore father generation in the olden days by the British. The only good thing about scamming is that it has drastically reduced the rate of armed robbery in the country.

Military scamming is the most popular and widely used dating scam and it is something that you need to be trained to do. After my training with the Boss, he provided me all the documents I needed to conduct the military scam. When I went onto SinglesBee and bombed to get prospective clients, Diana Garren was one of the women I was able to bring over to messenger. She became my client. She knew I was about to try to scam her. Once she got the information of where to send the money she told me she knew all along that I was a scammer, and told me what she was doing to educate people so they would not fall victim to online dating scams. She then told me things about life and made me realize some reasons why I have to live a good life. I already knew the truth that no one can be a scammer for life. This encounter and relationship with Diana has changed the course of my life. I am not who I use to be and I am no longer scamming.

This man also taught me about the military scam and through him, the second book 'Is It a Real Soldier Behind the Screen?' was birthed. This book provides details about the military scams.

I knew to make sure this chapter was forensically sound I had to not only put together the information I learned through years of chatting with scammers and my extensive research, but I had to have a minimum of three inside sources that provided me the same answers to my questions and at least one source to verify the information they provided. The man below verified the information provided.

Bobo Ighosogie Ogbomo

My name is Bobo Ighosogie Ogbomo and I live in Nigeria. Over two years ago I met Diana Garren on a Twitter. As we got to know each other she learned that I worked for the Nigerian Government and told me about the books and awareness program she was doing, and asked me if I knew anything about the romance scams that happened on the Internet in Nigeria. I told her I had an idea about what she was talking about. She then asked me if I could help her verify information about how the scamming world worked. I told her I would try. She then started feeding me information to verify. I then identified and befriended several professional scammers and learned detailed facts from about how they ran the scams and provided this information to Diana. My hope is that the information I have provided her will help bring awareness worldwide and stop people from getting their heart broken and losing their money.

Below is information that came from a man in Nigeria I met on Twitter. We became friends and he is not a scammer. He helped me decipher many things the scammers told me and translated Pidgin English for me. He wanted to contribute what he knew about scamming for this book.

Two years ago, I went to visit my friend (course mate, I'll use "Jay" as his name), to collect my "field note book". When I arrived at his house, his protector gate was locked but his generator was on, so I knew he was inside. I called him to let him know was in front of his house, so he came out and opened the protector gate and welcomed me.

When I entered, I saw three other course mates, all busy with laptops. So we greeted, I asked "What's so serious about what you guys are doing". . . . One replied, "We're doing business." So I observed. I learned that Jay was a novice in the business. I asked questions and they confided in me and did not hide anything from me.

ENVIRONMENT: A quiet estate, self-contained, a standby generator. They were always indoors.

EQUIPMENT: laptops, iPhone and a contact abroad.

Since Jay was a novice, he started by hacking people's PayPal Accounts. They buy over a thousand people's username and password from sources, and start accessing their accounts one by one. Some accounts are dormant, some have little money and some have a lot of money. They would immediately withdraw the money and buy things online. In three months' time Jay became a big boy on campus, bought a Blackberry, new clothes, watch and glasses. I think many scammers start like this.

Two other friends and I went to visit Jay, but this time he wasn't at his house but at a neighbor's house who was a known scammer. Jay is now doing online dating scams and now has several magas in the US. Jay was telling us how his friends who are fellow scammers gave him half of what his maga paid. So how I understood it, Jay poses as being in d US. So when the maga paid, Jay's friend received the money because he had a contact in US that would forward the money to Nigeria.

How did Jay get the money from his maga? He told her about a business proposal and that he needed a certain amount for the proposal and she gave Jay $500.

They were talking about one of the fellow scammer who has gone to Lagos to make it big with "Yahoo plus". These guys use spiritualist to cast spells on the women to get their money. These dudes will sleep in coffins for days and do certain rituals and whatever it takes to get their maga to give them whatever they ask for. I think these are the dudes that own the expensive real estate and expensive cars. I said to them if I were them I would invest the money and quit. One said they will not invest because more money always comes in.

With what Jay is doing, he doesn't make enough to buy a house or expensive car, so we joked: hope you will not join the Yahoo Plus dudes. Jay laughed and said, "he is ok wit what he is doing".

Jay had an iPhone, he said with the iPhone, when he called his maga they would see the number as though it was from within the US. I don't know how he did that. Jay told me his mom almost suspected him because he's constantly busy with his laptop from morning till night but he lied and told her he is doing his assignments.

I observed that these scammers womanize, they hardly help their fellow guy friends financially, but they will buy expensive wines and food, lodge in expensive hotels, buy watches, phones and clothing but they will never have cash.

CONCLUSION: Scamming damages the image of Nigeria. People then generalize all "Nigerians are scammers". They have made us to lose our trust abroad. Peer groups influence people to become scammers very fast. I have had a couple of bad friends but have never been influenced to do this. I thank God for this and the way I was raised in a real Christian home.

This is all I have encountered. I hope this helps.

NEU

Additional Information

On correspondences from cell phones, watch for the carrier to be listed. Sometimes the scammer will forget to remove that. Nigerian phone carriers are MTN, Glo Mobile, Airtel, Etisalat, Visafone, Starcomms, Multilinks Telkom, Zoom and Mtel. New carriers can be added. To check Nigerian carriers go to:

http://www.indexmundi.com/nigeria/cell-phone-companies-in-nigeria.html

You can find a complete listing of carriers for the United Kingdom at

http://en.wikipedia.org/wiki/List_of_mobile_network_operators_of_Europe

You can find a complete listing of carriers for the United States at

http://en.wikipedia.org/wiki/List_of_United_States_wireless_communications_service_provid
ers

Nigeria has earned a reputation for scamming and the number "419" that refers to the article of the Nigerian Constitution Criminal Code (part of Chapter 38: Obtaining Property by false pretences; Cheating) that states "Any person who by any false pretence, and with intent to defraud, obtains from any other person anything capable of being stolen, or induces any other person to deliver to any person anything capable of being stolen, is guilty of a felony, and is liable to imprisonment for three years. If the thing is of the value of one thousand naira or upwards, he is liable to imprisonment for seven years. It is immaterial that the thing is obtained or its delivery is induced through the medium of a contract induced by the false pretence. The offender cannot be arrested without warrant unless found committing the offence."

http://www.nigeria-law.org/Criminal%20Code%20Act-art%20VI%20%20to%20the%20end.htm

In 2003 the Economic and Financial Crimes Commission (EFCC) was established in Nigeria, partially in response to pressure from the Financial Action Task Force on Money Laundering (FATF), which named Nigeria as one of 23 countries non-cooperative in the international community's efforts to fight money laundering.

Some scammers actually advance fee fraud to write e-mails to earlier victims, posing as EFCC representatives, claiming they can help them get their money back, in order to scam them once more.

http://en.wikipedia.org/wiki/Economic_and_Financial_Crimes_Commission

The Economic and Financial Crimes Commission (EFCC) is a Nigerian law enforcement agency that investigates financial crimes and money laundering.

http://www.assetrecovery.org/kc/node/7be38a65a34611dcbf1b335d0754ba85.0;jsessionid=3
33F3884490E8861B423E761E682F564

The Financial Action Task Force (FATF) is an inter-governmental body established in 1989 by the Ministers of its Member jurisdictions. The objectives of the FATF are to set standards and promote effective implementation of legal, regulatory and operational measures for combating money laundering, terrorist financing and other related threats to the integrity of the international financial system.

The FATF is therefore a "policy-making body" which works to generate the necessary political will to bring about national legislative and regulatory reforms in these areas.

http://www.fatf-gafi.org/pages/aboutus/

CHAPTER 8

THE UNKNOW HIDDEN DANGERS OF ONLINE DATING

When it comes to the world of the "Romance Scam" I see a circle of death for both you and the scammer. It is a lose-lose situation. If you give money to a scammer you not only hurt yourself, you also hurt the scammer. I see this whole thing as a circle of death, one that none of us need to partake in.

I was told not to include the spiritual coercion/hypnotism in this chapter because it might tarnish my credibility, but I felt I had to or I would be doing you a disservice. Many things exist in this world, and who is to say if they are effective or not? My goal in this book is to make sure I provide you everything I know. My job is not to say if what you read in this chapter works or not; however, I surely don't want to take the chance of withholding something that could be important for you. The inner world of scamming and how it's done is so vast that I don't know all of it, but I believe I have learned enough to keep you safe.

From what my one Nigerian source taught me and my two other sources from Nigeria corroborated, and I confirmed with my in-depth research, there very well could be unknown dangers to be considered when online dating, dangers you may never think exist, but are in fact very real.

Spiritual Coercion/Hypnotism

It is said that a scammer can take control of you by using black magic/hypnotism, and it is nothing to play with. I have seen this happen to a woman just as my source said it would, so I believe this can work. You need to remember that a scammer is a criminal whose main goal is to make money at all costs. He may do things to you without your knowledge or consent, and you may not even know it.

One of the hidden dangers of online dating is *"spiritual coercion"* called *"Oracle Plus Plus"* or *"Yahoo Plus Plus"*. This is extremely dangerous and can be life altering for both you and the scammer. To many, *"Oracle Plus Plus"* or *"Yahoo Plus Plus"* are just other terms for *"Money Ritual"* or *"Blood Money"*. All of these terms mean the use of "Voodoo". Voodoo is a charm, spell or fetish involved in voodoo worship or rituals. Those unfamiliar with African culture might be particularly surprised to learn that many scammers make regular use of voodoo to get their victims (you) to give them money not only once, but to continue to give them money on a regular basis.

As one Yahoo Boy said, "The Voodoo thing exists for real, I have used it but I have stopped because of the fear of repercussion. With the aid of Voodoo the money comes faster. I have friends that still use it, they can collect money twice or thrice a week and it helps. I have a friend that uses a calabash filled with black substance; he hides it in his room and says incantations."

http://www.newscientist.com/blogs/onepercent/2012/02/meet-the-yahoo-boyshtml

An article I found online dated March 29, 2014 titled "How I Upgraded from Yahoo-Yahoo to Yahoo Plus – Internet Fraudster" featured the confession of a 25-year old alleged Internet fraudster who said that what he did went beyond mere conversation and emotional chat, and that he also used fetish means to hypnotize his victims to get what he wanted from them. He said, "You may not believe me but it is true. Those who are into yahoo plus use charms to hypnotize their victims. This is because the ordinary yahoo no longer yields the desired result. Our targets are getting wiser and no longer fall prey. When I noticed that I was not making any headway in the yahoo business, I decided to inquire from some of my friends who were in same business but were living better off."

I have learned that since the early 1990's many scammers have gone to a spiritualist or juju priest for assistance of charms to obtain money from their victim (you). This has become more prevalent since 2006 when it became more difficult for scammers to obtain money due to the sluggish economy.

Scammers perform various rituals, including sleeping in a cemetery or coffin, bathing in a river, eating certain types of fruit, delivering human menstrual blood (obtained from a girlfriend, friend or family member), or any other payment the spiritualist or priest requests to increase the scammer's chances of hypnotizing his victims (you). Once you are hypnotized, you will keep remitting money to the scammer no matter where you live in the world. Distance does not make a difference.

http://diaryofageek.com/yahoo-plus-face-nigerian-scams-419/

I am told by my source that what is needed to make the spell effective is your full maiden name, your picture and for the scammer to talk to you over the telephone. Spells might even be put on a gift of clothing that is sent to you and as soon as you put the clothing on, the spell begins and you will send the scammer whatever he asks for. My sources tell me they have seen this work many times.

Once the spell is cast the scammer might be instructed to keep his feet on a tortoise whenever he chats with you. He may make incisions in his fingertips or wrists. He may have an animal horn prepared for him by a fetish priest, which is filled with human body parts that he has to put on his tongue when chatting with you.

The range of payments and specific instructions for a scammer to follow is vast. He undertakes this because the payment and instructions are essential to the spell, and once the spell is cast you are guaranteed to keep remitting money to the scammer. You will find yourself doing whatever the scammer commands. You will sell things, beg, borrow and even steal to get him what he asks for. My source tells me Oracle Plus Plus and Yahoo Plus Plus are short-term spells, and there are others that last long-term. They are called "Yahoo Extreme" or "Yahoo Final". According to my research it is the next level, and a scammer will actually provide a child or part of a child for sacrifice to increase his chances of success. My source tells me that if a scammer uses "Yahoo Extreme" or "Yahoo Final" they will take control of the victim (you) forever, and when the victim (you) can no longer give the scammer what he wants, the victim (you) will commit suicide.

My source tells me that the spell is wrapped around the picture and voice of the scammer and the false promises the scammer makes to his victim (you). He says that to break the spell you need to remove the scammer's picture from your mind, realize that the promises the scammer made to you are false and will never come to fruition and remove them from your mind, stop chatting with the scammer, no longer read anything sent to you by the scammer, remove from your possession everything sent to you by the scammer, and never talk to the scammer again.

Other methods used to influence the victim (you) are listed below:

"*ASE* is a Yoruba word that means "command", "power", or "authority", depending on the context in which it is used. It can also mean *ability to make whatever statement you make come to pass or happen*".

http://www.arcane-archive.org/religion/african/ase-power-over-nature-1.php

"*Mayehun* Means "Refuse me not." It is used when you want a person to grant your request. It could be used to woo a person or request money. Note that it must be in a polite manner. There is a simple incantation that goes with some Mayehun formulas. In Yoruba Language: *Orun Lo ngba towo omode Orun Lo ngba towo agba*. Translation: *Sleep takes from the young. Sleep takes from the old.* Part of the preparation goes thusly: You put a cowry (cowrie shells) in each hand when going to sleep. The following morning they will have dropped from your hands. Pick them up and pound them (to powder) with specific herbs."

http://www.arcane-archive.org/religion/african/ase-power-over-nature-1.php

"*Afose Afose* means "Speak and come to pass" or "Speak and happen." This is a quite advanced form of ASE. It is usually prepared with black soap and put inside an animal horn; it can be a ram's, cow's, antelope's, etc. There are various formulas and some are quite powerful. Note that it is not a general rule that all Afose be mixed in black soap and kept in horns. Whatever is spoken might happen immediately or in the future, depending on the potency of the charm or the nature of the issue the ASE is addressing. A chameleon usually plays a prominent role in the preparation of Afose Afose, and at times the head of a black cobra is also used."

http://www.arcane-archive.org/religion/african/ase-power-over-nature-1.php

"*Gbetugbetu* is more of a "hypnotizing charm". The person under the spell doesn't really know what he or she is doing. It is used to compel people to do the most improbable things, things they would naturally not do or would refuse to do. It is somewhat difficult to prepare, but there are some simple formulas that vary in degree of potency. The powerful ones have as an ingredient a rope that a man used to hang himself."

http://www.arcane-archive.org/religion/african/ase-power-over-nature-1.php

"*Olugbohun* is believed to be a powerful spirit that picks whatever is said and makes it happen, if not immediately, then very soon. (Even if you mistakenly curse your children out of frustration.) It will create a situation that will cause your request to be met. It is not kept in the house, but far away in the bush and is consulted only once in a while. It is very powerful, and can be used in the arts and practice of black magic, if the owner of the Olugbohun is a bad person."

http://www.arcane-archive.org/religion/african/ase-power-over-nature-1.php

One of my sources encouraged me to not just focus on Nigeria for this book, because Ghana is also home to many scammers and scammers operate from every country worldwide. Nigeria is ranked third and Ghana is ranked sixth in the world for incidents of scamming. When researching for this chapter I learned about Ghanan scammers from a well put together documentary, *Sakawa Boys* (Safo, 2009). In Ghana they are not called Yahoo Boys, they are called the "Sakawa Boys". In the 1970's during the Nigerian oil boom many young men from Ghana went to Nigeria to work. While there they learned about a pen pal scam, and when they brought it home to Ghana they combined it with black magic. In 1993 it became prevalent to use black magic with romance scams. The black magic is called Juju, and it is a traditional West African religion. They pay the spirits to give them power. Today, Sakawa is a full blown culture in Ghana complete with movies and music. Sakawa Boys use human blood for their rituals. The reason for the rise in black magic and scamming is the same in Ghana as in Nigeria – there is no work for these boys and the government is corrupt. They say the police, soldiers and politicians all get their pockets greased with this money. Charles Nelson with Youth Against Cyber Crime (YACC) said "the scammer is both villain and victim, because the more desperate the boys become the more they lean on the occult and move from one spiritualist to another to help them get money." He said "the perceived occult dimension is able to destroy the lives and even kill the scammers and even their sisters, girlfriends or mothers, and **_no good comes from it_**. _If a scammer stops paying the charm, spiritualist or juju priest, the spell is reversed and the scammer can go insane, contract AIDS, and even die_".

To further my research I went onto Google Nigeria and found the information below. Remember that Africa is a different continent with a very different culture and beliefs, so we do not know what we might get ourselves into when online dating because all we see is a computer screen and have NO IDEA who is behind the screen.

I heard the term "Blood Money," so I wanted to learn and educate you about what this is. The article posted on News in Nigeria on February, 18 2013, "Everything You Need To Know About Blood Money In Nigeria: Victims of Ritual Murders Tell Their Stories," said "virtually every day, police stations nationwide in the South West part of Nigeria are inundated with reports of missing persons. Available records show that 10 percent of these people return home and 90 percent of them are not found; those that are found have often been mutilated and had their vital organs removed. The belief is that the majority of the victims are used for rituals, because the poor want to get rich with effortless ease. Native doctors assure them that if they bring more listed human parts, they can cross over to the other side where there is less dirt and more sunshine. On the other hand, the superstitious rich and affluent in the society wants to acquire more riches and political power, and are told that there can be no easier way than to sacrifice the lives of fellow human beings."

http://www.nigerianeye.com/2013/02/everything-you-need-to-know-about-blood.html

According to the article, checks by Sunday Sun revealed that "the most vulnerable are school children, young ladies, pregnant women and elderly people. Most of the ritual killers target children because it is believed that most children are virgins and more potent. Female virgins were also said to be in high demand for rituals. Amadi Okereafor, the chief priest of Umuohoko community in Ngor Okpala council area of Imo State said, "it is a sacrilege in Igbo land for anyone to terminate the life of another." He said that in the days of their ancestors if a man killed his brother or neighbor, he would automatically be banished from the community. Then he pointed out that the rising incidence of ritual killings was due to the inordinate ambition of the new generation of Ndigbo who think that money is the ultimate and said, "today life is nothing as people kill in the name of anything". He also blamed the upsurge in ritual killings on politicians who are ready to do anything to win political office."

One of the oldest men in Ohuhu, Chief Onukwube Anyanwu told Sunday Sun, "rituals are nothing, but sacrifices made to enhance one's chances and opportunities. Different types of people in the society perform rituals and sacrifices to make strong charms for protection, fame, success, riches, etc. The highest of all the charms that can be made by man are those that demand human sacrifice. They are the major causes of ritual killings. There are many people within the society who are in a hurry to attain a particular height. They are not ready to wait for God's time and for that reason, they want to push the hand of the clock to move faster. When the native doctors or herbalists see such people, they give them very hard conditions like the provision of human parts in order to get what they want. Human blood, whether we like it or not, is the costliest of all things mankind can possess. That is the reason many people seem to be succeeding in ritual practices. But whether they like it or not, those who embark on such things have ways of paying back sooner or later".

http://www.nigerianeye.com/2013/02/everything-you-need-to-know-about-blood.html

"In Igbo land, rituals are believed to enhance the chances of those who perform it to have one gain over the other. People consult an oracle and the oracle proclaims that the only thing that will make them succeed is to bring specific human parts. A chief priest, Kanu Nwaohamuo, said "ritual killing was not new in that part of the country. He said it started in the early days when able-bodied men, especially slaves and at times those that have offended the land were sacrificed to appease the gods. Children were not used for that purpose and ritual killings were not for moneymaking. It was done to either appease the gods of the land or as a mark of respect for a fallen king or great man in a community and were seldom done." The chief priest expressed regret that these days, ritual murder of even innocent children has become rampant in Igbo land, and mostly for moneymaking, and he described the frequency of such cases as alarming."

http://www.nigerianeye.com/2013/02/everything-you-need-to-know-about-blood.html

"A traditionalist, Ifamoye Eniola, told Sunday Sun "killing human beings for various rituals is real and common among Africans. Ifamoye who denied any involvement in ritual killing said humans are often used for rituals for money making, promotion, trading and securing appointments. However, he berated herbalists and other traditionalists involved in ritual killings." Ifamoye attributed the alarming rate of ritual killing to the tendency of people wanting to become rich at all costs and even at the expense of their parents and other blood relations. He added: *"Not only herbalists and traditionalists are involved in ritual killings as generally believed in the country. Some evil- minded marabouts and prophets especially the white garment group, use human parts as sacrifice for desperate politicians, businessmen and women and some internet fraudsters called "yahoo boys".*

http://www.nigerianeye.com/2013/02/everything-you-need-to-know-about-blood.html

In Their Own Words

I offer the following insights and information about Yahoo Boys and other scammers from the scammers themselves. Here is the inside scoop… *in their own words*.

http://timimaryz.blogspot.com/2012/07/yahoo-yahoo-boys-i-dont-think-i-should.html#!
/2012/07/yahoo-yahoo-boys-i-dont-think-i-should.html

July 25, 2012

YAHOO!!! YAHOO!!! BOYS

I don't think I should be seeing confused faces with this topic? It is a slugger knows by every countries and races in the entire world. Many people have fallen victim to this people. Let me call them the "underworld" for their actives aren't legal.

Long before this time, it is just few people can afford to use the internet back in my growing up days in Nigeria. To visit the café then was expensive and anyone who runs such business is considered very rich. I can still remember vividly sometimes 1992… not most people are familiar with email and setting it up too would require that someone that is already advance on internet will assist you with a fee. Has things began to get advance people started using email as a means of communication and to chat online too. Girls then are freely boosting of having an email, you can hear them say things like "do you have an email", "can you add me on yahoo messenger? It got so serious that if you don't have an email as a guy, it is sure you aren't going to get the girl.

Yahoo mail became popular among older and the younger ones that the cafés are always filled and you will have to wait to have a free system to use. My current email cost me $300 to open back then as a matter of fact. This is just a brief history of internet back in my growing up.

Now let us get to the business, Yahoo!!! Yahoo!!! It is a slugger like I actually said earlier; it is used by people who are involved in scamming, fraud and every other internet related crime. You might wonder how this found its way into our system. Other people might have a different way to put it, but for me I believed that it started with our ladies. Our women, I must say are very intelligent and knows how to get anything they want. 70% of people using the internet back in the 1990s were women, before the Yahoo boyz took over. Lots of women set up profile, frequent the yahoo messenger chat rooms and other social websites to make contacts. While online the ladies share their number freely with men who made interest of marriage with them—you don't need me to tell you the rest of the stories.

One particular day, I was in the café surfing without knowing what to search for, only that the joy of being on net and learning how to browse was more to me than learning what they really does. Beside me was a lady sitting next to me, because the desktop were arrange in rows. I became inquisitive, so I peep on the lady's conversation with a white man. From the conversation the lady in question has been getting money and gifts from the white man all the while. In conclusion, it was these activities of the ladies the guys took advantage of and started to pose on net using a female picture and data to get their desperate victims. It became a good business that many lazy bones start to use the net to get free money and gifts from their victims. As times goes on; with more research on how to making money in a dubious ways emerge, e.g : buying things on net, paying for a house rent, ordering clothes, shoes, watches, handset(mobile phone), just to name little from the Cyber crime our young guys now involves themselves.

YAHOO PLUS!!! Funny name you would say? The addition of the plus is to tell you that something else has been added or joined, isn't that so? And what was this thing that was added? Voodoo! Some called it black power, some called it juju. I chose to call it voodoo so you can understand where I am going to. Some five to six years back, when the cyber business had begun to fail the yahoo boyz; they had to think of something. Some turn to stealing; while some became arm robbers; some set of them turned to voodoo. A Yahoo plus' victims are been put under their spell of voodoo, they command them for money at will and only free them when their victims has no more left. This voodoo was a very powerful spells that when cast on a victim can make him or her unaware of what he/she is doing. Only the desperate yahoo plus engaged in such voodoo knowing the repercussion is bad. Some became a total beggar after everything failed them, some can go mad, and some their life became miserable and they began to sell everything they had. Like they say; 'not all that glitter is gold'.

YAHOO PLUS PLUS!!! After the introduction of voodoo into cyber crime, the coming up ones had to change the dimension of the Yahoo plus and came up with something that is not that powerful but effective after it has been applied. They went back to the origin of the yahoo yahoo system of posing like a lady and the buying and selling on net but with a charm to draw people who view or get in touch with them. There is no much to talk of about the yahoo plus plus, because it is a new system of operation among our youths. One last thing before I close this topic for good or perhaps if there is something new. If you think 'western union money transfer' is save, it is better you think twice. Banks are now begun to work along with the yahoo boyz to pick up people's money, long as they have the code without the question and answer security.

See you at the other side of failure!

YAHOO! Plus Boy Shows Off Money Ritual Shrine, Lots Of Dollars & Calls It Bastard Money All On Facebook

http://unclenaira.com/yahoo-plus-boy-shows-off-money-ritual-shrine-lots-of-dollars-calls-it-bastard-money-all-on-facebook/

Please keep in mind that once you open yourself up to a scammer, you have opened your life up to a criminal and anything bad can happen…

Your Pictures and Video Could Be Used

Once you give a scammer your pictures they may be used to scam someone else. If you give the scammer risqué pictures or show your body on camera the scammer can use these to not only scam others, but they can use them to exploit you for money. If you don't pay them the money, they will place your pictures on the web and your video on Youtube.

Phishing

Once in communication with a scammer they can lead you to a website or send you an email masquerading as a trustworthy entity. Their goal is to acquire your personally identifying and sensitive information such as usernames, passwords, social security number and credit card details (and sometimes, indirectly, money).

Among the websites and emails commonly used as lures are popular social media web sites, auction sites, banks, online payment processors or IT administrators.

Phishing emails may contain links to websites that are infected with malware. Phishing is typically carried out by email spoofing or instant messaging and it often directs you to enter details at a fake website whose look and feel are almost identical to the legitimate one it copies.

A phisher sends phishing email disguised as official email from a (fictional) bank, attempting to trick you into revealing confidential information by "confirming" it at what is actually the *phisher's* website. The email contains what appears to be a legitimate URL of the bank's webpage; in actuality, the hyperlink actually leads to the phisher's webpage.

Phishing emails often contain misspelled words. You can find more information about phishing at:

http://en.wikipedia.org/wiki/Phishing

Your Email Can Be hacked

Once a scammer knows your email address he can easily hack your email. He can then send emails or messages to your friends and family and may be able to post on your social media accounts.

Your Phone Number Can Be Used

Once a scammer knows your phone number you will need to change your phone number to get him to stop calling. If you use the messenger service "whatsapp" that works from phone numbers, he will have access to contact you on this service.

Open Yourself Up To Other Scammers

If his yahoo account gets hacked, other scammers will also have access to your information, and you had better believe they too will try to scam you.

Social Media

If a scammer infiltrates your social media accounts, he can use all your pictures, create a new account, and pretend to be you and create havoc on your life and your friends and family's life.

References:

http://diaryofageek.com/yahoo-plus-face-nigerian-scams-419/

http://www.nigerianeye.com/2014/03/how-i-upgraded-from-yahoo-yahoo-to.html

http://www.nairaland.com/782345/juju-black-magic-nigeria-blood

http://www.nigerianeye.com/2013/02/everything-you-need-to-know-about-blood.html

http://www.arcane-archive.org/religion/african/ase-power-over-nature-1.php

http://www.newscientist.com/blogs/onepercent/2012/02/meet-the-yahoo-boys.html

http://www.gistmania.com/talk/topic,129110.0.html

http://en.wikipedia.org/wiki/Phishing

Safo, Socrate. 2009. Sakawa Boys, four parts. 2009. Directed by Socrate Safo. Movie Africa Productions. Ghana. VCD - http://topdocumentaryfilms.com/sakawa-boys-internet-scamming-ghana/

CHAPTER 9

THE ROOT CAUSE OF ROMANCE SCAMS

E verything has a root cause. After spending over two and a half years in correspondence with scammers in Nigeria, I wanted to know the root cause of why these men felt it was perfectly ok to steal other peoples pictures, pretend to be someone they were not, and steal money from hard working innocent people all over the world.

They said they scam because they are suffering from the selfishness and corruption of their leaders in Nigeria. I have personally been to Niger but not Nigeria, Africa. While in Niger I saw for myself what it is like to live in a third world country. It is a very difficult life, to say the least. My experience in Niger made me appreciate what I have and where I live. So much so that every day when I wake up I am thankful I was born in the United States. I like to think that I would not steal from others no matter how difficult my life became. But none of us know for sure what we would do if we were hungry day in and day out and had nothing to feed our family.

My purpose of this book is three-fold: first, to educate people so they no longer fall prey to the online dating scammers; second, to call upon all people who have been scammed to step up and share their story and help me educate others; and third, to reveal the root cause in hopes of evoking change for the poverty-stricken people of Nigeria. (But please know that dating scams are conducted from all over the world, often for the same root causes as in Nigeria).

Let's talk first about **greed.** According to Dictionary.com, greed is excessive or rapacious desire, especially for wealth or possessions.

In "Nigerians are Greedy and Selfish – Rwanda" (http://thenews-chronicle.com/nigerians-are-greedy-and-selfish-rwanda/) the High Commissioner of Rwanda to Nigeria, Joseph Habineza, said, "The first disease Nigeria has is greed with selfishness." He also stated "The fact is there are bad politicians and there are good politicians, but the bad ones are so evil; they can use all means to get what they want."

In "Greed: The Root Cause of Nigerian Menace" Nigerian citizen and article author Benedict C. Onyeso writes, "greed is the root cause for the condition of Nigeria" and said "It is sad enough that no sector is left uncontaminated by this fiery monster." Onyeso came to the same conclusion I did when he said, "Tracing the event (sic) of history, in the Judeo-Christian account of creation, Cane had to kill his brother Abel, because of his greed expressed in the light of jealously; thus bearing the testimony of greed as an age-long menace, not only in Nigeria, but in the periphery of the whole human nature everywhere man exists as a being.

Following this line of thought, I feel exculpated from accusation and criticism when I say that greed being an inevitable attribute of human nature is a substantial make-up of any given society in the world. Explicitly unveiling, there is no society free from greed. It is intrinsically in every society and in man, for man is an insatiable being"

http://www.academia.edu/7549917/GREED_THE_ROOTCAUSE_OF_NIGERIAN_MENACE

In his article "Greed: Season of Greeds and Political Misfortunes" Bukhari Muhammed Bello Jega writes, "Naturally, this country (Nigeria) ought not to be poor country; but, outright stealing and pauperization of the people by its leaders has render this promising giant into a state of dwarf among comity of nations. A nation at independent, which promised to be a beckoned of hope for Africans, has become an embarrassment to her African brothers and sisters. A country with huge resources both mineral and manpower, but yet all these resource is of no benefit to the majority of its inhabitants except some tiny few; who not only plunder and raped the country but are also destroying the fabrics of the society." To learn more go to the source:

http://www.gamji.com/article8000/NEWS8673.htm

Clearly the greed starts with the leaders of Nigeria. Fredrick Nwabufo states this well in his article "Greed and Ego in Nigerian Politics." He writes, "Greed and ego are no doubt defining qualities of Nigerian politicians. These are congenital and acquired traits exhibited in unconscionable degrees by Nigerian politicians. By greed and ego being congenital traits in relation to Nigerian politicians, I mean, some Nigerian politicians are helpless and irredeemable, their greed and ego maladies are incurable. In fact, they are born to exude odorous fumes of the depraved traits. And by greed and ego being acquired traits in relation to Nigerian politicians, I imply, some level-headed persons who had rigid moral principles prior to joining the Nigerian political circus, but the egregious and corrupting political system of Nigeria has soiled them so bad that they give off more awful stench of the odoriferous traits than the scrum of Nigerian politicians whose greed and ego are congenital and atavistic."

This illustrates how greed infects good people and erodes a society. Nwafubo writes, "Greed and ego explain their lack of character, principles and morals; greed and ego explain their lack of direction, purpose and focus; greed and ego explain their corrupt state of mind, malfeasance and thievery." Where there are good leaders who lead by exemplary behavior, the citizens will follow.

Where there are bad leaders who lead by unconscionable behavior, some citizens will follow. Nigeria's leaders have created a national culture rife with greed and theft, and *it is spreading injury all over the world*. The people are following the lead of their leaders."

http://www.modernghana.com/news/494545/1/greed-and-ego-in-nigerian-politics.html

I found in my research that the greed in Nigeria affects economies all over the world. Every dollar a scammer steals is removed from the economy of the victim's country and funneled into the economy of Nigeria and other countries that participate in the scam culture.

I now ask ALL countries around the globe to help me win this war. Help me educate your people. Work to reduce or eliminate online dating scams. Help your citizens keep their money and strengthen your country's economy. We have only one weapon in this war – education. It is the only weapon we need to defeat this epidemic. If would-be victims refuse to give money to scammers, the scamming culture will wither and die.

Let's talk now about *corruption*. According to Dictionary.com, corruption is the act of corrupting or state of being corrupt; moral perversion, depravity; perversion of integrity; corrupt or dishonest proceedings; bribery.

Corruption is not new and it is not just in Nigeria; it is a global problem. However, corruption is pandemic in Nigeria. Her leaders and their followers are as corrupt as they are greedy.

Corruption takes many forms, all of them insidious. Corruption fuels the poverty and misery of the Nigerian population. It elevates personal gain and profit above all else and drives those infected by it to secure wealth, power and private gain through illegal means and at the expense of the public. In Nigeria, the stolen public funds are counted in billions of U.S. dollars and Nigeria Naira. Corruption appears to be the main means by which to accumulate quick wealth in Nigeria.

Victor E. Dike details the types and effects of corruption prevalent in Nigeria today. The following is excerpted from his Africa Economic Analysis, "Corruption in Nigeria: A New Paradigm for Effective Control":

"You have *political* corruption. This occurs at the highest levels of political authority. It occurs when the politicians and political decision-makers establish and implement the laws in the name of the people, are themselves corrupt. It also occurs when policy formulation and legislation is tailored to benefit politicians and legislators. Political corruption is seen similar to greed and affects decision making, manipulates political institutions, rules of procedure, and distorts the institutions of the government.

Then you have bureaucratic corruption. This type of corruption usually occurs at street level and the citizens encounter it daily at places like schools, hospitals, licensing offices, police and such. Some call it petty corruption.

Then there is *electoral* corruption which includes purchase of votes with money, promises of office or special favors, coercion, intimidation and interference with freedom of election. In Nigeria votes are bought, people are killed and maimed all for the votes. Payments are disguised in the forms of gifts, legal fees, employment, favors and social influence all at the cost to the public interest and welfare of the people.

Then you have other forms of corruption such as the following:

Bribery: The payment (in money or kind) that is taken or given in a corrupt relationship. These include *kickbacks, gratuities, pay-off, sweeteners, and greasing palms*. There was a time where one of my sources friends got arrested for online dating scams and many of the other Yahoo Boyz pitched in to pay-off the authorities and he walked away scott free.

Fraud: It involves some kind of trickery, swindle and deceit, counterfeiting, racketing, smuggling and forgery. This is the category that all scams fall under.

Embezzlement: This is theft of public resources by public officials. It is when a state official steals from the public institution in which he/she is employed. In Nigeria the embezzlement of public funds is one of the most common ways of wealth.

Extortion: This is money and other resources extracted by the use of coercion, violence or threats to use force. The Yahoo Boyz also use extortion to obtain money from their victims.

Favoritism: This is a mechanism of power abuse implying a highly biased distribution of state resources. However, this is seen as a natural human proclivity to favor friends, family and anybody close and trusted.

Nepotism: This is a special form of favoritism in which an office holder prefers his/her *kinfolk* and family members.

For anything to change in Nigeria, they must develop a culture of openness instead of secrecy and create employment and distribution of natural resources."

http://www.africaeconomicanalysis.org/articles/gen/corruptiondikehtm.html

More insight into corruption can be found in Femi Aribisala's "Why PDP politicians are thieves, but corrupt when decamp to APC," published at www.osundefender.org/?p=179039. The current President of Nigeria, Jonathan Goodluck is quoted as saying "What many Nigerians refer to as corruption is actually stealing. Stealing is not the same thing as corruption." As if to say that even if corruption is wrong, stealing isn't corruption, so it's not wrong. What? No wonder scammers think they are doing nothing wrong when they steal from innocent people. Their President endorses it.

We have talked about the first two causes – greed and corruption. Taken together they create the third cause (and the scamming), which is **poverty**. According to Dictionary.com, poverty is the state or condition of having little or no money, goods, or means of support; condition of being poor; deficiency of necessary or desirable ingredients, qualities, etc.; scantiness; insufficiency.

In his April 7, 2014 piece "Is Nigeria A Poor Country Of Rich Men Or A Rich Country Of Poor Men," Sam Nda-Isaiah writes that seventy percent of Nigerians are desperately poor. Nda-Isaiah is the former chairman of Leadership Group and he notes "Nigeria has the highest number of private jet owners on the African continent…the same Nigeria has the largest number of desperately poor people in Africa and one of the largest in the world." "Of the 174 million people in Nigeria, *122 million people live in desperate poverty, using the acceptable extreme poverty line of $1.25 a day.*" He also states that *in the last 20 years Nigeria has added 105 million new desperately poor people, and in just the last seven years Nigeria added nearly 50 million people to the list of extremely poor people.* According to Nda-Isaiah, "Nigeria urgently needs a leader that will quickly engage the nearly 50 million unemployed people and tackle the current 80 per cent graduate unemployment by modifying our education system into one that produces graduates who would be employers of labour instead of seekers of good jobs" http://leadership.ng/columns/363727/nigeria-poor-country-rich-men-rich-country-poor-men

If the average wage in Nigeria is $1.25 a day and there are 30 days in the month, the average Nigerian would make $37.50 a month. I think it would be very difficult to live on $37.50 a month. With these numbers and an extremely high rate of unemployment, I believe Nigeria is in great pain. However, I also know there are some better paying jobs and many people in Nigeria *do not* scam for a living.

In my opinion, worse than the scammers stealing "only what they need to survive" is them stealing in excess of what they truly need and wasting their ill-gotten gains on women, alcohol, drugs, expensive clothes, shoes, jewelry and other luxuries. Once they get a taste of quick, easy money and are able to afford things they want, it becomes very difficult to let go of the lifestyle. Thus they themselves move from poverty to greed and find it very hard to return to poverty.

In truth, all countries host poverty, greed, corruption and scamming of some sort. Nigeria and Ghana are hotbeds of scamming activity, and increasing awareness of the root causes is the first step to eradicating this plague.

Consider the economic problems all over the world – lack of infrastructure to support a strong economy, high unemployment rates, and widespread corruption – and ask yourself how close other countries, including America, are to becoming a third world country where people are in survival mode.

I ask the people and leaders of the world, *"When are we going to do a better job of looking out for our fellow man instead of our own greed? When will the corruption of people in power stop?"* When these two things happen, scamming will also stop. If these two things don't happen, the scamming epidemic will only gather strength, and the fabric of our society will continue to erode.

We all need to do our part to keep greed and corruption out of the government. As Pratibha Patil says, "Corruption is the enemy of development, and of good governance. It must be got rid of. Both the government and the people at large must come together to achieve this national objective."

In the meantime, we need to stop romance scams at a grassroots level. We have the power; we need to exert it. In the next chapter I explain how we can work together for change and save people from the heartbreak and financial loss of romance scams. I need each and every one of you in order to stop this!

Below you will see a visual circle of the root causes of scamming. Notice that the cycle is unending. The root causes have not only spawned scamming, they keep scamming alive and thriving!

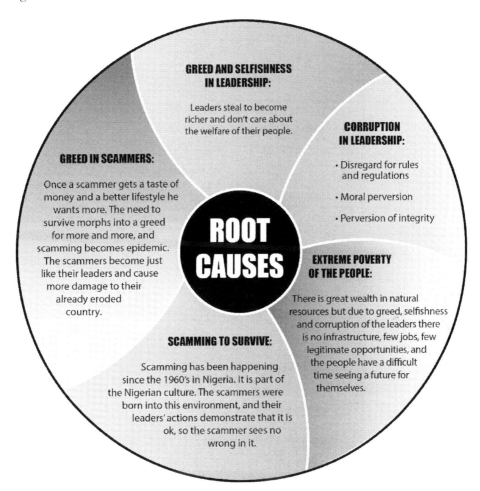

GREED AND SELFISHNESS IN LEADERSHIP:

Leaders steal to become richer and don't care about the welfare of their people.

CORRUPTION IN LEADERSHIP:

- Disregard for rules and regulations
- Moral perversion
- Perversion of integrity

GREED IN SCAMMERS:

Once a scammer gets a taste of money and a better lifestyle he wants more. The need to survive morphs into a greed for more and more, and scamming becomes epidemic. The scammers become just like their leaders and cause more damage to their already eroded country.

ROOT CAUSES

EXTREME POVERTY OF THE PEOPLE:

There is great wealth in natural resources but due to greed, selfishness and corruption of the leaders there is no infrastructure, few jobs, few legitimate opportunities, and the people have a difficult time seeing a future for themselves.

SCAMMING TO SURVIVE:

Scamming has been happening since the 1960's in Nigeria. It is part of the Nigerian culture. The scammers were born into this environment, and their leaders' actions demonstrate that it is ok, so the scammer sees no wrong in it.

CHAPTER 10

TOGETHER WE CAN MAKE A CHANGE

I nertia is powerful. When inertia keeps people from taking corrective action, negative, dysfunctional, dangerous, and damaging things continue to harm. In the case of Internet dating scams, many people think the problem is too massive and they are too small to make a difference. Some people give up before they even begin, believing that "nothing" can stem the tide of online dating fraud. When I got scammed, I did not find one division of law enforcement willing to take my statement, let alone help me. It's out of our jurisdiction. There's nothing we can do. If you were a victim of an online dating scam and tried to get help, I am sure you had a similar experience and was possibly even victimized again by law enforcement. So just because something is difficult or overwhelming or beyond your professional scope, you should do nothing? Nothing? I did something and you can too. We must. If law enforcement cannot do anything about it from a legal standpoint, we must!

Too many people have had their hearts broken, their bank accounts emptied, their self-confidence and trust in others demolished, not to mention the victims that have committed suicide because of online dating scams. This wicked crime perpetrates a negative and lasting effect on people and their lives. How can we remain silent and let the online dating scammers succeed at their ploys? We cannot. What we can do is take action and force a change. We cannot stop scammers from scamming, but we can speak out and educate people so they stop being scammed. Perhaps, when scammers can no longer scam people through the romance scams, they will move onto another type of scam. Time will tell. But with your help word will travel quickly within the scamming world that the romance scam is no longer profitable because people are educated and no longer falling for it.

I spent two years chatting with scammers and collecting information for this book and the following book, "Is It a Real Soldier Behind the Screen? Online Dating: How to Protect Your Heart and money." Every minute of every hour of those years men and women all over the world were being victimized by online romance scams at the exact time that I was conducting research into the scams. This knowledge fueled me to keep going and to dig deeper. It is what gave me the strength to stay up late and still be able to work my business during the day. It gave me the ability to role play with unsuspecting scammers and stay "in character" when everything in me wanted to cut loose and tell these men how despicable they were and that I knew they were scammers from the first time I saw their profiles. This book was written for all the people who have been scammed and for those out on dating websites looking for love. Thoughts of all of you gave me the courage to come forth with my own story and gather information for this book. The road was long, but every bit worth it. Thank you for encouraging me every step of the way!

What I did was just the start. *TOGETHER*, we can be more courageous and *WE CAN* make a change. I am not being unrealistic. I know we cannot rid the world of all things horrible, but if we work together at the grass roots level we can stop *this* horrible crime known as the "romance scam". Paul Price, who wrote the foreword for this book, worked in law enforcement for 20 years and now owns a digital forensic company by the name of Beyond IT. While in law enforcement his investigations focused on online fraud, and he always knew that the key to stopping it was education. This is why he is a strong supporter of this book and the corollary awareness program. Let's do what others wouldn't or couldn't do. *Let's educate the world*. As Desmond Tutu says, "Do your little bit of good where you are; it's those little bits of good put together that overwhelm the world." So together, let's overwhelm the world and put a stop to online dating scams once and for all!

To make Internet dating sufficiently unprofitable for scammers we need to do two things; first, if you have been scammed, please talk about it and second, educate others.

Please help me spread the word…

I know how stupid, foolish, embarrassed and ashamed you can feel after being scammed, because it is exactly how I felt. These feelings make us want to hide our experience. However, if we don't tell anyone, we remain victims, and the scammer continue to tantalize our thoughts and spirits. We continually say to ourselves, "How did this just happen?" "What the hell did I miss?" "How could I have not known?" "How could I have been so stupid?" I am here with wonderful news for you. It doesn't have to be like this. We should not be doing this to ourselves at all. We should not be silent. We need to *BREAK THE SILENCE* and become *VICTORIOUS*. We need to *TELL THE WORLD*. It is only through talking about it that we can heal and move forward with our lives and with our heads held high. It is only through talking about it that we can educate people and stop this vicious crime. We owe it not only to ourselves to talk about it, we also owe it to others so they don't get caught in the same trap.

The only thing we did wrong was trust someone untrustworthy. All we had was a computer screen, his picture and his sweet words. We did not anticipate that he might be a scammer. We wanted to know if he might be a potential partner, a prince charming. How on earth could we protect ourselves against something we didn't even know existed? I never heard anything about the romance scam until after I was scammed, and I have worked with fraud investigators for well over a decade! Once I was scammed, I actively researched the topic online and then learned a lot about it. However, if you never knew about the romance scam, why would you go looking for the red flags about it before you went online dating? You wouldn't! Most dating sites surely don't have warnings front and center to educate you. If they do have them they are buried within the website. I will work diligently to have this changed because scammers are on EVERY dating website. I want to applaud everyone who has information out there about the romance scam. You are doing great work at putting information out there. The only problem is, most people are learning after they have been scammed instead of before. We want everyone to learn before instead of after.

We have to realize that we were manipulated and we were not on an even playing ground. Scammers have lots of practice scamming people; we have no practice being scammed until it happens. Most of us in the target age bracket (44-70) are not as Internet savvy as younger generations who grew up with the Internet. That's one reason we are targeted. Scammers are skilled at using our personal characteristics against us to get to our money. It is time we leverage our personal characteristics – our intelligence, our instincts, our confidence, our sense of self – to defeat the romance scam.

We cannot change the fact that we were scammed and *"molested for money"*, but we can change what we do with the experience. We can remain silent and be a victim or we can *HAVE*

A VOICE and *BE VICTORIOUS.* We *CAN* prevent others from this kind of hurt, shame and embarrassment. If we all speak out and help educate others, we will be a greater army than the scammers. For illustration, I am going to work with very low numbers. Let's say there are 100,000 scammers and each scammer scams 25 people a year. That is 2,500,000 people a year getting scammed. If all these people talk about it, our army will definitely increase compared to theirs and we will win the war on online dating fraud. If you have been scammed, please come and join our army. Please take your power back and talk about it. Help educate others. Help stop this horrible crime.

If you have been scammed and you want to finally tell someone who will understand and not judge you, or you want to become part of this movement to stop the romance scam by educating others, please contact our awareness program at info@silentvictimnomore.com.

The next chapter is a quick guide on how to protect yourself when dating online. My hope is that by the time you finish this book, you already know the red flags, but the next chapter provides a quick reference in a few short pages.

CHAPTER 11

QUICK GUIDE ON HOW TO PROTECT YOURSELF WHEN ONLINE DATING

My first inclination is to beseech you NOT to date online because the dangers are great. However, I know millions of people date online every day and most will still continue to do so because it's a good avenue to meet new people. If you are going to date online, I pray you have learned from the chapters of this book what you need to do to keep your heart and money safe from scammers. I realize this may be redundant, but I do want to give you a review guideline for quick reference.

In Preparation to Date Online

1. Do not venture into online dating until you know the red flags to look for.
2. Set up an email address through Yahoo!, Gmail or Hotmail that you will use specifically for online dating only. Always use this email address until you are absolutely sure of who you are chatting/talking with.
3. Purchase a cheap cellphone that you can throw away if you come in contact with a scammer. This prevents people from finding out where you live by your phone number. Remember, you NEVER know who is behind that screen.
4. Never, ever give your personal details out to anyone on the Internet. This is especially true for your last name, bank account details, credit card numbers, addresses and social security numbers.
5. Be careful about opening things people send you on the Internet. It can be malware or spyware that can attack your computer and reveal your personal information.
6. Once you meet someone you are interested in an have doubt, please call us at 678-583-0401.

Your Profile

1. When filling out your profile, it is natural to want to share a lot about yourself. After all, you are online dating to find your Prince Charming. However, I encourage you not to share much, because scammers use the information in your profile to manipulate you. Be mysterious. Both men and women are intrigued by mystery. Put something very brief and intriguing in your profile and then end it with "If I told you everything, what would we have to talk about?" Do not put in your profile, "I am new to online dating," "If you are a scammer don't bother," "If you travel or live outside the country, don't bother," or "I'm not into games." Phrases like these attract the "professional scammer" like blood attracts a shark. This terminology tells them that you have either been scammed or dealt with a scammer before, and they will take you on as a personal challenge.
2. Be careful what pictures you put on the dating sites. Remember that once you put a picture out on the Internet it can be almost impossible to remove. As tempted as you are to upload many pictures, it is best to only upload one. Scammers look at the way you are dressed and the background of your picture to decipher if you have money. It is always best to appear that you don't have money. Remember, they want rich clients!
3. If you are widowed and/or retired, do not specify this. Scammers love to go after women who are widowed/retired.

Their Profiles

- ✓ Scammers use different types of pictures but if he looks like a model it is very likely he is a scammer. Remember, if it seems too good to be true, it probably is.
- ✓ Many scammers do not use a picture at all. The absence of a picture is a red flag.
- ✓ Pay attention to his age compared to the age of the woman he is looking for. Scammers typically seek women from their mid 40's to 70.
- ✓ Pay attention to his height. If he is from Africa, he may know only the metric system and may make errors when reporting his height.
- ✓ He may leave a lot of blanks in his profile. It depends if he has taken time to generate this information.
- ✓ If his occupation is in engineering, construction, oil, geology, business, or something else that requires traveling country to country, you can just about guarantee he is a scammer. He will not tell you he is a doctor, teacher, factory worker or anything else stable that doesn't involve traveling.
- ✓ He claims to be widowed or divorced. Now, many sincere and good people are widowed and divorced, so you need to look at all the categories to see if there are other red flags to go with this one.
- ✓ He gives only attractive details about himself.
- ✓ He says he is new to online dating.
- ✓ He demonstrates poor spelling, grammar and punctuation.
- ✓ He says in his profile that he is educated, but when you read what he writes, it doesn't appear as if an educated person wrote it.
- ✓ The words in his sentences are out of order.
- ✓ He does not capitalize "I's" or the names of cities or states, and he may misspell the names of cities and states.
- ✓ Throughout his profile description both capital and lower case "I's" are used where they should all be capitalized.
- ✓ Look for unusual repetition and incongruities.
- ✓ Look for the wrong pronouns.
- ✓ Look for him saying things that are typically said by a woman.
- ✓ He types "know" for "now."

Do not leave the dating site for a couple weeks to go to Yahoo! messenger, any other messenger, text or email. If you notice any of these items, DISCONNECT IMMEDIATELY and DO NOT SEND ANYONE MONEY!

If none of the above are found in his profile and you start chatting, pay attention for the following:

1. If his first email to you starts out with "Hi Pretty".
2. The need to travel; any type of illness, investment opportunity or banking delays come up. He may claim to be traveling and unable to cash his check for many days; he needs money temporarily, and he promises to pay it back to your account with interest.
3. He has some kind of dramatic grandiose story, and he needs you to help by sending him money.
4. He has no family, business associates or close friends to turn to; he only has you.
5. He asks you to assist with a personal transaction such as depositing funds or shipping merchandise.
6. He asks you to wire money through a bank, Western Union or Money Gram.
7. He says he is new to online dating.
8. He has a child in school in a different country.
9. He has a nanny who is taking care of his child somewhere other than where he is.
10. He only has a few pictures to send you.
11. The pictures he sends have the same number file with a different letter of the alphabet following, such as 198765A, 198765B, 198765C, etc. or his name followed by a number such as 1, 2, 3, etc.
12. His profile is incongruent with what he tells you now.
13. His answers to your questions are vague.
14. He claims to be from the United States but calls his Mom, Mum.
15. He sends you an invitation with his IM on the second or third contact and asks you to join him there or asks for your personal email address. There are exceptions to this where he will ask you to meet him on Yahoo! messenger the first contact. It all depends on his style.
16. He calls you his queen.
17. He refers to you as his wife.
18. His messages/emails are addressed to someone else.
19. His personal story reads like a magazine or news story.
20. He sends a very sugar coated and heart winning love letter email right away instead of one that says, "Hi, how are you? I would like to get to know you."
21. He replies to your email very quickly.
22. He changes his Yahoo! ID to be both of your names.
23. He puts your picture with a love message on his Yahoo! ID
24. He asks you to close your account on the dating site.
25. He disappears from the dating site or Yahoo! messenger and reappears with a different name and tells you his account has been hacked. (Nine times out of ten, he was reported as a scammer.)
26. He spends an inordinate amount of time chatting with you.

27. Within the first week or two he says it was "destiny" or "fate" that brought you together.

28. He sends you flowers, candy, teddy bears, jewelry, etc. He might even send you money so you think he has money and will not be suspicious when he asks you for money.

29. He asks for your mother's full name.

30. In the first or second email or chat he calls you baby, darling, babe, hun, my love, honey, and other endearing names.

31. He says "I love you" very quickly. Usually within the first or second chat.

32. He talks quickly about getting married.

33. He asks if you are chatting with other men.

34. He uses God and Scripture to gain your trust. He says he is "God Fearing". Do not feel safe just because someone appears to be a Christian and knows scripture. Remember, Satan knows scripture too. Knowing it doesn't mean you believe or walk it.

35. He sends love letters that he copies and pastes from other sites like www.lovingyou.com, www.lovelysms.com, www.1001loveletters.com and www.lovepoemsandquotes.com.

36. He frequently asks "So what do you think of me?"

37. He asks if you live alone, if you own or rent, and if you work.

38. He does not want you to tell friends or family members about your relationship with him.

39. The words in his sentences are out of order.

40. Some scammers say they are from abroad and then intentionally use bad grammar to make you think they really are from abroad and that English is their second language.

41. He uses Nigerian vernacular, such as "I slept off", "I'm going to bath now" or "my parents (mother or father or siblings) are late", "happy family", "loving kind", "brave heart", "I love you with all my life", "I promise I will never fail you", "Your heart is safe with me", "it got spoiled", "tell me your true mind", "you rule my world and my life", "soonest", "your kind of woman", "more better", "you own me", "I will not disappoint", "It all good", "I am very strong" (meaning sexually. Remember, most of them are in their 20's.)

42. For punctuation purposes, in their written correspondence scammers characteristically type an ellipses with only two periods (..) instead of the more common three (...).

43. He misspells the names of cities and states.

44. When he wants your attention he hits the "BUZZ" on Yahoo! messenger a lot.

45. He doesn't understand English slang.

46. When chatting, he gives details that contradict his profile, especially his age, date of birth, where he is from, height, eye and hair color.

47. He refers to the United States as the USA or the States and does not know much about the United States.

48. He talks a lot about current events that he just saw on CNN.

49. He IMs, texts and calls you at unusual hours.

50. If you ask what time it is where he is, he might give you the wrong time because he didn't calculate time zones properly. The world clock www.timeanddate.com/worldclock/ will help you figure out different time zones.

51. If you chat at night and he is tired. This is because it is the middle of the night in his time zone.

52. His correspondence sometimes has someone else's name other than yours or uses "him" when it should say "her" and "her" when it should say "him".

53. There are lapses in conversation on IM.

54. He tells you he is in a remote place to work, or in the desert if it's a military scam, and that the network isn't strong. He purposely logs in and out just so you think he has a bad network and to cover up the bad network in Africa.

55. He sends the same IM message two or more times in a row because he is copying and pasting and mistakenly hits the send button.

56. He gets booted off the computer a lot and tells you it is because of a bad network.

57. He always wants you to come on camera but tells you his web camera doesn't work, he doesn't have one or he is on his phone.

58. If he comes on camera briefly, it is probably a fake cam.

59. He does not answer personal and specific questions you ask him.

60. You do not hear from him for a couple days.

61. If he calls you, you have a hard time understanding him because of his accent and background noise. He may even say it is a friend of his calling on his behalf.

62. You are not able to get through when you call the number he gave you.

63. If he gives you a +44 70 number, it is a scammer.

64. He sends you a (fictitious) passport to prove his identity.

65. He sends you a (fictitious) social security number to gain your trust and make you believe that he is who he says he is.

66. He tries to make you feel guilty. "If you love me you will send money to help me."

67. He becomes verbally abusive if you refuse to send money.

68. If you accuse him of being a scammer he denies it and acts deeply offended.

69. He asks you to open a new account to transfer money.

70. He sends you a log in and password for a bank account.

71. He sends you copies of (fraudulent) checks and money orders when conducting an advance-fee scam to gain or further solidify your trust in the validity of the scam.

72. He sends you money (a couple thousand dollars) through wire transfer to gain your trust.

73. He may create accounts on Linked In, White Pages, Switchboard and Checkmate to make his fictitious identity appear real if you do an Internet search for him.

74. He has many (fictitious) identities, emails and IM accounts at one time.
75. He usually uses web-based email service (because it does not require valid identifying information and lets him mask his IP address).
76. If he has a website he might email you from that website domain.
77. He wants the relationship to progress very quickly.
78. He wants to have sex chats.
79. He tells you a dream he had about you.
80. He requests your home or work address to send you something. Professional scammers might research and find your address online and surprise you with gifts.
81. He wants you to compromise your principles.
82. If you ask too many questions or seem suspicious, he tries to put *you* in the hot seat.
83. He blames other for troubles in his life.
84. If he asks you to show your private body parts on the camera
85. He says customs is holding him. Customs cannot hold a person; only goods. Only immigration can hold a person.
86. If he reminds you of the scars of your past and tries to console you.
87. If he asks you to tell him all your secrets.
88. He tells you customs is holding his goods for his contract or for high taxes.
89. He tells you customs is going to put him in jail if he doesn't pay because he brought something he shouldn't have in his suitcase into a country.
90. If he sends you a lot of songs and/or poetry.
91. If he asks you to describe the perfect first date.
92. If he is extremely attentive.
93. If he totally sweeps you off your feet in the first week of chatting with him.
94. He says the bank won't cash his check.
95. His phone calls drop
96. When he calls the caller ID says private number

If you don't find any of the above, you might have met someone who is "genuine" and not a scammer. But *always* do your due diligence.

If you get scammed

1. Know that you were manipulated.
2. DISCONNECT IMMEDIATELY.
3. Change all your contact information.
4. Visit us at *www.silentvictimnomore.com. We can help you work through it because we have been there and we understand.*
5. If you are in the United States report it to IC3 at www.ic3.gov.

If a Scammer Shows You His Real Identity

Usually when a scammer shows you who he really is, it is just another scam. He will do whatever he can to get money or goods such as phones, laptops and such from you and this includes showing you who he really is. Do not believe that he is genuine. A scammer always has a motive and will turn your life upside down and inside out. He will destroy you emotionally, mentally and wipe you out financially. If you want to understand how this happens, please watch the following video. https://www.youtube.com/watch?v=53A0zfaab0s

If you are going to date online, please be extremely safe and please educate all the people you know who are online dating about the red flags. Share this book with them so they understand how scammers operate and don't get caught in their ploy.

Please also read our book, "Is It a Real Soldier Behind the Screen? Online Dating: How To Protect Your Heart and Money" to learn about the military scams. Military scams are totally different than the dating scams you have read about in this book. A person in uniform may be a scammer, not military personnel. Many times people trust them just because they are in uniform. The military dating scams are used a lot by scammers.

Thank you for giving me the opportunity to educate you and joining the army of people armed with information. Best of luck.

ABOUT THE AUTHOR

D L Garren is the Founder and CEO of True Perceptions, Inc®, a business consulting and perception management firm based in the United States of America. For more than a decade she has consulted in the areas of business development, sales, marketing, branding, and perception management for investigative agencies, many who are fraud investigators, retired Law Enforcement, FBI, CIA and Secret Service, security companies, process serving companies, and attorneys.

Through her work with investigators Garren learned investigative skills and techniques, which she leveraged to gather facts for this book.

D L Garren is a well-known speaker throughout the United States. She is widely regarded as a thought leader about the power of perception in every aspect of life. She is known for her sincerity, enthusiasm, and her no-nonsense approach. She speaks *truth* because she knows it is *truth* that makes a change. D L Garren can be reached to learn speaking availability at www.trueperceptions.com, www.dlgarren.com and www.silentvictimnomore.com.

Made in the USA
Middletown, DE
22 September 2020

19502050R00442